EIGHTH EDITION

RACE, ETHNICITY, GENDER, & CLASS

Sara Miller McCune founded SAGE Publishing in 1965 to support the dissemination of usable knowledge and educate a global community. SAGE publishes more than 1000 journals and over 800 new books each year, spanning a wide range of subject areas. Our growing selection of library products includes archives, data, case studies and video. SAGE remains majority owned by our founder and after her lifetime will become owned by a charitable trust that secures the company's continued independence.

Los Angeles | London | New Delhi | Singapore | Washington DC | Melbourne

EIGHTH EDITION
RACE, ETHNICITY, GENDER, & CLASS

The Sociology of Group Conflict and Change

JOSEPH F. HEALEY
Christopher Newport University

ANDI STEPNICK
Belmont University

EILEEN O'BRIEN
Saint Leo University, Virginia

Los Angeles | London | New Delhi
Singapore | Washington DC | Melbourne

FOR INFORMATION:

SAGE Publications, Inc.
2455 Teller Road
Thousand Oaks, California 91320
E-mail: order@sagepub.com

SAGE Publications Ltd.
1 Oliver's Yard
55 City Road
London EC1Y 1SP
United Kingdom

SAGE Publications India Pvt. Ltd.
B 1/I 1 Mohan Cooperative Industrial Area
Mathura Road, New Delhi 110 044
India

SAGE Publications Asia-Pacific Pte. Ltd.
3 Church Street
#10-04 Samsung Hub
Singapore 049483

Acquisitions Editor: Jeff Lasser
Content Development Editor: Sarah Dillard
Editorial Assistant: Tiara Beatty
Production Editor: Andrew Olson
Copy Editor: Gretchen Treadwell
Typesetter: C&M Digitals (P) Ltd.
Proofreader: Theresa Kay
Indexer: Will Ragsdale
Cover and Interior Designer: Gail Buschman
Marketing Manager: Kara Kindstrom

Library of Congress Cataloging-in-Publication Data

Names: Healey, Joseph F., author. | Stepnick, Andi, author. | O'Brien, Eileen, author.

Title: Race, ethnicity, gender, & class : the sociology of group conflict and change / Joseph F. Healey, Christopher Newport University, Andi Stepnick, Belmont University, Eileen O'Brien, Saint Leo University. Other titles: Race, ethnicity, gender, and class

Description: Eighth Edition. | Thousand Oaks : SAGE Publications, [2018] | Revised edition of Race, ethnicity, gender, & class, [2015] | Includes bibliographical references and index.

Identifiers: LCCN 2017048145 | ISBN 9781506346946 (pbk. : alk. paper)

Subjects: LCSH: Minorities--United States. | Ethnicity—United States. | Group identity—United States. | Social conflict—United States. | United States—Race relations. | United States—Ethnic relations. | United States—Social conditions.

Classification: LCC E184.A1 H415 2018 | DDC 305.800973—dc23
LC record available at https://lccn.loc.gov/2017048145

This book is printed on acid-free paper.

Printed in Canada.

18 19 20 21 22 10 9 8 7 6 5 4 3 2 1

Only when lions have historians will hunters cease to be heroes.

—African Proverb

Not everything that is faced can be changed, but nothing can be changed until it is faced.

—James Baldwin

BRIEF CONTENTS

DETAILED CONTENTS

PART I: AN INTRODUCTION TO THE STUDY OF MINORITY GROUPS IN THE UNITED STATES

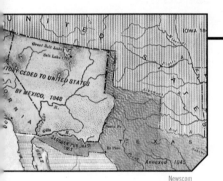

Newscom

PART II: THE EVOLUTION OF DOMINANT–MINORITY RELATIONS IN THE UNITED STATES

LOC

4. The Development of Dominant–Minority Group Relations in Preindustrial America: The Origins of Slavery 116

PART III: UNDERSTANDING DOMINANT–MINORITY RELATIONS IN THE UNITED STATES TODAY

Newscom

7. Native Americans: From Conquest to Tribal Survival in a Postindustrial Society   224

8. Hispanic Americans: Colonization, Immigration, and Ethnic Enclaves   262

Everett Collection/Newscom

Wikimedia

9. Asian Americans: Model Minorities? 312

LOC

10. New Americans, Assimilation, and Old Challenges 354

PART IV: OTHER GROUPS, OTHER PATTERNS

11. Gender   392

National Portrait Gallery, Public domain

12. Lesbian, Gay, and Bisexual Americans   430

Getty

LOC

13. Dominant–Minority Relations in Cross-National Perspective   462

PART V: CHALLENGES FOR THE PRESENT AND THE FUTURE

LOC

PREFACE

Of the challenges confronting the United States today, those relating to dominant–minority group relations continue to be among the most urgent and the most daunting. The history of our country is, in part, a story of discrimination and the rejection of "others." Along with equality, freedom, and justice, prejudice, racism, and sexism seem to be some of our oldest values. Every part of our society, and virtually every item on the national agenda—"welfare" and health care reform, policing, crime and punishment, family, education, defense, foreign policy, and terrorism—have some connection with dominant–minority relations.

This textbook contributes to our ongoing national discussion by presenting information, raising questions, and deeply examining relevant issues. Our intent is to help you increase your knowledge, improve your understanding of the issues, and clarify your thinking about social inequalities related to race, ethnicity, gender, class, and sexual orientation. We have written for undergraduate students—sociology majors and nonmajors alike. We assume little about your knowledge of history or sociological concepts, and we present the material in an accessible way. For example, we use a unified set of themes and concepts throughout the text, even as we examine multiple sociological perspectives and different points of view. We introduce most of the conceptual framework in the first four chapters. Then, in Chapters 5 through 13, we apply these concepts and analytical themes to a series of minority groups that we refer to as case studies. In the last chapter, we review our main points, consider present challenges, and speculate about the future.

Our analysis is, generally, macro and comparative. That is, we focus on large groups and social structures—such as social institutions and stratification system. We systematically compare and contrast the experiences of America's many minority groups over time. The book follows in the tradition of conflict theory, but it is not a comprehensive statement of that tradition. We introduce and apply other perspectives, but we do not attempt to explain everything, give equal attention to all current sociological paradigms, or include all possible viewpoints. Rather, our goals are (1) to present the sociology of minority-group relations in a way that you will find intellectually challenging but also understandable and (2) to address the issues (and tell the stories behind the issues) in a way that demonstrates the power and importance of sociological thinking.

To help tell these stories, Narrative Portraits in Chapters 1 through 12 explore the thoughts and experiences of a wide variety of people: minority group members including immigrants, journalists, sociologists, racists, and slaves, among others. These excerpts reinforce our sociological analysis personally, dramatically, and memorably. Comparative Focus features will help you think about these issues in relation to other societies. Additionally, photos throughout the text help document the experiences of minority groups and the realities of prejudice, racism, sexism, and discrimination. Timelines at the start of each chapter provide a brief overview of key events related to the chapter topic.

In addition to examining diversity across minority groups (e.g., Native Americans and Hispanic Americans), we stress the diversity of experiences *within* each minority group (e.g., Puerto Ricans and Cubans). Additionally, we use an intersectional perspective to explore the ways race, ethnicity, social class, gender, and sexual orientation influence one another, creating ever-shifting constellations of dominance and subordination. We give unique attention to gender as it relates to social beliefs, values, norms, and social structures. For example, we pay attention to how enslaved women in the antebellum South were oppressed in unique ways as a result of their gender and race.

Finally, we stress the ways American minority groups are inseparable from the American experience—from the early days of colonial settlements to the present day. The relative success of our society is due to the contributions of minority groups as well as those of the dominant group. The nature of the minority-group experience has changed as U.S. society has changed. To understand America's minority groups is to understand some elemental truths about America. To raise the issues of difference and diversity is to ask what it means, and what it has meant, to be an American.

The issues we face will not disappear; nor will they be resolved easily or quickly. People's feelings about these issues can be intense, and controversy, indifference, and bitterness can overshadow objective analysis and calm reason. We have little hope of resolving our nation's dilemmas until we address them openly and honestly. This book explores topics that involve conflict between groups. That history is tinged with pain. We discuss topics that can be challenging to learn. And, at times, we quote directly from sources that use language that may be offensive or painful to hear. We have included it because we cannot seek to understand (or change) things we do not face.

CHANGES IN THIS EDITION

This edition of *Race, Ethnicity, Gender, and Class* retains and updates popular features from our earlier editions, including the following:

- *Opening Vignettes* foreshadow the chapter content and stimulate student interest.
- *Learning Objectives* focus student attention on what they will know and be able to do after learning the chapter material.
- *Questions for Reflection* guide an analysis of the material.
- *Questions to Consider* help apply chapter concepts to each Narrative Portrait and Comparative Focus feature.
- *Applying Concepts* activities use key ideas in easy, creative ways.
- *Chapter Summaries* help students identify major points.
- *Key Terms* are defined and offset within the text for ease of reference.

In addition, the authors have thoroughly revised the text to make it fresher, more relevant, and more accessible to undergraduates. This edition incorporates the latest and best research and more than 100 new and updated tables, maps, and figures and more than 90 new photos that clearly illustrate sociological concepts. In addition to new content on gender and sexual orientation, the authors emphasize an intersectional approach to provide a more complex understanding of social inequalities related to race, ethnicity, gender, and class. To broaden students' awareness of dominant–minority group relations in the United States and around the world, each chapter incorporates relevant current events and offers examples of social change.

A sample of new or expanded topics in this edition are:

- Racial discrimination in the criminal justice system (e.g., policing and violence)
- Social policy changes including the proposed border wall, DACA/DREAMers, and the proposed ban on transpersons in the U.S. military
- The rise of the "alt-right" and trends in hate crimes, including those against Muslim, immigrant, and LGBT+ Americans
- Activism including Black Lives Matter, bended-knee protest at NFL and other sporting events, the 2016 Dakota Access Pipeline protest, and hashtag activism (e.g., #metoo/sexual assault)
- Women's participation in social movement activism (e.g., Delores Huerta, Rosa Parks)

- The social construction of race over time and place (e.g., U.S. Brazil, Puerto Rico, Australia, South Africa)

CHANGES IN CONTINUING FEATURES

Internet Activities (by Andi Stepnick) and Public Sociology Assignments (by Linda Waldron). Many sociologists have called for a more "public sociology," a sociology that is engaged in the community, the society, and the world. Although not all sociologists would endorse a call for activism and involvement, the study of American race relations will, for many people, stimulate an impulse to address social problems directly and personally. To facilitate that involvement, we have developed a number of projects for students that will lead them into their communities and the larger society and provide them with opportunities to make a positive difference in the lives of others.

The projects are presented at our website (edge.sagpub.com/healey8e), and each assignment is keyed to a specific chapter.

These assignments should be regarded as outlines and suggestions, and participants will likely have to improvise and respond to unanticipated challenges as they arise. Nonetheless, these assignments will allow students to bridge the (sometimes large) gap between the classroom and the community and to develop and practice their own public sociology. Each assignment could be the basis for a semester-long project for individual or teams of students.

OTHER CHANGES

- Research findings and data have been updated. This edition relies on the latest information from the U.S. Census Bureau, among other sources.
- There is an increased intersectional emphasis, particularly in Chapters 1, 6, 7, 8, 9, 11, and 12. For example, Chapter 4 addresses the experiences of enslaved women that result from interlocking systems of racial and gender oppression. The Chapter 8 Narrative Focus features gay Latino men.
- There is an increased emphasis on immigration, particularly in Chapter 1 and Chapters 8 through 10.
- Several new Narrative Portraits have been added to Chapters 1, 2, 4, 8, and 9 to make this feature more current. Others have been updated.
- The Comparative Focus and Applying Concepts features have been updated.
- The Internet Research Projects have been updated in Chapters 2, 4, and 6 through 10.
- More than 40 new Internet activities encourage students to apply chapter concepts to the "real

world" by exploring oral history archives, viewing online art exhibits, applying concepts to YouTube videos, TED Talks, and more.

ANCILLARIES

$SAGE edge™

http://edge.sagepub.com/healey8e

SAGE edge offers a robust online environment featuring an impressive array of tools and resources for review, study, and further exploration, keeping both students and instructors on the cutting edge of teaching and learning. SAGE edge content is open access and available on demand. Learning and teaching has never been easier!

SAGE edge FOR STUDENTS

SAGE edge for Students provides a personalized approach to help students accomplish their coursework goals in an easy-to-use learning environment.

- Mobile-friendly **eFlashcards** strengthen understanding of key terms and concepts.
- Mobile-friendly practice **quizzes** allow for independent assessment by students of their mastery of course material.
- **Learning Objectives** reinforce the most important material.
- Carefully selected chapter-by-chapter **video links** and **multimedia content** enhance classroom-based explorations of key topics.
- **Current Debates** present two or more opposing statements from scholars and analysts on controversial questions raised in the chapters (Are Indian Sports Team Mascots Offensive? Should Children Be Raised Genderless? etc.).
- **Public Sociology Assignments** encourage students to go beyond the classroom and engage with people, organizations, and resources in their local communities to learn more about minority groups and issues.
- **Internet Research Projects** refer students to selected public websites, or direct them on guided Internet research, in order to gather data and apply concepts from the chapter.

- EXCLUSIVE access to full-text **SAGE** journal articles that have been carefully selected to support and expand on the concepts presented in each chapter.

SAGE edge FOR INSTRUCTORS

SAGE edge for Instructors supports teaching by making it easy to integrate quality content and create a rich learning environment for students.

- **Test banks** provide a diverse range of prewritten options as well as the opportunity to edit any question and/or insert your own personalized questions to effectively assess students' progress and understanding.
- **Sample course syllabi** for semester and quarter courses provide suggested models for structuring your courses.
- Editable, chapter-specific **PowerPoint® slides** offer complete flexibility for creating a multimedia presentation for your courses.
- Carefully selected chapter-by-chapter **video links** and **multimedia content** enhance classroom-based explorations of key topics.
- **Current Debates** resource presents two or more opposing statements from scholars and analysts on controversial questions raised in the chapters (Are Indian Sports Team Mascots Offensive? Should Children Be Raised Genderless? etc.).
- **Public Sociology Assignments** encourage students to go beyond the classroom and engage with people, organizations, and resources in their local communities to learn more about minority groups and issues.
- **Internet Research Projects** refer students to selected public websites, or direct them on guided Internet research, in order to gather data and apply concepts from the chapter.
- A **common course cartridge** includes all of the instructor resources and assessment material from the student study site, making it easy for instructors to upload and use these materials in learning management systems such as Blackboard™, Angel®, Moodle™, Canvas, and Desire2Learn™.
- EXCLUSIVE access to full-text **SAGE** journal articles that have been carefully selected to support and expand on the concepts presented in each chapter.

ACKNOWLEDGMENTS

It has been a great privilege to work on this edition with Andi Stepnick. She has strengthened this text in countless ways and it has been an enormous pleasure to work with a coauthor who brings such unflagging professionalism, scholarship, and attention to detail. I also thank professors Edwin H. Rhyne and Charles S. Green, the teacher–scholars who inspired me as a student, and Eileen O'Brien, who has contributed enormously to the development of this project. Finally, I thank my colleagues, past and present, in the Department of Sociology and Anthropology at Christopher Newport University: Stephanie Byrd, Cheri Chambers, Robert Durel, Marcus Griffin, Mai Lan Gustafsson, Jamie Harris, Kai Heidemann, Michael Lewis, Marion Manton, Lea Pellett, Eduardo Perez, Iris Price, Virginia Purtle, Tracey Rausch, Andria Timmer, Linda Waldron, and Ellen Whiting. They have been unflagging in their support of this project, and I thank them for their academic, logistical, and intellectual assistance.

—Joseph F. Healey

I am grateful to Joe Healey for inviting me to participate in this project, for being such a thoughtful partner, and for inspiring me with his passion for sociology and social justice. I am grateful to the sociologists and activists who paved the way for this work and who, through various means, fought for the democratic ideals of equality and justice for all. I am indebted to many people for their support throughout the years and, especially, while I was working on this book. I owe special thanks to Drs. Patricia Y. Martin and Irene Padavic for helping me become a better sociological thinker, researcher, writer, and teacher. I thank my colleagues at Belmont University as well as Jerry Adams, Catherine Bush, Kris De Welde, Jennifer Hackett, Jennifer James, Wendy Marsh, Anna Randolph, Shari Stepnick, Jennifer Thomas, Ashley Virgin, the "Book Women," and the "Wild Women." I appreciate the many kinds of support that my parents have given me over the years. My father, Robert J. Stepnick, deserves special attention for listening to countless project updates and for offering encouragement when the going got tough. Lastly, I am grateful for my students, who remind me why I do this work.

—Andi Stepnick

I thank my department chair, Janis Prince; associate dean, Heather Parker; and dean Mary Spoto: Their confidence in my abilities has allowed me to spread my wings toward this project. Feeling supported by my superiors is something I shall never take for granted. I am also thankful for the camaraderie of my wonderful Saint Leo sociology faculty colleagues—Chris Snead and Patricia Campion. I also thank Mike Armato for his enduring friendship, and assistance with suggested readings, as well as Charles Benbow at the Coffeehouse who always inquired how the writing was going! I am so grateful for my amazing beautiful children—Kaya Faith and Kaden Robert—who remind me every day what is important, and give me hope for the future of this fragile world. I give special thanks to their father Kendall whose fully involved coparenting makes much of this possible. But above all, I am grateful to my coauthor Joe Healey, for this wonderful opportunity, for doing more than his share, and for giving me something to look forward to by watching his example.

— Eileen O'Brien

We all thank Jeff Lasser, Adeline Wilson, Sarah Dillard, Gretchen Treadwell, and Andrew Olson of SAGE Publishing for their invaluable assistance in the preparation of this manuscript, and Dave Repetto, Ben Penner, and Steve Rutter, formerly of SAGE Publishing, for their help in the development of this project.

This text has benefited in innumerable ways from the reactions and criticisms of a group of reviewers who proved remarkably insightful about the subject matter and about the challenges of college teaching. We thank them for the countless times when their comments led to significant improvements in the scholarship and clarity of this project. The shortcomings that remain are, of course, our responsibility, but whatever quality this text has is a direct result of the insights and expertise of these reviewers. We thank the following people:

FIRST EDITION REVIEWERS

Audwin Anderson, *University of South Alabama*
Donna Barnes, *University of Wyoming*
Norma Burgess, *Syracuse University*
Steven Cornell, *University of California, San Diego*

Gerry R. Cox, *Fort Hays State University*
Kevin Delaney, *Temple University*
Raul Fernandez, *University of California, Irvine*
Timothy Fiedler, *Carroll College*
Ramona Ford, *Southwest Texas State University*
Joni Fraser, *University of California, Davis*
Nicole Grant, *Ball State University*
Anne Hastings, *University of North Carolina, Chapel Hill*
Michael Hodge, *Georgia State University*
Ray Hutchison, *University of Wisconsin, Green Bay*
Joseph J. Leon, *California State Polytechnic University, Pomona*
Seymour Leventman, *Boston College*
Wendy Ng, *San Jose State University*
Carol Poll, *Fashion Institute of Technology*
Dennis Rome, *Indiana University*
Gerald Rosen, *California State University, Fullerton*
Ellen Rosengarten, *Sinclair Community College*
A. Seals, *Kentucky State University*
Charles Smith, *Florida A&M*
Susan Takata, *University of Wisconsin, Parkside*
Joyce Tang, *City University of New York, Queens College*
Maura I. Toro-Morn, *Illinois State University*
Diana Torrez, *University of Texas, Arlington*
Robert Williams, *Jackson State University*
Min Zhou, *University of California, Los Angeles*

SECOND EDITION REVIEWERS

JoAnn DeFiore, *University of Washington*
Linda Green, *Normandale Community College*
Jeremy Hein, *University of Wisconsin–Eau Claire*
David Matsuda, *Chabot College*
Victor M. Rodriguez, *Concordia University*
Craig Watkins, *University of Texas, Austin*
Norma Wilcox, *Wright State University*
Luis Zanartu, *Sacramento City College*
Min Zhou, *University of California, Los Angeles*

THIRD EDITION REVIEWERS

Rick Baldoz, *University of Hawaii, Manoa*
Jan Fiola, *Minnesota State University, Moorhead*
David Lopez, *California State University, Northridge*

Peggy Lovell, *University of Pittsburgh*
Gonzalo Santos, *California State University, Bakersfield*
Carol Ward, *Brigham Young University*

FOURTH EDITION REVIEWERS

Herman DeBose, *California State University, Northridge*
Abby Ferber, *University of Colorado, Colorado Springs*
Celestino Fernandez, *University of Arizona*
Samuel Leizear, *West Virginia University*
Gregory J. Rosenboom, *University of Nebraska/Nebraska Wesleyan University*
Peggy A. Shifflett, *Radford University*
Debbie Storrs, *University of Idaho*
Carol Ward, *Brigham Young University*
Norma Wilcox, *Wright State University*
Earl Wright, *University of Central Florida*

FIFTH EDITION REVIEWERS

Sharon Allen, *University of South Dakota*
Cathy Beighey, *Aims Community College*
Wendy H. Dishman, *Santa Monica College*
Bruce K. Friesen, *University of Tampa*
Susan E. Mannon, *Utah State University*
David McBride, *Pennsylvania State University*
Pam Brown Schachter, *Marymount College, Palos Verdes*
John Stone, *Boston University*
Merwyn L. Strate, *Purdue University*
Leigh A. Willis, *The University of Georgia*

SIXTH EDITION REVIEWERS

Tennille Allen, *Lewis University*
Steven L. Arxer, *University of Texas at Dallas*
Leslie Baker-Kimmons, *Chicago State University*
Melanie Deffendall, *Delgado Community College*
Sophia DeMasi, *Montgomery County Community College*
Creaig A. Dunton, *State University of New York, Plattsburgh*
Lisa A. Eargle, *Francis Marion University*

Kimberly H. Fortin, *Cayuga Community College*
Matasha L. Harris, *John Jay College of Criminal Justice*
C. Douglas Johnson, *Georgia Gwinnett College*
Chris Keegan, *State University of New York at Oneonta*
Janice Kelly, *Molloy College*
Patricia E. Literte, *California State University, Fullerton*
Marci B. Littlefield, *Indiana University-Purdue University*
Teri Moran, *Jackson Community College*
Gerald D. Titchener, *Des Moines Area Community College*
Deidre Ann Tyler, *Salt Lake Community College/The University of Utah*
Elsa Valdez, *California State University, San Bernardino*
Margaret A. M. Vaughan, *Metropolitan State University*
Elijah G. Ward, *Saint Xavier University*
Kathy Westman, *Waubonsee Community College*

SEVENTH EDITION REVIEWERS

Walter F. Carroll, *Bridgewater State University*
Wendy Dishman, *Santa Monica College*

Ramon Guerra, *University of Texas–Pan American*
Jason Hale, *Montclair State University*
Gina Logan, *Norwich University*
Yvonne Merchen Moody, *Chadron State College*
Lisa Speicher Muñoz, *Hawkeye Community College*
Deena Shehata, *Western International University*
Deidre Tyler, *Salt Lake Community College*
Judith Ann Warner, *Texas A&M International University*
Kathleen Westman, *Waubonsee Community College*

EIGHTH EDITION REVIEWERS

Joyce Altobelli, *Western Technical College*
Maria Aysa-Lastra, *Winthrop University*
Robert L. Dahlgren, *SUNY Fredonia*
Jo Beth DeSoto, *Wayland Baptist University*
Elsa Dias, *Metro State University at Denver*
Christopher Gullen, *Westfield State University*
Rose Suggett, *Southeast Community College–Lincoln, NE*
Pelgy Vaz, *Fort Hays State University*

ABOUT THE AUTHORS

Joseph F. Healey is Professor Emeritus of Sociology at Christopher Newport University in Virginia. He received his BA and MA from the College of William and Mary and his PhD in sociology and anthropology from the University of Virginia. An innovative and experienced teacher of numerous race and ethnicity courses, he has written articles on minority groups, the sociology of sport, social movements, and violence, and he is also the author of *Statistics: A Tool for Social Research* (11th ed., 2016).

Andi Stepnick is Professor of Sociology at Belmont University in Tennessee. She earned her PhD from Florida State University. In addition to other publications, she coedited *Disrupting the Culture of Silence: Confronting Gender Inequality and Making Change in Higher Education* (with Kris De Welde, 2014), which CHOICE named an Outstanding Academic Title in 2015. She earned Belmont University's Presidential Faculty Achievement Award for

significant contributions to students' intellectual, personal, and professional needs and was named its 2015 Simmons Distinguished Lecturer for excellence in teaching and scholarship.

Eileen O'Brien is Associate Professor of Sociology at Saint Leo University's Virginia campus. Her BA, MA, and PhD degrees, all in sociology, are from the College of William and Mary, Ohio State University, and University of Florida, respectively. Her books include *Whites Confront Racism: Antiracists and their Paths to Action* (2001); *White Men on Race: Power, Privilege and the Shaping of Cultural Consciousness* (with Joe Feagin, 2003); and *The Racial Middle: Latinos and Asian Americans Living Beyond the Racial Divide* (2008). She has published several pieces on race and hip hop with Dr. Ninochka McTaggart (including a *Sociological Inquiry* article), and they have a forthcoming title on white privilege together with Cognella Press.

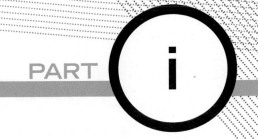

AN INTRODUCTION TO THE STUDY OF MINORITY GROUPS IN THE UNITED STATES

The United States is a nation of groups as well as individuals. These groups vary in many ways, including their size, wealth, education, race, culture, religion, and language. Some groups have been part of U.S. society since colonial days while others have formed fairly recently.

Questions of unity and diversity are among the most pressing issues facing the United States. How should groups relate to one another? Should we preserve the many cultural heritages and languages that currently exist and embrace our diversity? Should we encourage everyone to adopt Anglo-American culture and strive to become more similar? Who should be considered American?

We begin to address these issues in Chapters 1 and 2. Our goal throughout the text is to help you develop a broader, more informed understanding of the past and present forces that have created and sustained the groups that make up U.S. society.

Chapter 3 addresses prejudice and discrimination—feelings, attitudes, and actions that help maintain and reinforce the dividing lines that separate us into groups. How and why do these negative feelings, attitudes, and actions develop? How are prejudice and discrimination related to inequality and competition between groups? How can we reduce or eliminate them?

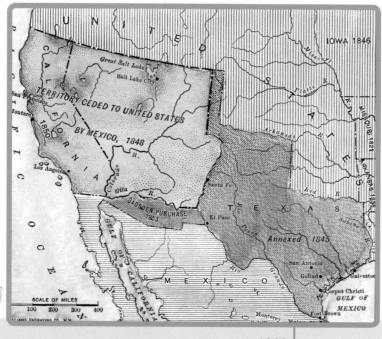

timeline

1790
The first naturalization law passes, restricting immigration to "free white persons" and excluding American Indians, indentured servants, slaves, free blacks, and Asians.

1848
Treaty of Guadalupe Hidalgo expands the U.S. borders to the Pacific. Mexican residents are given the option of declaring U.S. or Mexican citizenship.

1868
Fourteenth Amendment grants citizenship to African Americans born in the U.S.

1924
Johnson-Reed Act creates annual immigration quotas to limit the numbers of immigrants from Eastern Europe, the Mediterranean, and Asia.

1790   1820   1835   1865   1880   1925

1798
Alien and Sedition Acts allow for the deportation of "dangerous aliens."

1819
First federal immigration legislation requires reporting of all entries.

1830
Indian Removal Act leads to the deportation of 100,000 Native Americans to west of the Mississippi.

1882
Chinese Exclusion Act prohibits entry of Chinese immigrants for 10 years.

Who am I? . . . Where do I fit into American society? . . . For most of my 47 years, I have struggled to find answers to these questions. I am an American of multiracial descent and culture [Native American, African American, Italian American, and Puerto Rican]. In this aspect, I am not very different from many Americans [but] I have always felt an urge to feel and live the intermingling of blood that runs through my veins. American society has a way of forcing multiracial and biracial people to choose one race over the other. I personally feel this pressure every time I have to complete an application form with instructions to check just one box for race category.

—Butch, a 47-year-old man[1]

Actually, I don't feel comfortable being around Asians except for my family . . . I couldn't relate to . . . other Asians [because] they grew up in [wealthier neighborhoods]. I couldn't relate

[1] Schwartzbaum, Sara E., and Anita J. Thomas. 2008. *Dimensions of Multicultural Counseling: A Life Story Approach*. Thousand Oaks, CA: SAGE, p. 92.

LEARNING OBJECTIVES

By the end of this chapter, you will be able to:

1.1 Explain the increasing racial and ethnic diversity of the United States.

1.2 Understand the concept of a minority group.

1.3 Explain the sociological perspectives that will guide this text, especially as they relate to the relationships between inequality and minority-group status.

1.4 Explain how race and gender contribute to minority-group status.

1.5 Comprehend four of the key concepts in dominant–minority relations: prejudice, discrimination, ideological racism, and institutional discrimination.

1.6 Apply a global perspective to the relationship between globalization and immigration to the United States.

LOC

1952
The Immigration and Nationality Act establishes limited quotas for Asian countries and other areas from which immigrants had been excluded.

1986
The Immigration Reform and Control Act provides a method for undocumented aliens to legalize their status.

2002
Terrorist attacks on September 11, 2001, led to the Border Security and Visa Entry Reform Act. In addition to adding Border Patrol agents, schools must report foreign students.

2012
Deferred Action for Childhood Arrivals (DACA) protects people who entered the U.S. as undocumented minors for deportation.

1940   1955   1985   2000   2010   2015   2020

1942
The Bracero Program begins, allowing Mexican citizens to work temporarily in the United States as a source of low-cost labor. The program ends in 1964.

1990
Immigration Act of 1990 increases the diversity of the immigrant flow by admitting immigrants from underrepresented countries.

2008
Barack Obama is the first African American to be elected president.

2016
Donald Trump is elected president after campaigning to "Build a Wall" on the U.S-Mexico border and crack down on immigration.

1996
Illegal Immigration Reform and Immigrant Responsibility Act creates more stringent immigration laws pertaining to admission and deportation.

Wikimedia

Wikimedia

Public domain/NA

to the whole "I live in a mansion" [attitude]. This summer, I worked in a media company and it was kind of hard to relate to them [other Asians] because we all grew up in a different place . . . the look I would get when I say "Yeah, I'm from [a less affluent neighborhood]" they're like, "Oh, Oh," like, "That's unfortunate for your parents, I'm sorry they didn't make it."

—Rebecca, a 19-year-old
Macanese-Chinese-Portuguese woman[2]

Yeah, my people came from all over—Italy, Ireland, Poland, and others too. I don't really know when they got here or why they came and, really, it doesn't matter much to me. I mean, I'm just an American . . . I'm from everywhere . . . I'm from here!

—Jennifer, a 25-year-old
white American woman[3]

What do the people in the chapter opening have in common? How do they differ? They think about their place in U.S. society in very different ways. All are connected to a multitude of groups and traditions but not all find this fact interesting or important. One feels alienated from the more affluent members of her group, one seeks to embrace his multiple memberships, and one dismisses the issue of ancestry as irrelevant and is comfortable being "just an American."

Today, the United States is becoming more diverse in culture, race, religion, language, and other ways. The number of Americans who can connect themselves to diverse cultural traditions is increasing, as is the number of Americans of mixed race. Where will this lead us? Will increasing diversity lead to greater tolerance and respect for one another? Can we overcome the legacies of racism and inequality that stretch back to colonial days? Will we fragment along these lines of difference and dissolve into warring ethnic enclaves (the fate of more than one modern, apparently unified nation)?

This text raises a multitude of questions about the past, present, and future of group relationships in U.S. society. What historical, social, political, and economic forces shaped those relationships in the past? How do racial and ethnic groups relate to each other today? What kind of society are we becoming because of immigration? What kind of society can we become? What is an American? •

---

[2] O'Brien, Eileen. 2008. *The Racial Middle: Latinos and Asian Americans Living Beyond the Racial Divide.* New York: New York University Press, p. 45.

[3] Personal communication, June 2009.

The United States is a nation of immigrants and groups. Today, about 13% of the U.S. population was born in some other nation. Some states (e.g., California) are more than 25% foreign-born, and some cities (e.g., New York) are more than 35% foreign-born. Since the infancy of our society Americans have been arguing, often passionately, about inclusion and exclusion and about unity and diversity. Every member of our society is, in some sense, an immigrant or the descendant of immigrants. Even American Indians migrated to this continent, albeit thousands of years ago. We are all from somewhere else, with roots in other parts of the world. Some Americans came here in chains; others came on ocean liners, on planes, busses, and even on foot. Some arrived last week, while others have had family here for centuries. Each wave of newcomers has altered the social landscape of the United States. As many have observed, our society is continually being created.

Today, the United States is remaking itself yet again. Large numbers of immigrants are arriving from all over the world, and their presence has raised questions about who belongs, what it means to be an American, who should be granted U.S. citizenship, and how much diversity is best for society. How do immigrants affect the United States? Are they bringing new energy and revitalizing the economy? Are they draining resources such as school budget, health care, and jobs? How do they affect African Americans, Native Americans, and other groups? Are they changing what it means to be an American? If so, how?

In 2008, Americans elected Barack Obama to become our nation's first African American president. To some, this victory suggested that the United States has finally become what people often claim it to be: a truly open, "color-blind" society where one succeeds based on merit. In 2016, Americans elected Donald Trump to the presidency. Some see the rise of racist and xenophobic speech and actions that emerged during our most recent election season as a kind of backlash—not just against Democrats or the political system, but against diversity initiatives that expanded under the Obama administration.

Even as we debate the implications of immigration, other long-standing issues about belonging, fairness, and justice remain unresolved. American Indians and African Americans have been a part of this society since its start, but they have existed largely as outsiders—as slaves, servants, laborers, or even enemies—to the mainstream, dominant group. In many ways, they have not been treated as "true Americans" or full citizens, either by law or custom. The legacies of racism and exclusion continue to affect these groups today and, as you'll see in the chapters to come, they and other American minority groups continue to suffer from inequality, discrimination, and marginalization.

Even a casual glance at our schools, courts, neighborhoods, churches, corporate boardrooms—indeed, at any nook or cranny of our society—reveals pervasive patterns of inequality, injustice, and unfairness and different opportunities. So, which is the "real" America: the land of acceptance and opportunity or the one of insularity and inequity?

Some of us feel intensely connected to people with similar backgrounds and identify closely with a specific heritage. Others embrace multiracial or multi-ethnic identities. Some people feel no particular connection with any group or homeland. Others are unsure where they fit in the social landscape. Still, elements of our identity influence our lives and perceptions. The groups to which we belong affect our understanding of many social and political issues. Group membership including our race or ethnicity, class, and sexual orientation shape how we think about U.S. society, the world, and ourselves. Additionally, group membership shapes the opportunities available to us and to others in our society.

How do we understand these contrasts and divisions? Should we celebrate our diversity or stress the need for similarity? How can we incorporate all groups while avoiding fragmentation and division? What can hold us together as a nation? The United States may be at a crossroads. Throughout this book, you have an opportunity to reexamine the fundamental questions of citizenship and inclusion in our society. This chapter reviews the basic themes to help you do that effectively.

New Americans celebrating at a naturalization ceremony.

Department of Labor/Wikimedia

SOME AMERICAN STORIES

To illustrate the range of these group memberships, consider each person described in the following paragraphs. They represent millions of other people, and each exemplifies part of what it means to be an American.

• *Kim Park* is a 24-year-old immigrant from Korea. He arrived in New York City three years ago to work in his uncle's grocery store. Kim typically works a 12-hour shift, six days a week. His regular duties include stocking and cleaning, but he operates the register when necessary and is learning how to do the bookkeeping. Instead of wages, Kim receives room and board and some spending money.

Kim is outgoing and gregarious. His English is improving, and he practices it whenever possible. He has twice enrolled in English language classes, but the demands of his job prevented him from completing the courses.

Eventually, Kim wants to become a U.S. citizen, bring his siblings to America, get married and start a family, and manage the store when his uncle retires.

Over the years, many different minority groups have called Kim's neighborhood home. As recently as the 1950s, the area was almost exclusively Jewish. The Jewish residents have since died or moved, and were replaced by African Americans and different Hispanic and Asian groups. Today, the neighborhood continues to change.

• One of Kim's regular customers is *Juan Yancy*, who is about Kim's age. Juan works in maintenance at a downtown hotel. Since the unemployment rate in the neighborhood is high, he considers himself lucky to have a job. Despite Kim's halting English, the two men usually exchange greetings and neighborhood news when Juan shops at the grocery store.

Juan's mother is Puerto Rican. His father is Filipino and African American. In terms of ethnicity, Juan thinks of himself mostly as Puerto Rican but he also identifies with his father's ancestry. He resents the pressure from the larger society—on employment applications and other administrative forms, for example—to choose a single group membership.

• Juan lives in the apartment building where *Shirley Umphlett*, an African American, spent much of her childhood. In the 1920s, Shirley's family moved from Alabama to New York in search of work. Her grandfather and father were construction workers, but because most labor unions and employers were "white-only," they had no access to the better paying, more stable jobs and were often unemployed. Shirley's mother worked as a house cleaner to help meet family expenses. Shirley did well in school, attended college on scholarship, and is now a successful executive with a multinational corporation. She is in her 40s, married, and has two children. She is committed to helping other African

Americans and poor Americans, in general. She volunteers in several community action programs and maintain memberships in three national organizations that represent and serve African Americans.

- Shirley's commitment to service is partly a response to the fate of her nephew, *Dennard Umphlett*. When he was 16, Dennard was convicted of possession of crack cocaine with intent to distribute and was sentenced to a prison term of 20 years to life. Now, at age 22, he languishes in prison. He can't imagine spending another 14 more years—or longer—in prison. Dennard is losing all hope for life, but hangs on because of support from Shirley and a few other family members.

- Shirley's two children attend public school. One of their teachers is *Mary Farrell*, a fourth-generation Irish Catholic. Mary's great-grandparents came to New York as young adults in the 1880s. Her great-grandfather found work on the docks, and her great-grandmother worked as a housekeeper before marrying. They had seven children and 23 grandchildren, and Mary has more than 50 cousins living within an hour of New York City. Each generation of Mary's family tended to do a little better educationally and occupationally. Mary's father was a firefighter, and her sister is a lawyer.

Several years ago, Mary's relations with her family were severely strained when she told them that she was a lesbian and would be moving in with her long-time partner, Sandra. Mary's parents, traditional Catholics, found it difficult to accept her sexual orientation, as did many of her other relatives. She brought Sandra to several family gatherings, but they both found the tension too unpleasant to bear. Mary now either attends family events alone or skips them altogether. While she has been open with her family (much to their discomfort), she mostly stays "in the closet" at work, fearing the potential repercussions from parents and administrators. Still, she and Sandra are planning to marry soon.

- *George Snyder* was one of Mary's fourth-grade students. He is a young Native American born on a reservation in upstate New York, but his family moved to the city when he was a baby, driven away by the high unemployment rate. Mary kept in touch with George's family after he left elementary school. George and his parents stopped by occasionally to visit Mary. Then, when George reached high school, he became rebellious and his grades began to slip. He was arrested for shoplifting and never finished school. The last time they met, Mary tried to persuade him to pursue a GED, but she got nowhere with him. She pointed out that he was still young and there were many things he could do in the future. He responded, "What's the use? I'm an Indian with a record—I've got no future."

- George's parole officer is *Hector Gonzalez*. Hector's parents came to the United States from Mexico. Every year, they crossed the border to join the stream of agricultural migrant laborers and then returned to their village in Mexico at the end of the season. With the help of a cousin, Hector's father eventually got a job as a cabdriver in New York City, where Hector was raised. Hector's mother never learned much English but worked occasionally in a garment factory in her neighborhood.

With the help of his parents, Hector worked his way through college in seven years, becoming the first member of his family to earn a bachelor's degree. Hector thinks of himself as American but is interested in his parents' home village back in Mexico, where most of his extended family still lives. Hector is bilingual and has visited the village several times. His grandmother still lives there, and he calls her once a month.

Hector is married and has a child. He and his wife are very close and often refer to each other as "best friends." Hector is bisexual and has had relationships with men in the past, a fact that his wife accepts but that he keeps hidden from his parents and grandmother.

- Hector regularly eats lunch at a restaurant around the corner from his office. Two of the three managers of the restaurant are white, most of the servers are black, and the kitchen workers are Latino. One of the kitchen helpers who often clears Hector's table, *Ricardo Aldana*, is in the country illegally. He left his home village in Guatemala five years ago, traveled the length of Mexico on freight trains and on foot, and crossed the border in Texas. He lives in a tiny apartment with five others and sends 40% of his wages to his family in Guatemala. He enjoys living in the United States but is not particularly interested in legalizing his status. His most fervent wish is to go home, get married, and start a family.

- The restaurant is in a building owned by a corporation headed by *William Buford III*, a white American. William invests the bulk of his fortune in real estate and owns land and buildings throughout the New York metropolitan area. The Bufords have a three-story luxury townhouse in Manhattan but rarely go into town, preferring to spend their time on their rural Connecticut estate. William attended the finest private schools and graduated from Harvard University. At age 57, he is semiretired, plays golf twice a week, vacations in Europe, and employs a staff of five to care for himself and his family. He was raised a Mormon but is not religious and has little interest in the history of his family.

These individuals belong to groups that vary along some of the most consequential dimensions within our society—ethnicity, race, immigration status, social class, sexual orientation, gender, and religion—and their lives have been shaped by these affiliations (some more than others, of course). Some of these statuses (such as William's membership in the upper class) are privileged and envied, while others (e.g., Ricardo's undocumented status) are disadvantaged and can evoke rejection and contempt from others.

Each person's statuses are mixed. For example, in spite of his elite status, William has occasionally felt the sting of rejection because of his Mormon background. Dennard and George rank low on race and class but enjoy some of the advantages of being a man, while Mary's chances for upward mobility in the school system are reduced by her gender and sexual orientation. Each of these individuals is privileged in some ways and limited in others—as are we all.

Finally, note that each of our group memberships can affect how we perceive others, our opportunities, the way we think about ourselves, and our view of American society and the larger world. They affect our perception of what it means to be American.

QUESTIONS FOR REFLECTION

1. Clearly, William—the wealthy, white real-estate mogul—is the highest-ranking person in this group. How would you rank the others from high to low? Which would weigh more in such a ranking: class, gender, sexual orientation, or race and ethnicity?

2. Taking your own gender, sexual orientation, racial and ethnic background, and social class into account, where would you rank yourself relative to these nine people? At this stage of your life, are you more "privileged" or more "disadvantaged"? Would you rank yourself higher or lower than your parents and grandparents and why?

MINORITY GROUPS: TRENDS AND QUESTIONS

The group memberships discussed in the previous section can shape the choices we make in the voting booth and in other areas of social life. Members of different groups will evaluate these decisions in different ways due to their divergent experiences, group histories, and present situations. The debates over which direction our society should take are unlikely to be meaningful or even mutually intelligible without some understanding of the variety of ways someone can be an American.

INCREASING DIVERSITY

The choices about our society's future are especially urgent because the diversity of U.S. society is increasing dramatically,

largely due to high rates of immigration. Since the 1960s, the number of immigrants arriving in the United States each year has more than tripled and includes groups from all over the globe.

People's concerns about increasing diversity are compounded by other unresolved issues and grievances. For example, charts and graphs in Part 3 of this text document continuing gaps in income, poverty rates, and other measures of affluence and equality between minority and dominant groups. In fact, in many ways, the problems of African Americans, American Indians, Hispanic Americans, and Asian Americans today are just as formidable as they were a generation (or more) ago. How can our society successfully incorporate people from diverse cultures?

To gauge the dimensions of diversity in our nation, consider the changing makeup of U.S. society. Figure 1.1 presents the percentage of the total U.S. population in each of five largest groups. First, we will consider this information "on its face" and analyze some of its implications. Then, we will consider (and question) the framing of this information.

The figure reports the relative sizes of the groups from 1980 through 2010 and it offers the projected relative sizes of each group through 2060. The declining numbers of non-Hispanic whites reflect increasing diversity in the United States. As recently as 1980, more than 8 out of 10 Americans were non-Hispanic whites but, by the middle of this century, non-Hispanic whites will become a numerical minority. Several states (Texas, California, Hawaii, and New Mexico) already have "majority-minority" populations. And for the first time in history, most babies born in the United States (50.4%) are members of minority groups (U.S. Census Bureau, 2012a).

African Americans and Native Americans will grow in absolute numbers but are projected to remain about the

FIGURE 1.1 The U.S. Population by Race and Ethnicity, 1980–2060 (Projected)

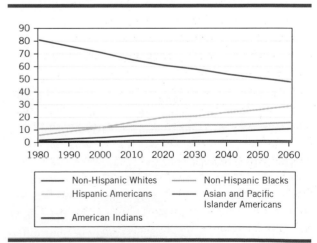

SOURCE: U.S. Bureau of the Census (2015a).

NOTE: "Hispanics" may be of any race.

same in terms of relative size. Hispanic American, Asian American, and Pacific Islander populations, on the other hand, will grow dramatically. Asian American and Pacific Islander groups together constituted only 2% of the population in 1980, but that will grow to 10% by midcentury. The most dramatic growth, however, will be among Hispanic Americans. This group became the largest minority group in 2002, surpassing blacks, and is projected to make up almost 30% of the U.S. population by 2060.

Projections about the future are just educated guesses based on documented trends; but, they suggest profound change. Our society will grow more diverse racially and culturally, becoming less white and less European, and more like the world as a whole. Some people see these changes as threats to "traditional" white, middle-class American values and lifestyles. Other people view them as an opportunity for other equally legitimate value systems and lifestyles to emerge. Which of these viewpoints are most in line with your own and why?

WHAT'S IN A NAME?

Let's take a moment to reflect on the categories used in Figure 1.1. The group names we used are arbitrary, and none of these groups have clear or definite boundaries. We use these terms because they are familiar and consistent with the labels used in census reports, much of the sociological research literature, and other sources of information. So, while such group names are convenient, this does not mean that they are "real" in any absolute sense or equally useful in all circumstances. In fact, these group names have some serious shortcomings. For example, group labels reflect social conventions whose meanings change from time to time and place to place. To underscore the *social construction* of racial and ethnic groups, we use group names interchangeably (e.g., blacks and African Americans; Hispanic Americans and Latinos). Further issues remain.

First, the race/ethnic labels suggest groups are largely homogeneous. However, while it's true that people within one group may share some general, superficial physical or cultural traits (e.g., language spoken), they also vary by social class, religion, gender, sexual orientation, and in many other ways. People within the Asian American and Pacific Islander group, for example, represent scores of different national backgrounds (Japanese, Pakistanis, Samoans, Vietnamese, and so forth), and the category "American Indian or Alaska Native" includes people from hundreds of different tribal groups. If we consider people's other social statuses such as age and religious affiliation, that diversity becomes even more pronounced. Any two people *within* one of these groups (e.g., Hispanics) might be quite different from each other in some respects while being similar to people from "different" racial/ethnic groups (e.g., whites).

QUESTIONS FOR REFLECTION

3. Savannah is a white, 27-year-old woman who was raised in Georgia but now lives in South Dakota. She is an Episcopalian, has a degree in computer science, and makes $60,000 a year. She is married to Tom, her "college sweetheart." Winona is a 40-year-old woman and a member of the Lakota nation. She was raised in South Dakota, but moved to California to pursue her career as a pharmacist. She is married to Robert and they have one child. Although the census would classify Savannah and Winona as belonging to different racial/ethnic groups, they are similar in many ways. In what ways are their similarities more significant than their differences?

Second, people do not necessarily use these labels when they think about their own identity. In this sense, the labels are not "real" or important for all the people in these racial/ethnic groups. For example, many whites in the United States (like William Buford, mentioned in the "Some American Stories" part of this chapter) think of themselves as "just American." A Hispanic American (like Hector Gonzalez or Juan Yancy) may think of themselves more in national terms, as Mexicans or Cubans or, even more specifically, they may identify with a particular region or village in their homeland. Gay or lesbian members within these groups may identify themselves more in terms of their sexual orientation than their race or ethnicity. Thus, the labels do not always reflect the ways people think about themselves, their families, or where they come from. The categories are statistical classifications created by researchers and census takers to help them organize information and clarify their analyses. They do not grow out of or always reflect the everyday realities of the people who happen to be in them.

Third, even though the categories in Figure 1.1 are broad, several groups don't neatly fit into them. For example, where should we place Arab Americans and recent immigrants from Africa? These groups are relatively small (about 1 million people each), but there is no clear place for them in the current categories. Should Arab Americans be included as "Asian," as some argue? Should recent immigrants from Africa be placed in the same category as African Americans? Should there be a new group such as Middle Eastern or North African descent (MENA)? Of course, we don't need to have a category for every person, but we should recognize that classification schemes like the one used in Figure 1.1 (and in many other contexts) have boundaries that can be somewhat ambiguous.

A related problem with this classification scheme will become increasingly apparent in the years to come: there is no category for the growing number of people who (like Juan Yancy) are members of more than one racial or ethnic group. The number of "mixed-group" Americans is relatively small today, about 3% of the total population (U.S. Bureau of the Census, 2015a). However, the number of people who chose more than one racial or ethnic category on the U.S. Census to describe themselves increased by 32% (from 2.4% to 2.9% of the total population) between 2000 and 2010 (Jones & Bullock, 2012) and is likely to continue to increase rapidly because of the growing number of marriages across group lines.

To illustrate, Figure 1.2 shows dramatic increases in the percentage of "new" marriages (couples that got married in the year prior to the survey date) and all marriages that unite members of different racial or ethnic groups (Livingston & Brown, 2017). Obviously, the greater the number of mixed (racial or ethnic) marriages, the greater the number of "mixed" Americans. One study estimates that the percentage of Americans who identify with "two or more races" will more than double between 2014 (when it was 2.5%) and 2060 (when it will be 6.2%) (Colby & Ortman, 2015, p. 9).

Finally, we should note that these categories and group names are **social constructions**,[4] created in particular historical circumstances and reflective of particular power relationships. For example, the group called "American Indians" today didn't exist prior to the period of European exploration and colonization of North America. Before the arrival of Europeans, hundreds of separate indigenous societies lived across the North American continent, each with its own language and culture. American Indians thought of themselves

---

Social constructions are perceptions shared by a group. These perceptions become real for the people who share them.

FIGURE 1.2 Interracial and Interethnic Marriages in the United States, 1967–2015

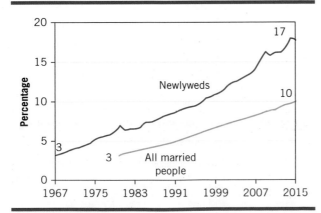

SOURCE: Livingston and Brown, 2017.

---

[4]The boldface terms in the text are defined in the glossary at the end of the book.

primarily in terms of their tribe and had little or no awareness of the other groups spread across the vast expanse of the North American continent. However, European conquerors constructed them as one group that was similar: the enemy. The fact that people today often view Native Americans as a single group reflects their historical defeat and subordination by white European colonists. This outcome led to their status as a minority group in a largely white society.

In the same way (although through different processes), African, Hispanic, and Asian Americans came to be seen as separate groups as the result of an unequal interaction with white Americans. These groups have become "real" because they are seen as real from a particular perspective—that of the dominant group in U.S. society: white Americans. We use these familiar group labels to facilitate our discussion of complex topics throughout this book (e.g., see the chapter titles in Part 3), rather than as a reflection of some unchangeable "truth" or reality regarding racial or ethnic groups.

QUESTIONS FOR REFLECTION

4. If you were asked for your group membership, which of the groups listed in Figure 1.1 (if any) would you choose? Do you feel that you belong to just one group or several? How important are these groups in your self-image? Do you think your group membership affects your view of the world or shapes your circle of friends? Explain your answers.

5. Over the past 5 to 10 years, what signs of increasing diversity have you seen in your home community or high school? How has increasing diversity enriched everyday life in these areas? What problems or issues have arisen from rising diversity?

QUESTIONS ABOUT THE FUTURE, SOCIOLOGY, AND THE PLAN OF THIS BOOK

Although the labels in Figure 1.1 reflect social constructions, the trends displayed there have important implications for the future of the United States. What kind of society are we becoming? What does it mean to be American? At its inception, the law only recognized white Anglo-Saxon Protestant men of elite classes as full citizens with specific rights (e.g., voting) and opportunities for success (e.g., college education). As our nation has changed, others have gained access to those rights and opportunities, at least to some degree. Given the changing U.S. population, how inclusive should the definition of an "American"

On Being American

Carla, now in her 20s, is the adopted daughter of an affluent white family. She grew up in the suburbs and enjoyed a comfortable middle-class lifestyle. She has never met her birth parents but knows that her biological mother was Korean American, and just 16 years old at the time of her birth. She knows nothing about her birth father. Carla is beginning to reconcile herself to how most Americans perceive her.

For much of her life, Carla has felt caught between her biological heritage and that of her adopted family. She often hesitates when people ask about her family or where she is from. Is she Asian American, in the terms of the U.S. Census (Figure 1.1)? Or, should she identify herself to people (or when she fills out employment applications) as "non-Hispanic white" because the only lifestyle she has ever known is white, suburban, middle class? For her, the social construction of race is very real and, at the same time, false.

Here is part of what she has to say about her identity:

When I was growing up, my parents would try to teach me about my Korean heritage. We would read books about Korean history and culture, my mom learned to prepare some Korean dishes, and we even discussed taking a trip to Korea—but never did. Looking back, I really appreciate what they were trying to do, but it all felt foreign to me, you know? Like we were discussing Bolivia or Kenya . . .

But then, someone would make assumptions about me based on my looks. They would think that I was good at math or nerdy or couldn't speak English. I can't tell you how many times someone has asked me, "Where are you from?" When I said, "I'm from here," most people wouldn't believe me and would ask, "No, where are you *really* from?"

Sometimes I tried to "be Korean" and even attended some meetings of the Asian Student Association when I was in school, but it felt wrong—it just wasn't me. But then, something would happen. . . . Like one time I was just walking through the mall, and some old white guy came up and said, out of the clear blue sky, "You people are ruining this country!" I mean, who did he think I was?

So, yeah, it took a long time to make peace with who I am and how others perceive me. But, now I think that I'm just me, you know? People can look at me one way and put me in all those different categories, but that's their problem. It's not who I am. It's not me!

SOURCE: Personal communication to the authors. Carla's name and exact circumstances have been fictionalized to preserve her privacy.

Questions to Consider

1. Is Carla's confusion about her identity a result of her social and physical characteristics? Or, does is it result from how other people see her? Explain.
2. How might Carla's situation change if she were a man? What if her birth mother were Hispanic or black?

---

be? Who "counts"? At what point, could diversity threaten societal cohesion? Could narrow definitions of what it means to be an American unjustly and unnecessarily stifle cultural diversity? Should our nation stress unity or celebrate diversity? Can we do both?

We've raised a lot of complex questions in these first few pages. The answers are not obvious or easy to come by. Indeed, there is no guarantee that we, as a society, will be able or willing to resolve all the issues related to intergroup relations in the United States. However, we will never make progress unless we confront the issues honestly and with an accurate base of knowledge and understanding. Certainly, these issues will not resolve themselves or disappear if we ignore them. The purpose of this book is to help you develop thoughtful, informed positions on these issues.

In the course of our inquiry, we will rely on sociology and other social sciences for concepts, theories, and information to gain a greater understanding of the issues. The first three chapters introduce and define many of the ideas that will guide our investigation. Part 2 explores how relations between the dominant group and minority groups have evolved in American society. Part 3 analyzes the current situation of U.S. racial and ethnic minority groups. In Part 4, we examine group divisions based on gender and sexual orientation, and patterns of group relationships around the globe. In Part 5, the final section of the book, we explore many of the challenges and issues facing our society (and the world) and see what conclusions we can glean from our investigations and how they might shape the future.

WHAT IS A MINORITY GROUP?

A common vocabulary will help us understand and discuss the issues. We begin with the term **minority group**. The mathematical connotation of this term is a bit misleading because it implies that minority groups are small. In reality, a minority group can be quite large and can even be a numerical majority of the population. Women, for example,

---

A **minority group** experiences systematic disadvantage and has a visible identifying trait. The group is self-conscious, and membership is usually determined at birth. Members tend to form intimate relations within the group.

are sometimes considered a minority group, even though they are a numerical majority of the U.S. population. As in many nations created by European colonization whites are a numerical minority in South Africa, accounting for less than 10% of the population (Central Intelligence Agency, 2017). However, whites have been the most powerful and affluent group by far. Despite changes resulting from the end of Apartheid, whites retain their advantage in many ways (e.g., economically, politically). Therefore, we would consider them the majority group.

Minority status has more to do with the distribution of resources and power than with the size of the group. We use the definition of minority group developed by Wagley and Harris (1958) that emphasizes these characteristics:

1. The members of the group experience a pattern of *disadvantage or inequality*.
2. The members of the group share a *visible trait or characteristic* that differentiates them from other groups.
3. Minority-group members are aware that they share their status with other members of the group.
4. Membership in the group is usually *determined at birth*.
5. Members tend to *form intimate relationships* (close friendships, dating partnerships, and marriages) *within the group*.

We will briefly examine these five defining characteristics next. A bit later, we will return to examine the first two—inequality and visibility—in greater detail, because they are the most important characteristics of minority groups.

1. Inequality. The first and most important defining characteristic of a minority group is *inequality*—that is, some pattern of disadvantage. The degree of disadvantage varies over time and location and include such slight irritants as a lack of desks for left-handed students or a policy of racial or religious exclusion at an expensive country club. (Note, however, that you might not agree that the irritant is slight if you are a left-handed student awkwardly taking notes at a right-handed desk or if you are a golf aficionado who happens to be African American or Jewish American.) The most significant types of inequalities include exploitation, slavery, and **genocide** (the intentional killing of a group such as the mass execution of Jews, Slavs, Roma, gays and lesbians, and others under Nazi rule in Germany).

Whatever its scope or severity, whether it affects people's ability to gain jobs, housing, wealth, political power, police protection, health care, or other valued resources, the pattern of disadvantage is the key characteristic of a minority group. Because the group has less of what society values, some people refer to minority groups as *subordinate groups*.

The pattern of disadvantage members of the minority group experience results from the actions of another group that benefits from and tries to sustain the unequal arrangement. This core group is the **dominant group**. We use the latter term most frequently because it reflects the patterns of inequality and the power realities of minority-group status. Keep in mind that the inequalities we observe today were always established in the past, sometimes centuries ago or even longer. Privilege exists even when the beneficiaries are unaware of it.

2. Visibility. The second defining characteristic of a minority group is some *visible trait* or characteristic that sets members of the group apart and that the dominant group holds in low esteem. The trait can be cultural (language, religion, speech patterns, or dress styles), physical (skin color, stature, or facial features), or both. Groups defined primarily by their cultural characteristics such as Irish Americans and Jewish Americans are called **ethnic minority groups**. Groups defined primarily by their physical characteristics, such as African Americans and Americans Indians, are **racial minority groups**. These categories overlap. So-called ethnic groups may also have (or may be thought to have) distinguishing physical characteristics (e.g., the stereotypical Irish red hair or "Jewish nose"). Racial groups may also have (or are thought to have) cultural traits that differ from the dominant group (e.g., differences in dialect, religious values, or cuisine).

These distinguishing traits help identify minority-group members and separate people into distinct groups. Thus, they help to maintain the patterns of disadvantage. That is, the dominant group has (or at one time had) sufficient power to create the distinction between groups and thus solidify a higher position for itself. These markers of group membership are crucial. Without visible signs, it would be difficult or impossible to identify who was in which group, and the system of minority-group oppression would soon collapse.

It is important to realize that the characteristics marking the boundaries between groups usually are not significant in and of themselves. They are selected for their

---

Genocide is the deliberate attempt to exterminate an entire group.

A **dominant group** is the group that benefits from minority-group subordination.

Ethnic minority groups are distinguished by cultural traits.

Racial minority groups are distinguished by physical traits.

FIGURE 1.3 Do Black Americans Have the Same Chances as White Americans to Obtain the Same Level of Employment? 1963–2016

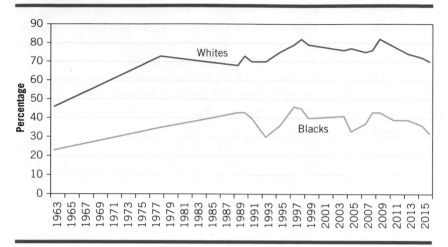

SOURCE: Gallup, 2017.

ACTUAL QUESTION: In general, do you think that black people have as good a chance as white people in your community to get any kind of job for which they are qualified, or do you think they do not have as good a chance?

visibility and convenience and, objectively, may be trivial and unimportant. For example, scientists now conclude that skin color and other so-called racial traits have little scientific, evolutionary, medical, or biological importance (Gannon, 2016; Yudell, Roberts, DeSalle, & Tishkoff, 2016). For example, darker skin color reflects the body's response to sunlight. In areas with greater sunlight (closer to the equator), people's bodies produce melanin to protect the skin. As we shall see in future chapters, skin color is an important marker of group membership in our society that emerged through a complex and lengthy historical process, not because it has any inherent significance. These markers of minority-group membership are social constructions that become important because people in a society attribute significance to them such as superiority or inferiority.

3. Awareness. A third characteristic of minority groups is that the members are aware of their differentiation from the dominant group and their shared disadvantage. This shared social status can provide the basis for strong intra-group bonds and a sense of solidarity, and can lead to views of the world that are markedly different from those of the dominant group and other minority groups. Minority and dominant groups can live in different cultural worlds. For example, public opinion polls frequently show sizeable differences between dominant and minority groups in their views of the seriousness and extent of discrimination in American society. Figure 1.3 shows persistent and size-able gaps in the percentage of nationally representative samples of whites and blacks who agree that blacks and whites have equal job opportunities. As would be expected, given their different histories, experiences, and locations in the social structure, black Americans have much more

negative views of racial equality. Even after the election of President Obama in 2008, the percentage of black Americans who perceived that racial opportunity was equal was about half the corresponding percentage of white Americans. Both groups have become more pessimistic about equal opportunity in recent years. A national Gallup poll conducted in 2016 showed just 71% of Americans believed black children have the same opportunity as white children to get a good education. This is the lowest percentage on record since Gallup began asking that question in 1962, less than a decade after the Supreme Court voted to desegregate public schools in *Brown v. the Board of Education* (1954). Just 70% believe black Americans have equal opportunities to get housing, which is the lowest rating on this question since 1989 (Jones, 2016).

4. Ascription. A fourth characteristic of minority groups is that, in general, membership is an **ascribed status** given to them, often at birth. The traits that identify minority-group membership are typically not easy to change. Thus, minority-group status is usually involuntary and for life.

In some cases—with "racial" minority groups, for example—this defining characteristic may seem obvious and hardly worth mentioning. Remember, however, that group labels are social constructions, based on particular historical circumstances and shared cultural perceptions. Thus, group membership can be negotiable and change-able, and a person's status at birth is not necessarily constant throughout his or her lifetime. A member of a racial minority may be able to "pass" as a member of a different group, and a member of a religious minority may be able to change status by changing his or her faith.

It's important to keep in mind the qualification that minority status is *generally* a matter of birth. There are important exceptions to the general rule and a great deal more ambiguity regarding group membership than may appear at first glance. Also, for some groups—gays and lesbians in particular—the notion of membership by ascription is debated. Some say homosexuality is inborn while others say it is learned. We will address this issue in Chapter 12.

An **ascribed status** is involuntary and usually acquired at birth.

5. Intimate Relationships. Finally, group members tend to *form emotionally close bonds with people like themselves.* That is, members tend to choose each other as close friends, dating partners, and partners (legal spouses or cohabitational partner). (Members of the dominant group do this, too.)

Pervasive racial and ethnic segregation of U.S. neighborhoods, schools, and other areas of social life influence who one meets or spends time with on a regular basis. In some cases, the dominant group dictates this pattern. For example, many states outlawed interracial marriages until the U.S. Supreme Court declared laws against **miscegenation** unconstitutional in 1967 in the case of *Loving v. Virginia* (Bell, 1992).

The Wagley and Harris (1958) multipart definition of a minority group encompasses "traditional" minority groups such as African Americans and American Indians, but can be applied to other groups. For instance, women as a group fit the first four criteria and can be analyzed with many of the same concepts and ideas that guide our analysis of other minority groups. Similarly, we can apply this concept to Americans who are gay, lesbian, bisexual, and transgender; to Americans who are differently abled; to Americans who are left-handed; to Americans who are very old, very short, very tall, or very obese. We will consider some of these groups in Part 4. For now, just note that the analyses developed in this book can be applied more broadly than you might realize at first. We hope this leads you to some fresh insights about a wide variety of groups and people.

QUESTIONS FOR REFLECTION

6. Consider one of the groups mentioned in the prior paragraph. Do they fit all five parts of this definition of minority groups? Why or why not?

PATTERNS OF INEQUALITY

As mentioned earlier, the most important defining characteristic of minority-group status is inequality. As we show in upcoming chapters, minority-group membership can affect access to jobs, education, wealth, health care, and housing. It is associated with a lower (often much lower) proportional share of goods and services and more limited (often much more limited) opportunities for upward mobility.

Miscegenation is marriage or sexual relations between members of racial groups that a society defines as different and unequal.

Stratification, or the unequal distribution of valued goods and services, is a feature of U.S. society. Every human society, except perhaps the simplest hunter-gatherer societies, is stratified to some degree. That is, society distributes its valued resources so that some people get more while others get less. We can visualize these divisions as horizontal layers (or strata) that differ from one another by the amount of resources they command. Economic stratification results in different **social classes**; Figure 1.4 shows one view of the American social class system. Many criteria (such as education, age, gender, and talent) may affect a person's social class position and his or her access to goods and services. Minority-group membership is one of these criteria, and it has a powerful impact on the distribution of resources in the United States and other societies.

The next section considers different theories about the nature and dimensions of stratification. Then, it focuses on how minority-group status relates to stratification.

THEORETICAL PERSPECTIVES

Sociology (and other social sciences such as economics, history, and political science) has been concerned with stratification and human inequality since the formation of the

FIGURE 1.4 Class in the United States (Gilbert–Kahn Model)

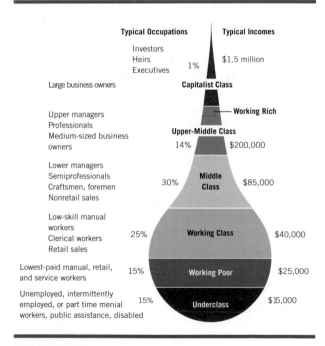

Typical Occupations		Typical Incomes
Investors Heirs Executives	1%	$1.5 million
Large business owners	**Capitalist Class**	
		Working Rich
Upper managers Professionals Medium-sized business owners	**Upper-Middle Class** 14%	$200,000
Lower managers Semiprofessionals Craftsmen, foremen Nonretail sales	30% **Middle Class**	$85,000
Low-skill manual workers Clerical workers Retail sales	25% **Working Class**	$40,000
Lowest-paid manual, retail, and service workers	15% **Working Poor**	$25,000
Unemployed, intermittently employed, or part time menial workers, public assistance, disabled	15% **Underclass**	$15,000

SOURCE: Gilbert, 2011.

Stratification is the system of unequal distribution of valued resources in society.

Social classes consist of people who have similar levels of access to valued goods and services.

Karl Marx (1818–1883) contributed to the founding of sociology and was one of the authors of the *Communist Manifesto*.

discipline in the 19th century. We highlight the work of four significant thinkers in this section. An early and important contributor to our understanding of the nature and significance of social inequality was Karl Marx, the noted social philosopher and revolutionary. Half a century later, sociologist Max Weber (pronounced Mahks Vay-ber), a central figure in the development of sociology, critiqued and elaborated on Marx's view of inequality. Gerhard Lenski was a modern sociologist whose ideas about the influence of economic and technological development on social stratification is relevant for comparing societies and understanding the evolution of intergroup relations. Finally, we consider another modern sociologist, Patricia Hill Collins, who argues for an intersectional approach to inequality. That is, we need to view inequalities based on class, race or ethnicity, gender (and so on) as a single, interlocking system of inequality.

Karl Marx. Although best known as the father of modern communism, Karl Marx was also the primary architect of a political, economic, and social philosophy that has played a major role in world affairs for more than 150 years. Marxism is a complex theory of history and social change in which inequality is a central concern.

Marx argued that the most important source of inequality in society was the system of economic production. He focused on the **means of production**, or the materials, tools, resources, and social relationships by which the society produces and distributes goods and services. In an industrial society, the means of production include factories, commercial enterprises, banks, and transportation systems, such as railroads.

In Marx's view, all societies include two main social classes that struggle over the means of production. In an industrial society, one class, the **bourgeoisie**, or capitalist class, owns or controls the means of production. It benefits from that arrangement and exploits and oppresses the **proletariat** or working class. Marx believed that conflict between these classes was inevitable and that, ultimately, the working class would successfully revolt against the bourgeoisie and create a society without exploitation, coercion, or inequality. In other words, it would create a classless society.

Scholars and others have extensively critiqued or modified Marx's ideas over the past century and a half. Still, modern social science owes a great deal to Marx's views on inequality and his insights on class struggle and social conflict. As you will see in later chapters, Marxism remains an important body of work and a rich source of insight concerning group relations in industrial society (Marx & Engels, 1848/1967).

Max Weber. One of Marx's major critics was Max Weber, a German sociologist who did most of his work around the turn of the 20th century. Weber thought that Marx's view of inequality was too narrow. Marx saw social class as a matter of economic position or relationship to the means of production, but Weber argued that inequality was more complex and included dimensions other than just the economic. Individuals could be members of the elite in some ways but not in others. For example, an aristocratic family that has fallen on hard financial times might belong to the elite in terms of family lineage and prestige but not in terms of wealth. Or, a major figure in the illegal drug trade could enjoy substantial wealth but be held in low esteem.

Weber expanded on Marx's view of inequality by identifying three separate stratification systems. First, economic inequality is based on ownership or control of wealth (such as property) and income (money from employment, interest on bank holdings, or other payments). This is similar to Marx's concept of class, and Weber used the term *class* to identify this form of inequality.

The **means of production** are the materials, resources, and social relationships by which society produces and distributes goods and services.

The **bourgeoisie** are the elite or ruling class that owns the means of production in an industrial society. The **proletariat** are the workers.

A second system of stratification revolves around differences in **prestige**, or the amount of honor, esteem, or respect given to us by others. Class position is one factor that affects the amount of prestige a person enjoys. Other factors that influence prestige include family lineage, athletic ability, and physical appearance. In the United States and other societies, the groups to which people belong affect prestige. Members of minority groups typically have less prestige than members of the dominant group. Thus, wealthy minority-group member might be ranked high on class, but low on prestige.

Weber's third stratification system is **power**, or the ability to influence others, impact the decision-making process of society, and pursue and protect one's self-interest and achieve one's goals. One source of power is a person's standing in politically active organizations, such as labor unions or pressure groups, that lobby state and federal legislatures. Some politically active groups have access to great wealth and can use their riches to promote their causes. Other groups may rely more on their size and ability to mobilize large demonstrations to achieve their goals. Political groups and the people they represent vary in their abilities to affect the political process and control decision making. That is, they vary in the power they can mobilize.

Typically, these three dimensions of stratification go together: wealthy, prestigious groups will be more powerful (more likely to achieve their goals or protect their self-interest) than low-income groups or groups with little prestige. However, power is a separate dimension: even very impoverished groups have sometimes found ways to express their concerns and pursue their goals.

Gerhard Lenski. Gerhard Lenski is a contemporary sociologist who expands on Weber's ideas by analyzing stratification in the context of societal evolution, or the **level of development** of a society (Nolan & Lenski, 2004). He argues that the degree of inequality or the criteria affecting a group's position is closely related to **subsistence technology**, the means by which the society satisfies basic needs such as hunger and thirst. For example, preindustrial agricultural societies rely on human and animal labor

Max Weber (1864–1920) was a major figure in the establishment of sociology. He took issue with many of Marx's ideas in publications such as *The Protestant Ethic* and *The Spirit of Capitalism*.

to generate the food necessary to sustain life. Inequality in these types of societies centers on control of land and labor because they are the most important means of production for that level of development.

In modern industrial societies, land ownership is not as crucial as control of financial, manufacturing, and commercial enterprises. Because the control of capital is more important than control of land for those societies, level of development, and the nature of inequality, would be different.

The United States and other societies have entered still another stage of development, often referred to as **postindustrial society**. In this type of society, developments in new technology, computer-related fields, information processing, and scientific research create economic growth. In postindustrial societies, economic success is closely related to specialized knowledge, familiarity with new technologies, and formal education (Chirot, 1994, p. 88; see also Bell, 1973).

Prestige is honor, esteem, or respect.

Power is the ability to affect the decision-making process of a social system.

The **level of development** is the stage of evolution of a society, including agrarian, industrial, and postindustrial.

A **subsistence technology** is the system by which a society satisfies basic needs.

A **postindustrial society** is dominated by service work, information processing, and high technology.

These changes in subsistence technology, from agriculture to industrialization to the "information society," alter the stratification system. As the sources of wealth, success, and power change, so do the relationships between minority and dominant groups. For example, the shift to an information-based, "high-tech," postindustrial society means that the advantages conferred by higher levels of education are magnified. Groups that have less access to schooling will likely rank low on all dimensions of stratification.

Patricia Hill Collins. Sociologist Patricia Hill Collins (2000) calls for an approach to the study of inequality and group relations that recognizes the multiplicity of systems of inequality and privilege that operate in society. Some stratification systems are based on social class, while others rank people by their gender, race, ethnicity, sexuality, age, disability, and other criteria. Most people have mixed statuses, some more privileged and some less privileged. For example, Hector, the Mexican American parole officer mentioned in the "American Stories" at the start of this chapter, is a college-educated man with a professional job. His gender and class (education and occupation) rank high in the United States. On the other hand, he is Mexican American and bisexual. These latter statuses put him at a disadvantage in a society where whiteness and heterosexuality are more valued.

Collins stresses **intersectionality**, a view that acknowledges that everyone—like Hector—has multiple group memberships and that these crisscross and create different experiences for people with varying combinations of statuses. The realities faced by gay, white-collar, Mexican American men are very different from those faced by heterosexual, blue-collar Puerto Rican women, even though both would be counted as "Hispanic" in Figure 1.1. From this perspective, you can see that no singular, uniform Hispanic American (or African American or Asian American) experience exists. Thus, we need to recognize how gender, class, sexual orientation, and other factors intersect with and reinforce one another.

Collins and other intersectional theorists critique the tendency to see inequality in terms of separate simple dichotomous systems, based on class (blue collar vs. white collar), race (black vs. white), gender (men vs. women), or some other criterion. An intersectional approach analyzes how these statuses link together and form a "matrix of domination." For example, white Americans are not a homogenous "dominant group." Some segments that this

Photo courtesy of Patricia Hill Collins

Patricia Hill Collins is a major contributor to the ongoing attempts by American social scientists to analyze inequality and group relations.

group, such as women or poor whites, occupy are privileged in terms of their race (white) but subordinate in terms of their gender (women) or class (poor). Who is the oppressed and who is the oppressor changes across social contexts, and people can occupy privileged and subordinated statuses simultaneously.

The separate systems of domination and subordination overlap and reinforce one another. This matrix of domination shapes people's opportunities, experiences, and their perceptions. As we'll see in later chapters, race and gender interact with each other and create especially disadvantaged positions for people who rank lower on both dimensions simultaneously (e.g., see Figure 6.5, which shows that black women consistently earn less income than either black men who share the same race and white women who share the same gender).

Likewise, stereotypes and other elements of prejudice are gendered. That is, they are attached to men or women, not to the entire group. For example, some stereotypical traits might be applied to all African Americans (such as laziness; see Figure 3.3), but others are applied only to women (e.g., the "welfare queen" or "mammy") or men (e.g., the "thug" or "buffoon").

Intersectionality stresses the linked inequalities in a society and the multiplicity of statuses all people occupy.

An intersectional approach stresses the multiplicity of the systems of inequality and analyzes the links among them. Groups are seen as differentiated and complex, not uniform. In this text, one of our main concerns will be to use an intersectional lens to explore how class and gender influence racial and ethnic minority-group experiences. However, you can apply an intersectional approach to other dimensions of power and inequality, including disability, sexual orientation, and religion.

MINORITY-GROUP STATUS AND STRATIFICATION

The theoretical perspectives we have just reviewed raise three important points about the connections between minority-group status and stratification. First, minority-group status affects access to wealth and income, prestige, and power. In the United States, minority-group status has been and continues to be one of the most important and powerful determinants of one's life chances, health, wealth, and success (e.g., education). We explore these complex patterns of inequality in Part 3, but observation of U.S. society will reveal that minority groups control proportionately fewer resources and that minority-group status and stratification are intimately and complexly intertwined. Second, although social class and minority-group status are correlated, they are different dimensions of inequality and they vary independently. The degree to which one status affects the other varies from group to group. Some groups, such as Irish or Italian Americans, have experienced considerable upward **social mobility** (or movement) within the class stratification system even though they faced considerable discrimination in the past. Furthermore, as stressed by the intersectional approach, each minority group is internally divided by systems of inequality based on class, status, or power. Some members of a minority group can be successful economically, wield great political power, or enjoy high prestige even though the vast majority of their group experiences poverty and powerlessness. Likewise, members of the same social class vary by ethnicity or race, gender, sexual orientation, and other social statuses.

Third, dominant–minority group relationships are created by struggle over the control of valued goods and services. Minority-group structures (such as slavery) emerge so that the dominant group can control commodities such as land or labor, maintain its position in the stratification system, or eliminate a perceived threat to its well-being. Struggles over property, wealth, prestige, and power lie at the heart of every dominant–minority relationship. Marx

---

Social mobility is movement up and down the stratification system.

---

believed that all aspects of society and culture were shaped to benefit the elite or ruling class and sustain the economic system that underlies its privileged position. The treatment of minority groups throughout American history provides a good deal of evidence to support Marx's point, as we'll see in upcoming chapters.

VISIBLE DISTINGUISHING TRAITS: RACE AND GENDER

In this section, we focus on the second defining characteristic of minority groups: the visible traits that represent membership. The boundaries between dominant and minority groups have been established along a wide variety of lines, including religion, language, skin color, and sexuality. Next, let's consider race and gender, two of the more physical and permanent—and thus more socially visible—markers of group membership.

RACE

In the past, race has been widely misunderstood, but the false ideas and exaggerated importance people have attached to race have not just been errors of logic that were subject to debate. At various times and places, ideas about race have resulted in some of the greatest tragedies in human history: immense exploitation and mistreatment, slavery, and genocide. Myths about race survive in the present though in diluted form. It is important to cultivate accurate understandings about race to decrease the likelihood of further tragedies.

Thanks to advances in the sciences of genetics, biology, and physical anthropology, we know more about what race is and, more important, what race is not. We cannot address all the confusion in these few pages, but we can establish a basic framework and use the latest scientific research to dispel some of the myths.

Race and Human Evolution. Our species first appeared in East Africa more than 160,000 years ago. Our ancient ancestors were hunters and gatherers who slowly wandered away from their ancestral region in search of food and other resources. Over the millennia, our ancestors traveled across the entire globe, first to what is now the Middle East and then to Asia, Europe, Australia, and North and South America (see Figure 1.6) (Gugliotta, 2008; Hirst, 2017).

"Racial" differences evolved during this period of dispersion, as our ancestors adapted to different environments and ecological conditions. For example, consider skin color, the most visible "racial" characteristic. As noted earlier, skin color derives from a pigment called melanin. In areas with

FIGURE 1.5 Skin Color Variation by Latitude

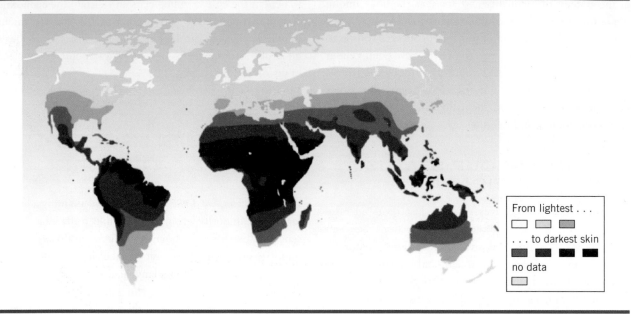

From lightest . . .

□ □ □

. . . to darkest skin

■ ■ ■

no data

□

SOURCE: Chapman, 2004.

intense sunlight, at or near the equator, melanin screens out the sun's ultraviolet rays helping to prevent sunburn and, more significantly, skin cancer. Thus, people from equatorial locations produce higher levels of melanin and have darker skin compared to people who live farther away from the equator (Jablonski & Chaplin, 2010). This almost certainly means that the first humans were dark skinned and that lighter skin colors are the more recent adaptation reflecting migration away from the equator (see Figure 1.5).

The lower concentration of melanin in peoples adapted to areas with less intense sunlight may also be a biological adaptation to a particular ecology. Lighter skin maximizes vitamin D synthesis, which is important for the absorption of calcium and protection against health problems such as rickets. In other words, the skin color of any group reflects the melanin in their skin that helps them balance the need for vitamin D against the need to protect their skin from ultraviolet rays (Jablonski & Chaplin, 2010).

The period of dispersion and differentiation, depicted in Figure 1.6, began to end about 10,000 years ago, when some of our hunting and gathering ancestors developed a new subsistence technology and established permanent agricultural villages. Over the centuries, some of these settlements grew into larger societies, kingdoms, and empires that conquered and absorbed neighboring societies, some of which differed culturally, linguistically, and racially from each other. The great agricultural empires of the past—Roman, Egyptian, Chinese, Aztec—united different peoples, reversed the process of dispersion and differentiation, and began a phase of consolidation and merging of human cultures and genes. Over the next 10,000 years following the first settlements, human genes were intermixed

and spread around the globe, eliminating any "pure" races (if such ever existed).

The differentiation created during the period of global dispersion was swamped by consolidation, a process that was greatly accelerated starting about 500 years ago when European nations began to explore and conquer much of the rest of the world (e.g., India, Africa). This consolidation of groups continues today. For example, in the United States, we can see it with the increasing numbers of people who claim "mixed-race" descent. We see similar patterns across the globe and throughout recent history.

Race and Western Traditions. Europeans had been long aware of racial variation, but aided by breakthroughs in navigation and ship design, the nations of Western Europe began regularly traveling to Africa, Asia, and eventually North and South America in the 1400s. The contact with the peoples of other continents resulted in greater awareness and curiosity about observable physical differences such as skin color.

European travel required tremendous time and resources. The goal wasn't exploration for exploration sake, but to lay claim to valued resources (like gold) that existed elsewhere. In the process, European nations such as England, France, Spain, and Russia conquered, colonized, and sometimes destroyed the peoples and cultures they encountered. This political and military domination (e.g., English colonization of India, French colonization of West and North Africa) required an ideology, or belief system to support it. From the beginning, Europeans linked physical variation with judgments about the relative merits of other races: people from conquering nations thought they were

FIGURE 1.6 The Migration of Anatomically Modern Humans

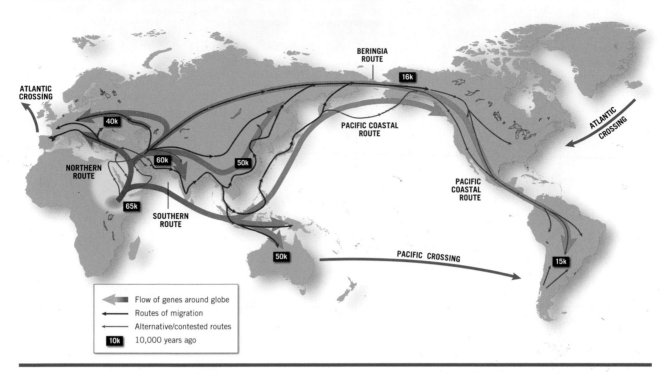

SOURCE: Gugliotta, 2008.

racially and culturally superior to the nations and peoples they conquered.

Since then, other countries have justified military conquest, genocide, exploitation, and slavery with similar racist and xenophobic thinking. But, the toxic form of racism that bloomed during the expansion of European power continues to haunt the world today. It was the basis for the concept of race that took root in the United States.

Race and Biology. Europeans primarily used race to denigrate, reject, and exclude nonwhites. However, as the tools of modern science developed, some people attempted to apply the principles of scientific research to the concept of race. These investigations focused on constructing typologies or taxonomies to classify every person of every race into a category. Some of these typologies were quite elaborate with numerous races and sub-races. For example, the "Caucasian" race was often subdivided into Nordics (blond, fair-skinned northern Europeans), Mediterraneans (dark-haired southern Europeans), and Alpines (people falling between the first two categories).

One major limitation of these systems of classification is that the dividing lines between the so-called racial groups are arbitrary. There is no clear or definite point where, for example, "black" skin color stops and "white" skin color begins. The characteristics used to define race blend imperceptibly into one another. Additionally, one racial trait (skin color) can appear with others (e.g., hair texture) in an infinite variety of ways. A given individual might have a skin color that people associate with one race, the hair texture of a second, the nasal shape of a third, and so forth.

Although people undeniably vary in their physical appearance, these differences do not sort themselves out in a way that permits us to divide people into neat and tidy groups like species of animals. The differences between the so-called human races are not at all like the differences between elephants and butterflies. The ambiguous and continuous nature of racial characteristics makes it impossible to establish categories that have clear, nonarbitrary boundaries. Even the most elaborate racial typologies could not address the fact that many individuals fit into more than one category while others do not fit into any of them. So, who gets to decide how many groups exist and what racial group people belong to?

Over the past several decades, advances in genetic research have provided new insights into race that negate the validity of racial typologies and racial myths associated with them. Perhaps the most important finding is that genetic variation *within* the "traditional" racial groups is *greater* than the variation *between* those groups (American Sociological Association, 2003). In other words, any two randomly selected members of the "black" race will probably vary genetically from each other *at least* as much as they do from a randomly selected member of the "white" race. This finding refutes traditional, non-scientific ideas that racial categories accurately reflect groups of homogeneous people. In other words, the traditional American perception of race as based primarily on skin color has no scientific validity.

FIGURE 1.7   Changes in Racial and Ethnic Categories Over the Past 220 Years

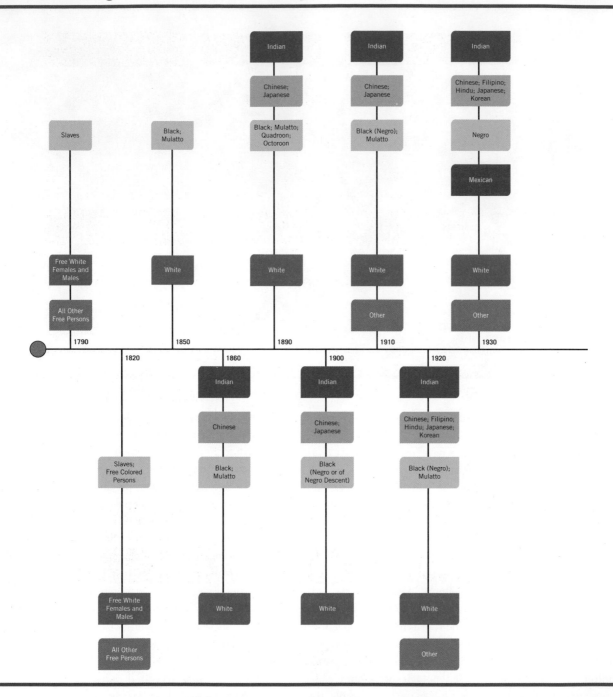

The Social Construction of Race. Sociologist W.E.B. Du Bois (who you will read about in Chapter 5) wrote that the "problem of the twentieth century is the problem of the color line" ([1903] 1997, page 45 c.f. Lee & Bean, 2007). He argues that our nation's history of slavery and the resulting discrimination and inequalities were critical to how U.S. race relations have evolved and, by extension, to how they affect society today.

You can begin to understand the social construction of this "color line" when you examine the U.S. Census race/ethnicity categories over time. The U.S. Constitution (Section 2, Article 1) requires a census (or population count) every decade (Blank, Dabady, & Citro, 2004, p. 206). A state's population influences its political representation in the U.S. House of Representatives, its taxation, and the federal resources it receives (Anderson & Fienberg, 1999).

The census also gatherers important demographic data about household members such as their race, age, gender, occupation, level or education, marital status, and if they own their residence. The first census in 1790 used just three racial categories. (If you consider gender, four subcategories exist; if you include age, there are five categories.) These categories reflect the de facto color line (and gender/age lines) operating in U.S. society at that time:

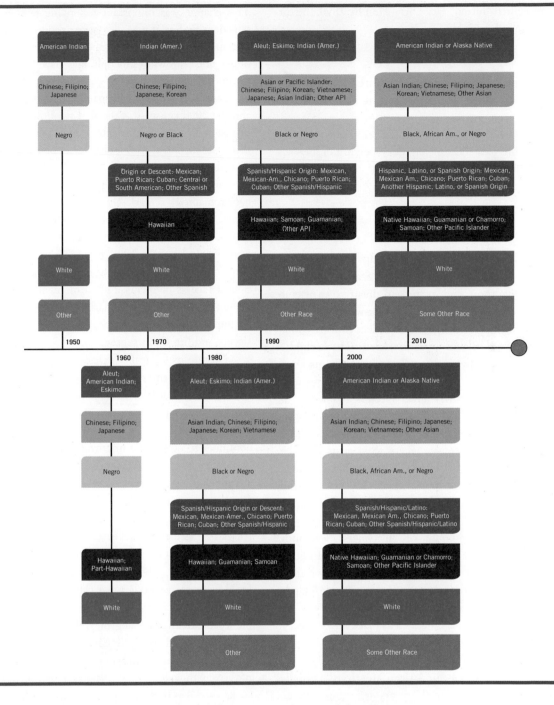

| 1950 | 1960 | 1970 | 1980 | 1990 | 2000 | 2010 |

- Free whites (males under 16 years old, males over 16 years old, females)
- All other free persons (e.g., Native Americans who paid taxes and free blacks)
- Slaves

Although southern states fought to define slaves as property in all other matters (e.g., see *Missouri v. Celia* in Chapter 4), they argued the opposite about census counts because states with more people would get more political power and resources. Such an arrangement would advantage slave holding states and, presumably, give them a

reason to enslave more people (Blank, Dabady, & Citro, 2004). Northern and southern states made a compromise to count slaves as three fifths of a person to distribute power more equitably, writing that "direct Taxes shall be apportioned among the several States . . . by adding to the whole Number of free Person sexcluding Indians not taxed, three fifths of all other Persons" (Blank, Dabady, & Citro, 2004, p. 206).

In addition to telling us about the population, census categories also tell us how people think about race at any given time. For example, the first census taken after slavery ended (1870) used these categories: White, Black, Mulatto, and Indian. (The category of "Mulatto" applied to people with unspecified "mixed" racial heritage.) By 1890, the categories changed, again, to:

- White
- Black (a person who is more than three-fourths black)
- Mulatto (a person who is three-eighths to five-eighths black)
- Quadroon (*quad* meaning four, or one-fourth black)
- Octoroons (*octo* meaning eight, one eighth or any other amount of "black blood")
- Indian
- Chinese
- Japanese

The addition of Chinese and Japanese categories reflects Asian immigration to the United States. The subcategories of "quadroon" and "octoroon" illustrate an attempt to precisely measure race along a black-white dichotomy (Blank, Dabady, & Citro, 2004), and reflect concerns about the impact of free slaves on U.S. society (Hochschild & Powell, 2008). Specifically, lawmakers sought "to ascertain and exhibit the physical effects upon offspring resulting from the amalgamation of human species" and see if "the mulattoes, quadroons, and octoroons are disappearing and the race becoming more purely Negro" (Hochschild & Powell, 2008). While census takers were advised to "be particularly careful to distinguish between blacks, mulattoes, quadroons, and octoroons," they were not told how to determine those specific fractions of "black blood" (Hochschild & Powell, 2008).

Identifying the amount of "blackness" was more complicated than it sounded; thus, the census did not use those categories again. However, southern states continued efforts to do so by introducing the "one-drop rule." Under this law, a person with any trace of black ancestry, even "one drop" of African blood, was defined as black and subject to the limitations of extreme racial inequality. Thus, it rigidly solidified the black-white color line in law and in custom.

The racial categories for African Americans and other groups have changed over the years—most notably for African Americans (see Figure 1.7). The Census Bureau continues to add ethnic categories as new immigrants have come to our country that, for now, fall under one of these primaries categories: Whites, Black/African American, American Indian/Alaskan Native, Asian (e.g., Chinese, Japanese, Native Hawaiian), and other. The Census Bureau notes that "Hispanic origins are not races" and thus, it asks people of Hispanic origin to identify their place of origin such as Cuba, Puerto Rico, or Mexico. The census has changed in other ways, too. In 1960, the Census Bureau mailed its form to urban residences and for the first time respondents could choose their racial identity. (In prior

decades, the census taker determined each person's race. This change was important for giving people agency to self-identify; but, it may also have produced more accurate information. That is, given the prejudice and discrimination against nonwhites, people may have been more likely to choose "white" when the census taker was nearby.) The first census to ask about Hispanic origin happened in 1980 and the 2000 census was the first to allow people to identify as multiracial by selecting more than one category (Lowenthall, 2014). For example, someone could identify as white and Cuban.

Yet even with these changes, the category of "white" has remained remarkably consistent over time (see Figure 1.7). Nor has it included gradations of "whiteness"; that is, there are no subcategories of "whiteness" as there were of "blackness" in 1890, for example (Blank, Dabady, & Citro, 2004). Thus, we might consider the U.S. construction of race as involving a white-nonwhite color line (i.e., white is a dominant, nonchanging category) that reflects assumptions of black inferiority made at the heart of U.S. slavery and Jim Crow segregation.

Despite its scientific uselessness, the idea of race continues to shape intergroup relations in the United States and around the world. Race, along with gender, is one of the first things people notice about one another. Because race is still a significant way of differentiating people, it continues to be socially important. In addition to discrimination by out-group members, ideas about race can also shape relations *within* a perceived racial group. For example, people within groups and outside of them may treat "light-skinned" African Americans better than "dark" African Americans. Walker (1983) named this colorism. Such discrimination reflects the dominant racial hierarchy that preferences lighter skin tone and presumed European facial features and body types (Harris, 2008, p. 54). While an important area of study, we (like other researchers) focus on broadly defined racial groups that affect all group members (see Blank, Dabady, & Citro, 2004, p. 29).

So, how does the idea of race remain relevant? Because of the way they developed, Western concepts of race have a social as well as biological dimension. Sociologists consider race a social construction whose meaning has been created and sustained not by science but by historical, social, economic, and political processes (see Omi & Winant, 1986; Smedley, 2007). For example, in Chapter 4, we will analyze the role of race in the creation of American slavery and you will see that the physical differences between blacks and whites became important *as a result* of that system of inequality. The elites of colonial society needed to justify their unequal treatment of Africans and seized on the obvious differences in skin color, elevated it to a matter of supreme importance, and used it to justify the enslavement of blacks. In other words, the importance of race was

FIGURE 1.8 Gender Inequality Worldwide

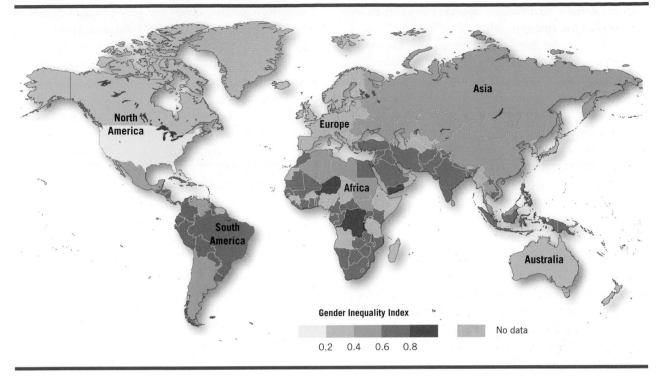

Gender Inequality Index

0.2 0.4 0.6 0.8   No data

SOURCE: Florida (2012).

socially constructed as the result of a particular historical conflict, and it remains important not because of objective realities, but because of the widespread, shared social perception that it is important.

GENDER

You have already seen that minority groups can be internally differentiated by social class and other factors. An additional source of differentiation is gender. Like race, gender has biological and social components that allow it to be a convenient way to sort people and organize social life. Historically, people have used visible biological characteristics such as genitalia to assign people into two sexes (i.e., female, male). Those ascribed statuses then become the basis for **gender norms**, or societal expectations about proper behavior, attitudes, and personality traits. In the contemporary United States, people have stressed the importance of nurturance, interpersonal skills, and "emotion work" (Hochschild, 1979) for girls, while people expect boys to be assertive and independent.

Gender norms vary across time and from one society to another, but sociologists and other social scientists have

---

Gender norms are societal expectations for behavior based on one's gender status (e.g., girl, boy). The social characteristics associated with males or females.

---

documented the close relationship between gender and inequality. Typically, men (as a group) possess more property, prestige, and power than women. Figure 1.8 provides some perspective on the variation in gender inequality across the globe. The map shows the Gender Inequality Index, a statistic that measures the amount of inequality between women and men based on variables such as education, health, labor market participation, and political representation. As you can see, gender equality is generally highest in the industrialized nations of North America and Western Europe and lowest in the less developed, more agricultural nations of sub-Saharan Africa.

Western European and North American societies rank relatively high on gender equality, but gender discrimination continues to be a major issue, as you'll see throughout this text (Chapter 11 in particular). For example, there is a consistent—and large—gender income gap in these societies, and women are decidedly underrepresented in the most lucrative and powerful occupations (e.g., see Figure 11.1). While many societies have made progress, gender equality will continue to be an issue for generations to come.

Part of the problem is that all societies, including Western Europe and North America, have strong traditions of **patriarchy**, or men's dominance. In a patriarchal society, men have more control over the economy and more access to leadership roles in business, politics, education, and

---

Patriarchy is men's dominance.

---

other institutions. Parallel to forms of racism that sought to justify and continue racial inequality, women have been subjected to **sexism**, an ideology that "explains" inequality based on gender. For example, people in some cultures viewed women as "delicate flowers," too emotional, and physically weak for the harsh demands of "manly" occupations outside the home. (In the United States and other societies, this social construction was racialized, applying only to white women. The same men who placed white women "on a pedestal" did not hesitate to send women of color into the fields to perform the most difficult, physically demanding, "unfeminine" tasks during slavery.)

Even in the most progressive societies, women continue to possess many characteristics of a minority group (namely, a pattern of disadvantage based on group membership marked by a physical characteristic). Thus, women could be, and in many ways should be, treated as a separate minority group. We will do this in Chapter 11, but throughout the text, we will address the divergent experiences of men and women within each minority group. We will consider how the interests and experiences of women of different groups and classes coincide with and diverge from one another and from those of the men in their groups. For example, on some issues African American women might have interests identical to those of white women and opposed to those of African American men, and on other issues the constellations of interests might be reversed. As stressed in the intersectionality approach, the experience of minority-group membership varies by gender (along with other criteria), and the way gender is experienced is not the same for every group.

Those in power generally write about history from their own standpoint—ignoring, forgetting, or trivializing minority-group experiences. For instance, much of the history of slavery has been told from the viewpoint of the slave owners. Laws against education kept slaves illiterate, leaving few mechanisms for recording their thoughts or experiences. A more accurate picture of slavery began to emerge only since the mid-20th century, when scholars started to dig beneath the written records and memoirs of the slave owners and reconstruct the experiences of African Americans from nonwritten documentation—such as oral traditions including folklore and songs—and from physical artifacts—such as quilts, pottery, and religious objects (e.g., see Levine, 1977).

However, despite these advances, the experiences of women minorities are much less well known and documented than men's experiences. One of the important trends in contemporary scholarship is to correct this skewed

---

Sexism refers to belief systems that label women as inferior and rationalize their lower status.

---

focus and systematically incorporate gender as a vital factor for understanding minority-group experiences (Baca Zinn & Thornton Dill, 1994; Espiritu, 1996).

The Social Construction of Gender. Social scientists see race as a social construction created under certain historical circumstances (such as the era of European colonialism) when it was needed to help justify the unequal treatment of nonwhite groups. What about gender? Is it also merely a social creation designed to rationalize the higher status of men and their easier access to power, prestige, and property? Figure 1.8 shows that all contemporary nations have some degree of gender inequality. Is this because—as many people believe—boys and men are "naturally" more aggressive and independent, and girls and women are "naturally" more gentle and dependent? What is the basis of these distinctions? What role, if any, do the distinctions have with people's biology (e.g., genes, hormones)?

First, the traits people commonly see as "typical" for women or men are not disconnected, separate categories. Every person has them to some degree. To the extent that gender differences exist at all, they are manifested not in absolutes but in averages, tendencies, and probabilities. Many people consider aggressiveness to be a masculine characteristic, but many women are more aggressive than many men. Likewise, people tend to associate "emotionality" with women but many men are more emotional than many women. As with race, research shows that there is more variation *within* categories than among them—a finding that seriously undermines the view that gender differences are genetic or biological (Basow, as cited in Rosenblum & Travis, 2002).

Second, gender as a social construction is illustrated by the fact that what is thought to be "appropriate" gender behavior varies over time period and from society to society. The behavior people expected from a woman in Victorian England isn't the same as those for women in 21st-century America. Likewise, the gender norms for men in 500 CE China are different from those in Puritan America. This variability makes it difficult to argue that the differences between the genders are "hardwired" in the genetic code; if they were, the variations over time and place would be nonexistent.

Third, the relationship between subsistence technology and gender inequality illustrates the social nature of gender norms. As we noted previously, our species evolved in East Africa and relied on hunting and gathering to satisfy their need for food. Our distant ancestors lived in small, nomadic bands that relied on cooperation and sharing for survival. Societies at this level of development typically divide adult labor roles by gender (with men hunting and women gathering), and, although they may tend toward patriarchy, women and women's work are highly valued and gender inequality is minimal. The subordination of women is more closely associated with settled agricultural communities, the first of which appeared about 10,000 years ago in what is now the Middle East. Survival in preindustrial farming societies requires the combined efforts of many people; thus, large families are valued as a cheap labor force. Women are consigned to household and domestic duties, with a strong emphasis on producing and raising children. Because the infant mortality rate in these societies is high (approximately 50% or more), women spend much of their lives confined and secluded, pregnant or nursing young children, far removed from the possibility of contending for leadership roles in their communities.

Industrialization and urbanization, linked processes that began in the mid-1700s in Great Britain, changed the cost-benefit ratios for childbearing. The expenses associated with having children rose in the city, and the nature of industrial work increasingly required education and literacy—qualities and abilities available to both genders. Thus, gender inequality probably reached its peak in preindustrial agrarian societies and has tended to decline as societies industrialized. It is no accident of timing that the push for gender equality and the Women's Liberation Movement are associated with industrial societies and that gender equality is highest today in industrial and postindustrial societies (see Figure 1.8).

Biology may shape one's personality to some degree, and researchers continue to explore the links between genetics and gender norms (e.g., see Hopcroft, 2009; Huber, 2007; Udry, 2000) as well as the interaction between them. However, at its core, gender is social, not biological (Booth, Granger, Mazur, & Kivligham, 2006, pp. 167–191; see also Ridgeway, 2011, pp. 18–23). Gender, like race, is a social construction, especially when people treat the supposed differences between men and women as categorical, "natural," and fixed, and then use those ideas to deny opportunity and equality to women.

QUESTIONS FOR REFLECTION

7. Are gender and race *merely* social constructions? Aren't they *real* in some ways? In what ways do they exist apart from people's perception of them? Are they both social constructions in the same way? Are they *equally* matters of perception?

KEY CONCEPTS IN DOMINANT–MINORITY RELATIONS

Whenever people raise sensitive issues such as dominant–minority group relations, the discussion often turns to matters of prejudice and discrimination. We need to clarify these terms. This section introduces and defines four concepts that will help you understand dominant–minority relations in the United States.

This book addresses how individuals from different groups interact, as well as how groups interact with each other. Thus, we need to distinguish between what is true for individuals (the more psychological level of analysis) and what is true for groups or society as a whole (the sociological level of analysis). Beyond that, we must attempt to trace the connections between these two levels of analysis.

At the individual level, what people think and feel about other groups may differ from how they actually behave toward members of another group. A person might express negative feelings about other groups in private but deal fairly with members of the group in face-to-face interactions. Groups and entire societies may display this same kind of inconsistency. A society may express support for equality in its official documents or formal codes of law and simultaneously treat minority groups in unfair and destructive ways. An example of this kind of inconsistency is the contrast between the commitment to equality stated in the Declaration of Independence ("All men are created equal") and the actual treatment of black slaves, Anglo-American women, and American Indians at that time.

At the individual level, social scientists refer to the "thinking/feeling" part of this dichotomy as prejudice and the "doing" part as discrimination. At the group level, the term **ideological racism** describes the thinking/feeling dimension and **institutional discrimination** describes the doing dimension. Table 1.1 depicts the differences among these four concepts.

TABLE 1.1 Four Concepts in Dominant–Minority Relations

DIMENSION	LEVEL OF ANALYSIS	
	Individual	**Group or Societal**
Thinking/feeling	Prejudice	Ideological racism
Doing	Discrimination	Institutional discrimination

Ideological racism refers to societal belief systems that label certain groups as inferior.

Institutional discrimination is a pattern of unequal treatment of a group built into the daily operation of society.

PREJUDICE

Prejudice is the tendency of an individual to think about other groups in negative ways, to attach negative emotions to those groups, and to prejudge individuals based on their group memberships. Individual prejudice has two aspects: **cognitive prejudice**, or the thinking aspect, and **affective prejudice**, or the feeling part. A prejudiced person thinks about other groups in terms of **stereotypes** (cognitive prejudice), generalizations that he or she thinks apply to group members. Examples of familiar stereotypes include notions such as "women are emotional," "Jews are stingy," "blacks are lazy," "the Irish are drunks," and "Germans are authoritarian." A prejudiced person also experiences negative emotional responses to other groups (affective prejudice), including contempt, disgust, arrogance, and hatred.

People vary in their levels of prejudice, and levels of prejudice vary in the same person from one time to another and from one group to another. We can say that people are prejudiced to the extent that they use stereotypes in their thinking about other groups or have negative emotional reactions to other groups.

Generally, the two dimensions of prejudice are highly correlated with each other; however, they are distinct and separate aspects of prejudice and can vary independently. One person may think entirely in stereotypes but feel no particular negative emotional response to any group. Another person may feel a very strong aversion toward a group but be unable to articulate a clear or detailed stereotype of that group.

Individual prejudice, like all aspects of society, evolves and changes. In the past, American prejudice was strongly felt, overtly expressed, and laced with clear, detailed stereotypes. Overt forms declined after the civil rights era of the 1950s and 1960s but did not disappear, and vast numbers of Americans came to view them as problematic. In modern societies that emphasize mutual respect and tolerance, people tend to express prejudice in subtle, indirect ways. For example, prejudice might manifest in language that functions as a kind of code; for instance, when people associate "welfare cheats" or criminality with certain minority groups. We will explore these modern forms of prejudice in Chapter 3,

---

Prejudice is the tendency of individuals to think and feel negatively toward others.

The **cognitive dimension of prejudice** refers to how people *think* about members of other groups.

The **affective dimension of prejudice** refers to how people *feel* about members of other groups.

Stereotypes are generalizations thought to characterize groups as a whole.

In 2017, hundreds of white nationalists marched on the University of Virginia campus. Note the shirt's triangular "dragon's eye" symbol of the white nationalist group, Identity Evropa.

Samuel Corum/Anadolu Agency/Getty Images

but we need to be clear that the relative absence of blatant stereotyping or expressions of strong public emotions against minority groups in modern society does not mean that we have eliminated individual prejudice in the United States. In more recent years, many of the traditional forms have reasserted themselves, as we'll discuss in future chapters.

DISCRIMINATION

Discrimination is the unequal treatment of people based on their group membership; for example, an employer doesn't hire someone because he or she is African American (or Puerto Rican, Jewish, Chinese, etc.). If the unequal treatment is based on the individual's group membership (e.g., race/ethnicity, gender, sexual orientation, religion), the act is discriminatory.

Just as the cognitive and affective aspects of prejudice can be independent, discrimination and prejudice do not necessarily occur together. Even highly prejudiced individuals may not act on their negative thoughts or feelings. In social settings regulated by strong egalitarian codes or laws (e.g., restaurants and other public facilities), people who are highly bigoted in their private thoughts and feelings may follow these norms in public. On the other hand, when people approve of prejudice in social situations, such support can produce discrimination from otherwise unprejudiced individuals. In the southern United States during the height of segregation, and in South Africa during the period of state-sanctioned racial inequality called apartheid, it was usual and customary for whites to treat blacks in discriminatory ways. Regardless of individuals' actual level of prejudice, they faced strong social pressure to conform to the official forms of racial superiority and discrimination.

Discrimination is the unequal treatment of a person based on his or her group membership.

Several actual events are listed below. In the space provided, classify each as an example of cognitive prejudice, affective prejudice, individual discrimination, ideological racism, or institutional discrimination, and briefly explain your reasoning. Some incidents may include elements that reflect more than one concept.

Note: Your instructor may ask you to complete this assignment with others as a group discussion.

	INCIDENT	CONCEPT	EXPLANATION
1	Upon learning that the house next door will be purchased by an Asian American family, Mrs. Smith, a white American, says, "Well, at least they're not black."		
2	Three friends decide to put bacon on the door of mosque. They spray-paint "Muslims not wanted" on the door.		
3	The U.S. Secret Service settles a class action lawsuit with black agents for repeatedly passing them over for promotions.		
4	Tom Smith, the CEO of Smith's Bank, did not hire Judy Washington as the head of his Human Resources (HR) Department. He worries that she might focus too much on "family issues." Although he thinks she seems like a "tough broad," he fears she might get "too emotional" in decision making and in carrying out difficult tasks like firing people.		
5	A task force investigation finds that the city police disproportionately focused on African Americans. African Americans make up about one-third of the city's population but were 72% of all "investigative street stops." Further, 74% of the 404 people shot by the police between 2008 and 2015 were black.		
6	Professor Jones is talking with Professor Jimenez and says, "I just can't stand it anymore. Students today are so lazy. They won't read for class. They don't seem to care about their homework. They don't want to listen in class—they just want to text all day. It's disgusting."		

TURN THE PAGE TO FIND OUR ANSWERS.

QUESTIONS FOR REFLECTION

8. Like most Americans, you are probably familiar with the stereotypes associated with various groups. Does this mean you are prejudiced against those groups? Does it mean you have negative emotions about those groups and are likely to discriminate against them? Explain.

IDEOLOGICAL RACISM

Ideological racism is a belief system asserting that a particular group is inferior; it is the group or societal equivalent of individual prejudice. Members of the dominant group use ideological racism to legitimize or rationalize the unequal status of minority groups. Through the process of socialization, such ideas pass from generation to generation, becoming incorporated into the society's culture. It exists separately from the individuals who inhabit the society (Andersen, 1993, p. 75; See & Wilson, 1988, p. 227). An example of a racist ideology is the elaborate system of beliefs and ideas that attempted to justify slavery in the American South. The exploitation of slaves was "explained" in terms of the innate racial inferiority of blacks and the superiority of whites.

In later chapters, we will explore the relationship between individual prejudice and racist ideologies at the societal level. For now, we can make what is probably an obvious point: people socialized into societies with strong racist ideologies are likely to absorb racist ideas and be highly prejudiced. It should not surprise us that a high level of personal prejudice existed among whites in the antebellum American South or in other highly racist societies, such as in South Africa under apartheid. Yet, it's important

	CONCEPT	EXPLANATION
1	Cognitive prejudice	Mrs. Smith seems to be thinking in terms of the traditional stereotype regarding the desirability of African Americans and Asian Americans.
2	Discrimination	These hostile behaviors are targeted toward members of the local mosque because of their membership in the group, "Muslims." The sign on the door is clear; the bacon reflects Islamic guidelines against eating pork.
3	Institutional discrimination	In this case, the Secret Service appears to have been following a discriminatory policy. This is larger in scope than just an individual act.
4	Cognitive prejudice	Mr. Smith appears to be using stereotypical thinking about women as being more interested in "family issues" than other issues that an HR director might need to address. Although he identifies Ms. Washington as a "tough broad" he puts her in the category of "emotional women."
5	Institutional discrimination	The specifics for this example come from an analysis of Chicago policing that pointed to a pattern of unequal treatment for blacks in the city. Institutional discrimination can be overt (such as laws requiring segregated schools). At other times, it is less obvious. The behaviors that lead to inequality do not have to be intentional to be discriminatory.
6	Affective prejudice	Professor Jones is expressing strong feelings of anger and contempt for students. (She's also stereotyping them all as "lazy.")

to remember that ideological racism and individual prejudice are different phenomena with different causes and different locations in the society. Racism is not a prerequisite for prejudice; prejudice may exist even in the absence of an ideology of racism.

INSTITUTIONAL DISCRIMINATION

Institutional discrimination is the societal equivalent of individual discrimination. It refers to a pattern of unequal treatment, based on group membership, built into the daily operations of society, whether or not it is consciously intended. Public schools, the criminal justice system, and political and economic institutions can operate in ways that can discriminate against some groups, disadvantaging its members.

Institutional discrimination can be obvious and overt. For many years following the American Civil War, practices such as poll taxes and rigged literacy tests (designed to ensure failure) prevented African Americans in the South from voting. For nearly a century, well into the 1960s, elections and elected offices in the South were restricted to whites only. The purpose of this blatant pattern of institutional discrimination was widely understood by African American and white Southerners alike: it existed to disenfranchise the African American community and to keep it politically powerless (Dollard, 1937).

At other times, institutional discrimination may operate subtly and without conscious intent. For example, if schools use biased aptitude tests to determine which students get to take college preparatory courses, and the tests favor the dominant (white) group, then the outcomes are discriminatory—even if everyone involved sincerely believes that they are merely applying objective criteria in a rational way. If a decision-making process has unequal consequences for dominant and minority groups, institutional discrimination may well be at work.

Although individuals may implement and enforce a particular discriminatory policy, it is more appropriate to recognize it as an aspect of the institution as a whole. For example, election officials in the South during segregation did not, and public school administrators today do not, have to be personally prejudiced to implement these discriminatory policies.

However, a major thesis of this book is that racist ideologies and institutional discrimination are created to sustain the stratification system. Widespread institutional discrimination maintains the relative advantage of the dominant group day to day. Members of the dominant group who are socialized into communities with strong racist ideologies and a great deal of institutional discrimination are likely to be personally prejudiced and to routinely engage in acts of individual discrimination. The mutually reinforcing patterns of prejudice, racism, and discrimination on the

NARRATIVE PORTRAIT

A White Man Reflects on Privilege

Tim Wise is a prominent antiracism activist.

In this passage, Tim Wise—lecturer, writer, and antiracism activist—reflects on his whiteness. He points out that racial privilege is largely invisible to whites because, unlike minority-group members, they don't have to deal with its restrictions. Our racist cultural traditions make whiteness "normal," the standard against which "others" are contrasted and differentiated. From the perspective of whites, only nonwhites have race and ethnicity. Does the same dynamic mean that the restrictions of traditional gender norms are visible only to women?

What does it mean to be white, especially in a nation created for the benefit of people like you? We [white people] don't often ask this question, mostly because we don't have to. Being [white] . . . allows one to ignore how race shapes one's life. For those of us called white, whiteness . . . becomes . . . the unspoken . . . norm, taken for granted, much as water can be taken for granted by a fish.

In high school, whites are sometimes asked to think about race, but rarely about whiteness. In my case, we read John Howard Griffin's classic book, *Black Like Me*, in which the author recounts his experiences in the Jim Crow South in 1959, after taking a drug that turned his skin brown and allowed him to experience apartheid for a few months from the other side of the color line.

It was a good book, especially for its time. Yet I can't help but find it a bit disturbing that it remains one of the most assigned volumes on summer reading lists dealing with race. [This popularity seems to signal] the extent to which race is considered a problem of the past . . . surely there are some more contemporary racial events students could discuss. . . . [By reading the book,] whites are encouraged to think about race from the perspective of blacks, . . . but *Black Like Me* leaves another aspect of the discussion untouched: namely, the examination of the white experience.

[To] be white in the United States . . . is to have certain common experiences based solely upon race. These experiences have to do with advantage, privilege . . . , and belonging. We are, unlike people of color, born to belonging, and have rarely had to prove ourselves deserving of our presence here. . . .

While some might insist that whites have a wide range of experiences, and [that] it isn't fair to make generalizations . . . , this is a dodge, and not a particularly artful one at that. Of course we're all different, sort of like snowflakes, which come to think of it are also white. None of us have led the exact same life. But, [regardless], all whites were placed above all persons of color when it came to the economic, social, and political hierarchies that were to form in the United States, without exception. This formal system of racial preference was codified in law from the 1600s until at least 1964, at which time the Civil Rights Act was passed. . . .

Prior to that time we didn't even pretend to be a nation based on equality. Or rather we did pretend, but not very well; at least not to the point where the rest of the world believed it, or to the point where people of color in this country ever did. Most white folks believed it, but that's simply more proof of our privileged status. Our ancestors had the luxury of believing those things that black and brown folks could never take as givens: all that stuff about life, liberty, and the pursuit of happiness. [Today,] whites can, indeed *must*, still believe it, while people of color have little reason to join the celebration, knowing as they do that there is still a vast gulf between who we say we are as a nation and people, and who we really are.

In other words, there is enough commonality about the white experience to allow us to make some general statements about whiteness and never be too far from the mark. Returning to the snowflake analogy: although . . . no two white people are exactly alike, it is also true that few snowflakes have radically different experiences from those of the average snowflake. Likewise, we know a snowflake when we see one, and in that recognition we intuit, almost always correctly, something about its life experience.

SOURCE: Wise (2008, pp. 2–4). Copyright © 2011 by Tim Wise from *White Like Me: Reflections on Race from a Privileged Son*. Reprinted by permission of Counterpoint.

Questions to Consider

1. Recall Carla's issues with identity in the previous Narrative Portrait. Is Tim more certain about who he is? Why?
2. How might Tim's statement change if he were a woman? Working class? Gay?
3. How is racial identity "invisible" to whites? What does the author mean when he says that whiteness is "the norm" in U.S. society? How does racial privilege permit whites to ignore race?

---

individual and institutional levels preserve the respective positions of dominant and minority groups over time.

Institutional discrimination is just one way members of a minority group can be denied access to goods and services, opportunities, and rights (such as voting). That is, institutional discrimination helps sustain and reinforce the unequal positions of racial and ethnic groups in the stratification system.

A GLOBAL PERSPECTIVE

In the chapters that follow, we will focus on developing a number of concepts and theories and applying those ideas to the minority groups of the United States. However, it is important to expand our perspective beyond the experiences of just a single nation and consider the experiences and histories of other peoples and places. Thus, we will take time throughout this text to apply our ideas to other societies and non-American minority groups. Also, in Chapter 13, we will systematically examine group relationships around the globe. If the ideas and concepts developed in this text can help us make sense of these situations, we will have some assurance that they have some general applicability and that the dynamics of intergroup relations in the United States are not unique.

On another level, we must also take account of the ways in which group relations in the United States are shaped by economic, social, and political forces beyond our borders. As you'll see, the experiences of this society cannot be understood in isolation. The United States is part of the global system of societies, and now, more than ever, we must systematically take account of the complex interconnections between the domestic and the international, particularly with respect to issues related to immigration. The world is indeed growing smaller, and we must see our society as one part of a larger system. The next section explores one connection between the global and the local.

IMMIGRATION AND GLOBALIZATION

Immigration is a major concern in our society today, and we will address the issue in the pages to come. Here, we will point out that immigration is a global phenomenon that affects virtually every nation in the world. About 244 million people—a little more than 3% of the world's population—live outside their countries of birth, and the number of migrants has increased steadily over the past several decades (United Nations Department of Economic and Social Affairs, Population Division, 2015). Figure 1.9 depicts the major population movement from 1990 to 2000 and clearly demonstrates the global nature of immigration. Note that Western Europe is a major destination for immigrants, as is the United States.

What has caused this massive population movement? One very important underlying cause is globalization, or the increasing interconnectedness of people, groups, organizations, and nations. This process is complex and multidimensional, but perhaps the most powerful dimension of globalization—especially for understanding contemporary immigration—is economics and the movement of jobs and opportunity from place to place. People flow from areas of lower opportunity to areas with greater opportunity.

To illustrate, consider the southern border of the United States. For the past several decades, there has been an influx of people from Mexico and Central America, and the presence of these newcomers has generated a great deal of emotional and political heat, especially because many of these migrants are undocumented.

FIGURE 1.9 Major Global Migration Flows, 1990–2000

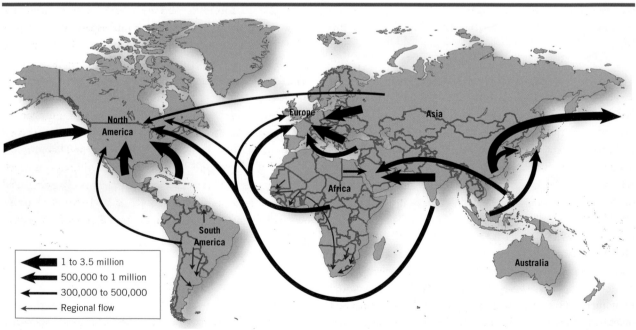

SOURCE: Adapted from *Stalker's Guide to Migration*, Peter Stalker.

FIGURE 1.10 Immigrant Deaths on the Southern Border, 2000–2010

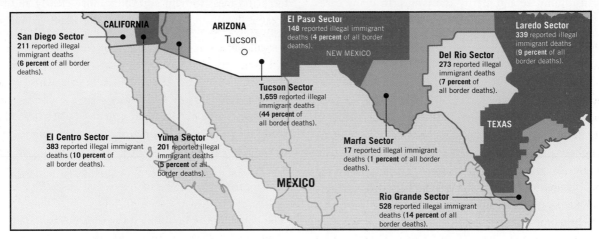

San Diego Sector
211 reported illegal immigrant deaths (**6 percent** of all border deaths).

CALIFORNIA

ARIZONA
Tucson

El Paso Sector
148 reported illegal immigrant deaths (**4 percent** of all border deaths).

NEW MEXICO

Laredo Sector
339 reported illegal immigrant deaths (**9 percent** of all border deaths).

Del Rio Sector
273 reported illegal immigrant deaths (**7 percent** of all border deaths).

Tucson Sector
1,659 reported illegal immigrant deaths (**44 percent** of all border deaths).

TEXAS

El Centro Sector
383 reported illegal immigrant deaths (**10 percent** of all border deaths).

Yuma Sector
201 reported illegal immigrant deaths (**5 percent** of all border deaths).

Marfa Sector
17 reported illegal immigrant deaths (**1 percent** of all border deaths).

MEXICO

Rio Grande Sector
528 reported illegal immigrant deaths (**14 percent** of all border deaths).

Illegal immigrant deaths, by Border Patrol sector: Covering 262 miles, the Tucson Sector has recorded nearly half of all deaths along the U.S.-Mexico border in the last decade.

SOURCE: Arizona Daily Star.

Some Americans see these newcomers as threats to traditional American culture and the English language, and others associate them with crime, violence, and drug smuggling. Others see them simply as people trying to survive as best they can, desperate to support themselves and their families. Few, however, see these immigrants as the human consequences of the economic globalization of the world.

What is the connection between globalization and this immigrant stream? The population pressure on the southern border has been in large part a result of the North American Free Trade Agreement (NAFTA), implemented in 1994. NAFTA united the three North American nations in a single trading bloc—economically "globalizing" the region—and permitted goods and capital (but not people) to move freely between Canada, the United States, and Mexico.

Among many other consequences, NAFTA opened Mexico to the importation of food products produced at very low cost by the giant agribusinesses of Canada and the United States. This cheap food (corn in particular) destroyed the livelihoods of many rural Mexicans and forced them to leave their villages in search of work. Millions pursued the only survival strategy that seemed remotely sensible: migration north. Even the meanest job in the United States pays many times more than the average Mexican wage.

Even as NAFTA changed the economic landscape of North America, the United States became increasingly concerned with the security of its borders (especially after the terrorist attacks of September 11, 2001) and attempted to stem the flow of people, partly by building fences and increasing the size of the Border Patrol. The easier border crossings were quickly sealed, but this did not stop the pressure from the south. Migrants moved to more difficult

and dangerous crossing routes, including the deadly, forbidding Sonoran Desert in southern Arizona, resulting in an untold number of deaths on the border since the mid-1990s. Border immigration has continued to be a concern for Americans since then. Most recently, President Donald Trump used this concern as one of his major appeals to voters in his 2016 election campaign.

Figure 1.10 displays one estimate of recent deaths along the southern U.S. border, but these are only the bodies that were discovered. Some estimates put the true number at 10 deaths for every recovered corpse, suggesting thousands of deaths along the border between the mid-1990s and the present.

The relationship between NAFTA and immigration to the United States is just one aspect of a complex global relationship. Around the globe, people are moving in huge numbers from less developed nations to more developed, more affluent economies. The wealthy nations of Western Europe, including Germany, Ireland, France, and the Netherlands, are also receiving large numbers of immigrants, and the citizens of these nations are concerned about their jobs, communities, housing, and language—as well as the integrity of the national cultures—in much the same ways as Americans. The world is changing, and contemporary immigration must be understood in terms of changes that affect many nations and, indeed, the entire global system of societies.

CONCLUSION

This chapter raises many questions. Our goal in writing this book is to teach you how to apply the sociological perspective to the world around you. With the concepts, theories, and body of research developed over the years, we can illuminate and clarify the issues. In many cases, we can identify approaches and ideas that are incorrect as well as those that hold promise. Sociology can't answer all questions, but it provides important research tools and ideas to help you think more clearly and with greater depth and nuance about the issues facing our society.

SUMMARY

We've organized this summary around the Learning Objectives at the beginning of the chapter.

 1.1 Explain the increasing racial and ethnic diversity of the United States.

Rates of immigration are high, and, as shown in Figure 1.1, non-Hispanic white Americans are declining in relative size. By mid-century, they will no longer be a numerical majority of the U.S. population. (Which groups are increasing in relative size? What will America look like in the future in terms of ethnicity, race, culture, language, and cuisine?)

Rates of marriage across group lines are also increasing, along with the percentage of the population that identifies with more than one racial or ethnic group. Groups that do not fit into the categories in Figure 1.1 (e.g., Arab Americans, immigrants from Africa) are growing in size.

Many of the grievances and problems that affect American minority groups (e.g., African Americans, Native Americans, and Hispanic Americans) have not been resolved, as we shall see in Part 3 of this text.

 1.2 Understand the concept of a minority group.

A minority group has five characteristics. Members of the group

- experience a pattern of disadvantage, which can range from mild (e.g., casual snubs or insults) to severe (e.g., slavery or genocide);

- have a socially visible mark of identification which may be physical (e.g., skin color), cultural (e.g., dress, language), or both;

- are aware of their disadvantaged status;

- are generally members of the group from birth; and

- tend to form intimate associations within the group.

Of these traits, the first two are the most important.

 1.3 Explain the sociological perspectives that will guide this text, especially as they relate to the relationships between inequality and minority-group status.

A stratification system has three different dimensions (class, prestige, and power), and the nature of inequality in a society varies by its level of development. Minority groups and social classes are correlated in many complex ways. Minority groups generally have less access to valued resources and opportunity. However, minority status and inequality are separate and may vary independently. Members of minority groups can be differentiated by gender, social class, and many other criteria; likewise, members of a particular social class can vary by gender, race, ethnicity, and along many other dimensions.

 1.4 Explain how race and gender contribute to minority-group status.

Visible characteristics such as skin color or anatomy are widely used to identify and differentiate people (e.g., woman/man, black/white/Native American/Asian/Latino). So-called racial characteristics, such as skin color, evolved as our ancestors migrated from East Africa and spread into new ecologies. During the period of European colonization of the globe, racial characteristics became important markers of "us and them," conqueror and conquered.

Race and gender are socially constructed ideas that become filled with social meaning (e.g., strong, nurturing, smart, lazy). These meanings change over time and across geographic location. Although they are just ideas, these social constructions feel "natural" and "real." Thus, they powerfully influence the way we think about one another. They influence minority-group membership and, therefore, one's life chances such as access to resources and privilege (e.g., education, legal rights, pay, prestige). Sexism and racism attempt to explain patterns of gender and racial inequality in terms group members' "inferiority."

Comprehend four of the key concepts in dominant–minority relations: prejudice, discrimination, ideological racism, and institutional discrimination.

This text analyzes dominant–minority relationships at both the individual and societal levels. Prejudice refers to individual feelings and thoughts while discrimination is different treatment of people based on their group membership. Individual discrimination is behavior done by individuals. Ideological racism and institutional discrimination are parallel concepts that refer to prejudice and discrimination at the societal level.

 Apply a global perspective to the relationship between globalization and immigration to the United States.

A global perspective means that we will examine dominant–minority relations not just in the United States but in other nations as well. We will be sensitive to the ways group relations in the United States are affected by economic, cultural, political, and social changes across the global system of societies. The relationship between NAFTA and immigration to the United States illustrates one of the many connections between domestic and international processes.

KEY TERMS

affective dimension of prejudice 26

ascribed status 12

bourgeoisie 14

cognitive dimension of prejudice 26

discrimination 26

dominant group 11

ethnic minority groups 11

gender norms 23

genocide 11

ideological racism 25

institutional discrimination 25

intersectionality 16

level of development 15

means of production 14

minority group 10

miscegenation 13

patriarchy 23

postindustrial society 15

power 15

prejudice 26

prestige 15

proletariat 14

racial minority groups 11

sexism 24

social classes 13

social constructions 9

social mobility 17

stereotypes 26

stratification 13

subsistence technology 15

REVIEW QUESTIONS

1. What is the significance of Figure 1.1? What are some of the limitations and problems with the group names used in this graph? Are the group names "social constructions"? How? In your view, does the increasing diversity of American society represent a threat or an opportunity? Should we acknowledge and celebrate our differences, or should we strive for more unity and conformity? What possible dangers and opportunities are inherent in increasing diversity? What are the advantages and disadvantages of stressing unity and conformity?

2. What groups should be considered "minorities"? The five-part definition presented in this chapter was developed with racial and ethnic minorities in mind. Does it apply to gay and lesbian Americans? How? In what ways does it apply to religious groups such as Mormons or Muslims? What about left-handed people or people who are very overweight or very tall or very short? Explain your answers.

3. What is a social construction? As social constructions, how are race and gender the same

and how do they differ? What does it mean to say, "Gender becomes a social construction—like race—when it is treated as an unchanging, fixed difference and then used to deny opportunity and equality to women"? Consider the changing social constructions of race over time suggested by the Census Bureau categories. What do you make of them? Which categories "make sense" to you and why? How do those categories reflect particular meanings or ways of thinking at the time?

4. Define and explain each of the terms in Table 1.1. Cite an example of each from your own experiences. How does ideological racism differ from prejudice? Which concept is more sociological? Why? How does institutional discrimination differ from discrimination? Which concept is more sociological? Why?

5. Why is it important to look beyond the United States when analyzing dominant–minority relations? What can we learn by taking a global perspective? Besides immigration, what other effects does globalization have on American dominant–minority relations?

$SAGE edge™

Sharpen your skills with SAGE edge at edge.sagepub.com/healey8e

SAGE edge for students provides a personalized approach to help you accomplish your coursework goals in an easy-to-use learning environment.

The following resources are available at SAGE edge:

Current Debates: Birthright Citizenship: Who Should Be an American?

The policy of birthright citizenship means that any baby born on American soil is automatically a citizen of the United States, regardless of the parents' citizenship. What are the implications of this policy? What costs does it create? Do undocumented immigrants take advantage of it? What would be the consequences of ending birthright citizenship?

On our website you will find an overview of the topic, the clashing points of view, and some questions to consider as you analyze the material.

Public Sociology Assignments

Public Sociology Assignments provide opportunities for students to address directly and personally some of the issues raised in this text.

The first two public sociology assignments on our website will lead students to confront diversity in their community. In the first assignment, you will investigate your hometown to see if you can document increases in racial and ethnic diversity consistent with Figure 1.1. In the second assignment, you will study graffiti: Does it express stereotypes and prejudice? What does it reflect about local group hierarchies?

Contributed by Linda M. Waldron

CHAPTER-OPENING TIMELINE CREDITS

1848: North Wind Picture Archives / Alamy Stock Photo

1882: Library of Congress Prints and Photographs Division

1924: Library of Congress Prints and Photographs Division

1942: Dorothea Lange / Oakland Museum of California / Wikimedia Commons

1952: Library of Congress Prints and Photographs Division

1965: Library of Congress Prints and Photographs Division

2008: Pete Souza, The Obama-Biden Transition Project / Wikimedia Commons

2016: Hillebrand Steve / U.S. Fish and Wildlife Service / Wikimedia Commons

ASSIMILATION AND PLURALISM

From Immigrants to White Ethnics

Wikipedia

1826
German Jews begin entering the U.S. By 1850, the Jewish population had risen from 6,000 to 50,000. Ten years later the population is 150,000.

1881–1885
1 million Germans immigrate to the U.S.

1820   1830   1840   1850   1860   1870   1880

1845–1852
Irish potato famine leads to mass immigration to the U.S.

Wikimedia Commons

1848
Serfdom ends in parts of Europe, freeing many peasants to move to the U.S.

1854
The Know-Nothings, a nativist political party seeking to restrict immigration, win significant victories in Congress, a sign of popular dissatisfaction with growing immigration from Catholic Ireland.

LOC

1862
The Homestead Act provides free plots of western land to settlers, spurring an influx of immigrants from Europe seeking land of their own.

LOC

We have room for but one flag, the American flag. . . . We have room for but one language and that is the English language, . . . and we have room for but one loyalty and that is a loyalty to the American people.

—Theodore Roosevelt, 26th president of the United States, 1907

If we lose our language [Ojibwa] . . . , I think, something more will be lost. . . . We will lose something personal. . . . We will lose our sense of ourselves and our culture. . . . We will lose beauty—the beauty of the particular, the beauty of the past and the intricacies of a language tailored for our space in the world. That Native American cultures are imperiled is important and not just to Indians. . . . When we lose cultures, we lose American plurality— the productive and lovely discomfort that true difference brings.

—David Treuer (2012, pp. 304–305)

Welcome to America. Now, speak English.

—Bumper sticker, 2017

LEARNING OBJECTIVES

By the end of this chapter, you will be able to do the following:

2.1 Explain types of assimilation and pluralism, including Anglo-conformity, the "melting pot," the "traditional" model of assimilation, cultural pluralism, and structural pluralism.

2.2 Discuss and explain other types of group relationships such as separatism.

2.3 Describe the timing, causes, and volume of European immigration to the United States, and explain how those immigrants became "white ethnics."

2.4 Understand the European patterns of assimilation and major variations in those patterns by social class, gender, and religion.

2.5 Describe the status of the descendants of European immigrants today, including the "twilight of white ethnicity."

2.6 Analyze contemporary immigration using sociological concepts in this chapter. Explain how the traditional model of assimilation does or does not apply to contemporary immigrants.

1890
The demographic trends in immigration shift as immigration from southern and eastern Europe substantially increases, while the relative proportion of immigration from northern and western Europe begins to decrease.

1917
The U.S. enters World War I with anti-German sentiment rising at home.

1948
The Displaced Persons Act opens American doors to more than 200,000 Europeans who could not return to their homes after World War II.

1980–2000
Economic turmoil in the Soviet Union leads to a massive exodus of Russian and Ukrainian Jews. More than 200,000 eventually settle in the U.S.

1895   1910   1925   1940   1955   1970   1985   2000

1881–1920
2 million Eastern European Jews immigrate to the U.S.

1911
The Dillingham Commission publishes a report warning that the "new" immigration from southern and eastern Europe threatens to subvert American society.

1911–1920
2 million Italians immigrate to the U.S.

1924
The Johnson–Reed Act limits annual European immigration to 2% of the number of people from that country living in the U.S. in 1890. The act greatly reduces immigration from southern and eastern European nationalities that had only small populations in the U.S. in 1890.

1965
The Hart-Celler Act produces major changes in patterns of immigration to the U.S., eventually reducing the percentage of immigrants from Europe.

In the United States, people speak more than 300 different languages, including more than 150 different Native American languages. Although most of these languages are spoken by small numbers of people, the sheer number of languages suggest the scope of contemporary American diversity.

Consider the quotations at the start of this chapter. What do you think? Does the range of languages and cultures they reflect create confusion and inefficiency in our society? Is there room for just one language as Roosevelt suggested? Or, does a diversity of language and culture enrich society? How much does it matter if a language disappears? Would we, as Treuer suggests, lose culture, beauty, and the "productive and lovely discomfort" of difference?

Americans (and the citizens of other nations) must consider such questions as we address issues of inclusion and diversity. Should we encourage groups to retain their unique cultural heritage, including their language, or should we stress conformity? How have we addressed these issues in the past? And, how should we approach them in the future? •

This chapter continues to look at the ways ethnic and racial groups in the United States relate to each other. Two key sociological concepts, assimilation and pluralism, can help us understand the variety of ways groups can relate to each other.

Assimilation is a process in which formerly distinct and separate groups come to share a common culture and merge socially. As a society undergoes assimilation, differences among groups decrease.

Pluralism, on the other hand, exists when groups maintain their individual identities. In a pluralistic society, groups remain separate, and their cultural and social differences persist over time.

In some ways, assimilation and pluralism are different processes, but they aren't mutually exclusive. They may occur together in a variety of combinations within a particular society or group. Some groups in a society may assimilate while others maintain (or even increase) their differences. As we'll see in Part 3, virtually every minority group in the United States has, at any given time, some members who are assimilating and others who are preserving or reviving traditional cultures. Some Native American groups for example, are pluralistic. They live on or near reservations, are strongly connected to their heritage, practice the "old ways" as much as they can, and speak their native languages. Other Native Americans are mostly assimilated into the dominant society: They live in urban areas, speak English only, and know relatively little about their traditional cultures. Both assimilation and pluralism are important forces in the everyday lives of Native Americans and most other minority group members.

American sociologists became concerned with these processes, especially assimilation, due to a massive migration from Europe to the United States that occurred between the 1820s and the 1920s. More than 31 million people crossed the Atlantic during this time, and a great deal of energy has been devoted to documenting, describing, and understanding the experiences of these immigrants and their descendants. These efforts have resulted in the development of a rich and complex body of research that seeks to explain how newcomers are incorporated into U.S. society. We will call this the "traditional" perspective.

This chapter begins with a consideration of the "traditional" perspective on assimilation and pluralism, and a brief examination of other possible group relationships. Then, we apply concepts and theories of the traditional perspective to European immigrants and their descendants, and we develop a model of American assimilation based on these experiences. We will use this model in our analysis of other minority groups throughout this book, especially in Part 3.

Since the 1960s, the United States has experienced a second mass immigration. A particularly important issue is whether the theories, concepts, and models based on the first mass immigration to the United States (from the 1820s to the 1920s) apply to this second wave. The newest immigrants to the United States differ in many ways from those who came earlier. Therefore, the ideas and theories based on the earlier immigration experiences won't necessarily apply to the present. We will briefly note some of these issues in this chapter and will explore them in detail in Part 3.

Finally, we will consider the implications of these first two chapters for the exploration of intergroup relations throughout this text. By the end of this chapter, you will be familiar with many of the concepts that will guide us as we examine the variety of possible dominant–minority group situations and the directions our society (and the groups within it) can take.

Assimilation is a process in which separate groups come to share a common culture and merge socially.

In **pluralism**, groups maintain separate identities, cultures, and organizational structures.

ASSIMILATION

We begin with the topic of assimilation because the emphasis in U.S. group relations has historically focused

The melting pot has been a popular and powerful image for Americans.

American minority groups (Abrahamson, 1980, pp. 152–154). Some groups—especially the racial minority groups—were largely excluded from the "melting" process resulting in a melting pot with a distinctly Anglocentric flavor: "For better or worse, the white Anglo-Saxon Protestant tradition was for two centuries—and in crucial respects still is—the dominant influence on American culture and society" (Schlesinger, 1992, p. 28).

Contrary to the melting-pot image, assimilation in the United States has primarily been a one-sided process more accurately called **Americanization** or **Anglo-conformity**. As reflected in the quote from President Roosevelt that opened this chapter, the leaders of American society, with the support of the public, designed assimilation to maintain the English language and the British-type institutional patterns created during the early years of American society.

The quote from President Roosevelt that opens this chapter also reflects the historic emphasis on Anglo-conformity. Many Americans today agree with Roosevelt. In a recent survey, 72% of respondents—the overwhelming majority—agreed that "it is essential that immigrants living in the United States learn to speak English." It may surprise you that 58% of Hispanic Americans agreed with this statement (compared with 67% of blacks and 77% of whites) (Jones, 2013). The apparent agreement between these groups may reflect different orientations and motivations. For some whites, the response may mix prejudice against non-English speakers with support for Americanization. The Hispanic responses may reflect their direct—possibly challenging—experiences navigating the monolingual institutions of American society.

Under Anglo-conformity, immigrant and minority groups are expected to adapt to Anglo-American culture as a precondition of acceptance and access to better jobs, education, and other opportunities. This type of assimilation means that minority groups have had to give up their traditions and adopt Anglo-American culture. To be sure, many groups and individuals were (and continue to be) eager to undergo Anglo-conformity, even if it meant losing much or all of their heritage. For others, the emphasis on Americanization created conflict, anxiety, demoralization, and resentment. In Part 3, we consider how different minority groups have experienced and responded to the pressures of Anglo-conformity.

on the goal of assimilation rather than pluralism. This section presents some of the most important sociological theories and concepts used to describe and analyze the assimilation of the 19th-century European immigrants into the United States.

TYPES OF ASSIMILATION

Assimilation is a general term for a process that can follow a number of different pathways. The metaphor of the **melting pot** is one form of assimilation in which different groups come together and contribute in roughly equal amounts to create a common culture and a new, unique society. This view of assimilation emphasizes sharing and inclusion and sees this process as benign and egalitarian. People often think of the United States as a "melting pot" and stress the ways diverse peoples contributed to American culture and society.

Although it is a popular idea, the melting pot is not an accurate description of how assimilation occurred for

---

The **melting pot** is a type of assimilation in which all groups contribute in roughly equal amounts to a new culture and society.

Americanization (or **Anglo-conformity**) is a type of assimilation in which the dominant culture pressures other groups to conform to Anglo-American culture.

THE "TRADITIONAL" PERSPECTIVE ON ASSIMILATION: THEORIES AND CONCEPTS

As noted earlier, the traditional perspective on assimilation emerged from research about European immigrants who came to the United States between the 1820s and the 1920s. The scholars in this tradition made invaluable contributions, and their thinking is impressively complex and comprehensive. This does not mean, of course, that they have exhausted the possibilities or answered (or asked) all the questions. Theorists working in the pluralist tradition and contemporary scholars studying the experiences of recent immigrants have questioned many aspects of traditional assimilation theory and have made a number of important contributions of their own.

Robert Park. Robert Park's research provided the foundation for many theories of assimilation. In the 1920s and 1930s, Park was one of a group of scholars who played a major role in establishing sociology as an academic discipline in the United States. Park felt that intergroup relations go through a predictable set of phases that he called a **race relations cycle**. When groups first come into contact (e.g., through immigration, conquest) relations are conflictual and competitive. However, the process, or cycle, eventually moves toward assimilation, or the "interpenetration and fusion" of groups (Park & Burgess, 1924, p. 735).

Park argued further that assimilation is inevitable in a democratic and industrial society. That is, in a political system based on democracy, fairness, and impartial justice, all groups should eventually secure equal treatment under the law. Additionally, in industrial societies, people's abilities and talents—rather than their ethnicity or race—will be the criteria used to judge them. Park believed that as the United States continued to modernize, urbanize, and industrialize, race and ethnicity would gradually lose their importance allowing the boundaries between groups to eventually dissolve. The result, he thought, would be a more "rational" and unified society (see also Geschwender, 1978, pp. 19–32; Hirschman, 1983).

Social scientists have examined, analyzed, and criticized Park's conclusions for decades. One frequent criticism is that he did not specify a time frame for the completion of assimilation. Therefore, his idea that assimilation is "inevitable" cannot be tested. Until the exact time when assimilation is deemed complete, we won't know whether his theory is wrong or whether we have not waited long enough. An additional criticism of Park's theory is that he does not describe the nature of the assimilation process in much detail. How would assimilation proceed? How would everyday life change? Which aspects of the group would change first? What do you think about these criticisms?

Milton Gordon. Sociologist Milton Gordon sought to clarify some of the issues Park left unresolved. He made a major contribution to theories of assimilation in his book *Assimilation in American Life* (1964). Gordon broke down the overall process of assimilation into seven subprocesses; we will focus on the first three. Before considering these phases of assimilation, we need to consider some new concepts.

Gordon makes a distinction between the cultural and the structural components of society. **Culture** encompasses all aspects of the way of life associated with a group of people. It includes language, religious and other beliefs, customs and rules of etiquette, and the values and ideas people use to organize their lives and interpret their existence. The **social structure**, or structural components of a society, includes networks of social relationships, groups, organizations, stratification systems, communities, and families. The social structure organizes the work of the society and connects individuals to one another and to the larger society.

It is common in sociology to separate the social structure into primary and secondary sectors. The **primary sector** includes interpersonal relationships that are intimate and personal, such as families and groups of friends. Groups in the primary sector are small. The **secondary sector** consists of groups and organizations that are more public, task oriented, and impersonal. Organizations in the secondary sector are often very large and include businesses, factories, schools and colleges, and bureaucracies.

Now we can examine Gordon's earliest stages of assimilation, which are summarized in Table 2.1.

The **race relations cycle** is the idea that group relations follow a predictable cycle starting with conflict but leading to eventual assimilation.

Culture includes all aspects of the way of life of a group of people, including beliefs, values, norm, symbols, technology, and many other components.

Social structure is the networks of relationships, groups, organizations, and institutions that organize society and connect individuals to one another.

The **primary sector** of a social structure consists of close, intimate relations.

The **secondary sector** of a social structure consists of impersonal, goal-oriented relations.

---

1. **Acculturation** or **cultural assimilation.** Members of the minority group learn the culture of the dominant group. For groups that immigrate to the United States, acculturation to the dominant Anglo-American culture may include changes both great and small, including learning the English language, changing eating habits, adopting new value systems and gender norms, and altering the spelling of the family surname.

2. **Integration** or **structural assimilation.** The minority group enters the social structure of the larger society. Integration typically begins in the secondary sector and gradually moves into the primary sector. That is, before people can form friendships with members of other groups (integration into the primary sector), they must first become acquaintances. The initial contact between groups often occurs in public institutions such as schools and workplaces (integration into the secondary sector). The greater their integration into the secondary sector, the more equal the minority group will be to the dominant group in income, education, and occupational prestige. Once a group has entered the institutions and public sectors of the larger society, according to Gordon, integration into the primary sector and the other stages of assimilation will follow inevitably (although not necessarily quickly). Measures of integration into the primary sector include the extent to which people have acquaintances, close friends, or neighbors from other groups.

3. **Intermarriage** or **marital assimilation.** When integration into the primary sector becomes substantial, the basis for Gordon's third stage of assimilation is established. People are most likely to select spouses from among their primary relations. Thus, in Gordon's view, primary structural integration typically comes before intermarriage.

Gordon argued that acculturation was a prerequisite for integration. Given the stress on Anglo-conformity, a member of an immigrant or minority group would not be able to compete for jobs or other opportunities in the

---

Acculturation or **cultural assimilation** is the process by which one group learns the culture of another.

Integration or **structural assimilation** is the process by which a group enters the social structure of the larger society.

Intermarriage or **marital assimilation** is marriage between members of different groups.

---

secondary sector of the social structure until he or she had learned the dominant group's culture. Gordon recognized, however, that successful acculturation does not automatically ensure that a group will begin the integration phase. The dominant group may still exclude the minority group from its institutions and limit the opportunities available to the minority group. Gordon argued that "acculturation without integration" (or Americanization without equality) is a common situation in the United States for many minority groups, especially the racial minority groups.

In Gordon's theory, movement from acculturation to integration is the crucial step in the assimilation process. Once integration occurs, the other subprocesses would inevitably occur, although movement through the stages could be very slow. Gordon's idea that assimilation runs a certain course in a particular order echoes Park's ideas about inevitability of the process.

Recent scholarship calls Gordon's conclusions about American assimilation into question. For example, the individual subprocesses that Gordon saw as occurring in a certain order can happen independently of one another (Yinger, 1985, p. 154). For example, a group may integrate before acculturating. Also, many researchers no longer think of the process of assimilation as necessarily linear or one-way (Greeley, 1974). Groups (or segments thereof) may "reverse direction" and become less assimilated over time, by reviving parts of their traditional culture such as language, or by revitalizing ethnic organizations or associations like the Irish Social Club of Boston.

Ngo (2008), among others, offers critiques of assimilationist models like Gordon's suggesting that a one-size-fits-all, unidirectional (stage) approach to acculturation overlooks a number of important issues. Because immigrants differ, it's logical to think that their assimilation process would, too. An intersectional approach might help us understand this critique and the diversity of immigration experiences. For example, how might the immigration and assimilation process be for a 16-year-old, middle-class, heterosexual Catholic girl from Russia moving to Nashville, TN? How would that experience be different for a 40-year-old gay Muslim man from Nigeria? How would age, sexual orientation, religious affiliation, gender, and class shape not just their immigration process, but their lives?

Gans (1997, c.f. Ngo, 2008) observes that many early scholars of assimilation were white men who had little experience with immigrants or speaking foreign languages. Thus, their conceptualization of the assimilation process may reflect their own backgrounds and perhaps ethnocentric assumptions that assimilation into the dominant culture is desirable and completely possible. Critics point out that such models ignore power dynamics, as if assimilation is just a matter of one's effort and will. Do all immigrants have an equal chance at full assimilation? To what degree

TABLE 2.1 Gordon's Stages of Assimilation

STAGE	PROCESS
1. Acculturation	The group learns the culture of the dominant group, including language and values.
2. Integration (structural assimilation)	
a. At the secondary level	Members of the group enter the public institutions and organizations of the dominant society.
b. At the primary level	Members of the group enter the cliques, clubs, and friendship groups of the dominant society.
3. Intermarriage (marital assimilation)	Members of the group marry with members of the dominant society on a large scale.

SOURCE: Adapted from Gordon (1964, p. 71).

should we consider structural and cultural inequities that immigrants face? For example, can people fully assimilate if those in the host culture don't want them there? As we'll see in future chapters, the degree to which minority groups have assimilated into the dominant culture varies. Thus, it may be useful to keep these critiques in mind.

Some scholars suggest that idealizing assimilation models such as Gordon's—for example by using it as the framework for national immigration policy—is akin to a form of colonization (see Ngo, 2008). They point out, also, that cultures influence one another. Because of such critiques, scholars have developed other models. For example, Berry (1980) offers a bidimensional model and argues that we need to consider people's cultural identity and connection to or participation in the host society. When one takes these two factors into account, four possibilities result: (1) assimilation, which he defines as a desire to interact with the new culture and low interest in retaining one's ethnic heritage, (2) separation (immigrants maintain the culture of their heritage and reject the host culture), (3) integration (immigrants keep their heritage culture but also adopt the receiving culture), and (4) marginalization (where the immigrant rejects the culture of his or her heritage and that of the host nation).

These critiques and others are useful to consider because as social life changes, our theoretical models for understanding them may need to change, too. Nonetheless, Gordon's model continues to guide our understanding of the assimilation process. For example, research on contemporary immigrants often involves assessing their experiences in Gordon's terms (Alba & Nee, 1997). In fact, Gordon's model will provide a major organizational framework for the case study chapters in Part 3 of this text.

Human Capital Theory. Why did some European immigrant groups acculturate and integrate more rapidly than others? Although not a theory of assimilation per se, **human capital theory** offers one possible answer to this question. This theory states that status attainment, or the level of success an individual achieves in society, is a direct result of educational attainment, personal values and skills, and other individual characteristics and abilities. From this perspective, education is an investment in human capital, similar to an investment a business might make in machinery or new technology. The greater the investment in a person's human capital, the higher the probability of success. Blau and Duncan (1967), in their pioneering statement of status attainment theory, found that even the relative advantage that comes from having a high-status father is largely mediated through education. In other words, high levels of affluence and occupational prestige aren't so much due to being born into a privileged status as they are the result of the superior education that affluence makes possible.

Human capital theory answers questions about the differing pace of upward mobility for immigrant groups in terms of the resources and cultural characteristics of the members of the groups, especially their levels of education and familiarity with English. From this perspective, people or groups who fail have not tried hard enough, have not made the right kinds of educational investments, or have values or habits that limit their ability to compete with others and move up the social class ladder.

Human capital theory is consistent with traditional American ideals. Both frame success as an individual phenomenon, a reward for hard work, sustained effort, and good character. Both tend to assume that success is equally available to everyone and that the larger society is neutral in its distribution of rewards and opportunity. Both tend to see assimilation as a highly desirable, benign process that blends diverse peoples and cultures into a strong, unified society. Thus, people or groups that resist Americanization or question its benefits are seen as threatening or illegitimate.

On one level, human capital theory is an important theory of success and upward mobility, and we will use it occasionally to analyze the experiences of minority and immigrant groups. However, because human capital theory resonates with American "common sense" views of success and failure, people may use it uncritically, ignoring flaws in the theory.

We will offer a final judgment on the validity of human capital theory at the end of this book, but you should be aware of its major limitations. First, human capital theory is an incomplete explanation of minority group experience

---

Human capital theory is the view that upward mobility is a direct result of effort, personal values and skills, and investment in education.

because it does not take account of all the factors that affect mobility and assimilation. Second, its assumption that U.S. society is equally open and fair to all groups is simply wrong. We will illustrate this issue and point out other strengths and limitations of this perspective as we move through the text.

QUESTIONS FOR REFLECTION

1. What are the limitations of the melting-pot view of assimilation?

2. Why does Gordon place acculturation as the first step in the process of assimilation? Could one of the other stages occur first? Why or why not?

3. What does human capital theory leave out? In what ways is it consistent with American values?

PLURALISM

Sociological discussions of pluralism often begin with a consideration of Horace Kallen's work. In articles published in *The Nation* magazine in 1915, Kallen argued that people should not have to surrender their culture and traditions to become full participants in American society. He rejected the Anglo-conformist, assimilationist model and contended that the existence of separate ethnic groups, even with separate cultures, religions, and languages, was consistent with democracy and other core American values. In Gordon's terms, Kallen believed that integration and equality were possible without extensive acculturation and that American society could be a federation of diverse groups, a mosaic of harmonious and interdependent cultures and peoples (Kallen, 1915a, 1915b; see also Abrahamson, 1980; Gleason, 1980).

Assimilation has been such a powerful theme in U.S. history that in the decades following the publication of Kallen's analysis, support for pluralism was low. In more recent decades, however, people's interest in pluralism and ethnic diversity has increased, in part because the assimilation that Park expected (and that many Americans assumed would happen) has not occurred. Perhaps we have not waited long enough, but as the 21st century unfolds, social distinctions among the racial minority groups in our society

show few signs of disappearing. In fact, some people question whether assimilation is desirable or not. Also, more surprising perhaps, white ethnicity has not disappeared, although it has changed in form and grown weaker. We review some of these changes at the end of this chapter.

An additional reason for the growing interest in pluralism is the everyday reality of the increasing diversity of U.S. society, as seen in Figure 1.1 (in Chapter 1). Controversies over issues such as "English-only" language policies, bilingual education, and eligibility for government benefits for immigrants are common and often bitter. Many Americans feel that diversity or pluralism has exceeded acceptable limits and that the unity of the nation is at risk.

Finally, developments around the globe have stimulated interest in pluralism. Several nation-states have re-formed into smaller units based on language, culture, race, and ethnicity. Recent events in India, the Middle East, former Yugoslavia, the former USSR, Canada, and Africa, to mention a few, have provided dramatic and often tragic evidence of how ethnic identities and hostilities can persist for decades (or even centuries) of submergence and suppression in larger national units.

In contemporary debates, discussions of diversity and pluralism are often couched in the language of **multiculturalism**, a general term for a variety of programs and ideas that stress mutual respect for all groups and for

Multiculturalism is a general term for pluralistic views that stress inclusion, mutual respect, and a celebration of group diversity.

Mulberry Street, New York City, around 1900, a bustling marketplace for Italian immigrants.

the multiple heritages that have shaped the United States. Some aspects of multiculturalism are controversial and have evoked strong opposition. In many ways, however, these debates merely echo a recurring argument about the character of American society, a debate that will be revisited throughout this text.

TYPES OF PLURALISM

We can distinguish various types of pluralism by using some of the concepts introduced in the discussion of assimilation. **Cultural pluralism** exists when groups have not acculturated and each maintains its own identity. The groups might speak different languages, practice different religions, and have different value systems. The groups are part of the same society and might even live in adjacent areas, but in some ways, they live in different worlds. Many Native Americans are culturally pluralistic and are committed to preserving their traditional culture. The Amish, a religious community sometimes called the Pennsylvania Dutch, are a culturally pluralistic group, also. They are committed to a way of life organized around farming, and they maintain a culture and an institutional life that is largely separate from the dominant culture (see Hostetler, 1980; Kephart & Zellner, 1994; Kraybill & Bowman, 2001).

Following Gordon's subprocesses, a second type of pluralism exists when a group has acculturated but not integrated. That is, the group has adopted the Anglo-American culture but does not have full and equal access to the institutions of the dominant society. In this situation, called **structural pluralism**, cultural differences are minimal, but the groups occupy different locations in the social structure. The groups may speak with the same accent, eat the same food, pursue the same goals, and subscribe to the same values, but they may also maintain separate organizational systems, including different churches, clubs, schools, and neighborhoods.

Under structural pluralism, groups practice a common culture but do so in different places and with minimal interaction across group boundaries. An example of structural pluralism occurs on Sunday mornings in the Christian churches of the United States, where local congregations are often identified with specific ethnic groups or races. What happens in the various churches—the rituals, expressions of faith, statements of core values and beliefs—is similar and expresses a common, shared culture. Structurally,

however, this common culture is expressed in separate buildings and by separate congregations.

A third type of pluralism reverses the order of Gordon's first two phases: integration without acculturation. This situation is exemplified by a group that has had some material success (e.g., measured by wealth or income) but has not become fully Americanized (become fluent in English, adopted uniquely American values and norms, etc.). Some immigrant groups have found niches in U.S. society in which they can survive and occasionally prosper economically without acculturating very much.

Two different situations can be used to illustrate this pattern. An **enclave minority group** establishes its own neighborhood and relies on a set of interconnected businesses, each of which is usually small in scope, for its economic survival. Some of these businesses serve the group, whereas others serve the larger society. The Cuban American community in South Florida and Chinatowns in many larger American cities are examples of ethnic enclaves.

A similar pattern of adjustment, the **middleman minority group**, also relies on small shops and retail firms, but the businesses are more dispersed throughout a large area rather than concentrated in a specific locale. Some Chinese American communities fit this second pattern, as do Korean American grocery stores and Indian American–owned motels (Portes & Manning, 1986). We discuss these types of minority groups further in Part 3.

The economic success of enclave and middleman minorities is partly due to the strong ties of cooperation and mutual aid within their groups. The ties are based on cultural bonds that would weaken if acculturation took place. In contrast with Gordon's idea that acculturation is a prerequisite to integration, whatever success these groups enjoy is due in part to the fact that they have *not* Americanized. Kim Park, who you read about in the Chapter 1 Some American Stories section, is willing to work in his uncle's grocery store for room and board and the opportunity to learn the business. His willingness to forgo a salary and subordinate his individual needs to the needs of the group reflects the strength of his relationship to family and kin. At various times and places, Jewish, Chinese, Japanese, Korean, and Cuban Americans have been enclave or middleman minorities as we'll see in future chapters (see Bonacich & Modell, 1980; Kitano & Daniels, 2001).

Under **cultural pluralism**, groups have not acculturated or integrated and each maintains a distinct identity.

Under **structural pluralism**, a group has acculturated but not integrated.

An **enclave minority group** establishes its own neighborhood and relies on a set of interconnected businesses for economic survival.

A **middleman minority group** relies on interconnected businesses, dispersed throughout a community, for economic survival.

The situation of enclave and middleman minorities—integration without acculturation—can be considered either a type of pluralism (emphasizing the absence of acculturation) or a type of assimilation (emphasizing the relatively high level of economic equality). Keep in mind that assimilation and pluralism are not opposites; they can occur in a variety of combinations. It is best to think of acculturation, integration, and the other stages of assimilation (or pluralism) as independent processes.

QUESTIONS FOR REFLECTION

4. Is the United States becoming more pluralistic? Explain. What are some of the costs and some of the benefits of increasing pluralism?

5. What are the differences between middleman and enclave minority groups? Do these groups challenge the idea that assimilation moves step-by-step in a certain order?

OTHER GROUP RELATIONSHIPS

This book concentrates on assimilation and pluralism because they are the most typical forms of group relations in the U.S. experience. Two other minority group goals include separatism and revolution (Wirth, 1945). The objective of **separatism** is for the group to sever political, cultural, and geographic ties with the larger society. Thus, separatism goes well beyond pluralism. Some Native Americans such as the Lakota have expressed both separatist and pluralist goals. Other ethnically based groups, such as Native Hawaiians and the Nation of Islam, have pursued separatism. Outside of the United States, one can find separatist groups in French Canada, Scotland, Chechnya, Cyprus, southern Mexico, and scores of other places, too.

A minority group promoting **revolution** seeks to become the dominant group or create a new social order, sometimes in alliance with members of the dominant group. Although some American minority groups (e.g., the Black Panthers) have pursued revolution, this goal has been relatively rare in the United States. Revolutionary minority groups are more commonly found where one nation has

Separatism is a minority-group goal. A separatist group wishes to sever all ties with the dominant group.

Revolution is a minority-group goal. A revolutionary group wishes to change places with the dominant group and establish a new social order.

conquered and controlled another racially or culturally different nation such as African countries colonized by France and the United Kingdom (e.g., Morocco).

Additionally, the dominant group may pursue goals other than assimilation and pluralism, including forced migration or expulsion, extermination or genocide, and continued subjugation of the minority group. Chinese immigrants were the victims of a policy of expulsion, beginning in the 1880s, when the Chinese Exclusion Act (1882) closed the door on further immigration and concerted efforts were made to encourage Chinese people to leave the United States (see Chapter 9). Native Americans have been the victims of expulsion, too. In 1830, the U.S. government forced all tribes living east of the Mississippi to migrate to a new territory in the West (see Chapters 4 and 7). The most infamous example of genocide is the Holocaust in Nazi Germany, during which six million Jews and millions of other minority-group members such as the Roma (or gypsies) and gay people were murdered. Tragically, many other examples of genocide exist.

Continued subjugation occurs when the dominant group exploits a minority group and seeks to keep them powerless. The system of slavery in the antebellum South is an example. Dominant groups may simultaneously pursue different policies with different minority groups and may change policies over time.

FROM IMMIGRANTS TO WHITE ETHNICS

In this section, we will explore the experiences of the minority groups that stimulated the development of what we are calling the traditional perspective on assimilation. A massive immigration from Europe began in the 1820s, and over the next century, millions of people made the journey from the Old World to the New. They came from every corner of the European continent: Germany, Greece, Ireland, Italy, Poland, Portugal, Russia, Ukraine, and scores of other nations and provinces. They came as young men and women seeking jobs, as families fleeing religious persecution, as political radicals fleeing the police, as farmers seeking land and a fresh start, and as paupers barely able to scrape together the cost of their passage. They came as immigrants, became minority groups upon their arrival, experienced discrimination and prejudice in all its forms, went through all the varieties and stages of assimilation and pluralism, and eventually merged into the society that had once rejected them so viciously. Figure 2.1 shows the major European sending nations.

These immigrants were a diverse group, and their experiences in the United States varied along crucial sociological dimensions. Some groups (Italians and other southern

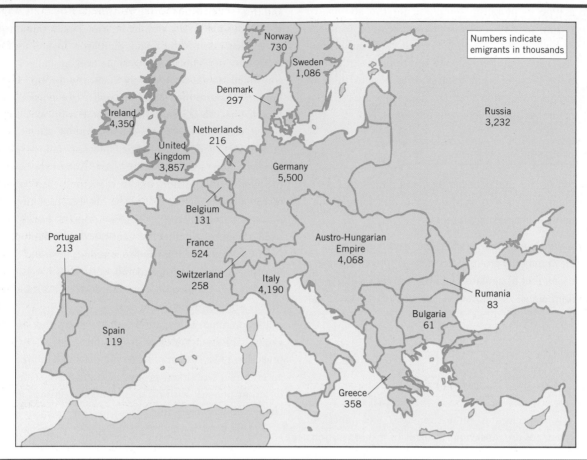

Europeans) were seen as racially inferior, while others (Irish Catholics and Jews from Eastern Europe) were rejected and marginalized because of their religion. The immigration experience—from start to finish—was shaped by gender and was decidedly different for women and men.

Social class was another major differentiating factor: Many European immigrants brought few resources and very low human capital. They entered U.S. society at the bottom of the economic ladder and often remained on the lowest occupational and economic rungs for generations. Other groups brought skills or financial resources that led them to a more favorable position and faster rates of upward mobility. All these factors—race, gender, and class—affected their experiences and led to very different outcomes in terms of social location, mobility paths, and acceptance within U.S. society.

This first mass wave of immigrants shaped the United States in many ways. When the immigration started in the 1820s, the United States was an agricultural nation clustered along the East Coast, not yet 50 years old. The nation was just coming into contact with Mexicans in the Southwest, slavery was flourishing in the South, and conflict with Native Americans was intense and brutal. When this period of intense immigration ended in the 1920s, the

U.S. population had increased from fewer than 10 million to more than 100 million. Society had industrialized, stretched from coast to coast, established colonies in the Pacific and the Caribbean, and become a world power.

It was no coincidence that America's industrialization and rise to global prominence occurred simultaneously with European immigration. These changes were intimately interlinked, the mutual causes and effects of one another. Industrialization fueled the growth of U.S. military and political power, and the industrial machinery of the nation depended heavily on the flow of labor from Europe. By World War I, for example, 25% of the U.S. labor force was foreign born, and more than half the workforce in New York, Detroit, and Chicago consisted of immigrant men. Immigrants were the majority of the workers in many important sectors of the economy, including coal mining, steel manufacturing, the garment industry, and meatpacking (Martin & Midgley, 1999, p. 15; Steinberg, 1981, p. 36).

In the sections that follow, we explore the experiences of these groups, beginning with the forces that caused them to leave Europe and come to the United States and ending with an assessment of their present status in American society.

INDUSTRIALIZATION AND IMMIGRATION

What forces stimulated this mass movement of people? Like any complex phenomenon, immigration from Europe had a multitude of causes, but underlying the process was a massive and fundamental shift in subsistence technology: the **industrial revolution**. We mentioned the importance of subsistence technology in Chapter 1. Dominant–minority relations are intimately related to the system a society uses to satisfy its basic needs, and those relations change as the economic system changes. The immigrants were pushed out of Europe as industrial technology wrecked the traditional agricultural way of life, and they were drawn to the United States by the jobs created by the spread of the very same technology. Let's consider the impact of this fundamental transformation of social structure and culture.

Industrialization began in England in the mid-1700s, spread to other parts of Northern and Western Europe and then, in the 1800s, to Eastern and Southern Europe. As it rolled across the continent, the industrial revolution replaced people and animal power with machines and new forms of energy (steam, coal, and eventually oil and gas), causing an exponential increase in the productive capacity of society. (See pages 48–49 for a detailed timeline.)

At the dawn of the industrial revolution, most Europeans lived in small, rural villages and survived by traditional farming practices that had changed very little over the centuries. The work of production was **labor-intensive**, done by hand or with the aid of draft animals. Productivity was low, and the tasks of food production and survival required the efforts of virtually the entire family working ceaselessly throughout the year.

Industrialization destroyed this traditional way of life as it introduced new technology, machines, and sources of energy to the tasks of production (e.g., steam engines) The new technology was **capital-intensive** or dependent on machine power. As agriculture modernized, the need for human labor in rural areas decreased. During this time, landowners consolidated farmland into larger and larger tracts for the sake of efficiency, further decreasing the need for human laborers. Yet, even as survival in this rapidly changing rural economy became more difficult, the rural population began to grow.

In response to these challenges, peasants began to leave their home villages and move toward urban areas. Factories were being built in or near the cities, opening up opportunities for employment. The urban population tended to increase faster than the job supply. Thus, many migrants could not find work and had to move on; many of

---

The **industrial revolution** is the shift in subsistence technology from labor-intensive agriculture to capital-intensive manufacturing.

Labor-intensive production is a form of work in which most of the effort is provided by people working by hand.

Capital-intensive technology replaces hand labor with machine labor. Large amounts of capital are required to develop, purchase, and maintain the machines.

FIGURE 2.2 Legal Migration to the United States by Region of Origin, 1820–2015

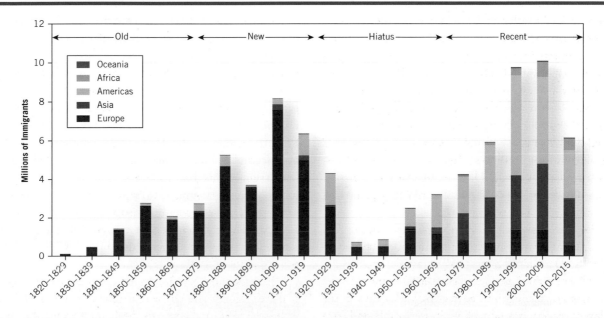

SOURCE: Data from Table 2, Persons Obtaining Legal Permanent Resident Status by Region and Selected Country of Last Residence: Fiscal Years 1820 to 2015. 2015 Yearbook of Immigration Statistics. U.S. Department of Homeland Security.

FIGURE 2.3 Timeline of the Industrial Revolution, 1712–1903

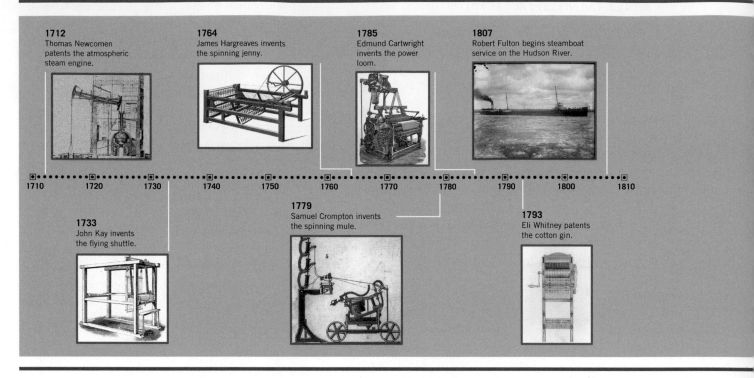

1712
Thomas Newcomen patents the atmospheric steam engine.

1764
James Hargreaves invents the spinning jenny.

1785
Edmund Cartwright invents the power loom.

1807
Robert Fulton begins steamboat service on the Hudson River.

1710 1720 1730 1740 1750 1760 1770 1780 1790 1800 1810

1733
John Kay invents the flying shuttle.

1779
Samuel Crompton invents the spinning mule.

1793
Eli Whitney patents the cotton gin.

SOURCE: Timeline of Industrial Revolution, 1700–1900 is adapted from Industrial Revolution: Timeline, Facts, and Resources, Research by B. Sobey, TheFreeResource.com.

them responded to opportunities in the United States. At the same time, the abundance of frontier farmland encouraged people to move westward, sustaining a fairly constant demand for labor in the East Coast areas that were easiest for Europeans to reach. As industrialization took hold on both continents, the population movement to European cities and then to North America eventually grew to become one of the largest in human history.

The timing of migration from Europe followed the timing of industrialization. The first waves of immigrants, often called the **Old Immigration**, came from Northern and Western Europe starting in the 1820s. A second wave, the **New Immigration**, began arriving from Southern and Eastern Europe in the 1880s. Figure 2.2 shows both waves and the rates of legal immigration up to 2015. Note that the New Immigration was much more voluminous than the Old Immigration, and that the number of immigrants declined drastically after the 1920s. We will explore the reasons for this decline later in this chapter and discuss in detail the more recent (post-1965) increase in immigration—overwhelmingly from the Americas (mostly Mexico) and Asia—in Chapters 8 through 10.

EUROPEAN ORIGINS AND CONDITIONS OF ENTRY

The immigrants from Europe varied from one another in innumerable ways. They followed a variety of pathways into the United States, and their experiences were shaped by their cultural and class characteristics, their countries of origin, and the timing of their arrival. Some groups encountered much more resistance than others, and different groups played different roles in the industrialization and urbanization of America. To discuss these diverse patterns systematically, we distinguish three subgroups of European immigrants: Protestants from Northern and Western Europe, the largely Catholic immigrant laborers from Ireland and from Southern and Eastern Europe, and Jewish immigrants from Eastern Europe. We look at these subgroups in the approximate order of their arrival. In later sections, we will consider other sociological variables such as social class and gender that further differentiated the experiences of people in these groups.

NORTHERN AND WESTERN PROTESTANT EUROPEANS

Northern and Western European immigrants included Danes (from Denmark), Dutch, English, French, Germans,

The **Old Immigration** was from Northern and Western Europe to the United States from the 1820s to the 1880s.

The **New Immigration** was from Southern and Eastern Europe to the United States from the 1880s to the 1920s.

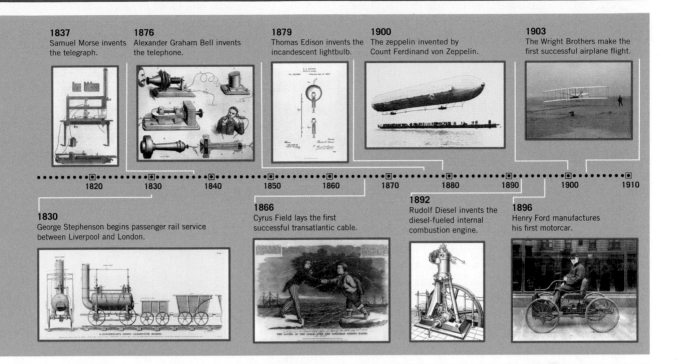

1837
Samuel Morse invents the telegraph.

1876
Alexander Graham Bell invents the telephone.

1879
Thomas Edison invents the incandescent lightbulb.

1900
The zeppelin invented by Count Ferdinand von Zeppelin.

1903
The Wright Brothers make the first successful airplane flight.

1820   1830   1840   1850   1860   1870   1880   1890   1900   1910

1830
George Stephenson begins passenger rail service between Liverpool and London.

1866
Cyrus Field lays the first successful transatlantic cable.

1892
Rudolf Diesel invents the diesel-fueled internal combustion engine.

1896
Henry Ford manufactures his first motorcar.

Norwegians, Swedes, and Welsh. These groups were similar to the dominant group in their racial and religious characteristics. They also shared many American values, including the **Protestant ethic**—which stressed hard work, success, and individualism—and support for the principles of democratic government. These similarities eased their acceptance into a society that was highly intolerant of religious and racial differences until well into the 20th century. These immigrant groups experienced a lower degree of ethnocentric rejection and racist disparagement than did the Irish and immigrants from Southern and Eastern Europe.

Northern and Western European immigrants came from nations that were just as developed as the United States. Thus, these immigrants tended to be more skilled and educated than other immigrant groups, and often brought money and other resources with which to secure a comfortable place for themselves in their new society. Many settled in the sparsely populated Midwest and in other frontier areas, where they farmed the fertile land that became available after the conquest and removal of Native Americans and Mexican Americans (see Chapter 4). By dispersing throughout the midsection of the country, they lowered their visibility and their degree of competition with dominant-group members. Two brief case studies, first of Norwegians and then of Germans, outline the experiences of these groups.

Protestant ethic stressed hard work, success, and individualism, and was analyzed by Max Weber (see Chapter 1) in his sociological classic *The Protestant Ethic and the Spirit of Capitalism.*

Newly arrived Ruthenian immigrant.

Immigrants From Norway. Norway had a small population base, and immigration from this Scandinavian nation to the United States was never large in absolute numbers. However, "America fever" struck here as it did elsewhere in Europe, and on a per capita basis, Norway sent more immigrants to the United States before 1890 than any other European nation except Ireland (Chan, 1990, p. 41).

The first Norwegian immigrants were moderately prosperous farmers searching for cheap land. They found abundant acreage in upper-Midwest states, such as Minnesota and Wisconsin, and then found that the local labor supply was too small to cultivate the available land effectively. Many turned to their homeland for assistance and used their relatives and friends to create networks and recruit a labor force. Thus, chains of communication and migration linking Norway to the Northern Plains were established, supplying immigrants to these areas for decades (Chan, 1990, p. 41). Today, a strong Scandinavian heritage is still evident in the farms, towns, and cities of the upper Midwest.

Immigrants From Germany. The stream of immigration from Germany was much larger than that from Norway. In the latter half of the 19th century, at least 25% of the immigrants each year were German (Conzen, 1980, p. 406) and they left their mark on the economy, political structure, and cultural life of their new land. In 2015, about 45 million Americans (14.2%) traced their ancestries to Germany, more than to any other country (ACS, 2015).

The German immigrants who arrived in the early 1800s moved into the newly opened farmland and the rapidly growing cities of the Midwest, as had many Scandinavians. By 1850, large German communities could be found in Milwaukee, St. Louis, and other Midwestern cities (Conzen, 1980, p. 413). Some German immigrants followed the trans-Atlantic route of the cotton trade between Europe and the southern United States and entered through the port of New Orleans, moving from there to the Midwest and Southwest.

German immigrants arriving later in the century were more likely to settle in urban areas, in part because fertile land was less available. Many of the city-bound German immigrants were skilled workers and artisans, and others found work as laborers in the rapidly expanding industrial sector. The double penetration of German immigrants into the rural economy and the higher sectors of the urban economy is reflected by the fact that by 1870, most employed German Americans were involved in skilled labor (37%) or farming (25%) (Conzen, 1980, p. 413).

German immigrants took relatively high occupational positions in the U.S. labor force, and their sons and daughters were able to translate that relative affluence into economic mobility. By the dawn of the 20th century, large numbers of second-generation German Americans were finding their way into white-collar and professional careers. Within a few generations, German Americans had achieved parity with national norms in education, income, and occupational prestige.

Assimilation Patterns. By and large, assimilation for Norwegian, German, and other Protestant immigrants from Northern and Western Europe was consistent with the traditional model discussed earlier in this chapter. Although members of these groups felt the sting of rejection, prejudice, and discrimination, their movement from acculturation to integration and equality was relatively smooth, especially when compared with the experiences of racial minority groups. Table 2.3, later in this chapter, illustrates their relative success and high degree of assimilation.

IMMIGRANT LABORERS FROM IRELAND AND SOUTHERN AND EASTERN EUROPE

The relative ease of assimilation for Northern and Western Europeans contrasts sharply with the experiences of non-Protestant, less-educated, and less-skilled immigrants. These "immigrant laborers" came in two waves. The Irish were part of the Old Immigration that began in the 1820s, but the bulk of this group—Bulgarians, Greeks, Hungarians, Italians, Poles, Russians, Serbs, Slovaks, Ukrainians, and scores of other Southern and Eastern European groups—made up the New Immigration that began in the 1880s.

Peasant Origins. Most of the immigrants in these nationality groups (like many recent immigrants to the United States) were peasants or unskilled laborers, with few resources other than their willingness to work. They came from rural, village-oriented cultures in which family and kin took precedence over individual needs or desires. Family life for them tended to be patriarchal and autocratic; that is, men dominated decision making and controlled family resources. Children were also expected to subordinate their personal desires and to work for the good of the family as a whole. Arranged marriages were common. This cultural background was less consistent with the industrializing, capitalistic, individualistic, Protestant, Anglo-American culture of the United States and was a major reason that these immigrant laborers experienced a higher level of rejection and discrimination than the immigrants from Northern and Western Europe.

The immigrant laborers were much less likely to enter the rural economy than were the Northern and Western European immigrants. Much of the better frontier land had already been claimed by the time these new immigrant groups began to arrive, and a large number of them had been permanently soured on farming by the oppressive and exploitative agrarian economies from which they were trying to escape (see Handlin, 2002).

Regional and Occupational Patterns. The immigrant laborers of this time settled in the cities of the industrializing Northeast and found work in plants, mills, mines, and factories. They supplied the armies of laborers needed to power the industrial revolution in the United States, although their view of this process was generally from the bottom looking up. They arrived during the decades in which the American industrial and urban infrastructure was being constructed. They built roads, canals, and railroads, as well as the buildings that housed the machinery of industrialization. For example, the first tunnels of the New York City subway system were dug, largely by hand, by laborers from Italy. Other immigrants found work in the coalfields of Pennsylvania and West Virginia and the steel mills of Pittsburgh, and they flocked by the millions to the factories of the Northeast.

Like other low-skill immigrant groups, these newcomers took jobs in which strength and stamina were more important than literacy or skilled labor. In fact, the minimum level of skills required for employment actually declined as industrialization proceeded through its early phases. To keep wages low and take advantage of what seemed like an inexhaustible supply of cheap labor, industrialists and factory owners developed technologies and machines that required few skills and little knowledge of English to operate. As mechanization proceeded, unskilled workers replaced skilled workers. Not infrequently, women and children replaced men because they could be hired for lower wages (Steinberg, 1981, p. 35).

Assimilation Patterns. Eventually, as the generations passed, the prejudice, systematic discrimination, and other barriers to upward mobility for the immigrant laborer groups weakened, and their descendants began to rise out of the working class. Although the first and second generations of these groups were largely limited to jobs at the unskilled or semiskilled level, the third and later generations rose in the American social class system. As Table 2.3 shows (later in this chapter), the descendants of the immigrant laborers achieved parity with national norms by the latter half of the 20th century.

EASTERN EUROPEAN JEWISH IMMIGRANTS AND THE ETHNIC ENCLAVE

Jewish immigrants from Russia and other parts of Eastern Europe followed a third pathway into U.S. society. These

Many "breaker boys" who worked in coal mines came from immigrant families.

immigrants were a part of the New Immigration and began arriving in the 1880s. Unlike the immigrant laborer groups, who were generally economic refugees and included many young, single men, Eastern European Jews were fleeing religious persecution and arrived as family units intending to settle permanently and become citizens. They settled in the urban areas of the Northeast and Midwest. New York City was the most common destination, and the Lower East Side became the best-known Jewish American neighborhood. By 1920, about 60% of all Jewish Americans lived in the urban areas between Boston and Philadelphia, with almost 50% living in New York City. Another 30% lived in the urban areas of the Midwest, particularly in Chicago (Goren, 1980, p. 581).

Urban Origins. In Russia and other parts of Eastern Europe, Jews had been barred from agrarian occupations and had come to make their livelihoods from jobs in the urban economy. For example, almost two thirds of the immigrant Jewish men had been tailors and other skilled laborers in Eastern Europe (Goren, 1980, p. 581). When they immigrated to the United States, these urban skills and job experiences helped them find work in the rapidly industrializing U.S. economy of the early 20th century.

Other Jewish immigrants joined the urban working class and took manual labor and unskilled jobs in the industrial sector (Morawska, 1990, p. 202). The garment industry in particular became the lifeblood of the Jewish community and provided jobs to about one third of all Eastern European Jews residing in the major cities (Goren, 1980, p. 582). Women and men worked in the garment industry. Jewish women, like the women of more recent immigrant laborer groups, created ways to combine their jobs and their domestic responsibilities. As young girls, they worked in factories and sweatshops, and after marriage, they did the same work at home, sewing precut garments together or

Hester Street, New York City, was the center of the Jewish immigrant enclave a century ago.

doing other piecework such as wrapping cigars or making artificial flowers, often assisted by their children (Amott & Matthaei, 1991, p. 115).

An Enclave Economy. Unlike most European immigrant groups, Jewish Americans became heavily involved in commerce. Drawing on their experience in the "old country," many started businesses and small independent enterprises. Jewish neighborhoods were densely populated and provided a ready market for all kinds of services such as bakeries, butcher and candy shops, and other retail enterprises.

Capitalizing on their residential concentration and close proximity, Jewish immigrants created an enclave economy founded upon dense networks of commercial, financial, and social cooperation. The Jewish American enclave survived because of the cohesiveness of the group; the willingness of wives, children, and other relatives to work for little or no monetary compensation; and the commercial savvy of the early immigrants. Also, a large pool of cheap labor and sources of credit and other financial services were available within the community. The Jewish American enclave grew and provided a livelihood for many of the children and grandchildren of the immigrants (Portes & Manning, 1986, pp. 51–52). As with other enclave groups that we will discuss in future chapters, including Chinese Americans and Cuban Americans, Jewish American economic advancement preceded extensive acculturation. That is, they made significant strides toward economic equality before they became fluent in English or were otherwise Americanized.

Americanized Generations. One way an enclave immigrant group can improve its position is to develop an educated and acculturated second generation. The Americanized, English-speaking children of these immigrants used their greater familiarity with the dominant society and their language facility to help preserve and expand the family enterprise. Furthermore, as the second generation appeared, the American public school system was expanding, and education through the college level was free or inexpensive in New York City and other cities (Steinberg, 1981, pp. 128–138). There was also a strong push for the second and third generations to enter professions, and as Jewish Americans excelled in school, resistance to and discrimination against them increased. By the 1920s, many elite colleges and universities, such as Dartmouth, had established quotas that limited the number of Jewish students they would admit (Dinnerstein, 1977, p. 228). These quotas were not abolished until after World War II.

Assimilation Patterns. The enclave economy and the Jewish neighborhoods the immigrants established proved to be an effective base from which to integrate into American society. The descendants of the Eastern European Jewish immigrants moved out of the ethnic neighborhoods years ago, and their positions in the economy—their pushcarts, stores, and jobs in the garment industry—have been taken

Chinatowns were the centers of social and economic life for Chinese immigrants.

up by more recent immigrants. When they left the enclave economy, many second- and third-generation Eastern European Jews did not enter the mainstream occupational structure at the bottom, as the immigrant laborer groups tended to do. They used the resources generated through the hard work, skills, and entrepreneurship of the early generations to gain access to prestigious and advantaged social class positions (Portes & Manning, 1986, p. 53). Today, Jewish Americans, as a group, surpass national averages in levels of education and income (Masci, 2016) as well as occupational prestige (Sklare, 1971, pp. 60–69; see also Cohen, 1985; Massarik & Chenkin, 1973). The relatively higher status of Russian Americans shown in Table 2.3 (later in this chapter) is due, in part, to the fact that many are of Jewish heritage.

CHAINS OF IMMIGRATION

All immigrant groups tend to follow "chains" established and maintained by group members. Some versions of the traditional assimilation perspective (especially human capital theory) treat immigration and status attainment as purely individual matters. To the contrary, scholars have demonstrated that immigration to the United States was in large measure a group (sociological) phenomenon. Immigrant chains stretched across the oceans, held together by the ties of kinship, language, religion, culture, and a sense of connection (Bodnar, 1985; Tilly, 1990).

Here is how chain immigration worked (and, although modified by modern technology, continues to work today): Someone from a village in, for instance, Poland would make it to the United States. This successful immigrant would send word to the home village, perhaps by hiring a letter writer. Along with news and adventure stories, they would send their address. Within months, another immigrant from the village, another relative perhaps, would show up at the address of the original immigrant. After months of experience in the new society, the original immigrant could lend assistance, provide a place to sleep, help with job hunting, and orient the newcomer to the area.

Before long, others would arrive from the village in need of the same sort of introduction to the mysteries of America. The compatriots would tend to settle close to one another, in the same building or on the same block. Soon, entire neighborhoods were filled with people from a certain village, province, or region. In these ethnic enclaves, people spoke the old language and observed the old ways. They started businesses, founded churches or synagogues, had families, and began mutual aid societies and other organizations. There was safety in numbers and comfort and security in a familiar, if transplanted, set of traditions and customs.

Immigrants often responded to U.S. society by attempting to re-create as much of their old world as possible within the bustling metropolises of the industrializing Northeast and West Coast. They did so, in part, to avoid the harsher forms of rejection and discrimination and also for solidarity and mutual support. These Little Italys, Little Warsaws, Little Irelands, Greektowns, Chinatowns, and Little Tokyos were safe havens that insulated the immigrants from the dominant U.S. society and helped them to establish bonds with one another, organize group life, pursue their own group interests, and have some control over the pace of their adjustment to American culture. For some groups and in some areas, the ethnic subcommunity was a short-lived phenomenon. For others (like the Jewish enclave discussed earlier, for example), the neighborhood became the dominant structure of their lives, and the networks continued to function long after the arrival of group members in the United States.

THE CAMPAIGN AGAINST IMMIGRATION: PREJUDICE, RACISM, AND DISCRIMINATION

Today, it may be hard to conceive of the bitterness and intensity of the prejudice that greeted the Irish, Italians, Jews, Poles, and other new immigrant groups. Even as they were becoming an indispensable segment of the American workforce, Americans castigated, ridiculed, attacked, and disparaged them. The Irish were the first immigrant laborers to arrive; thus, they were the first to feel this intense prejudice and discrimination. White Americans waged campaigns against them; mobs attacked Irish neighborhoods and burned Roman Catholic churches and convents. Some employers blatantly refused to hire the Irish, often posting signs that read "No Irish Need Apply." Until later arriving groups immigrated and pushed them up, the Irish were mired at the bottom of the job market (Blessing, 1980; Dolan, 2010; Potter, 1973; Shannon, 1964).

Other groups felt the same sting of rejection as they arrived. Italian immigrants were particularly likely to be the victims of violent attacks, one of the most vicious of which took place in New Orleans in 1891. The city's police chief was assassinated, and rumors of Italian involvement in the murder were rampant. The police arrested hundreds of Italians, and nine were brought to trial. All were acquitted. Yet within this context, anti-Italian sentiment was running so high that a mob lynched 11 Italians while police and city officials did nothing (Higham, 1963; Zecker, 2011).

Anti-Catholicism. Much of the prejudice against the Irish and the new immigrants was expressed as anti-Catholicism. Prior to the mid-19th century, Anglo-American society had been almost exclusively Protestant. Catholicism, with its celibate clergy, Latin masses, and cloistered nuns, seemed

NARRATIVE PORTRAIT

The Lost Boys of Sudan

Children in a refugee camp in Kakuma, Kenya.

The "Lost Boys of Sudan[1]" are youth who escaped the Second Sudanese Civil War (1983–2005), which killed more than two million people and injured and displaced many more (The Lost Boys of Sudan, IRC). To survive, between 20,000–25,000 of them, most between 8 to 18 years old, walked nearly 1,000 miles from South Sudan to Ethiopia. They suffered from exhaustion, hunger and starvation, dehydration, exposure to the elements, and threats to their lives from animals and people. They occasionally crossed into war zones where some were captured, threatened, and beaten. Some were conscripted into the army as "child soldiers." They stayed in Ethiopia for about five years until war drove them out (personal communication with author). They walked to Kenya and resettled in the Kakuma Refugee Camp where they lived for years. Only about half of the original group made it there (Rose, n.d.). Of those, about 3,000 were girls (Jack, 2010, p. 22).

Gender affects people's experience of war. In this case, boys were more likely to escape the war because they were tending cows away from their villages making it easier to run or hide. Some girls managed to escape, but when they arrived in Ethiopia, gender conventions influenced the decision to segregate them from the boys, usually by placing them in foster families. Thus, they typically could not take advantage of education, counseling, or sports programs in the camp. When the U.S. government decided to accept some of these refugees, they stipulated that they be orphans. Because the girls had been living with families for several years, they did not meet that requirement. Hence, of the 2,000 South Sudanese refugees to settle in the United States, only 89 were girls (Jack, 2010, p. 22).

As new immigrants, the Lost Boys faced many challenges of adapting to American culture while trying to maintain their cultural identities as Dinka and Nuer. The following excerpt describes John Bul Dau's arrival to the United States.

The airport hummed with so much activity, so many people moving so fast in so many directions. My first look at Americans in America, I thought. What do they look like? So many of them were short by Dinka standards, and they walked like crazy, almost as if they were running. They seem to all be in a hurry. The woman behind the immigration desk asked for papers by saying, "Next." That was all she said. "Next. Next. Next." I gave her my precious, sealed envelope. She opened it and looked it over. She signed my name to some documents and gave me more papers. Then she motioned me through, very fast. "Next," she said.

I had questions about how to find the waiting area. Sometimes, busy Americans don't even speak to answer. They just pointed . . . we were hungry and tired, and I felt sick from the malaria medicine . . . I walked into the men's room at LaGuardia and saw the toilets and fancy sinks. I had seen pictures of them at orientation, but they still seemed strange. I have watched a lesson on how to work a toilet, and I used it without incident. But the sink was another matter. It had no faucets. I needed to wash my hands . . . without warning, when I moved my hands . . . the water came on by itself. This is a magic country, I thought, and white people—that's how I thought of Americans—are so cunning. They make things easy for themselves; they make things work for them. I wondered if that made it tempting to be lazy.

. . . I had no bags . . . I stepped into a brightly lit room and spotted three Lost Boys, now Sudanese Americans, who had come to greet me. There were some white people, including a woman and her son . . . "Welcome," said the woman who first greeted me, and everyone joined in.

Welcome to Syracuse. Welcome to America. Welcome.

Questions to Consider

1. What concepts from the text thus far seem most applicable to this passage and why?

2. What are the most significant challenges the Lost Boys will face in the United States and why?

3. The Lost Boys are what some call "deserving immigrants" who differ from "undeserving immigrants" who enter the country illegally (Aptekar, 2015, p. 112). What do you make of this dichotomy? What are the most important factors we, as a society, should consider when deciding which immigrants we let in. How important are "merits" such as English fluency, education, religion, etc.? How should "merit" be balanced with human needs (e.g., safety, work)?

4. Most of the Sudanese refugees worked extremely hard to assimilate—working, taking classes, and adopting American norms. Yet, many have struggled to find good jobs and attain financial security. Discuss this in light of human capital theory.

---

[1]This name is a reference to Peter Pan and the "lost boys" who took care of one another in Never Never Land. The name is problematic because it linguistically erases girls. Interviews with the refugees suggest mixed appeal. A common negative response was similar to this one, "I don't like the name because we are not lost. Being called lost means that you don't know where you come from. If I were to change the name I would make it the 'Young Generation of Sudan.'" (Muhindi & Nyakato, 2002, p. 12).

alien, exotic, and threatening. The growth of Catholicism, especially because it was associated with non-Anglo immigrants, raised fears that the Protestant religions would lose status. There were even rumors that the pope was planning to move the Vatican to America and organize a takeover of the U.S. government.

Although Catholics were often stereotyped as a single group, they also varied along a number of dimensions. For example, the Catholic faith as practiced in Ireland differed significantly from Catholicism practiced in Italy, Poland, and other countries. Catholic immigrant groups often established their own parishes, with priests who could speak the old language. These cultural and national differences often separated Catholic groups, despite their common faith (Herberg, 1960).

Anti-Semitism. Jews from Russia and Eastern Europe faced intense prejudice and racism (or **anti-Semitism**) as they began arriving in large numbers in the 1880s. Biased sentiments and negative stereotypes of Jews have, unfortunately, been common for centuries. For nearly two millennia, Christians chastised and persecuted European Jews as the "killers of Christ" and stereotyped them as materialistic moneylenders and crafty business owners (Cohen, 1982).

The stereotype that links Jews and money lending has its origins in the fact that in premodern Europe, the Church forbade Catholics to charge interest for loans. Jews were under no such restriction, and they filled the gap within the economy (Frankel, 1997, p. 16; Jaher, 1996, p. 64). The most dreadful episode in the long history of European anti-Semitism was, of course, the Nazi Holocaust, in which six million Jews died. European anti-Semitism did not end with the demise of the Nazi regime, and it remains a prominent concern throughout Europe and Russia today (see Chapter 13).

Before the mass immigration of Eastern European Jews began in the late 1800s, anti-Semitism in the United States was relatively mild, perhaps because the group was so small. As European immigration continued and the Jewish population in the United States grew, anti-Semitism increased in intensity and viciousness. Many Americans accepted the European stereotype of Jews as cunning, dishonest merchants. In the late 19th century, whites began to ban Jews from social clubs and summer resorts, businesses such as hotels (Kennedy, 2001) and other organizations (Meenes, 1941; The Jew and the Club, 1924). Some began posting notices such as, "We prefer not to entertain Hebrews" (Goren, 1980, p. 585) and "Patronage of Jews is Declined" (Bernheimer, 1908, p. 1106). Such language was an attempt to mask blatant discrimination and hints at forms of modern racism to come.

By the 1920s and 1930s, the Ku Klux Klan and other extreme racist groups espoused anti-Semitism. Because many of the political radicals and labor leaders of the time were Jewish immigrants, anti-Semitism became fused with a fear of Communism and other anti-capitalist doctrines. Anti-Semitism became prominent among American prejudices and some well-known Americans espoused anti-Semitic views, including Henry Ford, the founder of Ford Motor Company; Charles Lindbergh, the first aviator to fly solo across the Atlantic; and Father Charles Coughlin, a Catholic priest with a popular radio show (Selzer, 1972).

Anti-Semitism reached a peak before World War II and tapered off in the decades following the war, shifting into more subtle forms. As we shall see in Chapter 3, it remains a part of U.S. society (Anti-Defamation League, 2000; Benowitz, 2017; Borstelmann, 2009; Nirenberg, 2014). Anti-Semitism also remains significant in the ideologies of a variety of extremist groups that have emerged in recent years, including "skinheads" and various contemporary incarnations of the Ku Klux Klan. Some of this targeting of Jews seems to increase during economic recession and may be related to the stereotypical view of Jewish Americans as extremely prosperous and materialistic as often depicted in film and television (Cohen, 1982).

A Successful Exclusion. The prejudice and racism directed against the immigrants also found expression in organized, widespread efforts to stop the flow of immigration. A variety of anti-immigrant organizations appeared almost as soon as the mass European immigration started in the 1820s. The strength of these campaigns waxed and waned, largely in harmony with the strength of the economy and the size of the job supply. Anti-immigrant sentiment intensified, and the strength of its organized expressions increased during hard times and depressions, and tended to soften when the economy improved.

The campaign ultimately triumphed with the passage of the National Origins Act in 1924, which established a quota system limiting the number of immigrants that the United States would accept each year from each sending nation. This system was openly racist. For example, the quota for European nations was based on the proportional representation of each nationality in the United States as of 1890. Legislators chose this year because it predated the bulk of the New Immigration and, therefore, gave nearly 70% of the available immigration slots to the nations of Northern and Western Europe, despite the fact that immigration from those areas had largely ended by the 1920s.

Moreover, the National Origins Act banned immigration from Asian nations altogether. At this time, almost all

---

Anti-Semitism is prejudice or ideological racism directed specifically toward Jews.

parts of Africa were still the colonial "possessions" of various European nations and received no separate quotas. In other words, the quota for African immigrants was zero.

The National Origins Act drastically reduced the number of immigrants that would be admitted into the United States each year. Figure 2.3 shows the effectiveness of the numerical restrictions. By the time the Great Depression took hold of the American economy in the 1930s, immigration had dropped to the lowest level in a century. The National Origins Act remained in effect until 1965.

QUESTIONS FOR REFLECTION

6. What forces motivated people to leave Europe and come to North America? How did these motives change from time to time and from place to place?

7. What motivated the forces of resistance and discrimination in the United States? How did the "exclusionists" finally triumph? What roles did class play in these processes?

8. Look at the interactive map called Here's Everyone Who's Immigrated to the U.S. Since 1820 at http://metrocosm.com/animated-immigration-map/. What ideas from the chapter help you understand these changing patterns? Do the changing patterns offer any useful insights for debates about current immigration? How?

PATTERNS OF ASSIMILATION

In this section, we will explore some of the common patterns in the assimilation process followed by European immigrants and their descendants. Research conducted in the traditional perspective documents these patterns as being consistent with Gordon's model of assimilation. They include assimilation by generation, ethnic succession, and structural mobility. We discuss each separately in this section.

THE IMPORTANCE OF GENERATIONS

People today—social scientists, politicians, and ordinary citizens—often fail to recognize the time and effort it takes for a group to become completely Americanized. For most European immigrant groups, the process took generations, and it was the grandchildren or the great-grandchildren (or even great-great-grandchildren) of the immigrants who finally completed acculturation and integration. Mass immigration from Europe ended in the 1920s, but the

assimilation of some European ethnic groups was not completed until late in the 20th century.

Here is a rough summary of how assimilation proceeded for these European immigrants: The first generation, the actual immigrants, settled in ethnic neighborhoods, such as Little Italy in New York City, and made only limited movement toward acculturation and integration. They focused their energies on the network of family and social relationships encompassed within their own groups. Of course, many of them—most often the men—had to leave their neighborhoods for work and other reasons, and these excursions required some familiarity with the larger society. Some English had to be learned, and taking a job outside the neighborhood is, almost by definition, a form of integration. Nonetheless, the first generation lived and died largely within the context of the old country, which had been re-created within the new.

The second generation, or the children of the immigrants, found themselves in a position of psychological or social marginality: They were partly ethnic and partly American but full members of neither group. They were born in America but in households and neighborhoods that were ethnic, not American. They learned the old language first and were socialized in the old ways. As they entered childhood, however, they entered the public schools, where they were socialized into the Anglo-American culture.

Often, the world the second generation learned about at school conflicted with the world they inhabited at home. For example, the old country family values often expected children to subordinate their self-interests to the interests of their elders and of the family as a whole. Parents arranged marriages, or at least heavily influenced them; marriages were subject to parents' approval. Needless to say, these customs conflicted sharply with American ideas about individualism and romantic love. Differences of this sort often caused painful conflict between the ethnic first generation and their Americanized children.

As the second generation progressed toward adulthood, they tended to move out of the old neighborhoods. Their geographic mobility was often motivated by desires for social mobility. They were much more acculturated than their parents, spoke English fluently, and enjoyed a wider range of occupational choices and opportunities. Discriminatory policies in education, housing, and the job market sometimes limited them, but they were upwardly mobile, and in their pursuit of jobs and careers, they left behind their ethnic communities and many of their parents' customs.

The members of the third generation, or the grandchildren of the immigrants, were typically born and raised in non-ethnic settings. English was their first (and often their only) language, and their values and perceptions were thoroughly American. Although family and kinship ties with grandparents and the old neighborhood often remained strong, ethnicity for this generation was a relatively minor part of their daily realities and self-images. Visits on weekends and holidays, and family rituals revolving around the cycles of birth, marriage, and death—these activities might have connected the third generation to the world of their ancestors, but in terms of their everyday lives, they were American, not ethnic.

The pattern of assimilation by generation progressed as follows:

- The first generation began the process and was at least slightly acculturated and integrated.
- The second generation was very acculturated and highly integrated (at least into the secondary sectors of the society).
- The third generation finished the acculturation process and enjoyed high levels of integration at both the secondary and the primary levels.

Table 2.2 illustrates Italian American patterns of the structural assimilation. The educational and occupational characteristics of this group converge with those of white Anglo-Saxon Protestants (WASPs) as the generations change. For example, the percentage of Italian Americans with some college shows a gap of more than 20 points between the first and second generations and WASPs. Italians of the third and fourth generations, though, are virtually identical to WASPs on this measure of integration in the secondary sector. The other differences between Italians and WASPs shrink in a similar fashion from generation to generation.

The first five measures of educational and occupational attainment in Table 2.2 illustrate the generational pattern

of integration (or structural assimilation). The sixth measures marital assimilation, or intermarriage. It displays the percentage of men of "unmixed," or 100%, Italian heritage who married women outside the Italian community. Note once more the tendency for integration, now at the primary level, to increase across the generations. The huge majority of first-generation men married within their group (only 21.9% married non-Italians). By the third generation, 67.3% of the men were marrying non-Italians.

This model of step-by-step, linear assimilation by generation fits some groups better than others. For example, immigrants from Northern and Western Europe (with the exception of the Irish) were generally more similar, culturally, to the dominant group and tended to be more educated and skilled. They experienced relatively easier acceptance and tended to complete the assimilation process in three generations or less.

In contrast, immigrants from Ireland and from Southern and Eastern Europe were mostly uneducated, unskilled people who were more likely to join the huge army of industrial labor that operated the factories, mines, and mills. These groups were more likely to remain at the bottom of the American class structure for generations (and have only recently risen to middle-class prosperity in the second half of the 20th century). As mentioned earlier, Eastern European Jews followed a distinctly different pathway of assimilation. Although widespread anti-Semitic attitudes and policies limited them, they formed an enclave that served as a springboard to launch the second and third generations into the larger society.

It is important to keep generational patterns in mind when examining current immigration to the United States. It is common for people to criticize contemporary newcomers (especially Hispanics) for their "slow" pace of

TABLE 2.2 Some Comparisons Between Italians and WASPs

INDICATORS:	WASPS*	GENERATION		
		First	Second	Third and Fourth
1. Percentage with some college	42.4%	19.0%	19.4%	41.7%
2. Average years of education	12.6	9.0	11.1	13.4
3. Percentage white collar	34.7%	20.0%	22.5%	28.8%
4. Percentage blue collar	37.9%	65.0%	53.9%	39.0%
5. Average occupational prestige	42.5	34.3	36.8	42.5
6. Percentage of "unmixed" Italian men marrying non-Italian women	N/A	21.9%	51.4%	67.3%

SOURCE: Adapted from Alba (1985, Tab. 5-3, 5-4, 6-2). Data are originally from the NORC General Social Surveys (1975–1980) and the Current Population Survey (1979). Copyright © 1985 Richard D. Alba.

NOTE: *White Anglo-Saxon Protestants (WASPs) were not separated by generation, and some of the differences between groups may be the result of factors such as age. That is, older WASPs may have levels of education more comparable to first-generation Italian Americans than to those of WASPs as a whole.

assimilation. But, this process should be seen in the light of the generational time frame for assimilation followed by European immigrants. Modern forms of transportation allow immigration to happen quickly. Assimilation, on the other hand, is slow by nature.

ETHNIC SUCCESSION

A second factor that shaped the assimilation experience is captured in the concept of **ethnic succession**, or the ways European ethnic groups unintentionally affected one another's positions in the social class structure of the larger society. The overall pattern was that each European immigrant group tended to be pushed to higher social class levels and more favorable economic situations by the groups that arrived after it. As more experienced groups became upwardly mobile and moved out of the neighborhoods that served as their "ports of entry," new groups of immigrants replaced them and began the process all over again. Some cities in the Northeast served as a type of ethnic neighborhood—the first safe haven in the new society—for a variety of successive groups. Some places, like the Lower East Side of New York City, continue to fill this role today.

This process of ethnic succession can be understood in terms of the second stage of Gordon's model: integration at the secondary level (see Table 2.1), or entry into the public institutions and organizations of the larger society. Three pathways of integration tended to be most important for European immigrants: politics, labor unions, and the church. We will discuss each in turn, illustrating with the Irish, the first immigrant laborers to arrive in large numbers; but, the general patterns apply to all white ethnic groups.

Politics. The Irish tended to follow the Northern and Western Europeans in the job market and social class structure and were, in turn, followed by the wave of new immigrants. In many urban areas of the Northeast, they moved into the neighborhoods and took jobs left behind by German laborers. After a period of acculturation and adjustment, the Irish began to create their own connections with mainstream American society and improve their economic and social positions. They were replaced in their neighborhoods and at the bottom of the occupational structure by Italians, Poles, and other immigrant groups arriving after them.

As the years passed and the Irish gained more experience, they began to forge more links to the larger society.

Ethnic succession is the process by which white ethnic groups affected one another's positions in the social class structure.

In particular, they allied themselves with the Democratic Party and helped construct the political machines that dominated many city governments in the 19th and 20th centuries, including Boston, Philadelphia, and Chicago (Erie & Kogan, 2016). Machine politicians were often corrupt and even criminal, regularly subverting the election process, bribing city and state officials, using city budgets to fill the pockets of the political bosses and their followers, and giving public jobs in exchange for favors and faithful service. Although not exactly models of good government, the political machines provided valuable social services for their constituents and loyal followers. Machine politicians, such as Boss Tweed of Tammany Hall in New York City, could find jobs, provide food and clothing for the destitute, aid victims of fires and other calamities, and intervene in the criminal and civil courts (Golway, 2014; Warren, 2008).

Much of the urban political machine power derived from their control of the city budgets. The leaders of the machines used municipal jobs and the city budget as part of a "spoils" or patronage system that reaped rewards for their supporters and allies. The faithful Irish party worker might be rewarded for service to "the machine" with a job in the police department or some other city agency. Private businesspeople might be rewarded with lucrative contracts to supply services or perform other city business (Menes, 2001).

The political machines served as engines of economic opportunity and linked Irish Americans to a central and important institution of the dominant society. Using the resources controlled by local government as a power base, the Irish (and other immigrant groups after them) began to integrate themselves into the larger society and carve out a place in the mainstream structures of American society (Menes, 2001), as illustrated in the following Narrative Portrait.

Labor Unions. The labor movement provided a second link between the Irish, other European immigrant groups, and the larger society. Although virtually all white ethnic groups had a hand in the creation and eventual success of the movement, many of the founders and early leaders were Irish. For example, Terence Powderly, an Irish Catholic, founded one of the first U.S. labor unions, and in the early years of the 20th century, about one third of union leaders were Irish and more than 50 national unions had Irish presidents (Bodnar, 1985; Brody, 1980).

As the labor movement grew in strength and gradually acquired legitimacy, the leaders of the movement also gained status, power, and other resources, while the rank-and-file membership gained job security, increased wages, and improved fringe benefits. The labor movement provided another channel through which resources, power, status, and jobs flowed to the white ethnic groups.

Ethnicity, Prejudice, and the Irish Political Machine

David Gray grew up a Welsh Protestant in Scranton, Pennsylvania, during the 1930s and 1940s. At that time, this coal-mining town was split along ethnic lines, and Gray (1991) recounts his socialization into the realities of in-groups and out-groups. He also describes how Scranton's Irish Catholic community responded to the Great Depression and how they used the local political machine to protect their own, generating resentment and prejudice among the Welsh.

Gray eventually earned a PhD in sociology, and became a college professor and an accomplished and respected sociologist. Among his many admiring students was one of the authors of this textbook, who grew up in Scranton's Irish Catholic community a generation after Gray.

Shadow of the Past

David Gray

I did not ask to be born Welsh Protestant in Scranton, Pennsylvania. No more than [my friend] Eddie Gilroy . . . asked to be born Irish Catholic. But there we both were in the heart of the anthracite coal region . . . during the years of the Great Depression. . . . We were friends, good friends. [After school], he played second base and I played shortstop. . . . We thought we were a good double-play combination and, beyond the baseball field, we respected and liked each other as well.

But, there was something wrong with Eddie Gilroy. At age ten I didn't know exactly what it was. He didn't make many errors and we often shared whatever pennies we had . . . at the corner candy store. Still, there was something wrong with him—vague, general, apart from real experience, but true all the same.

His fundamental defect came into sharper focus at the age of twelve. Sunday movies had just arrived in Scranton. . . . I wanted to go with Eddie . . . [but] I couldn't.

"Why?"

"Because Protestants don't go to the movies on Sunday"—nor play cards, football or baseball . . . .

"How come Eddie and Johnny can go?"

"They're Catholic."

No one quite used the word "immoral" but . . . the implication was clear: if Catholics did such bad things on Sunday, they surely did a lot of bad things on other days as well.

No matter, then, that Gilroy might sacrifice for even a Protestant runner to go to second, . . . or share his candy. . . . His Catholicism . . . permeated his being, . . . muting his individual qualities . . . .

. . . Little Welsh Protestant boys and girls learned that Catholics were somehow the enemy. . . .

But, quite unfortunately from their vantage point, the Welsh of Scranton were not the only ones in town. While they had come to the coal regions in large numbers, others, in even larger numbers, had come also. Irish, Italian, Polish, German. . . . With [some] exception[s]. . ., most were Catholic. . . .

In this communal setting . . . the Great Depression arrived with particular force. [The region suffered from massive unemployment.] The coal industry . . . was gone. . . . The public sector . . . became the primary possibility for . . . jobs.

And the Irish . . . controlled political power. . . . [They] did their best to take care of their . . . own. . . .

In Scranton's public life, the intimate relationship of religion, politics, and economics was clear. . . . From the Mayor's office to trash collectors, . . . the public payroll included the names of O'Neill, Hennigan, Lydon, Kennedy, Walsh, Gerrity, and O'Hoolihan. . . . Welsh Protestants came to know . . . that Lewis, Griffiths and Williams need not apply.

. . . Among the Welsh, the general feeling of resentment on more than one occasion was punctuated with: "Those goddam Irish Catholics."

. . . Jobs, homes, and lives were at stake, and religious affiliation was relevant to them all. Irish Catholic political power was a fact from which Welsh Protestant resentment followed. Prejudice there certainly was—deeply felt, poignantly articulated, . . . and, unfortunately, communicated to the young.

SOURCE: Gray (1991, pp. 34–38).

Questions to Consider

1. According to this passage, do the Welsh and Irish seem equally acculturated? Are they equally integrated?

2. What boundaries separate the Welsh and the Irish? How are their differences maintained? In what ways are they integrating with each other?

Because of the way in which jobs were organized in industrializing America, union work typically required communication and cooperation across ethnic lines. The American workforce at the turn of the 20th century was multiethnic and multilingual, and union leaders had to coordinate and mobilize the efforts of many different language and cultural groups to represent the interest of the workers as a social class. Thus, labor union leaders became important intermediaries between the larger society and European immigrant groups.

Women were heavily involved in the labor movement and helped lead some of the most significant events in American labor history. Immigrant women were among the most exploited segments of the labor force often relegated to the lowest paying jobs in difficult or unsafe working conditions. (Today we would call these "sweat shops.") For example, one of the first victories of the Union Movement is The Uprising of 20,000 (also known as the New York Shirtwaist Strike of 1909). Thousands of mostly Jewish and Italian girls and women (many in their teens) staged a strike opposing the garment industry's abusive working conditions (Kheel Center, 2017). Despite factory owners and "machine bosses" hiring people to attack the strikers and the local police unlawfully assaulting the participants, the strike managed to last four months. The strikers eventually won recognition of the union from many employers, a reversal of a wage decrease, and a reduction in the 56- to 59-hour workweek (Goren, 1980, p. 584).

One of the greatest tragedies in U.S. labor history also involved European immigrant women. In 1911, a fire swept through the Triangle Shirtwaist Company, a garment industry shop located on the 10th floor of a building in New York City. The fire spread rapidly, fueled by paper and fabric scraps. Because of management concerns that workers would take breaks or steal fabric, they locked and guarded the doors (von Drehle, 2004, p. 265). Overcrowding, a lack of exits (including a collapsed fire escape) made escape nearly impossible. Many leaped to their deaths to avoid being killed by fire. One hundred forty-six people were killed, 120 of them were young immigrant women, the youngest only 14 years old. The disaster outraged the public, and more than a quarter of a million people attended the victims' funerals. The incident fueled a drive for reform and improvement of work conditions and safety regulations (Amott & Matthaei, 1991, pp. 114–116; see also Kheel Center, 2017, and Schoener, 1967).

European immigrant women also filled leadership roles in the labor movement and served as presidents and in other offices, although usually in women-dominated unions. One of the most important union activists was Mother Jones, an Irish immigrant who worked tirelessly to organize miners:

> *Until she was nearly one hundred years old, Mother Jones was where the danger was greatest—crossing militia lines, spending weeks in damp prisons, incurring the wrath of governors, presidents, and coal operators—she helped to organize the United Mine Workers with the only tools she felt she needed: "convictions and a voice." (Forner, 1980, p. 281)*

Women workers often faced opposition from men workers as well as from employers. The major unions were not only racially discriminatory but also hostile to organizing women. For example, companies required women laundry workers in San Francisco at the start of the 20th century to live in dormitories and work from 6 a.m. until midnight. When they applied to the international laundry workers union for a charter, men union members blocked

Women striking for a 40-hour work week.

them. The women eventually went on strike and won the right to an eight-hour workday in 1912 (Amott & Matthaei, 1991, p. 117).

Religion. Religious institutions provided a third avenue of mobility for the Irish and other white ethnic groups. The Irish were the first large group of Catholic immigrants to come to the United States, and therefore were in a favorable position to dominate the church's administrative structure. The Catholic priesthood became largely Irish and, as these priests were promoted through the Church hierarchy, they eventually became bishops and cardinals. The Catholic faith was practiced in different ways in different nations. As other Catholic immigrant groups began to arrive, conflict within the Irish-dominated church increased. Both Italian and Polish Catholic immigrants demanded their own parishes in which they could speak their own languages and celebrate their own customs and festivals. Dissatisfaction was so intense that some Polish Catholics broke with Rome and formed a separate Polish National Catholic Church (Lopata, 1976, p. 49).

The other Catholic immigrant groups eventually began to supply priests and other religious functionaries and to occupy Church leadership positions. Although the Irish continued to disproportionately influence the Church, it served as a power base for other white ethnic groups to gain acceptance and become integrated into the mainstream American society (McCook, 2011).

Other Pathways. Besides party politics, the Union Movement, and religion, European immigrant groups forged other not-so-legitimate pathways of upward mobility. One alternative to legitimate success was offered by crime, a pathway that has been used by every ethnic group to some extent. Crime became particularly lucrative and attractive when Prohibition, the attempt to eliminate all alcohol use in the United States, went into effect in the 1920s. The criminalization of liquor failed to lower the demand, and Prohibition created an economic opportunity for those willing to take the risks involved in manufacturing and supplying alcohol to the American public.

Italian Americans headed many of the criminal organizations that took advantage of Prohibition. Criminal leaders and organizations with roots in Sicily, a region with a long history of secret antiestablishment societies, were especially important (Alba, 1985, pp. 62–64). The connection between organized crime, Prohibition, and Italian Americans is well known, but it is not widely recognized that ethnic succession operated in organized crime as it did in the legitimate opportunity structures. The Irish and Germans had been involved in organized crime for decades before the 1920s. The Italians competed with these established gangsters and with Jewish crime syndicates for control of bootlegging and other criminal enterprises. The patterns of ethnic succession continued after the repeal of Prohibition in 1933, and members of groups newer to urban areas, including African Americans, Jamaicans, and Hispanic Americans, have recently challenged the Italian-dominated criminal "families."

Ethnic succession can also be observed in the institution of sports. Since the beginning of the 20th century, sports have offered a pathway to success and affluence that has attracted countless millions of young men and women. Success in many sports requires little in the way of formal credentials, education, or English fluency, and sports have been particularly appealing to the young men and in minority groups that have few resources or opportunities.

For example, at the turn of the 20th century, the Irish dominated the sport of boxing, but boxers from the Italian American community and other new immigrant groups eventually replaced them. Each successive wave of boxers reflected the concentration of a particular ethnic group at the bottom of the class structure. The succession of minority groups continues to this day, with boxing now dominated by African American and Latino fighters (Rader, 1983, pp. 87–106). A similar progression, or "layering," of ethnic and racial groups can be observed in other sports and in the entertainment industry.

The institutions of American society, whether legitimate or illegal, reflect the relative positions of minority groups at a particular moment in time. Just a few generations ago, European immigrant groups dominated both crime and sports because they were blocked from legitimate opportunities. Now, the racial minority groups still excluded from the mainstream job market and mired in the urban underclass are supplying disproportionate numbers of young people to these alternative opportunity structures.

CONTINUING INDUSTRIALIZATION AND STRUCTURAL MOBILITY

We have already mentioned that dominant–minority relations tend to change along with changes in subsistence technology, and we can find an example of this relationship in the history of the European immigrant groups across the 20th century. Industrialization is a continuous process. As it proceeded, the nature of work in America evolved and changed and created opportunities for upward mobility for the white ethnic groups. One important form of upward mobility throughout the 20th century, called **structural mobility**, resulted more from changes in the structure of the economy and the labor market than from any individual effort or desire to "get ahead."

Structural mobility is the result of the continuing mechanization and automation of the workplace. As machines replaced people in the workforce, the supply of manual, blue-collar jobs that had provided employment for so many first- and second-generation European immigrant laborers dwindled. At the same time, the supply of white-collar jobs increased, but access to the better jobs depended heavily on educational credentials. For white ethnic groups, a high school education became much more available in the 1930s, and college and university programs began to expand rapidly in the late 1940s, spurred in large part by the educational benefits made available to World War II veterans. Each generation of white ethnics, especially those born after 1925, was significantly more educated than the previous generation, and many were able to translate their increased human capital into upward mobility in the mainstream job market (Morawska, 1990, pp. 212–213).

The descendants of European immigrants became upwardly mobile not only because of their individual ambitions and efforts but also because of the changing location of jobs and the progressively greater opportunities for education available to them. Of course, the pace and timing of this upward movement was highly variable from group to group and from place to place. Ethnic succession continued to operate, and the descendants of the most recent immigrants from Europe (Italians and Poles, for example)

Structural mobility refers to rising occupational and social class standing that is a result of changes in the structure of the economy and labor market, as opposed to individual efforts.

tended to be the last to benefit from the general upgrading in education and the job market.

Still, structural mobility is key to the eventual successful integration of all ethnic groups. Later in this chapter, Table 2.3 shows differing levels of educational attainment and income for white ethnic groups. During these same years, racial minority groups, particularly African Americans, were excluded from the dominant group's educational system and from the opportunity to compete for better jobs. We'll discuss this more in Chapter 6.

QUESTIONS FOR REFLECTION

9. Why is generation important for understanding assimilation?

10. What were the major institutional pathways through which European immigrants adapted to U.S. society? Can you cite evidence from your home community of similar patterns for immigrant groups today?

VARIATIONS IN ASSIMILATION

In the previous section, we discussed patterns that were common to European immigrants and their descendants. Now we address some of the sources of variation and diversity in assimilation, a complex process that is never exactly the same for any two groups. Sociologists have paid particular attention to the way degree of similarity, religion, social class, and gender shaped the overall assimilation of the descendants of the mass European immigration. They have also investigated the way in which immigrants' reasons for coming to this country have affected the experiences of different groups.

DEGREE OF SIMILARITY

Since the dominant group consisted largely of Protestants with ethnic origins in Northern and Western Europe and especially in England, it is not surprising to learn that the degree of resistance, prejudice, and discrimination encountered by the different European immigrant groups varied, in part by the degree to which they differed from these dominant groups. The most significant differences included religion, language, cultural values, and, for some groups, physical characteristics (which were often seen as "racial"). Thus, Protestant immigrants from Northern and Western Europe experienced less resistance than the English-speaking Catholic Irish, who in turn were accepted more readily than the new immigrants, who were both non–English speaking and overwhelmingly non-Protestant.

The preferences of the dominant group correspond roughly to the arrival times of the immigrants. The most similar groups immigrated earliest, and the least similar tended to be the last to arrive. Because of this coincidence, resistance to any one group of immigrants tended to fade as new groups arrived. For example, anti-German prejudice and discrimination never became particularly vicious or widespread (except during the heat of the World Wars) because the Irish began arriving in large numbers at about the same time. Concerns about the German immigrants were swamped by the fear that the Catholic Irish could never be assimilated. Then, as the 19th century drew to a close, immigrants from Southern and Eastern Europe—even more different from the dominant group—began to arrive and made concerns about the Irish seem trivial.

In addition, the New Immigration was far larger than the Old Immigration (see Figure 2.3). Southern and Eastern Europeans arrived in record numbers in the early 20th century. The sheer volume of the immigration raised fears that American cities and institutions would be swamped by hordes of what were seen as racially inferior, unassimilable immigrants, a fear that resonates today in our debates about modern immigrants.

Thus, a preference hierarchy was formed in American culture that privileged Northern and Western Europeans over Southern and Eastern Europeans, and Protestants over Catholics and Jews. These rankings reflect the ease with which the groups have been assimilated and have made their way into the larger society. This hierarchy of ethnic preference is still a part of American prejudice, as we shall see in Chapter 3, although it is much more muted today than in the peak of immigration.

RELIGION

A major differentiating factor in the experiences of the European immigrant groups, recognized by Gordon and other students of American assimilation, was religion. Protestant, Catholic, and Jewish immigrants lived in different neighborhoods, occupied different niches in the workforce, formed separate networks of affiliation and groups, and chose their marriage partners from different pools of people.

One important study that documented the importance of religion for European immigrants and their descendants (and also reinforced the importance of generations) was conducted by sociologist Ruby Jo Kennedy (1944). She studied intermarriage patterns in New Haven, Connecticut, over a 70-year period ending in the 1940s and found that the immigrants generally chose marriage partners from a pool whose boundaries were marked by ethnicity and religion. For example, Irish Catholics married other Irish Catholics, Italian Catholics married Italian Catholics, Irish

Protestants married Irish Protestants, and so forth across all the ethnic and religious divisions she studied.

She also found that the pool of marriage partners for the children and grandchildren of the immigrants continued to be bound by religion but not so much by ethnicity. Thus, later generations of Irish Catholics continued to marry other Catholics but were less likely to marry other Irish. As assimilation proceeded, ethnic group boundaries faded (or "melted"), but religious boundaries did not. Kennedy described this phenomenon as a **triple melting pot**: a pattern of structural assimilation within each of the three religious denominations (Kennedy, 1944, 1952).

Will Herberg (1960), another important student of American assimilation, also explored the connection between religion and ethnicity. Writing in the 1950s, he noted that the pressures of acculturation did not affect all aspects of ethnicity equally. European immigrants and their descendants were strongly encouraged to learn English, but they were not as pressured to change their religious beliefs. Very often, their religious faith was the strongest connection between later generations and their immigrant ancestors. The American tradition of religious tolerance allowed the descendants of the European immigrants to preserve this tie to their roots without being seen as "un-American." As a result, the Protestant, Catholic, and Jewish faiths eventually came to occupy roughly equal degrees of legitimacy in American society.

Thus, for the descendants of the European immigrants, religion became a vehicle through which their ethnicity could be expressed. For many members of this group, religion and ethnicity were fused, and ethnic traditions and identities came to have a religious expression. For example, Mary Farrell, the Irish American schoolteacher introduced in Chapter 1, attends Mass regularly even though the Catholic Church rejects homosexuality and gay marriage. Despite this conflict, she still feels connected to the church, in part, because her family has always been Catholic. Regardless of the conflict about the legitimacy/acceptance of the lesbian, bisexual, gay, and transgender (LGBT+)[1] community, participating in church rituals helps her feel connected to her family's history with the Catholic Church. For Mary, it is not just that she is Irish Catholic American but that—for her and millions of others—being Catholic is part of being Irish in America.

SOCIAL CLASS

Social class is a central feature of social structure, and it is not surprising that it affected the European immigrant groups in a number of ways. First, social class combined with religion to shape the social world of the descendants of the European immigrants. In fact, Gordon (1964) concluded that U.S. society in the 1960s actually incorporated not three, but four melting pots (one for each of the major ethnic or religious groups and one for black Americans), each of which was internally subdivided by social class. In his view, the most significant structural unit within American society was the **ethclass**, defined by the intersection of the religious, ethnic, and social class boundaries (e.g., working-class Catholic, upper-class Protestant). Thus, people were not "simply American" but tended to identify with, associate with, and choose their spouses from within their ethclasses.

Second, social class affected structural integration. The huge majority of the post-1880s European immigrants were working class, and because they "entered U.S. society at the bottom of the economic ladder, and . . . stayed close to that level for the next half century, ethnic history has been essentially working class history" (Morawska, 1990, p. 215; see also Bodnar, 1985). For generations, many groups of Eastern and Southern European immigrants did not acculturate to middle-class American culture but to an urban working-class, blue-collar set of lifestyles and values. Even today, ethnicity for many groups remains interconnected with social class factors, and a familiar stereotype of white ethnicity is the hard-hat construction worker.

GENDER

Anyone who wants to learn about the experience of immigration will find a huge body of literature incorporating every imaginable discipline and genre. The great bulk of this material, however, concerns the immigrant experience in general or focuses specifically on men immigrants. The experiences of women immigrants have been much less recorded and hence far less accessible (Weinberg, Gabaccia, Diner, & Seller, 1992; Gabaccia, 1991 also notes the system of knowledge production within the academy has played a role because the topic of "women" hasn't "belonged" to any one place). Many immigrant women came from cultures with strong patriarchal traditions. Thus, they had much

---

The **triple melting pot** is the idea that structural assimilation for white ethnic groups took place within the context of the three major American religions.

---

[1]We use LGBT+ to acknowledge gender and sexual diversity beyond those represented by LBGT (lesbian, bisexual, gay, and transgender). For example, people who identify as gender fluid, asexual, or pansexual. Chapters 11 and 12 will address these topics.

Ethclass is the group formed by the intersection of social class and ethnic or racial group.

---

less access to leadership roles, education, and prestigious, high-paying occupations. As is the case with women of virtually all minority groups, the voices of immigrant women have been muted. The research that has been done, however, shows that immigrant women played multiple roles both during immigration and during the assimilation process. As would be expected in patriarchal societies, the roles of wife and mother were central, but immigrant women were involved in myriad other activities as well.

In general, men immigrants tended to precede women, and it was common for the men to send for the women only after they had secured lodging, jobs, and a certain level of stability. However, women immigrants' experiences were quite varied, often depending on the economic situation and cultural traditions of their home societies. In some cases, women not only were prominent among the "first wave" of immigrants but also began the process of acculturation and integration. During the 19th century, for example, a high percentage of Irish immigrants were young, single women. They came to the United States seeking jobs and often wound up employed in domestic work, a role that permitted them to live "respectably" in a family setting. In 1850, about 75% of all employed Irish immigrant women in New York City worked as servants; the rest were employed in textile mills and factories. As late as 1920, 81% of employed Irish-born women in the United States worked as domestics. Factory work was the second most prevalent form of employment (Blessing, 1980; see also Steinberg, 1981).

Because the economic situation of immigrant families was typically precarious, it was common for women to be involved in wage labor. The type and location of the work varied from group to group. Whereas Irish women were concentrated in domestic work and factories and mills, it was rare for Italian women to work outside the home. Italian culture had strong patriarchal norms, and "one of the culture's strongest prohibitions was directed against contact between women and male strangers" (Alba, 1985, p. 53). Thus, acceptable work situations for Italian women were likely to involve tasks that could be done at home: doing laundry, taking in boarders, and doing piecework for the garment industry. Italian women who worked outside the home were likely to find themselves in single-sex settings among other immigrant women. Thus, women immigrants from Italy tended to be far less acculturated and integrated than those from Ireland.

Eastern European Jewish women represent still another pattern of assimilation. They were refugees from religious persecution, and most came with their husbands and children in intact family units. According to Steinberg (1981), "few were independent bread-winners, and when they did work, they usually found employment in the . . . garment industry. Often they worked in small shops with other family members" (p. 161).

Generally, immigrant women, like working-class women in general, were expected to work until they married, after which time it was expected that their husbands would support them and their children. In many cases, however, immigrant men could not earn enough to support their families, and their wives and children were required by necessity to contribute to the family budget. Immigrant wives sometimes continued to work outside the home, or they found other ways to make money. They took in boarders, did laundry or sewing, tended gardens, and were involved in myriad other activities that permitted them to contribute to the family budget and still stay home and attend to family and child-rearing responsibilities.

A 1911 report on Southern and Eastern European households found that about half kept lodgers and that the income from this activity amounted to about 25% of the husbands' wages. Children contributed to the family income by taking after-school and summertime jobs (Morawska, 1990, pp. 211–212). Compared with the men, immigrant women were more closely connected to home and family, less likely to learn to read or speak English or otherwise acculturate, and significantly more influential in preserving the heritage of their groups.

When they sought employment outside the home, they found opportunities in the industrial sector and in clerical and sales work, occupations that were quickly stereotyped as "women's work." Women were seen as working only to supplement the family treasury, and this assumption

Woman worker at a textile mill, early 20th century.

was used to justify a lower wage scale. Evans (1980) reports that in the late 1800s, "whether in factories, offices, or private homes . . . women's wages were about half of those of men" (p. 135).

Finally, in addition to the myriad other roles they played, women tended to function as the primary keepers of cultural traditions from the old country. Husbands were often more involved in the larger society and had greater familiarity with Anglo culture and the English language. Women, even when they were employed, tended to be more oriented to home, children, family, and the neighborhood, and more likely to maintain the traditional diet and dress, speak to their children in the old language, and observe the time-honored holidays and religious practices. Thus, in addition to their economic roles, the women of the immigrant groups performed crucial cultural and socialization functions and tended to be more culturally conservative and more resistant to Anglo values and practices than were the men. These gender role patterns are common in immigrant groups today, not only in the United States but also in Western Europe.

SOJOURNERS

Some versions of the traditional perspective and the "taken-for-granted" views of many Americans assume that assimilation is desirable and therefore desired. However, immigrant groups from Europe were highly variable in their interest in Americanization, a factor that greatly shaped their experiences.

Some groups were very committed to Americanization. Eastern European Jews, for example, came to America because of religious persecution and planned to make America their home from the beginning. They left their homeland in fear for their lives and had no plans and no possibility of returning. They intended to stay, for they had nowhere else to go. (The nation of Israel was not founded until 1948.) These immigrants committed themselves to learning English, becoming citizens, and familiarizing themselves with their new society as quickly as possible.

Other immigrants had no intention of becoming American citizens and therefore had little interest in Americanization. These **sojourners**, or "birds of passage," were oriented to the old country and intended to return once they had accumulated enough capital to be successful in their home villages or provinces. Because immigration records are not very detailed, it is difficult to assess the exact numbers of immigrants who returned to the old country (see Wyman, 1993). We do know, for example, that a large

---

Sojourners are immigrants who intend to return to their country of origin.

---

percentage of Italian immigrants were sojourners. Although 3.8 million Italians landed in the United States between 1899 and 1924, around 2.1 million departed during the same interval (Nelli, 1980, p. 547).

QUESTIONS FOR REFLECTION

11. What are some of the most important variations in the ways European immigrants adjusted to U.S. society?

12. What was the "triple melting pot," and how did it function?

13. What important gender role differences existed in European immigrant groups? Would you guess that men or women would be more likely to be sojourners? Why?

THE DESCENDANTS OF THE IMMIGRANTS TODAY

GEOGRAPHICAL DISTRIBUTION

Figure 2.4 shows the geographical distribution of 15 racial and ethnic groups across the United States. The map displays the single largest group in each county. The map offers great detail, but we will focus on some of the groups mentioned in this chapter, including Norwegian, German, Irish, and Italian Americans. (The Jewish population is too small to appear on this map. You'll also notice that this map, unlike others in this text, is somewhat "old." The most recent census [2010] did not ask people about their ancestry. Unfortunately, we can't provide a newer "snapshot." This is one example of why it's important to collect data.)

As noted earlier in the chapter, the single largest ancestry group in the United States is German American. This is reflected in Figure 2.4 by the predominance of dark gray from Pennsylvania to the West Coast. Note also how the map reflects the original settlement areas for this group, especially in the Midwest. Norwegian Americans (and Swedish Americans) are numerically dominant in some sections of the upper Midwest (e.g., northwestern Minnesota and northern North Dakota). Irish Americans and Italian Americans are also concentrated in their original areas of settlement, with the Irish in Massachusetts and the Italians more concentrated around New York City.

Thus, almost a century after the end of mass immigration from Europe, many of the descendants of the immigrants have not wandered far from their ancestral locales. Of course, the map shows that the same point could be made for other groups, including blacks (concentrated in the "black belt" across the states of the old

FIGURE 2.4 Ancestry With Largest Population in Each County, 2000

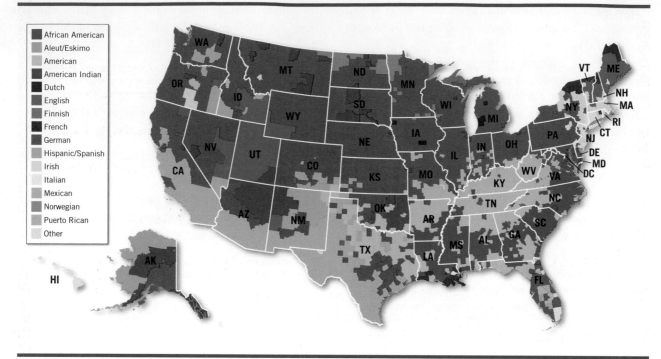

SOURCE: U S Census Bureau (2004a).

Confederacy), Mexican Americans (concentrated along the southern border from Texas to California), and Native Americans (their concentration in the upper Midwest, eastern Oklahoma, and the Southwest reflects the locations of the reservations into which they were forced after the end of the Indian wars).

Given all that has changed in American society over the past century—industrialization, population growth, urbanization, and massive mobility—the stable location of white ethnics (and other ethnic and racial groups) seems remarkable. Why aren't people distributed more randomly across the nation's landscape?

The stability is somewhat easier to explain for some groups. African Americans, Mexican Americans, and Native Americans have been limited in their geographic as well as social mobility by institutionalized discrimination, racism, and limited resources. We will examine the power of these constraints in detail in later chapters.

For white ethnics, on the other hand, the power of exclusion and rejection waned as the generations passed and the descendants of the immigrants assimilated and integrated. Their current locations are perhaps more a reflection of the fact that the United States is a nation of groups as well as individuals. Our group memberships, especially family and kin, exert a powerful influence on our decisions about where to live and work and, despite the transience and mobility of modern American life, can keep people connected to their relatives, the old neighborhood, their ethnic roots, and the sites of their ancestors' struggles.

INTEGRATION AND EQUALITY

Perhaps the most important point about white ethnic groups (the descendants of the European immigrants) is that they are on the verge of being completely assimilated today. Even the groups that were the most despised in earlier years (e.g., the Irish) are now acculturated, integrated, and thoroughly intermarried.

To illustrate this point, consider Table 2.3, which shows the degree to which nine of the more than 60 white ethnic groups had been integrated as far back as 1990. The groups include the two largest white ethnic groups (German and Irish Americans) and seven more chosen to represent a range of geographic regions of origin and times of immigration (U.S. Census Bureau, 2008).

The table shows that by 1990, all nine of the groups selected were at or above national norms ("all persons") for all measures of equality. Some variation exists among the groups, but all exceeded the national averages for both high school and college education and had dramatically lower poverty rates, usually less than half the national average. All nine groups exceed the national average for median household income, some—Russians, for example, many of whom are Jewish—by a considerable margin.

In other areas, the evidence for assimilation and equality is also persuasive. For example, the distinct ethnic neighborhoods that these groups created in American cities (Little Italy, Greektown, Little Warsaw, etc.) have faded away or been taken over by other groups, and the rate of intermarriage between members of different white ethnic groups is

To practice using Gordon's model of assimilation (see Table 2.1), we've written some questions about immigrant assimilation experiences that we'd like you to consider. As sociologists, we document social patterns. Yet each of you has a unique family history of one form or another. Therefore, we've provided you with some options based on what's most appropriate for you:

1) If you happen to be a third or fourth generation immigrant whose family came from Europe, you may be able to interview your grandparents or great-grandparents about your families' assimilation experiences. That would make this exercise particularly meaningful, interesting, and fun.

2) If your family is not from Europe but, you have older family members that you can interview (e.g., grandparents, great grandparents), you can still interview them about their immigration experience.

3) You can interview older people that you know such as teachers or neighbors.

4) You can imagine what answers a third or fourth generation immigrant might say based on what you've learned in this chapter.

Some of the questions you might ask are listed below. We'd like you to identify which part of Gordon's model that it tests. If you think of other questions that would fit, consider them, too. Place the letter of each question in the appropriate row of the box below.

A. What language did you speak at home when you were growing up?

B. What was your total household income last year?

C. (If married/partnered) Does your spouse/partner share your religious faith?

D. (If married/partnered) Does your spouse/partner share your ethnic background?

E. Did your parents have the same ethnic background? How about your grandparents?

F. Did you vote in the most recent presidential election?

G. What percentage of your friends share your ethnic background?

H. What percentage of your friends share your religious faith?

I. What is the highest level of education you have achieved?

J. Has your family name been changed or "Americanized"? If so, what was the original name and what did it become? How and why did that name change occur?

STAGE	ITEMS
Acculturation	
Integration (secondary level)	
Integration (primary level)	
Marital assimilation	

TURN THE PAGE TO FIND OUR ANSWERS.

quite high. For example, based on data from the 1990 census, about 56% of all married whites have spouses whose ethnic backgrounds do not match their own (Alba, 1995, pp. 13–14).

THE EVOLUTION OF WHITE ETHNICITY

Absorption into the American mainstream was neither linear nor continuous for the descendants of European immigrants. Over the generations, white ethnic identity sporadically reasserted itself in many ways, two of which are especially notable. First, there was a tendency for later generations to be more interested in their ancestry and ethnicity than were earlier generations. Marcus Hansen (1952) captured this phenomenon in his **principle of third-generation interest**: "What the second generation tries to forget, the third generation tries to remember" (p. 495). Hansen observed that the children of immigrants tended

STAGE	ITEMS
Acculturation	A, J
Integration (secondary level)	B, F, I
Integration (primary level)	G, H
Marital assimilation	C, D, E

to minimize or deemphasize ("forget") their ethnicity to avoid the prejudice and intolerance of the larger society and compete on more favorable terms for jobs and other opportunities. As they became adults and started families of their own, the second generation tended to raise their children in nonethnic settings, with English as their first and only language.

By the time the third generation reached adulthood, especially the New Immigrant groups that arrived last, the larger society had become more tolerant of white ethnicity and diversity. Having little to risk, the third generation tried to reconnect with its grandparents and roots. These descendants wanted to remember their ethnic heritage and understand it as part of their personal identities, their sense of who they were and where they belonged in the larger society. Thus, interest in the "old ways" and the strength of identification with the ancestral group was often stronger in the more Americanized third generation than in the more ethnic second. Ironically, of course, the grandchildren of the immigrants could not recover much of the richness and detail of their heritage because their parents had spent their lives trying to forget it. Nonetheless, the desire of the third generation to reconnect with its ancestry and recover its ethnicity shows that assimilation is not a simple, one-dimensional, or linear process.

In addition to this generational pattern, the strength of white ethnic identity also responded to the changing context of American society and the activities of other groups. For example, in the late 1960s and early 1970s,

---

The **principle of third-generation interest** is the idea that the grandchildren of immigrants will stress their ethnicity much more than will the second generation.

The **ethnic revival** was an increase in the interest in heritage that occurred among white ethnics in the 1960s and 1970s.

---

there was a notable increase in the visibility of and interest in white ethnic heritage, an upsurge often referred to as the **ethnic revival**. The revival manifested itself in a variety of ways. Some people became more interested in their families' genealogical roots, and others increased their participation in ethnic festivals, traditions, and organizations. The "white ethnic vote" became a factor in local, state, and national politics, and appearances at the churches, meeting halls, and neighborhoods associated with white ethnic groups became almost mandatory for candidates for office. Demonstrations and festivals celebrating white ethnic heritages were organized, and buttons and bumper stickers proclaiming the ancestry of everyone from Irish to Italians were widely displayed. Politicians, editorialists, and intellectuals endorsed the revival (e.g., see Novak, 1973), reinforcing the movement and giving it additional legitimacy.

The ethnic revival may have been partly fueled, à la Hansen's principle, by the desire to reconnect with ancestral roots, even though most groups were well beyond their third generations by the 1960s. More likely, the revival was a reaction to the increase in pluralistic sentiment in the society in general and the pluralistic, even separatist assertions of other groups. In the 1960s and 1970s, virtually every minority group generated a protest movement (Black Power, Red Power, Chicanismo, etc.) and proclaimed a recommitment to its own heritage and to the authenticity of its own culture and experience. The visibility of these movements for cultural pluralism among racial minority groups helped make it more acceptable for European Americans to express their own ethnicity and heritage.

Besides the general tenor of the times, the resurgence of white ethnicity had some political and economic dimensions that bring us back to issues of inequality and competition for resources. In the 1960s, a white-ethnic urban working class made up largely of Irish and Southern and Eastern European groups still remained in the neighborhoods

TABLE 2.3 Median Household Income, Percent of Families Living in Poverty, and Educational Attainment for Selected White Ethnic Groups, 1990

	MEDIAN HOUSEHOLD INCOME	PERCENTAGE OF FAMILIES LIVING IN POVERTY	PERCENTAGE WHO COMPLETED HIGH SCHOOL OR MORE	PERCENTAGE WHO RECEIVED AN UNDERGRADUATE DEGREE OR MORE
All Persons	**$30,056**	**10%**	**75.2%**	**20.3%**
Russian	$45,778	3.6%	90.8%	49%
Italian	$36,060	4.9%	77.3%	21%
Polish	$34,763	4.3%	78.5%	23.1%
Ukrainian	$34,474	4%	77.5%	28.3%
Swedish	$33,881	4.5%	87.3%	27.4%
German	$32,730	5.5%	82.7%	22%
Slovak	$32,352	3.8%	78.2%	21.6%
Norwegian	$32,207	5.1%	85.9%	26%
Irish	$31,845	6.5%	79.6%	21.2%

SOURCE: U.S. Census Bureau (2008).

of the industrial Northeast and Midwest and continued to breathe life into the old networks and traditions (see Glazer & Moynihan, 1970; Greeley, 1974). At the same time that cultural pluralism was becoming seen as more legitimate, this ethnic working class was feeling increasingly threatened by minority groups of color. In the industrial cities, it was not unusual for white ethnic neighborhoods to adjoin black and Hispanic neighborhoods, putting these groups in direct competition for housing, jobs, and other resources.

Many members of the white ethnic working class saw racial minority groups as inferior and perceived the advances being made by these groups as unfair, unjust, and threatening. Additionally, they reacted to what they saw as special treatment and attention being accorded on the basis of race, such as school busing and affirmative action. They had problems of their own (the declining number of good, unionized jobs; inadequate schooling; and deteriorating city services) and believed that their problems were being given lower priority and less legitimacy because they were white. The revived sense of ethnicity in the urban working-class neighborhoods was in large part a way of resisting racial reform and expressing resentment for the racial minority groups. Thus, among its many other causes and forms, the revival of white ethnicity that began in the 1960s was fueled by competition for resources and opportunities. As you'll see throughout this text, such competition commonly leads to increased prejudice and a heightened sense of cohesion among group members.

THE TWILIGHT OF WHITE ETHNICITY?[2]

As the conflicts of the 1960s and 1970s faded and white ethnic groups continued to leave the old neighborhoods and rise in the class structure, the strength of white ethnic identity resumed its slow demise. Today, several more generations removed from the tumultuous 1960s, white ethnic identity has become increasingly nebulous and largely voluntary. It is often described as **symbolic ethnicity** or as an aspect of self-identity that symbolizes one's roots in the "old country" but is otherwise minor. The descendants of the European immigrants feel vaguely connected to their ancestors, but this part of their identities does not affect their lifestyles, circles of friends and neighbors, job prospects, eating habits, or other everyday routines (Gans, 1979; Lieberson & Waters, 1988). For the descendants of the European immigrants today, ethnicity is an increasingly minor part of their identities that is expressed only occasionally or sporadically. For example, they might join in ethnic or religious festivals (e.g., St. Patrick's Day for Irish Americans, Columbus Day for Italian Americans), but these activities are seasonal or otherwise peripheral to their lives

Symbolic ethnicity is superficial, voluntary, and changeable.

[2]This phrase comes from Alba (1990).

and self-images. The descendants of the European immigrants have choices, in stark contrast to their ancestors, members of racial minority groups, and recent immigrants: They can stress their ethnicity, ignore it completely, or maintain any degree of ethnic identity they choose. Many people have ancestors in more than one ethnic group and may change their sense of affiliation over time, sometimes emphasizing one group's traditions and sometimes another's (Waters, 1990).

In fact, white ethnic identity has become so ephemeral that it may be on the verge of disappearing. For example, based on a series of in-depth interviews with white Americans from various regions of the nation, Gallagher (2001) found a sense of ethnicity so weak that it did not even rise to the level of "symbolic." His respondents were the products of ancestral lines so thoroughly intermixed and intermarried that any trace of a unique heritage from a particular group was completely lost. They had virtually no knowledge of the experiences of their immigrant ancestors or of the life and cultures of the ethnic communities they had inhabited, and for many, their ethnic ancestries were no more meaningful to them than their states of birth. Their lack of interest in and information about their ethnic heritage was so complete that it led Gallagher (2001) to propose an addendum to Hansen's principle: "What the grandson wished to remember, the great-granddaughter has never been told."

At the same time, as more specific white ethnic identities are disappearing, they are also evolving into new shapes and forms. In the view of many analysts, a new identity is developing that merges the various "hyphenated" ethnic identities (German American, Polish American, etc.) into a single, generalized "European American" identity based on race and a common history of immigration and assimilation. This new identity reinforces the racial lines of separation that run through contemporary society, but it does more than simply mark group boundaries. Embedded in this emerging identity is an understanding, often deeply flawed, of how the white immigrant groups succeeded and assimilated in the past and a view, often deeply ideological, of how the racial minority groups should behave in the present. These understandings are encapsulated in "immigrant tales": legends that stress heroic individual effort and grim determination as key ingredients leading to success in the old days. These tales feature impoverished, victimized immigrant ancestors who survived and made a place for themselves and their children by working hard, saving their money, and otherwise exemplifying the virtues of the Protestant Ethic and American individualism. They stress the idea that past generations became successful despite the brutal hostility of the dominant group and with no government intervention, and they equate the historical difficulties faced by immigrants from Europe with those suffered by racial minority groups (slavery, segregation, attempted genocide, etc.). They strongly imply—and sometimes blatantly assert—that the latter groups could succeed in America by simply following the example set by the former (Alba, 1990; Gallagher, 2001).

These accounts mix versions of human capital theory and traditional views of assimilation with prejudice and racism. Without denying or trivializing the resolve and fortitude of European immigrants, equating their experiences and levels of disadvantage with those of African Americans, Native Americans, and Mexican Americans is widely off the mark, as we shall see in the remainder of this text. These views support an attitude of disdain and lack of sympathy for the multiple dilemmas faced today by the racial minority groups and many contemporary immigrants. They permit a more subtle expression of prejudice and racism and allow whites to use these highly distorted views of their immigrant ancestors as a rhetorical device to express a host of race-based grievances without appearing racist (Gallagher, 2001).

Alba (1990) concludes as follows:

> The thrust of the [emerging] European American identity is to defend the individualistic view of the American system, because it portrays the system as open to those who are willing to work hard and pull themselves out of poverty and discrimination. Recent research suggests that it is precisely this individualism that prevents many whites from sympathizing with the need for African Americans and other minorities to receive affirmative action in order to overcome institutional barriers to their advancement. (p. 317)

What can we conclude? The generations-long journey from immigrant to white ethnic to European American seems to be drawing to a close. The separate ethnic identities are merging into a larger sense of "whiteness" that unites descendants of the immigrants with the dominant group and provides a rhetorical device for expressing disdain for other groups, especially African Americans and undocumented immigrants.

QUESTIONS FOR REFLECTION

14. In what concrete ways are the descendants of the European immigrants successful?

15. What is Hansen's principle, and why is it significant? What is Gallagher's addendum to this principle, and why is it important?

16. Does white ethnic identity have a future? Why or why not?

NARRATIVE PORTRAIT

Lucky to Be Here

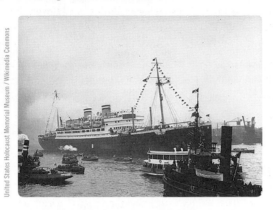

In 1939, over 900 Jewish refugees left Germany on the S.S. St. Louis, but were denied entry by Cuba, the U.S., and Canada. About one-fourth died in the Holocaust.

The following narrative is from Lucky To Be Here, *about the life of Werner Auerbach. Auerbach and his family are Jewish and fled Nazis during World War II. Auerbach is just eight years old when his family leaves Cologne, Germany, where they'd led a relatively comfortable life. They board a passenger ship and make their way to the United States, eventually settling in Toledo, Ohio. In the excerpt below, Werner considers a discussion that his parents have about changing their name. His father wants to change it so they have a better chance of fitting in, presumably so they will not have to deal with anti-Semitic prejudice or discrimination. However, his mother is concerned that if the family changes its name, their relatives may never be able to find them again. This concern stems from the fact that she has not heard from her relatives in Europe. He writes:*

"Mom and dad . . . haven't laughed much lately, anyway, not since the Germans invaded Holland. They are very worried about our family there. We used to get some letters from grandma and uncle Alfred, but not anymore. Mom and dad keep writing, but don't know if their letters get there."

"[Mother said] We don't even know if they are still at the same address, Gustav. It all seems so futile. If only we could get some sign of life from them."

"I know, I know."

"Mom and dad wait every day for the mailman, but he never brings any letters from Holland. We only get mail from uncle Julius in New York . . . The other thing they keep talking about is changing our family name so that it sounds more American. That's dad's idea, but mom doesn't want to do it.

"I just can't, Gustav," she says. "Then we might never get mail from the family. I don't want to take the chance."

"Dad wants to change our name to Meadowbrook. That's what it would be if it were translated into English. I'm not sure if he's serious about it because he smiles a little when he says, "we'd sound really Anglo-Saxon then: the Meadowbrooks of Northgate Manor. We make a break with the past that way, but I guess it's not that important."

"I know why he wants to do it—because we'll be even safer then. But he also knows how mom worries all the time, so I guess our name will always be Auerbach.

"Dad also told me that Werner means 'strong, brave warrior.' It's an old German name. Names are funny. I never knew what it meant, and I don't feel like a fighter. I don't like fights."

[Werner asks his mother about an advice column in the local paper where someone wrote in to ask:]

"As a Jew I have often been puzzled what to answer when confronted with the request for either my nationality or my religion. Since I was born here, my nation is America, and I do not follow the doctrines of any religion. Yet I am considered deceptive by some and replying American to my nationality and None to my religion. What do you, as an American and a Christian, think my response should be, and then in what manner do you consider me to be a Jew?"

Werner's mother believes he must be concerned about what his answer should be if someone asks about his "Jewish identity." Although his family are not observant Jews, they attended services on high holy days out of a sense of tradition. Werner is thinking about having a bar mitzvah, an important ritual for boys when they turn 13. As a child fleeing Nazi persecution, he may be concerned about negative consequences he and his family may suffer as a result.

Over time, the family assimilates more and more into their community. At the end of one summer, the family enjoys a picnic at the local park complete with hot dogs, marshmallows, and softball. The adults begin a discussion about the end of the war, which "everyone agreed was eminent." This is a conversation between Gustav's parents and two friends.

"We always wanted to see what California was like . . . I hear the schools are very good out there, and it might be the right time to take the plunge. Edith wondered where they might take the plunge. Not only would Gustav be out of work, but they would have to look for another apartment again, and they didn't have a house trailer to drive to California. . . . [Irv says] They're going to be a lot of jobs, even with men coming home from the service. Just think of all the housing they're going to need. Construction work, that'll be the field. The war has done one good thing for America, it's taking us out of the depression for good. That's for sure."

"You folks are eligible for American citizenship next year, aren't you?" Agnes asked.

"That's right, the five years are almost up," Gustav replied "that'll be a good feeling for all of us."

Questions to Consider

1. Consider the discussion between Gustav's parents about changing their name. How do you understand this within the context of anti-Semitism in Europe that caused them to flee Germany as well as

(Continued)

anti-Semitism in the United States? If you and your family are not Jewish, imagine that you were in the same position. What do you think you would do and why? What are some of the pros and cons you might consider in your decision-making process? Consider the chapter reading before answering. If you and your family are Jewish, how does this narrative compare with your family's assimilation experience?

2. You've read about different models of assimilation. Many people lately seem to prefer the idea of "Anglo-conformity" and want immigrants that come to the United States to conform to the dominant culture. Consider faith traditions as part of that culture. The United States has a Christian tradition and many of its citizens are Christian. Should immigrants like the Auerbachs have to conform to this aspect of society?

Why or why not? Is religious conformity different than other kinds of conformity such as the ability to speak English? If your answer is "no," does this hold for all religions equally? Why or why not? If your answer is "yes," how would it be for you to change your beliefs (including atheism) to assimilate into a host society where you were seeking refuge? How does power (or lack of it) factor in?

CONTEMPORARY IMMIGRANTS: DOES THE TRADITIONAL PERSPECTIVE APPLY?

Does the traditional perspective—based as it is on the experiences of European immigrants and their descendants—apply to more recent immigrants to the United States? Will contemporary immigrants duplicate the experiences of earlier groups? Will they acculturate before they integrate? Will religion, social class, and race be important forces in their lives? Will they take three generations to assimilate? More than three? Fewer? What will their patterns of intermarriage look like? Will they achieve socioeconomic parity with the dominant group? When? How?

Sociologists (as well as the general public and policymakers) are split in their answers to these questions. Some social scientists believe that the "traditional" perspective on assimilation does not apply and that the experiences of contemporary immigrant groups will differ greatly from those of European immigrants. They believe that assimilation today is fragmented, known as **segmented assimilation**, and will have a number of different outcomes. Some contemporary immigrant groups will integrate into the middle-class mainstream, but others will find themselves permanently mired in the impoverished, alienated, and marginalized segments

of racial minority groups. Still others may form close-knit enclaves based on their traditional cultures and become successful in the United States by resisting the forces of acculturation (Portes & Rumbaut, 2001, p. 45).

In stark contrast, other theorists believe that the traditional perspective on assimilation is still relevant and that contemporary immigrant groups will follow the established pathways of mobility and assimilation. Of course, the process will be variable from group to group and from place to place, but even the groups that are today the most impoverished and marginalized will, in time, move into mainstream society.

How will the debate be resolved? We cannot say at the moment, but we can point out that this debate is reminiscent of the critique of Park's theory of assimilation. In both cases, the argument is partly about time: Even the most impoverished and segmented groups may find their way into the economic mainstream eventually, at some unspecified time in the future. Other levels of meaning in the debate exist, however, related to one's perception of the nature of modern U.S. society. Is U.S. society today growing more tolerant of diversity, more open and equal? If so, this would seem to favor the traditionalist perspective. If not, this trend would clearly favor the segmented-assimilation hypothesis. Although we will not resolve this debate in this text, we will consider the traditional and segmented views on assimilation as a useful framework to understand the experiences of these groups (see Chapters 8, 9, and 10).

Segmented assimilation has multiple outcomes. Some groups may eventually enter the middle class, but others may be permanently excluded, marginalized, and impoverished.

QUESTIONS FOR REFLECTION

17. What is segmented assimilation, and why is this an important concept? How would social class and gender relate to the debate over whether contemporary assimilation is segmented?

COMPARATIVE FOCUS

Immigration and Ireland

FIGURE 2.5 Migration Into and Out of Ireland, 1987–2014

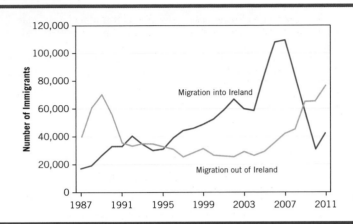

SOURCE: Central Statistics Office [Ireland], 2014.

Just as the United States has been a major receiver of immigrants for the past 200 years, Ireland has been a major supplier. Mass immigration from Ireland began with the potato famines of the 1840s and continued through the end of the 20th century, motivated by continuing hard times, political unrest, and unemployment. This mass out-migration—combined with the death toll of the famines—cut the 1840 Irish population of 7 million in half, and the population today is still only about 4.5 million.

History rarely runs in straight lines, however. In the 1990s and into the 21st century, after nearly 200 years of supplying immigrants, Ireland (along with other nations of Northern and Western Europe) became a consumer. As Figure 2.5 shows, the number of newcomers entering Ireland soared between 1987 and 2007, and the number of people leaving decreased. Starting in about 2007, however, the trend reversed: The number of newcomers plummeted, and the historic pattern of out-migration reappeared.

What explains these patterns? Answers are not hard to find. The influx of immigrants starting in the late 1980s was largely a response to rapid economic growth. The Irish economy—the so-called Celtic Tiger—had entered a boom phase, spurred by investments from multinational corporations and the benefits of joining the European Economic Union. Irish nationals who had left seeking work abroad returned home in large numbers, and people from Europe and other parts of the globe also began to arrive. In addition, Ireland began to receive refugees and people seeking asylum from Africa, the Middle East, and other trouble spots.

The changes that started in 2007 have an equally obvious cause. The global economy faltered badly in that year, and the Irish economy followed suit: Banks failed, companies went bankrupt, the housing market collapsed, and jobs disappeared. The Irish returned to their historic role as a supplier of immigrants to other economies around the world.

Although the era of in-migration lasted only a few decades, it may have created some permanent changes in Irish society. For example, the number of Irish of African and Asian descent has increased by a factor of 8 since 1996 (although both groups are less than 2% of the total population). Over the centuries, many different groups (e.g., Vikings, Spanish, and Anglo-Normans) have become part of Ireland, but, for the first time in their history, the Irish are dealing with issues of racial diversity.

Questions to Consider

1. What similarities can you see between immigration to Ireland and immigration to the United States?
2. Do you suppose that immigrants to Ireland will be assimilated in the same way as immigrants to the United States? If you could travel to Ireland, what questions would you ask about the assimilation process?

IMPLICATIONS FOR EXAMINING DOMINANT–MINORITY RELATIONS

Chapters 1 and 2 have introduced many of the terms, concepts, and themes that form the core of the rest of this text. Although the connections between the concepts are not simple, some key points can be made to summarize these chapters and anticipate the material to come.

First, minority-group status has much more to do with power and the distribution of resources than with simple numbers or the percentage of the population in any particular category. We saw this notion expressed in Chapter 1 in the definition of *minority group* and in our exploration of inequality. The themes of inequality and differentials in status were also covered in our discussion of prejudice, racism, and discrimination. To understand minority relations, we must examine some basic realities of human society: inequalities in wealth, prestige, and the distribution of power. To discuss changes in minority group status, we must be prepared to discuss changes in the way society does business, makes decisions, and distributes income, jobs, health care, and opportunities.

A second area that we will focus on in the rest of the book is the question of how our society should develop. Assimilation and pluralism, with all their variations, define two broad directions. Each has been extensively examined and discussed by social scientists, by leaders and decision makers in American society, and by ordinary people from all groups and walks of life. The analysis and evaluation of these two broad directions is a thread running throughout this book.

SUMMARY

This summary is organized around the Learning Objectives listed at the beginning of this chapter.

 2.1 Explain and analyze the concepts of assimilation and pluralism, including Anglo-conformity, the "melting pot," the "traditional" model of assimilation, cultural pluralism, and structural pluralism.

Assimilation and pluralism are two broad pathways of development for intergroup relations. Assimilation is a process by which groups grow more similar, and in the United States, it has generally meant Americanization or Anglo-conformity. In the traditional model, assimilation includes a number of stages: acculturation, integration at the secondary and primary levels, and intermarriage. Under pluralism, group differences are maintained through time. In cultural (or "full") pluralism, groups differ both culturally and structurally. Under structural pluralism, groups share essentially the same culture but occupy different locations in the social structure.

 2.2 Discuss and explain other group relationships such as separatism.

Group relations other than assimilation and pluralism include separatism, revolution, forced migration and expulsion, genocide, and continued subjugation.

 2.3 Describe the timing, causes, and volume of European migration to the United States, and explain how those immigrants became "white ethnics."

The period of mass European immigration stretched from the 1820s to the 1920s and included both "Old" (from Northern and Western Europe) and "New" (from Southern and Eastern Europe) phases. More than 30 million people made the journey from Europe to the United States during this time. People moved for many reasons, including the pursuit of religious and political freedom, but the underlying motive force was industrialization and urbanization. Immigrants from Europe were minority groups at first but, over a series of generations, assimilated, became upwardly mobile and integrated, and Americanized. Their experiences varied by gender, "race," and class, but, generally, most groups followed the "traditional" model of assimilation (which was based on these groups).

 2.4 Understand the European patterns of assimilation and major variations in those patterns by social class, gender, and religion.

Assimilation for European immigrant groups generally followed a three-generation pattern, with the grandchildren of the original immigrants completing the process. Ethnic succession occurred when newly arrived groups of immigrants pushed older groups up in the occupational structure. The three major pathways of integration were politics, labor unions, and religion, but others included organized crime and sports. Structural mobility occurred as the American industrial economy matured and changed. Continuing mechanization and automation changed the nature of work, creating more opportunities in the middle-class, white-collar areas. The descendants of the immigrants were generally able to take advantage of expanding opportunities for education and move higher in the class structure than their parents and grandparents did. The experience of assimilation varied by the physical appearance of the group, its religion, social class, gender, and extent of sojourning.

 2.5 Describe the status of the descendants of European immigrants today, including the "twilight of white ethnicity."

These groups are, on average, at or above national norms for affluence and success. White ethnicity seems to be fading and may be in its twilight, although it remains a significant force for some people.

2.6 Analyze contemporary immigration using sociological concepts in this chapter. Explain how the traditional model of assimilation does or does not apply to contemporary immigrants.

Research is ongoing, but, at least for some immigrant groups, assimilation today may be segmented and may have outcomes other than equality with and acceptance into the middle class. We will consider these possibilities in depth in Part 3.

KEY TERMS

acculturation or cultural assimilation 41
Americanization (or Anglo-conformity) 39
anti-Semitism 55
assimilation 38
capital-intensive 47
cultural pluralism 44
culture 40
enclave minority group 44
ethclass 63

ethnic revival 68
ethnic succession 58
human capital theory 42
industrial revolution 47
integration or structural assimilation 41
intermarriage or marital assimilation 41
labor-intensive 47
melting pot 39

middleman minority group 44
multiculturalism 43
New Immigration 48
Old Immigration 48
pluralism 38
primary sector 40
principle of third-generation interest 67
Protestant ethic 49
race relations cycle 40

revolution 45
secondary sector 40
segmented assimilation 72
separatism 45
social structure 40
sojourners 65
structural mobility 61
structural pluralism 44
symbolic ethnicity 69
triple melting pot 63

REVIEW QUESTIONS

1. Summarize Gordon's model of assimilation. Identify and explain each stage and how the stages are linked together. Explain Table 2.2 in terms of Gordon's model.

2. "Human capital theory is not so much wrong as it is incomplete." Explain this statement. What does the theory leave out? What are the strengths of the theory? What questionable assumptions does it make?

3. What are the major dimensions along which the experience of assimilation varies? Explain how and why the experience of assimilation can vary.

4. Define pluralism, and explain the ways it differs from assimilation. Why has interest in pluralism increased? Explain the difference between and cite examples of structural and cultural pluralism and cite examples of each. Describe enclave minority groups in terms

of pluralism and in terms of Gordon's model of assimilation. How have contemporary theorists added to the concept of pluralism?

5. Define and explain segmented assimilation, and explain how it differs from Gordon's model. What evidence is there that assimilation for recent immigrants is not segmented? What is the significance of this debate for the future of U.S. society? For other minority groups (e.g., African Americans)? For the immigrants themselves?

6. Do American theories and understandings of assimilation apply to Ireland? Do you suppose that immigrants to Ireland will assimilate in the same way as immigrants to the United States? If you could travel to Ireland, what questions would you ask about the assimilation process?

STUDENT STUDY SITE

⑤SAGE edge™

Sharpen your skills with SAGE edge at edge.sagepub.com/healey8e

SAGE edge for students provides a personalized approach to help you accomplish your coursework goals in an easy-to-use learning environment.

The following resources are available at SAGE edge:

Current Debates: English Only?

Should English be made the official language of the United States? Should immigrants be required to be fluent in English? Would "English-only" policies exclude and marginalize immigrants?

On our website you will find an overview of the topic, the clashing points of view, and some questions to consider as you analyze the material.

Public Sociology Assignments

Public Sociology Assignments provide opportunities for students to address directly and personally some of the issues raised in this text.

The first two public sociology assignments on our website will lead students to confront diversity in their community. In the first assignment, you will investigate your hometown to see if you can document increases in racial and ethnic diversity consistent with Figure 1.1. In the second assignment, you will study graffiti: Does it express stereotypes and prejudice? What does it reflect about local group hierarchies?

Contributed by Linda M. Waldron

Internet Research Project

For the Internet Research Project for this chapter, you will use information from the U.S. Census to assess the relative assimilation of several groups, including some white ethnic groups. Your investigation will be guided by a series of questions, and your instructor may ask you to discuss the issues in small groups.

For Further Reading

Please see our website for an annotated list of important works related to this chapter.

CHAPTER-OPENING TIMELINE PHOTO CREDITS

1845–1852: Mary Frances Cusack / Wikimedia Commons

1854: Library of Congress Prints and Photographs Division

1862: Library of Congress Prints and Photographs Division

1881–1885: Harper's Weekly/Wikimedia Commons

1881–1920: Library of Congress Prints and Photographs Division

1911–1920: Library of Congress Prints and Photographs Division

1917: Sackett & Wilhelms Corp N.Y. / Wikimedia Commons

1980–2000: SVEN NACKSTRAND/AFP/Getty Images

3 PREJUDICE AND DISCRIMINATION

1862
The "Anti-Coolie" Act discourages Chinese immigration to California by requiring Chinese workers pay a hefty monthly tax taking more than half their pay.

1880
Jim Crow laws mandate racial segregation in all public facilities in southern states.

1896
The Supreme Court rules in *Plessy v. Ferguson* that "separate but equal" accommodations are constitutional.

1815   1830   1845   1860   1875   1890   1905

1830
The Indian Removal Act leads to the forced removal of 100,000 Native Americans to west of the Mississippi.

1857
The Dred Scott decision mandates that African Americans cannot be citizens.

1866
The Ku Klux Klan is founded.

1836
The U.S. House of Representatives passes the first "gag rule," designed to prevent the introduction, reading, or discussion of any antislavery bill or petition.

1863
The Anti-Miscegenation laws passed by individual states prohibit interracial marriage and interracial sex.

In 2012, Wade Michael Page walked into a Sikh[1] temple in Oak Creek, Wisconsin, and started shooting. He killed six people and wounded four others before taking his own life. In 2015, Dylann Roof walked into a prayer service at the Emanuel African Methodist Episcopal Church in Charleston, South Carolina. He killed nine people and injured six others. In 2016, Omar Mateen killed 49 people and injured 58 others at popular gay club in Orlando, Florida, making it the second deadliest shooting by a single person in U.S. history.

How can we understand why these men wanted to kill so many people? If we use our sociological imaginations, we can identify some of the sociological processes at work (Mills, 1959). Further, we can see how these shootings connect to larger patterns of hate crimes in the United States. All three shooters

---

[1]The Sikh religion was founded in the Punjab region of India 500 years ago.

1943
In Los Angeles, U.S. sailors attack Mexican American boys wearing "zoot suits." Similar attacks occur in other cities.

1996
The Federal Defense of Marriage Act denies same-sex couples the right to have their partnerships recognized by the government. This prevents them from receiving the benefits heterosexual couples receive such as insurance, tax, or social security benefits.

2004
The Minuteman Project begins to organize anti-immigrant activists at the U.S./Mexico border. The group considers itself a citizens' border patrol.

1920   1935   1950   1965   1980   1995   2010

1942
Approximately 110,000 Japanese Americans are sent to internment camps.

1992
Riots erupt in Los Angeles after a jury acquits four white police officers for the videotaped beating of African American Rodney King.

1998
Matthew Shepard, a 21-year-old gay college student, is brutally murdered, bringing hate crimes against gays into the national spotlight.

2001
Hate crimes against Arab and Asian Americans spike after the terrorist attacks of September 11.

2012
Trayvon Martin, a 17-year-old African American, is fatally shot by George Zimmerman, renewing new debates about racial profiling.

were born in the United States. Page, age 40, became radicalized while serving in the U.S. Army. He became a white supremacist, a neo-Nazi, and a member of several white-power bands (Romell, 2012). He called nonwhites "dirt people" and wanted whites to have a homeland. He targeted a sacred setting that was populated by nonwhites, non-Christians, and recent immigrants. Like Page, Roof, age 21, was a white supremacist and a neo-Nazi. He had concerns that "Blacks were taking over the world" (Mindock, 2015) and wanted to start "a race war" (Payne & Botelho, 2015). Mateen, age 30, viewed himself as an "Islamic soldier." He told a police negotiator that America had "to stop bombing Syria and Iraq. They are killing a lot of innocent people" (Harris, 2016).

The United States has changed a lot over the past 100 years: from a time when blatant racism was common and racial discrimination was legal, to a nation that has twice elected a black president and that has seen much broader acceptance of people who are LGBTQ+. What can the mass shootings by Page, Roof, and Mateen tell us about how people become socialized to see others as not just different but problematic? What is the connection between prejudicial ideas and discrimination? •

Some people say that the election of Barack Obama to the presidency of the United States proves that prejudice, skin color, and group membership are no longer relevant in our society. Others, particularly social scientists, are less willing to pronounce the death of racism. They argue that prejudice has not decreased so much as it has changed to subtler, indirect forms. What do you think? What does the evidence suggest?

In this chapter, we explore these and a variety of other issues. Social scientists have conducted a significant amount of research on prejudice and discrimination and developed an impressive array of theories. We will review some of their most important conclusions and arguments.

We will begin by restating the difference between prejudice and discrimination, and then we will explore the two dimensions of prejudice (affective and cognitive). As we do so, we will examine some of the important individual-level theories of prejudice (see Table 3.1). We will then cover some of the central sociological perspectives on prejudice and discrimination. The emphasis will be on prejudice, but we will examine discrimination on many occasions in this chapter and in future ones.

Toward the end of the chapter, we will return to the issues introduced above: How has American prejudice evolved and changed over the recent past? We will conclude with a look at hate crimes, one of the most vicious manifestations of bigotry and antiminority sentiment.

TABLE 3.1 Four Relationships Between Prejudice and Discrimination in Individuals

	DOES NOT DISCRIMINATE	DOES DISCRIMINATE
Unprejudiced	Unprejudiced nondiscriminator (all-weather liberal)	Unprejudiced discriminator (fair-weather liberal)
Prejudiced	Prejudiced nondiscriminator (timid bigot)	Prejudiced discriminator (all-weather bigot)

SOURCE: Adapted from Merton (1968).

PREJUDICE AND DISCRIMINATION

Let's begin with definitions. Recall from Chapter 1 that prejudice is the tendency of individuals to think and feel in negative ways about members of other groups. Discrimination, on the other hand, is an action. An easy way to remember it is, "discrimination is differential doing" or DDD. Individual discrimination occurs when people treat someone differently because of the group to which they belong. Institutional discrimination is built into society, for example, in policies or procedures of the education, the criminal justice, or economic systems. Although prejudice and discrimination are related, they do not always occur together or have a causal relationship with each other.

Table 3.1 presents four combinations of individual prejudice and discrimination. In two cases, the relationship between prejudice and discrimination is consistent. The "all-weather liberal" is *not* prejudiced and does *not* discriminate, while the "all-weather bigot" *is* prejudiced and *does* discriminate. The other two combinations, however, are inconsistent. The "fair-weather liberal" discriminates without prejudice, while the "timid bigot" is prejudiced but does not discriminate. These combinations illustrate that prejudice and discrimination can be independent of each other. These inconsistencies between attitudes and behavior are not uncommon and may be caused by a variety of social pressures, including the desire to conform to the others' expectations. In this chapter, we focus more on prejudice than on discrimination, but we will address the relationship between the two concepts on several occasions and throughout the book.

PREJUDICE

American social scientists have made prejudice a primary concern of their research and have produced thousands of articles and books on the topic, asking a wide array of different questions from a variety of theoretical perspectives. One firm conclusion is that prejudice is not a single, unitary phenomenon. No single theory has emerged that can explain prejudice in all its complexity. It has a variety of probable causes (some more psychological and individual, others more sociological and cultural) and can present itself in a variety of forms (some blatant and vicious, others subtle and indirect). In keeping with the macrosociological approach of this text, we will focus on the theories related to culture, social structure, and group relationships.

THE AFFECTIVE DIMENSION

Individual prejudice is partly a set of feelings or emotions that people attach to groups, including their own. The emotions can run a wide gamut from mild to intense. For example, someone may have a negative, stereotypical view of the Irish and call them "a worthless bunch of drunks." Someone else might think, "I don't like Muslims" or "fat people are disgusting." The extreme hatred expressed by Wade Michael Page, Dylann Roof, and Omar Mateen in the chapter opening represent the other end of the continuum. What makes these emotions part of prejudice is their generalized association with an entire group, often in the complete absence of any actual experience with group members, and their element of prejudgment (which is, after all, the literal meaning of prejudice). Several psychological and social-psychological research traditions focus on the emotional or affective aspect of prejudice. Here, we will briefly examine two of these theories: the **scapegoat hypothesis** and the theory of the **authoritarian personality**.

The Scapegoat Hypothesis. This theory links prejudice to feelings of frustration and aggression. People sometimes deal with personal failure or disappointment by expressing their anger against a substitute target (or scapegoat), not against the actual object or person that caused their frustration. For example, someone who has been demoted at work might attack a family member rather than the boss. Or a student who earns a low grade on a test might "take it out" on a friend or pet rather than on the professor. Generally, the actual cause of the frustration (boss, professor) has more

---

The **scapegoat hypothesis** holds that people sometimes express their frustrations against substitute targets. When the substitutes are other groups, prejudice increases.

The theory of the **authoritarian personality** links prejudice to childhood experiences with stern, severe parents.

---

power than the substitute targets (family, friends, pets), which is why it's "safer" to attack the substitute instead.

Minority groups can make excellent substitute targets because they, by definition, have less power and other resources. Members of the dominant group target minority groups as the recipients of anger and aggression that, for whatever reason, cannot be directed at the real cause of a person's frustration. For example, as you'll see in Chapters 8 and 9, it may be easier to hate the Chinese or Mexicans because of the perception that they are "taking our jobs" rather than seeing them as being "hired to fill jobs" at lower wages. In this case, it benefits company owners to hire workers for less money. But it may be hard to see company owners as "the enemy" and it's risky to attack them if you need a job. When released against a minority group, displaced aggression is expressed as or accompanied by prejudice.

Many researchers have produced scapegoating against minority groups in laboratory settings. In a typical experiment, subjects are purposely frustrated, perhaps by being asked to complete a task that the researchers have made sure is impossible. Then, the subjects are offered the opportunity to release their anger as prejudice, sometimes by completing a survey that measures their feelings about various minority groups. Many people respond to this situation with increased feelings of rejection and disparagement against other groups (see Berkowitz, 1978; Dollard, Miller, Doob, Mowrer, & Sears, 1939; Miller & Bugleski, 1948).

Outside the laboratory, researchers use scapegoat theory to explain a variety of political, social, and economic events such as the rise of the Nazi Party in Germany in the 1930s. At that time, Germany was trying to cope with its defeat in World War I, a powerful economic recession, rampant unemployment, and horrific inflation. According to this line of analysis, the success of the extremely racist, violently anti-Semitic Nazi Party resulted, in part, because of its ability to capture people's intense anxieties and fears and redirect them against Jews and other minorities (see Dollard et al., 1939).

Along the same analytical lines, Hovland and Sears (1940) argued that the rate of lynching of African Americans in the South between 1882 and 1930 correlated with fluctuations in cotton prices. Lynching increased during hard times when cotton prices were low, resulting in widespread economic distress and increasing people's frustrations. (For a different, more sociological view, see Beck & Clark, 2002, and Beck & Tolnay, 1990.)

Finally, scapegoating has been implicated in many hate crimes in the United States, including seemingly random attacks on Middle Easterners following the terrorist attacks of September 11, 2001. We will return to the topic of hate crimes at the end of this chapter.

Malnourished Jewish prisoners in the Buchenwald concentration camp. Jews were a favorite scapegoating target for the Nazis.

The Theory of the Authoritarian Personality. This theory links stern, highly punitive styles of parenting in childhood with the development of prejudice and an authoritarian personality (Adorno, Frenkel-Brunswik, Levinson, & Sanford, 1950). On the surface, the children of authoritarian families respect and love their parents. Internally, however, they resent and fear their severe and distant parents. They can't consciously admit these negative feelings; instead, they scapegoat their fear and anger by expressing these emotions as prejudice against minority groups. Thus, prejudice provides people with authoritarian personalities a way of coping with their conflicted feelings for their parents.

Research on the authoritarian personality theory stretches back to before World War II, but reached its peak of popularity in the 1950s and 1960s, inspired, in part, by a desire to understand Hitler and high–ranking Nazi officials (Zillmer et al., 1995). More recent research has examined the links between authoritarianism and gender norms (Peterson & Zurbriggen, 2010), child abuse (Rodriguez, 2010), attitudes toward international students (Charles-Toussaint & Crowson, 2010), and even leisure activities (Peterson & Pang, 2006).

Authoritarian personality theory has contributed to our understanding of individual prejudice, but it has been widely criticized for several flaws—for example, for focusing solely on the internal dynamics of personality without taking sufficient account of the social settings in which an individual acts. Some individuals use prejudice as a tool for handling their personality problems, but to fully understand prejudice, we need to see its connections with social structure, social class, and the context and history of group relations. The sociological perspective, as we shall see, takes a broader approach and incorporates the social world in which the individual acts.

1. Identify some examples of scapegoating that you've seen or experienced. What substitute targets were selected? What were the actual causes of people's frustration? Does the theory fit your examples?

2. Is scapegoating always expressed as prejudice? Explain. If not, how is it expressed?

3. Identify an example where authoritarian personality theory might apply. What does the theory of the authoritarian overlook that might be helpful to consider?

4. Consider the scapegoat hypothesis and the theory of authoritarian personality as they apply to Nazi Germany. How can both ideas offer a more useful explanation than just one of them? Can you think of more recent examples where these ideas could be helpful for understanding prejudice? Explain. (If you don't find these ideas particularly helpful, consider what is lacking and why it's important to understanding prejudice.)

THE COGNITIVE DIMENSION: STEREOTYPES

The cognitive dimension of prejudice includes stereotypes about people in other groups. Stereotypes are oversimplified generalizations that are said to apply to all group members (e.g., all Christians, all feminists, all Southerners) regardless of individual characteristics. Stereotypes tend to emphasize just a few traits and they are resistant to disproof (Pettigrew, 1980, p. 822; see also Jones, 1997, pp. 164–202). That is, people often maintain their stereotypes despite contradictory evidence.

Stereotypes can change over time, however. For example, as you'll see in Chapter 9, Americans used to think of Asians as lazy, stupid, and dangerous but the dominant stereotype today is that Asians are hardworking and smart—the "model minority." Note that this stereotype doesn't distinguish between different Asian groups, of which there are many such as Bangladeshi, Pakistani, Laotian, Korean, and Indian. Nor does the model-minority stereotype account for variation within specific Asian groups. An intersectional view may encourage us to think about how people might vary by age, religion, sexual orientation, political affiliation, geographic region, gender, and other characteristics.

Yet, you might find yourself thinking, "But, Asians really are smart and hardworking!" Although that's a positive stereotype, what's problematic about that statement? For example, where did you get your ideas? And, what are some possible negative consequences that could result from a positive stereotype?

TABLE 3.2 Americans, Japanese See Each Other Through Different Lenses

Which characteristics do you associate with _____?

	AMERICAN VIEWS OF JAPANESE %	JAPANESE VIEWS OF AMERICANS %
Hardworking	94	25
Inventive	75	67
Honest	71	37
Intolerant	36	29
Aggressive	31	50
Selfish	19	47

SOURCE: 2015 Pew Research Center survey, Q4a-f.

Americans share a common set of images of the prominent ethnic, racial, religious, and other groups that make up U.S. society. Less prejudiced people are probably familiar with these images but pay little attention to them, and they do not use them to judge the worth of others. More prejudiced people will think in stereotypes, apply them to all members of a group, make sweeping judgments about the worth of others, and even commit acts of violence based solely on people's group membership. Just as Americans have certain stereotypes, people in other countries do, too. A recent survey conducted by the Pew Research Center, a nonpolitical "fact tank" (About Pew Research Center, n.d.), found that Americans and Japanese see each other differently. For example, Americans tend to see Japanese people as hardworking (94%), inventive (75%), and honest (71%) while Japanese respondents viewed Americans as inventive (67%), aggressive (50%), and selfish (47%) (Stokes, 2015). Now, consider the viewpoints presented in Table 3.2. What surprises you about these findings? Do the stereotypes about Americans apply to you? If not, how does it make you feel to be associated with them? Knowing what you know about prejudice, stereotypes, and discrimination, how might stereotypes about Americans affect you—perhaps without your even knowing it?

For the prejudiced individual, stereotypes are an important set of cognitive categories. Once people learn a stereotype, it can shape perceptions to the point that the individual pays attention only to information that confirms that stereotype. **Selective perception**, the tendency to see only what one expects to see, can reinforce and strengthen stereotypes to the point that the highly prejudiced individual simply does not accept evidence that challenges his

or her views. Thus, these overgeneralizations can become closed perceptual systems that screen out contrary information and absorb only the sensory impressions that ratify the original bias.

Types of Stereotypes and Dominant–Minority Relations. Stereotypes are, by definition, exaggerated overgeneralizations. At some level, though, even the most simplistic and derogatory stereotype can reflect some of the realities of dominant–minority group relationships. The content of a stereotype flows from the actual relationship between dominant and minority groups and is often one important way the dominant group tries to justify or rationalize that relationship.

For example, Pettigrew (1980) and others have pointed out two general stereotypes of minority groups. The first attributes extreme inferiority (e.g., laziness, irresponsibility, or lack of intelligence) to minority-group members and tends to be found in situations (such as slavery) in which a minority group is being heavily exploited and held in an impoverished and powerless status by the dominant group. This type of stereotype is a rationalization that helps justify dominant-group policies of control, discrimination, or exclusion.

The second type of stereotype occurs when power and status differentials are less extreme, particularly when the minority group has succeeded in gaining some control over resources, has experienced some upward mobility, and has had some success in school and business. In this situation, credulity would be stretched too far to label the group "inferior," so their relative success is viewed in negative terms: They are seen as *too* smart, *too* materialistic, *too* crafty, *too* sly, or *too* ambitious (Pettigrew, 1980, p. 823; see also Simpson & Yinger, 1985, p. 101).

A team of psychologists has documented a similar pattern of stereotypes in the United States and other nations.

How accurate is this stereotype of Americans? What does it overlook? How might stereotypes of Americans affect you?

Selective perception is the tendency to see only what one expects to see.

They find that perceptions of groups can be arrayed in a two-dimensional space defined by perceptions of competence and feelings of warmth. Interestingly, they include groups other than minority groups in their research.

Figure 3.1 presents multiple survey results from U.S. respondents. The circled clusters of scores show similar stereotypes. Among other findings, the researchers note two groups of ambivalent stereotypes: Some groups (the elderly, the disabled) are labeled "LC–HW" (low competence–high warmth) because they are viewed as helpless (low on competence) but also with positive affect (high on warmth). Others (Jews, Asians) are regarded as high on competence (HC) but low on warmth (LW): They are seen as capable but cunning (Cuddy et al., 2009, p. 4). The latter stereotype echoes the characterization of groups that people see as *too* successful, a pattern these researchers label as an "envious" prejudice.

Note that African Americans and other racial minority groups fall in the same "moderately competent–moderately warm" (MC–MW) cluster as, among others, gay men and Muslims, and that "whites" are seen as more competent and warmer than the racial minorities but as less competent than the "envied" minority groups. Consistent with traditional American values, the lowest rated groups are the poor, welfare recipients, and the homeless—groups whose presumed characteristics are often seen as overlapping with those of African Americans.

While these patterns are important, you should also realize that stereotypes and prejudice can exist apart from the context of actual group relationships or the relative "success" or social standing of groups. Research shows that some individuals will readily stereotype groups about which they have little or no information. In fact, some individuals will express prejudice against groups that do not even exist! In one test, researchers asked respondents how closely they would associate with "Daniereans, Pireneans,

and Wallonians"—all fictitious groups. A number of white respondents apparently reacted to the "foreign" sound of the names, rejected these three groups, and indicated that they would treat them about the same as other minority groups (Hartley, 1946). Clearly, the negative judgments about these groups were not made on the basis of personal experience or a need to rationalize some system such as slavery. The subjects exhibited a tendency to reject minority groups of all sorts.

The Content of American Stereotypes. A series of studies with Princeton University undergraduates provides some interesting perspectives on the content of American stereotypes. In 1933, researchers (Katz & Braley, 1933) gave students a list of 84 words and asked them to select the best descriptors for 10 different groups (e.g., Jews, African Americans, Irish, Germans). The researchers were interested in the cultural basis of stereotypes, that is, how stereotypes are socially constructed. For example, did students' stereotypes reflect media portrayed of the day (e.g., magazines)? Or, did students base stereotypes on their experiences with various kinds of people? Researchers repeated the study in 1951 and 1967 (Karlins, Coffman, & Walters, 1969) to investigate the staying power of stereotypes.

It is unusual to have comparable data covering such an extended period, which makes these studies significant even though Princeton undergraduates are hardly a representative sample of Americans. Several findings are worth noting. First, the content of the stereotypes echoed ideas from the larger society. For example, students consistently saw the English as sportsmanlike and conventional, Italians as passionate and musical, and Jews as shrewd and industrious. Second, the students' perceptions reflect the two kinds of stereotypes discussed in the prior section, Types of Stereotypes. That is, students saw African Americans as extremely inferior ("lazy," "ignorant") while seeing Jews in a tempered way: "intelligent" *but* "mercenary" and "shrewd." Third, although some stereotypes stayed constant across all three studies (Jews as "shrewd," Americans as "industrious," blacks as "musical") a recent readministration of the test (Fiske et al., 2009) showed some change. For example, respondents still described African Americans as "musical," but also saw them positively ("loyal to family" and "religious") and negatively ("loud").

Most students had little experience with people from the groups they evaluated. In 1951 and 1967, students were a bit more reluctant to generalize, especially about groups with whom they had little or no contact. Nevertheless, they repeated many of the stereotypes the students held in 1933. This suggests that people learn stereotypes through socialization and come to believe what they hear from different agents of socialization such as parents, friends, media, religious leaders, and politicians rather than through personal

FIGURE 3.1 American Stereotypes

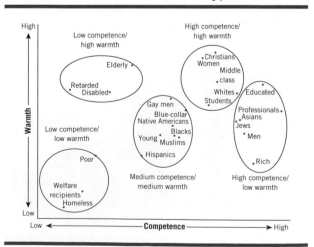

NOTE: See Cuddy et al. (2009) and Fiske, Bergsieker, Russell, and Williams (2009).

experience. Additionally, it seems that minority groups (e.g., Jews, African Americans) were socially constructed as "other"—somehow not fully "American." Importantly, this research shows the significance of social context for understanding prejudiced and stereotypical thinking. For example, in 1933, students labeled the Japanese as intelligent, industrious, progressive, shrewd, and sly. In 1951, just a few years after World War II , the stereotypes became quite negative: imitative, sly, extremely nationalistic, and treacherous. By 1967, the labels reflect the "model minority" stereotype: industrious, ambitious, efficient, intelligent, and progressive (Fishbein, 2014, p. 10).

Researchers have conducted similar studies of stereotypical thinking on other campuses in more recent years. Clark and Person (1982) measured white stereotypes of African Americans among undergraduates at two Southeastern universities in the early 1980s. They found some continuity in the content of the stereotypes from earlier studies but also found that their subjects were more likely to characterize African Americans as having positive traits such as "loyal to family" (Clark & Person, 1982). In contrast, a study conducted by Wood and Chesser (1994) found that white students at a large Midwestern university had more negative stereotypes of African Americans. The top five most common traits selected by the sample were uniformly negative and included "loud," "aggressive," and "lazy" (Wood & Chesser, 1994).

These studies are informative, but, because they are based on college students, they may have little applicability to the attitudes of Americans in general. Fortunately, we can learn more about stereotypical thinking among Americans in general by reviewing research based on representative samples. One important study (Bobo & Kluegal, 1997) examined prejudice in the 1990s, and we can get a sense of how American stereotypes have changed by comparing their findings with those of a 2016 survey. In both years, respondents were asked to rate "the characteristics of people in a group" on a number of scales, including an "intelligent–unintelligent" scale and a "hard working–lazy" scale. Results for white Americans are presented in Figures 3.2 and 3.3. The first figure displays perceptions of whites and blacks as "unintelligent," and the second does the same for perceptions of "laziness." In both years, more than 95% of the respondents answered the question, indicating that the willingness to label entire groups is widespread.

Let's begin by looking at the 1990 results for "unintelligent." About 30% of whites applied this term to blacks, but only about 6% applied it to their own group, a differential of about 24%. We can think of the size of the differential as a measure of the strength of this aspect of the traditional antiblack stereotype (Bobo & Kluegal, 1997, p. 101). In 2016, the willingness to apply this negative trait to blacks was dramatically lower (less than 13% of whites

FIGURE 3.2 White Americans' Perceptions of Intelligence by Race, 1990 and 2016

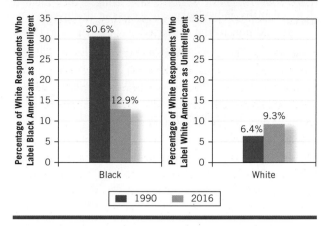

SOURCE: Adapted from Bobo and Kluegal, 1997, and National Opinion Research Council (1972–2016).

endorsed the stereotype), as was the differential between perceptions of blacks and whites (about 4%). This result might be taken as evidence of the declining strength of antiblack stereotypes among whites.

Figure 3.3 presents a less optimistic picture. Compared with the stereotype of "unintelligent," the stereotype of black laziness was more widespread in 1990 (more than 46% of whites applied this characterization to blacks) and the differential was much larger (about 42%). By 2016, the percentage of whites willing to apply this trait to blacks had declined, as had the differential (about 16%). Still, about 27% of whites saw blacks as lazy, a result that indicates that this aspect of the traditional "negative" stereotype of blacks persists in American society.

Overall, these results support the idea that elements of traditional stereotypical thinking persist in the United States. The declines reflected in Figure 3.2 may reflect decreasing levels of prejudice or a growing unwillingness to verbalize prejudice, possibilities we will discuss later in this chapter.

FIGURE 3.3 White Americans' Perceptions of Laziness by Race, 1990 and 2016

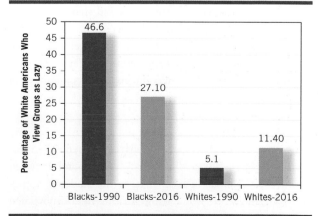

SOURCE: Adapted from Bobo and Kluegal, 1997, and National Opinion Research Council (1972–2016).

COGNITIVE AND AFFECTIVE DIMENSIONS OF STEREOTYPES

Remember that individual prejudice has an affective dimension in addition to the cognitive. Robert Merton (1968), a prominent American sociologist, makes this distinction between dimensions dramatically. Merton analyzed stereotypical perceptions of Abraham Lincoln, Jews, and Japanese. In the following passage, he argues that the three "stereotypes" are identical in content but vastly different in emotional shading:

> *The very same behavior undergoes a complete change of evaluation in its transition from the in-group Abe Lincoln to the out-group Abe Cohen or Abe Kurokawa. Did Lincoln work far into the night? This testifies that he was industrious, resolute, perseverant, and eager to realize his capacities to the full. Do the out-group Jews or Japanese keep these same hours? This only bears witness to their sweatshop mentality, their ruthless undercutting of American standards, their unfair competitive practices. Is the in-group hero frugal, thrifty, and sparing? Then the out-group villain is stingy, miserly, and penny-pinching. All honor is due to the in-group Abe for his having been smart, shrewd and intelligent, and, by the same token, all contempt is owing the out-group Abes for their being sharp, cunning, crafty, and too clever by far. (p. 482)*

The stereotype of all three Abes is identical; what varies is the affect, or the emotional tone, reflected in the descriptive terms. Thus, the same stereotype evokes different emotional responses for different groups or in different individuals.

INTERSECTIONS OF RACE, GENDER, AND CLASS

The affective and cognitive dimensions of prejudice vary not only by race and ethnicity but also by gender and class, the major axes that define social life and shape minority-group experience. For example, the stereotypes and feelings attached to black men differ from those attached to black women, and feelings about lower-class Mexican Americans are different from those evoked by upper-class members of the same group. We can get a sense of some of this variation by briefly reviewing three studies.

The first study asked white students at Arizona State University about their perceptions of women (Weitz & Gordon, 1993). Sharp distinctions were found between "women in general" (a label that, to the students, apparently signified white women) and African American women in particular. When asked to select traits for "American women in general," the responses were overwhelmingly positive and included "intelligent," "sensitive," and "attractive." Of the 10 most commonly selected traits, only 2 ("materialistic" and "emotional") might have had some negative connotations.

The students selected very different terms to describe African American women. The single most commonly selected trait was "loud," and only 22% of the sample saw African American women as "intelligent." Of the 10 most commonly selected traits, 5 (e.g., "talkative," "stubborn") seemed to have at least some negative affect attached to them.

The second study explores race/gender dynamics in the context of the relationships between hip-hop music and Asian American–Pacific Islanders (AAPIs) (McTaggart & O'Brien, 2013). From its origins as an expression of black, urban culture, hip-hop has grown into a diverse, global art form that transcends race, culture, language, gender, and age. A West Coast version of hip-hop began to flourish early in the movement and has long had a connection with AAPI groups, partly because it provides ways of negating dominant-group stereotypes of Asians. These stereotypes are gender specific: They depict AAPI men as soft, effeminate, and asexual, while AAPI women are seen as desirable, docile, and pliable (the ultimate fantasy of many men).

The study, based on in-depth interviews, found that for AAPI men, the hypermasculinity that is a part of hip-hop culture can be a way of compensating for and resisting the dominant-group stereotype, in much the same way as they might regard the success of NBA star Jeremy Lin as an antidote to the stereotype of AAPI men as nonathletic. For AAPI women, the youthful, urban, global aspects of hip-hop provide opportunities to break out of the narrow constraints of dominant-group images and to express themselves, even though they still have to contend with sexism and even misogyny. Thus, for its AAPI aficionados, hip-hop provides a more liberated space for self-expression and freedom from dominant-group culture.

Finally, a study by sociologist Edward Morris (2005) further illustrates how race, gender, and class can intersect in shaping feelings and thoughts of other groups. He studied an urban high school and focused on how various types of students were perceived and disciplined by school administrators and faculty. Morris found that, consistent with the notion of a "matrix of domination," mentioned in Chapter 1, stereotypes varied "not just through gender, or just through race, or just through class, but through all of these at once" (p. 44). For example, school administrators and faculty saw black boys as *too* masculine, extremely aggressive, and dangerous, and in need of careful watching. In contrast, they saw black girls as not feminine enough, too loud and aggressive, and in need of being molded into more compliant and deferential women. Other groups in the school—Latinas, Asian men, white men and women—were also the objects of stereotypical thinking and feelings.

Significantly, they tended to be subjected to forms of discipline that, ultimately, tended to reproduce the systems of inequality in the larger society.

QUESTIONS FOR REFLECTION)

5. Why are Jews and Asians grouped together in the "high competence–low warmth" category of Figure 3.1? What stereotypical traits do they allegedly share? Why?

6. How have white perceptions of blacks changed over time? What do you think these changes mean?

7. How are stereotypes specific to race/gender? Have you heard similar examples from your family or friends, or from the media? What other social categories (e.g., sexual orientation, religion) might influence stereotypes? Explain, using an example to illustrate your point.

8. Consider the role that social context plays in shaping stereotypes. For example, the way that World War II negatively affected stereotypes about the Japanese. What other group stereotypes have changed over time—positively or negatively—as the result of significant social change?

9. Consider the stereotypes that you've heard, seen, or believe. Where did they come from? How have they changed over time (if they have)? What chapter concepts best explain them?

SOCIOLOGICAL CAUSES OF PREJUDICE

Prejudice is a complex phenomenon with multiple causes and manifestations. In this section, we will take a macro-sociological approach and examine theories about prejudice that are related to culture, social structure, and group relationships.

GROUP COMPETITION

Every form of prejudice—even the most ancient—started at some specific point in history. If we go back far enough in time, we can find a moment that predates antiblack prejudice, anti-Semitism, negative stereotypes about Native Americans or Hispanic Americans, or antipathy against Asian Americans. What sorts of conditions create prejudice? The most important single factor in the origin of prejudice is competition between groups: Prejudice originates in the heat of that competition and is used to justify and rationalize the privileged status of the winning group. If we go back far enough, we can always find some instance in which one group successfully dominates, takes resources from, or eliminates a perceived threat by another group. The successful group becomes the dominant group, and the other becomes the minority group.

Why is group competition associated with the emergence of prejudice? Typically, prejudice doesn't cause group competition; it results from it. Prejudice functions to mobilize emotional energy for conflict, justify rejection and attack, and rationalize the structures of domination, like slavery or segregation, that result from the competition. Groups react to the competition and to the threat presented by other groups with antipathy and stereotypes about the "enemy" group. Prejudice emerges from the high levels of emotion but then can solidify and persist for years (even centuries) after the end of the conflict. In chapters to come—and particularly in Chapter 4—we will often focus on the relationships between group competition and prejudice.

Robber's Cave. The relationship between prejudice and competition has been demonstrated in a variety of settings and situations ranging from labor strikes to international war to social psychology labs. In the chapters to come, we will examine the role of prejudice during the creation of slavery in North America, as a reaction to periods of high immigration, and as an accompaniment to myriad forms of group competition. Here, to illustrate our central point about group competition and prejudice, we will examine a classic experiment from the sociological literature. The experiment was conducted in the 1950s at a summer camp for 11- and 12-year-old boys known as Robber's Cave.

The camp director, social psychologist Muzafer Sherif, divided the campers into two groups, the Rattlers and the Eagles (Sherif, Harvey, White, Hood, & Sherif, 1961). The groups lived in different cabins, and the staff continually pitted them against each other in a wide range of activities. They set up games, sports, and even housekeeping chores in a competitive way so that winners would earn individual and group prizes. As the competition intensified, the boys in each group developed and expressed negative feelings (prejudice) against the other group. Competition and prejudicial feelings grew quite intense, for example, in episodes of name-calling, taunting, and raids on the "enemy" group and burning of each other's flags.

In another phase of the experiment, Sherif attempted to reduce the boys' negative feelings for one another by bringing the campers together in various pleasant situations featuring food, movies, and other treats. But, the rival groups did not get on well and tensions remained high. Then, Sherif created situations that required the members of the rival groups to work cooperatively with each other. For example, the researchers deliberately sabotaged some plumbing to create a drinking water "emergency." Camp staff blamed "vandals." Both groups worked together to resolve the problem. As a result of these cooperative activities, intergroup "prejudice" declined and, eventually, friendships were formed across groups.

In the Robber's Cave experiment, as in many actual group relationships, prejudice (negative feelings and stereotypes about other campers) arose to help mobilize feelings and justify rejection and attacks, both verbal and physical, against the out-group. When group competition was reduced, the levels of prejudice abated and eventually disappeared, again demonstrating that prejudice is caused by competition, not the other way around.

Although the Robber's Cave experiment illustrates our central point, we must be cautious in generalizing from these results. The experiment was conducted in an artificial environment with young boys (all white) who had no previous acquaintance with one another and no history of grievances or animosity. Thus, these results may be only partially generalizable to group conflicts in the "real world." Nonetheless, Robber's Cave illustrates a fundamental connection between group competition and prejudice that we will observe repeatedly in the chapters to come. Competition and the desire to protect resources and status, as well as to defend against threats from other groups—perceived or real—are the primary motivations for the creation of prejudice and structures of inequality that benefit the dominant group.

THEORETICAL PERSPECTIVES ON GROUP COMPETITION AND PREJUDICE: POWER/CONFLICT MODELS

Many theorists have examined the dynamics of group competition and the results for prejudice and discrimination. Here we examine three of the most influential sociological perspectives on this topic.

Marxist Analysis. In Chapter 1, we discussed Marxism as a theory that sees class inequality as a result of the capitalist economic system. Under capitalism, a small group (the bourgeoisie) exploits the masses (the proletariat). A key reason capitalism continues is because the elites control ideas. Marx and Engels (1848/1967) wrote, "What else does the history of ideas prove, than that intellectual production changes its character in proportion as material production is changed? The ruling ideas of each age have ever been the ideas of its ruling class" (p. 102). In other words, the elites who control the means of production (e.g., factories, mills, mines) in a society also control the belief systems and intellectual activity of the society. They do so to support their dominance. When new elites come into control, these belief systems may change.

Elite classes who subordinate or exploit a minority group will develop and institutionalize ideologies to justify or "explain" social arrangements. Marx and Engels (1932/1972) wrote:

> The production of ideas, of conceptions, of consciousness, is at first directly interwoven with the material activity and the material intercourse of men, the language of real life. Conceiving, thinking, the material intercourse of men appear at this stage as the direct efflux of their material behavior . . . Men are the producers of their conceptions, ideas, etc. . . . (p. 47)

Although Marx didn't write much about racism, he would probably argue that it is a product of capitalism. After all, as you learned in Chapter 1, race is an *idea*—a social construction where the meanings of race vary over time and place. People create ideas about race, which then become embedded in social structures (e.g., norms, social institutions).

The history of the United States (and other nations) includes many situations in which elites used ideas to maintain their privileged position. For example, slave owners in the South used antiblack prejudice to justify the exploitation of the slaves to themselves and others. If people believed that blacks were inferior to whites, slavery would seem less oppressive and unjust. If slavery was seen as unjust, then people would be more likely to oppose it. By accepting ideas of black inferiority, people who benefitted most from that system helped to keep their advantage.

Another example of elites using a belief system for their own benefit is the way some slave owners used Christianity to encourage slaves to accept their status, for example, by emphasizing Biblical virtues of meekness and humility and by telling slaves that God wanted them to "obey your earthly masters with fear and trembling" (Ephesians 6:5) or "to be submissive to their masters" (Titus 2:9) (Glancy, 2002, p. 148). Religion could also focus slaves' attention on the promise of future rewards in heaven, rather than the misery and injustice of this life.

In a more industrial example, the history of the United States for the past 150 years is replete with instances of struggle between the capitalists who control the means of production and workers. For example, early in the 20th century, industrialists commonly tried to weaken labor unions by splitting the working class along racial lines. The greater the extent to which black and white workers fought each other, the less likely there would be a unified uprising against the capitalist class. The capitalist class controlled the racially mixed working class by following a strategy of "divide and conquer" (Cox, 1948; Reich, 1986).

Split Labor Market Theory. This theory agrees with the Marxist idea that prejudice and racist ideologies serve the interest of a specific class, but it identifies a different beneficiary. In split labor market theory, there are three actors in the economic sector of an industrial society. First are the elites, the capitalists who own the means of production. The other two groups are segments of the working class. The labor market is divided (or split) into higher-priced labor and cheaper labor. It is in the economic self-interest of the capitalist class to use cheaper labor whenever possible. Recent immigrants and minority groups often fill the role of cheaper labor.

Higher-priced labor (usually consisting of members of the dominant group) will attempt to exclude cheaper labor from the marketplace whenever it can. Such efforts include barring minority groups from labor unions, violent attacks on minority-group communities, support for discriminatory laws, and efforts to exclude groups from the United States entirely. Prejudice is used by higher-priced labor to arouse and mobilize opposition to the cheaper labor pool represented by the minority group. The economic nature of the competition and the economic self-interests of higher-priced labor are obscured by appeals to racial or cultural unity against the "threat" represented by the minority group. The major beneficiary of prejudice is not the capitalist class but the more powerful elements of the working class (Bonacich, 1972; Bonacich & Modell, 1980).

Group Interests. American sociologist Herbert Blumer (1958) began a similar line of analysis. He argued that prejudice is activated when groups feel that they are threatened by other groups they see as beneath them (see also Bobo & Tuan, 2006). The dominant group—which, by definition, has the highest status in a society—is particularly likely to use prejudice as a weapon when it feels that its privileges, its sense of entitlement and high position, are in peril.

We saw in Chapter 1 that sociologist Max Weber argued that there are three separate stratification systems in society: property (the economic system that includes jobs and income), power (control of decision making and the political institution at all levels), and prestige (the allocation of honor, esteem, and respect). Perceived threat could involve any of these dimensions or any combination of the three.

An example of these dynamics can be found in the reaction of many Southern (and other) whites to the black Civil Rights Movement of the 1950s and 1960s. We will

discuss this era of race relations in some detail in Chapter 6, but, for now, we can point out that the movement challenged the Southern system of race-based privilege that was institutionalized during slavery and perpetuated during segregation, a system that granted even the lowest-status white a position superior to all blacks.

Prejudice was an important part of the attempt by whites to resist racial change. Politicians and other leaders of the white community used the most vicious stereotypes (e.g., black men as sexual threats to white women) and the most negative emotional rhetoric to motivate whites to attempt to defeat demands for racial equality and an end to segregation. Sometimes, prejudice was used to foment or justify violence—bombings, lynchings, and beatings—but even milder forms of resistance were motivated by the perceived need to maintain the superior power, prestige, and property of whites in the South, and protect their racial privilege.

Contemporary examples of how prejudice has been used to help defend group position are not difficult to locate. For example, many Americans today feel threatened by immigration (particularly by undocumented immigrants), the rising tide of diversity (see Figure 1.1), and various global threats, including the rise of China and terrorist groups such as Al Qaeda. Predictably, politicians and media figures of all persuasions have exploited—and perhaps intensified—these feelings, particularly in election campaign ads designed to (sometimes blatantly) mobilize people's fears, prejudices, and sense of threat. One widely criticized example comes from the 2010 election campaign of Senator David Vitter of Louisiana. He accused his opponent of being soft on illegal immigration and border security, and his campaign ran a TV advertisement in which immigrants were shown sneaking across the border and being welcomed with checks, limousine rides, and other benefits, presumably the result of the policies advocated by his opponent. (See the original ad, Welcome Prize, at www.youtube.com/watch?v=9uvp0Jljh6U.) Vitter won the election by a wide margin.

> **Split labor market theory** argues that higher-priced dominant-group labor uses prejudice and discrimination to limit the ability of lower-priced minority-group labor to compete for jobs.

A clear expression of group preferences.

SUMMARY AND LIMITATIONS

These theories share the conclusion that prejudice flows from struggles to control or expand a group's share of scarce resources. The primary beneficiary of prejudice is sometimes the elite class (e.g., capitalists, plantation owners, high-status groups) and sometimes another segment of the dominant group (e.g., higher-priced labor). In general, though, these perspectives agree that prejudice exists because someone or some group gains by it.

These points are persuasive and help us understand why prejudice originates in the first place, but they cannot account for prejudice in all its forms. No theory can explain everything, especially something as complex as prejudice. The origins of prejudice can be found in culture, socialization, family structure, and personality development, as well as in politics and economics. As the authoritarian personality theory reminds us, prejudice can have important psychological and social functions independent of group power relationships.

To illustrate these limitations, consider an analysis of attitudes toward immigrants. Consistent with the idea that prejudice is stimulated by group competition, Burns and Gimpel (2000) found that opposition to immigration is greater when times are hard and people feel economically threatened. However, they also found that anti-immigration prejudice cannot be explained by economics alone and that it persists even when economic conditions improve, a finding consistent with the idea that prejudice is shaped by cultural and personality factors in addition to conflict over scarce resources.

QUESTIONS FOR REFLECTION

10. How are the ideas presented in this section sociological? How do they differ from more psychological theories of prejudice and discrimination?

THE PERSISTENCE OF PREJUDICE

Prejudice originates in group competition, but often outlives the conditions of its creation. It can persist, full-blown and intense, long after the episode that sparked it has faded from memory. How does prejudice persist through time?

THE VICIOUS CYCLE

In his classic analysis of American race relations, *An American Dilemma* (1944/1962), Swedish economist Gunnar Myrdal proposed the idea that prejudice is perpetuated through

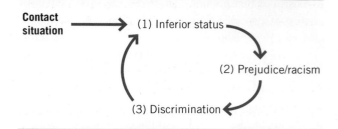

FIGURE 3.4 Myrdal's Vicious Cycle

time by a self-fulfilling prophecy or a **vicious cycle**, as illustrated in Figure 3.4. The dominant group uses its power to force the minority group into an inferior status, such as slavery, as shown in the diagram in Area 1. Partly to motivate the construction of a system of racial stratification and partly to justify its existence, individual prejudice and racist belief systems are invented and accepted by the dominant group, as shown in Area 2. Individual prejudices are reinforced by the everyday observation of the inferior status of the minority group. The fact that the minority group is impoverished, enslaved, or otherwise exploited confirms and strengthens the attribution of inferiority. The belief in inferiority motivates further discrimination and unequal treatment, as shown in Area 3 of the diagram, which reinforces the inferior status, which then validates the prejudice and racism, which justifies further discrimination, and so on. Over a few generations, a stable, internally reinforced system of racial inferiority becomes an integral, unremarkable, and (at least for the dominant group) accepted part of everyday life.

Culture is slow to change, and once created, prejudice will be sustained over time just like any set of attitudes, values, and beliefs. Future generations will learn prejudice in the same way and for the same reasons they learn any other aspect of their culture. Thus, prejudice and racism come to us through our cultural heritage as a package of stereotypes, emotions, and other ideas. We learn which groups are "good" and which are "bad" in the same way we learn table manners and religious beliefs (Pettigrew, 1958, 1971, p. 137; Simpson & Yinger, 1985, pp. 107–108). When prejudice is part of the cultural heritage, individuals learn to think and feel negatively toward other groups as a routine part of socialization, even if that socialization doesn't seem overt or intended. Much of the prejudice expressed by Americans—and the people of many other societies—is the typical result of typical socialization in families, communities, and societies that are, to some degree, racist. Given our

In the **vicious cycle**, minority-group inferiority is assumed and then forces are set in motion to create and perpetuate it.

long history of intense racial and ethnic conflict, it probably isn't surprising that Americans continue to manifest resentment toward and stereotypical ideas about other groups.

THE DEVELOPMENT OF PREJUDICE IN CHILDREN

Research on the development of prejudice in children confirms that prejudice is learned through socialization. Studies generally show that children become aware of group differences (e.g., black vs. white) at a very early age, even as early as six months (Katz, 2003, p. 898). By age three or younger, they recognize the significance and the permanence of racial groups and can accurately classify people on the basis of skin color and other cues (Brown, 1995, pp. 121–136; Katz, 1976, p. 126). Once children mentally establish the racial or group categories children begin the process of learning the "proper" attitudes and stereotypes to associate with the various groups, and both affective and cognitive prejudice begin to grow at an early age.

Children can acquire prejudice even when parents and other caregivers do not teach it overtly or directly. Adults control the socialization process and valuable resources (food, shelter, praise), and children are motivated to seek their approval and conform to their expectations (at least in the early years). Additionally, children face strong pressure to learn and internalize the perceptions of the older generation, and even a casual comment or an overheard remark can establish or reinforce negative beliefs or feelings about members of other groups (Ashmore & DelBoca, 1976). Children need not be directly instructed about presumed minority-group characteristics; it is often said that racial attitudes are "caught and not taught."

Additionally, research shows that children are actively engaged in their learning and that their levels of prejudice reflect their changing intellectual capabilities. Children as young as five to six months old can make some simple distinctions (e.g., by gender or race) between categories of people. The fact that this capability emerges so early in life suggests that it is not simply a response to adult teaching. "Adults use categories to simplify and make sense of their environment; apparently children do the same" (Brown, 1995, p. 126). Gross, simplistic distinctions between people may help very young children organize and understand the world around them. The need for such primitive categorizations may decline as the child becomes more experienced in life and more sophisticated in his or her thinking. Doyle and Aboud (1995), for example, found that prejudice was highest for younger children and actually decreased between kindergarten and the third grade. The decline was related to increased awareness of racial similarities (as well as differences) and diverse perspectives on race (see also Black-Gutman & Hickson, 1996; Bronson & Merryman,

2009; Brown, 1995, pp. 149–159; Cristol & Gimbert, 2008; Powlishta, Serbin, Doyle, & White, 1994; Van Ausdale & Feagin, 2001). Thus, changing levels of prejudice in children may reflect an interaction between children's changing mental capacities and their environment rather than a simple or straightforward learning of racist cultural beliefs or values.

SOCIAL DISTANCE SCALES: THE CULTURAL DIMENSIONS OF PREJUDICE

Further evidence for the cultural nature of prejudice is provided by research on the concept of **social distance**, which is related to prejudice but is not quite the same thing. Social distance is the degree of intimacy that a person is willing to accept in his or her relations with members of other groups. On this scale, the most intimate relationship is close kinship, and the most distant is exclusion from the country. The seven degrees of social distance, as specified by Emory Bogardus (1933), the inventor of the scale, are as follows:

1. To close kinship by marriage
2. To my club as personal chums
3. To my street as neighbors
4. To employment in my occupation
5. To citizenship in my country
6. As visitors only to my country
7. Would exclude from my country

Research using social distance scales demonstrates that Americans rank other groups in similar ways across time period and geographic location. This consistency indicates a common frame of reference or set of perceptions that suggest socialization into a common culture.

Table 3.3 presents some results of several administrations of the scale to samples of Americans from 1926 to 2011. The groups are listed by the rank order of their scores for 1926. In that year, the sample expressed the least social distance from the English and the most distance from Asian Indians. Whereas the average social distance score for the English was 1.02, indicating virtually no sense of distance, the average score for Asian Indians was 3.91, indicating a distance between "to employment in my occupation" and "to my street as neighbors."

As you inspect the table, note, first of all, the stability in the rankings. The actual scores (not shown) generally decrease from decade to decade, indicating less social distance and presumably a decline in prejudice over the years.

Social distance refers to the degree of intimacy a person is willing to accept for members of other groups.

The group rankings, however, tend to be the same year after year. Considering the changes that society experienced between 1926 and 2011 (the Great Depression; World War II, the Korean War, the Vietnam War, and the Cold War with the USSR; the Civil Rights Movement; the resumption of large-scale immigration; etc.), this overall continuity in group rankings is remarkable.

Second, note the nature of the ranking: Groups with origins in Northern and Western Europe are ranked highest, followed by groups from Southern and Eastern Europe, with racial minorities near the bottom. These preferences reflect the relative status of these groups in the U.S. hierarchy of racial and ethnic groups, which, in turn, reflects the timing of immigration and the perceived "degree of difference" from the dominant group (see Chapter 2). The rankings also reflect the relative amount of exploitation and prejudice directed at each group over the course of U.S. history.

Although these patterns of social distance scores support the general point that prejudice is cultural, this body of research has some important limitations. The respondents were generally college students from a variety of campuses, not representative samples of the population, and the differences in actual scores from group to group are sometimes very small.

Still, the stability of the patterns cannot be ignored: The top groups are always Northern European, Poles and Jews are always ranked in the middle third, and Koreans and Japanese always fall in the bottom third. African Americans and American Indians were also ranked toward the bottom until the most recent rankings.

Finally, note how the relative positions of some groups change with international and domestic relations. For example, both Japanese and Germans fell in the rankings at the end of World War II (1946). Comparing 1977 with 1946, Russians fell and Japanese rose, reflecting changing patterns of alliance and enmity in the global system of societies. The dramatic rise of African Americans in 2011 may reflect declining levels of overt prejudice in American society, and the low rankings of Muslims and Arabs in 2011 probably reflect the negative feelings generated by the terrorist attacks on September 11, 2001.

How do we explain the fact that group rankings generally are so stable from the 1920s to 2011? The stability strongly suggests that Americans view these groups through the same culturally shaped lens. A sense of social distance, a perception of some groups as "higher" or "better" than others, is part of the cultural package of intergroup prejudices we acquire from **socialization** into

---

Socialization is the process of physiological and social development by which a person learns his or her culture.

American society. The social distance patterns illustrate the power of culture to shape individual perceptions and preferences and attest to the fundamentally racist nature of American culture.

The Narrative Portrait on page 95 illustrates the power of culture to shape our perceptions.

SITUATIONAL INFLUENCES

As a final point in our consideration of the persistence of prejudice, we should note the importance of the social situation in which attitudes are expressed and behavior occurs. What people think and what they do is not always the same. Even intense prejudice may not translate into discriminatory behavior, and discrimination is not always accompanied by prejudice (refer back to Table 3.1).

One of the earliest demonstrations of the difference between what people think and feel (prejudice) and what they actually do (discrimination) was provided by sociologist Robert LaPiere (1934). In the 1930s, he escorted a Chinese couple on a tour of the United States. At that time, Chinese and other Asians were the victims of widespread discrimination and exclusion, and anti-Chinese prejudice was quite high, as demonstrated by the social distance scores in Table 3.3. However, LaPiere and his companions dined in restaurants and stayed in hotels without incident for the entire trip, and experienced discrimination only once.

Six months later, LaPiere wrote to every establishment the group had patronized and inquired about reservations. He indicated that some of the party were Chinese and asked if that would be a problem. Of those establishments that replied (about half), 92% said that they would not serve Chinese and would be unable to accommodate the party.

Why the difference? Although not a definitive or particularly sophisticated method of data gathering (for example, there was no way to tell whether the correspondents were the same persons LaPiere and his associates had dealt with in person), this episode exemplifies the difference between saying and doing and the importance of taking the situation into account. On LaPiere's original visit, anti-Asian prejudice may well have been present but was not expressed, perhaps to avoid making a scene. In a different situation, the more distant interaction of written correspondence, the restaurant and hotel staffs may have allowed their prejudice to be expressed in open discrimination because the potential for embarrassment was much less.

The situation a person is in shapes the relationship between prejudice and discrimination. In highly prejudiced communities or groups, the pressure to conform may cause

Do you have a sense of social distance from people in other groups—groups to which you don't belong? Has it changed over the past 10 years? Use the seven degrees of social distance to indicate the level of intimacy you would feel comfortable sharing with members of each of the groups listed. Also, estimate the degree of social distance you would have felt for each group 10 years ago. The scale is:

1. To close kinship by marriage
2. To my club as personal chums
3. To my street as neighbors
4. To employment in my occupation
5. To citizenship in my country
6. As visitors only to my country
7. Would exclude from my country

GROUP	YOUR SOCIAL DISTANCE SCORE TODAY	YOUR SOCIAL DISTANCE SCORE 10 YEARS AGO
Americans (white)		
Irish		
Russians		
Italians		
American Indians		
Jews		
Mexicans		
African Americans		
Chinese		
Muslims		

When you're done, consider the following questions: How did you acquire your sense of social distance? Was it from your family or community, or is it based on actual experience with members of these groups? Do you think it was "caught and not taught"? Why has it changed over the past 10 years (if it has)?

TURN TO TABLE 3.3 ON THE NEXT PAGE TO SEE HOW GROUP RANKINGS HAVE CHANGED OVER TIME. HOW DO YOUR SCORES COMPARE?

relatively unprejudiced individuals to discriminate. For example, if an ethnic or racial or gender joke is told in a group of friends or relatives, all might join in the laughter. Even a completely unprejudiced person might smile or giggle to avoid embarrassing or offending the person who told the joke.

On the other hand, situations in which there are strong norms of equal and fair treatment may stifle the tendency of even the most bigoted individual to discriminate. For example, if a community vigorously enforces antidiscrimination laws, even the most prejudiced merchant might refrain from treating minority-group customers unequally. Highly prejudiced individuals may not discriminate so they can "do business" (or at least avoid penalties or sanctions) in an environment in which discrimination is not tolerated or is too costly.

TABLE 3.3 Social Distance Scores of Selected Groups (Ranks for Each Year)

GROUP	1926	1946	1977	2011
English (British)	1	3	2	4
Americans (white)	2	1	1	1
Canadians	3	2	3	3
Irish	5	4	7	5
Germans	7	10	11	8
Russians	13	13	29	20
Italians	14	16	5	2
Poles	15	14	18	14
American Indians	18	20	10	12
Jews	19	19	15	11
Mexicans	21	24	26	25
Japanese	22	30	25	22
Filipinos	23	23	24	16
African Americans	24	29	17	9
Turks	25	25	28	—
Chinese	26	21	23	17
Koreans	27	27	30	24
Asian Indians	28	28	27	26
Vietnamese	—	—	—	28
Muslims	—	—	—	29
Arabs	—	—	—	30
Mean (all scores)	2.14	2.12	1.93	1.68
Range from highest to lowest scores	2.85	2.57	1.38	1.08

SOURCE: 1926 to 1977—Smith and Dempsey (1983, p. 588); 2011—Parrillo and Donoghue (2013).

NOTE: Values in the table are ranks for that year. To conserve space, we've eliminated some groups and ranks.

SUMMARY AND LIMITATIONS

The theories and perspectives examined in this section help us understand how prejudice can persist through time. Prejudice becomes a part of the culture of a society and is passed along to succeeding generations along with other values, norms, and information.

Although cultural causes of prejudice are obviously important, considering only cultural factors may lead us to the mistaken belief that all members of the same society have similar levels of prejudice. On the contrary, no two people have the same socialization experiences or develop exactly the same prejudices (or any other attitude, for that matter). Differences in family structure, parenting style,

school experiences, attitudes of peers, and a host of other factors affect the development of an individual's personality and attitude.

Furthermore, socialization is not a passive process; we are not neutral recipients of a culture that is simply forced down our throats. Our individuality, intelligence, and curiosity affect the nature and content of our socialization experiences. Even close siblings may have very different experiences and, consequently, different levels of prejudice. People raised in extremely prejudicial settings may moderate their attitudes as a result of experiences later in life, just as those raised in nonprejudiced settings may develop stronger biases as time passes.

NARRATIVE PORTRAIT

The Cultural Sources of Prejudice

In The Crazyladies of Pearl Street, *best-selling novelist Trevanian (2005) recounts his experiences growing up Irish Catholic in a poor neighborhood in Albany, New York, in the 1930s. Here, he recalls how his mother decided to apply for public assistance after her husband had abandoned them. Trevanian, then a boy of eight, advised her to enlist the assistance of Mr. Kane, the local grocer who had already extended them credit to buy food and other essentials. The young Trevanian saw Mr. Kane as kindly, but his mother focused on the fact that he was Jewish.*

For the author, his mother is a powerful and heroic figure. She is also, as are we all, a product of her culture. She inherited a set of attitudes and emotions about other groups and especially about Jews.

THE CRAZYLADIES OF PEARL STREET

Trevanian

Here's how things were: We were marooned on this slum street . . . where we didn't know anybody and . . . we had only a little more than five bucks to our name. But we weren't beaten. Not by a damn sight. Nobody beats [my mother]! No, sir! . . . Her pride had never let her seek public assistance, and it burned her up to have to do so now, but she . . . couldn't let pride stand in the way of us kids having food on the table. There must be agencies and people that she could turn to, just until we were on our feet again. First she'd contact them and ask them for help . . . make them help us, goddammit! Then she'd look for work as a

waitress.... But first, she had to find out the addresses of the welfare agencies. If only she knew someone she could ask about things like this.

"What about Mr. Kane?" I suggested.

"The grocery man? Oh, I don't know. I don't think we want any more favors from his sort."

". . . His sort?"

She shrugged.

"But he's nice," I said. "And smart, too."

She thought about that for a moment. She didn't like being beholden to strangers, but . . . Oh, all right, she'd go over to thank him for giving us credit. That was just common courtesy. . . .

"You know, come to think of it, this Mr. Kane of yours just might help us out because if he doesn't, we won't be able to pay what we owe him. You can only count on these people if there's something in it for them."

"He'd help us anyway. He's nice.". . .

She often said, and honestly believed, that she was not prejudiced—well, except in the case of Italian mobsters and drunken Irish loafers and stupid Poles and snooty Yankee Protestants, but then who wasn't? Among the cultural scars left by her early years in convent school was a stereotypical view of "the people who slew Jesus." "On the other hand," she said, always wanting to be fair, "I served some very nice Jewish people in the Lake George Restaurant last season. They always chose my station. Real good tippers. But then they had to be, didn't they? To make up for things."

I accompanied her across the street, and Mr. Kane spent half the morning looking up the appropriate

welfare agencies and using the pay phone at the back of his shop to call people and make appointments for my mother. . . .

She thanked him for his help, [and] as we crossed the street back to [the apartment] she told me that I must always be careful with these people.

"But Mr. Kane was just trying to be . . ."

"They have a way of worming things out of you."

"He wasn't worming any—"

"You just be careful what you tell them, and that's final. Period!"

Later that month, when we were able to begin paying something against our slate, my mother felt vindicated in her mistrust of "these people." She discovered that Mr. Kane had charged her a nickel for each call he made on her behalf. I explained that this was only fair because he had put a nickel into the slot for each call, but she waved this aside, saying she was sure he made a little something on each call. Why else would he have a phone taking up space in his shop? No, they work every angle, these people. . . .

SOURCE: Trevanian (2005). *The Crazyladies of Pearl Street*, pp. 31–33. New York: Crown Books. Copyright © 2005 by Trevanian. Used by permission of Crown Publishers, a division of Random House, Inc.

Questions to Consider

1. What stereotypes about Jewish people does Trevanian's mother believe?
2. How does she exemplify the concept of "selective perception"? Is there anything Mr. Kane could have done to negate her assumptions about him?

The development of prejudice is further complicated by the fact that, in the United States, we also learn egalitarian norms and values as we are socialized. Myrdal (1944/1962) was referring to this contrast when he titled his landmark study of race relations in the United States *An American Dilemma*. We learn norms of fairness and justice along with norms that condone or even demand unequal treatment based on group membership. Typically, people develop more than one attitude about other groups, and these multiple attitudes are not set in concrete. They can change from time to time and place to place, depending on the situation and a variety of other variables. The same point could be made about other attitudes besides prejudice; people have an array of attitudes, beliefs, and values about any particular subject, and some of them are mutually contradictory.

FIGURE 3.5 Declining Traditional Prejudice of White Americans Against African Americans, 1942–2016

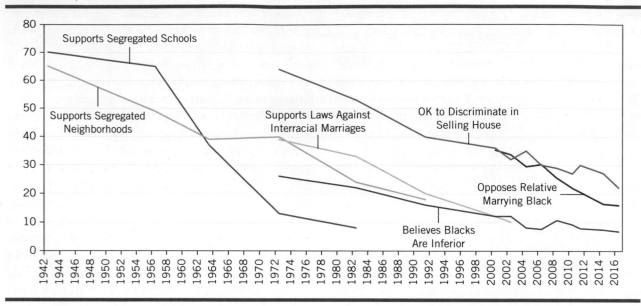

SOURCE: 1942, 1956, and 1963—Hyman and Sheatsley (1964); 1972 to 2016—National Opinion Research Council (NORC) (1972–2016).

RECENT TRENDS: TRADITIONAL PREJUDICE AND MODERN RACISM

At the beginning of this chapter we asked, "Is prejudice still a problem in the United States?" A great deal of research shows a decline in "traditional" prejudice: the blatant, overt feelings and ideas that have characterized American prejudice virtually from the birth of the nation. However, many social scientists argue strongly that prejudice has *not* declined but has evolved into subtler, less obvious, but just as consequential form. This new form of prejudice has been called a number of things, including **modern racism**, symbolic racism, and color-blind racism. Further, prejudice can take forms that seem positive such as "affectionate paternalism," which is when people treat an adult with "special" care—as if they were a child—which suggests they are weaker, less competent, or less able to deal with a particular task or situation. (In Chapter 11, we'll talk about a gender-specific type of affectionate paternalism called "benevolent sexism.") If we conceptualize prejudice only as overtly negative, we can overlook the other forms it takes (Dovidio, Glick, Rudman, 2008, p. 10).

In this section, we will first explore the decline in traditional prejudice and consider possible reasons for this decline. Then, we will consider the research about modern racism.

TRADITIONAL PREJUDICE: CHANGING ATTITUDES?

Some of the strongest evidence that traditional, overt prejudice is declining comes from public opinion research. Since the 1940s, researchers have polled representative samples of U.S. citizens about prejudice. These polls document a consistent decrease in support for prejudicial statements.

Figure 3.5 shows data gathered from white Americans who participated in several research studies over a 64-year period. On the far left, you'll see two topics that people were asked about in 1942: segregated schools and segregated neighborhoods. The huge majority—a little more than 70%—of white Americans thought that black and

---

Modern racism is a more subtle and indirect form of traditional prejudice.

---

white children should attend different schools. Forty years later, in 1982, less than 10% of Americans said they supported separate schools. People's support for segregated neighborhoods also decreased significantly over time.

The overall trend in Figure 3.5 is unmistakable: There has been a dramatic decline in support for prejudiced statements since World War II. By 2016, only 7% of white Americans said that they believed that blacks were inferior and only 16% opposed interracial marriage. Less than 25% supported discrimination in housing sales, down from 64% in 1972.

Of course, these polls also show that prejudice has not vanished. Some white Americans continue to endorse prejudicial sentiments and opinions on such issues as fair housing practices and interracial marriage.

Let's examine these changing attitudes in more detail. Note that, from 1972 to 2002, the percentage of white Americans who supported laws against interracial marriage dropped almost 30 percentage points, from 39% to 10%. Similarly, we see a tremendous decrease in the number of white Americans who opposed "a relative marrying an African American." Both trend lines suggest progress towards racial equality. Yet, they also suggest some contradictions worth considering. The question about laws banning interracial marriage captures prejudice about something somewhat abstract (a law) compared with a question about "a relative marrying an African American," which is more specific and brings the issue closer to home. Further, the former question might reflect people's attitudes about government regulation of one's personal life as well as their feelings about interracial marriage. In other words, the data might suggest that many Americans wouldn't want a relative to marry an African American, but they don't want the government to tell them they can't.

In 2017, a survey of a representative sample of all Americans (not just whites) asked participants if they thought that interracial marriage was a "good thing" or a "bad thing" for society or if it "doesn't make much difference" (Livingston & Brown, 2017). About 40% saw intermarriage as a positive change in society while 9% said it negatively affected society. (The other 52% said it didn't make a difference.) An intersectional lens might prompt you to wonder about *which* Americans feel positively or negatively about interracial marriage. Younger people had more favorable attitudes than older people: More than half (54%) of 18- to 29-year-olds felt positively about interracial marriage compared with 26% of those over 65. Education had a positive influence on people's attitudes: Over half (54%) of respondents with a college degree or more felt that intermarriage was good for society compared with only 26% of those with a high school degree or less. Finally, the data showed differences by place of residence. People living in urban areas were more likely to favor intermarriage

(45%) than people that lived in the suburbs (38%) and in rural areas (24%). These findings about the positive impact of age, education, and place of residence on prejudiced thinking are consistent with other the long-term research (Hyman & Sheatsley, 1964; NORC 1972–2012; See Bobo, Charles, Krysan, & Simmons, 2012, p. 42). You'll want to keep that in mind when reading the next section on Explaining the Decline of Traditional Prejudice.

We should also note another factor that affects the way people respond to sensitive survey items. In *The Presentation of Self in Everyday Life* (1959), sociologist Erving Goffman argues that when interacting with others, people try to present themselves in a favorable light. Otherwise, they risk social consequences (e.g., not getting hired, not being liked or accepted). In research, this tendency may influence participants to answer questions in ways that they perceive as appropriate or expected. Social scientists call this "social desirability bias." Social desirability bias is likely to increase when people are asked about stigmatized or sensitive topics such as drug use, cheating, or racial prejudice. Therefore, you should remember that survey research we just discussed shows only what people *say* they feel and think, which might be different from what they truly believe. One indicator that participants are aware of social norms regarding racial prejudice may be seen in the increasing number of people who answered questions (in Figure 3.5) with [I] "don't know." In the research by Hyman and Sheatsley (1964), participants were quite certain about their attitudes; less than 4% of them answered questions with [I] "don't know." However, about 10% to 20% of National Opinion Research Council participants answered questions that way (Bobo et al., 2012, p. 43). This may suggest that participants in the later research (1972–2012) knew that norms about racial attitudes tended to be more egalitarian and integrationist, but that they didn't want to agree with them. Of course, it's entirely possible that during times of great social change, people are unsure how they feel.

That said, if the general trends are reasonably valid, what sociological factors led to this attitudinal change? Next, we investigate two possible reasons: rising levels of education and increasing contact across racial lines.

EXPLAINING THE DECLINE OF TRADITIONAL PREJUDICE 1: THE ROLE OF EDUCATION

One possible cause of declining prejudice is that Americans have become much more educated during the time period covered in Figure 3.5 (1942–2016). Education has repeatedly been singled out as the single most effective cure for prejudice and discrimination (Tsai & Venkataramani, 2015; Weil, 1985). Education, like travel, is said to "broaden one's perspective" and encourage a more sophisticated view of human

FIGURE 3.6 High School and College Graduates in the United States, Age 25 and Older, 1950–2016

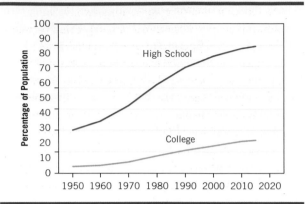

SOURCE: U.S. Bureau of the Census, 2017. Educational Attainment in the United States.

FIGURE 3.7 Prejudicial Views of White Americans by Level of Education, 2016

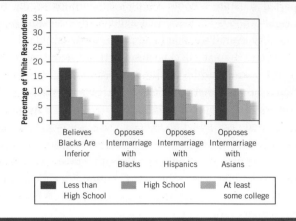

SOURCE: National Opinion Research Council (1972–2016).

affairs. People with higher levels of education are more likely to view other people in terms of their competence and abilities and not in terms of physical or ethnic characteristics. In some theories of assimilation (see Chapter 2), education is identified as one of the modernizing forces that will lead to a more rational, competency-based social system.

Figure 3.6 shows the percentage of the U.S. population with high school degrees increased almost 2.5 times between 1950 and 2016, from about 34% to 88%. In the same period, the percentage of the population with college degrees rose at an even faster rate (five times), from about 6% to 31%. Could it be merely coincidental that prejudice declined so dramatically during the same period?

Many studies have also found statistical correlations between an individual's level of prejudice and level of education (Hyman & Sheatsley, 1964; NORC 1972–2012; See Bobo, Charles, Krysan, & Simmons, 2012, p. 42). Figure 3.7 shows the relationships between various measures of prejudice and level of education for a representative sample of white Americans in 2016. The graph shows that prejudice decreases as education increases. White respondents with less education express greater support for the belief that blacks are inferior, and they are more opposed to marriage across group lines with blacks, Hispanics, and Asians.

The correlation between increased education and decreased prejudice supports the common wisdom that education is the enemy of (and antidote to) prejudice, but we need to consider some caveats and qualifications before we come to any conclusions. First, correlation is not the same thing as causation, and just because education and prejudice change together over time and are statistically associated does not prove that one is causing the change in the other. Perhaps people are still highly prejudiced and are simply hiding their true feelings from the public opinion pollsters, a trend that would be consistent with the arguments that traditional prejudice has morphed into modern racism.

Second, the limited set of possible responses offered to respondents (e.g., "agree" or "disagree") might not record the full range, subtlety, or complexity of people's feelings. People typically have many attitudes about a subject, especially one as emotionally charged as prejudice. As we have seen, different situations may activate different sets of attitudes, and public opinion surveys may evoke more tolerant responses. The more educated are particularly likely to be aware of the "correct" responses and more likely to express socially acceptable opinions or social desirability bias. The bottom line is that it is hard to determine how much of the apparent reduction in prejudice has been genuine and how much is due to conformity to the prevailing and fashionable attitudes of the day (see Cribbs & Austin, 2011; Jackman, 1978, 1981; Jackman & Muha, 1984; Smith & Seelbach, 1987; Weil, 1985).

EXPLAINING THE DECLINE OF TRADITIONAL PREJUDICE 2: THE CONTACT HYPOTHESIS

Like education, contact and increased communication between groups have often been suggested as remedies for prejudice, misunderstandings, discrimination, and hostile race and ethnic relations. A broad statement of this view might read something like this: "If people would get together and really talk to one another, they would see that we're all the same, all human beings with hopes and dreams." Such sentiments are common, and many organizations are devoted to opening and sustaining a dialogue between groups. How effective are such efforts? Does increased contact between group members reduce prejudice and discrimination? If so, under what conditions?

First, contact between groups is not, in and of itself, an automatic antidote for prejudice. Contact can have a variety of outcomes and can actually increase prejudice, depending on the situation. When contact occurs in situations of group inequality, such as during American slavery or segregation, prejudice is likely to be reinforced, not reduced. On the other hand, certain forms of intergroup contact can reduce prejudice (and stereotyping and discrimination).

One theory that addresses this relationship is the **equal status contact hypothesis** (often called the contact hypothesis). This theory specifies four conditions under which intergroup contact can reduce prejudice: The groups must have (1) equal status and (2) common goals, and (3) they must interact intensively in noncompetitive, cooperative tasks, and (4) have the active endorsement of authority figures (Dovidio, Glick, & Rudman, 2008; Pettigrew, 1998, pp. 66–67). Each of these four conditions is crucial to the reduction of prejudice.

1. *Equal status.* Only in situations in which all groups have equal resources, experiences, and prestige are people likely to view one another as individuals, not as representatives of their respective groups. When the people involved in intergroup contacts are unequal in status, they are more likely to keep or even intensify their prejudice. During slavery, for example, there was a high level of contact across racial lines because of the nature of agricultural work. However, the interactions between blacks and whites happened in a context of massive inequality and the contact did not encourage (to say the least) an honest and open sharing of views. Under the system of Jim Crow segregation that followed slavery, the frequency of interracial contact declined as blacks and whites were separated into different and unequal communities. By World War II, segregation was so complete that whites and blacks hardly saw each other except in situations in which blacks were lower in status such as housekeepers (Woodward, 1974, p. 118).

2. *Common goals.* The most effective contact situations for reducing prejudice are those in which members of different groups come together in a single group with a common goal. Additionally, it helps if contact involves enough time for people to feel comfortable with one another. Examples of effective groups include athletic teams working toward a winning season (Brown, Brown, Jackson, Sellers, & Manuel, 2003; Chu & Griffey, 1985); study groups of students helping one another prepare for tests throughout the semester (Aronson & Patnoe, 1997); soldiers fighting a battle (Amir, 1994); and community groups

organized to build a playground, combat crime, raise money for cancer research, and so forth.

3. *Intergroup cooperation and intensive interaction.* To reduce prejudice, contact must occur in an atmosphere free from threat or competition between groups. When intergroup contact is motivated by competition for scarce resources, prejudice tends to increase and may even be accompanied by hatred and violence. Recall the Robber's Cave experiment earlier in the chapter and the levels of prejudice that occurred when the groups ("Rattlers" and "Eagles") competed for prizes. Remember, also, how the need to fix the water supply brought them together to solve a common problem and resulted in connection and friendship. If people are bound together by cooperative behavior across group lines and are motivated to achieve a common goal, they are much more likely to come to regard one another as individuals, not as caricatures or stereotypical representatives of their groups.

   Furthermore, the contact has to be more than superficial. It must "lead to the perception of common interests and common humanity between different groups" (Allport, 1954, p. 281). The situation must last for a significant length of time, and the participants must be fully involved. Standing next to one another at a bus stop or eating at adjoining tables in a restaurant does not meet this criterion; people of different groups must deal with one another face-to-face and on a personal level.

4. *Support of authority, law, or custom.* Recall our discussion about the role socialization plays in creating prejudice. The reverse is also true. Intergroup contact that takes place with strong support from authority figures such as politicians, teachers, and ministers is more likely to have a positive impact on prejudicial attitudes and stereotypes. Further, it helps if the contact is supported by moral codes or values that encourage friendly, helpful, egalitarian attitudes and condemn ingroup-outgroup comparisons.

One of the most persuasive illustrations of the contact hypothesis is the Robber's Cave experiment, discussed earlier in this chapter (Sherif et al., 1961). As you recall, rival groups of campers were placed in competitive situations and became prejudiced as a result. It was not until the researchers created some situations in which the rival groups had to actively cooperate to achieve common goals that prejudice began to decline. Contact, in and of itself, did not affect intergroup attitudes. Only contact that required the goal-oriented cooperation of equals in status could reduce the prejudice that the staff had created through competition.

The **equal status contact hypothesis** argues that, under certain conditions, cooperative contacts between groups will tend to reduce prejudice.

The Robber's Cave experiment provides dramatic support for the contact hypothesis, but we must be cautious in evaluating this evidence. The experiment was conducted in a "pristine" environment in which the campers had no prior acquaintance with one another and brought no backlog of grievances and no traditions of prejudice to the situation. The study illustrates and supports the contact hypothesis but cannot prove the theory. For additional evidence, we turn to everyday life and more realistic intergroup contact situations.

In another classic study, Deutsch and Collins (1951) studied the anti-black prejudices of white residents of public housing projects. This study is significant because Deutsch and Collins were able to eliminate the problem of self-selection. In other studies, participation in the contact situation is typically voluntary. The people who volunteer for experiments in interracial contacts are usually not very prejudiced in the first place or at least are more open to change. Thus, any change in prejudice might be due to the characteristics of the people involved, not to the contact situation itself. By contrast, in the Deutsch and Collins study, some of the white participants were randomly assigned to live close to black families. The participants had no control over their living arrangement and thus were not self-selected for lower prejudice or openness to change.

A total of four public housing projects were studied. In two of the projects, black and white families were assigned to separate buildings or areas. In the remaining two, dwelling units were assigned regardless of race, and black and white families lived next to one another. As a result of proximity, the white subjects in these two housing projects had higher rates of contact with their black neighbors than did the white families assigned to "segregated" units.

The researchers interviewed the mothers of the white families and found that those living in the integrated projects were less racially prejudiced and much more likely to interact with their African American neighbors than were those living in the segregated setting. Deutsch and Collins (1951) concluded that the higher volume of interracial contact had led to lower prejudice.

More recent studies have been based on surveys administered to large, representative samples of black and white Americans and have generally supported the contact hypothesis. For example, one review of more than 500 tests conducted in a variety of nations concluded that contact has a powerful and consistent effect on prejudice, not only for racial and ethnic minorities but also for other outgroups, including gays and lesbians, and that the effects hold across nations, genders, and age groups (Pettigrew, Tropp, Wagner, & Christ, 2011, p. 271). (For more on the contact hypothesis, see Aberson, Shoemaker, & Tomolillo, 2004; Dixon, 2006; Dixon & Rosenbaum, 2004; Forbes, 1997; Katz & Taylor, 1988; Miller & Brewer, 1984; Pettigrew, 1998; Pettigrew & Tropp, 2006; Powers & Ellison, 1995; Sigelman & Welch, 1993; Smith, 1994; Wittig & Grant-Thompson, 1998; Yancey, 1999, 2007.)

Recent Trends in Intergroup Contact. Since the 1950s, concerted attempts have been made to reduce discrimination against minority groups in virtually every American social institution. In Gordon's (1964) terms, these efforts increased structural assimilation or integration (see Chapter 2) and provided opportunities for dominant- and minority-group members to associate with one another. Compared with the days of slavery and segregation, there is considerably more contact across group lines today in schools and colleges, workplaces, neighborhoods, and social gatherings.

As we have seen, some of this increased contact has reduced prejudice. In other instances, contact situations that seem on paper to be likely to reduce prejudice have had no effect or have made matters worse. For example, schools and universities across the country have been officially integrated for decades, but these situations do not always lead to increased acceptance and the growth of friendships across group boundaries. The groups involved—whites, African Americans, Latinos, Asians, or Native Americans—sometimes minimize face-to-face interaction and contact across the social dividing lines. To illustrate, you need only visit the cafeteria of many university campuses during mealtime and observe how the seating pattern follows group lines (see Cowan, 2005; Lewis, 2012; Schofield, Hausmann, Ye, & Woods, 2010).

The contact hypothesis offers a possible explanation for this pattern of separation within integration. The student body in many schools and colleges is organized along lines that meet some, but not all, of the conditions necessary for a contact situation to lower prejudice. Even when students from the various racial and ethnic groups are roughly equal in status, they do not engage in many cooperative activities that cross group lines. Classrooms themselves are typically competitive and individualistic; students compete for grades and recognition on a one-by-one basis. Cooperation among students (either within or across groups) is not required and is not, in fact, particularly encouraged. The group separation and the lack of opportunities for cooperation often extend beyond the classroom into clubs, sports, and other activities (for an application of the contact hypothesis to high school sports teams, see Brown, Brown, Jackson, Sellers, & Manuel, 2003).

The separation might be reduced and positive contacts increased by encouraging cooperative activities among members of different groups—for example, by imitating the plumbing "emergency" fabricated during the Robber's Cave experiment. One successful attempt to increase cooperation and positive contact was made using a cooperative learning technique called the **jigsaw method** (Aronson & Gonzalez, 1988).

In this experiment, the students in a fifth-grade class were divided into groups. A certain learning task was divided into separate parts, like a jigsaw puzzle. Researchers ensured that each jigsaw group included both dominant- and minority-group children. Each student in the jigsaw group was responsible for learning one part of the lesson and then teaching his or her piece to the other students. Everyone was tested on all the pieces, not just his or her own. Each study group needed to make sure that everyone had all the information necessary to pass the test. This goal could be achieved only through the cooperation of all members of the group.

Unlike typical classroom activities, the jigsaw method satisfies all the characteristics for a positive contact experience: Students of equal status are engaged in a cooperative project in which mutual interdependence is essential for the success of all. As Aronson and Gonzalez (1988) point out, the students do not need to be idealistic, altruistic, or motivated by a commitment to equality for this method to work.

Rather, the students are motivated by pure self-interest; without the help of every member of their group, they cannot pass the test (Aronson & Gonzalez, 1988, p. 307). As we would expect under true equal status contact, the results of the jigsaw method included reductions in prejudice (Aronson & Gonzalez, 1988, p. 307; see also Aronson & Patnoe, 1997). For a website devoted to this teaching method, see www.jigsaw.org.

Limitations of the Contact Hypothesis. Evidence from a variety of sources and nations supports the contact hypothesis (Pettigrew et al., 2011). In some cases, the reduction in prejudice may be situational; that is, the changed attitudes in one situation (e.g., the workplace) may not necessarily generalize to other situations (e.g., neighborhoods). Nonetheless, equal status cooperative contact does seem to reduce prejudice and discrimination. The true challenge may be to increase the number of intergroup contacts in societies, such as the United States, that remain so segregated in so many areas of social life.

QUESTIONS FOR REFLECTION

13. What experiences have you had that are consistent with the equal status contact hypothesis? Did these situations meet all four conditions of the hypothesis? How? Did they reduce prejudice? Did the reduction seem specific to that situation, or do you think it generalized to other situations?

14. Have you had intergroup contacts that *increased* your negative feelings about other groups? What features of these situations accounted for this increase in prejudice and how do they relate to the four conditions of the contact hypothesis?

MODERN RACISM: THE NEW FACE OF PREJUDICE?

Many scholars are investigating the idea that, rather than declining, prejudice is simply changing forms. These new forms of prejudice are called symbolic, color-blind, or modern racism. Rather than the overt kinds of hostility in older forms of prejudice, modern racism is a more subtle, complex, and indirect way of thinking or expressing negative feelings about minority groups or about one's opposition to changes in dominant–minority relations (see Bobo, 1988, 2001; Bobo, Charles, Krysan, & Simmons, 2012; Bonilla-Silva, 2001, 2006; Kinder & Sears, 1981; Kluegel & Smith, 1982; McConahy, 1986; Sears, 1988; for a review, see Quillian, 2006).

According to sociologist Eduardo Bonilla-Silva (2006), a leading researcher in this area, people express prejudice in seemingly neutral or "objective" terms. For example, the "modern racist" might attribute the underrepresentation of people of color in high-status positions to cultural factors ("'they' don't emphasize education enough") rather than biological ones ("they're just not as smart as whites"). Or, they might explain continuing residential and school segregation by the "natural" choices people make, such as "they would rather be with their own kind.") The language modern racists use is telling. Because most Americans reject overt racism, people can't openly say things like "we don't want blacks in our neighborhoods." Instead, says Bonilla-Silva, they might cloak their prejudicial feelings as expressions of concern about issues such as crime, property values, and schools (c.f. Blake, 2014).

Modern racism rationalizes the status quo, thereby not just permitting inequality, but reproducing it. For example, this type of thinking encourages dominant-group members to live in segregated neighborhoods and send their children to segregated schools without guilt or hesitation (Bonilla-Silva, 2006, p. 28). It obscures the many social forces that created segregated schools, neighborhoods, and other

---

The **jigsaw method** is a learning technique that requires cooperation among students.

manifestations of racial inequality in the first place—and that maintain them today (e.g., see Satter, 2009). Finally, "color-blind" thinking prevents whites from acknowledging the privileges that systemic racism give them because of their membership in the dominant group. Therefore, it seemingly absolves them of responsibility for eliminating inequality (Chavez-Dueñas, Adames, & Organista, 2013; Wise, 2008a; Wise, 2010).

Modern racism has been defined in a variety of ways, but it tends to be consistent with some tenets of the traditional assimilation perspective discussed in Chapter 2, especially human capital theory and the Protestant ethic, the traditional American value system that stresses individual responsibility and the importance of hard work. Modern racists resent and even fear minorities (especially African Americans), but they express their prejudiced attitudes and emotions indirectly. Modern racists believe the following:

- They are not prejudiced.
- Serious racial, ethnic, or religious discrimination in American society no longer exists.
- Because inequality no longer exists, efforts to reduce inequality such as affirmative action are unjustified and unfair. (They may also believe minority groups—especially African Americans—have already gotten more than they deserve.)
- Any remaining racial or ethnic inequality is the fault of members of the minority group, who simply are not working hard enough or who suffer from other, largely self-imposed, cultural disadvantages.

The last tenet is particularly important: Cultural explanations that explain inequality as the result of the behavior or values of minority group members have largely replaced the traditional biological explanations of "racial inferiority." For example, the election of President Obama in 2008 has been taken as a sign that the United States has become a society in which race no longer mattered, despite "substantial evidence to the contrary" (Dawson & Bobo, 2009, p. 247). If the United States is now "post-racial," then racial problems are the results of the values and behaviors of minority groups, not the powerful historical processes and policy choices of the dominant group which we will examine in future chapters. The problems lie with "them," not the larger society (Bonilla-Silva, 2006; Dawson & Bobo, 2009; Schorr, 2008; see Chavez-Dueñas, Adames, & Organista, 2013).

To illustrate the difference between traditional and modern racism, consider the results of a recent (2016) public opinion survey administered to a representative sample of Americans (National Opinion Research Council, 1972–2016). Respondents were asked to choose from among four explanations of why black people, on average, have "worse jobs, income, and housing than white people." Respondents could choose as many explanations as they wanted.

One explanation, consistent with traditional or overt antiblack prejudice, attributes racial inequality to the genetic or biological inferiority of African Americans ("The differences are mainly because blacks have less inborn ability to learn"). Less than 7% of the white respondents chose this explanation. A second explanation attributes continuing racial inequality to discrimination and a third to the lack of opportunity for education. Of white respondents, 38% chose the former and 50% chose the latter.

A fourth explanation, consistent with modern racism, attributes racial inequality to a lack of effort by African Americans ("The differences are because most blacks just don't have the motivation or willpower to pull themselves up out of poverty"). Of the white respondents, 42% chose this explanation, the second most popular of the four.

Thus, the survey found support for the idea that racial inequality was the result of discrimination and lack of educational opportunities, views that are consistent with the analysis presented in this book, and relatively little support for traditional antiblack prejudice based on genetic or biological stereotypes.

However, the second most endorsed explanation was that the root of the problem of continuing racial inequality lies in the African American community, not the society as a whole. Modern racism asserts that African Americans could solve their problems themselves but are not willing to do so. Modern racism deflects attention away from centuries of oppression and continuing institutional discrimination in modern society. It stereotypes African Americans and other minority groups and encourages the expression of negative attitudes against them.

Researchers have consistently found that modern racism is correlated with opposition to policies and programs intended to reduce racial inequality (Bobo, 2001, p. 292; Bobo et al., 2012; Quillian, 2006). In the 2016 survey summarized earlier, for example, respondents who blamed continuing racial inequality on the lack of motivation or willpower of blacks—the "modern racists"—were the least likely to support affirmative action programs and government help for blacks. In fact, they were less supportive than traditional racists (those who chose the "inborn ability" explanation) (see Figure 3.10).

Figure 3.11 shows that the willingness to endorse traditional stereotypes is also associated with the explanation for racial inequality. Note the split in the graph: The traditional and modern racists (represented by the "ability" and "motivation" bars) are much more likely to endorse the perception that blacks are lazy and unintelligent than are

COMPARATIVE FOCUS

The Contact Hypothesis and European Prejudice

Much of the research on the contact hypothesis has been conducted in the United States. How well does it explain prejudice in other societies? Rather well, according to sociologist Lauren McLaren (2003). McLaren used data from representative samples of citizens drawn from 17 European societies to study anti-immigrant sentiment.

Globally, immigration is at record highs (United Nations International Migration Report Highlights, 2016, p. 1). Like the United States, European nations have experienced a sharp increase in immigration in recent decades. In fact, Europe is the most popular destination for migrants, hosting 76 million foreign-born people (United Nations International Migration Report Highlights, 2016, p. 1). In 2014, nearly 20 million migrants were refugees seeking to escape war, starvation, and oppression. More than half (53%) came from Syria (3.9 million people), Afghanistan (2.6 million people), and Somalia

(1.1 million people) (United Nations International Migration Report 2016 Highlights, p. 9). In 2016, that number increased to 22.5 million refugees, according to the United Nations Refugee Agency (2017).

Necessity and geography compel these Syrian immigrants to head across land and over the border or across the Mediterranean Sea into Turkey (see Figure 3.8), which took in 1.6 million of them—more than any country in the world (United Nations International Migration Report Highlights, 2016, p. 9). Because of an agreement between the European Union and Turkey, Turkey now has the right to refuse entry, putting pressures on nearby countries, especially Italy and Greece. (This is similar to Cuban refugees who crossed the ocean to seek asylum in the United States, which you'll read about in Chapter 8.)

Many Europeans feel concerned about the impact of these newcomers. Some Europeans wish to exclude immigrants completely,

while others want to help them find their way into their new societies. What social factors explain these varying responses?

The contact hypothesis suggests that people who have more equal status contacts with immigrants will be more tolerant and less likely to support immigrant expulsion. To examine this, McLaren (2003) measured attitudes toward legal immigrants on a 5-point scale: The higher the score on this scale, the more negative the view of immigrants. Equal status contact was measured by asking respondents if they had "no," "some," or "many" friends among immigrant groups (see Figure 3.9).

McLaren (2003) found significant differences in support for expulsion by the number of immigrant friends in 16 of the 17 nations tested (the exception was Greece). Figure 3.9 shows results for 10 of the 17 nations studied. For each nation, the average score for the respondents with "no friends" was higher than the average score for respondents with "some

FIGURE 3.8 Main Migration Routes From Syria (After September 15, 2015)

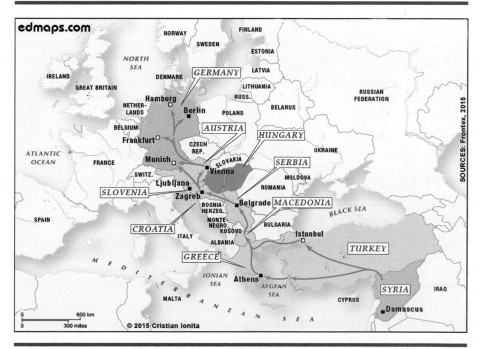

SOURCES: Frontex, 2015

(Continued)

(Continued)

FIGURE 3.9 Support for Excluding Immigrants From European Society Based on Levels of Friendship With Immigrants in Selected Nations, 2003

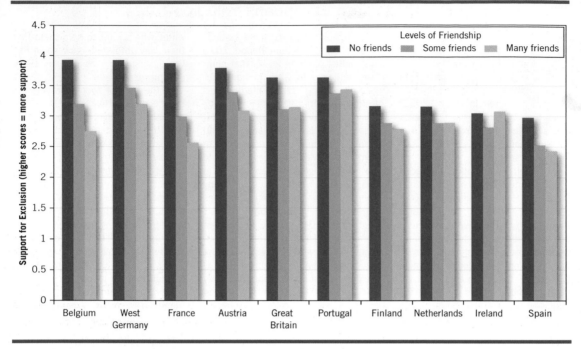

SOURCE: McLaren, 2003, p. 921.

friends," and the latter score was generally higher than the score for people with "many friends." This pattern is very (but not perfectly) consistent with the predictions of the equal status contact hypothesis.

Research done in Luxembourg produced similar findings. Luxembourg is an interesting case study because it has nearly an even mix of minority-(immigrant) and majority-group members. However, most of the foreign residents are European and fairly similar to the native-born population. It also has the highest gross domestic product, or GDP, per capita compared with the other 27 countries in the European Union (EU).

The researchers wanted to understand how contact with an out-group affects "threat perceptions" or concerns about immigrants, for example, that they will "take jobs," change the culture, "make crime worse," or drain welfare resources such as education, health care, or child care (Callens, Meuleman, & Valentová, 2015, p. 11). Participants were asked ". . . how much contact do you have with friends who are ____?" For example, Portuguese, Germans, and ex-Yougoslavs. Answer options included: "none, "a few," "some,"

or "a lot" (Callens, Meuleman, & Valentová, 2015). The results showed that "more intense contact with immigrant friends significantly reduces the threat perceptions . . . and increased support for multiculturalism" (Callens, Meuleman, & Valentová, 2015, p. 17).

This type of attitudinal change happens through a process that allows people to learn about one another and revisit their preconceived notions about the other group (Callens, Meuleman, & Valentová, 2015, p. 7). The contact hypothesis stresses optimal conditions: (1) equal status, (2) common goals, (3) intergroup cooperation and sustained interaction, and (4) support from authority figures or within the culture or legal system. Because immigrants in Luxembourg tend to be European, we can say they are of "equal status." Residents believe immigrants help run the country (Fetzer, 2011; cf CMV, 2015), which meets Criteria 2 of having a common goal. Luxembourg is financially strong compared to other EU nations and it has typically enjoyed high levels of employment. In other words, there is low competition between immigrants and native-born people. Finally, its population believes in open borders and a welcoming culture. Its three official

languages suggest that, too. Thus, we can say it meets the fourth criteria.

Our confidence in the equal status contact hypothesis is increased by its strong performance in a non-U.S. arena. We will build on this discussion in the Comparative Focus section in Chapter 8. Specifically, we'll consider threat perceptions in countries that have taken in large numbers of refugees who do not meet the "equal status" criteria: Greece, Italy, Sweden, and Germany, and also in areas where feelings of competition for national resources is high.

We should keep this research in mind as we consider prejudice, stereotyping, and discrimination in the United States. How can we develop the optimal conditions in keeping with contact hypothesis?

Questions to Consider

1. Why would interpersonal contact reduce prejudice? What processes are involved in causing people to rethink their feelings and beliefs?

2. These results show that, in some cases, greater contact leads to less support for exclusion. What would explain these "negative" results? What processes might be involved?

FIGURE 3.10 White American's Level of Support for Government Intervention Based on Explanation of Racial Inequality, 2016

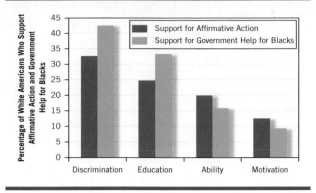

SOURCE: NORC, 1972–2016.

FIGURE 3.11 Belief in Stereotypical Views of Blacks by Explanation of Racial Inequality, 2016

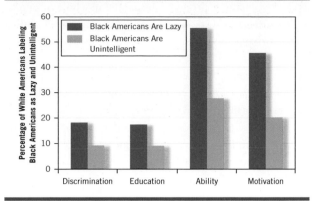

SOURCE: NORC, 1972–2016.

respondents who believe that racial inequality is due to discrimination or lack of education. In fact, the similarly stereotypical views of traditional and modern racists support the idea that the latter form of prejudice is, at least in part, a more subtle manifestation of the former.

In the view of many researchers, modern racism has taken the place of traditional or overt prejudice. If this view is correct, the "report card" on progress in the reduction of racial hostility in the United States must be mixed. On one hand, we should not understate the importance of the fading of blatant, overt prejudice. On the other hand, we cannot ignore the evidence that antiblack prejudice has changed in form rather than declined in degree. Subtle and diffuse prejudice is probably preferable to the blunt and vicious variety, but it should not be mistaken for prejudice's demise. In fact, there is considerable reason to believe that "old-fashioned," blatant racism lives on and, in some ways, is thriving. We consider this possibility in the last section of this chapter.

LIMITATIONS

As many critics have pointed out, theories of modern racism seem to confound prejudice with political conservatism. One of the classic tenets of American conservatism, for example, is that government should be minimal in size and scope. So, in Figure 3.10, when people object to "government help for blacks," are they expressing prejudice against blacks or are they objecting to "big government"? The survey item is "double-barreled" and measures *both* kinds of beliefs, and it is difficult to isolate the prejudice component from political conservatism (Quillian, 2006, p. 313).

There are (at least) two possibilities here. If the item confounds prejudice with a certain political philosophy, then researchers need to do a better job of separating the two components. On the other hand, the problem may be that—at least for some people—racism has become so thoroughly intermixed with political conservatism that it can't (or shouldn't) be separated. The Current Debate at the website for this text considers the latter possibility.

QUESTIONS FOR REFLECTION

15. What are the key differences between modern racism and traditional prejudice? Which would be the more challenging to identify and measure? Why?

Mourners in Wellington, New Zealand, hold a vigil in support of the victims of the 2016 Orlando Pulse Nightclub shooting.

HATE CRIMES

The FBI defines a **hate crime** as a "criminal offense against a person or property motivated in whole or in part by an offender's bias against a race, religion, disability, sexual orientation, ethnicity, gender or gender identity" (Farivar, 2017). They are attacks or other acts of intimidation motivated by the group membership of the victim or victims. Victims can be chosen randomly and are often strangers to their assailants. Perpetrators of hate crimes chose their victims because of their group membership (e.g., women, Jews, transpeople), not because of who they are as individuals.

Some people suggest that we don't need to record "hate crimes" separately from "crime." Brian Levin, a criminologist and director of the Center for the Study of Hate and Extremism at California State University–San Bernardino, argues that we do need a separate category because nuanced measurement is fundamental to understanding the complexities of social life. Killing someone for their wallet and killing someone because they are gay, for example, are two very different things. It's true that they both result in deaths and both deaths would be tragic. However, to improve any kind of situation, we must first understand it. For example, if we want to reduce unemployment in this country, we have to first understand some basic patterns. What are the demographics of the unemployed? Are they young or old? What's their level of education? What's their race, ethnicity, and gender?

We also want to place the demographic patterns in a social context. For example, are there jobs where they live but they don't have the education or skills to do that work? Does something else prevent them from working near where they live or getting the necessary training—such as lack of reliable transportation or child care, or chronic illness? If there aren't jobs in a particular area, what keeps unemployed people from moving? Could companies be encouraged to move to high unemployment areas?

We can probably all agree that unemployment isn't good. But, if we don't know the patterns of unemployment, our efforts to reduce it will waste a lot of time and money without the desired effect. Similarly, to prevent any kind of crime we first need to observe crime patterns. Who are crime victims and perpetrators, for example? Only with a clear measure of what is and what isn't a "hate crime" can we hope to prevent them.

Hate crime is a criminal offense against a person or property motivated in whole or in part by an offender's bias against a race, religion, disability, sexual orientation, ethnicity, gender, or gender identity.

These crimes are expressions of hatred or disdain, strong prejudice, and blatant racism, and are not committed for profit or gain. In recent years, they have included mass homicides such as those by Wade Michael Page, Dylann Roof, and Omar Mateen mentioned in the chapter opening. One highly publicized incident that occurred in 1998 illustrates this point. Matthew Shepard, a gay college student in Wyoming, was severely beaten, tied to a fence post, and left to die. He was robbed, but that was not the reason for this brutal attack.

Hate crimes include attacks on the symbols or buildings of out-groups in addition to attacks on individuals. Recent examples include arson or vandalism against black churches, Jewish synagogues, and Muslim mosques. They include cross burnings, nooses prominently tied to office doors of black university professors, and many other acts of intimidation and harassment.

Individuals carry out hate crimes, but as we saw in the chapter opening, people learn racists ideas from other people, including openly racist groups such as skinheads, the Ku Klux Klan (KKK), White Aryan Resistance (WAR), the Minutemen, the Aryan Nations, and many more. They not only exist but are thriving, thanks, in part, to the Internet, which has allowed them to spread their message easily and cheaply. Additionally, the Internet allows members to communicate with one another—even internationally—through online forums and through other electronic communication, which creates a sense of shared purpose and solidarity.

Does the recent increase in hate crimes contradict the notion that blatant prejudice is on the decline? Do they balance the shift to modern racism with an opposite shift to overt, violent racism? What causes these attacks? What are the implications?

As we will see in upcoming chapters, racial violence, hate crimes, and extremist racist groups aren't new to the United States. Violence between whites and nonwhites began in the earliest days of this society (e.g., conflicts with American Indians, the kidnapping and enslavement of Africans) and has continued, in one form or another, to the present. At the organizational level of society, we see groups like the KKK, for example, that was founded a little over 150 years ago, shortly after the Civil War. "The Klan" has since played a significant role in local and state politics at various times and places—and not just in the South. During the turbulent 1920s, the KKK reached what was probably the height of its popularity. It had a membership in the millions and was said to openly control many U.S. senators, governors, and local politicians. As sociologists trying to understand contemporary hate crimes in all their manifestations, we should consider them part of a historical trajectory. Today's groups are deeply rooted in America's past.

The Federal Bureau of Investigation (FBI) has been collecting and compiling information on hate crimes since 1996. Yet, not all localities report these incidents or classify them in the same way, and perhaps more important, not all hate crimes are reported to the police or other officials, often out of fear. Thus, the actual volume of hate crimes may be many times greater than the "official" rate compiled by the FBI. In fact, a recent report by the U.S. Bureau of Justice Statistics suggests that nearly two-thirds of hate crimes went unreported (Farivar, 2017). (For a recent analysis, see Fears, 2007.)

Keeping these limitations in mind, here is some of what the data suggest. Figure 3.12 reports the breakdown of hate crime victims in 2015 and shows that most incidents were motivated by race, ethnicity, or ancestry. In the majority (52%) of these racial cases, the victims were black Americans. White Americans were 19% of the victims and Hispanics or Latinos were 10%. Most of the religious incidents (52%) involved Jewish victims, and the majority (62%) of the attacks motivated by the sexual orientation of the victims were directed against gay men (FBI, 2017). Although the highest number of hate crimes involves race or ethnicity, when we account for their size in the population, people who are LGBT+ had a higher chance of being targeted. Of hate crimes involving LGBT+ people, the majority were against transpeople of color (Park & Mykhyalyshyn, 2016).

The Southern Poverty Law Center (SPLC) also tracks hate groups and hate crimes. In August 2017, it identified 917 active hate groups (SPLC Hate Map, 2017b) that are defined as groups that "have beliefs or practices that attack or malign an entire class of people, typically for their immutable characteristics" (Potok, 2013). These groups include the KKK, various skinhead and white-power groups, and black groups such as the Nation of Islam. The SPLC maintains a map at its website showing the locations of the known hate groups which we've reproduced in Figure 3.13. As you'll see, hate groups (and hate crimes) are not limited to a particular region; they exist throughout the nation and can be found in all states.

Figure 3.14 displays the number of hate groups documented by the Southern Poverty Law Center since the turn of the century. According to their analysis, the numbers rose dramatically after 2000 because of anger over illegal Hispanic immigration and concerns that U.S. society was quickly becoming non-Anglo. They attribute the decline after 2012 to a tendency of these groups to move to the Internet rather than conduct "on-the-ground" activities and the more recent increase to the 2016 Trump presidential campaign, which "flirted heavily with extremist ideas" (SPLC, 2017a).

What causes hate crimes? According to some analysts, there are two main types. Many hate crimes are motivated by

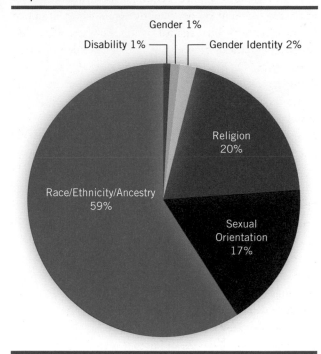

FIGURE 3.12 Breakdown of the 7,121 Single-Bias Hate Crime Incidents Reported in 2015

SOURCE: FBI (2017).

"thrill seeking" or the quest for excitement. These offenses are often committed by groups that search out random victims in gay bars, synagogues, or minority neighborhoods. The second common type of hate crime is "defensive": The perpetrators feel that their territory has been invaded or that members of the other group are threatening their resources or status. They strike to punish or expel the invaders, recover their rightful share of resources, or restore their prestige (Gerstenfeld, 2004, pp. 73–75).

One possible explanation for at least some hate crimes is that they are fueled by frustration and fear. Some white Americans believe that minority groups are threatening their position in society and making unfair progress at their expense. They feel threatened by what they perceive to be an undeserved rise in the status of minority groups and fear that they may lose their jobs, incomes, neighborhoods, and schools to what they see as "inferior" groups.

Given the nature of American history, it is logical to suppose that the white Americans who feel most threatened and angriest are those toward the bottom of the stratification system: lower-class and working-class whites. There is evidence that men from these classes commit the bulk of hate crimes and are the primary sources of membership for the extremist racist groups (Schafer & Navarro, 2004). In the eyes of the perpetrators, attacks on minorities may represent attempts to preserve status and privilege. Some of these dynamics are illustrated in the second Narrative Portrait in this chapter.

FIGURE 3.13 Location of Hate Groups in the United States, 2017

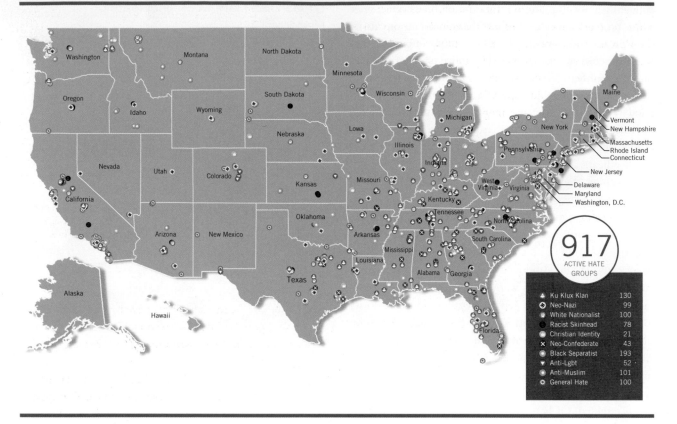

917 ACTIVE HATE GROUPS

▲	Ku Klux Klan	130
✪	Neo-Nazi	99
◉	White Nationalist	100
●	Racist Skinhead	78
◎	Christian Identity	21
✕	Neo-Confederate	43
◉	Black Separatist	193
▼	Anti-Lgbt	52
◉	Anti-Muslim	101
◎	General Hate	100

SOURCE: www.splcenter.org/hate-map.

The connection between social class and hate crimes might also reflect some broad structural changes in the economy, especially the shift from an industrial, manufacturing economy to a postindustrial, information-processing economy. This change has meant a decline in the supply of secure, well-paying, blue-collar jobs. Many manufacturing jobs have been lost to other nations with cheaper workforces; others have been lost to automation and mechanization.

The tensions resulting from the decline in desirable employment opportunities for people with lower levels of education have been exacerbated by industry downsizing,

FIGURE 3.14 Number of Hate Groups, 1999–2016

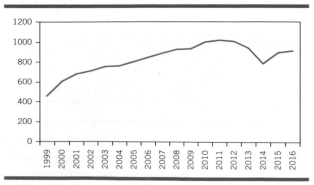

SOURCE: SPLC, 2017b, www.splcenter.org/hate-map.

increasing inequality in the class structure, and rising costs of living. These economic forces have squeezed the middle and lower ranges of the dominant group's class system, creating considerable pressure and frustration, some of which may be directed at immigrants and minority groups.

The idea that many hate crimes involve scapegoating is also supported by the spontaneous, unplanned, and highly emotional nature of these crimes. Consider how these themes of economic dislocation and scapegoating are illustrated in the 1982 murder of Vincent Chin, a frequently cited example of an American hate crime. Chin, who was Chinese American, was celebrating at a club in Detroit eight days before he was to be married. Two drunken autoworkers who blamed Japanese auto companies for their unemployment confronted him. Making no distinction between Chinese and Japanese (or American and Japanese), the autoworkers attacked and murdered Chin with a baseball bat. Apparently, any Asian would have served as a scapegoat for their resentment and anger (Levin & McDevitt, 1993, p. 58; see also U.S. Commission on Civil Rights, 1992, pp. 25–26).

Several studies support these ideas. One study found that at the state level, the rate of hate crimes increased as unemployment rose and as the percentage of the population between 15 and 19 years old increased. Also, the rate fell as average wages rose (Medoff, 1999, p. 970; see also Jacobs &

Wood, 1999). Another study, based on county-level data gathered in South Carolina, found a correlation between white-on-black hate crimes and economic competition (D'Alessio, Stolzenberg, & Eitle, 2002). Finally, Arab Americans have been victimized by a rash of violent attacks since September 11, 2001 (Ibish, 2003). These patterns are exactly what one would expect if the perpetrators of hate crimes tended to be young men motivated by a sense of threat and economic distress.

QUESTIONS FOR REFLECTION

16. Which theories of prejudice provide the most convincing explanations of hate crimes? Why?

17. How do you understand differing rates of hate crime for different groups of people (e.g., transpeople, Muslims, whites)? What are some possible explanations for the regional distribution of hate groups displayed in Figure 3.12?

18. How can an intersectional approach help us better understand hate crimes?

THE SOCIOLOGY OF PREJUDICE

We can summarize this chapter by considering the key points of the sociological approach to prejudice.

1. Prejudice has its origins in competition between groups, and it is more a result of that competition than a cause. It is created at a certain time in history to help mobilize feelings and emotional energy for competition and to rationalize the consignment of a group to minority status. It then is absorbed into the cultural heritage and is passed on to later generations as part of their taken-for-granted world, where it helps shape their perceptions and reinforce the very group inferiority that was its original cause.

2. Changes in the social environment, rising levels of education, or changing levels of intergroup contact will have relatively little impact on some types of prejudice. Prejudice that is caused by scapegoating or authoritarian personality structures, for example, is motivated by processes internal to the individual and may not respond to changes in the environment. It may be difficult to reduce these types of prejudice and impossible to eliminate them altogether. A more realistic goal might be to discourage their open expression. The greater the extent to which culture, authority figures, and social situations discourage

Anti-Semitic vandals knocked down and defaced headstones at a Jewish cemetery in Rochester, New York, in March of 2017. Governor Andrew Cuomo announced an investigation into the rise in crimes and threats against Jewish organizations in the state.

prejudice, the more likely that even people with strong personality needs for prejudice can be turned into prejudiced nondiscriminators, or "timid bigots" (see Table 3.1).

3. Culture-based or "traditional" prejudice can be just as extreme as personality-based prejudice. This type of prejudice differs not in intensity but in the degree to which it is resistant to change. A person who learns prejudice because he or she was socialized in racist environments should be more open to change than authoritarian personalities and more responsive to education and contact with members of other groups. To create more "all-weather liberals," situations that encourage or reward prejudice and discrimination must be minimized, and public opinion, the views of community and societal leaders, and the legal code must all promote tolerance. The reduction in overt prejudice over the past five or six decades, documented in Figure 3.5, is probably mainly due to a decline in traditional prejudice.

4. Intergroup conflict produces vicious, even lethal, prejudice and discrimination, but the problems here are inequality and access to resources and opportunity, not prejudice. Group conflicts and the prejudices they stimulate will continue as long as society is stratified along the lines of race, ethnicity, religion, and gender. Efforts to decrease hostile attitudes without also reducing inequality and exploitative relationships treat the symptoms rather than the disease.

5. Reducing prejudice will not necessarily change the situation of minority groups. The fundamental problems of minority-group status are inequality and systems of institutional discrimination and privilege that sustain the advantages of dominant groups.

The Dynamics of Racial Hatred

An expression of racial hatred and intimidation.

Brian Patterson was the product of a broken home and a racist father. He fell in with some racist groups and was involved in a variety of hate crimes. At the lowest point in his life, he was assisted by a black man, a complete stranger to him, and managed to turn his life around.

THE MAKING (AND UNMAKING) OF A SKINHEAD

Interview by Robert Steinback

Where were you reared and where did this story start?

I was born in. . . Mississippi. . . . My dad was racist, very racist. All of his friends and everybody that I was around was racist. . . . He was in the Klan. So was my grandfather and pretty much everybody I grew up knowing. [My father] . . . was violent. He liked to fight.

So violence was a part of life?

Yeah, it was routine. We were raised to be tough.. . . Around age 9, me and my brother and my mother moved to Pensacola, Florida. . . . I wound up going back to Tupelo at 11. I went and lived with my father until I was 15. That's where [the hate] really took root. During that time I really got indoctrinated. All of the kids in the area were indoctrinated into that way of thinking. We went to Klan rallies, and we loved it. We thought it was great. . . .

These Klan rallies were just like camp-fire parties to you?

Exactly. . . . I think they took the idea from Hitler Youth-type shit, you know. Get them while they're young. . . . [Then], at 15, . . . I wound up back in Florida. . . . So I'm basically on the streets from 15 to 18. You got the punk rock scene and the skinhead scene and that's where I wound up. . . . We had National White Resistance and WAR, White Aryan Resistance. The Klan was real big there, too. . . . I had fallen in with a violent group of skinheads. There were things that I did that I'm not proud of. . . . There was a lot of fighting, a lot of beatings.

Beatings of strangers?

Mostly gang confrontations. . . . You know, trying to keep blacks out of the neighborhoods that were predominantly white. . . .

But then you found yourself alone. How did that happen?

I . . . basically wound up by myself and stuck on Pensacola Beach. They left me there. . . . We got into it, and they left me. . . . I'm footin' it. No money, no food. . . . I'm just kind of drifting around. . . getting a little help. . . at the shelter. I was afraid to stay in the city. . . . I went to the country. . . . I got no food; I got no money; it's cold. I got no winter clothes, no blanket. So I'm sleeping in this patch of woods by this lodge. . . .

How close to the edge were you that night?

I was thinking heavy thoughts by that time, brother. I was thinking, "I'm going to do whatever it takes from this point on to feed myself. . . . The next motherfucker I come across is going to get it.". . . That was like the cross-roads right there.

What happened when morning arrived?

I wake up, and I smell food. And there's a blanket on me. . . . I look up, and there's this black guy. . . . He's got a fire built. This dude has done throwed a blanket on me. He sees my bald head. He sees my red suspenders and my red shoelaces in my boots and my Nazi patch. This dude sees this. He still goes back to his house and gets a blanket and some food and brings it back to me. . . . But I wake up and he's sitting there cooking me something to eat. . . . It was his kindness [that won me over]. It was the way this man helped me despite what I was. It probably saved my life. Had he not been there, there's no telling what I would have done. . . .

SOURCE: Southern Poverty Law Center (2010).

Questions to Consider

1. What ideas or theories about prejudice presented in this chapter does this passage illustrate?
2. How does prejudice begin? How is it sustained? How can it be changed?

Prejudice is a problem, but it is not the only problem. Reducing prejudice will not, by itself, eliminate minority-group poverty or unemployment, or end institutional discrimination in schools or in the criminal justice system.

6. Individual prejudice and discrimination are not the same as racism and institutional discrimination (see Chapter 1), and any one of these variables can change independently of the others. Thus, we should not confuse the recent reductions in overt, traditional prejudice with the resolution of American minority-group problems. Prejudice is only part of the problem and, in many ways, not the most important part.

The key points in this chapter are reflected in some key trends of the past several decades: Ethnic and racial inequalities persist (and may be increasing in some ways) despite the declines in overt prejudice. The verbal rejection of extreme or overt prejudice has been replaced by the subtleties of modern racism, combined with an unwillingness to examine the social, political, and economic forces that sustain minority-group inequality and institutional discrimination. Unless there are significant changes in the structure of the economy and the distribution of opportunities, we may have reached the limits of tolerance in America.

SUMMARY

This summary is organized around the Learning Objectives stated at the beginning of this chapter.

 3.1 Understand the sociological concepts of prejudice, discrimination, and racism.

Prejudice is the tendency to think and feel negatively about the members of other groups. Discrimination refers to negative acts motivated by a person's group membership. Prejudice and discrimination commonly occur together, but they are distinct concepts and do not necessarily cause each other.

 3.2 Understand the different forms and dimensions of prejudice, and the theories and research related to each.

Prejudice takes multiple forms and has a variety of causes, and no one theory accounts for all forms of prejudice. Some affective forms of prejudice are reactions to frustrations (scapegoating), and others are fundamental parts of a person's makeup (authoritarian personality). Stereotypes (the cognitive dimension) are related to the status of the minority group in the larger society. American stereotypes are plentiful and long lasting, although perhaps somewhat muted in their expression in recent decades. Some stereotypes are alleged to apply to entire groups, but others have strong gender and class dimensions.

 3.3 Explain how prejudice persists through time, including the role of group competition.

Prejudice can almost always be traced to a particular moment in history that featured a competition between groups over scarce resources. Prejudice can mobilize energy for the struggle and justify the treatment of the group that loses the competition. Once created, prejudice becomes a part of the culture of the dominant group, reinforced by the discriminatory treatment of the minority group and passed on to succeeding generations as part of their "taken-for-granted" world. Also, prejudice can be highly situational.

 3.4 Assess changing patterns of "traditional" prejudice, and explain "modern" racism as it relates to "traditional" prejudice.

Traditional, overt, blatant prejudice is less commonly expressed in modern U.S. society today, and its decline can be measured and documented with public opinion surveys. Some of the possible reasons for this decline include rising levels of education and intergroup contact.

However, many analysts believe that prejudice is simply changing form rather than declining. Modern racism is more subtle and indirect in its expression, and more likely to attribute continuing minority-group inequality to cultural rather than biological or genetic factors. However, so-called modern racists tend to be opposed to racial and ethnic change and fearful of and threatened by minority groups.

 3.5 Understand modern hate crimes and be able to explain some possible reasons for their persistence.

Hate crimes and hate groups have always been a part of U.S. society and continue into the present. Hate crimes can be motivated by the search for "excitement" or by the felt need to defend a territory or status. They are commonly associated with lower-status, less-educated men who have limited prospects for success in the conventional economy.

KEY TERMS

authoritarian
   personality 81
equal status contact
   hypothesis 99

hate crime 106
jigsaw method 101
modern racism 96
scapegoat hypothesis 81

selective
   perception 83
social distance 91
socialization 92

split labor
   market theory 89
vicious cycle 90

REVIEW QUESTIONS

1. Distinguish between prejudice and discrimination, and explain clear examples of both. Explain the different dimensions of prejudice and differentiate between them. What are stereotypes? What forms do stereotypes take? How are stereotypes formed and maintained?

2. Explain the various causes of prejudice, including the theoretical perspectives presented in this chapter. Explain and evaluate the research evidence that has been presented. Which theories seem most credible in terms of evidence? Why? Try to think of an incident—from your own experience, the news, or popular culture—that illustrates each theory.

3. How does prejudice persist through time? What are children taught about other groups? What were you taught by your parents? How did this compare with what you learned from friends? How would your socialization experience have changed if you had been raised in another group? Have your views been changed by education or intergroup contact? How?

4. Is prejudice really decreasing, or are the negative emotions and attitudes changing into modern racism? What evidence is most persuasive in leading you to your conclusion? Why?

5. Interpret the information presented in Figure 3.10. Does this graph support the notion that modern racism is an important cause of resistance to racial change? How?

6. What forms of prejudice are involved in hate crimes? What are the roles of group competition and scapegoating? Develop an explanation for hate crimes based on these connections.

STUDENT STUDY SITE

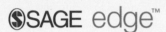

Sharpen your skills with SAGE edge at edge.sagepub.com/healey8e

SAGE edge for students provides a personalized approach to help you accomplish your coursework goals in an easy-to-use learning environment.

The following resources are available at SAGE edge:

Current Debates: Modern Racism on Television?

How common are expressions of modern racism on television? How often are minority groups blamed for their own victimization? How do the media reflect and reinforce modern racism in the larger society?

On our website you will find an overview of the topic, the clashing points of view, and some questions to consider as you analyze the material.

Public Sociology Assignments

Public Sociology Assignments provide opportunities for students to address directly and personally some of the issues raised in this text.

The first two public sociology assignments on our website will lead students to confront diversity in their community. In the first assignment, you will investigate your hometown to see if you can document increases in racial and ethnic diversity consistent with Figure 1.1. In the second assignment, you will study graffiti: Does it express stereotypes and prejudice? What does it reflect about local group hierarchies?

Contributed by Linda M. Waldron

Internet Research Project

For the Internet Research Project for this chapter, you will investigate the idea that prejudice is a largely unconscious set of feelings that, nonetheless, greatly affect thoughts and actions. You will test your own "implicit" prejudice and review some of the information that has been amassed on the subject. Your investigation will be guided by a series of questions, and your instructor may ask you to discuss the issues in small groups.

For Further Reading

Please see our website for an annotated list of important works related to this chapter.

Chapter 4   The Development of Dominant–Minority Group Relations in Preindustrial America: The Origins of Slavery

Chapter 5   Industrialization and Dominant–Minority Relations: From Slavery to Segregation and the Coming of Postindustrial Society

The chapters in Part 2 explore several questions: Why do some groups become minorities? How and why do dominant–minority relations change over time? These are more than casual or merely academic questions. Understanding the dynamics that created and sustained prejudice, racism, discrimination, and inequality in the past will build understanding about group relations in the present and future. This knowledge is crucial if we want to deal effectively with these problems. By understanding these dynamics, you can help be a part of social change. Both chapters in Part 2 feature African Americans as the primary case study. Chapter 4 focuses on the preindustrial United States and the creation of slavery but also considers the fate of Native Americans and Mexican Americans during the same time. Chapter 5 analyzes how the Industrial Revolution changed group relations. Specifically, it focuses on the shift from slavery to segregation for African Americans and their migration out of the South. Throughout the 20th century, industrial technology continued to evolve and shape group relationships in the United States. We begin to explore the consequences of these changes in Chapter 5. Throughout the next two chapters, you will use the concepts that you learned in Chapters 1 through 3. And we'll introduce you to some important new concepts and theories. By the end of Part 2, you will be familiar with virtually the entire conceptual framework that will guide us through the remainder of this book.

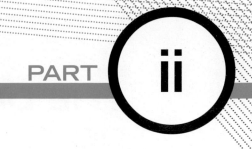

PART ii

THE EVOLUTION OF DOMINANT–MINORITY RELATIONS IN THE UNITED STATES

A Note on the Morality and the History of Minority Relations in America: Guilt, Blame, Understanding, and Communication

Very often, when people confront the kind of material presented in the next few chapters, they react on a personal level. Some might feel a sense of guilt for the troubling aspects of America's history of group relations. Others might respond with anger about the injustice and unfairness that remains in the United States. Still others might respond with denial or indifference or they might argue that the events discussed in Chapters 4 and 5 have no importance today.

These reactions—guilt, anger, denial, and indifference—are common. We ask you to think about them as you read these chapters. First, the awful things we will discuss did happen, and they were done largely by members of a particular racial and ethnic group: white Europeans and their descendants. No amount of denial or distancing can make these facts go away. African Americans, Native Americans, Mexican Americans, and other minority groups were victims, and they paid a terrible price for the early growth and success of white American society.

Yet, European Americans do not have a monopoly on greed, bigotry, or viciousness. Some minority-group members facilitated this domination and exploitation. The slave trade relied on black African slavers and their agents. Some Native Americans bought and sold slaves (both captured native people from other tribes and black Africans) when the slave market made it more profitable than keeping them as indentured servants. They helped Europeans in other ways, aiding the establishment of white society. And some Mexicans cheated other Mexicans out of their land. Many of the ideas and values on which the United

States was founded (justice, equality, liberty) have origins in European intellectual traditions. Minority group protest has often involved little more than insisting that the nation live up to these ideals.

At times throughout our history, members of the dominant group fought to end the oppression, bigotry, and racial stratification that you'll read about in this book. For example, some white Southerners opposed slavery and fought for the abolition of "our peculiar institution" (Stephens, 1861). Likewise, segments of the white community were appalled at the treatment of Native Americans and Mexicans in our nation's past and attempted to stop it. Some people devoted (and sometimes gave up) their lives for these causes.

Our point is to urge you to avoid a "good-guy/bad-guy" approach to this subject matter. Guilt, anger, denial, and indifference do little to advance understanding, inhibit communication between members of different groups, and can prevent us from making the necessary social change that will allow us to fully live up to our nation's ideals. We believe that an understanding of America's racial past is vitally important for understanding the present. The historical background and concepts we present in these chapters will give you a useful perspective on the intergroup complexities in our country today.

We will present the facts as neutrally as possible. As student-scholars, your goals should be to learn the realities of American society and American minority groups, understand relevant sociological concepts and principles, and apply them to your own life and the society around you—not to indulge in elaborate moral denunciations of American society, develop apologies for the past, or deny the realities of what happened.

THE DEVELOPMENT OF DOMINANT–MINORITY GROUP RELATIONS IN PREINDUSTRIAL AMERICA

The Origins of Slavery

4

Wikimedia Creative Commons

timeline

1641
Massachusetts becomes the first colony to legalize slavery.

1663
In Gloucester County, Virginia, the first documented slave rebellion in the colonies takes place.

1694
Rice cultivation is introduced into Carolina. Slave importation increases dramatically.

1788
The U.S. Constitution is officially adopted and includes the "three-fifths" clause by which each slave is considered three-fifths of a person for the purposes of congressional representation and tax apportionment.

1615   1635   1655   1675   1695   1715   1735

1619
Approximately 20 Africans arrive in Virginia, the first Africans in the British North American colonies.

1636
Colonial North America's slave trade begins when the first American slave carrier, *Desire,* is built and launched in Massachusetts.

LOC

1676
In Virginia, black slaves and black and white indentured servants band together to participate in Bacon's Rebellion.

1705
The Virginia Slave Code defines all slaves as real estate, acquits masters who kill slaves during punishment, forbids slaves and "free colored people" from physically assaulting whites, and denies slaves the right to bear arms or move abroad without written permission.

Wikipedia

The year was 1781, and the Zong, with its cargo of 442 African slaves, had been sailing for nearly three months. The overcrowded ship had just 17 crewmembers and that made it difficult to maintain proper sanitation and prevent the spread of disease. By the time the ship approached its destination in the New World, 50 slaves and seven crew had died, others were sick, and water was running short. The captain, believing that the sickest slaves would probably die, ordered 54 of them to be chained together and thrown overboard. Over the next two days, the crew killed another 78 slaves by throwing them into the sea. Several jumped to their deaths.

As was the practice of the day, slaves were insured as property. The captain knew that the

LEARNING OBJECTIVES

By the end of this chapter, you will be able to do the following:

4.1 Explain the two themes stated at the beginning of the chapter.

4.2 Explain the political, economic, and social forces that led to the creation of slavery in British America.

4.3 Explain the importance of the contact situation and the relevance of the Noel and Blauner hypotheses for the development of slavery in colonial America.

4.4 Apply the concepts of paternalism, power, inequality, discrimination, prejudice and racism, and assimilation to the American system of slavery.

4.5 Explain the dynamics of gender relations under American slavery.

4.6 Apply the Noel and Blauner hypotheses and other concepts to the creation of minority-group status for Native Americans and Mexican Americans.

4.7 Compare and contrast the three contact situations analyzed in this chapter. How do they differ? What are the implications of these different contact situations for relations in the present?

Cincinnati Art Museum

National Portrait Gallery

1804
The Underground Railroad is officially established in Pennsylvania.

1850
A second fugitive slave law strengthens the rights of slave owners and threatens the rights of free blacks.

1859
A group of whites and blacks, led by John Brown, conducts an unsuccessful raid on Harper's Ferry, Virginia, in an attempt to undermine slavery in the South.

1755   1775   1795   1815   1835   1855   1875   1895

1793
The first fugitive slave law is passed, allowing slave owners to cross state lines in the pursuit of fugitives and making it a penal offense to assist runaway slaves.

1800
Congress prohibits U.S. citizens from exporting slaves.

1808
Importing slaves is prohibited.

1831
Nat Turner, an enslaved Baptist preacher, leads a violent rebellion in Southampton, Virginia. At least 57 whites are killed.

HORRID MASSACRE IN VIRGINIA
LOC

1857
The Dred Scott decision mandates that African Americans cannot be citizens.

Wikipedia

1860
The slave population is now nearly four million, making the ratio of free to enslaved Americans approximately 7:1.

1861
Harriet Jacobs's *Incidents in the Life of a Slave Girl* is the first published autobiography of an African American woman.

Wikipedia

ship's insurance policy would cover losses due to drowning but not "natural causes."[1]

—Walvin, [data]

The slave trade that brought Africans to the New World was a business, subject to the calculation of profit and loss and covered by the same insurance companies that backed farmers, bankers, and merchants. To the captain and owners of the *Zong*, and to others involved in the slave trade, the people who were thrown overboard were just cargo, entries in a ledger book. Those books often recorded the enslaved person's height, gender, African origin, ship name, voyage ID, and embarkation and disembarkation points. The ledgers also recorded names and ages: Magee (aged 6), Amana (aged 7), Surboo (aged 12), Sarlar (aged 11), Hoodan (aged 8), Warday (aged 11), Okawho (aged 12), and Kesongo (aged 6). These children were just some of 15 million people who were part of the largest forced migration in history (Emory University, 2013).

What led to this cold, businesslike approach to trafficking in human beings? Was the same calculating eye for profit and efficiency behind the decision to use Africa as a source for slaves? How did the slave trade get linked to the British colonies that, eventually, became the United States? How could a nation that, from its earliest days, valued liberty and freedom be founded on slavery? Why does the institution of slavery matter today? •

From the first settlements in the 1600s until the 19th century, most people living in what was to become the United States relied directly on farming for food, shelter, and other necessities of life. In an agricultural society, land and labor are central concerns, and the struggle to control these resources led directly to the creation of minority group status for three groups: African Americans, Native Americans, and Mexican Americans. Why did the colonists create slavery? Why were Africans enslaved more than Native Americans or others? Why did Native Americans lose their land and most of their population by the 1890s? How did the Mexican population in the Southwest become "Mexican Americans"? How did the experience of belonging to a subordinated minority group vary by gender?

---

[1]This account is based on *The Zong: A Massacre, the Law and the End of Slavery* by James Walvin. Walvin notes that the number of slaves on board and killed was debated when the case came to court. Walvin put the count at 442 slaves on board and 132 dead—the number the court settled on. Other scholars put the counts higher or lower, but generally in that range.

In this chapter, we'll use the concepts introduced in Part 1 to answer these questions. We'll introduce some new ideas and theories, and by the end of the chapter, we will have developed a theoretical model to understand the process leading to the creation of a minority group. We will use the establishment of black slavery in colonial America, arguably the single most significant event in the early years of this nation, to illustrate this process. We will also consider the subordination of Native Americans and Mexican Americans—two more historical events of great significance—as additional case studies. We will follow the experiences of African Americans through the days of segregation (Chapter 5) and into the contemporary era (Chapter 6). The story of the development of minority group status for Native Americans and Mexican Americans will be picked up again in Chapters 7 and 8, respectively.

Two broad themes underlie this chapter and, indeed, the remainder of the text:

1. The nature of dominant–minority group relations at any point in time is largely a function of the characteristics of the society as a whole. The situation of a minority group reflects the realities of everyday social life and particularly the subsistence technology (the means by which the society satisfies basic needs, such as food and shelter). As explained by Gerhard Lenski (see Chapter 1), the subsistence technology of a society acts as a foundation, shaping and affecting every other aspect of the social structure, including minority group relations.

2. The contact situation—the conditions under which groups first come together—is the single most significant factor in the creation of minority-group status. The nature of the contact situation has long-lasting consequences for the minority group and the extent of racial or ethnic stratification, the levels of

Slaves were kidnapped in Africa and transported to provide labor in the New World. The "Middle Passage" across the Atlantic could take months.

FIGURE 4.1 Slave Trade Routes, 1518–1850

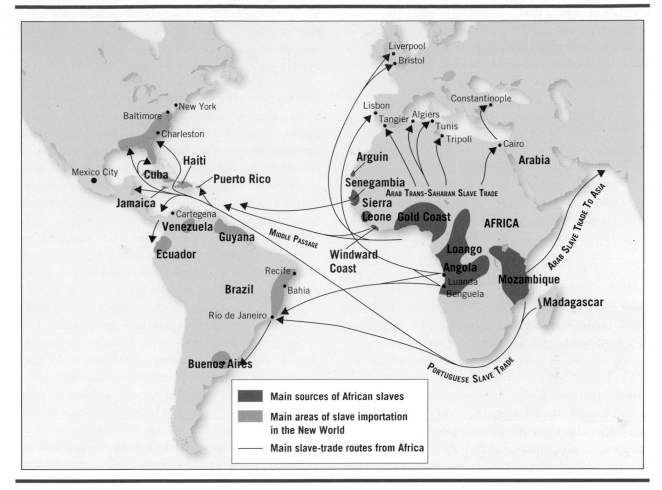

Main sources of African slaves

Main areas of slave importation in the New World

Main slave-trade routes from Africa

SOURCE: *Macmillan Encyclopedia of World Slavery*, edited by Paul Finkelman and Joseph C. Miller. Copyright © 1998 by Simon and Schuster Macmillan. Macmillan Reference USA.

racism and prejudice, the possibilities for assimilation and pluralism, and virtually every other aspect of the dominant–minority relationship.

THE ORIGINS OF SLAVERY IN AMERICA

By the early 1600s, the Spanish had conquered much of Central and South America, and the influx of gold, silver, and other riches from the New World had made Spain a powerful nation. Following Spain's lead, England proceeded to establish its presence in the Western Hemisphere, but its efforts at colonization were more modest than those of Spain. By the early 1600s, the English had established only two small colonies: Plymouth, settled by pious Protestant families, and Jamestown, populated primarily by men seeking their fortunes.

By 1619, the British colony at Jamestown, Virginia, had survived for more than a decade. The residents of the settlement had fought with the local natives and struggled continuously to eke out a living from the land. Starvation, disease, and death were frequent visitors, and the future of the enterprise continued to be in doubt.

In August of that year, a Dutch ship arrived. The ship needed provisions and the captain offered to trade his only cargo: about 20 black Africans (PBS, 1998a). Many of the details of this transaction have been lost, and we probably will never know exactly how these people came to be chained in the hold of a ship (National Park Service, 2014). Regardless, this brief episode was a landmark event in the formation of what would become the United States. In combination with the strained relations between the English settlers and Native Americans, the presence of these first few Africans raised an issue that has never been fully resolved: How should different groups in this society relate to each other?

The colonists at Jamestown had no ready answer. In 1619, England and its colonies did not practice slavery, so these first Africans were probably incorporated into colonial society as **indentured servants**, contract laborers who

---

Indentured servants are contract laborers who are obligated to serve another person for a specified length of time, usually without pay but in exchange for free passage to a new country.

are obligated to serve a master for a specific number of years. At the end of the indenture, or contract, the servant became a free citizen (PBS, 1998e). The colonies depended heavily on indentured servants from the British Isles for labor, and this status apparently provided a convenient way of defining the newcomers from Africa, who, after all, had been treated as commodities and exchanged for food and water (Wolfe & McCartney, 2015) (see Figure 4.1).

The position of African indentured servants in the colonies remained ambiguous for several decades. American slavery evolved gradually and in small steps; in fact, there was little demand for African labor during the years following 1619. By 1625, there were still only 23 black people in Virginia, and that number had increased to perhaps 300 by midcentury (Franklin & Moss, 1994, p. 57). In the decades before the dawn of slavery, we know that some African indentured servants did become free citizens. Some became successful farmers and landowners and, like their white neighbors, purchased African and white indentured servants themselves (Smedley, 2007, p. 104). Between 1630 and 1680, a steady influx of about 50,000 indentured servants from the British Isles arrived to the Virginia colonies (Wolfe & McCartney, 2015). As their arrival began to slow, needs for labor increased leading to changes in both laws and customs that made it legal for African Americans (and their offspring) to be treated as property, as slaves (Morgan, 1975, p. 154). The first colony to recognize slavery was Massachusetts in 1641. In 1705, the Virginia General Assembly declared:

> *All servants imported and brought into the Country . . . who were not Christians in their native Country . . . shall be accounted and be slaves. All Negro, mulatto and Indian slaves within this dominion . . . shall be held to be real estate. If any slave resists his master . . . correcting such slave, and shall happen to be killed in such correction . . . the master shall be free of all punishment . . . as if such accident never happened.* ("*From Indentured Servitude to Racial Slavery,*" 1998)

In the century that followed, hundreds of additional laws were passed to clarify and formalize the status of Africans in colonial America (see Wolfe & McCartney, 2015). By the 1750s, slavery was clearly defined in law and in custom, and the idea that a person could own another person—not just the labor or the energy or the work of a person, but the actual person—had been thoroughly institutionalized.

What caused slavery? The gradual evolution of and low demand for indentured servants from Africa suggest that slavery was not somehow inevitable or preordained. Why did the colonists deliberately create this repressive system? Why did they reach out all the way to Africa for their slaves? If they wanted to create a slave system, why didn't they enslave the Native Americans nearby or the white indentured servants already present in the colonies?

THE LABOR SUPPLY PROBLEM

American colonists of the 1600s saw slavery as a solution to several problems they faced. The business of the colonies was agriculture, and farm work at this time was labor-intensive, performed almost entirely by hand. The Industrial Revolution (see Chapter 2) would not occur for another two centuries, and there were few machines or labor-saving devices available to ease the burden of everyday work such as harvesting crops.

As colonial society grew and developed, a specific form of agricultural production began to emerge. The **plantation system** was based on cultivating and exporting crops such as sugar, tobacco, and rice grown on large tracts of land using a large, cheap labor force. Profit margins tended to be small, so planters—those who owned many slaves as opposed to farmers who owned none or few (Kolchin, 1993, p. xiii)—sought to stabilize their incomes by keeping the costs of production as low as possible. Profits in the labor-intensive plantation system could be maximized if landowners could maintain a large, disciplined, and cheap workforce (Curtin, 1990; Morgan, 1975).

At about the same time as the plantation system began to emerge, the supply of white indentured servants from the British Isles began to dwindle. Furthermore, every few years, the white indentured servants who had come to the colonies had to be released from their indenture. Land was available, and these newly freed citizens tended to strike out on their own. Thus, landowners who relied on white indentured servants had to deal with high turnover rates in their workforces and faced a continually uncertain supply of labor.

Attempts to solve the labor supply problem by using Native Americans failed. The colonies sometimes exploited the closest tribes for their labor power. However, by the time the plantation system had evolved the local tribes had dwindled in numbers as a result of warfare and, especially, disease. Other Indian nations across the continent retained enough power to resist enslavement, and it was relatively easy for Native Americans to escape back to their kinfolk.

This left black Africans as a potential source of labor power. The slave trade from Africa to the Spanish and

The **plantation system** is a form of labor-intensive agriculture that requires large tracts of land and a large, highly controlled labor force. This was the dominant form of agricultural production in the American South before the Civil War.

Portuguese colonies of South America had been established in the 1500s and could be expanded to fill the needs of the British colonies as well. The colonists came to see slaves captured in Africa as the most logical, cost-effective way to solve their vexing shortage of labor. The colonists created slavery to cultivate their lands and generate profits, status, and success. Thus, the paradox at the core of U.S. society had been established: The construction of a society devoted to freedom and individual liberty in the New World "was made possible only by the revival of an institution of naked tyranny foresworn for centuries in the Old" (Lacy, 1972, p. 22).

THE CONTACT SITUATION

The conditions under which groups first come into contact determine the immediate fate of the minority group and shape intergroup relations for years to come. In Chapter 3, we discussed the role of group competition in creating prejudice. Here, we develop these ideas by introducing two theories that will serve as analytical guides toward understanding the contact situation.

The Noel Hypothesis. Sociologist Donald Noel (1968) identified three features of the contact situation that in combination lead to some form of inequality between groups. The Noel hypothesis states, "*If two or more groups come together in a contact situation characterized by ethnocentrism, competition, and a differential in power, then some form of racial or ethnic stratification will result*" (p. 163). Some dominant–minority group structure will be created if the contact situation has all three of those characteristics.

Noel's first characteristic, **ethnocentrism**, is the tendency to judge other groups, societies, or lifestyles by the standards of one's own culture. Ethnocentrism may be a universal component of human society. Some degree of ethnocentrism helps people identify with a group in relation to another group thereby creating and maintaining social solidarity and cohesion. Without some minimal level of pride in and loyalty to one's own society and cultural traditions, there would be no particular reason for people to observe the informal norms and laws, honor the sacred symbols, or cooperate with others to do the daily work of society (see Sumner, 1906).

Yet, ethnocentrism can have negative consequences. At its worst, it can lead to the view that other cultures and peoples are not just different, but inferior. At the very least, ethnocentrism creates a social boundary line that group members recognize and observe. When ethnocentrism exists to any degree, people will tend to sort themselves along group lines and identify characteristics that differentiate "us" from "them."

Noel's second factor, **competition**, is a struggle over a scarce commodity. As we saw in Chapter 3, competition between groups often leads to harsh negative feelings (prejudice) and hostile actions (discrimination). In competitive contact situations, the victorious group becomes the dominant group and the losers become the minority group. The competition may center on land, labor, jobs, housing, educational opportunities, political office, or anything else that both groups desire or that one group has and the other group wants.

Competition provides the eventual dominant group with the motivation to establish superiority. The dominant group serves its own interests by ending the competition and exploiting, controlling, eliminating, or otherwise dominating the minority group.

The third feature of the contact situation is a **differential in power** between the groups. Power, as you recall from Chapter 1, is the ability of a group to achieve its goals despite opposition from other groups. The amount of power a group commands is a function of three factors:

- First, the size of the group can make a difference. All other things being equal, larger groups tend to be more powerful.
- Second, the degree of organization, discipline, and quality of group leadership can make a difference in a group's ability to pursue its goals.
- Third, resources matter. Anything that can help the group achieve its goals allows the group to exercise its power. Resources can include anything from land to information to money. The greater the number and variety of resources at a group's disposal, the greater that group's potential ability to dominate other groups.

Thus, a larger, better-organized group with more resources will generally be able to impose its will on smaller, less well-organized groups with fewer resources. The Noel hypothesis is diagrammed in Figure 4.2.

In Figure 4.2, note the functions of each of the three factors in shaping the contact situation and producing racial or ethnic inequality. If ethnocentrism is present, the

---

Ethnocentrism is the tendency to judge other groups by the standards of one's own group, culture, or society.

Competition is a struggle between two or more parties for control of some scarce resource.

A differential in power is any difference between groups in their ability to achieve their goals.

FIGURE 4.2 The Noel Hypothesis: A Model of the Establishment of Minority Group Status

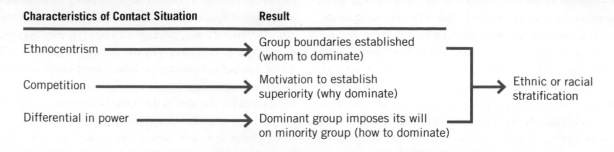

Characteristics of Contact Situation	Result	
Ethnocentrism	Group boundaries established (whom to dominate)	
Competition	Motivation to establish superiority (why dominate)	Ethnic or racial stratification
Differential in power	Dominant group imposes its will on minority group (how to dominate)	

groups will recognize their differences and maintain their boundaries. If competition is also present, the group that eventually dominates will attempt to maximize its share of scarce commodities by controlling or subordinating the group that will eventually become the "minority" group. The differential in power allows the dominant group to succeed in establishing a superior position. Ethnocentrism tells the dominant group *whom* to dominate, competition tells the dominant group *why* it should establish a structure of dominance, and power is *how* the dominant group imposes its will on the minority group.

The Noel hypothesis can be applied to the creation of minority groups in a variety of situations. We will also use the model to analyze changes in dominant–minority structures over time.

The Blauner Hypothesis. Sociologist Robert Blauner also analyzes the contact situation in his book *Racial Oppression in America* (1972). Blauner identifies two different initial relationships—colonization and immigration. His analysis is complex and nuanced but, for our purposes, we can summarize his thinking in terms of what we will call the **Blauner hypothesis**, which states, *minority groups created by colonization will experience more intense prejudice, racism, and discrimination than those created by immigration. Furthermore, the disadvantaged status of colonized groups will persist longer and be more difficult to overcome than the disadvantaged status faced by groups created by immigration* (Blauner, 1972, pp. 52–75).

Colonized minority groups, such as African Americans, are forced into minority status by the dominant group's greater military and political power. At the time of contact, the dominant group attacks the colonized group's culture and subjects them to massive inequalities. The dominant group assigns minority group members to positions, such as slaves, from which any form of assimilation is extremely difficult and perhaps even forbidden by the dominant group. Frequently, members of the minority group are identified by highly visible physical characteristics that help maintain and reinforce the oppressive system. Thus, minority groups created by colonization experience

harsher and more persistent rejection and oppression than groups created by immigration.

Immigrant minority groups are, at least to some degree, voluntary participants in the host society. That is, although the decision to immigrate may be motivated by extreme pressures, such as famine or political persecution, immigrant groups have at least some control over their destinations and their positions in the host society. As a result, they do not occupy positions that are as markedly inferior as those of colonized groups. They retain enough internal organization and resources to pursue their own self-interests, and they commonly experience more rapid acceptance and easier movement to equality. The boundaries between groups are not so rigidly maintained, especially when the groups are racially similar. In discussing European immigrant groups, for example, Blauner (1972) states that entering American society

> involved a degree of choice and self-direction that was for the most part denied to people of color. Voluntary immigration made it more likely that . . . European . . . ethnic groups would identify with America and see the host culture as a positive opportunity. (p. 56)

Acculturation and, particularly, integration were significantly more possible for European immigrant groups than for the groups formed under conquest or colonization as you'll see in future chapters.

The **Blauner hypothesis** states that minority groups created by colonization will experience more intense prejudice, racism, and discrimination than those created by immigration.

Colonized minority groups are created by conquest or colonization by the dominant group.

Immigrant minority groups are created by their more or less voluntary movement into the territory of the dominant group.

Blauner (1972) stresses that the initial differences between colonized and immigrant minority groups have consequences that persist long after the original contact. For example, based on measures of equality—or integration into the secondary sector, the second step in Gordon's model of assimilation (see Chapter 2)—such as average income, years of education, and unemployment rate, descendants of European immigrants are equal with national norms today (see Chapter 2 for specific data). In contrast, descendants of colonized and conquered groups (e.g., African Americans) are, on the average, below the national norms on virtually all measures of equality and integration (see Chapters 6–9 for specific data).

We should think of Blauner's two types of minority groups as opposite ends of a continuum, with intermediate positions between the extremes. Enclave and middleman minorities hold one such intermediate position (see Chapter 2). These groups often originate as immigrant groups who bring some resources and, thus, have more opportunities than colonized minority groups. However, they are usually racially distinct from Anglos, and certain kinds of opportunities are closed to them.

For example, until World War II, laws expressly forbid immigrants from China from U.S. citizenship. Federal laws restricted the entrance of Chinese immigrants, and state and local laws restricted their opportunities for education, jobs, and housing. For these and other reasons, we cannot equate Asian and European immigrant experiences or immigrant patterns (Blauner, 1972, p. 55). Because enclave and middleman minority groups combine characteristics of both the colonized and the immigrant minority group experience, we can predict that in terms of equality, they will occupy an intermediate status between the more assimilated white ethnic groups and the colonized racial minorities.

Blauner's typology has proven to be an extremely useful conceptual tool for the analysis of U.S. dominant–minority relations, and we use it extensively throughout this book. In fact, we arrange the case studies that compose Part 3 in approximate order from groups created by colonization to those created by immigration. Of course, it is difficult to measure the extent of colonization precisely and the exact order of the groups is somewhat arbitrary.

THE CREATION OF SLAVERY IN THE UNITED STATES

The Noel hypothesis helps explain why colonists enslaved black Africans instead of white indentured servants or Native Americans. First, all three groups were the objects of ethnocentric feelings on the part of the elite groups that dominated colonial society. Black Africans and Native Americans were perceived as being different for religious and racial reasons. Many white indentured servants were Irish Catholics, criminals, and often the very poor. (Overlap exists between those groups, too.) They not only occupied a lowly status in society but the British Protestants who dominated colonial society perceived them as different and inferior.

Second, competition of some sort existed between the colonists and all three groups. The competition with Native Americans was direct and focused on control of land. Competition with indentured servants, white and black, was more indirect. These groups were the labor force that the landowners needed to work on their plantations and to become successful in the New World.

Noel's third variable, differential in power, is the key variable that explains why Africans were overwhelmingly enslaved instead of the other groups. During the first several decades of colonial history, the balance of power between the colonists and Native Americans often favored Native Americans (Lurie, 1982, pp. 131–133). They outnumbered the colonists by a considerable margin and were highly organized, comfortable in their homeland, and experienced warriors. In fact, they mounted devastating attacks on the colonists (e.g., 1622 in Virginia) and may have had the ability to eliminate the English population—or come close to it—for some decades after first contact. However, as you'll see in Chapter 7, their power shrank as the colonies grew in size and resources and as European diseases took their toll. Still, the Indian wars lasted until the late 19th century, at least in the western half of the nation. If you view the relationship between indigenous Americans and the colonists over time, the power differential shifts. It was low at first but grew as the colonists established early American society and began systematically depriving the tribes of their land and resources, culminating in the massive population loss noted later in this chapter and again in Chapter 7.

White indentured servants, on the one hand, had the advantage of being preferred over black indentured servants (Noel, 1968, p. 168). Their greater desirability gave them bargaining power to negotiate better treatment and more lenient terms than could black indentured servants. If the planters had attempted to enslave white indentured servants, this source of labor would have dwindled even more rapidly.

Africans, on the other hand, did not freely choose to enter the British colonies. They became indentured servants by force and coercion. In Blauner's terms, they were a colonized group. Thus, they had no bargaining power. Unlike Native Americans, they had no nearby relatives, no knowledge of the countryside, and no safe havens to which to escape.

Table 4.1 summarizes the impact of these three factors on the three potential sources of labor in colonial America.

TABLE 4.1 The Noel Hypothesis Applied to the Origins of Slavery

POTENTIAL SOURCES OF LABOR	THREE CAUSAL FACTORS		
	Ethnocentrism	Competition	Differential in Power During Contact Period
White indentured servants	Yes	Yes	No
Native Americans	Yes	Yes	No
Black indentured servants	Yes	Yes	Yes

SOURCE: From "A Theory of the Origin of Ethnic Stratification" by Donald Noel in *Social Problems*, vol. 16, no. 2, Autumn 1968. Reprinted by permission of The University of California Press, via the Copyright Clearance Center.

QUESTIONS FOR REFLECTION

1. How do the concepts of subsistence technology and contact situation help clarify the origins of slavery in colonial America?

2. How do the three concepts in the Noel hypothesis apply to the decision to create slavery?

3. Blauner identifies two types of minority groups. How does this distinction apply to Africans in colonial America?

4. Why were African indentured servants—not white indentured servants or Native Americans—selected as the labor supply for slavery?

PATERNALISTIC RELATIONS

Recall the first theme stated at the beginning of this chapter: The nature of intergroup relationships will reflect the characteristics of the larger society. The most important and profitable unit of economic production in the colonial South was the plantation, and the region was dominated by a small group of wealthy landowners. A society with a small elite class and a plantation-based economy will often develop a form of minority relations called **paternalism** (van den Berghe, 1967; Wilson, 1973).

The key features of paternalism are vast power differentials and huge inequalities between dominant and minority groups, elaborate and repressive systems of control over the minority group, caste-like barriers between groups, elaborate and highly stylized codes of behavior and communication between groups, and low rates of overt conflict.

Chattel Slavery. As slavery evolved in the colonies, the dominant group shaped the system to fit its needs. To solidify control of the labor of their slaves, the plantation elite designed and enacted an elaborate system of laws and customs that gave masters nearly total legal power over slaves.

These laws defined slaves as **chattel**, or personal property, rather than as persons. As such, they were accorded no civil or political rights. Slaves could not own property, sign contracts, bring lawsuits, or even testify in court (except against another slave). The law gave masters legal authority to determine almost every aspect of a slave's life, including work schedules and conditions, living arrangements, and even names (Elkins, 2013; Franklin & Moss, 1994; Genovese, 1974; Jordan, 1968; Stampp, 1956). (See both Narrative Portraits in this chapter.)

The law permitted the master to determine the type and severity of punishment for misbehavior. Slaves were forbidden by law to read or write, and marriages between slaves were not legally recognized. Masters could separate husbands from wives and parents from children if it suited them. Slaves had little control over their lives or the lives of their loved ones.

A Closed System. In colonial America, slavery became synonymous with race. Race, slavery, inferiority, and powerlessness became intertwined in ways that still affect the ways black and white Americans think about each other (Hacker, 1992). Slavery was a **caste system**, or closed stratification system. In a caste system, there is no mobility between social positions, and the social class you are born into (your ascribed status) is permanent. Slave status was for

---

Paternalism is a form of dominant–minority relations marked by extreme inequality in power, property, and prestige. It is often associated with labor-intensive agrarian technology.

A **chattel** is a moveable item of personal property. A system of chattel slavery defines slaves as property, not people.

A **caste system** is a system of stratification in which there is virtually no movement or mobility between social positions or levels.

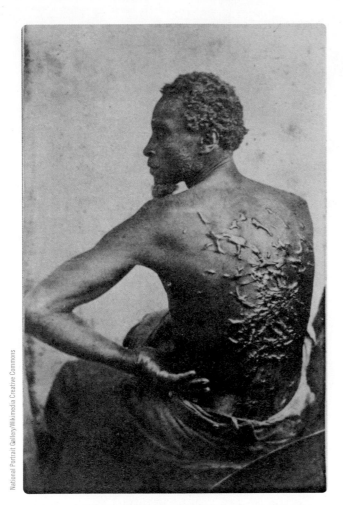

Slavery was founded on and maintained by violence. This slave, Gordon, shows the scars from multiple whippings.

often could not hate their owners as much as they hated the system that constrained them. The system defined slaves as pieces of property owned by their masters—yet they were, undeniably, human beings. Thus, slavery was founded, at its heart, on a contradiction.

> *The master learned to treat his slaves both as property and as men and women, the slaves learned to express and affirm their humanity even while they were constrained in much of their lives to accept their status as chattel. (Parish, 1989, p. 1)*

Powerlessness and Resistance. The slaves' powerlessness made it difficult for them to directly challenge the institution of slavery or their position in it. Open defiance could result in severe punishment, including death. In general, masters would not be prosecuted for such acts.

One of the few slave revolts that occurred in the United States illustrates the futility of overt challenge and the degree of repression built into the slavery system. In 1831, in Southampton County, Virginia, a slave named Nat Turner led an uprising during which 57 whites were killed. The revolt was starting to spread when the state militia met the growing slave army in battle. More than 100 slaves died in the armed encounter, and Nat Turner and 13 others were later executed for their role.

This rebellion, the deadliest in U.S. history, alarmed white Southerners, especially slave owners. Consequently they tightened the system of control over slaves, making it even more repressive (Franklin & Moss, 1994, p. 147). Unfortunately, the result of Nat Turner's attempt to lead slaves to freedom was greater oppression and control by the dominant group.

Others were more successful in resisting the system. Some, especially in the states bordering the free states of the North, ran away. The difficulty of escape and the low likelihood of successfully reaching the North did not deter thousands from attempting it, some of them repeatedly (see the Henry Walton Bibb Narrative Portrait later in this chapter). Many runaway slaves received help from the Underground Railroad, an informal network of safe houses supported by African Americans and whites involved in **abolitionism**, the movement to abolish slavery. The Underground Railroad, which operated from 1830 to 1861, was just one of the tactics abolitionists used (National Park Service, n.d.).

Besides running away and open rebellion, slaves resisted slave owners (and, by extension, the system of slavery) in other ways, too. For example, they resisted by learning to read and write, by stealing from their masters

life and was passed on to any children a slave might have. Whites, no matter what they did, could not become slaves.

In a paternalistic system, rigid, strictly enforced codes of etiquette governed the interactions between members of the dominant and minority groups. Whites expected slaves to show deference and humility and visibly display their lower status when interacting with whites. Plantation and farm work required close and frequent contact between blacks and whites. These rigid behavioral codes made it possible for blacks and whites to work together without threatening the power and status differentials inherent in the system. In the U.S. system of slavery, status differentials were maintained by social rather than by geographical separation.

Pseudotolerance. The frequent but unequal interactions allowed the elites to maintain a pseudotolerance, an attitude of benevolent despotism, toward their slaves. Their prejudice and racism were often expressed as positive emotions of affection for their black slaves. The attitude of the planters toward their slaves was often paternalistic and even genteel (Wilson, 1973, pp. 52–55). For their part, black slaves

---

Abolitionism is the movement to abolish slavery.

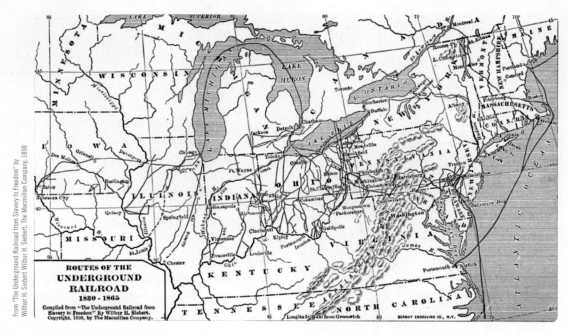

Routes of the Underground Railroad, 1830–1865.

or destroying their property, or by impeding work production by sabotaging machinery or damaging crops. Some slaves turned to violence, fighting and sometimes killing their masters. Still others, tragically, injured themselves to reduce their "property value," and the most desperate committed suicide ("Conditions of Antebellum Slavery," n.d.). As historian Peter Parish (1989) points out, it is difficult to separate "a natural desire to avoid hard work [from a] conscious decision to protest or resist" (p. 73), and much of this behavior may fall more into the category of noncooperation than of deliberate political rebellion. Nonetheless, these behaviors were widespread and document the rejection of the system by its victims. These escapes created legends and heroic figures, including Frederick Douglass and Harriet Tubman. The Narrative Portraits in this chapter present the experiences of two ex-slaves who eventually escaped to the North.

An African American Culture. On an everyday basis, the slaves managed their lives and families as best they could. Most slaves were neither docile victims nor unyielding rebels. As the institution of slavery developed, a distinct African American experience accumulated, and traditions of resistance and accommodation developed. Most slaves worked to create a world for themselves within the confines and restraints of the plantation system, avoiding the more vicious repression as much as possible while attending to their own needs and those of their families. African Americans forged their culture in response to the realities of slavery and it was manifested in folklore, music, religion, family and kinship structures, and other aspects of everyday life (Blassingame, 1972; Genovese, 1974; Gutman, 1976).

QUESTIONS FOR REFLECTION

5. How did the plantation system shape slavery in colonial America?

6. Define the terms *chattel slavery* and *caste system*. Explain how they apply to the American system of slavery. Does the United States still have a racial caste system? Explain.

7. How did slaves resist their oppression? What were the risks associated with resistance?

THE DIMENSIONS OF MINORITY-GROUP STATUS

The situation of African Americans under slavery can be understood more completely by applying some of the concepts you learned in Part 1.

Power, Inequality, and Institutional Discrimination. The key concepts for understanding the creation of slavery are power, inequality, and institutional discrimination. The plantation elite used its greater power resources to consign black Africans to an inferior status. The system of racial inequality was implemented and reinforced by institutionalized discrimination and became a central aspect of everyday life in the antebellum South. The legal and political institutions of colonial society were shaped to benefit the landowners and give them almost total control over their slaves.

Prejudice and Racism. What about the attitudes and feelings of the people involved? What was the role of personal

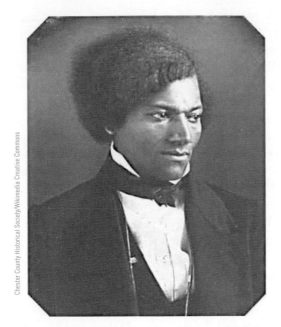

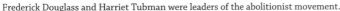
Frederick Douglass and Harriet Tubman were leaders of the abolitionist movement.

prejudice? How and why did the ideology of antiblack racism start? As we discussed in Chapter 3, individual prejudice and ideological racism are not as important as causes of the creation of minority-group status, but are more the results of systems of racial inequality (Jordan, 1968, p. 80; Smedley, 2007, pp. 100–104). Colonists did not enslave black indentured servants because they were prejudiced or because they disliked blacks or thought them inferior. They did it to resolve a labor supply problem. The primary roles of prejudice and racism in the creation of minority-group status are to rationalize and "explain" the emerging system of racial and ethnic advantage (Wilson, 1973, pp. 76–78).

Prejudice and racism helped mobilize support for the creation of minority-group status and helped stabilize the system as it emerged. Prejudice and racism can provide convenient and convincing justifications for exploitation. They can help insulate a system such as slavery from questioning and criticism and make it appear reasonable and even desirable. Thus, the intensity, strength, and popularity of antiblack Southern racism actually reached its height almost 200 years after slavery began to emerge. During the early 1800s, the American abolitionist movement brought slavery under heavy attack, and in response, the ideology of antiblack racism was strengthened (Wilson, 1973, p. 79). The greater the opposition to a system of racial stratification or the greater the magnitude of the exploitation, the greater the need of the beneficiaries and their apologists to justify, rationalize, and explain.

Once created, dominant-group prejudice and racism become widespread and common ways of thinking about the minority group. In the case of colonial slavery, antiblack beliefs and feelings became part of the standard package of

knowledge, understanding, and truths shared by members of the dominant group. As the decades wore on and the institution of slavery solidified, prejudice and racism were passed on from generation to generation. For succeeding generations, antiblack prejudice became just another piece of information and perspective on the world learned during socialization. Antiblack prejudice and racism began as part of an attempt to control the labor of black indentured servants, became embedded in early American culture, and were established as integral parts of the socialization process for future generations (see Myrdal's "vicious cycle" in Chapter 3).

We show these conceptual relationships in Figure 4.3. Racial inequality arises from the contact situation, as specified earlier in the Noel hypothesis. As the dominant–minority relationship begins to take shape, prejudice and racism arise as rationalizations. Over time, a vicious cycle develops as prejudice and racism reinforce the pattern of inequality between groups, which was the cause of the prejudice and racism in the first place. Thus, as the Blauner hypothesis states, the subordination of colonized minority groups is perpetuated through time.

FIGURE 4.3 A Model for the Creation of Prejudice and Racism

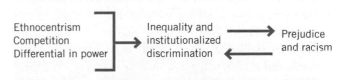

Ethnocentrism
Competition
Differential in power

→ Inequality and institutionalized discrimination ←

→ Prejudice and racism

Assimilation. An enormous amount of literature documents American slavery, and research on the characteristics and meaning of this system continues today. Some issues remain unsettled; one of the more controversial, consequential, and interesting of these concerns the effect of slavery on the slaves.

Apologists for the system of slavery and some historians of the South writing early in the 20th century accepted the rationalizations stemming from antiblack prejudice. They argued that slavery was actually beneficial for black Africans. According to this view, British American slavery operated as a "school for civilization" (Phillips, 1918) that rescued savages from the jungles of Africa and exposed them to Christianity and Western civilization. Some argued that slavery was benevolent because it protected slaves from the evils and exploitation of the factory system of the industrial North. These racist views were most popular a century ago, early in the development of the social sciences. Since that time, scholars have established a number of facts (e.g., Western Africa, the area from which most slaves came, had been the site of a number of powerful, advanced civilizations) that make this view untenable by anyone but the most dedicated racist thinkers.

At the opposite extreme, historian Stanley Elkins 2013 [orig. 1959] compared slavery with Nazi concentration camps that he likened to a "perverted patriarchy" in his book *Slavery: A Problem in American Institutional and Intellectual Life* (p. 104). For example, Elkins compares the below deck areas of slave ships with the cattle cars that took Jews to concentration camps. However, instead of asking moral questions about slavery, he pondered its psychological impact on slaves (Rodriguez, 1997, p. 245). He asserted that slavery brainwashed, emasculated, and dehumanized slaves, stripping them of their heritage and culture. Like people in concentration camps who sought to appease Nazis, enslaved people sought to please plantation owners (Rodriguez, 1997, p. 564). Some regard Elkins's argument as overstated at best and highly problematic at worst, saying, at the very least, that Elkins relied too heavily on plantation owners' views and not enough on evidence regarding the lived experiences of enslaved peoples. Recent scholarship on slavery has attempted to refute or at least modify Elkins's ideas. Despite the debate stirred by his work, the general questions that Elkins asks about the characteristics of the institution of slavery and its impact on enslaved people are useful to consider.

A third view of the impact of slavery that emerged after Elkins's publication says that through all the horror and abuse of enslavement, slaves retained a sense of self and a firm anchor in their African traditions. This point of view stresses the importance of kinship, religion, and culture in helping African Americans cope; it has been presented most poignantly in Alex Haley's (1976) semi-autobiographical

family history, *Roots* (see Blassingame, 1972; Genovese, 1974). Archeologists provide evidence of this symbolic connection; for example, in the blue beads, carved crosses, pottery, and other artifacts unearthed throughout the South. Such objects may appear ordinary to the untrained eye, but they link the users of these pieces to the spiritual traditions of their ethnic roots. For example, crossed lines carved into pottery (see page 129) or coins suggests the cosmology of the BaKongo people who originate from what was then called the Congo-Angolan region in central Africa (Fennell, 2013; Orser, 1994). The vertical line represents a demarcation of the earthly and spirit worlds. The horozontal line reflects the passage of the sun that is repeated each day and the directions of East and West. Symbolically, it represents the cycle of birth and death (Fennell, 2013, p. 6; for a more complete description of the cosmogram, see Fennell, 2013).

In addition to connecting individuals to their ethnic roots, such symbolic objects served to unite enslaved people from many cultural backgrounds who may not have spoken the same language but who had similar belief systems (Fennell, 2013, p. 11). These religious elements survived. Although some enslaved people adopted some Christian ideas, archeologists and anthropologists believe slaves merged these components with their original beliefs about the universe (Fennell, 2013, p. 13). This process of cultural transformation is called *syncretism*. When it occurs under oppressive conditions such as slavery, the cultural components most likely to survive are those that are like those of the oppressors (Davidson, 2004, p. 35). Early scholarship typically framed such objects within the traditional, unidirectional model of acculturation, probably because scholars did not understand the original cultural meanings of objects and symbols. New interpretations that incorporate greater cultural awareness suggest that acculturation is not unidirectional (Davison, 2004).

The debate over the impact of slavery continues (see the Current Debates section at the website for this text), and we cannot hope to resolve the issues here. However, it is clear that African Americans, in Blauner's (1972) terms, were a "colonized" minority group who were extensively—and coercively—acculturated. Language acculturation began on the slave ships, where people from dozens of different tribal and language groups were shackled together. Though physically linked, their ability to communicate across groups was limited, which lowered the potential for resistance and revolt (Hall, 2009, p. 45; Mannix, 1962).

The plantation elite, their agents, and other colonists needed to communicate with their workforce. Because they had little ability to recognize or understand the variety of African languages spoken by their slaves, they insisted on using English. For example, historic records describe J. F. D. Smyth (1784) who sold his slave because he could

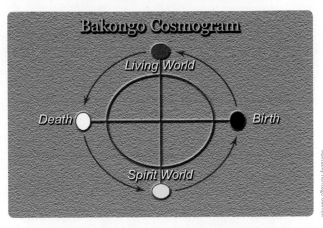

The crossed lines on pottery reflect Bakongo beliefs about the nature of the universe, while the Bakongo cosmogram represents the cycle of birth and death and the connection between the earthly and spirit worlds.

"'not understand . . . one syllable . . . of his [a slave's] language'" (Dillard, 2014, p. 60). This caused African language use to all but die out within a generation or two. However, some African words and language patterns continue to the present day. For example, throughout the Gullah/ Geechee Cultural Heritage Corridor, (from Wilmington, North Carolina, to Jacksonville, Florida), people speak in a way that closely parallels the Creole spoken in the Bahamas, Barbados, and Belize. Creole reflects a variety of linguistic traditions from many African ethnic groups as well as from English. It has survived, in part, because the Gullah/Geechee were protected by the unique geography of the coastal barrier islands that limited contact from people outside of their communities (Gullah/Geechee Cultural Heritage Corridor Cultural Heritage, n.d.). Other components of Gullah/Geechee culture exist (and are appreciated widely) today—such as foodways, music, textiles, and sweet grass baskets—and connect them back to their African roots (Sengova, 2016, pp. 139–141). These cultural remnants are a sign that acculturation is not solely a one-way process. However, these limited cultural survivals are trivial compared with the coerced adoption of English. To the extent that culture depends on language and belief systems, Africans under slavery experienced massive acculturation.

Acculturation through slavery was clearly a process that was forced on African Americans. Because they were a colonized minority group and unwilling participants in the system, they had little choice but to adjust to the conditions established by the plantation elite. Whites suppressed slaves' expression of their home cultures, and sharply constrained their options in other ways. Indeed, most slaves' survival depended on acculturation. Although slaves developed new cultural forms and social relationships in response to this acculturation process, they had few (rarely any) options (Blauner, 1972, p. 66). Some African cultural elements survived the institution of slavery, but, given the power differentials inherent in the system, African Americans had few choices regarding their manner of adjustment.

Southern agrarian society developed into a complex social system stratified by race, gender, and class. As you'll see in Table 4.2 on page 131, slaves made up almost 40% of the southern population in 1860, but that rate varied by geographical location. In Arkansas, about 1 in 4 (26%) people were enslaved; in South Carolina and Mississippi, the rate was more than double that (57% and 55% respectively). Note, also, that in South Carolina and Mississippi, slaves outnumbered the free population, a reminder that minority groups status is about power, not numbers (Minnesota Population Center, 2016).

In the seven Deep South states where the agricultural economy depended on slave labor (Alabama, Florida, Georgia, Louisiana, Mississippi, South Carolina, and Texas), a little less than half the total population—an estimated 2,312,352 people—was enslaved (Census, 1860; also see Hall, 2011, and Dubrulle, 2016). The rate of families owning slaves varied by region, also, generally mirroring the overall pattern described earlier. That is, the highest rates of slave ownership by family was in the Deep South states with 46% of families in South Carolina owning slaves and 49% of families in Mississippi owning slaves. The lowest rates were in Arkansas (20%), Tennessee (25%), and Virginia (26%).

Contrary to popular belief, it wasn't just the wealthiest people who owned slaves. While it's true that in 1850, for example, only 1% of families (the "large planters") owned more than 100 slaves each, it's also true that 25% of southern whites did, too. Teasing out the patterns further illustrates this class-based social hierarchy. The plantation elite, small in number but wealthy and politically powerful, were at the top of the structure. Most whites in the South were small farmers, and relatively few of them owned slaves. Of those who did, half owned between one to four slaves,

NARRATIVE PORTRAIT

The Lives of Enslaved People

Bentley Historical Library/Wikimedia Creative Commons

Henry Bibb

Henry Walton Bibb's memoir, like those of other enslaved people, is an important source for understanding the power dynamics of the U.S. system of slavery. As you'll see, Bibb suffered great cruelty and loss in his lifetime. He was owned by James Bibb, a prominent Kentucky politician and landowner who was also his biological father. Henry's mother was Mildred Jackson, one of James Bibb's slaves. It might seem shocking that Bibb Sr., like other men of his time, could enslave his own child. That reality underscores the complex, dehumanizing nature of the slavery system.

Walton Bibb was bought and sold many times in his early life. At 19, he married an enslaved woman named Malinda who, soon after, had a daughter. At the age of 22, Bibb escaped, but agonized over leaving his family in bondage. Six months later, he returned in an attempt to rescue them but was captured. Amazingly, he managed to escape the next day. He made several more rescue attempts but was recaptured each time. Ultimately, he found safety in Canada, but was unable to reunite with his family. He became a well-known abolitionist speaker and writer, which is, largely, how we know about him today.

NARRATIVE OF THE LIFE AND ADVENTURES OF HENRY WALTON BIBB

I was born May 1815 . . . in Shelby County, Kentucky. . . . I was taken away from my mother, hired out to labor for various persons, eight or ten years in succession . . . It was then my sorrows and sufferings commenced . . . I was a wretched slave, compelled to work under the lash without wages, and often without clothes enough to hide my nakedness . . . I have often worked without half enough to eat, both late and, early, by day and by night. I have often laid my wearied limbs down at night to rest upon a dirt floor, or a bench, without any covering at all, because I had no where else to rest my wearied body, after having worked hard all the day. I have also been compelled in early life, to go at the bidding of a tyrant, through all kinds of weather, hot or cold, wet or dry, and without shoes frequently, until the month of December, with my bare feet on the cold frosty ground, cracked open and bleeding as I walked. Reader, believe me when I say that no tongue, nor pen ever has or can express the horrors of American Slavery.

[*Next, Bibb recalls his later life, including his marriage and the birth of his daughter. He also recounts the abuses he and his family suffered because of their status as slaves.*]

Not many months [after getting married] Malinda made me a father. The dear little daughter was called Mary Frances. . . . Malinda's business was to labor out in the field the greater part of her time, and there was no one to take care of poor little Frances while her mother was toiling in the field. She was left at the house to creep under the feet of an unmerciful old mistress, Mrs. Gatewood (Malinda's owner's wife).

[We] came in from the field one day . . . and poor little Frances . . . [had] . . . large tear drops standing in her dear little eyes. . . . Her little face was bruised black with the whole print of Mrs. Gatewood's hand . . . But oh! this darling child was a slave; born of a slave mother . . . Who can imagine the feelings of a mother and father, when looking upon their infant child whipped and tortured with impunity, and they placed in a situation where they could afford it no protection? . . .

On this same plantation, I was compelled to stand and see my wife shamefully scourged and abused by her master; and the manner in which this was done was so violent and inhuman that I despair in finding decent language to describe the bloody act of cruelty. . . .

I could never look upon [my daughter] without being filled with sorrow and fearful apprehensions, of being separated by slaveholders, because she was a slave, regarded as property. . . . But Oh! When I remember that my daughter, my only child, is still there . . . it is too much to bear. . . .

SOURCE: *Narrative of the Life and Adventures of Henry Bibb, An American Slave* . . . Accessed from the UNC-CH digitization project, Documenting the American South. http://docsouth.unc.edu/neh/bibb/bibb.html (1849, pp. 54–65, 80–81).

and 75% didn't own any (Franklin & Moss, 1994, p. 123; "Conditions of antebellum slavery," n.d.) (see Table 4.3).

To understand the *system* of slavery, we can't limit our discussion to slave owning elites. Doing so obscures how many people benefitted from slavery, regardless of whether or not they personally owned slaves. For example, farmers who couldn't afford to own slaves occasionally rented them to help on an as needed basis. Likewise, many white women who didn't technically own slaves still relied on slaves to help with labor intensive "cooking, caring, and cleaning" (Anderson 2000). Coates (2010) explains how far-reaching the system of slavery was:

TABLE 4.2 Slave Ownership in the South

	TOTAL POPULATION	TOTAL SLAVES	FREE POPULATION	% SLAVES	NUMBER SLAVEHOLDERS	TOTAL NUMBER FAMILIES	% FAMILIES OWNING SLAVES
Alabama*	964,201	435,080	529,121	45.12%	33,730	96,603	35%
Arkansas*	435,450	111,115	324,335	25.52%	11,481	57,244	20%
Florida*	140,424	61,745	78,679	43.97%	5,152	15,090	34%
Georgia*	1,057,286	462,198	595,088	43.72%	41,084	109,919	37%
Louisiana*	708,002	331,726	376,276	46.85%	22,033	74,725	29%
Mississippi*	791,305	436,631	354,674	55.18%	30,943	63,015	49%
North Carolina	992,622	331,059	661,563	33.35%	34,658	125,090	28%
South Carolina*	703,708	402,406	301,302	57.18%	26,701	58,642	46%
Tennessee	1,109,801	275,719	834,082	24.84%	36,844	149,335	25%
Texas*	604,215	182,566	421,649	30.22%	21,878	76,781	28%
Virginia	1,596,318	490,865	1,105,453	30.75%	52,128	201,523	26%
South:	9,103,332	3,521,110	5,582,222	38.68%	316,632	1,027,967	32%
Deep South:	4,969,141	2,312,352	2,656,789	46.53%	181,521	494,775	37%

SOURCE: 1860 Census.

NOTE: *indicates the Deep South states where agriculture depended heavily on slave labor and where almost half (46.53%) of the population were enslaved people. The percentage of families owning slaves is calculated by the number of slave holders (i.e., head of household)/number of families.

Slave labor was as much a part of life in the antebellum South as heat in the summer . . . Southerners who didn't own slaves could not but avoid coming in regular, frequent contact with the institution. They hired out others' slaves for temporary work. They did business with slaveholders, bought from or sold to them. They utilized the products of others' slaves' labor. They traveled roads and lived behind levees built by slaves. Southerners across the Confederacy, from Texas to Florida to Virginia, civilian and soldier alike, were awash in the institution of slavery.

Gender Relations. The principal line of differentiation in the antebellum South was race, which had become synonymous with slave versus nonslave status. However, each of the racial groups was also stratified by gender. White women were subordinate to the men of the plantation elite. Gendered and racialized ideologies of the day

TABLE 4.3 The Structure of Free Southern Society (1860)

GROUP	SIZE	NOTES
Large planters (1000 or more acres)	< 1% of white families	The wealthiest class who had disproportionate social and political power compared to their size. Most owned 50+ slaves.
Planters (100–1000 acres)	Approx. 3% of white families	Owned 20–49 slaves. This group also controlled a great deal of wealth in the South; many politicians were from this group.
Small slaveholders	Approx. 20% of white families	Owned < 20 slaves. Most were farmers; a few were merchants.
Nonslaveholding whites	Approx. 75% of white families	This group farmed small plots of land, generally to feed their families. About 1/5 of them didn't own land. Some were day laborers.
Free blacks	3% of all free families	Free blacks in the South were small in number. Most lived in the upper South (e.g., Maryland). Due to legal and social restrictions, they had limited opportunity for economic advancement. Many were tenant-farmers or day laborers.
Slaves	Approximately 3.5 million	75% worked on plantations and medium-sized farms. Another 10% did hard physical labor. Considered "below whites."

SOURCE: Adapted from Goldfield et al., 2002.

NARRATIVE PORTRAIT

Ain't I a Woman?

Sojourner Truth

SOJOURNER TRUTH

Sojourner Truth pointed out the contradictory views of black and white women in her famous speech before the 1851 Women's Rights Convention. The attendees were primarily white women interested in the subject of women's suffrage (voting rights). At the time, the nation was hotly debating rights for women and people of color. Some of the suffragettes were concerned that their cause (white women's rights) would be hurt by Truth's ideas about abolition.

In the antebellum South, enslaved women, by virtue of their race, were not defined in law or custom as "real women." Truth's speech beautifully illustrates her intersectional perspective. She notes that white women get certain privileges ("to have the best place") while women of color were expected to bear immense costs (e.g., "the lash"). Truth's refrain, "And ain't I a woman?" asks listeners to consider that paradox.

Well, children, where there is so much racket there must be something out of kilter. I think that 'twixt the negroes of the South and the women at the North, all talking about rights, the white men will be in a fix pretty soon. But what's all this here talking about?

That man over there says that women need to be helped into carriages, and lifted over ditches, and to have the best place everywhere. Nobody ever helps me into carriages, or over mud-puddles, or gives me any best place! And ain't I a woman? Look at me! Look at my arm! I have ploughed and planted, and gathered into barns, and no man could head me! And ain't I a woman? I could work as much and eat as much as a man—when I could get it—and bear the lash as well! And ain't I a woman? I have borne thirteen children, and seen most all sold off to slavery, and when I cried out with my mother's grief, none but Jesus heard me! And ain't I a woman?

Then they talk about this thing in the head; what's this they call it? [Someone whispers, "intellect"]What's that got to do with women's rights or negroes' rights? If my cup won't hold but a pint, and yours holds a quart, wouldn't you be mean not to let me have my little half measure full?

Then that little man in black there [a minister], says women can't have as much rights as men, 'cause Christ wasn't a woman! Where did your Christ come from? Where did your Christ come from? From God and a woman! Man had nothing to do with Him.

If the first woman God ever made was strong enough to turn the world upside down all alone, these women together ought to be able to turn it back, and get it right side up again! And now they is asking to do it, the men better let them . . .

---

idealized southern white women and placed them on a pedestal. The gender hierarchy of slave communities echoed the same patriarchal pattern seen among whites, except that the degree of gender inequality among blacks was sharply truncated by the fact that slaves had little autonomy and few resources.

As we will see in future chapters, women of color are at risk for "double jeopardy." That is, they occupy a disadvantaged social location based on their gender *and* their race or ethnicity. For black women slaves, the constraints were triple. As White (1985) noted, enslaved women were "Black in a white society, slave in a free society, women in a society ruled by men, female slaves had the least formal power and were perhaps the most vulnerable group of antebellum America" (p. 15).

The romanticized conception of femininity that elite white women were expected to fulfill was quite inconsistent with the roles women slaves had to play. Besides domestic roles, enslaved women also worked in the fields and did their share of the hardest, most physically demanding, and least "feminine" farm work. Southern ideas about feminine fragility and daintiness could not simultaneously exist with these realities. If they had, plantation life would have been damaged, seriously decreasing the potential profit to be made from slave labor (Amott & Matthaei, 1991, p. 146).

As you saw in the Narrative Portrait from Henry Walton Bibb, one of the most horrific abuses enslaved women suffered was their rape by white men. The next Narrative Portrait from Harriet Jacobs also documents this experience. An intersectional approach can help us better understand the specific kinds of domination that reflected their vulnerability and powerlessness—not just as slaves but also as women. Men raped enslaved women for a variety of reasons. First, to satisfy their own sexual desires. However, like rape today, this was not the primary reason. Second, because of the principle of *partus sequitur ventrem*, the law that classified children born to enslaved women as slaves, even if their fathers were white (Curtis, 2012, p. 139), some white men raped enslaved women to produce more slaves to sell. Yet, this was not its primary purpose, either (Whisnant, 2017). Roberts (1997, 29-30, c.f. Whisnant section 3.3) argues that

> the rape of slave women by their masters was primarily a weapon of terror that reinforced whites' domination over their human property. Rape was an act of physical violence designed to stifle Black women's will to resist and to remind them of their servile status .... Whites' sexual exploitation of their slaves, therefore, should <u>not</u> be viewed simply as either a method of slave-breeding or the fulfillment of slave-holders' sexual urges.

While some enslaved men and white women also experienced rape, scholars have documented a widespread pattern of rape experienced by enslaved women. John Blassingame (1972) explained their vulnerability to sexual victimization saying

> Many white men considered every slave cabin a house of ill-fame. Often through "gifts" but usually by force, white overseers and planters obtained the sexual favors of black women. Generally speaking, the women were literally forced to offer themselves "willingly" and receive a trinket for their compliance rather than a flogging for their refusal. (p. 83)

Some historical accounts misrepresent the rape of slave women when describing them as "mistresses." This linguistic construction suggests a romantic liaison between two equal partners. It obscures slave women's lack of power that prevented their full consent.

Moreover, enslaved women usually had no recourse under law if they were raped. For example, although Missouri law made rape illegal in 1845 and gave white women protection in cases of self-defense, this law didn't apply to enslaved women. The landmark case, *Missouri v. Celia*, illustrates this point. In 1850, Robert Newsome purchased Celia, a 14-year-old girl. He raped her, repeatedly, over the next five years. She had two of his children. She later fell in love with a slave who refused to continue seeing her if the situation with Newsome continued. So, she asked Newsome's daughters for help, and she asked Newsome to stop. He refused. Ultimately, she killed him.

Slaves could not give testimony in court and the prosecution lawyers fought against the notion that Celia killed him in self-defense. Her lawyer argued that she should be protected under law. However, the judge cited *Missouri*

Slave Code (1804) to the jury. It says that one can't "intrude on his own property." A jury of white men found Celia guilty and she was sentenced to death by hanging.

Gender and Daily Life. The routines of work and everyday life differed for men and women slaves. Although they sometimes worked with the men, especially during harvest time, women more often worked in sex-segregated groups organized around domestic as well as farm chores. In addition to working in the fields, they attended the births and cared for the children of both races, cooked and cleaned, wove cloth and sewed clothes, and did the laundry. The women often worked longer hours than the men, doing housework and other chores long after the men had retired for the night (Robertson, 1996, p. 21; White, 1985, p. 122).

The group-oriented nature of their tasks gave women slaves an opportunity to develop bonds and relationships with other slave women. Women cooperated in their chores, in caring for their children, in the maintenance of their quarters, and in myriad other domestic and family chores.

These networks and interpersonal bonds could be used to resist the system. For example, slave women sometimes induced abortions rather than bring more children into bondage. They often controlled the role of midwife and were able to effectively deceive slave owners and disguise the abortions as miscarriages (White, 1985, pp. 125–126). The networks of relationships among the women slaves provided mutual aid and support for everyday problems, solace and companionship during the travails of a vulnerable and exploited existence, and some ability to buffer and resist the influence and power of the slave owners (Andersen, 1993, pp. 164–165).

Slaves in the American system were brutally repressed and exploited, but women were even more subordinated than men. Also, their oppression and exclusion sharply differentiated women slaves from white women. The white "Southern Belle," chaste, untouchable, and unremittingly virtuous, had little in common with African American women under slavery.

QUESTIONS FOR REFLECTION

8. Explain and evaluate this statement: *The key concepts for understanding American slavery are power and inequality, not prejudice or racism.*

9. Were American slaves acculturated? Were they integrated? Under what conditions? How do these concepts relate to Blauner's distinction between immigrant and colonized minorities?

10. What, if anything, did black and white women have in common under slavery? How were their gender norms similar? How were they different?

Life as a Slave Girl

Harriet Jacobs

Below, Harriet Jacobs recounts some of her experiences as a young slave. Her narrative illustrates the gendered dynamics of power within the U.S. system of slavery. Specifically, she offers an intersectional understanding of the unique subordination that slave women experienced, particularly in terms of their rape by white men.

Like Walton Bibb (in the first narrative), Harriet and her brother John were born into slavery, as their mother was enslaved. Her mother, Delilah Horniblow, was held by John Horniblow. Like Bibb, she escaped from her bondage and penned an account of her experiences. It was one of the first books to address the specific struggles of enslaved women.

HARRIET ANN JACOBS (FEBRUARY 11, 1813 – MARCH 7, 1897)

During the first years of my service in Dr. Flint's family, I was accustomed to share some indulgences with the children of my mistress. . . . But I now entered on my fifteenth year—a sad epoch in the life of a slave girl. My master began to whisper foul words in my ear. . . . I tried to treat them with indifference or contempt . . . .

He was a crafty man, and resorted to many means to accomplish his purposes. Sometimes he had stormy . . . ways that made his victims tremble; sometimes he assumed a gentleness that he thought must surely subdue. . . . He tried his utmost to corrupt the pure principles my grandmother had instilled. He peopled my young mind with unclean images, such as only a vile monster could think of.

I turned from him with disgust and hatred. But he was my master. . . . I saw a man forty years my senior daily violating the most sacred commandments of nature. He told me I was his property; that I must be subject to his will in all things. My soul revolted against the mean tyranny. But where could I turn for protection? . . . There is no shadow of law to protect [me] from insult, from violence, or even from death; all these are inflicted by fiends who bear the shape of men. . . .

SOURCE: "The Trials of Girlhood," reprinted by permission of the publishers from *Incidents in the Life of a Slave Girl: Written by Herself* by Harriet A. Jacobs, edited and with an introduction by Jean Fagan Yellin, pp. 27–30, Cambridge, Mass.: Harvard University Press, Copyright 1987, 2000 by the President and Fellows of Harvard College.

Questions to Consider

1. How do the experiences of Bibb and Jacobs (in the Narrative Portraits) illustrate the paternalism of the slave system?

2. How do the concepts of institutional discrimination and power apply to these narratives?

3. How do these narratives illustrate the need for an intersectional approach to understanding social life?

THE CREATION OF MINORITY STATUS FOR NATIVE AMERICANS AND MEXICAN AMERICANS

Two other groups became minorities during the preindustrial period. In this section, we will review the dynamics of these processes and make some comparisons with African Americans. As you will see, both the Noel and Blauner hypotheses provide some extremely useful insights for understanding these experiences.

NATIVE AMERICANS

As Europeans entered the New World, they encountered hundreds of societies that had lived on this land for thousands of years. American Indian societies were highly variable in culture, language, size, and subsistence technology. Some were small, nomadic hunter-gatherer bands, whereas others were more developed societies in which people lived in settled villages and tended large gardens. Regardless of their exact nature, the relentless advance of white society eventually devastated them all. Contact began in the East and established a pattern of conflict and defeat for Native Americans that continued until the last of the tribes were finally defeated in the late 1800s. The continual expansion of white society into the West allowed many settlers to fulfill their dreams of economic self-sufficiency, but Native Americans, who lost not only their lives and their land but also much of their traditional way of life, paid an incalculable price.

An important and widely unrecognized point about Native Americans is that there is no such thing as *the* American Indian. Rather, there were—and are—hundreds

How much slave labor exists today? Where does it exist? How many people are being victimized? Who are they?

The ancient institution of slavery lives on, although its dynamics are rather different, of course, from the system developed in colonial America. Slavery has been outlawed in much of the world, and modern technology has lessened the need for labor-intensive forms of work, at least in more-developed nations. However, machines have not entirely replaced people, and the moral consensus that made slavery illegal has not spread everywhere.

Below is a brief quiz on modern slave labor, and the Internet Research Project at the end of this chapter follows up on this topic. Most people would not have the information required to answer all these questions correctly—this exercise is meant to pique your interest as well as test your knowledge.

1. How many people are modern-day slaves? _____

2. In what form of work are most modern-day slaves involved?

    a. Agricultural labor

    b. Sex work

    c. Other

3. Who are the primary slave owners?

    a. Governments

    b. Private business

    c. Individuals

4. What region of the world has the most slaves? _____

5. What group is the most vulnerable to slavery?

    a. Men

    b. Women

    c. Children

TURN THE PAGE TO FIND OUR ANSWERS.

of different tribes or nations, each with its own language, culture, home territory, and unique history. There are, of course, similarities from tribe to tribe, but there are also vast differences between, for example, the forest-dwelling tribes of Virginia, who lived in longhouses and cultivated gardens, and the nomadic Plains tribes, who relied on hunting to satisfy their needs. Each tribe was and remains a unique blend of language, values, and social structure. Because of space constraints, we will not always be able to consider all these differences. Nonetheless, it is important to be aware of that diversity and to be sensitive to the variety of peoples and histories within the category of "American Indian."

A second important point is that many American Indian tribes no longer exist or are vastly diminished in size. When Jamestown was established in 1607, it is estimated that there were anywhere from several million to 10 million or more Native Americans living in what became the United States. By 1890, when the Indian Wars finally ended, the number of Native Americans had fallen to fewer than 250,000. By the end of the nearly 300-year-long "contact situation," American Indian populations had declined by at least 75% and perhaps as much as 95% (Mann, 2011; Wax, 1971, p. 17; see also McNickle, 1973).

Very little of this population loss was due directly to warfare and battle casualties. The greatest part was caused by European diseases brought by the colonists and by the destruction of the food supplies on which American Indian societies relied. Native Americans died by the thousands from measles, influenza, smallpox, cholera, tuberculosis, and a variety of other infectious diseases (Wax, 1971, p. 17; see also Oswalt & Neely, 1996; Snipp, 1989). Expanding American society took over traditional hunting grounds and garden plots, and slaughtered game such as the buffalo to the point of extinction. The result of the contact situation for Native Americans very nearly approached genocide.

Native Americans and the Noel and Blauner Hypotheses. We have already used the Noel hypothesis to analyze why Native Americans were not enslaved during the colonial era. Their competition with whites centered on land, not labor, and the Indian nations were often successful in resisting domination (at least temporarily). As American

society spread to the West, competition over land continued, and the growing power, superior technology, and greater resource base of the dominant group gradually pushed Native Americans to near extinction.

Various attempts were made to control the persistent warfare, the most important of which occurred before independence from Great Britain. In 1763, the British Crown ruled that the various tribes were to be considered "sovereign nations with inalienable rights to their land" (see Lurie, 1982; McNickle, 1973; Wax, 1971). In other words, each tribe was to be treated as a nation-state, like France or Russia, and the colonists could not simply expropriate tribal lands. Rather, negotiations had to take place, and treaties of agreement had to be signed by all affected parties. The tribes had to be compensated for any loss of land.

After the American Revolution, the newborn federal government continued this policy in theory but often ignored it in reality. The principle of sovereignty is important because it established a unique relationship between the federal government and Native Americans. Because white society ignored the policy and regularly broke the treaties, Native Americans have legal claims against the federal government that are unique.

East of the Mississippi River, the period of open conflict was brought to a close by the Indian Removal Act of 1830, a policy of forced emigration. The law required all tribes in the East to move to lands west of the Mississippi. Some of the affected tribes went without resistance, others fought, while some fled to Canada rather than move to the new territory. Regardless, the Indian Removal Act "solved" the perceived Indian problem in the East. Today, we continue to see the impact of this law in the relative scarcity of Native Americans in the eastern United States. The majority of Native Americans live in the western two thirds of the nation.

In the West, the grim story of competition for land accompanied by rising hostility and aggression repeated itself. Wars were fought, buffalo were killed, territory was expropriated, atrocities were committed on both sides, and the fate of the tribes became more and more certain. By 1890, the greater power and resources of white society had defeated the Indian nations. All the great warrior chiefs were dead or in prison, and almost all Native Americans were living on reservations controlled by agencies of the federal government. The reservations consisted of land set aside for the tribes by the government during treaty negotiations. Often,

These photos illustrate just some of the diversity among Native American women.

these lands were not the traditional homelands and were hundreds or even thousands of miles away from what the tribe considered to be "home." It is not surprising that the reservations were usually on undesirable, often worthless, land.

The 1890s mark a low point in American Indian history, a time of great demoralization and sadness. The tribes had to find a way to adapt to reservation life and new forms of subordination to the federal government. Although elements of the tribal way of life have survived, the tribes were impoverished and without resources, and had little ability to pursue their own interests.

Native Americans, in Blauner's terms, were a colonized minority group who faced high levels of prejudice, racism, and discrimination. Like African Americans, they were controlled by paternalistic systems (the reservations) and, in a variety of ways, were coercively acculturated. Furthermore, according to Blauner, the negative consequences of colonized minority-group status persist long after the contact situation has been resolved. As we will see in Chapter 7, the experiences of this group after the 1890s provide a great deal of evidence to support Blauner's prediction.

Gender Relations. In the centuries before contact with Europeans, American Indian societies distributed resources and power in a wide variety of ways. At one extreme, some American Indian societies were highly stratified, and many practiced various forms of slavery. Others stressed equality, sharing of resources, and respect for the autonomy and dignity of each individual, including women and children (Amott & Matthaei, 1991, p. 33). American Indian societies were generally patriarchal and followed a strict gender-based division of labor, but this did not necessarily mean that women were subordinate. In many tribes, women held positions of great responsibility and controlled the wealth. For example, among the Iroquois (a large and powerful federation of tribes located in the Northeast), women controlled the land and the harvests, arranged marriages, supervised the children, and were responsible for the appointment of tribal leaders and decisions about peace and war (Oswalt & Neely, 1996, pp. 404–405). It was not unusual for women in many tribes to play key roles in religion, politics, warfare, and the economy. Some women even became highly respected warriors and chiefs (Amott & Matthaei, 1991, p. 36).

Gender relations were affected in a variety of ways during the prolonged contact period. In some cases, the relative status and power of women rose. For example, the women of the Navajo tribe (located mainly in what is now Arizona and New Mexico) were traditionally responsible for the care of herd animals and livestock. When the Spanish introduced sheep and goats into the region, the importance of this sector of the subsistence economy increased, and the power and status of women grew along with it.

In other cases, women were affected adversely. The women of the tribes of the Great Plains, for example, suffered a dramatic loss following the contact period. The gendered division of labor in these tribes meant that women were responsible for gardening while men hunted. When horses were introduced from Europe, the productivity of the men hunters greatly increased. As their economic importance increased, men became more dominant and women lost status and power.

Women in the Cherokee Nation—a large tribe whose original homelands were in the Southeast—similarly lost considerable status and power under the pressure to assimilate. Traditionally, Cherokee land was cultivated, controlled, and passed down from generation to generation by the women. This matrilineal pattern was abandoned in favor of the European pattern of men's ownership when the Cherokee attempted (futilely, as it turned out) to acculturate and avoid relocation under the Indian Removal Act of 1830 (Evans, 1989, pp. 12–18).

Summary. By the end of the contact period, the surviving American Indian tribes were impoverished, powerless, and clearly subordinate to white society and the federal government. Like African Americans, Native Americans were sharply differentiated from the dominant group by race, and, in many cases, the tribes were internally stratified by gender. As was the case with African American slaves, the degree of gender inequality within the tribes was limited by their overall lack of autonomy and resources.

QUESTIONS FOR REFLECTION

11. What was the nature of the competition between British colonists and Native Americans? How did this differ from the competition between Anglos and blacks? What were the consequences of these differences?

12. In Blauner's terms, were Native Americans a colonized minority group? Explain.

13. How did gender relations vary from tribe to tribe? How were these relationships affected by contact with Anglo society?

MEXICAN AMERICANS

As the population of the United States increased and spread across the continent, contact with Mexicans inevitably occurred. Spanish explorers and settlers had lived in what is now the southwestern United States long before the wave of American settlers broke across this region. For example, Santa Fe, New Mexico, was founded in 1598, nearly a decade before Jamestown. As late as the 1820s, Mexicans and Native Americans were almost the sole residents of the region.

By the early 1800s, four areas of Mexican settlement had developed, roughly corresponding with what would become Texas, California, New Mexico, and Arizona. These areas were sparsely settled, and most Mexicans lived in what was to become New Mexico (Cortes, 1980, p. 701). The economy of the regions was based on farming and herding. Most people lived in villages and small towns or on ranches and farms. Social and political life was organized around family and the Catholic Church, and tended to be dominated by an elite class of wealthy landowners.

Texas. Some of the first effects of U.S. expansion to the West were felt in Texas early in the 1800s. Mexico was no military match for its neighbor to the north, and the farmland of East Texas was a tempting resource for the cotton-growing interests in the American South. Anglo-Americans began to immigrate to Texas in sizable numbers in the 1820s, and by 1835, they outnumbered Mexicans 6 to 1. The attempts by the Mexican government to control

these immigrants were clumsy and ineffective and eventually precipitated a successful revolution by the Anglo-Americans, with some Mexicans also joining the rebels. At this point in time, competition between Anglos and Texans of Mexican descent (called Tejanos) was muted by the abundance of land and opportunity in the area. Population density was low, fertile land was readily available for all, and the "general tone of the time was that of intercultural cooperation" (Alvarez, 1973, p. 922).

Competition between Anglo-Texans and Tejanos became increasingly intense. When the United States annexed Texas in the 1840s, full-scale war broke out, and Mexico was defeated. Under the Treaty of Guadalupe Hidalgo in 1848, Mexico ceded much of its southwestern territory to the United States. In the Gadsden Purchase of 1853, the United States acquired the remainder of the territory that now composes the southwestern United States. As a result of these treaties, the Mexican population of this region had become, without moving an inch from their traditional villages and farms, both a conquered people and a minority group.

Following the war, intergroup relations continued to sour, and the political and legal rights of the Tejano community were often ignored in the hunger for land. Increasingly impoverished and powerless, the Tejanos had few resources with which to resist the growth of Anglo-American domination. They were badly outnumbered and stigmatized by the recent Mexican military defeat. Land that had once been Mexican increasingly came under Anglo control, and widespread violence and lynching reinforced the growth of Anglo dominance (Moquin & Van Doren, 1971, p. 253).

California. In California, the Gold Rush of 1849 spurred a massive population movement from the East. Early relations between Anglos and Californios (native Mexicans in the state) had been relatively cordial, forming the basis for a multiethnic, bilingual state. The rapid growth of an Anglo majority after statehood in 1850 doomed these efforts, however, and the Californios, like the Tejanos, lost their land and political power.

Laws were passed encouraging Anglos to settle on land traditionally held by Californios. In such situations, the burden was placed on the Mexican American landowners to show that their deeds were valid. The Californios protested the seizure of their land but found it difficult to argue their cases in the English-speaking, Anglo-controlled court system. By the mid-1850s, a massive transfer of land took place, moving land into Anglo-American hands (Mirandé, 1985, pp. 20–21; see also Pitt, 1970).

Other laws passed in the 1850s made it increasingly difficult for Californios to retain their property and power as Anglo-Americans became the dominant group and the majority of the population. Anglo-Americans suppressed the area's Mexican heritage and eliminated it from public life and institutions such as schools and local government. For example, in 1855, California repealed a requirement in the state constitution that all laws be published in Spanish and English (Cortes, 1980, p. 706). Anglo-Americans used violence, biased laws, discrimination, and other means to exploit and repress Californios, and the new wealth generated by gold mining flowed into Anglo hands.

Arizona and New Mexico. The Anglo immigration into Arizona and New Mexico was less voluminous than that into Texas and California, and both states retained Mexican numerical majorities for a number of decades. In Arizona, most of the Mexican population were immigrants themselves, seeking work on farms, on ranches, in the mines, and on railroads. The economic and political structures of the state quickly came under the control of the Anglo population.

Only in New Mexico did Mexican Americans retain some political power and economic clout, mostly because of the relatively large size of the group and their skill in mobilizing for political activity. New Mexico did not become a state until 1912, and Mexican Americans continued to play a prominent role in governmental affairs even after statehood (Cortes, 1980, p. 706).

Thus, the contact situation for Mexican Americans was highly variable by region. Although some areas were affected more rapidly and more completely than others, the ultimate result was the creation of minority-group status for Mexican Americans (Acuña, 1999; Alvarez, 1973; Gomez, 2008; McLemore, 1973; McWilliams, 1961; Moore, 1970; Stoddard, 1973).

Mexican Americans and the Noel and Blauner Hypotheses. The causal model we have applied to the origins of slavery and the domination of Native Americans also provides a way of explaining the development of minority group status for Mexican Americans. Ethnocentrism was clearly present from the very first contact between Anglo immigrants and Mexicans. Many American migrants to the Southwest brought with them the prejudices and racism they had acquired with regard to African Americans and Native Americans. In fact, many of the settlers who moved into Texas came directly from the South in search of new lands for the cultivation of cotton. They readily transferred their prejudiced views to at least the poorer Mexicans, who were stereotyped as lazy and shiftless (McLemore, 1973, p. 664).

The visibility of group boundaries was heightened and reinforced by physical and religious differences. Mexicans were "racially" a mixture of Spaniards and Native Americans, and the differences in skin color and other physical characteristics provided a convenient marker of group membership. In addition, the vast majority of Mexicans were Roman Catholic, whereas the vast majority of Anglo-Americans were Protestant.

A California 49er. The 1849 Gold Rush brought huge numbers of people from the East causing competition between Mexican American landowners and Anglo-Americans.

Competition for land began with the first contact between the groups. However, for many years, population density was low in the Southwest, and the competition did not immediately or always erupt into violent domination and expropriation. Nonetheless, the loss of land and power for Mexican Americans was inexorable, although variable in speed.

The size of the power differential between the groups was variable and partly explains why domination was established faster in some places than in others. In both Texas and California, the subordination of the Mexican American population followed quickly after a rapid influx of Anglos and the military defeat of Mexico. Anglo-Americans used their superior numbers and military power to acquire control of the political and economic structures and expropriate the resources of the Mexican American community. In New Mexico, the groups were more evenly matched in size, and Mexican Americans were able to retain a measure of power for decades.

Unlike the case of Native Americans, however, the labor as well as the land of the Mexicans was coveted. On cotton plantations, ranches, and farms, and in mining and railroad construction, Mexican Americans became a vital source of inexpensive labor. During times of high demand, this labor force was supplemented by workers who were encouraged to emigrate from Mexico. When demand for workers decreased, these laborers were forced back to Mexico. Thus began a pattern of labor flow that continues to the present.

As in the case of African Americans and Native Americans, the contact period clearly established a colonized status for Mexican Americans in all areas of the Southwest. Their culture and language were suppressed even as their property rights were abrogated and their status lowered. In countless ways, they, too, were subjected to coercive acculturation. For example, California banned the use of Spanish in public schools, and severely restricted bullfighting and other Mexican sports and recreational activities (Moore, 1970, p. 19; Pitt, 1970).

In contrast to African Americans, however, Mexican Americans were in close proximity to their homeland and maintained close ties with villages and families. Constant movement across the border with Mexico kept the Spanish language and much of the Mexican heritage alive in the Southwest. Nonetheless, 19th-century Mexican Americans fit Blauner's category of a colonized minority group, and the suppression of their culture was part of the process by which the dominant culture was established.

Anglo-American economic interests benefited enormously from the conquest of the Southwest and the colonization of the Mexican people. Growers and other businessmen came to rely on the cheap labor provided by Mexican Americans and immigrant and day laborers from Mexico. The region grew in affluence and productivity, but Mexican Americans were now outsiders in their own land and did not share in the prosperity. The Anglo-American land grab of the 1800s and the conquest of the indigenous Mexican population are one of the roots shaping Mexican American relations with the dominant U.S. society today.

Gender Relations. Prior to the arrival of Anglo-Americans, Mexican society in the Southwest was patriarchal and maintained a clear gender-based division of labor. These characteristics tended to persist after their conquest and the creation of minority group status.

Most Mexican Americans lived in small villages or on large ranches and farms. The women devoted their energies to the family, child rearing, and household tasks. As Mexican Americans were reduced to a landless labor force, women along with men suffered the economic devastation that accompanied military conquest by a foreign power. The kinds of jobs available to the men (mining, seasonal farm work, railroad construction) often required them to be away from home for extended periods of time, and women, by default, began to do the economic and other tasks traditionally performed by men.

Poverty and economic insecurity placed the family structures under considerable strain. Traditional cultural understandings about men's dominance and patriarchy became moot when the men were absent for long periods of time, and the decision-making power of Mexican American women increased. Also, women were often forced to work outside the household for the family to survive economically. The economics of conquest led to increased matriarchy and more working mothers (Becerra, 1988, p. 149).

For Mexican American women, the consequences of contact were variable, even though the ultimate result was a loss of status within the context of the conquest and colonization of the group as a whole. Like black women slaves, Mexican American women became the most vulnerable part of the social system.

QUESTIONS FOR REFLECTION

14. What was the nature of the competition between Anglos and Mexican Americans? How did this compare and contrast with the competition between Anglos and Native Americans and between Anglos and black Americans?

15. In Blauner's terms, were Mexican Americans a colonized or immigrant minority group? Why?

16. How were Mexican American gender relations affected by contact with Anglo society?

COMPARING MINORITY GROUPS

Native Americans and black slaves were the victims of the explosive growth of European power in the Western Hemisphere that began with Columbus's voyage in 1492. Europeans needed labor to fuel the plantations of the mid–17th century American colonies and settled on slaves from Africa as the most logical, cost-effective means of resolving their labor supply problems. Black Africans had a commodity the colonists coveted (labor), and the colonists

A depiction of one of the many battles between Native Americans and U.S. soldiers.

COMPARATIVE FOCUS

Mexico, Canada, and the United States

Spanish conquistadors confront the Aztec leadership in the Aztec capital city.

How do the experiences of the Spanish and the French in the Western Hemisphere compare with those of the British in what became the United States? What roles did the contact situation and subsistence technology play?[1]

The Spanish conquered much of what is now Central and South America about a century before Jamestown was founded. In 1521, they defeated the Aztec Empire, located in what is now central Mexico. The Aztec Empire was large and highly organized. The emperor ruled over scores of subject nations, and the great majority of his subjects were peasants who farmed small plots of land.

When the Spanish defeated the Aztecs, they destroyed cities and temples, but not the social structure; rather, they absorbed it and used it for their own benefit. For example, the Aztec Empire had financed its central government by collecting taxes and rents from citizens. The Spanish simply grafted their own tax collection system onto this structure and diverted the flow from the Aztec elite classes (which they had, at any rate, destroyed) to themselves (Russell, 1994, pp. 29–30).

The Spanish tendency to absorb rather than destroy operated at many levels. Thus, Aztec peasants became Spanish (and then Mexican) peasants, occupying roughly the same role in the new society as they had in the old,

save for paying their rents to different landlords. Additionally, there was extensive intermarriage between the groups, but, unlike the English in their colonies to the north, the Spanish recognized the resultant racial diversity. They recognized as many as 56 different racial groups, including whites, mestizos (mixed European Indians), and mulattoes (mixed European Africans) (Russell, 1994, p. 35).

The society that emerged was highly race conscious, and race was highly correlated with social class: the elite classes were white, and the lower classes were nonwhite. However, the large-scale intermarriage and the official recognition of mixed-race peoples did establish the foundation for a racially mixed society. Today, the huge majority of the Mexican population is mestizo, although the elite positions continue to be monopolized by people of "purer" European ancestry.

The French began to colonize Canada at about the same time as the English established their colonies farther south. The dominant economic enterprise in the early days was not farming but trapping and the fur trade, and the French developed cooperative relations with some tribes to develop this enterprise. They, like the Spanish in Mexico, tended to absorb Native American social structures, and there was also a significant amount of intermarriage, resulting in a mixed-race group, called the Metís, who had their own identities and, indeed, their own settlements along the Canadian frontier (Russell, 1994, p. 39).

Note the profound differences in these three contact situations. The Spanish confronted a large, well-organized social system and found it expeditious to adapt Aztec practices to their own benefit. The French

developed an economy that required cooperation with at least some Native American tribes, and they, too, found benefits in adaptation. The tribes the English encountered were much smaller and much less developed than the Aztecs, and there was no particular reason for the English to adapt to or absorb their social structures. Furthermore, because the business of the English colonies was agriculture (not trapping), the competition at the heart of the contact situation was for land, and Native Americans were seen as rivals for control of that most valuable resource.

Thus, the English tended to exclude Native Americans, keeping them on the outside of their emerging society and building strong boundaries between their own "civilized" world and the "savages" that surrounded them. The Spanish and French colonists adapted their societies to fit with Native Americans, but the English faced no such restraints. They could create their institutions and design their social structure to suit themselves (Russell, 1994, p. 30).

As we have seen, one of the institutions created in the English colonies was slavery based on African labor. Slavery was also practiced in New Spain (Mexico) and New France (Canada), but the institution evolved in very different ways in those colonies and never assumed the importance that it did in the United States. Why? As you might suspect, the answer has a lot to do with the nature of the contact situation. Both the Spanish and French attempted large-scale agricultural enterprises that might have created a demand for imported slave labor. In the case of New Spain, however, there was a ready supply of Native American peasants available and, although Africans became a part of the admixture that shaped modern Mexico racially and socially, demand for black slaves never matched that in the English colonies. Similarly, in Canada, slaves from Africa were sometimes used, but farmers there tended to rely on labor from France

---

[1]This section is largely based on Russell (1994).

(Continued)

(Continued)

to fill their agricultural needs. The British opted for slave labor from Africa over indentured labor from Europe, and the French made the opposite decision.

Finally, we should note that many of the modern racial characteristics of these three neighboring societies were foreshadowed in their colonial origins (e.g., the greater concentration of African Americans in the United States and the more racially intermixed population of Mexico). The differences run much deeper than race alone, of course, and include differences in class structure and relative levels of industrialization and affluence. For our purposes, however, this brief comparison of the origins of dominant–minority relations underscores the importance of the contact situation in shaping group relations for centuries to come.

Questions to Consider

1. What were the key differences in the contact situations in New Spain, New France, and the British colonies? How do the concepts of competition and power apply?
2. What are some contemporary differences between Mexico, the United States, and Canada that might be traced to the contact situation?

---

subsequently constructed a system to control and exploit this commodity.

To satisfy the demand for land created by the stream of European immigrants to North America, the threat represented by Native Americans had to be eliminated. Once their land was expropriated, Native Americans ceased to be of much concern. The only valuable resource they possessed—their land—was under the control of white society by 1890, and Native Americans were thought to be unsuitable as a source of labor.

Mexico, like the United States, had been colonized by a European power—in this case, Spain. In the early 1800s, the Mexican communities in the Southwest were a series of outpost settlements, remote and difficult to defend. Through warfare and a variety of other aggressive means, Mexican citizens living in this area were conquered and became an exploited minority group.

African Americans, Native Americans, and Mexican Americans, in their separate ways, became involuntary players in the growth and development of European and, later, American economic and political power. None of these groups had much choice in their respective fates; all three were overpowered and relegated to an inferior, subordinate status. Many views of assimilation (such as the "melting pot" metaphor discussed in Chapter 2) have little relevance to these situations. These minority groups had little control over their destinies, their degree of acculturation, or even their survival as groups. These three groups were coercively acculturated in the context of paternalistic relations in an agrarian economy. Meaningful integration (structural assimilation) was not a real possibility, especially for African Americans and Native Americans. In Milton Gordon's (1964) terms (see Chapter 2), we might characterize these situations as "acculturation without integration" or structural pluralism. Given the grim realities described in this chapter, Gordon's terms seem a little antiseptic, and Blauner's concept of colonized minority groups seems far more descriptive.

SUMMARY

This summary is organized around the Learning Objectives listed at the beginning of this chapter.

 4.1 Explain the two themes stated at the beginning of the chapter.

These themes are explored throughout the chapter and, indeed, in much of the remainder of this text:

- Dominant–minority relations are shaped by the characteristics of society as a whole. In particular, the nature of the subsistence technology will affect group relations, culture, family structure, and virtually all aspects of social life.

- The contact situation is the single most important factor in the development of dominant–minority relations, and it will have long-term consequences.

 4.2 Explain the political, economic, and social forces that led to the creation of slavery in British America.

Slavery developed as a solution to a labor supply problem in the context of a plantation economy and labor-intensive subsistence technology. Africans became the source of slave labor in the British colonies in large part because they had less power than white indentured servants and Native Americans.

 4.3 Explain the importance of the contact situation and the relevance of the Noel and Blauner hypotheses for the development of slavery in colonial America.

In colonial America, the contact situation for Anglos and Africans featured ethnocentrism, competition, and a differential in power. African Americans were a colonized minority group, created by conquest and the superior power of Anglos.

 4.4 Apply the concepts of paternalism, power, inequality, discrimination, prejudice and racism, and assimilation to the American system of slavery.

Paternalistic systems of group relationships such as American slavery are characterized by extreme inequalities between groups, especially in terms of power. The minority group is controlled by a comprehensive system of discrimination and is the victim of high levels of prejudice and racism. Assimilation is not a realistic possibility in such systems, except in terms of acculturation. For example, slaves were required to learn English and adapt to British systems of work and family life.

 4.5 Explain the dynamics of gender relations under American slavery.

While white women tended to be idealized as symbols of virtue and purity, black women were often required to perform the most difficult, least "feminine" tasks.

Black women had little in common with the "Southern Belle" and tended to be the most exploited and powerless segment of society. When not working in the fields, they performed domestic and family chores for their white owners and often worked the longest hours of any group.

 4.6 Apply the Noel and Blauner hypotheses and other concepts to the creation of minority-group status for Native Americans and Mexican Americans.

The competition with Native Americans centered on control of the land. American Indian tribes were conquered and pressed into a paternalistic relationship with white society. Native Americans became a colonized minority group and were subjected to forced acculturation. Mexican Americans were the third minority group created during the preindustrial era. Mexican Americans competed with white settlers over both land and labor. Like African Americans and Native Americans, Mexican Americans were a colonized minority group subjected to forced acculturation.

 4.7 Compare and contrast the three contact situations analyzed in this chapter. How do they differ? What are the implications of these different contact situations for relations in the present?

The three situations vary in terms of the nature of the competition (land vs. labor), the size of the power differential, and along many other dimensions. All three groups were victims of the expansion of British power in what became the United States, and all three were colonized minority groups, subjected to paternalism and coercive acculturation.

KEY TERMS

abolitionism 125
Blauner hypothesis 122
caste system 124
chattel 124

colonized minority groups 122
competition 121
differential in power 121

ethnocentrism 121
immigrant minority groups 122
indentured servants 119

paternalism 124
plantation system 120

REVIEW QUESTIONS

1. State and explain the two themes presented at the beginning of the chapter. Apply each to the contact situations between white European colonists, African Americans, Native Americans, and Mexican Americans. Identify and explain the key differences and similarities among the three situations.

2. Explain what a plantation system is and why this system of production is important for understanding the origins of slavery in colonial America. Why are plantation systems usually characterized by (a) paternalism, (b) huge inequalities between groups, (c) repressive systems of control, (d) rigid codes of behavior, and (e) low rates of overt conflict?

3. Explain the Noel and Blauner hypotheses and how they apply to the contact situations covered in this chapter. Explain each of the following key terms: *ethnocentrism*, *competition*, *power*, *colonized minority group*, and *immigrant minority group*. How did group conflict vary when competition was over land rather than labor?

4. Explain the role of prejudice and racism in the creation of minority-group status. Do prejudice and racism help cause minority-group status, or are they caused by minority-group status? Explain.

5. Compare and contrast gender relations in each of the contact situations discussed in this chapter. Why do the relationships vary?

6. What does it mean to say that, under slavery, acculturation for African Americans was coerced? What are the implications for assimilation, inequality, and African American culture given this type of acculturation?

7. Compare and contrast the contact situations of Native Hawaiians and Native Americans. What were the key differences in their contact situations? How are these differences reflected in the groups' current situations?

8. Compare and contrast the contact situations in colonial America, Canada, and Mexico. What groups were involved in each situation? What was the nature of the competition, and what were the consequences?

STUDENT STUDY SITE

Sharpen your skills with SAGE edge at edge.sagepub.com/healey8e

SAGE edge for students provides a personalized approach to help you accomplish your coursework goals in an easy-to-use learning environment.

The following resources are available at SAGE edge:

Current Debates: How Did Slavery Affect the Origins of African American Culture?

Did the institution of slavery permanently flaw African American culture? Or did African Americans create sufficient space within their subjugation to develop and sustain positive cultural norms and self-images? How was the experience of slavery different for women and men?

On our website you will find an overview of the topic, the clashing points of view, and some questions to consider as you analyze the material.

Public Sociology Assignments

Public Sociology Assignments provide opportunities for students to address directly and personally some of the issues raised in this text.

The public sociology assignments designed for Part 2 on our website will lead students to a study of the persistence of prejudice and discrimination in society today. The first assignment is an investigation of children's books and focuses on the depiction of race, gender, and ethnicity. Are children's books as diverse as the larger society? The second assignment analyzes patterns of cross-group interaction in local eateries, and the third looks at the depiction of historical events in contemporary cinema. How are movies based in the past affected by contemporary understandings?

Contributed by Linda M. Waldron

Internet Research Project

For the Internet Research Project for this chapter, you will investigate modern slavery. As you saw in this chapter's Applying Concepts section, slavery is a worldwide phenomenon and can be found in societies at all levels of development, including the United States. Who are the victims of modern slavery? Where are they? Who are the slave owners?

As always, this project will be guided by a series of questions, and your instructor may ask you to discuss your findings in small groups.

For Further Reading

Please see our website for an annotated list of important works related to this chapter.

5

INDUSTRIALIZATION AND DOMINANT–MINORITY RELATIONS

From Slavery to Segregation and the Coming of Postindustrial Society

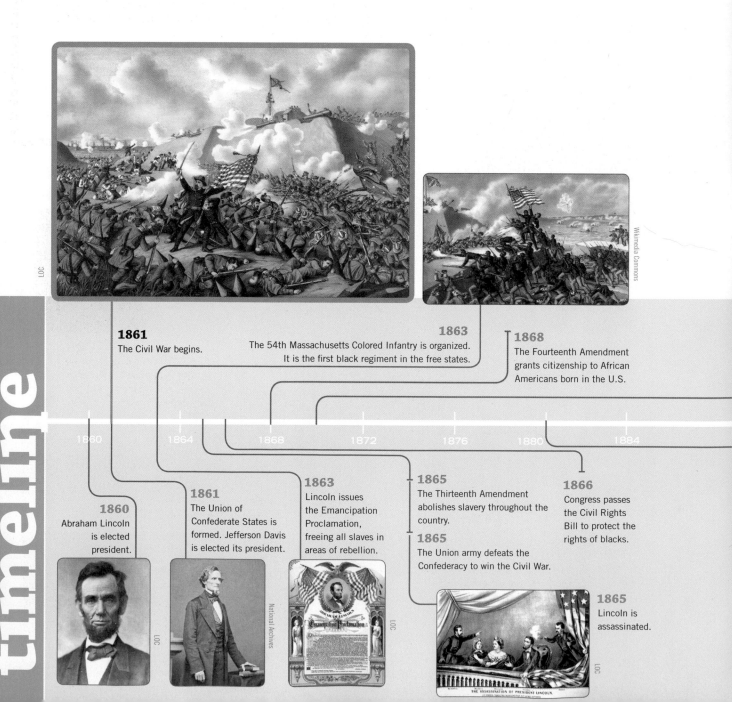

timeline

1861
The Civil War begins.

1863
The 54th Massachusetts Colored Infantry is organized. It is the first black regiment in the free states.

1868
The Fourteenth Amendment grants citizenship to African Americans born in the U.S.

1860   1864   1868   1872   1876   1880   1884

1860
Abraham Lincoln is elected president.

1861
The Union of Confederate States is formed. Jefferson Davis is elected its president.

1863
Lincoln issues the Emancipation Proclamation, freeing all slaves in areas of rebellion.

1865
The Thirteenth Amendment abolishes slavery throughout the country.

1865
The Union army defeats the Confederacy to win the Civil War.

1866
Congress passes the Civil Rights Bill to protect the rights of blacks.

1865
Lincoln is assassinated.

Wikimedia Commons

LOC

National Archives

LOC

"All railroads carrying passengers in the state (other than street railroads) shall provide equal but separate accommodations for the white and colored races, by providing two or more passenger cars for each passenger train, or by dividing the cars by a partition, so as to secure separate accommodations."

—Tennessee, 1891

"It shall be unlawful for any white prisoner to be handcuffed or otherwise chained or tied to a negro prisoner."

—Arkansas, 1903

"Any person . . . presenting for public acceptance or general information, arguments or suggestions in favor of social equality or of

LEARNING OBJECTIVES

By the end of this chapter, you will be able to do the following:

5.1 Explain the corollary to the main themes of Chapter 4: specifically, that dominant–minority group relations change as the subsistence technology of the society changes.

5.2 Understand the complexity of Jim Crow segregation in the South, why it was created, and its effects.

5.3 Explain the significance of the Great Migration and the origins of black protest.

5.4 Apply the concepts of acculturation, integration, and intersectionality to the time frame covered in this chapter.

5.5 Explain the important trends created by the shifts to industrial and postindustrial subsistence technology, and describe how these trends affected dominant–minority relations.

5.6 Explain what is meant by the shift from paternalistic to rigid to fluid competitive group relations.

5.7 Apply the concept of modern institutional discrimination to contemporary black–white relations, and understand why affirmative action policies were created to combat it.

1870
The Fifteenth Amendment is ratified, securing the right to vote for African American men.

1896
The Supreme Court rules in *Plessy v. Ferguson* that "separate but equal" accommodations are constitutional.

1914
Marcus Garvey founds the Universal Negro Improvement Association in 1914 in his native Jamaica and founds the first U.S. branch in 1916.

| 1888 | 1892 | 1896 | 1900 | 1904 | 1908 | 1912 | 1916 |

1880s
Jim Crow laws mandate racial segregation in public facilities.

1890–1930
An estimated 3.5 million African Americans move away from the South to escape Jim Crow and search for higher wages in the Northeast and Midwest.

1909
The National Association for the Advancement of Colored People (NAACP), a civil rights organization, is founded.

intermarriage between whites and negroes, shall be guilty of a misdemeanor and subject to a fine not exceeding five hundred dollars or imprisonment not exceeding six months or both fine and imprisonment in the discretion of the court."

—Mississippi, 1920

"Separate free schools shall be established for the education of children of African descent; and it shall be unlawful for any colored child to attend any white school, or any white child to attend a colored school."

—Missouri, 1929

"It shall be unlawful for a negro and white person to play together or in company with each other in any game of cards or dice, dominoes or checkers."

—Birmingham, Alabama, 1930

SOURCE: Jim Crow Laws. Smithsonian National Museum of American History.

The last Negro has left Decatur, Ind. . . . About a month ago a mob of 50 men drove out all the Negroes who were then making that city their home. Since that time the feeling against the Negro race has been intense, so much so that an Anti-Negro Society was organized.

The colored man who has just left came about three weeks ago, and since that time received many threatening letters. When he appeared on the streets he was insulted and jeered at. An attack was threatened.

The anti-negroites declare that as Decatur is now cleared of Negroes they will keep it so, and the importation of any more will undoubtedly result in serious trouble.

—New York Times, July 14, 1902
(Loewen, 2005, p. 90)

Decatur was not alone. The excerpt above illustrates a little known phenomenon: Between the 1890s and late 1960s, thousands of American towns, cities, and counties—almost all outside the South—expelled their nonwhite population. Some locales prominently posted signs warning nonwhites to be outside city limits by the time the sun set, earning them the name "sundown towns" (Loewen, 2005).

Such practices make it clear that the pervasive racial residential segregation between whites and nonwhites didn't "just happen." It was created intentionally and supported by violence (or threats of violence) as well as by "peaceful" means such as

legislation that made it illegal for people of color to buy or rent property in certain areas. Real-estate agents, property owners, city leaders, and others colluded to maintain it (Massey, 2007; Russell, 2010; Taylor, 2014, p. 202).

But why did such practices emerge years *after* the Civil War in 1865 and the end of the Reconstruction in 1877? And why does any of that matter now? As you'll see in this and future chapters, this massive racial segregation resulted in the exclusion of nonwhites from opportunities for schooling and jobs and provided the foundation for today's racial inequalities (Coates, 2014; Rothstein, 2017). •

In the beginning of Chapter 4, you learned that the subsistence technology of a society affects group relations, culture, family structure, and virtually all aspects of social life. Specifically, agrarian technology and the desire to control land and labor profoundly shaped dominant–minority relations in the formative years of the United States. The agrarian era ended in the 1800s, and the United States experienced two major transformations in subsistence technology since that time, each of which has transformed dominant–minority relations and required the creation of new structures and processes to maintain racial stratification and white privilege. In this chapter, we'll explore a corollary of that theme: *Dominant–minority group relations change as the subsistence technology changes.*

The first transformation, the industrial revolution, began in the early 19th century when machine-based technologies began to develop, especially in the North. In the agrarian era, work was labor intensive, done by hand or with the aid of draft animals. During industrialization, work became capital-intensive (see Chapter 2), and machines replaced people and animals.

The new industrial technology rapidly increased the productivity and efficiency of the U.S. economy and quickly began to change all other aspects of society, including the nature of work, politics, communication, transportation, family life, birth and death rates, the system of education, and, of course, dominant–minority relations. The groups that had become minorities during the agrarian era (e.g., African Americans, Native Americans, and Mexican Americans) faced new possibilities and new dangers, but industrialization also created new minority groups, new forms of exploitation and oppression, and, for some, new opportunities to rise in the social structure and succeed in America. In this chapter, we will explore this transformation and illustrate its effects on the status of African Americans, focusing primarily on the construction of Jim Crow

The assembly line at a Ford Motor company plant.

TABLE 5.1 Three Subsistence Technologies and the United States

TECHNOLOGY	KEY TRENDS AND CHARACTERISTICS	DATES
Agrarian	Labor-intensive agriculture. Control of land and labor are central.	1607 to early 1800s
Industrial	Capital-intensive manufacturing. Machines replace animal and human labor.	Early 1800s to mid-1900s
Postindustrial	Shift from manufacturing to a service economy. The "information society."	Mid-1900s to the present

segregation in the South during the 1870s. The impact of industrialization on other minority groups will be considered in the case studies presented in Part 3.

The second transformation in subsistence technology brings us to more recent times. In the mid-20th century, the United States (and other advanced industrial societies) entered the postindustrial era, also called **deindustrialization**. This shift in subsistence technology was marked by (1) a decline in the manufacturing sector of the economy and a decrease in the supply of secure, well-paid, blue-collar, manual-labor jobs, and (2) an expansion in the service and information-based sectors of the economy and an increase in the relative proportion of white-collar and "high-tech" jobs.

Like the 19th-century industrial revolution, these changes have profound implications for every aspect of modern society, not just for dominant–minority relations. Indeed, every characteristic of American society—work, family, politics, popular culture—is being transformed as the subsistence technology continues to evolve. In the latter part of this chapter, we examine this most recent transformation in general terms and note some of its implications for minority groups. We will examine some new concepts—especially **modern institutional discrimination**—to help us understand group relations in this new era. Last, we will establish some important groundwork for the case studies in Part 3, in which we consider in detail the implications of postindustrial society for America's minority groups.

Deindustrialization is the shift from a manufacturing economy to a service-oriented, information-processing economy.

Modern institutional discrimination is a more subtle and covert form of institutional discrimination.

Table 5.1 summarizes the characteristics of the three major subsistence technologies considered in this text. As U.S. society moved through these stages, group relations and the nature of racial stratification changed.

INDUSTRIALIZATION AND THE SHIFT FROM PATERNALISTIC TO RIGID COMPETITIVE GROUP RELATIONS

As we noted in Chapter 2, the Industrial Revolution began in England in the mid-1700s and spread to the rest of Europe, to the United States, and eventually to the rest of the world. The key innovations associated with this change in subsistence technology were the application of machine power to production and the harnessing of inanimate sources of energy, such as steam and coal, to fuel the machines. As machines replaced humans and animals, work became much more productive, the economy grew, and the volume and variety of goods produced increased dramatically.

In an industrial economy, the close, paternalistic control of minority groups found in agrarian societies becomes irrelevant. Paternalistic relationships such as slavery exist in societies with labor-intensive technologies and help organize and control a large, involuntary, and geographically immobile labor force. An industrial economy, in contrast, requires a workforce that is geographically and socially mobile, skilled, and literate. Furthermore, with industrialization comes urbanization, and close, paternalistic controls are difficult to maintain in cities.

Thus, as industrialization progresses, agrarian paternalism gives way to **rigid competitive group** relations (see Table 5.2 later in this chapter). Under this system, minority-group members are freer to compete for jobs and other valued commodities with dominant-group members, especially those in the lower-class segments. As competition increases, the threatened members of the dominant group become more hostile, and attacks on the minority groups tend to increase.

Whereas paternalistic systems seek to directly dominate and control the minority group (and its labor), rigid competitive systems are designed to eliminate threats and defend the privilege of the dominant group. The threatened segments of the dominant group seek to minimize or eliminate minority-group competition for jobs, housing, or other valuable goods or services (van den Berghe, 1967; Wilson, 1973).

Paternalistic systems such as slavery required minority group members to participate, although involuntarily. Rigid competitive systems, in contrast, limit the ability of minority group members to participate in the job market, schools, politics, and other areas. In some cases, competition from the minority group is eliminated entirely.

In Chapter 2, we saw an example of a dominant group attempting to protect itself from a threat by passing the National Origins Act in the 1920s to stop European immigration in hopes of protecting Americans' jobs and wages. In this chapter, we consider similar dominant-group attempts as the United States shifted from an agricultural to an industrial base. Specifically, will examine efforts to keep African Americans powerless and impoverished—to maintain the system of black–white racial stratification.

THE IMPACT OF INDUSTRIALIZATION ON THE RACIAL STRATIFICATION OF AFRICAN AMERICANS: FROM SLAVERY TO SEGREGATION

Industrial technology began to transform American society in the early 1800s, but its effects were not felt equally in all regions. The northern states industrialized first, while the plantation system and agricultural production continued to dominate the South. This economic diversity was one of the underlying causes of the regional conflict that led to the Civil War. Because of its more productive technology, the North had more resources and defeated the Confederacy in a bloody war of attrition. Slavery was abolished, and black–white relations in the South entered a new era when the Civil War ended in April 1865.

Union soldiers at the Battle of Fredericksburg.

The southern system of race relations that ultimately emerged after the Civil War was designed in part to continue the control of African American labor that was institutionalized under slavery. It was intended, also, to eliminate any political or economic threat from the African American community.

This rigid competitive system grew to be highly elaborate and inflexible, partly because of the long history of African American powerlessness in the South and their racial visibility and partly because of the particular needs of southern agriculture. In this section, we look at black–white relations from the end of the Civil War through the ascendance of segregation in the South and the mass migration of African Americans to the industrializing cities of the North.

RECONSTRUCTION (1865 TO THE 1880S)

The period of **Reconstruction** was a brief respite in the long history of oppression and exploitation of African Americans. The federal government focused on reintegrating the southern states of the former Confederacy back into the Union, establishing rights for newly freed African Americans, and rebuilding the fractured nation. The Union Army and other agencies of the federal government, such as the Freedmen's Bureau, enforced racial freedom in the defeated Confederacy.

A **rigid competitive group system** of group relations is one in which the dominant group seeks to exclude the minority group or limit its ability to compete for scarce resources.

Reconstruction followed the Civil War and lasted from 1865 until the 1880s. Many racial reforms were instituted during this time, but all were reversed during the Jim Crow era.

Though the law of the land had moved toward equality, black Southerners faced great opposition as they pursued new opportunities such as the right to vote (see Foner, 2011). Blacks had been organizing for voting rights before Reconstruction—in Norfolk, Virginia, Atlanta, Georgia, Lexington, Kentucky, Mobile, Alabama, and in other cities across the United States. They raised moral arguments as well as political ones, noting, for example, that as citizens they were subject to taxes and to being drafted (Foner, 2011, p. 5). In 1868, William Murphey, a former slave, spoke before the Arkansas constitutional convention. He questioned why black men who had fought for the Union could be denied political representation, saying, "Has not the man who conquers upon the field of battle, gained any rights? Have we gained none by the sacrifice of our brethren?" (Foner, 2011, p. 10).

Black (men) in the South took advantage of the Fifteenth Amendment to the Constitution, passed in 1870, which says that the right to vote cannot be denied on the grounds of "race, color, or previous condition of servitude." They registered to vote in large numbers and more than a half-million voted in the 1870s (women were not given that right until 1920.) (Constitutional Rights Foundation, n.d.). They didn't just vote—they also ran for office. More than 1,400 blacks held offices during Reconstruction, including 600 in lower levels of state legislature and 16 members of Congress (Smithsonian National Museum of American History, n.d.). They also began to serve as police officers and in other positions from which they had previously been excluded (Lawson, 2009 pp. 6–7).

In 1865, the Bureau of Refugees, Freedmen, and Abandoned Lands (known as the Freedmen's Bureau) was established and provided crucial necessities such as food, shelter, and medical aid to millions of formerly enslaved people. It opened 3,000 schools and colleges such as Fisk Free Colored School (now Fisk University) in Nashville, Tennessee, and Hampton Normal and Agricultural Institute (now Hampton University) in Virginia. It offered legal and other kinds of family assistance as well. For example, it helped people negotiate employment contacts, start businesses, locate relatives, and legalize marriages (Washington, 2005; Wormser, n.d.).

Congress voted to renew the Bureau's funding in 1866, but President Andrew Johnson (serving due to Lincoln's assassination) vetoed it. He said the costs would be too great and because not all the southern states had been admitted back into the Union, and therefore did not have Congressional representation, the bill would unfairly interfere with those states' rights. Though slaves had suffered from discrimination for hundreds of years, Johnson also believed aid would unfairly advantage one group (former slaves) over another (whites, especially poor ones) who

THE FIRST COLORED SENATOR AND REPRESENTATIVES.
In the 41ˢᵗ and 42ⁿᵈ Congress of the United States.

First black members of Congress.

had not had similar support. He also feared it would encourage idleness and reliance on the government (Freedmen's Bureau, n.d.; "Veto of the Freedmen's Bureau Bill," 2015c). Congress passed the bill anyway. However, after several years of pressure from white Southerners, Congress ended the program in 1872 (Wormser, n.d.).

Reconstruction began to end when the federal government demobilized its armies of occupation and turned its attention to other matters. By the 1880s, the federal government had withdrawn from the South, Reconstruction was over, and black Southerners quickly became victimized by a new system of exploitation and inequality.

Reconstruction was too brief to change two of the most important legacies of slavery. First, the centuries of bondage left black Southerners impoverished, largely illiterate and uneducated, and with few and limited resources. When new threats of racial oppression appeared, African Americans found it difficult to defend their group interests. These developments are consistent with the Blauner hypothesis: Colonized minority groups face greater difficulties in improving their disadvantaged status because they confront greater inequalities and have fewer resources at their disposal.

Second, although slavery had become illegal, the culture that supported it had not changed. For the most part, white communities throughout the country held onto the racist beliefs, values, and norms that had long dominated U.S. society. The contention about the Freedman's Bureau provides an example of this, as well as an opportunity to revisit the contact hypothesis from Chapter 3. Recall that the contact hypothesis says that for prejudice to decrease, four conditions need to be maximized: (1) equal status between groups including resources and prestige; (2) common goals; (3) cooperation and significant, meaningful interaction between groups that occurs in an atmosphere free from threat or competition; and (4) support from authority, law, or custom. As we seek to understand the racial violence and exclusion that emerged with Reconstruction (such as the "sundown towns" noted in the chapter opening) it may be helpful to acknowledge that none of these conditions had been met.

Antiblack prejudice and racism originated as rationalizations for slavery but had taken on lives of their own over the generations. After two centuries of slavery, the heritage of prejudice and racism was thoroughly ingrained in southern culture. White Southerners were predisposed by this cultural legacy to see racial inequality and exploitation of African Americans as normal and desirable. They were able to construct a social system based on the assumption of racial inferiority after Reconstruction ended and the federal government withdrew. As Douglas Blackmon (2009) argues in his Pulitzer Prize winning book, *Slavery by Another Name: The Re-Enslavement of Black Americans from the Civil War to World War II*, this was the "Age of Neo-slavery" during which, "White Southerners initiated an extraordinary campaign of defiance and subversion against the new biracial social order" (p. 42).

DE JURE SEGREGATION

The system of race relations that replaced slavery in the South was **de jure segregation**, sometimes referred to as the **Jim Crow system**. Under this type of segregation, the minority group is physically and socially separated from the dominant group and consigned to an inferior position in virtually every area of social life. The term *de jure* ("by law") means that the system is sanctioned and reinforced by the legal code; the inferior status of African Americans was actually mandated or required by state and local laws. For example, southern cities during this era had laws requiring African Americans to ride at the back of the bus. If an African American refused to comply with this seating arrangement, he or she could be arrested.

De jure segregation came to encompass all aspects of southern social life. Neighborhoods, jobs, stores, restaurants, and parks were segregated. When new social forms, such as movie theaters, sports stadiums, and interstate buses, appeared in the South, they, too, were quickly segregated.

The Statue of Liberty opened in 1886. Because it is elevated, many visitors are unaware of the broken chain next to her foot, a symbol in support of abolition.

The logic of segregation created a vicious cycle (see Figure 3.4). The more African Americans were excluded from the mainstream of society, the greater their objective poverty and powerlessness became. The more inferior their status and the greater their powerlessness, the easier it was to mandate more inequality. High levels of inequality reinforced racial prejudice and made it easy to use racism to justify further separation. The system kept turning on itself, finding new social niches to segregate and reinforcing the inequality that was its starting point. For example, at the height of the Jim Crow era, the system had evolved to the point that some courtrooms maintained separate Bibles for African American witnesses to swear on (Woodward, 1974, p. 118). Some additional examples of Jim Crow laws are listed in the chapter opening.

What were the causes of this massive separation of the races? Once again, the concepts of the Noel hypothesis prove useful. Because strong antiblack prejudice was already in existence when segregation began, we do not need to account for ethnocentrism. The post-Reconstruction competition between the racial groups was reminiscent of the origins of slavery, in that black Southerners had something that white Southerners wanted: labor. In addition, a free black electorate threatened the political and economic dominance of the elite segments of the white community. Finally, after the withdrawal of federal troops and the end of Reconstruction, white Southerners had sufficient power resources to end the competition on their own terms and construct repressive systems of control for black Southerners.

THE ORIGINS OF DE JURE SEGREGATION

Although the South lost the Civil War, its basic class structure and agrarian economy stayed intact. The plantation elite remained dominant, and they were able to use their power to build a system of racial stratification to replace slavery.

De jure segregation is racial segregation that is institutionalized in local and state law.

The **Jim Crow system** was the system of rigid competitive race relations in the American South that lasted from the 1880s until the 1960s.

Control of Black Labor. The plantation elite kept ownership of huge tracts of land, and cotton remained the primary cash crop in the South. The landowners needed a workforce, yet it was hard to imagine doing it without massive amounts of forced labor (Blackmon, 2009). Because of the economic disruption and physical destruction caused by the Civil War, the plantation elite were short on cash and liquid capital. Moreover, they were "not just financially but intellectually bereft" because slaves had the experience and knew the ins and outs of cotton production; but with emancipation, those resources were gone (Blackmon, 2009, p. 26).

Almost as soon as the war ended, southern legislatures attempted to force African Americans back into involuntary servitude by passing a series of laws known as the "Black Codes." For example, most southern states made it illegal for blacks to engage in what they called "vagrancy." These laws stemmed from the same stereotypes that President Johnson and others invoked about blacks being shiftless and prone to dependency as reason to close the Freedman's Bureau. In general, any blacks "not [working] under the protection of a white man" could be arrested (Blackmon, 2009, p. 53). In Florida, this included able-bodied blacks seen "wandering or strolling about or leading an idle, profligate, or immoral course of life." Penalties for breaking these laws included a fine "not exceeding $500 dollars," imprisonment for up to a year, or being sold to the highest bidder for as much as twelve months" (Dyke & Sparhawk, 1865, p. 29).

The Black Codes provided the foundation for "neo-slavery" (Blackmon, 2009) and the "new Jim Crow" (Alexander, 2012) because they allowed states to arrest blacks and, then, rent them out in the form of "convict labor." (This threat of arrest and imprisonment compelled many black sharecroppers to sign oppressive contracts with plantation owners.) This practice was (and is) legal under the Constitution's Thirteenth Amendment, ratified on December 6, 1865, which states that "Neither slavery nor involuntary servitude, *except as a punishment for crime whereof the party shall have been duly convicted*, shall exist within the United States, or any place subject to their jurisdiction" ("13th Amendment," 1865).

The plantation elite solved their labor problem by developing a system of **sharecropping** in which former slaves would work the land in return for "shares" of profit once the crop was sold. Millions of former slaves needed jobs and now were seemingly in competition with poor white day laborers for work (Blackmon, 2009). With

---

Under the **sharecropping** system of farming, the sharecropper (often black) worked the land and split the profits with the landowner.

This iconic image of imprisoned Black men picking cotton in Texas in 1968 harkens back to slave labor and sharecropping.

few options, approximately 75% to 80% of former slaves pursued this line of work (Boyer, Clark, Hawley, Kett, & Rieser, 2008, p. 369). The agreements between both parties varied, but in general, landowners would supply a place to live, food, and clothing on credit. After the harvest, tenant and landowner would split the profits (sometimes very unequally). Then, tenant's debts for land, tool use, irrigation, and other expenses would be deducted from their share. Landowners kept the accounts, and they could cheat and take advantage of tenants with great impunity. With few or no political and civil rights, black sharecroppers found it difficult to keep unscrupulous white landowners honest. Landowners could inflate the indebtedness of sharecroppers and claim that they were still owed money even after profits had been split.

Plantation owners usually required contracts that many former slaves would not have been able to read. Some wanted these to be "lifetime contracts" and refusing to sign could bring devastating consequences for blacks (Blackmon, 2009, p. 27). Annual contracts were more common. To earn pay, workers would have to stay the season. This stipulation may seem reasonable. However, contracts often imposed significant limits on blacks' newfound freedom and mirrored the oppressive conditions of slavery. For example, they could not leave the owner's property without written permission and they had to obey all the supervisor's commands. They were expected to follow social norms of humility and "servile manner" and when rules were broken, whites could impose any punishments they desired, including whipping (Blackmon, 2009, p. 27). Under this system, sharecroppers had few opportunities to improve their situations and could be bound to the land for years until their "debts" were paid off (Geschwender, 1978, p. 163).

By 1910, more than half of all employed African Americans worked in agriculture, and more than half of the remainder (25% of the total) worked in domestic occupations, such as maid or janitor (Geschwender, 1978, p. 169).

The labor shortage in southern agriculture was solved, and the African American community once again found itself in a subservient status. At the same time, the white southern working class was protected from direct job competition with African Americans. As the South began to industrialize, white workers were able to exclude black workers and reserve the better-paying jobs using a combination of whites-only labor unions and strong antiblack laws and customs. White workers took advantage of the new jobs industrialization created, while black Southerners remained a rural peasantry, excluded from participation in the modernizing job structure.

In some sectors of the changing southern economy, the status of African Americans actually fell lower than it had been during slavery. For example, in 1865, 83% of the artisans, or skilled craftsmen, in the South were African Americans; by 1900, this percentage had fallen to 5% (Geschwender, 1978, p. 170). The Jim Crow system confined African Americans to the agrarian and domestic sectors of the labor force, denied them the opportunity for a decent education, and excluded them from politics. The system was reinforced by still more laws and customs that drastically limited the options and life opportunities available to black Southerners.

Political and Civil Rights Under Jim Crow. A final force behind the creation of de jure segregation was political. As the 19th century drew to a close, a wave of agrarian radicalism known as populism spread across the country. This anti-elitist movement was a reaction to changes in agriculture caused by industrialization. The movement attempted to unite poor whites and blacks in the rural South against the traditional elite classes.

The economic elite were frightened by the possibility of a loss of power and split the incipient coalition between whites and blacks by fanning the flames of racial hatred. The strategy of "divide and conquer" proved to be effective (as it often has both before and since this time), and the white elite classes in states throughout the South eliminated the possibility of future threats by depriving African Americans of the right to vote (Woodward, 1974).

The disenfranchisement of the black community was accomplished by measures such as literacy tests, poll taxes, and property requirements. The literacy tests were officially justified as promoting a better-informed electorate but were shamelessly rigged to favor white voters. The requirement that voters pay a tax or prove ownership of a certain amount of property could also disenfranchise poor whites, but again, the implementation of these policies was racially biased (Constitutional Rights Foundation, n.d.).

The policies were extremely effective, and by the early 20th century, the political power of the southern black community was virtually nonexistent. For example, as late as 1896 in Louisiana there had been more than 100,000 registered African American voters, and they were a majority in 26 parishes (counties). In 1898, the state adopted a new constitution with stiff educational and property requirements for voting—unless the voter's father or grandfather had been eligible to vote as of January 1, 1867. At that time, the Fourteenth and Fifteenth Amendments, which guaranteed suffrage for black men, had not yet been passed. Such "grandfather clauses" made it easy for white men to register while disenfranchising blacks. By 1900, just four years later, only about 5,000 African Americans were registered to vote in Louisiana, and African American voters were not a majority in any parish. A similar decline occurred in Alabama where an electorate of more than 180,000 African American men decreased to 3,000 by provision of a new state constitution. This story repeated itself throughout the South, and African American political powerlessness was a reality by 1905 (Franklin & Moss, 1994, p. 261; Lawson, 2009, p. 14). Black representation at the federal (and state) level took a hit as well. George H. White of North Carolina left his position in government in 1901. He was the last black congressman from the South until the 1970s (Lawson, 2009, p. 14).

This system of legally mandated racial privilege was approved by the U.S. Supreme Court, which ruled in the case of *Plessy v. Ferguson* (1896) that it was constitutional for states to require separate facilities (schools, parks, etc.) for African Americans as long as the separate facilities were fully equal. The southern states paid close attention to "separate" but ignored "equal."

Reinforcing the System. Under de jure segregation, as under slavery, the subordination of the African American community was reinforced and supplemented by an elaborate system of racial etiquette. Everyday interactions between blacks and whites involved highly

The Jim Crow system of segregation encompassed water fountains and restrooms.

Jim Crow Segregation and South African Apartheid

Apartheid legislation impacted all areas of life.

Systems of legalized, state-sponsored racial segregation like Jim Crow can be found in many nations, and one the most infamous of these systems was South African apartheid. We will discuss more about apartheid in Chapter 13, but here we will note some of its many similarities to Jim Crow segregation.

First, and most important, both apartheid and American de jure segregation were deliberately constructed by the dominant group (whites) to control and exploit the minority group (blacks) and to keep them powerless. In both systems, segregation was comprehensive and encompassed virtually every area of life, including neighborhoods, schools, movie theaters, parks, public buildings, buses, and water fountains.

In both systems, whites benefited from a cheap, powerless labor supply in agriculture and in business. Domestically, even white families of modest means could afford servants, gardeners, and nannies.

Blacks in both systems were politically disenfranchised and closely controlled by police and other agencies of the state. For example, blacks were controlled in where they could live, who they could marry, and so on. Their low status was reinforced by violence and force, sometimes administered by the police, sometimes by extralegal vigilante and terrorist groups.

Elaborate rituals and customs governed interaction between the races: All were intended to overtly display and reinforce the power differential between the groups. Under both apartheid and Jim Crow segregation, blacks generally lived in abject poverty, with incomes a tiny fraction of those of the white community.

In both cases, protest movements formed in the black community and helped end the systems of racial segregation. The protests were met with extreme violence and repression from the state, and the ensuing struggles created heroes such as Martin Luther King Jr. and Nelson Mandela, among others. Also, in both cases, state-sponsored racial oppression ended only after prolonged, intense conflict. Apartheid was dismantled in the early 1990s.

Of course, there were differences between the two systems, and we will explore these in Chapter 13. For now, we can note that apartheid was more repressive than Jim Crow segregation and more viciously defended by the white dominant group. Why? Part of the reason is simple arithmetic. Whites in South Africa were a numerical minority (no more than 10% of the total population) and felt that their privileged status was under extreme threat from the black majority. White South Africans had a "fortress mentality" and feared that they would be swamped by the black majority if they allowed even the slightest lapse in the defense of their racial privilege.

Today, South Africa continues to deal with the legacies of racial segregation, as does the United States. In both nations, racial divisions run deep, and neither has been able to completely resolve its myriad issues of fairness, justice, and equality. We will return to these concerns in Chapter 13.

Questions to Consider

1. Why did whites in South Africa and the American South respond so violently to black protest movements? What was at stake, as they saw it?
2. What other differences, besides the numerical one, can you identify between the two situations? For example, is it important that one system was regional and the other national? What are the implications of this difference?

stylized and rigidly followed codes of conduct intended to underscore African Americans' inferior status within the stratification system. Whites were addressed as "mister" or "ma'am," whereas African Americans were called by their first names or, perhaps, by an honorific title such as "aunt," "uncle," or "professor." Whites expected blacks to assume a humble and deferential manner, for example, by removing their hats, looking downward, and enacting the role of the subordinate in all interactions with whites. If an African American had reason to call on anyone in the white community, he or she was expected to go to the back door.

These expectations and "good manners" for black Southerners were systematically enforced. Anyone who ignored them ran the risk of reprisal, physical attacks, and even death by lynching. Between 1877 and 1950, 4,084 blacks (primarily men) were lynched (Equal Justice Initiative, n.d.). They averaged almost one every other day (Equal Justice Initiative, n.d.; Franklin & Moss, 1994, p. 312). The bulk of this violent terrorism was racial and

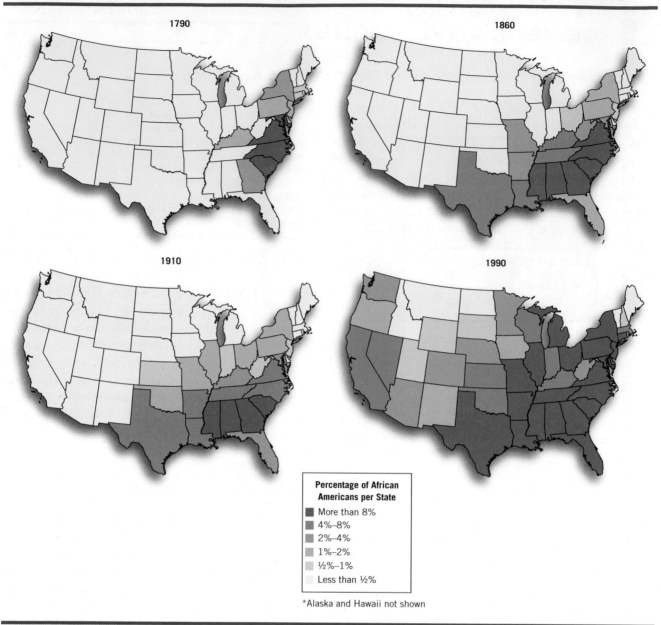

1790

1860

1910

1990

Percentage of African Americans per State

- More than 8%
- 4%–8%
- 2%–4%
- 1%–2%
- ½%–1%
- Less than ½%

*Alaska and Hawaii not shown

SOURCE: Bureau of the census, U.S. Department of Commerce.

intended to reinforce the system of racial advantage more than to punish real or imagined transgressors. Also, various secret organizations, such as the Ku Klux Klan, engaged in terrorist attacks against the African American community and anyone else who failed to conform to the dictates of the white supremacist system (Equal Justice Initiative, n.d.).

Increases in Prejudice and Racism. As the system of racial advantage formed and solidified, levels of prejudice and racism increased (Wilson, 1973, p. 101). The new system needed justification and rationalization, just as slavery did, and antiblack sentiment, stereotypes, and ideologies of racial inferiority grew stronger. At the start of the 20th century, the United States in general—not just the South—was a very racist and intolerant society. This spirit of rejection

and scorn for all out-groups coalesced with the need for justification of the Jim Crow system and created an especially negative brand of racism in the South.

QUESTIONS FOR REFLECTION

1. How does the concept of subsistence technology clarify the shift from a paternalistic to a rigid competitive system of race relations?

2. How do the concepts of competition and differential in power in the Noel hypothesis apply to the creation of the Jim Crow system of segregation?

3. From a sociological point of view, what were the most important features of de jure segregation?

THE GREAT MIGRATION (1916–1970)

Although African Americans lacked the power resources to withstand the resurrection of southern racism and oppression, they did have one option that had not been available under slavery: freedom of movement. African Americans were no longer legally tied to a specific master or to a certain plot of land. In the early 20th century, a massive population movement, often called the Great Migration, began out of the South. Slowly at first, African Americans began to move to other regions of the nation and from the countryside to the city. The Great Migration—like the European immigration discussed in Chapter 2—happened in waves. By the end of 1919, approximately one million blacks had moved away from the South and by 1978, almost 6,000,000 had left. The movement increased when hard times hit southern agriculture and slowed down during better times. In discussing the Great Migration, it has been said that African Americans voted against southern segregation with their feet.

As Figure 5.1 shows, the black population was highly concentrated in the South as recently as 1910, a little more than a century ago. By 1990, African Americans had become much more evenly distributed across the nation, spreading to the Northeast and the upper Midwest. Since 1990, the distribution of the black population has remained roughly the same, although there has been some movement back to the South.

Figure 5.2 shows that, in addition to movement away from the South, the Great Migration was also a movement from the countryside to the city. A century ago, blacks were overwhelmingly rural, but today more than 90% are urban.

Thus, an urban black population living outside of the South is a 20th-century phenomenon. The significance of this population redistribution is manifold. Most important, perhaps, was the fact that by moving out of the South and into urban areas, African Americans moved from areas of great resistance to racial change to areas of lower resistance. In the northern cities, for example, it was far easier to register and vote. Black political power began to grow and eventually provided many of the crucial resources that fueled the Civil Rights Movement of the 1950s and 1960s.

LIFE IN THE NORTH

What did African American migrants find when they got to the industrializing cities of the North? There is no doubt that life in the North was better for the vast majority of them. The growing northern African American communities relished the absence of Jim Crow laws and oppressive racial etiquette, the relative freedom to pursue jobs, and the greater opportunities to educate their children. Inevitably, however, life in the North fell far short of utopia. Many

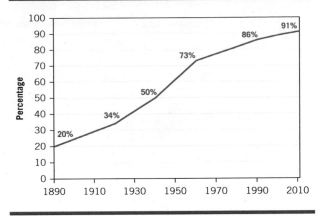

FIGURE 5.2 Percentage of African Americans Living in Urban Areas, 1890–2010

SOURCE: 1890 to 1960; Geschwender (1978); 1980 & 1990: Pollard and O'Hare (1999); 2000: U.S. Census Bureau (2000b); 2010: U.S. Census Bureau (2013f).

aspects of African American culture—literature, poetry, music—flourished in the heady new atmosphere of freedom, but on other fronts, northern African American communities faced massive discrimination in housing, schools, and the job market. Along with freedom and such cultural flowerings as the Harlem Renaissance came black ghettos and new forms of oppression and exploitation. In Chapter 6, we will explore these events and the workings of what has been called de facto segregation.

COMPETITION WITH WHITE ETHNIC GROUPS

It is useful to see the movement of African Americans out of the South in terms of their resultant relationships with other groups. Southern blacks began to move to the North at about the same time as the New Immigration from Europe (see Chapter 2) began to end. By the time substantial numbers of black Southerners began arriving in the North, European immigrants and their descendants had had years, decades, and even generations to establish themselves in the job markets, political systems, labor unions, and neighborhoods of the North. Many of the European ethnic groups had also been the victims of discrimination and rejection. And, as we discussed in Chapter 2, their hold on economic security and status was tenuous for much of the 20th century. Frequently, they saw the newly arriving black migrants as a threat to their status, a perception that was reinforced by the fact that industrialists and factory owners often used African Americans as strikebreakers and scabs during strikes. The white ethnic groups responded by developing defensive strategies to limit the dangers presented by these migrants from the South. They tried to exclude African Americans from their labor unions and other associations and limit their impact on the political system. Often they successfully attempted to maintain segregated

NARRATIVE PORTRAIT

The Kitchenette

Library of Congress Prints and Photographs Division

Richard Wright, one of the most powerful writers of the twentieth century.

Richard Wright (1908–1960), one of the most powerful writers of the 20th century, lived through and wrote about many of the social changes discussed in this chapter. He grew up in the South during the height of the Jim Crow system, and his passionate hatred for segregation and bigotry is expressed in his major works, Native Son *(1940) and the autobiographical* Black Boy *(1945). In 1941, Wright helped produce* 12 Million Black Voices, *a folk history of African Americans. A combination of photos and brief essays, the work is a powerful commentary on three centuries of oppression.*

The following selection is adapted from "Death on the City Pavements," which expresses Wright's view of the African American migration out of the South, a journey he himself experienced. This bittersweet migration often traded the harsh, rural repression of the South for the overcrowded, anonymous ghettos of the North. Housing discrimination, both overt and covert, confined African American migrants to the least desirable, most overcrowded areas of the city—in many cases, the neighborhoods that had first housed immigrants from Europe. Unscrupulous landlords subdivided buildings into the tiniest possible apartments ("kitchenettes"), and as impoverished newcomers who could afford no better, African American migrants were forced to cope with overpriced, substandard housing as best they could. Much of this passage, incidentally, could have been written about any 20th-century minority group.

DEATH ON THE CITY PAVEMENTS[1]

Richard Wright

And the Bosses of the Buildings take these old houses and convert them into "kitchenettes," and then rent them to us at rates so high that they make fabulous fortunes. . . . Because we have been used to sleeping several in a room on the plantations in the South, we rent these kitchenettes and are glad to get them. . . .

A war sets up in our emotions: One part of our feelings tells us it is good to be in the city, that we have a chance at life here, that we need but turn a corner to become a stranger, that we need no longer bow and dodge at the sight of the Lords of the Land. Another part of our feelings tells us that, in terms of worry and strain, the cost of living in the kitchenettes is too high, that the city heaps too much responsibility on us and gives too little security in return.

The kitchenette is the author of the glad tidings that new suckers are in town, ready to be cheated, plundered, and put in their places.

The kitchenette is our prison, our death sentence without a trial,

_____
[1]From *Twelve Million Black Voices* by Richard Wright. Copyright 1941 by Richard Wright. Published by Thunder's Mouth Press, an imprint of Avalon Publishing Group Incorporated.

the new form of mob violence that assaults . . . all of us, in its ceaseless attacks.

The kitchenette, with its filth and foul air, with its one toilet for thirty or more tenants, kills our black babies so fast that in many cities twice as many of them die as white babies. . . .

The kitchenette scatters death so widely among us that our death rate exceeds our birth rate, and if it were not for the trains and autos bringing us daily into the city from the plantations, we black folk who dwell in northern cities would die out entirely over the course of a few years. . . .

The kitchenette throws desperate and unhappy people into an unbearable closeness of association, thereby increasing latent friction, giving birth to never-ending quarrels of recrimination, accusation, and vindictiveness, producing warped personalities.

The kitchenette injects pressure and tension into our individual personalities, making many of us give up the struggle, walk off and leave wives, husbands, and even children behind to shift as best they can. . . .

The kitchenette reaches out with fingers of golden bribes to the officials of the city, persuading them to allow old firetraps to remain standing and occupied long after they should have been torn down.

The kitchenette is the funnel through which our pulverized lives flow to ruin and death on the city pavement, at a profit.

SOURCE: Wright (1941/1988, pp. 104–111).

Questions to Consider

1. Given the grim realities described in this passage, why do you think African Americans continued to move out of the South?

2. What concepts can you apply to this passage? How does it illustrate the dynamics of this period of history?

neighborhoods and schools (although the legal system outside the South did not sanction overt de jure segregation).

This competition led to hostile relations between black southern migrants and white ethnic groups, especially the lower- and working-class segments of those groups. Ironically, however, in another chapter of the ethnic succession discussed in Chapter 2, the newly arriving African Americans actually helped white ethnic groups become upwardly mobile. Dominant-group whites became less contemptuous of white ethnic groups as their alarm over the presence of African Americans increased. The greater antipathy of the white community toward African Americans made the immigrants more desirable and, thus, hastened their admission into the institutions of the larger society. For many white ethnic groups, the increased tolerance of the larger society coincided happily with the coming of age of the more educated and skilled descendants of the original immigrants, further abetting the rise of these groups in the U.S. social class structure (Lieberson, 1980).

For more than a century, each new European immigrant group had helped to push previous groups up the ladder of socioeconomic success and out of the old, ghettoized neighborhoods. Black Southerners got to the cities after immigration from Europe had been curtailed, and no newly arrived immigrants appeared to continue the pattern of succession for northern African Americans. Instead, American cities developed concentrations of low-income blacks that were economically vulnerable and politically weak and whose position was further solidified by antiblack prejudice and discrimination (Wilson, 1987, p. 34).

THE ORIGINS OF BLACK PROTEST

As we pointed out in Chapter 4, African Americans have always resisted their oppression and protested their situation. Under slavery, however, the inequalities they faced were so great and their resources so meager that their protest was ineffective. With the increased freedom following the abolition of slavery, a national African American leadership developed and spoke out against oppression and founded organizations that eventually helped lead the fight for freedom and equality. Even at its birth, the black protest movement was diverse and incorporated a variety of viewpoints and leaders.

Booker T. Washington was the most prominent African American leader prior to World War I. Washington had been born in slavery and was the founder and president of Tuskegee Institute, a college in Alabama dedicated to educating African Americans. His public advice to African Americans in the South was to be patient, to accommodate to the Jim Crow system for the time being, to raise their levels of education and job skills, and to take full advantage of whatever opportunities became available. This nonconfrontational stance earned Washington praise and support from the white community and widespread popularity in the nation. Privately, he worked behind the scenes to end discrimination and implement full racial integration and equality (Franklin & Moss, 1994, pp. 272–274; Hawkins, 1962; Washington, 1965).

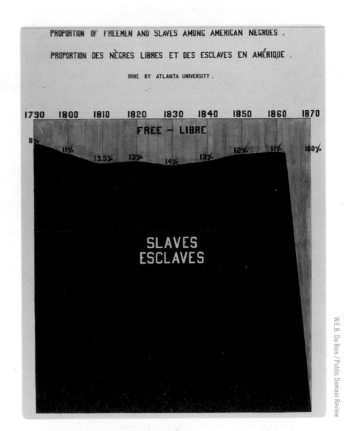

A drawing by sociologist W.E.B. Du Bois based on his research.

Washington's most vocal opponent was W. E. B. Du Bois, an activist and intellectual trained in sociology—in fact, many argue he is the "father" of American sociology (see Morris, 2015). Du Bois was born in the North and educated at some of the leading universities of the day. Among his many other accomplishments, Du Bois was part of a coalition of blacks and white liberals who founded the National Association for the Advancement of Colored People (NAACP) in 1909. Du Bois rejected Washington's accommodationist stance and advocated immediate pursuit of racial equality and a direct assault on de jure segregation (Morris, 2015). Almost from the beginning of its existence, the NAACP filed lawsuits that challenged the legal foundations of Jim Crow segregation (Du Bois, 1961). As we shall see in Chapter 6, this legal strategy was eventually successful and led to the demise of the Jim Crow system.

Washington and Du Bois may have differed on matters of strategy and tactics, but they agreed that the only acceptable goal for African Americans was an integrated, racially equal United States. A third leader emerged early in the 20th century and called for a very different approach to the problems of U.S. race relations. Marcus Garvey was born in Jamaica and immigrated to the United States during World War I. He argued that the white dominated U.S. society was hopelessly racist and would never truly support integration and racial equality. He advocated

Three early leaders of African American protest: Booker T. Washington, W.E.B. Du Bois, and Marcus Garvey.

separatist goals, including a return to Africa. Garvey founded the Universal Negro Improvement Association in 1914 in his native Jamaica and founded the first U.S. branch in 1916. Garvey's organization was very popular for a time in African American communities outside the South, and he helped to establish some of the themes and ideas of black nationalism and pride in African heritage that would become prominent again in the pluralistic 1960s (Essien-Udom, 1962; Garvey, 1969, 1977; Vincent, 1976).

These early leaders and organizations established some of the foundations for later protest movements, but prior to the mid-20th century they made few actual improvements in the situation of African Americans in the North or South. Jim Crow was a formidable opponent, and the African American community lacked the resources to successfully challenge the status quo until the century was well along and some basic structural features of American society had changed.

THE DIMENSIONS OF MINORITY-GROUP STATUS

ACCULTURATION AND INTEGRATION

During this era of southern segregation and migration to the North, assimilation was not a major factor in the African American experience. Rather, the black–white relations of the time are better described as a system of structural pluralism combined with great inequality. Excluded from the mainstream but freed from the

limitations of slavery, African Americans constructed a separate subsociety and subculture. In all regions of the nation, African Americans developed their own institutions and organizations, including separate neighborhoods, churches, businesses, and schools. Like immigrants from Europe in the same era, they organized their communities to cater to their own needs and problems and pursue their agenda as a group.

During segregation, a small African American middle class emerged based on leadership roles in the church, education, and business. A network of black colleges and universities was constructed to educate the children of the growing middle class, as well as other classes. Through this infrastructure, African Americans began to develop the resources and leadership that in the decades ahead would attack, head-on, the structures of racial inequality.

GENDER AND RACE

For African American men and women, the changes wrought by industrialization and the population movement to the North created new possibilities and new roles. However, as African Americans continued to be the victims of exploitation and exclusion in both the North and the South, African American women continued to be among the most vulnerable groups in society.

Following emancipation, there was a flurry of marriages and weddings among African Americans, as they were finally able to legitimate their family relationships (Staples, 1988, p. 306). African American women continued to have primary responsibility for home and children. Historian Herbert Gutman (1976) reports that it was common for married women to drop out of the labor force and attend solely to household and family duties, because a working wife was too reminiscent of a slave role. This pattern became so widespread that it created serious labor shortages in many areas (Gutman, 1976; see also Staples, 1988, p. 307).

Former slaves were hardly affluent, however, and as sharecropping and segregation began to shape race relations in the South, women often had to return to the fields or to domestic work for the family to survive. One former slave woman noted that women "do double duty, a man's share in the field and a woman's part at home" (Evans, 1989, p. 121). During the bleak decades following the end of Reconstruction, southern black families and black women in particular lived "close to the bone" (p. 121).

In the cities and in the growing African American neighborhoods in the North, African American women played a role that in some ways paralleled the role of immigrant women from Europe. The men often moved north first and sent for the women after they had attained some level of financial stability or after the pain of separation became too great (Almquist, 1979, p. 434). In other cases, African American women by the thousands left the South to work as domestic servants; they often replaced European immigrant women, who had moved up in the job structure (Amott & Matthaei, 1991, p. 168).

In the North, discrimination and racism created constant problems of unemployment for the men, and families often relied on the income supplied by the women to make ends meet. It was comparatively easy for women to find employment, but only in the low-paying, less desirable areas, such as domestic work. In both the South and the North, African American women worked outside the home in larger proportions than did white women. For example, in 1900, 41% of African American women were employed, compared with only 16% of white women (Staples, 1988, p. 307).

In 1890, more than a generation after the end of slavery, 85% of all African American men and 96% of African American women were employed in just two occupational categories: agriculture and domestic or personal service. By 1930, 90% of employed African American women were still in these same two categories, whereas the corresponding percentage for employed African American men had dropped to 54% (although nearly all the remaining 46% were unskilled workers; Steinberg, 1981, pp. 206–207). Since the inception of segregation, African American women have had consistently higher unemployment rates and lower incomes than African American men and white women (Almquist, 1979, p. 437). These gaps, as we shall see in Chapter 6, persist to the present day.

During the years following emancipation, some issues divided men and women, within both the African American

African American women were often forced to work in the fields to help make ends meet.

community and the larger society. Prominent among these was suffrage, or the right to vote, which was still limited to men only. The abolitionist movement, which had been so instrumental in ending slavery, also supported universal suffrage. Efforts to enfranchise women, though, were abandoned by the Republican Party and large parts of the abolitionist movement to concentrate on efforts to secure the vote for African American men in the South. Ratification of the Fifteenth Amendment in 1870 extended the vote, in principle, to African American men, but the Nineteenth Amendment enfranchising women would not be passed for another 50 years (Almquist, 1979, pp. 433–434; Evans, 1989, pp. 121–124).

QUESTIONS FOR REFLECTION

4. Why did African Americans begin to migrate to the North in the early 20th century? Did this move improve their situation? Explain.

5. What African American strategies for protest were developed early in the 20th century? How were these strategies shaped by the overall situation of the group?

6. Did African Americans become more or less acculturated and integrated during the Jim Crow era? Explain.

7. How was the experience of African Americans shaped by gender during this time period?

INDUSTRIALIZATION, THE SHIFT TO POSTINDUSTRIAL SOCIETY, AND DOMINANT–MINORITY GROUP RELATIONS: GENERAL TRENDS

The processes of industrialization that began in the 19th century continued to shape the larger society and dominant–minority relations throughout the 20th century. Today, the United States bears little resemblance to the society it was a century ago. The population has more than tripled in size and has urbanized even more rapidly than it has grown. New organizational forms (bureaucracies, corporations, multinational businesses) and new technologies (computers, the Internet, cell phones) dominate everyday life. Levels of education have risen, and the public schools have produced one of the most literate populations and best-trained workforces in the history of the world.

Minority groups grew in size during this period, and most became even more urbanized than the general population. Minority group members have come to participate in an increasing array of occupations, and their average levels of education have risen, too.

Despite these real improvements, however, virtually all U.S. minority groups continue to face racism, poverty, discrimination, and exclusion. As industrialization proceeded, the mechanisms for maintaining racial stratification also evolved, morphing into forms that are subtle and indirect, but, in their way, as formidable as Jim Crow segregation.

In this section, we outline the social processes that began in the industrial era and continue to shape the postindustrial stage. We note the ways these processes have changed American society and examine some of the general implications for minority groups. We then summarize these changes in terms of a transition from the rigid competitive Jim Crow era to a new stage of group relations called *fluid competitive* relations. The treatment here is broad and intended to establish a general framework for the examination of the impacts of industrialization and deindustrialization on group relations in the case studies that make up Part 3 of this text.

URBANIZATION

We have already noted that urbanization made close, paternalistic controls of minority groups irrelevant. For example, the racial etiquette required by southern de jure segregation, such as African Americans deferring to whites on crowded sidewalks, tended to disappear in the chaos of an urban rush hour.

Besides weakening dominant group controls, urbanization also created the potential for minority groups to mobilize and organize large numbers of people. As stated in Chapter 1, the sheer size of a group is a source of power. Without the freedom to organize, however, size means little, and urbanization increased both the concentration of populations and the freedom to organize.

OCCUPATIONAL SPECIALIZATION

One of the first and most important results of industrialization, even in its earliest days, was an increase in occupational specialization and the variety of jobs available in the workforce. The growing needs of an urbanizing population increased the number of jobs available in the production, transport, and sale of goods and services. Occupational specialization was also stimulated by the very nature of industrial production. Complex manufacturing processes could be performed more efficiently if they were broken down into the narrower component tasks. It was easier and more efficient to train the workforce in the simpler, specialized jobs. Assembly lines were invented, work was subdivided, the division of labor became increasingly complex, and the number of different occupations continued to grow.

The sheer complexity of the industrial job structure made it difficult to maintain rigid, caste-like divisions of labor between dominant and minority groups. Rigid competitive forms of group relations, such as Jim Crow segregation, became less viable as the job market became more diversified and changeable. Simple, clear rules about which groups could do which jobs disappeared.

As the more repressive systems of control weakened, job opportunities for minority group members sometimes increased. However, conflict between groups also increased as the relationships between group memberships and positions in the job market became more blurred. For example, as we have noted, African Americans moving from the South often found themselves in competition for jobs with members of white ethnic groups, labor unions, and other elements of the dominant group.

BUREAUCRACY AND RATIONALITY

As industrialization continued, privately owned corporations and businesses came to have workforces numbering in the hundreds of thousands. Gigantic factories employing thousands of workers became common. To coordinate the efforts of these huge workforces, bureaucracy became the dominant form of organization in the economy and, indeed, throughout the society.

Bureaucracies are large-scale, impersonal, formal organizations that run "by the book." They are governed by rules and regulations (i.e., "red tape") and are "rational" in that they attempt to find the most efficient ways to accomplish their tasks. Although they typically fail to attain the ideal of fully rational efficiency, bureaucracies tend to recruit, reward, and promote employees on the basis of competence and performance (Gerth & Mills, 1946).

The stress on rationality and objectivity can counteract the more blatant forms of racism and increase the array of opportunities available to members of minority groups. Although they are often nullified by other forces (see Blumer, 1965), these antiprejudicial tendencies do not exist at all or are much weaker in preindustrial economies.

The history of the concept of race illustrates the impact of rationality and scientific ways of thinking. Today, virtually the entire scientific community rejects the traditional idea that race is an important determinant of intelligence or personality traits such as dependability or competence. These conclusions are based on decades of research. These scientific findings undermined and contributed to the destruction of the formal systems of privilege based solely on race (e.g., segregated school systems) and traditional prejudice, which is based on the assumption that race is a crucial personal characteristic.

GROWTH OF WHITE-COLLAR JOBS AND THE SERVICE SECTOR

Industrialization changed the composition of the labor force. As work became more complex and specialized, the need to coordinate and regulate the production process increased, and as a result bureaucracies and other organizations grew larger still. Within these organizations, white-collar occupations—those that coordinate, manage, and deal with the flow of paperwork—continued to expand throughout much of the century. As industrialization progressed, mechanization and automation reduced the number of manual or blue-collar workers, and white-collar occupations became the dominant sector of the job market in the United States.

The changing nature of the workforce can be illustrated by looking at the proportional representation of three different types of jobs:

1. **Extractive (or primary) occupations** are those that produce raw materials, such as food and agricultural products, minerals, and timber. The jobs in this sector often involve unskilled manual labor, require little formal education, and are generally low paying.

2. **Manufacturing (or secondary) occupations** transform raw materials into finished products ready for sale in the marketplace. Like jobs in the extractive sector, these blue-collar jobs involve manual labor, but they tend to require higher levels of skill and are more highly rewarded. Examples of occupations in this sector include the assembly line jobs that transform steel, rubber, plastic, and other materials into finished automobiles.

3. **Service (or tertiary) occupations** do not produce "things"; rather, they provide services. As urbanization increased and self-sufficiency decreased, opportunities for work in this sector grew. Examples of tertiary occupations include police officer, clerk, waiter, teacher, nurse, doctor, and cabdriver.

The course of industrialization is traced in the changing structure of the labor market depicted in Figure 5.3. In 1850, when industrialization was just beginning in the United States, most of the workforce (almost 70%) was in the extractive sector, with agriculture being the dominant occupation. As industrialization progressed, the manufacturing, or secondary, sector grew, reaching a peak around World War II. Today, in the postindustrial era, the large majority of U.S. jobs are in the service, or tertiary, sector.

As noted earlier in the chapter, this shift away from blue-collar jobs and manufacturing since the 1960s is sometimes referred to as deindustrialization, or the shift to a postindustrial subsistence technology. The U.S. economy has lost millions of unionized, high-paying factory jobs since the 1960s, and the downward trend continues. The industrial jobs that sustained so many generations of American workers have moved to other nations where wages are considerably lower than in the United States. Additionally, jobs have been eliminated by robots or other automated manufacturing processes (see Rifkin, 1996).

The changing structure of the job market helps clarify the nature of intergroup competition and the sources of wealth and power in society. Job growth in the United States today is largely in the service sector, and these occupations are highly variable. At one end are low-paying jobs with few, if any, benefits or chances for advancement (e.g., washing dishes in a restaurant). At the other end are

Extractive (or primary) occupations are those that produce raw materials such as food, minerals, or timber.

Manufacturing (or secondary) occupations are those that transform raw materials into finished products ready for the marketplace.

Service (or tertiary) occupations provide services.

FIGURE 5.3 The Changing U.S. Workforce: Distribution of Jobs From 1850 to 2010

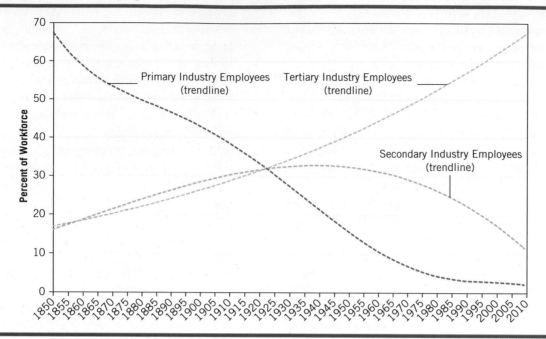

high-prestige, lucrative positions, such as Supreme Court justice, scientist, and financial analyst.

The new service-sector jobs are either highly desirable technical, professional, or administrative jobs with demanding entry requirements (e.g., physician or nurse) or low-paying, low-skilled jobs with few benefits and little security (e.g., receptionist, nurse's aide). Over the past half century, job growth in the United States has been either in areas where educationally deprived minority-group members find it difficult to compete or in areas that offer little compensation, upward mobility, or security. As we will see in Part 3, the economic situation of many contemporary minority groups reflects these fundamental trends.

THE GROWING IMPORTANCE OF EDUCATION

Education has been an increasingly important prerequisite for employability in the United States and in other advanced industrial societies. A high school or, increasingly, a college degree has become the minimum entry-level requirement for employment. However, opportunities for high-quality education are not distributed equally across the population. Some minority groups, especially those created by colonization, have been systematically excluded from the schools of the dominant society, and today they are less likely to have the educational backgrounds needed to compete for better jobs.

Access to education is a key issue for all U.S. minority groups, and the average educational levels of these groups have been rising since World War II. Still, minority children continue to be much more likely to attend segregated,

underfunded, deteriorated schools and to receive inferior educations (see Orfield & Lee, 2007).

A DUAL LABOR MARKET

The changing composition of the labor force and increasing importance of educational credentials has split the U.S. labor market into two segments or types of jobs. The **primary labor market** includes jobs usually located in large, bureaucratic organizations. These positions offer higher pay, more security, better opportunities for advancement, health and retirement benefits, and other amenities. Entry requirements include college degrees, even when people with fewer years of schooling could competently perform the work.

The **secondary labor market**, sometimes called the competitive market, includes low-paying, low-skilled, insecure jobs. Many of these jobs are in the service sector. They do not represent a career, per se, and offer little opportunity for promotion or upward mobility. Very often, they do not offer health or retirement benefits, have high rates of turnover, and are part-time, seasonal, or temporary.

Many American minority groups are concentrated in the secondary job market. Their exclusion from better jobs is perpetuated not so much by direct or overt discrimination

The **primary labor market** includes jobs that are better paying, higher status, and more secure.

The **secondary labor market** includes jobs that are lower paying, lower status, and less secure.

as by their lack of access to the educational and other credentials required to enter the primary sector. The differential distribution of educational opportunities, in the past as well as in the present, effectively protects workers in the primary sector from competition from minority groups.

GLOBALIZATION

Over the past century, the United States became an economic, political, and military world power with interests around the globe. These worldwide ties have created new minority groups through population movement and have changed the status of others. Immigration to this country has been considerable for the past three decades. The American economy is one of the most productive in the world, and jobs, even those in the low-paying secondary sector, are the primary goals for millions of newcomers. For other immigrants, this country continues to play its historic role as a refuge from political and religious persecution.

Many of the wars, conflicts, and other disputes in which the United States has been involved have had consequences for American minority groups. For example, both Puerto Ricans and Cuban Americans became U.S. minority groups as the result of processes set in motion during the Spanish–American War of 1898. Both World War I and World War II created new job opportunities for many minority groups, including African Americans and Mexican Americans. After the Korean War in the early 1950s, international ties were forged between the United States and South Korea, and this led to an increase in immigration from that nation. In the 1960s and 1970s, the military involvement of the United States in Southeast Asia led to the arrival of Vietnamese, Cambodians, Hmong, and other immigrant and refugee groups from that region. The most recent war in Iraq has also produced new communities of immigrants and refugees.

Dominant–minority relations in the United States have been increasingly played out on an international stage, as the world has effectively "shrunk" in size and become more interconnected by international organizations, such as the United Nations; by ties of trade and commerce; and by modern means of transportation and communication. In a world in which two thirds of the population is nonwhite and many important nations (such as China, India, and Nigeria) are composed of peoples of color, the treatment of racial minorities by the U.S. dominant group has come under increased scrutiny. It is difficult to preach principles of fairness, equality, and justice—which the United States claims as its own—when domestic realities suggest an embarrassing failure to fully implement these standards. Part of the incentive for the United States to end blatant systems of discrimination such as de jure segregation came from the desire to maintain a leading position in the world.

POSTINDUSTRIAL SOCIETY AND THE SHIFT FROM RIGID TO FLUID COMPETITIVE RELATIONSHIPS

The coming of postindustrial society brought changes so fundamental and profound that they are often described in terms of a revolution: from an industrial society, based on manufacturing, to a postindustrial society, based on information processing and computer-related or other new technologies. As the subsistence technology evolved, so did American dominant–minority relations. The rigid competitive systems (such as Jim Crow) associated with earlier phases of industrialization gave way to **fluid competitive systems** of group relations.

In fluid competitive relations, formal or legal barriers to competition—such as Jim Crow laws or South African apartheid—no longer exist. Both geographic and social mobility are greater in the newer system, and the limitations imposed by minority group status are less restrictive and burdensome. Rigid caste systems of stratification, in which group membership determines opportunities, adult statuses, and jobs, are replaced by more open class systems, in which the relationships between group membership and wealth, prestige, and power are weaker. Because fluid competitive systems are more open and the position of the minority group is less fixed, the fear of competition from minority groups becomes more widespread in the dominant group, and intergroup conflict increases. Table 5.2 compares the characteristics of the three systems of group relations.

Compared with previous systems, the fluid competitive system is closer to the American ideal of an open, fair system of stratification in which effort and competence are rewarded and race, ethnicity, gender, religion, and other "birthmarks" are irrelevant. However, as we will see in chapters to come, race and ethnicity continue to affect life chances and limit opportunities for minority-group members even in fluid competitive systems. As suggested by the Noel hypothesis, people continue to identify themselves with particular groups (ethnocentrism), and competition for resources continues to play out along group lines. Consistent with the Blauner hypothesis, the minority groups that were formed by colonization remain at a disadvantage in the pursuit of opportunities, education, prestige, and other resources.

In **fluid competitive systems** of group relations, minority-group members are freer to compete for jobs and other scarce resources.

TABLE 5.2 Characteristics of Three Systems of Group Relationships

| | SYSTEMS OF GROUP RELATIONS | | |
| | Paternalistic | Competitive | |
		Rigid	Fluid
Subsistence technology	**Agrarian**	**Industrial**	**Postindustrial**
Stratification	**Caste.** Group determines status.	**Mixed.** Elements of caste and class. Status largely determined by group.	**Variable.** Status strongly affected by group. Inequality varies within groups.
Division of labor	**Simple.** Determined by group.	**More complex.** Job largely determined by group, but some sharing of jobs by different groups.	**Most complex.** Group and job are less related. Complex specialization and great variation within groups.
Contact between groups	**Common**, but statuses unequal.	**Less common,** and mostly unequal.	**More common.** Highest rates of equal-status contact.
Overt intergroup conflict	**Rare**	**More common**	**Common**
Power differential	**Maximum.** Minority groups have little ability to pursue self-interests.	**Less.** Minority groups have some ability to pursue self-interests.	**Least.** Minority groups have more ability to pursue self-interests.

SOURCE: Based on Farley (2000, p. 109).

QUESTIONS FOR REFLECTION

8. Why did black–white relations shift from a rigid to a fluid competitive system? What was the role of subsistence technology in the shift?

9. What are the key changes in the shift to postindustrial subsistence technology? What are the implications of these changes for American minority groups?

MODERN INSTITUTIONAL DISCRIMINATION

In general, American minority groups continue to lag behind national averages in income, employment, and other measures of equality, despite the greater fluidity of group relations, the end of legal barriers such as Jim Crow laws, the dramatic declines in overt prejudice (see Chapter 3), and the introduction of numerous laws designed to ensure that all people are treated without regard to race, gender, or ethnicity. After all this change, shouldn't there be more equality and less racial stratification?

As we saw in Chapter 3, many Americans attribute the persisting patterns of inequality to a lack of willpower or motivation to get ahead on the part of minority-group members. In the remaining chapters of this text, however, we argue that the major barriers facing minority groups in postindustrial, post–Jim Crow America are pervasive, subtle, but still powerful forms of

discrimination that together can be called modern institutional discrimination.

As you read in Chapter 1, institutional discrimination is built into the everyday operation of the social structure of society. The routine procedures and policies of institutions and organizations are arranged so that minority-group members are automatically put at a disadvantage. In the Jim Crow era in the South, for example, African Americans were deprived of the right to vote by overt institutional discrimination and could acquire little in the way of political power.

The forms of institutional discrimination that persist in the present are more subtle and difficult to document than the blatant, overt customs and laws of the Jim Crow system. In fact, they are sometimes unintentional or unconscious and are manifested more in the results for minority groups than in the intentions or prejudices of dominant-group members. Modern institutional discrimination is not necessarily linked to prejudice, and the decision makers who implement it may sincerely think of themselves as behaving rationally and in the best interests of their organizations.

THE CONTINUING POWER OF THE PAST

Many forces conspire to maintain racial stratification in the present. Some are the legacies of past discriminatory practices. Consider, for example, **past-in-present institutional discrimination**, which involves practices in the present that have discriminatory consequences because of some pattern of discrimination or exclusion in the past (Feagin & Feagin, 1986, p. 32).

How have the trends discussed in this section affected you and your family? If the United States had not industrialized, where would your family live? What kind of career would your parents and grandparents have had? Would you have had the opportunity for a college education?

You can get some insight on the answers to these questions by researching your family history over the past several generations and completing the table below. You may not have all the information requested, but that might be a good reason to give your parents or grandparents a call! If you know nothing at all about your family history and have no way to get the information, perhaps you can find someone—a roommate or friend—to interview for this exercise.

To complete the table, pick *one* ancestor from each generation, perhaps the one about which you know the most. To get you started and provide a comparison, the table is completed for two of the authors. When you get to the bottom row of the table, fill in the blanks in terms of your desires or plans. Would you rather live in the city, suburbs, or country? What is your ideal job or the career for which you are preparing? What degree are you pursuing?

HEALEY			
Generations	**Residence**	**Education**	**Occupation**
Great-grandparent	City	Unknown, perhaps as much as six years	Coal miner, board member of labor union
Grandparent	City	High School	Miner, clerk for the city
Parent	City	High school, some college	Agent for the Internal Revenue Service
Healey	Suburbs	PhD	College professor

STEPNICK			
Generations	**Residence**	**Education**	**Occupation**
Great-grandparent	Rural	2 years	Road supervisor
Grandparent	Rural	9 years	Coal miner, machinist
Parent	City	DDS	Periodontist; captain in the Navy
Stepnick	City	PhD	College professor

YOU			
Generations	**Residence**	**Education**	**Occupation**
Great-grandparent			
Grandparent			
Parent			
You			

TURN THE PAGE TO SEE THE PATTERNS WE PREDICT.

One form of this discrimination is found in workforces organized around the principle of seniority. In these systems, which are quite common, workers who have been on the job longer have higher incomes, more privileges, and

---

Past-in-present institutional discrimination involves patterns of inequality or unequal treatment in the present that are caused by some pattern of discrimination in the past.

---

other benefits, such as longer vacations. The "old-timers" often have more job security and are designated in official, written policy as the last to be fired or laid off in the event of hard times. Workers and employers alike may think of the privileges of seniority as just rewards for long years of service, familiarity with the job, and so forth.

Personnel policies based on seniority may seem perfectly reasonable, neutral, and fair; however, they can have discriminatory results in the present because in the past members of minority groups and women were excluded from specific occupations by racist or sexist labor unions, discriminatory employers, or both. As a result, minority-group workers and women may have fewer years of experience than do dominant-group workers and men, and may be the first to go when layoffs are necessary. The adage "last hired, first fired" describes the situation of minority-group and women employees who are more vulnerable not because of some overtly racist or sexist policy but because of the routine operation of the seemingly neutral principle of seniority.

Racial differences in home ownership provide a second example of the myriad ways in which the past shapes the present and maintains the moving target of racial stratification. Today, about 72% of non-Hispanic whites own their own homes, and these houses have a median value of $179,000. In contrast, only 44% of non-Hispanic blacks are homeowners, and the median value of their homes is $125,900 (U.S. Census Bureau, 2013a). Homeownership is an important source of family wealth, because home equity can be used to establish credit, to finance businesses and other purchases and investments, and to fund education and other sources of human capital for the next generation. What is the origin of these huge differences in family wealth?

Part of the answer lies in events that date back 80 years. As you know, President Franklin D. Roosevelt's administration responded to the Great Depression of the 1930s, in part, by instituting the New Deal: a variety of programs that provided assistance to distressed Americans. What is not so widely known is that these programs were racially discriminatory and provided few or no benefits to African Americans (Massey, 2007, p. 60; see also Katznelson, 2005; Lieberman, 1998).

One of the New Deal programs was administered by the Federal Housing Administration (FHA): The agency offered low-interest mortgages and made home ownership possible for millions of families. However, the FHA sanctioned racially restrictive covenants that forbade whites to sell to blacks and helped institutionalize the practice of "redlining" black neighborhoods, which prevented banks from making home loans in these areas. Together, these and other discriminatory practices effectively excluded black Americans from homeownership (Massey, 2007, pp. 60–61; Massey & Denton, 1993, pp. 53–54). Thus, another racial divide was created that, over the generations, has helped countless white families develop wealth and credit but made it impossible for black families to qualify for homeownership, the "great engine of wealth creation" (Massey, 2007, p. 61).

More broadly, racial residential segregation—which is arguably the key factor in preserving racial stratification in the present—provides another illustration of modern institutional discrimination. The overt, Jim Crow–era laws and customs that created racially segregated neighborhoods and towns in the past were abolished decades ago, and racial discrimination in selling and renting houses has been illegal since the passage of the Fair Housing Act in 1968. However, blacks continue to be concentrated in all or mostly black neighborhoods (see, e.g., Figure 5.4), many of which are also characterized by inadequate services and high levels of poverty and crime. How is racial residential segregation maintained in an era of fair housing laws?

Some of the practices that preserve racial residential segregation have been documented by audit studies. In this technique, black and white (and sometimes Latino and Asian) individuals with carefully matched background credentials (education, employment and credit histories, and finances) are sent to test the market for racial fairness. Characteristically, the black customer is steered away from white neighborhoods, required to furnish larger down payments or deposits, charged higher interest rates, or otherwise discouraged from securing a successful sale or rental. Sometimes the black customer may be told that a unit is already sold or rented, or otherwise given false or misleading information (see Pager & Shepherd, 2008, for a review).

The result is that blacks are discouraged from breaking the housing color line but not directly, blatantly, or in ways that clearly violate the fair housing laws. The gatekeepers (e.g., real-estate agents, landlords, mortgage bankers) base their behavior not on race per se but on characteristics associated with race—accent, dialect, home address, and so forth—to make decisions about what levels of service and responsiveness to provide to customers. Sociologist Douglas Massey (2000) has even demonstrated racially biased treatment based on the use of "Black English" in telephone contacts (p. 4).

Audit studies have also documented racial discrimination in the job market (e.g., see Bertrand & Mullainathan, 2004). Other forms of modern institutional discrimination include the use of racially and culturally biased standardized tests in school systems, the pattern of drug arrests that sends disproportionate numbers of black teenage boys and young men to jail and prison (see Chapter 6 for more on this trend), and decisions by businesspeople to move their operations away from center-city neighborhoods. Part of what makes modern institutional discrimination so challenging to document is that race, ethnicity, or gender may not be a conscious or overt part of these decision-making processes. Still, the results are that blacks and other minorities—in the past as in the present—are filtered away from opportunities and resources, and racial stratification is maintained, even in the new age of a supposedly color-blind society.

Modern institutional discrimination routinely places black Americans in less desirable statuses in education, residence and home ownership, jobs, the criminal justice system—indeed, across the entire expanse of the socioeconomic system. The result is racial stratification maintained not by monolithic Jim Crow segregation or slavery, but by a subtle and indirect system that is the "new configuration of inequality" (Katz & Stern, 2008, p. 100). We will apply the concept of modern institutional discrimination throughout the case study chapters in Part 3 of this text.

AFFIRMATIVE ACTION

Modern institutional discrimination is difficult to identify, measure, and eliminate, and some of the most heated disputes in recent group relations have concerned public policy and law in this area. Among the most controversial issues is **affirmative action**, a group of programs that attempt to reduce the effects of past discrimination or increase diversity in the workplace and in schools. In the 1970s and 1980s, the Supreme Court found that programs designed to

FIGURE 5.4 Concentration of Whites, Blacks, and Hispanics in Chicago, 2008

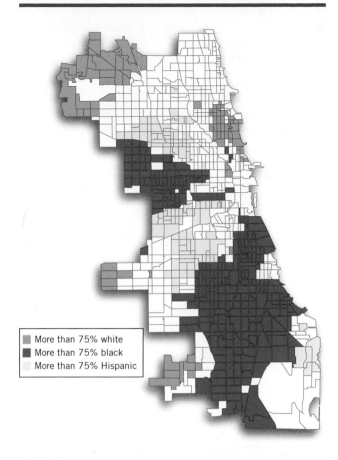

More than 75% white
More than 75% black
More than 75% Hispanic

SOURCE: Center for Governmental Studies, Northern Illinois University.

favor minority employees as a strategy for overcoming past discrimination were constitutional (e.g., *Firefighters Local Union No. 1784 v. Stotts*, 1984; *Sheet Metal Workers v. EEOC*, 1986; *United Steelworkers of America, AFL-CIO-CLC v. Weber*, 1979).

Virtually all these early decisions concerned blatant policies of discrimination, which are becoming increasingly rare as we move farther away from the days of Jim Crow. Even so, the decisions were based on narrow margins (votes of five to four) and featured acrimonious and bitter debates. More recently, the Supreme Court narrowed the grounds on which such past grievances could be redressed (e.g., *Adarand Constructors Inc. v. Pena*, 1995).

A Case of Discrimination? The most recent case involving affirmative action programs in the workplace is

Affirmative action refers to programs that are intended to reduce the effects of past discrimination or increase diversity in workplaces and schools.

Ricci v. DeStefano, 2009, involving firefighters in New Haven, Connecticut. In 2003, the city administered a test for promotion in the city's fire department. More than 100 people took the test but no African American scored high enough to qualify for promotion. The city decided to throw out the test results on the grounds that its dramatically unequal racial results strongly suggested that it was biased against African Americans.

This decision is consistent with the legal concept of *disparate impact*. That is, if a practice has unequal results, federal policy and court precedents tend to assume that the practice is racially biased. The city feared that using these possibly "tainted" test scores might result in lawsuits by black and other minority firefighters. Instead, a lawsuit was filed by several white and Hispanic firefighters who *had* qualified for promotion, claiming that invalidating the test results amounted to reverse racial discrimination. In 2009, the Supreme Court ruled in favor of the white and Hispanic plaintiffs in a five to four ruling.

This case illustrates some of the difficult issues that accompany attempts to address modern institutional discrimination. The issue in *Ricci v. DeStefano* is not overt, Jim Crow discrimination, but rather a test that might be discriminatory in its results, although not in its intent. New Haven was attempting to avoid racial discrimination. How far do employers need to go to ensure racial fairness? Should policies and procedures be judged by their outcomes or their intents? What does "fairness" and "equal treatment" mean in a society in which minority groups have only recently won formal equality and still have lower access to quality schooling and jobs in the mainstream economy? Did the city of New Haven go too far in its attempt to avoid discrimination? (Five of the Supreme Court Justices thought so.) Can there be a truly fair, race-neutral policy for employment and promotion in the present when opportunities and resources in the past were so long allocated on the basis of race? If the problem is color coded, can the solution be color neutral?

Higher Education and Affirmative Action. Colleges and universities have been another prominent battleground for affirmative action programs. Since the 1960s, many institutions of higher education have implemented programs to increase the number of minority students on campus at both the undergraduate and graduate levels, sometimes admitting minority students who had lower grade point averages (GPAs) or test scores than those of dominant-group students who were turned away. In general, advocates of these programs have justified them in terms of redressing the discriminatory practices of the past or increasing diversity on campus and making the student body a more accurate representation of the surrounding society. To say the least, these programs have been highly controversial and the targets of frequent lawsuits, some of which have found their way to the highest courts in the land.

Recent decisions by the U.S. Supreme Court have limited the application of affirmative action to colleges and universities. In two lawsuits involving the University of Michigan in 2003 (*Grutter v. Bollinger* and *Gratz v. Bollinger*), the Supreme Court held that the university's law school *could* use race as one criterion in deciding admissions but that undergraduate admissions *could not* award an automatic advantage to minority applicants. In other words, universities could take into account an applicant's race but only in a limited way, as one factor among many.

In more recent cases involving affirmative action in higher education, the Supreme Court further narrowed the ability of universities to consider race in admissions decisions. One case, decided in June 2013, was *Fisher v. University of Texas at Austin*. The University of Texas (UT) had been using a unique admissions system according to which the top 10% of the student body in each high school in Texas were automatically admitted. Because of the residential segregation in towns and cities across the state, the student body at many high schools is disproportionately black, white, or Hispanic, and the 10% rule guarantees substantial diversity in the UT student body. Some 80% of the students are selected by this method. The remaining 20% are selected using a variety of criteria, including race and ethnicity. It is common for selective institutions such as UT to use many criteria—not just test scores—to diversify their student body.

The case was brought by Amy Fisher, a white student who was not admitted to UT. She argued that some of the admitted minority students had lower GPAs and test scores than she did. The university argued that the educational benefit of a diverse student body justified its partial and limited use of race as one admission criterion among many.

The Supreme Court sent the case back to the federal appeals court with instructions to apply a strict standard: Race could be used as an admission criterion only if there were no workable race-neutral alternatives that would result in a diverse student body. The decision was not a death blow to affirmative action, but it appeared to continue the trend of limiting the circumstances under which affirmative action policies could be applied.

In the second recent decision (*Schuette v. BAMN*), decided in April 2014, the Supreme Court upheld an amendment to the state constitution of Michigan that banned the use of race as a factor in admissions and hiring decisions in all state agencies. This decision effectively ended affirmative action, in any form, in Michigan and in several other states with similar laws. Combined with the 2013 *Fisher* decision, it seems that the role of affirmative action in higher education has been severely curtailed.

The Future of Affirmative Action. What lies ahead for affirmative action? On one hand, there is a clear trend in court decisions to narrow the scope and applicability of these programs. Also, there is very little public support for affirmative action, especially for programs that are perceived as providing specific numerical quotas for minority groups in jobs or university admissions. For example, in 2016, a representative sample of Americans was asked in a survey if they supported "preferential hiring and promotion of blacks." Only 18% of white respondents expressed support. Somewhat surprisingly, less than half (41%) of black respondents supported preferential hiring (National Opinion Research Council, 1972–2016).

On the other hand, although white (and many minority group) Americans object to fixed quotas, people support programs that expand the opportunities available to minority groups, including enhanced job training, education, and recruitment in minority communities (Wilson, 2009, p. 139). Programs of this sort are more consistent with traditional ideologies and value systems that stress individual initiative, personal responsibility, and equality of opportunity.

Many businesses and universities are committed to the broad principles of affirmative action and see the need to address past injustices and the usefulness and desirability of creating diversity in the workplace and classroom. Thus, they are likely to sustain their programs to the extent allowed by court decisions and legislation into the future. Some affirmative action programs, especially those that stress equality of opportunity, may continue in some limited form for some time. On the other hand, the Trump administration has signaled that it is not enthusiastic about affirmative action. For example, in August 2017, the U.S. Department of Justice announced that it would investigate colleges and universities that discriminated against white students in their admissions programs (Savage, 2017).

QUESTIONS FOR REFLECTION

10. What is *modern* institutional discrimination, and how does it differ from *traditional* or blatant institutional discrimination? What are some of the common forms of modern institutional discrimination?

11. What is affirmative action, and what are some of the ways it has been used to combat modern institutional discrimination?

SOCIAL CHANGE AND MINORITY-GROUP ACTIVISM

This chapter has focused on the continuing Industrial Revolution and its impact on minority groups in general and black–white relations in particular. For the most part, changes in group relations have been presented as the results of the fundamental transformation of the U.S. economy from agrarian to industrial to postindustrial. However, the changes in the situation of African Americans and other minority groups did not "just happen" as society modernized. Although the opportunity to pursue favorable change was the result of broad structural changes in American society, the realization of these opportunities came from the efforts of the many who gave their time, their voices, their resources, and sometimes their lives in pursuit of racial justice in America. Since World War II, African Americans have often been in the vanguard of protest activity, and we focus on the contemporary situation of this group in the next chapter.

SUMMARY

This summary is organized around the Learning Objectives listed at the beginning of this chapter.

 5.1 Explain the corollary to the main themes of Chapter 4: specifically, that dominant–minority group relations change as the subsistence technology of the society changes.

Group relations change as the subsistence technology and the level of development of the larger society change. As nations industrialize and urbanize, dominant–minority relations change from paternalistic to rigid competitive forms.

Industrialization continued throughout the 20th century and has continued to shape dominant–minority relations.

As a postindustrial society began to emerge, group relations in the United States shifted from rigid to fluid competitive.

 5.2 Understand the complexity of Jim Crow segregation in the South, why it was created, and its effects.

In the South, slavery was replaced by de jure segregation, a system that combined racial separation with great inequality. The Jim Crow system was intended to control the labor of African Americans and eliminate their political power. It was reinforced by coercion and intense racism and prejudice.

5.3 Explain the significance of the Great Migration and the origins of black protest.

Black Southerners responded to segregation, in part, by moving to urban areas outside the South, particularly in the Northeast and Midwest. The African American population enjoyed greater freedom and developed some political and economic resources away from the South, but a large concentration of low-income, relatively powerless African Americans developed in the ghetto neighborhoods.

Various strategies for combatting Jim Crow segregation and improving the status of African Americans began to emerge in the early 20th century, along with protest organizations and leaders. The resources and relative freedom of blacks living outside the South became an important foundation for the various movements that dramatically changed American race relations, starting in the middle of the 20th century.

 5.4 Apply the concepts of acculturation, integration, and gender to the time frame covered in this chapter.

In response to segregation, the African American community developed a separate institutional life centered on family, church, and community. An African American middle class emerged, as well as a protest movement. Combining work with family roles, African American women were employed mostly in agriculture and domestic service during the era of segregation and were one of the most exploited groups.

 5.5 Explain the important trends created by the shifts to industrial and postindustrial subsistence technology, and describe how these trends affected dominant–minority relations.

Urbanization, specialization, bureaucratization, the changing structure of the occupational sector, the increasing importance of education, and other trends have changed the shape of race relations. The shifts in subsistence technology created more opportunity and freedom for all minority groups but also increased the intensity of struggle and conflict.

 5.6 Explain what is meant by the shift from paternalistic to rigid to fluid competitive group relations.

The basic features of these systems of group relations are summarized in Table 5.2. Paternalistic systems are associated with an agrarian subsistence technology and the desire to control a large, powerless labor force. Under industrialization, group relationships feature more competition for jobs and status, and lower levels of contact between groups. As a postindustrial society began to emerge, group relations in the United States shifted from rigid to fluid competitive. The postindustrial subsistence technology is associated with the highest levels of openness and opportunity for minorities, along with continuing power differentials between groups.

 5.7 Apply the concept of modern institutional discrimination to contemporary black–white relations and understand why affirmative action policies were created to combat it.

Modern institutional discrimination consists of subtle, indirect, difficult-to-document forms of discrimination that are built into society's daily operation. These forms include past-in-present discrimination and other policies, such as the use of racially biased school aptitude tests and drug laws, that are more punitive for minority groups. Affirmative action policies are intended, in part, to combat these forms of discrimination.

KEY TERMS

affirmative action 169
de jure segregation 152
deindustrialization 149
extractive (or primary)
   occupations 163
fluid competitive
   systems 165

Jim Crow system 152
manufacturing
   (or secondary)
   occupations 163
modern institutional
   discrimination 149

past-in-present
   institutional
   discrimination 167
primary labor market 164
Reconstruction 150
rigid competitive group
   system 150

secondary labor
   market 164
service (or tertiary)
   occupations 163
sharecropping 153

REVIEW QUESTIONS

1. The opening paragraph of this chapter offers a corollary to two themes from Chapter 4: *dominant–minority group relations change as the subsistence technology changes.* How does the material in this chapter illustrate the usefulness of that idea?

2. Explain paternalistic and rigid competitive relations and link them to industrialization. How does the shift from slavery to de jure segregation illustrate the dynamics of these two systems?

3. What was the Great Migration to the North? How did it change American race relations?

4. Explain the transition from rigid to fluid competitive relations and explain how this transition is related to the coming of postindustrial society. Explain the roles of urbanization, bureaucracy, the service sector of the job market, and education in this transition.

5. What is modern institutional discrimination? How does it differ from traditional institutional discrimination? Explain the role of affirmative action in combating each.

6. Explain the impact of industrialization and globalization on gender relations. Compare and contrast these changes with the changes that occurred for racial and ethnic minority groups.

7. What efforts have been made on your campus to combat modern institutional discrimination? How effective have these programs been?

STUDENT STUDY SITE

Learning Resources on the Web

Sharpen your skills with SAGE edge at edge.sagepub.com/healey8e

SAGE edge offers a robust online environment featuring an impressive array of free tools and resources for review, study, and further exploration, keeping both instructors and students on the cutting edge of teaching and learning.

The following resources are available at SAGE edge:

Current Debates: Affirmative Action in Higher Education (the "Mismatch" Hypothesis)

Are minority students with lesser academic credentials who are admitted to elite universities being placed in a position where they cannot hope to succeed? Are they being set up to fail? Does affirmative action create a "mismatch" between high expectations and low preparation for some of its beneficiaries?

On our website you will find an overview of the topic, the clashing points of view, and some questions to consider as you analyze the material.

Public Sociology Assignments

Public Sociology Assignments provide opportunities for students to address directly and personally some of the issues raised in this text.

The public sociology assignments designed for Part 2 on our website will lead students to a study of the persistence of prejudice and discrimination in society today. The first assignment is an investigation of children's books and focuses on the depiction of race, gender, and ethnicity. Are children's books as diverse as the larger society? The second assignment analyzes patterns of cross-group interaction in local eateries, and the third looks at the depiction of historical events in contemporary cinema. How are movies based in the past affected by contemporary understandings?

Contributed by Linda M. Waldron

Internet Research Project

For this Internet Research Project, you will visit a website that documents and explores the dynamics of the Jim Crow system in the American South. You will visit each of the five sections of the website and take a quiz to assess the amount of information you have absorbed. Your analysis will be guided by a series of questions, and your instructor may ask you to discuss your findings in small groups.

For Further Reading

Please see our website for an annotated list of important works related to this chapter.

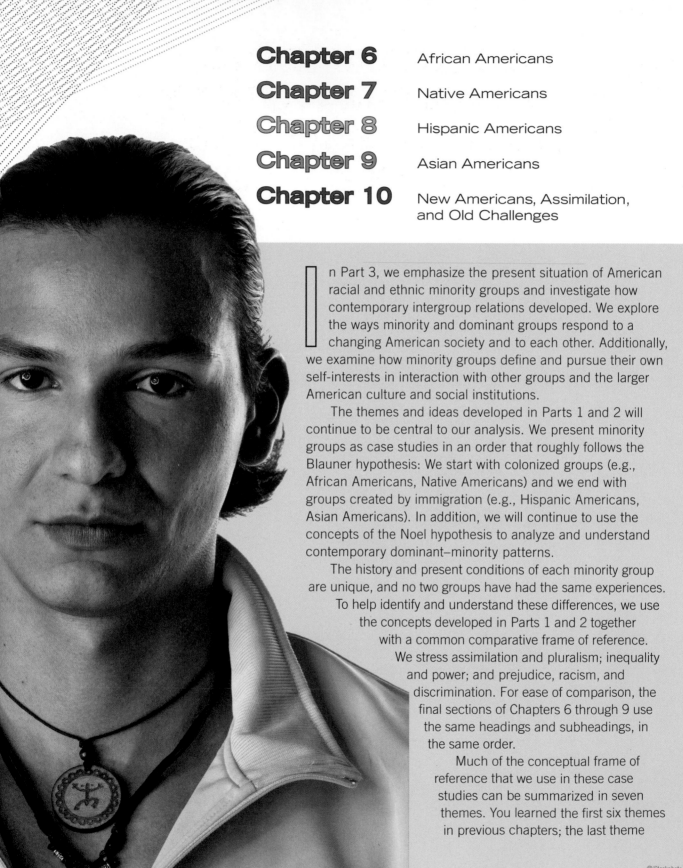

In Part 3, we emphasize the present situation of American racial and ethnic minority groups and investigate how contemporary intergroup relations developed. We explore the ways minority and dominant groups respond to a changing American society and to each other. Additionally, we examine how minority groups define and pursue their own self-interests in interaction with other groups and the larger American culture and social institutions.

The themes and ideas developed in Parts 1 and 2 will continue to be central to our analysis. We present minority groups as case studies in an order that roughly follows the Blauner hypothesis: We start with colonized groups (e.g., African Americans, Native Americans) and we end with groups created by immigration (e.g., Hispanic Americans, Asian Americans). In addition, we will continue to use the concepts of the Noel hypothesis to analyze and understand contemporary dominant–minority patterns.

The history and present conditions of each minority group are unique, and no two groups have had the same experiences. To help identify and understand these differences, we use the concepts developed in Parts 1 and 2 together with a common comparative frame of reference. We stress assimilation and pluralism; inequality and power; and prejudice, racism, and discrimination. For ease of comparison, the final sections of Chapters 6 through 9 use the same headings and subheadings, in the same order.

Much of the conceptual frame of reference that we use in these case studies can be summarized in seven themes. You learned the first six themes in previous chapters; the last theme

PART iii

UNDERSTANDING DOMINANT–MINORITY RELATIONS IN THE UNITED STATES TODAY

is covered in the forthcoming chapters. We list these themes below:

1. Consistent with the Noel hypothesis, the present conditions of America's minority groups reflect their contact situations, especially the nature of their competition with the dominant group (e.g., competition over land versus competition over labor) and the size of the power differential between groups at the time of contact.

2. Consistent with the Blauner hypothesis, minority groups created by colonization experience economic and political inequalities that have lasted longer and been more severe than those experienced by minority groups created by immigration.

3. Power and economic differentials and barriers to upward mobility are especially pronounced for groups identified by racial or physical characteristics, as opposed to cultural or linguistic traits.

4. Consistent with the themes stated in Chapters 4 and 5, dominant–minority relations reflect the economic and political characteristics of the larger society and change as those characteristics change. Changes in the subsistence technology of the larger society are particularly consequential for dominant–minority relations. The shift from a manufacturing to a service economy (deindustrialization) is one of the key factors shaping dominant–minority relations in the United States today.

5. As we saw in Chapter 3, the "mood" of the dominant group over the past four decades combines a rejection of blatant racism with the belief that the modern United States is nondiscriminatory and that success is attainable for all who are willing to work hard enough. It is also common for dominant-group Americans to believe that further reforms of the larger society or special programs or treatment for minorities are unnecessary and unjustified. Efforts to address contemporary minority-group problems must deal with the pervasive "modern racism" of the dominant group.

6. The development of group relations, both in the past and for the future, can be analyzed in terms of assimilation (more similarity) and pluralism (more diversity). Group relations in the past (e.g., the degree of assimilation permitted or required of the minority group) reflected mainly dominant group needs and wishes. Although the pressure for Americanization remains considerable, there is more flexibility and variety in group relations today.

7. Since World War II, minority groups have gained significantly more control over the direction of group relationships. This trend reflects the decline of traditional prejudice in the larger society and the successful efforts of minority groups to protest, resist, and change patterns of exclusion and domination. These successes have been possible in large part because American minority groups have increased their share of political and economic resources.

6 AFRICAN AMERICANS

From Segregation to Modern Racism and Institutional Discrimination

1965
Malcolm X, black Nationalist and founder of the Organization of Afro-American Unity, is assassinated.

1954
Brown v. Board of Education of Topeka, Kansas overturns *Plessy v. Ferguson* (1896) and declares that racial segregation in schools is unconstitutional.

1960
Sit-In Movement begins.

1964
President Johnson signs the Civil Rights Act, prohibiting discrimination based on race, color, religion, or national origin.

1950   1955   1960   1965   1970

1955
Rosa Parks refuses to give up her seat on a bus to a white passenger, spurring the Montgomery bus boycott.

1965
Congress passes the Voting Rights Act of 1965, making it easier for southern blacks to register to vote.

1965
In six days of rioting in Watts, a black section of Los Angeles, 34 people are killed.

1967
The Supreme Court rules in *Loving v. Virginia* that laws prohibiting interracial marriage are unconstitutional.

LOC

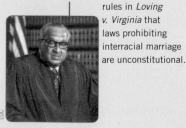

1963
The March on Washington for Jobs and Freedom is attended by about 250,000 people. Martin Luther King Jr. delivers his famous "I Have a Dream" speech.

1967
Thurgood Marshall becomes the first African American Supreme Court Justice.

timeline

When I was out with my oldest daughter, who's [four years old], we were in a shopping mall, in a garage in Los Angeles . . . and there was a lady, who was with her husband. And I could tell they were just really nervous around me. And then we went to an ATM — I had to get some money — and there's another couple and I heard the woman say "Hurry up, let's go, let's go." Like I was going to rob them, and my daughter was all like "What happened dad? What was that all about?" And I have to go into this conversation, "Well honey, sometimes people look at the color of my skin and they think I am a threat to them."

Sometimes if I am walking down a street or something, I am whistling Frozen songs just to prove that . . . "Hey I have kids, I am not a threat to you. I just want to go home to my

LEARNING OBJECTIVES

By the end of this chapter, you will be able to do the following:

6.1 Explain the forces that led to the end of de jure segregation, including relevant organizations, leaders, and legal changes.

6.2 Compare and contrast the Civil Rights Movement with the Black Power Movement.

6.3 Explain the most important issues and trends pertaining to black–white relations since the 1960s, including

a. the relationship between the criminal justice system and the black community,

b. class inequality within the black community,

c family forms and family as a social institution,

d. new racial identities,

e. prejudice, and

f. individual and institutional forms of discrimination.

6.4 Analyze the contemporary situation for African Americans using the concepts of assimilation and pluralism, especially in terms of

a. acculturation,

b. secondary structural assimilation, and

c. primary structural assimilation.

6.5 Use sociological concepts and evidence from the chapter to evaluate the *overall* situation for African Americans today. Evaluate the progress made compared with remaining problems. (Is the glass half empty or half full?)

Getty

1968
Martin Luther King Jr. is assassinated.

1978
In the case of *Bakke v. Regents of the University of California,* the U.S. Supreme Court upholds the constitutionality of affirmative action, but outlaws specific racial quotas.

1992
After a jury acquits four white police officers for the brutal beating of Rodney King, riots erupted in south-central Los Angeles.

2009
Barack Obama becomes the first African American to be elected president of the United States.

2013
Black Lives Matter is founded to fight systemic racism and violence.

2014
Police officer Darren Wilson kills Michael Brown. When he is not indicted, protests emerge in Ferguson, Missouri, and throughout the United States.

2016
The National Museum of African-American History and Culture opens in Washington, DC.

Wikimedia Commons

2017
In the wake of protests, cities and colleges begin to reassess Civil War monuments. Many are removed.

Wikimedia Commons

1980   1990   2010   2015   2020

family." So often people just view this as, "Oh gosh, you're just whining," or "they are just making excuses or pulling out some mythical race card that doesn't exist." This is a real thing.

—Doyin Richards (a blogger who writes about fathers and fathering)

It's like we are seen as animals. Treated like animals. It's not easy.

—William Jones (high-end retail worker)

[I was] walking home in my beautiful upper-middle-class neighborhood in D.C., when the cops start following me—kind of like this cat and mouse thing. They are in their car, and you know, every time I move they move. And we get up to my house and I just stop on the street and say "what are you doing?" And then they say "what are you doing?" I say "I live here." They say "prove it." They made me go to my porch, and then when I got there I said, "you know what, I don't have to prove anything." I knew this because I am a law professor. They said, "we are not leaving until you go in the house, because we think you're a burglar." I say "you're doing this because I am black." They said, "no, we are not, were black too," and that was true. These were African-American officers. Even they were racial profiling me, another black man . . .

—Paul Butler (law professor)

Every day, I live and operate with that feeling of fragility, that feeling that I could be taken out at any time. I am a chokehold away from being Eric Garner.

—Ben Saunders (psychology professor)

It is common for African American men to experience the sense of "otherness," the presumption of guilt, threat, and danger described in the opening narratives. Shopkeepers watch them with special attention; police routinely stop, question, and frisk black (and other minority group) men; and white pedestrians may cross the street when they see black men approaching.

Some people might say that you can't control what other people think about you, and that's true. However, these views of black men are more than "just an annoyance" or "something to learn to live with." One only needs to read the news to find cases where interactions, shaped by a presumption about black men's (and women's) "dangerousness," can escalate quickly and, in some cases, turn deadly. The 2012 case of Trayvon Martin, a young black man shot and killed while walking home from the store, provides just one example. The shooter, George Zimmerman, stopped Martin because he "looked suspicious," and their confrontation quickly turned deadly. Zimmerman was acquitted of homicide charges in July 2013. (We'll discuss this case further later in the chapter.)

The opening narratives reflect what research repeatedly shows—on many levels, many people continue to see African Americans as "different" from other Americans. For example, people see black men as bigger than they really are compared with comparable size white men (Wilson, Hugenberg, & Rule, 2017). Black boys over the age of 10 are seen as older than they are—by about 4.5 years—and "less innocent" compared with other children (Goff et al., 2014). According to the U.S. Department of Education, black boys are punished more frequently and more harshly compared with white boys. Boys of color who have disabilities are disproportionately restrained at school compared with whites (Lewin, 2012). Even black *preschoolers* are more likely to be suspended and expelled compared to white preschoolers (U.S. Department of Education Office for Civil Rights, 2014). (We see similar patterns for African American girls, too.)

Certainly, U.S. society has made progress toward racial justice and inclusion, but African Americans still suffer from race-based inequalities. As you read this chapter, consider the historical trajectory and how what we see in the present may be connected to the past. For example, consider what you've learned so far about the social construction of African Americans as "inferior" to white people. How might those ideas, part of our American consciousness for centuries, shape present-day stereotypes, prejudice, and discrimination? How might they influence everything from interactions like those described in the opening narratives to widespread patterns of inequality related to education, employment, and incarceration? And, where do we begin if we want to make change? •

At the start of the 20th century (more than 100 years ago), African Americans primarily lived in the rural South. The legal and civil rights they had briefly enjoyed during Reconstruction (1865–1880s) were stripped away by Jim Crow segregation. They had limited access to quality education and had few occupational choices. They were exploited by the sharecropping system of agriculture, and blocked from the better-paying industrial and manufacturing jobs in urban areas. They possessed few political rights and had few means of expressing their grievances to the larger society or the world.

Since then, the United States has seen greater equality between the dominant and minority groups, including African Americans. Perhaps the single most significant sign of progress is the election of Barack Obama to the presidency of the United States. If we take a "glass half-full" perspective, we see signs of this progress in almost every area of social life. African Americans are earning advanced degrees in greater numbers than ever before and contributing to every occupation. They have reached the highest levels of American society, serving on the Supreme Court and in other important government positions, leading some of the most important American corporations (e.g., American Express, Time Warner), and teaching at our most prestigious universities. Some of the best-known, most successful, most respected people in the world are African American: Martin Luther King Jr., Malcolm X, Michael Jordan, Toni Morrison, Beyoncé (Knowles-Carter), Michael Jackson, Maya Angelou, Muhammad Ali, Oprah Winfrey, Serena and Venus Williams, Colin Powell, Ta-Nehisi Coates, LeBron James, Kanye West, and Neil deGrasse Tyson to name just a few.

African Americans continue to break barriers. For example, in 2012, Ana Duverney became the first black woman to win the Best Director award at Sundance Film Festival (Hall & Renee, 2016). In 2015, Misty Copeland became the first African American woman to become the lead dancer for the world-renowned American Ballet Theatre ("The Root 100," 2016). That same year, Vincent R. Stewart became the first African American director of the U.S. Defense Intelligence Agency, Loretta Lynch became the first black woman to serve as the U.S. attorney general (Chung, 2015), and Michael Curry became the first black presiding bishop of Episcopal church (The Associated Press, 2015). In 2016, Maurice Ashley became the first African American grandmaster nominated to the U.S. Chess Hall of Fame. Finally, Simone Biles won four gold medals (and a bronze medal) in women's gymnastics, making her the first American woman to do so at a single Olympic games (Hall & Renee, 2016).

Compared with 100 years ago, the situation of black Americans today is much improved. However, sociologists, like other scientists, caution against using a few examples (or personal experiences) as representative of larger societal patterns. The journey to racial equality in the United States is far from accomplished. As we shall see in this chapter, a large percentage of African Americans continue to experience exclusion and persistent inequalities in education, health care, housing, employment, and other areas of social life. Even the more fortunate segments of the black community remain in a tenuous situation: They have fewer resources to fall back on in hard times and weaker connections to the sources of power and privilege. The glittering success stories of some obscure the continuing struggles of the many, and racism, prejudice, and discrimination continue to be significant problems.

To understand contemporary black–white relations, we must comprehend the watershed events of the recent past: the end of de jure segregation, the triumphs (and limitations) of the Civil Rights Movement of the 1950s and 1960s, the urban riots and Black Power Movement of the 1960s, and the continuing racial divisions within U.S. society since the 1970s. Behind these events, we can see the powerful pressures of industrialization and modernization, the shift from rigid to fluid competitive group relations, deindustrialization and modern institutional discrimination, changing distributions of power and forms of intergroup competition, the shift from traditional prejudice to modern racism, and new ideas about assimilation and pluralism. Black–white relations changed as a direct result of protest, resistance, and the concerted actions of thousands of individuals, both black and white.

THE END OF DE JURE SEGREGATION

As a colonized minority group, African Americans entered the 20th century facing extreme inequality, relative powerlessness, and sharp limitations on their freedom. Their most visible enemy was the system of de jure segregation in the South, the rigid competitive system of group relations that controlled the lives of most African Americans.

Why and how did de jure segregation—segregation by law—end? Recall from Chapter 5 that dominant–minority relationships change as the larger society and its subsistence technology change. As the United States industrialized and urbanized during the 20th century, a series of social, political, economic, and legal processes were set in motion that ultimately destroyed Jim Crow segregation.

The mechanization and modernization of agriculture in the South had a powerful effect on race relations. As farm work became less labor-intensive and machines replaced people, the need to maintain a large, powerless workforce declined (Geschwender, 1978, pp. 175–177). Thus, one of the primary motivations for maintaining Jim Crow segregation and the sharecropping system of farming lost force.

In addition, the modernization of southern agriculture helped spur the migration northward and to urban areas, as we discussed in Chapter 5. Outside the rural South, African Americans found it easier to register to vote and pursue other avenues for improving their situations. The weight of the growing African American vote was first felt in the 1930s and was large enough to make a difference in local, state, and even national elections by the 1940s. In 1948, for example, President Harry Truman recognized that he could not be reelected without the support of African American voters. As a result, the Democratic Party adopted a civil rights plank in the party platform—the first time since Reconstruction that a national political party had taken a stand on race relations (Wilson, 1973, p. 123).

The weight of these changes accumulated slowly, and no single date or specific event marks the end of de jure segregation. The system ended as it had begun: gradually and in a series of discrete episodes and incidents. By the mid-20th century, resistance to racial change was weakening and the power resources of African Americans were increasing. This enhanced freedom and strength fueled a variety of efforts that sped the demise of Jim Crow segregation. Although a complete historical autopsy is not necessary here, a general understanding of the reasons for the death of Jim Crow segregation is essential for an understanding of modern black–white relations.

WARTIME DEVELOPMENTS

One of the first successful applications of the growing stock of black power resources occurred in 1941, as the United States was mobilizing for war against Germany and Japan. Despite the crisis atmosphere, racial discrimination was common, even in the defense industry. A group of African Americans, led by labor leader A. Philip Randolph, head of the Brotherhood of Sleeping Car Porters, threatened to march on Washington to protest the discriminatory treatment (Brown, 2015).

To forestall the march, President Franklin D. Roosevelt signed an Executive Order banning discrimination in defense-related industries, and created a watchdog federal agency, the Fair Employment Practices Commission, to oversee compliance with the new anti-discriminatory policy (Franklin & Moss, 1994, pp. 436–437; Geschwender, 1978, pp. 199–200). President Roosevelt's actions were significant in two ways. First, a group of African Americans not only had their grievances heard at the highest level of society but also succeeded in getting what they wanted. Underlying the effectiveness of the planned march was the rising political and economic power of the African American community outside the South and the need to mobilize all segments of the population for a world war. Second, the federal government made an unprecedented commitment to fair employment rights for African Americans. This alliance between the federal government and African Americans was tentative, but it foreshadowed some of the dynamics of racial change that would occur in the 1950s and 1960s.

THE CIVIL RIGHTS MOVEMENT

The **Civil Rights Movement** was a multifaceted campaign to end legalized segregation and ameliorate the massive inequalities faced by African Americans. The campaign lasted for decades and included lawsuits and courtroom battles as well as protest marches and demonstrations. We begin our examination with a look at the movement's successful challenge to the laws of racial segregation.

Brown v. Board of Education of Topeka. In 1954, the U.S. Supreme Court delivered the single most powerful blow to de jure segregation in their ruling on *Brown v. Board of Education of Topeka*. They reversed the *Plessy v. Ferguson* decision of 1896 (see Chapter 5) and ruled that racially separate facilities are inherently unequal and therefore unconstitutional. Segregated school systems—and all other forms of legalized racial segregation—would have to end.

The landmark *Brown* decision was the culmination of decades of planning and effort by the National Association for the Advancement of Colored People (NAACP) and individuals such as Thurgood Marshall, the NAACP's chief counsel (who was appointed to the Supreme Court in 1967). The strategy of the NAACP was to dismantle the unjust Jim Crow laws by finding instances in which the civil

---

The **Civil Rights Movement** was the organized effort of African Americans and their allies in the 1950s and 1960s to end de jure segregation in the South.

A demonstration protesting school segregation organized by the NAACP.

REFLECTIONS FROM ROSA PARKS

Library of Congress Prints and Photographs Division

Rosa Parks's handwritten account of the contradictory social norms regarding segregation.

"In Montgomery Alabama, the cradle of the Confederacy, Heart of Dixie there exists some strange and varied customs of racial segregation and Jim Crow laws. There is much evidence everywhere of integration being practiced between the races somewhere and sometimes for a long, long time. Night time integration and daytime segregation makes this a very mixed up place. It is not easy to remain rational and normal mentally in such a setting where even in our airport in Montgomery County, there is a white waiting room, none for colored except an unmarked seat in the entrance. It doesn't say who should take this seat. There are restroom facilities for White Ladies and Colored Women, white men and colored men. We stand outside after being served at the same ticket counter instead of sitting on the inside. Also there is only one drinking fountain. We board the plane and find no segregation.

"On arrival in B'ham [Birmingham], we note one waiting room, but white and colored drinking fountains . . .

"This time gives me a little while to go back in my mind to my home in Montgomery and its unique position today. Where segregation was the order of the day, way of life and accepted patterns apparently taken for granted by all with the exception of a few persons who were called radicals, sore heads, agitators, troublemakers to name just a few terms given them. The masses seemed not to put forth too much effort to struggle against the status quo."

rights of an African American had been violated and then bringing suit against the relevant governmental agency.

The NCAAP intended for the impact of these lawsuits to extend far beyond the specific case being argued. The goal was to persuade the courts to declare segregation unconstitutional not only in the specific instance being tried but in all similar cases. The *Brown* (1954) decision was the ultimate triumph of this strategy. The significance of the Supreme Court's decision was not that Linda Brown— the child in whose name the case was argued—would attend a different school or even that the school system of Topeka, Kansas, would be integrated. Instead, the significance was in the rejection of the principle of de jure segregation in the South and, by implication, throughout the nation.

Southern states' response to the *Brown* (1954) decision was to mount campaigns of massive resistance. Jim Crow laws remained on the books for years. Most white Southerners strongly supported the system of racial privilege and attempted to forestall change through a variety of means, including violence and intimidation. The Ku Klux Klan (KKK), largely dormant since the 1920s, reappeared, along with other racist and terrorist groups such as the White Citizens' Councils. White politicians and other leaders competed with one another to express the most adamant statements of racist resistance (Wilson, 1973, p. 128). One locality, Prince Edward County in central Virginia, chose to close its public schools rather than integrate. The schools remained closed for five years. During that time, white children attended private, segregated academies created to keep segregated schooling alive. The county provided no schooling at all for African American children (Franklin, 1967, p. 644). If they wanted to attend school, they needed to travel outside of the county, but most black families did not have the resources to do so.

Nonviolent Direct Action Protest. The principle established by *Brown* (1954) was assimilationist: It ordered the educational institutions of the dominant group to open freely and equally to all. Southern states and communities overwhelmingly rejected the principle of equal access and shared facilities. Centuries of racist tradition and privilege were at stake, and it would take considerable collective effort to overcome southern defiance and resistance to the changes brought about by *Brown*. The central force in this struggle was a protest movement that we often trace to Montgomery, Alabama. There, on December 1, 1955, Rosa Parks was riding the city bus home from her job as a department store tailor. As the bus filled, the driver ordered her to surrender her seat to a white man who had just boarded the bus. When she refused, the police were called and Parks was arrested for violating a local segregation ordinance.

Most Americans know the basic story of Rosa Parks. However, there's much more to know. At the time of her arrest, Parks had been active in the fight for equal rights as a member of the Montgomery chapter of the NAACP. When she joined the organization in 1943, she "was the only woman there" (Theoharis, 2015, p. 17). She first served as the organization's secretary, and over the next decade engaged in other types of activism, such as voter registration and documenting African Americans' experiences of discrimination. Just months before her arrest, Parks attended a desegregation workshop at the Highlander Folk School in Tennessee (now called the Highlander Research and Education) (Theoharis, 2015).

But, it was her work for the NAACP in 1944 that helped lay the foundations for the powerful civil rights protest to come and, according to Parks, that motivated her actions on the bus that day. As you learned in Chapters 4 and 5, sexualized violence (or the threat of it) against enslaved women was a mechanism of social control in the antebellum South and it remained so under Jim Crow. In 1944, in Abbeville, Alabama, six white men stopped Recy Taylor and Fannie and West Daniels as they walked home from church. The men abducted Taylor, a 24-year-old African American woman, at gunpoint, took her to a secluded area, and raped her. The police identified the men but did not arrest them. Police did not arrange for a suspect lineup and Taylor could not identify the men by name. Though the case went to trial, the jury of white men deliberated only for a few minutes before finding the accused men "not guilty" (McGuire 2010). After the trial, Taylor and her family received threats including an attack on their home. The case sent shockwaves through the black community, so the NAACP sent Parks to investigate. The information she gathered helped inspire the Committee for Equal Justice

to document African American women's experience of violence at the hands of white men (McGuire, 2010, p. 13).

Although Parks says she did not plan her act of civil disobedience on the bus that day, her training and activism helped to prepare her for that moment. Her case galvanized the African American community, which organized a boycott of the city buses, with the Reverend Martin Luther King Jr., the new minister of a local Baptist church, leading the boycott. However, it took collective, sustained effort to make the boycott successful. Participants set up car pools, shared taxis, and walked (in some cases, for miles) to and from work, worship services, or other places they needed to go. (Some white allies supported the boycott, too. For example, white women who employed women of color as their housekeepers drove them to and from work so that they would not need to take the buses. Others, like long-time white civil rights activist, Virginia Durr, believe that most white women who did so were motivated not by a desire to support the boycott but to ensure they had assistance in their homes. See Chappell, 1996, p. 78.) The boycott lasted for more than a year, until the United States Supreme Court declared that segregated city buses in Montgomery, and throughout Alabama, were unconstitutional.

As we have noted, many people know about Rosa Parks. However, many courageous individuals, before and after Parks, resisted similar treatment and participated in nonviolent civil disobedience. For example, 50 years before the Montgomery bus boycott, African Americans in Nashville, Tennessee, effectively boycotted the city's streetcars for a year (from 1905–1906) (Cardona, 2015). Due to space limitations, we can't name all the individuals who paved the way for Parks and the Montgomery bus boycott, but here are some:

- **1946—Irene Morgan**, a 27-year-old from Maryland, was recuperating from a miscarriage at her mother's home in Virginia. Morgan needed to see her doctor and took the bus back to Maryland. Although she was sitting in the "colored section," the bus got crowded and the driver asked her (and another passenger) to move farther back. When Morgan refused, the driver drove to the jail where the sheriff produced a warrant for her arrest. Morgan tore it up and threw it out the bus window. Morgan wasn't trained in nonviolent civil disobedience and when an officer grabbed her she fought back. A court found her guilty of resisting arrest and ordered her to pay a $100 fine, equivalent to more than $1,200 in 2017 (Inflation Calculator, n.d.). She pleaded "not guilty" to violating Virginia's segregation laws, and was convicted and fined another $10, but would not pay it. The NAACP provided a legal team under the leadership of Thurgood Marshall and William Hastie who took the case before the Supreme Court (*Morgan v. Commonwealth of Virginia*). Morgan won with the Court ruling that segregated seating by race on *interstate* travel was "an undue burden on commerce" (Pilgrim, 2007).

- **1947—Bayard Rustin,** a gay activist who had worked with A. Philip Randolph (mentioned earlier in the chapter), was serving as a field representative for the Fellowship of Reconciliation (FOR) (King Encyclopedia, n.d.). FOR helped found an important civil rights organization, the Congress of Racial Equality (CORE) ("Fellowship of Reconciliation," n.d.), and took an intersectional approach to nonviolent civil disobedience to "bring about equality for all people regardless of race, creed, sex, age, disability, sexual orientation, religion or ethnic background" (Congress of Racial Equality, n.d.). Although *Morgan v. the Commonwealth of Virginia* ruled that segregation on *interstate* transportation was unconstitutional, many southern *private* bus companies avoided obeying this ruling by passing their own segregation guidelines. To put an end to segregated interstate travel, 16 men from CORE, 8 black and 8 white, traveled on what they called a Journey of Reconciliation. The white men sat in the "colored section" of the buses and African American men sat in the "white section." Several of the men were arrested and jailed. The court sentenced Rustin to 30 days on a chain gang and, ever the activist, he published a report about his experiences, *Twenty-Two Days on the Chain Gang at Roxboro, North Carolina*, that led to prison reforms (Rustin, 1947). The CORE bus rides provided a model for the Freedom Rides of 1961 ("King Encyclopedia," n.d.).

- **1952—Sarah Louise Keys** was traveling by bus from New Jersey where she was serving in the Women's Army Corps. She was headed home, to North Carolina, to enjoy a furlough. For part of the trip, she had been sitting in a row toward the front of the bus. However, when a new driver came on board, he asked her to move to the back. She refused. The driver then instructed the other passengers to get on a new bus, but he would not allow Keys to get on. The police arrested, fined, and jailed Keys overnight. When a North Carolina court upheld her conviction, she sought help from the NAACP. Less than a week before Rosa Parks refused to go to the back of the bus, the Supreme Court ruled in favor of Keys (McCabe & Roundtree, 2009; Richardson & Luker, 2014, pp. 267–268). The case was monumental in its impact because the Court did not stand by the "separate but equal" doctrine established in *Plessy vs. Ferguson*. Because of its importance, the case was hailed as a "symbol of a movement that cannot be held back" (McCabe & Roundtree, 2009, p. 154).

From these beginnings sprang the protest movement that eventually defeated de jure segregation. The central strategy of the movement involved **nonviolent direct action**, a method by which people confronted the system of de jure segregation head-on, not in the courtroom or in the state legislature but in the places where they experienced it, such as the bus, the shop, the movie theater, or the street. The movement's principles of nonviolence were adopted from the tenets of Christianity and from the teachings of Mohandas K. Gandhi, Henry David Thoreau, and others. Dr. King, who earned his undergraduate degree in sociology from Morehouse College before earning his theology degree, expressed this basic philosophy in a number of books and speeches (King, 1958, 1963, 1968). In short, he believed that nonviolent protest should confront the forces of evil rather than the people who happened to be doing evil. In other words, nonviolent direct action sought to change the unjust social structure including social institutions like the education system, the economy, the justice system, and government. Dr. King believed that these actions could shift America's culture toward beliefs, values, and norms that were more in line with the egalitarian democratic ideas. King asserted the movement should attempt to win the friendship and support of its enemies rather than seeking to defeat or humiliate them. Above all, nonviolent protest required courage and discipline; as he said, it was not a method for cowards (King, 1958, pp. 83–84).

The movement used different tactics for different situations, including sit-ins at segregated restaurants, protest marches and demonstrations, prayer meetings, and voter registration drives. The police and terrorist groups such as the KKK often responded to these protests with brutal repression and violence, and protesters were routinely imprisoned, beaten, and attacked by police dogs. The violent resistance sometimes escalated to acts of murder, including the 1963 bombing of a black church in Birmingham, Alabama, which took the lives of four little girls, and the 1968 assassination of Dr. King. Resistance to racial change in the South was intense. It would take more than protests and marches to end de jure segregation, and the U.S. Congress finally provided the necessary tools to do so (see D'Angelo, 2001; Halberstam, 1998; Killian, 1975; King, 1958, 1963, 1968; Lewis, 1999; Morris, 1984).

Nonviolent direct action was the central tactic used by the Civil Rights Movement to confront de jure segregation.

Rosa Parks is fingerprinted following her arrest for violating the Montgomery, Alabama, bus segregation law. The U.S. Congress later called her "the first lady of civil rights" and "the mother of the freedom movement."

Landmark Legislation. The successes of the protest movement, combined with changing public opinion and the legal principles established by the Supreme Court, coalesced in the mid-1960s to stimulate the passage of two laws that together ended Jim Crow segregation. In 1964, at the urging of President Lyndon B. Johnson, the U.S. Congress passed the Civil Rights Act of 1964, banning discrimination on the grounds of race, color, religion, national origin, or gender.

The law applied to publicly owned facilities such as parks and municipal swimming pools, businesses and other facilities open to the public, and any programs that received federal aid.

Congress followed this up with the Voting Rights Act in 1965, also initiated by President Johnson, which required that the same standards be used to register all citizens in federal, state, and local elections. The act banned literacy tests, whites-only primaries, and other practices that had been used to prevent African Americans from registering to vote. This law gave the franchise back to black Southerners for the first time since Reconstruction and laid the groundwork for increasing black political power. The landmark federal legislation, in combination with court decisions and the protest movement, finally succeeded in crushing Jim Crow.

We cannot overstate the significance of these two laws for ending state-sponsored racial discrimination and furthering the commitment of the nation to equality and justice. The principles of the Civil Rights Act are now firmly implanted in American culture and law, and the double standards of the past that granted equal rights only to whites seem like outdated relics.

The Voting Rights Act (VRA) was equally crucial in ending de jure segregation, but, unlike the Civil Rights Act, it was specifically designed to remedy discriminatory practices occurring in certain states in the mid-1960s. Congress has renewed the VRA periodically, and did so, most recently in 2006 with bipartisan support, a huge majority in the House of Representatives, and a unanimous vote in the Senate (Hagler, 2015).

However, in 2013, the U.S. Supreme Court ruled in a 5-to-4 decision that parts of the Voting Rights Act are unconstitutional, arguing that the specific discriminatory voting practices such as poll taxes or literacy tests no longer exist. Chief Justice John Roberts noted that in most of the states originally covered by the law in 1965, African Americans voted at higher rates than whites in the 2012 presidential election (Liptak, 2013).

As you've learned, social change does not always happen easily or in a linear fashion. Rather, it often emerges from struggle between different groups. Following the Court's 2013 ruling, a variety of states created new voting restrictions. For example, in 2013 North Carolina passed legislation that eliminated same-day voter registration, required photo IDs, and shortened the early voting period. The Fourth Circuit Court of Appeals later struck down those changes saying they "target[ed] African Americans with almost surgical precision" (Vicens, 2016). Likewise, in 2014, legislation in Ohio eliminated its "Golden Week" when voters could simultaneously register and vote early (Hurley, 2016). Historically, people of color and lower-income individuals are less likely to vote (Pew Research Center, 2014). This may be, in part, due to restricted ability to get to polling places or to take time off from work to do so and from feelings of disenfranchisement from the political system. Thus, a federal district court judge later ruled that changes such as those enacted in North Carolina and Ohio violated part of the Voting Rights Act regarding discrimination on the "basis of race, color, or membership in one of the language minority groups" (Vicens, 2016, para. on Ohio). Ohio Secretary of State Jon Husted challenged that ruling, but a 2016 decision by the Supreme Court left the restrictions in place. Similar legislation was passed in other states including Wisconsin, Kansas, Virginia, Texas, Arizona, and North Dakota (Vicens, 2016). In 2015, legislators proposed changes to the Voting Rights Act but Congress did not vote on them (Actions Overview H.R.2867, 2015). We will consider some of the implications of this decision later in the chapter when we discuss African American political power.

The Success and Limitations of the Civil Rights Movement. Why did the Civil Rights Movement succeed? A comprehensive list of reasons would be lengthy, but we can cite some of the most important causes of its success, especially those consistent with the general points about dominant–minority relations that have been made in previous chapters.

1. *Changing subsistence technology.* The continuing industrialization and urbanization of the society as a whole—and the South in particular—weakened the Jim Crow, rigid competitive system of minority group control and segregation. We made this point in Chapter 5 when we discussed the impact of the changing subsistence technology and the end of paternalistic controls (see Table 5.2).

2. *An era of prosperity.* Following World War II, the United States enjoyed a period of prosperity that lasted into the 1960s. Consistent with the Noel hypothesis, this was important because it reduced the intensity of intergroup competition, at least outside the South. During prosperous times, resistance to change tends to weaken. If the economic "pie" is expanding, the "slices" minority groups claim can increase without threatening the size of anyone else's portions, and the prejudice generated during intergroup competition (à la Robber's Cave, Chapter 3) is held in check. Thus, these "good times" muted the sense of threat in the dominant group sparked by the demands for equality made by the Civil Rights Movement.

3. *Increasing resources in the black community.* Some of the economic prosperity of the era found its way into African American communities and increased their pool of economic and political resources. Networks of independent, African American–controlled organizations and institutions, such as churches and colleges, were created or grew in size and power. The increasingly elaborate infrastructure of the black community included protest organizations, such as the NAACP (see Chapter 5), and provided material resources, leadership, and "people power" to lead the fight against segregation and discrimination.

4. *Assimilationist goals.* The Civil Rights Movement embraced the traditional American values of liberty, equality, freedom, and fair treatment. It demanded civil, legal, and political rights for African Americans, rights available automatically to whites. Thus, many whites did not feel threatened by the movement because they saw it as consistent with mainstream American values, especially in contrast to the intense, often violent resistance of southern whites.

5. *Coalitions.* The perceived legitimacy of the goals of the movement also opened up the possibility of alliances with other groups (e.g., white liberals, Jews, college students). The support of others was crucial because black Southerners had few resources of their own other than their numbers and courage. By mobilizing the resources of other, more powerful groups, black Southerners forged alliances and created sympathetic support that was brought to bear on their opposition.

6. *Mass media.* Widespread and sympathetic coverage from the mass media, particularly television, was crucial to the success of the movement. The oft-repeated scenario of African Americans being brutally attacked while demonstrating for their rights outraged many Americans and reinforced the moral consensus that eventually rejected "traditional" racial prejudice along with Jim Crow segregation (see Chapter 3).

The southern Civil Rights Movement ended de jure segregation but found it difficult to survive the demise of its primary enemy. The confrontational tactics that had been so effective against the Jim Crow system proved less useful when attention turned to the actual distribution of jobs, wealth, political power, and other valued goods and services. Outside the South, the allocation of opportunity and resources had always been the central concern of the African American community. Let's take a look at these concerns.

QUESTIONS FOR REFLECTION

1. What social forces led to the end of Jim Crow segregation? What was the role of broad social changes such as changing subsistence technology? How important were the contributions of individuals and organizations?

2. Explain the Supreme Court decision and laws that ended de jure segregation.

3. How do the concepts of competition and differential in power in the Noel hypothesis apply to the demise of the Jim Crow system of segregation?

4. List and explain the important reasons for the success of the Civil Rights Movement.

DEVELOPMENTS OUTSIDE THE SOUTH

DE FACTO SEGREGATION

Chapter 5 discussed some of the difficulties African Americans encountered as they left the rural South. Discrimination by labor unions, employers, industrialists, and white ethnic groups was common. Racial discrimination outside the South was less overt but still pervasive, especially in housing, education, and employment.

The pattern of racial separation and inequality outside the South during this time of our history is called **de facto segregation**: segregation resulting from what seems to be, at first glance, peoples' choices or personal preferences. As opposed to the Jim Crow system in the South or apartheid in South Africa, under de facto segregation, no public laws mandate racial separation. Thus, people often assume that de facto segregation "just happened" as people and groups made decisions about where to live and work; or, that it resulted from some benign tendency of people to be "with their own kind."

On the contrary, de facto segregation was intentional. You could consider it de jure segregation in disguise. Racial segregation outside the South was the direct result of intentionally racist decisions made by governmental and quasi-governmental agencies, such as real estate boards, school boards, and zoning boards (see Massey & Denton, 1993, pp. 74–114; also see Loewen, 2005). De facto segregation was created when local and state authorities actively colluded with private citizens behind the scenes, ignored racist practices within their jurisdictions, and "simply refrained from enforcing black social, economic, and political rights so that private discriminatory practices could do their work" (Massey, 2007, p. 57). For example, shortly after World War I, the real estate board in the city of Chicago adopted a policy that required its members, on penalty of "immediate expulsion," to enforce racial residential segregation (Cohen & Taylor, 2000, p. 33; Rothstein, 2014). The city itself passed no Jim Crow laws but the result was the same: Black Americans were consigned to a separate and unequal status.

African Americans outside the South faced more poverty, higher unemployment, and lower-quality housing and schools than did whites, but there was no clear equivalent of Jim Crow to attack or blame for these patterns of inequality. Thus, the triumphs of the Civil Rights Movement had little impact on their lives. In the 1960s, the African American community outside the South expressed its frustration over the slow pace of change in two ways: urban unrest and a movement for change that rose to prominence as the Civil Rights Movement faded.

URBAN UNREST

In the mid-1960s, the frustration and anger of urban African American communities erupted into a series of violent uprisings. The riots began in the summer of 1965 in Watts, a black neighborhood in Los Angeles, California, and over the next four years, virtually every large black urban community experienced similar outbursts. Racial violence was hardly a new phenomenon in America. Race riots had existed as early as the Civil War, and various times had seen racial violence of considerable magnitude.

The riots of the 1960s were different, however. Most race riots in the past had been attacks by whites against African Americans, often including the invasion and destruction of African American neighborhoods (e.g., see D'Orso, 1996; Ellsworth, 1982). The urban unrest of the 1960s, in contrast, consisted largely of attacks by African Americans against white-owned businesses operating in black neighborhoods and against the police, who were seen as an army of occupation and whose excessive use of force often precipitated the riots (Conot, 1967; Mozingo & Jennings, 2015; National Advisory Commission, 1968).

THE BLACK POWER MOVEMENT

The urban riots of the 1960s were an unmistakable sign that the problems of race relations had not been resolved with the end of Jim Crow segregation. Outside the South, the problems were different and called for different solutions. Even as the Civil Rights Movement was celebrating its victory in the South, a new protest movement rose to prominence. The **Black Power Movement** was a loose coalition of organizations and spokespersons that encompassed a variety of ideas and views, many of which differed sharply from those of the Civil Rights Movement. Some of the central ideas included racial pride ("Black is beautiful" was a key slogan of the day), interest in African heritage, and Black Nationalism. In contrast to the assimilationist goals of the Civil Rights Movement, Black Power groups worked to increase African American control over schools, police, welfare programs, and other public services operating in black neighborhoods.

Most adherents of the Black Power Movement believed that white racism and institutional discrimination, forces buried deep in the core of American culture and society, were the primary causes of racial inequality in America. Thus, if African Americans were ever to be truly empowered, they would have to liberate themselves and do it on their own terms. Some Black Power advocates specifically rejected the goal of assimilation into white society, arguing

---

De facto segregation is racial separation and inequality that appears, on the surface, to result from voluntary choice. Often, de facto segregation is really a disguised form of de jure segregation.

The **Black Power Movement** rose to prominence in the 1960s as a coalition of groups. Some of the central themes of the movement were Black Nationalism, autonomy for African American communities, and pride in heritage.

Growing Up as a Black Girl in the Jim Crow South

Feminist intellectual bell hooks was born in Kentucky in the 1950s, at the height of the Jim Crow system. Her family was rural and poor, but she rose from these humble beginnings to earn her doctorate in English. She teaches at Berea College, and she has written more than 35 books and has devoted her life to a passionate critique of white supremacy, capitalism, and patriarchy. The name under which she writes is a pseudonym, and she does not capitalize it, to stress that her ideas are more important than her name or any other aspect of her identity. In addition to race, what class, gender, and other differentiating factors can you identify in the passage? What is the young bell hooks learning about herself and her world?

BONE BLACK

bell hooks

We live in the country. We children do not understand that that means we are among the poor. We do not understand that the outhouses behind many of the houses are still there because running water came here long after they had it in the city. . . . Because we are poor, because we live in the country, we go to the country school—the little white wood-frame building where all the country kids come. They come from miles and miles away. They come so far because they are black. As they are riding the school buses they pass school after school where children who are white can attend without being bused, without getting up in the wee hours of the morning, sometimes leaving home in the dark. . . .

School begins with chapel. There we recite the Pledge of Allegiance to the Flag. We have no feeling for the flag but we like the words; said in unison, they sound like a chant. We then listen to a morning prayer. We say the Lord's Prayer. It is the singing that makes morning chapel the happiest moment of the day. It is there I learn to sing "Red River Valley." It is a song about missing and longing. I do not understand all the words, only the feeling—warm wet sorrow, like playing games in spring rain. After chapel we go to classrooms. . . .

Here at the country school we must always work to raise money—selling candy, raffle tickets, having shows for which tickets are sold. Sold to our parents, neighbors, friends, people without money who are shamed into buying little colored paper they cannot afford, tickets that will help keep the school going. . . .

We learn about color with crayons. We learn to tell the difference between white and pink and a color they call Flesh. The flesh-colored crayon amuses us. Like white it never shows up on the thick Manila paper they give us to draw on, or on the brown paper sacks we draw on at home. Flesh we know has no relationship to our skin, for we are brown and brown and brown like all good things. . . .

I must sell tickets for a Tom Thumb wedding, one of the school shows. . . . We get to dress up in paper wedding clothes and go through a ceremony for the entertainment of the adults. The whole thing makes me sick but no one cares. Like every other girl I want to be the bride but I am not chosen. It has always to do with money. The important roles go to the children whose parents have money to give, who will work hard selling tickets. I am lucky to be a bridesmaid, to wear a red crepe paper dress made just for me. I am not thrilled with such luck. I would rather not wear a paper dress, not be in a make-believe wedding. They tell me that I am lucky to be lighter skinned, not black black, not dark brown, lucky to have hair that is almost straight, otherwise I might not be in the wedding at all, otherwise I might not be so lucky.

This luck angers me and when I am angry things always go wrong. We are practicing in our paper dresses, walking down the aisle while the piano music plays a wedding march. We are practicing to be brides, to be girls who will grow up to be given away. My legs would rather be running, itch to go outdoors. My legs are dreaming, adventurous legs. They cannot walk down the aisle without protest. They go too fast. They go too slow. They make everything slow down. The girl walking behind me steps on the red dress; it tears. It moves from my flesh like wind moving against the running legs. I am truly lucky now to have this tear. I hope they will make me sit, but they say No we would not think of taking you out of the show. They know how much every girl wants to be in a wedding. The tear must be mended. The red dress like a woman's heart must break silently and in secret.

Questions to Consider

1. How does this passage illustrate aspects of the Jim Crow era? Be specific and identify several of them.
2. Use an intersectional approach to explain the gender and class dynamics in this memoir. In what ways do they affect hook's childhood experiences differently from African American boys, black girls of higher economic status, or white girls of the same class background?

that integration would require African Americans to become part of the very system that had for centuries oppressed, denigrated, and devalued them and other peoples of color.

The Nation of Islam. The themes of Black Power voiced so loudly in the 1960s were decades, even centuries, old. Marcus Garvey had popularized many of these ideas in the 1920s. In the 1960s, the Nation of Islam, popularly known as the Black Muslims, embraced and further developed them. The Black Muslims, one of the best-known organizations within the Black Power Movement, were angry and outspoken. They denounced the hypocrisy, greed, and racism of American society and advocated staunch resistance and racial separation. The Black Muslims did

Malcolm X, one of the most charismatic representatives for the Black Power Movement. Rosa Parks called him her "personal hero."

Muhammad, the leader of the Nation of Islam, Malcolm X founded his own organization, in which he continued to express and develop the ideas of Black Nationalism. In 1965, like so many other protest leaders of the era, Malcolm X was assassinated (Marable, 2011).

Black Power leaders such as Malcolm X advocated autonomy, independence, and a pluralistic direction for the African American protest movement. They saw the African American community as a colonized, exploited population in need of liberation from the unyielding racial oppression of white America, not integration into the system that was the source of its oppression.

PROTEST, POWER, AND PLURALISM

THE BLACK POWER MOVEMENT IN PERSPECTIVE

By the end of the 1960s, the riots had ended, and the most militant and dramatic manifestations of the Black Power Movement had faded. In many cases, the passion of Black Power activists had been countered by the violence of the police and other agencies such as the FBI. Many of the most powerful spokespersons of the movement were dead, in jail, or in exile. The nation's commitment to racial change wavered and weakened as other concerns, such as the Vietnam War, competed for public attention. Richard M. Nixon was elected president in 1968 and made it clear that his administration would not ally itself with the black protest movement. Pressure from the federal government for racial equality was reduced. The boiling turmoil of the mid-1960s faded, but the idea of Black Power had become thoroughly entrenched in the African American community.

more than talk, however. Pursuing the goals of autonomy and self-determination, they worked hard to create a separate, independent African American economy within the United States. They opened businesses and stores in African American neighborhoods and tried to deal only with other Muslim-owned firms. Their goal was to develop the African American community economically and supply jobs and capital for expansion using solely their own resources (Essien-Udom, 1962; Lincoln, 1961; Malcolm X, 1964; Marable, 2011; Wolfenstein, 1993).

The Nation of Islam and other Black Power groups distinguished between racial separation and racial segregation. The former is a process of empowerment whereby a group grows stronger as it becomes more autonomous and self-controlled. The latter is a system of inequality in which the African American community is powerless and controlled by the dominant group. Thus, the Black Power groups were working to find ways African Americans could develop their own resources and deal with the dominant group from a more powerful position, a strategy similar to that followed by minority groups that form ethnic enclaves (see Chapter 2).

Malcolm X is the best-known representative for the Nation of Islam and was one of the most charismatic figures of the 1960s. Malcolm X forcefully articulated the themes of the Black Power Movement. Born Malcolm Little, he converted to Islam and joined the Nation of Islam while serving a prison term. He became the chief spokesperson for the Black Muslims and a well-known but threatening figure to many white Americans. After a dispute with Elijah

Buildings burning during a riot in the Watts area of Los Angeles, 1965.

In some part, the pluralistic themes of Black Power were a reaction to the failure of assimilation and integration in the 1950s and 1960s. Laws had been passed; court decisions had been widely publicized; and promises and pledges had been made by presidents, members of Congress, ministers, and other leaders. For many African Americans, though, little had changed. Their parents' and grandparents' problems continued to constrain and limit their lives and, as far into the future as they could see, the lives of their children. The pluralistic Black Power ideology was a response to the failure to go beyond the repeal of Jim Crow laws and fully implement the promises of integration and equality.

Black Nationalism, however, was and remains more than simply a reaction to a failed dream. It was also a different way of defining what it means to be black in America. In the context of black–white relations in the 1960s, the Black Power Movement served a variety of purposes. First, along with the Civil Rights Movement, it helped to offer a new way of seeing African Americans. The cultural stereotypes of black Americans (see Chapter 3) emphasized their supposed laziness, irresponsibility, and inferiority. The Black Power Movement rejected these ideas. The black protest movement emphasized African American power, assertiveness, seriousness of purpose, intelligence, and courage.

Second, Black Power served as a new rallying cry for solidarity and unified action. Following the success of the Civil Rights Movement, these new themes and ideas helped to focus attention on "unfinished business": the black–white inequalities that remained in U.S. society.

Finally, the ideology offered an analysis of the problems of American race relations in the 1960s. The Civil Rights Movement, of course, had analyzed race relations in terms of integration, equality of opportunity, and an end to exclusion. After the demise of Jim Crow, that analysis became less relevant. A new language was needed to describe and analyze the continuation of racial inequality. Black Power argued that the continuing problems of U.S. race relations were structural and institutional, not individual or legal. Taking the next steps toward actualizing racial equality and justice would require a fundamental and far-reaching restructuring of society. Ultimately, white Americans, as the beneficiaries of the system, would not support restructuring. The necessary energy and commitment had to come from African Americans pursuing their own self-interests.

Memphis sanitation workers on strike for better wages, working conditions, and dignity. Many had served the country fighting overseas yet returned to racial inequality as had black soldiers before them who fought in the Civil War, World War I, and World War II. Whites, for example, often called them "boy." The I AM A MAN signs speak to that indignity. They also harken back to Sojourner Truth's "Ain't I a Woman" speech (Chapter 4), which built on the 1787 abolitionist campaign, Am I Not a Man and a Brother? Dr. Martin Luther King Jr., who led the march, was assassinated just a few days after this photo was taken.

The nationalistic and pluralistic demands of the Black Power Movement evoked defensiveness and a sense of threat in white society. By questioning the value of assimilation and celebrating a separate African heritage equal in legitimacy with white European heritage, the Black Power Movement questioned the legitimacy and worth of Anglo-American values. In fact, many Black Power spokespersons condemned Anglo-American values fiercely and openly and implicated them in the creation and maintenance of a centuries-long system of racial repression. Today, almost 50 years after the success of the Civil Rights Movement, assertive and critical demands by the African American community continue to be perceived as threatening.

GENDER AND BLACK PROTEST

The Civil Rights and Black Power Movement organizations reflected widely held stereotypical ideas about gender that existed at the time and, which remain to some degree today (e.g., men are "naturally better" leaders or "naturally more intelligent" compared with women). Thus, as with other areas of social life (e.g., workplaces, schools, places of worship) men dominated the leadership and many members often viewed women as supporters of men rather than equal partners in the fight for racial equality. For example, when Rosa Parks joined the NCAAP in 1943, the local leader, Edgar Nixon, reportedly said "women don't need to be nowhere but the kitchen" (Theoharis, 2013, p. 28). However, he needed a secretary and asked Parks to help with those duties. (In Chapter 8, note how a very similar statement was made to Jessie Lopez De La Cruz, an activist in the Chicano Movement.) The Nation of Islam emphasized girls' and women's subservience, imposed a strict code of behavior and dress for women, and separated people by gender in many activities.

Thus, the battle against racism and the battle against sexism were separate struggles with separate and often contradictory agendas (Amott & Matthaei, 1991, p. 177; Theoharis, 2013). Even getting resources to do their work was a struggle, according to activist Gwendolyn Zoharah Simmons who said the women in the movement "had to fight for resources" such as "good typewriters and a good car . . . because the guys would get first dibs on everything" (Simmons, 2011). Some women in these groups actively worked to challenge sexism. For example, the women in the Student Nonviolent Coordinating Committee (SNCC) wrote position papers to protest their relegation to clerical positions and frequently being called "girls" (Andersen, 1993, p. 284).

Although women were denied organizational leadership roles and decision-making positions, they were key participants in the Civil Rights Movement and the Black Power Movement. When the protest movements began, African American women were already heavily involved in community and church work, and used their organizational skills and energy to further the cause of racial equality. Many people view African American women as the backbone of the movement, even if they were often relegated to less glamorous but vital organizational work (Evans, 1979). Fannie Lou Hamer, an African American who became a prominent leader in the Civil Rights Movement, illustrates the importance of the role played by women. Born in 1917 to sharecropper parents, Hamer's life was so circumscribed that until she attended her first rally at the beginning of the Civil Rights Movement she was unaware that African Americans could—even theoretically—register to vote. The day after the rally, she quickly volunteered to register:

> I guess I'd had any sense I'd a-been a little scared, but what was the point of being scared? The only thing they could do to me was kill me and it seemed like they'd been trying to do that a little bit at a time ever since I could remember. (Evans, 1989, p. 271)

Because of her activism, Hamer lost her job, was evicted from her house, and was jailed and beaten on a number of occasions. She devoted herself entirely to the Civil Rights Movement and founded the Freedom Party, which successfully challenged the racially segregated Democratic Party and the all-white political structure of the State of Mississippi (Evans, 1979; Hamer, 1967). Much

Bettmann / Getty Images

Fannie Lou Hamer, a leader of the Civil Rights Movement in Mississippi. Among other notable accomplishments, she founded the Freedom Party, which challenged the racially segregated state Democratic Party.

of the energy that motivated black protest was forged in the depths of segregation and exclusion, a system of oppression that affected all African Americans. Not all segments of the community had the same experience; the realities faced by the black community, as always, were differentiated by class as well as gender as you read in the bell hooks Narrative Portrait earlier in this chapter.

QUESTIONS FOR REFLECTION

5. How did de facto segregation differ from de jure segregation? Were the differences merely cosmetic? Why or why not?

6. How and why did the Black Power Movement differ from the Civil Rights Movement?

7. To what degree did the Black Power Movement succeed in achieving its goals? Explain.

8. What were some of the important gender dimensions of black protest movements?

9. Compare and contrast women's experiences under Jim Crow segregation with that of the antebellum South. How did women's experiences during both times reflect the larger society?

10. What were you most surprised to learn so far in this chapter? Why might that be useful to understand?

11. Consider what you've learned so far throughout this book. What connections do you see between the past and present?

BLACK–WHITE RELATIONS SINCE THE 1960s: ISSUES AND TRENDS

Black–white relations have changed since the 1960s, but the basic outlines of black inequality and white dominance persist. To be sure, improvements have been made in integrating society and eliminating racial inequality. Barack Obama's election to the presidency—which would have been unimaginable just a few decades ago—stands as one unmistakable symbol of racial progress. In fact, it was a breakthrough so stunning that many Americans claimed that the United States had become a "post-racial" society and that the color of people in this society no longer influenced their lives. As trends and statistics will show in this chapter, that argument doesn't hold up to the evidence.

Without denying the signs of progress, the situation of the African American community today has stagnated in many dimensions, and the problems that remain are deep rooted and inextricably mixed with the structure and functioning of modern American society. As was the case in earlier eras, we cannot address contemporary racism and racial inequality apart from changes in the larger society, especially changes in subsistence technology. This section examines the racial separation that continues to characterize so many areas of U.S. society and applies many of the concepts from previous chapters to present-day black–white relations.

CONTINUING SEPARATION

Just over 50 years ago, a presidential commission charged with investigating black urban unrest warned that the United States was "moving towards two societies, one black, one white, separate and unequal" (National Advisory Commission, 1968, p. 1). We could object to the commission's use of the phrase "moving towards," with its suggestion that U.S. society was at one time racially unified, but the warning still seems prophetic.

While race relations are better today, African Americans and white Americans, in many ways, continue to live in separate worlds. The separation is especially complete when race is compounded with class and residence: The black poor lead lives that barely intersect with the lives of the more affluent whites.

The social construction of race, patterns of inequality, and power differentials between the two groups that are the legacy of our racist past structure everyday reality so that many white people see African Americans as "invaders" pushing into areas where they "do not belong" and are not wanted. Sometimes, the reactions to these perceived intrusions are immediate and bloody, as you'll learn later in the chapter. Sociological research suggests that attempts to exclude African Americans continue to be part of everyday life. It can be intentional or unintentional, but the result is the same: profound negative effects for African Americans that often lead to cumulative disadvantage. For example, you read about redlining practices that result in mortgage loans being denied to African Americans or to African Americans being charged much higher rates compared with white loan applicants with similar credit scores (see Chapter 5). In 2016, the Department of Justice and the Consumer Financial Protection Bureau brought charges against a Mississippi-based bank for its widespread discriminatory lending practices. Compared with white counterparts, the bank denied personal and business loans twice as often for African American applicants than for comparable whites and charged blacks higher percentage rates, costing them more over time and, potentially, making it harder to pay back their loans. Moreover, the bank "structur[ed] its business to avoid and discourage consumers in minority neighborhoods from accessing mortgages" (Lane, 2016).

Evidence of continuing discrimination is abundant and the files of the U.S. Equal Employment Opportunity Commission (EEOC) document many cases. The EEOC is charged with investigating and attempting to resolve charges of different types of discrimination (e.g., by race, gender, disability, age) related to hiring, unequal pay and promotion, and hostile work environments. To illustrate, a 2012 case involving an environmental services company found that African American employees were subjected to physical threats, implied threats via the repeated displays of nooses, disrespect, and disparagement by being repeatedly called the "N-word," among other forms of harassment. Several plaintiffs claimed the company fired them because of their race. One supervisor said that he could fire "that . . . N*****" ("*EEOC v. WRS Infrastructure*," 2012). Additionally, several white

COMPARATIVE FOCUS

Race in Another America

FIGURE 6.1 Main Ethnic Groups in Brazil

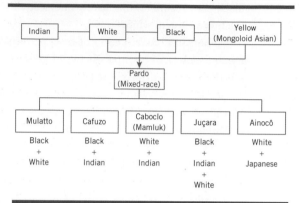

SOURCE: https://commons.wikimedia.org/wiki/File:Main_ethnic_groups_in_brazil.JPG

The dichotomous, white/black social construction of race in the United States contrasts sharply with many other nations. For example, throughout Central and South America, people perceive race as a broad continuum of combinations. One instructive and useful comparison is between Brazil and the United States. Although the racial histories of these two nations run parallel in many ways, they perceive race very differently. Figure 6.1 shows some of the racial categories in Brazil.

To understand the perception of race in Brazil, it may help to consider the demographic differences as long ago as 1880. At the time, the U.S. population was predominantly white (86.5%). African Americans were the second biggest group (13.3%) and Native Americans, Asians, and Hispanics were just 0.3% of the population (Gibson & Jung, 2005, p. 115). Brazil's population was more diverse. Most importantly, "white" and "black" (including "pardo" and "preto" or multiracial) groups were similar in size.

Race in Brazil is based largely on self-identification (Telles, 2002). To illustrate, in 1976, the government asked people to describe their race and this resulted in 134 categories, including "Pinkish white," "Burnt yellow," and "cinnamon," among others (Garcia-Navarro, 2015). Besides skin color, qualities such as hair texture, eye color, ethnicity, and social

class (e.g., education, occupation, income) can affect one's race (Caldwell, 2008; Flavia, et al., 2003). For example, people with higher class status are considered "whiter" than those of lower status, regardless of actual skin color (Bucciferro, 2015; Wade, 1997). Additionally, people may be seen as "whiter" when they marry lighter-skinned person (Hernandez, 2007).

Past scholarship has likened Brazil to a racial utopia (Freyre, 1946) and Brazil has taken pride in being called a "racial democracy." Yet, more expansive constructions of race do not mean that Brazil is egalitarian. Indeed, the Brazilian construction of race that connects whiteness to wealth, education, and "success" also associates blackness with poverty, lack of refinement, and other negative qualities.

The legacy of slavery is strong in Brazil and skin color and social status are highly correlated. For example, black and mixed-race Brazilians have higher illiteracy, unemployment, and poverty rates, and are less likely to have access to a university education compared with white Brazilians (Bourcier, 2012; Gradin, 2007). Additionally, they are more likely than whites to experience police-based violence (Salhani, 2015). Whites dominate the more prestigious and lucrative occupations and the leadership positions in the economy and in politics, while black Brazilians are concentrated at the bottom of the

class system, with mixed-race people in between (Haan & Thorat, 2012; Marteleto, 2012).

People in the United States and Brazil perceive race differently and this is consistent with the notion that race is a social construction. Yet prejudice, discrimination, and racial inequalities are significant parts of both societies' past and present. They take different forms, and this reflects different contact situations and national histories. Brazilian sociologist Antonio Risério put it this way, "It's clear that racism exists in the US. It's clear that racism exists in Brazil. But they are different kinds of racism" (Risério, 2007, p. 17; c.f. Reid, 2014, p. 181).

We will explore this topic further in Chapter 13. For now, consider these points:

The foundation for contemporary race relations in Brazil was laid in the distant past. The Portuguese, the colonial conquerors of Brazil, were mostly single men. They intermarried with people from other racial/ethnic groups and produced "mixed-race" children.

In Brazil, people did not equate slavery as thoroughly with race as in the United States, where slavery, blackness, and inferiority were tightly linked in the dominant ideology. However, Brazilians did link "blackness" with inferiority, which contributed to the social construction of race (including the tendency to "self-whiten"). Contemporary social inequalities reflect these racial ideologies.

After slavery ended, Brazil did not go through a period of legalized racial segregation like the Jim Crow system in the U.S. South or apartheid in South Africa. Mixing between groups had always been common (Affirming a Divide, 2012).

Questions to Consider

1. Compare the social constructions of race in the United States and in Brazil. Why do the differences exist?

2. Think back to the Noel hypothesis. How does contact situation shape contemporary race relations in these two societies?

employees reported being harassed and fired in retaliation for supporting their African American coworkers. As with many other cases of discrimination, the company not only allowed this systemic, repeated discrimination but they did not acknowledge, prevent, or rectify it, even when notified by employees. Management even ignored the "extreme symbolism of a noose" intended to intimidate African Americans. Lastly, they did not provide a "written policy forbidding racial harassment to its employees, post it at the job-site, or train the employees about what constitutes harassment and how to report it," which allowed the harassment to continue ("*EEOC v. WRS Infrastructure*," 2012).

Many cases brought before the courts involve widespread institutional discrimination—discrimination built into organizational policies and procedures—rather than one individual discriminating against another. The largest class action racial discrimination lawsuit to date (*Pigford v. Glickman*) was brought before U.S. District Court for the District of Colombia in 1999 by 13,000 black farmers who charged the U.S. Department of Agriculture (USDA) with widespread discrimination between 1983 and 1997. Evidence showed that the U.S. Department of Agriculture (USDA) systematically discriminated against black farmers in a variety of ways. For example, it was much less likely to give loans to black farmers to buy necessary farm supplies (e.g., equipment, fertilizer) and black farmers had to wait three times as long for loan approval compared with white farmers who applied for similar loans. Additionally, the USDA often "supervised" black farmers, requiring them to get an approval signature from a USDA official before taking their money out of the bank.

When one group is discriminated against, another group is advantaged—even if the group that benefits is not aware of their advantage and did not seek it. By some accounts, decades of preferential treatment for white farmers pushed black farmers out of agriculture. Although USDA policies were "colorblind" the loan application and approval process occurred at the county level. Evidence showed that although many of the counties had majority black populations, almost no people of color were included on local county loan approval committees. The court awarded nearly $1 billion of payments to the farmers. However, because the suit did not include 70,000 black farmers who had been affected, Congress approved another $1.2 billion in restitution payments in 2010.

As the goals of full racial equality and integration continue to seem remote, frustration and anger continue to run high and many African Americans mirror the hostility of whites. While Barack Obama's election created strong optimism and positive attitudes about the future in the black community, the more current, typical mood is pessimistic. (Recall our discussion of public opinion poll results and the differences in black and white perceptions of U.S. race relations from Chapter 1.)

In the last few chapters, you learned about the experiences of African Americans from our nation's founding until the present day. The vast majority of resistance toward racial inequality has been peaceful protest and other kinds of direct nonviolent action (e.g., the Underground Railroad, sit-ins, the Nashville and Montgomery bus boycotts, lawsuits). At times, however, the discontent and frustration have manifested in violence and riots. One of the most widely publicized modern examples occurred in Los Angeles in 1992 when police officers were videotaped beating Rodney King. The police attempted to pull King (and his passengers) over on the highway and he attempted to evade them, eventually pulling off into a residential area. The police approached and ordered them out of the car. Passengers Bryant Allen and Freddie Helms appear to have been hit, kicked, and threatened. However, it was the attack on King, filmed by local residents, that stunned the nation. National and international news outlets covered the incident widely, showing video of the police using a Taser, kicking, and hitting King with a nightstick, even as he lay on the ground. (You could consider this the first "viral video" that occurred at a time before cell phones were ever-present.)

The officers were charged with assault with a deadly weapon and use of excessive force. Contrary to the expectations of most people who saw the video, an all-white jury acquitted the police officers of almost all charges. On April 29, 1992, on hearing word of the acquittals, communities in several cities erupted in violence. The worst disturbance occurred in the Watts section of Los Angeles where more than 60 people died (LATimes Staff, 2012) and 2,300 were injured. Police arrested about 12,000 people and 1,100 buildings, valued between $785 million and $1 billion, were destroyed (Kim & Kim, 1999; Lee, 2015; Wilkens, 1992).

Although the riot was sparked by the Rodney King verdict, it occurred within a larger historical context of racial and class inequality. In 1965, Watts had experienced similar rioting—sometimes called the Watts Rebellion—after police stopped an African American man, Marquette Frye, on suspicion of drunk driving (Alonso, 1998). The situation between police, Frye, and his family members quickly escalated. Accounts differ about what happened. The police claimed that Mr. Frye resisted arrest. Frye said that when his mother attempted to stop the police from impounding their vehicle, the police "roughed [her] up" and knocked him unconscious. During the altercation, a large crowd gathered and quickly grew angry, viewing the situation as yet another example of excessive force by the police (UPI, 1986). The riot lasted five days. More than $40,000,000 of property were destroyed, 34 people died, 1,032 people were injured, and almost 4,000 people were arrested (Alonso, 1998; Hinton, 2016, pp. 68–72).

This 1965 riot should also be contextualized. Remember that due to the Great Migration (Chapter 5), large numbers of African Americans left the South to live in other parts of the country. Between 1940 in 1965, the black population of Los Angeles increased almost 5.5 times (Simpson, 2012). Like other parts of the country, Los Angeles was racially segregated due to redlining and other kinds of housing-related discrimination (e.g., higher rents). Additionally, real estate covenants barred people of color from renting or buying certain properties (see Chapter 5). As a result, in 1940, African Americans (and Asians) were restricted to just 5% of the residential area of Los Angeles, which contributed to overcrowding in those parts of the city (Alonso, 1998).

As more African Americans (and Asian and Hispanics) moved into Los Angeles, pressures to find housing increased. Minorities attempted to move into other neighborhoods, but were subjected to violence or threat of violence (e.g., cross burnings) from whites who wanted to keep them out of "their" neighborhoods. During this time, the Los Angeles suburbs were growing and white families left the city, in mass, as people of color began to move in. This phenomenon is known as "white flight" (see Woldoff, 2011) and it also occurred throughout the country.

In an effort to address widespread patterns of discrimination, the Rumford Fair Housing Act of 1963 made it illegal for landlords to deny housing to anyone on the basis of race, ethnicity, gender, physical ability, religion, and so on. However, in 1964, Californians approved Proposition 14, which, essentially, legalized discrimination by giving landlords the right to "decline to sell, lease or rent such property to such person or persons as he, in his absolute discretion, chooses" (Brilliant, 2010, p. 193). In 1966, Proposition 14 was ruled unconstitutional. Some scholars (Alsonso, 1998; Theoharis, 2006) argue that Proposition 14 contributed to the 1965 riots.

What's important for you to take away from this discussion is that protest doesn't occur in a vacuum. Contemporary civil unrest is built on patterns of the past. Both the 1965 and 1992 L.A. riots illustrate common ingredients: residential segregation, economic disparity, problematic policing, and other forms of social inequality.

Today, cell phones and dashboard cameras often provide visual evidence of police interactions making it easy to forget the social context in which these interactions occur. For example, in 2009 in Oakland, California, Oscar Grant, a 23-year-old black man, was returning from New Year's Eve celebrations in San Francisco when he was caught up in a subway station fight.[1] Police had Grant down on the ground when Officer Johannes Mehserle shot him in the back. Grant was not handcuffed, and Mehserle claimed that Grant was reaching for his waistband—possibly for a gun—when he fired the fatal shot. In fact, Grant was unarmed.

Individuals recorded the shooting on their cell phones and official police cameras also recorded it. The videos quickly went viral on the Internet. Many people saw Grant's death as intentional and unprovoked; yet, the court found Mehserle guilty of a lesser charge of involuntary manslaughter (McKinley, 2010). The community—primarily African American but also including whites, Asians, and Hispanics—responded with both peaceful protests and violent rioting. Mehserle was sentenced to a two-year prison term, but the punishment seemed a mere slap on the wrist to many and provoked further protest, both peaceful and violent (Bulwa, 2010; Egelko, 2009).

In recent years, similar unrest has followed the police-related killings of black boys and men, including (but not limited to) the following:

- Eric Garner (killed on July 17, 2014, in Staten Island, New York)
- Michael Brown (killed on August 9, 2014, in Ferguson, Missouri)
- Tamir Rice (killed on November 22, 2014, in Cleveland, Ohio)
- Tony Robinson (killed March 6, 2015, in Madison, Wisconsin)
- Walter Scott (killed on April 4, 2015, in Charleston, South Carolina)
- Freddie Gray (killed on April 12, 2015, in Baltimore, Maryland)
- Philando Castile (killed on July 6, 2016, in Falcon Heights, Minnesota)
- Sylville Smith (killed on August 13, 2016, in Milwaukee, Wisconsin)
- Terence Crutcher (killed on September 16, 2016, in Tulsa, Oklahoma)
- Keith Scott (killed on September 20, 2016, in Charlotte, North Carolina)

The shooting of Michael Brown in Ferguson, Missouri, sparked some of America's most significant race-related protests to date, gaining international attention and leading to investigations by Amnesty International and the U.S. Department of Justice. Nearly all of the research on Ferguson points to racial tensions in the community including those related to discriminatory policing practiced by a nearly all-white police department in a community that is predominately black. As with other police-related shootings, initial reports about what happened vary (Lowery, Leonnig, & Berman, 2014). What is not in dispute is that Brown's body lay in the street for several hours, in mid-day

---

[1]This incident is the basis for the 2013 feature-length film *Fruitvale Station*.

summer heat. Though the mayor acknowledged that the policy is to immediately cover and then remove the body, that didn't happen in this case. Police say a delay occurred because they weren't able to "quiet the situation" enough to get their investigation underway (Bosman & Goldstein, 2014). Neighbors and other community members interpreted the delay in removing Brown's body as a sign of disrespect—and as a threat, a suggestion of what can happen. Compounding matters, Brown's relatives heard about the shooting from a friend, not from the police. When they arrived at the scene, police did not provide them with information or let them see their son's body (Bosman & Goldstein, 2014; Follman, 2014).

Soon after the shooting, community members began arriving at the location where Brown died, leaving flowers, candles, stuffed animals, notes, and other gifts to memorialize the 18-year-old. Then, several factors changed the direction of this originally peaceful gathering: Police reportedly let one of their dogs urinate on the makeshift memorial. Then, they began to block off the area, driving over some of the memorial's flowers and candles (Follman, 2014; Mathis-Lilley, 2014). The evening of the shooting, community members held a candlelight vigil. Several hundred people went to the police headquarters, held their hands in the air, and said, "Hands up, don't shoot" (Lurie, 2014). (This phrase and gesture became incorporated into later protests and in popular culture.) Police became concerned about "unruly" individuals and brought in 150 police officers with riot gear. People began to vandalize vehicles, break windows, loot stores, and confront the police (Tribune Wire Reports, 2014). In an attempt to control the situation, the police used riot gear and other crowd control tactics; yet, over the next several days, the crowds increased and the situation between community members and police escalated. Thus, Missouri Governor Jay Nixon turned the situation over to the Missouri State Highway Patrol (MSHP) who took a different approach. They arrived without riot gear, vowed not to block the streets, and promised to listen to people's concerns (Hartman, 2014).

Over the next several months, racial tensions in Ferguson continued and smaller protests continued to take place. Anticipating potential problems related to the upcoming grand jury verdict in the case, the governor declared a state of emergency on November 17, 2014. On November 24, when the grand jury did not indict the officer in question, both peaceful protest and angry clashes resumed, setting off a second wave of protest that lasted eight days, including tens of thousands of people protesting in 170 U.S. cities (Almasy & Yan, 2014), Canada, England, and elsewhere (Yan & Almasy, 2014). Crowds adopted the phrase "Black Lives Matter" to emphasize disproportionate violence against blacks, and people engaging in "hashtag activism" adopted #BlackLivesMatter. Though #BlackLivesMatter originated in 2013 near the time when George Zimmerman shot Trayvon Martin, it was only used 48 times until the Brown shooting. In the four hours after the grand jury announcement in the Brown case, people used it 92,784 times on social media (Freelon, McIlwain, & Clark, 2016).

How do we understand racialized violence that follows a historical pattern? The instances described above (going back before the 1965 Watts Rebellion) suggest systemic problems related to race and policing that occur within a larger social context of prejudice, discrimination, racial segregation, and poverty. A U.S. Department of Justice's investigation into Ferguson agreed, finding "a pattern or practice of unlawful conduct within the Ferguson Police Department that violates the First, Fourth, and Fourteenth Amendments to the United States Constitution, and federal statutory law." Further, the report's authors wrote that "officers expect and demand compliance even when they lack legal authority" (Department of Justice, 2015, p. 2). Additionally, "they are inclined to interpret the exercise of free-speech rights as unlawful disobedience, innocent movements as physical threats, indications of mental or physical illness as belligerence" (Department of Justice, 2015, p. 2).

These are complex matters and even with video recording police, protesters, and others may have radically different perceptions of what happened in Ferguson. You only need to read a paper, get on Twitter, or listen to the news to know that Americans are deeply divided about this and other race-related issues. For example, some feel the Black Lives Matter (BLM) protesters should focus on violence within the African American community. Others suggest that focusing on violence against people of color is problematic and they have taken up #AllLivesMatter. Finally, some suggest that BLM protestors are antipolice, and in response, they've started #BlueLivesMatter.

In some ways, recent unrest is similar to the 1960s protests and riots that emerged out of the Civil Rights Movement. The protests and mass violence were spontaneous and expressed diffuse but bitter discontent with the racial status quo. They signaled the continuing racial inequality, urban poverty and despair, and the reality of separate communities, unequal and hostile.

Continuing Separation: Envisioning the Past and Future. Though the shooting of Michael Brown is one of many similar events, something about his death and police-related violence against people of color hit a nerve and became a conduit for broader discussions about racial inequalities, for example, about Civil War monuments and other Confederate-era symbols prominently displayed in town squares, on college campuses, and on city buildings.

Many people question their appropriateness, especially in public spaces. The concern is not just that they suggest a limited history of the South focused narrowly on the Civil War. It's that, devoid of sociohistorical context, such symbols seem to honor people who supported the system of slavery. Further, their continued presence suggests formal and continuing approval of what they represent to many Americans. The mayor of New Orleans articulated these concerns in his May 2017 speech about the removal of its remaining Civil War monuments:

> . . . it immediately begs the questions, why there are no slave ship monuments, no prominent markers on public land to remember the lynchings or the slave blocks; nothing to remember this long chapter of our lives; the pain, the sacrifice, the shame . . . So for those self-appointed defenders of history and the monuments, they are eerily silent on what amounts to this historical malfeasance, a lie by omission. There is a difference between remembrance of history and reverence of it. (Landrieu, 2017)

Throughout this book, we've talked about race as a social construction; however, people collectively *create* meaning about all sorts of things (e.g., beauty, time, gender, age). Because people have different social locations (e.g., race/ethnicity, class, gender, sexual orientation, age, nationality), they may experience the world quite differently. Accordingly, they may construct different, sometimes conflicting, interpretations of social life. Over time, those meanings come to feel "true" and "natural." That's why, when someone has a very different social construction of reality, you might be tempted to call them "crazy."

Social life is complex and it can be helpful to remember the social construction of reality when trying to understand race-related issues. In August 2017, one of the largest white nationalist (WN) gatherings in decades took place in Charlottesville, Virginia. Members of different groups participated including the Ku Klux Klan, neo-Nazis, neo-Confederates (sometimes called Southern Nationalists), the Proud Boys, various militia (Morlin, 2017), as well as groups calling themselves "Anti-Communists" and Fascist/National Socialists ("Flags and Other Symbols," 2017). Violent clashes broke out between the white nationalists and counter protestors. Three people died and dozens were injured. The governor declared a state of emergency (Stolberg & Rosenthal, 2017).

Recently, these groups have become known, collectively, as the "Alt-Right"—a name that suggests they are merely an innocuous "alternative." The Alt-Right name is part of a larger effort "to become more integrated and more mainstream" (Kovaleski et al., 2016). As one neo-Nazi website founder wrote, "we need to be extremely conscious of . . . how we present ourselves" (Anglin, 2017). Thus, in a similar move, one major group (the National Socialist Movement) has replaced the swastikas on its uniforms and banners with the Odal (or Othala) Rune (⚭), a lesser known symbol used by the Nazis (Kovaleski et al., 2016). Other groups have followed suit.

The rally, on the surface, was to protest the city's plan to remove a statue of Robert E. Lee from a local park. Participants carried torches, confederate flags, and signs saying, for example, "you will not replace us." This phrase is a reference to the statue's planned removal and to the WN interpretation of the nation's changing demographics (see Chapter 10). Specifically, they see whites as losing their numerical majority and "being replaced" by people of color, calling it "white genocide" (Kessler, 2017; Law, 2017). From their perspective, it is crucial to "unite the right" and organizers hoped the Charlottesville rally would build a coalition of white Americans who might otherwise have felt divided due to ethnic heritage (e.g., Irish, French) or region (e.g., Northerners, Southerners). As one speaker put it, "We are all White, and that means we are all in the same boat now" (Law, 2017).

Because people collectively construct meaning, the statue of Robert E. Lee simultaneously exists as a symbol of all that is good about the South, sacrifice in war, and southern heritage, *as well as* a symbol of racial hatred, oppression, inequality, and coercion. Its removal—or continued placement—threatens people's beliefs, values, and norms. For example, consider protests about the 2015 decision to remove the Confederate flag from the South Carolina statehouse grounds (Rosenblatt & Siemaszko, 2017). While some supporters of the Confederate flag claim its removal is a misguided attempt to erase history, a study by the Georgia state senate noted that until the 1940s, the flag "largely went away" (Strother, Ogorzalek, & Piston, 2017) except in Civil War re-enactments or to honor the dead or in Confederate veterans' parades (Bruzgulis, 2015). However, the flag's meaning, and its presence, changed with the 1948 "Dixiecrat revolt" when white Southerners walked out of the Democratic National Convention to protest the party's civil rights goals—a schism that had been brewing between conservatives and liberals within the party since the early 1930s.

During the Jim Crow era, some southern states incorporated aspects of the Confederate flag into their flags as visible reminders of white resistance to racial change (Coski, 2009). These efforts increased with the 1954 *Brown v. Board of Education* ruling in favor of desegregation. For example, Georgia changed its state flag two years after the *Brown* decision. The official resolutions to add the confederate emblem to the Georgia state flag framed it as a desire to honor southern "tradition." It did not mention the Civil War or Confederate soldiers as part of its motivation. Rather,

Removal of Robert E. Lee statue in New Orleans in May 2017.

A Biased Criminal Justice System? The perception of bias is not without justification. As this text has documented, the police and other elements of the criminal justice system have a long tradition of abuse, harassment, and mistreatment of people of color. Within this context, it seems understandable that African Americans would be more likely than whites to view the police and the criminal justice system with suspicion. For example, a 2016 nationally representative poll found that 76% of black respondents thought that the American criminal justice system is biased against blacks compared with 45% of whites (Newport, 2016a). Gallup Poll data for 2011–2016 (combined) showed a similar pattern regarding racialized perception of the police: 58% of whites have "a great deal or quite a lot" of confidence in the police compared with 29% of blacks (Newport, 2016a).

The vast majority of social science research has documented the continuing bias of the criminal justice system, at all levels, against African Americans (and other minorities). In a comprehensive summary of this research, Rosich (2007) concluded that, while blatant and overt discrimination has diminished over the past few decades, the biases that remain have powerful consequences for the black community, even though they often are more subtle and harder to tease out. Even slight acts of racial discrimination can have a cumulative effect throughout the stages of processing in the criminal justice system and can result in large differences in racial outcomes (Rosich, 2007).

The magnitude of these racial differences is documented by a report that found that, while African Americans make up 16% of all young people, they account for 28% of juvenile arrests, 34% of youths formally processed by the courts, and 58% of youths sent to adult prison (National Council on Crime and Delinquency, 2007, p. 37; see also Mauer, 2011). Civil rights advocates and other spokespersons for the black community charge that there is a dual justice system in the United States and that African Americans, adults as well as juveniles, are more likely to receive harsher treatment than are whites charged with similar crimes.

The greater vulnerability of the African American community to the criminal justice system is further documented in two recent studies. The first (Pettit & Western, 2004) focused on men born between 1965 and 1969, and found that 20% of African Americans, compared with 3% of whites, had been imprisoned by the time they were 30 years old. Also, the study found that education was a key variable affecting the probability of imprisonment: Nearly 60% of African American men in this cohort who had not completed high school went to prison.

The second study (Neal & Rick, 2014) concluded that black men, especially those with lower levels of education, have been the major victims of the growth in American incarceration rates over the past several decades. As many

it identified school integration as "an affront and challenge to [those] traditions" and vowed "to protect and maintain the segregation of the races in our schools" (Strother, Ogorzalek, & Piston, 2017). Georgia redesigned its state flag in 2003 to remove any trace of the Confederate flag.

Instead of redesigning its state flag, South Carolina began flying the Confederate flag on top of its statehouse in 1961, ostensibly to celebrate the Confederate War Centennial. Taken as a whole, we can see the incorporation of the Confederate flag into state flags (or city buildings) as resistance to racial equality in general and to federal civil rights laws, specifically (Bruzgulis, 2015; Coski, 2009; Strother, Ogorzalek, & Piston, 2017). Likewise, we can interpret contemporary battles about race-related objects and events as a struggle between groups to define history and enforce laws and informal norms.

THE CRIMINAL JUSTICE SYSTEM AND AFRICAN AMERICANS

No area of race relations seems more volatile and controversial than the relationship between the black community and the criminal justice system. There is considerable mistrust and resentment of the police among minorities, especially African Americans, and the perception that the entire criminal justice system is stacked against them is common.

Trayvon Martin, another victim of a racially biased criminal justice system?

as a third of black male high school dropouts age 26 to 29 in 2010 have been imprisoned or otherwise institutionalized. As a result, black men, relative to white men, face far worse prospects in the labor market today than they did as recently as the 1980s (Neal & Rick, 2014, p. 80).

The War on Drugs. Perhaps the most important reason for these racial differences is that, since the 1980s, black men have been much more likely than white men to get caught up in the national "get tough" policy on drugs, especially for crack cocaine. Crack cocaine is a cheap form of the drug, and the street-level dealers who have felt the brunt of the national antidrug campaign disproportionately have been young African American men from less affluent areas. Affluent whites tend to use the powder form of cocaine.

Some see the "war on drugs" as a not-so-subtle form of racial discrimination. For example, until 2010, federal law required a mandatory prison term of five years for possession of five grams of crack cocaine, a drug much more likely to be dealt by poor African Americans. In contrast, comparable levels of sentencing for dealing powder cocaine—the more expensive form of the drug—are not reached until the accused possesses a minimum of 500 grams (Rosich, 2007). Originally, it was thought that crack was much more addictive than powder cocaine and sentencing guidelines reflected this idea. The result is that many more poor

minorities are serving lengthy prison sentences compared to whites who used the powdered form of cocaine.

In 2010, the sentencing disparity was reduced by congressional action, and the mandatory five-year prison term for simple possession of crack cocaine was eliminated (Eckholm, 2010), yet Figure 6.2 illustrates the much higher drug arrest rate for black since the early 1980s. Notice that the arrest rate for African Americans spiked in the late 1980s, when the war on drugs began.

Another recent study focused on marijuana arrests and found huge racial disparities in the nation as a whole, in every state except Hawaii, and in the great majority of counties (American Civil Liberties Union, 2013). Nationally, in 2010, African Americans were arrested at a rate of about 700 per 100,000 population, while the white arrest rate was slightly less than 200 per 100,000 population. Thus, African Americans were roughly 3.5 times more likely to be arrested for this crime. Is this because black Americans use the drug more than do white Americans? Decidedly not. There was virtually no difference in the rate of use for African Americans and whites either in the populations as a whole or among younger people.

If there is no racial difference in marijuana use, what accounts for the huge racial disparity in arrests? Like the narratives that opened this chapter, African Americans are more likely to be policed, watched, stopped and frisked, and profiled than are whites. Their greater vulnerability to

FIGURE 6.2 Drug Abuse Arrests by Race, 1980–2015

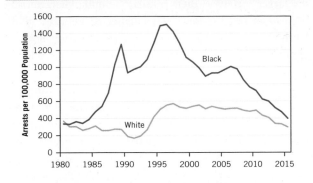

SOURCE: National Center for Juvenile Justice, 2017. "Juvenile Arrest Rates by Offence, Race, and Sex, 1980–2015."

arrest for this relatively minor offense is echoed in patterns throughout the criminal justice system and reflects the continuing "otherness" of African Americans in U.S. society.

Racial Profiling. The racial differences in vulnerability to arrest are captured by the concept of racial profiling: the police use of race as an indicator when calculating whether a person is suspicious or dangerous (Kennedy, 2001b, p. 3). The tendency to focus more on African Americans and disproportionately to stop, question, and follow them is a form of discrimination that generates resentment and increases the distrust (and fear) many African Americans feel toward their local police forces.

According to some, humiliating encounters with police (e.g., being stopped and questioned for "driving while black") are virtually a rite of passage for black men (Kennedy, 2001b, p. 7). According to one national survey, 17% of young black men felt that they had been "treated unfairly" in dealings with the police within the previous 30 days (Newport, 2013b).

The charges of racial profiling and discrimination in the war on drugs can be controversial, but these patterns sustain the ancient perceptions of African Americans as dangerous outsiders, and in the African American community they feed the tradition of resentment and anger toward the police.

The New Jim Crow? Many of the ideas in this section are presented in a thought-provoking, important book, *The New Jim Crow: Mass Incarceration in the Age of Colorblindness* (Alexander, 2012). Alexander argues that the racial differentials in the war on drugs amount to a new racial control system that has halted Civil Rights era advances. The millions of black men who have been convicted under the racially biased drug laws are not only sent to prison; they also carry the stigma of a felony conviction for their entire lives. Their prospects for legitimate employment are miniscule, they lose the right to vote, and they are ineligible for many government programs, including student loans for college. Like the entire black population under de jure

segregation, they are marginalized, excluded, second-class citizens highly controlled by the state.

INCREASING CLASS INEQUALITY

As black Americans moved out of the rural South and as the repressive force of de jure segregation receded, social class inequality within the African American population increased. Since the 1960s, the black middle class has grown, but black poverty continues to be a serious problem.

The Black Middle Class. A small African American middle class, based largely on occupations and businesses serving only the African American community, had been in existence since before the Civil War (Frazier, 1957). Has this more affluent segment benefited from increasing tolerance in the larger society, civil rights legislation, and affirmative action programs? Has the black middle class continued to increase in size and affluence?

The answer to these questions appears to be no. Any progress that might have been made since the civil rights era seems to have been wiped out by the downturn in the American economy that began in 2007.

In actuality, it seems that the size and prosperity of the black middle class was always less than is sometimes assumed. Two studies illustrate this point. One (Kochhar, 2004) found that between 1996 and 2002, the percentage of African Americans that could be considered middle and upper class never exceeded 25% of the black population. The comparable figure for whites was almost 60%. Thus, according to this study, the black middle and upper classes were less than half the size of the white middle and upper classes.

The other study (Oliver & Shapiro, 2006) indicates that, prior to the 2007 economic disruption, the African American middle class was not only smaller than the white middle class but also much less affluent. The researchers studied racial differences in wealth, which includes not only income but all other financial assets: the value of houses, cars, savings, other property, and so forth.

Figure 6.3 compares the wealth of African Americans and whites, using two different definitions of middle class and two different measures of wealth. Middle-class status is defined, first, in terms of level of education, with a college education indicating middle-class status, and, second, in terms of occupation, with a white-collar occupation indicating middle-class status.

Wealth is defined first in terms of net worth, which includes all assets (houses, cars, and so forth) minus debt. The second measure, net financial assets, is the same as net worth but excludes the value of a person's investments in home and cars. This second measure is a better indicator of the resources that are available to invest in educating the next generation or financing new businesses (Oliver & Shapiro, 2006, pp. 60–62).

FIGURE 6.3 Wealth by Definition of the Middle Class by Race

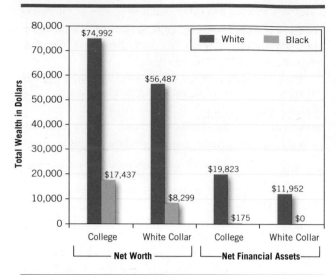

SOURCE: Based on Oliver & Shapiro (2006, p. 96).

By either definition, the black middle class was at a distinct disadvantage. There are huge differentials in net worth between African Americans and whites, and even greater differences in net financial assets. Note, in fact, that the figure for net financial assets of African Americans in white-collar occupations is exactly zero. Once their equity in houses and cars is subtracted out, they are left with no wealth at all, a statistic that strongly underscores the greater precariousness of middle-class standing for African Americans.

The bad economic times that began in 2007 have affected virtually all Americans, but they have had a disproportionally harsh effect on African Americans. In 2013, the net worth of white households was $144,200, slightly less than in 2007 but 13 times greater than the new worth ($11,200) of black households (Pew Research Center, 2016, p. 25; see also Shapiro, Meschede, & Osoro, 2013, p. 2; see also Kochhar, Fry, & Taylor, 2011).

These economic differences are due partly to discrimination in the present and partly to the racial gaps in income, wealth, and economic opportunity inherited from past generations. As we mentioned in Chapter 5, racial differences in homeownership are a key component of the racial gap in wealth (Shapiro et al., 2013, p. 4). The greater economic marginality of the African American middle class today is a form of past-in-present institutional discrimination (see Chapter 5). It reflects the greater ability of white parents (and grandparents), in large part rooted in higher rates of homeownership, to finance higher education and subsidize business ventures and home mortgages (Oliver & Shapiro, 2006).

Not only is their economic position more marginal, but middle-class African Americans commonly report that they are unable to escape the narrow straitjacket of race.

No matter what their level of success, occupation, or professional accomplishments, race continues to be seen by the larger society as their primary defining characteristic (Benjamin, 2005; Cose, 1993; Hughes & Thomas, 1998). Without denying the advances of some, many analysts argue that the stigma of race continues to set sharp limits on the life chances of African Americans.

There is also a concern that greater class differentiation may decrease solidarity and cohesion within the African American community. There is greater income inequality among African Americans than ever before, with the urban poor at one extreme and some of the wealthiest, most recognized figures in the world—millionaires, celebrities, business moguls, politicians, and sports and movie stars—at the other. Will the more affluent segment of the African American community disassociate itself from the plight of the less fortunate and move away from the urban neighborhoods, taking with it its affluence, articulateness, and leadership skills? If this happens, it would reinforce the class division and further seal the fate of impoverished African Americans, who are largely concentrated in urban areas.

Urban Poverty. African Americans have become an urban minority group, and the fate of the group is inextricably bound to the fate of America's cities. The issues of black–white relations cannot be successfully addressed without dealing with urban issues, and vice versa.

As we saw in Chapter 5, automation and mechanization in the workplace have eliminated many of the manual labor jobs that sustained city dwellers in earlier decades (Kasarda, 1989). The manufacturing, or secondary, segment of the labor force has declined in size, and the service sector has continued to expand. The more desirable jobs in the service sector have more and more demanding educational prerequisites. The service-sector jobs available to people with lower educational credentials pay low wages—often less than the minimum necessary for the basics, including food and shelter, and offer little in the way of benefits, little security, and few links to more rewarding occupations. This form of past-in-present institutional discrimination constitutes a powerful handicap for colonized groups such as African Americans, who have been excluded from educational opportunities for centuries.

Furthermore, many of the blue-collar jobs that have escaped automation have migrated away from the cities. Industrialists have been moving their businesses to areas where labor is cheaper, unions have less power, and taxes are lower. This movement to the suburbs, to the Sunbelt, and out of the country has been devastating for the inner city. Poor transportation systems, the absence of affordable housing outside the center city, and outright housing discrimination have combined to keep urban poor people of color confined to center-city neighborhoods, distant from opportunities for jobs and economic improvement (Feagin, 2001, pp. 159–160; Kasarda, 1989; Massey & Denton, 1993).

Sociologist Rogelio Saenz (2005) analyzed the situation of African Americans in the 15 largest metropolitan areas in the nation and found that they are much more likely than whites to be living in highly impoverished neighborhoods, cut off from the "economic opportunities, services, and institutions that families need to succeed" (para. 2). Saenz found that the greater vulnerability and social and geographical isolation of African Americans is pervasive, however, and includes not only higher rates of poverty and unemployment but also large differences in access to cars and even phones, amenities taken for granted in the rest of society. In the areas studied by Saenz, African Americans were as much as three times more likely not to have a car (and, thus, no means to get to jobs outside center-city areas) and as much as eight times more likely not to have a telephone.

Furthermore, after some improvements in the late 20th century, the racial concentration of poverty has increased since 2000. Jargowsky (2015) reports that, since 2000, the percentage of African Americans living in "high poverty neighborhoods" (defined as a neighborhood in which more than 40% of the population was below the poverty level) has increased from 19% to 25%. Comparatively, only about 8% of whites lived in high poverty neighborhoods in 2015 (Jargowsky, 2015, p. 6).

Some of these industrial and economic forces affect all poor urbanites, not just minority groups or African Americans in particular. The dilemma facing many African Americans is not only due to racism or discrimination; the impersonal forces of evolving industrialization and social class structures contribute in some part as well. However, when immutable racial stigmas and centuries of prejudice (even disguised as modern racism) are added to these economic and urban developments, the forces limiting and constraining many African Americans become extremely formidable.

For the past 60 years, the African American poor have been increasingly concentrated in narrowly delimited urban areas ("the ghetto") in which the scourge of poverty has been compounded and reinforced by a host of other problems, including joblessness, high rates of school dropout, crime, drug use, teenage pregnancy, and welfare dependency. These increasingly isolated neighborhoods are fertile grounds for the development of oppositional cultures, which reject or invert the values of the larger society. The black urban counterculture may be most visible in music, fashion, speech, and other forms of popular culture, but it is also manifested in widespread lack of trust in the larger society, and whites in particular. An

urban underclass, barred from the mainstream economy and the primary labor force and consisting largely of poor African Americans and other minority groups of color, has become a prominent and perhaps permanent feature of the American landscape (Kasarda, 1989; Massey & Denton, 1993; Wilson, 1987, 1996, 2009).

Consider the parallels and contrasts between the plight of the present urban underclass and black Southerners under de jure segregation:

- In both eras, a large segment of the African American population was cut off from opportunities for success and growth.
- In the earlier era, African Americans were isolated in rural areas; now, they are isolated in urban areas, especially center cities.
- In the past, escape from segregation was limited primarily by political and legal restrictions and blatant racial prejudice; escape from poverty in the present is limited by economic and educational deficits and a more subtle and amorphous prejudice.

The result is the same: Many African Americans remain as a colonized minority group—isolated, marginalized, and burdened with a legacy of powerlessness and poverty.

MODERN INSTITUTIONAL DISCRIMINATION

The processes that maintain racial inequality in the present are indirect and sometimes difficult to document and measure. They often flow from the patterns of blatant racial discrimination in the past but are not overtly racial in the present. They operate through a series of cumulative effects that tend to filter black Americans into less desirable positions in education, housing, the criminal justice system, and the job market. To better understand this, we will consider two areas where racial class inequalities are perpetuated: employment networks that were closed in the past and remain shut today, and the greater vulnerability of the black community to economic hardships in the larger society.

Closed Networks and Racial Exclusion. The continuing importance of race as a primary factor in the perpetuation of class inequality is dramatically illustrated in a research project conducted by Royster (2003), who interviewed

The **urban underclass** refers to African Americans and other minority groups of color who are marginalized and separated from the economic mainstream.

FIGURE 6.4 Unemployment Rate by Race, United States 1972–2016

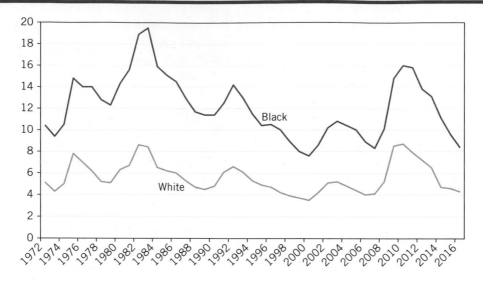

SOURCE: Bureau of Labor Statistics. 1972–2013: Labor Force Characteristics by Race and Ethnicity http://www.bls.gov/opub/reports/cps/race_ethnicity_2013.pdf 2014–2016: Bureau of Labor Statistics, 2016 "Employment Status of Civilian Noninstitutionalized Population by Sex, Age, and Race https://www.bls.gov/cps/cpsaat05.pdf.

black and white graduates of a trade school in Baltimore. Her respondents had all completed the same curricula and earned similar grades. In other words, they were nearly identical in terms of the credentials they brought to the world of work. Nonetheless, the black graduates were employed less often in the trades for which they had been educated, had lower wages, and fewer promotions, and experienced longer periods of unemployment. Virtually every white graduate found secure and reasonably lucrative employment. The black graduates, in stark contrast, usually were unable to stay in the trades and became, instead, low-skilled, low-paid workers in the service sector.

What accounts for these differences? Based on extensive interviews with the subjects, Royster (2003) concluded that the differences could not be explained by training or personality characteristics. Instead, she found that what really mattered was not "what you know" but "who you know." The white graduates had access to networks of referrals and recruitment that linked them to the job market in ways that simply were not available to black graduates. In their search for jobs, whites were assisted more fully by their instructors and were able to use intraracial networks of family and friends, connections so powerful that they "assured even the worst [white] troublemaker a solid place in the blue-collar fold" (p. 78).

Needless to say, these results run contrary to some deeply held American values, most notably the widespread, strong support for the idea that success in life is due to individual effort, self-discipline, and the other attributes enshrined in the Protestant Ethic. The strength of this faith is documented in a recent survey that was administered to a representative sample of adult Americans. The respondents were asked whether they thought people got ahead by hard

work, luck, or a combination of the two. The majority of the sample, 69%, chose "hard work," and another 20% chose "hard work and luck equally" (National Opinion Research Council, 1972–2016). This overwhelming support for the importance of individual effort is echoed in human capital theory and many "traditional" sociological perspectives on assimilation (see Chapter 2).

Royster's (2003) results demonstrate that the American faith in the power of hard work alone is simply wrong. To the contrary, access to jobs is controlled by networks of personal relationships that are decidedly not open to everyone. These subtle patterns of exclusion and closed intraracial networks are more difficult to document than the blatant discrimination that was at the core of Jim Crow segregation, but they can be just as devastating in their effects and just as powerful as mechanisms for perpetuating racial gaps in income and employment.

The Differential Impact of Hard Times. Because of their greater vulnerability, African Americans are more likely to suffer the more virulent form of any illness—economic or otherwise—that strikes society: They will tend to feel the impact earlier, experience higher levels of distress, and be the last to recover. As we have seen, the 2007 recession has affected almost everyone in one way or another. Americans everywhere suffered job loss, increasing poverty, home foreclosures, loss of health care coverage, and other disasters. How has the recession affected the black community?

Consider the unemployment rate, which generally runs twice as high for blacks as for whites. During the recession, the rate rose for all groups but, as displayed in Figure 6.4, it rose earlier for blacks, rose at a steeper angle to a much higher peak, and leveled off and began to fall later than for

FIGURE 6.5 Composition of Family Households in the United States, 1970–2016

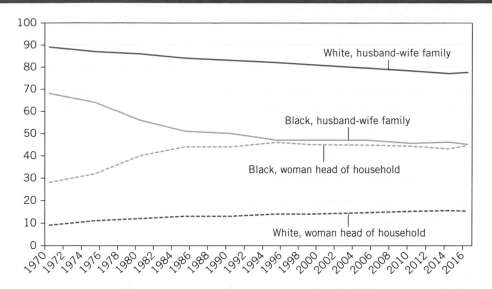

SOURCE: U.S. Bureau of the Census, 1978, p. 43, 2007, p. 56, 2016b.

whites. The highest rate for whites was 8.7%, about 55% of the peak rate of 15.8% for blacks.

The white unemployment rate leveled off and began to fall in early 2010, but the rate for African Americans did not begin to decline until nearly two years later. These hard times affected all groups, across the board, but created a deeper economic hole for black Americans.

Another crucial area in which African Americans have been disproportionately affected by the recession is homeownership, which, as we have noted on several occasions, is a crucial source of wealth for the average American. Income enables families to get along, but financial assets such as homeownership help families get ahead, escape poverty, and become socially mobile (Oliver & Shapiro, 2008, p. A9).

Not surprisingly, black Americans suffered more in this area during the recent recession, as they did in unemployment. In addition to the "redlining" noted earlier in the chapter, one report (Oliver & Shapiro, 2008) found that black Americans and other minority groups of color, compared with whites, were more than three times as likely to be victimized by toxic "subprime" home loans and more than twice as likely to suffer foreclosure as a result. Subprime home loans were new financial instruments that enabled many previously ineligible people to qualify for home mortgages. Predatory lenders marketed the loans especially to more vulnerable populations, and the deals had hidden costs, higher interest rates, and other features that made keeping up with payments difficult. One result of the housing market's collapse was "the greatest loss of financial wealth" in the African American community (Oliver & Shapiro, 2008, p. A11). By 2017, only 43% of African Americans were home owners, compared to 72% of whites (U.S. Bureau of the Census, 2017, p. 9).

Thus, a group that was already more vulnerable and economically marginal suffered the greatest proportional loss—an economic collapse that will take years to recover from. Societal disasters such as the recent recession are not shared equally by everyone, but are especially severe for the groups that are the most vulnerable and have the most tenuous connections with prosperity and affluence. Thus, racial inequality persists decades after the end of blatant, direct, state-supported segregation.

THE FAMILY INSTITUTION AND THE CULTURE OF POVERTY

The state of African American families as a social institution has been a continuing source of public concern and controversy. On one hand, some analysts see the African American family as structurally weak, a cause of continuing poverty and a variety of other problems. No doubt the most famous study in this tradition was the Moynihan (1965) report, which focused on the higher rates of divorce, separation, desertion, and children born out of marriage among African American families and the fact that black families were far more likely to be headed by women than white families. Moynihan concluded that the fundamental barrier facing African Americans was a family structure that he saw as crumbling, a condition that would perpetuate the cycle of poverty entrapping African Americans (p. iii). Today, many of the differences between black and white heterosexual couples identified by Moynihan are even more pronounced. Figure 6.5, for example, compares the percentage of households headed by women (black and white) with the percentage of heterosexual households headed by married

FIGURE 6.6 Median Income for Full-Time, Year-Round Workers by Race and Gender, 1955–2015

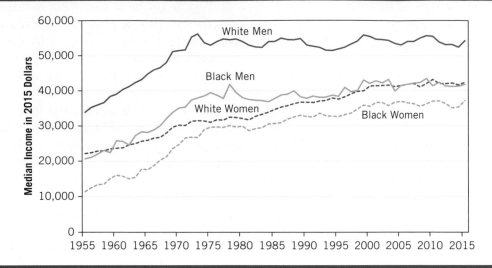

SOURCE: U.S. Bureau of the Census, 2016. Table P-36 Historical Income Tables: People Full-Time Year Round Workers by Median Income and Sex, https://www.census.gov/data/tables/time-series/demo/income-poverty/historical-income-people.html.

couples. (Note that the trends seem to have stabilized since the mid-1990s.)

The line of analysis implicit in the Moynihan (1965) Report locates the problem of urban poverty in the characteristics of the African American community, particularly in African American families. These structures are "broken" in important ways and need to be "fixed." This argument is consistent with the **culture of poverty theory**, which argues that poverty is perpetuated by the particular characteristics of the poor. Specifically, poverty is said to encourage **fatalism** (the sense that one's destiny is beyond one's control) and an orientation to the present rather than the future. The desire for instant gratification is a central trait of the culture of poverty, as opposed to the ability to defer gratification, which is thought to be essential for middle-class success. Other characteristics include violence, school failure, authoritarianism, and high rates of alcoholism and family desertion by men (Lewis, 1959, 1965, 1966; for a recent reprise of the debate over the culture of poverty concept, see Small, Harding, & Lamont, 2010; Steinberg, 2011).

The culture of poverty theory leads to the conclusion that the problem of urban poverty would be resolved if woman-headed family structures and other cultural characteristics correlated with poverty could be changed.

Culture of poverty theory argues that poverty creates certain personality traits—such as the need for instant gratification—that, in turn, perpetuate poverty.

Fatalism is the view that one's destiny is beyond one's control.

Note that this approach is consistent with the traditional assimilationist perspective and human capital theory: The poor have "bad" or inappropriate values. If they could be equipped with "good" (i.e., white, middle-class) values, the problem would be resolved.

An opposed perspective, more consistent with the concepts and theories that underlie this text, sees the matriarchal structure of the African American family as the *result* of urban poverty—rather than a cause—and a reflection of pervasive, institutional racial discrimination and the scarcity of jobs for urban African American men. In impoverished African American urban neighborhoods, the supply of men able to support a family is reduced by high rates of unemployment, incarceration, and violence, and these conditions are, in turn, created by the concentration of urban poverty and the growth of the "underclass" (Massey & Denton, 1993; Wilson, 1996, 2009). Thus, the burden of child rearing tends to fall on women, and woman-headed households are more common than in more advantaged neighborhoods.

Woman-headed African American families tend to be poor, not because they are weak in some sense but because of the lower wages accorded to women in general and to African American women in particular, as documented in Figure 6.6. Note that Figure 6.6 includes only full-time, year-round workers and that wages are presented in 2015 dollars, to control for the effects of inflation. Black woman workers have the lowest wages throughout the time period. Also note that the gap between black women and white men has narrowed over the years. In 1955, black women earned about a third of what white men earned. In 2015, the gap stood at about 68% (after shrinking to just under 70% in 2005), largely because men's wages (for African Americans as well as whites) have been relatively flat since the 1970s, while women's wages (again for both whites and African Americans) have risen. This pattern reflects the impact of deindustrialization: the shift away from manufacturing, which has eliminated many good blue-collar jobs, and the rise of employment sectors in which women tend to be more concentrated.

The poverty associated with black women-headed households reflects the interactive effects of sexism and racism on black women, not some weakness in the black family. African American urban poverty is the result of the complex forces of past and present institutional discrimination, American racism and prejudice, the precarious position of African American women in the labor force, and continuing urbanization and industrialization. The African American family is not in need of "fixing," and the attitudes and values of the urban underclass are more the results of impoverishment than they are the causes. The solution to African American urban poverty lies in fundamental changes in the urban industrial economy and sweeping alterations in the distribution of resources and opportunities.

MIXED RACE AND NEW RACIAL IDENTITIES

As we have discussed, Americans traditionally see race as a simple dichotomy: People are either black or white, with no intermediate categories. In the past, the social convention of the "one-drop rule" meant that people of mixed racial descent were classified as black. To illustrate, consider the story of Gregory Williams (known then as Billy), a white boy growing up in the segregated South in the late 1940s and early 1950s (Williams, 1995). When Billy was 10, his father revealed that he was "half-colored." Under the one-drop rule, that made Billy black. He at first refused to believe his father: "I'm not colored, I'm white! I look white! I've always been white! I go to the 'whites only' school, 'whites only' movie theaters, and 'whites only' swimming pool" (p. 34). Gradually, he came to realize that his life—not just his life chances and his relations with others but his very identity—had been transformed by the revelation of his father's race.

In the past, mixed-race people such as Williams had few choices: Others classified him as black, and the rigid social conventions of the day forced him to accept that identity, with all its implications. Today, five decades after the formal end of Jim Crow segregation, Americans are confronting the limitations of this dichotomous racial convention. People of mixed-race descent are increasing in number and, in fact, are some of the most prominent and well-known people in society. President Obama is an obvious example of a highly visible mixed-race person, but others include professional golfer Tiger Woods (who defines himself—tongue in cheek—as Cablanasian: Caucasian,

black, American Indian, and Asian), vocalist Mariah Carey, Yankees baseball star Derek Jeter, and actress Halle Berry.

How do people of multiracial descent define themselves today? How do others define them? Have the old understandings of race become irrelevant? Is there still pressure to place people in one and only one group? There has been a fair amount of research on this issue, and we can begin to formulate some ideas.

One important study illustrates some of the possible identities for mixed-race individuals. Rockquemore and Brunsma (2008; Brunsma, 2005) interviewed several hundred mixed-race college students, confining their attention to people who had one white and one black parent. They found that, in contrast to the definition of racial identity faced by Billy Williams, today the meaning of mixed-race identity is conceptually complex and highly variable (Rockquemore & Brunsma, 2008, p. 50). They identified four main categories that their respondents used to understand their biracialism, and we present these in order from most to least common. However, the sample they assembled was not representative, so we can't assume that these same percentages would characterize all biracial Americans.

1. The most common racial identity in the sample was the *border identity*. These respondents (58% of the sample) didn't consider themselves to be either black or white. They define themselves as members of a third, separate category that is linked to both groups but is unique in itself. One respondent declared, "I'm not black, I'm biracial" (Rockquemore & Brunsma, 2008, p. 43). The authors make a further distinction:

    a. Some border identities are "validated" or recognized and acknowledged by others. These respondents see themselves as biracial, and they are also seen that way by family, friends, and the community.

    b. Other border identities are "unvalidated" by others. These individuals see themselves as biracial but are classified by others as black. For example, one respondent said, "I consider myself biracial but I experience the world as a black person" (p. 45). This disconnect may be the result of the persistence of traditional dichotomous racial thinking and the fact that some people do not recognize or understand the category of "biracial." According to the authors, people in this category are of special interest because of the tensions created by the conflict between their self-image and the way they are defined by others.

2. The second most common identity in the sample was the *singular identity*. These individuals saw themselves not as biracial, but as exclusively black (13%) or

exclusively white (3%). As Williams's case illustrated, the singular black identity is most consistent with American traditional thinking about race. The authors argue that the fact that this identity is *not* the most common in their sample illustrates the complexity of racial identity for biracial people today.

3. A third identity was the *transcendent identity* (15%). The respondents in this category rejected the whole notion of race, along with the traditional categories of black and white, and insisted that they should be seen as unique individuals and not placed in a category, especially because those categories carry multiple assumptions about character, personality, intelligence, attitudes, and a host of other characteristics. Respondents with the transcendent identity were in a constant battle to avoid classification in America's highly race-conscious society. One respondent's remarks are illustrative:

> *I'm just John, you know? . . . I'm a good guy, just like me for that. . . . When I came here (to college), it was like I was almost forced to look at other people as being white, black, Asian, or Hispanic. And so now, I'm still trying to go, "I'm just John," but uh, you gotta be something. (Rockquemore & Brunsma, 2008, p. 49)*

4. The final racial identity is the least common (4%) but perhaps the most interesting. The authors describe the racial identity of these individuals as *protean*, or changing as the individual moves from group to group and through the various social contexts of everyday life. There are different "ways of being" in groups of African Americans versus groups of whites, and individuals with the protean racial identity slip effortlessly from one mode to the next and are accepted by both groups as insiders. The authors point out that most people adjust their *behavior* to different situations (e.g., a fraternity party vs. a family Thanksgiving dinner), but these individuals also change their *identity* and adjust who they are to different circumstances. Respondents with the protean identity felt empowered by their ability to fit in with different groups and felt they were endowed with a high degree of "cultural savvy" (p. 47). In our increasingly diverse, multicultural, and multiracial society, the ability to belong easily to multiple groups may prove to be a valuable strength.

What can we conclude? Racial identity, like so many other aspects of our society, is evolving and becoming more complex. Traditions such as the one-drop rule live on but in attenuated, weakened form. Also, racial identity, like other aspects of self-concept, can be situational or contingent on

social context, not permanent or fixed. Given the world in which he lived, Williams had no choice but to accept a black racial identity. Today, in a somewhat more tolerant and pluralistic social environment, biracial people have choices and some space in which to carve out their own, unique identity. According to Rockquemore and Brunsma (2008), these identity choices are contingent on a number of factors, including personal appearance, but they are always made in the context of a highly race-conscious society with long and strong traditions of racism and prejudice.

QUESTIONS FOR REFLECTION

12. This section examined several issues and trends in contemporary black–white relations. In your opinion, which of these is most important? Why?

13. To what extent do African Americans and whites live in different worlds? Is it fair to characterize contemporary black–white relations as "continuing separation"? Why or why not?

14. How has racial identity evolved in modern America? How is racial identity for biracial Americans different today?

PREJUDICE AND DISCRIMINATION

Modern racism, the subtler form of prejudice that seems to dominate contemporary race relations, was discussed in Chapter 3. Although the traditional, more overt forms of prejudice have certainly not disappeared, contemporary expressions of prejudice are often amorphous and indirect. For example, the widespread belief among whites that racial discrimination has been eliminated in the United States may be a way of blaming African Americans—rather than themselves or the larger society—for the continuing reality of racial inequality.

As we saw in Chapter 5 and earlier in this chapter, a parallel process of evolution from blunt and overt forms to more subtle and covert forms has occurred in patterns of discrimination. The clarity of Jim Crow has yielded to the ambiguity of modern institutional discrimination and the continuing legacy of past discrimination in the present.

How can the pervasive problems of racial inequality be addressed in the present atmosphere of modern racism, low levels of sympathy for the urban poor, and subtle but powerful institutional discrimination? Many people advocate a "color-blind" approach to the problems of racial inequality: The legal and political systems should simply ignore skin color and treat everyone the same. This approach seems sensible to many people because, after all, the legal and overt barriers of Jim Crow discrimination are long gone and, at least at first glance, there are no obvious limits to the life chances of African Americans.

In the eyes of others, however, a color-blind approach is doomed to failure. To end racial inequality and deal with the legacy of racism, society must follow race-conscious programs that explicitly address the problems of race and racism. Color-blind strategies amount to inaction. All we need to do to perpetuate (or widen) the present racial gap is nothing. This issue is taken up in the Current Debates feature introduced at the end of this chapter.

ASSIMILATION AND PLURALISM

In this section, we will use the major concepts of the Gordon model of assimilation to assess the status of African Americans. To facilitate comparisons, the same format and organization will be used in the following three chapters. Of course, we will not be able to address all aspects of these patterns or go into much depth, so these sections should be regarded as overviews and suggestions for further research.

ACCULTURATION

The Blauner hypothesis states that the culture of groups created by colonization will be attacked, denigrated, and, if possible, eliminated, and this assertion seems well validated by the experiences of African Americans. African cultures and languages were largely eradicated under slavery. As a powerless, colonized minority group, slaves had few opportunities to preserve their heritage, even though traces of African homelands have been found in black language patterns, kinship systems, music, folk tales, and family legends (see Levine, 1977; Stuckey, 1987).

Cultural domination continued under the Jim Crow system, albeit through a different structural arrangement. Under slavery, slaves and their owners worked together, and interracial contact was common. Under de jure segregation, intergroup contact diminished and African Americans and whites generally became more separate. After slavery ended, the African American community had somewhat more autonomy (although still few resources) to define itself and develop a distinct culture.

The centuries of cultural domination and separate development have created a unique black experience in America. African Americans share language, religion, values, beliefs, and norms with the dominant society, but have developed distinct variations on the general themes.

The acculturation process may have been slowed (or even reversed) by the Black Power Movement. On one hand, since the 1960s, there has been an increased interest in African culture, language, clothing, and history, and a more visible celebration of unique African American experiences (e.g., Kwanzaa) and the innumerable contributions of African Americans to the larger society. On the other hand, many of those traditions and contributions have been in existence all along. Perhaps all that really changed was the degree of public recognition.

SECONDARY STRUCTURAL ASSIMILATION

Structural assimilation, or integration, involves two different phases. Secondary structural assimilation refers to integration in more public areas, such as the job market, schools, and political institutions. We can assess integration in this area by comparing residential patterns, income distributions, job profiles, political power, and levels of education of the different groups. Each of these areas is addressed in the next sections. We will then discuss primary structural assimilation (integration in intimate associations, such as friendship and intermarriage).

Residential Patterns. After a century of movement out of the rural South, African Americans today are highly urbanized and much more spread out across the nation. As we saw in Chapter 5 (see Figures 5.1 and 5.2), about 90% of African Americans are urban and a slight majority of African Americans continue to reside in the South. About 35% of African Americans now live in the Northeast and Midwest, overwhelmingly in urban areas. Figure 6.7 clearly shows the concentration of African Americans in the states of the old Confederacy; the urbanized East Coast corridor from Washington, D.C., to Boston; the industrial centers of the Midwest; and, to a lesser extent, California.

Residential segregation between African Americans and whites peaked toward the end of the Jim Crow era, in the 1960s and 1970s, and has decreased in recent decades (Logan & Stults, 2011). This pattern is displayed in Figure 6.8, which shows levels of residential segregation between white and black Americans for the past four census years. Scores for residential segregation between white and Hispanic Americans and white and Asian Americans are also included in the graph. We will focus on black Americans here and discuss the other groups in Chapters 8 and 9, respectively.

Figure 6.8 uses a statistic called the **dissimilarity index**, which shows the degree to which groups are *not* evenly spread across neighborhoods or census tracts. Specifically, the index is the percentage of each group that would have

The **dissimilarity index** is a measure of residential segregation. The higher the score, the greater the segregation; scores above 60 are considered to indicate extreme segregation.

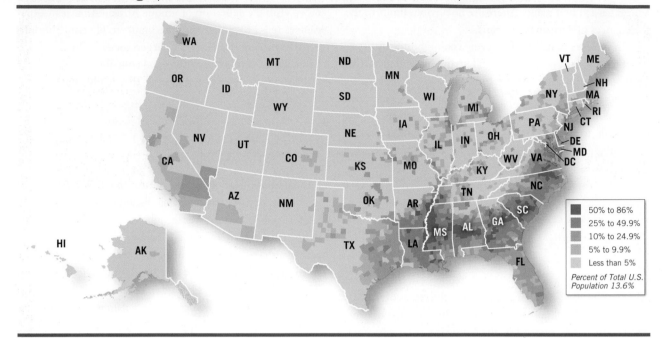

50% to 86%
25% to 49.9%
10% to 24.9%
5% to 9.9%
Less than 5%

*Percent of Total U.S.
Population 13.6%*

SOURCE: Rastogi, Johnson, Hoeffel, and Drewery, 2011, p. 11.

to move to a different tract to achieve integration. A score above 60 is considered to indicate extreme segregation.

Those seeking evidence of improving relations between African Americans and whites ("the glass is half full") will note the falling scores for racial residential segregation between 1980 and 2010 and, especially, that the dissimilarity index actually dipped to slightly below 60 in the most recent year. However, those with a more negative frame of mind ("the glass is half empty") might point out how the graph shows racial residential segregation continuing

FIGURE 6.8 Residential Segregation for Black, Hispanic, and Asian Americans, 1980–2010 (Dissimilarity Index)

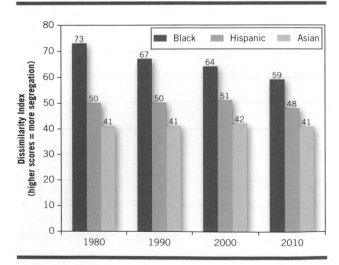

SOURCE: Logan and Stutts, 2011, p.5.

to be the norm and that African Americans are much more segregated from whites than are the other two groups.

As we saw in Chapter 5 and earlier in this chapter, the continuing patterns of residential segregation are reinforced by a variety of practices, including racial steering (guiding clients to same-race housing areas) by real estate agents and barely disguised discrimination. The Great Migration out of the South did little to end residential segregation, which tends to be highest in the older industrial cities of the Northeast and upper Midwest. In fact, the five most residentially segregated large metropolitan areas in 2010 were not in southern or border states but were (in rank order) in Detroit, Milwaukee, New York, Newark, and Chicago (Logan & Stults, 2011, p. 6).

Contrary to popular belief among whites, an African American preference for living in same-race neighborhoods plays a small role in perpetuating these patterns. For example, studies generally find that African Americans prefer to live in areas split 50/50 between African Americans and whites but that whites much prefer neighborhoods with low percentages of African Americans or Latinos (e.g., see Krysan & Farley, 2002, p. 949; Lewis, Emerson, & Klineberg, 2011, Havekes, Bader, & Krysan, 2016). The social class and income differences between African Americans and whites are also relatively minor factors in perpetuating residential segregation, as the African American middle class is just as likely as the African American poor to be segregated (Stoll, 2004, p. 26; see also Dwyer, 2010).

School Integration. In 1954, the year of the landmark *Brown* desegregation decision, the great majority of African Americans lived in states operating segregated school

The table below lists 10 metropolitan areas from across the nation in alphabetical order. Based on what you have learned in this chapter and Chapter 5, which ones do you think have the highest levels of racial residential segregation?

Cities in the South? Cities in the Northeast or the West? Cities with a higher or lower black population? Why?

What's your best guess? Rank order the cities from 1 (most segregated) to 10 (least segregated).

	CITY	REGION	PERCENTAGE BLACK, 2010*	RANK
1	Atlanta, Georgia	South	32%	
2	Baltimore, Maryland	Border	29%	
3	Boston, Massachusetts	Northeast	7%	
4	Dallas–Fort Worth, Texas	Southwest	15%	
5	Kansas City, Kansas	Midwest	13%	
6	Pittsburgh, Pennsylvania	Northeast	8%	
7	Richmond, Virginia	South	38%	
8	San Diego, California	West	5%	
9	San Francisco, California	West	8%	
10	Washington, D.C.	South/Border	26%	

*Percentage in entire metropolitan area, including suburbs. Data from U.S. Census Bureau (2012c, p. 31).

TURN THE PAGE TO SEE THE ACTUAL RANKS AND SCORES.

systems. Compared with white schools, Jim Crow schools were severely underfunded and had fewer qualified teachers, shorter school years, and inadequate physical facilities. School integration was one of the most important goals of the Civil Rights Movement in the 1950s and 1960s, and,

In 1942, white tenants in a Detroit housing project erected this sign to deter people of color from moving in.

aided by pressure from the courts and the federal government, considerable strides were made toward this goal for several decades.

In recent decades, however, the pressure from the federal government has eased, and school integration is slowing and, in many areas, has even reversed. The high point in the desegregation of public schools was in 1988, nearly four decades ago. In that year, less than 6% of public schools were "intensely segregated" or had an enrollment that was 90% to 100% nonwhite. In the decades following, this percentage has tripled to over 18% (Oldfield, Ee, Frankenberg, & Siegel-Hawley, 2016, p. 3).

Not only has the goal of school desegregation not been achieved, but African American children (and other minority groups of color) have been increasingly concentrated in schools that are segregated by social class as well as by race. Figure 6.9 shows that, since the 2000–2001 school year, the percentage of African American students that attended "High Poverty" schools has risen 16 percentage points, from 32% to 48%. Thus, African American students are doubly isolated: by social class as well as by race. Needless to say, this increasing economic and racial separation is a deep betrayal of the visions and goals of the Civil Rights Movement.

Here are those 10 metro areas listed from most to least segregated. Many American cities are more segregated than Pittsburgh, and some are less segregated than San Diego. These 10 cities were selected to represent a variety of regions and race relations histories, and are not, of course, representative of the society as a whole.

	CITY	SCORE (DISSIMILARITY INDEX)
1	Pittsburgh, Pennsylvania	64.9
2	Baltimore, Maryland	62.2
3	Kansas City, Kansas	57.7
4	Boston, Massachusetts	57.6
5	Washington, D.C.	56.1
6	Atlanta, Georgia	54.1
7	San Francisco, California	50.5
8	Richmond, Virginia	49.6
9	Dallas–Fort Worth, Texas	47.5
10	San Diego, California	38.6

SOURCE: Data from Glaeser and Vigdor (2012).

What accounts for the failure to integrate public schools? One very important cause is the declining number of whites in the society as a whole (see Figure 1.1) and in public schools in particular. In the 2013 school year, whites were 50% of all students, down from almost 80% in the early 1970s (Orfield, Ee, Frankenberg, & Siegel-Hawley, 2016, p. 2).

Another cause is the widespread residential segregation mentioned previously. The challenges for school integration are especially evident in those metropolitan areas that consist of a largely black-populated inner city surrounded by largely white-populated rings of suburbs.

Without a renewed commitment to integration, American schools will continue to resegregate. This is a particularly ominous trend, because it directly affects the quality of education. Years of research demonstrate that the integration of schools—by social class as well as race—is related to better educational experiences and improved test scores (e.g., see Orfield et al., 2016).

FIGURE 6.9 Percentages of Students by Poverty and Race, Selected School Years

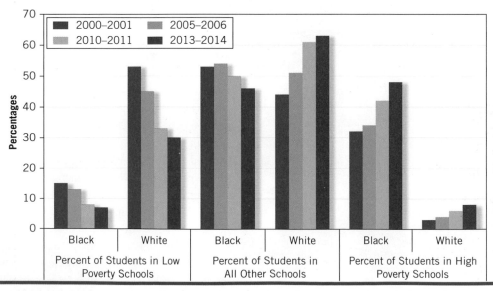

SOURCE: U.S. Government Accountability Office, 2016.

NOTE: "Low Poverty" schools are those in which less than 25% of students were eligible for free or reduced-price lunch.
"High Poverty" schools are those in which 75% to 100% of students were eligible for free or reduced-price lunch.

FIGURE 6.10 High School Graduation Rates of People 25 Years and Older in the United States, 1940–2015

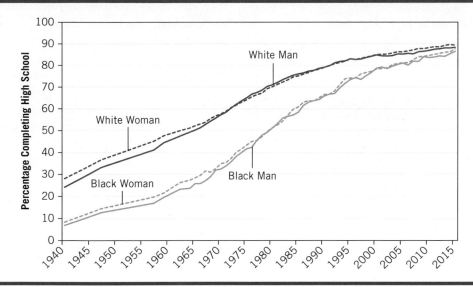

SOURCE: U.S. Bureau of the Census, 2017. Table A-2.

In terms of the quantity of education, the gap between whites and African Americans has generally decreased over the past several decades. Figure 6.10 displays the change from 1940 to 2015 in the percentage of the population older than 25 years, by race and gender, with high school diplomas; there is a dramatic decline in racial differences. Given the increasing demands for higher educational credentials in the job market, it is ironic that the nation has nearly achieved racial equality in high school education at a time when this credential matters less.

At the college level, the trends parallel the narrowing gap in levels of high school education, as shown in Figure 6.11. In 1940, white men held a distinct advantage over all other race/gender groups: They were about three times more likely than African American men and women to have a college degree. By 2015, the advantage of white men had shrunk, but they were still about 1.5 times more likely than black men and women to have a college degree. These racial differences grow larger with more advanced degrees, however, and differences such as these will be increasingly serious in an economy in which jobs more frequently require an education beyond high school.

Political Power. Two trends have increased the political power of African Americans since World War II. One is the movement out of the rural South, a process that concentrated African Americans in areas where it was easier for them to register to vote. As the black population outside

FIGURE 6.11 College Graduation Rates of People 25 Years and Older in the United States, 1940–2015

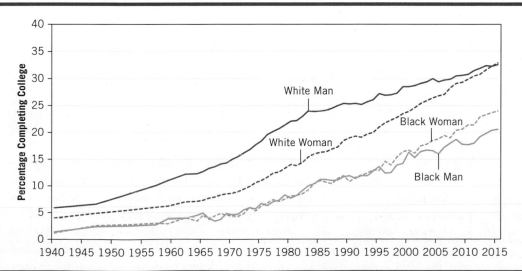

SOURCE: U.S. Bureau of the Census, 2017. Table A-2.

the South grew, so did their representation at the national level. The first African American representative to the U.S. Congress (other than those elected during Reconstruction) was elected in 1928, and by 1954, there were still only three African American members in the House of Representatives (Franklin, 1967, p. 614). In 2013, there were 44, still less than the proportional share of the national population (13%) (Manning, 2013, p. 8). Fifty-one African Americans are serving in Congress during the current session (2017–2019) ("Black-American Representatives and Senators by Congress, 1870–Present," n.d.).

When Barack Obama was elected to the Senate in 2004, he was only the fifth African American senator since Reconstruction to serve in that role. Since then, five more African Americans have been elected to the Senate: Roland Burris (Illinois, 2009), Tim Scott (South Carolina, 2013), Mo Cowan (Massachusetts, 2013), Corey Booker (New Jersey, 2013), and Kamala Harris (California, 2017).

The number of African American elected officials at all levels of government increased from virtually zero at the turn of the 20th century to about 10,500 in 2011 (Eilperin, 2013). In Virginia in 1989, Douglas Wilder became the first African American to be elected to a state governorship, and both Colin Powell and Condoleezza Rice have served as Secretary of State, the highest governmental office—along with Supreme Court justice and excluding the presidency—ever held by an African American.

African American communities are virtually guaranteed some political representation because of their high degree of geographical concentration at the local level. Today, most large American cities, including Los Angeles, Chicago, Atlanta, New York, and Washington, D.C., have elected African American mayors.

The other trend that has increased black political power is the dismantling of the institutions and practices of disenfranchisement that operated during Jim Crow segregation (see Chapter 5). As we discussed earlier, the Voting Rights Act of 1965 specifically prohibited many of the practices (poll taxes, literacy tests, and whites-only primaries) traditionally used to keep African Americans politically powerless.

Since the 1960s, the number of African Americans in the nation's voting-age population has increased from slightly less than 10% to about 13%. But this increasing potential for political power has not always been fully mobilized in the past, and actual turnout has generally been lower for African Americans than for whites. In the hotly contested presidential races of 2000, 2004, and 2008, however, a variety of organizations (such as the NAACP) made a concerted and largely successful effort to increase turnout among African Americans. In these years, black turnout was comparable to that of whites, and in the 2012 presidential election, the black turnout (66.2%) was slightly larger than the white turnout (64.1%) (File, 2013). However, after steadily increasing from 1996 through 2012, the African Americans turnout dropped sharply to 59.6% in the Trump-Clinton election of 2016, 6 percentage points below that of white voters (Krogstad & Lopez, 2017).

Overall, black American political power has tended to increase over the past several decades on the national, state, and local levels. One potentially ominous threat to this trend is the growth of restrictions on voting in many states in recent years. Well over half the states have considered or have passed various measures that could decrease the size of the electorate in general and disproportionately lower the impact of the African American vote. For example, many states may require voters to show a government-issued photo ID—such as a driver's license—before allowing them to cast a ballot. For a variety of reasons (e.g., their relative poverty) African Americans—and other minority groups of color—are less likely to possess official forms of identification.

One of the possible consequences of the Supreme Court's decision to rule the 1965 Voting Rights Act unconstitutional is enabling states and localities to enact measures to restrict voting rights and suppress the voting power of a variety of groups. Shortly after the decision, Texas announced that a voter identification law, previously blocked, would go into effect immediately (Liptak, 2013), and North Carolina passed one of the most restrictive laws since the Jim Crow era (Brennan Center for Justice, 2013). The latter was declared unconstitutional by the courts on the grounds that it blatantly targeted African American voters (Liptak & Wines, 2017).

Proponents of restrictive voting measures argue that they prevent voter fraud, and the new laws do not, of course, mention African Americans or other minority groups, as is typical of modern institutional discrimination. The result may be a dramatically lower turnout on Election Day for groups that are less likely to have driver's licenses, passports, or similar documentation, including not only African Americans but also other minority groups of color, low-income groups, senior citizens, and younger voters (see Brennan Center for Justice, 2013, for a list of efforts to restrict voting).

Jobs and Income. Integration in the job market and racial equality in income follow the trends established in many other areas of social life: The situation of African Americans has improved since the end of de jure segregation but has stopped well short of equality. Among men, whites are much more likely to be employed in the highest-rated and most lucrative occupational areas, whereas African Americans are overrepresented in the service sector and in unskilled labor (U.S. Census Bureau, 2016a). One comprehensive analysis of race/gender employment trends found that, after some

FIGURE 6.12 Median Household Income by Race, 1967–2015

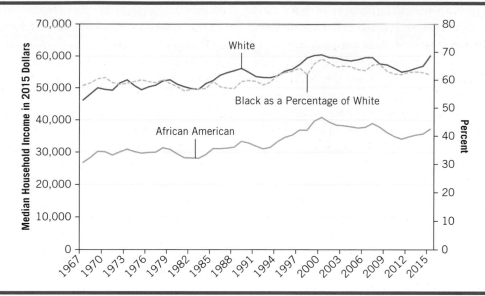

SOURCE: U.S. Census Bureau, 2017. "Race and Hispanic Origins of Householder–Households by Median and Mean Income, Table H-5," http://www.census.gov/hhes/www/income/data/historical/household/index.html.

gains in the years following the passage of the landmark legislation of the mid-1960s, employment gains for black men and women (and white women) have been slight, and that white men continue their disproportionate hold on better jobs (Stainback & Tomaskovic-Devey, 2012, pp. 155–177).

Although huge gaps remain, we should note that the present occupational distribution represents a rapid and significant upgrading, given the fact that as recently as the 1930s the majority of African American men were unskilled agricultural laborers (Steinberg, 1981, pp. 206–207). A similar improvement has occurred for African American women. In the 1930s, about 90% of employed African American women worked in agriculture or in domestic service (Steinberg, 1981, pp. 206–207). The percentage of African American women in these categories has dropped dramatically, and the majority of African American women are employed in the two highest occupational categories, although typically at the lower levels of these categories. For example, in the top-rated "managerial and professional" category, women are more likely to be concentrated in less well-paid occupations, such as nurse or elementary school teacher (see Figure 11.1), whereas men are more likely to be physicians and lawyers.

Figure 6.12 depicts the racial income gap in terms of the median, an average that shows the difference between "typical" white and black households. It reflects racial differences in education and occupations, which result in a persistent racial income gap. The graph presents two kinds of information: the median household incomes for African Americans and whites (in 2015 dollars) over the time period (read these from the left vertical axis) and the percentage of black to white household income (read this from the right vertical axis). Additionally, Figure 6.12 shows that

median incomes for black and white households generally moved together over the time period and that both trended upward until the turn of this century. At that point, both lines flattened and then fell, a reflection of hard economic times after 2000 and especially after 2007. In the most recent years, household incomes have risen once again, with white income rising more rapidly.

Also note that incomes for black households remained well below those of white households throughout the time period. In the late1960s, black household income was about 58% of white household income. The gap remained relatively steady through the 1980s, closed during the boom years of the 1990s, and, since the turn of the century, has widened again, especially in the most recent years. The gap was smallest in 2000 (68%) and, in the most recent year, has grown to 62%, reflecting the differential effects of the recession on minority groups of color, as we discussed previously.

Figure 6.13 supplements this information by comparing the distribution of income within each racial group for 2015, and highlights the differences in the percentage of each group in low-, middle-, and upper-income categories. To read this graph, note that income categories are arrayed from top to bottom and that the horizontal axis has zero points in the middle of the graph. The percentage of white households in each income category is represented by the bars to the left of the zero point, and the same information is presented for black households by the bars to the right of the zero point.

Starting at the bottom, note that the bars representing black households are considerably wider than those for white households. This reflects the fact that black Americans are more concentrated in the lower income brackets. For example, 13.4% of black households were in the lowest two income categories (less than $10,000); this

FIGURE 6.13 Distribution of Household Income for White and Black Americans, 2015

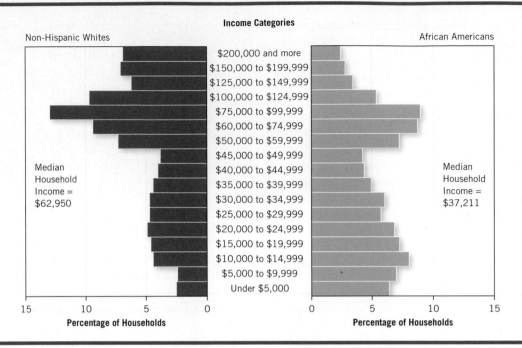

Income Categories

Non-Hispanic Whites / African Americans

- $200,000 and more
- $150,000 to $199,999
- $125,000 to $149,999
- $100,000 to $124,999
- $75,000 to $99,999
- $60,000 to $74,999
- $50,000 to $59,999
- $45,000 to $49,999
- $40,000 to $44,999
- $35,000 to $39,999
- $30,000 to $34,999
- $25,000 to $29,999
- $20,000 to $24,999
- $15,000 to $19,999
- $10,000 to $14,999
- $5,000 to $9,999
- Under $5,000

Median Household Income = $62,950

Median Household Income = $37,211

Percentage of Households

SOURCE: U.S. Census Bureau, 2017. "Age of Householder–Households by Total Money Income, Type of Household, Race and Hispanic Origin of Householder, Table HINC-02," https://www.census.gov/data/tables/time-series/demo/income-poverty/cps-hinc/hinc-02.html.

figure is 2.7 times greater than the percentage of white households (4.9%) in this range.

As we move upward, notice the clustering of both black and white households in the $50,000 to $124,000 categories, income ranges that would be associated with a middle and upper-middle-class lifestyle. In this income range, however, it is the white households that are overrepresented: 39% of white households versus only 30% of black households had incomes in this range. The racial differences are even more dramatic in the two highest income ranges: About 14% of white households had incomes greater than $150,000 versus only 5% of black households. While African Americans can be found at all income levels, graphs such as this convincingly refute the notion, common among "modern racists" and many other Americans, that there are no important racial inequalities in the United States today.

Finally, poverty affects African Americans at much higher rates than it does white Americans. Figure 6.14 shows the

FIGURE 6.14 Families and Children Living in Poverty in the United States, 1967–2015

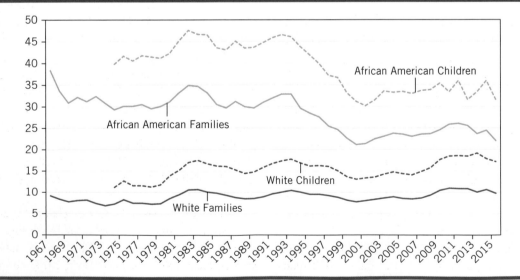

African American Children

African American Families

White Children

White Families

SOURCE: U.S. Census Bureau, 2017. "Poverty Status, Tables 3 and 4," https://www.census.gov/data/tables/time-series/demo/income-poverty/historical-poverty-people.html.

NOTE: Family poverty rates and child poverty rates are computed using different units of analysis. Family rates represent the percentage of all families below the poverty line. The rates for children are the percentage of all people younger than 18 in poverty.

percentage of white and black American families living below the federally established, "official" poverty level from 1967 through 2015. The poverty rate for African American families runs about 2.5 to 3 times higher than the rate for whites.

Note that there was a dramatic decrease in black poverty during the boom years of the 1990s, only to be followed by an even more sudden rise after 2000. The poverty rates for both groups trended upward between 2000 and 2012, with a sharp spike in black poverty following the 2007 recession before decreasing in the most recent years Tragically, the highest rates of poverty continue to be found among children, especially African American children. Like Figures 6.12 and 6.13, this graph refutes the notion that serious racial inequality is a thing of the past for U.S. society.

Library of Congress Prints and Photographs Division

An integrated school, one of the few in the United States in 1955.

PRIMARY STRUCTURAL ASSIMILATION

Interracial contact in the more public areas of society, such as schools or the workplace, is certainly more common today. As Gordon's model of assimilation predicts, this has led to increases in more intimate contacts across racial lines. To illustrate, one study looked at changing intimate relationships among Americans by asking a nationally representative sample about the people with whom they discuss "important matters." Although the study did not focus on black–white relations per se, the researchers did find that the percentage of whites that included African Americans as intimate contacts increased from 9% to more than 15% between 1984 and 2004 (McPherson, Smith-Lovin, & Brashears, 2006). While this increase would be heartening to those committed to a more integrated, racially unified society, these low percentages could also be seen as discouraging because they suggest that about 85% of white Americans maintain racially exclusive interpersonal networks of friends and acquaintances.

A more recent study (Cox, Navarro-Rivera, & Jones, 2016) found similar racial patterns in people's social networks. Respondents were asked to name the people with whom they "discussed important matters" and then identify these contacts by race. The vast majority of white respondents maintained racially homogenous networks: 91% of their close contacts were also white. Black respondents reported less racial exclusiveness: 83% of their close contacts were also black. This difference in the racial composition of social networks is partly a result of simple math: Because white Americans outnumber black Americans, they have more choices for friends and acquaintances and, as the dominant group, they can more easily maintain racial exclusiveness.

Another interesting study (Fisher, 2008), which reflects some of the same patterns, looked at interracial friendships on a sample of 27 college campuses across the nation. First-year students were interviewed at the end of their second semester and asked about the group membership of their 10 closest friends on campus. The study found that cross-group friendships were common but that white students had the least diverse circles of friends. For whites, 76% of their friends were also white, a much higher percentage of in-group exclusiveness than Asian students (51%), Hispanic students (56%), and black students (27%).

Obviously, these percentages reflect the racial composition of the campuses (all were majority white), but it is significant that cross-group choices were positively related to more tolerant attitudes and a history of having a friend from another group in high school. Most interesting, perhaps, was that cross-group choices were positively related to greater diversity on campus. This finding supports the contact hypothesis and Gordon's assertion that integration at the secondary level leads to integration at the primary level.

Consistent with the decline in traditional, overt prejudice, Americans are much less opposed to interracial dating and marriage today. As we noted in Chapter 3, a recent national poll (Livingston & Brown, 2017) found that only 9% of Americans felt that interracial marriage is "a bad thing" for society. Almost 40% felt interracial marriages were "a good thing" (up from 24% in 2010) and the majority (52%) felt that it didn't "make much difference" (p. 24). Support for interracial marriage was especially high among young people (54% of 18- to 29-year-olds said it was "a good thing" vs. only 26% of respondents over 65), the college educated (54% of the college educated said it was "a good thing" vs. only 26% of respondents with a high school degree), and urbanites (45% of city dwellers said it was "a good thing" vs. only 24% of rural respondents) (Livingston & Brown, 2017, p. 25).

Behavior appears to be following attitudes, as the rates of interracial dating and marriage are increasing. A number of studies find that interracial dating is increasingly common (see Wellner, 2007; Keels & Harris, 2014), and marriages between African Americans and whites are also increasing in number, although still a tiny percentage of all marriages. According to the U.S. Census Bureau, there were 65,000

TABLE 6.1 Percentage Married to a Person of the Same Race, 1980 and 2008

YEAR	WHITES		AFRICAN AMERICANS	
	Men	**Women**	**Men**	**Women**
1980	96%	95%	93%	97%
2008	93%	92%	77%	88%

SOURCE: Qian and Lichter (2011, p. 1072). Copyright © 2011 National Council on Family Relations. Reprinted with permission.

black–white married couples in 1970 (including persons of Hispanic origin), about 0.10% of all married couples. By 2010, the number of black–white married couples had increased by a factor of 8.5, to 558,000, but this is still less than 1% (0.9%) of all married couples (U.S. Census Bureau, 2012b, p. 54; see also Livingston & Brown, 2017).

Finally, a study comparing intermarriage based on the 1980 and 2008 censuses found a slight trend toward decreasing in-marriage, particularly for black men. The results are summarized in Table 6.1. Most black men who married outside their race were married to whites (14.4%) and Hispanics (4.8%). Black women who married outside their group showed a similar pattern: 6.5% were married to whites and 2.3% to Hispanics.

QUESTIONS FOR REFLECTION

15. This section examines a variety of dimensions of acculturation and integration for African Americans. Which is most important? Why?

16. In which of these areas has there been the most progress over the past 50 years? Explain.

17. What evidence can you cite for the claim that "black–white relations are the best they've ever been"? What evidence can you cite against this claim?

IS THE GLASS HALF EMPTY OR HALF FULL?

The contemporary situation of African Americans is perhaps what might be expected for a group so recently "released" from exclusion and subordination. Figure 6.15 visually represents the length of the periods of subjugation and the brevity of time since the fall of Jim Crow. The average situation of African Americans improved vastly during the latter half of the 20th century in virtually every area of social life. As demonstrated by the data presented in this

chapter, however, racial progress has stopped well short of equality.

In assessing the present situation, one might stress the improved situation of the group (the glass is half full) or the challenges that remain before full racial equality and justice are achieved (the glass is half empty). While African Americans have occupied the highest levels of the society (including the Oval Office and the Supreme Court), a large percentage of the African American population have merely traded rural peasantry for urban poverty and face an array of formidable and deep-rooted problems.

The situation of African Americans is intimately intermixed with the plight of our cities and the changing nature of the labor force. It is the consequence of nearly 400 years of prejudice, racism, and discrimination, but it also reflects broader social forces, such as urbanization and industrialization. Consistent with their origin as a colonized minority group, the relative poverty and powerlessness has persisted for African Americans long after other groups (e.g., the descendants of the European immigrants who arrived between the 1820s and the 1920s) have achieved equality and acceptance. African Americans were enslaved to meet the labor demands of an agrarian economy, became rural peasants under Jim Crow segregation, were excluded from the opportunities created by early industrialization, and remain largely excluded from the better jobs in the emerging postindustrial economy.

Progress toward racial equality has slowed since the heady days of the 1960s, and in many areas, earlier advances seem hopelessly stagnated. Public opinion polls indicate that there is little support or sympathy for the cause of African Americans (see Chapter 3). Traditional prejudice has declined only to be replaced by modern racism. In the court of public opinion, African Americans are often held responsible for their own plight. Biological racism has been replaced with indifference to racial issues or with blaming the victims.

FIGURE 6.15 Timeline of American Slavery and Segregation

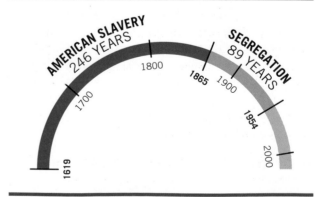

SOURCE: http://zerflin.com/2016/04/06/client-highlight-how-white-supremacy-attempts-to-make-slavery-and-segregation-soooo-long-ago/.

Of course, real improvements have been made in the lives of African Americans. Compared with their counterparts in the days of Jim Crow, African Americans today on the average are more prosperous and more politically powerful, and some are among the most revered of current popular heroes (the glass is half full). However, the increases in average income and education and the glittering success of the few obscure a tangle of problems for the many—problems that may well grow worse. Poverty, unemployment, a failing educational system, residential segregation, subtle racism, and continuing discrimination persist as inescapable realities for millions of African Americans. In many African American neighborhoods, crime, drugs, violence, poor health care, malnutrition, and a host of other factors compound these problems (the glass is half empty).

Given this gloomy situation, it should not be surprising to find in the African American community significant strength in pluralistic, nationalistic thinking, as well as resentment and anger. Black Nationalism and Black Power remain powerful ideas, but their goals of development and autonomy for the African American community remain largely rhetorical sloganeering without the resources to bring them to actualization.

The situation of the African American community in the early 21st century might be characterized as a combination of partial assimilation, structural pluralism, and inequality—a depiction that reflects the continuing effects, in the present, of a colonized origin. The problems that remain are less visible (or perhaps just better hidden from the average white middle-class American) than those of previous eras. Responsibility is more diffused, and the moral certainties of opposition to slavery or to Jim Crow laws are long gone. Contemporary racial issues must be articulated and debated in an environment of subtle prejudice and low levels of sympathy for the grievances of African Americans. Urban poverty, modern institutional discrimination, and modern racism are less dramatic and more difficult to measure than an overseer's whip, a lynch mob, or a sign that reads "Whites Only," but they can be just as real and just as deadly in their consequences.

SUMMARY

This summary is organized around the Learning Objectives listed at the beginning of this chapter.

 Cite and explain the forces that led to the end of de jure segregation, including organizations, leaders, and legal changes.

The system of de jure segregation ended because of changing economic, social, legal, and political conditions. Continuing industrialization in the South lessened the need for a large, powerless labor force, but southern resistance to racial change was intense. Crucial events included the threat of a march on Washington during World War II (led by A. Philip Randolph), the *Brown v. Board of Education of Topeka* Supreme Court decision, the Montgomery bus boycott, and the triumphs of the Civil Rights Movement, led by Martin Luther King Jr. and many others. The legal basis for the Jim Crow system ended with the passage of two landmark bills by the U.S. Congress: the Civil Rights Act of 1964 and the Voting Rights Act of 1965.

 Compare and contrast the Civil Rights Movement with the Black Power Movement.

The Civil Rights Movement was primarily a southern phenomenon designed to combat legalized, state-sponsored racial segregation. Outside the South, problems were different and the strategies that had worked in the South had less relevance. Other movements, organizations, and leaders—including the Black Muslims and Malcolm X—arose to articulate these issues and channel the anger of the urban, northern black population. The Civil Rights Movement was primarily assimilationist, but the Black Power Movement had strong elements of pluralism and even separatism. Both movements relied heavily on the energy and courage of black women but tended to be dominated by men.

 Explain the most important issues and trends that have animated black–white relations since the 1960s, including

a. the relationship between the criminal justice system and the black community,
b. class inequality within the black community,
c. family forms and family as a social institution,
d. new racial identities,
e. prejudice, and
f. individual and institutional forms of discrimination.

Black–white relations since the 1960s have been characterized by continuing inequality, separation, and hostility, along with substantial improvements in status for some African Americans.

a. Relations with the criminal justice system continue to be problematic, and the black community has been victimized by the "war on drugs" on several levels.

b. The African American middle class has less financial security than the white middle class, and urban poverty continues as a major problem. Class differentiation within the African American community is greater than ever before.

c. The African American family has been perceived as weak, unstable, and a cause of continuing poverty. Culture of poverty theory attributes poverty to certain characteristics of the poor. An alternative view sees problems such as high rates of family desertion by men as the *result* of poverty, rather than the cause.

d. New racial identities continue to emerge as cross-racial and cross-ethnic marriages continue to increase

e. and f. Antiblack prejudice and discrimination are manifested in more subtle, covert forms (modern racism and institutional discrimination) in contemporary society.

 6.4 Analyze the contemporary situation of African Americans using the concepts of assimilation and pluralism, especially in terms of

a. acculturation,

b. secondary structural assimilation, and

c. primary structural assimilation.

a. African Americans are largely acculturated, but centuries of separate development have created a unique black experience in American society.

b. There have been real improvements for many African Americans, but the overall secondary structural assimilation remains low for a large percentage of the group. Evidence of continuing racial inequality in residence, schooling, politics, jobs, income, unemployment, and poverty is massive and underlines the realities of the urban underclass.

c. In the area of primary structural assimilation, interracial interaction and friendships appear to be rising. Interracial marriages are increasing, although they remain a tiny percentage of all marriages.

6.5 Use sociological concepts and evidence from the chapter to evaluate the *overall* situation for African Americans today. Evaluate the progress made compared with remaining problems. (Is the glass half empty of half full?)

Compared with their situation at the start of the 20th century, African Americans have made significant improvements, but the distance to true racial equality remains considerable. What evidence of improvements in race relations is presented in this chapter? What evidence is provided for the argument that substantial problems remain? Which body of evidence is more persuasive? Why?

KEY TERMS

Black Power Movement 188

Civil Rights
  Movement 182

culture of poverty
  theory 206

de facto segregation 188

dissimilarity
  index 209

fatalism 206

nonviolent direct
  action 185

urban underclass 203

REVIEW QUESTIONS

1. What forces led to the end of de jure segregation? To what extent was this change a result of broad social forces (e.g., industrialization), and to what extent was it the result of the actions of African Americans acting against the system (e.g., the southern Civil Rights Movement)? By the 1960s and 1970s, how had the movement for racial change succeeded, and what issues were left unresolved? What issues remain unresolved today?

2. Describe the differences between the southern Civil Rights Movement and the Black Power Movement. Why did these differences exist? How are the differences related to the nature of de jure versus de facto segregation? Do these movements remain relevant today? How?

3. How does gender affect contemporary black–white relations and the African American protest

movement? Is it true that African American women are a "minority group within a minority group"? Explain.

4. According to an old folk saying, "When America catches a cold, African Americans get pneumonia." Evaluate this idea using the information, data, and analysis presented in this chapter. Is it true? Exaggerated? Untrue? What other kinds of information would be needed for a fuller assessment of the quote? How could you get this information?

5. What are the implications of increasing class differentials among African Americans? Does the greater affluence of middle-class African Americans mean they

are no longer a part of a minority group? Will future protests by African Americans be confined only to working-class and lower-class African Americans?

6. Regarding contemporary black–white relations, is the glass half empty or half full? Considering the totality of evidence presented in this chapter, which of the following statements would you agree with? Why? (1) American race relations are the best they've ever been; racial equality has been essentially achieved (even though some problems remain). (2) American race relations have a long way to go before society achieves true racial equality.

STUDENT STUDY SITE

Sharpen your skills with SAGE edge at edge.sagepub.com/healey8e

SAGE edge for students provides a personalized approach to help you accomplish your coursework goals in an easy-to-use learning environment.

The following resources are available at SAGE edge:

Current Debates: Should the United States Be Color-Blind?

To be "color-blind" is to treat everyone the same, ignoring gender, race, and ethnicity. Would color blindness increase fairness and justice in American society? Or would it perpetuate the advantage of the dominant group?

On our website you will find an overview of the topic, the clashing points of view, and some questions to consider as you analyze the material.

Public Sociology Assignments

Public Sociology Assignments provide opportunities for students to address directly and personally some of the issues raised in this text.

There are two assignments for Part 3 on our website. The first looks at patterns of self-segregation in school cafeterias, and in the second, students analyze the portrayal of the American family on television in terms of race, ethnicity, sexual orientation, and other sociologically relevant characteristics.

Contributed by Linda M. Waldron

Internet Research Project

For this Internet Research Project, you will use data gathered by the U.S. Census Bureau to assess the situation of African Americans relative to the population in general and to one of the white ethnic groups you investigated in the Chapter 2 Internet Research Project. The project will be guided by a series of questions related to course concepts, and your instructor may ask you to discuss your findings in small groups.

For Further Reading

Please see our website for an annotated list of important works related to this chapter.

NATIVE AMERICANS

From Conquest to Tribal Survival in a Postindustrial Society

Newscom

LOC

timeline

1838
Approximately 17,000 Cherokee are forcibly removed from North Carolina, Tennessee, Georgia, and Alabama to the Indian Territory, present-day Oklahoma, along the 1,200-mile "Trail of Tears." Some 4,000 to 8,000 Cherokee die during the removal process.

1876
Sitting Bull and Crazy Horse (Lakota) defeat George Custer at the Battle of the Little Bighorn.

1830   1845   1860   1875   1890   1905   1920

1830
The Indian Removal Act leads to the deportation of 100,000 Native Americans to west of the Mississippi.

1851
The Indian Appropriations Act of 1851 allocates funds to move tribes onto reservations.

1871
The Indian Appropriations Act of 1871 dissolves the status of tribes as sovereign nations.

1862
The Homestead Act essentially allows Americans to settle on Indian land.

1886
Apache leader Geronimo surrenders to U.S. troops.

1887
The Dawes Act allows government to divide Indian land into individually owned parcels in an attempt to establish private ownership of Indian lands.

1890
About 300 Sioux are killed at Wounded Knee in last battle between U.S. troops and Native Americans.

LOC

INDIAN LAND FOR SALE

GET A HOME OF YOUR OWN

EASY PAYMENTS

PERFECT TITLE

POSSESSION WITHIN THIRTY DAYS

FINE LANDS IN THE WEST
IRRIGATED   GRAZING   AGRICULTURAL
IRRIGABLE   DRY FARMING

Wikimedia Commons

LOC

Lorinda announced that the [Blessing Way ceremony for Lynette's unborn child] was about to start . . . [so we] walked into the hoghan. *A single light bulb lit the room dimly. Couches, futon mattresses, and large pillows were set against the walls for the night's sing. A coffee-maker, microwave, and crock-pot sat on a folding table against the northern wall for the midnight eating. This was the same Navajo adaptation I'd grown up seeing, the age-old ritual with modern technology.*

The hataałii *[shaman or healer] sat against the western wall. . . . He wore thick silver bracelets and a silk bandana across his brow, the knot tied off at his right temple in traditional style. A basket of* tádídíín *[corn pollen] sat at his left.*

LEARNING OBJECTIVES

By the end of this chapter, you will be able to do the following:

7.1 Explain the changing population characteristics and common cultural characteristics of Native Americans and Alaska Natives.

7.2 Summarize and explain the changing relationship between Native Americans and the U.S. federal government, especially the changes in laws and policies and their effects, and the dynamics of Indian resistance and protest.

7.3 Understand the most critical issues and trends that have influenced relations between Native Americans and the larger U.S. society in recent decades, including

  a. struggles over natural resources,

  b. attempts to bring jobs to reservations,

  c. broken treaties,

  d. gaming, and

  e. prejudice and discrimination.

7.4 Analyze the contemporary relations between Native Americans and whites using the concepts of prejudice, discrimination, assimilation, and pluralism, especially in terms of

  a. acculturation,

  b. secondary structural assimilation, and

  c. primary structural assimilation.

7.5 Assess the overall situation of Native Americans today based on the concepts and information presented in this chapter.

1924
Federal law grants all Native Americans citizenship.

1968
The American Indian Movement, an advocacy group, is founded.

1988
Federal legislation legalizes reservation gambling.

2005
The National Collegiate Athletic Association bans use of "hostile and abusive" American Indian mascots in postseason tournaments.

1935   1950   1965   1980   1995   2010   2020

1934
The Indian Reorganization Act decreases federal control of Indian affairs and re-establishes self-governance for many tribes.

1972
The American Indian Movement sponsors the Trail of Broken Treaties, a cross-country protest presenting a 20-point list of demands from the federal government.

1978
The American Indian Movement leads the Longest Walk, a spiritual walk across the country for tribal sovereignty and to protest anti-Indian legislation.

2012
Revenue from gaming on reservations reaches almost $28 billion.

2016–2017
Thousands protest the Dakota Access Pipeline.

[There were] gifts: . . . a stethoscope, that the baby would have good health and might be a healer; . . . a pair of running shoes, that the child would be a strong runner; dollar bills . . . to wish the child a wealthy life; cowboy boots and work gloves so that the child would be a hard worker. . . .

The hataałii *spoke in quiet Navajo as he passed the basket of* tádídíín *to Dennis, who sprinkled the yellow pollen at each corner of the* hoghan, *first East, South, West, then North. Then he passed the basket around the room in a clockwise order; when it came to me, I did what the others had done: I placed a pinch inside my lower lip, pressed a second pinch to my forehead, then spread the pollen in the air above in a small arch to resemble the rainbow that promises life and beauty.*

The hataałii *began the sing. Brandon and the two burly men entered the chant with accenting rhythms as articulate as wind chimes, but with the resonance of distant thunder. . . .*

Lorinda leaned forward and rocked slowly, speaking her own prayer: I heard the word hózhó *sung many times. There is no English equivalent, but mostly it means "beautiful harmony." Christians might call it grace.*

—Jim Kristofic (2011, pp. 183–184)

At the end of first grade, Jim Kristofic found himself moving from western Pennsylvania to the Navajo reservation in Arizona where his mother had taken a job as a nurse. Like many Americans, he had little information about indigenous people before getting to know them. As the new boy in school he was initially rejected and bullied by the Navajo kids. Eventually, he developed a deep respect for and understanding of the "Rez," the people, and the Navajo way of life. In the previous passage, he gives us a glimpse into a sacred Navajo ceremony called the Blessing Way that has been practiced for centuries. Can ancient traditions such as this—and the indigenous people that practice them—survive in the modern world? •

In Chapter 4, we discussed the contact period for Native Americans, which began in the earliest colonial days and lasted nearly 300 years. It ended with the final battles of the Indian Wars in the late 1800s. During that time, the many, diverse Indian[1] nations fought to preserve their cultures and to keep their land (see Chapter 4 for a review). The tribes had enough power to win many battles, but they eventually lost all of the wars. Nichols (1986, p. 128) suggests that the diversity of Native communities (including 250 different languages) contributed to the challenges of fighting whites (Regan, 2018, p. 239). The superior resources of the burgeoning white society made the eventual defeat of Native Americans almost inescapable (Diamond, 1998).

By 1890, the last of the tribes had been conquered, their leaders had been killed or were in custody, and their people were living on U.S. government-controlled reservations. By the start of the 20th century, Native Americans were, in Blauner's (1972) terms, a conquered and colonized minority group. Like African Americans on slave plantations, Native people living on reservations were subjected to live, by law, under a paternalistic system controlled by federally mandated regulations. Because the reservation system destroyed tribal governments, most lived under the supervision of U.S. appointed Indian agents who temporarily lived on the reservations and who supervised their acculturation into U.S. society in detail, for example, by governing everything including hair length, clothing, and language (Nichols, 1986, p. 135). For almost 150 years, as Jim Crow segregation, Supreme Court decisions, industrialization, and urbanization shaped the status of other minority groups, Native Americans lived on the fringes of development and change and had weaker links to the larger society than white ethnic groups and other minority groups. Thus, they were marginalized, relatively powerless, and isolated geographically and culturally. While other minority groups have maintained a regular presence in the national headlines, Native Americans have been generally ignored and unnoticed, except perhaps as mascots for sports teams (e.g., Washington Redskins, Atlanta Braves) or because of recent protests at the Standing Rock Reservation about the Dakota Access Pipeline (DAPL).

The last decades of the 20th century witnessed some improvement in the status of Native Americans in general,

----

[1]Columbus used the term *Indian* because he thought he had landed in India. We use the term *Native American*—rather than *American Indian*—to emphasize that such people are indigenous to the area that became the United States of America. The term Native American also applies to other indigenous peoples of the United States (e.g., in Alaska) as well as Canada and Central and South America. We focus on people indigenous to the U.S. mainland because their experiences most closely parallel the other mainland groups discussed in this book. Likewise, people debate the language of *tribes, nations,* or *communities.* Different indigenous people use different terms. As with other racial and ethnic groups, these labels highlight their socially constructed nature. We encourage you to learn more and decide what seems most accurate and respectful. In "real life," it's best to ask people what they like to be called instead of assuming.

Painting of the Battle of the Little Bighorn by Kicking Bear, a Native American healer who was born Oglala Lakota (Sioux). He became a subchief among the Minneconjou Sioux during the period known as the Sioux Wars (1854–1890).

ethnic groups, the Census Bureau's categories for Native Americans have changed over time. As you recall from Chapter 1, the first time people could claim membership in more than one racial or ethnic category on the census was in 2000. If we define Native Americans as consisting of people who identify themselves as *only* Native American, we will get one estimate. If we include people who claim mixed racial ancestry our estimate of group size will be much larger. Table 7.1, based on the most recent (2010) U.S. Census, shows this difference in size.

and some tribes, especially those with casinos and other gaming establishments, made notable progress toward parity with national standards (Spilde & Taylor, 2013; Taylor & Kalt, 2005). Also, the tribes now have more control over their own affairs, and many have effectively used their increased autonomy and independence to address problems in education, health, joblessness, and other matters. Despite the progress, large gaps remain between Native Americans and other groups, especially whites, in virtually every area of social and economic life. For example, some Native Americans living on reservations are among the poorest groups in U.S. society.

In this chapter, we will discuss the history of Native Americans up to the present and explore recent progress and persisting problems. Some of the questions we will discuss include: How does the situation of Native Americans compare with that of other colonized and conquered minority groups? What accounts for the inequalities this group has faced for much of the past century? How can we explain improvements, especially since the 1990s? What key problems remain? What strategies could close the remaining gaps between Native Americans and the larger society?

SIZE OF THE GROUP

How many Native Americans live in the United States? This question has several answers, partly because of the social and subjective nature of race and group membership. Historically and today, the U.S. government and individual tribes have defined the status of "Indian" in different ways. Sometimes those definitions have been based on specific percentages of "Indian blood" (Cohen, 1945, p. 5). At other times, they have defined Indian status broadly, even including individuals who joined tribal communities through marriage (Nichols, 1986, p. 128).

The answer also varies because of the way the Census Bureau collects information. As with other racial and

TABLE 7.1 Native Americans and Alaska Native Population, 2010

	ALONE	ALONE OR IN COMBINATION (2 OR MORE GROUPS)
All Native Americans & Alaska Natives	2,932,248	5,220,579
Native Americans	2,042,825	3,831,740
Alaska Natives	113,902	162,504
10 LARGEST TRIBAL GROUPINGS FOR NATIVE AMERICANS		
	One Tribe	**Two or More Tribes**
Cherokee	284,247	819,858
Navajo	286,731	332,129
Choctaw	103,910	195,764
Chippewa	112,757	170,742
Sioux	112,176	170,110
Apache	63,193	118,810
Blackfeet	27,279	105,304
Pueblo	72,270	91,242
Creek	48,352	88,332
Iroquois	40,570	81,002
Largest Tribal Groupings for Alaska Natives		
Yup'ik	27,329	33,868
Inupiat	20,941	25,687
Tlingit-Haida	8,547	13,486
Alaskan Athabascan	12, 318	16,665

SOURCE: Norris, Vines, and Hoeffel (2012).

If you look at the top row of Table 7.1, you'll see that more than five million people claimed at least *some* Native American or Alaska Native ancestry; if we define the group as people who select *only* Native American, the group is a little more than half that size. By either count, Native Americans are a small minority—about 1.6%—of the U.S. population. Table 7.1 presents information for the 10 largest tribal groupings of Native Americans and for the four largest tribal groupings of Alaska Natives but these categories only hint at the diversity of the group. We present them as separate groups because their vastly different geographical locations shaped the contact situation and, therefore, their group histories and also because tribal affiliation continues to matter to many members of this group (National Congress of American Indians, n.d.).

As you'll see in Figure 7.1, the Native American population has grown rapidly over the past several decades, but this fact needs to be seen in the full context of history. As you learned in Chapter 4, in 1492, there were anywhere from several million to more than 10 million or more Native Americans living in what is now the continental ("Lower 48") United States (Mann, 2011). By 1900, fewer than 250,000 American Indians remained due to deaths during the contact period—from disease, battles, and starvation due to loss of land and, therefore, the ability to hunt animals and gather plants, and nuts, and other resources.

Recent population growth is largely the result of changing definitions of race in the larger society and people's greater willingness to claim Indian ancestry (Wilson, 2000). This pattern also underscores the social character of race.

NATIVE AMERICAN CULTURES

The dynamics between Native Americans and Anglo-Americans have been shaped by the vast differences in culture between the two groups (e.g., beliefs, values, norms, language). These differences have hampered communication in the past and continue to do so in the present. Although we're discussing Native Americans as a group, as we noted in Chapter 4, there were (and are) almost 600 different tribes, each with its own heritage, social structure, and geography (National Congress of American Indians, n.d.; Regan, 2018). A comprehensive analysis of Native American cultures that takes such diversity into account is beyond the scope of this text. However, as Regan (2018) notes, we can identify some common cultural characteristics.

AGRICULTURE, VIEWS ON NATURE, AND LAND OWNERSHIP

Before exploring the content of their culture, recall Lenski's arguments about how subsistence technology profoundly shapes societies (see Chapter 1). Most Native American tribes that existed in what is now the U.S. relied on hunting, fishing, and gathering to satisfy their basic needs. As the text box on page 229 shows, many also cultivated gardens rich with squash, corn, beans, sunflower (for the oil-rich seeds), goosefoot (a starch), and other plants (George-Kanentiio, 2000; Nabhan, 2002; Nash & Strobel, 2006; Nelson, 2008; Park, Hongub, & Daily, 2016; Wessell, 1986).

FIGURE 7.1 Native American and Alaska Native Population, 1900–2015

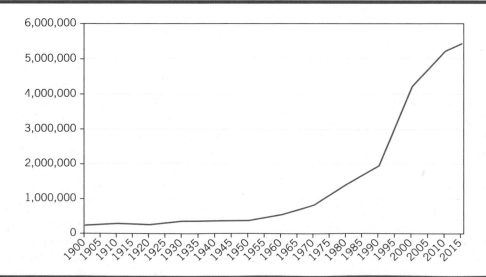

SOURCES: For data for 1900 to 1990, Thornton (2001, p. 142); 2000 and 2010, U.S. Census Bureau (2007, p. 14; 2010) and Norris et al. (2012), 2015 U.S. Census Bureau, 2015.

Below, William Strachey describes his travels to Virginia (in the English of the early 1600s) his travels to Virginia, including what Native Americans grew and ate each season and how food availability (or lack thereof) affected people. It illustrates the precariousness of the food supply: When food was plentiful people were fat and strong, but when food was scarce they would become lean and weak.

About their howses they have commonly square plotts of cleered grownd, which serve them for gardens, some one hundred, some two hundred foote square, wherein they sowe their tobacco, pumpons [pumpkins], and a fruit like unto a musk million, but less and worse, which they call macock gourds, and such like, which fruets *increase exceedingly, and ripen in the beginning of July, and contynue until September; they plant also the field apple, the maracock, a wyld fruit like a kind of pomegranette, which increaseth infinitelye, and ripens in August, contynuing untill the end of October, when all the other fruicts be gathered, but they sowe nether herb, flower, nor any other kynd of fruit.*

They neither ympale for deare, nor breed cattlle, nor bring up tame poultry, albeit they have great stoore of turkies, nor keepe birds, squirrells, nor tame patridges, swan, duck, nor goose. In March and April they live much upon their weeres [traps used to catch fish] and feed on fish, turkies, and squirrells; and then, as also sometymes in May, they plant their fields annd sett their corn, and live after those months *most of acrons [acorns], walnutts, chesnutts, chechinquarnins [a form of wild grain], and fish; but, to mend their dyett, some disperse themselves in small companeys, and live upon such beasts as they can kyll with their bows and arrows, upon crabbs, oysters, land-tortoyses, strawberryes, mulberries, and such like. In June, July, and August they feed upon the roots of tockohow [tuckahoe, or the arrow arum plant that grows in wetlands], berries, grownd nutts, fish, and greene wheate [corn], and sometyme upon a greene serpent, or greene snake, of which our people likewise use to eate.*

It is strange to see how their bodies alter with their dyett; even as the deare and wild beasts they seem fatt and leane, strong and weake (Strachey & Major, 1849, pp. 72–73).

Indeed, in 1607 when the colonists arrived in Virginia, their survival was due, in part, to Native Americans' crops and seeds as well as their willingness to share their knowledge about how to cultivate crops in the new world

Edward S. Curtis / Wikimedia Commons

Hupa man with spear, 1923.

(Smith, 2013, p. xv). Nevertheless, the food supply was unreliable and Native Americans (like colonists) often lived on the edge of hunger and want.

As is typical at the hunting-and-gathering level of development, Native American societies tended to be more oriented toward groups (e.g., the extended family, clan, or tribe) than toward individuals. Such communities stress values of sharing and cooperation which enable them to maintain strong bonds of cohesion and solidarity. In such communities, people subordinate self-interests to those of the group (Regan, 2018).

One important difference between Native Americans and European settlers involved their ideas about the relationship between human beings and the natural world. In the traditional Native American cultures, the universe is a unity. Humans are simply a part of a larger reality, no different from or more important than other animals, plants, trees, and the earth itself. Because the natural world is connected to the spiritual world, the goal of many Native American tribes was to live in harmony with nature (Regan, 2018, p. 240).

This framework influenced Native American beliefs about property which differed from European thinking. Contrary to popular stereotypes, Native Americans did own personal possessions. For example, Lakota men owned their horses, clothing, weapons, and spiritual objects. Indigenous women of Alaska marked their stored fish to show its ownership. Because many indigenous women were responsible for the tipis, they were considered their property. And, the Great Law of the Iroquois stated, "women shall be considered the Progenitors of the Nation. They shall own the land and soil" (cited from Andersen, 2016, p. 37).

Pretty Nose, an Arapaho war chief, sometimes referred to as Cheyenne. She fought in the Battle of the Little Bighorn. Photographed at Fort Keogh, Montana, in 1879.

Laton Alton Huffman / Wikimedia Commons

GENDER AND SOCIAL STRUCTURE

Egalitarianism, respect, and the worth of every person were other important values that organized many traditional Native American communities. Virtually all tribes had a division of labor based on gender, and often by age, and they valued work regardless of who did it. For example, Choctaw men and women both did food-related work: Men hunted for food and women supervised food production and distribution (Andersen, 2016). The gendered division of labor in many tribes was flexible, allowing people to do what fit with their gender identity and skills. For example, among the Yuma (or Quechan), a woman who had a dream about fighting could take on the role of a warrior and fight alongside the men of her tribe (Allen, 1992; Andersen, 2016, p. 35).

Women in many indigenous communities occupied important economic, political, and religious positions, and had much greater freedom than colonial women (who the law defined as dependents) (Anderson, 2016; George-Kanentiio, 2006; Hartman, n.d.). Among the Iroquois, a council of older women appointed the tribe's chiefs, had veto power over their decisions, and made decisions about when to wage war (Allen, 1992; Amott & Matthaei, 1991, pp. 34–35; Mann, 2008). Women could also impeach chiefs that did not make decisions in the interests of the group or live up to their standards (George-Kanentiio, 2006, p. 45; Mann, 2008, p. 191).

The colonists and Native Americans viewed gender differently, too. The colonists believed that one's gender came from God and that gender relations on earth should model the biblical account of Adam and Eve. For them, gender was a binary: A person is either a girl/woman or a boy/man. They linked gender to biological sex (e.g., anatomy) and saw women and men as having essential differences. In their interpretation of Genesis, God made woman from man. Thus, in colonial families, men were expected to be patriarchs ("fathers") who would rule families as God the Father is said to rule over creation—with ultimate power and authority. Women and children were expected to be subservient to them.

Because fathers are of the utmost importance in patriarchal societies like Great Britain and the American colonies, those societies are patrilineal. This means that people trace their name and lineage through the father's family line. Patriarchal societies also tend to be patrilocal. That is, when (heterosexual) couples get married, the woman would leave her father's (family) house to live with her husband and his family.

Native Americans also connected gender and the spiritual world, but their creation accounts are woman-centered and often emphasize women's ability to bring life into the world. For example, the Iroquois tell of Sky People who lived happily (in the sky) and for whom death

This phrasing, that women "own the land and soil," shows how indigenous Americans thought of land ownership; that is, land belongs to the group. This is partly why Tecumseh, a Shawnee chief, was incensed to find that a few men had sold land to settlers while he was away. He spoke to Governor William Henry about why this was problematic, saying,

> [the] Great Spirit that made them, to keep it, to traverse it, to enjoy its productions . . . it never was divided, but belongs to all for the use of each. For no part has a right to sell, even to each other, much less to strangers—those who want all, and will not do with less. (Tecumseh, 1810, as cited in Drake, 1845, p. 121)

Although the European notion of individuals owning, selling, and buying land went against this ethos (Andersen, 2016; Banner, 2005) Native Americans had a system of land tenure that served them for generations, somewhat like the English common gardens with which colonists may have been familiar (Banner, 2005; Craven, 1970, p. 107). Land was often given to individuals and those people had land use rights, but anyone could hunt or gather on unallocated land (Banner, 2005, p. 37). According to one Creek chief, "We have no suits about land titles because the title is not disputable" (Banner, 2005, p. 266).

did not exist. When a pregnant Sky Woman fell toward earth, the birds caught her and other animals helped, too. Together, they created the world (Allen, 1992; Anderson, 2016; Nash & Strobel, 2006, p. 40).

Because women are central to creation stories, Native Americans considered them central to everything on earth. Thus, the social organization of many tribes, such as the Iroquois, Tlingit, and Navajo, are matrilineal. In matrilineal societies people trace their name and lineage through the mother's family. Many of these tribes were also matrilocal. That is, when heterosexual couples got married, the man would move into his wife's (family) home rather than she moving to live in his (George-Kanentiio, 2006; Nash & Strobel, 2006).

Native Americans separated gender, sex, and sexual orientation which allowed for gender expression beyond the girl/woman and boy/man dichotomy of colonial America. (See Chapter 1 for a basic review and Chapters 11 and 12 for details.) Researchers have documented as many as 130 tribal communities that welcomed **two-spirit** people—formerly called *berdache* by anthropologists and *hermaphrodites* by Europeans (Roscoe, 2014)—who identify as *both* genders or who identify outside of the Western gender binary (Lang, 2010; Roscoe, 1991, p. 5; Thomas, 1997). Some people also use *two-spirit* to include diverse sexual orientations (e.g., lesbian/gay, queer). In reality, the two-spirit designation is more complex; it connects and cuts across gender and sexuality.

The number and type of two-spirit genders varied by tribal community including the winkte (Lakota), nádleehí (Navajo), kwidó (Tewa), tainna wa'ippe (Shoshone), dubuds (Paiute), and lhamana (Zuni). The Navajo, for example, had four genders (Thomas, 1997) while the Cree had five (Âpihtawikosisân, 2012), for example, a "feminine" male who lives as a woman and is viewed as a woman. Or, a "masculine" female who is socially defined and accepted as a man (Estrada, 2011; Lang, 2010; Mirandé, 2017; Thomas, 1997).

These labels may sound similar to contemporary ways of thinking about gender. For example, people display femininity and masculinity to varying degrees. However, in contemporary American society, people tend to think of a "feminine" male/man as a *man*. In traditional Native

George Catlin's "Dance to the Berdache."

communities, such a person could be recognized as a *woman* although they are biologically male. Keep in mind that these gender categories don't always translate well into English (Âpihtawikosisân, 2010). We may be tempted to think about them through a Western framework, seeing them as gender binary with additional options. Blackwood (1997) urges us not think this way because doing so privileges certain categories and presumed relationships (e.g., female/girl/woman, male/boy/man) over others (p. 288). Rather, she suggests, we need to think about the diversity of Native American genders as a holistic system of gender relations. (Also see Mirandé, 2017.)

BELIEF SYSTEMS AND GENDER

In every society, belief systems (ideologies) shape norms of behavior and other aspects of social structure. Native American communities believed that the Great Creator made everything, including two-spirit people. They were thought to have the qualities and skills of both women and men and, thus, were seen as uniquely sacred. This gender status gave them a special role in their communities for which they received appreciation and respect (Anderson, 2016; Cherry, 2012; Harrington, 2016; Mirandé, 2017; Roscoe, 1991). The "Old West" painter, George Catlin, documented the celebration of two-spirit people among the plains Indians in his painting, "Dance to the Berdache."

Mythology and religious beliefs encouraged acceptance of two-spirit people. For example, the Zuni have Ko'lhamana, a two-spirit god. Likewise, the Maricopa have Avialyxa (Lang, 2010), the Bella Coola have Sx'ints (or Skhints), and the Navajo have Begochiddy, described as a "cross-dressing shape-shifting bisexual Navajo

Two-spirit people identify as *both* genders or identify outside of the Western gender binary of girl/woman or boy/man.

George Catlin / Wikimedia Commons

We'Wha, a Zuni "Lhamana," is one of the best recognized two-spirit persons who also served as an ambassador for the Zuni people (Roscoe, 1991).

god . . . who is the son of the Sun and a creator of wild and domestic animals" (Roscoe, 1991, c.f. Brunnerová, 2016, p. 35). The Acoma-Laguna Pueblo have stories that describe the Storoka, an entire community of two-spirit people (Brunnerová, 2016; Cherry, 2012; Roscoe, 2014, p. 12). Lastly, the Bella Coola have a story that highlights the unique contributions of two-spirit people. It tells of Winwina, six supernatural birds, and Ala'yao, a two-spirit person, who go in search of food. Each bird finds a different type of salmon while Ala'yao gathers the first berries for people to eat (Bagemihl, 2000; Carlson-Ghost, 2016).

In contemporary language, we would say that Native Americans accepted gender fluidity. Someone could choose their gender based on a dream or their perceived skills (for example) rather than having to be the gender that

TABLE 7.2 Gender Role Change

TRIBE	OCCUPATIONS	CONTEXT
Shoshoni	Hunting, men's work in general	Sometimes men's clothing; one case: married, hunted; other case: wore only man's clothing
Sinkaietk	Hunting	Refused to marry; behavior not supported by the community
Thompson	Behaved "like men"	Rare cases; men's clothing
Ute	Men's work	Men's clothing
Wintu	Men's work, not clothing	Women's clothing; lived with women
Wiyot	Hunting	Men's clothing

SOURCE: "Masculine Role Aspects Taken Up by men-Women & Women," Lang 2010, p. 270–271.

"matched" a certain kind of anatomy (Anderson, 2016; Lang 2010; Mirandé, 2017). (Today, we call people with sex and gender congruence *cis gender*.) Among the Cocopah and Mohave, children's friends and preferences for play could, for example, influence one's gender. A biological female who preferred to play with boys or "boys' toys" could live as a boy (Allen, 1992; Gilley, 2006). They might adopt boys' clothing and do work assigned to boys and people would recognize them as a boy (rather than what we, today, might call a "tomboy"). Likewise, biological males might wear women's clothing and do women's work and be accepted as women (Mirandé, 2017).

Being two-spirit was normative within different indigenous communities until the 1890s. Community members did not see two-spirit people as acting, confused, or deviant. However, the influence of European culture, especially Christian beliefs about gender, changed that (Thomas, 1997, p. 156). Native American writer Leslie Silko describes that shift among the Laguna, saying, "before the arrival of Christian missionaries, a man could dress as a woman and work with the women, and even marry a man without any fanfare. Likewise, a woman was free to dress

Osh-Tisch (left), a Crow two-spirit person, born biologically male, in clothing typically worn by women. On the right is The Other Magpie, biologically female and who identified as a woman. (Today we could call her cisgender; see Chapter 11.) In this rare photo she wears men's attire, perhaps recreating the clothing she wore as a woman warrior. Both were afforded social status for their bravery in battle and for other contributions to their tribal communities.

like a man, to hunt and go to war with the men, and to marry a woman. In the old Pueblo world view, we are all a mixture of male and female, and the sexual identity is constantly changing" (Silko, 2013/1999, p. 67).

Table 7.2 illustrates what Lang (2010) calls gender role change. Some native women wanted to do "men's work" and were generally permitted to do so. Others had identities more aligned with two-spirit people or "men-women."

Anthropologist Sue-Ellen Jacobs says that most of the tribes she studied spoke about homosexuality in positive ways. The 11 tribes that denied the existence of homosexuality among their members were those with the "heaviest, lengthiest, and most severely puritanical white encroachment" (Anderson, 2016, p. 66).

Native Americans view of land ownership and their lack of experience with deeds, titles, contracts, and other Western legal concepts often made it difficult for them to defend their resources from Anglo-Americans. Over time, Christian missionaries and government representatives continued to pursue an assimilationist path. They tried to reverse the traditional Native American division of labor, in which women handled the gardening, because in the Western view, only men did farm work. Likewise, they pushed women out of the fur trade (Anderson, 2016). Military and political representatives of the dominant society usually ignored women tribal leaders and imposed Western notions of patriarchy and men leadership on the tribes (Amott & Matthaei, 1991, p. 39). According to Anderson (2016), George Washington said he planned "to turn Native men into industrious, republican farmers and women into chaste, orderly housewives" (p. 38). These cultural differences in thinking—about nature, land ownership, gender, sexuality, and family—compounded by the power differentials, often placed Native Americans at a disadvantage when dealing with the dominant group.

QUESTIONS FOR REFLECTION

1. Why are there different estimates for the size of the Native American and Alaska Native population? How do these differences support the idea that race is a social construction?

2. What are the key characteristics of Native American cultures? How do these vary from Anglo culture? Describe the conflicting notions regarding gender. How did these differences shape Anglo–Indian relations?

3. Describe the main tenets of colonists' and Native American belief systems. How did those ideas shape group life? How did they fuel tensions between the groups?

RELATIONS WITH THE FEDERAL GOVERNMENT AFTER THE 1890s

By the end of the Indian Wars in 1890, Native Americans had few resources with which to defend their self-interests. In addition to being confined to the reservations, most Native American groups were scattered throughout the western two thirds of the United States and split by cultural and linguistic differences. Politically, the power of the group was further limited by the facts that the huge majority of Native Americans were not U.S. citizens and most tribes lacked a cultural basis for understanding representative democracy as practiced in the larger society.

Economically, Native Americans were among the most impoverished groups in society. Reservation lands were generally of poor quality, traditional food sources such as buffalo and other game had been destroyed, and traditional hunting grounds and gardening plots had been lost to white farmers and ranchers. The tribes had few means of satisfying even their most basic needs. Many became totally dependent on the federal government for food, shelter, clothing, and other necessities.

Prospects for improvement seemed slim. Most reservations were in remote areas, far from sites of industrialization and modernization (see Figure 7.2), and Native Americans had few of the skills (knowledge of English, familiarity with Western work habits and routines) that would have enabled them to compete for a place in the increasingly urban and industrial American society of the early 20th century. Off the reservations, racial prejudice and strong intolerance limited them. On the reservations, they were subjected to policies designed either to maintain their powerlessness and poverty or to force them to Americanize. Either way, the future of Native Americans was in serious jeopardy, and their destructive relations with white society continued in peace as they had in war.

RESERVATION LIFE

As would be expected for a conquered and still hostile group, the reservations were intended to closely supervise Native Americans and maintain their powerlessness. Relationships with the federal government were paternalistic and featured a variety of policies designed to coercively acculturate the tribes.

Paternalism and the Bureau of Indian Affairs. The reservations were run not by the tribes, but by an agency of the federal government: the **Bureau of Indian Affairs (BIA)** of the U.S. Department of the Interior. The BIA and

FIGURE 7.2 Native American Reservations in the United States

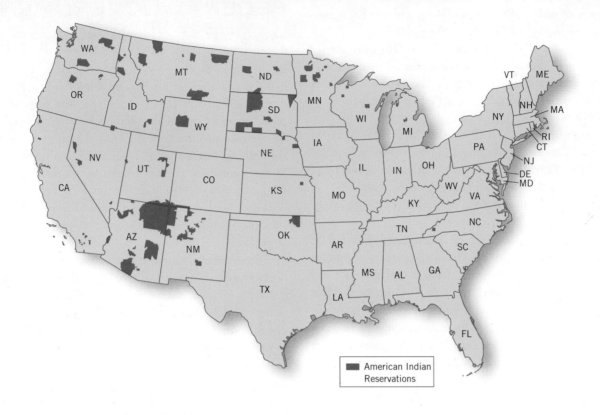

SOURCE: U.S. Parks Service. n.d. https://www.nps.gov/nagpra/DOCUMENTS/ResMAP.HTM.

its local superintendent controlled virtually all aspects of everyday life, including the reservation budget, the criminal justice system, and the schools. The BIA (again, not the tribes) even determined tribal membership.

The traditional leadership structures and political institutions of the tribes were ignored as the BIA executed its duties with little regard for, and virtually no input from, the people it supervised. The BIA superintendent of the reservations "ordinarily became the most powerful influence on local Indian affairs, even though he was a government employee, not responsible to the Indians but to his superiors in Washington" (Spicer, 1980, p. 117). The superintendent controlled the food supply and communications with the world outside the reservation. This control was used to reward tribal members who cooperated and punish those who did not.

Coercive Acculturation: The Dawes Act and Boarding Schools. Consistent with the Blauner hypothesis, Native Americans on the reservations were subjected to coercive acculturation or forced Americanization. Their culture was attacked, their languages and religions forbidden, and their institutions circumvented and undermined. The centerpiece

of U.S. Indian policy was the **Dawes Allotment Act of 1887**, a deeply flawed attempt to impose white definitions of land ownership that divided Native American land into smaller units that the government gave to individuals. The government would offer U.S. citizenship to those Native Americans who took the land and lived away from their tribal communities.

The intention was to give each Indian family the means to survive like their white neighbors and to encourage Native people to assimilate into the larger white society. Once the land had been allotted, the U.S. government then put the rest up for sale to non-Native settlers.

The **Bureau of Indian Affairs (BIA)** is the federal agency responsible for the administration of Indian reservations.

Dawes Allotment Act of 1887 was a key piece of U.S. government policy that divided Native American land into smaller units for individual ownership and moved indigenous people away from their tribal communities.

The U.S. Army encouraged massive hunts that nearly made bison extinct in the 1870s. One goal of the hunts was to force native people off Plains land and onto reservations.

U.S. Department of the Interior sold "Indian Land." This 1911 advertisement features Padani Kokipa Sni, also known as "Not Afraid of Pawnee," of the Yankton and Siouan (Sioux) Tribes.

Although the law might seem benevolent in intent (certainly, thousands of immigrant families would have been thrilled to own land), it was flawed by a gross lack of understanding of Native American cultures and needs, and in many ways, it was a direct attack on those cultures, in part, because of the way it reorganized tribal communities.

Many Native Americans had little or no concept of land as private property, and it was relatively easy for settlers, land speculators, and others to separate Indian families from the land allocated to them by this legislation. By allotting land to families and individuals, the legislation sought to destroy the broader kinship, clan, and tribal social structures and replace them with Western systems that featured individualism and the profit motive (Cornell, 1988, p. 80).

The U.S. government allotted about 140 million acres to Native Americans in 1887. By the 1930s, nearly 90 million of those acres—almost 65%—had been lost. Most of the remaining land was desert or otherwise nonproductive and would not be able to support their communities (Wax, 1971, p. 55). From the standpoint of the Indian nations, the Dawes Allotment Act was a disaster and a further erosion of their limited resources (for more details, see Josephy, 1968; Lurie, 1982; McNickle, 1973; Wax, 1971).

Additionally, coercive acculturation operated through a variety of other avenues. Whenever possible, the BIA sent Native American children to boarding schools, sometimes hundreds of miles away from parents and other kin, where they were required to speak English, convert to Christianity, and become educated in the ways of Western civilization such as dressing in western style clothing (Jacobs, 2009). Consistent with the Blauner (1972) hypothesis, tribal languages, dress, and religion were forbidden, and to the extent that native cultures were mentioned at all, they were attacked and ridiculed. Children of different tribes were mixed together as roommates to speed the acquisition of English. When school was

not in session, children were often boarded with local white families, usually as unpaid domestic helpers or farmhands, and prevented from visiting their families and revitalizing their tribal ties (Hoxie, 1984; Spicer, 1980; Wax, 1971).

Hastiin To'Haali, a Navajo (Diné) who became known as Tom Torlino. The photo on the left was taken when he entered Carlisle Boarding School in 1882. The photo on the right was taken three years later. Some suggest that photographers used filters and lighting to darken the "before" images and lighten the "after" images. He did not fully assimilate as the school hoped. Rather, he returned to his community and his life as a healer and rancher. He used his knowledge of English to help his community in dealing with Westerners.

NARRATIVE PORTRAIT

Civilize Them With a Stick

In recent decades, boarding schools for Native American children have been much improved. Facilities have been modernized and upgraded. The curriculum has been updated and often includes elements of Native American culture and language. Still, it was not that long ago that coercive acculturation at its worst was the daily routine.

In the following passage, Mary Crow Dog, a member of the Sioux tribe who became deeply involved in the Red Power Movement that began in the 1960s, recalls some of the horrors of her experiences at a reservation boarding school. As you read her words, keep in mind that she was born in 1955 and started school in the early 1960s, just a generation or two ago.

LAKOTA WOMAN

Mary Crow Dog

It is almost impossible to explain . . . what a typical old Indian boarding school was like; how it affected the Indian child suddenly dumped into it like a small creature from another world, helpless, defenseless, bewildered, trying desperately to survive and sometimes not surviving at all. Even now, when these schools are so much improved, when . . . the teachers [are] well-intentioned, even trained in child psychology—unfortunately the psychology of white children, which is different from ours—the shock to the child upon arrival is still tremendous. . . .

In the traditional Sioux family, the child is never left alone. It is always surrounded by relatives, carried around, enveloped in warmth. It is treated with the respect due to any human being, even a small one. It is seldom forced to do anything against its will, seldom screamed at, and never beaten. . . . And then suddenly a bus or car arrives full of strangers, who yank the child out of the arms of those who love it, taking it screaming to the boarding school. The only word I can think of for what is done to these children is kidnapping. . . .

The mission school at St. Francis was a curse for our family for generations. My grandmother went there, then my mother, then my sisters and I. At one time or another, every one of us tried to run away. Grandma told me about the bad times she experienced at St. Francis. In those days they let students go home only for one week every year. Two days were used up for transportation, which meant spending just 5 days out of every 365 with her family. . . . My mother had much the same experiences but never wanted to talk about them, and then there was I, in the same place. . . . Nothing had changed since my grandmother's days. I have been told that even in the '70s they were still beating children at that school. All I got out of school was being taught how to pray.

I learned quickly that I would be beaten if I failed in my devotions or, God forbid, prayed the wrong way, especially prayed in Indian to Wakan Tanka, the Indian creator. . . .

My classroom was right next to the principal's office and almost every day I could hear him swatting the boys. Beating was the common punishment for not doing one's homework, or for being late to school. It had such a bad effect upon me that I hated and mistrusted every white person on sight, because I met only one kind. It was not until much later that I met sincere white people I could relate to and be friends with. Racism breeds racism in reverse.

SOURCE: *Lakota Woman* (1990, pp. 28–34). Copyright © 1990 by Mary Crow Dog and Richard Erdoes. Used by permission of Grove/Atlantic, Inc.

Questions to Consider

1. How does this passage illustrate the concept of "coercive acculturation"? What other concepts seem applicable? Why?

2. What do you think about Mary Crow Dog's comment that "racism breeds racism in reverse"? Does this idea apply to other situations discussed in this text? How about to situations you have observed or experienced personally?

Native Americans were virtually powerless to change the reservation system or avoid the campaign of acculturation. Nonetheless, they resented and resisted coerced Americanization, and many languages and cultural elements survived the early reservation period, although often in altered form. For example, the traditional tribal religions remained vital throughout the period, despite the fact that by the 1930s, the great majority of Native Americans had affiliated with one Christian faith or another. Furthermore, many new religions were founded, some combining Christian and traditional elements (Spicer, 1980, p. 118). Mary Crow Dog's Narrative Portrait earlier in this chapter gives an intimate account of the dynamics of coercive acculturation.

The Indian Reorganization Act. By the 1930s, the failure of the reservation system and the policy of forced assimilation had become obvious to all who cared to observe. The quality of life for Native Americans had not improved, and there was little economic development, as well as fewer job opportunities, on the reservations. Health care was woefully inadequate, and education levels lagged far behind national standards.

The plight of Native Americans eventually found a sympathetic ear in the administration of Franklin D. Roosevelt, who was elected president in 1932, and John Collier, the man he appointed to run the BIA. Collier was knowledgeable about Native American issues and concerns, and was instrumental in securing the passage of the **Indian Reorganization Act (IRA)** in 1934.

This landmark legislation contained a number of significant provisions for Native Americans and broke sharply with the federal policies of the past. In particular, the IRA rescinded the Dawes Act of 1887 and the policy of individualizing tribal lands. It also provided means by which the tribes could expand their landholdings. Many of the mechanisms of coercive Americanization in the school system and elsewhere were dismantled. Financial aid in various forms and expertise were made available for the economic development of the reservations. In perhaps the most significant departure from earlier policy, the IRA proposed an increase in Native American self-governance and a reduction of the paternalistic role of the BIA and other federal agencies.

Although sympathetic to Native Americans, the IRA had its limits and shortcomings. Many of its intentions were never realized, and the empowerment of the tribes was not unqualified. The move to self-governance generally took place on the dominant group's terms and in conformity with the values and practices of white society. For example, the proposed increase in the decision-making power of the tribes was contingent on their adoption of Anglo-American political forms, including secret ballots, majority rule, and written constitutions. These were alien concepts to those tribes that selected leaders by procedures other than popular election (e.g., leaders might be chosen by councils of elders) or that made decisions by open discussion and consensus building (i.e., decisions required the agreement of everyone with a voice in the process, not a simple majority). The incorporation of these Western forms illustrates the basically assimilationist intent of the IRA.

The IRA had variable effects on Native American women. In tribes that were dominated by men, the IRA gave women new rights to participate in elections, run for office, and hold leadership roles. In other cases, new political structures replaced traditional forms, some of which, as in the Iroquois culture, had accorded women considerable power. Although the political effects were variable, the programs funded by the IRA provided opportunities for women on many reservations to receive education and training for the first time. Many of these opportunities were oriented toward domestic tasks and other roles traditionally done by Western women, but some prepared Native American women for jobs outside the family and off the reservation, such as clerical work and nursing (Evans, 1989, pp. 208–209).

In summary, the IRA of 1934 was a significant improvement over prior federal Indian policy, but was bolder and more sympathetic to Native Americans in intent than in execution. On the one hand, not all tribes were capable of taking advantage of the opportunities provided by the legislation, and some ended up being further victimized. For example, in the Hopi tribe, located in the Southwest, the Act allowed a Westernized group of Native Americans to be elected to leadership roles, with the result that dominant group firms were allowed to have access to the mineral resources, farmland, and water rights controlled by the tribe. The resultant development generated wealth for the white firms and their Hopi allies, but most of the tribe continued to languish in poverty (Churchill, 1985, pp. 112–113). On the other hand, some tribes prospered (at least comparatively speaking) under the IRA. One impoverished, landless group of Cherokee in Oklahoma acquired land, equipment, and expert advice through the IRA, and between 1937 and 1949, they developed a prosperous, largely debt-free farming community (Debo, 1970, pp. 294–300). Many tribes remained suspicious of the IRA, and by 1948, fewer than 100 tribes had voted to accept its provisions.

The Termination Policy. The IRA's stress on the legitimacy of tribal identity seemed "un-American" to many. There was constant pressure on the federal government to return to an individualistic policy that encouraged (or required) Americanization. Some viewed the tribal structures and communal property-holding patterns as relics of an earlier era and as impediments to modernization and development. Not so incidentally, some elements of dominant society still coveted the remaining Indian lands and resources, which could be more easily exploited if property ownership were individualized.

In 1953, the assimilationist forces won a victory when Congress passed a resolution calling for an end to the reservation system and to the special relationships between the tribes and the federal government. The proposed policy, called **termination**, was intended to get the federal government "out of the Indian business." It rejected the IRA and proposed a return to the system of private land ownership imposed on the tribes by the Dawes Act. Horrified at the notion of termination, the tribes opposed the policy strongly and vociferously. Under this policy, all special relationships—including treaty obligations—between the federal government and the tribes would end. Tribes would no longer exist as legally recognized entities, and tribal lands and other resources would be placed in private hands (Josephy, 1968, pp. 353–355).

The **Indian Reorganization Act**, passed in 1934, was intended to give Indians more autonomy.

Termination was a federal policy intended to end the reservation system and the special relationships between Indian tribes and the federal government.

About 100 tribes, most of them small, were terminated. In virtually all cases, the termination process was administered hastily, and fraud, misuse of funds, and other injustices were common. The Menominee of Wisconsin and the Klamath on the West Coast were the two largest tribes to be terminated. Both suffered devastating economic losses and precipitous declines in quality of life. Neither tribe had the business or tax base needed to finance the services (e.g., health care and schooling) formerly provided by the federal government, and both were forced to sell land, timber, and other scarce resources to maintain minimal standards of living. Many poor Native American families were forced to turn to local and state agencies, which placed severe strain on welfare budgets. The experience of the Menominee was so disastrous that, at the concerted request of the tribe, reservation status was restored in 1973; for the Klamath it was restored in 1986 (Raymer, 1974; Snipp, 1996, p. 394).

Relocation and Urbanization. At about the same time the termination policy came into being, various programs were established to encourage Native Americans to move to urban areas. The movement to the city had already begun in the 1940s, spurred by the availability of factory jobs during World War II. In the 1950s, the movement was further encouraged with programs of assistance and by the declining government support for economic development on the reservation, the most dramatic example of which was the policy of termination (Green, 1999, p. 265). Centers for Native Americans were established in many cities, and various services (e.g., job training, housing assistance, English instruction) were offered to assist in the adjustment to urban life.

The urbanization of the Native American population is displayed in Figure 7.3. Note the rapid increase in the movement to the city that began in the 1950s. More than 70% of all Native Americans are now urbanized, and since 1950, Indians have urbanized faster than the general population. Nevertheless, Native Americans are still the least urbanized minority group. The population as a whole is about 80% urbanized; in contrast, African Americans (see Figure 5.2) are about 90% urbanized.

Like African Americans, Native Americans arrived in the cities after the mainstream economy had begun to deemphasize blue-collar or manufacturing jobs. Because of their relatively low average levels of educational attainment and their racial and cultural differences, Native Americans in the city tended to encounter the same problems African Americans and other minority groups of color experienced: high rates of unemployment, inadequate housing, and all the other travails of the urban underclass.

Native American women also migrated to the city in considerable numbers. The discrimination, unemployment, and poverty of the urban environment often made it

FIGURE 7.3 Urbanization of Native Americans, 1900–2010

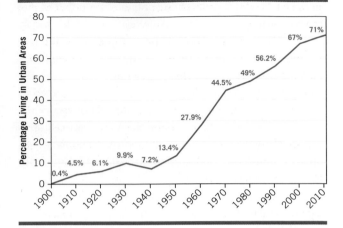

SOURCE: 1900–1990: Thornton, 2001, p. 142. 2000 and 2010: U.S. Bureau of the Census, 2013f.

difficult for the men of the group to fulfill the role of breadwinner, thus, the burden of supporting the family tended to fall on the women. The difficulties inherent in combining child rearing and a job outside the home are compounded by isolation from the support networks provided by extended family and clan back on the reservations. Nevertheless, one study found that Native American women in the city continue to practice their traditional cultures and maintain the tribal identity of their children (Joe & Miller, 1994, p. 186).

Native Americans living in the city are, on average, better off than those living on reservations, where unemployment can reach 80% or even 90%. The improvement is relative, however. Although many individual Native Americans prosper in the urban environment, income figures for urban Native Americans as a whole are comparable to those for African Americans and well below those for whites. Native American unemployment rates run much higher than the national average. For example, in the first half of 2010, unemployment for all Native Americans was about 15%, comparable to the figure for African Americans (see Figure 6.3) and 67% higher than that for whites (Austin, 2010). Thus, a move to the city often means trading rural poverty for the urban variety, with little net improvement in life chances.

Native Americans will probably remain more rural than other minority groups for years to come. Despite the poverty and lack of opportunities for schooling and jobs, the reservation offers some advantages in services and lifestyle. On the reservation, there may be opportunities for political participation and leadership roles that are not available in the cities, where Native Americans are a tiny minority. Reservations also offer kinfolk, friends, religious services, and tribal celebrations (Snipp, 1989, p. 84). Lower levels of education, work experience, and financial resources combine with the prejudice, discrimination, and racism of the larger society to lower the chances of success in the city, and will probably sustain a continuing return to the reservations.

Although the economic benefits of urbanization have been slim for the group as whole, other advantages have accrued from life in the city. It was much easier to establish networks of friendship and affiliation across tribal lines in the cities, and urban Indians have been one of the sources of strength and personnel for a movement of protest that began early in the 20th century. Virtually all the organizational vehicles of Native American protest have had urban roots.

Self-Determination. The termination policy aroused so much opposition from Native Americans and was such an obvious disaster that the pressure to push tribes to termination faded in the late 1950s, although the act itself was not repealed until 1975. Since the 1960s, federal Indian policy has generally returned to the tradition set by the IRA. Termination and forced assimilation continue to be officially rejected, and within limits, the tribes have been granted more freedom to find their own way, at their own pace, of relating to the larger society.

Several federal programs and laws have benefited the tribes during the past few decades, including the antipoverty and "Great Society" campaigns launched in the 1960s. In 1970, President Richard Nixon affirmed the government's commitment to fulfilling treaty obligations and the right of the tribes to self-governance. The Indian Self-Determination and Education Assistance Act was passed in 1975. This legislation increased aid to reservation schools and Native American students, and increased tribal control over the administration of the reservations, from police forces to schools to road maintenance.

The Self-Determination Act primarily benefited the larger tribes and those that had well-established administrative and governing structures. Smaller and less well-organized tribes have continued to rely heavily on the federal government (Snipp, 1996, p. 394). Nonetheless, in many cases, this new phase of federal policy has allowed Native American tribes to plot their own courses free of paternalistic regulation, and just as important, it gave them the tools and resources to address their problems and improve their situations. Decision making was returned to local authorities, who were "held more accountable to local needs, conditions, and cultures than outsiders" (Taylor & Kalt, 2005, p. xi).

In the view of many, self-determination is a key reason for the recent improvements in the status of Native Americans, and we will look at some of these developments after examining the Native American protest movement.

PROTEST AND RESISTANCE

EARLY EFFORTS

As BIA-administered reservations and coercive Americanization came to dominate tribal life in the early 20th century, new forms of Indian activism appeared. The modern protest movement was tiny at first and, with few exceptions, achieved a measure of success only in recent decades. In fact, the Native American protest movement in the past was not so much unsuccessful as simply ignored. The movement has focused on several complementary goals: protecting Native American resources and treaty rights, striking a balance between assimilation and pluralism, and finding a relationship with the dominant group that would permit a broader array of life chances without sacrificing tribal identity and heritage.

Formally organized Native American protest organizations have existed since the 1910s, but the modern phase of the protest movement began during World War II. Many Native Americans served in the military or moved to the city to take jobs in aid of the war effort and were thereby exposed to the world beyond the reservation. Also, political activism on reservations, which had been stimulated by the IRA, continued through the war years, as the recognition of growing problems that were shared across tribal lines grew.

These trends helped stimulate the founding of the National Congress of Native Americans (NCAI) in 1944. This organization was pan-tribal (i.e., included members from many different tribes); 50 different tribes and reservations attended its first convention (Cornell, 1988, p. 119). The leadership consisted largely of Native Americans educated and experienced in the white world. However, the NCAI's program stressed the importance of preserving the old ways and tribal institutions as well as protecting Indian welfare. An early victory for the NCAI and its allies came in 1946 when the federal government created an Indian Claims Commission. This body was authorized to hear claims brought by the tribes with regard to treaty violations. The commission has since settled hundreds of claims, resulting in awards of millions of dollars to the tribes, and it continues its work today (Weeks, 1988, pp. 261–262).

In the 1950s and 1960s, the protest movement was further stimulated by the threat of termination and by the increasing number of Native Americans living in the cities who developed friendships across tribal lines. Awareness of common problems, rising levels of education, and the examples set by the successful protests of other minority groups also increased readiness for collective action.

RED POWER

By the 1960s and 1970s, Native American protest groups were finding ways to express their grievances and problems to the nation. The Red Power Movement, like the Black Power Movement (see Chapter 6), encompassed a coalition of groups, many considerably more assertive than the NCAI, and a varied collection of ideas, most of which stressed self-determination and pride in race and cultural heritage. Red Power protests included a "fish-in" in Washington State in 1965, an episode that also illustrates the nature of Native American demands. The state of Washington had tried to limit the fishing rights of several different tribes because the supply of fish was diminishing and needed to be protected. The tribes depended on fishing for subsistence and survival, and they argued that their right to fish had been guaranteed by treaties signed in the 1850s and it was the pollution and commercial fishing of the dominant society that had depleted the supply of fish. They organized a "fish-in" in violation of the state's policy and were met by a contingent of police officers and other law officials. Violent confrontations and mass arrests ensued. Three years later, after a lengthy and expensive court battle, the tribes were vindicated, and the U.S. Supreme Court confirmed their treaty rights to fish the rivers of Washington State (Nabakov, 1999, pp. 362–363).

Another widely publicized episode took place in 1969, when Native Americans from various tribes occupied Alcatraz Island in San Francisco Bay, the site of a closed federal prison. The protesters were acting on an old law that granted Native Americans the right to reclaim abandoned federal land. The occupation of Alcatraz was organized in part by the American Indian Movement (AIM), founded in 1968. More militant and radical than the previously established protest groups, AIM aggressively confronted the BIA, the police, and other forces that were seen as repressive. With the backing of AIM and other groups, Alcatraz was occupied for nearly four years and generated a great deal of publicity for the Red Power Movement and the plight of Native Americans.

In 1972, AIM helped organize a march on Washington, D.C., called the Trail of Broken Treaties. Marchers came from many tribes and represented both urban and reservation Indians. The intent of the marchers was to dramatize the problems of the tribes. The leaders offered a 20-point position paper that demanded the abolition of the BIA, the return of illegally taken land, and increased self-governance for the tribes, among other things. When they reached Washington, some of the marchers forcibly occupied the BIA offices. Property was damaged (by which side is disputed), and records and papers were destroyed.

FIGURE 7.4 Map of the Dakota Access Pipeline

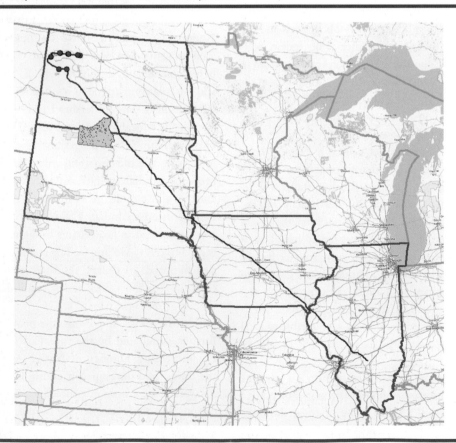

SOURCE: https://commons.wikimedia.org/wiki/File:Bakken_map_osm_basemap.png.

The marchers eventually surrendered, and none of their demands were met. The following year, AIM occupied the village of Wounded Knee in South Dakota to protest the violation of treaty rights. Wounded Knee was the site of the last armed confrontation between Native Americans and whites, in 1890, and was selected by AIM for its deep symbolic significance. The occupation lasted more than two months and involved several armed confrontations with federal authorities. Again, the protest ended without the federal government meeting any of the demands made by the Native American leadership (Olson & Wilson, 1984, pp. 172–175).

Demonstration against the Dakota Access Pipeline on December 4, 2016.

Photo by Andrew Lichtenstein/Corbis via Getty Images

THE DAKOTA ACCESS PIPELINE (DAPL)

In 2016, Native Americans carried out their biggest protest of the last 40 years in opposition the construction of the Dakota Access Pipeline (DAPL), a 1,172-mile oil pipeline that would run from North Dakota through parts of Illinois (see Figure 7.4).

Once built, the pipeline is expected to carry between 470,000 and 570,000 barrels of crude oil per day (Dakota Access, LLC; Healy, 2016a). The original route was rejected because it threated populous (mostly white) residential areas and city water systems, leading the U.S. Corps of Engineers to recommend an alternate route .55 miles north of the Standing Rock Sioux Reservation (Meyer, 2017) on land taken from them in 1958 (McKibben, 2016).

Initially "fast-tracked," DAPL received exemptions from the National Environmental Policy Act and the Clean Water Act. The company behind DAPL, Energy Transfer Partners (ETP), has said it will create thousands of jobs and be safer than pipelines now in use (McKibben, 2016; Meyer, 2017; Mufson, 2016). As early as 2014, the Standing Rock Sioux (SRS) expressed concerns about the potential impact of an oil spill on nearby land and water. Several federal agencies echoed the tribes' concerns; for example, the Department of the Interior said the proposed location was a "serious concern" and recommended an Environmental Impact Statement be conducted (Sammon, 2016).

The Great Sioux Nation tribes, including the Sioux, Lakota, Oglala, and others, say the pipeline threatens 380 archeological and sacred sites, including burial grounds, along its route (Matas, 2016). Thus, they argue, it threatens Native American culture(s) (McKibben, 2016). In protest, thousands of Native Americans from more than 100 tribes, and other indigenous people from around the world,

began living at three camps in North Dakota (McKibben, 2016; Sammon, 2016). They received support from nonindigenous supporters as well, including 2,100 U.S. military veterans offering to act as "human shields" in the wake of a "militarized police force" (Healy, 2016; Veterans for Standing Rock). Protests occurred throughout the United States and elsewhere and thousands of people donated money to help with legal fees and supplies such as generators, eye protection (against tear gas or water cannons), and medical supplies. More than a million people signed various online petitions asking the U.S. government to end the project and that banks end funding ETP and its partners (Amazon Watch, 2017).

This conflict illustrates familiar concerns about land treaties, Native American sacred sites, and cultural preservation. Calling themselves water protectors, the tribes have repeatedly sued the federal government, ETP, and its subsidiaries to prevent the pipeline's construction. The tribes argue that the land is theirs, noting that the U.S. Government has broken the 1851 and 1868 Laramie Treaties that gave them land west of the Missouri River. ETP says it purchased the land from private landowners (McKibben, 2016).

In September 2016, a court order temporarily halted DAPL construction. Tensions between protestors and law enforcement (and some area locals) often ran high with police turning to pepper spray, dogs, tear gas, and water cannons to quell protests. Hundreds of people were arrested and injured (Healy, 2016). As a preventative measure, the governor of North Dakota called in the National Guard (Sammon, 2016).

A federal judge rejected the Standing Rock Sioux's petition to end construction. In response, the Department of the Interior, Department of Justice, and the Department of the Army issued a statement asking ETP voluntarily to halt construction until it could confirm whether or not DAPL breaks National Environmental Policy Act rules (Sammon, 2016). The SRS made additional efforts to halt construction, each ultimately rejected by the courts. Citing costs due to delays and the need to dig before the ground froze in winter, ETP moved forward with the project, ignoring federal requests to wait.

In November, the governor ordered protestors to leave, saying that the camp is "not zoned for dwellings suitable for living in winter conditions, and also [does] not possess proper permanent sanitation infrastructure to sustain a living environment consistent with proper public health" (Yardley, 2016). Before leaving, the remaining protestors burned the camp. In June 2017, a judge ruled that the Corps' investigation of "the impacts of an oil spill on fishing rights, hunting rights, or environmental justice" was "particularly deficient" and ordered a new study (Meyer, 2017). As of fall 2017, the pipeline project had moved forward even as protests and legal efforts to stop the pipeline continued around the country (Hand, 2017; Hult, 2017; Sawyer, 2017).

PROTEST AND PRESERVATION OF NATIVE AMERICAN CULTURES

Ironically, the struggle for Red Power encouraged assimilation as well as pluralism. The movement linked members of different tribes and forced Indians of diverse heritages to find common ground, often in the form of a generic Native American culture. Inevitably, the protests were conducted in English, and the grievances were expressed in ways that were understandable to white society, thus increasing the pressure to acculturate even while arguing for the survival of the tribes. Furthermore, successful protest required that Native Americans be fluent in English, trained in the law and other professions, skilled in dealing with bureaucracies, and knowledgeable about the formulation and execution of public policy. Native Americans who became proficient in these areas thereby took on the characteristics of their adversaries (Hraba, 1994, p. 235).

As the pan-tribal protest movement forged ties between members of diverse tribes, the successes of the movement along with changing federal policy and public opinion encouraged a rebirth of commitment to tribalism and "Indianness." Native Americans were simultaneously stimulated to assimilate (by stressing their common characteristics and creating organizational forms that united the tribes) and to retain a pluralistic relationship with the larger society (by working for self-determination and enhanced tribal power and authority). Thus, part of the significance of the Red Power Movement was that it encouraged both pan-tribal unity and a continuation of tribal diversity (Olson & Wilson, 1984, p. 206). Today, Native Americans continue to seek a way of existing in the larger society that merges assimilation with pluralism.

Table 7.3 summarizes this discussion of federal policy and Indian protest. The four major policy phases since the end of overt hostilities in 1890 are listed on the left. The thrust of the government's economic and political policies are listed in the next two columns, followed by a brief characterization of tribal response. The last column shows the changing bases for federal policy, sometimes aimed at weakening tribal structures and individualizing Native Americans, and sometimes (including most recently) aimed at working with and preserving tribal structures.

TABLE 7.3 Federal Indian Policy and Indian Response

PERIOD	ECONOMIC IMPACT	POLITICAL IMPACT	INDIAN RESPONSE	GOVERNMENT APPROACH
Reservation late 1800s–1930s	Land loss (Dawes Act) and welfare dependency	Government control of reservation and coerced acculturation	Some resistance; growth of religious movements	Individualistic; creation of self-sufficient farmers
Reorganization (IRA) 1930s and 1940s	Stabilized land base and supported some development of reservation	Established federally sponsored tribal governments	Increased political participation in many tribes; some pan-tribal activity	Incorporated tribes as groups; creation of self-sufficient "Americanized" communities
Termination and Relocation late 1940s–early 1960s	Withdrawal of government support for reservations; promotion of urbanization	New assault on tribes; new forms of coercive acculturation	Increased pan-tribalism; widespread and intense opposition to termination	Individualistic; dissolved tribal ties and promoted incorporation into the modern, urban labor market
Self-Determination 1960s to present	Developed reservation economies; increased integration of Indian labor force	Support for tribal governments	Greatly increased political activity	Incorporated tribes as self-sufficient communities with access to federal programs of support and welfare

SOURCE: Based on Cornell, Kalt, Krepps, and Taylor (1998, p. 5).

3. What are the major phases in Indian–white relations since the 1890s? What laws and federal policies shaped these changes? How did Indians respond?

4. Compare and contrast the Red Power Movement with the Black Power Movement discussed in Chapter 6.

5. How were the similarities and differences shaped by the groups' situations?

CONTEMPORARY NATIVE AMERICAN–WHITE RELATIONS

Conflicts between Native Americans and the larger society are far from over. Although the days of deadly battle are (with occasional exceptions) long gone, the issues that remain are serious, difficult to resolve, and, in their way, just as much matters of life and death. Native Americans face enormous challenges in their struggle to improve their status, but, largely because of their greater freedom from stifling federal control since the 1970s, they also have some resources, some opportunities, and a leadership that is both talented and resourceful (Bordewich, 1996, p. 11).

NATURAL RESOURCES

Ironically, land allotted to Native American tribes in the 19th century sometimes turned out to be rich in resources that became valuable in the 20th century. These resources include oil, natural gas, coal, and uranium, basic sources of energy in the larger society. In addition (and despite the devastation wreaked by the Dawes Act of 1887), some tribes hold title to water rights, fishing rights, woodlands that could sustain a timber industry, and wilderness areas that could be developed for camping, hunting, and other forms of recreation. These resources are likely to become more valuable as the earth's natural resources and undeveloped areas are further depleted in the future.

The challenge Native Americans face is to retain control of these resources and to develop them for their own benefit. Threats to the remaining tribal lands and assets are common. Mining and energy companies continue to cast envious eyes on Native American land, and other tribal assets are coveted by real-estate developers, fishers (recreational as well as commercial), backpackers and campers, and cities facing water shortages (Harjo, 1996).

Some tribes have succeeded in developing their resources for their own benefit, in part because of their increased autonomy and independence since the passage of the 1975 Indian Self-Determination Act. For example, the White Mountain Apaches of Arizona own a variety of enterprises, including a major ski resort and a casino (Cornell & Kalt, 1998, pp. 3–4). On many other reservations, however, even richer stores of resources lie dormant, awaiting the right combination of tribal leadership, expertise, and development capital.

On a broader level, tribes are banding together to share expertise and negotiate more effectively with the larger society. For example, 25 tribes founded the Council of Energy Resource Tribes in 1975 to coordinate and control the development of the mineral resources on reservation lands. Since its founding, the council has successfully negotiated a number of agreements with dominant group firms, increasing the flow of income to the tribes and raising their quality of life (Cornell, 1988; Snipp, 1989). The council now encompasses more than 50 tribes and several Canadian First Nations (Council of Energy Resource Tribes, n.d.).

ATTRACTING INDUSTRY TO THE RESERVATION

Many efforts to develop the reservations have focused on creating jobs by attracting industry through such incentives as low taxes, low rents, and a low-wage pool of labor—not unlike the package of benefits offered to employers by less-developed nations in Asia, South America, and Africa. With some notable exceptions, these efforts have not been particularly successful (for a review, see Cornell, 2006; Vinje, 1996). Reservations are often so geographically isolated that transportation costs become prohibitive. The jobs that have materialized are typically low wage and have few benefits; usually, non-Indians fill the more lucrative managerial positions. Thus, the opportunities for building economic power or improving the standard of living from these jobs are sharply limited. These new jobs may transform "the welfare poor into the working poor" (Snipp, 1996, p. 398), but their potential for raising economic vitality is low.

To illustrate the problems of developing reservations by attracting industry, consider the Navajo, the second-largest Native American tribe. The Navajo reservation spreads across Arizona, New Mexico, and Utah, and encompasses about 20 million acres, an area a little smaller than either Indiana or Maine (see Figure 7.2). The reservation seems huge on a map, but much of the land is desert not suitable for farming or other uses. As they have for the past several centuries, the Navajo today rely heavily on the cultivation of corn and sheepherding for sustenance.

Most wage-earning jobs on the reservation are with the agencies of the federal government (e.g., the BIA) or with the tribal government. Tourism is a large industry, but the jobs are typically low wage and seasonal. There are reserves

Australian Aborigines and Native Americans

Bradshaw rock painting in the Kimberley region of Western Australia.

Each colonization situation has its unique history, but similar dynamics are at work. To illustrate, we will compare the impact of European colonization of Australian Aborigines and the indigenous peoples of North America.

Australia came under European domination in the late 1700s, nearly two centuries after colonization in the United States. Despite the time difference, the contact situations have commonalities: (1) Great Britain was the colonial power, (2) first contact occurred in the preindustrial era, and (3) indigenous groups were spread thinly across vast geographical areas, and lacked resources and technological development compared to the British (Diamond, 1998).

Aboriginal peoples lived in Australia 50,000 to 65,000 years before the British arrived (Australian Government, 2015). They were nomadic hunter-gatherers who lived in groups of 30 to 50 people connected by marriage or kinship and organized into 500 to 600 nations (Australian Government, 2015; Pettit, 2015). Aborigines shared a common culture, including a belief system called "The Dreaming" that explained the world and offered a moral framework (Australian Government, 2015; Bodley, 2013, p. 41; Pettit, 2015).

Although early relations between the English and the Aborigines were hospitable, competition for land and other resources soon led to conflict (Pettit, 2015; Reynolds, 2006, p. 69). The British equated "blackness" with inferiority (Smithers, 2008) and saw the Aborigines as "savages." They disliked much about them; for example, Aborigines' use of spears to hunt, bodily adornment, nomadic ways, and their lack of desire for material wealth (Buchanan, 2005; Grey, 1841).

The contact situation became violent—and included massacres, rape, and the forcible removal of indigenous people from their land. The Aborigines fought back, but lacked British fire power (Clements, 2014). Disease, violence, loss of land, and malnutrition killed 90% to 95% of the Aboriginal population (Reynolds, 2006, p. 127). Some people consider it genocide (Clements, 2014).

The British pushed the remaining Aborigines into missions, reserves, and stations (AIATSIS, n.d.). Church-established missions attempted to "civilize" Aborigines. The government created unmanaged reserves where Aborigines could live as they had prior to colonization. Eventually the government provided blankets and basic food—less out of concern than to keep Aborigines from killing settlers' cattle in "white areas" (AIATSIS, n.d., Peterson, 2005). Government-supervised stations provided housing and job training (e.g., as servants) (Choo, 2016, p. 111). However, station conditions were "appalling" and Aborigines suffered from malnutrition and poor health (Berndt & Berndt, 1987, p. xi; Peterson, 2005).

Between 1905 and 1969, the government took approximately 100,000[1] "half-caste" children from their families by "persuasion and threats" (Commonwealth of Australia, 1997, p. 34). Today, they are called "The Stolen Generation." The stated goals of child removal laws were to protect "neglected" children, teach them "European values and work habits," and make them employable (Commonwealth of Australia, 1997, p. 2).

The government focused on half-caste children it believed could "absorb" into the white population. It hoped that, over time, "full-blooded natives" would be "eliminated" (Commonwealth of Australia, 1997, p. 24). To ensure they "never saw their parents or families again" children's names were changed and they were taken far away (Commonwealth of Australia, 1997, p. 24). Their lives were strictly controlled. For example, their hair was cut and their possessions taken. They worked during the day or went to school. At sundown, they were "locked up in dormitories" to discourage running away (Commonwealth of Australia, 1997, p. 116). Breaking even minor rules resulted in the "strap" or being "put into jail" (e.g., solitary confinement) (Commonwealth of Australia, 1997, p. 71).

At the start of the 20th century, the Aboriginal population was less than 100,000. In 2014, it was 686,800—about 3% of Australia's total population. Numbers have increased, partly because of higher birth rates, but also because changing attitudes make it easier for people to claim their Aboriginal heritage. Sixty-two percent of Aboriginal people identified with "a clan, tribal, or language group"; 35% live in cities while only 21% live in remote areas (Australian Bureau of Statistics, 2014).

Compared with the general population, Aborigines have less access to health care and higher rates of alcoholism, malnutrition, unemployment, and suicide. Their life expectancy is 12 years lower and 65% reported long-term health conditions. Just 26% had completed 12th grade (up from 20% in 2008) and 18% lived in overcrowded housing. More than one third (39%) reported experiencing discrimination (Australian Bureau of Statistics, 2014).

[1]The Australian government's report notes that it's hard to estimate a number because many institutions didn't keep records or didn't record children's family history information as Aboriginal. It did "conclude with confidence that between one in three and one in ten Indigenous children were forcibly removed from their families and communities in the period from approximately 1910 until 1970. . . . and not one Indigenous family has escaped the effects of forcible removal" (Commonwealth of Australia, 1997, p. 3).

of coal, uranium, and oil on the reservation, but these resources have not generated many jobs. In some cases, the Navajo have resisted the damage to the environment that would be caused by mines and oil wells because of their traditional values and respect for the land. When exploitation of these resources has been allowed, the companies involved often use highly automated technologies that generate few jobs (Oswalt & Neely, 1996, pp. 317–351).

Figures 7.5 and 7.6 contrast Navajo income, poverty, and education with those of the total U.S. population. The poverty rate for the Navajo is more than two and a half times greater than the national norm, and they are below national standards in terms of education, especially in terms of college education. Also, median household income for the Navajo is

only about 67% of household income for all Americans, and their per capita income is only 53% of the national norm.

On the other hand, some tribes have managed to achieve relative prosperity by bringing jobs to their people. The Choctaw Nation of Mississippi, for example, is one of the 10 largest employers in the state. Tribal leaders have been able to attract companies such as McDonald's and Ford Motor Company by promising (and delivering) high-quality labor for relatively low wages. The tribe runs a variety of business enterprises, including two casinos. Incomes have risen; unemployment is relatively low; the tribe has built schools, hospitals, and a television station; and it administers numerous other services for its members (Mississippi Band of Choctaw Indians, 2017).

FIGURE 7.5 Poverty Rates and Educational Attainment for the Total Population, American Indians and Alaska Natives (AIAN), Navajo, and Choctaw, 2015

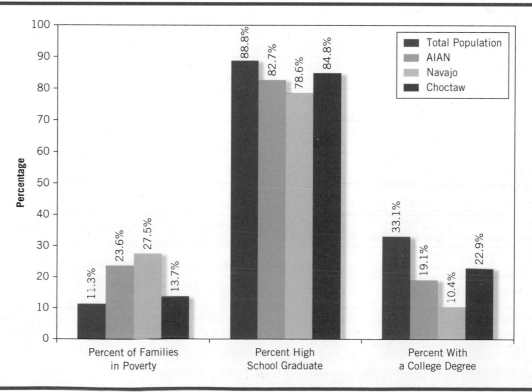

SOURCE: U.S. Bureau of the Census, 2015. 2015 American Community Survey, https://factfinder.census.gov/faces/nav/jsf/pages/index.xhtml.

FIGURE 7.6 Median Household Income and Per Capita Income for the Total Population, All American Indians and Alaska Natives (AIAN), Navajo, and Choctaw, 2015

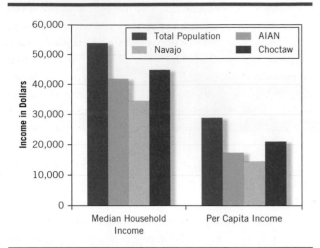

SOURCE: U.S. Bureau of the Census, 2015. 2015 American Community Survey, https://factfinder.census.gov/faces/nav/jsf/pages/index.xhtml.

FIGURE 7.7 Gaming Revenue From American Indian Gaming Establishments, 1995–2016

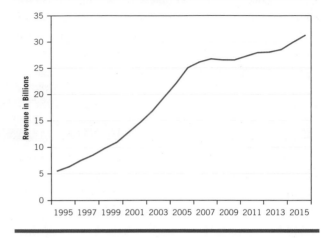

SOURCE: National Indian Gaming Commission, 2017.

The poverty rate for the Choctaw is about half that for the Navajo (although still higher than the national norm), and their educational level approaches the national standard for high school education and is much closer to the national standard for college education than are those of the Navajo or Native Americans as a whole. Median household income for the Choctaw is almost 90% of the national norm and more than $10,000 greater than the median income for the Navajo.

The Choctaw are not the most affluent tribe, and the Navajo are far from being the most destitute. They illustrate the mixture of partial successes and failures that typify efforts to bring prosperity to the reservations; together, these two cases suggest that attracting industry and jobs to the reservations is a possible—but difficult and uncertain—strategy for economic development.

It is worth repeating that self-determination, the ability of tribes to control development on the reservation, seems to be one of the important keys to success. Tribes such as the Choctaw are, in a sense, developing ethnic enclaves (see Chapter 2) in which they can capitalize on local networks of interpersonal relationships. As with other groups that have followed this strategy, success in the enclave depends on solidarity and group cohesion, not Americanization and integration (see Cornell, 2006).

BROKEN TREATIES

For many tribes, the treaties signed with the federal government in the 19th century offer another potential resource. These treaties were often violated by white settlers, the military, state and local governments, the BIA, and other elements and agencies of the dominant group, and many tribes are pursuing this trail of broken treaties and seeking compensation for the wrongs of the past. For example, in 1972 the Passamaquoddy and Penobscot tribes filed a lawsuit demanding the return of 12.5 million acres of land—an area more than half the size of Maine—and $25 billion in damages. The tribes argued that this land had been illegally taken from them more than 150 years earlier. After eight years of litigation, the tribes settled for a $25 million trust fund and 300,000 acres of land. Although far less than their original demand, the award gave the tribes control over resources that could be used for economic development, job creation, upgrading educational programs, and developing other programs that would enhance human and financial capital (Worsnop, 1992, p. 391).

Virtually every tribe has similar grievances, and if pursued successfully, the long-dead treaty relationship between the Indian nations and the government could be a significant fount of economic and political resources. Of course, lawsuits require considerable (and expensive) legal expertise and years of effort before they bear fruit. Because there are no guarantees of success, this avenue has some sharp limitations and risks.

GAMING AND OTHER DEVELOPMENT POSSIBILITIES

Another resource for Native Americans is the gambling industry, the development of which was made possible by federal legislation passed in 1988. There are currently almost 500 tribally owned gaming establishments (National Indian Gaming Commission, 2017), and the industry has grown many times over, from almost $5 million in revenues in 1995 to over $31 billion in 2016 (National Indian Gaming Commission, 2017). Figure 7.7 charts the growth of revenues from gaming on Native American reservations from 1995 to 2016.

Most operations are relatively small in scale. The 21 largest Indian casinos—about 5% of all Indian casinos—generate almost 40% of the total income from gaming, and the 74 smallest operations—about 17% of all Indian casinos—account for less than 1% of the income (National Indian Gaming Commission, 2011).

The single most profitable Indian gambling operation is the Foxwoods Casino in Connecticut, operated by the Pequot tribe. The casino is one of the largest in the world and generates more revenue than the casinos of Atlantic City. The profits from the casino are used to benefit tribal members in a variety of ways, including the repurchase of tribal lands, housing assistance, medical benefits, educational scholarships, and public services such as a tribal police force (Bordewich, 1996, p. 110). Other tribes have used gambling profits to purchase restaurants and marinas and to finance the development of outlet malls, manufacturing plants, and a wide variety of other businesses and enterprises (Spilde, 2001).

The power of gaming to benefit the tribes is suggested by the information displayed in Table 7.4, which shows that on a number of indicators, both gaming and nongaming reservations enjoyed significant improvements in their quality of life in the last decade of the 20th century but the gaming reservations improved more rapidly. For example, all reservations increased their per capita income faster than the nation as a whole (+11%), but gaming reservations improved faster (+36%) than nongaming reservations (+21%). (For a more pessimistic view of the benefits of gaming, see Guedel, 2014).

Various tribes have sought other ways to capitalize on their freedom from state regulation and taxes. Some have established small but profitable businesses selling cigarettes tax free. Also, because they are not subject to state and federal environmental regulations, some reservations are exploring the possibility of housing nuclear waste and other refuse of industrialization—a somewhat ironic and not altogether attractive use of the remaining Indian lands.

Clearly, the combination of increased autonomy, treaty rights, natural resources, and gambling means that Native Americans today have an opportunity to dramatically raise their standards of living and creatively take control of their own destinies. Some tribes have enjoyed enormous benefits, but for others, these assets remain a potential waiting to be actualized. Without denying the success stories or the improvements in recent years, the lives of many Native Americans continue to be limited by poverty and powerlessness, prejudice, and discrimination. We document these patterns in the next section.

PREJUDICE AND DISCRIMINATION

Anti-Indian prejudice has been a part of American society since first contact. Historically, negative feelings such as hatred and contempt have been widespread and strong, particularly during the heat of war, and various stereotypes of Indians have been common. One stereotype, especially strong during periods of conflict, depicts Indians as bloodthirsty, ferocious, cruel savages capable of any atrocity. The other image of Native Americans is that of "the noble Red Man," who lives in complete harmony with nature and symbolizes goodwill and pristine simplicity (Bordewich, 1996, p. 34). Although the first stereotype tended to fade away as hostilities drew to a close, the latter image retains a good deal of strength in modern views of Indians found in popular culture and among environmentalist and "new age" spiritual organizations.

A variety of studies have documented continued stereotyping of Native Americans in the popular press, textbooks, the media, cartoons, and various other places (e.g., see Aleiss, 2005; Bird, 1999; Meek, 2006; Rouse & Hanson, 1991). In the tradition of "the noble Red Man," Native Americans are often portrayed as bucks and squaws, complete with headdresses, bows, tepees, and other such "generic" Indian artifacts. These simplified portrayals obliterate the diversity of Native American culture and lifestyles.

Native Americans are often referred to in the past tense, as if their present situation were of no importance or, worse, as if they no longer existed. Many history books continue to begin the study of American history in Europe or with the "discovery" of America, omitting the millennia of civilization prior to the arrival of European explorers and colonizers. Contemporary portrayals of Native Americans, such as in the movie *Dances With Wolves* (Costner, 1990),

TABLE 7.4 Various Indicators of Improvement on Gaming vs. Nongaming Reservations, 1990–2000

INDICATOR	NONGAMING	GAMING	UNITED STATES
Per capita income	+21%	+36%	+11%
Family poverty	–7%	–12%	–1%
Unemployment	–2%	–5%	–1%
High school graduates	–1%	+2%	–1%
College graduates	+2%	+3%	+4%

SOURCE: Taylor and Kalt (2005, p. xi).

Protest against the Washington Redskins mascot.

are more sympathetic but still treat the tribes as part of a bucolic past forever lost, not as peoples with real problems in the present.

The persistence of stereotypes and the extent to which they have become enmeshed in modern culture is illustrated by continuing controversies surrounding the names of athletic teams (e.g., the Washington Redskins, the Cleveland Indians, and the Atlanta Braves) and the use of Native American mascots, tomahawk "chops," and other practices offensive to many Native Americans (for more, see the Current Debates section for this chapter). Protests have been held at athletic events to increase awareness of these derogatory depictions, but as was the case so often in the past, the protests have been attacked, ridiculed, or simply ignored.

Relatively few studies of anti-Indian prejudice exist within the social science literature. Therefore, it is difficult to fully understand the changes that may have occurred over the past several decades. We do not know whether there has been a shift to more symbolic or "modern" forms of anti-Indian racism, as there has been for antiblack prejudice, or whether the stereotypes of Native Americans have declined in strength or changed in content.

One of the few records of national anti-Indian prejudice over time is that of social distance scale results (see Table 3.2). When the scales were first administered in 1926, Native Americans were ranked in the middle third of all groups (18th out of 28), at about the same level as southern and eastern Europeans and slightly above Mexicans, another colonized group. The ranking of Native Americans remained stable until 1977, when there was a noticeable rise in their position relative to other groups. In the most recent

polls, the rankings of Native Americans have remained stable, at about the same level as Jews and Poles but below African Americans. These shifts may reflect a decline in levels of prejudice, a change from more overt forms to more subtle modern racism, or both. Remember, however, that the samples for the social distance research were college students, for the most part, and the results do not necessarily reflect trends in the general population (see also Hanson & Rouse, 1987; Smith & Dempsey, 1983).

Additionally, research is unclear about the severity or extent of discrimination against Native Americans. Certainly, the group's lower average levels of education limit their opportunities for upward mobility, choice of occupations, and range of income. This is a form of institutional discrimination in the sense that the opportunities to develop human capital are much less available to Native Americans than to much of the rest of the population.

In terms of individual discrimination or more overt forms of exclusion, there is simply too little evidence to sustain clear conclusions (Snipp, 1992, p. 363). The situation of Native American women is also underresearched, but Snipp reports that, like their counterparts in other minority groups and the dominant group, they "are systematically paid less than their male counterparts in similar circumstances" (p. 363).

The very limited evidence available from social distance scales suggests that overt anti-Indian prejudice has declined, perhaps in parallel with antiblack prejudice. A great deal of stereotyping remains, however, and demeaning, condescending, or negative portrayals of Native Americans are common throughout the dominant culture. Institutional discrimination is a major barrier for Native Americans, who have not had access to opportunities for education and employment.

Native Americans were the victims of systematic discrimination in a variety of institutions.

In this chapter, we've shown some of the diversity with-in the Native American population. To test your general knowledge about Native Americans as a group, here is a true/false quiz. You will be able to answer some questions from chapter information, but others ask you to consider ideas that you might have heard about Native Americans from popular culture or friends. How well do you think most Americans would do on this quiz? Why?

1. Native Americans have their college expenses paid for by their tribes or by the federal government.

2. Pocahontas was an Indian princess.

3. Native Americans scalped their slain enemies.

4. The term *powwow* is a derogatory, stereotypical term that shouldn't be used by non-Native people.

5. Native Americans practiced slavery and Native Americans were enslaved much like African Americans.

6. Native Americans use peyote in religious ceremonies.

7. Native Americans are getting rich from casinos.

8. Anyone with an Indian ancestor is automatically a member of that tribe.

9. Native Americans were always considered U.S. citizens.

10. Indian tribes are sovereign nations.

TURN THE PAGE TO FIND OUR ANSWERS.

QUESTIONS FOR REFLECTION

6. This section examined a number of issues in contemporary Indian–white relations. In your opinion, which of these is most important? Why?

7. Thinking about the concepts developed in this text, what is the single most important force shaping the situation of Native Americans over the past century? Why?

8. Compare and contrast antiblack prejudice with anti-Indian prejudice. How and why are the two forms of prejudice different? How has that prejudice influenced forms of discrimination?

9. Was the colonization of America a Native American genocide? Explain.

ASSIMILATION AND PLURALISM

In this section, we continue to assess the situation of Native Americans today using the same conceptual framework used in Chapter 6. Once again, please regard this material as an overview and as starting points for further research.

Compared with other groups, information about Native Americans is scant. Nonetheless, a relatively clear picture emerges. The portrait stresses a mixed picture: improvements for some combined with continued coloniza-tion, marginalization, and impoverishment for others. Like African Americans, Native Americans can be found at every status and income level in the United States, but Indians living on reservations continue as one of the most impov-erished, marginalized groups in society. Native Americans as a group face ongoing discrimination and exclusion, and continue the search for a meaningful course between assim-ilation and pluralism.

ACCULTURATION

Despite more than a century of coercive Americanization, many tribes have been able to preserve at least a portion of their traditional cultures. For example, many tribal lan-guages continue to be spoken on a daily basis. About 20% of Native Americans and Alaska Natives speak a language other than English at home, about the same percentage as the total population. Figure 7.8 suggests the extent of

answers to APPLYING CONCEPTS

Some answers may vary based on tribe or based on the differing opinions among the five million Native Americans currently living in the United States. If you live in an area near a tribal community or organization, we encourage you to use those resources to learn more about these topics. Otherwise, the Internet and your college or local library may have useful information.

(1) False. The "urban legend" that all Native Americans get a free ride to college is not true. Only 19% of Native Americans have a college degree. Some tribes offer scholarships to members and the number of tribal colleges has increased over time. Here's one funding organization that's trying to assist with scholarships: http://college fund.org/.

(2) False. Pocahontas was the daughter of Powhatan, the "paramount chief" of a large confederation of tribes in the Tidewater, Virginia area. So, she wasn't a "princess" (which is a British royal title). She was held in high regard and she may have saved the life of English colonist John Smith, as legend has it.

(3) True. Archaeological evidence dating back to pre-Columbian times suggest scalping was practiced, though the type and prevalence varied widely by tribal community and geographic region. Europeans transformed this indigenous practice into a kind of bounty hunting by encouraging native people to scalp Indians who were hostile to European interests. (See Axwell & Sturtevant, 1980.) Evidence of scalping has been found in Asia, Europe, and Mexico, too.

(4) True. Powwows are festivals that preserve and celebrate Native American culture and traditions, including sacred ones. Thus, use the phrase "have a powwow" to indicate a chat, meeting, or negotiation would be factually incorrect and, to some, inappropriate, insensitive, or rude.

(5) True. Precolonization, some tribes enslaved other Native Americans as war captives who could provide labor (including reproductive labor). However, they were not seen as an inferior race and often became integrated into tribes, for example, through marriage. Rushforth (2012) notes that "indigenous slavery moved captives 'up and in' toward full, if forced, assimilation" (p. 66). Some Southern Indian communities ritually adopted enslaved people who acted as a proxy for dead tribal members (Snyder, 2010, p. 103). For the Comanche, enslavement practices were strategic—to gain numbers. However, they "never draw a hard line between masters and slaves, and they possessed neither the necessary means to enforce unconditional submission nor a racist ideology to mentally suppress the slave population" (Hämäläinen, 2008, p. 251).

Native enslavement practices changed as the U.S. system of slavery developed. Additionally, they were intertwined with the Spanish system. The Spanish enslaved the majority of indigenous Americans to supply labor in the West (e.g., gold mining in Mexico) (Lowcountry, n.d.). As the British and Spanish systems of slavery developed, it became more lucrative for Native Americans to sell, rather than enslave, other Native Americans. However, widespread enslavement of Native Americans in the U.S. colonies was problematic. As discussed in Chapter 4, many indigenous Americans died due to lack of immunity to European diseases, reducing the potential labor pool. Additionally, indigenous Americans could escape more easily than African slaves because they possessed knowledge of the area and could often get help from other indigenous people (Lowcountry, n.d.). Because of this "flight risk," slave traders often took them to Brazil to be sold there. As the U.S. system of slavery developed, some tribes, especially in the Southeast, began to enslave Africans (Snyder, 2010) while others offered sanctuary to runaway African slaves. For example, researchers estimate that thousands of "Maroons" lived with Native Americans in the Great Dismal Swamp (Sayers, Burke, & Henry, 2007). In short, Native Americans did enslave other Native Americans and, at times, some African slaves. However, it was quite different from the chattel-oriented slave system developed in the United States (also see Madley, 2016; Reséndez, 2016, Trueur, 2012).

(6) True. For example, the Native American Church uses peyote as part of its rituals, as explained later in this chapter.

(7) False. While some tribes earn a lot of money from casinos, many do not. See the relevant sections of this chapter.

(8) False. Tribes have specific rules about membership eligibility, and an Indian ancestor is no guarantee of acceptance.

(9) False. Not all Native Americans were covered by the Fourteenth Amendment granting citizenship to persons "born or naturalized in the United States." The Indian Citizenship Act of 1924 granted citizenship; however, it didn't automatically give all rights to Native peoples. As with African Americans, some states refused to give Native Americans the right to vote.

(10) False. Tribes do, however, have considerable autonomy and the power to govern their own affairs under a variety of laws.

NARRATIVE PORTRAIT

An Indian View of White Civilization

Who's the savage? One stereotype of Native Americans portrays them as "cruel, barbaric, and savage." Is it possible, however, that Native Americans are more advanced than the dazzling sophisticates of urban America? In a 1972 interview, John Lame Deer, a Sioux, gives his view of the technologically advanced society that surrounds him. Through his words, we can hear the voices of the Indian cultures that have survived.

LISTENING TO THE AIR

John Lame Deer

You have made it hard for us to experience nature in the good way by being part of it. Even here [a Sioux reservation in South Dakota] we are conscious that somewhere out in those hills there are missile silos and radar stations. White men always pick the few unspoiled, beautiful, awesome spots for these abominations. You have raped and violated these lands, always saying, "gimme, gimme, gimme," and never giving anything back. . . . You have not only despoiled the earth, the rocks, the minerals, all of which you call "dead" but which are very much alive; you have even changed the animals, . . . changed them in a horrible way, so no one can recognize them.

There is power in a buffalo—spiritual, magic power—but there is no power in an Angus, in a Hereford.

There is power in an antelope, but not in a goat or a sheep, which holds still while you butcher it, which will eat your newspaper if you let it. There was great power in a wolf, even in a coyote. You made him into a freak—a toy poodle, a Pekinese, a lap dog. You can't do much with a cat, which is like an Indian, unchangeable. So you fix it, alter it, declaw it, even cut its vocal cords so you can experiment on it in a laboratory without being disturbed by its cries. . . .

You have not only altered, declawed, and malformed your winged and four-legged cousins; you have done it to yourselves. You have changed men into chairmen of boards, into office workers, into time-clock punchers. You have changed women into housewives, truly fearful creatures. . . . You live in prisons which you have built for yourselves, calling them "homes," offices, factories. We have a new joke on the reservations: "What is cultural deprivation?" Answer: "Being an upper-middle-class white kid living in a split-level suburban home with a color TV.". . .

I think white people are so afraid of the world they created that they don't want to see, feel, smell, or hear it. The feeling of rain or snow on your face, being numbed by an icy wind and thawing out before a smoking fire, coming out of a hot sweat bath and plunging into a cold stream, these things make you feel alive, but you don't want them anymore. Living in boxes that shut out the heat of the summer and the chill of winter, living inside a body that no longer has a scent, hearing the noise of the hi-fi rather than listening to the sounds of nature, watching some actor on TV have a make-believe experience when you no longer experience anything for yourself, eating food without taste—that's your way. It's no good.

Questions to Consider

1. Does Lame Deer's critique of mainstream American culture ring true? If you were in a debate with him, could you refute his points?
2. How does this passage support the idea that Native American culture has survived coercive acculturation and military conquest? Is there a future for the ideas Lame Deer expresses?

---

language preservation. For many tribes, less than 10% of their members speak the tribal language at home. Some tribes, however, continue to speak their native language, including about 30% of Apache and almost half of Navajo.

While some Native American languages have survived, it seems that even the most widely spoken of these languages is endangered. One study (Krauss, 1996) estimates that only about 11% of the surviving 200 languages spoken are being taught by parents to their children in the traditional way and that most languages are spoken on a daily basis only by the older generation. Few, if any, people are left who speak only a tribal language. One authority (A. Treuer, 2012, p. 80) reports that only 20 tribal languages in the United States and Canada are spoken by children in significant numbers. If these patterns persist, Native Americans languages will disappear as the generations change. A number of tribes have instituted programs to try to renew and preserve their language, along with other elements of their culture, but the success of these efforts is uncertain (Schmid, 2001, p. 25; see also D. Treuer, 2012, pp. 300–305).

Traditional culture is retained in other forms besides language. Religions and value systems, political and economic structures, and recreational patterns have all survived the military conquest and the depredations of reservation life, but each pattern has been altered by contact with the dominant group. Cornell (1987), for example, argues that the strong orientation to the group rather than the individual is being significantly affected by the "American dream" of personal material success.

The tendency to filter the impact of the larger society through continuing vital Native American culture is also illustrated by the Native American Church. The Native

FIGURE 7.8 Percentage of Total Population, All American Indians and Alaska Natives (AIAN), and Selected Tribes That Speak a Language Other Than English at Home, 2015

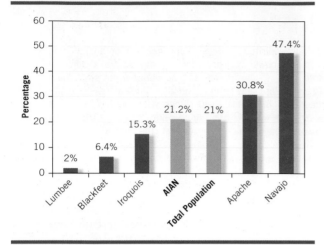

SOURCE: U.S. Bureau of the Census, 2017. American Community Survey, 2015.

American Church is an important Native American religion, with more than 100 congregations across the nation.

This religion combines elements from both cultures, and church services freely mix Christian imagery and the Bible with attempts to seek personal visions by using peyote, a hallucinogenic drug. The latter practice is consistent with the spiritual and religious traditions of many tribes but clashes sharply with the laws and norms of the larger society. The difference in traditions has generated many skirmishes with the courts, and as recently as 2004, the right of the Native American Church to use peyote was upheld by the Supreme Court of Utah ("Utah Supreme Court Rules," 2004).

Native Americans have been more successful than African Americans in preserving their traditional cultures, a pattern that is partly explained by the differences in the relationship between each minority group and the dominant group. African Americans were exploited for labor, whereas the competition with Native Americans involved land. African cultures could not easily survive because the social structures that transmitted the cultures and gave them meaning were largely destroyed by slavery and sacrificed to the exigencies of the plantation economy.

In contrast, Native Americans confronted the dominant group as tribal units, intact and whole. The tribes maintained integrity throughout the wars and throughout the reservation period. Tribal culture was attacked and denigrated during the reservation era, but the basic social unit that sustained the culture survived, albeit in altered form. The fact that Native Americans were placed on separate reservations, isolated from one another and the "contaminating" effects of everyday contact with the larger society, also supported the preservation of traditional languages and culture (Cornell, 1990). The second

Narrative Portrait in this chapter illustrates the persistence of a distinct Indian culture and point of view.

The vitality of Indian cultures may have increased in the current atmosphere of greater tolerance and support for pluralism in the larger society, combined with increased autonomy and lower government regulation on the reservations. However, a number of social forces are working against pluralism and the continuing survival of tribal cultures. Pantribalism may threaten the integrity of individual tribal cultures as it represents Native American grievances and concerns to the larger society. Opportunities for jobs, education, and higher incomes draw Native Americans to more developed urban areas and will continue to do so as long as the reservations are underdeveloped. Many aspects of the tribal cultures can be fully expressed and practiced only with other tribal members on the reservations. Thus, many Native Americans must make a choice between "Indian-ness" on the reservation and "success" in the city. The younger, more educated Native Americans will be most likely to confront this choice, and the future vitality of traditional Native American cultures and languages will hinge on which option they choose.

SECONDARY STRUCTURAL ASSIMILATION

This section assesses the degree of integration of Native Americans into the various institutions of public life, following the general outlines of the parallel section in Chapter 6.

Residential Patterns. Since the Indian Removal Act of 1830 (see Chapter 4), Native Americans have been concentrated in the western two thirds of the nation, as illustrated in Figure 7.9, although some pockets of population still can be found in the East. The states with the largest concentrations of Native Americans—California, Oklahoma, and Arizona—together include about 30% of all Native Americans. As Figure 7.9 illustrates, most U.S. counties have few Native American residents. The population is concentrated in eastern Oklahoma, the upper Midwest, and the Southwest (Norris et al., 2012, p. 8).

Because Native Americans are such a small, rural group, it is difficult to assess the overall level of residential segregation. An earlier study using 2000 Census data found that they were less segregated than African Americans and that the levels of residential segregation had declined since 1980 (Iceland, Weinberg, & Steinmetz, 2002, p. 23). More detailed data from the 2000 Census for the 10 metropolitan areas with the highest numbers of Native American residents shows that residential segregation was "extremely high" (dissimilarity index at or above 60) in four of the cities (New York, Phoenix, Albuquerque, and Chicago) but lower than the levels of black–white segregation. Also, a couple of the cities (Oklahoma City and Tulsa) had low scores, or

FIGURE 7.9 Percentage of County Population Choosing Native American or Alaska Native, Alone or in Combination, 2010

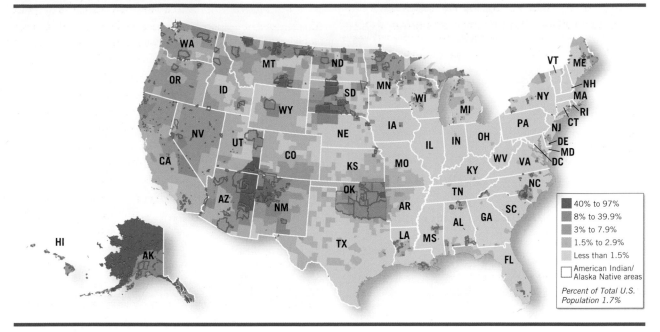

SOURCE: Norris, Vines, and Hoeffel, 2012.

a dissimilarity index at or below 30 (Social Science Data Analysis Network, n.d.).

What can we conclude? It seems that residential segregation for Native Americans is lower than it is for African Americans. However, it is difficult to come to firm conclusions because of the small size of the group and the fact that 30% of Native Americans live on rural reservations, where the levels of isolation and racial segregation are quite high.

School Integration and Educational Attainment. As a result of the combined efforts of missionaries and federal agencies, Native Americans have had a long but not necessarily productive acquaintance with Western education. Until the past few decades, schools for Native Americans were primarily focused on Americanizing children, not so much on educating them.

For many tribes, the percentage of high school graduates has increased in the recent past, but Native Americans' graduation rates as a whole are still somewhat below national rates and the rates of non-Hispanic whites, as shown in Figure 7.10. The differences in schooling are especially important because the lower levels of educational attainment limit mobility and job opportunities in the postindustrial job market.

One positive development for the education of Native Americans is the rapid increase in tribally controlled colleges. There are now 37 tribal colleges: All offer two-year degrees, six offer four-year degrees, and two offer master's degrees. These institutions are located on or near reservations; some have been constructed with funds generated in the gaming industry. They are designed to be more

sensitive to the educational and cultural needs of the group, and tribal college graduates who transfer to four-year colleges are more likely to graduate than are other Native American students (Pego, 1998; see also His Horse Is Thunder, Anderson, & Miller, 2013).

An earlier study found that Native American school children were less segregated than African American school children in the 2005–2006 school year, but that the levels of racial isolation might be increasing (Fry, 2007). Again, it is difficult to assess trends because of the small size of the group and their concentration in rural areas.

Political Power. The ability of Native Americans to exert power as a voting bloc or otherwise directly affect the political structure is limited by group size; they are a tiny percentage of the electorate. Furthermore, their political power is limited by their lower than average levels of education, language differences, lack of economic resources, and fractional differences within and between tribes and reservations. The number of Native Americans holding elected office is minuscule, far less than 1% (Pollard & O'Hare, 1999). In 1992, however, Ben Nighthorse Campbell, of Colorado, a member of the Northern Cheyenne tribe, was elected to the U.S. Senate and served until 2005.

Jobs and Income. Some of the most severe challenges facing Native Americans relate to work and income. The problems are especially evident on the reservations, where jobs traditionally have been scarce and affluence rare. As mentioned previously, the overall unemployment rate for all Native Americans is about double the rate for whites.

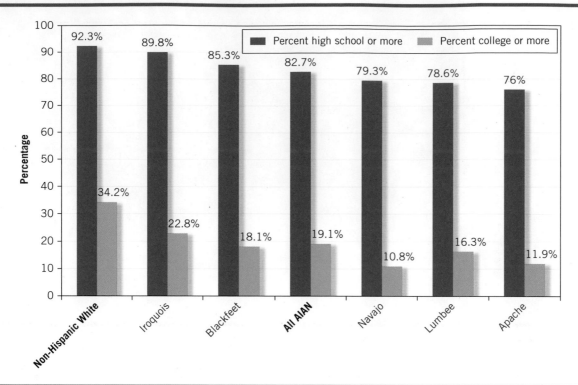

Legend: ■ Percent high school or more   ■ Percent college or more

- Non-Hispanic White: 92.3% / 34.2%
- Iroquois: 89.8% / 22.8%
- Blackfeet: 85.3% / 18.1%
- All AIAN: 82.7% / 19.1%
- Navajo: 79.3% / 10.8%
- Lumbee: 78.6% / 16.3%
- Apache: 76% / 11.9%

(Y-axis: Percentage, 0 to 100)

SOURCE: U.S. Bureau of the Census, 2017. American Community Survey, 2015.

For Indians living on or near reservations, however, the rate is much higher, sometimes rising to 70% to 80% on the smaller, more-isolated reservations (U.S. Census Bureau, 2010).

Nationally, Native Americans are underrepresented in the higher-status, more lucrative professions and overrepresented in unskilled labor and service jobs (U.S. Census Bureau, 2010). Like African Americans, Native Americans who hold white-collar jobs are more likely than whites to work in lower-income occupations, such as typist or retail salesperson (Ogunwole, 2006, p. 10).

Housing on reservations for Native Americans is often substandard. This dilapidated trailer is home for a family of Cheyenne Indians on the Standing Rock reservation in South Dakota.

Figure 7.11 shows median household income in 2015 for non-Hispanic whites, all Native Americans and Alaska Natives, and five of the larger tribes. Median household income for Native Americans and Alaska Natives is about 68% of that of non-Hispanic whites. There is a good deal of variability among the tribes, but again, none approach the incomes of non-Hispanic whites.

These income statistics reflect lower levels of education as well as the interlocking forces of past discrimination and lack of development on many reservations. The rural isolation of much of the population and their distance from the more urbanized centers of economic growth limit possibilities for improvement and raise the likelihood that many reservations will remain the rural counterparts to urban underclass ghettos.

Figure 7.12 supplements the information in Figure 7.11 by displaying the distribution of income for all Native Americans and Alaska Natives (AIAN) compared with non-Hispanic whites. This type of graph was introduced in Chapter 6, which covered African Americans, and its format is similar to the format of Figure 6.13. In both graphs, the pattern of income inequality is immediately obvious. Starting at the bottom, we see that Native Americans and Alaska Natives are overrepresented in the lowest income groups, as were African Americans. For example, over 13% of Native Americans and Alaska Natives have incomes less than $10,000—this is more than double the percentage for whites (5.6%) in this range.

Moving up the figure through the lower- and middle-income brackets, we see that Native American

FIGURE 7.11 Median Household Income for Non-Hispanic Whites, All American Indians and Alaska Natives (AIAN), and Selected Tribes, 2015

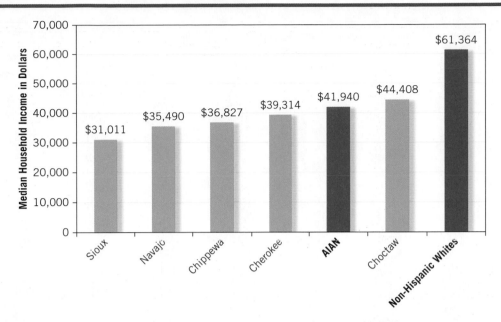

SOURCE: U.S. Bureau of the Census, 2017. American Community Survey, 2015.

and Alaska Native households continue to be overrepresented. There is a notable clustering of both groups in the $50,000 to $100,000 categories, but it is whites who are overrepresented at these higher-income levels. The income differences are especially obvious at the top of the figure. For example, almost 12% of non-Hispanic white households are in the two highest income categories, compared with only 4.2% 6 of AIAN households. Figure 7.12 also shows the median household incomes for the two groups: The

figure for non-Hispanic whites is more than $22,000 higher than that of American Indians and Alaska Natives.

Finally, Figure 7.13 shows the poverty levels for non-Hispanic whites, all Native Americans and Alaska Natives, and five of the larger tribes. The poverty rate for all Native American and Alaska Native families is almost triple the rate for non-Hispanic whites, and three of these tribes have an even higher percentage of families living in poverty. The poverty rates for children show a similar pattern, with very high rates for the Lumbee, Navajo, and Blackfeet. As a

FIGURE 7.12 Distribution of Household Income for Non-Hispanic Whites and American Indians and Alaska Natives (AIAN), 2015

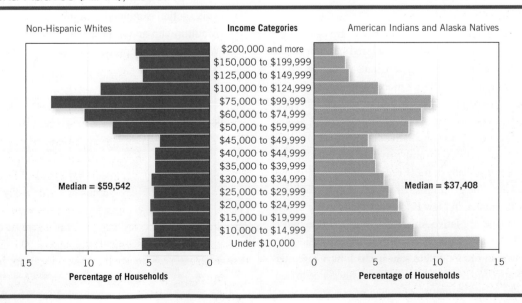

SOURCE: U.S. Census Bureau, 2013g.

FIGURE 7.13 Families and Children in Poverty for Non-Hispanic Whites, All American Indians and Alaska Natives (AIAN), and Selected Tribes, 2015

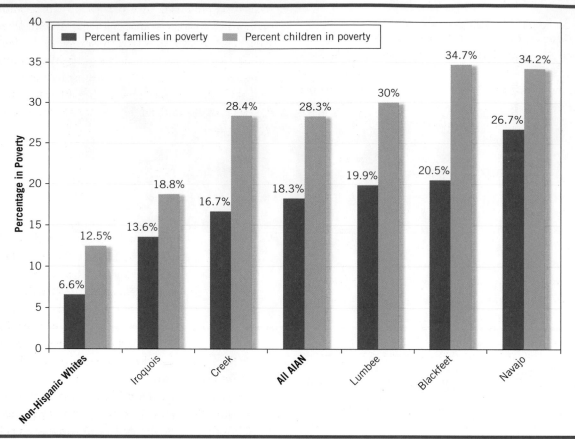

SOURCE: U.S. Census Bureau, 2013f.

NOTE: Family and child poverty rates are computed using different units of analysis. Family rates represent the percentage of all families in the group that are below the poverty line while the rates for children are the percentage of all people younger than 18 in the group who live in poverty.

whole, this information on income and poverty shows that despite the progress Native Americans have made over the past several decades, a sizable socioeconomic gap persists.

PRIMARY STRUCTURAL ASSIMILATION

Rates of out-marriage for Native Americans are quite high compared with other groups, as displayed in Table 7.5. While the overwhelming majority of whites were married to other whites in both years, a little more than 40% of Native Americans had marriage partners within the group. This pattern is partly the result of the small size of the group. As less than 1% of the total population, Native Americans are numerically unlikely to find dating and marriage partners within their own group, especially in those regions of the country and urban areas where the group is small in size. For example, an earlier study found that in New England, which has the lowest relative percentage of Native Americans of any region, more than 90% of Indian marriages were to partners outside the group. But even in the mountain states, which have a greater number of Native Americans who are also highly concentrated on reservations, only about 40% of Indian marriages involved

partners outside the group (Snipp, 1989, pp. 156–159). Also, the social and legal barriers to Indian-white intermarriages have been comparatively weak (Qian & Lichter, 2011).

QUESTIONS FOR REFLECTION

10. This section examined a variety of dimensions of acculturation and integration for Native Americans. Which is most important? Why?

11. In which of these areas has there been the most progress over the past 50 years? Explain?

TABLE 7.5 Percentage Married to a Person of the Same Race, 1980 and 2008

	WHITES		NATIVE AMERICANS	
YEAR	Men	Women	Men	Women
1980	96%	95%	41%	43%
2008	93%	92%	43%	42%

SOURCE: Qian, Zhenchao, and Lichter, Daniel. "Changing Patterns of Interracial Marriage in a Mulitracial Society." *Journal of Marriage and Family*, 75:1065–1084. Copyright © 2011 National Council on Family Relations. Reprinted with permission.

COMPARING MINORITY GROUPS

Comparing the experiences of Native Americans with those of other groups will further our understanding of the complexities of dominant–minority relationships and permit us to test the explanatory power of the concepts and theories that are central to this text. No two minority groups have had the same experiences, and our concepts and theories should help us understand the differences and the similarities. We will make it a point to compare groups in each of the chapters in this part of the text. We begin by comparing Native Americans with African Americans.

First, note the differences in the stereotypes attached to the two groups during the early years of European colonization. While Indians were seen as cruel savages, African Americans under slavery were seen as lazy, irresponsible, and in constant need of supervision. The two stereotypes are consistent with the outcomes of the contact period. The supposed irresponsibility of blacks under slavery helped justify their subordinate, highly controlled status, and the alleged savagery of Native Americans helped justify their near extermination by white society.

Second, both Native Americans and African Americans were colonized minority groups, but their contact situations were governed by very different dynamics (competition for labor vs. land) and a very different dominant group agenda (the capture and control of a large, powerless workforce vs. the elimination of a military threat). These differing contact situations shaped subsequent relationships with the dominant group and the place of the groups in the larger society.

For example, consider the situations of the two groups a century ago. At that time, the most visible enemy for African Americans was de jure segregation, the elaborate system of repression in the South that controlled them politically, economically, and socially (see Chapters 5 and 6). In particular, the southern system of agriculture needed the black population—but only as a powerless, cheap workforce. The goals of African Americans centered on assimilation, equality, and dismantling this oppressive system.

Native Americans, in contrast, were not viewed as a source of labor and, after their military defeat, were far too few in number and too dispersed geographically to constitute a political threat. Thus, there was little need to control them in the same way African Americans were controlled. The primary enemies of the tribes were the reservation system, various agencies of the federal government (especially the BIA), rural isolation, and the continuing attacks on their traditional cultures and lifestyles, which are typical for a colonized minority group. Native Americans had a different set of problems, different resources at their disposal, and different goals in mind. They always have been more oriented toward a pluralistic relationship with the larger society and preserving what they could of their autonomy, their institutions, and their heritage. African Americans spent much of the 20th century struggling for inclusion and equality; Native Americans were fighting to maintain or recover their traditional cultures and social structures. This difference in goals reflects the different histories of the two groups and the different circumstances surrounding their colonization.

PROGRESS AND CHALLENGES

What does the future hold for Native Americans? Their situation has certainly changed over the past 100 years, but is it "better" or just "different," as is the case for large segments of the African American community? As the group grows in size and improves its status, the answer seems to be a little of both. To reach some conclusions, we will look at several aspects of the situation of Native Americans and assess the usefulness of our theoretical models and concepts.

Since the 1960s, the decline of intolerance in society, the growth of pride in ancestry in many groups (e.g., Black Power), and the shift in federal government policy to encourage self-determination have all helped spark a reaffirmation of commitment to tribal cultures and traditions. Like the Black Power Movement, the Red Power Movement asserted a distinct and positive Indian identity, a claim for the validity of Native American cultures within the broad framework of the larger society. During the same period, the favorable settlements of treaty claims, the growth in job opportunities, and the growth of the gambling industry have enhanced the flow of resources and benefits to some reservations. In popular culture, Native Americans have enjoyed a strong upsurge of popularity and sympathetic depictions. This enhanced popularity accounts for much of the growth in population size as people of mixed ancestry resurrect and reconstruct their Indian ancestors and their own ethnic identities.

Linear or simplistic views of assimilation do not fit the current situation or the past experiences of Native Americans very well. Some Native Americans are intermarrying with whites and integrating into the larger society; others strive to retain a tribal culture in the midst of an urbanized, industrialized society; still others labor to use the profits from gaming and other enterprises for the benefit of the tribe as a whole. Members of the group can be found at every degree of acculturation and integration, and the group seems to be moving toward assimilation in some ways and away from it in others.

From the standpoint of the Noel and Blauner hypotheses, we can see that Native Americans have struggled with conquest and colonization, experiences made more difficult by the loss of so much of their land and other resources and by the concerted, unrelenting attacks on their culture and language. The legacy of conquest and colonization was poor health and housing, an inadequate and misdirected education system, and slow (or nonexistent) economic development. For most of the 20th century, Native Americans were left to survive as best they could on the margins of the larger society, too powerless to establish meaningful pluralism and too colonized to pursue equality.

Today, one key to further progress for some members of this group is economic development on reservation lands and the further strengthening of the tribes as functioning social units. Some tribes do have assets—natural resources, treaty rights, and the gambling industry—that could fuel development. However, they often do not have the expertise or the capital to finance the exploitation of these resources. They must rely, in whole or in part, on non-Indian expertise and white-owned companies and businesses. Thus, non-Indians, rather than the tribes, may be the primary beneficiaries of some forms of development (this would, of course, be quite consistent with American history). For those reservations for which gambling is not an option and for those without natural resources, investments in human capital (primarily education) may offer the most compelling direction for future development.

Urban Indians confront the same patterns of discrimination and racism that confront other minority groups of color. Members of the group with lower levels of education and job skills face the prospects of becoming part of a permanent urban underclass. More educated and more skilled Native Americans share with African Americans the prospect of a middle-class lifestyle that is more partial and tenuous than that of comparable segments of the dominant group.

The situation of Native Americans today is vastly superior to the status of the group a century ago, and this chapter has documented the notable improvements that have occurred since 1990. Given the depressed and desperate conditions of the reservations in the early 20th century, however, it would not take much to show an improvement. Native Americans are growing rapidly in numbers and are increasingly diversified by residence, education, and degree of assimilation. Some tribes have made dramatic progress over the past several decades, but enormous problems remain, both on and off the reservations. The challenge for the future, as it was in the past, is to find a course between pluralism and assimilation, pan-tribalism and traditional lifestyles that will balance the issues of quality of life against the importance of retaining an Indian identity.

SUMMARY

This summary is organized around the Learning Objectives listed at the beginning of this chapter.

 7.1 Explain the changing population characteristics and common cultural characteristics of Native Americans and Alaska Natives.

Although they remain a tiny numerical minority of the population (about 1%), Native American and Alaska Native populations are growing rapidly and, according to the 2010 Census, more than five million people now claim at least partial Native American or Alaska Native ancestry. The increase reflects, in part, the social nature of race and the changing definitions used in the census. Traditional Indian cultures were numerous and variable. As is typical for societies at the hunting-and-gathering level of development, they commonly stressed strong group ties, cooperation with others, and egalitarian relations.

 7.2 Summarize and explain the changing relationships between Native Americans and the federal government, especially the changes in laws and policies and their effects, and the dynamics of Indian resistance and protest.

After the end of armed hostilities, relations between Native Americans and the larger society were paternalistic and featured coercive acculturation. At the beginning of the 20th century, Native Americans faced the paternalistic reservation system, poverty and powerlessness, rural isolation and marginalization, and the Bureau of Indian Affairs. Native Americans continued to lose land and other resources. Some landmark legislation and federal policies included the Indian Reorganization Act (1934), termination, relocation, and, beginning in the 1970s, increasing self-determination. There have been organized protest movements since early in the 20th century, including a Red Power Movement. Native American protests achieved some successes and were partly assimilationist, even though they pursued some pluralistic goals and greater autonomy for the tribes.

7.3 Understand the most critical issues and trends that have influenced relations between Native Americans and the larger society in recent decades, including

a. struggles over natural resources,
b. attempts to bring jobs to reservations,
c. broken treaties,
d. gaming, and
e. prejudice and discrimination.

As a group, Native Americans and Alaska Natives have experienced some improvements in quality of life, especially since the 1970s, but the progress has been uneven and enormous challenges remain.

a. Some tribes and reservations have access to valuable natural resources, including oil, coal, clean water, and timber, which have sometimes been used to improve their situation.
b. Some tribes (e.g., the Choctaw Nation of Mississippi) have been able to attract industry, but many reservations are too remote and inaccessible to be viable sites for development and good jobs.
c. The legacy of broken treaties may provide the basis for successful lawsuits and give some tribes resources and opportunities.
d. The gaming industry has benefited some tribes and has the potential to benefit others.
e. Prejudice and discrimination remain potent forces limiting the opportunities for Native Americans and Alaska Natives. There is some indication that anti-Indian prejudice has shifted to more "modern" forms. Institutional discrimination and access to education and employment remain major problems confronting Native Americans.

 7.4 Analyze the contemporary relations between Native Americans and whites using the concepts of prejudice, discrimination, assimilation, and pluralism, especially in terms of

a. acculturation,
b. secondary structural assimilation, and
c. primary structural assimilation.

a. Native Americans have been able to retain more of their culture than have African Americans, and the tribal languages are still spoken on some reservations. However, the forces of pan-tribalism and especially the attractions of education and jobs in the larger society seem to be working against the survival of traditional cultures.
b. Despite recent improvements, the overall secondary structural assimilation of Native Americans remains low. Inequalities persist in schooling, jobs, income, unemployment, and poverty levels.
c. In terms of primary structural assimilation, intermarriages are high compared with other groups, largely as a function of the small size of the group.

7.5 Assess the overall situation of Native Americans today based on the concepts and information presented in this chapter.

The situation of Native Americans today is shaped by their origin as a colonized minority group, their history of competition with the dominant group for control of land, and their recent history on the reservations. Today, the group faces an array of problems similar to those faced by all American colonized minority groups of color, as they try to find ways to raise their quality of life and continue their commitment to their tribes and to an Indian identity.

With the recent increase in self-determination and the development of resources on some reservations, the situation of some members of the group and some tribes is improved, but many others are far from equality. What evidence of improvements is presented in this chapter? What evidence of continuing inequality is presented? How does this group compare with African Americans? What important similarities and differences can you identify?

KEY TERMS

Bureau of Indian Affairs 234

Dawes Allotment Act of 1887 234

Indian Reorganization Act 237

termination 237

two-spirit 231

REVIEW QUESTIONS

1. What were the most important cultural differences between Native American tribes and the dominant society? How did these affect relations between the two groups?

2. Compare and contrast the effects of paternalism and coercive acculturation on Native Americans after the end of the contact period with the effects on African Americans under slavery. What similarities and differences existed in the two situations? Which system was more oppressive and controlling? How? How did these different situations shape the futures of the groups?

3. How did federal Indian policy change over the course of the 20th century? What effects did these changes have on the tribes? Which were more beneficial? Why? What was the role of the Indian protest movement in shaping these policies?

4. What options do Native Americans have for improving their position in the larger society and developing their reservations? Which strategies seem to have the most promise? Which seem less effective? Why?

5. Compare and contrast the contact situations of Native Americans, African Americans, and Australian Aborigines. What are the most crucial differences in their situations? What implications did these differences have for the development of each group's situation after the initial contact?

6. Characterize the present situation of Native Americans in terms of acculturation and integration. How do they compare with African Americans? What factors in the experiences of the two groups might help explain contemporary differences?

7. What gender differences can you identify in the experiences of Native Americans? How do these compare with the gender differences in the experiences of African Americans?

8. Given the information and ideas presented in this chapter, speculate about the future of Native Americans. How likely are Native American cultures and languages to survive? What are the prospects for achieving equality?

9. Given their small size and marginal status, recognition of their situations and problems continues to be a central struggle for Native Americans. What are some ways the group can build a more realistic, informed, and empathetic relationship with the larger society, the federal government, and other authorities? Are there lessons in the experiences of other groups or in the various protest strategies followed in the Red Power Movement?

STUDENT STUDY SITE

Sharpen your skills with SAGE edge at edge.sagepub.com/healey8e

SAGE edge for students provides a personalized approach to help you accomplish your coursework goals in an easy-to-use learning environment.

The following resources are available at SAGE edge:

Current Debates: Are Indian Sports Team Mascots Offensive?

What messages are conveyed by team names such as the Indians, Braves, and, especially, Redskins? Are these mascots offensive? Do they perpetuate stereotypes and negative views of Native Americans? Or are they harmless tributes to virtues such as bravery and honor?

On our website you will find an overview of the topic, the clashing points of view, and some questions to consider as you analyze the material.

Public Sociology Assignments

Public Sociology Assignments provide opportunities for students to address directly and personally some of the issues raised in this text.

There are two assignments for Part III on our website. The first looks at patterns of self-segregation in school cafeterias, and, in the second, students analyze the portrayal of the American family on television in terms of race, ethnicity, sexual orientation, and other sociologically relevant characteristics.

Contributed by Linda M. Waldron

Internet Research Project

For this Internet Research Project, you will use data gathered by the U.S. Census Bureau to assess the situation of all Native Americans and a tribe of your choosing. You will add this information to the data you gathered previously on African Americans and the general population. You will also search the Internet for additional information on the specific tribe you selected. The project will be guided by a series of questions related to course concepts, and your instructor may ask you to discuss your findings in small groups.

For Further Reading

Please see our website for an annotated list of important works related to this chapter.

CHAPTER-OPENING TIMELINE PHOTO CREDITS

1838: Picture History/Newscom

1851: Library of Congress Prints and Photographs Division

1876: Library of Congress Prints and Photographs Division

1886: Library of Congress Prints and Photographs Division

1887: Wikimedia Commons

1890: Library of Congress Prints and Photographs Division

1978: Library of Congress Prints and Photographs Division

2005: Wikipedia

2012: Library of Congress Prints and Photographs Division

HISPANIC AMERICANS

Colonization, Immigration, and Ethnic Enclaves

Everett Collection/Newscom

LOC

LOC

timeline

1942
The Bracero Program begins, allowing Mexican citizens to work temporarily in the U.S. as a source of low-cost labor. The program ends in 1964.

1953–1958
Operation Wetback results in the deportation of more than 3.8 million undocumented Mexicans.

1965
César Chávez and Dolores Huerta found the United Farm Workers Association.

1910   1920   1930   1940   1950   1960   1970

1917
The Jones Act extends U.S. citizenship to Puerto Ricans.

1929
During the Great Depression, between 300,000 and 500,000 Mexicans and Mexican Americans are deported to Mexico.

1943
Los Angeles erupts in the Zoot Suit Riots. American sailors cruise Mexican American neighborhoods in search of "zoot-suiters," dragging people out of movie theaters and cafes, tearing their clothes off, and viciously beating them.

1966
The Cuban Refugee Act permits more than 400,000 people to enter the U.S.

1910
The Mexican Revolution begins; hundreds of thousands of Mexicans flee to the U.S.

Graham Avenue in [Brooklyn] was the broadest street I'd ever seen. . . . Most of these stores were . . . run by Jewish people [and] there were special restaurants called delis where Jewish people ate. . . . We didn't go into the delis because, Mami said, they didn't like Puerto Ricans in there. Instead, she took me to eat pizza.

"It's Italian," she said.

"Do Italians like Puerto Ricans?" I asked as I bit into hot cheese and tomato sauce that burned the tip of my tongue.

"They're more like us than Jewish people are," she said, which wasn't an answer.

In Puerto Rico the only foreigners I'd been aware of were Americanos. In two days in Brooklyn I had already encountered Jewish people, and now Italians. There was another group of people Mami had pointed out to me. Morenos [African Americans]. But they weren't foreigners, because they were American. They were black, but they didn't look like Puerto Rican negros. They dressed like Americanos but walked with a jaunty

LEARNING OBJECTIVES

By the end of this chapter, you will be able to do the following:

8.1 Understand the population characteristics of all Hispanic American groups.

8.2 Explain the history of Mexican Americans, including their cultural characteristics, their immigration patterns, their development in the United States, changing U.S. policy and laws affecting them, and their key organizations and leaders in social movement activism.

8.3 Explain the history of Puerto Ricans, including their immigration patterns.

8.4 Explain the history of Cuban Americans, including their immigration patterns and the dynamics and importance of the Cuban American ethnic enclave.

8.5 Analyze how different types of prejudice and discrimination affect Hispanic Americans.

8.6 Compare and contrast the differing situations for Hispanic Americans using the concepts of assimilation and pluralism, especially in terms of

a. acculturation,

b. secondary structural assimilation, and

c. primary structural assimilation.

8.7 Apply the concepts and information in this chapter to the overall situation of Hispanic Americans today, and assess their influence on U.S. society, including our understanding of race and ethnicity and what it means to be an American.

1974
The Equal Educational Opportunities Act allows for bilingual education.

1994
California's Proposition 187 is approved by voters, preventing undocumented immigrants from obtaining public services. Proposition 187 is ruled unconstitutional in 1996.

2004
Hispanic Americans become the largest minority group.

2017
Massive demonstrations occur around the U.S. in support of immigrant rights.

1975   1980   1985   1990   1995   2000   2005   2010

1980
Approximately 125,000 Cubans immigrate to the U.S. during the Mariel boatlift.

1986
The Immigration Reform and Control Act creates a process for undocumented immigrants to gain legal status and grants citizenship to about three million people.

2001
U.S. Senate considers the Development, Relief, and Education for Alien Minors Act, which would provide a legal path to citizenship for many undocumented immigrant minors who either attend college or serve in the military. The DREAM Act is later defeated.

2009
Sonia Sotomayor is sworn in as first Latina Justice of the U.S. Supreme Court.

2010
Arizona SB 1070 requires police to question people if there's reason to suspect they are in the U.S. illegally. Certain provisions of the law are later struck down by the Supreme Court.

hop that made them look as if they were dancing down the street, only their hips were not as loose as Puerto Rican men's were. According to Mami, they too lived in their own neighborhoods, frequented their own restaurants, and didn't like Puerto Ricans.

"How come?" I wondered, since in Puerto Rico, all of the people I'd ever met were either black or had a black relative somewhere in their family. I would have thought morenos would like us, since so many of us looked like them.

"They think we're taking their jobs."

"Are we?"

"There's enough work in the United States for everybody," Mami said.

—Esmeralda Santiago (1993)

Esmeralda Santiago moved from Puerto Rico to Brooklyn the summer before she began eighth grade. It was the 1950s, well before the surge of newcomers to the United States and New York City that began after the change in immigration policy in 1965. Still, she was overwhelmed with the variety of groups and cultures, cuisines, and languages she had to navigate. Like many Puerto Ricans who move to the mainland, she also had to deal with different ideas about the meaning of race and the importance of skin color.

Puerto Ricans have been U.S. citizens since 1917, but they often live in a different cultural world. Just as Santiago was changed by contact with U.S. culture, Puerto Rican and other Hispanic cultures were also influenced. Now, as we shall see in this chapter, a variety of fast-growing Hispanic American groups are changing and being changed by Anglo culture. •

Hispanic Americans are more than 17% of the total population, which makes them the nation's largest minority group. (African Americans are about 13% of the population.) Historically, they have been concentrated in the West and South (particularly in California, Texas, and Florida), reflecting the Mexican and Spanish histories of those areas. In recent decades, the Hispanic American population has grown rapidly and expanded into every region and state (Ennis, Rios-Vargas, & Albert, 2011, p. 6; Gutiérrez, n.d.). People in some areas are, for the first time, hearing Spanish in their communities and finding (and enjoying) what used to be thought of as "exotic" foods—tortillas, salsa, refried beans, and more—in their grocery stores and restaurants. Yet, not every community welcomes these changes. As Hispanic Americans join more communities, America is being remade, just as it has been by African Americans, white ethnic groups, and Native Americans. How will the increasing Hispanic American population change U.S. society in the future?

Of course, not all Hispanic American groups are newcomers. Some lived in North America before the Declaration of Independence was signed, before slavery began, and before European colonists founded Jamestown. As part of their colonization of the Americas, the Spanish landed in "La Florida" in 1513 (Hennesey, 1981), eventually forming a colony in St. Augustine in 1565. They went north (going as far as present-day Maine) and west—establishing communities in present-day Texas, New Mexico, Arizona, and California. Many Spanish-named cities reflect that history—San Antonio (St. Anthony), El Paso (The Pass), Las Cruces (The Crosses), San Diego (St. Diego), Los Angeles (The Angels), Sacramento (Sacrament), to name a few. Prior to Spanish colonization, indigenous Mexicans and Indians lived throughout these areas.

Hispanic American groups share a language and some cultural traits but they are diverse and distinct from one another in many ways. These groups connect themselves to a variety of cultural traditions; like U.S. society, they are dynamic and evolving. Because of this, Hispanic American groups do not think of themselves as a single social entity. Rather, many Hispanic Americans identify with their national origin group (e.g., Mexican American, Cuban, Columbian).

In this chapter, we look at the development of Hispanic American groups over the past century, examine their contemporary relations with the larger society, and assess their current status. We focus on the three largest Hispanic groups: Mexican Americans, Puerto Ricans, and Cuban Americans. (In Chapter 10, we will cover other, smaller Hispanic groups, such as Dominicans and Columbians, in more detail.)

Table 8.1 displays some information on the size and growth of Hispanic Americans and the 10 largest Latino groups as of 2015. Mexican Americans, the largest group, are almost 11% of the total U.S. population (and almost two thirds of all Hispanic Americans), but the other groups are small. Figure 8.1 shows the relative sizes of the 10 largest Latino groups in the United States.

The number of Mexican Americans increased by 2.6 times between 1990 and 2015, and the Hispanic American population in general has grown 2.4 times, almost twice as fast as the total population (1.3 times). Researchers expect this growth to continue well into the century. As a result, Hispanic Americans will become an increasingly important part of life in the United States. Today, 17.1 out of every 100

TABLE 8.1 Size and Growth of All Hispanic Americans and 10 Largest Groups by Origin, 1990–2015

COUNTRY OF ORIGIN	1990	2000	2015	GROWTH (NUMBER OF TIMES LARGER, 1990–2015)	PERCENTAGE OF TOTAL POPULATION, 2015
Total Hispanic American	22,355,990	35,305,818	54,232,205	2.4	17.1%
Mexico	13,496,000	20,640,711	34,640,287	2.6	10.9%
Puerto Rico*	2,728,000	3,406,178	5,174,554	1.9	1.6%
Cuba	1,044,000	1,241,685	2,014,010	1.9	<1%
El Salvador	565,081	655,165	1,719,678	3.0	<1%
Dominican Republic	520,521	764,945	2,022,687	3.9	<1%
Guatemala	268,779	372,487	1,296,634	4.8	<1%
Colombia	378,726	470,684	1,060,519	2.8	<1%
Honduras	131,066	217,569	785,332	6.0	<1%
Ecuador	191,198	260,559	377,183	2.0	<1%
Nicaragua	202,658	177,684	407,288	2.0	<1%
Percentage of U.S. Population	9.0%	12.5%	16.6%	17.1%	—
Total U.S. Population	248,710,000	281,421,906	316,515,021	1.3	—

SOURCES: For 1990, U.S. Census Bureau (1990); for 2000, Ennis et al. (2011, p. 3); for 2012, U.S. Census Bureau (2013a).

NOTE: *Living on mainland only.

FIGURE 8.1 Countries of Origin for Hispanic Population in the United States, 2015

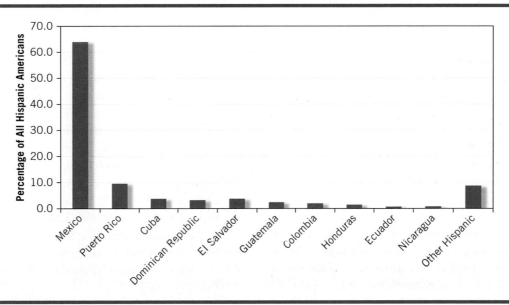

SOURCE: U.S. Census Bureau, 2017, American Community Survey, 2015, 5-Year Estimates.
NOTE: "Other Hispanic" include Costa Ricans, Venezualans, Argentinians, Bolivians, and many others.

Americans are Hispanic. Researchers project this ratio to rise to more than 29 out of every 100 by 2060 (see Figure 1.1). Latino groups are growing rapidly, partly because of their relatively high birthrates, but mainly because of immigration (Cohn, 2010). However, contrary to the assumptions of many, most Latinos are not immigrants: about two thirds are born in the United States (Stepler & Brown, 2016). Still the high rates of recent immigration mean that many members of these groups—in some cases, the vast majority—are foreign-born, as displayed in Figure 8.2.

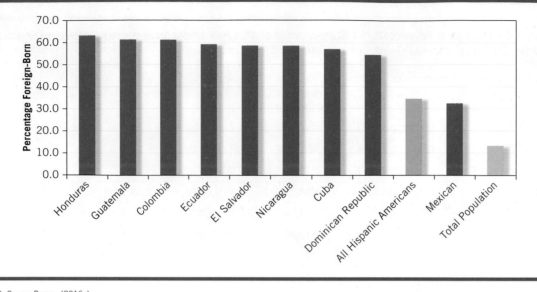

SOURCE: U.S. Census Bureau (2016a).

We discuss Hispanic Americans at this point in the book because they include both colonized and immigrant groups, and in that sense, they combine elements of the extremes of Blauner's typology of minority groups. We would expect the historically more colonized Hispanic groups to have more in common with African Americans and Native Americans today. Likewise, we expect Hispanic groups whose experiences lie closer to the "immigrant" end of the continuum to have different characteristics and follow different pathways of adaptation. We test these ideas by reviewing the groups' histories and by analyzing their current status and degree of acculturation and integration.

Before moving on, it's important to address a few more issues relevant to our discussion of Hispanic Americans:

- In Chapter 1, you learned about the U.S. Census and how its racial and ethnic categories have changed over time to reflect the immigration of different groups to this country and the ways people have thought about race at a particular time. In 1930, the Census Bureau added "Mexican" as a racial category. However, Latino civil rights groups successfully campaigned to change this classification because it implies that Hispanic groups are races and, specifically, that Mexicans cannot be white (Zócalo Public Square, 2009). The first census to ask about "Hispanic origin" occurred in 1980 (see Chapter 1). In recent censuses, most Latinos did not identify with a particular racial category and many chose "other" which the Census Bureau had to reclassify in order to analyze the data (Zócalo Public Square, 2009). In the last census (2010), people who claimed Spanish/Hispanic origin could choose: (1) Mexican, Mexican-American, Chicano;

(2) Puerto Rican; (3) Cuban; or they could write in an answer for (4) another Spanish/Hispanic group such as Argentinean, Colombian, or Dominican. This write-in category is important because, as seen in the 2014 National Survey of Latinos, just 25% of Hispanic Americans considered themselves Hispanic or Latino (Pew Research Center, 2015b). A 2011 survey found that most (51%) identified themselves by their family's country of origin while nearly one quarter (21%) most frequently thought of themselves simply as "American" (Taylor, Lopez, Martinez, & Velasco, 2012, p. 9). Further, research shows that people's identity varies by the primary language, generation, and education of the respondent. For example, almost two thirds of Spanish speakers and first-generation (foreign-born) Latinos prefer to identify themselves in terms of their countries of origin, whereas the "American" designation is most popular with the college educated, the third and higher generations, and English speakers (Taylor et al., 2012, pp. 12–13). To address these issues, the Census Bureau asks Hispanic Americans about their ethnicity; that is, their country of origin *and* about their race (e.g., white, black, Asian, native American or some combination) (Krogstad & Cohn, 2015). (See Figure 8.3.)

- The Census Bureau has been testing possible changes to its questions for the next census of 2020. In 2015, it conducted a trial run, asking people in 1.2 million U.S. households questions that combined Hispanic ethnicity with race. Additionally, people could pick as many categories as they liked. As a result, more than 70% of self-identified Hispanics identified as such. However, they tended not to choose a race in the

FIGURE 8.3 Questions on Hispanic Origin and Race from the 2010 Census

→ **NOTE: Please answer BOTH Question 8 about Hispanic origin and Question 9 about race. For this census, Hispanic origins are not races.**

8. **Is Person 1 of Hispanic, Latino, or Spanish origin?**

☐ **No,** not of Hispanic, Latino, or Spanish origin

☐ Yes, Mexican, Mexican Am., Chicano

☐ Yes, Puerto Rican

☐ Yes, Cuban

☐ Yes, another Hispanic, Latino, or Spanish origin — *Print origin, for example, Argentinean, Colombian, Dominican, Nicaraguan, Salvadoran, Spaniard, and so on.* ⇁

[grid of empty boxes]

9. **What is Person 1's race?** *Mark* ☒ *one or more boxes.*

☐ White

☐ Black, African Am., or Negro

☐ American Indian or Alaska Native — *Print name of enrolled or principal tribe.* ⇁

[grid of empty boxes]

☐ Asian Indian   ☐ Japanese   ☐ Native Hawaiian

☐ Chinese   ☐ Korean   ☐ Guamanian or Chamorro

☐ Filipino   ☐ Vietnamese   ☐ Samoan

☐ *Other Asian — Print race, for example, Hmong, Laotian, Thai, Pakistani, Cambodian, and so on.* ⇁   ☐ *Other Pacific Islander — Print race, for example, Fijian, Tongan, and so on.* ⇁

[grid of empty boxes]

☐ Some other race — *Print race.* ⇁

[grid of empty boxes]

→ **If more people were counted in Question 1, continue with Person 2.**

SOURCE: U.S. Census Bureau.

combined question. Yet this is a great improvement over the 8.4% of people in the prior census who self-identified as Hispanic but did not answer the race question about race (Cohn, 2017). These efforts highlight the complexities of people's identities and some of the challenges in studying race and identity. (Other countries face similar challenges. For example,

consider the Brazilian classifications discussed in the Chapter 6 Comparative Focus.)

• These changing group labels reflect the social construction of race and ethnicity. We recognize that no one term encompasses everyone. Therefore, we use the terms *Latino, LatinX,* and *Hispanic* interchangeably. No matter the label, Hispanic

Americans are often the victims of prejudice and racial discrimination in the United States. Perceived racial differences often (but not always) overlap with cultural distinctions and reinforce the separation of Hispanic Americans from Anglo-American society (Zócalo Public Square, 2009). As you'll learn later in the chapter, even members of the group who are completely acculturated may still experience discrimination based on their physical appearance, names, or other ethnic identifiers.

- Group names are important because they reflect power dynamics. In the last chapter, we discussed the labels of "Native Americans," "Indigenous Americans," and "American Indians." Similar debates exist about using the terms *Hispanic* and *Latino*. *Hispanic* emphasizes Spanish (European) heritage and language, but does not acknowledge the cultural roots of groups from Latin America (which are also connected to African and Native American civilizations). *Latino*, which is short for *Latino Americano*, stresses the common geographic origins of Latin American groups, and doesn't, therefore, include the Spanish people from Europe. Colonizing nations created both labels and neither Latino nor Hispanic applies to everyone. Further, some people mistakenly apply both labels to immigrant groups with French, Portuguese, or English traditions (e.g., Haitians, Brazilians, and Jamaicans, respectively).

- Like other Romance languages, Spanish is gendered. That means words can be "feminine" (e.g., *mesa* or table) or "masculine" (e.g., *bolso* or handbag). Spanish is also masculine dominant meaning that the masculine form is said to be gender neutral. For example, the label "Latino" refers to both women and men, but the term "Latina" only refers to women. Some people argue this convention is sexist (Kelly, 2012). Additionally, the labels Latino and Latina exclude gender-fluid and gender nonconforming people who don't identify as either girls/women or boys/men—or who identify as both, simultaneously. (We'll cover this more in Chapter 11 on gender.) In 2004, to help rectify this issue and to be more inclusive, people within the U.S. queer community began using *LatinX* (pronounced "Lah-teen-ex"). (The *X* is a nod to languages spoken by several indigenous peoples of Latin America.) In the 1990s, a similar attempt was made to use *Latin@* and, more recently, with *Latine*. Though not used widely, *LatinX* and *Latin@* reflect an intersectional approach to group identity that's becoming more mainstream (Cardenas, 2017; Demby, 2013; Reichard, 2017).

For example, *LatinX* is now in the *Oxford English Dictionary* and the University of Wisconsin, Madison, has a Department of Chican@ and Latin@ Studies. However, these words have also come under criticism for being "invented" words that don't reflect correct, formal Spanish (Reyes, 2016).

- Hispanic Americans are partly an ethnic minority group (i.e., identified by cultural characteristics such as language, foodways, and religious beliefs) and partly a racial minority group (i.e., related to their genetic makeup and loosely identified by physical appearance). Beginning in 2005, researchers with the Genographic Project began collecting DNA data from people around the world. Today, they have samples from more than a million people. Like other Americans, Hispanic Americans bring a variety of genetic and racial backgrounds to U.S. society that reflect the mingling between groups. Table 8.2 shows the key genomic backgrounds for Mexican Americans and Puerto Ricans. As you'll see, Mexican Americans primarily show indigenous American (67%) and European (17%) ancestries. Puerto Ricans, in contrast, show mostly European (54%) and African (29%) ancestries—with only 17% indigenous ancestry (National Geographic Society, 2017). The original inhabitants of Puerto Rico are the Taíno people who descend from the Arawak of South America and the Kalinago (formerly known as the Caribe) of the Caribbean. They lived on the island for 4,000 years before the Spanish arrived in 1492. Spanish colonization killed many of them though violence, disease, and loss of land (Taíno Museum, 2017). The African component, seen in the DNA data in Table 8.2, reflects enslaved Africans being brought to the island which had "a significant influence on the local genetic patterns on the island." There has been considerable intermarriage between groups (National Geographic Society, 2017).

TABLE 8.2 Key Genomic Backgrounds for Two Hispanic American Groups

Mexican Americans	Puerto Ricans
Native American 67%	Southern Europe 48%
Southern Europe 12%	Western & Central Africa 26%
Western & Central Europe 5%	Native American (Taino people) 17%
Jewish Diaspora 4%	Western & Central Europe 6%
Northern Africa 4%	Northern Africa 3%
Western & Central Africa 4%	
Asia Minor 2%	

SOURCE: National Geographic Society, 2017. "Reference Populations - Geno 2.0 Next Generation."

MEXICAN AMERICANS

In Chapter 4, we applied the Noel and Blauner hypotheses to Mexican Americans. Mexicans were conquered and colonized in the 19th century and used as a cheap labor force in agriculture, ranching, mining, railroad construction, and other areas of the dominant group economy in the Southwest. In the competition for control of land and labor, they became a minority group, and the contact situation left them with few power resources to pursue their self-interests.

By the dawn of the 20th century, the situation of Mexican Americans resembled that of American Indians in some ways. Both groups were small, numbering about 0.5% of the total population (Cortes, 1980, p. 702). Both differed from the dominant group in culture and language, and both were impoverished, relatively powerless, and isolated in rural areas distant from the centers of industrialization and modernization.

In other ways, Mexican Americans resembled African Americans in the South: They both supplied much of the labor power for the agricultural economy and were limited to low-paying occupations and subordinate status in the social structure. Europeans colonized all three groups, and, at least in the early decades of the 20th century, these groups lacked the resources to end their exploitation and protect their cultural heritages from continual attack by the dominant society (Mirandé, 1985, p. 32).

Perhaps the most important contrast is between Mexican Americans and African Americans. Because of the proximity of Mexico and the ease of travel across the border, it was much easier for Mexican Americans to maintain a distinct cultural heritage.

Mexicans and Mexican Americans planted, weeded, and harvested sugar-beets—once one of most labor-intensive crops in the United States.

CULTURAL PATTERNS

Mexican Americans are a large, diverse group and their cultural patterns can vary by length of residence in the United States, region, social class, urban versus rural residence, and along many other dimensions. Nonetheless, we can identify some differences between Mexican American and Anglo cultures.

Traditionally, Mexican Americans were overwhelmingly Catholic, in contrast with the larger society. Although the group is becoming more diverse religiously, most Mexican Americans (61%) remain Catholic while most non-Hispanics are Protestant (47%) or unaffiliated with any faith (23%) (Lopez, 2015). Although the Catholic Church remains one of the most important institutions in Mexican American communities, it appears to be losing some of its influence. For example, one report finds that, in just a three-year span (between 2010 and 2013) the percentage of Mexican Americans affiliated with the Catholic Church fell from 71% to 61% while the percentage of Evangelical Protestants rose from 10% to 13% and the percentage of those unaffiliated with any church rose from 11% to 20% (Pew Research Center, 2014).

Mexican Americans are not only growing more religiously diverse, they are also becoming more similar to other Americans. One study compared the values and opinions of Mexican Catholics with Mexican American Catholics and all U.S. Catholics. Mexican American Catholics as a group differed considerably in their views from Mexican Catholics. However, Mexican American Catholics born in the United States were quite similar to all U.S. Catholics. For example, while only 31% of Mexican Catholics agreed that the church should allow priests to marry, 65% of U.S.-born Mexican American Catholics agreed. The latter percentage is similar to the level of agreement among all U.S. Catholics of 72% (Donoso, 2014).

Another area of difference in values revolves around the notion of the "culture of poverty" that we discussed in Chapter 6. In the past, some researchers described everyday life among Mexican Americans in terms of this constellation of values. This description was based on anthropological research in several different Hispanic communities including Cuba, Puerto Rico, Mexico, and New York that was principally conducted by Oscar Lewis (see Lewis, 1959, 1965, 1966). Lewis claimed that a specific culture (i.e., beliefs, values, norms) existed among the poor that made it hard for them or their children to escape poverty. Lewis said the "culture of poverty" influenced people's families and mindsets, for example, by having children with different husbands, by not working full time, or by spending money instead of saving it. Though Lewis said "the culture of poverty is both an adaptation and a reaction of the poor classes to their marginal position in a class-stratified, highly individualistic, capitalistic society" (Lewis, 1965, p. xliv), many people overlook this connection to the broader economic system and interpret his research to be about the culture of specific groups, including Mexicans.

Most social scientists today find this stereotypical characterization as exaggerated or simply inaccurate. They point to studies showing little difference between the value systems of Mexican Americans and other Americans with similar length of residence in the United States, social class, and educational background (e.g., see Buriel, 1993; Moore & Pinderhughes, 1993; Pew Hispanic Center, 2005, p. 20; Valentine & Mosley, 2000). One recent survey found that Hispanic Americans were *more* supportive of "hard work" as a recipe for getting ahead—perhaps the central value in the American Creed—than was the U.S. population in general. About 75% of Hispanic Americans—versus only 58% of the general population—agreed that most people can "get ahead with hard work" (Taylor et al., 2012, pp. 18–19).

Another area of cultural difference involves **machismo**, a value system that stresses men's dominance, honor, virility, and violence. Stereotypical views of machismo emphasize its negative aspects and often fail to recognize positive ones such as being a good provider and a respected father (Arciniega, Anderson, Tovar-Blank, & Tracey, 2008; Falicov,

2010; Gutmann, 2006) Yet, similar attitudes exist in many cultures, including Anglo-American cultures, in varying ways (Moore & Pachon, 1985).

Some of these cultural differences have served as the basis for excluding Mexican Americans from the larger society. However, the differences have also provided a basis for group cohesion and unity that has sustained common action and protest activity among Mexican Americans. As you'll see in the next section, part of the divide between groups has to do with feelings about immigration.

IMMIGRATION

Although Mexican Americans originated as a colonized minority group, their situation since the early 1900s (and especially since the 1960s) has been largely shaped by immigration. The numbers of legal Mexican immigrants to the United States are shown in Figure 8.4. The fluctuations in the rate of immigration can be explained by conditions in Mexico; the varying demand for labor in the low-paying, unskilled sector of the U.S. economy; broad changes in North America and the world; and changing federal immigration policy. As you will see, competition, one of the key variables in Noel's hypothesis, has shaped the relationships between Mexican immigrants and the larger American society.

Push and Pull. Like the massive wave of immigrants from Europe that arrived between the 1820s and 1920s (see Chapter 2), Mexicans have been pushed from their homeland and toward the United States by a variety of sweeping

---

Machismo is a cultural value system that stresses men's dominance and honor.

FIGURE 8.4 Legal Immigration from Mexico, 1905–2015

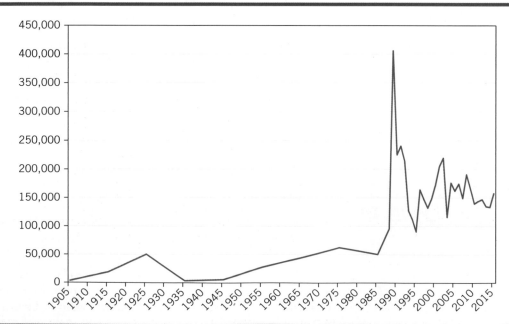

SOURCE: United States Department of Homeland Security. 2016 Yearbook of Immigration Statistics: 2015, https://www.dhs.gov/immigration-statistics/yearbook/2015.

NOTES: 1. The very high number of "immigrants" in the late 1980s and early 1990s was the result of people already in the United States legalizing their status under the provisions of the Immigration Reform and Control Act (IRCA).

2. Values are averages per year during each decade until 1989.

NARRATIVE PORTRAIT

The Meaning of Macho?

In Chapter 1 you learned about the social construction of race and ethnicity, the social construction of gender, and about the benefits of using an intersectional approach to studying social life. Recall that intersectionality involves looking at how different systems of inequality and privilege intersect and create different experiences for different types of people. For example, in Chapter 5 we looked at how systems of race and gender in the antebellum South affected enslaved women in specific ways. To understand those experiences, we can't just think about race because while their experiences are gendered, they are gendered differently from white women. (Consider Sojourner Truth's "Ain't I a Woman?" speech.) Further, we can't understand the experiences of enslaved women by only thinking about gender. Rather, we need to see how those systems interact.

This Narrative Portrait offers you a chance to practice using an intersectional lens. Specifically, you'll hear from several gay Latino undergraduates about what "machismo" means to them and how they construct and understand their identity. Peña-Talamantes (2013) argues that "the heavy emphasis on heterosexuality accompanying the concept of machismo becomes particularly detrimental to Latino men who may identify as, or be perceived as, homosexual" (p. 167). Further, he notes that the men in his study define machismo in relation to being "el maricon" or sissy. The label, "el maricon," represents "passivity, subordination, and devalued aspects of femininity" (p. 170).

Peña-Talamantes asks his participants about the most difficult thing surrounding being a gay Latino, the qualities of "machismo," and what it's like to be "el maricon." In keeping with research ethics, all names are pseudonyms.

Eduardo: "It's mainly the machismo, you know. Men have to be all powerful, they have to be able to defend themselves and exert a sort of power over everybody else, even other men who seem weaker, and they do it all the time, you know. You have to be ambitious, and very aggressive and walk with your chest out, riding those big trucks and motorcycles, basically running over anyone who tries to question your authority, but that's just the way it is . . ." [if you are "el maricon"] "other people just wouldn't want to have anything to do with you, cause it's kinda like you become sorta pathetic since you're this flimsy weakling that's like girly and unable to fend for themselves [sic]."

Adrian: "You know . . . the machos, I mean the machistamen, are the ones who are socially venerated and stuff, but the jotos or maricones, you know the sissies, are socially shunned, pobresitos [poor things] . . . it's true, there are machos and then there is the maricones which are so effeminate and weak that they are not even considered men anymore, it's what we are taught as little kids. Like my mother used to say *no te vayas a hacer de los otros* [you better not become one of the others], once you are a maricón you are socially shunned forever."

Hector: ". . . it's hard when you're gay and Latino you know. You are torn. The gay side calls for freedom and being not as masculine sometimes, you know, like you're radiating rainbow colors once in a while (laughs), but then, as a Latino, you can't do that, you're supposed to be more centered, more masculine, hiding every tear, every, like, emotion, you know. So as a gay Latino, I can't just be really macho or really flamey [flamboyant], I have to find my place somewhere in the middle but still be accepted."

Peña-Talamantes asks: Would you say you are more macho or maricón?

Mario: "Well, I'm not super macho but I'm definitely not a maricón, I mean, yeah sometimes people say it to tease you, but it's really hard to just say, 'are you this or that?', you know? I mean, there are so many possibilities and it's weird 'cause you just end up feeling like you're floating in masculine limbo."

Hector: ". . . There is a big divide between the real manly mans and the really gay guys. But for us, it's like playing with both extremes and trying to create a ribbon, like glue it together, kind of like this *Twilight* book . . . you know, the red ribbon is torn, but not really, it's still holding on with a couple of threads, and if you think about it, it can work backwards, we may work to sew the two parts back together."

Questions to Consider

1. In Chapter 1, you learned that most people have mixed statuses in society; some of those positions are likely to be more privileged than others. How does this Narrative Portrait illustrate that? What are the privileged statuses and how do you know?
2. How does this Narrative Portrait illustrate cultural differences between Anglos and Mexican Americans? How does it illustrate similarities?
3. In what ways might being a lesbian Latina be similar to or different from being a gay Latino man? In other words, do you think gender matters? If so, why? If not, why not?

changes both domestic and global. Industrialization, urbanization, and rapid population growth influenced European immigration. Similar broad social forces, including continuing industrialization and globalization, encourage Mexican immigration.

At the heart of the immigration lies a simple fact: The almost 2,000-mile-long border between Mexico and the United States is the longest continuous point of contact between a less developed nation and a more developed nation in the world. For the past century, the United States has developed faster than Mexico, moving from an industrial to a postindustrial society and sustaining a substantially higher standard of living. The continuing wage gap between the two nations has made even menial work in the North attractive to millions of Mexicans (and other Central and South Americans). Mexico has a large number of people who need work, and the United States offers jobs that pay more—often much more—than the wages available south of the border. To lend some numerical perspective to the size of the immigration, over 34 million people of Mexican descent live in the United States and, although many have had family in what is now the United States for centuries, about 30% of them are first generation (see Table 8.1 and Figure 8.2). Just as the air flows from high to low pressure, people move from areas of lower to higher economic opportunities. The flow is not continuous, however, and has been affected by conditions in both the sending and receiving nations.

Conditions in Mexico, Fluctuating Demand for Labor, and Federal Immigration Policy. Generally, for the past 100 years, Mexico has served as a reserve pool of cheap labor for the benefit of U.S. businesses, agricultural interests, and other groups, and the volume of immigration largely reflects changing economic conditions in the United States (Lanthemann, 2014). Immigration increases with good times in the United States and decreases when times are bad, a pattern reinforced by the policies and actions of the federal government. The most important events in the complex history of Mexican immigration to the United States are presented in Table 8.3, along with some comments regarding the nature of each event and its effects.

Prior to the early 1900s, the volume of immigration was generally low and largely unregulated. It wasn't until 1904 when President Teddy Roosevelt created the United States Immigration Service with just 75 men to patrol of the 2,300-mile southwest border (Johnson, 2014). People crossed the border—in both directions—as the need arose, informally and without restriction. The volume of immigration and concern over controlling the border began to rise with the increase of political and economic turmoil in Mexico in the early decades of the 20th century, but still remained a comparative trickle.

Immigration increased in the 1920s when federal legislation curtailed the flow of cheap labor from Europe. In 1924, the Border Patrol was established to prevent illegal immigration (though, at that time, the staff focused on Canada, not Mexico, fearing that illegal liquor was being smuggled in during prohibition [Johnson, 2014]). When hard times came to the United States (and the world) during the Great Depression, in the early 1930s, many Mexicans in the United States returned home, sometimes voluntarily, often by force. As competition for jobs increased, efforts

Mexican American migrant workers in California, 1935.

began to expel Mexican laborers, just as the Noel hypothesis would predict.

The federal government instituted a **repatriation** campaign aimed specifically at deporting illegal Mexican immigrants. In many localities, repatriation was pursued with great zeal, and the campaign intimidated many legal immigrants and U.S.-born Mexican Americans into moving to Mexico. The result was that the Mexican American population of the United States declined by an estimated 40% during the 1930s (Cortes, 1980, p. 711).

When the Depression ended and U.S. society began to mobilize for World War II, federal policy about immigrants from Mexico changed once more as employers again turned to Mexico for workers. In 1942, the Bracero Program was initiated to permit men as contract laborers, usually employed in agriculture and other areas requiring unskilled labor, to work in the United States for a limited time. When their contracts expired, the men were required to return to Mexico (Budech, 2014).

The Bracero Program continued for several decades after the war and was a crucial source of labor for the American economy. In 1960 alone, braceros supplied 26% of the nation's seasonal farm labor (Cortes, 1980, p. 703). The program generated millions of dollars of profit for

---

Repatriation was a government-sponsored campaign during the 1930s to deport undocumented immigrants back to Mexico.

TABLE 8.3 Significant Dates in Mexican Immigration

DATES	EVENT	RESULT	EFFECT ON IMMIGRATION FROM MEXICO
1910	Mexican Revolution	Political turmoil and unrest in Mexico	Increased
Early 20th century	Mexican industrialization	Many groups (especially rural peasants) displaced	Increased
1920s	Passage of National Origins Act of 1924	Decreased immigration from Europe	Increased
1930s	Great Depression	Decreased demand for labor and increased competition for jobs leading to repatriation campaign	Decreased; many return to Mexico
1940s	World War II	Increased demand for labor leading to Bracero Guest Worker Program	Increased
1950s	Concern over undocumented immigrants	Operation Wetback	Decreased; many return to Mexico
1965	Repeal of National Origins Act	With new immigration policy, high priority given to close family of citizens	Increased
1986	Immigration Reform and Control Act (IRCA)	Undocumented immigrants given opportunity to legalize their status	2.7 million undocumented immigrants gain legal status
1994	North American Free Trade Agreement (NAFTA)	Many groups in Mexico (especially rural peasants) displaced	Increased
2007	Recession in the United States	Widespread unemployment in the United States; shrinking job supply	Decreased

growers and other employers because they were paying braceros much less than they would have paid American workers (Amott & Matthaei, 1991, pp. 79–80).

While the Bracero Program permitted immigration from Mexico, other programs and agencies worked to deport undocumented (or illegal) immigrants, large numbers of whom entered the United States with the braceros. Government efforts reached a peak in the early 1950s with **Operation Wetback**, a program under which federal authorities deported almost four million Mexicans (Grebler, Moore, & Guzman, 1970, p. 521).

During Operation Wetback, raids on Mexican American homes and businesses were common, and authorities often ignored their civil and legal rights. In an untold number of cases, U.S. citizens of Mexican descent were deported along with undocumented immigrants. These violations of civil and legal rights have been a continuing grievance of Mexican Americans (and other Latinos) for decades (Mirandé, 1985, pp. 70–90).

In 1965, the overtly racist national immigration policy incorporated in the 1924 National Origins Act (see Chapter 2) was replaced by a new policy that gave a high

Los Angeles Times Photographic Archive/Wikimedia Commons

Some of the many Mexican agricultural laborers admitted into the United States under the government's Bracero program that ran from 1942–1964.

Operation Wetback was a government-sponsored campaign during the 1950s to deport undocumented immigrants from Mexico.

priority to immigrants who were family and kin of U.S. citizens. That is, there was no numerical limit on the immigration of the immediate family (parents, spouses, and children) of U.S. citizens. Some numerical restrictions were placed on the number of immigrants from each sending country, but about 80% of these restricted visas were reserved for other close relatives of citizens. The remaining 20% of the visas went to people who had skills needed in the labor force (Bouvier & Gardner, 1986, pp. 13–15, 41; Rumbaut, 1991, p. 215).

Immigrants have always tended to move along chains of kinship and other social relationships, and the new policy reinforced those tendencies. The social networks connecting Latin America with the United States expanded, and the rate of immigration from Mexico increased sharply after 1965 (see Figure 8.3) as immigrants became citizens and sent for family members.

Most of the Mexican immigrants, legal as well as undocumented, who have arrived since 1965 continue the pattern of seeking work in the low-wage, unskilled sectors of the labor market in the cities and fields of the Southwest. For many, work is seasonal or temporary, and it follows agricultural patterns with migrants moving to the South in the fall and North in the spring. When the work ends, they often return to Mexico, commuting across the border as they have done for decades in a pattern of circular migration (Passel & Cohn, 2017).

In 1986, Congress attempted to deal with undocumented immigrants, most of whom were thought to be Mexican, by passing the Immigration Reform and Control Act. This legislation allowed undocumented immigrants who had been in the country continuously since 1982 to legalize their status. According to the U.S. Immigration and Naturalization Service (1993), about 3 million people—75% of them Mexican—took advantage of this provision, but the program did not slow the volume of undocumented immigration (p. 17). In 1988, at the end of the amnesty application period, almost 3 million undocumented immigrants lived in the United States. In 2015, 11 million undocumented immigrants were in the United States, down from a high of 12 million in 2007 (Passel & Cohn, 2017).

Recent Immigration From Mexico. Mexican immigration to the United States continues to reflect the difference in level of development and standard of living between the two societies. Mexico remains a more agricultural nation and continues to have a lower standard of living, as measured by average wages, housing quality, health care, or any number of other criteria. To illustrate, the gross national income per capita for Mexico in 2016 was $16,383—much higher than in 2002 but nowhere near the comparable figure for the United States at $56,180. About half of the

Mexican population (53.2%) lives in poverty (World Bank, 2013). Almost half (48%) of Mexican immigrants come to enjoy a better life in the United States (Gonzalez-Barrera, 2015). Opportunities for work are scarce, 60% of Mexicans express dissatisfaction with the state of their economy (Pew Research Center, 2014c), and many Mexicans are drawn to the United States, in the hopes of finding employment or better wages. Given that the average length of schooling in their homeland is only about 8.6 years, Mexican immigrants have much lower levels of job skills than U.S. citizens and compete for work in the lower levels of the U.S. job structure (United Nations Development Programme, 2016). Furthermore, 79% cite crime and illegal drugs (72%) as very big problems in their homeland (Pew Research Center, 2014). Since 2006, 80,000 people have been killed in Mexico due to organized crime–related incidents (CNN, 2017a).

The globalization of the Mexican economy reinforced the impetus to immigrate. In the past, the Mexican government insulated its economy from foreign competition with a variety of tariffs and barriers. These protections have been abandoned over the past several decades, and Mexico, like many less developed nations, has opened its doors to the world economy. The result has been a flood into Mexico of foreign agricultural products (cheap corn, in particular, see Johnson, 2011), manufactured goods, and capital, which, while helpful in some parts of the economy, has disrupted social life and forced many Mexicans, especially the poor and rural dwellers, out of their traditional way of life.

The most significant changes to Mexican society have probably come from the 1994 North American Free Trade Agreement, or NAFTA. As discussed in Chapter 1, this policy united the three nations of North America into a single trading zone. U.S. companies began to move their manufacturing operations to Mexico, attracted by lower wages, less-stringent environmental regulations, and weak labor unions. They built factories (called *maquiladoras*) along the border and brought many new jobs to the Mexican economy. However, other jobs—no longer protected from global competition—were lost, more than offsetting these gains. Analysts estimate that 2 to 2.5 million jobs were lost, driving families—especially rural ones—out of the economy because they cannot compete with U.S. and Canadian agribusinesses (Faux, 2004; Johnson, 2011). Many of the men in those communities left to find work in the United States, leaving nearly empty villages or ones populated by women and children (Johnson, 2011). Mexican wages actually declined after the implementation of NAFTA, increasing the already large number of Mexicans living in poverty.

Thus, globalization in general and NAFTA in particular have reinforced the long-term relationship between the two nations. Mexico, like other nations of the less developed "South," continues to produce a supply of unskilled, less educated workers, while the United States, like other nations of the more developed and industrialized "North," provides a seemingly insatiable demand for cheap labor. Compared with what is available at home, the wages in *el Norte* are quite attractive, even when the jobs are at the margins of the mainstream economy or in the irregular, underground economy (e.g., day laborers paid off the books, illegal sweatshops in the garment industry, and sex work), and even when the journey requires Mexican immigrants to break American laws, pay large sums of money to "coyotes" to guide them across the border, and live in constant fear of raids by *la Migra* (the Border Patrol or other immigration authorities).

The movement of people from Mexico that began in the 1960s and accelerated in the 1990s was the largest immigration from a single nation to the United States in history (Passel, Cohn, & Gonzalez-Barrera, 2012, p. 6). Some 12 million people, about 51% unauthorized, crossed the border in this period.

More recently, the historic trend has reversed. As Figure 8.5 shows, immigration from Mexico has declined dramatically since 2005. The decline is due to multiple factors, including enhanced border enforcement efforts, the growing dangers of crossing illegally, and Mexico's declining birthrate (Passel, Cohn, & Gonzalez-Barrera, 2013, p. 6). Perhaps most central to the declining numbers is the U.S. economic recession and the weak job market (Gonzalez-Barrera, 2015). The pull that attracted immigrants in the past has weakened considerably, particularly after the collapse of the housing market in 2007. This relationship suggests that immigration may resume as the U.S. economy recovers.

The Continuing Debate Over Immigration Policy. Immigration has once again become a hotly debated issue in the United States. How many immigrants should be admitted? From which nations? With what skills? Should the relatives of U.S. citizens continue to receive a high priority? What about those facing the ravages of war or

A maquiladora in Mexico.

FIGURE 8.5 Number of Legal and Unauthorized Immigrants Arriving Each Year From Mexico, 1991–2010

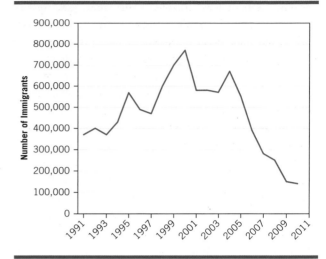

SOURCE: "Annual Immigration from Mexico to the U.S., 1991–2010," Fig. 2.5, p. 17 in Passel, Jeffrey, Cohn, D'Vera, and Gonzalez-Barrera, Ana. 2013. "Net Migration from Mexico Falls to Zero—and Perhaps Less." Pew Hispanic Center.

violence? The issue that seems to generate the most passion: What should be done about unauthorized immigrants? These questions—even those phrased in general, abstract terms—are mainly about the large volume of immigration along the U.S. southern border.

Many of immigration issues divide the nation. Public opinion polls over the past decade show that about 40% to 50% of all Americans would like to lower the volume of immigration but an almost equal percentage (30–40%) favor keeping present level (Morales, 2010; Newport, 2016b). In August 2016, a Gallup Poll yielded similar results: 38% of Americans want to decrease immigration and 38% would like to keep it at its current level. Interestingly, 21% wanted to increase immigration. Also, as shown in Figure 8.6, there

FIGURE 8.6 Attitudes of U.S. Adults Toward Immigration, 2001–2016

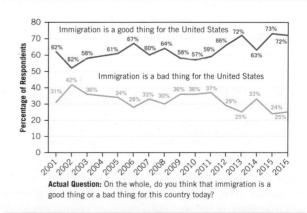

Actual Question: On the whole, do you think that immigration is a good thing or a bad thing for this country today?

SOURCE: Newport, Frank. 2016. "In US, Support for Decreasing Immigration Holds Steady," Gallup Polls, http://www.gallup.com/poll/194819/support-decreasing-immigration-holds-steady.aspx.

has been persistent support for immigration. Since 2001, the majority of Americans have endorsed the opinion that immigration is a "good thing" and this position has generally increased in popularity since 2010.

Since the 9/11 terrorist attack in 2001, the federal government has increased its attempt to reduce the flow of immigrants by extending the wall along the border with Mexico and beefing up the Border Patrol (BP), with increased personnel and more high-tech surveillance technology (see Table 8.4). In 2003, the Border Patrol became a part of Homeland Security and between 2003 and 2016, the number of Border Patrol agents more than doubled from 9,821 to 19,828 (down from a high of 21,444 in 2011) (United States Customs and Border Patrol, 2016). In 2006, the Secure Fence Act set aside money to build 700 miles of double-layered border fencing (though not all of it was completed) and in the years that followed, the government provided the BP with an "unprecedented level in resources," according to former Secretary of Homeland Security Jeh Johnson. By 2014, under President Obama, Border Patrol had a $3.5 billion budget and 23,000 support personnel in addition to border patrol agents (Johnson, 2014). Under President Trump, who campaigned on stricter border control and a promise to "build a wall," BP resources are expected to increase. In May 2017 Congress approved $1.5 billion maintenance on 650 miles of existing border fence (Ogrysko, 2017). The proposed 2018 budget requests funding for 500 more Border Patrol agents, 600 new support personnel (Ogrysko, 2017) new fencing along 74 miles of the southern border, and $4.4 billion for detention related programs, but primarily to increase the number of detention center beds (Washington Office on Latin America [WOLA], July 17, 2017). Additionally, it will provide for 1,000 more Immigration and Customs (ICE) agents, of the 10,000 requested, to enforce federal laws governing border control. Previously ICE agents focused on "serious criminals," but under the new administration, anyone suspected of being undocumented, including bystanders, which ICE calls "collateral" arrests, will be apprehended and deported (Kulish, Dickerson, & Nixon, 2017). Between January 22 and April 29, 2017, ICE arrested 41,318 people, up from 30,028 during that approximate time in 2016—roughly 400 more people per day (Dickerson, 2017).

Communities across the nation—not just in the southern border states—are feeling the impact of immigration and wondering how to respond. Some citizens support measures to close the borders through bigger, thicker walls, surveillance, and even the use of deadly force while others ponder ways to allow newcomers into the U.S. without negatively affecting local schools, medical facilities, or housing markets. Some people raise fiscal and humanitarian concerns, calling current efforts expensive, ineffective, and deadly (WOLA, 2017), noting the 6,023 migrants who have

TABLE 8.4 Growth in Border Patrol Resources, Fiscal Years 2000–2014

	2000*	2014*
Border Patrol agents dedicated to the southwest border	8,619	18,127
Fence (miles)	77	700
"Strategically placed" all-weather roads (miles)	17	145.7
"Strategically placed" lighting (miles)	29	70
Underground sensors	"few"	11,863
Aircraft	56	107
Arial surveillance vehicles (unstaffed)	0	8
Boats	2	84
Mobile surveillance systems	1	40
Mobile video surveillance systems	"Little if any"	178
Remote video surveillance systems	140	273
Night vision goggles	n/a	9,255
Thermal imaging capabilities	little or no	Over 600

SOURCE: Remarks by Secretary of Homeland Security Jeh Johnson: "Border Security in the 21st Century" - As Delivered https://www.dhs.gov/news/2014/10/09/remarks-secretary-homeland-security-jeh-johnson-border-security-21st-century, October 9, 2014.

*FISCAL YEAR

died between 2000 and 2016 trying to cross the border into Arizona, California, New Mexico, and Texas (Fernandes, 2017). Those estimates are probably low because finding bodies in such a vast landscape is difficult (International Organization for Migration, 2014).

The U.S. Southern border is, increasingly, crossed more frequently by non-Mexicans, especially Guatemalans, Hondurans, and Salvadorans who must cross multiple country borders (Bolter, 2017; Meyer & Isacson, n.d.). While attempts to cross have "decreased significantly" in the last 15 years, the head of Homeland Security recently noted that "border security alone cannot overcome the powerful push factors of poverty and violence that exist in Central America. Walls alone cannot prevent undocumented migration" (Johnson, 2016). In particular, people face violence not just from war, but from organized crime, gangs, or domestic violence, and human trafficking (UN, 2014). A recent concern is the large number of children traveling alone including 68,541 in 2014 and 59,692 in 2016 (Johnson, 2016). (See Figure 8.7.) Those numbers have declined in recent years because the U.S. pushed Mexico to crack down on non-Mexican Latinos crossing into Mexico (Meyer & Isacson, n.d.).

In addition to border control efforts, a variety of immigration reforms have been proposed and continue to be debated. One key issue is the treatment of undocumented immigrants: Should undocumented immigrants be immediately deported, or should some provision be made for them to legalize their status, as was done in the Immigration Reform and Control Act of 1986? If the latter, should the opportunity to attain legal status be extended to all or only to immigrants who meet certain criteria (e.g., those with steady jobs and clean criminal records)? Many feel that amnesty is unjust because immigrants who entered illegally have broken the law and should be punished. Others point to the economic contributions of these immigrants and the damage to the economy that would result from summary, mass expulsions. Still others worry about the negative impact undocumented immigrants may have on the job prospects for the less skilled members of the larger population, including the urban underclass that is disproportionately populated by minority group members. (We address some of these issues later in this chapter and in Chapters 9 and 10.)

Immigration, Colonization, and Intergroup Competition. We next focus on three points about Mexican immigration to the United States. First, the flow of population from Mexico was and is stimulated and sustained by powerful political and economic interests in the United States. Systems of recruitment and networks of communication and transportation have been established to routinize the flow of people and to provide a predictable labor source that benefits U.S. employers such as those in agriculture. This movement of people back and forth across the border was well established long before current efforts to regulate it. Depending on U.S. policy, this immigration is sometimes legal and encouraged and sometimes illegal and discouraged. Regardless of the label, it has been steadily flowing for decades in response to opportunities for work in the North (Gonzales-Barrera & Lopez, 2013; Portes, 1990, pp. 160–163).

FIGURE 8.7 Border Patrol Apprehensions of Unaccompanied Minors

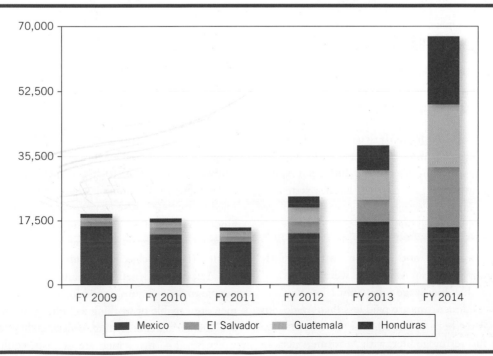

SOURCE: Meyer, Maureen and Adam Isacson. No date. "Border Security, Migration, and Humanitarian Concerns in South Texas." https://www.wola.org/files/1502_stx/index.html.

Second, Mexican immigrants enter a social system in which the group's colonized status has already been established. The paternalistic traditions and racist systems that were formed in the 19th century shaped the positions that were open to Mexican immigrants in the 20th century. Mexican Americans continued to be treated as a colonized group despite the streams of new arrivals, and the history of the group in the 20th century closely parallels those of African Americans and American Indians. Thus, Mexican Americans might be thought of as a colonized minority group that happens to have a large number of immigrants or, alternatively, as an immigrant group that incorporates a strong tradition of colonization.

Third, this brief review of the twisting history of U.S. policy on Mexican immigration should remind us that prejudice, racism, and discrimination increases as competition and the sense of threat between groups increases. The qualities that make Mexican labor attractive to employers have caused bitter resentment among segments of the Anglo population that feel that "their" jobs and financial security are threatened. Often caught in the middle, Mexican immigrants and Mexican Americans have not had the resources to avoid exploitation by employers or rejection and discrimination by others. The ebb and flow of the efforts to regulate immigration (and sometimes even deport U.S. citizens of Mexican descent) can be understood in terms of competition, differentials in power, and prejudice.

QUESTIONS FOR REFLECTION

1. How do Mexican American and Anglo cultures vary? How have these differences shaped relations between the groups?

2. Why has the volume of immigration from Mexico to the United States fluctuated?

DEVELOPMENTS IN THE UNITED STATES

As the flow of immigration from Mexico fluctuated with the need for labor, Mexican Americans struggled to improve their status. In the early decades of the 20th century, like other colonized minority groups, they faced a system of repression and control in which they were accorded few rights and had little political power.

Continuing Colonization and Gender Patterns. Early in the 20th century, Mexican Americans were largely limited to less desirable, low-wage jobs. Split labor markets, in which Mexican Americans are paid less than Anglos for the same jobs, have been common. The workforce often has been split further by gender, with Mexican American women filling the worst jobs and receiving the lowest wages (Takaki, 1993, pp. 318–319).

Men's jobs often took them away from their families to work in the mines and fields. In 1930, 45% of all Mexican American men worked in agriculture and 28% in unskilled nonagricultural jobs (Cortes, 1980, p. 708). Economic necessity often forced women to enter the job market. In 1930, they were concentrated in farm work (21%), unskilled manufacturing jobs (25%), and domestic and other service work (37%) (Amott & Matthaei, 1991, pp. 76–77). They were typically paid less than both Mexican American men and Anglo women. In addition to their job responsibilities, Mexican American women had to maintain their households and raise their children, often facing these tasks without a partner (Baca Zinn & Eitzen, 1990, p. 84).

As the United States industrialized and urbanized during the century, employment patterns became more diversified. Mexican Americans found work in manufacturing, construction, transportation, and other sectors of the economy. Some Mexican Americans, especially those of the third generation or later, moved into middle- and upper-level occupations, and some began to move out of the Southwest. Today, Mexican Americans can be found at all levels of affluence and poverty; however, they are disproportionately concentrated in lower level occupations and face higher levels of poverty (especially the more recent immigrants). For example, in 2015, Mexican Americans were twice as likely to be employed in agriculture and construction as non-Hispanic whites and only half as likely to be in management positions. Mexican American households had a median income $17,000 less than non-Hispanic whites ($42,098 vs. $59,542) and Mexican American families were three times more likely to be in poverty (23.4% vs. 7.1%) (U.S. Bureau of the Census, 2016a).

Sociologists and economists have long documented such occupational segregation by gender and race and demographic patterns in which people are concentrated in different types of jobs. Decreases in occupational segregation have occurred in some fields, primarily those requiring college degrees; but for people with less than a high school diploma, little has changed (Blau, Brummund, & Liu, 2012). Many occupations show remarkable consistency in their gender composition over time such as carpentry, civil engineering, and computer programming where most jobs continue to be filled by men. Likewise, women overwhelmingly fill jobs as kindergarten teachers, nurses, and dental hygienists; overall, those jobs have become *more* gender segregated since 1972, not less (Hegewisch & Hartmann, 2014).

Yet, it's not genetics or "natural abilities" that compel people to do such jobs. Social forces are involved. After all, men are capable of working as "administrative professionals," answering calls, typing, ordering supplies, and so on. Likewise, if so many men are dentists, couldn't they also

NARRATIVE PORTRAIT

In the Country We Love: My Family Divided

Diane Guerrero (actor on Orange Is the New Black *and* Jane the Virgin*) was born in the United States to Colombian parents. Below, she describes the frequent fears that many children of undocumented parents have about being found out. Before school on the day she describes below, she'd snapped at her mother who was trying to get her to eat breakfast. After school, she has drama practice and then goes to buy sneakers. She knows her parents will want to know when she'll be home, so she calls to let them know. This is what happened next.*

Ring. Ring. Ring. Ring. "You've reached Maria, Hector, and Diane," said my mother's voice on the machine. "We're not here right now. Please leave us a message." Beep. One of my parents was always home by this time. Always. And neither of them had mentioned having plans. Where could they be? With my hands trembling, I searched my pockets for a second quarter. Empty. I threw off my pack, unzipped the back compartment, and swept my fore-finger along the bottom edge. Bingo. I forced the coin into the slot and pressed hard on each digit. Ring. Ring. Ring. Ring. Again—no answer. All at once, I swung on my pack and jetted. I'd run these three blocks to our house dozens of times; I knew the route in my sleep. Let them be home, I prayed with every step. God, please— let them be there. The faster I sprinted, the slower I seemed to be moving. One block. One and a half. Two blocks . . . My right shoelace came undone. I didn't stop to retie it. When I made it onto our street, I saw my dad's Toyota station wagon in the driveway. Relief. They didn't hear the phone, I reassured myself. They've gotta be here. I rushed up to our porch and pulled out my set of keys, riffling through them until I got to the silver one. I slid it into the dead bolt, held my breath, and tried to brace myself for what I'd find beyond that door.

. . . For me, that moment came when I was fourteen . . . Deported. Long before I fully understood what that word meant, I'd learned to dread it. With every ring of my family's doorbell, with every police car passing on the street, a horrifying possibility hung in the air: My parents might one day be sent back to Colombia. That fear permeated every part of my childhood.

Day after day, year after year, my mom and dad tried desperately to become American citizens and keep our family together. They pleaded. They planned. They prayed. They turned to others for help. And in the end, none of their efforts were enough to keep them here in the country we love.

My story is heartbreakingly common. There are more than eleven million undocumented immigrants in America, and every day an average of seventeen children are placed in state care after their parents are detained and deported, according to US Immigration and Customs Enforcement (ICE). Those numbers don't take into account the scores of others who, like me, simply fell through the bureaucratic cracks. After my parents were snatched away, no government official checked up on me. No one seemed to care or even notice that I was on my own.

It's not easy for me to be so open about what happened in my family, especially after spending so many years hiding in the shadows. I've really struggled with putting my business out there. So why am I choosing to reveal so much now? Because on that afternoon when I came home to an empty house, I felt like the only child who'd ever dealt with something so overwhelming. And in the agonizing years that followed, it would've meant everything for me to know that someone, somewhere had survived what I was going through. For the thousands of nameless children who feel as forgotten as I did—this memoir is my gift to you. It's as much for your healing as it is for my own.

Just as one moment can bring despair, it can also lead to a powerful new beginning. A different life. A dream for moving onward and upward rather than backward. What you'll read in these pages is ultimately about that hope—the same desire that once led my family to this nation. That hope is the only thing that has sustained me through this frightening ordeal.

These days, we're surrounded by a lot of talk about immigration reform. Border security. A path to citizenship for the millions of undocumented workers who live among us. Behind every one of the headlines, there is a family. A mother and father. An innocent child. A real-life story that's both

deeply painful and rarely told. At last, I've found the courage to tell you mine.

Questions to Consider

1. What is the most interesting or useful idea you learned this Narrative Portrait? If you don't know any undocumented immigrants (you may not know if you do), what does this piece add to your understanding of immigration issues? If you know undocumented immigrants (or if you are undocumented), what similarities and differences do you see between their/your experiences and Guerrero's?

2. Like many children of undocumented immigrants, Guerrero was born in the U.S. So, the government cannot deport her. Under Deferred Action for Childhood Arrivals (DACA), 800,000 immigrants—illegally brought here as children—gained permission to stay and work in the United States. In September 2017 the government rescinded this policy. However, it allowed people whose permits were expiring before March 5, 2018, to renew them. Due to postal service delays, 900 applications did not reach Citizenship and Immigration Services by the October 5, 2017, deadline (Robbins, 2017). Once advised of this news, applicants have 30 days to reapply. What do you know about this policy? How should we deal with these children? At what point, if any, should the children of undocumented immigrants be deported and why? For example, if they've lived here less than a year? Five years? Ten? What do you know about the time, cost, and other criteria one must meet to apply for citizenship?

3. If you knew Diane Guerrero from watching *Orange Is the New Black* or *Jane the Virgin*, did it surprise you to learn that her parents are undocumented immigrants? Does this Narrative Portrait change the way you think about her as a person, positively or negatively?

become dental hygienists? (In 2014, 97.10% of all dental hygienists were women. See U.S. Department of Labor, 2014.) Interestingly, most of the highest paying jobs are predominantly filled by men and most of the lowest paying as primarily staffed by women (Hegewisch & Hartmann, 2014).

By 2015, 12 million immigrant women held jobs in the United States, making them just 7% of the labor force. Just over half (50.8%) came from Latin America and of those, 2.8 million (23.8%) came from Mexico (American Immigration Council, 2017). See Figure 8.8.

Immigrant women have increasingly worked outside the home, but historically their employment was limited to agriculture, domestic service, and the garment industry (Amott & Matthaei, 1991, pp. 76–79; Cortes, 1980, p. 708). Although women work in a variety of fields today such as transportation, office administration healthcare, and computing, they dominate "pink-collar" personal-service jobs that are "systematically underpaid," and that offer few (if any) benefits, low autonomy, and little opportunity for advancement (Stallard, Ehrenreich, & Sklar, 1983, p. 19). In 2015, nearly a third (32.5%) of immigrant women worked in these occupations with most (882,663) employed as housekeepers, health aides (501,740), cashiers (480,391), and building cleaners (364,494) (American Immigration Council, 2017). An intersectional lens can help us understand this phenomenon when we consider employment obstacles that women immigrants may face compared to white women or immigrant men.

As you read earlier, many Mexican immigrants have relatively low educational attainment compared with Anglo-Americans and only 66% of first-generation Mexican Americans (born in Mexico) are proficient in English (Gonzalez-Barrera & Lopez, 2013). These factors will strongly influence their job prospects. Additionally, women remain primarily responsible for child and elder care, and lack of support in those areas could negatively limit their employment options. Finally, lack of legal immigration status will strongly restrict the pool of potential employers (Hess, Henrici, & Williams, 2011; Hess & Henrici, 2013), and influences women's ability to get a driver's license which may be necessary to get to a job (especially in places with limited public transportation). Of course, they would need to be able to afford a car in the first place.

Women immigrants tend to work in jobs that are poorly compensated and many are underemployed. In 2013, about 20% of immigrant women looking for full-time work were unable to find it (Women's Labor Force Participation, n.d.). For those working full-time, year-round, median annual earnings were just $32,000. Mexican Americans who dominate low-wage work earned the least of all immigrant groups, averaging just $22,000 a year (Women's Labor Force Participation, n.d.). In 2015, 20.4% of immigrant women workers earned poverty-level wages of $11,770 per year. Another fifth (21%) earned more than $11,770 but less than 20,000. The majority of these women (62%) were Latin American, primarily from Mexico (American Immigration Council, 2017).

Like African Americans in the segregated South, laws and customs have excluded Mexican Americans from the institutions of the larger society for much of the 20th century. Though the census and law defined them as white, Anglo-American society—for the most part—didn't see them as white, and in many communities Mexican Americans were disenfranchised and given few legal or civil rights. Local governments created separate (and unequal) school systems for Mexican American children (later ruled unconstitutional in the 1947 court case of *Mendez v. Westminster*). There were "whites-only" primary elections

FIGURE 8.8 Foreign-Born Women Workers by Country of Origin, 2015

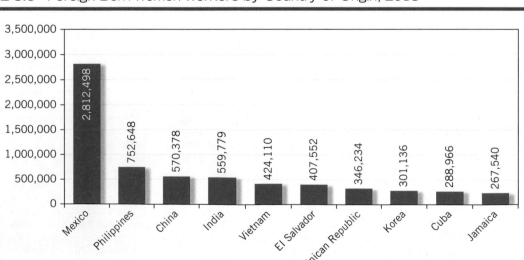

SOURCE: https://www.americanimmigrationcouncil.org/research/impact-immigrant-women-americas-labor-force.

Similar to Jim Crow, this sign reflects what is sometimes called "Juan Crow" — laws and customs intended to segregate Hispanics from whites.

modeled after the Jim Crow system—sometimes called Juan Crow—and residential segregation was (and remains) widespread (Echavarri & Bishop, 2016). The police and the court system generally abetted or ignored the rampant discrimination against the Mexican American community, and discrimination in the criminal justice system and civil rights violations have been continual grievances of Mexican Americans throughout the century.

Protest and Resistance. Like all minority groups, Mexican Americans have attempted to improve their collective position whenever possible. The beginnings of organized resistance and protest stretch back to the original contact period in the 19th century, when protest was usually organized on a local level. Regional and national organizations made their appearance in the 20th century (Cortes, 1980, p. 709).

Like those of African Americans, Mexican Americans' early protest organizations were integrationist and reflected the assimilationist values of the larger society. For example, one of the earlier and more significant groups was the League of United Latin American Citizens (LULAC), founded in Texas in 1929. LULAC promoted Americanization and greater educational opportunities for Mexican Americans and worked to expand civil and political rights for Mexican Americans. LULAC fought numerous court battles against discrimination and racial segregation (Moore, 1970, pp. 143–145).

The workplace has been a particularly conflictual arena for Mexican Americans. Split labor market situations increased anti–Mexican American prejudice; some labor unions tried to exclude Mexican immigrants to the United States, along with immigrants from Asia and Southern and Eastern Europe (Grebler et al., 1970, pp. 90–93).

At the same time, Mexican Americans played important leadership roles in the labor movement. Since early in the century, Mexican Americans have been involved in union organizing, particularly in agriculture and mining. When excluded by Anglo labor unions, they often formed their own unions to work for the improvement of working conditions. As the 20th century progressed, the number and variety of groups pursuing the Mexican American cause increased. During World War II, Mexican Americans served in the armed forces. As with other minority groups, this experience increased their impatience with the constraints on their freedoms and opportunities in the United States. That is, many went to fight in Europe where they were afforded broader rights and respect. After the war ended, they returned only to find the country they fought for didn't treat them equally under the law. This awareness led to new Mexican American organizations such as the Community Service Organization in Los Angeles and the American GI Forum in Texas. Compared with older organizations such as LULAC, the new groups were less concerned with assimilation per se, addressed a broad range of community problems, and attempted to increase Mexican American political power (Grebler et al., 1970, pp. 543–545).

Chicanismo. The 1960s were a time of intense activism and militancy for Mexican Americans. A protest movement—El

AMERICANOS TODOS ★ LUCHAMOS POR LA VICTORIA

★ AMERICANS ALL ★ LET'S FIGHT FOR VICTORY

During World War II, the U.S. Government created this poster calling for unity among Americans regardless of racial or ethnic identity.

Movimento—guided by an ideology called **Chicanismo** began at about the same time as the Black Power and Red Power Movements. Chicanismo encompassed a variety of organizations and ideas, united by a heightened militancy and impatience with the racism of the larger society and strongly stated demands for justice, fairness, and equal rights. The movement questioned the value of assimilation and sought to end the exploitation of Mexican Americans; it adapted many of the tactics and strategies (e.g., marches, rallies, voter registration drives) of the Civil Rights Movement of the 1960s.

Chicanismo is similar in some ways to the Black Power ideology (see Chapter 6) in that it emerged partly in reaction to the failure of U.S. society to fulfill the promises of integration and equality. Chicanismo rejected traditional stereotypes of Mexican Americans, proclaimed a powerful and positive group image and heritage, and analyzed the group's past and present situation in American society in terms of victimization, continuing exploitation, and institutional discrimination. Activists saw the inequalities that separated Mexican Americans from the larger society as the result of deep-rooted, continuing racism and the cumulative effects of decades of exclusion. According to Chicanismo, the solution to these problems lay in group empowerment, increased militancy, and group pride, not in assimilation to a culture that had rationalized and supported the exploitation of Mexican Americans (Acuña, 1988, pp. 307–358; Grebler et al., 1970, p. 544; Moore, 1970, pp. 149–154).

Some of the central thrusts of the 1960s protest movement are captured in the widespread adoption of the term **Chicanos**, which had been a derogatory term, as a group name for Mexican Americans. Other minority groups underwent similar name changes at about the same time. For example, African Americans shifted from *Negro* to *black* as a group designation. These name changes were not merely cosmetic—they marked fundamental shifts in group goals and desired relationships with the larger society. The new names came from the minority groups themselves, not from the dominant group, and they expressed the pluralistic themes of group pride, self-determination, militancy, and increased resistance to exploitation and discrimination.

Organizations and Leaders. The Chicano Movement saw the rise of many new groups and leaders: Reies López Tijerina, who formed the Alianza de Mercedes (Alliance of Land Grants) in 1963, was one of the most important. The goal of this group was to correct the unjust, illegal seizure of land from Mexicans during the 19th century. The Alianza was militant and confrontational, and the group seized and occupied federal lands to bring attention to their cause. Tijerina spent several years in jail as a result of his activities, and the movement eventually lost its strength and faded from view in the 1970s.

Another prominent Chicano leader was Rodolfo Gonzalez, who founded the Crusade for Justice in 1965. The crusade focused on abuses of Mexican American civil and legal rights and worked against discrimination by police and the criminal courts. In a 1969 presentation at a symposium on Chicano liberation, Gonzalez expressed some of the nationalistic themes of Chicanismo and the importance of creating a power base within the group (as opposed to assimilating or integrating):

> *Where [whites] have incorporated themselves to keep us from moving into their neighborhoods, we can also incorporate ourselves to keep them from controlling our neighborhoods. We . . . have to understand economic revolution. . . . We have to understand that liberation comes from self-determination, and to start to use the tools of nationalism to win over our barrio brothers. . . . We have to understand that we can take over the institutions within our community. We have to create the community of the Mexicano here in order to have any type of power. (Moquin & Van Doren, 1971, pp. 381–382)*

A third important leader was José Angel Gutiérrez, organizer of the party La Raza Unida (The People United). La Raza Unida offered alternative candidates and ideas to those of Democrats and Republicans. Its most notable success was in Crystal City, Texas, where, in 1973, it succeeded in electing its entire slate of candidates to local office (Acuña, 1988, pp. 332–451).

Without a doubt, the best-known Chicano leader of the 1960s and 1970s was the late César Chávez, who founded the National Farm Workers Association (NFWA). Long recognizing connections between workers, the NFWA joined the Filipino workers' union and became the United Farm Workers, UFW, the first union to successfully represent migrant workers (Rojas, 2011). Chávez was as much a labor leader as a leader of the Mexican American community, and the UFW sought to protect and advance the rights African American, Asian American, and Anglo-American workers. Migrant farm workers have few economic or political resources, and the migratory nature of their work isolates them in rural areas and makes them difficult to contact. In the 1960s (and still today), many were

---

Chicanismo was an ideology of the Mexican American protest movement that rose to prominence in the 1960s. It expressed militancy, impatience with injustice, and a number of pluralistic themes.

Chicanos is a group name for Mexican Americans that is associated with the ideology of Chicanismo.

César Chávez, cofounder of the United Farm Workers and leader of the grape boycott.

Like Dr. Martin Luther King Jr., Chávez was a disciple of Gandhi and a student of nonviolent direct protest (see Chapter 6). His best-known tactic was the boycott; in 1965, he organized a grape-pickers' strike and a national boycott of grapes. The boycott lasted five years and ended when the growers recognized the United Farm Workers as the legitimate representative of farm workers. Chávez and his organization achieved a major victory, and the agreement provided for significant improvements in the situation of the workers. (For a biography of Chávez, see Levy, 1975.)

Gender and the Chicano Protest Movement. Like African American women involved in the Civil Rights Movement, Chicano women encountered sexism and gender discrimination, even as they worked for the benefit of the group. Activist Sylvia Gonzales described their dilemmas:

> *Along with her male counterpart, she attended meetings, organized boycotts, did everything asked of her. . . . But, if she [tried to assume leadership roles] she was met with the same questioning of her femininity which the culture dictates when a woman is not self-sacrificing and seeks to fulfill her own needs. . . . . The Chicano movement seemed to demand self-actualization for only the male members of the group.* (as cited in Amott & Matthaei, 1991, p. 83)

undocumented immigrants who spoke little or no English and returned to the cities or to their countries of origin at the end of the season. As a group, farm workers were nearly invisible in the social landscape of the United States in the 1960s, and organizing this group was a demanding task. Chávez's success in this endeavor is one of the more remarkable studies in group protest.

Yet, when speaking about women's participation in the Chicano Civil Rights Movement, César Chávez voiced opposition to such sexism, saying, "The women have to be involved. They're the ones working out in the fields with their husbands, if you can take women into the fields with their husbands you can certainly take them to meetings," (c.f. Ortz, 2009, p. 260). Yet, within a culture steeped in machismo, not everyone believed as Chávez did.

Mural (by Yreina Cervántez) honors Dolores Huerta, cofounder of the National Farmworkers Association and lifetime activist.

Mexican American women were key to the success of the Chicano Movement, but they often had to fight to participate. Dolores Huerta and Jessie Lopez De La Cruz were central figures. As a child, Huerta's family (especially her grandfather) encouraged her to appreciate language and conversation and nicknamed her "*Siete Lenguas*" or Seven Tongues because of her affinity for talking (Beagle, 2016, p. 7). She later used that voice (and her intellect and fortitude) in negotiations with farm owners and politicians and also when bringing workers and community members together. For example, in her "Statement to the U.S. Senate Subcommittee on Migratory Labor" (1969), she skillfully spoke of the need to eliminate federal barriers that would allow farm workers to organize (Beagle, 2016). She is the originator of the phrase "*Sí se puede*" ("Yes, it can be done" or "Yes, you can") which other civil rights groups and politicians have used, most notably Barack Obama during his Senate and presidential campaigns. Although "it can be done," women in the movement faced unique struggles because of gender discrimination. Huerta possessed an intersectional view of the problem, saying, "It was very hard being a woman organizer. Many of our people my age and older were raised with the old customs in Mexico: Where the husband rules, he is king of his house. The wife obeys, and the children too. So when we first started it was a very, very hard. Men gave us the most trouble—neighbors there . . . were for the union, but they were not taking orders from women, they said" (Rose, 1990, p. 30).

Lopez De La Cruz's involvement in the Chicano Movement began when she and her husband opened their home for a UFW meeting. Like many women of her era, she was expected to be "in the kitchen." While the men talked about the issues in the other room, she listened in—until Chávez said it was important for her to join the group. Lopez De La Cruz, like other women activists, also experienced prejudice and gender discrimination. For example, she said that early in her activism, the founder of the Agricultural Workers Association "didn't want me to be involved. He said farm labor organizing was no place for a woman. So I kind of worked undercover, doing the work through my husband and my brother" (as cited in Budech, 2014, p. 16). She contributed a lot, including teaching English to migrant workers, serving on the California Rural Legal Assistance executive board to assist farm workers with legal matters, and she remained an activist until late in life. She may be known best for testifying against the use of *el cortito* (the short one), also known as *el brazo del diablo* (the devil's arm), a type of hoe with a short handle. Employers required lettuce and beet harvesters to use el cortito, claiming it was gentler on the crops. However, doing so meant that workers had to hunch over and twist all day, making it hard to stand at day's end. Using el cortito for weeks or months on end led to long term pain and disability, and it was particularly hard on children's bodies because they were still developing (Beagle, 2016, p. 120; Davis, 2008, p. 43). Lopez De La Cruz helped get it outlawed.

In addition to sexism within the UFW, Latina women faced it from outsiders, too. Huerta recalled her efforts to negotiate with growers regarding the Delano Grape Strike, saying "they weren't used to dealing with women . . . People like Jerry Cohen [also a negotiator] would say, 'You have to be polite.' And my thinking is, Why do we need to be polite to people who are making racist . . . [and] sexist comments? You have to call them on it" (as cited in Rosales, 1997, p. 143 c.f. Beagle, 2016, p. 117).

In addition to their employment obligations and activist work, women in the movement had to manage gendered expectations, especially about what many people viewed as "women's work." Many Latina activists had large families and they were expected to cook, clean, and tend to children's needs. To participate in the movement, some of these women thus brought their families with them: Maria Luisa Rangel relocated her family to Michigan to assist with the grape boycott. Juanita Valdez moved hers to Ohio to participate in the lettuce campaign. Herminia Rodriguez and her family went to Washington, D.C. for revived boycotts of lettuce, grapes, and Gallo wine (Rose, 1990, p. 29).

Women of the Chicano Civil Rights Movement possessed an intersectional view on civil rights. They saw connections between worker's rights, immigrant rights, and women's rights. Yet, some people (especially men) felt that this approach—along with Chicanas increasing prominence—undermined the movement (Beagle, 2016, p. 122). Further, some claimed that the "Chicana woman does not want to be liberated" (Beagle, 2016, p. 88). In response to this proclamation, more than 600 Chicana women met in 1971 to discuss key issues for women such as education, family/marriage, and sexuality. This meeting inspired further efforts toward gender equality and inspired the creation of the first Chicana journal (*Encuentro Femenil*) and a Chicana-focused newspaper (*Hijas de Cuauhtemoc*) to focus attention on women's issues and to pursue gender equality within Chicano culture and Chicano Civil Rights Movement (Beagle, 2016, pp. 121–122). They fought against "the triple burden of racial, gender, and economic discrimination" (Beagle, 2016, pp. 118). Despite the challenges they faced, Chicano women contributed widely to the movement, for example, by organizing poor communities and working for welfare reform. Today, they continue to work on issues including domestic violence, childcare, the criminal victimization of women, and other forms of racial and gender oppression that combine in specific ways to limit women of all minority groups (Amott & Matthaei, 1991, pp. 82–86; see also Mirandé & Enríquez, 1979, pp. 202–243).

MEXICAN AMERICANS AND OTHER MINORITY GROUPS

Like the Black Power and Red Power movements, Chicanismo began to fade from public view in the 1970s and 1980s. The movement could claim some successes, but perhaps the clearest victory was in raising the awareness of the larger society about the grievances and problems of Mexican Americans. Today, many Chicanos continue to face poverty, powerlessness, and exploitation as a cheap agricultural labor force. The less educated, urbanized segments of the group share the prospect of becoming a permanent urban underclass with other minority groups of color.

Over the course of the 20th century, the ability of Chicanos to pursue their self-interests has been limited by both internal and external forces. Like African Americans, the group has been systematically excluded from the institutions of U.S. society. Continuing immigration from Mexico has increased the size of the group, but these immigrants bring few resources with them that could be directly or immediately translated into economic or political power in the United States.

Unlike immigrants from Europe, who settled in the urban centers of the industrializing East Coast, Mexican Americans tended to work and live in rural areas distant from and marginal to urban centers of industrialization and opportunities for education, skill development, and upward mobility. They were a vitally important source of labor in agriculture and other segments of the economy but only to the extent that they were exploitable and powerless. As Chicanos moved to the cities, they tended to continue their historic role as a colonized, exploited labor force concentrated at the lower end of the stratification system. Thus, the handicaps discrimination created in the past were reinforced by continuing discrimination and exploitation in the present, perpetuating the cycles of poverty and powerlessness.

At the same time, however, the flow of immigration and the constant movement of people back and forth across the border kept Mexican culture and the Spanish language alive. Unlike African Americans under slavery, Chicanos were not cut off from their homeland and native culture and it was easier for Mexican American culture to survive. Clearly, the traditional model of assimilation—which was based largely on the experiences of European immigrant groups—does not effectively describe the experiences of Mexican Americans. They have experienced less social mobility than European immigrant groups but have maintained their traditional culture and language more completely. Like African Americans, the group is split along lines of social class. Although many Mexican Americans (particularly of the third generation and later) have acculturated and integrated, a large segment of the group continues to fill the same economic role as their ancestors did: an unskilled labor force for the development of the Southwest, augmented with new immigrants at the convenience of U.S. employers. For the less educated and for recent immigrants, cultural and racial differences combine to increase their social visibility, mark them for exploitation, and rationalize their continuing exclusion from the larger society.

QUESTIONS FOR REFLECTION

3. Are Mexican Americans a colonized or immigrant minority group? Both? Neither? Why?

4. Compare Chicanismo with Black and Red Power. How and why do these protest movements differ? Describe the key ideas, leaders, and organizations of Mexican American protest.

Mexican workers cultivating lettuce, 2013. Many migrant laborers are drawn to the United States by better wages than they can earn in their home countries. Lower labor expenses help keep food costs down for U.S. consumers.

Postage stamp commemorating *Mendez v. Westminster* (1947), which declared separate "Mexican schools" were illegal. It was the first ruling for school desegregation in the United States and laid the ground for *Brown v. Board of Education* (1954).

PUERTO RICANS

Puerto Rico ("Rich Port") became a territory of the United States in 1898 after the defeat of Spain in the Spanish–American War. While rich in natural resources, the island was small and relatively impoverished and powerless compared with the United States. It was difficult for Puerto Ricans to avoid U.S. domination as the following brief history shows.

In 1900, the Foraker Act made Puerto Rico the first unincorporated territory of the United States and replaced military rule on the island with a civil government (Santiago, 2001). It also replaced people's Spanish citizenship with a Puerto Rican one and sought to make English the official language, for example, by conducting all government matters such as court proceedings in English (Foraker Act, 1900; Leonard & Lugo-Lugo, 2015, p. 193). In 1906, President Roosevelt suggested that Puerto Ricans should become United States citizens, saying, "I cannot see how any harm can possibly result from it, and it seems to me a matter of right and justice to the people of Porto Rico. They are loyal, they are glad to be under our flag, they are making rapid progress along the path of orderly liberty. Surely we should show our appreciation of them, our pride in what they have done, and our pleasure in extending recognition for what has thus been done, by granting them full American citizenship" (Roosevelt, 1906).

While many embraced the new relationship with the United States—especially land owners and labor leaders—others did not. In 1914, the Puerto Rican House of Delegates unanimously voted for independence from the United States, but Congress rejected this idea (Gonzalez, 2011). A year later, Puerto Rico's governor, Arthur Yager, led a delegation to Washington and asked Congress to give the island greater autonomy. In 1917, Congress responded to these efforts for self-determination with the Jones-Shafroth Act, which awarded U.S. citizenship to all island-born residents. This meant that the United States could draft Puerto Rican men for military service in World War I, which some politicians thought would help "Americanize" them (Shaffer, 2013, p. 133). About 230,000 of them registered and 18,000 fought in battle. Additionally, the Jones-Shafroth Act created a bill of rights and a three-branch government (legislative, executive, and judicial) (Leonard & Lugo-Lugo, 2015).

This complex, often contested relationship has continued over the years. For example, in *Balzac v. Porto Rico* (1922) the U.S. Supreme Court affirmed Puerto Rico's status as a territory saying that the U.S. constitution did not apply in Puerto Rico (Chronology of Puerto Rico in the Spanish-American War, n.d.).

In 1947, Puerto Ricans were allowed to elect a governor. Today, Puerto Rico has a nonvoting member in the U.S. House of Representatives (called a Resident Commissioner) and while Puerto Ricans living on the mainland can vote in presidential elections, island inhabitants cannot (Krogstad, Starr, & Sandstrom, 2017; Murriel, 2016).

Therefore, while Puerto Ricans are not "foreigners," they do not have the rights of full American citizenship (Santiago, 2001). For decades, Puerto Ricans have debated their status as a U.S. territory and voted in several referendums about seeking statehood or becoming fully independent. In a June 2017 vote, just a few weeks after the government declared bankruptcy, 97% of Puerto Ricans voted to become the 51st state. The catch? While Puerto Rico typically has high voter participation (around 80%), only 23% of registered voters cast ballots in the referendum (Robles, 2017). How this issue develops will be interesting to watch and, no matter what happens, it is history in the making.

Thus, although Puerto Rico may move toward statehood, the initial contact between Puerto Ricans and U.S. society occurred in an atmosphere of war and conquest. By the time Puerto Ricans migrated to the mainland in large numbers, their relationship to U.S. society was largely that of a colonized minority group, and they generally retained that status on the mainland.

Professional football player Victor Cruz (left) and rapper/musician Frankie Cutlass (center) celebrate at the National Puerto Rican Day Parade.

Mr-Sam Elliot / Wikimedia Commons

MIGRATION (PUSH AND PULL) AND EMPLOYMENT

At the time of initial contact, the population of Puerto Rico was overwhelmingly rural and supported itself with subsistence farming and by exporting coffee and sugar. As the century wore on, U.S. firms began to invest in and develop the island economy, especially the sugarcane industry. These agricultural endeavors took more and more of the land. Opportunities for economic survival in the rural areas declined, and many people were forced to move into the cities (Portes, 1990, p. 163).

Movement to the mainland began gradually and increased slowly until the 1940s. In 1900, about 2,000 Puerto Ricans lived on the mainland. By World War II, this number had grown to only 70,000, a tiny fraction of the total population. Then, during the 1940s, the number of Puerto Ricans on the mainland increased more than fourfold, to 300,000. During the 1950s, it nearly tripled, to 887,000 (U.S. Commission on Civil Rights, 1976, p. 19).

This massive and sudden population growth was the result of a combination of circumstances. First, because Puerto Ricans are U.S. citizens, international boundaries or immigration restrictions did not impede their movements. Second, unemployment was a major problem on the island. The sugarcane industry continued to displace the rural population, urban unemployment was high, and the population continued to grow. By the 1940s, a considerable number of Puerto Ricans were available to work off the island and, like Chicanos, could serve as a cheap labor supply for U.S. employers.

Third, Puerto Ricans were pulled to the mainland by the same labor shortages that attracted Mexican immigrants during and after World War II. Whereas the latter responded to job opportunities in the West and Southwest, Puerto Ricans moved to the Northeast. The job profiles of these two groups were similar: Both were concentrated in the low-wage, unskilled sector of the job market. However, the Puerto Rican migration began decades after the Mexican migration, at a time when the United States was much more industrialized and urbanized. As a result, Puerto Ricans were more concentrated in urban labor markets than Mexican immigrants (Portes, 1990, p. 164).

In the late 1940s, affordable air travel between San Juan and New York City facilitated movement between the island and the mainland. New York had been the major center of settlement for Puerto Ricans on the mainland even before annexation. A small Puerto Rican community had been established in the city, and, like many other immigrant groups, Puerto Ricans established organizations and networks to ease the transition and help newcomers with housing, jobs, and other issues. Although they eventually dispersed to other regions and cities, Puerto Ricans on the mainland remain centered in New York City. About 53% now reside in the Northeast, with 23% in New York alone (Brown & Patten, 2013e, p. 2).

Economics and jobs were at the heart of the Puerto Rican migration to the mainland. The rate of Puerto Rican migration followed the cycle of boom and bust, just as the rate of Mexican immigration has. The 1950s, the peak decade for Puerto Rican migration, was a period of rapid U.S. economic growth. Migration was encouraged, and job recruiters traveled to the island to attract workers. By the 1960s, however, the supply of jobs in Puerto Rico expanded appreciably, reducing the average number of migrants from the peak of 41,000 per year in the 1950s to about 20,000 per year. In the 1970s, the U.S. economy faltered, unemployment grew, and the flow of Puerto Rican migration reversed itself, with the number of returnees exceeding the number of migrants in various years (U.S. Commission on Civil Rights, 1976, p. 25). However, movement to the mainland has continued, and in 2015 over five million Puerto Ricans (see Table 8.1 earlier in the chapter), about 60% of all Puerto Ricans, were living on the mainland. In 2016, 3.4 million lived in Puerto Rico (Krogstad, Starr, & Sandstrom, 2017).

In September 2017, a Category 5 hurricane hit Puerto Rico. It brought heavy winds and dumped almost three feet of water on portions of the island. It ravaged both the natural environment and much of the island's infrastructure including buildings, roads, water systems, and the electrical grid. Six days after the storm, most of the island remained without power, 85% of the hospitals remained closed, and more than 1.5 million Puerto Ricans were without safe drinking water (Meyer, 2017). The death toll is debated. Government officials suggest the numbers are low. However, using interviews with funeral directors, medical staff, and others, and by calculating and comparing monthly death estimates over time, researchers suggest as many as 1,000 people may have died (Barclay & Campbell, 2017).

Recovery efforts remained slow. By December 1, 2017, most people (93%) had water, but to be completely safe, they were advised to boil it. One third (33%) of Puerto Ricans were still without power and nearly a third (27%) of cell phone sites were not operable. Nearly a million cubic yards of debris needed to be removed (Holmes, 2017). The storm closed schools and businesses and destroyed vast amounts of agriculture—all of which further affected Puerto Rican life. Mental health professionals suggest that most Puerto Ricans likely suffer some degree of post-traumatic stress disorder (Dickerson, 2017). Given the slow pace of reconstruction, 200,000 people have left Puerto Rico. This mass migration will surely change the island and the U.S. mainland in ways that we do not yet understand (Alvarez, 2017; Holmes, 2017; Meyer, 2017).

As the U.S. economy expanded and migration accelerated after World War II, Puerto Ricans moved into a broad range of jobs and locations in society, and the group grew more economically diversified and more regionally dispersed. Still, the bulk of the group tends to be concentrated in lower-status jobs in the larger cities of the Northeast. Puerto Rican men have often found work as unskilled laborers or in service occupations, particularly in areas where English is not necessary (e.g., janitorial work). The women often have been employed as domestics, hotel housekeepers, or tailors for the garment industry in New York City (Portes, 1990, p. 164).

TRANSITIONS

Although Puerto Ricans are not immigrants, the move to the mainland involves a change in culture, including language (Fitzpatrick, 1980, p. 858). Despite more than a century of political affiliation, Puerto Rican and Anglo cultures differ along many dimensions. Puerto Ricans are overwhelmingly Catholic, but their religious practices and rituals on the mainland are quite different from those on the island. Mainland Catholic parishes often reflect the traditions and practices of other cultures and groups. On the island, "Religious observance reflects the spontaneous and expressive practices of the Spanish and the Italian and not the restrained and well-organized worship of the Irish and Germans" (p. 865). Also, a shortage of Puerto Rican priests and Spanish-speaking clergy exists on the mainland. Although the overwhelming majority of Latinos are Catholic, only about 6% of Catholic priests are Latinos (Olivo & Eldeib, 2013). Thus, members of the group often feel estranged from and poorly served by the Church (Fitzpatrick, 1987, pp. 117–138).

Like most Caribbean people, Puerto Ricans do not construct race as a white/nonwhite dichotomy. Compared with the U.S. mainland, slavery in Puerto Rico was less monolithic and total, and the island had no periods of systematic, race-based segregation like the Jim Crow system. Additionally, Puerto Rico has a long history of racial intermarriage as noted earlier in the chapter. Thus, although racial prejudice exists in Puerto Rico, it never has been as categorical as on the mainland. On the island, people perceive race as a continuum of possibilities and combinations, not as a simple dichotomy between white and black (Grant-Thomas & Ofield, 2008, p. 167; Hollinger, 2003). Goudreau (2000) notes that a woman might be called "*triguena, negra, india, de color o blanquita* (copper color, Black, Indian, colored, or white) by different people in different moments. Moreover, one person could use all these terms to refer to another one in the same conversation. The meaning of each category will depend on the social context in which it is used and on the relations among those talking" (p. 45, c.f. Grant-Thomas & Ofield, 2008, p. 167).

As you learned in the Chapter 6 Comparative Focus about race in Brazil, social class can affect perceptions of skin color, and people of higher status might be seen as lighter skinned. Puerto Ricans also possess a more nuanced, intersectional view of race. For example, people might call an upper-class woman *blanquita* (Grant-Thomas & Ofield, 2008, p. 167). Roughly translating as "little white woman," this term simultaneously constructs race, class, and gender. Other labels construct ethnicity in relation to geographic location. For example, Nuyoricans (Puerto Rican New Yorkers) are different from Boricuas (Puerto Ricans from Puerto Rico).

A study of Puerto Rican college students in New York City illustrates this racial construction. Researchers found dramatic differences between the personal racial identification of the students and their perceptions of how Anglos viewed them. When asked for their racial identification, most of the students classified themselves as "tan," with one third labeling themselves "white" and only 7% considering themselves "black." When asked how they thought Anglos classified them, none of the students used the "tan" classification. Fifty-eight percent believed they were seen as "white," and 41% believed they were seen as "black" (Rodriguez, 1989, pp. 60–61; see also Rodriguez & Cordero-Guzman, 1992; Vargas-Ramos, 2005).

Another study documented dramatic differences in the terms women on the mainland and those in Puerto Rico use to express racial identity. The latter identified their racial identities primarily in terms of skin color: black, white, or *trigueña* (which translates as "wheat-colored" and which is just one of many mixed-race categories) (Wells, 1992, p. 11). However, mainland women identified themselves in nonracial terms, such as Hispanic, LatinX, Hispanic American, or American. In the view of the researchers, these labels serve to deflect the stigma associated with black racial status on the mainland (Landale & Oropesa, 2002).

In the United States where race is less fluid, Puerto Ricans may feel they have no clear place or that they have to favor one aspect of their racial or ethnic identity over others (Quiros, 2009). They may be genuinely puzzled when they first encounter prejudice and discrimination based on skin color and feel uncertain about their own identities and self-image. Schachter's (2016) research suggests that whites viewed nonwhite people as dissimilar from them—symbolically not fully American. A recent example of this happened during discussions about U.S.-born Sonia Sotomayor being named to the U.S. Supreme Court. Some questioned whether her "immigrant background" would interfere with her ability to uphold the Constitution (Greenberg, 2015). The negative racial perceptions and stereotypes of the dominant culture threaten Puerto Ricans to the extent that they can be victimized by the same types of discrimination and disadvantage that affects African Americans and Native Americans (and other minority groups). Institutionalized racial barriers can be extremely formidable; they may combine with cultural and linguistic differences to sharply limit opportunities and mobility for Puerto Ricans.

PUERTO RICANS AND OTHER MINORITY GROUPS

Puerto Ricans arrived in Northeast cities long after the great wave of European immigrants and several decades after African Americans began migrating from the South. They have often competed with other minority groups for housing, jobs, and other resources. In some neighborhoods and occupational areas, a pattern of ethnic succession can be seen in which Puerto Ricans have replaced other groups that have moved out (and sometimes up).

Because of their more recent arrival, Puerto Ricans on the mainland were not subjected to the more repressive paternalistic or rigid competitive systems of race relations such as slavery or Jim Crow. However, the subordinate status of the group is manifested in their occupational, residential, and educational profiles and by the institutionalized barriers to upward mobility that they face. Puerto Ricans share many problems with other urban minority groups of color: poverty, failing educational systems, and crime. Like African Americans, Puerto Ricans find their fate to be dependent on the future of the American city, and a large segment of the group is in danger of becoming part of a permanent urban underclass.

Like Mexican Americans, Puerto Ricans on the mainland combine elements of immigrant and colonized minority experiences. The movement to the mainland is voluntary in some ways, but in others it is strongly motivated by the transformations in the island economy that resulted from modernization and U.S. domination. Since 2005, a historic number of people (almost half a million) have left Puerto Rico for the mainland because of economic recession (Krogstad, Starr, & Sandstrom, 2017). Given the current financial problems in Puerto Rico, it is likely we will see more islanders migrating to the mainland. Like Chicanos, Puerto Ricans tend to enter the labor force at the bottom of the occupational structure and face similar problems of inequality and marginalization. Also, Puerto Rican culture retains a strong vitality and is continually reinvigorated by the considerable movement back and forth between the island and the mainland.

QUESTIONS FOR REFLECTION

5. Would you say that Puerto Ricans are more an immigrant or colonized minority group? Why?

6. What are some of the key differences between Puerto Rican and Anglo cultures? How have these differences shaped relations between the groups?

CUBAN AMERICANS

The contact period for Cuban Americans, as for Puerto Ricans, dates to the Spanish–American War of 1898. At that time, even though Cuba was a Spanish colony, the United States had been involved in Cuban politics and economics for decades. When Cubans revolted against the Spanish, U.S. businesses and other interests were threatened and the United States declared war on Spain. The United States invaded Cuba and began a military occupation that lasted until 1902, when Cuba became an independent nation. However, U.S. troops occupied the island on two additional occasions (1906–1909 and 1917–1922). Today, the U.S. Navy still operates the Guantanamo Bay Naval Base on the island's southern border.

The development of a Cuban American minority group in the United States bears little resemblance to the experience of Mexican Americans or Puerto Ricans. Until the 1950s, few Cubans immigrated to the United States, even during times of labor shortages, and Cuban Americans were a very small group, numbering no more than 50,000 (Perez, 1980, p. 256).

IMMIGRATION (PUSH AND PULL)

Since the end of the Spanish–American War in 1898, Cuba has been heavily influenced by the U.S. government and by U.S. companies that helped develop the Cuban economy. By the 1950s, the Cuban political leadership and the more affluent classes were profoundly Americanized in their attitudes and lifestyles (Portes, 1990, p. 165). In 1959, a revolution that brought Fidel Castro into power created the conditions for mass immigration to the United States.

Castro's government was decidedly anti-American and it began to restructure Cuban society along socialist lines. The middle and upper classes lost political and economic power and the revolution made it impossible for Cuban capitalists to continue business as usual. Thus, the first Cuban immigrants to the United States were elites; most were affluent, powerful, and white (Pedraza, 1998) and their resources made it possible for them to leave. The U.S. government and the American public perceived them as refugees from Communist persecution (the immigration occurred at the height of the Cold War between the United States and the communist Soviet Union) and welcomed them warmly.

Prior social, cultural, and business ties pulled the immigrants in the direction of the United States. Because Cuba is only 90 miles from southern Florida, the U.S. mainland was a logical destination, and many immigrants hoped to return to Cuba someday (Pedraza, 1998). More than 215,000 Cubans arrived during this first wave of immigration, which ended in 1962, after an escalation of hostile relations, including the failed Bay of Pigs invasion, resulted in the cutoff of all direct contact between Cuba and the United States (Pedraza, 1998).

The second wave of immigrants came between 1965 and 1974, after the Cuban government seized 55,000 small businesses (Pedraza, 1998). With the aid of "Freedom Flights" sponsored by the U.S. government, 300,000 Cubans made the journey. When the air connection was terminated in 1973, immigration slowed to a trickle once more (Rusin, Zong, & Batalova, 2015). Portes, Clark, and Bach (1977) called this second wave of immigrants "those who search."

In 1980, the Cuban government permitted another period of immigration. Unlike the first two waves, most of these immigrants were young, working class, single, black men. Many were convicted criminals—some were political prisoners, including those who sought to leave Cuba (which was illegal until 2013 for those lacking government approval). Some had been imprisoned for being gay and others had mental illnesses. Castro labeled them "scum" (Flight From Cuba, 1994; Pedraza, 1998).

This wave brought almost 125,000 Cubans to Florida (Rusin, Zong, & Batalova, 2015). They crossed the ocean in a variety of boats, though the lucky ones came on large tankers paid for by Cuban Americans living in Florida (Flight From Cuba, 1994). Sometimes these immigrants were called **marielitos**, after the port of Mariel from which many of them departed; more typically, Americans called them "Cuban boat people." This wave of immigrants generated a great deal of controversy in the United States and their reception was decidedly less favorable than it had been for prior groups. Even some in the established Cuban American community distanced itself from the marielitos, who were born after the revolution, and with whom they lacked kinship or friendship ties (Portes & Shafer, 2006, pp. 16–17).

Like many island nations, Cuba needed to import resources. As a result of a U.S. embargo, Cuba became increasingly dependent on the Soviet Union. When the USSR collapsed, Cuba suffered a new economic crisis prompting another period of immigration starting in 1989. Portes, Clark, and Bach (1977) called this group of immigrants "those who despair."

In 1992, in hopes of pushing Cubans to overthrow Castro, the U.S. government escalated the embargo. Most Cubans were unable to obtain necessities, including food. This crisis prompted so many Cubans to flee that the government cracked down (Ackerman, n.d.) even sinking a tugboat and killing the 32 people on it (Ackerman, n.d.).

Fidel Castro, leader of the Cuban Revolution.

Cubans rioted and Castro temporarily lifted the travel ban. Unsure how long this window of opportunity would stay open, fleeing Cubans tried their luck on anything that would float, including homemade rafts and old tires (Pedraza, 1998; Taylor, 2014).

More than 32,000 Cubans left and boats were often overcrowded and undersupplied (without water or life jackets) making the 90-mile ocean journey perilous (Ackerman, n.d.). Many succeeded in reaching the United States; however, at least 16,000 died in the waters between Cuba and the United States (Ackerman, n.d.). The 1994 refugee crisis led to the Cuban Migration Agreement between the two countries, informally called the Wet Feet, Dry Feet policy.

Fleeing Cuba on a homemade raft. Under 2018 U.S. policy, Cubans found at sea are immediately returned to Cuba or sent to another country.

Marielitos were refugees from Cuba who arrived in the United States in 1980.

Gender Images of Latinas

One part of the minority-group experience is learning to deal with the stereotypes, images, and expectations of the larger society. Of course, everyone (even white men) has to respond to the assumptions of others, but given the realities of power and status, minority-group members have fewer choices and a narrower range in which to maneuver: The images imposed by society are harder to escape and more difficult to deny.

In her analysis, Judith Ortiz Cofer (1995), a writer, poet, professor of English, and Puerto Rican, describes some of the images and stereotypes of Latinas with which she has had to struggle and some of the dynamics that have created and sustained those images. She writes from her own experiences, but the points she makes illustrate many of the sociological theories and concepts that guide this text.

THE ISLAND TRAVELS WITH YOU

Judith Ortiz Cofer

On a bus trip . . . a young man . . . spotted me and as if struck by inspiration went down on his knees in the aisle. With both hands over his heart he broke into a . . . rendition of "María" from *West Side Story*. My . . . fellow passengers gave [him a] round of gentle applause. . . . I managed my version of an English smile: no show of teeth, no extreme contortions of the facial muscles. . . . But María had followed me to London, reminding me of a prime fact of my life: you can leave the Island, master the English language, and travel as far as you can, but if you are a Latina, . . . the Island travels with you. . . .

As a Puerto Rican girl growing up in the United States and wanting like most children to "belong," I resented the stereotype that my Hispanic appearance called forth from many people I met.

Our family lived in . . . New Jersey during the sixties. . . . We spoke in Spanish, we ate Puerto Rican food bought at the bodega, and we practiced strict Catholicism. . . .

As a girl, I was kept under strict surveillance, since virtue and modesty were . . . the same as family honor. As a teenager, I was instructed on how to behave as a proper señorita. But it was a conflicting message girls got, since the Puerto Rican mothers also encouraged their daughters to look and act like women and to dress in clothes our Anglo friends found too "mature" for our age. . . . At Puerto Rican festivals, neither the music nor the colors we wore could be too loud. I still experience a vague sense of letdown when I'm invited to a "party" and it turns out to be a marathon conversation in hushed tones rather than a fiesta with salsa, laughter, and dancing—the kind of celebration I remember from my childhood. . . .

Mixed cultural signals have perpetuated certain stereotypes—for example, that of the Hispanic woman as the "Hot Tamale" or sexual firebrand. . . .

It is custom, however, . . . that leads us to choose scarlet over pale pink. As young girls, we were influenced in our decisions about clothes and colors by the women—older sisters and mothers who had grown up on a tropical island where the natural environment was a riot of primary colors, where showing your skin was one way to keep cool as well as to look sexy. Most important of all, on the island, women perhaps felt freer to dress and move more provocatively, since . . . they were protected by the traditions, mores, and laws of a Spanish/Catholic system of morality and machismo whose main rule was: *You may look at my sister, but if you touch her I will kill you.* The extended family and church structure could provide a young woman with a circle of safety in her small pueblo on the island; if a man "wronged" a girl, everyone would close in to save her family honor. . . .

Because of my education and proficiency with the English language, I have acquired many mechanisms for dealing with the anger I experience. This [is] not . . . true for the many Latin women working at menial jobs who must put up with stereotypes about our ethnic group such as: "They make good domestics." . . . María, the housemaid or counter girl, is now indelibly etched into the national psyche. The big and the little screens have presented us with the picture of the funny Hispanic maid, mispronouncing words and cooking up a spicy storm in a shiny California kitchen. . . .

There are thousands of Latinas without the privilege of an education or the entrée into society that I have. For them, life is a struggle against the misconceptions perpetuated by the myth of the Latina as whore, domestic, or criminal. My personal goal in my public life is to try to replace the old pervasive stereotypes and myths about Latinas. . . . Every time I give a reading [of my poetry], I hope the stories I tell, the dreams and fears I examine in my work, can achieve some universal truth which will get my audience past the particulars of my skin color, my accent, or my clothes.

SOURCE: *From the Latin Deli: Prose & Poetry* by Judith Ortiz Cofer. Copyright 1993 by Judith Ortiz Cofer. Reprinted by permission of the University of Georgia Press.

Questions to Consider

1. What differences between Puerto Rican and Anglo culture are examined in this passage? How might these differences affect or distort communications between cultures?

2. How does this passage illustrate the idea, introduced in Chapter 3, that stereotypes can be "gendered"?

Balseros (rafters) who attempted to escape Cuba. Under the Wet Foot/Dry Foot policy (which ended in 2017), Cubans who made it to land could apply for residency. These men were unsuccessful.

In prior decades, the U.S. government allowed Cuban refugees to immigrate. Under the new agreement, refugees caught at sea ("wet feet") by the Coast Guard were sent back to Cuba. If they made it to land ("dry feet") they were granted a one-year stay and the opportunity to become legal permanent residents (Rusin, Zong, & Batalova, 2015).

In recent years, changes in political leadership have meant positive changes for Cubans, potentially affecting future migration to the United States. For example, in 2003, the Cuban government allowed citizens to start small businesses (Fernandes, 2017). (Because economics are a major driver of immigration, we might expect this to decrease the number of Cubans seeking to immigrate.) When Fidel Castro turned over power to his brother Raul in 2006, it opened the door for a new relationship between Cuba and the United States (Corral, Figueras, Nesmith, & Anaagasti, 2016). In 2014, the U.S. government began allowing small numbers of U.S. citizens to travel to Cuba and in 2015, the United States took Cuba off its terrorism list where it had been since 1982 (*L.A. Times* Editorial Board, 2015). Additionally, a U.S. Embassy opened in Cuba and a Cuban one opened in the United States (Sopel, 2015). In 2016, Fidel Castro died and in 2017 the United States ended the Wet Foot, Dry Foot policy. Since the election of President Trump, U.S. relations with Cuba are under scrutiny and trade and travel restrictions have tightened (Kahn, 2017). How relations between the two countries unfold may also impact life for Cuban Americans.

REGIONAL CONCENTRATIONS

The overwhelming majority of Cuban immigrants settled in southern Florida, especially in Miami and the surrounding Dade County. Today, Cuban Americans remain one of the most spatially concentrated minority groups in the United States, with 68% of all Cuban Americans residing in Florida (Lopez, 2015a). This dense concentration has led to many disputes between the Hispanic, Anglo, and African American communities in the area. Issues have centered on language, jobs, and discrimination by the police and other governmental agencies. The conflicts often have been intense, and on more than one occasion have erupted into violence and civil disorder.

SOCIOECONOMIC CHARACTERISTICS

Compared with other streams of immigrants from Latin America, Cubans are, on the average, unusually affluent and well educated. Among the early immigrants in the 1960s were large numbers of professionals, landowners, and businesspeople. In later years, as Cuban society was transformed by the Castro regime, the stream included fewer elites—largely because there were fewer left in Cuba—and more political dissidents and working-class people. Today (as displayed in the figures later in this chapter), Cuban Americans rank higher than other Latino groups on a number of dimensions, a reflection of the educational and economic resources they brought with them from Cuba and the favorable reception they enjoyed in the United States (Portes, 1990, p. 169).

These assets gave Cubans an advantage over Chicanos and Puerto Ricans, but the differences between the three Latino groups run deeper and are more complex than a simple accounting of initial resources would suggest. Cubans adapted to U.S. society in a way that is fundamentally different from the experiences of the other two Latino groups.

THE ETHNIC ENCLAVE

Most of the minority groups we have discussed to this point have been concentrated in the unskilled, low-wage segments of the economy in which jobs are not secure and not linked to opportunities for upward mobility. Many Cuban Americans have bypassed this sector of the economy and much of the discrimination and limitation associated with it. Like several other groups, such as Jewish Americans, Cuban Americans are an enclave minority (see Chapter 2). An ethnic enclave is a social, economic, and cultural subsociety controlled by the group itself. Located in a specific geographical area or neighborhood inhabited solely or largely by members of the group, the enclave encompasses sufficient economic enterprises and social institutions to permit the group to function as a self-contained entity, largely independent of the surrounding community.

The first wave of Cuban immigrants brought with them considerable human capital and business expertise. Although much of their energy was focused on ousting Castro and returning to Cuba, they generated enough economic activity to sustain restaurants, shops, and other small businesses that catered to the exile community.

As the years passed and the hope of a return to Cuba dimmed, the enclave economy grew. Between 1967 and 1976, the number of Cuban-owned firms in Dade County increased nine-fold, from 919 to about 8,000. Six years later, the number had reached 12,000. Most of these enterprises were small, but some factories employed hundreds of workers (Portes & Rumbaut, 1996, pp. 20–21). By 2001, more than 125,000 Cuban-owned firms existed in the United States and the rate of Cuban-owned firms per 100,00 people was 4 times greater than the rate for Mexican Americans and 14 times greater than the rate for African Americans (Portes & Shafer, 2006, p. 14).

Cuban-owned firms have become integrated within local economies and increasingly competitive with other firms involved in construction, manufacturing, finance, insurance, real estate, and an array of other activities in the larger society. The growth of economic enterprises has been paralleled by a growth in the number of other types of groups and organizations and in the number and quality of services available (schools, law firms, medical care, funeral parlors, etc.). The enclave has become a largely autonomous community capable of providing for its members from cradle to grave (Logan, Alba, & McNulty, 1994; Peterson, 1995; Portes & Bach, 1985, p. 59).

That the enclave economy is controlled by the group itself is crucial; it separates the ethnic enclave from "the ghetto," or neighborhoods that are impoverished and segregated. In ghettos, members of other groups typically control the local economy; the profits, rents, and other resources flow out of the neighborhood. In the enclave, profits are reinvested in the neighborhood. Group members can avoid the discrimination and limitations imposed by the larger society, and can apply their skills, education, and talents in an atmosphere free from language barriers and prejudice. Those who might wish to venture into business for themselves can use the networks of cooperation and mutual aid for advice, credit, and other forms of assistance. Thus, the ethnic enclave provides a platform from which Cuban Americans can pursue economic success independent of their degree of acculturation or English language ability.

The effectiveness of the ethnic enclave as a pathway for adaptation is illustrated by a study of Cuban and Mexican immigrants, all of whom entered the United States in 1973. At the time of entry, the groups were comparable in levels of skills, education, and English language ability. The groups were interviewed on several different occasions, and although they remained comparable on many variables, there were dramatic differences between the groups that reflected their different positions in the labor market. The majority of the Mexican immigrants were employed in the low-wage job sector. Less than 20% were self-employed or employed by someone of Mexican descent. Conversely, 57% of the Cuban immigrants were self-employed or employed by other Cubans (i.e., in the enclave economy). Among the subjects in the study, self-employed Cubans reported the highest monthly incomes ($1,495), and Cubans otherwise employed in the enclave earned the second-highest monthly incomes ($1,111). The lowest monthly incomes ($880) were earned by Mexican immigrants employed in small, non-enclave firms; many of them worked as unskilled laborers in seasonal, temporary, or otherwise insecure jobs (Portes, 1990, p. 173; see also Portes & Bach, 1985).

A more recent study confirms the advantages that accrue from forming an enclave. Using 2000 Census data, Portes and Shafer (2006) compared the incomes of several groups in the Miami–Fort Lauderdale metropolitan area, including the original Cuban immigrants (who founded the enclave), their children (the second generation), Cuban immigrants who arrived after 1980 (the marielitos and others), and several other groups. Some of the results of the study for men are presented in Figure 8.9.

The founders and primary beneficiaries of the Cuban enclave are the self-employed, pre-1980 Cuban immigrants, shown in the far-left bar in Figure 8.9. The income for this group is higher than for all other Cuban groups included in the graph, and only slightly less than for non-Hispanic whites (not shown). The sons of the founding generation (U.S.-born Cuban Americans) also enjoy a substantial benefit, both directly (through working in the

FIGURE 8.9 Family Incomes for Self-Employed and Wage/Salaried Men Workers From Three Cuban American Groups, 2000

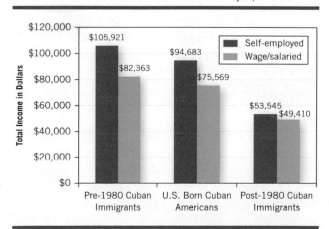

SOURCE: Portes and Shafer (2006, p. 42).

enclave firms started by their fathers) and indirectly (by translating the resources of their families into human capital, including education, for themselves). The incomes of post-1980 Cuban immigrants are the lowest on the graph and, in fact, are comparable to incomes for non-Hispanic blacks (not shown).

The ability of most Hispanic (and other) immigrants to rise in the class system and compete for place and position is constrained by discrimination and their own lack of economic and political power. Cuban immigrants in the enclave do not need to expose themselves to American prejudices or to rely on the job market of the larger society. They constructed networks of mutual assistance and support and linked themselves to opportunities more consistent with their ambitions and their qualifications.

The link between the enclave and economic equality (an aspect of secondary structural integration) challenges the predictions of some traditional assimilation theories and the understandings of many Americans. The pattern long has been recognized by some leaders of other groups, however, and is voiced in many of the themes of Black Power, Red Power, and Chicanismo that emphasize self-help, self-determination, nationalism, and separation.

However, ethnic enclaves cannot be a panacea for all immigrant or other minority groups. They develop only under certain limited conditions—namely, when business and financial expertise and reliable sources of capital are combined with a disciplined labor force willing to work for low wages in exchange for on-the-job training, future assistance and loans, or other delayed benefits. Enclave enterprises usually start on a small scale and cater only to other ethnic people. Thus, the early economic returns are small, and prosperity follows only after years of hard work, if at all. Most important, eventual success and expansion beyond the boundaries of the enclave depend on the persistence of strong ties of loyalty, kinship, and solidarity. The pressure to assimilate might easily weaken these networks and the strength of group cohesion (Portes & Manning, 1986, pp. 61–66).

CUBAN AMERICANS AND OTHER MINORITY GROUPS

The adaptation of Cuban Americans contrasts sharply with the experiences of colonized minority groups and with the "traditional" view of how immigrants are "supposed" to acculturate and integrate. Cuban Americans are neither the first nor the only group to develop an ethnic enclave, and their success has generated prejudice and resentment from the dominant group and from other minority groups. Puerto Ricans and Chicanos have been stereotyped as lazy, unmotivated, criminals, clowns, or "Latin lovers" (Mastro, Behm-Morawitz, & Ortiz, 2007). Yet, higher-status Cuban

Americans have been stereotyped as "too successful," "too clannish," and "too ambitious." The former stereotype commonly emerges to rationalize exploitative relationships; the latter expresses disparagement and rejection of groups that are more successful in the struggle to acquire resources (see Chapter 3). Nonetheless, the stereotype of Cubans is an exaggeration and a misperception that obscures the fact that poverty and unemployment are major problems for many members of this group, especially for the post-1980 immigrants (see the figures at the end of this chapter).

QUESTIONS FOR REFLECTION

7. Would you say that Cuban Americans are more an immigrant or colonized minority group? Why?

8. Are Cuban Americans an enclave minority? What are the most important advantages enjoyed by enclave minority groups? Are there any disadvantages?

PREJUDICE AND DISCRIMINATION

The American tradition of prejudice against Latinos was born in the 19th century conflicts that created minority-group status for Mexican Americans. The themes of the original anti-Mexican stereotypes and attitudes were consistent with the nature of the contact situation: As Mexicans were conquered and subordinated, they were characterized as inferior, lazy, irresponsible, low in intelligence, and dangerously criminal (McWilliams, 1961, pp. 212–214). Prejudice and racism, supplemented with the echoes of the racist ideas and beliefs brought to the Southwest by many Anglos, helped justify and rationalize the colonized, exploited status of the Chicanos.

These prejudices were incorporated into the dominant culture and transferred to Puerto Ricans when they began to arrive on the mainland. However, this stereotype does not fit the situation of Cuban Americans very well. Instead, their affluence has been exaggerated and perceived as undeserved or achieved by unfair or "un-American" means, a characterization similar to the traditional stereotype of Jews but just as prejudiced as perceptions of LatinX inferiority.

Some evidence suggests that the level of prejudice against Latinos has been affected by the decline of explicit American racism (discussed in Chapter 3). For example, social distance scales show a decrease in the scores for Mexicans, although their relative ranking remains fairly stable.

On the other hand, anti-Latino prejudice and racism tend to increase during times of high immigration.

As a child, Jane Hill used "mock Spanish" phrases such as "no problemo" and "buenos nachos" after learning them from popular culture. Now a linguistic anthropologist, Hill (1995) argues that mock Spanish is a form of covert racism.

To mock means to imitate; "mock" also implies disdain. Though people who use mock Spanish may intend it as funny, mock Spanish is problematic. For example, it oversimplifies Spanish—as if adding "-o" to an English word makes it Spanish. For example, consider "el stupido" or "el cheapo" (Hill, 1995). By extension, mock Spanish reduces Spanish-speaking people to simple or stupid caricatures while English speakers are presumed to be smarter or more sophisticated (Zentella, 2003).

Hill's (1995) and Zentella's (2003) analyses of mock Spanish reveal a linguistic double standard: Spanish speakers are often disparaged or ridiculed for using incorrect English; however, English speakers who misuse Spanish generally do so without consequence. Fought (c.f. Trotta, 2006) says, "It's perfectly fine for white people to say 'Hasta la vista, baby' [from the movie *Terminator 2: Judgment Day*] to each other, but there is no tolerance for Spanish speaking co-workers who say 'hasta la vista' to each other . . . There's a lot of negativity attached to the use of Spanish. It's associated with poverty and a lack of education." In other words, white people can use mock Spanish. However, as English-only legislation suggests, many people view speaking Spanish as problematic. Zimmer (2006) suggests that mock Spanish is "how people try to phonetically speak when they talk down to you."

Zentella (2003) argues that mock Spanish obscures the diversity of Hispanic/Latino groups and relies on and reinforces negative stereotypes (p. 52). For example, calling Mexicans "bad hombres" depends on the speaker and the listener having familiarity with the stereotype of Latino men as violent, criminal, or deviant. Similarly, "Es no my yob" builds on and may reinforce the stereotype of Latinos as lazy.

Mock Spanish is different from "Spanglish," which blends English and Spanish into a new language used by some bilingual speakers. For example, in Spanish, lunch menu is "menu de almuerzo." In Spanglish, it is "el menu de lonche" which blends *el menu* (Spanish) with the phonetic Spanglish *lonche* (Gonzales, n.d.). To the untrained listener, Spanglish might sound like a linguistic mash-up that results from someone being confused or uneducated. Linguists, however, see it positively (Zentella, 2003, p. 56).

Mock Spanish differs from "code switching" that occurs when bilingual speakers alternate between languages (Montes-Alcalá, 2000, p. 218; Leslie, 2016; Price, 2010). It helps people manage social situations, creates humor, prevents eavesdroppers from fully understanding private conversations, and reduces language barriers between speakers (Cromdal, 2004; Horasan, 2013, p. 14).

Now that you understand the difference between mock Spanish, Spanglish, and code switching, you may understand why some people view mock Spanish as problematic. What do you think? Consider the children's book *Skippyjon Jones* (2003). Skippyjon is an adorable white cat with big ears who speaks English. Skippyjon's alter ego is Skippito Friskito, a brown superhero Chihuahua that speaks in mock Spanish as we learn in the passage, "My ears are too beeg for my head. My head ees too beeg for my body. I am not a Siamese cat. . . . I am a chihuahua!"

Casillas (2014) and others find the book problematic for many of the reasons we've discussed. What do you think? Is the mock Spanish used in *Skippyjon Jones* problematic? Does it rely on and perpetuate stereotypes? Or, is *Skippyjon Jones* "just fun"? What about other examples of mock Spanish that you may have seen in greeting cards, magazines, newspapers, blogs, or heard around you? For example, "cinco de drinko" (not Cinco de Mayo)?

Some examples are listed below. Can you identify the sources and the speakers?*

(1) "I'll splain." "Ok splain."

(2) "Nurse Espinosa and her nursitas want more dinero."

(3) "I need a lift in your el trucko to the next towno . . ."

(4) "I'm promoting myself to 'El Tigre Numero Uno.'"

(5) "Correctomundo."

(6) "First-o, take a finger to the cream . . ." The goal is to achieve "El Messy Look."

*Some of these examples come from Teaching Linguistic Anthropology at teach.linguisticanthropology.org/tag/mock-Spanish.

TURN THE PAGE TO FIND THE ANSWERS

In particular, considerable though largely anecdotal evidence suggests that the surge of immigration that began in the 1990s sparked high levels of anti-Latino prejudice in the "borderlands," or the areas along the U.S.–Mexican border. Extreme, racist rhetoric was common, and media prominently featured hate group activities. Many observers see racism in Arizona's state-mandated ban on ethnic studies programs in public schools and in its widely debated State Bill 1070 that, in part, allows police to check anyone for proof of citizenship. In 2012, the Supreme Court upheld this component of the bill but struck down three other provisions, and in 2014, a federal judge rejected additional provisions. At any rate, the level of immigrant bashing and anti-LatinX sentiment along the border and in other parts of the United States demonstrates that American prejudice, although sometimes disguised as a subtle modern racism, is alive and well.

Even though immigration rates from Mexico and Latin America tended to decrease in recent years, prejudicial sentiments were a prominent feature of President Trump's presidential campaign and the early days of his administration. As we have seen, prejudice is not always a direct response to threat and group competition (see Chapter 3), but is also motivated by cultural and personality factors. Anti-Hispanic and anti-immigration sentiments were frequently expressed during Trump's campaign for the presidency. In fact, his campaign began with a speech in which he associated undocumented Mexican immigrants with drugs and rape, and one of the most prominent features of his campaign rhetoric was a promise to build a wall along the U.S.–Mexican border.

Furthermore, one of Trump's first acts as president was to initiate a ban on immigrants from seven predominantly Muslim nations (Singhvi & Parlapiano, 2017). This ban was overturned in the courts but a revised policy was tentatively permitted by the Supreme Court some months later (Barnes & Zapotosky, 2017).

In Chapter 5, we mentioned that audit studies have documented the persistence of discrimination against African Americans in the housing and job markets; many of the same studies also demonstrate anti-Hispanic biases (see Quillian, 2006, for a review). Discrimination of all kinds, institutional as well as individual, against Latino groups has been common, but it has not been as rigid or as total as the systems that controlled African American labor under slavery and segregation. However, discrimination against Latinos persists across the United States. Because of their longer tenure in the United States and their original status as a rural labor force, Mexican Americans probably have been more victimized by the institutionalized forms of discrimination than have other Latino groups.

ASSIMILATION AND PLURALISM

As in previous chapters, we will use the central concepts of this text to review the status of Latinos in the United States. Where relevant, we'll make comparisons between the major LatinX groups and the minority groups discussed in previous chapters.

One of the many organized demonstrations protesting Arizona Senate Bill 1070.

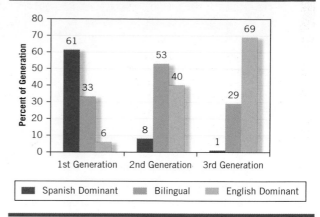

FIGURE 8.10 Primary Language by Generation for Hispanic Americans, 2012

SOURCE: Taylor, Paul, Lopez, Hugo, Martinez, Jessica, and Velasco, Gabriel, 2012. "When Labels Don't Fit: Hispanics and their Views of Identity," http://www.pewhispanic .org/2012/04/04/when-labels-dont-fit-hispanics-and-their-views-of-identity/.

ACCULTURATION

Latinos are highly variable in their extent of acculturation but are often seen as "slow" to change, learn English, and adopt Anglo customs. Contrary to this perception, research shows that Hispanics follow many of the same patterns of assimilation as European groups. Their rates of acculturation increase with length of residence and are higher for the native born (Espinosa & Massey, 1997; Goldstein & Suro, 2000; Valentine & Mosley, 2000).

The dominant trend for Hispanic groups, as for immigrants from Europe in the past (see Chapter 2), is that language acculturation increases over the generations, as the length of residence in the United States increases, and as education increases. A 2007 study of more than 14,000 respondents from six different surveys since 2000 (Hakimzadeh & Cohn, 2007) illustrates these points (see Figures 8.10 and 8.11).

A more recent study (Krogstad & Gonzalez-Barrera, 2015) came to similar conclusions. They found that the majority of Hispanics speak English only (25%) or are bilingual (36%) and that the percentage who mainly speak English increases with the generations: 42% of second-generation Hispanics speak mainly English, as do 76% of the third or higher generation.

An earlier study (Pew Hispanic Center, 2004) found that Anglo and Latino values become virtually identical as length of residence increases, generations pass, and English language ability increases. For example, the values of predominantly Spanish speakers (who were mostly foreign-born or first generation) are distinctly different from those of non-Latinos, especially on a survey item that measures support for the statement, "Children should live with their parents until they are married." Virtually all the predominantly Spanish speakers supported the statement, but English-speaking Latinos showed the more individualistic values of Anglos. A similar acculturation to American values occurred for the other three items that researchers studied.

A more recent study (Pew Research Center, 2014c) found similar acculturation trends on the "hot-button" issues of same-sex marriage and abortion (see Table 8.5). The attitudes of Hispanic Americans born in the United States are far more similar to the general public than are foreign-born Hispanic Americans.

Even while acculturation continues, however, immigration revitalizes Hispanic culture and the Spanish language. By its nature, assimilation is a slow process that can require decades or generations to complete. In contrast, immigration can be fast, often accomplished in less than

FIGURE 8.11 Percentage of Hispanic Americans Who Speak English "Very Well" by Years of Residence and Levels of Education, 2007

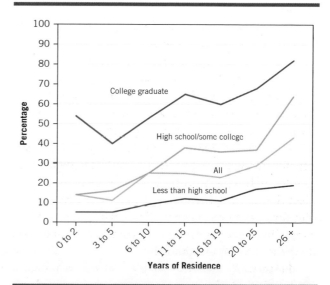

SOURCE: Hakimzadeh, Shirin, & Cohn, D'Vera. 2007. "English Language Usage Among Hispanics in the United States." Pew Hispanic Center, http://pewhispanic.org/files/reports/82.pdf.

TABLE 8.5 Opinions on Same-Sex Marriage and Abortion

ITEM	PERCENTAGE IN FAVOR		
	General Public	**U.S. Born Hispanics**	**Foreign-Born Hispanics**
"Gays and lesbians should be allowed to legally marry."	50%	58%	39%
"Abortion should be legal in all or most cases."	54%	49%	33%

SOURCE: Pew Research Center, 2014c.

a day. Thus, even as Hispanic Americans acculturate and integrate, Hispanic culture and language are sustained and strengthened. What is perceived to be slow acculturation for these groups is mostly the result of fast and continuous immigration.

Furthermore, colonized minority groups such as Chicanos and Puerto Ricans were not encouraged to assimilate in the past. Valued primarily for the cheap labor they supplied, they were seen as inferior, undesirable, and unfit for integration. For much of the 20th century, Latinos were excluded from the institutions and experiences (e.g., school) that could have led to greater equality and higher rates of acculturation. Prejudice, racism, and discrimination combined to keep most LatinX groups away from the centers of modernization and change and away from opportunities to improve their situation.

Finally, for Cubans, Dominicans, Salvadorans, and other groups, cultural differences reflect that they are largely recent immigrants. Their first generations are alive and well. As is typical for immigrant groups, they keep their language and traditions alive.

SECONDARY STRUCTURAL ASSIMILATION

In this section, we survey the situation of Latinos in the public areas and institutions of American society, following the same format as the previous two chapters. We begin with where people live.

Residence. Figure 8.12 shows the geographic concentrations of Latinos in 2010. The legacies of the varied patterns of entry and settlement for the largest groups are evident. The higher concentrations in the Southwest reflect the presence of Mexican Americans, those in Florida are the result of the Cuban immigration, and those in the Northeast display the settlement patterns of Puerto Ricans.

Figure 8.13 highlights the areas of the nation where the Latino population is growing fastest. A quick glance at the map reveals that many of the high-growth areas are distant from the traditional points of entry for these groups. In particular, the Hispanic American population is growing rapidly in parts of New England, the South, the upper Midwest, the Northwest, and even Alaska. This population movement is a response to (among many other forces) the availability of jobs in factories, mills, chicken-processing plants and slaughterhouses, farms, construction, and other low-skilled areas of the economy.

Within each of these regions, Latino groups are highly urbanized, as shown in Figure 8.14. With the exception of Mexican Americans, more than 90% of each of the 10 largest Hispanic American groups live in urban areas, and this percentage approaches 100% for some groups. Mexican Americans are more rural than the other groups, but the percentage of the group living in rural areas is tiny today, in sharp contrast to their historical role as an agrarian workforce.

The extent of residential segregation for Hispanic Americans was displayed in Figure 6.8 (see Chapter 6), using the dissimilarity index for each of the last four census years. Residential segregation is much lower for Hispanics than for African Americans: None of the scores for Hispanics in Figure 6.8 approach the "extreme" segregation denoted by a dissimilarity index of 60 or more.

Note that, contrary to the decreasing levels of black–white segregation, Hispanic–white residential segregation has held steady, with minor increases or decreases. Among other factors, this is a reflection of high rates of immigration and "chain" patterns of settlement, which concentrate newcomers in ethnic neighborhoods. In other words, levels of residential segregation for Hispanics remain relatively steady because weakening barriers to integration in the larger society are counteracted by the continuing arrival of newcomers, who tend to settle in predominantly Hispanic neighborhoods.

Education. Figure 8.15 displays the extent of school segregation for Hispanic Americans using the same format that Figure 6.9 used for African Americans. Four different school years are used and the figure displays trends quite similar

COMPARATIVE FOCUS

Immigration to Europe Versus Immigration to the United States

The volume of immigration in the world today is at record levels. As we pointed out in Chapter 1 ("Immigration and Globalization"), in 2015, 244 million people, just over 3.3% of the world's population, lived outside their countries of birth. That's a 41% increase since 2000 and almost every nation and region has been affected (United Nations International Migration Report Highlights, 2015, p. 1). In 2014, almost 20 million immigrants (about 8% of all migrants) were refugees fleeing war, famine, and persecution—the highest number since World War II (United Nations International Migration Report 2015 Highlights, p. 9).

The United States is a popular destination for immigrants. The United States now has 47 million, roughly 19% of the world's total (United Nations International Migration Report Highlights, 2015, pp. 7–8). Almost one million arrived here in 2015 (Lopez & Bialik, 2017). When examined relative to population size, or per capita, the U.S. ranking is near the middle for the number of migrants it hosts. In 2013, it ranked 65th (Siegel, 2014).

The issues of immigration and assimilation we debate so fervently in the United States echo across the globe. Almost two thirds of all migrants live in Asia (75 million) or Europe (76 million) (United Nations International Migration Report Highlights, 2015, p. 1).

The advanced industrial nations of Western Europe are prime destinations for immigrants. Germany and the Russian Federation each have about 12 million migrants. The United Kingdom hosts almost 9 million people (United Nations International Migration Report Highlights, 2015, p. 8). Like the United States, these nations have high standards of living and offer opportunities for economic survival, though the price may be to live at the margins of society or to take jobs scorned by the native born. Also, most Western European nations have very low birthrates, and in some cases (e.g., Spain, Germany), their populations are projected to decline in coming decades (Population Reference Bureau, 2014, p. 11). This decline will create labor force shortages, attracting immigrants to Europe for decades to come.

The immigrant stream to Europe is varied and includes people from all walks of life, from highly educated professionals to laborers. The most prominent flows include movements from Turkey to Germany, from Africa to Spain and Italy, and from many former British colonies (e.g., Jamaica, India, Nigeria) to the United Kingdom. This immigration is primarily an economic phenomenon motivated by the search for jobs and survival, but the stream also includes refugees and asylum seekers spurred by civil war, genocide, and political unrest. In 2014, Turkey hosted the most refugees of any country in the world—1.6 million people—followed by Pakistan (1.5 million), Lebanon (1.2 million), and the Islamic Republic of Iran (1.0 million) (United Nations International Migration Report Highlights, 2015, p. 1). In 2016, the United States took in 84,995 refugees (Lopez & Bialik, 2017).

In terms of numbers, the volume of immigration to Europe is smaller than the flow to the United States, but its proportional impact is comparable. About 13.4% of the U.S. population is foreign-born. That's three times as many as in the 1970s when immigrants were just 4.7% of the population. However, it's not the high we had in 1890 when 14.8% of the U.S. population were foreign-born (Lopez & Bialik, 2017). Many European nations (including Belgium, Germany, and Sweden) have a similar profile (Dumont & LeMaitre, 2011). Thus, in both cases immigration has generated major concerns and debates about how to handle newcomers and manage a pluralistic society, including national language policy, the limits of religious freedom, and the criteria for citizenship.

For example, since 2011, more than 60% of Syrians (12.5 million) have been displaced from their homes. This particular crisis has dramatically increased the proportion of refugees living in European countries and has resulted in disapproval of current European Union policies regarding immigrants, including refugees (Connor & Krogstad, 2017). Greeks, Swedes, and Italians express the highest dissatisfaction, reflecting the large proportions of refugees taken in by their countries. They are concerned that immigrants will "take" jobs and other social services such as education. Additionally, they fear the possibility of increased crime and terrorism (the latter concern is linked with negative attitudes about Muslims) (Poushter, 2016). These realities have resulted in increased nationalism, perhaps best exemplified by Britain's decision to exit (Brexit) the European Union (Stokes, 2016).

Germany has one of the largest immigrant communities of any European nation and has been dealing with a large foreign-born population for decades. Germany began to allow large numbers of immigrants to enter as temporary workers or "guest workers" (*Gastarbeiter*) to help staff its expanding economy beginning in the 1960s. Most of these immigrants came from Turkey, and Germans saw them as temporary workers only—that is, people who would return to their homeland when they were no longer needed. Thus, Germany saw no particular need to encourage immigrants to acculturate and integrate.

Contrary to this expectation, many immigrants stayed and settled permanently, and many of their millions of descendants today speak only German and have no knowledge of or experience with their "homeland." Although acculturated, they are not fully integrated. In fact—in contrast with the United States—they were denied the opportunity for citizenship until recently.

In recent years, discontent and protests about immigrants have been common across Western Europe, especially with the growth of Muslim communities. Many Europeans see Islamic immigrants as unassimilable, too foreign or exotic to ever fit in to

(Continued)

the mainstream of their society. In France, Germany, the Netherlands, and other countries, violence has punctuated these conflicts.

Struggles over the essential meaning of national identity are increasingly common throughout the developed world. Across Europe, just as in the United States (and Canada), nations wrestle with issues of inclusion and diversity: What should it mean to be German, or French, or British, or Dutch, or American? How much diversity can be accepted before national cohesion is threatened? What is the best balance between assimilation and pluralism?

Questions to Consider

1. What is the most important idea you learned in this section? What surprised you most? What are you now curious to know based on what you read?

2. What similarities and differences between the United States and Europe can you cite in terms of immigration?

3. Do you think the United States is more or less successful its approach to immigration than European nations? Why?

4. Consider issues facing immigrants generally and refugees in particular. If you were in charge of immigration policy, what would you want it to look like and why? (We realize the reality and the vision may be two different things. For now, just consider the ideas.) How might your ideas differ from an immigrant leaving a country where he or she could not find work or a refugee who was fleeing war? What, if anything, does that tell you about social location?

---

to those for African Americans. The percentage of Hispanic American students in "High Poverty" schools has risen to 48% in the 2013–2014 school year, exactly the same percentage as that of African American students. This increasing concentration of students by social class and ethnicity reflects high rates of immigration and the tendency of recent immigrants to seek out their co-ethnics in inner-city neighborhoods.

Levels of education for Hispanic Americans have risen in recent years but are far below national standards (see Figure 8.16). Hispanic Americans in general and all subgroups, except Colombian Americans, fall well below non-Hispanic whites for high school education. Note that 61% of Mexican Americans and only about half of Honduran, Salvadoran, and Guatemalan Americans have completed high school. At the college level, Colombian and Cuban Americans approximate national norms, but the other groups and Hispanic Americans as a whole are far below non-Hispanic whites.

FIGURE 8.12 Geographical Distribution of Hispanic Americans by County, 2010 (Percentage Share of County Population)

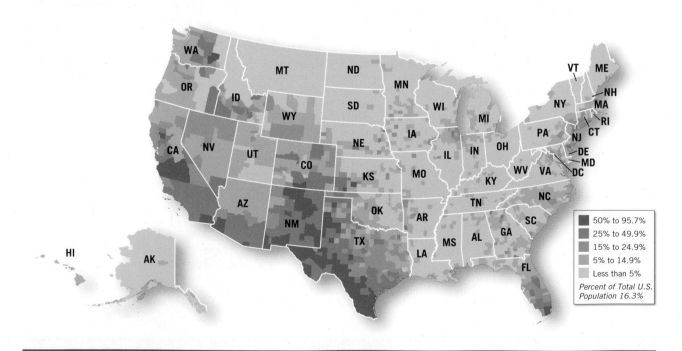

SOURCE: Ennis, Rios-Vargas, & Albert (2011, p. 10); U.S. Census Bureau (2011b).

FIGURE 8.13 Percentage Change in Hispanic Population by County, 2000–2010

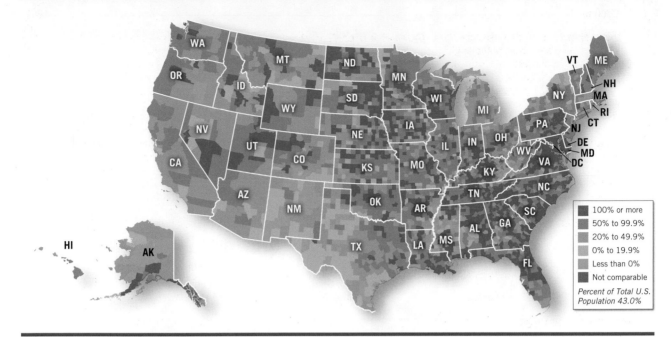

Legend:
- 100% or more
- 50% to 99.9%
- 20% to 49.9%
- 0% to 19.9%
- Less than 0%
- Not comparable

Percent of Total U.S. Population 43.0%

SOURCE: Ennis et al. (2011, p. 12); U.S. Census Bureau (2000b, 2011b).

The lower levels of education for Mexican Americans and Puerto Ricans are the cumulative results of decades of systematic discrimination and exclusion. These levels have been further reduced by the high percentage of recent immigrants from Mexico, the Dominican Republic, El Salvador, and other nations that have modest educational backgrounds.

Given the role that educational credentials have come to play in the job market, these figures are consistent with the idea that assimilation may be segmented for some Hispanic groups (see Chapters 2 and 10), who may contribute in large numbers, along with African Americans and Native Americans, to the growth of an urban underclass.

Political Power. The political resources available to Hispanic Americans have increased over the years, but the group is still proportionally underrepresented. Nationally, Hispanic Americans rose from about 6% of those eligible to vote in 1996 to almost 12% in 2016 (Krogstad, 2017) . However, this increase in potential political power was limited by lower rates of registration and lower voter turnout:

FIGURE 8.14 Percentage of 10 Largest Hispanic American Groups and Non-Hispanic Whites Living in Urbanized Areas, 2000

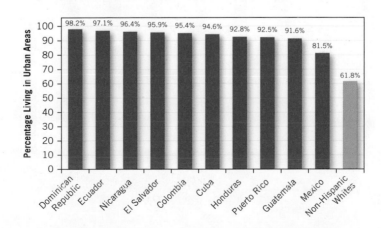

SOURCE: U.S. Census Bureau (2000b).

NOTE: An "urbanized area" is defined as an area with a minimal population density of 1,000 people per square mile and a minimum population of 50,000.

FIGURE 8.15 Percentages of Students by Poverty and Race, Selected School Years

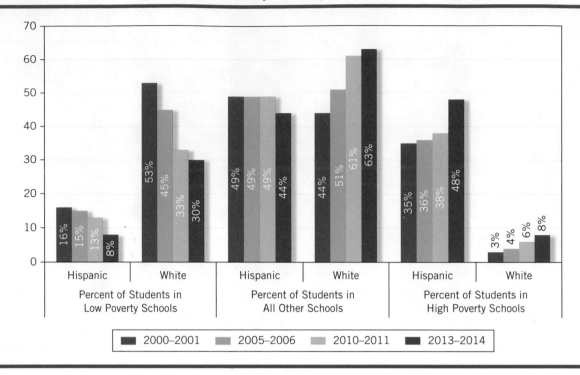

SOURCE: United States GAO, 2016. p. 59.

Less than half (48%) of Hispanic Americans eligible to vote cast a ballot in the 2016 presidential election (U.S. Bureau of the Census, 2017g). The impact of the LatinX vote on national politics will increase as the group grows in size, but participation is likely to remain lower than that of other groups for some time because of the large percentage of noncitizens and recent, non-English-speaking immigrants in the group.

FIGURE 8.16 Educational Attainment for All Hispanic Americans, Non-Hispanic Whites, and 10 Largest Hispanic American Groups, 2015

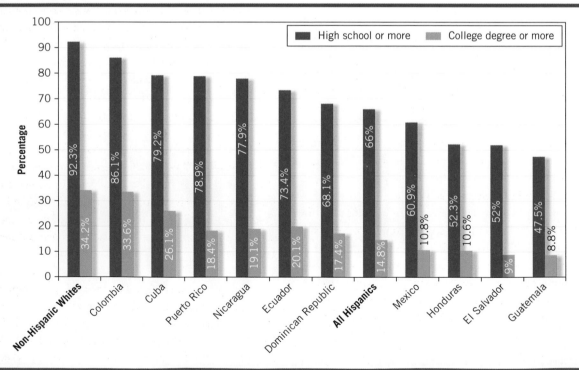

SOURCE: U.S. Census, 2015 American Community Survey, 1-Year Estimates, https://factfinder.census.gov/faces/tableservices/jsf/pages/productview.xhtml?pid=ACS_15_1YR_S0201&prodType=table.

At the national level, 45 Hispanic Americans serve in the U.S. Congress; this is more than double the number in 1990 and about 8% of the total membership. There are 40 Hispanic members of the House of Representatives[1] (29 of them Democrats and 10 are women) and 5 senators (3 of them Republicans and one of them a woman) (Manning, 2017). On the local and state levels, the number of public officials identified as Hispanic increased by more than 65% between 1985 and 2008, from 3,147 to 5,240 (U.S. Census Bureau, 2011a, p. 259).

Although Hispanic Americans are still underrepresented, these figures suggest that they will become increasingly important in American political life as their numbers continue to grow and their rates of naturalization rise. Even with a relatively small turnout, Hispanic voters were an important part of the coalition that elected President Barack Obama in 2008 and 2012. Not surprisingly, Hispanic voters voted overwhelmingly for Hillary Clinton (the Democratic candidate) in 2016: only 28% voted for Trump (Krogstad & Lopez, 2016). However, it seems probable that the competition between the Republican and Democratic parties for this growing segment of the electorate will continue.

Jobs and Income. The economic situation of Hispanic Americans is quite mixed. Many Latinos, especially those who have been in the United States for several generations, are doing "just fine. They have, in ever increasing numbers, accessed opportunities in education and employment and have carved out a niche of American prosperity for themselves and their children" (Camarillo & Bonilla, 2001, pp. 130–131). For others, however, the picture is not as promising. They face the possibility of becoming members of an impoverished, powerless, and economically marginalized urban underclass, like African Americans and other minority groups of color.

Occupationally, Hispanic Americans who are recent immigrants with modest levels of education and job skills are concentrated in the less desirable, lower-paid service and unskilled segments of the job market. Those with higher levels of human capital and education compare more favorably with the dominant group.

Unemployment, low income, and poverty continue to be issues for all Hispanic groups.

Figure 8.17 compares median household incomes for non-Hispanic whites and all Hispanic Americans across a 35-year period. The size of the income gap fluctuates but generally remains in the low to 70% range. In the most recent years, however, it has risen slightly to just over 70%.

As a group, Hispanic Americans historically have been intermediate between African Americans and whites in the

---

[1]One of the Hispanic members of Congress is also of Asian descent and one is also of African descent. This number includes the nonvoting member from Puerto Rico.

FIGURE 8.17 Median Household Incomes for Non-Hispanic White and All Hispanic Households, 1972–2015

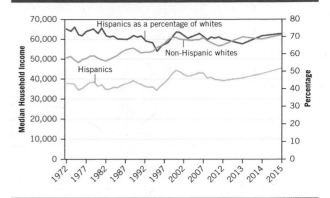

SOURCE: U.S. Census Bureau. 2016. "Race and Hispanic Origins of Householder - Households by Median and Mean Income Table H-5," http://www.census.gov/hhes/www/income/data/historical/household/index.html.

stratification system; this is reflected by the fact that the Hispanic–white income gap is smaller than the black–white income gap (which was 62% in 2015; see Figure 6.12). This smaller gap also reflects the more favorable economic circumstances of Hispanics (especially those more "racially" similar to the dominant group) who have been in the United States for generations and are thoroughly integrated into the mainstream economy.

Figure 8.18 shows that there is a good deal of income variability from group to group but that Hispanic Americans in general and all subgroups have, on the average, dramatically lower median household incomes than do non-Hispanic whites, especially the groups with large numbers of recent immigrants who bring low levels of human capital.

Figure 8.19 supplements the information on median income by displaying the overall distribution of income for Hispanic Americans and non-Hispanic whites for 2015. Although Hispanic Americans can be found at all income levels, the figure shows a greater concentration (wider bars) of Hispanics in the lower-income categories and a lower concentration (narrower bars) in the income groups at the top of the figure. There is a noticeable concentration of both groups in the $50,000 to $125,000 categories, but the percentage of whites is greater (39% to 35%) in these income ranges. In the three highest income categories, the percentage of whites is double that of Hispanic Americans (20% to 10%).

Recent detailed income information is not available for the separate subgroups. However, we can assume that, although all groups have members in all income categories, Mexican Americans, Dominican Americans, and Puerto Ricans would be disproportionately represented in the lowest income categories. Cuban Americans—especially those who benefit from the enclave economy—are disproportionately represented in the higher income groups.

FIGURE 8.18 Median Household Income for Non-Hispanic Whites, All Hispanic Americans, and 10 Largest Hispanic Groups, 2015

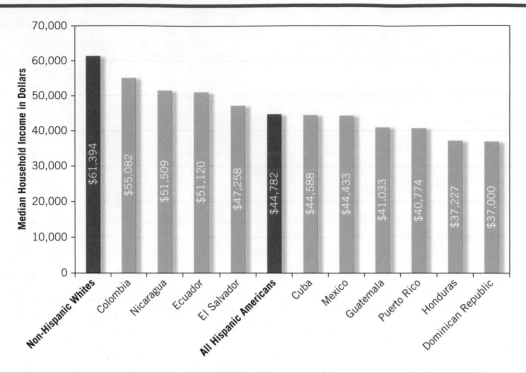

SOURCE: U.S. Census Bureau (2016). "Race and Hispanic Origins of Householder - Households by Median and Mean Income Table H-5," http://www.census.gov/hhes/www/income/data/historical/household/index.html.

Figure 8.20 finishes the socioeconomic profile for Hispanic Americans. It shows varying levels of poverty, a pattern that is consistent with the previous information on income and education. The poverty rate for all Hispanic families is more than three times the rate for non-Hispanic white families but lower than that of African Americans (see Figure 6.14). However, considerable diversity exists across the subgroups. The poverty rates for Colombians, Nicaraguans, and Cubans is closest to that of non-Hispanic whites; Dominicans and Hondurans are the most

FIGURE 8.19 Distribution of Household Income for Non-Hispanic Whites and Hispanic Americans, 2015

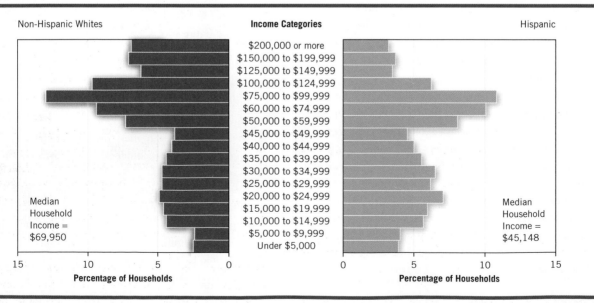

SOURCE: U.S. Census, 2015 American Community Survey, 1-Year Estimates, https://factfinder.census.gov/faces/tableservices/jsf/pages/productview.xhtml?pid=ACS_15_1YR_S0201&prodType=table.

FIGURE 8.20 Poverty Rates for Non-Hispanic Whites, All Hispanics, and 10 Largest Hispanic Groups, 2015

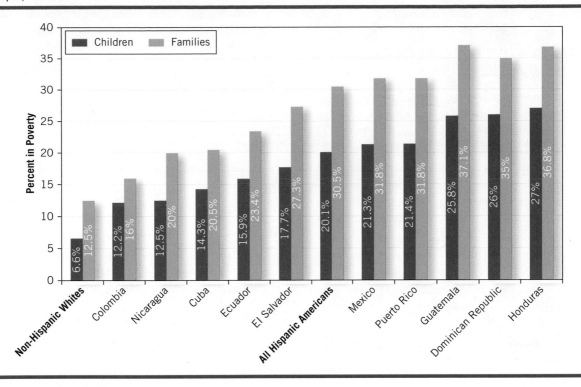

SOURCE: U.S. Census Bureau (2016).

NOTE: Family poverty rates and child poverty rates are computed using different units of analysis. Family rates represent the percentage of all families in the group that are below the poverty line while the rates for children are the percentage of all people younger than 18 in the group who live in poverty.

impoverished. For all groups, children have higher poverty rates than families. Recall that family poverty rates and child poverty rates are computed using different units of analysis.

These socioeconomic profiles reflect the economic diversity of Latinos. Some are "doing just fine," but others are concentrated in the low-wage sector of the economy. As a group, Cuban Americans rank higher than Mexican Americans and Puerto Ricans—the two other largest groups—on virtually all measures of wealth and prosperity. As we saw previously, this relative prosperity is even more pronounced for the earlier immigrants from Cuba and their children.

The income gap and the level of economic distress would be higher if we focused on recent immigrants, especially undocumented immigrants, who are concentrated in the informal economy. Employers frequently pay such workers less than minimum wage and "off the books." As discussed previously, recent immigrants typically live as frugally as possible to maximize the money they can send home, for example, by living 5 or even 10 people to a room. Because they tend to live "off the radar," they are less likely to be included in the data-gathering efforts that supply the information for the figures in this chapter. If they were included, the average wages for virtually all Latino groups would decrease and, thus, the rates of poverty would increase.

Gender and Inequality. As you've seen, the labor market is differentiated by race and ethnicity. It is also segmented by gender. Hispanic women—like minority group women in general—are among the lowest paid, least-protected, and, therefore, most-exploitable segments of the U.S. labor force. The impact of poverty is especially severe for Latino women because they often find themselves taking sole responsibility of caring for their children. In 2015, about 20% of all Hispanic American households were headed by women versus about 13% in the total population. This percentage ranged from a low of 15% for Cuban Americans to a high of about 33% for Dominicans (U.S. Census Bureau, 2016a). This pattern results from many factors, including Latino men's the status in the labor force. The jobs available to Latino men often do not pay enough to support a family because many jobs are seasonal, temporary, low wage, or otherwise insecure.

Women-headed LatinX families face a triple economic burden: They have only one wage earner whose potential income is limited by discrimination against both women and Latinos. These multiple disadvantages result in an especially high rate of poverty. Whereas 22% of non-Hispanic white, woman-headed households fall below the poverty line, it is almost double (38%) for Hispanic households headed by women (U.S. Census Bureau, 2016a).

Summary. The socioeconomic situation of Latinos is complex, diversified, and segmented. Many Latinos have successfully entered the mainstream economy, but others face poverty and exclusion. Highly concentrated in deteriorated urban areas, some people in these groups, like other minority groups of color, face the possibility of permanent poverty and economic marginality.

PRIMARY STRUCTURAL ASSIMILATION

Overall, the extent of intimate contact between Hispanic Americans and the dominant group probably has been higher than for either African Americans or American Indians (e.g., see Quillian & Campbell, 2003; Rosenfield, 2002). This pattern may reflect the fact that Latinos are partly ethnic minority groups and partly racial minority groups. Some studies report that contact is greater for the more affluent social classes, in the cities, and for the younger generations (who may be more "Americanized") (Fitzpatrick, 1976; Grebler et al., 1970, p. 397; Rodriguez, 1989, pp. 70–72). On the other hand, the extent of contact probably has been decreased by the rapid increase in immigration and the tendency of the first generation to socialize more with co-ethnics.

Rates of intermarriage are higher for Latinos than for African Americans, but neither is a very high percentage of all marriages. Black and white interracial couples make up less than 1% of all marriages, and the comparable figure for Latinos is 4% of all marriages (U.S. Census Bureau, 2012c, p. 54).

Table 8.6 shows that rates of in-marriage for Hispanics are lower than those for whites. This is partly a function of simple arithmetic: The larger group (white Americans) is more likely to find partners within the group. However, note that the rate of Latino in-marriage is also lower than that of blacks (see Table 6.1), a group of about the same size. This pattern may reflect the tenacity of racial (vs. ethnic) barriers to integration in this institutional area.

Also, note that nativity affects rates of in-marriage for Latinos. In both years, the foreign-born were more likely to marry within the group than were the U.S.-born. This pattern, like so many others, reflects the high rates of immigration and the tendency of recent immigrants to socialize within the ethnic subcommunity. For both years,

Hispanics who married outside their group were most likely to marry whites.

Finally, a 2017 study found that, for recently married couples, Hispanics were more likely to cross group boundaries (27%) than blacks (16%). However, the percentage of Hispanic newlyweds marrying across group lines was virtually the same as in 1980 (26%) while the percentage for black newlyweds had increased dramatically, from 5% to 18%. While these patterns and percentages varied by level of education, age, and urban versus rural residence, the overall trend seems to be toward more diversity and, as a result, an increasing percentage of "mixed-race" individuals (Livingston & Brown, 2017b).

QUESTIONS FOR REFLECTION

9. This section examined a variety of dimensions of acculturation and integration for Hispanic Americans. Which is most important? Why?

10. Which Hispanic groups have been more successful in U.S. society and why? Do you agree with the definitions of *success* used in this section? What other definitions might be useful, and how might these change your ideas about which group is most successful?

ASSIMILATION AND HISPANIC AMERICANS

As test cases for what we have called the traditional view of American assimilation, Latinos fare poorly. Almost two centuries after the original contact period, Mexican Americans tend to be concentrated in the low-wage sector of the labor market, a source of cheap labor for the dominant group's economy. Puerto Ricans, who are more recent arrivals, occupy a similar profile and position.

The fundamental reality faced by both groups, in their histories and in their present situations, is their colonized

TABLE 8.6 Percentage of Whites and Latinos Married to a Person of the Same Group, 1980 and 2008

| YEAR | WHITES | | LATINOS | | | |
| | | | Men | | Women | |
	Men	Women	Foreign-Born	U.S.-Born	Foreign-Born	U.S.-Born
1980	96%	95%	80%	67%	84%	70%
2008	93%	92%	83%	58%	83%	59%

SOURCE: Qian and Lichter (2011, p. 1072). Copyright © 2011 National Council on Family Relations. Reprinted with permission.

HISPANIC AMERICANS AND THE EVOLUTION OF THE AMERICAN RACIAL ORDER

The United States has, virtually since its birth, been organized into two communities: black and white, separate and unequal. This structural relationship has been reinforced and solidified by the traditional perception that there are *only* two races. What will happen to this tradition as groups that are neither black nor white—Latinos, Asian Americans, and others—continue to grow in numbers and significance in the everyday life of U.S. society?

One possibility, called the whitening thesis, hypothesizes that Latinos (and Asian Americans) eventually will be accepted as white, while African Americans remain relegated to the perpetual black (Vasquez, 2014). An opposing position, called the browning thesis, predicts that all "peoples of color" will band together and threaten the dominance of whites. We consider each of these views below, as well as a third possible future for the racial order of the United States.

WHITENING

In this model, Latinos and Asian Americans will become part of the white American racial group while African Americans will remain disproportionately unequal, powerless, and marginalized. The racial identities of Latinos and Asians will become "thinner," declining in salience for them as they increasingly access the privileges of whiteness, much like the Irish and Italians before them. As they assimilate, the "white" racial identity will grow more prominent and their sense of ethnicity will become largely symbolic.

This prediction is consistent with Gordon's assimilation model and the notion that immigrants move through a series of stages and become more incorporated into the dominant society in a relatively linear fashion. Once a group has completed acculturation, integration, and intermarriage, they will begin to racially identify with the dominant group.

George Yancey (2003) has tested the whitening thesis on a nationally representative data set, and his analysis places Latinos and Asian Americans in the middle stages of assimilation, because their residential patterns, marital patterns, and several key political beliefs align more closely with white Americans than they do with black Americans. If Gordon's model holds true, these groups will come to identify as white over the next several generations.

Another research project (Murguia & Foreman, 2003) focused on Mexican Americans and found that they tend to

This mural of people surrounding Our Lady of Guadalupe (the Virgin Mary) suggests the faith of many Mexican Americans. Note the references to the Chicano Movement and the Gallo wine boycott organized by the United Farm Workers.

status in U.S. society. Even while many Mexican Americans and Puerto Ricans have risen in the social class and occupational structure of the larger society, others share many problems with other urban minority groups of color.

Traditional views of the nature of assimilation, likewise, fail to describe the experiences of Cuban Americans. They are more prosperous, on the average, than either Mexican Americans or Puerto Ricans, but they became successful by remaining separate and developing an ethnic enclave in South Florida.

There is no single Hispanic American experience or pattern of adjustment to the larger society. We have focused mainly on three of the many LatinX groups in the United States, and the diversity of their experiences suggests the variety and complexity of what it means to be a minority group in U.S. society. Additionally, their experiences illustrate some of the fundamental forces that shape minority group experiences: the split labor market and the U.S. appetite for cheap labor, the impact of industrialization, the dangers of a permanent urban underclass, the relationships between competition and levels of prejudice and rejection, and the persistence of race as a primary dividing line between people and groups.

prefer spouses, neighbors, coworkers, and friends who are either Puerto Rican or white, not black. The researchers also found that Mexican Americans tend to endorse modern racism (see Chapter 3): the belief that racism is not much of a barrier to success and that people of color are largely responsible for their own hardships. This consistency with the ideology of the dominant group also positions Mexican Americans on the path to whiteness.

Finally, note that an important part of the whitening process is to distance oneself from the perpetually stigmatized black group. To the extent that a whitening process occurs for Latino and Asian Americans, these groups will tend to use both traditional and modern antiblack racism to emphasize their differences and align themselves more with the attitudinal and cultural perspectives of the dominant group. We discussed this type of dynamic in our coverage of the racial identity of Puerto Ricans who come to the mainland.

BROWNING

The browning thesis argues that whites will gradually lose their dominant status as Latino and Asian American groups grow in numbers. The balance of power will tip toward the nonwhite groups, who will use their greater numbers to challenge whites for position in the society.

Some theorists see the loss of white dominance as very negative, a threat to the integrity of Anglo-American culture. This version of the browning thesis has been presented by political scientist Samuel Huntington (2004), among many others (see the Current Debate at the end of this chapter). Some proponents of this perspective argue that Latinos are "unassimilable" due to their alleged unwillingness to learn English and absorb other aspects of U.S. culture, a view based largely on nativism, ethnocentrism, and prejudice, and refuted by much of the evidence presented in this chapter (e.g., see Figures 8.10 and 8.11). Nevertheless, this version of the browning thesis has gained momentum in popular culture and on some talk radio and cable TV shows. It also manifests itself in the political arena in debates over immigration policy and in the movement to make English the "official" language of the nation (see Chapter 2).

Some sociologists offer a different version of the browning thesis. For example, Feagin and O'Brien (2004) put a positive spin on the declining white numerical majority. They believe that as nonwhite groups grow in size, whites will be forced to share power in a more democratic, egalitarian, and inclusive fashion. This shift will be more likely if minority groups can forge alliances with one another as suggested by studies of generational differences in immigrants' racial attitudes. Specifically, this research suggests that native-born or second-generation Latinos and Asian Americans express more solidarity with African Americans than foreign-born and recently arrived

members of their group (Murguia & Foreman, 2003). In contrast to the whitening thesis, this view of the browning thesis expects Latinos and Asian Americans to embrace a more color-conscious worldview and find ways to leverage their growing numbers, in alliance with African Americans, to improve their status in American society.

This version of the browning thesis also adopts a more global perspective. It recognizes that the world is occupied by many more "people of color" than by whites of European descent and that the growing numbers of non-whites in the United States can be an important resource in the global marketplace. For example, people around the world commonly speak several languages. Because most Americans are monolingual they are at a disadvantage in a global marketplace. The United States might improve its position if it encourages the "fluent bilingualism" of its Latino, Asian American, and other citizens, rather than insisting on "English only" (see Chapter 2).

SOMETHING ELSE?

Another group of scholars challenges the browning and the whitening theses and foresees a three-way racial dynamic. These scholars focus on the tremendous diversity within the LatinX and Asian American communities in the United States in terms of relative wealth, skin color and other "racial" characteristics, religion, and national origins. This diversity leads them to conclude that only some Latino and Asian Americans will "whiten."

For example, Eduardo Bonilla-Silva (2003) sketches out a future racial trichotomy: whites, honorary whites, and the collective black. In this schema, well-off and light-skinned Latinos and Asians would not "become white" but would occupy an intermediary status as "honorary whites." This status would afford them much of the privilege and esteem not widely accorded to people of color, but it would still be a conditional status, which potentially could be revoked in times of economic crisis or at any other time when those in power found it necessary. Bonilla-Silva predicts that groups such as Chinese Americans and lighter-skinned Latinos would fit into the honorary white category, while darker-skinned Latinos and Asians would fit into the collective black category, along with, of course, African Americans.

Murguia and Foreman's (2003) study of Mexican Americans illustrates this process. They point out that skin color and educational levels make a difference in whether or not Latinos ally with African Americans. Mexican Americans with darker skin and higher educational levels and those born in the United States are less likely to hold the antiblack stereotypes of the larger culture and are more likely to recognize the racism in their own lives. Such attitudes and awareness may form the basis of future alliances between some Latinos, Asian Americans, and African Americans.

7. Describe the situation of the major Hispanic American groups in terms of acculturation and integration. Which groups are closest to equality? What factors or experiences might account for the differences between groups? In what ways might the statement "Hispanic Americans are remaining pluralistic even while they assimilate" be true?

STUDENT STUDY SITE

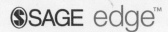

Sharpen your skills with SAGE edge at edge.sagepub.com/healey8e

SAGE edge for students provides a personalized approach to help you accomplish your coursework goals in an easy-to-use learning environment.

The following resources are available at SAGE edge:

Current Debates: Are Hispanic Americans Assimilating, or Are They Changing American Culture?

Will Hispanic immigrants—especially those from Mexico—ultimately adapt to American culture? Or will they transform the fundamental values of U.S. society? Is American society being "Hispanicized"?
On our website you will find an overview of the topic, the clashing points of view, and some questions to consider as you analyze the material.

Public Sociology Assignments

Public Sociology Assignments provide opportunities for students to address directly and personally some of the issues raised in this text.

There are two assignments for Part III on our website. The first looks at patterns of self-segregation in school cafeterias, and, in the second, students analyze the portrayal of the American family on television in terms of race, ethnicity, sexual orientation, and other sociologically relevant characteristics.

Contributed by Linda M. Waldron

Internet Research Project

For this Internet Research Project, you will use data gathered by the U.S. Census Bureau to assess the situation of all Hispanic Americans and a Latino group of your choosing. You will add this information to the data you gathered previously on African Americans, Native Americans, and the general population. The project will be guided by a series of questions related to course concepts, and your instructor may ask you to discuss your findings in small groups.

For Further Reading

Please see our website for an annotated list of important works related to this chapter.

CHAPTER-OPENING TIMELINE PHOTO CREDITS

1910: Library of Congress Prints and Photographs Division

1942: Los Angeles Times Photographic Archive/Wikimedia Commons

1943: Anthony Porter Collection / Hulton Archive / Getty Images

1965: Department of Labor

2001: Reuters/Jeff Topping

2007: ©iStockphoto.com/rrodrickbeiler

2009: Collection of the Supreme Court of the United States/ Steve Petteway

2010: ©iStockphoto.com/jcamilobernal

ASIAN AMERICANS

Model Minorities?

9

Wikimedia

LOC

1760 1850 1865 1880 1895 1910 1925

timeline

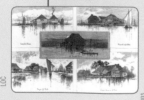

LOC

Wikimedia Commons

I had flown from San Francisco . . . and was riding a taxi to my hotel to attend a conference on multiculturalism. My driver and I chatted about the weather and the tourists. . . . The rearview mirror reflected a white man in his forties. "How long have you been in this country?" he asked. "All my life," I replied, wincing. "I was born in the United States." With a strong Southern drawl, he remarked: "I was wondering because your English is excellent!" . . . I explained: "My grandfather came here from Japan in the 1880s. My family has been here for over a hundred years." He glanced at me in the mirror. Somehow, I did not look "American" to him; my eyes and complexion looked foreign.

—Ronald Takaki (1993, p. 2), professor
of Asian American studies

LEARNING OBJECTIVES

By the end of this chapter, you will be able to do the following:

9.1 Understand the population characteristics of the 10 largest Asian American groups.

9.2 Explain the history of Chinese and Japanese Americans, including their cultural characteristics, their immigration patterns, their development in the United States, and the nature and importance of each enclave.

9.3 Explain the patterns of the recent immigration from Asia.

9.4 Understand how prejudice and discrimination affected Asian Americans in the past and today.

9.5 Apply the concepts of assimilation and pluralism to explain the contemporary situation of Asian Americans, especially

a. acculturation,

b. secondary structural assimilation, and

c. primary structural assimilation.

9.6 Assess the overall situation of Asian Americans today based on the concepts and information presented in this chapter, and assess the idea that Asian Americans are a "model minority." Are Asian Americans "whitening," "blackening," or becoming "honorary whites"?

1942
Approximately 110,000 Japanese Americans are sent to internment camps during World War II.

2001
Hate crimes against Arab and Asian Americans follow the September 11 terrorist attacks.

2016
Asian American actors and others protest "white washing" and fight for greater and less-stereotypical media representation.

| 1940 | 1955 | 1970 | 1985 | 2000 | 2015 | 2020 |

1943
Congress repeals Chinese Exclusion Act and grants naturalization rights.

1988
The Civil Liberties Act of 1988 pays surviving Japanese-American internees $20,000 each.

2012
Asians surpass Hispanics as the largest group of new immigrants in the U.S.

2016
Asian Americans strengthen political activism, for example, in fighting for immigrant rights.

These few seconds of Takaki's conversation speak deeply to U.S. perceptions of Asian Americans (and other minority groups). The taxi driver probably meant no insult, but his casual question revealed his view, widely shared, that the United States is a white European society. At the time of the conversation, Professor Takaki was a distinguished professor at a prestigious West Coast university and an internationally renowned expert in his area. Very possibly, his family had been in the United States longer than the taxi driver's family, yet the driver automatically assumed he was an outsider. •

Asian Americans, like other peoples of color, continually find themselves set apart, excluded, and stigmatized—whether during the 19th-century anti-Chinese campaign in California, after the 1922 Supreme Court decision (*Takao Ozawa v. United States*) that declared Asians ineligible for U.S. citizenship, or by the racist reactions to the crowning of Nina Davulari, an American of Indian descent, as Miss America in September 2013 (Oldenburg, 2013). The stereotypes are sometimes "positive"—as in the view that Asian Americans are "model minorities"—but the "othering" is real, painful, and consequential (Wu, 2015).

In this chapter, we begin with an overview of Asian American groups and then briefly examine the traditions and customs they bring with them to America. For much of the chapter, we will focus on the two oldest groups, Chinese Americans and Japanese Americans. Throughout, we will be especially concerned with people's perception that Asian Americans in general and Chinese and Japanese Americans, in particular, are "model minorities": successful, affluent, highly educated people who do not suffer from the problems usually associated with minority-group status. How accurate is this view? Have Asian Americans forged a pathway to upward mobility that could be followed by other groups? Do the concepts and theories that have guided our discussion so far (particularly the Blauner and Noel hypotheses) apply? Does the relative success of these groups mean that the United States is an open, fair, and just society and that challenges other minority groups face are the result of individual choices or abilities?

At least 30 different Asian American ethnic groups exist in the United States (Census, 2010) and they vary in their cultural and physical characteristics, and in their experiences in the United States. Some of these groups are relative newcomers, but others have roots in this country stretching back more than 200 years. As was the case with Native Americans and Hispanic Americans, "Asian American" is a convenient label imposed by the larger society (and by

TABLE 9.1 Size and Growth of Asian Americans* and 10 Largest Asian American Groups, by Origin, 1990–2012

GROUP	1990	2000	2015	GROWTH (NUMBER OF TIMES LARGER), 1990–2015	PERCENT OF TOTAL POPULATION, 2015
Total Asian American	6,908,638	11,070,913	20,416,808	3.0	6.5%
China	1,645,472	2,879,636	4,947,968	3.0	1.6%
India	815,447	1,899,599	3,982,398	4.9	1.3%
Philippines	1,406,770	2,364,815	3,898,739	2.8	1.2%
Vietnam	614,547	1,223,736	1,980,344	3.2	<1%
Korea	798,849	1,228,427	1,822,213	2.3	<1%
Japan	847,562	1,148,932	1,411,188	1.7	<1%
Pakistan	N/A	204,309	518,769	—	<1%
Cambodia	147,411	206,052	330,259	2.2	<1%
Hmong#	90,082	186,310	299,191	3.3	<1%
Laos	149,014	198,203	271,421	1.8	<1%
Percent of U.S. Population	2.8%	3.9%	6.5%	2.3	
Total U.S. Population	248,710,000	281,422,000	316,515,021	1.3	

SOURCES: 1990—U.S. Census Bureau (1990); 2000—U.S. Census Bureau (2000b); 2015 U.S. Census Bureau, 2015 American Community Survey, 5-Year Estimates.

* Asian Americans, alone and in combination with other groups.

The Hmong are from various Southeast Asian nations, including Laos, Vietnam, and Thailand.

government agencies such as the U.S. Census Bureau) that deemphasizes the differences between the groups. Table 9.1 lists some information about size and growth rates for the 10 largest Asian American groups. Figure 9.1 provides a snapshot of each group's size.

Several features of Table 9.1 are worth noting. First, Asian Americans are a small fraction of the total U.S. population. Even when combined, they account for only 6.5% of the total U.S. population. In contrast, African Americans and Hispanic Americans constitute 13% and 16%, respectively (Brown, 2014).

Second, most Asian American groups have grown dramatically since 1965 because of high rates of immigration due to changes in U.S. immigration policy. In 2015, 59% of Asian Americans were born outside of the United States (see Figure 9.2).

All the groups listed in Table 9.1 grew faster than the total population between 1990 and 2015. Japanese Americans grew at the slowest rate (largely because immigration from Japan has been low in recent decades), but the number of Asian Indians almost quintupled, and nearly all the other groups doubled or tripled their populations.

This rapid growth is projected to continue for decades to come, and the impact of the Asian American population on everyday life and American culture will increase accordingly. As you saw in Figure 1.1, by midcentury, 1 out of every 10 Americans will likely be of Asian descent. If projections hold, by 2065 they will be 14% of the population, more than twice their relative size today. No group will be a majority of the population: Non-Hispanic whites will be 46% of the population, Hispanics will be 24%, and African Americans will be 12% (Cohn, 2015).

Like Hispanic Americans, most Asian American groups have a high percentage of foreign-born members, as displayed in Figure 9.2, and even Japanese Americans, the lowest-ranked group, has almost double the national norm for foreign-born members. The vast majority of Asian Americans (88%) are either immigrants or their second-generation children (Pew Research Center, 2013c, p. 23).

We pointed out in Chapter 8 that most Hispanic Americans identify themselves in terms of their family's country of origin, and the same is true of Asian Americans. According to a recent survey, about 62% describe themselves in terms of their country of origin (e.g., "Chinese American"), about 20% describe themselves as "Asian American," and 14% describe themselves as just "American." There are large differences in self-description by nativity: Almost 70% of the foreign-born (vs. 43% of the native-born) describe themselves in terms of their country of origin (Pew Research Center, 2013c, pp. 88–89).

ORIGINS AND CULTURES

Asian cultures predate the founding of the United States by thousands of years and each has their own history. They vary politically, economically, and culturally. Their members speak many different languages and practice diverse religions including Buddhism, Confucianism, Islam, Hinduism, and Christianity. Asian American immigrants bring this diversity to the United States. Although no two

FIGURE 9.1 Asian American Groups in the United States by Countries of Origin, 2015

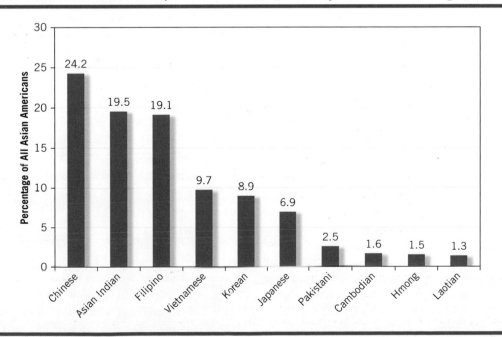

SOURCE: U.S Census Bureau, 2017. American Community Survey, 2015, One-Year Estimates.

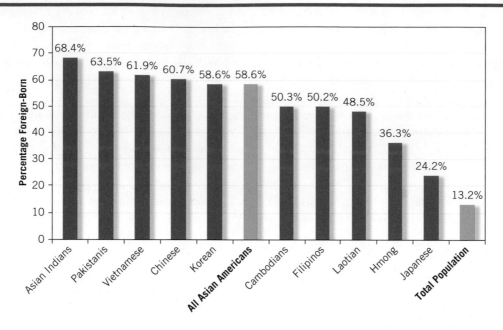

SOURCE: U.S Census Bureau, 2017. American Community Survey, 2015, 1-Year Estimates.

cultures are the same, they share some general similarities. These cultural traits have shaped Asian American behavior and dominant-group members' perceptions. Thus, these cultural characteristics are foundational to Asian American experiences in this country.

Asian cultures tend to stress group membership over individual self-interest. For example, Confucianism, which was the dominant ethical and moral system in traditional China and had a powerful influence on many other Asian cultures, counsels people to see themselves as elements in larger social systems and status hierarchies. Collectivist values and norms include loyalty to the group, conformity to societal expectations, living with kin, sharing property collectively, and respecting one's superiors. These contrast with the individualist values that dominate Western society and include individual rights (including property rights), individual achievement, and independent living (Leake & Black, 2005).

In traditional China, as in other Asian societies, the business of everyday life was organized around kinship relations, and most interpersonal relations were with family members and other relatives (Lyman, 1974, p. 9). The family or the clan often owned the land on which all depended for survival, and kinship ties determined inheritance patterns. The clan also performed a number of crucial social functions, including arranging marriages, settling disputes between individuals, and organizing festivals and holidays.

Asian cultures stress sensitivity to the opinions and judgments of others and the importance of avoiding public embarrassment and not giving offense. Especially when discussing Japanese culture, these cultural tendencies are often contrasted with Western practices in terms of "guilt versus shame" and the nature of personal morality (Benedict, 1946). In Western cultures, individuals are encouraged to develop and abide by a conscience, or an inner moral voice, and behavior is guided by one's personal sense of guilt.

In contrast, Asian cultures stress the importance of maintaining the respect and good opinion of others and avoiding shame and public humiliation. Group harmony, or *wa* in Japanese, is a central concern, and displays of individualism are discouraged. These characteristics are reflected in the Japanese proverb, "The nail that sticks up must be hammered down" (Whiting, 1990, p. 70). Asian cultures emphasize proper behavior, conformity to convention and the judgments of others, and avoiding embarrassment and personal confrontations ("saving face").

A manifestation of this tendency to seek harmony and avoid confrontation was documented by Chou and Feagin (2008) in interviews with Asian Americans from a variety of groups. They found that their subjects commonly used "compliant conformity" to cope with white racism, discrimination, and rejection (p. 222). Their respondents often expressed the belief that their conformity and hard work would bring recognition and acceptance from the larger society. The parents of the respondents, even those who had experienced substantial discrimination, commonly pressured their children to conform to white expectations and Anglo values in the hope that their success

The Japanese American Citizens League is one of the most significant Asian American civil rights organization in the United States. Part of its mission is to protect Asian Americans (and Pacific Islanders) from prejudice and discrimination. In 2009, it produced *Myths and Mirrors: Real Challenges Facing Asian American Students* to help educate the non–Asian American population about cultural differences and similarities between the two groups. This Applying Concepts activity is inspired by that publication.

Below is a series of statements you might hear on a college campus. Although any of them might be spoken by a student of any background, which do you think are more likely to be said by an Asian American student? Which are more reflective of Anglo culture? Consider what you learned about collectivist versus individualist cultures earlier in the chapter.

STATEMENT	ASIAN	ANGLO
"I really love the social life on this campus—I really enjoy chatting with all different kinds of people, making small talk, and trading gossip."		
"It's really important to show respect to our professors and the college administrators."		
"I was so proud to be recognized in front of the whole class for my research project."		
"I don't like to talk in class when I am directly called on."		
"I don't think that people should bottle their emotions—let it all hang out!"		
"I wouldn't dream of moving away from my family right after graduation. I have obligations to fulfill."		

TURN THE PAGE TO FIND OUR ANSWERS.

(e.g., in school) would protect them from negative treatment and stereotyping. Chou and Feagin suggest that this strategy has had limited success (at best) and that, ultimately, it sustains white prejudicial values and the conventional racial hierarchy in U.S. society by complying with rather than challenging racism (p. 222).

Traditional Asian cultures were dominated by men, and women were in subordinate roles. A Chinese woman was expected to serve first her father, then her husband, and, if widowed, her eldest son. Confucianism decreed that women should observe the Four Virtues: chastity and obedience, shyness, a pleasing demeanor, and skill in the performance of domestic duties (Amott & Matthaei, 1991, p. 200). Women of high status in traditional China (around the 10th or 11th century) symbolized their subordination by binding their feet. This painful, crippling practice began in early childhood (usually between the ages of 4 and 10) and required girls to wrap their feet tightly to keep them artificially small. The bones in the arch were broken so that the toes could be bent under the foot, further decreasing the size of the foot. Bound feet were considered beautiful, but they were intended to prevent girls and women from "wandering away" from domestic and household duties (Jackson, 2000; Takaki, 1993, pp. 209–210) by immobilizing them.

The experiences of Asian Americans in the United States modified these patriarchal values and traditional traits. For the groups with longer histories in U.S. society, such as Chinese Americans and Japanese Americans, the effects of these values on individual personality may be slight, but for more recently arrived groups, the effects can be more powerful.

The cultural and religious differences among the Asian American groups also reflect the recent histories of each of the sending nations. For example, Vietnam was a Chinese colony for 1,000 years, but for much of the past century it was a French colony. Although China has heavily influenced Vietnamese culture, many Vietnamese are Catholic, resulting from the efforts of the French to convert them. Western nations also colonized the Philippines and India—the former by Spain and then the United States, and the latter by Great Britain. As a result, many Filipinos are Catholic, and many Asian Indian immigrants speak English and are familiar with Anglo culture.

These examples are the merest suggestion of the diversity between these groups. Additionally, we see tremendous diversity within these groups when we take other social statuses into account, for example, by gender, class, sexual orientation, and age. In fact, Asian Americans, who share little more than a slight physical resemblance and some broad cultural similarities, are much more diverse than Hispanic Americans, who are overwhelmingly Catholic and share a

answers to APPLYING CONCEPTS

STATEMENT	ASIAN	ANGLO
"I really love the social life on this campus—I really enjoy chatting with all different kinds of people, making small talk, and trading gossip."		X
Asian American values place less emphasis on spontaneity, sociability, and flexibility, and more on self-control and discipline.		
"It's really important to show respect to our professors and college administrators."	X	
Asian Americans are more likely to stress obedience to authority, while Anglos are more likely to stress questioning authority.		
"I was so proud to be recognized in front of everyone—the entire class—for my research project."		X
Asian American values prize humility, cooperation with others, and shared responsibility, not individual achievement.		
"I don't like to talk in class when I am directly called on."	X	
In Anglo culture, individual visibility is acceptable, even encouraged. Asian American culture places more value on the collective.		
"I don't think that people should bottle their emotions—let it all hang out!"		X
Anglo culture places more stress on "telling it like it is" and openly expressing all emotions.		
"I wouldn't dream of moving away from my family right after graduation. I have obligations to fulfill."	X	
Asian Americans are more likely to stress loyalty and responsibility to kin groups over individual desires.		

Some Points to Consider

1. Do Asian Americans and Anglo-American students behave differently because of their cultural differences? If so, to what degree and in what kinds of situations? Could differences in values and norms be problematic for Asian American students, for example, in classes where teachers grade students for their verbal contributions to class discussion?

2. How might other factors such as personality, age, or social class affect people's values and norms? How might time of residency in the United States influence the way one thinks, talks, and behaves? For example, how might it matter if an Asian American came from a family who had lived here since the 1800s versus someone who became a citizen in 2017?

3. More broadly, what kinds of issues might arise in situations where students must make contact across ethnic or racial lines, face racism, or desire to date someone from another group? How? Realizing that your personal experiences aren't scientific, have you observed situations where cultural differences are problematic? Or, do people work cooperatively to overcome them? Or, do those differences seem minimal or nonexistent? Explain. You might also consider other ethnic groups. For example, many Native American communities possess similar collectivist ideals.

NOTE: This exercise is largely based on Japanese American Citizens League (2009).

common language and a historical connection with Spain (Min, 1995, p. 25).

QUESTIONS FOR REFLECTION

1. What are some of the key differences between Asian and Anglo cultures? How have these differences shaped relations between the groups?

2. Given what you've learned so far, which group do you think is the most diverse: African Americans, Native Americans, Hispanic Americans, or Asian Americans? Explain. Does it make sense to discuss each of these groups as a single entity? Why or why not?

CONTACT SITUATIONS AND THE DEVELOPMENT OF THE CHINESE AMERICAN AND JAPANESE AMERICAN COMMUNITIES

The earliest Asian groups to arrive in substantial numbers were from China and Japan. Their contact situations not only shaped their own histories but also affected the present situation of all Asian Americans in many ways. As we will see, the contact situations for both Chinese Americans and Japanese Americans featured massive rejection and discrimination. Both groups adapted to the racism of the larger society by forming enclaves, a strategy that eventually produced some major benefits for their descendants.

CHINESE AMERICANS

Early Immigration and the Anti-Chinese Campaign. Immigrants from China to the United States began to arrive in the early 1800s and were generally motivated by the same kinds of social and economic forces that have inspired immigration everywhere for the past two centuries (or more). Rapid population growth and European colonization disrupted traditional social relations and "pushed" Chinese immigrants to leave their homeland (Chan, 1990; Lyman, 1974; Tsai, 1986). At the same time, these immigrants were "pulled" to the West Coast of the United States by the Gold Rush of 1849 and by other opportunities that arose as the West developed. More than 20,000 Chinese immigrants lived in California by 1852 and though they lived in relative harmony with whites, that began to change as economic conditions deteriorated.

The Noel hypothesis (see Chapter 4) offers a useful way to analyze the contact situation that developed between Chinese and Anglo-Americans in the mid-19th century. As you may recall, Noel argues that racial or ethnic stratification will result when a contact situation has three conditions: ethnocentrism, competition, and a differential in power. Once all three conditions were met on the West Coast, a vigorous campaign against the Chinese began, and the group was pushed into a subordinate, disadvantaged position. For example, in 1862, Congress passed what became known as the Anti-Coolie Act or the Chinese Police Act, which required Chinese immigrants to pay a hefty monthly tax for working in California (Odo, 2002;

Soennichsen, 2011, p. 121). By some estimates, the tax took up between 60% to 80% of their wages. Police impounded and auctioned the belongings of those who could not pay and employers were held liable after that (Odo, 2002).

Ethnocentrism based on racial and cultural differences was present from the beginning, but at first, competition for jobs between Chinese immigrants and native-born workers was muted by a robust, rapidly growing economy and an abundance of jobs. At first, politicians, newspaper editorial writers, and business leaders praised the Chinese for their industriousness and tirelessness (Tsai, 1986, p. 17). For example, Denis Kearney, head of the Workingman's Party (WP) labor organization, once suggested that white workers should strive to be "thrifty and industrious like the Chinese" (Soennichsen, 2011, p. 52). Before long, however, the economic boom slowed and the supply of jobs began to dry up. The Gold Rush petered out, and the transcontinental railroad, which thousands of Chinese workers had helped build, was completed in 1869. The migration of Anglo-Americans from the East continued, and competition for jobs and other resources increased. As the West Coast economy changed, whites began to see the Chinese as a threat and they began to wonder about "the Chinese question" (see image on p. 320).

The Chinese were a small group—there were only about 100,000 in the entire country in 1870—and by law, they were not permitted to become citizens. Hence, they controlled few power resources with which to withstand these attacks. During the 1870s, whites limited their competition and forced Chinese workers out of most sectors of the mainstream economy. Yet, hostilities lingered and an anti-Chinese campaign of harassment, discrimination, and violent attacks began. In Los Angeles, for example, a mob of "several hundred whites shot, hanged, and stabbed 19 Chinese to death" in what is now called the 1871 Chinese Massacre (Tsai, 1986, p. 67). Other attacks against the Chinese occurred in Denver, Seattle, Tacoma, and Rock Springs, Wyoming (Lyman, 1974, p. 77).

"Chinese Coolies Crossing the Missouri River," by Leavitt Burnham shows Chinese men walking across the frozen river into Texas where they would be employed to build a railroad.

Rock Spring Massacre, one of many violent attacks against the Chinese in the 1870s.

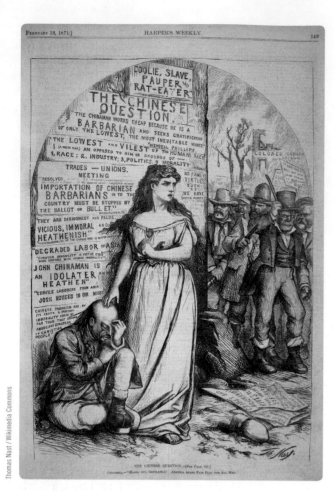

"The Chinese Question" (February 1871) by Thomas Nast.

China . . . rakes the slums of Asia to find the meanest slave on earth—the Chinese coolie—and imports him here to meet the free American in the Labor market, and still further widen the breach between the rich and the poor, still further to degrade white Labor. These cheap slaves fill every place. Their dress is scant and cheap. Their food is rice from China. They hedge twenty in a room, ten by ten . . . They are imported by companies, controlled as serfs, worked like slaves, and at last go back to China with all their earnings . . . Do not believe those who call us savages, rioters, incendiaries, and outlaws. We seek our ends calmly, rationally, at the ballot box . . . But, we know how false, how inhuman, our adversaries are . . . we have resolved that they shall not defeat us. We shall arm. We shall meet fraud and falsehood with defiance, and force with force, if need be. We are men, and propose to live like men in this free land, without the contamination of slave labor, or die like men, if need be, in asserting the rights of our race, our country, and our families. (Kearney, 1978)

In 1882, the anti-Chinese campaign experienced its ultimate triumph when the U.S. Congress passed the **Chinese Exclusion Act**, banning virtually all immigration from China. The act was one of the first restrictive immigration laws and was aimed solely at the Chinese. It established a rigid competitive relationship between the groups (see Chapter 5) and eliminated the threat presented by Chinese labor by excluding the Chinese from American society.

The **Chinese Exclusion Act**, passed by the U.S. Congress in 1882, banned virtually all immigration from China.

On the transcontinental railroad, as many as 9 out of 10 workers were Chinese. These indentured laborers, derogatorily called "coolies," became a prime target for criticism in the mid-19th century.

Kearney fanned these resentments by continuing to speak of Chinese men as "cheap working slave[s]" who created unfair competition for jobs. Part of his claims were true. Companies took advantage of the fact that it was legal to pay the Chinese workers less than white workers. Saxton (1966) estimates companies saved about 33% by hiring Chinese workers instead of native-born whites. Between 10,000 and 15,000 Chinese men helped build the transcontinental railway and although some eventually earned pay comparable to white men they often worked unpaid overtime. They also had to pay the company for rent, food, and tools—items that employers gave their white workers (Chinese Railroad Workers, n.d.). Despite discrimination against the Chinese, the Workingman's Party framed the Chinese as the problem rather than blaming the companies that profited from it. The Workingman's Party adopted "The Chinese must go!" as their motto and Kearney would say it at the end of every speech. Additionally, he subtly threatened company owners to beware of "Judge Lynch" if they didn't fire thousands of Chinese workers (Kearney, 1877 c.f. Pfaelzer, 2008, pp. 77–78).

In Kearney's view, the government was run by "money men" who didn't care about the "poor [white, man] Laborer" (Kearney, 1978). Thus, he believed that white workers should take matters into their own hands. He said:

The floating clouds, the fog, darken the sky.
The moon shines faintly as the insects chirp.
Grief and bitterness entwined are heaven sent.
The sad person sits alone, leaning by a window.
America has power, but not justice.

In prison, we were victimized as if we were guilty.
Given no opportunity to explain, it was really brutal.
I bow my head in reflection but there is nothing I can do.

—Poetry written on the walls of the Angel Island Immigration
Station by a detained immigrant

Consistent with the predictions of split labor market theory (see Chapter 3), the primary antagonists of Chinese immigrants were native-born workers and organized labor forces. White owners of small businesses, feeling threatened by Chinese-owned businesses, also supported passage of the Chinese Exclusion Act (Boswell, 1986). Other social classes, such as the capitalists who owned larger factories, might actually have benefited from the continued supply of cheaper labor created by immigration from China. Conflicts such as the anti-Chinese campaign could be especially intense because they confounded racial and ethnic antagonisms with disputes between different social classes.

The ban on immigration from China remained in effect until World War II, when China was awarded a yearly quota of 105 immigrants in recognition of its wartime alliance with the United States. Large-scale immigration from China did not resume until federal policy was revised in the 1960s.

Wikimedia Commons

This 19th-century political cartoon, "Uncle Sam kicks out the Chinaman," refers to the Chinese Exclusion Act.

Population Trends and the "Delayed" Second Generation. Following the Chinese Exclusion Act, the number of Chinese in the United States actually declined (see Figure 9.3) as some immigrants passed away or returned to China and were not replaced by newcomers. The huge majority of Chinese immigrants in the 19th century had been young adult men, sojourners who intended to work hard, save money, and return to their home villages in China (Chan, 1990, p. 66). After 1882, it was difficult for anyone from China, men or women, to enter the United States, and the Chinese community in the United States remained dominated by men for many decades. At the end of the 19th century, for example, men outnumbered women by more than 25 to 1, and the gender ratio did not approach parity for decades (Wong, 1995, p. 64; see also Ling, 2000). The scarcity of Chinese women in the United States delayed the second generation (the first generation born in the United States). It wasn't until the 1920s, 80 years after immigration began, that as many as one third of all Chinese in the United States were native-born (Wong, 1995, p. 64).

The delayed second generation may have reinforced the exclusion of the Chinese American community, which began as a reaction to the overt discrimination of the dominant group (Chan, 1990, p. 66). The children of immigrants are usually much more acculturated, and their language facility and greater familiarity with the larger society often permit them to represent the group and speak for it more effectively. In the case of Chinese Americans (and other Asian groups), members of the second generation were citizens of the United States by birth, a status from which the immigrants were barred, and they had legal and political rights not available to their parents. Thus, the decades-long absence of a more Americanized, English-speaking generation increased the isolation of Chinese Americans.

The Ethnic Enclave. The Chinese became increasingly urbanized as the anti-Chinese campaign and rising racism took their toll. Forced out of towns and smaller cities, they settled in larger urban areas, especially San Francisco, which offered the safety of urban anonymity as well as

FIGURE 9.3 Population Growth for Chinese and Japanese Americans, 1850–2015

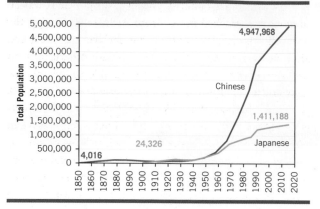

SOURCE: Hoeffel, Rastogi, Kim, and Shahid (2012, p. 4); Kitano (1980, p. 562); Lee (1998, p. 15), U.S. Bureau of the Census, 2017. American Community Survey, 2015.

ethnic neighborhoods where the old ways could be practiced and contact with Anglo society minimized. Chinatowns had existed since the start of the immigration, and they now took on added significance as safe havens from the storm of anti-Chinese venom. The Chinese withdrew to these neighborhoods and became an "invisible minority" (Tsai, 1986, p. 67).

These early Chinatowns were ethnic enclaves like those founded by Jews on the East Coast and the more recently founded Cuban community in Miami, and a similar process formed them. The earliest urban Chinese included merchants and skilled artisans who, like the early wave of Cuban immigrants, were experienced in commerce (Chan, 1990, p. 44). They established businesses and retail stores that were typically small in scope and modest in profits. As the number of urban Chinese increased, the market for these enterprises became larger and more spatially concentrated. New services were required, the size of the cheap labor pool available to Chinese merchants and entrepre-

neurs increased, and the Chinatowns became the economic, cultural, and social centers of the community.

Within the Chinatowns, elaborate social structures developed that mirrored traditional China in many ways. The enforced segregation of the Chinese in America helped preserve much of the traditional food, dress, language, values, and religions of their homeland from the pressures of Americanization. The social structure was based on a variety of types of organizations, including family and clan groups and huiguan, or associations based on the region or district in China from which the immigrants had come. These organizations performed various, often overlapping, social and welfare services, including settling disputes, aiding new arrivals from their regions, and facilitating the development of mutual aid networks (Lai, 1980, p. 221; Lyman, 1974, pp. 32–37, 116–118).

Life was not always peaceful in Chinatown, and there were numerous disputes over control of resources and the organizational infrastructure. In particular, secret societies called **tongs** contested the control and leadership of the merchant-led huiguan and the clan associations. These sometimes bloody conflicts were sensationalized in the American press as "Tong Wars," and they contributed to the popular stereotypes of Asians as exotic, mysterious, and dangerous (Lai, 1980, p. 222; Lyman, 1974, pp. 37–50).

Despite these internal conflicts, American Chinatowns evolved into highly organized, largely self-contained communities, complete with their own leadership and decision-making structures. The internal "city government" of Chinatown was the Chinese Consolidated Benevolent Association (CCBA). Dominated by the larger huiguan and clans, the CCBA coordinated and supplemented the activities of the various organizations and represented the interests of the community to the larger society.

The local CCBAs, along with other organizations, also attempted to combat the anti-Chinese campaign, speaking out against racial discrimination and filing numerous lawsuits to contest racist legislation (Lai, 1980, p. 223). The effectiveness of the protest efforts was handicapped by the lack of resources in the Chinese community and the fact that Chinese immigrants could not become citizens. Attempts were made to mobilize international pressure to protest the treatment of the Chinese in the United States. At the time, however, China was itself colonized and dominated by other nations (including the United States). The

Men in Chinatown, San Francisco, wearing traditional queues, or long, braided pigtails, 1895.

Huiguan were associations based on the region of China from which immigrants originated. They performed various social and welfare functions.

Tongs were secret societies in Chinatown that sometimes fought with each other and with other organizations for control of resources.

country was further weakened by internal turmoil and could mount no effective assistance for its citizens in the United States (Chan, 1990, p. 62).

Survival and Development. The Chinese American community survived despite the widespread poverty, discrimination, and pressures created by the unbalanced gender ratio. Members of the group began to seek opportunities in other regions, and Chinatowns appeared and grew in New York, Boston, Chicago, Philadelphia, and many other cities.

The patterns of exclusion and discrimination that began during the 19th-century anti-Chinese campaign were common throughout the nation and continued well into the 20th century. Chinese Americans responded by finding economic opportunity in areas where dominant group competition for jobs was weak, continuing their tendency to be an "invisible" minority group. Very often, they started small businesses that either served other members of their own group (e.g., restaurants) or relied on the patronage of the general public (e.g., laundries). The jobs these small businesses provided were the economic lifeblood of the community but were limited in the amount of income and wealth they could generate. Until recent decades, for example, most restaurants served primarily other Chinese, especially single men. Because their primary clientele was poor, the profit potential of these businesses was sharply limited. Laundries served the more affluent dominant group, but the returns from this enterprise declined as washers and dryers became increasingly common in homes throughout the nation. The population of Chinatown was generally too small to sustain more than these two primary commercial enterprises (Zhou, 1992, pp. 92–94).

As the decades passed, the enclave economy and the complex subsociety of Chinatown evolved. However, discrimination, combined with defensive self-segregation, ensured the continuation of poverty, limited job opportunities, and substandard housing. Relatively hidden from general view, Chinatown became the world in which the second generation grew into adulthood.

The Second Generation. The immigrant generation generally retained its native language and customs. However, the second generation was much more influenced by the larger culture. The institutional and organizational structures of Chinatown were created to serve the older (mostly men) immigrant generation. But younger Chinese Americans tended to look beyond the enclave to fill their needs. They came in contact with the larger society through schools, churches, and voluntary organizations such as the YMCA and YWCA.

This second generation of Chinese Americans abandoned many traditional customs and were less interested in the clan and regional associations that the immigrant generation had constructed. They founded organizations of their own that were more compatible with their Americanized lifestyles (Lai, 1980, p. 225).

As with other minority groups, World War II was an important watershed for Chinese Americans. During the war, job opportunities outside the enclave increased, and after the war, many of the 8,000 Chinese Americans who had served in the armed forces were able to take advantage of the GI Bill to further their education (Lai, 1980, p. 226). Thus, in the 1940s and 1950s, many second-generation Chinese Americans moved out of the enclave to pursue opportunities in the larger society. This group was mobile and "Americanized," and with educational credentials comparable to those of the general population, they were prepared to seek success outside Chinatown.

In another departure from tradition, second-generation Chinese women pursued education, also. As early as 1960, median years of schooling for Chinese American women were slightly higher than for Chinese American men (Kitano & Daniels, 1995, p. 48). Additionally, Chinese American women became more diverse in their occupational profile as the century progressed. In 1900, three quarters of all employed Chinese American women were employed doing domestic work or in manufacturing (usually in the garment industry or in canning factories). By 1960, less than 2% were in domestic work, 32% were in clerical occupations, and 18% held professional jobs, often as teachers (Amott & Matthaei, 1991, pp. 209–211).

The men and women of the second generation achieved considerable educational and occupational success, and helped establish the idea that Chinese Americans are a "model minority." A closer examination reveals, however, that the old traditions of anti-Chinese discrimination and prejudice continued to limit the life chances of even the best-educated members of this generation. Second-generation Chinese Americans earned less, on the average, and had less-favorable occupational profiles than did comparably educated white Americans, a gap between qualifications and rewards that reflects persistent discrimination. Kitano and Daniels (1995) conclude, for example, that although well-educated Chinese Americans could find good jobs in the mainstream economy, the highest, most lucrative positions—and those that required direct supervision of whites—were still closed to them (p. 50; see also Hirschman & Wong, 1984).

Furthermore, many Chinese Americans, including many of those who stayed in the Chinatowns to operate the enclave economy and the immigrants who began arriving after 1965, do not fit the image of success at all. A large percentage of these Chinese Americans face many of the same problems as do members of colonized, excluded, exploited minority groups of color. For survival, they rely on low-wage jobs in the garment industry, the service sector, and the small businesses of the enclave economy, and they are beset by poverty and powerlessness, much like the urban underclass segments of other groups.

Thus, Chinese Americans can be found at both ends of the spectrum of success and affluence, and the group is often said to be "bipolar" in its occupational structure (see Barringer, Takeuchi, & Levin, 1995; Min, 2006; Takaki, 1993, pp. 415–416; Wong, 1995, pp. 77–78; Zhou & Logan, 1989). Although a high percentage of Chinese Americans are found in more desirable occupations—sustaining the idea of Asian success—others, less visible, are concentrated at the lowest levels of society. Later in this chapter, we will again consider the socioeconomic status of Chinese Americans and the accuracy of the image of success and affluence.

JAPANESE AMERICANS

Immigration from Japan began to increase shortly after the Chinese Exclusion Act of 1882 took effect, in part, to fill the gap in the labor supply created by the restrictive legislation (Kitano, 1980). The 1880 Census counted only a few hundred Japanese in the United States, but the group increased rapidly over the next few decades. By 1910, the Japanese in the United States outnumbered the Chinese, and they remained the larger of the two groups until large-scale immigration resumed in the 1960s (see Figure 9.3).

The Anti-Japanese Campaign. The contact situation for Japanese immigrants resembled that of the Chinese. They immigrated to the same West Coast regions as the Chinese, entered the labor force in a similar position, and were a small group with few power resources. Predictably, the feelings and emotions generated by the anti-Chinese campaign transferred to them. By the early 1900s, an anti-Japanese campaign to limit competition was in full swing. Efforts were being made to establish a rigid competitive system of group relations and to exclude Japanese immigrants in the same way the Chinese had been barred (Kitano, 1980, p. 563; Kitano & Daniels, 1995, pp. 59–60; Petersen, 1971, pp. 30–55).

Japanese immigration was partly curtailed in 1907 when a "gentlemen's agreement" was signed between Japan and the United States limiting the number of laborers Japan would allow to emigrate (Kitano & Daniels, 1995, p. 59). This policy remained in effect until the United States changed its immigration policy in the 1920s and barred immigration from Japan completely. The end of Japanese immigration is largely responsible for the slow growth of the Japanese American population displayed in Figure 9.3.

Most Japanese immigrants, like the Chinese, were young men laborers who planned to return eventually to their homeland or bring their wives after they were established in their new country (Duleep, 1988, p. 24). The agreement of 1907 curtailed the immigration of men, but because of a loophole, women were able to continue immigrating until the 1920s. Thus, Japanese Americans were able to maintain a relatively balanced gender ratio, marry, and begin families, and a second generation of Japanese Americans began to appear without much delay. Native-born Japanese Americans numbered about half of the group by 1930 and were a majority of 63% on the eve of World War II (Kitano & Daniels, 1995, p. 59).

The anti-Japanese movement also attempted to dislodge the group from agriculture. Many Japanese immigrants were skilled agriculturists, and farming proved to be their most promising avenue for advancement (Kitano, 1980, p. 563). In 1910, between 30% and 40% of all Japanese in California were engaged in agriculture; from 1900 to 1909, the number of independent Japanese farmers increased from fewer than 50 to about 6,000 (Jibou, 1988, p. 358).

Most of these immigrant farmers owned small plots of land, and they made up only a minuscule percentage of West Coast farmers (Jibou, 1988, pp. 357–358). Nonetheless, their presence and relative success did not go unnoticed and eventually stimulated discriminatory legislation, most notably the **Alien Land Act**, passed by the California legislature in 1913 (Kitano, 1980, p. 563). This bill made aliens who were ineligible for citizenship (essentially only immigrants from Asia) also ineligible to own land. The legislation, however, did not achieve its goal of dislodging the Japanese from the rural economy. They were able to dodge the discriminatory legislation through various devices, mostly by putting land titles in the names of their American-born children, who were citizens by law (Jibou, 1988, p. 359).

A Japanese American unfurled this banner the day after the Pearl Harbor attack when many Americans began to question the "loyalty" of Japanese Americans, even those who had been here for many generations.

The **Alien Land Act**, passed by the California legislature in 1913, declared aliens ineligible for citizenship (meaning Asian immigrants) could not own land.

Big Little Man: In Search of My Asian Self

Photo courtesy of the University of Oregon School of Journalism and Communication

Alex Tizon

Alex Tizon was a Filipino-American who came to the U.S. with his family in 1964, prior to the first postwar wave of Asian immigration. His family struggled financially and moved a lot—and to diverse places such as Hawaii and New York City. He became an investigative journalist and was nominated for the 1990 Pulitzer for reporting on street subcultures, including youth gangs. His work (with Eric Nalder and Deborah Nelson) about corruption and mismanagement within the Federal Indian Housing Program earned him the 1997 Pulitzer Prize for investigative reporting. He taught in the School of Journalism and Communication at University of Oregon. Most recently, his article for The Atlantic, "My Family's Slave," received international attention. (See Chapter 4's Internet Research Project on Slavery.) It was the last thing he published before his death in 2017.

Much of Tizon's writing, both literary and journalistic, addresses issues of diversity. The following excerpt comes from his book, Little Big Man: In Search of My Asian Self. In it, he expands on these themes and gives us an opportunity to use an intersectional approach to understanding issues of gender, ethnicity, and class. Throughout the book Tizon shares his "struggle[s] as an Asian boy trying to figure how to be an Asian man," which he thought represented a collective experience shared by Asian American boys and men because they face "the deep-rooted Western notion,

perpetuated by entertainment media, that Asians are at the bottom of the food chain, the weakest, the smallest, the least masculine of men" (Tizon, 2016).

BECOMING AN AMERICAN MAN

Alex Tizon

At age four I was brought by my parents to America . . . It was hard work, becoming an American, and I felt I'd succeeded for the most part. Yet I was not "all-American." I could never be that. Most of us, when imagining an all-American, wouldn't picture a man who looked like me. Not even I would. You would have to take my word for it that more than a few times in my life I looked in a mirror and was startled by the person looking back. I could go a long time feeling blithely at home, until a single glance at my reflection would be like a slap on the back of the head. Hey! You are not of this land. Certainly during my growing-up years in America, many people, friends and strangers, intentionally and not, helped to embed in me like a hidden razor blade the awareness of being an outsider. I remember an encounter with a fellow student at JHS 79 in the Bronx, where my family lived in the 1970s. I was about thirteen. My school was just off the Grand Concourse on 181st, a five-story brick building with bars over all the windows and dark clanging stairwells that might as well have been back alleys. Some stairwells you did not dare travel alone, but I was new and didn't know better. One afternoon in one of these stairwells, an open hand with five impossibly long fingers fell hard against my chest and stopped me in my tracks.

"What you supposed to be, motherfukka?" the owner of the hand said.

"Wha?—??" I stammered.

"Are you deaf, boy? I said, What you supposed to be?" The owner of the hand was a tall black guy, Joe Webb,

who turned out to be the oldest and biggest member of my seventh-grade class, a man among boys. He was one of those guys whose muscles bulged like rocks sewn under skin, whose glare conveyed the promise of apocalyptic violence. "Are you a Chink, a Mehi-kan? What?"

Blacks, Puerto Ricans, and other Latinos made up the majority of students at the school. There were some whites and a handful of Chinese and Taiwanese. I was the only Filipino in the school, and a lot of students like Joe had never met one and knew nothing about the Philippines. I told him what I thought I was.

"You don't look American, bitch," he said. He eventually let me pass after I gave him the change from my pocket, which I would learn was really what he was after. Moving around the school meant paying certain tolls. Sweet scary Joe Webb. We ended up sitting next to each other in English, and he would copy off my test answers with my implicit consent. After he had found me acceptable six months into the school year, he became my friend and protector for the rest of my time at JHS 79. Sometime later that year, when another kid tried to shake me down in the very same stairwell, Joe loomed over him with those murderous eyes and long fingers rolled up into fists and the other kid melted into the darkness whence he came, never to bother me again.

Joe's original query was a question I've been asked in various, usually more tactful ways ever since I could remember. What you supposed to be? From where on this planet did you come? What are you? The person in the mirror was the color of coffee with two tablespoons of cream. The face was wide with hair so black it sometimes appeared blue. The eyes were brown and oval, the nose broad, the lips full.

Questions to Consider

1. When you hear "all-American," what thoughts or images come to mind? Make a quick list of them. What does an "all-American"

(Continued)

person look like (e.g., hair color, clothing)? What are their other qualities? What do they do for fun? What is their family like? Is there someone who exemplifies being "all-American"? When you're done with your list, add gender into the mix. For example, what comes to mind when you hear "all-American girl" or "all-American boy"? How does gender affect your ideas, if at all? What do you make of your answers? If you have an opportunity to share your answers with classmates, see if any patterns emerge.

2. Tizon writes, "I could never be that. Most of us, when imagining an all-American, wouldn't picture a man who looked like me. Not even I would." How does his comment relate to what you said in #1? Did you picture someone who looks like him (as described in his writing)? What does his comment suggest about the way people internalize societal messages about things like nationality/citizenship, gender, race/ethnicity, age, beauty, class, and so on?

3. How does this excerpt illustrate racialized stereotypes such as the "perpetual foreigner" discussed throughout this chapter?

4. In an interview, Tizon said, "As individuals, and as a society, we're always being asked: do we want to focus on the likenesses or the differences? We might be tempted to take one side and condemn the other. This is what mostly happens now. The messy answer, it might turn out, is that we should focus on our likenesses—except for those times when understanding our differences can be helpful in making our collective life better" (Tizon, 2016). What do you think of this statement? If you agree, how could you put that into practice? If you disagree, what approach might be more useful?

The Alien Land Act was one part of a sustained campaign against the Japanese in the United States. In the early decades of this century, the Japanese were politically disenfranchised and segregated from dominant group institutions in schools and residential areas. They were discriminated against in movie theaters, swimming pools, and other public facilities (Kitano & Daniels, 1988, p. 56). The Japanese were excluded from the mainstream economy and confined to a limited range of poorly paid occupations (see Yamato, 1994). Thus, there were strong elements of systematic discrimination, exclusion, and colonization in their overall relationship with the larger society.

The Ethnic Enclave. Spurned and disparaged by the larger society, the Japanese, like the Chinese, constructed a separate subsociety. The immigrant generation, called **Issei** (from the Japanese word *ichi*, meaning "one"), established an enclave in agriculture and related enterprises, a rural counterpart of the urban enclaves constructed by other groups we have examined.

By World War II, the Issei had come to dominate a narrow but important segment of agriculture on the West Coast, especially in California. Although the Issei were never more than 2% of the total population of California, Japanese American–owned farms produced as much as 30% to 40% of various fruits and vegetables grown in that state. As late as 1940, more than 40% of the Japanese American population was involved directly in farming, and many more were dependent on the economic activity stimulated by agriculture, including the marketing of their produce (Jibou, 1988, pp. 359–360). Other Issei lived in urban areas, where they were concentrated in a narrow range of businesses and services, such as domestic work and gardening,

some of which catered to other Issei and some of which served the dominant group (Jibou, 1988, p. 362).

Japanese Americans in both the rural and urban sectors maximized their economic clout by doing business with other Japanese-owned firms as often as possible. Gardeners and farmers purchased supplies at Japanese-owned firms, farmers used other members of the group to haul their produce to market, and businesspeople relied on one another and mutual credit associations, rather than dominant-group banks, for financial services. These networks helped the enclave economy to grow and also permitted the Japanese to avoid the hostility and racism of the larger society. However, these very same patterns helped sustain the stereotypes that depicted the Japanese as clannish and unassimilable. In the years before World War II, the Japanese American community was largely dependent for survival on their networks of cooperation and mutual assistance, not on Americanization and integration.

The Second Generation (Nisei). In the 1920s and 1930s, anti-Asian feelings continued to run high, and Japanese Americans continued to be excluded and discriminated against despite (or perhaps because of) their relative success. Unable to find acceptance in Anglo society, the second generation, called **Nisei**, established clubs, athletic leagues,

---

The **Issei** were first-generation immigrants from Japan.

The **Nisei** were second-generation Japanese Americans.

A map of World War II Japanese American detention camps. The "exclusion area" was the area from which the Japanese were barred by the presidential order of 1942.

churches, and a multitude of other social and recreational organizations within their own communities (Kitano & Daniels, 1995, p. 63). These organizations reflected the high levels of Americanization of the Nisei and expressed values and interests quite compatible with those of the dominant culture. For example, the most influential Nisei organization was the Japanese American Citizens League, whose creed expressed an ardent patriotism that was to be sorely tested: "I am proud that I am an American citizen.... I believe in [American] institutions, ideas, and traditions; I glory in her heritage; I boast of her history, I trust in her future" (Kitano & Daniels, 1995, p. 64).

Although the Nisei enjoyed high levels of success in school, the intense discrimination and racism of the 1930s prevented most of them from translating their educational achievements into better jobs and higher salaries. Many occupations in the mainstream economy were closed to even the best-educated Japanese Americans, and anti-Asian prejudice and discrimination did not diminish during the hard times and high unemployment of the Great Depression in the 1930s. Many Nisei were forced to remain within the enclave, and in many cases jobs in the produce stands and retail shops of their parents were all they could find. Their demoralization and anger over their exclusion were eventually swamped by the larger events of World War II.

The Detention Camps. On December 7, 1941, Japan attacked Pearl Harbor, killing almost 2,500 Americans. President Franklin D. Roosevelt asked Congress for a declaration of war the next day. The preparations for war stirred up a wide range of fears and anxieties among the American public, including concerns about the loyalty of Japanese Americans. Decades of exclusion and anti-Japanese prejudice had conditioned members of the dominant society to see Japanese Americans as sinister, clannish, cruel, unalterably foreign, and racially inferior. Fueled by the ferocity of the war itself and fears about a Japanese invasion of the mainland, the tradition of anti-Japanese racism laid the groundwork for a massive violation of civil rights.

Two months after the attack on Pearl Harbor, President Roosevelt signed Executive Order 9066, which led to the relocation of Japanese Americans living on the West Coast. By the late summer of 1942, more than 110,000 Japanese Americans, young and old, men and women—virtually the entire Japanese population from the West Coast—had been forcibly transported to **detention camps,** where they were

Japanese Americans were held at **detention camps** during World War II.

imprisoned behind barbed-wire fences patrolled by armed guards. The majority of these people were American citizens, yet the U.S. government made no attempt to distinguish between citizens and noncitizens. No trials were held, and no one was given the opportunity to refute the implicit charge of disloyalty. (The government forcibly relocated approximately 11,500 German American and 3,000 Italian American as well. Citing the need for hemispheric security, it also developed a deportation-internment that resulted in 2,000 Japanese Latin Americans being deported from Peru and Panama and held in camps in the United States. Others were sent from Mexico, Bolivia, Colombia, Nicaragua, Costa Rica, Cuba, Ecuador, Venezuela, and El Salvador [Mak, 2017].)

The U.S. government gave families little notice to prepare for removal and secure their homes, businesses, and belongings. They were allowed to bring only what they could carry and had to abandon many of their possessions. Businesspeople sold their establishments and farmers sold their land at panic-sale prices. Others locked up their stores and houses and walked away, hoping that the removal would be short-lived and their possessions undisturbed.

The detention lasted for nearly three and a half years, nearly the entire war. At first, Japanese Americans were not permitted to serve in the armed forces, but eventually more than 25,000 escaped the camps by volunteering for military service. Nearly all of them served in segregated units or in intelligence work with combat units in the Pacific Ocean. Two all-Japanese combat units served in Europe and became the most decorated units in American military history (Kitano, 1980, p. 567). Other Japanese Americans were able to get out of the camps by different means. Some, for example, agreed to move to militarily nonsensitive areas far away from the West Coast (and their former

homes). Still, about half the original internees remained when the camps closed at the end of the war (Kitano & Daniels, 1988, p. 64).

The strain of living in the camps affected Japanese Americans in a variety of ways. (The next Narrative Portrait summarizes the experiences of one Japanese American.) Lack of activities and privacy, overcrowding, boredom, and monotony were common complaints. The camps disrupted the traditional forms of family life, as people had to adapt to living in crowded barracks and dining in mess halls. Conflicts flared between people who counseled caution and temperate reactions to the incarceration and those who wanted to protest in more vigorous ways. Many of those who advised moderation were Nisei intent on proving their loyalty by cooperating with the camp administration.

Despite the injustice and dislocations of the incarceration, the camps did reduce the extent to which women were relegated to a subordinate role. Like Chinese women, Japanese women were expected to devote themselves to the care of the men of their family. In Japan, for example, education for women was not intended to challenge their intellect so much as to make them better wives and mothers. In the camps, however, pay for the few jobs available was the same for both men and women, and the mess halls and small living quarters freed women from some of the burden of housework. Many used this period of incarceration to take classes to learn more English and other skills. The younger women were able to meet young men on their own, weakening the tradition of family-controlled, arranged marriages (Amott & Matthaei, 1991, pp. 225–229).

Some Japanese Americans protested the incarceration from the start and brought lawsuits to end their forced relocation. Finally, in 1944 the Supreme Court ruled that detention was unconstitutional. As the camps closed, some Japanese American individuals and organizations sought compensation and redress for the economic losses the group had suffered. In 1948, Congress passed legislation to compensate Japanese Americans for lost wages and lost property. About 26,500 people filed claims and eventually settled for a total of about $38 million or about $1,434 per person (or about $14,565 in 2017)—much less than the actual economic losses for lost wages and property.

Demand for meaningful redress and compensation continued. In 1980, Congress began to study the impact of the camps and a 1982 report estimated total economic losses between $2.5 to $6.2 billion after adjusting for inflation. Further, it acknowledged that "the magnitude of the losses and injuries that come under the heading of 'pain and suffering' cannot be estimated objectively in an economic sense and we made no attempt to study them" (Pippert, 1983). In 1988, Congress passed a bill granting reparations of about $20,000 to each of the 60,000

Japanese Americans from Los Angeles, California, prepare to be taken to the Manzanar detention camp, approximately 250 miles away.

National Archives and Records Administration/Wikimedia Commons

NARRATIVE PORTRAIT

The Relocation

The barrack housing of the Manzanar detention camp. Dust from nearby dry lake beds "permeated . . . everything." It contained "heavy toxic minerals" that led to significant health problems including asthma and autoimmune diseases (Jensen, 2008).

Joseph Kurihara was born in Hawaii in 1895. He moved to California at age 20 and was a U.S. Army veteran (WWI). He completed college and became a businessman. He worked actively to promote acculturation and better relations with the larger society.

Like more than 10,000 other people, the government forced him to move to the Manzanar detention camp. Although he had never visited Japan and had no interest in or connection with his parents' birth country, his experiences in the camp were so terrible that he expatriated to Japan following the war.

WE WERE JUST JAPS

Joseph Kurihara

[The forced evacuation] . . . was really cruel and harsh. To pack and evacuate in 48 hours was an impossibility . . . Did the government of the United States intend to ignore [our] rights regardless of . . . citizenship? Those beautiful furnitures [*sic*] which the parents bought to please their sons and daughters, costing hundreds of dollars were robbed of them at the single command, "Evacuate!" . . . Having had absolute confidence in Democracy, I could not believe my very eyes what I had seen that day. America, the standard bearer of Democracy had committed the most heinous crime in its history. . . .

The desert [where Manzanar was located] was bad enough. The . . . barracks made it worse. The constant cyclonic storms loaded with sand and dust made it worst. After living in well-furnished homes with every modern convenience and suddenly forced to live the life of a dog is something which one cannot so readily forget. Down in our hearts we cried and cursed this government every time when we were showered with sand.

We slept in the dust; we breathed the dust; and we ate the dust. Such abominable existence one could not forget, no matter how much we tried to be patient, understand the situation, and take it bravely. Why did not the government permit us to remain where we were? Was it because the government was unable to give us protection? I have my doubt . . . It was because we were Japs! Yes, Japs!

After corralling us like a bunch of sheep . . . did the government treat us like citizens? No! We were treated like aliens regardless of our rights. Did the government think we were so without pride to work for $16.00 a month when people outside were paid $40.00 to $50.00 a week in the defense plants? . . .

My American friends . . . no doubt must have wondered why I renounced my citizenship. This decision . . . dates back to the day when General DeWitt ordered evacuation. It was confirmed when he flatly refused to listen even to the voices of the . . . veterans and it was doubly confirmed when I entered Manzanar. We . . . had proven our loyalty by serving in the last World War . . . The veterans asked for special consideration but their requests were denied . . . we were all alike. "A Jap's a Jap. Once a Jap, always a Jap." . . . I swore to become a Jap 100% and never to do another day's work to help this country fight this war. My decision to renounce my citizenship there and then was absolute.

SOURCE: Swaine and Nishimoto (1946).

Questions to Consider

1. Many Americans know little about Japanese American detention camps. Was this the case for you? What are possible consequences from not knowing this part of U.S. history? How is the general lack of education about the detention camps similar to or different from lack of education about other parts of history that you've learned about in this book (or elsewhere)?

2. What might it have been like to hear people say, "Japs must go!" and learn that you had 48 hours to store or sell your possessions? Could you sell everything that fast? What essentials would you take to the camp and why? If you have a family connection to the camps, what do you want classmates to know about it?

3. Manzanar housed more than 10,000 people in 504 barracks over 36 blocks . . . "surrounded by barbed wire and eight guard towers with searchlights and patrolled by military police." On each block, "200 to 400 people . . . shared men's and women's toilets and showers [. . . with no partitions; and showers with no stalls], a laundry room, and a mess hall." Eight people lived in " . . . a 20-by-25-foot room. An oil stove, a single hanging light bulb, cots, blankets, and mattresses filled with straw were the only furnishings provided" (National Park Service, 2015b). What practical, emotional, and other consequences would these conditions have on you, your family, and the community?

4. Some people have called for detention camps for American Muslims as a "preventative measure." Is this a reasonable, effective solution that could increase national security? If so, should we detain members of other groups that also have the potential to become radicalized or to harm the nation (e.g., white nationalists)? Explain. If you think this is a problematic plan, explain why.

5. Compare and contrast the forcible removal of Japanese Americans with that of Native Americans, with the legal segregation of black Africans under apartheid and African Americans under Jim Crow, and with the persecution of Jews, Roma, and gays under the Third Reich in Germany.

survivors and acknowledged the detention resulted from "racial prejudice, war hysteria and the failure of political leadership."

In 2004, The House of Representatives approved a National Day of Remembrance on February 19, the date Executive Order 9066 was signed. The Congressional Record notes that though national security should be the highest priority, we must "not again have a failure among our political leadership. We must not give in to war hysteria. We must not fall back to racial prejudice, discrimination and unlawful profiling. It is critical and important, more than ever, to speak up against possible unjust policies that may come before this body" (Congressional Record, 2007).

The World War II relocation devastated the Japanese American community and left it with few material resources. The emotional and psychological damage inflicted by this experience is incalculable. The fact that today, only seven decades later, the performance of Japanese Americans is equal or superior to national averages on measures of educational achievement, occupational prestige, and income is one of the more dramatic transformations in minority-group history.

Japanese Americans After World War II. In 1945, Japanese Americans faced a world very different from the one they had left in 1942. To escape the camps, nearly half the group had scattered throughout the country and lived everywhere but on the West Coast. As Japanese Americans attempted to move back to their former homes, they found their fields untended, their stores vandalized, their

Women work making military netting at the Manzanar detention camp.

possessions lost or stolen, and their lives shattered. In some cases, there was simply no Japanese neighborhood to return to; the Little Tokyo area of San Francisco, for example, was now inhabited by African Americans who had moved to the West Coast to take jobs in the defense industry (Amott & Matthaei, 1991, p. 231).

Japanese Americans themselves had changed as well. In the camps, the Issei had lost power to the Nisei. The English-speaking second generation had dealt with the camp administrators and held the leadership positions. Many Nisei had left the camps to serve in the armed forces or to find work in other areas of the country. For virtually every American minority group, the war brought new experiences and a broader sense of themselves, the nation, and the world. A similar transformation occurred for the Nisei. When the war ended, they were unwilling to rebuild the Japanese community as it had been before.

Like second-generation Chinese Americans, the Nisei had a strong record of success in school, and they also took advantage of the GI Bill to further their education. When anti-Asian prejudice began to decline in the 1950s and the job market began to open, the Nisei were educationally prepared to take advantage of the resultant opportunities (Kitano, 1980, p. 567).

The Issei-dominated enclave economy did not reappear after the war. One indicator of the shift away from an enclave economy was the fact that the percentage of Japanese American women in California who worked as unpaid family laborers (i.e., worked in family-run businesses for no salary) declined from 21% in 1940 to 7% in 1950 (Amott & Matthaei, 1991, p. 231). Also, between 1940 and 1990, the percentage of the group employed in agriculture declined from about 50% to 3%, and the percentage employed in personal services fell from 25% to 5% (Nishi, 1995, p. 116).

By 1960, Japanese Americans had an occupational profile very similar to that of whites except that they were actually overrepresented among professionals. Many were employed in the primary economy, not in the ethnic enclave, but there was a tendency to choose "safe" careers (e.g., in engineering, optometry, pharmacy, accounting) that did not require extensive contact with the public or supervision by whites (Kitano & Daniels, 1988, p. 70).

Within these limitations, the Nisei, their children (**Sansei**), and their grandchildren (**Yonsei**) have enjoyed relatively high status, and their upward mobility and prosperity have contributed to the perception that Asian Americans are a model minority group. An additional factor contributing to the high status of Japanese Americans

The **Sansei** and **Yonsei** are, respectively, third- and fourth-generation Japanese Americans.

Japan's "Invisible" Minority

As stated in Chapter 1, two of the most important characteristics of minority groups are that they: (1) are the objects of a pattern of disadvantage and (2) are easily identifiable, either culturally or physically. These two traits work in tandem: Members of the dominant group must be able to determine a person's group membership quickly and easily so the discrimination that is the hallmark of minority-group status can be practiced.

Visibility is such an obvious precondition for discrimination that it almost seems unnecessary to state it. However, every generalization seems to have an exception, and the members of at least one minority group, the Burakumin of Japan, have been victimized by discrimination and prejudice for hundreds of years but are virtually indistinguishable from the general population. How could such an "invisible" minority come into being? How could the disadvantaged status be maintained through time?

The Burakumin were created centuries ago, when Japan was organized into a caste system (see Chapter 4) based on occupation. The ancestors of today's Burakumin did work that brought them into contact with death (e.g., as gravediggers) or required them to handle meat products (e.g., as butchers). These occupations were regarded as very low in status, "unclean," or polluted.

The Burakumin were required to live in separate villages and to wear identifying leather patches (thus raising their social visibility). They were forbidden to marry outside their caste, and any member of the general population who touched a member of the Burakumin had to be ritually purified or cleansed of pollution (Lamont-Brown, 1993, p. 137).

The caste system was officially abolished in the 19th century, at about the time Japan began to industrialize, and most observers today agree that the overall situation of the Burakumin has improved (Ball, 2009). But the Burakumin maintain their minority status, and prejudice against them continues (Neary, 2003, p. 288).

The Burakumin are a small group, about 2% or 3% of Japan's population. About one million still live in traditional villages, and another two million or so live in non-Burakumin areas, mostly in larger cities. They continue to be seen as "filthy," "not very bright," and "untrustworthy"—stereotypical traits often associated with minority groups mired in subordinate and unequal positions. Also, as is the case for many American minority groups, the Burakumin have a number of protest organizations—including the Buraku Liberation League (www .bll.gr.jp/eng.html)—that are dedicated to improving conditions.

The situation of the Burakumin might seem puzzling. If the group is indistinguishable from the general population, why don't the Burakumin simply blend in and disappear? What keeps them attached to their group? Some Burakumin are proud of their heritage and refuse to surrender to the dominant culture. They have no intention of trading their identity for acceptance or opportunity. For others, even those attempting to pass, the tie to the group and a subtle form of social visibility are maintained by the ancient system of residential segregation. The identity of the traditional Burakumin areas of residence are well known, and this information—not race or culture—is what establishes the boundaries of the group and forms the ultimate barrier to Burakumin assimilation.

There are reports that Japanese firms use lists of local Burakumin addresses to screen out potential employees. Also, the telltale information may be revealed when applying to rent an apartment (some landlords refuse to rent rooms to Burakumin because of their alleged "filthiness") or purchase a home (banks may be reluctant to provide loans to members of a group that is widely regarded as "untrustworthy").

Another line of resistance can arise with marriage. It is common for Japanese parents to research the family history of a child's fiancé, a process that is sure to unearth any secret Burakumin connections. Thus, members of the Burakumin who pass undetected at work and in their neighborhood are likely to be "outed" if they attempt to marry outside the group.

This link to the traditional Burakumin residential areas means that this group is not really invisible: There is a way to determine group membership, a mark or sign of who belongs and who doesn't. Consistent with our definition, this "birthmark" is the basis for a socially constructed boundary that differentiates "us" from "them," and for the discrimination and prejudice associated with minority-group status.

Questions to Consider

1. What makes the Burakumin's situation unique? What other minority groups are similarly "invisible"?

2. Are the Burakumin advocacy groups justified in attempting to preserve the group's heritage? Should they be working for greater assimilation? Explain.

3. What do you suppose the future holds for the Burakumin? Will they disappear and assimilate into the larger society? Use ideas from the book to support your answer.

(and to the disappearance of Little Tokyos) is that unlike the Chinese American community, the Japanese American community has had few new immigrants, and the community has not had to devote many resources to newcomers. Furthermore, recent immigrants from Japan tend to be highly educated professionals whose socioeconomic characteristics add to the perception of success and affluence.

The Sansei and Yonsei are highly integrated into the occupational structure of the larger society. Compared with their parents, their connections with their ethnic past are more tenuous, and in their values, beliefs, and personal goals, they resemble dominant group members of similar age and social class (Kitano & Daniels, 1995, pp. 79–81; see also Spickard, 1996).

COMPARING MINORITY GROUPS

What factors account for the differences in the development of Chinese Americans and Japanese Americans and other racial minority groups? First, the dominant group had no desire to control the labor of these groups, as it had desired to control African Americans in the 1600s and Mexican Americans in the 1800s. The contact situation featured economic competition (e.g., for jobs) during an era of rigid competition between groups (see Table 5.2), and Chinese Americans and Japanese Americans were seen as a threat to security that needed to be eliminated, not as a labor pool that needed to be controlled.

Second, unlike Native Americans, Chinese and Japanese Americans in the early 20th century presented no military danger to the larger society; so, there was little concern with their activities once the economic threat had been eliminated. Third, Chinese Americans and Japanese Americans had the ingredients and experiences necessary to form enclaves. The groups were allowed to "disappear," but unlike other racial minority groups, the urban location of their enclaves left them with opportunities for starting small businesses and providing an education for the second and later generations. As many scholars argue, the particular mode of incorporation developed by Chinese Americans and Japanese Americans is the key to understanding the present status of these groups.

QUESTIONS FOR REFLECTION

3. What forces shaped the immigration of Chinese and Japanese Americans? Compare and contrast these patterns with those of Hispanic immigration and immigration from Europe between 1820 and 1920. What are the key differences and similarities?

4. Compare and contrast the development of the Chinese American community with the development of the Japanese American community. What are the most important differences and similarities? What accounts for these patterns? Did both groups form enclaves? Why and how?

5. Are Japanese and Chinese Americans colonized or immigrant groups? Why or why not?

CONTEMPORARY IMMIGRATION FROM ASIA

Figure 9.4 displays the volume of immigration from Asia since 1900. The green line represents the number of immigrants for each time period (read these values from the left vertical axis) and shows the decline in rates after the restrictive legislation of the 1920s—almost to zero—and the steep increases following the change in U.S. immigration policy in the mid-1960s. Immigration from Asia has steadily increased in volume since the 1960s and continued to increase even as the flow of immigrants from Hispanic nations has declined. Starting in 2009, Asia became the largest supplier of immigrants to the United States.

The blue line shows the percentage of all immigrants in each time period that came from Asia. This line (read from the right vertical axis) shows that Asian immigration was rare—less than 5% of all immigrants—until the mid-1960s. The percentage increased until the 1980s and then declined in the 1990s as the volume of immigration from Mexico and Central and South America exploded. The percentage has risen to about 40% in more recent years, a reflection of the continued flow from Asia and the declining flow of Hispanic groups.

Figure 9.5 shows that Asian immigration since the 1950s has been heaviest from China, India, and the Philippines but that Korea and Vietnam have also made sizable contributions. As noted previously, immigration from Japan has been relatively low since the initial influx a century ago (see Figure 9.3).

As is the case with Hispanic immigrants, the sending nations (other than Japan) are less economically developed than the United States, and the primary motivation for most

FIGURE 9.4 Immigration from Asia, 1900–2015

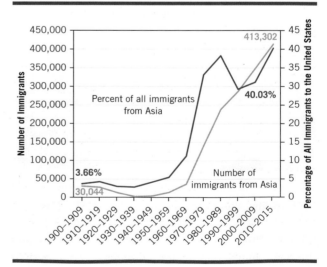

SOURCE: U.S. Department of Homeland Security, 2016.

FIGURE 9.5 Relative Size of Immigrant Groups From Asia, 1950–2015

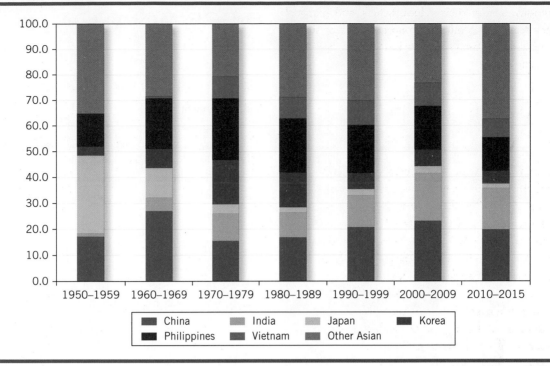

SOURCE: U.S. Department of Homeland Security, 2016.

of these immigrants is economic. However, unlike Hispanic immigration, the Asian immigrant stream also includes a large contingent of highly educated professionals seeking opportunities to practice their careers and expand their skills.

These more elite immigrants contribute to the image of "Asian success," but many Asian immigrants are less skilled and educated, and often undocumented. Thus, this stream of immigrants includes people from both the top and the bottom of the occupational and educational hierarchies.

Of course, other factors besides economics attract such immigrants. The United States has maintained military bases throughout the region (including in South Korea, Japan, and the Philippines) since the end of World War II. Many Asian immigrants to the United States are the spouses of American military personnel who were stationed in those parts of the world.

Also, U.S. involvement in the war in Southeast Asia in the 1960s and 1970s created interpersonal ties and governmental programs that drew refugees from Vietnam, Cambodia, and Laos, many of whom were escaping war and who lived in refugee camps and relocation centers for years before immigrating to the United States. The conditions of their escape meant they typically brought little in the way of human or material capital.

Among the refugee groups are the Hmong, people from Laos and other Southeast Asian nations who fought with the American forces in the Vietnam War. They are a relatively small group of immigrants (see Table 9.1) and face some unique challenges in adjustment to U.S. society. Their culture is very traditional and, in many ways, far removed from the modernized, Western world in which they find themselves.

Prior to the Vietnam War, the Hmong were at the hunter-gatherer level of subsistence technology and brought very little of what most Americans would call social or cultural capital with them. Anthropologist Anne Fadiman illustrates the complex challenges the Hmong face in acculturating to the United States in her 1998 account of an epileptic Hmong girl, Lia Lee. According to traditional Hmong cultural understandings, illness is caused by spirits and needs to be treated in the time-honored way, by traditional healers or shamans. Lia's parents loved her deeply. Lia's Californian doctors attempted to treat her with medicine, but linguistic barriers and cultural differences made it difficult for Lia's parents to understand and follow the instructions. The resultant tragedy underscores the distance between the Hmong and the Western world, and illustrates the challenges of acculturation for this group (Fadiman, 1998). Contrary to the stereotypical image of Asian American success, the Hmong generally display a socioeconomic profile more consistent with America's colonized minority groups.

Another striking contrast is between immigrants from India, many of whom are highly educated and skilled, and Vietnamese Americans, who have a socioeconomic profile that more resembles those of non-Asian racial minorities in the United States. Part of the difference between these two groups relates to their contact situations and can be illuminated by applying the Blauner hypothesis. Immigrants from India are at the "immigrant" end of Blauner's continuum.

Jonathan P Beck/Wikimedia Commons

A woman in a traditional Hmong dress in Seattle, Washington.

They tend to bring strong educational credentials and to be well equipped to compete for favorable positions in the occupational hierarchy.

The Vietnamese, in contrast, began their American experience as a refugee group fleeing the turmoil of war. Although they do not fit Blauner's "conquered or colonized" category, most Vietnamese Americans had to adapt to American society with few resources and few contacts with an established immigrant community. The consequences of these vastly different contact situations are suggested by the data presented in the figures at the end of this chapter. We will address some of these groups in more detail in Chapter 10.

QUESTIONS FOR REFLECTION

6. Identify the major groups of recent immigrants from Asia. How do they differ from Chinese and Japanese Americans?

7. How did the motivation for immigration vary for the different Asian groups? How have these differences affected their relationship with U.S. society and their experiences as immigrants?

8. Are these groups colonized or immigrant groups? Why?

PREJUDICE AND DISCRIMINATION

American prejudice against Asians first became prominent during the anti-Chinese movement of the 19th century. The Chinese were believed to be racially inferior, docile, and subservient, but also cruel and crafty, despotic, and threatening (Lai, 1980, p. 220; Lyman, 1974, pp. 55–58). The Chinese Exclusion Act of 1882 was justified by the idea that the Chinese could never fully assimilate into U.S. society. The Chinese were seen as a threat to the working class, to American democracy, and to other American institutions. Many of these stereotypes and fears transferred to the Japanese later in the 19th century and then to other groups as they, in turn, arrived in the United States.

The social distance scores presented in Table 3.3 provide the only long-term record of anti-Asian prejudice in society as a whole. In 1926, the five Asian groups included in the study ranked in the bottom third of the scale, along with other racial and colonized minority groups. Twenty years later, in 1946, the Japanese had fallen to the bottom of the rankings, and the Chinese had risen seven positions, changes that reflect America's World War II conflict with Japan and alliance with China. This suggests that anti-Chinese prejudice may have softened during the war as distinctions were made between "good" and "bad" Asians. For example, an item published in a December 22nd, 1941, issue of *Time* magazine, "How to Tell Your Friends From the Japs," provided some tips for identifying "good" Asians: "The Chinese expression is likely to be more placid, kindly, open; the Japanese more positive, dogmatic, arrogant. . . . Japanese are nervous in conversation, laugh loudly at the wrong time" (p. 33).

In more recent decades, the average social distance scores of Asian groups have fallen even though the ranking of the groups has remained relatively stable. The falling scores probably reflect the society-wide increase in tolerance and the shift from blatant prejudice to modern racism that we discussed previously. However, the relative position of Asians in the American hierarchy of group preferences has remained remarkably consistent since the 1920s. This stability may reflect the cultural or traditional nature of much of the anti-Asian prejudice in America.

As you saw in Chapter 3, the biggest rise in hate crimes was for Muslim Americans. However, numerous reports document an increase in violent attacks and other forms of harassment against Asian Americans (Chen, 2017), especially against recent immigrants. (These groups overlap, too.) Some of these incidents are extreme and overt, such as the killing of Vincent Chin in Detroit, in 1982, which we cited in Chapter 3 as an example of a hate crime. Though it happened decades ago, Chin's death is particularly notable because it highlights the group competition we've been discussing throughout this book. As you recall, Chin was beaten to death by white auto workers who had recently been laid off. They reportedly yelled, "It's because of you we're out of work" (Wu, 2012). Although they associated Chin with the Japanese auto industry that they blamed for their troubles, they were wrong: Chin was Chinese American. His death underscored the significance of being seen as a "perpetual foreigner"—something Robert Takaki spoke of in this chapter's opening narrative and that Japanese Americans imprisoned by the U.S. government during World War II also experienced.

Because hate crimes are under-reported (see Chapter 3), the nonprofit organization Asian Americans Advancing Justice (AAAJ) set up an online hate crime tracker in early 2017 to gather more comprehensive data. One particularly troubling report described a man making machine gun sounds while screaming "YELLOW [n-word]" threatening to rape the person and "ship [their] remains back to where [they] come from." Other people reported being followed, pushed, grabbed, threatened, or touched in other threatening or demeaning ways (AAAJ, 2017). The AAAJ data suggest that the perception of Asian Americans as "perpetual foreigners" is at the core of racist incidents against them (Chen, 2017).

Some respondents reported being told "to go back where [you] came from" and "I hate your f****** race. We're in charge of this country now." Another reported being called a "slant-eyed chink." Some researchers classify such incidents as a form of modern racism called microaggressions. Microaggressions are "brief and commonplace daily verbal, behavioral and environmental indignities, whether intentional or unintentional, that communicate hostile, derogatory or negative racial slights and insults that potentially have harmful or unpleasant psychological impact on the target person or group" (Sue et al., 2007, p. 72). Specifically, these examples from the AAAJ represent "microassaults" meant to hurt the target (Sue et al., 2007, p. 73).

Two other types of microaggressions include "microinsults" and "microinvalidations." Microinsults include offensive or degrading comments or actions while microinvalidations attempt to contradict or disavow people's experiences (Sue et al., 2007, p. 73). For example, Asian Americans being told "You speak good English" or being asked "Where are you really from?" are forms of microinsults that suggest "real" Americans are white/non-Asian. These incidents can be so subtle and so common, one might barely notice them.

Positive stereotypes regarding the presumed intellect of Asian Americans can be problematic, too. For example, high school and middle school students of Asian descent who are stereotyped as "high-achieving students who

During and after World War II, anti-Japanese prejudice was often openly expressed.

rarely fight back" become excellent candidates for bullying and scapegoating by other groups (Associated Press, 2005). Harassment at one high school in New York rose to such severe levels that the U.S. Department of Justice intervened at the request of school officials (Associated Press, 2005). Incidents such as these suggest that the tradition of anti-Asian prejudice is close to the surface and could be reactivated under the right combination of competition and threat.

On the other hand, a recent survey administered to a representative sample suggests that most Asian Americans do not perceive discrimination and prejudice as major problems. Only 13% of the Asian Americans interviewed said that discrimination was a "major problem," with results ranging from 24% for Korean Americans to only 8% for Japanese Americans (Pew Research Center, 2013c, p. 110). About 20% said they had personally experienced discrimination because of their Asian origin, and only 10% said they had been called offensive names (p. 114). These levels are far below those of African Americans and Hispanic Americans when asked similar questions. For example, 43% of a representative sample of African Americans said there was "a lot" of discrimination against their group, and 61% of Hispanic Americans said discrimination was a "major problem" for them (p. 115). What might account for these differences? One possibility is that Asian Americans downplay the extent of their negative experiences, in conformity with the cultural tendency to avoid confrontation and stress harmony.

Another possibility is that Asian Americans truly experience less discrimination than do other racial minorities. As we discussed in Chapter 8, some analysts argue that Asian Americans (along with lighter-skinned, more affluent Latinos) become "honorary whites," positioned between whites and blacks (and darker-skinned, less affluent Latinos) in the American racial order. If this is the case, we would expect Asian Americans to be somewhat less victimized than blacks and some Hispanic Americans.

A final possibility, closely related to the second, is that Asian Americans benefit from "positive" stereotypes and are seen in a more favorable light than other racial minorities. The perception of Asian Americans as a "model minority"—polite, successful, and deferential—could explain their lower levels of discrimination. As you'll see, the model-minority image is a stereotype, exaggerated and overstated. For some Asian American groups, the image is simply false. The label has been applied to these groups by the media, politicians, and others. It is not an identity the Asian American groups themselves have developed or advocated—in fact, many virulently oppose it because it obscures many of the problems that exist in Asian American communities. We will explore these issues later in this chapter.

ASSIMILATION AND PLURALISM

In this section, we continue to assess the situation of Asian Americans today using the same conceptual framework used in the previous three chapters.

ACCULTURATION

The extent of acculturation of Asian Americans is highly variable from group to group. Japanese Americans represent one extreme. They have been a part of American society for more than a century, and the current generations are highly acculturated. Immigration from Japan has been low and has not revitalized the traditional culture or language. As a result, Japanese Americans are the most acculturated of the Asian American groups, as illustrated in Figure 9.6, and have the lowest percentage of members who speak English "less than very well."

Filipino and Indian Americans also have low percentages of members who are not competent English speakers, but for different reasons. The Philippines has had a strong American presence since the Spanish–American War of 1898, while India is a former British colony in which English remains an important language for higher education and of the educated elite.

Chinese Americans, in contrast, are highly variable in the extent of their acculturation. Many are members of families who have been American for generations and are highly acculturated. Others, including many recent undocumented immigrants, are newcomers who have little knowledge of English or Anglo culture. On this dimension, as in occupations, Chinese Americans are "bipolar." This great variability within the group makes it difficult to characterize their overall degree of acculturation.

Also, note that the groups who are refugees from the 1960s and 1970s wars in Southeast Asia (Vietnamese, Cambodians, Hmong, and Laotians) are less acculturated. They, along with the Chinese and Koreans, have many foreign-born members (see Figure 9.2) and are still largely in their first generation.

Gender and Physical Acculturation: The Anglo Ideal. Anglo-conformity can happen on levels other than the cultural. A number of studies document the feelings of inadequacy and negative self-images that often result when

FIGURE 9.6 Percentage of Asian Americans Who Speak English Less Than "Very Well," 2015

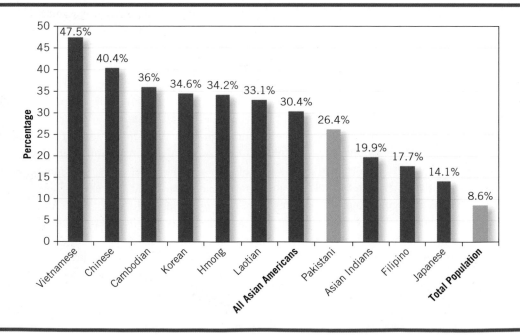

SOURCE: U.S Census Bureau, 2017. American Community Survey, 2015, 1-year Estimates.

minority group members—especially women—compare themselves with the Anglo standards of attractiveness and beauty that dominate U.S. culture.

Some of the studies in this tradition are classics of the social science literature, including the "doll studies" conducted by social psychologists Kenneth and Mamie Clark in the 1930s and 1940s (Clark & Clark, 1940, 1950). The Clarks showed pairs of white and black dolls to a sample of young African American children and asked them a series of questions, including "Which doll is pretty?" "Which doll is nice?" "Which doll would you like to play with?" and "Which doll is ugly?"

They documented a preference for the white doll, which they interpreted as evidence that the children had internalized white standards of beauty and developed negative self-images as a consequence. Contemporary projects inspired by the Clark doll study include a YouTube video titled "A Girl Like Me" (2005) by then 17-year-old Kiri Davis[1], and a documentary by Chris Rock titled *Good Hair* (2009).

Asian American women, like most women in modern U.S. society, are pressured by the cultural message that physical beauty should be among their most important concerns. As minorities, they are also subjected to the additional message that they are inadequate by Anglo standards and that some physical traits (e.g., "slanted" eyes and "flat" noses) are unattractive and in need of "fixing" (Kaw, 1997). For example, many African American women spend millions of dollars on hair straightening and skin bleaching.

_____
[1] See YouTube: http://www.youtube.com/watch?v=5f71JW2zJTU.

For Asian American women, the attempt to comply with Anglo standards of beauty may include cosmetic surgery to sculpt their noses or to "open" their eyes.

To study these experiences, Kaw (1997) conducted in-depth interviews with medical practitioners and with a small sample of Asian American women, most of whom had had surgery on their eyelids or noses. The women tended to see their surgeries as simply their personal choice, not unlike putting on makeup. However, Kaw found that they consistently described their presurgical features in negative terms. They uniformly said "that 'small, slanty' eyes and a 'flat' nose" suggest a person who is dull and passive "and a mind that is 'closed.'" For example, one subject said that she considered eyelid surgery while in high school to "'avoid the stereotype of the Oriental bookworm' who is 'dull and doesn't know how to have fun.'" Kaw concludes that racist stereotypes and patriarchal norms greatly influence Asian American women's decisions to undergo surgery: an attempt—common among all racial minority groups—to acculturate on a physical as well as cultural level.

SECONDARY STRUCTURAL ASSIMILATION

We cover this topic in the order followed in previous chapters.

Residence. Figure 9.7 shows the regional concentrations of all Asian Americans in 2010. The tendency to reside on either coast and around Los Angeles, San Francisco, and New York City stands out clearly. Note also the sizable

FIGURE 9.7 Distribution of Asian Americans, 2010 (Percentage of County Population)

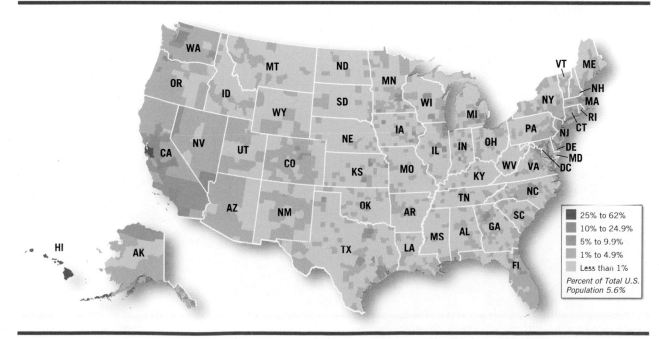

SOURCE: Hoeffel et al. (2012, p. 10).

concentrations in a variety of metropolitan areas, including Chicago, Atlanta, Miami, Denver, and Houston.

The various Asian American groups are concentrated in different regions, with the vast majority of Filipino and Japanese Americans residing in the West, along with about half of Chinese and Vietnamese Americans. Asian Indians have the highest percentage living in the Northeast (30%), and Vietnamese Americans have the highest percentage in the South (32%), mostly concentrated on the Texas and Louisiana coasts where they work in the fishing industry. The Hmong, alone among Asian American groups, are concentrated in the upper Midwest, especially in Wisconsin and Minnesota (Hoeffel et al., 2012, pp. 18–20).

Figure 9.8 shows that Asian Americans, like Hispanic Americans, are moving away from their "traditional" places of residence into new regions. Between 2000 and 2010, the Asian American population increased especially rapidly along the East and West Coast, in Arizona, and in some areas of the upper Midwest.

Between 2000 and 2010, the Asian population increased more than 50% in 30 of the 50 states, with 8 more closely approaching the 50% mark. In seven states (including Arizona, Nevada, Delaware, and North Carolina) the Asian population increased by more than 75% (Hoeffel et al., 2012, p. 7).

Asian Americans in general are highly urbanized, a reflection of the entry conditions of recent immigrants as well as the appeal of ethnic neighborhoods, such as Chinatowns, with long histories and continuing vitality. As Figure 9.9 shows, all but 2 of the 10 largest Asian American

groups were more than 90% urbanized in 2000, and several approach the 100% mark.

In Chapter 6, Figure 6.8 showed that Asian Americans are less residentially segregated than either African Americans or Hispanic Americans. The levels of residential segregation for Asian Americans have been well below "high" (dissimilarity scores greater than 60) but tend to be slightly higher in cities with more concentrated Asian populations. The level of residential segregation is holding steady, a reflection of high rates of immigration and the tendency of newcomers to settle close to other members of their group. Also, these lower scores may reflect the more favored position for Asian Americans—as opposed to blacks and darker-skinned Hispanic Americans—which we noted earlier when discussing their lower levels of reported discrimination. On the other hand, the residential segregation of Asian Americans, as for other groups, has been maintained by explicitly racist policies of the dominant group. For example, the racially restrictive real estate covenants in Seattle legally banned certain types of people from renting, leasing, buying, or residing in particular areas. (See Table 9.2.)

Asian Americans are also moving away from their traditional neighborhoods and enclaves and into the suburbs of metropolitan areas, most notably in the areas surrounding Los Angeles, San Francisco, New York, and other cities where the groups are highly concentrated. For example, Asian Americans have been moving in large numbers to the San Gabriel Valley, just east of downtown Los Angeles. Once a bastion of white, middle-class suburbanites, these areas have taken on a distinctly Asian flavor

FIGURE 9.8 Percentage Change in Asian American Population, 2000–2010

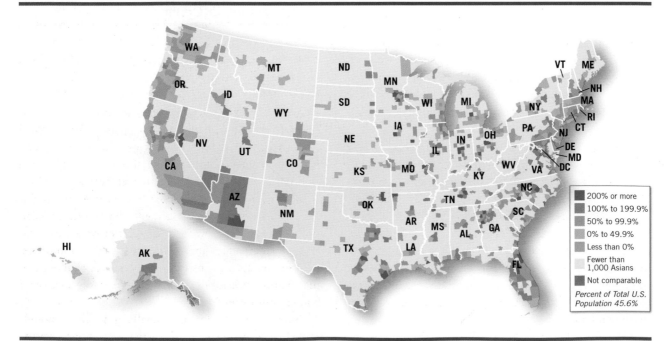

SOURCE: Hoeffel et al. (2012, p. 11).

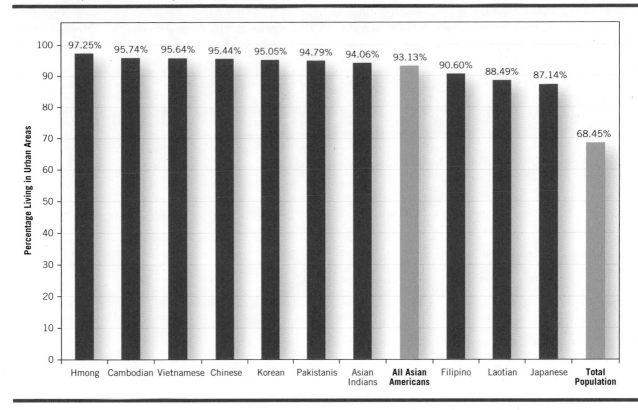

SOURCE: U.S. Census Bureau (2000a).

in recent years. Monterey Park, once virtually all white, is now majority Chinese American and is often referred to as "America's first suburban Chinatown" or the "Chinese Beverly Hills" (Fong, 2002, p. 49; see also Chowkwanyun & Segall, 2012).

Education. Asian American children experience less school segregation than Hispanic and black American children (Fry, 2007), although the extent of segregation for this population may have increased in recent years because of high rates of immigration and residential concentration, particularly in larger cities.

The extent of schooling for Asian Americans is very different from that for other U.S. racial minority groups, at least at first glance. Asian Americans as a whole compare favorably with society-wide standards for educational achievement, and they perform above those standards on many measures. Figure 9.10 shows that 3 of the 10 Asian American groups rank higher than non-Hispanic whites in completing high school, and 6 of 10 rank higher in completing college degrees, a pattern that has been reinforced by the high levels of education of many recent Asian immigrants.

A quick glance at Figure 9.10 might sustain the image of Asian American success, but note that several groups are relatively low in educational attainment. Asian Americans display a full range of achievement: While it is true that some groups (or at least some elements of some groups) are quite successful, others have profiles that are closer to those of colonized racial minority groups.

This more balanced view of Asian Americans is further explored in Figures 9.11 and 9.12. The former shows the percentage of each group with *less than* a high school education and includes Hispanic Americans, African Americans, Native Americans, and non-Hispanic whites for comparison. As we saw in Chapter 8, recent Hispanic immigrants tend to bring modest educational credentials, and the same point can be made for several of the Asian American groups, all of which have a high percentage of foreign-born members and include many refugees from the wars in Southeast Asia. On this measure of educational attainment, the Southeast Asian groups actually fare worse than African Americans and Native Americans, both colonized racial minorities. Information such as this presents a serious challenge to glib characterizations of Asian Americans as successful "model minorities."

Figure 9.12 further challenges the model-minority image by comparing the educational attainment of Chinese Americans and non-Hispanic whites.

TABLE 9.2 Example of Racially Restrictive Covenants in Seattle, 1927–1958

Beacon Hill-Mid Beacon Hill (1927)	No person **other than one of the Caucasian race** shall reside on any of said described premises excepting that a domestic servant in the actual employ of an occupant may reside in the home of his master.
Overland Park (1928)	That the said lots or buildings thereon shall never be rented, leased, or sold, transferred or conveyed to, nor shall the same be occupied by any **negro or colored person or person of negro blood, or persons of the Mongolian race.**
Licton Springs Park (1930)	. . . no part of the premises herein described shall at any time be leased, mortgaged, or conveyed in law or in equity to any person of **Chinese, Japanese, African or Hindu** descent or to any person, company or trustee for their use and benefit . . .
Maple Leaf (1940)	No person of any race other than the Caucasian race shall use or occupy any building or any lot, except that this covenant shall not prevent occupancy by domestic servants of a different race domiciled with an owner or tenant.
Inglewood (1945)	No title or interest or right of occupancy of said premises shall ever become invested in any person other than of the Caucasian race.
Marine Highlands (1947)	That neither the said premises or any house, building or improvement thereon erected, shall at any time be occupied by persons of the **Ethiopian race, or by Japanese or Chinese, or any other Malay** ["Malays" are Filipinos] **or Asiatic race**, save except as domestic servants in the employ of persons not coming within this restriction.
Queen Anne (1929; lasts until 1958)	No person or persons of Asiatic, African or Negro blood, lineage, or extraction shall be permitted to occupy a portion of said property, or any building thereon; except domestic servants may actually and in good faith be employed by white occupants of such premises.
Sea Tac (1937; lasts through 1956)	Nor shall the said property, or any part thereof, be used or occupied by any person of the **Malay or any Asiatic race or descent, or any person of the races commonly known as the Negro race, or of their descent**, and the grantee, his heirs, personal representatives or assigns shall not, at any time throughout said period, place any such person in the possession or occupancy of said property, excepting only employees in the domestic service . . .

SOURCE: Lind, Carolyn et al. "Restrictive Covenants Database." Seattle Civil Rights & Labor History Project, http://depts.washington.edu/civilr/covenants_database.htm.

FIGURE 9.10 Educational Attainment for All Asian Americans, 10 Largest Asian American Groups, and Non-Hispanic Whites, 2015

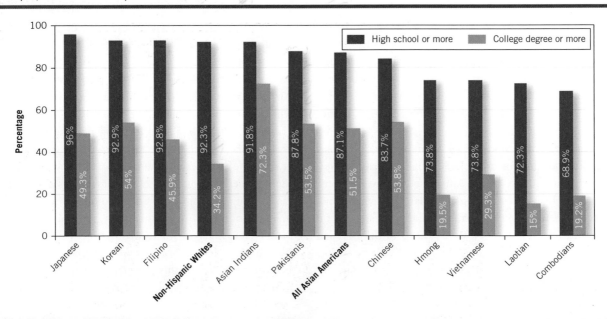

SOURCE: U.S Census Bureau, 2017. American Community Survey, 2015, 1-year Estimates.

FIGURE 9.11 Percentage Hispanic Americans, African Americans, Native Americans, Non-Hispanic Whites, All Asian Americans, and 10 Largest Asian American Groups With Less Than a High School Education, 2015

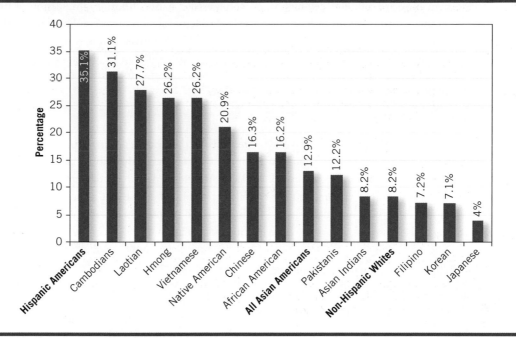

SOURCE: U.S Census Bureau, 2017. American Community Survey, 2015, 1-year Estimates.

More than 50% of Chinese Americans hold college and graduate degrees, far outnumbering whites (33%) at this level. Note, however, that Chinese Americans are also disproportionately concentrated at the lowest level of educational achievement. About 17% of the group has less than a high school diploma, as opposed to about 8% of non-Hispanic whites. Many of these less educated Chinese Americans are recent immigrants (many undocumented), and they supply the unskilled labor force—in retail shops, restaurants, and garment industry "sweatshops"—that staffs the lowest levels of the Chinatown economy.

FIGURE 9.12 Educational Attainment for Non-Hispanic Whites and Chinese Americans, 2015

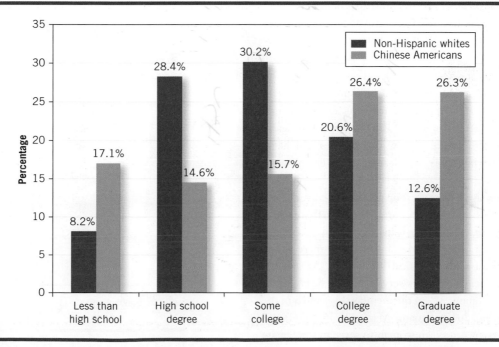

SOURCE: U.S Census Bureau, 2017. American Community Survey, 2011–2015, 1-year Estimates.

Assessments of Asian American success must also differentiate between the native-born and the foreign-born members of the groups. The native-born are generally better educated, and the foreign-born are split between highly educated professionals and those who bring lower levels of human capital. For example, according to a recent survey, almost all (98%) native-born Chinese Americans were high school graduates and 73% had college degrees. In contrast, only 77% of foreign-born Chinese Americans had finished high school and only 41% had earned a college degree (computed from Pew Research Center, 2013c).

As these examples illustrate, the image of success for Asian Americans needs to be balanced with the recognition that there is a full range of achievement in the group and average levels of educational attainment are inflated for some groups by recent immigrants who are highly educated, skilled professionals.

Political Power. The ability of Asian Americans to pursue their group interests has been sharply limited by a number of factors, including the relatively small size of the population, institutionalized discrimination, and the same kinds of racist practices that have limited the power resources of other minority groups of color. However, and contrary to the perception that Asian Americans are a "quiet" minority, the group has a long history of political action, including a civil rights movement in the 1960s and 1970s (Fong, 2002, pp. 273–281).

The political power of Asian Americans today is also limited by their high percentage of foreign-born members and, for some groups, lack of facility in English. Rates of political participation for the group (e.g., voting in presidential elections) are considerably lower than national norms. For example, as was the case with Hispanic Americans, less than half (49%) of Asian Americans voted in the 2016 presidential election (vs. about 64% of non-Hispanic whites and blacks) (U.S. Census Bureau, 2017g). This level of participation was about the same as in the 2008 presidential election, although slightly higher than in earlier presidential elections (File, 2013, pp. 3–5). Like Hispanic Americans, the impact of this group on national politics will likely increase as more members Americanize, learn English, and become citizens.

There are signs of the group's growing power, especially in areas where they are most residentially concentrated. Of course, Asian Americans have been prominent in Hawaiian politics for decades, but they are increasingly involved in West Coast political life as well. At present, 15 Asian and Pacific Islanders serve in the U.S. House of Representatives (about 2% of the membership) and 3 in the Senate (Manning, 2017). Senator Mazie Hirono of Hawaii was the first Asian American woman to serve in the Senate (Manning, 2013, p. 8).

Jobs and Income. The economic situation of Asian Americans is mixed and complex, as it is for Hispanic Americans. On some measures, Asian Americans as a whole exceed national norms, a reflection of the high levels of academic achievement combined with the impressive educational credentials of many new arrivals. However, overall comparisons can be misleading, and we must also recognize the economic diversity within the group of Asian Americans.

Starting with occupational profiles, the image of success is again sustained. Both men and women are overrepresented in the highest occupational categories, a reflection of the high levels of educational attainment for the group. Asian American men are underrepresented among manual laborers, but, otherwise, the group's occupational profiles are in rough proportion to society as a whole (U.S. Census Bureau, 2013a).

Figure 9.13 shows median household incomes for Asian Americans and non-Hispanic whites since 1987 and reveals that Asian Americans have *higher* median household incomes, a picture of general affluence that is in dramatic contrast to the other racial minority groups we have examined in this text. The gap fluctuates, but Asian Americans' median household income is generally 115% of whites.

This image of success, glittering at first glance, becomes more complicated and nuanced when we look at the separate subgroups within the Asian American community. Figure 9.14 displays median household incomes for all non-Hispanic whites, all Asian Americans, and the 10 largest subgroups. We can see immediately that economic success is not universally shared: Of the 10 Asian American groups, 4 are below the average income for non-Hispanic whites.

FIGURE 9.13 Median Household Income for Non-Hispanic Whites and All Asian Americans, 1987–2015

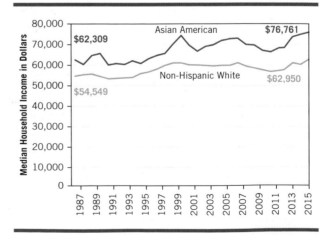

SOURCE: U.S. Census Bureau, 2017. Historical Income Tables, Table H-5, https://www.census.gov/data/tables/time-series/demo/income-poverty/historical-income-households.html.

FIGURE 9.14 Median Household Income for Non-Hispanic Whites, All Asian Americans, and 10 Largest Groups, 2015

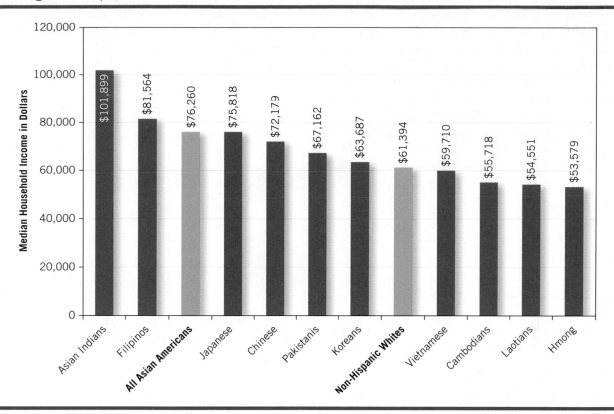

SOURCE: U.S Census Bureau, 2017. American Community Survey, 2015, 1-year Estimates.

A still more telling picture emerges when we consider income per capita (or per person) as opposed to median incomes for entire households. This is an important comparison because the apparent prosperity of so many Asian American families is linked to their ownership of small businesses in the enclave. These enterprises typically employ the entire family for many hours each day, with children adding their labor after school and on weekends and other relatives (many of them new immigrants, a percentage of which are undocumented) contributing as well. The household unit may post a high income as a result of these collective efforts, but, when spread across many family members, the glow of "success" is muted.

Figure 9.15 shows that, on per capita income, only one Asian American group exceeds non-Hispanic whites. The other nine groups (including Chinese and Korean Americans, the groups most dependent on small business ownership) enjoy much lower levels of relative prosperity. In particular, the Southeast Asian groups with high percentages of refugees from the Vietnam War (especially the Hmong) are below national norms on this measure.

Figure 9.16 provides additional evidence that the image of a so-called model minority—uniformly prosperous and successful—is greatly exaggerated. Asian Americans, unlike other racial minority groups, are overrepresented in the three highest income categories: 29% of all Asian Americans are in these categories compared with only 20% of non-Hispanic whites. However, note that Asian Americans are also overrepresented in the lowest income category, a reflection of the "bipolar" distribution of Chinese Americans and some other groups.

Figures 9.17 and 9.18 finish the economic portrait of Asian Americans and reinforce the picture of complexity and diversity. While the poverty levels of all Asian Americans, considered as a single group, are comparable to those of non-Hispanic whites, several of the groups have much higher rates of poverty, especially for children. As we have seen in other figures, Japanese Americans, Filipino Americans, and Asian Indian Americans are "successful" on this indicator, but other groups have poverty levels comparable to those of colonized racial minority groups.

Figure 9.18 examines the situation of several Asian Americans in terms of their nativity. Once again, we see the great diversity from group to group, with foreign-born Vietnamese Americans (largely refugees) and Korean Americans exhibiting the highest percentage of members earning less than $30,000. For all six groups, in fact, the native-born have much lower percentages of members with low incomes, and in some cases (e.g., for Chinese Americans) the difference is quite dramatic.

FIGURE 9.15 Per Capita Income for Non-Hispanic Whites, All Asian Americans, and 10 Largest Groups, 2015

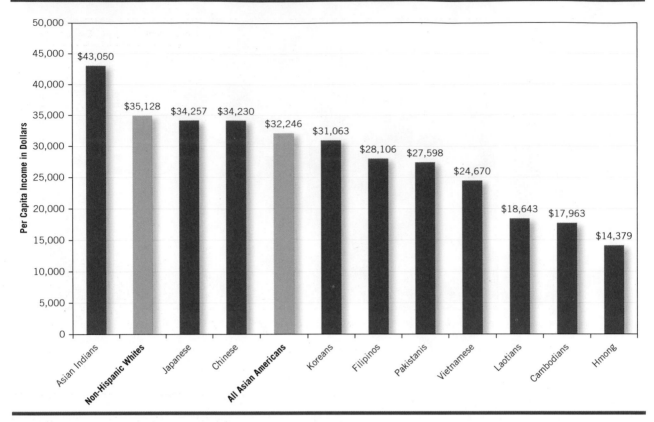

SOURCE: U.S Census Bureau, 2017. American Community Survey, 2015, 1-year Estimates.

FIGURE 9.16 Distribution of Household Income for Non-Hispanic Whites and Asian Americans, 2015

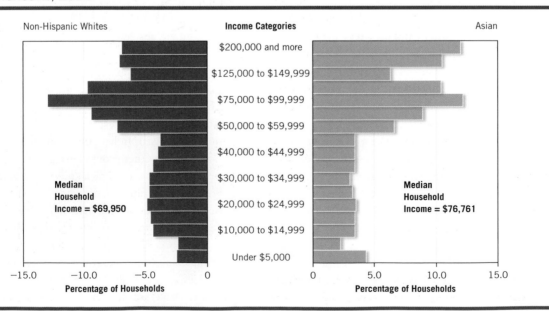

SOURCE: U.S. Bureau of the Census, 2016. "Age of Householder-Households, by Total Money Income, Type of Household, Race and Hispanic Origin of Householder, Table HINC-02," https://www.census.gov/data/tables/time-series/demo/income-poverty/cps-hinc/hinc-02.html.

FIGURE 9.17 Percentages of Families and Children in Poverty for Non-Hispanic Whites, All Asian Americans, and 10 Largest Asian American Groups, 2015

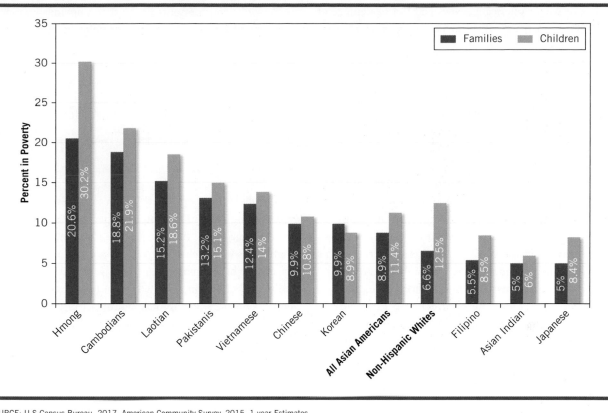

SOURCE: U.S Census Bureau, 2017. American Community Survey, 2015, 1-year Estimates.
NOTE: Family poverty rates and child poverty rates are computed using different units of analysis. Family rates represent the percentage of all families in the group that are below the poverty line while the rates for children are the percentage of all people younger than 18 in the group who live in poverty.

These socioeconomic profiles reflect the diversity of Asian American groups. Some are indeed prosperous and successful, and their financial wealth exceeds national norms, sometimes by a considerable margin. Other groups resemble other American racial minority groups. Japanese and Chinese Americans have the longest histories in the United States and generally rank at the top in measures of wealth and prosperity. Other groups—particularly those that include large numbers of refugees from Southeast Asia—have not fared as well and present pictures of poverty and economic distress. Some "bipolar" groups, such as Chinese Americans, fit in both categories. Additionally, we should note that the picture of economic distress for these groups would be much greater if we focused on undocumented immigrants, who are numerous in the community and concentrated in the informal, irregular economy.

PRIMARY STRUCTURAL ASSIMILATION

Levels of integration at the primary level for Asian Americans are, as in other areas, highly variable from group to group. Japanese Americans tend to be the most integrated on this dimension. One study found that, of the six Asian American

groups studied, Japanese Americans were the most likely to have friends outside their group and to marry across group lines (Pew Research Center, 2013d, pp. 32, 98). The same study found that, as would be expected, integration at the primary level was lower for the foreign-born and those with less English language ability.

FIGURE 9.18 Percentage of Selected Native-born and Foreign-born Asian American Groups and Non-Hispanic Whites With Incomes less than $30,000

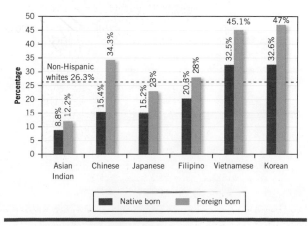

SOURCE: Computed from Pew Research Center, 2013d.

Generally, rates of primary integration tend to be higher than for other groups but are declining as the number of Asian Americans grows and the percentage of foreign-born increases (Passel, Wang, & Taylor, 2010, p. 17). This pattern reflects the tendency of newcomers to marry within their group.

Table 9.3 compares in-marriage trends of Asian Americans and whites in 1980 and 2008 following the same format used in earlier chapters. Asian Americans have much lower rates of in-marriage than do African Americans and Hispanic Americans, although they have somewhat higher rates than Native Americans. Again, this is partly a function of the relative sizes of these groups but also reflects the more favored position of Asian Americans in the dominant group's perceptions. However, nearly half (46%) of Asian Americans who cohabit do so with someone outside of their racial/ethnic group. This is almost twice as much as Hispanic Americans (24%) and African Americans (20%), and three times the rate of whites (12%). This difference between marriage and cohabitation may be related to being native-born versus foreign-born, which reflects the Asian American group's degree of assimilation. Of those who cohabit, a majority (59%) were born in the United States. As with other social trends, we see variation within the group. For example, people with more education are more likely to cohabit than those with less education (Livingston, 2017). Also, note that the percentage of foreign-born Asian Americans marrying within the group increased for both men and women. This is consistent with high rates of immigration in recent years and the idea that the first generation tends to socialize more with co-ethnics.

QUESTIONS FOR REFLECTION

9. In this section, we examined a variety of dimensions of acculturation and integration for Asian Americans. Which is most important? Why?

10. What evidence is presented to support the idea that Asian Americans are a "model minority"? What evidence is presented against this characterization? Which argument is more convincing? Why?

COMPARING MINORITY GROUPS: EXPLAINING ASIAN AMERICAN SUCCESS

To conclude this chapter, let's return to a question raised in the opening pages: How can we explain the apparent success of some Asian American groups? Relative affluence and high status are not characteristic of the other racial minority groups we have examined, and at least at first glance, there seems to be little in our theories and concepts to help us understand the situation of Asian Americans. Of course, as we have noted on several occasions, we need to recognize that the "success" label is simplistic and even incorrect for some groups, especially for Southeast Asian groups with a high percentage of refugees, who have profiles that resemble those of colonized racial minority groups. To better focus this discussion, we will concentrate on the groups with the longest histories in the United States: Chinese and Japanese Americans. We present several different views on the nature and causes of "success" for these groups. In this section, we compare Chinese and Japanese Americans with European immigrant groups and colonized minority groups. What crucial factors differentiate the experiences of these groups? Can we understand these differences in terms of the framework provided by the Blauner and Noel hypotheses and the other concepts developed in this text?

The debate over the causes of Asian American success often breaks down into two different viewpoints. One view offers a cultural explanation, which accepts the evidence of

TABLE 9.3 Percentage of Whites and Asian Americans Married to a Person of the Same Group, 1980 and 2008

| YEAR | WHITES | | ASIAN AMERICANS | | | |
| | | | MEN | | WOMEN | |
	Men	Women	Foreign-Born	U.S.-Born	Foreign-Born	U.S.-Born
1980	96%	95%	58%	57%	45%	51%
2008	93%	92%	77%	53%	55%	52%

SOURCE: Qian and Lichter (2011, p. 1072). Copyright © 2011 National Council on Family Relations. Reprinted with permission.

Art by Chinese American Tyrus Wong, a painter, lithographer, and designer. As a child, he was held at the Angel Island Immigration Station, the West Coast parallel of Ellis Island.

Asian American success at face value and attributes it to the "good values" of traditional Asian cultures that we briefly explored at the beginning of this chapter. These values—including respect for elders and authority figures, hard work and thriftiness, and conformity and politeness—are highly compatible with U.S. middle-class Protestant value systems and presumably helped Asian Americans gain acceptance and opportunities. The cultural explanation is consistent with traditional assimilation theory and human capital theory, and an example of it can be found in the selection by Professor Harry Kitano in this chapter's Current Debates section.

The second point of view stresses the ways in which Chinese Americans and Japanese Americans entered American society and their reactions to the barriers of racism and exclusion they faced. This approach could be called a "structural explanation," and it emphasizes contact situations, modes of incorporation, enclave economies, group cohesion, position in the labor market, and institutionalized discrimination, rather than cultural values.

Also, the structural approach questions the notion that Asian Americans are "successful" and stresses the realities of Asian American poverty and the continuing patterns of racism and exclusion. The structural approach is more compatible with the theories and concepts used throughout this text, and it identifies several of the important pieces needed to solve the puzzle of Asian "success" and put it in perspective. However, this is not to suggest that the cultural approach is wrong or irrelevant. The issues we raise are complex and will probably require many approaches and perspectives before they are fully resolved.

ASIAN AMERICANS AND WHITE ETHNICS

Chinese and Japanese immigrants arrived in America at about the same time as immigrants from Southern and Eastern Europe (see Chapter 2). Both groups consisted mainly of young men, many of them sojourners, who were largely unskilled, from rural backgrounds, and not highly educated. Immigrants from Europe, like those from Asia, encountered massive discrimination and rejection and were also victims of restrictive legislation. Yet the barriers to upward mobility for European immigrants (or at least for their descendants) fell away more rapidly than the barriers for immigrants from Asia. Why?

Some important differences between the two immigrant experiences are clear, the most obvious being the greater racial visibility of Asian Americans. Whereas the cultural and linguistic markers that identified Eastern and Southern Europeans faded with each passing generation, the racial characteristics of the Asian groups continued to separate them from the larger society.

Thus, Asian Americans are not "pure immigrant" groups (see Blauner, 1972, p. 55). For most of the 20th century, Chinese Americans and Japanese Americans remained in a less favorable position than did European immigrants and their descendants, excluded by their physical appearance from the mainstream economy until the decades following World War II.

Another important difference relates to position in the labor market. Immigrants from Southern and Eastern Europe entered the industrializing East Coast economy, where they took industrial and manufacturing jobs. Although such jobs were poorly paid and insecure, this location in the labor force gave European immigrants and their descendants the potential for upward mobility in the mainstream economy. At the very least, these urban industrial and manufacturing jobs put the children and grandchildren of European immigrants in positions from which skilled, well-paid, unionized jobs were reachable, as were managerial and professional careers.

In contrast, Chinese and Japanese immigrants on the West Coast were forced into ethnic enclaves and came to rely on jobs in the small business and service sector, and, in the case of the Japanese, in the rural economy. By their nature, these jobs did not link Chinese and Japanese immigrants or their descendants to the industrial sector or to better-paid, more secure, unionized jobs. Furthermore, their exclusion from the mainstream economy was reinforced by overt, racially based discrimination from both employers and labor unions (see Fong & Markham, 1991).

ASIAN AMERICANS AND COLONIZED RACIAL MINORITY GROUPS

Comparisons between Asian Americans and African Americans, Native Americans, and Hispanic Americans have generated a level of controversy and a degree of heat and passion that may be surprising at first. An examination of the issues and their implications, however, reveals that the debate involves some thinly disguised political and moral agendas and evokes sharply clashing views on the nature of U.S. society. What might appear on the surface to be merely an academic comparison of different minority groups turns out to be an argument about the quality of American justice and fairness and the very essence of the U.S. value system.

What is not in dispute in this debate is that some Asian groups (e.g., Japanese Americans) rank far above other racial minority groups on all the commonly used measures of secondary structural integration and equality. What is disputed is how to interpret these comparisons and assess their meanings. Of course, gross comparisons between entire groups can be misleading. If we confine our attention to averages (mean levels of education or median income), the picture of Asian American success is sustained. However, if we also observe the full range of differences within each group (e.g., the "bipolar" nature of occupations among Chinese Americans), we see that the images of success have been exaggerated and need to be placed in a proper context (see the selection by Min in this chapter's Current Debates section).

Even with these qualifications, however, discussion often slides on to more ideological ground, and political and moral issues begin to cloud the debate. Asian American success is often taken as proof that American society is truly the land of opportunity and that people who work hard and obey the rules will get ahead: In America, all people can be anything they want as long as they work hard enough.

When we discussed modern racism in Chapter 3, we pointed out that a belief in the openness and fairness of the United States can be a way of blaming the victim and placing the responsibility for change on the minority groups rather than on the structure of society or on past-in-present or institutionalized discrimination. Asian success is sometimes taken as a "proof" of the validity of this ideology. The none-too-subtle implication is that other groups (African Americans, Hispanic Americans, and Native Americans) could achieve the same success as Asian Americans but, for

various reasons, "choose" not to. Thus, the relative success of Chinese Americans and Japanese Americans has become a device for criticizing other minority groups.

A more structural approach to investigating Asian American success begins with a comparison of the history of the various racial minority groups and their modes of incorporation into the larger society. When Chinese Americans and Japanese Americans were building their enclave economies in the early part of the 20th century, African Americans and Mexican Americans were concentrated in unskilled agricultural occupations. Native Americans were isolated from the larger society on their reservations, and Puerto Ricans had not yet begun to arrive on the mainland. It follows, then, that social class differences between these groups today flow from their respective situations in the past.

Many of the occupational and financial advances made by Chinese and Japanese Americans have been due to the high levels of education achieved by the second generations. Although education is traditionally valued in Asian cultures, the decision to invest limited resources in schooling is also quite consistent with the economic niche occupied by these immigrants. Education is one obvious, relatively low-cost strategy to upgrade the productivity and profit of a small-business economy and improve the economic status of the group as a whole. Educated, English-speaking second-generation Chinese and Japanese Americans could act as intermediaries and bring expertise and business acumen to the family enterprises and lead them to higher levels of performance. Education might also be the means by which the second generation could enter professional careers. This strategy may have been especially attractive to an immigrant generation that was itself relatively uneducated and barred from citizenship (Hirschman & Wong, 1986, p. 23; see also Bonacich & Modell, 1980, p. 152; Sanchirico, 1991).

The efforts to educate the next generation were largely successful. Chinese Americans and Japanese Americans achieved educational parity with the larger society as early as the 1920s. One study found that for men and women born after 1915, the median years of schooling completed were actually higher for Chinese Americans and Japanese Americans than they were for whites (Hirschman & Wong, 1986, p. 11).

Before World War II, both Asian groups were barred from the mainstream economy and from better jobs. When anti-Asian prejudice and discrimination declined in the 1950s, however, the Chinese and Japanese American second generations had the educational background necessary to take advantage of the increased opportunities.

Thus, there was a crucial divergence in the development of Chinese and Japanese Americans and the colonized minority groups. At the time when native-born Chinese

Americans and Japanese Americans reached educational parity with whites, the vast majority of African Americans, Native Americans, and Mexican Americans were still victimized by Jim Crow laws and legalized segregation and excluded from opportunities for anything but rudimentary education. The Supreme Court decision in *Brown v. Board of Education of Topeka* (1954) was decades in the future, and most Native American schoolchildren were still being subjected to intense Americanization in the guise of a legitimate curriculum.

Today, these other racial minority groups have not completely escaped from the disadvantages imposed by centuries of institutionalized discrimination. African Americans have approached educational parity with white Americans only in recent years (see Chapter 6), and the educational achievements of Native Americans and Mexican Americans remain far below national averages (see Chapters 7 and 8, respectively).

The structural explanation argues that the recent upward mobility of Chinese and Japanese Americans is the result of the methods by which they incorporated themselves into American society, not so much their values and traditions. The logic of their enclave economy led the immigrant generation to invest in the education of their children, who would then be better prepared to develop their businesses and seek opportunities in the larger society.

As a final point, note that the structural explanation is not consistent with traditional views of the assimilation process. The immigrant generation of Chinese Americans and Japanese Americans responded to the massive discrimination they faced by withdrawing, developing ethnic enclaves, and becoming "invisible" to the larger society. Like Jewish Americans and Cuban Americans, Chinese Americans and Japanese Americans used their traditional cultures and patterns of social life to create and build their own subcommunities, from which they launched the next generation. Contrary to traditional ideas about how assimilation is "supposed" to happen, we see again that integration can precede acculturation and that the smoothest route to integration may be the creation of a separate subsociety independent of the surrounding community.

SUMMARY

This summary is organized around the Learning Objectives listed at the beginning of this chapter.

 9.1 Understand the population characteristics of the 10 largest Asian American groups.

Asian Americans and Pacific Islanders are diverse and have brought many different cultural and linguistic traditions to the United States. As a whole, Asian Americans are 5.6% of the population, but that percentage is expected to increase to 10% by mid-century. Like Hispanic Americans, Asian Americans have a high percentage of first-generation members and are growing more rapidly than the population as a whole. Asian Americans have accounted for the largest stream of immigrants to the United States since 2009, when they outpaced Hispanic Americans. The largest groups are Chinese, Filipino, and Indian Americans, and the groups with the longest history in the United States are Chinese Americans and Japanese Americans.

 9.2 Explain the history of Chinese and Japanese Americans, including their cultural characteristics, their immigration patterns, their development in the United States, and the nature and importance of each enclave.

Asian cultures tend to be less individualistic and more focused on maintaining harmonious interpersonal relations than is Anglo culture. Also, they tend to be more group and family oriented.

- Chinese Americans began immigrating in significant numbers in the 1840s. Tolerated at first, they became the victims of a massive campaign of discrimination and exclusion, to which they responded by constructing enclaves. Chinatowns became highly organized communities, largely run by the local Chinese Consolidated Benevolent Association and other groups. The second generation faced many barriers to employment in the dominant society, although opportunities increased after World War II.

- Japanese immigration began in the 1890s and stimulated a campaign that attempted to oust the group from agriculture and curtail immigration from Japan. The Issei formed an enclave, but during World War II, Japanese Americans were forced into relocation camps, an experience that devastated the group economically and psychologically. The group has since made a strong recovery and is, today, probably the most assimilated Asian American group.

 9.3 Explain the patterns of the recent immigration from Asia.

Recent immigration from Asia is diverse in terms of national origins, contact situation, levels of human capital, and mode of incorporation into U.S. society. Some immigrants are highly educated professionals, while others more closely resemble the "peasant laborers" who have come from Mexico in recent decades and from Italy, Ireland, Poland, and scores of other nations in the past.

 9.4 Understand how prejudice and discrimination affected Asian Americans in the past and today.

Overall levels of anti-Asian prejudice and discrimination have probably declined in recent years but remain widespread. A recent survey suggests that people perceive prejudice and discrimination as being less of a problem for Asian Americans than for other racial minority groups. This might reflect "positive" stereotypes of Asian Americans or the movement of the group toward "honorary" whiteness.

9.5 Apply the concepts of assimilation and pluralism to explain the contemporary situation of Asian Americans, especially

a. acculturation,
b. secondary structural assimilation, and
c. primary structural assimilation.

- Levels of acculturation are highly variable. Some groups, such as Japanese Americans, are highly acculturated, while others, especially those with many first-generation members, have barely begun the process. Continuing high levels of immigration help sustain the various Asian American cultures.
- Secondary structural assimilation is highly variable. Members of these groups whose families have been in the United States longer tend to be highly integrated. Recent immigrants from China, however,

are "bipolar": Many are highly educated and skilled, but a sizable number are "immigrant laborers" who bring modest educational credentials and are likely to be living in poverty.
- Levels of primary assimilation are highly variable. Asian Americans who have had family in the United States for a long time tend to rank high on primary assimilation, while recent immigrants who reside in the enclave tend to rank low. Rates of intermarriage with other groups are higher than for African and Hispanic Americans, but this is dependent on nativity, among other variables.

 9.6 Assess the overall situation of Asian Americans today based on the concepts and information presented in this chapter, and assess the idea that Asian Americans are a "model minority." Are Asian Americans "whitening," "blackening," or becoming "honorary whites"?

The notion that Asian Americans are a "model minority" is exaggerated, but comparisons with European immigrants and colonized minority groups suggest some of the reasons for the relative "success" of these groups. Asian American groups occupy various relations with the larger society, encompassing multiple forms of assimilation and pluralism. Some groups, or segments of groups, may be "whitening," others may be perpetuating an enclave, while still others are marginalized and, perhaps, moving toward a position in the urban underclass. At any rate, traditional, linear notions of assimilation do not describe the situations of these groups, at least at present.

KEY TERMS

Alien Land Act 324	detention	Issei 326	tongs 322
Chinese Exclusion	camps 327	Nisei 326	Yonsei 330
Act 320	huiguan 322	Sansei 330	

REVIEW QUESTIONS

1. Describe the cultural characteristics of Asian American groups. How did these characteristics shape relationships with the larger society? Did they contribute to the perception of Asian Americans as "successful"? How?

2. Compare and contrast the contact situations for Chinese Americans, Japanese Americans, and Cuban Americans (Chapter 8). What common characteristics led to the construction of ethnic enclaves for all three groups? How and why did these enclaves vary from one another?

3. In what sense was the second generation of Chinese Americans "delayed"? How did this affect the relationship of the group with the larger society?

4. Compare and contrast the campaigns that arose in opposition to the immigration of Chinese and Japanese people. Do the concepts of the Noel hypothesis help explain the differences? Do you see any similarities with the changing federal policy toward Mexican immigrants across the 20th century? Explain.

5. Compare and contrast the Japanese relocation camps with Indian reservations in terms of paternalism and coerced acculturation. What impact did this experience have on the Japanese Americans economically? How were Japanese Americans compensated for their losses? Does the compensation paid to Japanese Americans provide a precedent for similar payments (reparations) to African Americans for their losses under slavery? Why or why not?

6. How do the Burakumin in Japan illustrate "visibility" as a defining characteristic of minority-group status? How is the minority status of this group maintained?

7. What gender differences characterize Asian American groups? What are some of the important ways in which women's and men's experiences vary?

8. Describe the situation of the Chinese Americans and Japanese Americans in terms of prejudice and discrimination, acculturation, and integration. Are these groups truly "success stories"? How? What factors or experiences might account for this "success"? Are all Asian American groups equally successful? Describe the important variations from group to group. Compare the integration and level of equality of these groups with other American racial minorities. How would you explain the differences? Are the concepts of the Noel and Blauner hypotheses helpful? Why or why not?

STUDENT STUDY SITE

Sharpen your skills with SAGE edge at edge.sagepub.com/healey8e

SAGE edge for students provides a personalized approach to help you accomplish your coursework goals in an easy-to-use learning environment.

The following resources are available at SAGE edge:

Current Debates: Asian American "Success": What Are the Dimensions, Causes, and Implications for Other Minority Groups?

Considered as a whole, Asian Americans tend to exceed national norms in education, income, and other measures of success. How accurate is this picture? What truths are obscured by the myth of Asian success? What are the implications for other minority groups?

On our website you will find an overview of the topic, the clashing points of view, and some questions to consider as you analyze the material.

Public Sociology Assignments

Public Sociology Assignments provide opportunities for students to address directly and personally some of the issues raised in this text. There are two assignments for Part III on our website. The first looks at patterns of self-segregation in school cafeterias, and, in the second, students analyze the portrayal of the American family on television in terms of race, ethnicity, sexual orientation, and other sociologically relevant characteristics.

Contributed by Linda M. Waldron

Internet Research Project

For this Internet Research Project, you will use data gathered by the U.S. Census Bureau to assess the situation of all Asian Americans and an Asian American group of your choosing. You will add this information to the data you gathered previously on African Americans, Native Americans, Hispanic Americans, and the general population. The project will be guided by a series of questions related to course concepts, and your instructor may ask you to discuss your findings in small groups.

For Further Reading

Please see our website for an annotated list of important works related to this chapter.

CHAPTER-OPENING TIMELINE PHOTO CREDITS

1763: Library of Congress Prints and Photographs Division

1847: Wikimedia/Fred Hsu

1848: Wikimedia Commons

1882: Library of Congress Prints and Photographs Division

1924: Library of Congress Prints and Photographs Division

1942: Dorothea Lange/National Archives and Records Administration/Wikimedia Commons

1988: Ronald Reagan Presidential Library

2001: Ninjanabe/Wikimedia Commons

2016: Michael Loccisano/Getty Images Entertainment/Getty Images

10 NEW AMERICANS, ASSIMILATION, AND OLD CHALLENGES

1875
In search of opportunity, a small number of Arab Muslims emigrate from the Ottoman Empire and settle in New York.

1907
Executive Order 589 prevents Japanese and Koreans from entering the U.S. mainland.

1946
Luce-Celler Act permits Filipinos and Indians to immigrate and grants them naturalization rights.

1874   1886   1898   1910   1922   1934

1893
The first substantial migration of Muslims to the U.S. begins.

1924
The Supreme Court rules that Asian Indians cannot be naturalized.

1952
Muslims in the U.S. military sue the government to be allowed to identify themselves as Muslims. Until then, Islam was not recognized as a legitimate religion.

1952
The Immigration and Nationality Act drastically reduces the number of Caribbean farm workers allowed to enter the U.S.

Sade and four of his twenty-something friends are at a hookah cafe almost underneath the Verrazano-Narrows Bridge in Brooklyn. It's late, but the summer heat is strong and hangs in the air. They sit on the sidewalk in a circle, water pipes bubbling between their white plastic chairs.

Sade is upset. He recently found out that his close friend of almost four years was an undercover police detective sent to spy on him, his friends, and his community. Even the guy's name . . . was fake, which particularly irked the twenty-four-year-old Palestinian American. . . .

"I was very hurt," he says. "Was it friendship, or was he doing his job?" He takes a puff from his water pipe. "I felt betrayed." The smoke comes out thick and smells like apples. . . . He shakes his head. . . .

LEARNING OBJECTIVES

By the end of this chapter, you will be able to do the following:

10.1 Understand the volume and diversity of recent immigration to the United States.

10.2 Understand the general characteristics of recent immigrants, especially new Hispanic and Asian groups, groups from the Caribbean, Middle Eastern and Arab groups, and immigrants from Africa.

10.3 Characterize the new immigrant groups in terms of whether they are entering through the primary or secondary labor markets or through ethnic enclaves.

10.4 Explain the attitudes of the American public as well as the values and statistical characteristics of the immigrants.

10.5 Understand the various positions regarding the costs and benefits of immigration, undocumented immigrants, and DREAMers.

10.6 Explain the points of view and evidence regarding whether contemporary immigration will be segmented.

10.7 Place current immigration in the context of globalization, and cite some of the implications of immigration for "traditional" American minority groups.

1965
The Hart-Celler Act, a new immigration law, launches a new wave of immigration from the Caribbean. Pakistanis, Bangladeshis, and Arabs from the professional classes also immigrate, helping to establish Islam in America.

1977–1981
60,000 Haitians land in South Florida by boat, fleeing the brutal political repression of the Duvalier dictatorship. Thousands are returned to Haiti.

2001
Hate crimes against Arab and Asian Americans follow the September 11 terrorist attacks.

2017
Thousands of people across the United States protest Executive Order 13780 banning citizens of some Muslim-majority countries from entering the United States.

1946   1958   1970   1982   1994   2006   2018

1956
Dalip Singh Saund of California becomes the first Indian American in Congress.

1975
The Vietnam War ends, leading to a large migration of Southeast Asians.

1979–1992
During El Salvador's civil war, between 500,000 and one million immigrate to the U.S.

1980
Ethiopians become the largest group of Africans to immigrate to the U.S. under the provisions of the Refugee Act of 1980.

1986
40,000 Haitians seeking political asylum are given permanent resident status.

2008
The number of undocumented immigrants begins to decline in response to economic hard times in the U.S., falling to less than 11 million in 2012.

2012
The Obama administration creates a program by which the children of undocumented immigrants ("DREAMers") can apply to stay in the U.S. without fear of deportation.

Informants and spies are regular conversation topics [among Arab Americans] in the age of terror, a time when friendships are tested, trust disappears, and tragedy becomes comedy. If questioning friendship isn't enough, Sade has also had other problems to deal with. Sacked from his Wall Street job, he is convinced that the termination stemmed from his Jerusalem birthplace. Anti-Arab and anti-Muslim invectives were routinely slung at him there, and he's happier now in a technology firm owned and staffed by other hyphenated Americans. But the last several years have taken their toll. I ask him about life after September 11 for Arab Americans. "We're the new blacks," he says. "You know that, right?"

—Moustafa Bayoumi (2008, pp. 1–2)

Sade's comparison between Arab Americans and blacks may be overstated, but there is no question that America finds itself in a new era of group relations today. The "traditional" minority groups—black Americans, Mexican Americans, and others—have been joined by new groups from places that most Americans could not find on a map: Armenia, Zimbabwe, Bhutan, Guyana, and Indonesia, to name but a few.

What do these newcomers bring? What do they contribute, and what do they cost? How are they changing the United States? What will the country look like in 50 years? We asked at the beginning of this text: "What does it mean to be an American?" How will that question be answered in the future? •

The world is on the move as never before, and migration connects even the most remote villages of every continent in a global network of population ebb and flow. As we have seen, people are moving everywhere, but the United States remains the single most popular destination. Migrants will pay huge amounts of money—thousands of dollars, veritable fortunes in economies where people survive on dollars a day—and undergo considerable hardship for the chance to reach the United States.

What motivates this population movement? How does it differ from migrations of the past? What impact will the newcomers have on U.S. society? Will they absorb American culture? What parts? Will they integrate into American society? Which segments?

We have been asking questions like these throughout the text. In this chapter, we focus specifically on current immigrants and the myriad issues stimulated by their presence. We mentioned some groups of new Americans in Chapters 8 and 9. In this chapter, we begin by addressing recent immigration in general terms and then consider some additional groups of new Americans, including Hispanic, Caribbean, and Asian groups; Arabs and Middle Easterners; and immigrants from sub-Saharan Africa. A consideration of these groups will broaden your understanding of the wide variations in culture, motivations, and human capital of the current immigrant stream to the United States.

We will next discuss the most important and controversial immigration issues facing U.S. society and conclude with a brief return to the "traditional" minority groups: African Americans, American Indians, and other peoples of color who continue to face issues of equality and full integration, and who must now pursue their long-standing grievances in an atmosphere where public attention and political energy are focused on other groups and newer issues.

CURRENT IMMIGRATION

As you know, the United States has experienced three different waves of mass immigration. In Chapter 2, we discussed the first two waves (see Figure 2.2). As you recall, the first wave lasted from the 1820s to the 1880s and consisted of mostly Northern and Western European immigrants. The second, from the 1880s to the 1920s, brought primarily Southern and Eastern European immigrants. During these two periods, more than 37 million people immigrated to the United States, an average rate of about 370,000 per year. These waves of newcomers transformed American society on every level: its cities, its neighborhoods and

FIGURE 10.1 Number of Legal Immigrants to the United States, 1960–2015

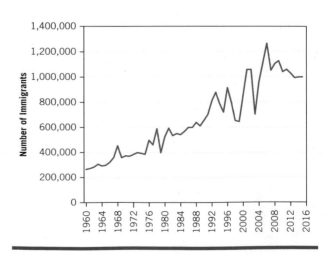

SOURCE: U.S. Department of Homeland Security, 2016.

parishes, its popular culture, its accents and dialects, its religion, its cuisine, and so much more.

The third wave of mass immigration promises to be equally transformative. This wave began after the 1965 change in U.S. immigration policy and includes people from every corner of the globe. Since the mid-1960s, over 30 million newcomers have arrived (not counting undocumented immigrants). This rate of more than 670,000 people per year is much higher than the earlier period, although the rate is lower as a percentage of the total population. Figure 10.1 shows that the number of legal immigrants per year has generally increased over this period, at least until the U.S. economy turned sour in more recent years.

The official record for most immigrants in a year was set in 1907, when almost 1.3 million people arrived in the United States. That number was almost equaled in 2006 and, if undocumented immigrants had been included in the count, the 1907 record would have been eclipsed several times since the 1960s.

The more recent wave of immigration is much more diverse than the first two. In 2015 alone, immigrants arrived from more than 200 separate nations—from Afghanistan and Albania to Zambia and Zimbabwe. Only 8.6% of the newcomers were from Europe, about 15% were from Mexico alone, and almost 40% were from Asia. Figure 10.2 lists the numbers for the top 25 sending nations for 2015. Note that the number of Mexican immigrants is more than double the number from China, the next-highest sending nation. Also, note the variety of nations and regions of origin. Immigration to the United States is truly a global phenomenon!

How will this new wave of immigration transform the United States? How will these new immigrants be transformed by living in the United States? What do they contribute? What do they cost? Will they adopt the ways of the dominant society? What are the implications if they don't?

We begin by reviewing several case studies of new Americans, focusing on information and statistics comparable to those used in Chapters 6 through 9. Each of the groups covered in this chapter has had some members in the United States for decades, some for more than a century. However, in all cases the groups were quite small until the latter part of the 20th century. Although they are growing rapidly now, all stay relatively small, and none composes more than 1% of the population. Nonetheless, some will have a greater impact on American culture and society in the future, and some groups—Muslims and Arab and Middle Easterner Americans—have already become a focus of concern and controversy because of the events of September 11 and the ensuing war on terrorism.

QUESTIONS FOR REFLECTION

1. What are some of the key differences between the first two waves of mass immigration from the 1820s to the 1920s and the current, post-1965 wave?

2. Why is the current wave of immigration so diverse? What are the implications of this diversity for the future of American society?

FIGURE 10.2 Number of Legal Immigrants for Top 25 Sending Nations, 2015

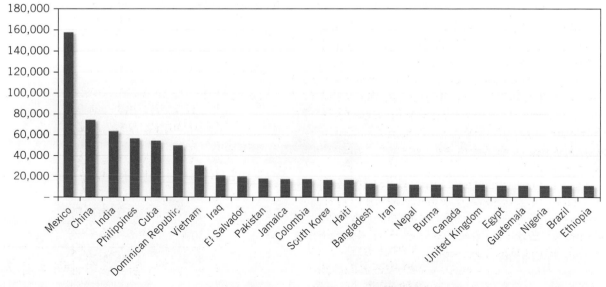

SOURCE: U.S. Department of Homeland Security (2016).

January 31, 2017. Thousands of people across the United States protest Executive Order 13780, which, in part, barred citizens of some Muslim-majority countries from entering the United States. The countries are Iran, Iraq, Libya, Somalia, Sudan, Yemen, and Syria—including Syrian refugees fleeing war.

NEW HISPANIC GROUPS: IMMIGRANTS FROM THE DOMINICAN REPUBLIC, EL SALVADOR, AND COLOMBIA

Immigration from Latin America, the Caribbean, and South America has been considerable, even excluding Mexico. As with other sending nations, the volume of immigration from these regions increased after 1965 and has averaged about 200,000 per year. Generally, Latino immigrants—not counting those from Mexico—have composed about 25% of all immigrants since the 1960s (U.S. Department of Homeland Security, 2016).

The sending nations for these immigrants are economically less developed, and most have long-standing relations with the United States. In Chapter 8, we discussed the roles that Mexico and Puerto Rico have played as sources of cheap labor and the ties that led Cubans to immigrate to the United States. Each of the other sending nations has been similarly linked to the United States, the dominant economic and political power in the region.

Although the majority of these immigrants bring educational and occupational qualifications that are modest by U.S. standards, they tend to be more educated, more urbanized, and more skilled than the average citizens of the nations from which they come. Contrary to widely held beliefs, these immigrants do not represent the poorest of the poor, the "wretched refuse" of their homelands. They tend to be rather ambitious, as evidenced by their willingness to attempt to succeed in a society that has not been notably hospitable to Latinos or people of color in the past. Most of these immigrants are not only fleeing poverty or joblessness but also are trying to pursue their ambitions and seek opportunities for advancement that are generally not available in their countries of origin (Feliciano, 2006; Portes & Rumbaut, 1996, pp. 10–11).

This characterization applies to legal and unauthorized immigrants alike. In fact, the latter may illustrate the point more dramatically, because the cost of illegally entering the United States can be considerable, much higher than the cost of a legal entry. The venture may require years of saving or the combined resources of a large kinship group. Forged papers and other costs of being smuggled into the country can easily amount to many thousands of dollars, a considerable sum in nations in which the usual wage is a tiny fraction of the U.S. average. Also, the passage can be extremely dangerous and can require a level of courage (or desperation) that many Americans do not often associate with undocumented immigrants.

TABLE 10.1 Selected Characteristics of Three Hispanic American Groups and Non-Hispanic Whites, 2015

GROUP	SIZE	PERCENTAGE WITH LESS THAN HIGH SCHOOL DIPLOMA	PERCENTAGE WITH COLLEGE DEGREE OR MORE	PERCENTAGE FOREIGN-BORN	PERCENTAGE WHO SPEAK ENGLISH LESS THAN "VERY WELL"	MEDIAN HOUSEHOLD INCOME	PERCENTAGE OF FAMILIES IN POVERTY
Non-Hispanic whites	—	8.2	34.2	4%	1.6	$61,394	6.6
Dominicans	1,719,678	31.0	16.9	54.8	42.7	$37,000	26
Salvadorans	2,022,687	49.0	8.6	59.3	50.1	$47,258	17.7
Colombians	1,081,838	14.0	33.6	61.1	35.9	$55,082	12.2

SOURCE: U.S. Census Bureau, 2016, American Community Survey, 2015, 5-year Estimates, https://factfinder.census.gov/faces/tableservices/jsf/pages/productview.xhtml?pid=ACS_15_SPT_DP02&prodType=table.

Rather than attempting to cover all South and Central American groups, we have selected three of the largest to serve as case studies: those from the Dominican Republic, El Salvador, and Colombia. In recent years, these three groups have made up 7% to 8% of all immigrants and about 30% of the immigrants from Central and South America and the Caribbean. These groups had few members in the United States before the 1960s, and all have had high rates of immigration over the past four decades. However, the motivation of the immigrants and the immigration experience has varied from group to group, as we shall see.

THREE CASE STUDIES

Table 10.1 presents some basic information about these three groups. Some of this information was also presented in Chapter 8 and is repeated here to provide a common frame of reference for the groups covered in this chapter.

Each of these groups has a high percentage of foreign-born members, and, predictably with so many members in the first generation, proficiency in English is an important issue. Although Colombian Americans approach national norms in education, the other two groups have relatively low levels of human capital (education). They are well below national norms for income and have higher rates of poverty.

Although these groups share some characteristics, there exhibit important differences. They differ in their "racial" characteristics, with Dominicans being more African in appearance, Colombians more European, and Salvadorans more Indian. The groups tend to settle in different places. Colombians are clustered in the South (49%), particularly in Florida, and the Northeast (33%), mostly in New York and New Jersey (Brown & Patten, 2013a, p. 2). Dominicans are concentrated in the Northeast (78%), with almost half living in New York alone (Brown & Patten, 2013c, p. 2). In contrast, Salvadorans tend to reside in the West (40%), mostly in California, and the South, mostly in Texas (Brown & Patten, 2013e, p. 2).

Finally, the groups differ in the conditions of their entry or contact situations—a difference that, as we have seen, is consequential. Salvadorans are more likely to be political refugees who fled a brutal civil war and political repression, while Dominicans and Colombians are more likely to be motivated by economics and the employment possibilities offered in the United States. Let's consider each of these groups briefly and further explore some of their differences.

Dominicans. The Dominican Republic shares the Caribbean island of Hispaniola with Haiti. The island economy is still largely agricultural, although the tourist industry has grown in recent years. Unemployment and poverty are major problems, and Dominicans age 25 and over average about five years of education (World Bank, 2017). Dominican immigrants, like those from Mexico, are motivated largely by economics, and they compete for jobs with Puerto Ricans, other immigrant groups, and native-born workers with lower levels of education and job skills.

Although Dominicans are limited in their job options by the language barrier, they are somewhat advantaged by their willingness to work for lower wages. They are concentrated in the service sector, as day laborers (men) or domestics (women). Dominican immigrants maintain strong ties with home and are a major source of income and support for the families left behind.

In terms of acculturation and integration, Dominicans are roughly similar to Mexican Americans and Puerto Ricans, although some studies suggest that they are possibly the most impoverished immigrant group (see Table 10.1 and Figures 8.18 and 8.20). A high percentage of Dominicans are undocumented, and many spend a great deal of money and take considerable risks to get to the United States. If these less visible members of the community were included in the official, government-generated statistics used in the figures and tables presented in this and previous chapters, the portrait of poverty and low levels of education and job skills likely would be even more dramatic.

Salvadorans. El Salvador, like the Dominican Republic, is a relatively poor nation, with a high percentage of the population relying on subsistence agriculture for survival. Approximately 35% of the population lives below the poverty level (Central Intelligence Agency, 2017) due to major problems with unemployment and underemployment. About 80% of the population is literate, and the average number of years of school completed in the population 25 years of age and older is about 6 (World Bank, 2017).

El Salvador, like many sending nations, has a difficult time providing sufficient employment opportunities for its population, and much of the pressure to migrate is economic. However, El Salvador also suffered through a brutal civil war in the 1980s, and many of the Salvadorans in the United States today are political refugees. The United States, under the administration of President Ronald Reagan, refused to grant political refugee status to Salvadorans and returned many of them to El Salvador. This federal policy resulted in high numbers of undocumented immigrants and stimulated a sanctuary movement, led by American clergy, to help Salvadoran immigrants, both undocumented and legal, stay in the United States. As is the case with Dominicans, if the undocumented immigrants from El Salvador were included in official government statistics, the picture of poverty would become more extreme.

TABLE 10.2 Selected Characteristics of Two Non-Hispanic Caribbean Groups and Non-Hispanic Whites, 2015

GROUP	SIZE	PERCENTAGE WITH LESS THAN HIGH SCHOOL DIPLOMA	PERCENTAGE WITH COLLEGE DEGREE OR MORE	PERCENTAGE FOREIGN-BORN	PERCENTAGE WHO SPEAK ENGLISH LESS THAN "VERY WELL"	MEDIAN HOUSEHOLD INCOME	PERCENTAGE OF FAMILIES IN POVERTY
Non-Hispanic whites	—	8.2	34.2	4	1.6	$61,394	6.6
Haitians	1,062,550	19.0	22.2	57.6	34.1	$47,751	17.0
Jamaicans	1,097,196	14.8	27.1	57.3	0.9	$50,935	12.5

SOURCE: U.S. Census Bureau (2013a).

Colombians. Colombia is somewhat more developed than most other Central and South American nations but has suffered from more than 40 years of internal turmoil, civil war, and government corruption. It is a major center for the production and distribution of drugs to the world in general and the United States in particular, and the drug industry and profits are complexly intertwined with domestic strife.

Colombian Americans are closer to U.S. norms of education and income than are other Latino groups (see Table 10.1, as well as Figures 8.16, 8.18, and 8.20). Recent immigrants are a mixture of less-skilled laborers and well-educated professionals seeking to further their careers. Colombians are residentially concentrated in urban areas, especially in Florida and the Northeast, and often settle in areas close to other Latino neighborhoods. Of course, the huge majority of Colombian Americans are law-abiding and not connected with the drug trade, but many must deal with the pervasive stereotype that portrays Colombians as gangsters and drug smugglers (not unlike the Mafia stereotype about Italian Americans).

NON-HISPANIC IMMIGRANTS FROM THE CARIBBEAN

Immigrants from the Western Hemisphere bring a variety of traditions to the United States other than Hispanic ones. Two of the largest non-Latino groups come from Haiti and Jamaica in the Caribbean. Both nations are much less developed than the United States, and this is reflected in the educational and occupational characteristics of their immigrants. A statistical profile of both groups is presented in Table 10.2, along with statistics for non-Hispanic whites for purposes of comparison.

TWO CASE STUDIES

Haitians. Haiti is the poorest country in the Western Hemisphere, and most of the population relies on small-scale subsistence agriculture for survival. An estimated 59% of the population lives below the poverty line, and the unemployment rate is about 40% (Central Intelligence Agency, 2017). About 40% of the population is illiterate, and Haitians average less than three years of formal education (World Bank, 2017). A massive earthquake in January 2010 intensified the already difficult conditions in Haiti and the tiny nation continues to suffer from the devastation.

Haitian migration was virtually nonexistent until the 1970s and 1980s, when thousands began to flee the brutal repression of the Duvalier dictatorship, which—counting both father ("Papa Doc") and son ("Baby Doc")—lasted until the mid-1980s. In stark contrast to its treatment of Cuban immigrants (see Chapter 8), the U.S. government

Haitian refugees attempting to sail to the Florida. Note the overcrowded, unsafe condition of their boat.

defined Haitians as economic refugees ineligible for asylum, and began an intense campaign to keep Haitians out of the United States. The U.S. government returned thousands of people to Haiti, some to face political persecution, prison, and even death. Others were incarcerated in the United States. In the view of some, "during the 1970s and 1980s, no other immigrant group suffered more U.S. government prejudice and discrimination than Haitians" (Stepick, Stepick, Eugene, Teed, & Labissiere, 2001, p. 236).

What accounts for this cold, negative reception? Some reasons are not hard to identify. Haitian immigrants brought low levels of human capital and education. This created concerns about their ability to support themselves in the United States and also meant that they had relatively few resources with which to defend their self-interests. In addition, although French is the language of the educated elite, most Haitians speak a version of Creole that is spoken only by Haitians, and a high percentage of Haitian immigrants speak English poorly or not at all. Perhaps the most important reason for the rejection is that Haitians are black and must cope with the centuries-old traditions of rejection, racism, and prejudice that are such an integral part of American culture (Stepick et al., 2001).

Haitian Americans today are still mostly first-generation, recent immigrants. Overall, they are comparable to Hispanic Americans in terms of measures of equality such as income and poverty (see Table 10.2, as well as Figures 8.18 and 8.20 for information on the status of Hispanic Americans). Still, research shows that some Haitians continue to face the exclusion and discrimination long associated with nonwhite ancestry.

One study of Haitians in Florida found several factors—their hostile reception, their poverty and lack of education, and their racial background—lead to the second generation (immigrants' children) having a relatively low level of academic achievement and a tendency to identify with the African American community. This suggests that some members of the second generation are unlikely to move into the middle class and that their assimilation will be segmented (Stepick et al., 2001, p. 261). In 2017, the U.S. government ended a program that granted Temporary Protected Status to nearly 60,000 Haitians who came to the U.S. after an earthquake displaced more than a million of them. This change will further impact the Haitian American community.

Jamaicans. The Jamaican economy is more developed than Haiti's, and this is reflected in the higher levels of education of Jamaican immigrants (see Table 10.2). However, like other economies throughout the less-developed world, the Jamaican economy has faltered in recent decades, and the island nation has been unable to provide full employment opportunities to its population. Jamaica is a former British colony, and its emigrants have journeyed to the United Kingdom in addition to the United States. In both cases, the immigrant stream tends to be more skilled and educated, and represents something of a "brain drain" on its home country. We have seen this phenomenon with other groups, including Asian Indians (Feliciano, 2006). Needless to say, the loss of the more educated Jamaicans to other nations exacerbates problems of development and growth on the island.

Jamaicans typically settle on the East Coast, particularly in the New York City area. Because they come from a former British colony, they have the advantage of speaking English as their native language. On the other hand, they are black, and like Haitians, they must face the barriers of discrimination and racism faced by nonwhite groups in the United States. On average, they possess significantly higher socioeconomic standing than Haitians (and native-born African Americans), but poverty and institutionalized discrimination limit upward mobility for a segment of the group. Some, like other groups of color in the United States, face the possibility of segmented assimilation and permanent exclusion from the economic mainstream. On the other hand, at least one study shows that many second-generation Jamaicans are moving into the mainstream economy and taking jobs comparable to those of others with their level of education, at least in New York City, where many of them live (Kasinitz, Mollenkopf, Waters, & Holdaway, 2008).

CONTEMPORARY IMMIGRATION FROM ASIA

Immigration from Asia has been considerable since the 1960s, averaging close to 300,000 people per year and running about 30% to 40% of all immigrants (U.S. Department of Homeland Security, 2016). Like the sending nations for Hispanic immigrants, the sending nations for Asians are considerably less economically developed than the United States, and the primary motivation for most of these immigrants is economic. As we pointed out in Chapter 9, however, the Asian immigrant stream is "bipolar" and includes many highly educated professionals along with the less skilled and less educated. Also, many Asian immigrants are refugees from the Vietnam War in Southeast Asia in the 1960s and 1970s. Others are the spouses of U.S. military personnel who have been stationed throughout the region.

As before, rather than attempting to cover all Asian immigrant groups, we will concentrate on four case studies and consider immigrants from India, Vietnam, Korea, and the Philippines. Together, these four groups make up about half of all immigrants from Asia (U.S. Department of Homeland Security, 2016).

FOUR CASE STUDIES

The four groups considered here are small and include a high percentage of foreign-born members. They vary in their backgrounds, occupational profiles, levels of education, and incomes. In contrast to Hispanic immigrants, they tend to have higher percentages of members who are fluent in English, members with higher levels of education, and relatively more members prepared to compete for good jobs in the American economy. A statistical profile of the groups is presented in Table 10.3, along with that of non-Hispanic whites for purposes of comparison.

The four groups vary in their settlement patterns. Most are concentrated along the West Coast, but Asian Indians are roughly equally distributed on the East and West Coasts, and Vietnamese have a sizable presence in Texas, in part related to the fishing industry along the Gulf Coast.

Asian Indians. India, home to more than 1.2 billion people, is the second most populous nation in the world. India has a wide variety of religions, ethnic groups, and languages (including 19 official languages). Overall, the level of education is fairly low: About 71% of the population is literate (Central Intelligence Agency, 2017) with an average of less than 5 years of formal schooling (World Bank, 2017). However, about 20% of the college-age Indian population is enrolled in some form of higher education ("College Enrollment," 2012). This means millions of educated Indians are looking for careers commensurate with their credentials. Because of the relative lack of development in the Indian economy, many college-educated Indians must search for career opportunities abroad, and not just in the United States.

Additionally, it is important to note that as a legacy of India's long colonization by the British, English is the language of the educated. Thus, Indian immigrants to the United States tend to be not only well educated, but English speaking, also (see Table 10.3).

Immigration from India to the United States was low until the mid-1960s, and the group was quite small at that time. The group almost quintupled in size between 1990 and 2015 (see Table 9.1), and Indians are now the second-largest Asian American group (Chinese Americans are the largest group).

Immigrants from India tend to be a select, highly educated, and skilled group, as shown in Table 10.3 and Figures 9.10 and 9.15. According to the 2000 Census, Indians are overrepresented in some of the most prestigious occupations, including computer engineering, medicine, and college teaching (U.S. Census Bureau, 2000b). Indian immigrants are part of a worldwide movement of educated peoples from less-developed countries to more-developed countries. One need not ponder the differences in career opportunities, technology, and compensation for long to get some insight into the reasons for this movement. Other immigrants from India are more oriented to commerce and small business, and there is a sizable Indian ethnic enclave in many cities (Dingra & Pawan, 2012; Kitano & Daniels, 1995, pp. 96–111; Sheth, 1995).

Koreans. Immigration from South Korea to the United States began early in the 20th century, when laborers were recruited to help fill the void in the job market left by the 1882 Chinese Exclusion Act that you read about in Chapter 9. This group was extremely small until the 1950s, when the rate of immigration rose because of refugees and "war brides" (women who married U.S. military personnel) after the Korean War (National Association of Korean Americans, 2003). Immigration did not become

TABLE 10.3 Selected Characteristics of Four Asian American Groups and Non-Hispanic Whites, 2012

GROUP	SIZE	PERCENTAGE WITH LESS THAN HIGH SCHOOL DIPLOMA	PERCENTAGE WITH COLLEGE DEGREE OR MORE	PERCENTAGE FOREIGN-BORN	PERCENTAGE WHO SPEAK ENGLISH LESS THAN "VERY WELL"	MEDIAN HOUSEHOLD INCOME	PERCENTAGE OF FAMILIES IN POVERTY
Non-Hispanic whites	—	8.2	34.2	4.0	1.6	$61,394	6.6
Asian Indians	3,982,398	8.2	72.3	68.4	19.9	$101,899	5
Koreans	1,822,213	7.1	54.0	58.6	34.6	$63,687	9.9
Filipinos	3,898,739	7.2	45.9	50.2	17.7	$81,564	5.5
Vietnamese	1,980,344	26.2	29.3	61.9	47.5	$59,710	12.4

SOURCE: U.S. Census Bureau, 2017. American Community Survey, 5-year estimates.

substantial, however, until 1965 when immigration law changed (Pew Research Center, 2013d). The number of Korean immigrants peaked in the late 1980s (Min, 2006, p. 232). The size of the group increased fivefold in the 1970s and more than doubled between 1990 and 2015 (see Table 9.1), although it is still much less than 1% of the total population.

Like the immigrant stream from India, South Korean immigrants include many middle-class, more educated, professional people, many of whom were "pushed" from their homeland by a repressive military government. Korea transitioned to a more Western-style democracy in the late 1980s, and immigration declined as a direct result (see Figure 9.5).

Although differences in culture, language, and race make Koreans visible targets of discrimination, the high percentage of Christians among them (about 70%) may help them appear more "acceptable" to the dominant group. Certainly, Christian church parishes play many important roles for the Korean American community, such as offering assistance to newcomers and the less fortunate, serving as a focal point for networks of mutual assistance, and generally assisting in the completion of the numerous additional chores to which immigrant communities must attend (e.g., government paperwork, registering to vote; see Kitano & Daniels, 2001, p. 123).

Korean American immigrants have formed an enclave, and group members are heavily involved in small businesses and retail stores—particularly fruit and vegetable retail stores or greengroceries. According to one study, Koreans had the second-highest percentage of self-employment among immigrant groups (Greeks were the highest), with about 23% of the group in this occupational category (Min, 2006, pp. 238–239; also see Pew Research Center, 2013d). However, Korean Americans are typically more visible than many other entrepreneurial groups because of their size and concentration in the largest metropolitan areas.

As is the case for other groups that have pursued this course, the enclave allows Korean Americans to avoid the discrimination and racism of the larger society and survive in an economic niche in which lack of English fluency is not a particular problem. (Though 43% of Korean American adults report speaking English "very well"; see Pew Research Center, 2013d.) However, the enclave has its perils and its costs. For one thing, the success of Korean enterprises depends heavily on the mutual assistance and financial support of other Koreans and the willingness of group members to work long hours for little or no pay (recall the story of Kim Park from Chapter 1). These resources would be weakened or destroyed by acculturation, integration, and the resultant decline in ethnic solidarity. Only by maintaining a distance from the dominant culture can the infrastructure survive.

Furthermore, the economic niches in which mom-and-pop greengroceries and other small businesses can survive are often in deteriorated neighborhoods populated largely by other minority groups. There has been a good deal of hostility and resentment expressed against Korean shop owners by African Americans, Puerto Ricans, and other urbanized minority groups. For example, anti-Korean sentiments were widely apparent in the 1992 Los Angeles riots that followed the acquittal of the policemen charged in the beating of Rodney King. Korean-owned businesses were some of the first to be looted and burned. When asked why, one looter said simply, "Because we hate' em. Everybody hates them" (Cho, 1993, p. 199). Pew Research Center data (2013d) suggests that almost one quarter of Korean Americans (24%) report that "discrimination is a major problem." Thus, part of the price of survival for many Korean merchants is to place themselves in positions in which antagonism and conflict with other minority groups is common (Kitano & Daniels, 1995, pp. 112–129; Light & Bonacich, 1988; Min, 2006; see also Hurh, 1998).

Filipino Americans. Ties between the United States and the Philippines were established in 1898 when Spain ceded the territory after its defeat in the Spanish–American War. The Philippines achieved independence following World War II, but the United States has maintained a strong military presence there for much of the past 60 years. The nation has been heavily influenced by American culture, and English remains one of two official languages. Thus, Filipino immigrants are often familiar with English, at least as a second language (see Table 10.3).

Today, Filipinos are the third-largest Asian American group, but their numbers became sizable only in the past few decades. In 1920, fewer than 1,000 Filipinos lived in the United States; by 1960, the group still numbered fewer than 200,000. Most of the recent growth has come from increased post-1965 immigration. The group almost tripled in size over the past several decades (see Table 9.1). Many of the earliest immigrants were agricultural workers recruited for the sugar plantations of Hawaii and the fields of the West Coast. Because the Philippines was a U.S. territory, Filipinos could enter without regard to immigration quotas until 1935, when the nation became a self-governing commonwealth.

The most recent wave of immigrants is diversified, and, like Chinese Americans, Filipino Americans are "bipolar" in their educational and occupational profiles. Many recent immigrants have entered under the family preference provisions of the U.S. immigration policy. These immigrants are often poor and compete for jobs in the low-wage secondary labor market (Kitano & Daniels, 1995, p. 94).

Since 1965, more than half of all Filipino immigrants have been professionals, many working in the health and medical fields. For example, more than 20,000 immigrant medical graduate (IMG) physicians from the Philippines work in the United States, the second largest of all immigrant groups (Hohn, Lowry, Witte, & Fernández-Pena, 2016). Many women immigrants were nurses actively recruited by U.S. hospitals to fill gaps in the labor force. In fact, nurses have become something of an export commodity in the Philippines. Thousands of trained nurses leave the Philippines every year to work all over the world. About one third of immigrant nurses working in the United States came from the Philippines (Hohn et al., 2016). Thus, the Filipino American community includes some members in the higher-wage primary labor market while others compete for work in the low-wage secondary sector (Agbayani-Siewert & Revilla, 1995; Espiritu, 1996; Kitano & Daniels, 1995, pp. 83–94; Min, 2006; Posadas, 1999).

Vietnamese. A flow of refugees from Vietnam began in the 1960s as a direct result of the war in Southeast Asia. The war began in Vietnam but expanded when the United States attacked communist forces in Cambodia and Laos. Social life was disrupted, and people were displaced throughout the region. In 1975, when Saigon (the South Vietnamese capital) fell and the U.S. military withdrew, many Vietnamese and other Southeast Asians who had collaborated with the United States and its allies fled in fear for their lives.

This group included high-ranking officials and members of the region's educational and occupational elite. Later groups of refugees tended to be less well educated and more impoverished. Many Vietnamese waited in refugee camps for months or years before being admitted to the United States, and they often arrived with few resources or social networks to ease their transition to the new society (Kitano & Daniels, 1995, pp. 151–152). The Vietnamese are the largest of the Asian refugee groups, and, contrary to Asian American success stories and notions of model minorities, they have incomes and educational levels that are somewhat comparable to those of colonized minority groups (see Table 10.3 and Figures 9.10, 9.11, 9.14, 9.15, and 9.17). The story of one Vietnamese refugee family is recounted in the following Narrative Portrait.

MIDDLE EASTERN AND ARAB AMERICANS

Immigration from the Middle East and the Arab world began in the 19th century but has never been particularly large. The earliest immigrants tended to be merchants and traders, and the Middle Eastern community in the United States has been constructed around an ethnic, small-business enclave. The number of Arab and Middle Eastern Americans has grown rapidly over the past several decades but still remains a tiny percentage of the total population. Table 10.4 displays some statistical information on the group, broken down by the ancestry subgroup with which individuals identify. The "Arab American" category is a general one and includes Lebanese, Egyptian, and Syrian Americans, along with many smaller groups.

Table 10.4 shows that these groups tend to rank relatively high in income and education. All groups rank higher than non-Hispanic whites in terms of college graduates, and some (Egyptians and Iranians) are far more educated. Although poverty is a problem (especially for the general "Arab American" category), most of these groups compare quite favorably to other U.S. residents in terms of median household income.

Many recent Middle Eastern immigrants are, like Asian immigrants, highly educated people who take jobs in the highest levels of the American job structure. Consistent with the heritage of being an enclave minority, the groups are overrepresented in sales and underrepresented in occupations involving manual labor. Compared with other ethnic groups, much less research has been conducted on Arab American women's employment. Read (2004) mailed a survey to a national sample of Arab American women and found that immigrant Arab American women have a very low rate of employment, the lowest of any immigrant group. The author's analysis of these data strongly suggests that this pattern is due to traditional ideas about gender and family norms, specifically regarding the "proper" role of women (Read, 2004).

Arab and Middle Eastern Americans are diverse and vary along many dimensions. For example, not all Middle Easterners are Arabic; Iranians, for example, are Persian. They bring different national traditions and cultures and vary in religion. Most are Muslim, but many are Christian. In 2017, 3.35 million Muslim Americans lived in the United States; 2.05 million of them are adults (Pew Research Center, 2017c). About two thirds of them are immigrants or children of immigrants, but no individual nation accounts for more than 15% of adult Muslim immigrants.

Similarly, Muslim American adults come from a variety of racial and ethnic backgrounds. Nearly half (41%) of all Muslims living in the United States identify as white, a category that includes Middle Eastern, Arab, Persian, and other ethnic groups. (See Chapter 1.) Nearly one third (28%) identify as Asian (including South Asia), and one fifth (20%) identify as black. Of U.S.-born Muslims, 35% identify as white, 32% as black, and 10% as Asian (Pew Research Center, 2017c, p. 35).

NARRATIVE PORTRAIT

Refugees

PH2 Phil Eggman/Wikimedia Commons

Vietnamese refugees are picked up by a U.S. Navy ship after spending eight days at sea.

C. N. Le was a young boy when his family left Vietnam. They were in the first wave of refugees who left their homeland as the U.S.-supported South Vietnamese government collapsed. Although they had to leave their possessions and their life savings behind, Le's family brought a number of resources, including the ability to speak English, and—unlike many refugee families—they made a successful transition to America. Notice the role played by ethnic networks and extended family in the adjustment process. Le became a sociologist and currently maintains the Asian-Nation website (www.asian-nation.org).

FROM SAIGON TO SUBURBIA

C. N. Le

Our "ticket" out of Viet Nam . . . was my mother's employment with the U.S. government. . . . Her superiors . . . arranged for us to be evacuated. We . . . were [picked up by] a cargo ship. . . .

As the ship approached, everyone tried to use whatever vessels they could find, steal, or rent to make their way to the ship. People were swimming in the sea and jumping from boat to boat in their efforts to board. . . . In this frantic confusion, my mother's mother and her brother and his family failed to get on

board and were left behind. She would not see them again for almost 20 years. . . .

Conditions were very crowded [on the ship]. . . . Because [we] had to leave all [our] possessions behind, my family literally had nothing besides the clothes on [our] backs. . . .

When I asked [them] how they felt [about being] relocated in the United States, . . . my mother said that she was quite distraught, depressed, and in a state of shock worrying over what would become of her brother and mother. . . . As she put it, her sadness overshadowed any feelings of coming to the United States.

My father was also very sad at having to leave his home, his business, and our life savings back in Viet Nam, and at the thought that he probably would never see Viet Nam again. . . . He also mentioned that he was worried about the prospects for a good life in the United States. As he put it, "I was thinking about whether my skills could feed a family of five and could my children get along in school speaking a different language and having a different culture." . . . His pragmatism and vision fortunately compensated for my mother's feelings of distress. . . .

We were flown to one of the four relocation centers that the U.S. government had set up to process the approximately 125,000 refugees who left Viet Nam. We . . . began our life in the United States on May 15, 1975. . . .

[My] family moved to Camp Pendleton in California to take custody of my 2-year-old cousin, who had become separated from her family. . . . Our sponsor agency . . . eventually found us an apartment [near] . . . Los Angeles, on September 25, 1975. We were part of a group of 16 other families that were settled in the same apartment complex, the first group of refugees being settled into that area. The sponsor agency arranged for our first month's rent, along with a supply of groceries.

Since my mother knew enough English, she began working as a teacher's aide in an English class that all refugees [had] to attend. . . . She went on to take . . . classes [and obtained] her GED. After my father's mother arrived to look after my sisters and me, she was able to . . . take nursing courses. . . . She became an RN in

1983. She now works as an auditor for the Los Angeles County hospital system.

My father also immediately went to find employment, riding the bus to the unemployment office and all around the greater metropolitan area. . . . After a month, he found a position as a mechanical drafter. Eventually, [he found work] as a mechanical and structural engineer.

My parents were able to borrow enough money from relatives so that, combined with their savings (which they regularly added to for just this occasion), we were eventually able to move to a . . . quiet, middle-class [neighborhood]. . . .

Everyone in our family is now a citizen of the United States, my parents having applied for citizenship in 1982, seven years after we came to the United States. When I asked each parent why they wanted to become citizens, my mother [said that] she wanted to be a citizen of a free country . . . with its better opportunities and benefits, which gave our family the chance to achieve the "American dream."

Since our arrival in the United States, we have sponsored two groups of Vietnamese immigrants. In 1981, we sponsored my father's niece and her husband [and] a year later . . . we sponsored my mother's cousin and her husband. To this day, both my parents are very active in the Vietnamese community . . . assisting recent immigrants and refugees.

SOURCE: Le (2005, pp. 348–351). Reprinted by permission of Pearson Education, Inc., Upper-Saddle River, NJ.

Questions to Consider

1. Compare and contrast Le's experience with those of other immigrants you've read about in this book, for example, the Lost Boys from Chapter 2. What differences and similarities can you identify? What are the implications for adjustment to the larger society?
2. Immigrants tend to move along chains of communication and interpersonal networks. How does this idea apply to Le's narrative?
3. Le's family had nothing but the clothes on their backs as they left Vietnam. What resources did they have that helped them adjust to the United States?

A 1979 protest in in Washington, D.C. during the Iran hostage crisis.

Almost one third (31%) of Muslims living in the United States have college or postgraduate degrees, which is comparable to educational attainment overall in the United States (Pew Research Center, 2017c, p. 23). However, Muslim immigrants have more education compared with U.S.-born Muslims. Specifically, 38% of foreign-born Muslims have a college degree or higher while only 21% of U.S.-born Muslims do (Pew Research Center, 2017c, p. 41).

A recent survey of Muslim Americans, a category that includes the huge majority of Arab and Middle Eastern Americans, finds them to be "middle class and mostly mainstream." They have a positive view of U.S. society and espouse distinctly American values (Pew Research Center, 2007).

Residentially, Arab and Middle Eastern Americans are highly urbanized, and almost 50% live in just five states (California, New Jersey, New York, Florida, and Michigan). This settlement pattern is not too different from that of other recent immigrant groups except for the heavy concentration in Michigan, especially in the Detroit area. These settlement patterns reflect chains of migration, some set up decades ago. Figure 10.3 shows the regional distribution of the group in 2000 and clearly displays the clusters in Michigan, Florida, and Southern California.

DETROIT'S ARAB AMERICAN COMMUNITY

Dr. Steven Gold

The greater Detroit area has long been a center of Arab American life. It continues to display vitality, with growing numbers of businesses, continued arrivals from the Middle East, and the creation of communal institutions such as the Arab American National Museum and the Islamic Center of America, the nation's largest Muslim house of worship. The population, which traces its local presence back 100 years, is large and continues to grow. However, due to recent arrivals, difficulties in enumeration, and the effects of intermarriage, estimates of the population are subject to debate. While the 2000 U.S. Census counted some 130,000 people of Arab and Middle Eastern origin in the tri-county Detroit area, the Zogby Worldwide polling firm pegs the community at more than 400,000.

Major nationality groups making up the Arab American population include Lebanese, Iraqi, Palestinian, and Yemeni. In addition, these groups reflect considerable

TABLE 10.4 Selected Characteristics of Arab Americans and Middle Eastern American and Non-Hispanic Whites, 2015

GROUP	SIZE	PERCENTAGE WITH LESS THAN HIGH SCHOOL DIPLOMA	PERCENTAGE WITH COLLEGE DEGREE OR MORE	PERCENTAGE FOREIGN-BORN	PERCENTAGE WHO SPEAK ENGLISH LESS THAN "VERY WELL"	MEDIAN HOUSEHOLD INCOME	PERCENTAGE OF FAMILIES IN POVERTY
Non-Hispanic whites	—	8.2	34.2	4.0	1.6	$61,394	6.6
Arab Americans	1,963,478	10.1	48.1	45.6	21.9	$55,117	18.1
Lebanese	508,054	6.5	51.4	21.6	7.2	$74,757	7.7
Egyptians	251,507	4.8	64.6	61.7	27.3	$61,344	17.1
Syrians	170,552	7.7	46.7	31.3	12.6	$66.965	10.9
Iranians	486,994	5.8	61.8	64.2	27.1	$72,345	9.7
Turks	203,996	9.5	53.7	56.3	23.5	$61,187	10.7

SOURCE: U.S. Census Bureau, 2016, American Community Survey, 2015, 5-year Estimates.

FIGURE 10.3 Regional Distribution of Arab Americans, 2000

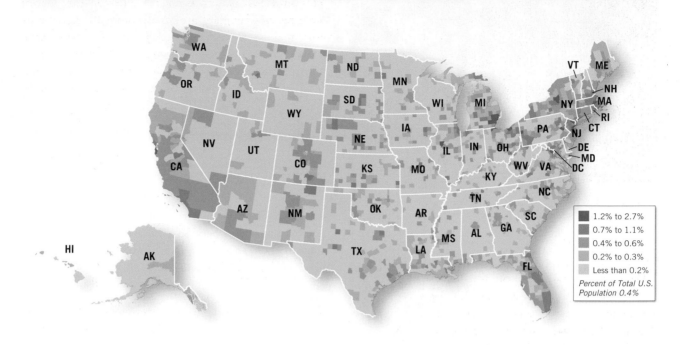

1.2% to 2.7%
0.7% to 1.1%
0.4% to 0.6%
0.2% to 0.3%
Less than 0.2%
*Percent of Total U.S.
Population 0.4%*

SOURCE: de la Cruz and Brittingham (2003, p. 6).

religious diversity associated with several traditions, including Chaldean, Melkite, Maronite, and Roman Catholics; Protestants and Orthodox Christians; as well as Sunni and Shi'a Muslims. Local enclaves based on nationality and religion can be found throughout Metro Detroit's three counties, revealing significant diversity in housing, class membership, and way of life.

Detroit's Arab Americans have created a broad array of organizations that address the population's social service, cultural, religious, health, educational, political, and economic needs. Among the most well-known is ACCESS (Arab Community Center for Economic and Social Services). Established in the early 1970s, ACCESS is the largest Arab American human services nonprofit in the United States. With eight locations and more than 100 programs, it caters to a diverse population. Ismael Ahamed, the organization's founder, has gone on to serve as the director of the Michigan Department of Human Services—the state government's second-largest agency—and is currently associate provost of the University of Michigan at Dearborn. While inclusive and large-scale organizations such as ACCESS maintain a communitywide focus, others reflect particular concerns associated with the population's varied subgroups.

Arab Detroit is noted for its extensive self-employment. The population is estimated to own some 5,000 enterprises—with Chaldeans (Iraqi Catholics) and Lebanese having especially high rates of entrepreneurship. The growth of Arab American businesses is most evident in Dearborn, where thousands of Arabic signs advertise a whole range of goods and services to local customers. At the same time, Arab-owned shops, restaurants, car dealerships, gas stations, and professionals serve consumer needs throughout the region in neighborhoods ranging from the inner city to affluent suburbs.

Business success is enabled by a wide range of resources, including familial and communal ties and personal experience with self-employment. In addition, the population's generally high levels of education and intact families are known to facilitate proprietorship. Indeed, Middle Eastern–origin groups have long revealed a propensity toward self-employment in the United States. In 1911, the Dillingham Commission of the U.S. Congress found that more than 75% of Syrian immigrant men (who would now be classified as Lebanese) in New York were self-employed. Recent evidence suggests that the trend endures. According to the 1990 U.S. Census, 6 of the 10 nationality groups with the highest rates of self-employment in the United States were from the Middle East.

Finally, a variety of ethnic organizations, including the Arab American Chamber of Commerce, Chaldean Federation of America, Arab American Women's Business Council, Chaldean American Chamber of Commerce, Chaldean American Bar Association, Chaldean American Association for Health Professionals, and Lebanese American Chamber of Commerce, provide services and contacts for Arab American entrepreneurs in Southeast Michigan.

Despite the community's size, wealth, and influence, a number of activists and observers contend that the population suffers from significant hostility and discrimination.

Images of the Arab American community in Detroit, Michigan.

This includes racial profiling and surveillance conducted by U.S. government agencies since September 11, 2001, as well as discrimination and violence from members of the American public. The net impact of these trends causes Arab Americans to feel unsafe in their own homes, deprecated for their national and religious origins, pressured to apologize for acts they had nothing to do with, and compelled to cooperate with intrusive surveillance activities.

Based on decisions made by federal agencies, South Asians and Middle Easterners in the United States are treated as a special population. In the years following the September 11 attacks, more than 1,200 persons—who were neither named nor charged with crimes—were detained, with about half being deported. At the same time, numerous ethnic and religious organizations representing the same nationalities have been accused of assisting terrorists—generally with little or no evidence—an action that permits the freezing of their assets and the criminalization of their members.

In addition to dealing with criminal justice and migration officials, Arab Americans also confront various forms of hostility, including insults, vandalism, and violence, as they go about their daily lives. This is evidenced by the cancellation of the Dearborn Arab International Festival in 2013, an event that for the previous 18 years brought together hundreds of thousands of people from throughout the United States and the world to enjoy Middle Eastern food and culture and family-friendly entertainment.

Fundamentalist Christian groups targeted the festival as a setting where they could confront Arabs and Muslims. These missionaries—who included Florida Pastor Terry Jones, best known for the public burning of a Quran (the Muslim holy book)—brought with them a pig's head and signs insulting Islam's prophet. When the fundamentalist protestors won a 2010 lawsuit protecting their First Amendment rights, the city of Dearborn withdrew its support of the festival. Instead, officials encouraged the festival's organizers to hold it in a park where public order could be more easily maintained.

Representatives of the Arab American community rejected this option because they favored the event's previous location, adjacent to numerous Arab businesses that have been vital to improving the city's (and region's) economic and cultural vitality. With too little time to make alternative arrangements, the popular and highly successful event had to be cancelled.

In sum, Detroit's Arab community continues to grow and prosper, bringing vitality and development to a location more commonly associated with economic decline and population loss. Yet, even as its members seek to celebrate their successful participation in American life, the circumstances of their religion, heritage, and regional origins often result in their being denied access to opportunities that groups with different origins might take for granted.[1]

9/11 AND ARAB AMERICANS

A faint strain of prejudice directed at Middle Easterners has always existed in American culture (e.g., see the low position of Turks in the 1926 social distance scales presented in Chapter 3). These feelings have intensified in recent

---

[1] Suggestions for further reading:

Bakalian, Anny, and Bozorgmehr Mehdi. 2009. *Backlash 9/11.* Berkeley, CA: University of California Press.

Gold, Steven J., and Bozorgmehr Mehdi. 2007. "Middle East and North Africa." pp. 518–533 in *The New Americans: A Guide to Immigration Since 1965,* edited by M. Waters and R. Ueda (with Helen B. Marrow). Cambridge, MA: Harvard University Press.

Schopmeyer, Kim. 2011. "Arab Detroit After 9/11: A Changing Demographic Portrait." pp. 29–63 in *Arab Detroit 9/11: Life in the Terror Decade,* edited by N. Abraham, S. Howell, and A. Shryock. Detroit, MI: Wayne State University Press.

Shryock, Andrew, Nabeel Abraham, and Sally Howell. 2011. "The Terror Decade in Arab Detroit: An Introduction." pp. 1–25 in *Arab Detroit 9/11: Life in the Terror Decade,* edited by N. Abraham, S. Howell, and A. Shryock. Detroit, MI: Wayne State University Press.

A protest against the construction of an Islamic Mosque in Temecula, California.

decades as relations with various Middle Eastern nations and groups have worsened. For example, in 1979, the U.S. Embassy in Tehran, Iran, was attacked and occupied, and more than 50 Americans were held hostage for more than a year. The attack stimulated a massive reaction in the United States, in which anti-Arab and anti-Muslim feelings figured prominently. Continuing anti-American activities across the Middle East in the 1980s and 1990s stimulated a backlash of resentment and growing intolerance in the United States.

These earlier events pale in comparison to the events of September 11, 2001. Americans responded to the attacks on the World Trade Center and the Pentagon by Arab terrorists with an array of emotions that included bewilderment, shock, anger, patriotism, and deep sorrow for the victims and their

families. Though the 19 attackers were from Saudi Arabia, the United Arab Emirates, Egypt, and Lebanon, research shows increased prejudicial rejection of Middle Easterners, Arabs, Muslims, and any group even vaguely associated with the perpetrators of the attacks. Specifically, in the nine weeks following September 11, more than 700 violent attacks were reported to the Arab American Anti-Discrimination Committee, followed by another 165 violent incidents in the first nine months of 2002 (Arab American Anti-Discrimination Committee, 2002). In this same period, there were more than 80 incidents in which Arab Americans were removed from aircraft after boarding because of their ethnicity, more than 800 cases of employment discrimination, and "numerous instances of denial of service, discriminatory service, and housing discrimination" (Ibish, 2003, p. 7). In 2015, anti-Muslim assaults came close to reaching 2001 levels (see Figure 10.4).

Thus, although the Arab and Middle Eastern American communities are small in size, they have assumed a prominent place in the attention of the nation. The majority of these groups denounce and reject terrorism and violence, but, like Colombians and Italians, many Americans hold strong stereotypes about them that, like other stereotypes, are often applied uncritically. A 2017 Pew Research Center survey asked participants to apply a "feeling thermometer" toward nine religious groups including Jews, Buddhists, Mormons, Hindus, and Catholics. The lower the score, the more negative the rating. Muslims had an average of 48 degrees, up from 40 in 2014. However, people still ranked them lower than any other group, including atheists who averaged 50 degrees in 2017, up from 41 in 2014

FIGURE 10.4 Anti-Muslim Assaults from 2000–2015

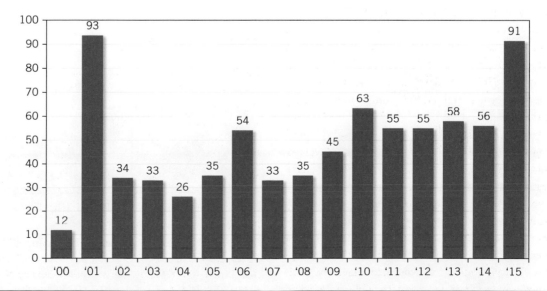

Anti-Muslim Assaults at Highest Level Since 2001

Anti-Muslim Assaults Reported to the FBI

SOURCE: Kishi, 2016. "Anti-Muslim assaults reach 9/11-era levels, FBI data show."

(Pew Research Center, 2017c). This evaluation of Islam as less desirable compared to other religions is reflected in Figure 10.5. As you'll see, a majority of Muslim Americans (62%) feel Islam is not accepted as "mainstream."

U.S. Muslims are very concerned about becoming scapegoats in the war on terror. As Figure 10.5 shows, half (50%) say that it became more difficult to be a Muslim in the United States in recent years (Pew Research Center, 2017c) compared with 53% responding that way after 9/11 (Pew Research Center, 2007). Furthermore, almost three-fourths of American Muslims (71%) are "at least somewhat concerned about extremism in the name of Islam occurring in the U.S." (Abdo, 2017).

There is overlap between the Arab American and Muslim American communities, but the two are not identical. Both groups face problems of prejudice and discrimination. As Figure 10.5 shows, three quarters of American Muslims surveyed said there is "a lot of discrimination" against members of their group. Being perceived as Arab or Muslim—for example, based on appearance (e.g., wearing a hijab), name (e.g., Ahmad, Abboud), or language or accent—may lead to individual discrimination such as interpersonal microaggressions (see Chapter 9). Or, it may include verbal threats and physical violence of the kind documented by the FBI and shown in Figure 10.4. At the macrolevel of society, customs and laws may be discriminatory, even if they are not intended as such. For example, the USA Patriot Act, passed in 2001, allows for long-term detention of suspects and a wider scope for searches and surveillance, including profiling at airport security checks. Similarly, it led to greater restrictions on entering the country as did the 2017 Executive Order 13769, "Protecting the Nation from Foreign Terrorist Entry into the United States," also called the "Muslim Ban." These and other policies have caused concern for many Americans about violations of due process and suspension of basic civil liberties for Arab Americans and/or Muslim Americans.

Relations between Arab Americans and the larger society are certainly among the most tense and problematic for any minority group. Given the U.S. invasions of Iraq and Afghanistan following 9/11, the threat of further terrorist attacks, and the recent decision by the U.S. government to deploy more American troops to Afghanistan, it is likely such tensions will not ease anytime soon.

As we learned about the contact hypothesis in Chapter 3, intergroup contact can reduce or increase prejudice (and, therefore, increase or decrease possible discrimination) under certain conditions: equal status, common goals, intergroup cooperation and meaningful interaction, and support by authority, law, or custom. Research by the Southern Poverty Law Center shows that prejudice intensified during the most recent presidential campaign. Specifically, they identify a threefold increase of anti-Muslim hate groups: In 2015, 34 groups were on the SPLC's radar, but that spiked to 101 in 2016 (Southern Poverty Law Center, 2017a). Some may liken President Trump's actions and rhetoric to those of Dennis Kearney's Working Man's Party of the 1870s (see Chapter 9). That is, they see a parallel between the "Chinese Must Go," "Build That Wall," and "no Muslims wanted." As we learned in Chapter 9 about the Japanese detention centers during World War II, while U.S. security is paramount, we must "be cautious to not fall back to racial prejudice and war hysteria" (Congressional Record, 2007, p. 3721). We discuss some of the consequences of these relationships in the next Narrative Portrait. Given what we know about the contact hypothesis, we encourage you to find ways to increase the meaningful interaction you have with members of the groups discussed in this text.

FIGURE 10.5 U.S. Muslims' Concerns

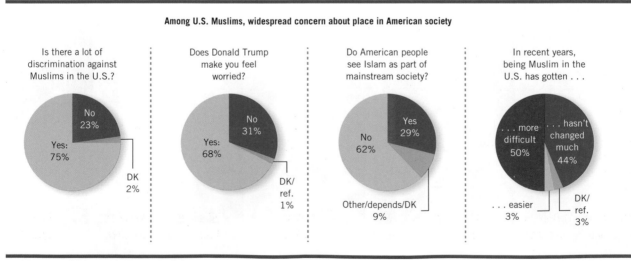

Among U.S. Muslims, widespread concern about place in American society

Is there a lot of discrimination against Muslims in the U.S.?
No 23%
Yes: 75%
DK 2%

Does Donald Trump make you feel worried?
No 31%
Yes: 68%
DK/ref. 1%

Do American people see Islam as part of mainstream society?
Yes 29%
No 62%
Other/depends/DK 9%

In recent years, being Muslim in the U.S. has gotten . . .
. . . more difficult 50%
. . . hasn't changed much 44%
. . . easier 3%
DK/ref. 3%

SOURCE: http://www.pewforum.org/2017/07/26/findings-from-pew-research-centers-2017-survey-of-us-muslims/.

Mark Ralston/AFP/Getty Images

"Taco Trucks at Every Mosque" started as a way bring Muslims and Latinos together during Ramadan.

IMMIGRANTS FROM AFRICA

Our final group of new Americans consists of immigrants from Africa. Immigration from Africa has been quite low over the past 50 years. However, there was the usual increase after the 1960s, and Africans were about 5% of all immigrants after 1960 and have been almost 10% since 2000.

Table 10.5 shows the total number of sub-Saharan Africans in the United States in 2015, along with the two largest national groups. The number of native Africans in the United States has more than doubled since 1990. This rapid growth suggests that these groups may have a greater impact on U.S. society in the future.

The category "sub-Saharan Africans" is extremely broad and encompasses people as diverse as destitute black refugees from African civil wars (e.g., the Lost Boys of

Sudan discussed in Chapter 2) and relatively affluent white South Africans. In the remainder of this section, we will focus on Nigerians and Ethiopians rather than on this very broad category.

Although their numbers may be growing, Nigerians and Ethiopians are tiny minorities: Neither group is as much as 0.1% of the total population. They are recent immigrants and have a high representation of first-generation members. Nigerian and Ethiopian immigrants tend to be highly skilled and educated, and they bring valuable abilities and advanced educational credentials to the United States. Both compare favorably to national norms for education; thus, they provide another example of a "brain drain" from their countries of origin. Like some other groups, many of the immigrants from Nigeria and Ethiopia are motivated by a search for work, and they compete for more desirable positions in the U.S. job structure.

Nigeria is a former British colony, so the relatively high level of English fluency among its immigrants is not surprising. Table 10.5 shows that, on average, members of the group have been able to translate their relatively high levels of human capital and English fluency into a favorable position in the U.S. economy. They compare quite favorably with national norms in their income levels.

Compared with Nigerians, Ethiopians rank lower in their English fluency and are more mixed in their backgrounds. They include refugees from domestic unrest along with the educated elite (see Table 10.5). Although Ethiopians compare favorably with national norms in education, they have much lower levels of income and, therefore, much higher rates of poverty. These contrasts suggest that Ethiopians are less able to translate their educational credentials into higher-ranked occupations in the United States.

TABLE 10.5 Selected Characteristics of Sub-Saharan African Groups and Non-Hispanic Whites, 2015

GROUP	SIZE	PERCENTAGE WITH LESS THAN HIGH SCHOOL DIPLOMA	PERCENTAGE WITH COLLEGE DEGREE OR MORE	PERCENTAGE FOREIGN-BORN	PERCENTAGE WHO SPEAK ENGLISH LESS THAN "VERY WELL"	MEDIAN HOUSEHOLD INCOME	PERCENTAGE OF FAMILIES IN POVERTY
Non-Hispanic whites		8.2	34.2	4.0	1.6	$61,394	6.6
All sub-Saharan Atricans	3,482,384	12.2	33.3	37.8	13.4	$43,682	19.4
Ethiopians	280,439	13.9	30.2	68.6	32.5	$41,736	19.1
Nigerians	390,255	4.3	59.3	61.5	10.3	$61,086	11.6

SOURCE: U.S. Census Bureau, 2016, American Community Survey, 2015, 5-year Estimates (2013a).

CHAPTER 10 • NEW AMERICANS, ASSIMILATION, AND OLD CHALLENGES

NARRATIVE PORTRAIT

9/11 and Middle Eastern Americans

Amir Marvasti and Karyn McKinney are sociologists who, between 2002 and 2004, conducted in-depth interviews with 20 Middle Eastern Americans. The interviews covered a variety of topics, but most centered on the reactions of the respondents to the attacks of 9/11, the ensuing public reaction, and their own rethinking of what it means to be an American. What follows are the personal reactions of the respondents, knit together by the narrative written by Marvasti and McKinney.

MIDDLE EASTERN AMERICANS AND THE AMERICAN DREAM

Amir Marvasti and Karyn McKinney

Difficulty with cultural assimilation is a common experience for most ethnic groups, but being designated public enemy number one is not. In the hours following the tragic attacks of September 11, 2001, being or just looking Middle Eastern became an instant offense. For members of this group, this was a turning point in terms of both the way they were viewed by others and the way they defined themselves. While the feeling of shock is similar to what everyone must have felt that day, in the case of Middle Eastern Americans, there was also a feeling of impending doom, the knowledge that their lives would never be exactly the same. . . .

As the day went by, a chasm began to form between Middle Eastern Americans and their fellow citizens. The perception that Middle Easterners were the aggressors and Americans the victims began to take hold, and out of this perception grew anger:

> Wherever you went you always—that day even among my friends there was talk about anger and they looked really angry. . . . There was talk about "We should bomb Palestine." And "Who cares about these people now." In a way, I understood their anger because of what had just happened. I guess it was kind of lonely that day.

In the days following the attacks, Middle Eastern Americans had to accept the fact that they were seen by many as legitimate targets of anger. The news media were full of messages about hate being an acceptable emotion under the circumstances. In that atmosphere, it was indeed very "lonely" to be Middle Eastern American. . . .

Perhaps the most significant realization for many Middle Eastern Americans was the awareness that their right to be part of the American Dream could be taken away for actions that they were not in any way responsible for. With this realization came the sense of not belonging and the real possibility of being physically separated from the rest of society and placed in an internment camp. One young Middle Eastern American remembered,

> I really thought I was going to be sent to like a camp. . . . It didn't—for those couple of days—it didn't feel like we were going to be back to normal again. . . . I thought my life was never going to be the same. I no longer had a home here.

As this respondent puts it, realizing that one no longer has a home here was tantamount to realizing that the American Dream applied to some more than others. . . .

September 11 was an important turning point in the psyche of Middle Eastern Americans to the extent that it caused them to reevaluate their place in American society and its promises of freedom and equality. Consider, for example, how this Pakistani American woman . . . rethinks her status as an American in light of how she and her family have been treated since September 11:

> My brother was assaulted three days after September 11th. It was part of the backlash. . . . I feel I'm even considered an outsider a lot of the times. I sound just as American as anyone else, and I was born and raised here. . . . [After September 11] I think a lot of people thought that if you're not going to consider me American, why am I going to consider myself an American. . . .

According to this respondent, . . . it became particularly apparent that the ideals of equality in the American Dream did not apply to her and her family. Her ethnicity transcends her identity as an American and places her in the position of a second-class citizen. . . .

One of the most profound effects of September 11 on the lives of Middle Eastern Americans was the realization that their daily routines . . . would be subjected to scrutiny and potentially make them vulnerable to acts of violence. An Iranian American man describes how September 11 affected his life:

> I actually canceled a trip. . . . And that's when I realized there's a difference in this war [the war on terrorism]. There is a new order. . . . We can't go somewhere and play our own music. We like our own music, we like our own dance, we like our own food and tradition so we couldn't do that therefore I canceled that trip. That's when it occurred to me there's a difference.

Collectively, these post-9/11 experiences have caused some Middle Eastern Americans to question the meaning of the American Dream and the extent to which its lofty promises apply to them. They have recognized that full assimilation into American culture will not provide protection against acts of ignorance and that their future in this country is uncertain.

SOURCE: Marvasti and McKinney (2004, pp. 121–126). Copyright © 2004 by Rowman & Littlefield Publishers Inc.

Questions to Consider

1. What theories of prejudice and discrimination (see Chapter 3) can you apply to the experiences described in this narrative?

2. In the passage that opened this chapter, Sade says that Arabs are "the new blacks." Does this narrative—and other material in this chapter—tend to support or refute that comparison? How?

MODES OF INCORPORATION

As the case studies included in this chapter (and in Chapters 8 and 9) demonstrate, recent immigrant groups occupy a wide array of different positions in U.S. society. One way to address this diversity is to look at the contact situation, especially the characteristics the groups bring with them (e.g., their race and religion, the human capital with which they arrive) and the reaction of the larger society. There are three main modes of incorporation for immigrants in the United States: entrance through the primary labor market, the secondary labor markets (see Chapter 5), or the ethnic enclave. We will consider each pathway separately and relate them to the groups discussed in this chapter.

Immigrants serving in the U.S. military say the Pledge of Allegiance at a naturalization ceremony April 25, 2003, in Los Angeles, California. More than 4,000 new immigrants took the U.S. citizenship oath during Secretary of Homeland Security Tom Ridge's three-day visit to southern California.

IMMIGRANTS AND THE PRIMARY LABOR MARKET

The primary labor market consists of more desirable jobs with greater security, higher pay, and more benefits, and the immigrants entering this sector tend to be highly educated, skilled professionals and businesspeople. Members of this group are generally fluent in English, and many were educated at U.S. universities. They are highly integrated into the global urban-industrial economy, and, in many cases, they are employees of multinational corporations transferred here by their companies. These immigrants are affluent, urbane, and dramatically different from the peasant laborers so common in the past (e.g., from Ireland and Italy) and in the present (e.g., from the Dominican Republic and Mexico). The groups with high percentages of members entering the primary labor market include Indian, Egyptian, Iranian, and Nigerian immigrants.

Because they tend to be affluent, immigrants with professional backgrounds tend to attract less notice and fewer racist reactions than their more unskilled counterparts. Although they come closer to Blauner's pure immigrant group than most other minority groups we have considered, racism can still complicate their lives. In addition, Arab American Islamic group members must confront discrimination and prejudice based on their religious affiliation.

IMMIGRANTS AND THE SECONDARY LABOR MARKET

This mode of incorporation is more typical for immigrants with lower levels of education and fewer job skills. Jobs in this sector are less desirable and command lower pay, little security, and few benefits and are often seasonal or in the underground or informal economy. This labor market includes jobs in construction or the garment industry, in which workers are paid "off the books," and working conditions are unregulated by government authorities or labor unions; domestic work; and some forms of criminal or deviant activity, such as drug sales and sex work. The employers who control these jobs often prefer to hire undocumented immigrants because they are easier to control and less likely to complain to the authorities about abuse and mistreatment. The groups with high percentages of members in the secondary labor market include Dominicans, Haitians, and the less-skilled and less-educated kinfolk of the higher-status immigrants.

IMMIGRANTS AND ETHNIC ENCLAVES

As we have seen, some immigrant groups—especially those that can bring financial capital and business experience—have established ethnic enclaves. Some members of these groups enter U.S. society as entrepreneurs and become owners of small retail shops and other businesses; their less-skilled and less-educated co-ethnics serve as a source of cheap labor to staff the ethnic enterprises. The enclave provides contacts, financial and other services, and social support for the new immigrants of all social classes. Korean Americans and some Arab American groups, like Cuban Americans and Jewish Americans in the past, have been particularly likely to follow this path.

SUMMARY

This classification suggests some of the variety of relationships between the new Americans and the larger society. The contemporary stream of immigrants entering the United States is extremely diverse and includes people from the most sophisticated and urbane to the most desperate and despairing. This variety can be seen in a list of occupations in which recent immigrants are overrepresented. For men, the list includes biologists and other natural scientists, taxi drivers, farm laborers, and waiters. For women, the list includes chemists, statisticians, produce packers, laundry workers, and domestics (Kritz & Girak, 2004).

QUESTIONS FOR REFLECTION

3. List and describe the characteristics of the largest groups of immigrants from Central America, the Caribbean, Asia, the Middle East, and Africa.

4. Which of these groups is most likely to assimilate into the primary labor market? Why? Which group is most likely to be incorporated into the secondary labor market? Why? Which is most likely to be an enclave minority? Why?

IMMIGRATION: ISSUES AND CONTROVERSIES

THE ATTITUDES OF AMERICANS

One factor that affects the fate of immigrant groups is the attitude of the larger society, particularly of the groups that have the most influence with governmental policymakers. Overall, American public opinion is split on the issue of immigration. Today, the majority of Americans regard immigration as a positive force, and this percentage has increased in the past few years (see Figure 8.6). In a Pew Research Center survey released in March 2017, more than half (59%) of Americans said immigrants strengthened the country, while 33% described them as a burden. Interestingly, those findings are nearly the opposite of public opinion in 1994. At that time, 63% of Americans viewed immigrants as a burden compared with 31% who thought they strengthened the country (Jones, 2016). That said, many Americans are vehemently opposed to immigration and immigrants.

The history of this nation is replete with anti-immigrant and nativist groups and activities, including those that opposed the immigration from Europe (Chapter 2), Mexico (Chapter 8), and China and Japan (Chapter 9). The present is no exception: As immigration increased over the past several decades, so have the number and visibility of anti-immigrant groups, particularly in the states along the Mexican border.

The contemporary anti-immigrant movements have generated a number of state laws. One of the most controversial and widely publicized of these has been State Bill

1070, passed by the Arizona legislature and signed into law in April 2010. Among other provisions, the law required law enforcement officers to check the immigration status of anyone they stopped, detained, or arrested if they had a "reasonable" suspicion that the person might be in the country illegally. Supporters of the legislation argued that it would help control illegal immigration while opponents raised fears of racial profiling and legalized anti-Hispanic discrimination. Some people expressed considerable concern that the legislation would deter Hispanic Americans from reporting crimes or otherwise cooperating with the police.

In June 2012, the Supreme Court invalidated most of the provisions of Arizona S.B. 1070, by which time several other states had passed similar bills. In 2011, Alabama's House passed Bill 56, considered by some to be particularly punitive. Among other provisions, it required schools to verify the immigration status of students in grades K–12, banned undocumented immigrants from soliciting work, and made it a crime to give the undocumented rides or rent apartments to them. However, most of the provisions of the law were repealed in the fall of 2013 (Vock, 2013).

Consistent with the idea that Americans are ambivalent about immigration, other states passed legislation favorable to immigrants during the same period. Some states (e.g., Colorado and Oregon) extended in-state tuition to undocumented immigrants who graduated from their high school system, and others (e.g., Georgia and Illinois) began to allow them to get driver's licenses (Wogan, 2013).

What factors might account for people's view of immigration? Researchers have identified a number of important causes, many of them consistent with the ideas we have examined throughout this text. Prejudice and racism are linked to competition between groups for scarce resources (jobs, political power, control of neighborhoods, and so forth) and a sense of threat. Guided by the results of the Robber's Cave experiment (Chapter 3) and the Noel hypothesis (Chapter 4), we would expect that negative feelings toward immigrants would be strongest among the most economically vulnerable Americans and those who feel most threatened by the increase in immigration over the past several decades (e.g., see Wallace & Figueroa, 2012).

On the other hand, some research (Hainmueller & Hiscox, 2010; Reyna, Dobria, & Wetherell, 2013) finds little correlation between a person's anti-immigrant feelings and personal economic situation. Rather, they found that both high- and low-status respondents were less concerned with their own pocketbooks and more focused on the potential costs of low-skill immigrants—for schooling, health care, and other services—and their impact on the U.S. economy in general. So, while the issue of resources still plays a role in one's attitudes, the concern is at a broader level, not a personal one.

Of course, "competition" can be much broader than fights over jobs and votes. Many opponents to immigration in the United States (and Europe) seem to be motivated by a collective sense of threat, the idea that the newcomers will compromise the way of life and cultural integrity of the host nation. These defensive forms of prejudice can stimulate powerful emotions, as we have seen repeatedly throughout this text.

Finally, we have seen that prejudice and negative feelings toward other groups can be motivated by a variety of factors, not just competition. Anti-immigrant attitudes are highly correlated with other forms of prejudice and are caused by the same processes we examined in Chapter 3—for example, exposure to racist cultural norms and values during childhood, and low levels of education (Pettigrew, Wagner, & Christ, 2007).

Is everyone who has reservations and questions about immigration a racist? Absolutely not. While anti-immigrant feelings, prejudice, and a sense of threat seem to be linked, this does not mean that all who oppose immigration are bigots or that all proposals to decrease the flow of immigrants are racist. These are serious and complex issues, and it is not helpful simply to label people as bigots or dismiss their concerns as prejudiced.

On the other hand, we need to clearly recognize that anti-immigrant feelings—particularly the most extreme—are linked to some of the worst, most negative strains of traditional American culture: the same racist and prejudicial views that helped justify slavery and the near genocide of American Indians. In popular culture, on some talk radio and cable TV "news" shows, in letters to the editor, and so forth, these views are regularly used to demonize immigrants, blame them for an array of social problems, and stoke irrational fears and rumors, such as the idea that Latino immigrants are aiming to return parts of the Southwest to Mexico. At any rate, when American traditions of prejudice and racism are linked to feelings of group threat and individual insecurity, the possibilities for extreme reactions, hate crimes, and poorly designed policy and law become formidable.

THE IMMIGRANTS

One survey of immigration issues (National Public Radio, 2004) included a nationally representative sample of immigrant respondents. Not surprisingly, the researchers found that the immigrants' attitudes and views differed sharply from those of native-born respondents on a number of dimensions. For example, immigrant respondents were more likely to see immigration as a positive force for the larger society and more likely to say that immigrants work hard and pay their fair share of taxes. The survey also showed that immigrants are grateful for the economic opportunities available in the United States, with 84% agreeing that there are more opportunities to get ahead here than in their countries of origin.

A more recent survey (Taylor, Cohn, Livingston, Funk, & Morin, 2013) documents the willingness of immigrants to take advantage of opportunities through a commitment to hard work. Large majorities of both Hispanic (78%) and Asian (68%) immigrants supported the idea that hard work results in success, an endorsement of the Protestant ethic that exceeds that of the general public (58%) (p. 85). On the other hand, the survey also showed that some immigrants are ambivalent about U.S. culture and values. For example, only 32% of Hispanic immigrants and 14% of Asian immigrants believed that the family is stronger in the United States than in their homelands, and less than half (44% of Hispanic and 36% of Asian immigrants) said that moral values are better in the United States (p. 77).

Another helpful report (Motel & Patten, 2013) used census data to compile a statistical portrait of the 40 million Americans—about 13% of the total population—who are foreign-born or first-generation immigrants. As you would expect, Mexicans are the single largest segment of this group (29%), with Asian immigrants being the second largest (25%). Almost 40% of the foreign-born immigrated before 1990 (this category includes the surviving members of the last great wave of European immigrants), but an almost equal percentage (36%) are true newcomers, having arrived since 2000.

Based on this study, most (58%) of the foreign-born are married (vs. 47% of the native-born), and they have a higher fertility rate than the general population. As we have seen, facility with English is an important issue for immigrants: Only about one third of immigrants speak English "very well." As we have also seen, there is a great deal of diversity among the foreign-born in terms of education. Overall, 16% of the foreign-born (vs. 18% of the native-born) are college educated, but this percentage varies from about 4% for immigrant Mexican Americans to almost 30% for immigrants from Asia. Occupation, income, and poverty are also highly variable from group to group.

What can we conclude? Synthesizing the information in this and previous chapters, we can say that the immigrant stream is highly diversified and that the United States is growing more diverse as a result. The "typical immigrant" is from Mexico, China, or another Asian or Central American nation, and is motivated primarily by economics and the absence of viable opportunities at home. Those who come from less-developed nations bring little human capital, education, or job skills, but others bring glowing educational and professional credentials.

As is typical of the first generation, they are often more oriented to their homes than to the United States. Many, especially the "low-skilled" immigrants, don't have the time, energy, or opportunity to absorb much of Anglo culture or the English language, while others—the more skilled and educated—move easily between their native cultures and American lifestyles. Like past waves of immigrants, even the least skilled and educated are determined to find a better way of life for themselves and their children, even if the cost of doing so is living on the margins of the larger society.

QUESTIONS FOR REFLECTION

5. How welcoming are Americans of newcomers? What are some of the ways that states have attempted to deal with immigrants, particularly the undocumented? Have these attempts been successful? Offer examples to illustrate your point.

6. What are some of the causes of anti-immigrant sentiment? Is it fair to label Americans as prejudiced against immigrants? Why or why not?

7. What characteristics do immigrants bring? What are their motivations for immigrating?

COSTS AND BENEFITS

Many Americans believe that immigration is a huge drain on the economic resources of the nation. Common concerns include the ideas that immigrants take jobs from native-born workers, strain societal institutions including schools, housing markets, and medical facilities, and do not pay taxes. These issues are complex and hotly debated at all levels of U.S. society—so much so that passion and intensity of feeling on all sides often compromises the objective analysis of data.

The debate is further complicated because conclusions about these economic issues can vary depending on the type of immigrants being discussed and the level of analysis being used. For example, conclusions about costs and benefits can be very different depending on whether we focus on less-skilled or undocumented immigrants or the highly educated professional immigrants entering the primary job market. Immigrants in their 20s and 30s are more likely to make a net contribution (especially if they have no children) than those who are over 65 and out of the workforce. Also, national studies might lead to different conclusions than studies of local communities, because the former spreads the costs of immigrants over the entire population while the latter concentrates those costs in a specific locality.

Contrary to widespread beliefs, many studies, especially those done at the national level, find that immigrants to the United States are not a particular burden. For one thing, most immigrants are ineligible for most publically funded services (such as Medicaid and food

stamps), and undocumented immigrants are ineligible for virtually all such services. The exceptions are the children of immigrants, who are eligible for many programs targeted at children and schools—U.S. schools must educate all children regardless of legal status (West, 2011, pp. 433–434).

Two recent studies illustrate some of the common conclusions and controversies regarding the impact of undocumented immigration. One study (National Academies of Sciences, Engineering, and Medicine, 2017) found that immigration had both positive and negative consequences for the larger society. For example, the study concluded that the impact of immigration on wages and employment is slight and felt mostly by prior immigrants and native-born high school dropouts (p. 266). Thus, the widespread belief that immigrants take jobs away from the native-born has little support. However, the report also found that the impact of immigration varied widely across the nation and that there may be a substantial tax burdens on many states and localities.

The second study (Gee, Gardner, & Wiehe, 2016) found that undocumented immigrants pay a substantial amount in local and state and state taxes, totaling over 11 billion dollars a year. The study found that the undocumented pay about 8% of their income in state and local taxes compared to the richest 1% of Americans whose tax rate is only 5.4% (p. 1).

Many studies find that immigrants are a positive addition to the economy. They add to the labor supply in areas as disparate as the garment industry, agriculture, domestic work, and higher education. Other researchers find that low-skilled immigrants tend to find jobs in areas of the economy in which few U.S. citizens work or in the enclave economies of their own groups, taking jobs that would not have existed without the economic activity of their co-ethnics and thus do not have a negative effect on the employment of native-born workers (Bean & Stevens, 2003; Kochhar, 2006; Meissner, 2010).

Another concern is the strain immigrants place on taxes and services such as schools and welfare programs. Again, these issues are complex and far from settled, but many research projects show that immigrants generally "pay their own way." Taxes are automatically deducted from their paychecks (unless, of course, they are being paid "under the table"), and their use of public services is actually lower than their proportional contributions. This is particularly true for undocumented immigrants, whose use of services is sharply limited by their vulnerable legal status (Marcelli & Heer, 1998; Simon, 1989). Bean and Stevens (2003) found that immigrants are not overrepresented on the welfare rolls. Rather, the key determinant of government aid use is refugee status. Groups such as Haitians, Salvadorans, and Vietnamese—who arrive without resources and, by definition, are in need of assistance on all levels—are the most likely to be on the welfare rolls (pp. 66–93).

In general, immigrants—undocumented as well as legal—pay local, state, and federal taxes and make proportional contributions to Social Security and Medicare. The undocumented are the most likely to be paid "off the books" and receive their wages tax-free, but estimates are that the vast majority (50%–75%, depending on the study) pay federal and state taxes through payroll deduction (White House, 2005). Also, *all* immigrants pay sales taxes and other consumption taxes (e.g., on gas, cigarettes, and alcohol). (See this chapter's Current Debates section for a reprise of many of these issues.)

Some evidence suggests that immigrants play a crucial role in keeping the Social Security system solvent. This source of retirement income is being severely strained by the "baby boomers"—the large number of Americans born between 1945 and 1960 who are now retiring. This group is living longer than previous generations and, because the U.S. birthrate has stayed low over the past four decades, there are relatively fewer native-born workers to support them and replace the funds they withdraw as Social Security and Medicare benefits. Immigrants may supply the much-needed workers to take up the slack in the system and keep it solvent. In particular, most undocumented immigrants pay into the system but (probably) will never draw any money out, because of their illegal status. They thus provide a tidy surplus—perhaps as much as $7 billion a year or more—to help subsidize the retirements of the baby boomers and keep the system functioning (Porter, 2005; see also Dewan, 2013).

Conclusions about the impact and costs of immigration must await the findings of ongoing research, and there is no question that many local communities experience distress as they try to deal with the influx of newcomers in their housing markets, schools, and health care facilities. Concerns about the economic impact of immigrants are not unfounded, but they may be exaggerated by prejudice and racism directed at newcomers and strangers. The current opposition to immigration may be a reaction to "who" as much as to "how many" or "how expensive."

Finally, we can repeat the finding of many studies (e.g., Bean & Stevens, 2003) that immigration is generally a positive force in the economy. As they have for decades, immigrants—legal and undocumented—continue to find work and niches in American society in which they can survive. The highly skilled immigrants fill gaps in the primary labor market and in schools and universities, corporations, hospitals, and hundreds of other sectors of the economy. Less-skilled immigrants provide cheap labor for the low-wage secondary job market; frequently, the primary beneficiaries of this long-established system are not the immigrants (although they are often grateful for the opportunities) but employers, who benefit from a less expensive, more easily exploited workforce, and American consumers, who benefit from lower prices in the marketplace and reap the benefits virtually every time they go shopping, have a meal in a restaurant, pay for home repairs or maintenance, or place a loved one in a nursing home (for an overview, see Griswold, 2012).

UNDOCUMENTED IMMIGRANTS

Americans are particularly concerned with undocumented immigrants but, again, are split in their attitudes. A recent poll (Saad, 2010) asked about people's concerns regarding undocumented immigrants and found that 61% of respondents were concerned with the burden on schools, hospitals, and government services, 55% were concerned that "illegal immigrants might be encouraging others to move here illegally," and 53% were concerned that undocumented immigrants are lowering wages for native-born workers. At the same time, 64% of respondents proclaimed themselves to be "very" or "somewhat" sympathetic toward undocumented immigrants. Only 17% said they were "very unsympathetic."

The high level of concern is certainly understandable because the volume of illegal immigration has been huge over the past few decades. As displayed in Figure 10.6, the estimated number of undocumented immigrants increased from 8.4 million in 2000 to a high of 12 million in 2007, an increase of more than 40%. The number has declined during the recession and is now about 10.7 million. About 55% of all unauthorized immigrants are from Mexico (Passel, Cohn, & Gonzalez-Barrera, 2013).

Some undocumented immigrants enter the country on tourist, temporary worker, or student visas and simply remain in the nation when their visas expire. In 2012 alone, the Department of Homeland Security processed

FIGURE 10.6 Estimated Total and Mexican Undocumented Immigrants, 1990–2012

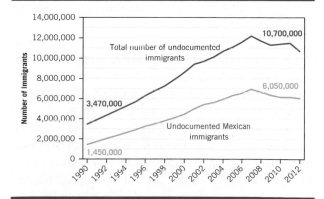

SOURCE: Passel et al. (2013).

The border fence splits a beach on the U.S. Mexican border.

more than 181 million nonimmigrant admissions for tourists, businesspeople, temporary workers, and foreign students entering the United States (Teke & Navarro, 2016). These numbers suggest how difficult it is to keep tabs on this source of illegal immigration. Others cross the border illegally in the hopes of evading the Border Patrol and finding their way into some niche in the American economy. The fact that people keep coming suggests that most succeed.

One of the reasons the supply of unauthorized immigrants is so high is the continuing demand for cheap labor in the U.S. economy. As we have noted on several occasions, the Global South—and Mexico in particular—has functioned as a reserve labor force for the U.S. economy for decades. Even in 2010, after several years of economic recession, undocumented immigrants provided a sizable percentage of the workforce in many states and were as much as 10% of the workers in several (see Figure 10.7).

The demand for cheap (undocumented) labor varies by the sector of the economy, and one of the biggest users has been the agricultural sector. Arturo Rodriguez (2011), president of the United Farm Workers of America (the union founded by César Chávez and mentioned in Chapter 8), estimates that as much as 70% of the two million agricultural workers in the United States—the people who pick the crops and prepare them to be shipped to market—are undocumented immigrants. U.S. agriculture and the food supply would collapse without the contributions of undocumented workers.

A variety of efforts continue to be made to curtail and control the flow of illegal immigrants. Various states have attempted to lower the appeal of the United States by limiting benefits and opportunities. Other than the aforementioned State Bill 1070 in Arizona, one of the best known

FIGURE 10.7 Unauthorized Immigrants as Share of Labor Force by State, 2010

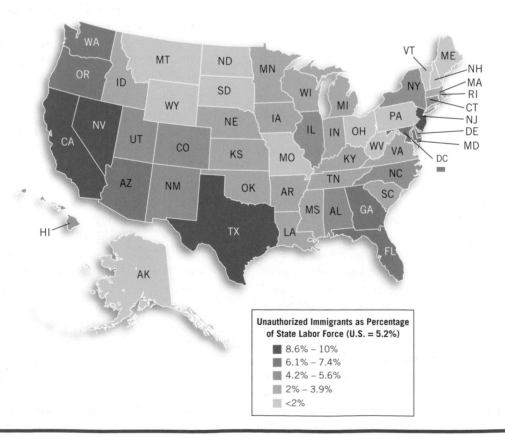

Unauthorized Immigrants as Percentage of State Labor Force (U.S. = 5.2%)
- 8.6% – 10%
- 6.1% – 7.4%
- 4.2% – 5.6%
- 2% – 3.9%
- <2%

SOURCE: Passel and Cohn (2011).

of these attempts occurred in 1994, when California voters passed Proposition 187, which would have denied educational, health, and other services to illegal immigrants. The policy was declared unconstitutional, however, and never implemented.

Other efforts to decrease the flow of illegal immigration have included proposals to limit welfare benefits for immigrants, denial of in-state college tuition to the children of illegal immigrants, increases in the size of the Border Patrol, and, most prominently in recent years, the construction of a taller and wider wall along the border with Mexico. Over the past decade, a variety of proposals to reform the national immigration policy have been hotly debated at the highest levels of government, but none has been passed.

Although Americans will continue to be concerned about this problem, many people wonder if much can be done (within the framework of a democratic, humane society) to curtail the flow of people. The social networks that deliver immigrants—legal as well as illegal—are too well established, and the demand for cheap labor in the United States is simply insatiable. In fact, denying services, as envisioned in Proposition 187, may make illegal immigrants *more* attractive as a source of labor by reducing their ability to resist exploitation. For example, if the children of illegal immigrants were not permitted to attend school, they would become more likely to join the army of cheap labor on which some employers depend. Who would benefit from barring access to public schools or denying in-state college tuition for the children of illegal immigrants?

DREAMERS

In 2001, the U.S. Senate considered the Development, Relief, and Education for Alien Minors (DREAM) Act. This act, like so many attempts to address immigration issues, stalled and was never passed, but it did give a name (DREAMers) to a population that has increased in size since that time and remains a continuing concern: the children of undocumented immigrants who were brought to the United States as young children.

DREAMers are in the United States illegally but not because of any choice of their own. They are not citizens of the United States (unlike the children born to undocumented immigrants in the United States), and, in many ways, they are not citizens of their "native" land either. Many have never visited their "homeland" and are unfamiliar with its customs or even its language.

As you saw in Chapter 8, this part of the population is caught in the middle—residents of the United States but not citizens, strangers to the homelands of their parents. They live in fear of deportation, and their illegal status can prevent them from competing for jobs in the primary

On September 5, 2017, demonstrators in Chicago, Illinois displayed American and Mexican flags while protesting the announced end to the Deferred Action for Childhood Arrivals (DACA) program.

labor market, getting a driver's license, attending college, or receiving unemployment benefits or food stamps. Where do the roughly two million DREAMers (most of them Mexican) belong?

Attempts to revive the 2001 bill have failed, as did various alternative measures. Because of the political gridlock at the highest levels of government, many members of the group feared that their situation would never be reasonably addressed, let alone resolved.

Then, in June 2012, the Obama administration enacted a program under which the children of undocumented immigrants could apply to stay in the United States without threat of deportation. Those who met the conditions of the program (e.g., they must be high school graduates with no significant criminal violations) can get driver's licenses and work permits, as well as attend college. More than 500,000 people applied to and were approved for the program.

The program grants a two-year, renewable reprieve from deportation for the DREAMers (but not for their parents and other relatives). It does not offer permanent legal status or a pathway to citizenship. Despite its limited scope, the program is controversial. President Trump promised to end it during his campaign for the presidency (because it was created by the executive order of one president, it can be rescinded by the executive order of succeeding presidents). And, in the fall of 2017, he acted to do so (Harte, Julia, 2017). He has since signaled a possible willingness to compromise on this issue and the fate of the DREAMers remains uncertain (Stolberg & Alcindor, 2017).

QUESTIONS FOR REFLECTION

8. Do immigrants cost more than they contribute? What are some of the factors that have to be taken into account in dealing with this issue?

9. Has the number of undocumented immigrants grown in recent years? What factors affect the size of this population? Will it continue to grow in the future?

10. Who are the DREAMers? What should be done to resolve their situation, if anything?

IS CONTEMPORARY ASSIMILATION SEGMENTED?

In Chapter 2, we reviewed the patterns of acculturation and integration that typified the adjustment of Europeans who immigrated to the United States before the 1930s. Although their process of adjustment was not smooth or simple, these groups eventually acculturated and achieved levels of education and affluence comparable to national norms.

Will contemporary immigrants experience similar success? Will their children and grandchildren rise in the occupational structure to positions similar to those of the dominant group? Will their cultures and languages fade and disappear?

Final answers to these questions must await future developments. In the meantime, there is considerable debate on these issues. Some analysts argue that the success story of the white ethnic groups will not be repeated and that assimilation for contemporary immigrants will be segmented: Some will enjoy success and rise to middle-class prosperity, but others will become mired in the urban underclass, beset by crime, drugs, school failure, and marginal, low-paid menial jobs (Haller, Portes, & Lynch, 2011, p. 737).

Other analysts find that the traditional perspective on assimilation—particularly Milton Gordon's model of assimilation—continues to provide a useful framework for describing the experience of contemporary immigrants. They argue that these groups will be successful like earlier immigrants. Next, we will review the most important and influential arguments from each side of this debate. Finally, we will attempt to come to some conclusions about the future of assimilation.

THE CASE FOR SEGMENTED ASSIMILATION

This thesis has many advocates, including some of the most important researchers in this area of the social sciences. Here, we will focus on two of the most important works. The first presents an overview and the second is based on an important, continuing research project on the second generation, the children of contemporary immigrants.

Assimilation Now Versus Then. Sociologist Douglas Massey (1995) argued that there are three crucial differences between past (before the 1930s) and contemporary (after the mid-1960s) assimilation experiences. Each calls the traditional perspective into question.

First, the flow of immigrants from Europe to the United States slowed to a mere trickle after the 1920s because of restrictive legislation, the worldwide depression of the 1930s, and World War II (see Figure 2.2). Immigration in the 1930s, for example, was less than 10% of the flow in the early 1920s. Thus, as the children and grandchildren of the European immigrants Americanized and grew to adulthood in the 1930s and 1940s, few new immigrants fresh from the old country replaced them in the ethnic neighborhoods. European cultural traditions and languages weakened rapidly with the passing of the first generation and the Americanization of their descendants.

It is unlikely, argues Massey, that a similar hiatus will interrupt contemporary immigration. For example, as we saw in Figure 10.6, the number of undocumented immigrants remained high even after the economic recession that began in 2007. Massey argues that immigration has become continuous, and as some immigrants (or their descendants) Americanize and rise to success and affluence, new immigrants will replace them and keep the ethnic cultures and languages vital and whole.

Second, the speed and ease of modern transportation and communication will maintain cultural and linguistic diversity. A century ago, immigrants from Europe could maintain contact with the old country only by mail, and many had no realistic expectation of ever returning. Modern immigrants, in contrast, can return to their homes in a day or less and can use telephones, television, e-mail, and the Internet to stay in intimate contact with the families and friends they left behind. Thus, the cultures of modern immigrants can be kept vital and whole in ways that were not available (or even imagined) 100 years ago.

Third, and perhaps most important, contemporary immigrants face an economy and a labor market that are vastly different from those faced by European immigrants of the 19th and early 20th centuries. The latter group generally rose in the class system as the economy shifted from manufacturing to service (see Figure 5.3). Today, rates of upward mobility have decreased, and the children of contemporary immigrants—especially those whose parents are undocumented—face myriad challenges in securing access to a quality education (Massey, 1995, pp. 645–646).

For the immigrants from Europe a century ago, assimilation meant a gradual rise to middle-class status and suburban comfort, a process often accomplished in three generations. Massey fears that assimilation today is segmented, and that a large percentage of the descendants of contemporary immigrants—especially many of the "peasant immigrants," such as some Hispanic groups, Haitians, and other peoples of color—face permanent membership in a growing underclass population and continuing marginalization and powerlessness.

The Second Generation. An analysis of the second generation of recent immigrant groups (Haller et al., 2011) also found support for the segmented assimilation model. The researchers interviewed the children of immigrants in the Miami and San Diego areas at three different times— in the early 1990s (when they were at an average age of 14), 3 years later, and 10 years later, when the respondents were at an average age of 24. The sample was large (more than 5,000 respondents at the beginning) and representative of the second generation in the two metropolitan areas where the study was conducted. This is an important study because its longitudinal design permits the researchers to track these children of immigrants in precise detail.

Haler and colleagues (2011) argue, consistent with Massey (1995) and with many of the points made previously in this text, that contemporary immigrants face a number of barriers to successful adaptation, including racial prejudice (because the huge majority are nonwhite), a labor market sharply split between a primary sector that requires high levels of education and a secondary sector that is low paid and insecure, and a widespread criminal subculture, based on gangs and drug sales, that provides a sometimes attractive alternative to the conventional pursuit of success through education.

Whether immigrants and their descendants can overcome these obstacles depends decisively on three factors (listed at the far left of Figure 10.8). Figure 10.8 also depicts several different projected pathways of mobility across the generations. Immigrants who arrive with high levels of human capital enter the primary labor market, and their descendants generally have entered the economic and social mainstream by the third generation (see the top row of Figure 10.8). The descendants of immigrants with lower levels of human capital can succeed if they benefit from strong families and strong co-ethnic communities that reinforce parental discipline. This pathway, depicted in the middle row of Figure 10.8, also results in full acculturation and integration in the economic mainstream by the third generation.

The bottom row of the figure outlines a very different pathway for a large percentage of some contemporary immigrant groups. The mode of incorporation for these immigrants does not place them in a strong co-ethnic community. Further, they may experience weaker family structures, sometimes because of their undocumented status or because the family is split between the United States and their home country. The result is lower educational achievement and economic marginalization and, potentially, assimilation into gangs, drug subcultures, and similar groups.

The researchers present a variety of evidence to support segmented assimilation theory. For example, the

FIGURE 10.8 Paths of Immigrant Mobility Across Generations

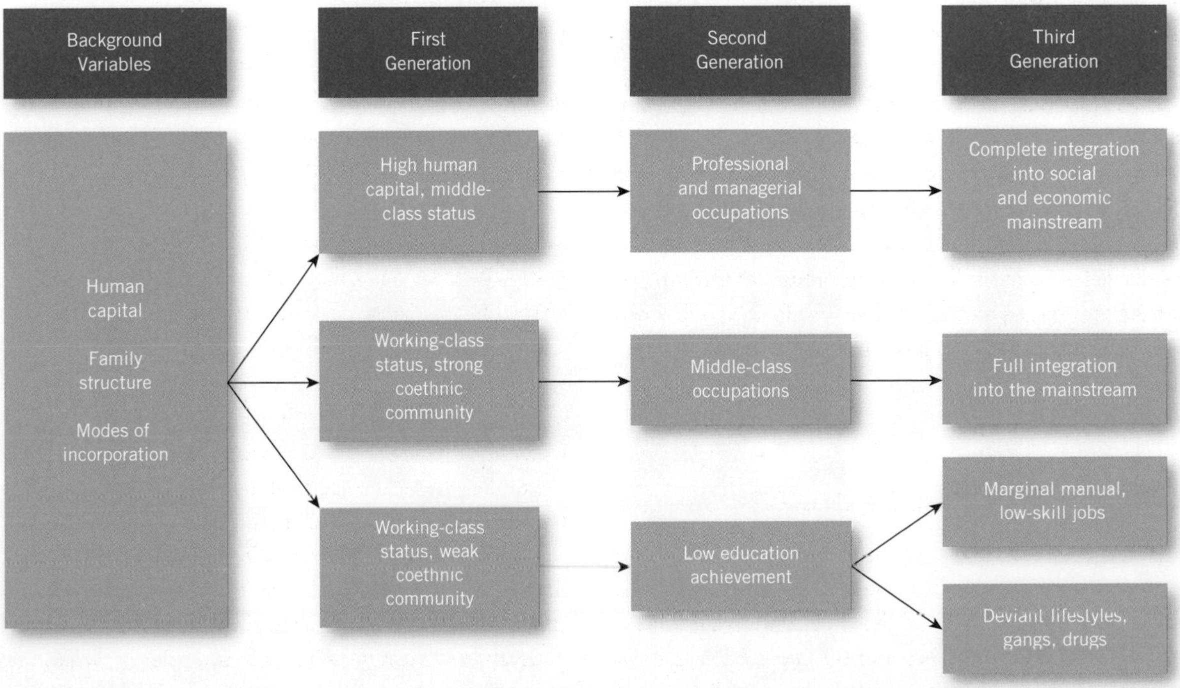

SOURCE: Based on Haller et al. (2011, p. 738).

second generations of different groups have different experiences in school, different income levels, and different interactions with the criminal justice system. Some of these differences are presented in Figure 10.9 and illustrate the large variations in the percentage of second generation individuals (by ethnic group) who do *not* pursue education beyond high school. Figure 10.10 shows patterns of incarceration by group.

These patterns are not random. Rather they reflect large differences in the human capital of the immigrant generation and variations in modes of incorporation (especially in terms of legal status and racial prejudice). They show that large percentages of the second (and third and later) generations of some groups are likely to assimilate into low-status, marginalized, or deviant sectors of American society, in direct contradiction to the patterns predicted by some versions of traditional assimilation theory.

Another important recent study reinforces some of these points. Sociologists Telles and Ortiz (2008) studied a sample of Mexican Americans who were interviewed in 1965 and again in 2000. They found evidence of strong movements toward acculturation and integration on some dimensions (e.g., language) but not on others. Even

fourth-generation members of their sample continued to live in "the barrio" and marry within the group, and did not reach economic parity with Anglos. The authors single out institutional discrimination (e.g., underfunding of public schools that serve Mexican American neighborhoods) as a primary cause of the continuing separation, a point consistent with Massey's (1995) conclusion regarding the decreasing rates of upward mobility in American society.

THE CASE FOR "TRADITIONAL" ASSIMILATION THEORY

Other recent studies come to a very different conclusion regarding the second generation: They are generally rising relative to their parents. This contradicts the segmented assimilation thesis and supports traditional assimilation theories. These studies (e.g., Alba & Nee, 2003; Bean & Stevens, 2003; Kasinitz et al., 2008; White & Glick, 2009) argue that contemporary assimilation will ultimately follow the same course that it followed for European immigrant groups 100 years ago, as described in Gordon's theory (see Chapter 2).

FIGURE 10.9 Percentage of Second-Generation Americans With a High School Diploma or Less

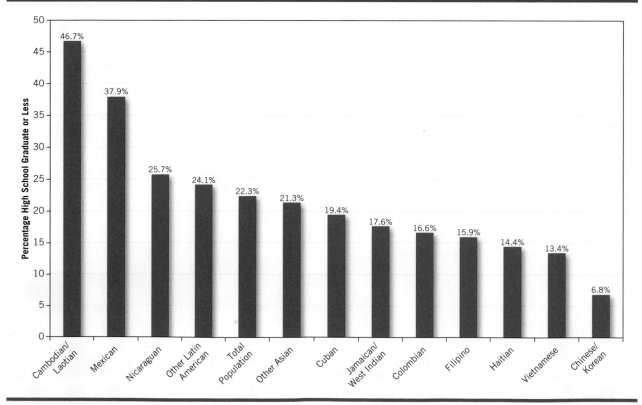

SOURCE: Based on Haller et al. (2011, p. 742).

NOTES:

Chinese and Korean Americans were combined, as were Cambodian and Laotian Americans, because of similar patterns and in order to create groups large enough for statistical analysis.

"Other Latin American" consists mostly of Salvadoran and Guatemalan Americans.

"Other Asian" is a diverse group that includes many nationalities.

FIGURE 10.10 Percentage of Second-Generation Men Incarcerated

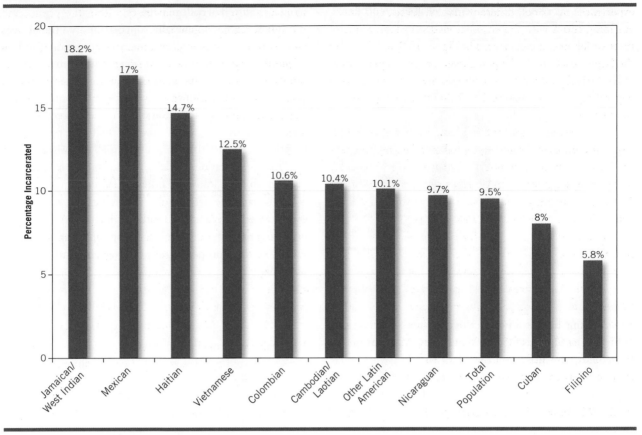

SOURCE: Based on Haller et al. (2011, p. 742).

NOTES:

Chinese and Korean Americans were combined, as were Cambodian and Laotian Americans, because of similar patterns and in order to create groups large enough for statistical analysis.

"Other Latin American" consists mostly of Salvadoran and Guatemalan Americans.

For example, two studies (Alba & Nee, 2003; Bean & Stevens, 2003) find that most contemporary immigrant groups are acculturating and integrating at the "normal" three-generation pace. Those groups that appear to be lagging behind this pace (notably Mexicans) may take as many as four to five generations, but their descendants will eventually find their way into the primary job market and the cultural mainstream.

Studies of acculturation show that immigrants' values become Americanized and that English language proficiency grows with time of residence and generation (Bean & Stevens, 2003, p. 168). We discussed some of these patterns in Chapter 8 (see Figures 8.10 and 8.11).

In terms of structural integration, contemporary immigrant groups may be narrowing the income gap over time, although many groups (e.g., Dominicans, Mexicans, Haitians, and Vietnamese) are disadvantaged by low levels of human capital at the start (Bean & Stevens, 2003, p. 142). Figures 10.11 and 10.12 illustrate this process with respect to wage differentials between Mexican and white non-Hispanic men and women of various generations and levels of education. (As you look at these figures, remember that complete income equality with non-Hispanic whites

would be indicated if the bar touched the 100% line at the top of the graph.)

FIGURE 10.11 Wage Differential of Mexican American Workers Relative to Whites, Men

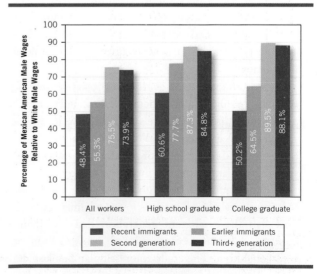

SOURCE: Bean and Stevens (2003, p. 139).

FIGURE 10.12 Wage Differentials of Mexican American Workers Relative to Whites, Women

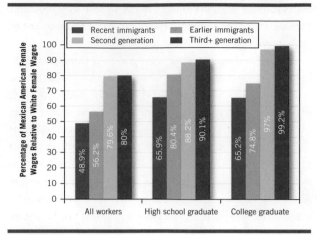

SOURCE: Bean and Stevens (2003, p. 139).

levels of human capital brought by the immigrant generation (e.g., 50% had college degrees).

These patterns generally support the traditional perspective on assimilation. Income and education tend to improve by generation, even though the pattern is not linear or complete. The second and third generations, on average, seem to be moving toward the economic mainstream, even though they do not close the gap completely. Bean and Stevens (2003) conclude that the patterns in Figures 10.11 and 10.12 are substantially consistent with the "three-generation model." The assimilation trajectory of Mexican Americans and other recent immigrant groups is not toward the urban poor, the underclass, or the disenfranchised, disconnected, and marginalized. Assimilation is not segmented, but is substantially repeating the experiences of the European groups on which Gordon (1964) based his theory.

SUMMARY

How can we reconcile the directly contradictory conclusions supported by the segmented and traditional perspectives on assimilation? In large part, this debate concerns the type of evidence and judgments about how much weight to give various facts and trends. On one hand, Massey's (1995) points about the importance of the postindustrial economy, declining opportunities for less-educated workers, and the neglect that seems typical of inner-city schools are well taken. Other studies provide evidence to support the segmented assimilation thesis.

On the other hand, it seems that even the least-educated immigrant groups have been able to find economic niches in which they and their families can manage long enough for their children and grandchildren to rise in the social structure, a pattern that has been at the core of the American immigrant experience for almost two centuries.

This debate will continue, and new evidence and interpretations will appear. Ultimately, however, these disputes may continue until immigration stops (which is very unlikely to happen, as Massey points out) and the fate of the descendants of the last immigrant groups is measured.

Looking first at all men workers (the leftmost bars in Figure 10.11), it is evident that recent Mexican immigrants earned a little less than half of what white men earned. The difference in income is smaller for earlier immigrants and even smaller for second and third generations of Mexicans. Separating out men with high school diplomas (the middle bars) and college degrees (the rightmost bars), the wage differential is generally lower for the more educated members of each generation. In other words, income equality tends to increase over the generations and as education increases.

On the other hand, note that third-generation men do not rise relative to their parents' generation. This contradicts the view that assimilation will proceed in a linear, stepwise fashion across the generations and is reminiscent of the findings of Telles and Ortiz (2008), noted earlier. For women (Figure 10.12), the wage differential also shrinks as the generations pass and level of education increases. Note that for third-generation, college-educated women, the wage differential shrinks virtually to zero, indicating integration on this variable (at least compared with dominant group women).

Another study (Taylor et al., 2013) used census data to compare immigrants and their children, and generally found that the latter rose in the society relative to the former. The second generation had higher incomes and levels of education, and lower levels of poverty. For example, for Hispanics, median household income rose from $34,600 for the immigrant generation to $48,400 for the second generation. Levels of education showed a similar upgrade: Almost half the immigrant generation had less than a high school education compared with only 17% of the second generation. The study found similar but less dramatic improvements for Asians, largely because of the high

QUESTIONS FOR REFLECTION

11. What are the arguments and evidence for the segmented assimilation model and traditional assimilation theory?

12. Which of these perspectives is more convincing? Why? What questions would have to be answered before one of them could be discarded?

RECENT IMMIGRATION IN HISTORICAL AND GLOBAL CONTEXT

The current wave of immigration to the United States is part of a centuries-old process that spans the globe. Underlying this immense and complex population movement are the powerful forces of continuing industrialization, economic development, and globalization. The United States and other advanced industrial nations are the centers of growth in the global economy, and immigrants flow to the areas of greater opportunity. In the 19th century, population moved largely from Europe to the Western Hemisphere. Over the past 50 years, the movement has been from the Global South to the Global North. This pattern reflects the simple geography of industrialization and opportunity and the fact that the more developed nations are in the Northern Hemisphere.

The United States has been the world's dominant economic, political, and cultural power for much of the past 100 years, and the preferred destination of most immigrants. Newcomers from around the globe continue the collective, social nature of past population movements (see Chapter 2). The direction of their travels reflects contemporary global inequalities: Labor continues to flow from the less-developed nations to the more-developed nations. The direction of this flow is not accidental or coincidental. It is determined by the differential rates of industrialization and modernization across the globe. Immigration contributes to the wealth and affluence of the more-developed societies and particularly to the dominant groups and elite classes of those societies.

The immigrant flow is also a response to the dynamics of globalization, particularly since the 1980s (Sen & Mamdouh, 2008). The current era of globalization has been guided by the doctrine of neoliberalism, or free trade, which urges nations to eliminate barriers to the movement of goods and capital. The North American Free Trade Agreement (NAFTA), mentioned on several occasions in this book, is an example of a neoliberal policy. These policies open less-developed nations such as Mexico to consumer goods manufactured and controlled by large, transnational corporations. These corporations often undersell goods made in those countries, which often drives small-scale local farmers and manufacturers out of business.

In addition, the international agencies such as the International Monetary Fund (IMF) that regulate the global economy pressure nations to reduce the size of their governmental sector. This often means that a country's budget for health and education is slashed and that services once controlled and subsidized by the government (e.g., water, electricity) are sold to private businesses, which then raise prices beyond what many people can afford. The combined result of these global forces is an increasingly vulnerable population in less-developed nations, unable to provide for themselves, educate their children, or afford the simplest of daily necessities.

Americans tend to see immigrants as individuals acting of their own free will and, often, illegally. ("They chose to come to the United States and break the law.") However, that picture changes when we see immigration as the result of these powerful, global economic and political forces. While domestic economies and social systems crumble, the victims of neoliberal globalization are left with few choices: They cross borders into the United States and to other advanced industrial nations. They do so illegally, if they have to, because "it is the best choice to achieve a dignified life—if not for themselves, then for their children" (Sen & Mamdouh, 2008, p. 7).

When viewed through the lens of globalization, it is clear that this population movement will continue because immigrants simply have no choice. It is unlikely that they can be stopped by further militarization of the border or by building bigger and taller walls. Immigrants come to the United States in such numbers, as they did in the past, because the alternatives in their home countries are unacceptable or nonexistent.

This perspective suggests that the tendency to reject, demonize, and criminalize immigrants is self-defeating. Punitive, militaristic policies will not stem the flow of people from the Global South to the Global North. Globalization, in its neoliberal form, is incomplete: It allows for the free movement of goods and capital but not of people. It benefits transnational corporations and the mega-businesses that produce consumer goods but victimizes the vulnerable citizens of the less-developed nations. As long as these forms of globalization hold, the population pressure from South to North will continue.

NEW IMMIGRANTS AND OLD ISSUES

In this chapter, we focused on some of the issues raised by high levels of immigration since the 1960s. As we discuss, debate, and consider these issues, we need to remember a fundamental fact about modern American society: The issues of the "traditional" minority groups—African Americans and American Indians, for example—have not been resolved. As we saw in earlier chapters, these groups have been a part of American society from the beginning, but they remain, in many ways, distant from achieving complete equality and integration.

Many of the current issues facing these groups relate to class and race. The urban underclass is disproportionately made up of peoples of color and continues to have marginal access to education and job opportunities, decent housing, and good health care when compared with the dominant Anglo society. While it is probably true the United States is more open and tolerant than ever before, we must not mistake a decline in blatant racism or a reduction in overt discrimination with its demise. As we have seen, abundant evidence shows that racism and discrimination have not declined, but have merely changed form, and that the patterns of exclusion and deprivation sustained in the past continue in the present.

Similarly, gender issues and sexism remain on the national agenda. Blatant sexism and overt discrimination against women are probably at historic lows, but, again, we cannot mistake change for disappearance. Most important, minority women remain the victims of a double jeopardy and are among the most vulnerable and exploited segments of society. Many women members of the new immigrant groups find themselves in similarly vulnerable positions.

Some societal trends exacerbate these problems of exclusion and continuing prejudice and sexism. For example, the continuing shift in subsistence technology away from manufacturing to the service sector privileges groups that, in the past as well as today, have had access to education. The urban underclass consists disproportionately of groups that have been excluded from education in the past and have unequal access in the present.

New immigrant groups have abundant problems of their own and need to find ways to pursue their self-interests in their new society. Some segments of these groups—the well-educated professionals seeking to advance their careers in the world's most advanced economy—will be much more likely to find ways to avoid the harshest forms of American rejection and exclusion. Similarly, the members of the "traditional" minority groups that have gained access to education and middle-class status will enjoy more opportunities than previous generations could have imagined. (As we have seen, however, their middle-class position will be more precarious than that of their dominant-group counterparts.)

Will we become a society in which ethnic and racial groups are permanently segmented by class, with the more favored members enjoying a higher, if partial, level of acceptance while other members of their groups languish in permanent exclusion and segmentation? What does it mean to be an American? What *should* it mean?

SUMMARY

This summary is organized around the Learning Objectives listed at the beginning of this chapter.

 Understand the volume and diversity of recent immigration to the United States.

The third wave of mass immigration to the United States began in the mid-1960s. This wave surpasses the first two in both number of immigrants per year (especially if undocumented immigrants are included in the count) and diversity. While the earlier waves were mostly European, contemporary immigrants are much more global and come from every continent and nearly every society.

 Understand the general characteristics of recent immigrants, especially new Hispanic and Asian groups, groups from the Caribbean, Middle Eastern and Arab groups, and immigrants from Africa.

Recent immigrant groups include Salvadorans, Dominicans, Haitians, Vietnamese, Filipinos, Syrians, Lebanese, Nigerians, and literally scores of other groups. Most new Hispanic and Caribbean groups tend to resemble the "peasant laborers" of old and have characteristics similar to those of Mexicans. Other groups tend to be "bipolar," including less-skilled laborers and refugee groups as well as highly educated professionals. All together, these groups bring an impressively diverse array of languages, cultural norms, background experiences, and desires. They also face multiple issues, including institutionalized discrimination, racism, and a changing U.S. economy. Arab Americans remain a special target for hate crimes, discrimination, and rejection.

 Characterize the new immigrant groups in terms of whether they are entering through the primary or secondary labor markets or through ethnic enclaves.

The primary labor market consists of more desirable jobs with higher pay and greater security. Immigrants entering this sector are highly educated professionals and businesspeople, and include, among others, many immigrants from India, Iran, and Nigeria. Jobs in the secondary sector are less desirable and command lower pay, little security, and few benefits. These jobs are filled by immigrants with lower levels of education and job skills, including Dominicans and Haitians. Some groups, including Korean and Arab Americans, have established ethnic enclaves consisting mostly of small retail shops and other businesses. The pathway of each group is strongly influenced by the amount of human capital its members bring, their racial background, the attitude of the larger society, and many other factors.

 10.4 Explain the attitudes of the American public as well as the values and statistical characteristics of the immigrants.

Relations between immigrants and the larger society are animated by a number of issues, including the relative costs and benefits of immigration, concerns about undocumented immigrants, and the speed of assimilation. Most Americans see immigration as positive, but there is a large and vociferous opposition. The contemporary anti-immigrant movement has sponsored various bills at the state level. Group competition and a sense of threat may be important motivators for those opposed to immigration. The immigrants are eager to exploit the economic opportunities offered in the United States but often have reservations about American values. The immigrant stream is highly diversified in terms of education, occupation, and motivation.

 10.5 Understand the various positions regarding the costs and benefits of immigration, undocumented immigrants, and DREAMers.

Prominent immigration issues include relative costs and benefits, the fate of undocumented immigrants, and the situation of DREAMers. Immigration is thought to be a generally positive force in the economy, but research continues to explore this controversial and complex issue.

The size of the undocumented population seems to have fallen in recent years, but there is still a great deal of debate over public policy on this matter. DREAMers are illegal immigrants who were brought to the United States as children. An executive order in 2012 allows DREAMers who meet certain criteria to stay in the United States for a renewable two-year term, without fear of deportation, but the future of this policy is in question.

 10.6 Explain the points of view and evidence regarding whether contemporary immigration will be segmented.

Segmented assimilation theory, in contrast to traditional assimilation theory, predicts that not all immigrants will rise to the middle class but that some will become part of a permanent, marginalized underclass. At present, evidence supports both theories.

 10.7 Place current immigration in the context of globalization, and cite some of the implications of immigration for "traditional" American minority groups.

Current immigration to the United States is part of a global population movement that reflects global inequalities and is stimulated, in part, by neoliberal globalization. Goods and capital but not people are free to move internationally. Also, national governments in the Third World are being pressured to open their borders and reduce the protections they offer their people. Immigration is partly a response to globalization.

REVIEW QUESTIONS

1. What differences exist among these new Americans in terms of their motivations for coming to the United States? What are the implications of these various "push" factors for their reception and adjustment to the United States?

2. Compare and contrast the Hispanic and Asian immigrant groups discussed in this chapter. What important differences and similarities can you identify in terms of modes of incorporation and human capital? What are the implications of these differences for the experiences of these groups?

3. Compare Arab and Middle Eastern immigrant groups with those from the Caribbean. Which group is more diverse? What differences exist in their patterns of adjustment and assimilation? Why do these patterns exist?

4. Compare and contrast African immigrants with immigrants from other groups. How do they differ? What are the implications of these differences for their adjustment to the larger society?

5. What, in your opinion, are the most important issues facing the United States in terms of immigration and assimilation? How are these issues playing out in your community? What are the implications of these issues for the future of the United States?

6. Will assimilation for contemporary immigrants be segmented? After examining the evidence and arguments presented by both sides, and using information from this and previous chapters, which side of the debate seems more credible? Why? What are the implications of this debate? What will the United States look like in the future if assimilation is segmented? How will the future change if assimilation follows the "traditional" pathway? Which of these scenarios is more desirable for immigrant groups? For society as a whole? For various segments of U.S. society (e.g., employers, labor unions, African Americans, consumers, the college educated, the urban underclass)?

Sharpen your skills with **SAGE edge** at edge.sagepub.com/healey8e

SAGE edge for students provides a personalized approach to help you accomplish your coursework goals in an easy-to-use learning environment.

The following resources are available at SAGE edge:

Current Debates: Is Immigration Harmful or Helpful to the United States?

What do immigrants cost American taxpayers? What do they contribute to the economy? Do the costs exceed the contributions?

On our website you will find an overview of the topic, the clashing points of view, and some questions to consider as you analyze the material.

Public Sociology Assignments

Public Sociology Assignments provide opportunities for students to address directly and personally some of the issues raised in this text.

There are two assignments for Part III on our website. The first looks at patterns of self-segregation in school cafeterias, and, in the second, students analyze the portrayal of the American family on television in terms of race, ethnicity, sexual orientation, and other sociologically relevant characteristics.

Contributed by Linda M. Waldron

Internet Research Project

For this Internet Research Project, you will choose any two of the new American groups covered in this chapter and use data gathered by the U.S. Census Bureau to assess their situation. You will add this information to the data you gathered previously on African Americans, Native Americans, Hispanic Americans, Asian Americans, and the general population. The project will be guided by a series of questions related to course concepts, and your instructor may ask you to discuss your findings in small groups.

For Further Reading

Please see our website for an annotated list of important works related to this chapter.

CHAPTER-OPENING TIMELINE PHOTO CREDITS

OTHER GROUPS, OTHER PATTERNS

I n Part IV, we go beyond minority groups defined by race and ethnicity, and beyond the United States. Chapter 11 considers gender as a dimension of minority-group status, and Chapter 12 analyzes minority groups defined by sexual orientation: lesbian, gay, and bisexual (LGB) Americans. Chapter 13 examines dominant–minority group situations across the globe, in nations from a variety of regions. We continue to apply the analytical framework (with some modifications) developed in the first three parts of the book.

It may be helpful to say a word about labels and our use of the LGB acronym in Chapter 12. As noted in Chapter 3, people often identify gender and sexual orientation minorities with the acronyms LGBT, LGBTQ+, or LGBTQIA, or with a variety of other labels. We use LGB in Chapter 12 for several reasons. We discuss transgender people in Chapter 11 on gender. Our focus in Chapter 12 is on lesbian and gay Americans and, to a lesser extent, bisexual Americans because data and other information are more available for these groups. However, all the categories are important because they reflect people's lived experiences and highlight the evolving, socially constructed nature of gender identity and sexual orientation.

11

GENDER

National Portrait Gallery, Public domain.

Wikimedia Commons

Wikimedia Commons

Wikipedia

timeline

1843
Isabella Baumfree takes the name Sojourner Truth and goes on to become a famed abolitionist and women's rights activist.

1881
Clara Barton founds the American Red Cross.

1920
The Nineteenth Amendment gives women the right to vote.

1840   1852   1864   1876   1888   1900   1912   1924   1936

1839
Mississippi becomes the first state to grant married women the right to hold property in their own names, independent of their husbands.

1848
The first women's rights convention is held in Seneca Falls, N.Y.

1869
The first law giving women the right to vote is passed in Wyoming.

1872
Susan B. Anthony is arrested for trying to vote.

1890
Wyoming becomes the first state to grant women the right to vote in all elections.

1932
Amelia Earhart becomes the first woman to fly solo across the Atlantic.

Maria's parents always told her she could grow up to be anything she wanted to be. She and her brother, Malcolm, were bright students, but Malcolm sometimes struggled with behavioral issues, and Maria earned better grades. Maria knew that girls and boys were equally smart, strong, and capable, but her life was not the same as her brother's. While she babysat neighborhood kids for $3 to $5 an hour, Malcolm was mowing the neighbors' lawns for $25 to $50 each. Malcolm's curfew was later than hers, and her parents set stricter limits on her social life.

Maria and Malcolm were both interested in math and computer science, and although Maria got into the "better" college, they both enrolled in the same major. But Maria's computer classes were dominated by men, and

LEARNING OBJECTIVES

By the end of this chapter, you will be able to do the following:

11.1 Explain the difference between sex and gender and understand the social context of the latter.

11.2 List and explain key historical and economic events that have shaped gender relations.

11.3 Understand feminism as a social movement, its varieties, its achievements, and its challenges.

11.4 Identify and explain the key evidence and causes of gender inequality today.

11.5 Describe how race, class, sexual orientation, and religion impact gender inequality.

11.6 Explain how the concepts of assimilation and pluralism apply to women's experiences as a minority group in U.S. society.

Wikimedia Commons

1938
The Fair Labor Standards Act establishes minimum wage without regard to gender.

1963
The Equal Pay Act is passed by Congress to close gender pay gap.

1963
Betty Friedan's *The Feminine Mystique* is published.

1964
Title VII of Civil Rights Act of 1964 prohibits employment discrimination on basis of race, color, religion, national origin, or gender.

1972
Title IX bans gender discrimination in schools.

1973
In *Roe v. Wade*, the Supreme Court protects a woman's right to end pregnancy.

1981
Sandra Day O'Connor becomes the first woman Supreme Court justice.

1982
For the first time, more women than men receive bachelor's degrees.

1998
The Supreme Court rules that employers are liable for workplace sexual harassment.

2009
President Obama signs into law the Lilly Ledbetter Fair Pay Act, intended to reduce the pay gap between men and women.

2017
First women soldiers graduate from U.S. Army infantry training.

2016
Hillary Clinton becomes the first woman in U.S. history to win the nomination of a major political party.

2016
The U.S. military lifts its ban on transgender service members and allows eligible women to serve in any position, even combat.

2017
The Trump administration revokes federal policies allowing transgender students to use bathrooms consistent with their gender identity. It also begins the process of prohibiting transpeople from serving in the military.

1948   1960   1972   1984   1996   2008   2016   2020

Getty

Wikimedia Commons

White House Photographic Office

she struggled to form a social network among her peers. She had always loved working with children, so she picked up a second major in education. When the two siblings graduated from college, within a year of each other, Malcolm took a job as a computer programmer, starting at $65,000 a year, and Maria took a job teaching high school math and computers for $35,000 a year.

Maria and Malcolm both want to marry and have children eventually. They both also happen to be multiracial (Latino, African American, and white). Both attended predominantly white colleges, but while Malcolm enjoyed an active dating life, Maria did not conform to the "white" standard of beauty confronting her in media images and the surrounding culture, and thus had a harder time finding suitable mates.

Maria feels more pressure to conform to a certain "look" than Malcolm ever did. Both wonder whether their future relationships will bear any resemblance at all to their parents' marriage. Their family was able to get by primarily on their father's income, while their mother worked part-time and was heavily involved in their schooling and extracurricular activities. Right now, not even Malcolm would be able to buy a house on his own without some additional income or assets, much less Maria . . .

Siblings can be drastically different, even when raised by the same parents, due to variations in personality and temperament. However, what other social factors are at play here, influencing the two siblings' divergent paths? How much of their different lifestyles can we attribute to their biochemical makeup and how much to socialization, culture, or the structure of society? What, if anything, can be done to change these inequalities? Does anything need to be changed? •

This chapter examines how gender shapes stratification and inequality in American society. While certain biological factors distinguish the sexes of the human species from each other, the gender dynamics in everyday life are the outcomes of human social arrangements (e.g., institutions, laws). As with other types of stratification that we have analyzed in this book, when a society designates certain groups (in this case, women) as minorities, it impacts how people relate to one another.

First, we explain some basic concepts related to the sociology of gender. Next, we examine the history and background of gender relations. Specifically, we will analyze how

society's economic development and transitions have had a significant impact on how gender relations are structured in each period. Then, we will examine the various protest and resistance movements that have sought to lessen gender stratification. These efforts toward social change and gender equality are often referred to in the modern context as **feminism**. However, we will also consider the diversity of what is meant by the term *feminism* and the sometimes-problematic relationship between the ideals of feminism and the various individuals and groups that have sought gender equality.

As with the racial and ethnic minorities we have already studied, research documents continued discrimination against women in terms of their economic and political power as a worldwide minority group. We will examine a few examples from the United States (and worldwide) of how gender discrimination continues to impact women's lives, thereby exemplifying the relationship between sexism and modern society. Because gender relations operate quite differently depending on one's race, class, sexual orientation, age, and other factors, we will use an intersectional approach in our examination of sexism. Not all men benefit from sexism equally, nor do all women feel its oppression in the same ways.

Finally, at the end of the chapter, we will apply the concepts of assimilation and pluralism to evaluate how women as a minority group have been similar to and different from other groups we have studied in this book. By the end of this chapter, you will be familiar with historical as well as contemporary gender relations and will be able to understand how stratification operates in this particular area of social life.

THE SOCIOLOGY OF GENDER: THE BASICS

The term **sex** refers to human biological variation based on genitalia, hormones, and chromosomes. Most people are female or male. However, biologists and medical practitioners have documented variation besides just the male/female dichotomy around which most societies are organized. For example, almost 2% the U.S. population are intersex. That is, they have biological characteristics from more than one sex category (Fausto-Sterling, 2000).

Feminism refers to ideas and movements that have sought to achieve gender equality.

Sex refers to people's biological characteristics based on genitalia, hormones, and chromosomes.

Intersex people have the biological characteristics of more than one sex.

A year after women won full voting rights, these women joined in the St. Patrick's Day Parade on Fifth Avenue on March 27, 1921.

For example, someone who has an X or Y chromosomal pattern that deviates from the XX (female) and XY (male) forms. To put that figure in perspective, about 1% to 2% of Americans are also born with red hair (Organization Intersex International, 2015).

While sex is biological, **gender** refers to the social meanings or characteristics that people "attach" to males and females. People in the United States primarily recognize two dominant **gender statuses**: boy/man and girl/woman. Typically, medical professionals assign a person's gender based on genitalia seen in ultrasounds or at birth. They do so based on presumed congruence between sex and gender. For example, when a fetal ultrasound for sex shows a penis, people declare, "It's a boy!" From that point onward, the gendering process begins: by picking out "boy names," buying clothing in baby (boy) blue, or decorating the baby's room in "boy colors" or with gendered décor such as a baseball glove lamp, rather than a sparkly "princess" lamp. Gender is so important that people have started having "gender reveal" parties. An August 2017 review of "gender reveal themes" on one popular website included "Pearls or Bow ties?", "Pirate or Mermaid?", "Rifles or Ruffles?", "Quarterback or Cheerleader?", "Lures or

Lace?", and "Wheels or Heels?", among others. These themes tell us that Americans construct gender as a binary (girl or boy) and that the construction is so important that people often refer to girls/women and boys/men as the "opposite sex." Additionally, these gender reveal themes offer insight into the **gender socialization** process that teaches people gender-related beliefs and norms and through which they develop their gender identity.

Norms are societal prescriptions for behavior that come from beliefs and values. (Norms are not necessarily what is "typical" or "normal" in a society.) As you learned in Chapter 1, gender norms are the societal expectations for what boys/men and girls/women should be like or do. (Or, conversely, what they should *not* be like or do.) Societies label certain qualities (e.g., nurturing) or activities (e.g., wearing makeup) as "masculine" or "feminine." The "gender reveal" party themes suggest that the "masculine" things boys should like include rifles, football, fishing, cars, acting like pirates, and wearing bow ties. The normative expectations for girls seem quite different: they should

"Gender reveal" parties illustrate the importance of gender for organizing social life.

Gender refers to the socially defined meanings or characteristics (e.g., masculine, feminine).

Gender statuses are positions in the social structure based on gender (e.g., girl, boy).

Gender socialization is the process by which people learn societal beliefs and norms related to gender and through which they develop a gender identity.

like lace, pearls, ruffles, high heels, and being cheerleaders (presumably for boy football players). These themes also subtly suggest that boys should be active; they should do things with their bodies. Girls, on the other hand, should spend time looking a certain way (for others to see) or serving in support roles, such as cheering for football players. (We realize, of course, that cheering involves athleticism and creativity and can be quite dangerous and that some boys cheer, too.) So, what happens if a girl likes guns, pirates, and fishing significantly more than lace, pearls, or heels? Depending on her family and other social groups (e.g., peer group, school), she might be labeled a "tomboy" or be sanctioned negatively.

For tomboys (or others), doing "boy things" probably reflects personal taste, similar to preferring tacos to hamburgers or the beach to the mountains. They are not indicators of **gender identity**; that is, one's feeling of being a girl/woman, boy/man, or some other gender. Most Americans are **cisgender**. That is, their gender identity "matches" the biological sex they were assigned at birth. However, a small percentage of the U.S. population identify as **transgender**. Transgender people have gender identities that differ from societal prescriptions for sex-gender correspondence, for example, someone with male sex characteristics (e.g., testes) and who identifies as (feels like) a girl or woman.

To achieve congruence between one's body and gender identity, transgender people may change their name, hairstyle, or clothing to be in line with the social norms for boys/men or girls/women. Additionally, some transgender people may change biological aspects of their bodies to be more congruent with their gender identity. For example, by binding breast tissue to lay flat against the torso or by taking hormones to stop facial hair growth or to increase breast size. (Males have breasts though Americans constructs tend to call them "pecs"—a linguistic construction that suggests difference.) Though some (25%) transgender people have surgery (e.g., facial reconstruction, breast augmentation/reduction, or genital procedures), most do not (James et al., 2016). Such individual changes highlight gender as a social construction, but do not alter the dominant binary gender system.

We can't possibly address the diversity of gender that exists throughout the world and in the United States in this short book, but it may be helpful to review some of them. For example, people who are **gender fluid** feel like both genders and their gender expression shifts easily between "masculine" and "feminine." They might "feel like a woman" one day—and dress as such—choosing an extremely feminine **gender display** by wearing a short, tight-fitting dress, heels, and makeup. However, the next day they may feel "like a man" and wear baggy jeans, a loose T-shirt, and a baseball cap. Most people display gender through their actions most of the time, for example, by

Social media activist Jeffrey Marsh identifies as gender fluid.

how they walk and talk (and what they talk about). Gender and gender displays are not just a category to which one belongs, but something a person actively does to indicate one's gender status to others. Yet, people are usually not aware that they "**do gender**" because gender identity and gender norms are strongly internalized. Thus, what one feels or does feels natural—believing them to just be personal preferences (West & Zimmerman, 1987). In terms of gender fluidity, identifying with more than one gender is key. A woman might wear loose clothing and a baseball cap one day because it's raining out and she just pulled an all-nighter. The next evening, she might dress up for a date in a tight dress, heels, and makeup. This behavior doesn't make her gender fluid because she identifies with a particular gender status (i.e., "woman"). Her gender identify doesn't shift and change.

Gender identity is one's sense of being a girl/woman, boy/man, or some other gender.

Cisgender refers to people whose gender identity "matches" the biological sex they were assigned at birth.

Transgender people have a gender identity different from their assigned sex.

Gender fluid people identify with more than one gender and easily shift between them.

Gender displays are indicators (e.g., clothing, hobbies) of one's gender status.

Doing gender involves actions to display one's gender status.

Alternatively, people who identify or express their gender in nonconforming ways may call themselves **genderqueer**. Still others prefer the term "pangender" whose root word ("pan") means "all." Other people don't identify with any gender and may call themselves agender, gender free, genderless, or post-gender. Or, they may not label their gender at all. It can surprise you to learn who identifies outside the gender binary. For example, guitar legend Pete Townshend (of The Who) once said, "I know how it feels to be a woman because I am a woman. And I won't be classified as just a man" (Giuliano, 2002, p. 241). (As we discuss in Chapter 12, people with non-binary gender identities have a variety of sexual orientations.)

Because Americans are socialized within a binary-dominant gender system (girl/woman, boy/man), it can be hard for some people to understand identities and practices that differ from that system. For example, the language that people use to describe themselves (e.g., genderqueer) may seem complicated, unnecessary, or strange. It may be helpful to note how these gender descriptors parallel racial or ethnic identity (see Chapters 1, 5, 6, 7, 8, and 9). For example, people from the same country might identify as Hispanic, Latino, or by their specific country of origin. Still others may identify as multiracial or refuse to label their ethnicity or race at all.

To say that gender is a social construction means that people "create" gender-related beliefs, norms, and practices through their interactions. As with race, these interactions occur within a larger social context of ideologies and institutional practices. For example, if a dominant belief in society is that men are (and should be) strong, one related norm might be "don't cry, even when hurt." People might encourage this behavior by complimenting little boys for "being a strong little man." Or, they might negatively sanction boys and men who cry by calling them names like "sissy," or by saying "boys don't cry."

Changing gender norms also illustrate that gender is a social construction. For example, the photo on this page shows a child with long hair, wearing a white dress with a big lace collar. They wear shiny patent leather "Mary Janes" and hold a hat adorned with feathers and a big bow. The child is Franklin Delano Roosevelt, and he grew up to become our 32nd president. If you're surprised that this is a boy, that's because we construct gender differently today. The symbols of "dress," "Mary Janes," "lace," and "bows" are now associated with girls and femininity.

Prior to the 1940s, gender-specific colors didn't exist as they do now. Girls and boys wore white because it was

Franklin Delano Roosevelt (FDR) at age 2 1/2, illustrating typical gender-neutral clothing in 1884. Gender-specific colors and styles didn't emerge until later.

easy to clean with chemicals. Girls had no "natural" attraction to pink—it hadn't been defined as a "girl" color as is it today. Marketers had to teach these ideas to adults. For example, in 1918, Earnshaw's Infants' Department trade publication wrote that, "The generally accepted rule is pink for the boys, and blue for the girls. The reason is that pink, being a more decided and stronger color, is more suitable for the boy, while blue, which is more delicate and dainty, is prettier for the girl" (Maglaty, 2011). That's right—the gender-related colors then were the opposite of today's. Likewise, norms about cheerleading have changed. In 1911, people thought of cheerleading as masculine so much so that "the reputation of having been a valiant 'cheer-leader' is one of the most valuable things a boy can take away from college. As a title to promotion in professional or public life, it ranks hardly second to that of having been a quarterback" (Adams & Bettis, 2003, p. 76).

Finally, you can see how gender is socially constructed by noticing how gender norms vary by religion, social class, sexual orientation, age, and other social factors. To "be a man" meant something different for an 80-year-old Japanese American man in the 19th century compared to what it means for a 12-year-old Latino boy in the 21st century. Similarly, the "feminine" ideal for a 40-year-old straight, white, working-class woman in the 19th century may be quite different from that of a 20-year-old, bisexual,

---

Genderqueer is an umbrella term that includes anyone whose sexual orientation, gender identity, or gender expression deviates from the gender binary of girl/woman or boy/man.

upper-class Latina woman today. (Sojourner Truth's "Ain't I a Woman?" speech in Chapter 4 made this observation, too.)

While gender seemingly proscribes everyday life, it is not an inescapable straightjacket. A young girl in Afghanistan may find it inconceivable to envision a life where she receives a formal education, chooses a well-paid profession, and selects her own life partner. A young man in urban America may find it impossible to cry when he is sad, to choose to become a professional ballet dancer, or to stay at home with his children while his partner fulfills the role of breadwinner. But because gender is a social construction, it is also possible to create social change—both within the cultural expectations for gendered behaviors and in the social structures that assign differential rewards and life chances based on gender. Some changes can be attained through hard-won political and legal struggles, while others will have to be addressed more creatively through the processes by which we socialize people and in the cultural norms we uphold throughout various institutions—the family, religion, schools, and media, just to name a few.

QUESTIONS FOR REFLECTION

1. Consider what different agents of socialization taught you about gender during childhood. What subtle and overt messages did you hear from family members, friends, teachers, the media, and others? Did any of those messages conflict or reinforce one another? How did you display your gender to others and did you conform to social expectations?

2. Consider times when you or someone you knew broke gender norms. What happened and how did people react? Did social context such as age or setting make a difference? For example, was it okay for a 4-year-old boy to cry when hurt, but not for an 18-year-old or 50-year-old? Can boys/men cry at home, but not in public? What are the rules and how did you learn them?

3. Consider the ways we construct gender difference between boys/girls and men/women (e.g., clothing, names). What ideologies support the the social construction of gender difference? How is this process similar to the social construction of racial difference?

HISTORY AND BACKGROUND OF GENDER RELATIONS

Although gender relations in any society often seem taken for granted, as if things have always operated that way, a

quick review of history allows us to examine how gender stratification can be organized quite differently depending on the society's primary mode of subsistence. Typically, as global economic shifts happen, gender relations shift accordingly.

HUNTING AND GATHERING

Only recently in human history have societies moved away from hunting and gathering in favor of growing their own food. A few small hunting-and-gathering societies remain, but this is an all-but-disappeared mode of social organization. When humans rely on hunting and gathering for their primary resources, they cannot easily settle anywhere permanently, for when the food source depletes, they must move.

The nomadic nature of hunting-and-gathering societies means that their population growth stays low, so reproductive activities are a relatively small part of the total life course. This is significant to gender relations because so much of the inequality that develops in more modern economies revolves around the women's and men's divergent relationships to childbirth and child rearing. Forming huge families, with the time and space dedicated to them, is a luxury that hunter-gatherers cannot afford.

Out of necessity and practicality, the organization of hunting-and-gathering societies involved men and women engaging in parallel activities. Food had to be produced daily and clan members had to produce food and cooperate to survive. Men engaged primarily in hunting and fishing, and though animal products accounted for only a small percentage of the people's diets, they provided important nutrients and calories. Women tended to be in charge of foraging for seeds, nuts, berries, and other sources of food. Because of the level of development, hunter-gatherer societies lacked any type of surplus. With few resources to acquire and horde, it was extremely difficult for anyone to gain any power over others (Lenski, 1984).

These characteristics of hunting-and-gathering societies are important to sociologists of gender stratification because they challenge the ideological basis of the argument that a man breadwinner and a woman caregiver is the traditional, natural, or primal gender arrangement. Indeed, this historical (and for some, current) mode of subsistence illustrates that it is possible for men and women to have relatively equal power in society and to work cooperatively toward survival.

AGRARIAN

As societies shifted from hunting and gathering toward the development of agriculture, the household became a place of domestic production. The division of labor within families became organized by gender and age. For example, men tended to be involved in field work such as plowing, harvesting crops like wheat, and caring for large animals such as cattle and sheep. Girls and women grew vegetables, tended chickens, prepared and preserved food (e.g., canning), and spun yarn from sheep's wool. Yet, all family members were needed for survival, and this division of labor in and of itself didn't necessarily lead to gender inequality (Kulikoff, 1992).

This gendered division of labor (i.e., women primarily inside the home, men outside) may have emerged, in part, because some tasks required greater physical strength, though women did heavy labor such as building and plowing when their husbands or fathers were ill. The need for women to breastfeed and care for infants also played a role. However, the emergence of private property was the most fundamental shift that led to this gendered organization of family life. In agrarian societies people domesticated animals and produced their own food—sometimes even accumulating a surplus. With the ability to have private property came the emergence of capitalism. In this new economic system, people no longer just exchanged goods; selling goods became a way to make money to buy more goods.

People needed to keep track of their property and because property was passed down from fathers to sons (usually only the first son), men needed to be certain which children "belonged" to them (Engels, 1884/2010). One way to do this was to control women's sexuality through monogamous marriage. Thus, the patriarchal family was born. The structure of the patriarchal family form reflects the intersection of three institutions: the economy, the system of gender relations, and religion. The word *patriarchal* comes from *pater*, meaning "father." In patriarchal families, men were to rule their families like god, the father. That is, with ultimate power and authority. (Not all agrarian societies are patriarchal. For an interesting take on Lenski's argument that considers gender inequality see Blumberg, 2004.)

The patriarchal family brought the beginnings of the ideology of "separate spheres." This ideology asserted that man's place is primarily in the field and the marketplace, while women's activities should be concentrated within the domestic sphere. Women certainly made ample contributions to production (e.g., milking cows, cooking, sewing), but their activities were less likely to engage the marketplace directly. Families also began to have more children, who were more likely than ever to survive to adulthood, which meant a greater proportion of women's time had to be spent in child-rearing activities, further confining them to the domestic sphere (Gray, 2000).

Despite the gender inequality and gendered division of labor in agrarian societies, agricultural work required all participants to contribute, and the outputs of labor were immediately tangible in their impact. Men and women,

girls and boys alike were up early doing chores, and the various tasks that needed doing continued into nightfall. It was not until industrialization that a distinct labor force—with categories of employed and unemployed—emerged, fusing unpaid labor with the domestic sphere and paid labor with the public sphere, and thus further entrenching sexism in the ideology of separate spheres (Padavic & Reskin, 2002). Although there can be some variation, many societies today are organized around the agricultural mode of production and the resultant gender inequality.

INDUSTRIAL

By the middle of the 19th century, with the advent of the sewing machine, telegraph, transcontinental railroad, and automobile, the industrial revolution was in full swing and, with it, so was urbanization. Work was no longer just out in the field or the local marketplace; it was now in a central city that required some travel time to reach, and it typically excluded young children. As employment became urbanized, women's and children's participation in the paid labor force declined. Thus, in an industrialized, urbanized society, the workplace became decidedly gendered as a "masculine" space (Padavic & Reskin, 2002). Because men earned a wage while women often did not, men's power within families became further solidified (Gottlieb, 1993).

With industrialization came a labor force with a tiered wage structure. In the United States and other Western societies, employers reserved the highest-paying jobs for white men. Unions developed to curb labor exploitation and fight for humane working conditions, but, as we have seen in previous chapters, unions also functioned to restrict those on the lower end of the stratification ladder from entering the skilled labor pool. Those persons excluded from unions for much of the early history of labor in the United States include women, immigrants, and nonwhites.

Along with the new vision of the ideal worker (i.e., white men) came the practice of paying a "family wage." Employers such as Henry Ford of Ford Motor Company realized that to retain good employees, they could pay their men workers a wage sufficient to support their entire families, ideally eliminating the need for wives and children to work. Because it would lessen the likelihood of employees migrating in search of better work, the "family wage" was a rational decision from the perspective of business owners. However, it assumed a two-parent family headed by a man. As a result, single or widowed women trying to support themselves (and possibly children), as well as women supplementing the family income, earned substantially lower wages than men counterparts.

Only a small minority of middle and upper classes could afford to approximate this ideal family structure of the "man as breadwinner" and "woman as homemaker."

Immigrant and nonwhite women, whether single or married, continued to labor at low-wage work, as their income was sorely needed to supplement the poorly compensated labor of the men in their families.

This ideal family structure was held up as universally desirable, but it was an unrealistic standard for many. It deepened the "separate spheres" ideology that drew stark contrasts between masculinity and femininity. The ideal husband should be a "good provider" whose domain was outside the home in the economic and political areas of society. Men were not expected to show interest or emotion about home life. Juxtaposed with this was the "cult of true womanhood," which emphasized four qualities for women: purity, piety, domesticity, and submissiveness (Welter, 1966, p. 152). The ideal woman was expected to be a "good" wife and mother, an "angel of consolation" after a hard day's work (p. 169). By definition, some women could not embody this gender ideal (e.g., poor women who worked outside of the home for money and unmarried women).

As historian Stephanie Coontz (1997) notes, "The resulting identification of masculinity with economic activities and femininity with nurturing care, now often seen as the 'natural' way of organizing the nuclear family, was in fact a historical product of this 19th-century transition from an agricultural household economy to an industrial wage economy" (pp. 55–56). Such ideals were

Images such as this encouraged and celebrated the contributions of women to the war effort during World War II.

much more than mere stereotypes; they were encoded into law, and sanctions existed for those who deviated from them. For example, until the 1970s when "no-fault" divorce laws became enacted, a person needed "grounds" for a divorce. With this, a man could divorce his wife for not being an adequate "homemaker." Similarly, a wife could divorce her husband if he was not an adequate "breadwinner" (Schwartz & Scott, 1997).

Despite informal and formal norms, as the industrial era continued to roll forward, significant events contributed to the slow but steady increase in the involvement of women in all institutional areas of society. For example, in 1920, after a suffrage movement that had been active for decades, American women gained the right to vote.

Women's involvement in the paid labor force also rose over the decades. As was the case with many other minority groups we have discussed, the job opportunities available to women increased during World War II. Their contributions were encouraged and celebrated with wartime propaganda such as the now-famous image of Rosie the Riveter.

The Civil Rights and feminist movements of the 1960s also encouraged more women toward employment and financial independence. However, until the passage of the Civil Rights Act of 1964, employers could fire women in certain types of jobs such as teaching when they got married (or pregnant). The broader U.S. culture also discouraged the hiring of married women. These practices, called the "marriage bar," primarily affected white, educated women. Likewise, as late as the 1970s, a married woman in some states could not get a driver's license, credit card, or even library card unless it was in her husband's name. It was not until the 1970s, with the advent of deindustrialization, that women's participation in the labor force dramatically increased.

GENDER INEQUALITY IN A GLOBALIZING, POSTINDUSTRIAL WORLD

Deindustrialization and globalization transformed gender relations along with relations among racial and ethnic groups. Everywhere, even in the most patriarchal societies, women have been moving away from their customary wife and mother roles, taking on new responsibilities, and facing new challenges. In the United States, the transition to a postindustrial society has changed gender relations and the status of women on a number of levels.

Women and men are now generally equal in terms of education levels (for example, see Figures 6.10 and 6.11), and the shift to fluid competitive group relations has weakened the barriers to gender equality, along with those to racial equality, although formidable obstacles remain. The changing role of women is also shaped by other characteristics of a modern society: smaller families, higher divorce rates, and rising numbers of single mothers who must work to support their children as well as themselves.

One of the most fundamental changes in U.S. gender relations has been the increasing participation of women in the paid labor force, a change related to both demographic trends (e.g., lower birthrates) and changing aspirations. Women are now employed at almost the same levels as men. In 2016, for example, 70% of unmarried women (vs. about 82% of unmarried men) and about 66% of married women (vs. about 91% of married men) had jobs outside the home. Furthermore, between 1970 and 2009, the workforce participation of married women with children increased from a little less than 40% to over 70% (U.S. Bureau of Labor Statistics, 2017).

One reflection of changing aspirations is that U.S. women are entering a wider variety of careers. In the past, women were largely concentrated in a relatively narrow range of women-dominated jobs such as nurse and elementary school teacher. Figure 11.1 focuses on four pairs of careers and illustrates both the traditional pattern and recent changes. Each pair includes an occupation dominated by women and a comparable but higher-status, more lucrative, occupation traditionally dominated by men. While the "women's" jobs remain largely done by women,

the percentage of women in the higher-status occupations has increased dramatically (even though, except for university professor, the more lucrative careers remain disproportionately filled by men).

The changing status of women in postindustrial society is also reflected in other measures of secondary structural integration. We will analyze these trends later in this chapter, following much the same format as used in the chapters in Part III.

QUESTIONS FOR REFLECTION

4. Is the glass half-empty or half-full for women today? Consider how the comparison group we choose—for example, women of the past or men of the present—might influence our answer to that question.

5. Consider how race, class, sexual orientation, and religion might have affected the gender advances and restrictions described in this section. For example, to what degree do men of every class, race, and ethnicity have privileges over comparable women? Are all women able to take advantage of educational and occupational opportunities, regardless of religion, sexual orientation, and other social statuses?

FIGURE 11.1 Percentage of Women in Selected Occupations, 1983–2010

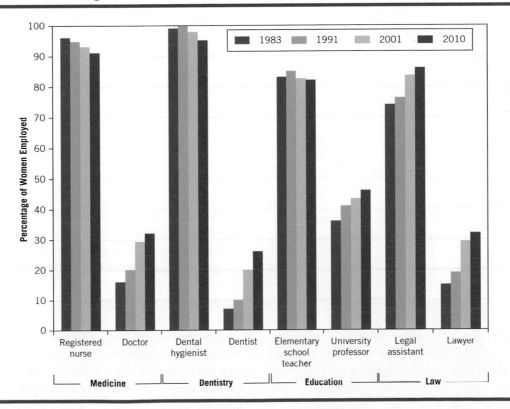

SOURCE: 1983 and 1991—calculated from U.S. Census Bureau (1993, pp. 392–393); 2001—calculated from U.S. Census Bureau (2002, pp. 587–588); 2010—calculated from U.S. Census Bureau (2012c, pp. 393–394).

MOVEMENTS FOR GENDER EQUALITY

Although it was not until after 1970 that women's labor force participation increased in the United States and the gender gap in earnings began to decline, it was not for women's lack of trying in earlier periods. Several movements for gender equality have been making strides for more than 170 years, marked by periods of significant social change and legal achievements alternating with "doldrum" periods, when women were still organizing but more quietly and under more repression (Rupp & Taylor, 1987).

The term *feminism* has come to represent various social movements for gender equality, and historians have identified three major "waves" of feminism. The first wave consisted of the suffragists—women who worked for gender equity in the United States and several other Western industrialized nations during the late 19th and early 20th centuries. Their main goal was to secure the vote for women (or suffrage) and the right of women to run for political office (see Figure 11.2 for a timeline of when women won the right to vote in various nations). However, as you learned in Chapter 4, the early feminist movement was also connected with the abolitionist movement.

The late 1960s to early 1970s brought the second wave, and this is the period when the word *feminist* emerged. This wave culminated in various achievements, including the Equal Pay Act, the acceptance of women into virtually all previously men's-only colleges and universities, and Title IX, which addresses gender equality in school and university sports.

The third wave is generally dated from the 1980s to the present. Third-wave feminists are the first to take advantage of the many legal and other institutional advances for which the second wave fought. The third-wave period is also characterized by a heightened diversity of gender experiences—encompassing multiracial feminism, postmodern feminism, and transgender activism, among others. Below we consider each wave in turn.

FIRST WAVE: SUFFRAGISTS

In the mid-1800s, women who were engaged in the abolitionist movement to end slavery began to consider the question of human equality under the law more broadly. In 1848, the Seneca Falls Convention was held, and Elizabeth Cady Stanton, Lucretia Mott, Frederick Douglass, and many others drafted the Declaration of Sentiments, which included demands for women's right to vote (Kraditor, 1981). The document also included a number of statements that reflected compromises between the delegates and were the results of heated debates and negotiations. Not all abolitionists believed in gender equality, and not all suffragists endorsed racial equality (Davis, 1983).

The abolitionist movement met its primary goal during the Civil War. Although it is often said that the 1865 Emancipation Proclamation granted black men the right to vote in the United States—55 years before women attained the same legal right in 1920—the reality was that the Jim Crow terrorism that followed the war in the South (see Chapter 5) made it virtually impossible for black men to exercise that right, nor were black women able to do so in many states even after 1920. It would take the concerted efforts of the second wave of feminists to secure voting rights for all women, not just in theory but in practice.

However, the first wave was concerned with much more than just voting rights. Women's economic independence was also a central concern. In the United States, women could not own property, and it was perfectly legal to pay women much less than men for the same work.

Moreover, particularly for women in the white upper classes—who had the most time, resources, and education to be the voice of the early movement—their reproductive capacity and homemaking seemed to be their only source of societal worth. Sociologist Charlotte Perkins Gilman wrote eloquently during the late 1800s and early 1900s about the excessive "sex distinction" between men and women. While acknowledging that women were the only ones capable of giving birth to children, Gilman critiqued a society that relegated so many of the other domestic tasks to women, when either men or women could easily perform them. She further argued that keeping half the human race from engaging in productive mental and public labor was limiting the progress of humans as a species. She also pointed out that, due to lack of economic independence, women were reduced to using "sex attraction" to pursue a gold ring (marriage), because at that time the only way women could access property and various other rights was through their husbands (Appelrouth & Edles, 2012).

Without the ability to control their own reproductive capacities, women's economic independence would continue to prove elusive. Recognizing this connection, Margaret Sanger opened the first birth-control clinic in the United States in 1916, shortly before the Nineteenth Amendment to the U.S. Constitution granted women the right to vote. Not unlike the racial tensions inherent in the struggle for suffrage, women's involvement in the fight for access to birth control was tainted by its association with the eugenics movement. Finding herself a target of hostility and death threats for her work and desperate for allies, Sanger accepted support from white supremacists who saw birth control as an ideal way to curb the reproduction of those

In 1971, psychologist Sandra Bem wanted to understand the degree to which people identified with masculine or feminine traits and "gender roles." She needed a way to measure that variation and created what is now known as the Bem Sex-Role Inventory. Bem was particularly interested in **androgynous** people whom she defined as having relatively high amounts of "masculine" and "feminine" qualities. (Sometimes the term *androgyny* is also used to describe people without overt displays of masculinity or femininity and who may seem gender ambiguous, for example, Prince,

Tilda Swinton, Jenny Shimizu, Ruby Rose, and Erika Linde. *Androgyny* is used less today than in the 1970s and 1980s as our understanding of gender has become more nuanced and led to newer conceptualizations such as "gender fluid.")

Bem argued that four "gender role" orientations existed: androgynous, feminine, masculine, and "undifferentiated." This latter category represents people who scored low for both masculine and feminine traits. Rank the traits below as to how well they describe you by using the following scale:

1 = Never or almost never true

2 = Usually not true

3 = Sometimes but infrequently true

4 = Occasionally true

5 = Often true

6 = Usually true

7 = Always or almost always true

_____ Adaptable	_____ Affectionate	_____ Aggressive
_____ Conceited	_____ Compassionate	_____ Assertive
_____ Conscientious	_____ Eager to soothe hurt feelings	_____ Defends own beliefs
_____ Conventional	_____ Gentle	_____ Dominant
_____ Jealous	_____ Loves children	_____ Forceful
_____ Moody	_____ Sensitive to the needs of others	_____ Has leadership abilities
_____ Reliable	_____ Sympathetic	_____ Independent
_____ Secretive	_____ Tender	_____ Strong personality
_____ Tactful	_____ Understanding	_____ Willing to take a stand
_____ Truthful	_____ Warm	_____ Willing to take risks

TURN THE PAGE TO CALCULATE YOUR SCORE.

they deemed "lesser races," including Jews, blacks, eastern Europeans, many other immigrants, Native Americans, and anyone else not fitting their limited ideas of "racial purity" (Davis, 1983). Although it is debated whether her allies' ideology corresponded with her own personal views, the public affiliation between the two movements separated white women and women of color, a division that continued to be of considerable consequence during the second and even third wave of the movement.

Androgynous refers to a combination of "masculine" and "feminine" traits.

SECOND WAVE: WOMEN'S LIBERATION MOVEMENT

Although it was the vision of their foremothers in the 1800s that women be able to own property independent of their husbands, women continued to be subjected to men in various areas of social life, both domestic and public, well into the mid-1950s. Gender equality was not a popular political issue, particularly during the "doldrum" period of 1945 to 1960 (Rupp & Taylor, 1987). During this time, the "cult of domesticity" reigned supreme. "Ideal" womanhood meant a stay-at-home mother complete with all the trappings of a suburban household, such as a refrigerator, washing machine, and even dishwasher. While industrial society

answers to APPLYING CONCEPTS

First, calculate your score:

Total the second and third columns.

The first column is what might be called a dummy column, meant to keep you from skewing the test while you're taking it.

Total from the second column is Score A.

Total from the third column is Score B.

Subtract Score B from Score A for the Difference Score.

Second, use the following table to determine your gender trait score:

For instance,

if your A score is 90 and your B score is 70, it would be 90–70 = +20 (positive 20);

if your A score is 70 and your B score is 90, it would be 70–90 = –20 (negative 20).

Masculine	–20 and under
Nearly masculine	–19 to –10
Androgynous	–9 to +9
Nearly feminine	+9 to +19
Feminine	+20 and over

If you scored in the "masculine" range, (–10 or below) you were presumed to be assertive and independent. Scores of +10 or more classified you in the "feminine" range with assumed qualities of being affectionate and empathy.

Note that this is just one way that scientists have attempted to measure gender identity and "gender role" adherence. Others have used word association, ink blot tests, and so on. For example, Terman and Miles created the Attitude-Interest Analysis Test (AIAT) in 1936 to measure what they called "mental masculinity and femininity." The test had several different sections including one that asked participants to answer a series of items such as "Things cooked in grease are: (a) boiled, (b) broiled, (c) fried, or (d) roasted." Can you guess which answers the researchers labeled as being "appropriate" for boys versus girls? The correct answer—which most of you probably know—is (c) fried. Picking answer "c" added six points to the participant's score. The answers "boiled," "broiled," and "roasted" earned 0, +10, and –6, respectively. Another item concerned where "most of our anthracite coal" comes from. The answers included Alabama (–8), Colorado (–5), Ohio (–11), and Pennsylvania (+18). The correct answer is Pennsylvania.

Sometimes people get a score that they don't like. Remember that such tests are made by humans who are socialized into the same societal ideas about gender as their research participants. The questions about frying and coal aren't tapping into anything inherent. Rather, they are evaluating stereotypical knowledge for a specific time and place—when girls/women did much more cooking than boys/men. Terman and Miles (1936) wanted to see how "males and females differed" (p. 3). Based on assumptions about difference and about "appropriate" masculinity and femininity, girls who got the answer wrong lost "feminine" points because they were expected to know about frying while boys who knew the right answer lost "masculine" points because, presumably, they shouldn't be interested enough in cooking to know about it. Scoring for the item about coal was similar. Researchers assumed that boys would know (or should know) about coal. Those

who didn't know the correct answer lost "masculine" points and girls who got the answer wrong lost "feminine" points. Masculine answers also included showing dislike for foreigners, thin women, being alone, and women "cleverer than you are." Girls gained femininity points for dislike of riding bicycles, bald men, and giving advice (Morawski, 1998, p. 461).

Questions to Consider

1. The AIAT was ground-breaking and Terman and Miles's research laid the foundation for future work like Bem's. Both tests are limited in many ways. On what grounds might we question their validity?

2. What assumptions do you see about gender difference in Bem's (1971) and Terman and Miles's (1936) test? What does this tell you about the social construction of gender as well as the social construction of difference? Why do you suppose we don't talk very much about the tremendous similarity between boys/girls or women/men? Or, why don't we talk very much about the amount of variation within one gender group of "all men" or "all women"? How might these areas of focus/ areas we ignore relate to the dominant gender ideology in the U.S.?

3. Terman and Miles's research identified two groups of gay men—one with high "masculinity" scores and one with "high femininity" scores (Sanfort, 2005). Eventually, the test was given to help identify gay boys (and lesbians) in order to help "correct" their sexual orientation, for example, by recommending such boys take up sports (Kimmel, 1997). Given what you know about the test, what do you make of this prescription? What does it tell you about how people conflate gender and sexual orientation? Do people still make such assumptions? If so, why? If not, why not?

FIGURE 11.2 When Women Won the Right to Vote in Selected Countries

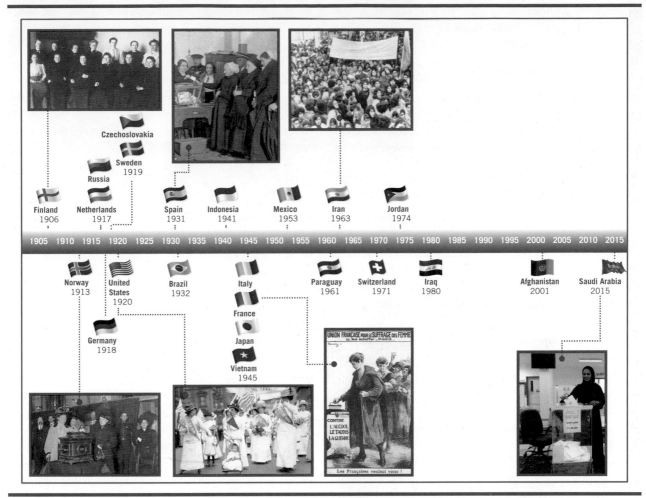

Czechoslovakia
Sweden
1919
Russia
Finland
1906
Netherlands
1917
Spain
1931
Indonesia
1941
Mexico
1953
Iran
1963
Jordan
1974

1905 1910 1915 1920 1925 1930 1935 1940 1945 1950 1955 1960 1965 1970 1975 1980 1985 1990 1995 2000 2005 2010 2015

Norway
1913
United
States
1920
Brazil
1932
Italy
France
Japan
Vietnam
1945
Germany
1918
Paraguay
1961
Switzerland
1971
Iraq
1980
Afghanistan
2001
Saudi Arabia
2015

seemed to be advancing rapidly, a woman was still clearly the property of her husband. The concept of "marital rape" was still an oxymoron—husbands did not need consent from their wives. And an unmarried woman past a certain age was still socially stigmatized and shunned.

A number of factors converged to spur the rise of the second wave against these oppressive conditions. Young women were heavily involved in the student liberation movements and civil rights movement in the South during the 1960s, not unlike the abolitionist movements of the previous era. Yet many women fought sexism within these social movements (see Chapter 6) as they struggled to be taken as seriously as the men with whom they worked (Evans, 1980).

While some young, unmarried women were growing restless with their subordinate status in the Civil Rights Movement, some married women were becoming restless with their suburban domesticity. The publication of Betty Friedan's *Feminine Mystique* in 1963 gave voice to many women's dissatisfaction with being reduced to homemaking without a choice and is often cited as one of the catalysts for the second wave.

Some leaders of the women's movement—including Billie Jean King, Bella Abzug, and Betty Friedan—participate in the passing of a torch that was carried by runners from New York to Houston for the 1977 Women's Convention.

This "women's liberation movement" that began in the 1960s had many goals. For years, the loftiest aim (never achieved) was an Equal Rights Amendment to the U.S. Constitution. This amendment would have made unequal treatment for men and women unconstitutional, with far-reaching implications for jobs, income, education, and virtually every other area of social life. The amendment passed both the houses of Congress but failed to generate the required approval of 38 of the 50 states.

However, many other victories were achieved by the movement and its activists. Between 1963 and 1968, several measures strengthened women's economic independence, including the Equal Pay Act (1963), the 1967 executive order that applied what is known as "affirmative action" to employment for women, and a 1968 Supreme Court ruling that finally made illegal the practice of separate "Help Wanted: Men" and "Help Wanted: Women" job ads. Besides these employment measures, several legal reforms having to do with gender equality in education were achieved in the 1970s, such as the Women's Educational Equity Act and Title IX, which attempted to equalize funding for women's and girls' athletics.

Like the first wave, the second wave continued to push for greater reproductive rights and domestic equality. In 1965, the U.S. Supreme Court in *Griswold v. Connecticut* finally outlawed the state bans on use of birth control by married couples, and in the 1970s, no-fault divorce laws began, doing away with the gender-specific grounds for divorce described earlier in this chapter. By the mid-1970s, several U.S. states began adopting laws against marital rape and opening domestic violence and rape crisis centers.

Such legal reforms, though, were only part of what the second-wave feminists aimed to accomplish. **Cultural feminism** also sought to change the values and norms associated with patriarchal societies, where "masculine" traits are considered superior and "feminine" traits are devalued. Within patriarchy, women are negatively sanctioned for being tough and independent, even though those are precisely the traits associated with success in the dominant society.

Likewise, men in a patriarchal society are negatively sanctioned for displaying qualities considered feminine—such as being emotional, crying, or appearing too docile. Feminists who advocated cultural as well as legal changes could often be found protesting in social spaces where women were treated as devalued sex objects. For example, feminist journalist Gloria Steinem became famous for her undercover work as a Playboy bunny after she wrote scathing exposés on the sexist treatment of women in that environment, and Robin Morgan led the first of many protests of the Miss America beauty pageant.

Some of the diversity of the second wave is captured by sociologist Judith Lorber's (2001) distinction among three different types of feminism: gender reform, gender resistance, and gender rebellion. The first two types were prominent during the second wave, and the third emerged during the third wave.

The first type includes feminists whose work aimed primarily at making sure institutions treated women and men equally. These reformers would include liberal, Marxist, and postcolonial feminists.

On the other hand, the gender-resistance feminists—who become more prominent in the second wave—focused not just on legal change but also on cultural change. While gender-reform feminists generally see the existing social structure and institutions as suitable provided that women can participate as equals alongside men, gender-resistance feminists take issue with many of the premises on which American society is based. Indeed, these feminists might argue that if a patriarchal structure were replaced with some of the socially defined "feminine" values—for instance, cooperation and consensus building—as opposed to cutthroat competitiveness—the world would be a better place.

Thus, while gender-reform feminists were fighting to get women equal footing in politics and the economy, gender-resistance feminists were demanding woman-centered spaces, such as rape crisis centers and battered women's shelters, where the unique needs of women could be considered. They also created cultural spaces such as *Ms. Magazine* and eventually women's studies programs at colleges and universities to focus on the unique contributions women have made to society—overlooked and overshadowed by a patriarchal curriculum (Lorber, 2001).

The achievements of the second-wave feminists cannot be overstated, nor can the weight of the societal resistance they had to overcome. Their efforts coincided with a historical moment that was ripe for civil rights and a time when the economy was relatively stable. Yet even with these factors on their side, those in power often subscribed to a chauvinism that was difficult to sidestep. Feminists, and their men allies in the movement, often took stances that were unpopular with the mainstream simply to earn basic rights that many of today's young women now take for granted. The stigma of the "feminist" label that existed in this middle era continues into the modern period—the third wave—where many new names and terms are emerging to represent those who continue to struggle for gender equality.

THIRD WAVE: POSTMODERN AND POSTINDUSTRIAL MOVEMENTS FOR GENDER EQUALITY

While the second wave made great strides toward equality, some felt that the movement did not speak for everyone. For

---

Cultural feminism is the movement to change the values and norms of patriarchal societies.

example, the National Organization for Women pushed for abortion rights, but many women of color believed that their major reproductive rights struggle was to control their own fertility, not be involuntarily sterilized, and avoid situations as domestic workers where they had to raise other women's children. Women of color were more interested in having and caring for their own children, a right they had often been effectively denied by the power of Jim Crow state institutions or the economic exigencies of their lives.

These were altogether different problems from the typical white suburban housewife's plight as described in Friedan's *Feminine Mystique* (e.g., being discouraged from paid labor while staying home to raise children and not having access to the legal right to birth control). Women of color, even when married, did not have the luxury of dropping out of the paid labor force to raise their children because of the large discrepancy between white men's salaries and the incomes of men of color (see Figure 6.6). It seemed that the issues of white middle-class women were defining the feminist movement's agenda, while the pressing social and economic gender-related concerns were left unaddressed by the movement at large (Davis, 1983).

In response, a "womanist" movement was born. In the mid- to late 1980s, scholars/activists such as Angela Davis (1983), Barbara Smith (1983/2000), bell hooks (1984/2000), and Gloria Anzaldúa (1987/1999), among others, published a flurry of works that became the foundation for what Lorber (2001) calls *multiracial feminism*. These women argued that one cannot simply speak of "men" and "women" without taking into account the myriad differences within those categories—age, class, race, sexual orientation, religion, and so on. By the 1990s, this approach became known as intersectionality, which we introduced in the opening chapter of this text and have used throughout.

Though intersectionality became a relevant scholarly lens, it emerged only after the powerful social movement for change that preceded it. Black women had been arguing since the early 1970s that neither the black liberation movement nor the women's movement fully addressed their struggles. By 1983, Alice Walker had coined the term *womanist* to refer to "a black feminist or feminist of color" but also to someone who is "committed to survival and wholeness of entire people, male *and* female" (p. xii; emphasis in original). Walker's quote characterizes the mood of the third-wave generation: "Womanist is to feminist as purple is to lavender" (p. xii). The third wave saw second-wave feminists as narrowly focused on empowering suburban white women and sought to be more inclusive and broader in its agenda.

If the first wave was about women *being equal* to men in the existing structure and the second wave emphasized *dismantling* that patriarchal structure, the third wave *questions* the very idea of "men" and "women" altogether. Acknowledging the vastly different experiences of white

Third-wave feminism sought a broader focus, including inclusion of women of color and greater acknowledgment of their gendered and racialized experience such as the right to have and care for their own children.

men and men of color, for example, multicultural feminists ask the questions, "Which men?" and "Which women?"

However, other types of feminists in Lorber's (2001) "gender rebellion" category (the third wave) remind us that the social constructions of "man" and "woman" serve to greatly reduce the substantial diversity of humanity that exists between and beyond these two categories. For example, social-constructionist feminists stress that we "do" gender as performance, as opposed to the idea of gender flowing directly out of biological sex. Postmodern feminists likewise challenge the gender binary, suggesting that gender is fluid and people can occupy different gender spaces depending on context.

Transgender activists, in particular, have been a force shaping these more recent feminist issues. Of course, there have been "gender benders" throughout human history, but as we shall see in the next chapter, the gay liberation movement gained traction and broadened to include transgender persons within its range of advocacy. The existence of transgender people encourages us to think more critically about why we socialize people and divide societal resources along the lines of male/female, girl/boy, man/woman, and feminine/masculine when such a range of diversity exists between those two poles.

Thus, for reasons that are biological, social, or both, more people than many of us realize do not fit comfortably into either gender "box." Third-wave feminists in particular are more likely to take issue not just with gender inequality or patriarchy but with the entire dichotomous gender structure. They may advocate for changes such as unisex restroom options in public places and more than two "sex" options on government forms such as birth certificates and driver's licenses.

Some college campuses—such as the University of Iowa, University of Pennsylvania, and University of

Missouri–Kansas City—have been at the forefront of these social changes, allowing for multiple gender categories on applications and even providing dormitory spaces for transgender people. For example, they use the term *cisgender* and *non-cisgender* to refer to individuals for whom the relationship between biological sex and gender identity is not as clear-cut (Schulman, 2013).

The contribution of transgender and multiracial feminists to the third-wave movement is that they question the simple assertion that "men" have it better than "women" in contemporary societies. They also alert us to the fact that, in a postmodern world, efforts to achieve gender equality must be context and society specific. Just as we cannot see an individual man and assume he is a privileged oppressor—his class, race, or sexual orientation might not place him in the dominant/majority group—we also cannot assume that someone who appears to be a "man" was born that way sexually or has had a relatively easy time being accepted by society due to his gender.

In the same way, we cannot assume that someone who appears to be a "woman" has led a linear life of being biologically female or faces the same gender-related struggles as any other woman. If the slogan of the second wave was "sisterhood is powerful," the third wave insists that feminism be "multigendered" as well as "multiracial, multicultural, and multi-issue" (www.thirdwavefoundation.org). The shift in terminology for university academic departments (founded as a result of second-wave activism) once called "women's studies" and now called "gender studies" is also indicative of the historical transition from second- to third-wave feminist ideals. A dichotomous notion of women versus the patriarchy is no longer viable within the diverse landscape of the third wave.

The diversity of gender expression along with that of racial, class, and sexual orientation issues that encompass third-wave feminism sometimes lead to multiple, complex positions. For example, while second-wave feminism was characterized by a relatively homogenous voice speaking out against pornography and sex work as exploitation of women, the third wave includes some "sex-positive" feminists who may view sex work as empowering when undertaken freely and without coercion.

At the same time, third-wave feminists would wholeheartedly reject sex slavery and human trafficking, where the notion of choice is virtually nonexistent. Third-wave feminists include "girlie" young women espousing girl power alongside masculine women and/or women of color who reject makeup and high heels as oppressive (Baumgardner & Richards, 2000). One important goal of these modern feminists is that all human beings be able to freely choose their own forms of productive work, their own relationships, their own life, liberty, and pursuit of happiness, without regard to their gender, race, class, or other form of difference. This "postmodern" version of feminism acknowledges that issues of gender inequality are complex and diverse and that a one-size-fits-all feminist agenda is no longer viable in a postindustrial, globalized world.

QUESTIONS FOR REFLECTION

6. Before reading this section, what pictures would come into your head when you heard the word *feminist*? Where do you think these images come from? Are they stereotypes? How would you revise your previously held picture after reading this brief history?

7. What examples of second- or third-wave feminism from your campus or home community can you cite? To find examples, you might look at university documents that deal with sex discrimination or at the titles, course descriptions, or syllabi of courses.

INSTITUTIONAL GENDER DISCRIMINATION

Institutional discrimination refers to a pattern of inequality that is built into the daily operation of an organization or a society. For example, in the Applying Concepts section of Chapter 1, we mentioned two recent examples of institutional discrimination based on race: The U.S. Secret Service repeatedly passing over black agents for promotions and the Chicago police disproportionately focusing on African Americans (e.g., in "investigative street stops"). In cases of institutional discrimination, organizational leaders (e.g., managers) often ignore systemic discrimination, which, in turn, perpetuates it. In other instances, organizations may have "off-the-record" policies that allow certain types of discrimination to thrive.

Class action lawsuits are one way to fight institutional discrimination and achieve some restitution for victims. For example, in Chapter 6, you read about *Pigford v. Glickman*, a class action lawsuit brought by 13,000 black farmers against the U.S. Department of Agriculture. Approximately 1.6 million women employees and former employees of Wal-Mart have been fighting a similar, ongoing battle over charges of companywide gender discrimination in the landmark Supreme Court case *Dukes v. Wal-Mart Stores, Inc.*

In 2001, a middle-aged African American woman named Betty Dukes, an ordained minister from California, became the first woman employee to legally charge Wal-Mart with gender discrimination. Although the official basis of her legal case was gender discrimination, Dukes felt compelled to speak on behalf of low-wage workers everywhere and she also identified discriminatory incidents at Wal-Mart that may have been racially motivated (Elias, 2010;

NARRATIVE PORTRAIT

Growing Up Transgender

At her birth in 1949, Leslie Feinberg was identified as a girl. Early on, however, she realized that there was, in our terms, a mismatch between her sex and her gender. She grew up in the 1950s, well before the rigid rules of racial and gender conformity would be challenged by the movements for black, gay, and women's liberation. She struggled to find a clear sense of herself and longed for acceptance. Feinberg survived her conflicted childhood and became a novelist, journalist, and transgender activist.

I Must Be a Martian

Leslie Feinberg

When I was born in 1949, the doctor confidently declared, "It's a girl." That might have been the last time anyone was so sure. I grew up a very masculine girl. It's a simple statement to write, but it was a terrifying reality to live.

I was raised in the 1950s—an era marked by rigidly enforced social conformity and fear of difference. . . .

I tried to mesh two parallel worlds as a child—the one I saw with my own eyes and the one I was taught. For example, I witnessed powerful adult women in our working-class [housing] projects handling every challenge of life, while coping with too many kids and not enough money. Although I hated seeing them so beaten down by poverty, I loved their laughter and their strength. But, on television I saw women depicted as foolish and not very bright. Every cultural message taught me that women were only capable of being wives, mothers, housekeepers—seen, not heard. So, was it true that women were the "weak" sex? . . .

And I learned very early on that boys were expected to wear "men's" clothes, and girls were not. When a man put on women's garb, it was considered a crude joke. By the time my family got a television, I cringed as my folks guffawed when "Uncle Miltie" Berle donned a dress. It hit too close to home. I longed to wear the boys' clothing I saw in the Sears catalog.

My own gender expression felt quite natural. I liked my hair short and I felt most relaxed in sneakers, jeans and a t-shirt. However, when I was most at home with how I looked, adults did a double-take or stopped short when they saw me. The question, "Is that a boy or a girl?" hounded me throughout my childhood. The answer didn't matter much. The very fact that strangers had to *ask* the question already marked me as a gender outlaw.

My choice of clothing was not the only alarm bell that rang my difference. If my more feminine younger sister had worn "boy's" clothes, she might have seemed stylish and cute. Dressing all little girls and all little boys in "sex-appropriate" clothing actually called attention to our gender differences. Those of us who didn't fit stuck out like sore thumbs.

Being different in the 1950s was no small matter. McCarthy's anti-communist witch hunts were in full frenzy. Like most children, I caught snippets of adult conversations. . . .

The lesson seeped down: keep your mouth shut; don't rock the boat. . . .

. . . learned that my survival was my own responsibility. From kindergarten to high school, I walked through a hail of catcalls and taunts in school corridors. I pushed past clusters of teenagers on street corners who refused to let me pass. I endured the stares and glares of adults. It was so hard to be a masculine girl in the 1950s that I thought I would certainly be killed before I could grow to adulthood. Every gender image—from my Dick and Jane textbooks in school to the sitcoms on television—convinced me that I must be a Martian.

SOURCE: Feinberg (1996, pp. 3–6).

Questions to Consider

1. How does Leslie's Narrative Portrait compare with those of Carla ("On Being American") and Tim Wise ("A White Man Reflects on Privilege") in Chapter 1? What about the Latino American men in "The Meaning of Macho?" (Chapter 8) or Alex Tizon's Narrative Portrait, "Big Little Man: In Search of My Asian Self" (Chapter 9)? What similarities and differences are worth noting?

2. Do you suppose that Leslie would have comparable difficulties if she were growing up today? Why or why not? How about if she were black or Hispanic instead of white? Would that compound or lessen her discomfort?

Jamieson, 2012). Thus, *Dukes v. Wal-Mart Stores, Inc.* suggests how race, class, and gender intersect to produce specific forms of discrimination (Corkery, 2017).

In the course of investigating Dukes' allegations, her attorneys found that such discrimination was not an isolated event. Women of various backgrounds followed Dukes's lead and joined a class action suit against the corporation. Statisticians revealed a troubling pattern of discrimination against women at the company. Even though women generally had lower turnover rates, stayed with the company longer, and had higher average performance evaluations, Wal-Mart paid women, on average, less than men in similar positions. Additionally, the company didn't have a formal system for posting job announcements that would have allowed qualified applicants equal opportunity to advance. Rather, informal mechanisms such as word-of-mouth tracked men into management training programs and promoted them at higher rates than women employees (Drogin, 2003). Thus, what first appeared as a simple case of individual discrimination, upon inspection, revealed a larger, systematic pattern of institutional discrimination. Lawyers for the plaintiffs argued that such discrimination violated Title VII of the 1964 Civil Rights Act of 1964.

Before the U.S. Supreme Court decided the *Dukes* case, similar class action suits reached state and local level courts. For example, in 2010, the federal Equal Employment Opportunity Commission (EEOC) successfully secured $11.7 million in back wages and damages for a group of women Wal-Mart employees in Kentucky. The court found that Wal-Mart routinely hired men—even when women applicants were more qualified—in part because of stereotypical thinking that men were more appropriate for the positions. The company was also required to improve its hiring processes so that qualified women applicants would have a fair chance of being hired in the future (EEOC, 2010; Hines, 2012; Jamieson, 2012).

The U.S. judicial system has struggled with how to deal fairly with such massive cases of discrimination. In a 5–4 ruling in June 2011, the Supreme Court threw out *Dukes v. Wal-Mart Stores, Inc.*, but not because the case didn't have merit. Rather, it said that the 1.6 million women (with different managers in more than 3,400 stores) had "little in common but their sex and this lawsuit" and that "proof of commonality necessarily overlaps with respondents' merits . . ." (Corkery, 2017; *Wal-Mart v. Dukes*, p. 2). In other words, the group was too diverse to qualify as a single class. By 2012, almost 2,000 women in 48 states filed gender discrimination claims against Wal-Mart with the EEOC (Hines, 2012) and lawyers on both sides continued to pursue legal action. In 2016, several women involved in the original *Dukes v. Wal-Mart* suit settled privately out of court with Wal-Mart while others filed new state and regional lawsuits (McGowan, 2016). For example, one case addresses gender discrimination against women who worked at nearly 300 Wal-Mart and Sam's Clubs stores in California and more than a dozen other states between 1998 and 2004 (McGowan, 2016; Norman, 2016). In November 2017, women in Florida brought a similar suit claiming discrimination in pay and promotion (Campbell, 2017).

By singling out Wal-Mart as an employer whose influence and scope is so widespread, proponents of gender equality hoped to send an amplified message about battles they have long fought on many fronts. Yet many companies appear to be in a "race to the bottom" in the postindustrial, globalized economy, seeking to cut their labor costs in any way possible, including, perhaps, discrimination (Pincus, 2011). As you will see in a subsequent section on jobs and income, the glass ceiling that blocks women from receiving promotions and salary increases within corporations existed well before Wal-Mart entered the corporate landscape.

Because employment discrimination law is handled only in civil court, the penalties are monetary. While financial awards provide some compensation for injustice and for the time, energy, and expenses necessary to pursue legal action, such sanctions do little to alter the dominance of corporations like Wal-Mart in the global economic landscape.

Rather, successfully litigation is largely symbolic and serves primarily as a warning to others who may be harder hit by penalties for institutional discrimination. Unfortunately, research and lawsuits continue to document widespread discrimination against women in a variety of industries, most notably of late in Silicon Valley's tech and "startup" industries. In addition to complaints about sexist, hostile cultures, Twitter, Facebook, Uber, Google, and Microsoft have been recently involved in litigation for alleged gender discrimination.

In 2016, to demonstrate the problem of sexual harassment and assault, writer Kelly Oxford tweeted "Women: tweet me your first assaults . . . they aren't just stats" using the #NotOkay hashtag (Domonoske, 2016). It struck a nerve and within 24 hours, Oxford had reportedly received nearly 1 million replies with almost 10 million tweets using #NotOK or #NotOkay (CBS News/Associated Press, 2016; Domonoske, 2016). While many people seemed surprised at the breadth of these reports, little social change came from it. In October 2017, the cultural tide appeared to shift after several women accused film producer Harvey Weinstein of sexual harassment and assault. Actor Alyssa Milano tweeted "If all the women who have been sexually harassed or assaulted wrote 'Me too' as a status, we might give people a sense of the magnitude of the problem." By October 17th, 850,000 people had used the hashtag, and Facebook reported more than 4.7 million people using the hashtag worldwide in more than 12 million posts within just 24 hours (Santiago & Criss, 2017).

As this book went to press, allegations and sanctions had been levied against many more men in the field of entertainment such as talk show hosts Bill O'Reilly, Matt Lauer, and Charlie Rose, comedian Louis C.K., and producer Chris Savino. Soon, similar allegations were brought against men in other fields including: (1) business (e.g., Roy Price of Amazon, Uber CEO Travis Kalanick, Binary Capital cofounder Justin Caldbeck), (2) government (e.g., President Donald Trump, former president George Bush, Senator Al Franken, Representatives Al Moore and John Conyers), and (3) sports (e.g., Olympic gymnastics team physician Larry Nassar, swim coach Jack Nelson) (Almukhtar, Buchanan, & Gold, 2017; Associated Press, 2017; Hobson & Rich, 2017; Sumagaysay & Ross, 2017). The long-term impact of #MeToo activism remains to be seen. Facebook's chief operating officer, Sheryl Sandberg, is just one business leader worried about a potential backlash against women saying that she hears people saying, "This is why you shouldn't hire women" rather than seeing some men's behavior as problematic and more women in business and government as one part of the solution (Peck, 2017). For now, the focus appears positive and significant. *Time Magazine* calls the women who came forward "the Silence Breakers" and has named them their "Person of the Year" (Zacharek, Dockterman, & Edwards, 2017).

Note that the U.S. government's EEOC requires that cases meet stringent criteria before seeking legal redress for claimants. In some instances, cases might not seem like "that big of a deal." For example, in a suit against a pizza restaurant in Kansas (Civil Action No. 2:17-cv-02513) brought by Jenson Walcott, Walcott applied for a job together with her friend, Jake Reed. They had the same experience and both got job offers, but his starting pay was 25 cents more an hour than hers. For some people, that $520 annual pay difference (based on a 40-hour week) doesn't seem worth the effort and expense of a lawsuit. In this case, however, the pay inequality allegation was compounded by the fact that when Reed complained about the pay gap, they fired her—and her friend. Such retaliation is also protected by the Equal Pay Act of 1963 (EEOC, 2017). Similarly, the EEOC brought another case against Denton County, Texas, for violating the Equal Pay Act by paying a woman physician $34,000 less a year than a man performing the same job. Over 15 years of employment, that would add up to more than half-a-million dollars. The cases brought by individuals are just part of the large pattern—one that also involves Merck & Co., which also has been accused of underpaying women sales representatives. The lawsuit is seeking at least $250 million in damages.

In the last few years, the courts have also seen more cases brought by transgender employees, such as the 2016 case *Roberts v. Clark Cty. Sch. Dist.* in which an employer banned a transgender school police officer from using the women's bathroom at work. Specifically, "It banned Roberts from the women's bathroom because he no longer behaved like a woman. This alone shows that the school district discriminated against Roberts based on his gender and sex stereotypes. And the department also admits that it banned Roberts from the men's bathroom because he is biologically female" (*Roberts v. Clark Cnty. Sch. Dist*). The court ruled in the officer's favor, citing illegal sex discrimination (EEOC, 2017).

SEXUAL HARASSMENT AND ASSAULT IN THE MILITARY

Just as institutional discrimination is not limited to a single corporation, the evidence is clear that sexual harassment and assault exist in many other organizations and institutions including the U.S. military. The military provides an interesting case study for students of social inequalities because of its relatively high level of racial integration. For this reason, the military has often been held up as a model of equal opportunity—especially for those who cannot afford higher education (Moskos & Butler, 1997).

Protestors rally to denounce the decision by Air Force General Franklin to overturn the conviction of Lt. Col. Wilkerson for sexual assault.

Because the military emphasizes promotion based on uniform standards and rank rather than demographic distinctions, some people regard the U.S. military as one of few meritocratic institutions where anyone can "make it." Though it has been a long struggle toward gender equality, women have made tremendous progress since World War I when they were first allowed to join the military. Almost 100 years later, in 2016, women who met eligibility requirements became allowed to serve in any position, even in combat roles that are crucial to promotion. In 2017, women reached another milestone—graduating from U.S. Army infantry training for the first time in U.S. history.

Transgender people have experienced similar challenges toward full and equal integration in the U.S. military. One significant change came in June 2016 when the military lifted its ban forbidding openly transgender people from service effective July 1, 2017. However, on June 30, 2017, Defense Secretary Mattis postponed the policy's start date. On July 26, 2017, President Trump announced in a series of tweets that he was barring transpeople from serving "in any capacity." He claimed concerns about "tremendous medical costs and disruption that transgender in the military would entail." Yet, a 2016 Pentagon-sponsored study contradicted these concerns, finding that transgender soldiers had "minimal impact on readiness and health care costs." Since then, the military has continued studying the implications of the proposed ban (Hirschfeld & Cooper, 2017).

As with other cases of institutional discrimination, the courts are helping to shape organizational practices. In October 2017, a judge ruled that proposed changes to the military's policy were based on "disapproval of transgender people generally" and that there was "absolutely no support for the claim that the ongoing service of transgender people would have any negative effective on the military." Rather, "banning of such individuals would have such effects." As such, the military has been ordered to follow its earlier policy, effective January 1, 2018 (Phillips, 2017).

Only time will tell how the military's policies and procedures will develop. Yet students of social inequalities might find it useful to compare these debates with similar concerns about African American men serving alongside white men and about women serving together with men. At their core, all involved assumptions of difference between people that were presumed to involve expense (e.g., for separate facilities for women) and disruption of the military's mission.

Some research shows that white women in the military report greater job satisfaction and self-assessed quality of life than their civilian counterparts (Lundquist, 2008). Yet even with these great strides in inclusiveness, the military culture remains patriarchal in some respects that, historically, has created an atmosphere that makes the reporting and sanctioning of sexual assault and harassment cases extremely difficult (Steinhauer, 2013). In recent years, in the wake of troubling increases in sexualized violence, the military has taken steps to address these issues by changing policies and attempting to shift the culture, largely through education (Department of Defense, 2017).

Sometimes people misunderstand sexual assault and sexual harassment as being motivated by sexual attraction. Yet research shows these crimes are primarily about the perpetrator's (or perpetrators') desire for power, control, and dominance. In addition to being assaulted, victims (women and men) must deal with a culture that often blames and silences them, making it extremely challenging to bring perpetrators to justice.

In 2012, U.S. armed forces documented 26,000 cases of "unwanted sexual contact." Of those, fewer than one in seven victims (about 14% or 3,374 people) reported the attack. Only 10% of those cases went to trial and even fewer brought convictions (Nieves, 2014). In 2013, 5,061 incidents were reported; about 10% (484) went to trial, resulting in 376 convictions (Cooper, 2014).

Army Soldier 1st Lt. Shaye Haver (right) takes part in mountaineering training at the U.S. Army Ranger School on Mount Yonah, in Fort Benning, Georgia. U.S. Army Capt. Kristen Griest and 1st Lt. Shaye Haver were the first women soldiers to graduate from Ranger School.

Unfortunately, the measure of "unwanted sexual contact" is a bit lacking because it includes more serious offenses such as rape along with other types of unwanted touching such as being grabbed in the genital area. To better document the problem, a Defense Department study used more specific (and more difficult to hear) language in their 2014 questionnaire. They found that many of the 20,000 incidents experienced by respondents went well beyond what would have been previously classified as "unwanted sexual contact." Rather, they were notably violent acts (Kime, 2014).

The Uniform Code of Military Justice defines sexual assault as "intentional sexual contact characterized by the use of force, threats, intimidation, or abuse of authority or when the victim does not or cannot consent" (Cornell University, n.d.). In 2015 and 2016, the number of victims reporting sexual assault increased to 6,082 and 6,172, respectively—a "record high" (Reuters, 2017). What these numbers don't convey readily, though the official reports do, is that most victims reported being assaulted more than once (Protect Our Defenders, 2017). Mirroring sexual assault research in other contexts, anonymous surveys of armed forces personnel conducted for the Department of Defense found rates more than double what was officially reported—though they decreased some over anonymous reports in 2014. A majority of victims (58%) expressed concerns over retaliation should they come forward. While the general increase in assaults is troubling, the military hopes it might also indicate some positive change—specifically that new reporting procedures have helped some assault victims gain trust in the process (Reuters, 2017).

In a time of repeated deployments due to ongoing conflicts in Iraq and Afghanistan, government officials grew increasingly outspoken about this troubling pattern of sexual abuse among service members, fearing it could pose threats to their ability to complete their missions effectively. With the military handling complaints and punishments for sexual abuse "in house," it is perhaps not surprising that more than half of those surveyed who did report abuse felt that they had experienced some type of retaliation for coming forward (O'Toole, 2013; Reuters, 2017).

Certain expressions of power become institutionalized, or at least tacitly accepted, within the ranks of such authoritarian organizational cultures. Not unlike the situation of police officers of color who participate in racial profiling of blacks and other minorities, some men offenders in the military also choose to sexually victimize other men. While women service members have higher rates of sexual assault, approximately 6,300 service members reporting sexual assault were men (Protect Our Defenders, 2017). A broad analysis of the data over the past several years shows that most of the offenders were heterosexual men (Dao, 2013; Lundquist, 2008).

Guilt and shame often work to silence victims of all genders, and cultural sexual scripts about what behaviors are socially acceptable contribute to the problem. Failure of leadership matters, too. Research shows that in military units in which commanders initiate or even just tolerate sexual harassment, the likelihood of sexual assault triples or quadruples. What is clear is that the cultural belief systems trickle down from commanders. Sadler, Booth, Cook, and Doebbeling (2003) found that when commanding officers start or condone sexual harassment, the sexual assault rate increases by 300% to 400%.

A congressional bill (S.1752), introduced in both the U.S. House and Senate in 2013, was intended to reform the military structure of reporting so that victims could report assaults to independent military prosecutors rather than their commander. The hope was that, regardless of gender, offenders would be more likely to be brought to justice (Briggs, 2013). However, that effort failed in 2014 (Cooper, 2014). A related bill (S.2992) was "read the second time" and "placed on senate legislative calendar" in late 2014. No additional action has been taken (Coooper, 2014).

The problem of sexual harassment and assault that plagues the larger society nevertheless stands out as a major issue for the U.S. military where racial and gender gaps in promotions, pay equity, and job satisfaction are smaller than in the civilian sector. Due to the global reach of the nation's military, even those analysts who do not particularly identify as feminists agree that, from a national security standpoint, this acute problem cannot remain publicly unaddressed.

REPRODUCTIVE RIGHTS AND FREEDOMS

Establishing control over one's own reproductive capacities is hardly a new gender inequality issue. As we noted previously, feminists of the first, second, and third waves all tackled various legal and cultural barriers to achieving reproductive freedom. In societies where women are unable to give legal consent to sexual activity and/or control the timing of childbirth, men are able to exert great dominance over women. Reproductive freedom continues to be a political issue of paramount importance both nationally and globally.

Political junkies in the United States might equate the term "reproductive rights" to abortion and the now four-decades-old *Roe v. Wade* (1973) Supreme Court ruling that preserved a woman's right to privacy in first trimester abortions. The 2012 presidential campaign and subsequent Obama term featured plenty of political mudslinging along these lines—including one political commentator referring to a law student who wanted birth control pills covered by health insurance as a "slut" and a "prostitute" (Geiger, 2012),

and a congressman erroneously claiming that "legitimate rape" would somehow automatically protect a woman from unwanted pregnancy (Whiteman, 2012).

However, across the globe, reproductive rights are defined much more broadly than just as access to abortions and contraceptives. Reproductive freedom includes a woman's right to access maternal health care—as in the landmark case of a poor Afro-Brazilian woman whose death during childbirth could have been prevented, a case that was taken up pro bono by the Center for Reproductive Rights as a symbol of the struggles of women everywhere to receive adequate care in pregnancy and childbirth (Cook, 2013). Reproductive freedom also includes the right to resist child marriage, which tends to be most common in the least-developed nations, where poverty is widespread and the education rate for women and girls is dismally low (Prois, 2013).

Indeed, most advocates for women's equality globally argue that the key factor in reducing gender inequality, particularly in developing countries, is ensuring that women have more control over their reproductive functions. For example, during a speaking engagement in Saudi Arabia—a country that ranks close to last in gender equality among nations—Bill Gates was asked about what could be done to advance the nation technologically. The founder of Microsoft and one of the world's richest person bluntly replied that Saudi Arabia would be handicapped in its development efforts as long as half the population was not allowed to participate in the creative process of the economy. As long as Saudi women were restricted to the roles of wives and mothers, the nation would never reach its full potential for growth (Quigley, 2013).

The same point can be made for Western democracies such as the United States: Being married off at an early age and/or quickly forced into childbirth and parenting without a chance to educate and better oneself further deepens gender inequality and limits development and growth. Greater access to contraceptive education and services is of paramount importance in many societies around the world. Although the most critical areas of public policy vary from nation to nation, the unifying concern of reproductive rights, broadly defined, will continue to be a pressing issue of gender inequality as long as the economic, political, and educational inequalities we discuss in the following sections persist.

QUESTIONS FOR REFLECTION

8. How might current civil rights legislation be reformed to better address the ongoing problem of institutional discrimination, since the current model expects plaintiffs to file individual lawsuits suing for damages against the company responsible for the discrimination?

9. What do you suspect would affect greater reductions in sexual assaults in the military—changes to the culture of military life or organizational changes to the punitive structure for such offenses? Why?

10. Develop a systematic list of reproductive rights and freedoms, for both women and men. Which seem to be of greater concern among your peers and local community, and which tend to get less media/popular attention? Why?

SEXISM AND DISCRIMINATION

Some people argue that there is no longer a need for feminism or gender-related social change. Despite the evidence we review in this chapter—showing that women are a minority in areas such as the economy, political power, and even some aspects of education—there are those who claim that as many stereotypes exist about men as about women, and that men have no particular overall advantages in society. Yet social science evidence supports the existence of sexism—that is, a system of oppression that confers overall advantages to men over women in social life.

To convey the systemic nature of sexist oppression, feminist writer Marilyn Frye (1983) uses the metaphor of a bird cage. She points out that if we focus only on one wire in the cage, we may wonder why the bird simply does not fly around that wire. Yet if we step back and take a wider view, we realize that each single wire on its own adds up to a network that cannot be easily subverted.

The advantaged group in an oppressive system may face some isolated wires but nothing it cannot get around. Frye notes that some confuse examples such as "men aren't allowed to cry" as oppression, but it is more appropriate to think about the drawbacks men face as unfortunate limitations. If they "fly" the other way, not crying at all, they will be socially approved—allowing them to get around that one single wire. In contrast, a minority group faces a **double bind**: No matter what choice is made, there are negative consequences. For women in a patriarchal society, crying earns them the stigma of being too emotional or irrational, yet *not* crying opens them to accusations of being frigid, uptight, or even a "bitch" (Frye, 1983).

Additionally, as we noted in several earlier chapters (Chapters 1 and 4, for example), oppressive systems are held in place by an ideology. The ideology that undergirds sexism tells us that those traits, characteristics, behaviors, and activities associated with men are more highly valued. Thus, taking the "men can't cry" example a bit further, some point out that U.S. society today is harder on boys because there is no longer much stigma associated with girls who want to "cross" the gender divide and become more athletic or play with cars. Boys who want to play dress-up or with dolls, on the other hand, are harassed, bullied, and taunted. What this example really demonstrates, however, is the relative value society continues to place on people's activities. Because "masculine" activities are more valued, women can enact them with little or no stigma, but men enacting the less valued "feminine" activities receive far stronger sanctions and much more stigma.

In Chapter 3, we discussed how stereotypes exist for many different racial groups, and how many of us hold prejudices about different groups, whether majority or minority. Likewise, there indeed exist negative stereotypes about both sexes and prejudices about what they can and cannot do; for example, men are assumed not to know how to cook or clean properly, and women are assumed to be useless when it comes to machinery. Yet, taken together, the assumptions add up to a collective advantage for men, both culturally and structurally, by elevating whatever is deemed "masculine" and attaching greater material rewards to that category.

One of the most striking examples of this pattern can be found in the research of Christine Williams (1992, 2013), who examined the experience of men in traditionally women-dominated, or **pink collar**, occupations such as nurse, librarian, social worker, and elementary school teacher (also see Chapter 8). We know that sometimes society attaches negative stigmas to men who choose these professions. The popular films *Meet the Parents* and *Meet the Fockers* famously depict this, as Robert DeNiro's character relentlessly ridicules Ben Stiller's character about his "feminine" career choice of nurse.

Likewise, some of Williams's interviewees reported facing negative prejudices, including being called "sissy" and enduring antigay slurs. Yet these men ironically experienced a **glass escalator** in their respective professions. That is, they were often fast-tracked to the upper-level (higher-paying) spots in their profession, well ahead of women counterparts with more experience. Men elementary school teachers were quickly moved to principal or the school board office; Men librarians were quickly moved away from the desk and shelves and toward the more prestigious position of library director. Despite the

---

A **double bind** is a situation in which negative consequences ensue regardless of the choice that is made.

Pink collar occupations are those that have been predominantly held by women.

The **glass escalator** (as opposed to the glass ceiling) is an occupational setting in which the dominant group (e.g., men) enjoys a distinct advantage.

---

negative stigma attached to the pursuit of "women's" occupations, the power and privilege of being a member of the dominant group asserted themselves.

Analyzing sexism and discrimination in modern times is complex. Much like modern racism, official legal barriers to employment discrimination against women have been removed, but inequalities persist. Token women have achieved greater successes than ever before—heads of state, Fortune 500 CEOs—but an overall pattern of women's disadvantage in these fields is undeniable. Not unlike color-blind racism (see Chapter 3), this seeming paradox leads some to use **modern sexism** to explain continued gender inequality. Modern sexism, like modern racism, assumes that gender discrimination is a thing of the past and that any continuing inequalities are the fault of the minority group.

The modern sexist has negative feelings but expresses them indirectly and symbolically. The old-fashioned sexist believes that gender inequality is natural and even desirable; the modern sexist denies the existence of gender discrimination and inequality, and trivializes or dismisses the concerns of women. Modern sexism is harder to detect and measure, in part because it is often expressed in the language of equality and fairness. For example, the modern sexist might express opposition to affirmative action programs for women by arguing that such programs are unfair to men, rather than invoking notions of women's inferiority or incompetence (Beaton, Tougas, & Joly, 1996).

Some research findings suggest that modern sexism is one important factor in the continued maintenance of gender inequality. These studies indicate that modern sexists are less likely to perceive instances of sexist discrimination and more likely to dismiss complaints of sexism as trivial (e.g., see Barreto & Ellemers, 2005; Cameron, 2001; Swim, Mallett, & Stangor, 2004). Also, modern sexists are less likely to identify instances of sexist discrimination and more likely to use sexist language.

Another study (Swim & Cohen, 1997) examined reactions to several situations involving charges of sexual harassment (e.g., an offer to trade career assistance for sexual favors and a work situation in which men employees displayed sexually explicit photos or made sexual comments to women employees). The subjects in the study, all men, were asked to judge the seriousness of these various scenarios. Subjects who scored higher on modern sexism were less likely to classify the incidents as sexual harassment, had less sympathy for victims, were more likely to see the women victims as overreacting, and were less likely to recommend harsh punishments for perpetrators.

Modern sexism, like modern racism, is an indirect, more subtle way of expressing prejudice against women.

Of course, men are not the only ones who subscribe to modern sexism. Just as people of color can internalize racism, women also can adopt to this lens to interpret the relative lack of success of their own group. One example of a modern sexist belief is the assumption that women simply choose restricted career paths, either because they are not as ambitious or they have other priorities, such as marriage and family. The chief operating officer of Facebook, Sheryl Sandberg (2013), notably perpetuated this argument with her book *Lean In*. Although she argues that women are capable of being just as successful as men in business, she mainly implicates individual women's choices rather than the structure of society for continued gender inequality. For example, she suggests women need to be smarter in selecting partners who will share domestic tasks equally. Also, women need to fight harder for themselves in corporate negotiations. Factors such as institutional discrimination, particularly in the low-wage sector of the economy, and sexual harassment receive notably less attention in Sandberg's "manifesto" (hooks, 2013). Modern sexism can distract our attention from the more systematic transformations needed to bring about greater gender equality in society.

QUESTIONS FOR REFLECTION

11. In the context of sexism and gender oppression, what are double binds and how do they limit women more than men? Why is it less stigmatizing for women to cross the gender divide than for men?

12. What is the "glass escalator," and how does it benefit men?

13. What is modern sexism, and how does it help maintain the structures of men's privilege? Can women be modern sexists? How?

ASSIMILATION AND PLURALISM

In this section, we use the major concepts of Gordon's model of assimilation to assess the status of women, as we have done in previous chapters with other minority groups.

ACCULTURATION

In previous chapters, we discussed acculturation in terms of Americanization or Anglo conformity (the process of the minority group learning the dominant-group culture), or the degree of similarity between the languages, values systems, and norms of the minority and dominant groups. Obviously, this approach does not fit the cultural differences between men and women. Instead, we will focus on how culture influences boys/men and girls/women through socialization.

In a society where gender was no longer the basis for social stratification, insults such as "You throw like a girl" or descriptors such as "Mr. Mom" would have no meaning. Yet, despite the removal of multiple legal barriers to gender equality in many modern societies, gender norms—society's expectations for how women and men should behave—continue to exist. As we mentioned at the start of the chapter, these expectations are reinforced through gender socialization that is often unnoticed and taken for granted. These agents include parents, teachers, peers, and media, among many others. Next, we will build on our discussion at the start of the chapter by further discussing these influences throughout the life cycle and in light of sociological research.

Infancy and Childhood. Even before birth, parents and others attach myriad assumptions about the physical and psychological makeup of their baby once they find out its sex, based on the cultural assumptions attached to that gender in their society. (See the Current Debates section for this chapter to consider a case in which parents tried to deflect these cultural assumptions.) Experimental studies in which adults are informed or misinformed of a baby's sex and then asked to describe the baby often produce highly stereotypical descriptions of the baby and its behavior (e.g., Delk, Madden, Livingston, & Ryan, 1986). For example, when told that a baby is a boy, people are likely to say that the child is tough, strong, and adventurous. Given the tendency of children to want to live up to their parents' expectations, we can easily see how these gender norms become self-fulfilling prophecies in the lives of many.

If parents were the only socialization agent in the primary process, some dedicated parents with feminist ideals might be able to subvert this gender stereotyping altogether. However, the media, the economy (especially toy marketing), teachers/schools, and peer groups all contribute to reinforcing the internalization of these societally sanctioned gender norms. Despite the rising number of women athletes in the wake of Title IX, an athletic girl might still be considered a "tomboy" and a nonathletic throw is still known as "throwing like a girl." And even the most open-minded of parents are likely to be concerned when their son shows too much interest in items culturally marked as "feminine"—such as nail polish, makeup, dolls, and dresses. Both positive and negative sanctions work together to quickly steer us away from activities and interests that do not fit our gender norm proscriptions and toward those that do.

Before we know it, such gender norms—clearly originating externally from our society's proscriptions—become so ingrained in us that it is difficult to tell where our own interests and proclivities end and where society's begin. Mattel was once forced to recall a Barbie doll that said, "math class is tough," because it perpetuated the stereotype that women are not good at math. Yet, despite evidence of equal math abilities between the genders, society's stereotypes persist; not only do teachers assume boys are better at math, but young men and women tend to underestimate or overestimate their abilities according to the stereotypes (Correll, 2004; Quaid, 2008). There is concern that these gender stereotypes influence young adults in their choice of careers, and some tangible results of this can be seen in Figure 11.1 earlier in this chapter.

Adolescence and Adulthood. What begins in infancy and childhood continues into adolescence and adulthood. As dating begins, **sexual scripts**—gender-based blueprints for sexual behavior—and their sexual double standard become evident. For example, Tanenbaum (1999) noted that a young man with multiple partners is more likely to be deemed within the realm of masculine acceptability—a stud, a player, a Romeo—while a young woman with the same number of partners is often labeled much more negatively (e.g., slut, whore). More recent research, however, paints a fuzzier picture. Researchers asked college students how much they agreed/disagreed with the following statement: "If (men/women) hook up or have sex with lots of people, I respect them less." Most students (35% of men and 55% of women) said they would lose respect for *both* women and men who did this; in contrast, 25% of women and 31% men said they wouldn't lose respect for *either* one. In terms of gendered views, almost one third (28%) of men and 4% of women said they would lose respect for women only (but not for men) while 16% of women and 6% of men said the opposite—they would lose respect for men, but not for women (Allison & Risman, 2013).

Other norms are changing, too. Girls and woman learn quickly that others will judge them based on appearance and that this will matter more for her in life than for similar men. Research on self-esteem for girls shows that it plummets by puberty, which some link to expectations for dating and desirability on the "mate market." Indeed, studies of personal ads and dating sites have shown that while women tend to seek financial security in men partners, men tend to seek physical attractiveness as the primary characteristic in potential women partners (Davis, 1990; Hitsch, Hortacsu, & Ariely, 2010). Seeking men who are financially well off reflects their historic position as breadwinners since the economic shift away from hunting and gathering.

Sexual scripts are gender-based dating expectations.

Men's Invisible Privilege

As we have noted on several occasions, white privilege tends to be invisible to its beneficiaries, largely because Western and U.S. cultural traditions make whiteness "normal."

This point was notably made by Peggy McIntosh (1989) in her classic article "White Privilege: Unpacking the Invisible Knapsack," in which she listed 50 ways whites are privileged in everyday life.

A parallel point can be made about men's privilege. In this passage, Barry Deutsch adapts McIntosh's list and describes some of the everyday privileges that boys and men may have that girls and women do not. To fit this space, we have edited his original list to only 15 items.

A CHECKLIST OF MEN'S PRIVILEGE

Barry Deutsch

In 1990, Wellesley College professor Peggy McIntosh wrote an essay [in which she] observes that whites in the U.S. are "taught to see racism only in individual acts of meanness, not in invisible systems conferring dominance. . . ." To illustrate these . . . systems, McIntosh wrote a list of . . . invisible privileges whites benefit from.

As McIntosh points out, men also tend to be unaware of their own privileges. . . . In the spirit of McIntosh's essay, I . . . compile[d] a list . . . focusing on the invisible privileges benefiting men.

Since I first compiled . . . the list . . . critics (usually, but not always, male) have pointed out men have disadvantages too—being drafted into the army, being expected to suppress emotions, and so on. These are indeed bad things—but I never claimed that life for men is all ice cream sundaes. . . .

Pointing out that men are privileged in no way denies that sometimes bad things happen to men.

Several critics have also argued that the list somehow victimizes women. I disagree; pointing out problems is not the same as perpetuating them. It is not a "victimizing" position to acknowledge that injustice exists; on the contrary, without that acknowledgment it isn't possible to fight injustice.

An . . . acquaintance of mine once wrote, "The first big privilege which whites, males, people in upper economic classes, the able bodied, the straight . . . can work to alleviate is the privilege to be oblivious to privilege." This checklist is, I hope, a step towards helping men to give up the "first big privilege."

THE MEN'S PRIVILEGE CHECKLIST

1. I can be confident that my co-workers won't think I got my job because of my sex [gender]—even though that might be true.
2. I am far less likely to face sexual harassment at work than my female [women] co-workers are.
3. On average, I am taught to fear walking alone after dark in . . . public spaces much less than my female counterparts are.
4. If I have children but do not provide primary care for them, my masculinity will not be called into question.
5. When I ask to see "the person in charge," odds are I will face a person of my own sex. The higher-up in the organization the person is, the surer I can be.
6. As a child, chances are I was encouraged to be more active and outgoing than my sisters.
7. If I'm careless with my driving it won't be attributed to my sex [gender].
8. Even if I sleep with a lot of women, there is no chance that I will be seriously labeled

a "slut," nor is there any male counterpart to "slut-bashing."
9. If I'm not conventionally attractive, the disadvantages are relatively small and easy to ignore.
10. I can be loud with no fear of being called a shrew. I can be aggressive with no fear of being called a bitch.
11. My ability to make important decisions and my capability in general will never be questioned depending on what time of the month it is.
12. The decision to hire me will not be based on assumptions about whether or not I might choose to have a family sometime soon.
13. Most major religions argue that I should be the head of my household, while my wife and children should be subservient to me.
14. If I have children with my girlfriend or wife, I can expect her to do most of the basic childcare such as changing diapers and feeding.
15. I have the privilege of being unaware of my male [gender] privilege.

SOURCE: Deutsch (n.d.).

Questions to Consider

1. Can you add to Deutsch's list? What unconscious or "invisible" men's privilege have you observed?
2. Some might criticize lists such as this as frivolous or trivial. Do you agree? Why or why not?
3. How would you respond to Deutsch's point (quoting McIntosh) about racism (and sexism) as "individual acts" versus "invisible systems"? Which of these levels of analysis is emphasized in this chapter and this text? How?

Another study (Toma & Hancock, 2010) found that while women and men in online dating profiles both wanted to appear attractive, being attractive was more significant for women in two ways: (1) men sought "more attractive" women compared to those deemed "less attractive" and (2) women realized the importance of being perceived as "pretty," internalized those ideals, and actively responded to that social pressure. For example, women offered more

COMPARATIVE FOCUS

Women's Status in Global Perspective

On October 9, 2012, in the Swat region of Pakistan, an armed assailant attacked 15-year-old Malala Yousafzai while she was riding a bus to school. Her attacker sought her out and even asked for her by name. He shot at her three times, one bullet passing through her left eye and out her shoulder.

The reason for the attack? Malala wanted an education and was an outspoken advocate for schooling for girls. The gunman was sent by the Taliban to punish Malala because she flouted, publicly and repeatedly, the organization's ideas regarding the proper place of women.

Malala survived the attack and was transported to the United Kingdom, where she underwent a lengthy and painful recovery. Far from being intimidated, she resumed her advocacy for education and was frequently featured by the mass media in Western Europe, the United States, and around the globe. In recognition of her courage, eloquence, and passion, she was nominated for the Nobel flouted, Peace Prize in 2013, becoming the youngest person to be so recognized.

Why was Malala willing to risk her life? How oppressed are women in Pakistan? How does the status of Pakistani women compare to that of women in other nations?

In Pakistan and around the globe, women are moving out of their traditional and often highly controlled and repressed status. According to United Nations statistics (United Nations Department of Economic and Social Affairs, Population Division, 2013),

rates of early marriage and childbirth are falling, and education levels and participation in the paid labor force are rising. Today, almost 50% of all women worldwide are in the paid labor force (vs. 72% of all men), although they still tend to be concentrated in lower-status, less-lucrative, and more-insecure jobs everywhere (pp. 8, 20–22).

The women of Pakistan are not as repressed as women in many other nations, including Saudi Arabia, where women won the legal right to drive only in 2017 and the right to vote only in 2015. Some simple statistics will illustrate the range of possibilities. Table 11.1 provides information on women's status in four nations representing various levels of development, locations, and religious backgrounds.

As we have noted, the status of women is partly a function of subsistence technology. Mali is the most agricultural of these four nations (with 80% of its workforce in farming), and the women there have more children, earlier in life, and are far more likely to die in childbirth. They are also much less educated than the women of other nations and the men of their own nation.

Pakistan is less agricultural than Mali, and the status of women is relatively higher, although they are indeed much less likely than men to be educated. Note, also, that the statistics suggest that Pakistani women are still largely focused on producing and maintaining large families.

Women's status generally rises as industrialization and urbanization proceed, as indicated by the profiles

of Chile and Sweden. Sweden is more industrialized than Chile, and Swedish women have fewer children, later in life, and are just as educated as men in their nation.

Why does the status of women generally improve as societies move away from agricultural subsistence technology? One reason, no doubt, is the changing economies of childbearing: Large families are useful in the labor-intensive economies of agrarian nations, but children become increasingly expensive in modern urban-industrial economies. Also, consistent with Malala's point, more-educated women tend to make different choices about career and family and about their own life goals.

Questions to Consider

1. From the statistics presented in Table 11.1, what can you infer about the lives of women in Mali? Would they live in the city or countryside? Would they attend school at all? What power would they have regarding decisions about family size? What kinds of activities would they pursue during the day? What dreams would they have for their daughters? For their sons? How would their lives compare with those of women in Sweden?

2. How important is Malala's cause? What effect would higher levels of education have on women in less-developed nations? Why?

TABLE 11.1 Status of Women in Select Nations, 2017

VARIABLES	NATION			
	Mali	Pakistan	Chile	Sweden
Percentage of labor force in agriculture	80	42.3	9.2	1.7
Mother's mean age at first birth	18.8	23.4	23.7	28.9
Maternal mortality rate (deaths of mothers per 100,000 live births)	587	178	22	4
Total fertility rate (average number of children per woman, lifetime)	5.95	2.68	1.81	1.88
Percentage literate				
Men	48	70	98	99
Women	29	46	97	99

SOURCE: Central Intelligence Agency (2017).

descriptors of their appearance and attractiveness compared to men, particularly when they were evaluated as "less attractive." Additionally, women "enhance[d]" their photos more than men (p. 343). Finally, Hitsch, Hortacsu, and Ariely's (2010) study reaffirms much of the prior research on dating preferences, with women being much more interested in men's income than looks. More broadly, their research suggests that even if online daters expect women and men to look a particular way, they fall in line with gendered expectations. Specifically, heterosexual women wanted men to be tall and economically well-off and they preferred slightly overweight men to thinner ones. In contrast, straight men preferred women who were slightly underweight and who were not taller than they were. Do you see how people's desires for size and shape reflect, at least to some degree, the way we conceptualize women and men? For example, if the normative expectation is for (straight) men to be "big" and "strong," this may be hard for a man to achieve—symbolically—if the woman he is dating is several inches taller. In contrast, a "slightly underweight" woman would make him seem bigger while dating a woman of the same size or larger would not.

Likewise, research on gender in the corporate world reveals that physical attractiveness and normative height/weight ratios matter far less for men's career success than women's (Quast, 2012). As a result, gender socialization nudges women to pay close attention to their appearance. This is the cultural sexism that the second-wave feminists fought so hard to undo. They argued that if women were able to spend less time on primping and more on cultivating their minds and talents, the world would be a better place (Wolf, 2002).

The near-impossible standard of beauty elevated in many Western cultures has been blamed for alarmingly high incidences of eating disorders—with sometimes deadly consequences—among modern young women (Thompson, 1996). Third-wave feminists have critiqued unrealistic body images in advertising by creating alternative ad campaigns, such as The Body Shop's campaign centered on a voluptuous doll named Ruby ("There are 3 billion women who don't look like supermodels and only 8 who do") and Dove's Real Beauty campaign featuring average-sized women wearing plain white cotton undergarments and little to no makeup (Bahadur, 2014; Callimachi, 2005).

Despite these alternative voices, young women and girls continue to evaluate themselves against mass media images of beauty. Interestingly, in one study, both white teens and teenagers of color found such images to be unrealistic, but the white teens incorporated those negative evaluative schemas into their own self-concepts, chastising themselves for not being able to achieve the depicted ideal. By contrast, nonwhite young women had a clearer sense that they were never going to achieve the depicted ideal and thus substituted more attainable standards of beauty for themselves (Milkie, 1999).

Studies of men and gender norms also exhibit great variability with respect to race and class. While toughness and aggressiveness are associated with masculinity in general, the boundaries within which one is permitted and expected to express these traits are often defined by one's social status. There exists a **hegemonic masculinity**—the expression of masculinity that is most privileged in society—and this is usually associated with middle- to upper-class white, heterosexual men. When men of color or men of lower socioeconomic status exhibit an "over-the-top" bravado or machismo, it may be considered cartoonish or buffoonish and not "refined" enough for the hegemonic ideal.

Michael Messner's (1990) study of how young men constructed their masculinities through organized sports, for example, demonstrated how middle- to upper-class white boys knew at some level that doing sports was but one avenue of expression for them and that educational and economic success was another. In contrast, the youth of lower socioeconomic status were not socialized to believe that there were multiple avenues of success for them, so they often pursued sports with a one-dimensional intensity, and with all the "feel-no-pain" ethic that comes with that arena. Men's studies, an outgrowth of third-wave feminism, has joined multiracial feminism in pointing out how much of the cultural sexism that undergirds gender inequality is also influenced by race, class, and sexual orientation.

Young men and women grow up to form families of their own, and gender socialization continues. Again, even with the best of intentions, men and women who desire an egalitarian ideal struggle with societal pressures and cultural expectations for what their family role should be (Gerson, 2009). Despite the rising number of dual-earner couples and even stay-at-home fathers, the task of child rearing is still assumed to be the mother's primary role, lending meaning to the label "Mr. Mom"—a man performing what is assumed to be the feminine parenting role in society. Mass-media images still reinforce the notion of a feminine domestic sphere. Progressive men brought attention to this cultural sexism by critiquing (and boycotting) a 2012 Huggies diapers ad that depicted men as clueless when it came to taking care of babies—not unlike an image of several confused-looking men on cell phones in the baby food aisle that PBS Parents posted to its Facebook page the same year (Belkin, 2012).

Hegemonic masculinity is the privileged, dominant expression of masculinity in a society.

Other lingering concerns include societal tolerance for what has been termed **rape culture,** which contributes to the high level of sexual victimization of American women by (mostly straight) men. The broader population mirrors what we discussed earlier about sexual assault in the military: it is a pervasive problem and the vast majority of sexual assaults (approximately 70%) go unreported. Underreporting occurs for several reasons, including the fear of not being believed by police or being re-traumatized in a court of law. Other victims are aware of low conviction rates and don't believe that reporting will get them justice. For example, when factoring in nonreported rapes, just 2% of rapists serve jail time (French, 2015). Still other victims are concerned about potential stigma, for example, problematic claims that they were "asking for it" or "wanted it" in some way. And, of course, many survivors—including boys and men—don't report their assaults for *all* of those reasons.

Rape culture is a patriarchal culture in which boy's and men's violence and rape are tolerated. The highly publicized Brock Turner case illustrates rape culture and such concerns about the judicial system. Turner, a then Stanford University undergraduate, raped an unconscious woman behind a dumpster on the university's campus. Fortunately, two Swedish graduate students observed the incident and questioned Turner. When he ran, they restrained him while waiting for police (see Bever, 2016). Turner offered a statement that, while acknowledging his responsibility, indicated his behavior was the result of peer pressure, a drinking culture, and "sexual promiscuity." Additionally, he said the woman had consented to having sex—though she was unconscious. Turner's father angered many by saying, among other things, that his son's life had been ruined for "20 minutes of action." Turner was found guilty, but the outrage people across the country felt was worsened by his six-month jail sentence for a crime that carries a maximum penalty of 14 years (Stack, 2016). He served just half that time. This case was also unusual in that the victim not only pursued legal recourse, but offered an incredibly powerful statement about her experience that went "viral." In it, she highlighted how sexual assault is much more than a physical injury, saying "You took away my worth, my privacy, my energy, my time, my intimacy, my confidence, my own voice" (Bever, 2016).

The U.S. Department of Justice estimates that between 2009 and 2013, 293,066 girls and women over 12 years of age were raped or sexually assaulted *each year*. More than 20 million women (18% of all U.S. women) report being raped at some point in their lifetime. Girls and women are the vast majority of victims (17.7 million) but about 3% of boys/men experience sexual assault, too (U.S. Department of Justice, n.d.). In teasing out patterns, we see variation by social location. For example, younger people are more likely

Students assemble to raise awareness of sexual violence and rape on college campuses.

to be raped than older people: Almost one third (28%) of boys who were raped were victimized when they were 10 years old or younger. Native American women and "mixed race" women are more likely to be raped than white women.

A 2015 study by the Association of American Universities reported more than one in four (27%) women college seniors had at least some kind of unwanted sexual contact since starting college (Mastropasqua, 2015). (For college women, that number was significantly lower with only 12% of rapes being reported to law enforcement. This may reflect what some say are pressures from colleges and universities to handle sexual assaults "in house.")

Taken as a whole, these issues (e.g., beauty standards, assault, pay inequality) are of particular concern to feminists, because even when legal barriers are removed, these very strong gender expectations in Western and U.S. culture continue to exert pressure and negative sanctions on those who dare to subvert them. Public policy such as laws against gender-based wage discrimination, against rape, and for gender-neutral family leave are obviously important. However, if gender norms remain so prominent in our culture's fabric, policies alone will not be able to do the work of achieving gender equity.

SECONDARY STRUCTURAL ASSIMILATION

This section will cover the various dimensions of secondary structural assimilation in the same order as the chapters in Part III did, although some topics (residential and school segregation, for example) are not relevant here.

Rape culture: Beliefs, values, and norms that encourage, condone, or minimize the rape of girls and women by boys and men.

Education. Today, the men and women of every group we have considered in this text are equal in terms of levels of education. We saw in Figures 6.10 and 6.11 that there is virtually no gender gap in high school or college education for either blacks or whites (although a notable gap remains between the races). The same holds true for the other groups we discussed in Part III: Although the groups vary with respect to each other (e.g., Hispanic Americans are lower and Asian Americans are higher), there are no gender gaps within the groups (U.S. Census Bureau, 2012c, p. 151).

On the other hand, sexism persists in education in sometimes subtle ways. The tradition of patriarchy in Western society tends to place more weight on the education of men, even in these relatively enlightened times. In elementary school classrooms, for example, boys tend to be called on more than girls, praised more, and given more attention from the teacher (Sadker & Zittleman, 2009). Also, at all levels of education, girls tend to be steered toward traditionally woman-dominated fields of study (e.g., nursing, education, social work) and away from such areas as engineering, physics, and math. The result is continuing sex segregation of college majors and adult occupations, as we discussed in connection with Figure 11.1.

Political Power. As we have mentioned, U.S. women acquired the right to vote in 1920 with the ratification of the Nineteenth Amendment and have been increasing their involvement in politics ever since. In fact, since 1980, women have tended to vote at higher rates than men, at least in presidential elections (Center for American Women and Politics, 2017). For example, 63.3% of eligible women voted in the 2016 presidential election, slightly down from 2012 (63.7%). Nearly 60% of men voted in the 2016 presidential election, about the same as in 2012 (Center for American Women and Politics, 2017; Roper Center, 2012).

Women's voting power may be equal to that of men—or perhaps greater, if they exercise the right to vote more than men. However, women are less represented in elected office. In 2017, 105 women served in the U.S. Congress: 21 as senators and 84 as state representatives. That's 19.6% of 535 seats. Women make up 25% of all state legislators, holding 1,844 of 7,383 positions. They hold just 75 statewide elective executive positions: 6 governors, 12 lieutenant governors, 57 other elective offices such as states attorney general, comptroller, and treasurer. That's almost no change from 71 who held such positions in 2010. However, the number of women serving in state legislatures has more than quintupled since 1971 (around 4% of all elected state and local public offices across the nation). Representation in state legislatures ranged from lows of 10% (South Carolina) and 11% (Oklahoma) to highs of almost 40% (Nevada) and 39% (Colorado and Vermont) (Center for American Women and Politics, 2018a).

Overall, the political power of women is increasing, but continued imbalances in representation remain, especially at the highest levels of power. The first woman Supreme Court justice (Sandra Day O'Connor) was nominated in 1981, and today three of the nine justices are women. In 2008, Sarah Palin became only the second woman candidate of a major political party for the vice presidency of the United States. (Geraldine Ferraro was the first, in 1984.) Also, Hillary Clinton was the first woman to be selected by a major national party as its presidential candidate. As of writing, 10 women serve in high-level positions including U.N. Ambassador Nimrata "Nikki" Haley who is also notable as one of just two Indo-Americans elected as a state governor. (Her parents are from India.) Another is Kellyann Conway who serves as counselor to the president and is the first woman to manage a presidential campaign (Center for American Women and Politics, 2018b). Clearly, some barriers remain to the election of women into political offices, especially the highest ones. Only time will tell if they will fall in the next few election cycles.

Jobs and Income. As is the case with many other minority groups, the economic status of women has improved over the past few decades but has stopped well short of equality. For example, as displayed in Figure 11.3, there is a persistent, although decreasing, gender gap in income. Notice the median incomes (in 2015 dollars to control for inflation) for both men and women (read from the left vertical axis) and the percentage of men's incomes that women earn (read from the right vertical axis). Note that only full-time, year-round workers are included in the graph.

On the average, women workers today earn about 80% of what men earn, up from about 64% in 1955. The relative increase in women's income is due to a variety of factors, including the movement of women into more lucrative careers, as reflected in Figure 11.1. Another cause of women's rising income is that some of the occupations in which women are highly concentrated have benefited from deindustrialization and the shift to a service economy. For example, job opportunities in the FIRE (finance, insurance, and real estate) sector of the job market have expanded rapidly since the 1960s, and because a high percentage of the workers in this sector are women, this has tended to elevate average salaries for women in general (Farley, 1996, pp. 95–101).

A third reason for the narrowing gender income gap has more to do with men's wages than women's, as we have seen in previous chapters. Before deindustrialization began to transform U.S. society, men monopolized the more desirable, higher-paid, unionized jobs in the manufacturing sector. For much of the 20th century, these blue-collar jobs paid well enough to subsidize a comfortable lifestyle, a house in the suburbs, and vacations, with enough left over to save for a rainy day or the kids' college education. However, with

SOURCE: U.S. Census Bureau, 2017. "Historical Income Tables, Table P-36." https://www.census.gov/data/tables/time-series/demo/income-poverty/historical-income-people.html.

deindustrialization, many of these desirable jobs were lost to automation and cheaper labor forces outside the United States, and were replaced, if at all, by low-paying jobs in the service sector. The result, reflected in Figure 11.3, is that while women's wages increased steadily between the 1950s and about 2000, men's wages have remained virtually level since the early 1970s.

These large-scale, macrolevel forces have tended to raise the status of women and narrow the income gap, but they have not equalized gender relations. Far from it! For example, although women and men are now equal in terms of education, women tend to get lower returns on their investment in human capital. Figure 11.4 compares men and women who were full-time workers in 2013 and shows a wage gap at every level of education. Wages rise as education rises for both women and men, but the wage gap persists. Generally, the wage gap increases as education rises, which may, in part, reflect the fact that wages for workers with lower education (especially less than high school) are so low to begin with.

A recent study showed that the gender wage gap for each level of education appears to be reproduced for jobs that require different skill levels. The researchers divided jobs into three skill levels, based on criteria used by the U.S. Department of Labor. Researchers classified jobs as being men-dominated if more than 75% of jobs were filled by men, woman-dominated if more than 75% were done by women, and "mixed" if rates fell between these two categories.

Table 11.2 shows a sizable gender gap in pay for each skill level, with the largest gap for high-skilled jobs. The researchers note that this gender gap between occupations compounds the gap within occupations, creating a kind of double income jeopardy for women: Women earn less than comparably qualified men in the same occupation and are paid less because they are in jobs dominated by women (Hegeswisch, Liepmann, Hayes, & Hartmann, 2010, p. 13).

FIGURE 11.4 Mean Annual Income for Full-Time, Year-Round Workers Age 25–64 by Gender and Educational Attainment, 2015

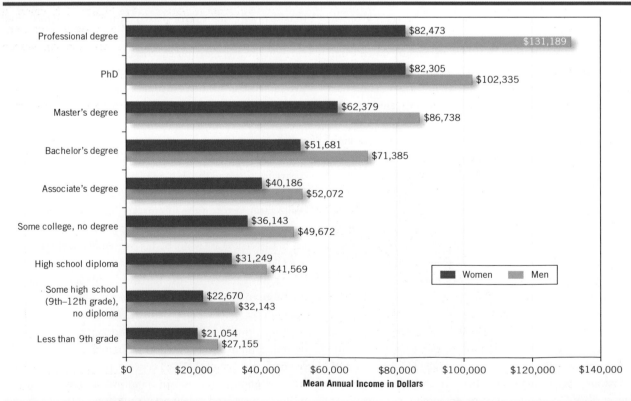

SOURCE: U.S. Census Bureau (2017).

TABLE 11.2 Median Weekly Earnings in Occupations by Skill Level and Gender Composition, 2009

SKILL LEVEL	MEN-DOMINATED	MIXED	WOMEN-DOMINATED	EARNINGS IN WOMEN-DOMINATED OCCUPATIONS AS A PERCENTAGE OF EARNINGS IN MEN-DOMINATED OCCUPATIONS
Low	$553	$435	$408	73.8
Medium	$752	$735	$600	79.8
High	$1,424	$1,160	$953	66.9

SOURCE: Hegeswisch et al. (2010, p. 10). Based on IWPR analysis of data from U.S. Department of Labor, Bureau of Labor Statistics. 2009. "Household Data Annual Averages. Table 39."

Continuing gender income inequality is also documented in Figure 11.5, which compares the income distribution for men and women workers in 2015. This figure is similar to income pyramids in earlier chapters (e.g., see Figure 6.13) and shows that, as with most minority groups, women tend to be overrepresented in the lower income categories and notably underrepresented in the higher income brackets. For example, 10.0% of women workers earn less than $20,000 per year (vs. only 6.8% of men), and less than 10% of women workers are in the highest income group (vs. more than 20% of men).

The size of the gap varies from group to group and from time to time. To illustrate, Table 11.3 shows the gender income gap for various groups, along with the gap between each group and non-Hispanic white men. Hispanic and black Americans have the smallest gender income gaps,

perhaps because the men and women of both groups are overrepresented in the low-wage, low-skill sectors of the economy (see Chapters 6 and 8).

Asian American men and women have the highest average incomes of their respective genders for these four groups, a reflection of the higher levels of education of both the native-born and immigrants (but remember the "bipolar" nature of many Asian American groups, as discussed in Chapter 9). But even in this most "successful" group, a gender gap in income persists, roughly equal in size to the gap for non-Hispanic whites.

The continuing gender income gap is partly a function of the persistent concentration of women in less-well-paid occupations, illustrated in Figure 11.1, which, in turn, is partly the result of outright occupational discrimination and the pervasive pressure to funnel young women

FIGURE 11.5 Distribution of Income for Men and Women (Full-Time, Year-Round Workers Only), 2015

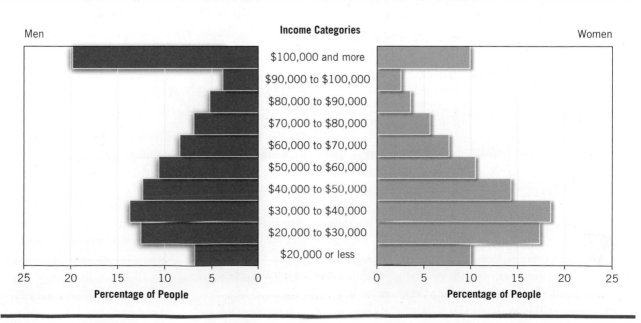

SOURCE: U.S. Census Bureau, 2017f.

TABLE 11.3 Median Incomes for Full-Time, Year-Round Workers by Gender and Racial or Ethnic Group, 2016

GROUP	MEDIAN INCOME	PERCENTAGE OF WHITE MEN	PERCENTAGE OF WOMEN TO MEN IN THEIR GROUP
Non-Hispanic white men	$60,750	—	81.2
Non-Hispanic white women	$45,694	81.2*	
Black men	$41,677	74.1	89.0
Black women	$37,097	66.0	
Asian men	$63,444	112.8	78.9
Asian women	$50,034	89.0	
Hispanic men	$35,973	64.0	88.0
Hispanic women	$31,657	56.3	

SOURCE: U.S. Census Bureau, 2017. Selected Characteristics of People 15 Years and Over, by Total Money Income, Work Experience, Race, Hispanic Origin, and Sex. Table PINC-01, https://www.census.gov/data/tables/time-series/demo/income-poverty/cps-pinc/pinc-01.html#par_textimage_14.

NOTE: Blacks and Asians are "alone and in combination" with other groups.

*This gap is not strictly comparable with the one reported in Figure 11.3. The two data sources are slightly different, as are the groups involved (all women and men in Figure 11.3 vs. non-Hispanic white men and women in Table 11.3).

into "appropriate" jobs, as mentioned earlier. This pattern is also a result of the choices women make to balance the demands of their jobs and family obligations. Whereas men are expected to make a total commitment to their jobs and careers, women have been expected to find ways to continue fulfilling their domestic roles even while working full-time, and many "women's" jobs offer some flexibility in this area. For example, some women become elementary school teachers because the job offers long summer breaks, which can help women meet their child-care and other family responsibilities. We see this demonstrated in the divergent paths of the similarly educated siblings Maria and Malcolm in the opening vignette of this chapter. This pattern of gender occupational segregation testifies to the persistence of minority status for women and the choices they make to reconcile the demands of career and family.

Women, along with minority groups in general, are also limited by the **glass ceiling**, or the discriminatory practices that limit opportunities to rise to higher levels in their careers, qualify for promotions, and earn higher salaries. These practices are, today, usually subtle, unspoken, and unwritten but effective in maintaining gender inequality, including income inequality. Decisions about promotions or raises will not overtly mention gender, but the glass ceiling is maintained, for example, by giving women less access to key mentors or sponsors and fewer opportunities for training and other experiences needed to qualify for higher-level jobs (Federal Glass Ceiling Commission, 1995, p. 8; Ridgeway, 2011, pp. 109–117).

One recent cross-national study demonstrated the reality of gender discrimination in business. The researchers followed a group of men and women who held MBAs from prestigious universities and found that the women in the sample started in lower positions, earned less over the course of their careers, and were far less likely to rise to the top in their companies (Carter & Silva, 2010).

Another recent study of the Fortune 500 largest corporations found that women were woefully underrepresented among top business leaders and absent from the executive suites and boardrooms. Women made up almost half of the total workforce in these companies but were only about 15% of executive officers and board members, and less than 8% of top earners (Soares, Combopiano, Regis, Shur, & Wong, 2010).

PRIMARY STRUCTURAL ASSIMILATION

Gordon's model of assimilation cites marital assimilation as the final stage of the assimilation process, and we have applied this idea to a variety of American minority groups in previous chapters. For women and men, we must revise this routine, since the two groups already intermarry (even though the institution of marriage often has been the locus and even the very embodiment of women's oppression).

The **glass ceiling** refers to practices that limit opportunities for women or for other minority groups.

Instead, we will consider other areas of primary socialization and relationships in which women still fall short of full assimilation in society. Just because men and women marry each other does not mean that women are viewed and treated as equals in all areas of life.

Interestingly, some aspects of the contact hypothesis (see Chapter 3), which predicts that cross-group contact between status equals over a prolonged period of time can reduce intergroup prejudice, can be applied to gender relations as well. For example, some research suggests that boys who grow up with sisters are less likely to perpetuate violence against women than are those who grow up primarily with other boys as peers (Lefkowitz, 1998).

Also, research shows that some college fraternities are more misanthropic and "rape-prone" than others. One key factor in determining negative attitudes and behaviors toward women is the extent to which cross-gender socialization is encouraged on campus: The more gender segregation is encouraged, the more likely abuse is to occur (Boswell & Spade, 1996). This evidence has led some universities to consider encouraging more coed fraternities—even doing away with single-gender fraternities altogether—as a way to cut down on campus sexual assaults (Theen & Staley, 2012).

Patterns forged in adolescence and early adulthood continue into adults' occupational lives as well. Consider workplace sexual harassment. As predicted by the contact hypothesis, the more men socialize with women as peers and equals, the less likely they will be to objectify them and treat them as pawns to be manipulated sexually in the workplace. Cohen (2013) points out that highly gender-segregated careers—such as auto mechanic or airline pilot—are more prone to cases of sexual harassment. Interestingly, one study found that claims of sexual harassment by white women had actually begun to go down slightly by the early 2000s, yet the numbers of such claims were going up for women of color (Joyce, 2004). Because the informal networks of white men include even fewer women of color than they do white women, this evidence would seem to support the hypothesis that the absence of cross-gender socialization in informal platonic settings creates an atmosphere where abuses—particularly of the less familiar (to white men) women of color—are more likely to occur.

As we have explored throughout this text, discrimination can occur in overt acts—such as abuse and harassment—but also in more subtle ways, through the conference of privilege and advantage, whereby members of the more dominant groups continue doing what has always been more comfortable for them and thus marginalizing those left outside the network of privilege. As a case in point, consider the typical golf course in the United States. It is known to be an arena where business and political contacts are solidified, and even where deals are made. Yet, for the majority of the nation's history, most golf courses excluded both women and nonwhites, thus barring members of these groups from opportunities for deal making and socializing.

In one study of corporate employees, about half of businesswomen surveyed named lack of access to informal networks as the most important obstacle to their success, and the top informal network cited was golf (Andrews, 2012). Elliott and Smith (2004) refer to this as **homosocial reproduction** and point out that white men have greater access to these informal networks of power than do any other race/gender group. This social network advantage pays dividends in terms of promotion advances. For example, Gail McGuire's study of one of the United States' largest financial institutions found that even where level of experience and tenure with the company were the same, men were able to parlay their informal network connections into promotions with the firm in a way that women could not (Reaney, 2010).

Access and position in these networks not only affect one's pace of advancement within the workplace but also determine whether one learns about job opportunities at all. Particularly at the highest levels, research shows that white men have greater access to job availability information than any other group, due to their routine conversations with informal-network peers (McDonald, Lin, & Ao, 2009). These inequalities in contacts are highly problematic because they cannot be legislated away through public policy and will require more innovative solutions to remedy. Yet the evidence is clear: The more cross-gender socialization occurs in platonic/intimate spaces, in addition to romantic/marriage relationships, the more attainable gender equality will be.

QUESTIONS FOR REFLECTION

14. According to the evidence, in which areas of social life or in which social institutions would you say women have come closest to full assimilation? Alternatively, which areas seem to need the most work or attention?

15. In the vignette that opened this chapter, we discussed Maria and Malcolm. If you were their parents, what actions, if any, might you have taken to bring greater equality to the siblings' experiences? (Keep in mind that some actions might be on the micro level in terms of your individual parenting choices, but others would require you to get involved in politics and public policy.)

Homosocial reproduction is the tendency of elite men to select candidates for advancement who are most like themselves.

CONCLUSIONS AND IMPLICATIONS FOR DOMINANT–MINORITY RELATIONS

In Chapter 6, after considering the situation of African Americans, we asked if the glass was half empty or half full, and the same question can be asked of women. Considerable progress toward equality has been made over the past few decades, but enormous challenges remain at every level of society and in every institutional sector.

It is clear that generalizations about "all women" or "all men" need to be carefully qualified. For example, the size of the gender income gap varies by racial and ethnic group, as we have seen, as do levels of education and occupational segregation. Systems of gender inequality and oppression are not the same for all women, and the quality and nature of gender privilege is not the same for all men. Nor do the terms *women* and *men* alone capture all people's gendered experiences, as the writers of the third wave of the feminist movement have pointed out. At any rate, women of all groups and social classes—and all those who are not included in the dominant gender—face considerable resistance to further progress, especially in the context of economic recession, globalization of employment, and deindustrialization. We should be careful not to let our celebration of progress in some areas blind us to the barriers that remain throughout the social structure and across the life course.

SUMMARY

This summary is organized around the Learning Objectives listed at the beginning of this chapter.

 11.1 Explain the difference between sex and gender and the social context of the latter.

Sex refers to biological differences between males and females, yet much of what we observe in everyday life as differences between these two groups is a result of gender distinctions rather than solely biological sex. Gender socialization is so all encompassing, we may begin to perceive this social conditioning as natural and immutable. Gender norms also vary greatly by race, class, religion, and nationality.

 11.2 List and explain key historical and economic events that have shaped gender relations.

Shifts from hunting-and-gathering societies to agrarian economies to industrial-based economies to the postindustrial globalized service economies have all affected transitions in gender relations worldwide. Societies create ideologies for culturally acceptable divisions of labor that rationalize various inequalities and divides. For example, industrial society emphasized a "separate spheres" doctrine that in some ways was even more damaging to gender equality than were the ideologies of eras that came before it. And when the economy becomes more globally interdependent, new forms of gender exploitation emerge that capitalize on readily available cheap labor. At the same time, historical events such as women in other industrialized nations obtaining the right to vote and the 1960s Civil Rights Movement for African Americans have pushed the United States to take legal and political strides toward greater gender equality.

 11.3 Understand feminism as a social movement, its varieties, its achievements, and its challenges.

Feminism is generally defined as the social movement for gender equality, though it exists in many different forms. Lorber's distinctions between gender reform, gender resistance, and gender rebellion movements are useful, and correspond roughly to the historic periods of the first, second, and third waves of feminism. The first wave accomplished voting rights and some economic and reproductive reforms, while the second wave extended more economic and reproductive gains, along with a host of cultural shifts in terms of how women were regarded by the patriarchal society. The ongoing third wave conceptualizes gender as less dichotomous and more fluid, and is more cognizant of gender diversity. Some are reluctant to identify with feminism for fear of appearing too radical, or because they do not think the movement addresses their group's unique gender concerns. Others hold the misconception that gender equality has already been achieved and feminism is no longer needed. However, a plethora of feminist organizations exist today, both domestically and internationally, concentrating on a host of varied gender-related issues.

 11.4 Identify and explain the key evidence and causes of gender inequality today.

While women in postindustrialized nations experience many signs of equality that, relative to the past and industrializing nations, are unparalleled historically, they nonetheless continue to face barriers to full equality. Such inequalities are evidenced in statistics such as the wage gap and the percentages of women in the highest political and corporate offices. Yet women worldwide, regardless of type of society, continue to face the threat of sexual violence and to lack full reproductive control. Various forms of cultural sexism, exacerbated by gender socialization as well as institutional sex discrimination, all contribute to these continued inequalities.

 11.5 Describe how race, class, sexual orientation, and religion impact gender inequality.

Although men are generally considered privileged in patriarchal societies, many gay men, men of color, poor/working-class men, and men who are members of religious minority groups may not feel very privileged. Structurally, examining the gender wage gap, white men tend to enjoy a comfortable wage advantage over all other groups, whether men or women. Culturally, boy's and men's gender socialization that encourages dangerous risk-taking behavior tends to be more pronounced for boys and men in communities of color and lower socioeconomic status. Heterosexual marriage privileges accord elite white women (often married to elite white men) a degree of social status that women of other backgrounds (e.g., lesbians, women of color) cannot as readily access. And certain

religions' norms and values are particularly damaging to gender equality. Sweeping generalizations about all women or all men are seldom accurate—the data show us that such statements usually need to be contextualized by race, class, sexual orientation, and religion, among other characteristics.

 11.6 Explain how the concepts of assimilation and pluralism apply to women's experiences as a minority group in U.S. society.

Gender socialization creates very different cultural expectations for boys/men and girls/women at each stage of the life cycle, although these experiences are mediated by social class, race, and ethnicity. These expectations remain powerful forces in social life, in spite of the efforts of public policy to encourage gender neutrality. In the United States (and many other advanced industrial nations), women and men are equal in terms of years of education, but persistent and important gender gaps remain in the quality of education, occupational profiles, income, political power, and virtually every institutional area. The extent of gender inequality varies by social class, race, and ethnicity. In terms of primary structural assimilation, patterns of inequality persist in terms of access to the informal social networks that often control upward mobility.

KEY TERMS

androgynous 403

cisgender 396

cultural feminism 406

doing gender 396

double bind 414

feminism 394

gender 395

gender displays 396

gender fluid 396

gender identity 396

gender status 395

gender socialization 395

genderqueer 397

glass ceiling 424

glass escalator 414

hegemonic masculinity 419

homosocial reproduction 425

intersex 394

modern sexism 415

pink collar 414

rape culture 420

sex 394

sexual scripts 416

transgender 396

REVIEW QUESTIONS

1. Define and explain the difference between sex and gender. What does it mean to say that someone is "outside the binary"?

2. What does it mean to say that gender is a "social construction"? Give examples of ways that people socially construct gender, ideally from your own life and observations.

3. How do changes in subsistence technology affect gender relations? At what level of development are gender relations most unequal? Why?

4. Define and explain androgyny. What advantages does androgyny bring in modern Western urban-industrial society? Would these same advantages apply to non-Western societies or those at lower levels of development? Why or why not?

5. What movements for gender equality have been active over the past several centuries? What were the goals of these movements? What are the three waves of feminism? Did each succeed? How?

6. Summarize and explain each of the three recent gender trends and issues cited in this chapter. What public policies might be developed to better address these issues?

7. With regard to gender relations today, is the glass half empty or half full? What evidence of persistent gender inequality is presented in this chapter? How serious are these problems? What are some useful approaches to addressing these problems?

STUDENT STUDY SITE

Sharpen your skills with SAGE edge at edge.sagepub.com/healey8e

SAGE edge for students provides a personalized approach to help you accomplish your coursework goals in an easy-to-use learning environment.

The following resources are available at SAGE edge:

Current Debates: Should Children Be Raised Genderless?

Should all children be raised in the same way, without regard to their biological sex? Should children be free to choose their own gender expressions? Is it possible to socialize boys and girls outside of societal gender expectations? On our website you will find an overview of the topic, the clashing points of view, and some questions to consider as you analyze the material.

Public Sociology Assignments

Public Sociology Assignments provide opportunities for students to address directly and personally some of the issues raised in this text.

There are four assignments for Part IV on our website. In the first assignment, students will use the information available from the Pew Research Center to examine religion as a source of diversity in American life. In the second assignment, groups of students will analyze the lyrics of popular songs. Do the lyrics reflect stereotypes of racial or ethnic groups? What messages are being conveyed about gender or sexual orientation?

The third assignment focuses on a film and website that probe the reality of bullying in America's schools. The fourth assignment is an analysis of the thousands of languages around the world that are in danger of becoming extinct.

Contributed by Linda M. Waldron

Internet Research Project

For this Internet Research Project, you will use information gathered by the U.S. Census Bureau to learn more about gender differences and gender inequality for all Americans and two groups of your own choosing. The groups you choose can be any racial or ethnic group or subgroup covered in this text, including white ethnics, black Americans, Native Americans, Hispanic or Asian Americans, or one of the "New American" groups covered in Chapter 10. The project will be guided by a series of questions related to course concepts, and your instructor may ask you to discuss your findings in small groups.

For Further Reading

Please see our website for an annotated list of important works related to this chapter.

12

LESBIAN, GAY, AND BISEXUAL AMERICANS

Getty

Wikimedia Commons

timeline

1955
The Daughters of Bilitis, a lesbian organization, is founded.

1969
A police raid on a popular gay bar, the Stonewall Inn, led to riots. To safeguard LGB community members from intimidation and violence, people organized, making this one of the most important events in modern LGB history.

1979
An estimated 75,000 people participate in the National March on Washington for Lesbian and Gay Rights.

1940   1946   1952   1958   1964   1970   1976

1943
The U.S. military bars gays and lesbians from serving in the Armed Forces.

1953
Executive order bans homosexuals from working for the federal government or any of its private contractors.

1960
The first U.S. public gathering of lesbians occurs at San Francisco's Daughters of Bilitis national convention.

1973
The board of the American Psychiatric Association votes to remove homosexuality from its list of mental illnesses.

1978
Harvey Milk, an openly gay San Francisco city council member and promoter of gay rights, is murdered.

1948
The Kinsey Report finds that 4% of men identify as exclusively homosexual while 37% have had sexual relationships with other men.

LOC

Associated Press

1987
The National March on Washington for Lesbian and Gay Rights draws over 500,000 people, making it the largest civil rights demonstration in U.S. history.

Evelyn and Hope Johnson have been together for 20 years and have two children—Mariah and Paul. The Johnson parents tried to be as involved as possible in their children's schooling but occasionally were met with palpable hostility by certain teachers and administrators—including one teacher who said that it was against her religion to welcome both of Mariah's parents to the classroom party at the end of the year. Usually, reactions were more "subtle" but equally frustrating. Some teachers would make eye contact with one parent but ignore the other during conferences, and forms and class projects almost always included references to "mom" and "dad." The result was that the children were often uncomfortable sharing the details of their loving family with their classmates and teachers.

LEARNING OBJECTIVES

By the end of this chapter, you will be able to do the following:

 12.1 Identify and analyze the difference between sexual orientation, sexual identity, and sexual behavior or practices.

 12.2 List and explain the key events that have impacted how lesbian, gay, and bisexual persons are viewed by society and have experienced society.

 12.3 Describe key moments in the struggle for gay liberation.

12.4 Identify and explain the patterns of sexual-orientation inequality in society today.

 12.5 Describe how race, class, gender, and religion impact sexual-orientation inequality.

National Institutes of Health

Wikipedia

Wikimedia Commons

1987
The Names Project unveils the AIDS Memorial Quilt on the Capitol Mall in Washington, D.C.

1998
Matthew Shepard, a 21-year-old gay college student, is murdered, bringing hate crimes against gays into the national spotlight.

2008
California voters approve Proposition 8, making same-sex marriage in California illegal. In 2010, Prop 8 is found unconstitutional.

2014
18 states plus Washington, D.C., allow gay marriage.

2015
The Supreme Court (*Obergefell v. Hodges*) strikes down various state laws that define marriage in terms of heterosexuality; it legalizes adoptions and foster care by gay couples, and secures equal rights for same-sex couples in a variety of medical, legal, and other areas of family life.

1988   1994   2000   2006   2012   2018

1993
The Department of Defense enacts the "Don't Ask, Don't Tell" policy for military applicants.

2004
Massachusetts becomes the first state to legalize same-sex marriage.

2009
The Matthew Shepard Act is passed, expanding the 1969 U.S. Federal Hate Crime Law to include crimes motivated by a victim's sexual orientation.

2010
The "Don't Ask, Don't Tell" policy is repealed, allowing gays and lesbians to serve openly in the U.S. military.

2013
The Boy Scouts lift ban on gay members.

2013
The U.S. Supreme Court strikes down DOMA (see 1996).

1996
President Clinton signs the Federal Defense of Marriage Act (DOMA), denying same-sex couples the right to have their unions/partnerships recognized by the federal government.

Flickr

2016
49 people are killed and 58 injured at Pulse, a popular gay club in Orlando, Florida; the deadliest shooting by a single person in U.S. history.

The White House

This lack of acceptance came to a head several years ago when Evelyn was in a car accident and spent several weeks in the hospital in critical condition. Because the hospital records showed that it was Hope who gave birth to Mariah and Paul, hospital staff would not allow the children to visit their critically ill mother, despite the fact that Evelyn is a legal guardian and shares their last name. (Because of the laws of their state at that time, Evelyn was unable to formally adopt the children she has coparented and provided for since birth.) Scarier still, it took several days of legal battles and heartache before even Hope was allowed to be at Evelyn's bedside, because the hospital did not consider her "family."

Evelyn and Hope got married in New York, but they lived in North Carolina, which did not recognize their marriage at the time of the accident. Their medical bills were astronomical because they had to carry the cost of two different family health insurance policies. The Johnsons tried to shield their children as much as possible from these struggles, but as the children got older, they came to understand how many people in their town viewed their family. Both children are passionate about fighting sexual-orientation discrimination, and are now majoring in public policy and law. They are heavily involved with several organizations working to eliminate the bias and discrimination that LGB people and families experience.

Globally, many types of families exist. What many people call the "traditional" nuclear family—husband and wife with children—is only one of many possibilities. What challenges did the Johnsons face that other types of families did not? What dynamics of prejudice and discrimination described in the opening vignette resemble those faced by the racial/ethnic minorities we have studied thus far? Which are different? In this chapter, we will explore these and many other related questions. •

This chapter examines how society is stratified by sexual orientation—in its culture and social structure (e.g., social institutions). We will review the various, often unconscious privileges heterosexual individuals enjoy because they are members of the dominant group. We'll also examine the societal stigma placed on lesbians, gays, and bisexuals (LGBs). While some major cultural shifts have occurred in the United States and some other nations in recent years, particularly in the younger generations, inequalities and differences in treatment based on sexual orientation continue across virtually all areas of social life.

We begin this chapter by considering the difference between sexual orientation, sexual identity, and sexual behavior. Then, we will examine the history of sexual orientation as an organizing principle for stratification. We will analyze how changes in subsistence technology and level of development have affected the patterns of inequality for LGB individuals, and we'll review various protest movements that have sought to eliminate stratification based on sexual orientation.

We will also consider some of the issues that are central to relations between LGB persons and the larger society. Following our usual approach, we will end the chapter by applying some of the concepts we have used throughout the text to compare LGB people, as a group, to other minority groups we have studied. Throughout the chapter, we will use an intersectional approach to examine the relationships between sexual orientation and inequality. Antigay prejudice and the marginalization of LGB persons operate quite differently depending on race, class, and gender. Not all heterosexuals benefit from heterosexism equally, nor do all LGB people experience homophobia in the same way.

As with the other types of inequality that we have studied, discrimination against LGB people exists globally. Homophobia affects all social institutions including family, religion, politics, education, media, and the economy. For example, in many places, LGB relationships are criminalized and LGB people face harsh penalties including fines, jail, torture, and death. Antigay hate crimes occur even in societies with laws that guarantee equality or that seem relatively more tolerant. Heterosexual families often receive privileges that gay and lesbian families do not. Additionally, although research documents increased equality for LGB people in some areas of social life, popular culture and the media often project a more optimistic view. By the end of this chapter, you will be familiar with issues of central concern in the history and development of sexual orientation inequality, and will be able to understand how stratification operates in this area of social life.

SEXUAL ORIENTATION, SEXUAL IDENTITY, AND SEXUAL BEHAVIOR

Sexual orientation refers to the gender or genders to which a person is predominantly attracted—physically or emotionally. It may help to think about sexual orientation as a continuum. People who are attracted to the "opposite" gender are at one end of the spectrum and are called heterosexual or straight. Women and men who feel

People may have more than one sexual orientation and sexual identity as suggested by the variety of boxes (e.g., gay, asexual, straight).

same-gender attraction are at the other end of the spectrum and are called homosexual or gay. (Women who are attracted to other women are also called lesbians.) People who feel attraction for both men and women are bisexual. As you'll learn, other sexual orientations exist, too.

These definitions might seem simple enough, but people don't always fall into one and only one category. For example, in Chapters 7 and 11, you learned that a person's biological sex does not always match his or her gender. For example, what is the sexual orientation of a transgender person who is physically male, but who identifies and lives as a woman, and who feels attracted only to women? Is this individual a lesbian? Heterosexual? Bisexual? What about the bisexual person who chooses to be celibate? These are probably not the images that come to mind when you think about sexual orientation, but they serve to illustrate the range of possibilities.

Sexual identity refers to the way people think about themselves as sexual beings and it differs from sexual orientation. A person who identifies as a "straight" may occasionally feel physically attracted to members of the same gender and someone who identifies as gay may sometimes be attracted to the "opposite" gender.

Sexual orientation and sexual identity are closely connected, but neither has a one-to-one correspondence with the other or with actual sexual behavior. For example, many virgins or celibate people (behavior) identify as heterosexual (identity) and feel attracted to members of the "opposite" gender (orientation). Some people may think of themselves as "bicurious" or "heteroflexible" if they have had only or predominantly heterosexual relations but have considered or imagined—but not necessarily engaged in—sexual activity with people with the same gender.

Sexual orientation refers to the gender or genders to which a person is attracted.

Sexual identity refers to the way people think about themselves sexually.

Still other people may engage in sexual behavior that does not correspond with their stated sexual orientation, for example, a bisexual man who, because of social norms, marries a woman and only has sex with her (like Hector in Chapter 1), or a straight woman who sometimes feels attracted to other women and has sex with them to satisfy that physical need. Remember that sexual orientation can include emotional attraction, too. People's emotional or physical attractions aren't always consistent with each other.

Figure 12.1 explores the relationship between sexual orientation and sexual identity. Researchers asked a representative sample of LGB individuals to identify their sexual orientation with the question, "Who are you attracted to?" Their responses are organized by their stated sexual identity (gay, lesbian, or bisexual). The results illustrate our point that sexual orientation and sexual identity are closely but not perfectly connected.

Virtually all gay men (91%) said that they are attracted "only or mostly" to other men; 80% of lesbians said they were "only or mostly" attracted to other women and 13% said they were "somewhat" more attracted to women than to men. Interestingly, about 3% of the self-identified lesbians said they were equally attracted to both men and women, and perhaps even more surprising, 2% said they were more attracted to men.

The self-identified bisexuals were, as their sexual identity suggests, quite variable in their sexual orientation. Roughly equal percentages of bisexual men were more sexually attracted to men (32%), to women (32%), and to both genders equally (28%). In contrast, a substantial number of bisexual women (34%) were more attracted to men,

FIGURE 12.1 Sexual Attraction by Sexual Identity (LGB Individuals Only)

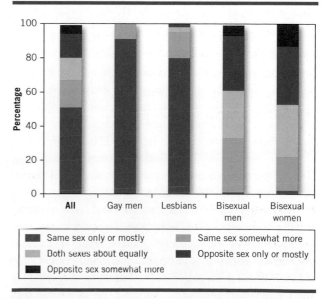

Legend:
- Same sex only or mostly
- Both sexes about equally
- Opposite sex somewhat more
- Same sex somewhat more
- Opposite sex only or mostly

SOURCE: Pew Research Center (2013d, p. 81). Reprinted with permission of Pew Research Center.

while 20% were more attracted to women and 31% were attracted to both genders equally.

If nothing else, these results suggest that the relationship between sexual orientation and sexual identity is neither simple nor straightforward. As with race, ethnicity, and gender, the terms *heterosexual, lesbian, gay,* and *bisexual* are socially constructed identities and social statuses that are by no means exhaustive or mutually exclusive in terms of representing the range of human sexuality. Nonetheless, the social divisions between those who are heterosexual and those who are not affects the allocation of societal resources—particularly in the institutions of politics, the economy, family, and religion. This chapter focuses on these inequalities.

SEXUAL ORIENTATION INEQUALITIES, MINORITY-GROUP STATUS, AND IDENTITY

As with other minority group classifications, being a member of a sexual minority group can result in stigma, marginalization, and discrimination. Fear of these consequences makes some people reluctant to publicly identify as anything other than "straight," which can complicate the relationship between sexual identity and sexual behavior. To illustrate, recall the cases of Mary Farrell and Hector Gonzalez in Chapter 1. Mary identifies as a lesbian and is in a long-term, committed relationship with another woman. But Mary is not "out" in her role as schoolteacher. Hector is married and his wife is his best friend. He is bisexual, a sexual orientation he has shared with his wife but not his parents or grandmother. Mary and Hector are comfortable with their sexual identities. However, they are mindful about who they share this information with. This might be similar to how an African American who "passes" for white might be cautious about revealing all of their personal information.

Research on sexual behavior and desires, undertaken by Alfred Kinsey and his colleagues as early as the 1940s, revealed that nearly 40% of the population admitted to experiencing some kind of same-sex desire and/or behavior, and this estimate has been replicated fairly consistently in subsequent studies (Ellis, Burke, & Ames, 1987; Kinsey, 1948). This research suggests that nonheterosexual desires and behaviors are quite common.

In recognition of the complicated and uncertain relationship between sexual orientation, sexual identity, and actual sexual behavior, many scholars argue that sexual orientation should be regarded as a continuum rather than a series of discrete categories (e.g., straight or gay). This framework more accurately describes the variety of sexualities that exist in the world. However, the gay/straight dichotomy has become a significant dimension of social differentiation that, in turn, affects people's access to societal resources. Because of this influence (and partly as a matter of linguistic convenience), we will use the language of gay/straight throughout this chapter though we realize reality is more complex.

In Chapter 11, we discussed how some women prefer the term *womanist* rather than *feminist*. They feel the term "feminist" is inadequate because it does not account for the many crucial differences—by race, age, class, region, and so forth—between the genders. Likewise, we cannot simply discuss gays, lesbians, and bisexuals as if they are homogeneous groups; we must recognize the significance of other intersecting social categories. For example, research finds that people of color are more reluctant to identify themselves as *gay* and *lesbian* than whites (Pathela et al., 2006; Wolitski, Jones, Wasserman, & Smith, 2006). People of color may instead refer to themselves as "same-gender loving," "in the life," and "on the down low" to refer to their sexual identities and practices. Boykin (2006) suggests they do so, in part, to avoid taking on another stigmatized identity in addition to being racial minorities.

VISIBILITY AND IDENTITY: GENDER TRAITS AND SEXUAL ORIENTATION

We should note some of the similarities and differences between the social visibility of members of the LGB minority and other minority groups we have considered in other chapters. Compared with people of color who typically have no control over their social visibility, it may seem that LGB people have more options to remain "invisible" and avoid the potential sanctions that come with their minority group status.

As we have discussed, however, many multiracial persons are assumed to be one race but are another (or a mix of others). Likewise, some LGB people may attempt to conceal their sexual orientation, but if they exhibit traits that are stereotypically identified with being gay, others may presume it.

Many people incorrectly conflate gender and sexual orientation. In many cultures, men who others regard as "feminine" may be assumed to be gay. Likewise, people may assume that a woman who appears "masculine" must be a lesbian. In fact, that was one of the assumptions in the Attitude-Interest Analysis Test (AIAT) we discussed in the Chapter 11 Applying Concepts section. A popular sitcom from the late 1990s/early 2000s (and "rebooted" in 2017), *Will and Grace*, provides a token example of this assumption. A character named Jack, a man, exhibits more feminine behavior than his more masculine friend, Will. Yet, both men are gay. Neither men are fully "in the closet," but if

NARRATIVE PORTRAIT

Black or Gay?

Keith Boykin, author of *One More River to Cross: Black and Gay in America*.

Keith Boykin is a lawyer, best-selling author, columnist, TV commentator, and gay rights advocate. He is the cofounder and president of the National Black Justice Coalition, an organization committed to fighting racism and homophobia. Additionally, he has worked as a media consultant in the Clinton White House and as a political science professor. Boykin "came out" when he was in law school. In this passage, he describes his relationships with African Americans, the gay community, and his family.

ONE MORE RIVER TO CROSS

Keith Boykin

I have often been asked by blacks and gays alike which group I most closely identify with. I have been black for far longer than I have known I am gay, so I think I understand African-American culture better than gay culture. In addition, the gay community . . . has long been dominated by white men, so as a black person I have felt ostracized by that world. But at the same time, I do not believe many in the black community fully understand or accept me either. As a result, I've spent a great deal of my time and energy as an openly gay black man shuttling back and forth between my two identities.

It took time to learn about the dark realities of both communities.

I had felt so liberated when I first came out that I began to immerse myself in the so-called gay lifestyle, slowly, unknowingly, and destructively absorbing characteristics of a culture that devalued me because of my color. I later learned how white gays had excluded African Americans, denying them entry into nightclubs, ignoring their contributions to the gay political movement, and reinforcing straight society's stereotypes and prejudices.

At the same time, the black community made my life difficult as well. When I lived in the closet, I suffered the oppression of living a lie, and once I came out, I faced a different prejudice, one based on fear and dislike. The more out I was, the more at risk I became. At first, some "straight" black men I knew observed me from afar with both curiosity and trepidation, as though they were examining a dangerous animal in the jungle. Others seemed afraid even to talk to me, apparently fearing that they, too, would be labeled gay by their association with me. When I hung out with certain black male classmates in law school, some would almost immediately begin talking about their girlfriends, as if to let me know they were straight. Being out, I learned, sometimes meant being marginalized by one's own communities. . . .

Ultimately, it was the black lesbian and gay community that reaffirmed my existence . . . and taught me to love myself as a mirror image of these others. Within this group, I felt I could be a whole person rather than just a gay man or just a black man. I felt the comfort of unqualified love and acceptance that I had never really felt in other communities. Many of the black lesbians and gay men I met came from backgrounds different from my own. We had different jobs, interests, and desires. Yet I did not feel ostracized for not being "black enough" or for not being "gay enough.". . .

Years of hiding my sexual identity from myself and others had diminished my sense of self-worth. But in the black gay community I found a support group, if not a family, willing to love me and accept my love for them regardless of our differences. . . . On the one hand, I wanted to return home to my family and to the black community; but on the other hand, I was unsure whether I would be welcomed by either once they learned who I really was. I followed the road in my heart, and I started on my way home.

I soon learned that the assumptions I had made were not always accurate. By assuming my family would react negatively to my homosexuality, I made this reality somewhat self-fulfilling. By dodging and tiptoeing around the issue, I thought I could protect both myself and them from . . . painful and bitter discussions. . . . Instead, by not challenging anyone to confront the reality of my identity and my place in the family, I only made it harder for us all. But as I began to come out to family members, I learned to do something I had never been able to do before—to love. I learned to love myself enough so that I could open up and love other people, and I learned to love my family enough to be honest with them in spite of the consequences.

SOURCE: Boykin (1997, pp. 26–28).

Questions to Consider

1. Compare Boykin's experiences with Leslie Feinberg's from Chapter 11 and with Carla's and Tim Wise's from Chapter 1. What similarities and differences can you find in these memoirs? Who is the least uncertain about who they are? Who is the most? Why?

2. How do Boykin's experiences and thoughts illustrate the importance of the intersectionality perspective? How would his story change if he were uneducated? A girl or woman? Hispanic? Why?

they wanted to be, it's likely that Will would be more successful because he conforms to masculine norms.

In Chapter 7 we discussed the diversity of gender identity and expression in Native American communities. In Chapter 11, we discussed gender diversity more broadly in the United States and elsewhere. We see this diversity within the LGB population, too. While people may stereotypically view lesbians as "man-ish," many lesbians embrace "femininity." (Some people call them "lipstick lesbians" or "femmes.") Porta de Rossi, Ellen Page, Raven-Symoné, Sarah Paulson, and Traci Dinwiddie are examples. Likewise, some gay men are quite masculine while others are not. Consider, for example, the six openly gay college football players who started the 2017 season. It's unlikely that anyone would consider them "feminine." Because they conform to gender norms, if they weren't "out of the closet" most people might assume they were straight. The LGB population is diverse in other ways, too. For example, almost one fifth (17%) consider religion "very important" in their lives and within this group, 41% report attend weekly religious services. (See Pew Research Center, 2013a.)

Assumptions about gendered behavior and sexual orientation are at the root of some "anti-gay" hate crimes. (See Chapter 3.) Some assailants have interpreted gender-nonconforming behavior as "gay" and attacked people based on these assumptions—even when the victims were heterosexual (Mooney, Knox, & Schacht, 2010). In other words, people may confer a minority sexual-orientation status onto others that is not necessarily accurate. The variable relationship between sex, gender identity, gender displays, and sexual orientation is one reason why we chose to discuss transgender people in Chapter 11 (on gender)—because transgender people can be of any sexual orientation.

HISTORY AND BACKGROUP OF SAME-SEX RELATIONSHIPS

Same-sex relations have existed throughout time, but a distinct social identity based on sexual orientation—and even the word *homosexual*—did not emerge until the latter part of the 19th century (Pincus, 2011). In reviewing the history of same-sex relations, it becomes clear that a crucial determining factor of how such relationships are conceptualized—and an interesting connection with the preceding chapter on gender—is society's relative degree of openness toward women's economic independence. A society's views toward same-sex relations are deeply influenced by whether women are seen as fully intelligent and capable human beings and whether they are able to support themselves without men's companionship.

ANCIENT GREECE

Ancient Greece was a patriarchal society. Men made the rules and rarely acknowledged or respected women's humanity. Greeks (women and men) generally viewed women as intellectually inferior to men, and men were socialized to expect little more than idle conversation with them. Rather, Greek society encouraged men to form strong emotional and physical bonds with other men. When men courted women, it was primarily to secure a wife with whom they would procreate. As seems to be the case across different eras and geographical locations, men were expected to choose younger women for these purposes.

In ancient Greece, relations between same gender individuals were just one of many ways to explore sexual desire and emotional attachment. Social norms dictated appropriate ways that older men could mentor younger people though these norms varied by social class and by the gender of the protégé. Particularly among the elite, it was acceptable for older men to "woo" young men. If the older man was of high social standing, such a relationship could bring prestige to the younger one (Hubbard, 2003). Sappho's writing, particularly her poems, indicate similar erotic yearnings and relationships between women in ancient Greece. Sappho grew up on the Greek island, Lesbos and ran a school for girls there. The word *lesbian*,

A representation of Sappho, the Greek poet whose residence on the isle of Lesbos may be the origin of the term "lesbian."

coined in the 20th century, is said to reflect Sappho's heritage (Sappho & Lombardo, 2002).

As with most societies where women were marginal figures in political and public life, women in ancient Greece who desired an education pursued their studies in a sex-segregated environment, where they forged emotional connections with one another through learning and sharing their intellectual curiosity, not unlike the relationships among educated men described by Plato. However, the fact that Sappho's poetry describes erotic feelings for women as well as for men underscores the conclusion drawn by most scholars of about men's relationships in ancient Greece: People did not define same-gender relations as deviant and they existed alongside a range of other forms of sexual and romantic expression.

By today's standards, one might observe the intimate relations of ancient Greece and categorize them as "bisexual"; however, doing so would misinterpret history and apply a modern concept that does not really fit the social structure and norms of that period (Halperin, 1989). Because sexual behavior is governed by both biological drives and social constraints, it would be more accurate to say that certain forms of same-sex relations were approved and encouraged, particularly when they fostered political and intellectual connections, because they did not pose a threat to procreation. As one translator of Sappho's poetry noted, the poet seemed to have loved men, women, and music, in equal measure (Sappho & Carson, 2003).

The writings that have survived from ancient times frame various aspects of life with passionate language of longing and desire, heartache and heartbreak, and the genders of the various protagonists and antagonists in the stories are not always of central concern. However, once social ideologies—religious, political, and otherwise—began to confine people's relationships in particular ways, a quite different framing of what forms of sexuality were considered appropriate began to appear. People's behaviors adapted accordingly.

SEPARATE SPHERES: AGRARIAN TO INDUSTRIAL SOCIETY

As we have seen, agrarian societies need high levels of fertility and larger families to supply the labor power required for the level of economic development. In agrarian societies, sexual behaviors were primarily sanctioned within the marital unit. Victorian and Puritan societies featured highly restrictive social norms regarding sexuality. For example, sexual intercourse outside of heterosexual marriage was viewed as a sin and, often, a crime (D'Emilio, 1998).

Within these rigid boundaries, same-sex intimacy continued. In Victorian England, where women were almost entirely isolated from men, women created intimate bonds and desires for other women, sometimes even consummated in what they referred to as "marriage" to each other (Marcus, 2007).

By the late 19th century, many of the women involved in the suffrage movement and those who had the economic means to pursue a profession were realizing they could not do the work they found most meaningful while fulfilling the duties of a "wife." Some of these unmarried women—negatively labeled as "spinsters" by society—found emotional and sometimes physical companionship with other women. The founding of several elite women's colleges (Vassar, Smith, Wellesley, and Bryn Mawr) in the late 1800s facilitated these connections among independent-minded women. Some of these affluent women even formed households that were sometimes referred to as "Boston marriages." Records left behind by the participants in these relationships demonstrate that emotional bonds definitely existed, though the exact nature of the sexual relations in these households cannot always be determined (Faderman, 1991).

Late-19th-century developments in same-sex relations can also be tied to the emergence of urbanization, industrialization, and capitalism. Rigid norms regarding sexuality and gender relations still ruled society, but the decline of the agrarian family and the movement of the population from rural villages to urban areas allowed people—mainly men but women as well—some latitude in developing their sexual identities. With the shift from labor-intensive agrarian technology to capital-intensive industrial technology, a man did not need a house full children to help farm the land and survive economically.

These forces combined in many cities to create a distinctly "gay" subculture among men—primarily in New York, San Francisco, and Washington, D.C. By the 1920s, there were certain urban areas where men could find each other for intimate relations (D'Emilio, 1998). Not all women were elite enough to fashion themselves an educated "Boston marriage," but there are records of working-class women who lived in "marriages" with each other—one disguised as a man to find work in the city (D'Emilio, 1998; Faderman, 1991). Key figures of the Harlem Renaissance have left behind writings to attest to the fact that this urban center included same-sex relations among people of color as well (Schwarz, 2012).

These men and women, increasingly labeled "homosexual" by their society, knew they were engaging in behavior that bucked conventional norms. The aforementioned Puritanical church law, as well as state law, labeled their behavior sinful, criminalized it, and relegated homosexuals to the fringes of "respectable" society—or well beyond those fringes. At the same time, science and medicine were coming to see homosexuality as a disease. Bolstered by the shared rejection of same-sex relations across institutions, the state and law enforcement authorities repressed, censored, and arrested persons who engaged in homosexual behavior or who advocated for understanding and tolerance. The result was that the "gay community" remained largely invisible, underground, and covert.

FROM WORLD WAR II AND THE MCCARTHY ERA TO CIVIL RIGHTS

World War II was a watershed for nonheterosexual minority groups, as it was for so many others. The war increased opportunities for many types of same-sex relations. With men away at war and women encouraged by the political propaganda of the day to do their patriotic duty and enter the workplace en masse, same-gender associations—some intimate and sexual—practically became the rule rather than the exception. Even people who did not live in larger cities began to be exposed to opportunities for nonheterosexual relations. For nonheterosexuals who had previously lived quietly, privately tormented by their own desires, this period provided them the possibility of no longer feeling alone with their secret.

Yet repression loomed large, both during the war and into the years that followed. At best, psychoanalysts strove to "cure" those deemed "homosexual" of their "illness"; at worst, the political "witch hunts" of the 1940s and 1950s, led by U.S. Senator Joe McCarthy, pulled them from their jobs and threw them in jail. Although McCarthy is best remembered for targeting suspected communists, close to 5,000 Americans were dismissed from military and civilian positions between 1947 and 1950 due to their alleged sexual orientation (Faderman, 1991).

Bars that were undercover gay/lesbian gathering places continued to be subjected to police raids and harassment in the 1940s and 1950s. Because the people found at these bars were widely framed as "sexual perverts" and deviants, there was not much societal concern for the police abuses and injustices that took place during and after these raids. Both men and women were routinely sexually abused by officers, and their word was often disregarded in courts of law. There was little legal recourse for those targeted by these raids (D'Emilio, 1998; Faderman, 1991).

A political consciousness began to form in the gay community at this time, and some key protest organizations were founded as people started to speak out publicly against these injustices. However, severe social stigmas were still attached to LGB persons, and no legal protections existed in any state to shield those living with same-sex partners from being fired from their jobs or even jailed for their private activities. Thus, those who dared to be "out" often faced severe repercussions. Even when people were beaten and killed for their sexual orientation, the justice system remained unsympathetic to those they considered "perverts" and "outcasts" (D'Emilio, 1998). In fact, not until after the turn of the present century would same-sex behavior even in private be decriminalized at the federal level.

THE 1960s AND BEYOND: GROWING VISIBILITY, BACKLASH, AND HIV/AIDS

Intolerance of LGB people began to soften in the latter half of the 20th century, as did other forms of prejudice and racism (see Chapter 3). One major milestone occurred in 1973 when the American Psychiatric Association removed homosexuality from its list of mental illnesses, where it had been for nearly a century (Bayer, 1987). This decision helped reduce the stigma attached to gays and lesbians, and removed one of the primary rationales for their exclusion and marginalization in the larger society.

Several pioneering sociological works, including Howard Becker's *Outsiders* (1963) and Erving Goffman's *Stigma* (1963), also helped reduce prejudice against gays and lesbians by presenting compelling arguments about the crucial role of social construction in deciding what is deviant and what is not. These works encouraged open conversations about various forms of human behavior and relationships previously considered taboo in the larger society.

Furthermore, the fact that sexual activity between adults was not always aimed at procreation was made more public by Supreme Court decisions such as *Griswold v. Connecticut* (1965), which made it legal for married couples to obtain contraception, and *Eisenstadt v. Baird* (1972), which made contraception available to unmarried persons (Dudley, 2006).

Developments such as these challenged the traditional societal consensus regarding gays and lesbians just as the civil rights movements began to raise cultural awareness about injustice against minorities. Several states began to decriminalize same-sex behavior in the 1970s (D'Emilio, 1998), and LGB people became more socially visible across a range of cultural and institutional spaces.

This increasing tolerance was hardly unanimous, however. A movement of political and religious conservatism often called the Religious Right rose to prominence and influence in the 1980s. Led by men such as Jerry Falwell, a Baptist preacher and the founder of Liberty University, and Pat Robertson, chair of the Christian Broadcasting Network, this movement targeted gay and lesbian behavior as one of many social ills to which it was morally opposed. There were also legal setbacks. In 1986, for example, the U.S. Supreme Court, in the case of *Bowers v. Hardwick*, upheld a Georgia state law that criminalized private, consensual same-sex behavior, a victory for those groups and

National Institutes of Health

Quilts memorialize victims of the AIDS epidemic.

a setback for gays and lesbians (Carpenter, 2012). Thus, it seemed the gains of the 1960s and 1970s threatened to be reversed, and echoes of the pariah and "pervert" stigmatization of the McCarthy era returned to prominence.

The most important development in the antigay backlash of the 1980s, on many levels, was the HIV/AIDS epidemic. The disease became associated in the public consciousness with gay men, despite the fact that many types of people carried and spread the virus, and transmitted it in many other ways besides through intimate relations.

The stark losses of the AIDS-related epidemic provoked concern in the hearts of not only LGB persons but others as well. This sympathetic concern was strengthened by the case of Ryan White, a young boy who had hemophilia and passed away after contracting HIV/AIDS through a blood transfusion, and by Elizabeth Taylor's publicly expressed support for victims of the disease, one of whom was her good friend and fellow actor Rock Hudson. These were just two of many voices that worked in the 1980s to raise national and global awareness about AIDS.

In the view of many, the social stigma associated with HIV/AIDS hampered the medical community's ability to develop public health solutions. In response, playwright Larry Kramer founded the organization ACT UP (AIDS Coalition to Unleash Power) in New York City in 1987 (U.S. Department of Health and Human Services, 2011). As the organization's name suggests, there was an urgency among both LGB persons and their allies to take to the streets to raise public awareness about the disease. Thus, the health crisis renewed the social stigma attached to gays and lesbians but also brought together those concerned about injustice against LGB persons.

COMING OUT

Increasing AIDS awareness, growing visibility of the LGB minority, and increasing tolerance in the larger community led many people, both famous and ordinary, to publicly reveal their sexual orientation during the last decades of the 20th century. Note that "**coming out**" refers only to nonheterosexuals: The term highlights both the privileged status of heterosexuality and the relative invisibility of sexual orientation as a social status and dimension of inequality. Just as whiteness is often assumed to be the unspoken norm, so, too, is heterosexuality in most cultures around the world. Essentially, the act of coming out transforms an invisible minority status into a visible one.

The first National March on Washington for Gay and Lesbian Rights was held on October 11, 1987. In commemoration of that date, October 11 was chosen to celebrate the first National Coming Out Day a year later. By 1990, Coming Out Day was recognized in all 50 states (Human Rights Campaign, 2013).

One of the most important causes addressed by the organizers of the national coming out campaign was civil rights protection for gays and lesbians. At that time, hardly any U.S. state or city included sexual orientation in its civil rights laws, making employment discrimination against LGB persons perfectly legal. The organizers thought that the courage required to "come out," and the risks incurred by those who did, would attract allies, make LGB people more visible, and build momentum for the expansion of civil rights law to include this "new" minority.

This strategy is supported by research—consistent with the contact hypothesis introduced in Chapter 3—that shows one of the strongest predictors of support for gay rights is a personal relationship with someone who is gay or lesbian (Hinrichs & Rosenberg, 2002). Although the LGB population is still a small minority, it is probable that many people are acquainted with someone who is LGB, even

Coming out refers to the act of a nonheterosexual person publicly disclosing his or her sexual identity.

The first national march on Washington for gay and lesbian rights, 1987.

though they may not be aware of it (Leff, 2011; Pincus, 2011; Sullivan, 2015). The logic of National Coming Out Day is to increase visibility and cause more people to recognize their connections to LGB people. The more widespread this recognition, the greater the support for civil rights protection.

RECENT DEVELOPMENTS

LGB visibility is much greater today than ever before in U.S. history, and because of the social movement activity we will outline in the next section, this group has experienced many political, legal, and cultural advances. Contemporary media portrayals contribute to LGB visibility and provide a broader range of representation than in the past. Portrayals are much more positive than in the past, too. Until the 1960s, few LGB characters were on television or in movies, but when they were, they were usually portrayed in a negative light (Steiner, Fejes, & Petrich, 1993). In 2016, broadcast network primetime series were expected to include 895 characters. Of those, 68 were LGB (plus three who were transgender)—43 (4.8%) as regular characters and 28 (3.1%) as recurring characters. Representation on primetime cable series included 142 LGBT regular or recurring characters. (Recall that T stands for transgender people and we include them here as the report addressed LGBT people as a group.) This is the highest number of LGBT characters to date and is fairly accurate in terms of the actual size of the LGB population of the United States. Of those characters, most (71% on networks, 72% on cable) were white, which, as you know by now, reflects overrepresentation. Due to these gains, more LGB persons feel comfortable coming out.

Research using a random sample of 1.6 million American adults estimates that just over 10 million identified as LGBT. That's 4.1% of the total U.S. population, up from 3.9% in 2015 (Gates, 2017). Thus, we might say that television representation is surprisingly accurate in terms of *proportional* representation. Yet, curiously, most Americans believe that there are many more gay and lesbian people than there actually are. In 2015, a Gallup poll asked Americans to estimate the size of the LGB population relative to the total U.S. population. In 2015, the mean size reported was 23% though one-third of respondents (33%) estimated the LGB population to be greater than 25%. These most recent findings are consistent with the 2002 and 2011 reports (Franke-Ruta, 2012; Newport, 2015). (Other surveys show that Americans also overestimate the proportion of the population that consists of African Americans and other people of color.) Some scholars suggest that this massive overestimation may be related to concerns about the LGB(andT) population.

Of course, media representation is different from acceptance, which varies markedly from region to region and between more rural and more metropolitan areas. This variation was demonstrated by an innovative research project conducted by Harvard economist Seth Stephens-Davidowitz (2013), based on a combination of Facebook, Google, and other data. The researcher looked at both rural and urban areas to see if gay men were "public" (e.g., stated their sexual orientation on their Facebook profiles) or "private" (e.g., searched the Internet for gay porn) and found that the key variable was residence in a "tolerant" state, or a state that supported gay marriage initiatives. Rhode Island was rated as the most tolerant (joined by several other northeastern and western states), and Mississippi (along with all other southern states except Florida) was the least tolerant. The findings suggest that many rural and southern Americans (and others) continue to remain in the closet due to fear of social stigma and other potential repercussions (Stephens-Davidowitz, 2013). At the same time, in some nations today, sex between two persons of the same sex is punishable by life in prison or even death (Crossley, Gourlay, & Spraggon, 2017).

A recent study of LGB life in rural America shows that members of the nonheterosexual minority deal with their surrounding communities in a variety of ways (Johnson, 2013). While some LGB persons—such as Evelyn and Hope, whose vignette opened this chapter—are fighting to have their families recognized legally, others are still struggling simply to live without fear of attack by fellow citizens. Everywhere, LGB activists and their allies continue to seek equal rights, both for themselves and for those who are unable to come out of the closet.

QUESTIONS FOR REFLECTION

1. Since same-sex relations have existed throughout human history, why was the term *homosexuality* coined only relatively recently?

2. What ideologies create societal resistance to homosexuality, and how have science and religion played a role? In what ways were these ideologies similar to and different from those that stigmatized people of color?

3. What factors converged to lessen social stigma against LGB persons over time, and where is such lessening most and least evident?

GAY LIBERATION MOVEMENTS

In this section, we review the various movements for gay liberation in the United States over the past century. There have been three distinct phases in these movements, and we use the Stonewall Rebellion of 1969—a direct and violent reaction to the police harassment of gay and lesbian bar patrons—as the benchmark to separate the first two. The third phase, which we date from the turn of the present century, encompasses many political achievements for gay rights both in the United States and worldwide.

PRE-STONEWALL: HOMOPHILE ORGANIZATIONS

We already mentioned the shift to an urban-industrial economy that, by the 1920s, created social spaces in which a distinct gay community could develop. In turn, these communities allowed for the growth of a **collective identity**, or a shared understanding of one's place in the social order, which is an important prerequisite for the formation of social movement organizations. With the rise of an urban gay culture, gays and lesbians became increasingly cognizant of the need to organize for social change. Knowing they were a small numerical minority, they understood that they would need to secure allies to reach their goals.

Spurred by the desire to challenge the McCarthy-era homosexual "witch hunt", the Mattachine Society first organized in 1951 in Los Angeles. This organization took its name from the masked mythological creatures of medieval times that were rumored to be homosexual. The Mattachine Society was founded by men who wanted to educate the public about gay men and convince society that they were just as deserving of the right to live and work without fear of harassment as were other Americans.

The Mattachine Society engaged with allies in the medical community, particularly sexuality researchers associated with Kinsey who were beginning to uncover the range of sexual desires present in the "normal" human psyche. Eventually, they would become known as part of the "homophile" movement. They engaged in public service to their community with the hopes of counteracting the caricature of them in the wider society that branded them as deviant and disposable (D'Emilio, 1998).

Although the Mattachine Society aspired to advocate for all, regardless of gender or race, its membership was mainly white men. Lesbians also began to organize for political and protest activity but responded to different social situations. For example, there was a social class divide between the elite educated women and the working-class lesbians who gathered in bars, often with one partner

being a "butch"—dressing in men's clothing and passing as a man—and the other a "femme." Middle- and upper-class lesbians of the day tended to look down on the lesbian working-class bar culture and instead sought to create an alternative gathering space for women similar to the social clubs where married women interacted and engaged in community service. Out of this desire, the Daughters of Bilitis formed in 1955 in San Francisco, just a few short years after the Mattachine Society (D'Emilio, 1998; Faderman, 1991).

The primary aim of both the Mattachine Society and the Daughters of Bilitis was assimilation into the wider society, and they strove to counteract the severe repression of the 1950s. Chapters of both organizations sprung up in several major cities across the country, connected by newsletters, but concerns for safety and retribution prevented the organizations from pursuing mass membership.

Then, the turbulent 1960s brought a change in tactics. Inspired by civil rights organizations such as the Student Nonviolent Coordinating Committee (SNCC) and Congress of Racial Equality (CORE), as well as feminist groups such as the National Organization for Women (NOW), new leadership challenged homophile organizations to be less "genteel" and more confrontational, more demanding of basic rights and respect.

This new direction eventually culminated in the Stonewall Rebellion, a spontaneous and violent reaction to a 1969 police raid on the Stonewall Inn, a bar in Greenwich Village, New York City. As we have noted, such raids were common in cities across the nation, but this time the gay community fought back. A crowd gathered and fought the police in the streets of Greenwich Village, and hostilities continued, sporadically, for several nights thereafter. The gay community had sent a message: It would no longer tolerate police harassment and mistreatment. The event has been compared to France's Bastille Day and the fall of the Berlin Wall, in terms of its significance for the gay rights movement (Carter, 2005; D'Emilio, 1998).

Perhaps most interesting about the Stonewall Rebellion is that those responsible represented a distinct shift from the socioeconomic profile of the homophile organizations that preceded it. The clientele at the Stonewall Inn, particularly those who fought back against the police, included mostly blacks, Latinos, and the working class.

The participants also did not fit the assimilationist profile that the homophile organizations strove to promote—educated, successful, and "just like heterosexuals" in every way but choice of partner. Rather, they were drag queens and other types that sought to accentuate their differences from the mainstream (Duberman, 1994). This is one of many reasons why the Stonewall Rebellion is considered a turning point for the movement.

Collective identity is the shared understanding of one's place in society.

The Stonewall Rebellion, 1969.

POST-STONEWALL: GAY LIBERATION MOVEMENT

The final three decades of the 20th century saw some progress toward inclusion and equal rights, but the movement was hardly linear. After Stonewall, the homophile organizations faded into the background, giving way to gay rights groups or coalitions. By the time an anniversary march honoring the Stonewall Rebellion took place in 1970 (eventually becoming an annual gay pride parade), two groups—the Gay Liberation Front and the Gay Activist Alliance—had formed. These groups often used direct-action tactics to confront politicians or institutions that refused to serve gay people (D'Emilio, 1998).

The 1970s saw the development of an array of major gay organizations—some cultural, others more political. The cultural organizations included gay/feminist bookstores, gay choruses, and gay or gay-friendly churches—specifically, the Metropolitan Community Church, United Church of Christ, and Unitarian Universalists. The latter two churches existed well before the 1970s but passed gay-inclusive resolutions and began to hire openly gay ministers. Periodical publications such as *The Empty Closet*, *The Advocate*, *The Lesbian Connection*, and *Journal of Homosexuality* all began circulation in the 1970s and are still in print today. Bisexual-focused organizations also appeared for the first time starting in this decade. The more community building that occurred, the more political organizing was possible (Eaklor, 2008).

Several political milestones were reached in the 1970s: an openly lesbian Massachusetts House representative, another on the Ann Arbor City Council, and an openly gay city supervisor in San Francisco named Harvey Milk, famously portrayed by Sean Penn in the 2008 film. The same year Milk was elected (1977), the White House held its first meeting with lesbian and gay leaders, and the Gay Rights National Lobby was founded in 1978 (Eaklor, 2008).

This greater visibility resulted in stronger alliances beyond the LGB community. For example, a group called Parents and Friends of Lesbians and Gays was started in New York City by the mother of a gay man and continues to have many chapters across the country—both urban and rural (Bernstein, 2008). Several municipalities and states began rescinding their antisodomy laws and adding sexual orientation to their antidiscrimination ordinances (Eaklor, 2008). The 1970s were the first decade of notable political and legal advancements in LGB equality.

If the 1970s were a decade of action, the 1980s were a time of reaction, mostly to the efforts, led by politically and religiously conservative elements, to resist the gay liberation movement. For example, ACT UP and National Coming Out Day were formed in resistance to the Supreme Court decision mentioned previously that upheld state antisodomy laws.

By the early 1990s, the momentum of the movement was reinvigorated. Embracing an identity outside of the mainstream but also committed to equal rights, groups such as Queer Nation and Lesbian Avengers formed, with an emphasis on lack of conformity with the status quo. These groups began to thrive, while at the same time, more politically centered organizations, such as the Human Rights Campaign, picked up the fight to become more involved with the political process. In 1992, the Human Rights Campaign endorsed its first presidential candidate, Democrat Bill Clinton (Eaklor, 2008).

During the Clinton era of the 1990s, the gay rights movement attracted many allies among heterosexuals. Just as the Civil Rights Movement enlisted support from white antiracists, the gay liberation movement also worked to gain heterosexual allies. From Clinton's campaign promise to end the ban on gays in the military (with Democratic Party support) to MTV's show *The Real World* featuring an openly gay cast member, the early 1990s clearly thrust LGB persons into the cultural and political mainstream. In the late 1990s, a variety of media events, including the coming out of Ellen DeGeneres in 1997, continued this pattern (Eaklor, 2008).

Allies are sometimes also activated in times of crisis, as with AIDS in the 1980s. In the 1990s, antigay hate crimes drew more media attention and outraged many people, regardless of their political and religious orientations. When gay (and HIV-positive) Wyoming college student Matthew Shepard was beaten to death in 1998, many allies—particularly among adolescents and college students—took note. Although the first gay–straight alliance had formed nearly a decade before, the number of youth gay–straight alliances (at both the university and high school levels) soared after Shepard's death (Miceli, 2005). Youth have been consistently more supportive of gay rights (Pew Research Center, 2013b), a pattern we also see with prejudice toward other types of minority groups (von Hippel, Silver, & Lynch, 2000). Yet youth are rarely in a position to shape public policy. Gay–straight alliances often faced resistance from parents, school administrators, and community members (Miceli, 2005).

While support for gay rights was gaining ground among the younger generation at the end of the 20th century, the baby-boom generation—which made up most of the political elite—was not as receptive. President Clinton's initial promises regarding civil rights for gays ended up in political compromises that were in some cases worse than before he took office. For example, Clinton had pledged to allow gays to serve openly in the military, but the compromise policy—"Don't Ask, Don't Tell"—that began in 1993 eventually resulted in more than 13,000 discharges. A disproportionate number of those discharged due to sexual orientation were also racial minorities and women (O'Keefe, 2010). Many in positions of power were not ready for significant policy changes that would remove discrimination from LGB persons' lives.

In the 1990s, it seemed that every step forward for LGB rights was countered by a step back. On one hand, the Hawaii Supreme Court ruled (in *Baehr v. Miike*, 1996) that it was unconstitutional to exclude same-sex couples from the right to marry, and a host of European countries (e.g., Denmark, Norway, Sweden, and the Netherlands) began to offer domestic partner benefits.

On the other hand, reactions to these advances resulted in President Clinton signing the Defense of Marriage Act (DOMA) in 1996 (Eaklor, 2008). This law disallowed any federal recognition of same-sex marriages whatsoever and also upheld states' rights to refuse to recognize same-sex marriages performed in other states, even though no state recognized same-sex marriage at the time (Hawaii voters had overturned the 1996 ruling by constitutional amendment by 1998). Also in 1996, the Employment Non-Discrimination Act failed to pass, by a narrow 49–50 vote in the U.S. Senate (Eaklor, 2008). This law would have banned discrimination based on sexual orientation or sexual identity.

Although the progress was spotty, by the close of the 20th century, the struggle for LGB equality was irrevocably on the national and global radar, particularly in the Western industrialized world. In the new millennium, the gay liberation movement would focus increasingly on mobilizing its allies, in both likely and unlikely places: from Log Cabin Republicans—a gay rights organization formed in a political party not typically supportive of the movement—to Coretta Scott King (Martin Luther King Jr.'s widow), who publicly encouraged civil rights activists to join the gay liberation movement. By the end of the century, the allies that had been collected would lay the groundwork for the successes to come in the next decades.

NEW MILLENNIUM: LGBT AND QUEER POLITICS

The new millennium is when the LGBT (lesbian, gay, bisexual, and transgender) movement began to reap the fruit of its labors from the prior decades. The youth who came of age in the 1990s, when mainstream pop culture opened significantly toward nonheterosexuals, had grown old enough to begin to exert some political influence, and the movement began to center its efforts on the state rather than federal level. Vermont became the first state to offer civil unions to same-sex couples in 2000, and Massachusetts became the first state to allow gay marriage in 2004, with New Hampshire, Vermont, Connecticut, Iowa, and Washington, D.C., following by the end of the decade (PBS, 2011). In the meantime, several nations that had already been granting civil unions and partnerships moved to full marriage equality: The Netherlands was the first (2001), followed by Belgium (2003), Spain and Canada (2005), South Africa (2006), Norway and Sweden (2009), and Portugal, Iceland, and Argentina (2010) (BBC News, 2013).

Marriage equality was not the only priority of the movement, however. Not every person in the LGBT community aspired to mimic heterosexual lifestyles, and many, in a variety of U.S. states and other nations, remained focused on very basic issues: the right not to be fired from their jobs or attacked, jailed, or even murdered because of their sexual orientation. The work of building a safe society, where the rights of LGBTs are truly protected across all institutions, continues—often at the local level and often with very small steps.

Victories for gay rights at the national level did begin to accrue, however. In 2003, for example, the U.S. Supreme Court, in the case of *Lawrence v. Texas*, overturned the 1986 ruling that upheld state antisodomy laws (Eaklor, 2008). Also, the election of President Barack Obama in 2008 set the stage to move beyond the Clinton presidency's compromises on gay rights.

For example, in a partial reversal of DOMA, Obama signed an act in 2009 that allowed same-sex partners of federal employees to receive some of the benefits routinely available to marital partners. In the same year, Obama signed the Matthew Shepard Act, which updated the 1969 federal hate crimes law to include gender expression, sexual identity, and disability. By the close of the decade, with the support of the Senate, Obama also repealed the Don't Ask, Don't Tell law that effectively excluded gays from the U.S. military (PBS, 2011). Upon his election for a second term, Obama also made history by being the first president to make mention of gay rights in an inaugural address, using "Selma, Seneca Falls, and Stonewall" to invoke black, women's, and gay liberation struggles, respectively (Walshe, 2013).

The single most important victory for the LGBT community occurred in 2015 when the Supreme Court (*Obergefell v. Hodges*) struck down various state laws that defined marriage in terms of heterosexuality and made same-sex marriage the law of the land in all 50 states. This ruling was a major step toward equality for the gay community and helped to limit the obstacles faced by couples such as Hope and Evelyn, whose vignette opened this chapter. The ruling also legalized adoptions and foster care by gay couples and secured equal rights for same sex couples in a variety of medical, legal, and other areas of family life. Even for LGB Americans who don't ever hope to marry, the ruling carried important symbolic weight, because it recognized LGB Americans as equal citizens, and as deserving of love and marriage, as straight ones.

Obergefell v. Hodges has garnered mixed response, including significant resistance. For example, many religious organizations, including affiliated media outlets such as the Christian Broadcasting Network, voiced disagreement with the ruling, either for moral reasons or because they interpreted the ruling as an infringement against religious freedom—or both. However, different denominations within the same faith tradition interpret holy texts (e.g., the Bible or Torah) and the Supreme Court's ruling in diverse ways. For example, in 1976, the Episcopal Church (USA) approved a resolution (1976-A069) proclaiming that "homosexual persons are children of God who have a full and equal claim with all other persons upon the love, acceptance, and pastoral concern and care of the Church" (The Episcopal Church, 1976). In July 2015, The Episcopal Church (USA) voted, with overwhelmingly support, to marry gay couples. It also approved a move to change gendered language in such services, changing "man and woman" to "the couple." However, these decisions brought sanction by the international Anglican Communion (Grundy, 2015). In August 2017, members of the Council on Biblical Manhood and Womanhood, drafted what they called the Nashville Statement (NS), named for the location where it was drafted. More than 150 evangelical Christian leaders signed the statement, which offered criticism and concern for what they saw as anti-Biblical shifts regarding sexuality and gender in 21st-century America. As such, it offered reaffirmation of its views. For example, the statement defined marriage as only for heterosexuals, "condemn[ed] infidelity," declared men and women of "equal worth" and noted that any gender differences were part of God's plan, and defined "transgenderism" and homosexuality as sinful (Showalter, 2017).

At the state and local levels, individuals and legislatures pushed back on the Supreme Court decision. For example, some states (e.g., Texas) passed resolutions that voiced opposition to the ruling and its attorney general suggested that state workers didn't have to grant marriage licenses to gay couples, saying, "this newly minted federal constitutional right to same-sex marriage can and should peaceably coexist with longstanding constitutional and statutory rights, including the rights to free exercise of religion and freedom of speech." Indeed, that sentiment has been widely expressed and city and state employees have refused to issue marriage licenses to gay and lesbian couples. Other states have simply stopped issuing marriage licenses or are considering it, shifting to having couples simply register their marriage (e.g., Alabama) (Gonzales, 2017). It is likely that this back and forth will continue between different groups, as has been the case for dominant–minority relations examined in prior chapters.

THE ROLE OF YOUTH AND QUEER LIBERATION

As with the black civil rights movement, the feminist movement, and other social movements, college students have often been the force propelling action in the gay liberation movement. While middle and high schools formed gay–straight alliances, LGBT and **queer** student groups organized at colleges and universities in the late 20th and early 21st century. The term *queer* is used in this context to represent an umbrella collection of people whose gender expression and/or sexual identity and practice do not fall in line with societal norms. While the "gay" rights movement typically brings to mind men attracted to men and/or women attracted to women, a "queer" movement is meant to bring to mind a wider range of possibilities. Indeed, organizing around the word *queer* can help supporters of "gay rights" come to see themselves as part of a broader, aggrieved minority group.

Barrie and Tony Drewitt-Barlow were the first gay couple in the United Kingdom to become fathers through surrogacy.

Queer refers to gender expressions and identities that do not conform to societal expectations.

Bisexual, transgender, and even some practicing heterosexual people may be more inclined to favor the "queer" label because they feel it is more inclusive of various forms of gender and/or sexual expression that fall outside the bounds of the traditional heterosexual norm. For example, a man who carries a purse, gets his nails done, dyes his hair, and wears earrings may proudly consider himself "queer" even though he identifies as a heterosexual and has always had women as sexual partners. A bisexual woman may consider herself queer and seek to distance herself from lesbians who appear to be trying to pass as straight in their everyday lives or to emphasize her commonality with other lesbians despite currently having a man for a partner. A female-to-male transgender person may still feel "queer" despite the fact that to the outside world, his choice of a woman partner may appear to make him a conforming heterosexual. The point is that the term *queer* can be used in many ways.

The practice of reclaiming words that were once used as derogatory slurs against them is a common practice of many minority groups, and LGBT people's use of the word *queer* falls in line with this pattern. As with other "reclaimed" slurs, not everyone in the minority group feels comfortable with embracing the term, as for some it may too strongly represent a painful history of oppression. Age, class, and education levels, among other experiences, are often related to a person's willingness to use the term *queer*. But even by using the acronym LGBT, as opposed to the "gay liberation" groups of a previous era, the newer movement indicated a historical transition.

And while youth are more supportive of gay rights than other groups, there is still much danger in being young and gay in a heteronormative society. According to the Centers for Disease Control (CDC) (2017), negative attitudes toward LGB persons increase risk of violence against LGB youth.

The widely publicized case of 18-year-old Rutgers student Tyler Clementi's suicide, after his roommate cyberbullied him about his sexual orientation, brought to light in 2010 a long-standing problem of antigay harassment among youth (Allen, 2010). The 2015 national Youth Risk Behavior Survey (YRBS) found that 34% of LGB youth experienced bullying at school, including 10% who were injured with a weapon on school property or experienced threats of violence. Compared with straight students, LGB students were 140% more likely to skip school due to fears about their safety.

Coming out is easier in some places than others, and some youth are kicked out of their homes when they come out to their parents, resulting in a disproportionate number of homeless youth being LGBT (Ray, 2006). Current estimates suggest that while LGBT youth make up just 5% to 10% of the youth population (under 18), they are 20% to 40%

Parents and Friends of Lesbians and Gays (PFLAG) participate in Capital Pride in Washington, D.C.

of the homeless youth population (Page, 2017). This, of course, exposes them to other hardships including sexual assault and depression. LGB youth are almost five times more likely (29%) to have attempted suicide compared with straight counterparts (6%) (YRBS, 2015). The rate is even higher if they are also nonwhite (Harrison-Quintana & Quach, 2013). Groups such as the National Gay and Lesbian Task Force, the Gay Lesbian Straight Education Network, and the It Gets Better Project continue to work to end chronic problems such as bullying, suicide, and homelessness among youth as the new millennium continues.

QUESTIONS FOR REFLECTION

4. What distinct connotations do the terms *homosexual*, *gay*, and *queer* suggest? What different goals would you predict for social movement organizations depending on which of the terms it uses (or used) to label itself?

5. Before reading this text, what was your impression of the gay rights movement and what it has accomplished? How would you revise your impression after reading this brief history?

6. In what ways have race, class, gender, and geographic location shaped the gay rights movement?

RECENT TRENDS AND ISSUES

Social change tends to come in spurts. While the biggest waves of political and legal victories for women and African Americans happened in earlier decades, most positive change for LGB persons, particularly in Western industrialized nations, has been more recent. Several public policy issues for gay men and lesbians hang in the balance today. Two particularly volatile areas are the legal recognition of same-sex families and the integration of LGB service members into the U.S. armed forces. Here we cover recent developments in both of these areas, as well as a third issue particularly relevant to the intersectionality lens we have carried throughout this text—how race and racism impact LGB communities and their struggle for civil rights.

SAME-SEX MARRIAGE

As our opening vignette about Hope and Evelyn demonstrates, marriage equality was a major issue for the American LGBT community. In 2013, 220,000 children in the United States were being raised by same-sex couples, down by 30,000 since 2011 (Gates, 2013; James, 2011). Hundreds of rights and privileges come to a couple upon marriage in the United States—including parental rights to any child born to or adopted by the other partner, federal tax benefits, immigration privileges, and spousal immunity (not having to testify against one's partner in court), just to name a few. These rights were unavailable to same-sex couples and this stark imbalance had motivated LGB activists to make marriage equality one of the movement's central goals.

Interestingly, the pathway that gay marriage has traveled resembles the road toward legalizing interracial marriage in the United States. Certain states were in the forefront of recognizing and affirming interracial marriage long before the U.S. Supreme Court struck down all state bans of interracial marriage in 1967 (*Loving v. Virginia*).

Couple marries in San Francisco City Hall within hours of the city being able to grant marriage licenses on June 28, 2013.

When the Supreme Court ruled that interracial marriage bans were unconstitutional, 17 states (mostly southern) still forbade it (Monifa, 2008). However, several states had already removed their interracial marriage bans—some immediately after the Civil War ended and others following the 1948 desegregation of the military and the end of World War II. When the Supreme Court ruled in favor of same-sex marriage, 18 states plus Washington, D.C., allowed gay marriage, and the vast majority (13) of those states changed their laws after 2010 (National Gay and Lesbian Task Force, 2014). Thus, changes were happening at a rapid-fire pace. Today, 10.2% of LGB(and T) adults are married to a same-sex spouse, up from 7.9% in 2015 (Jones, 2017).

The states that had approved gay marriage before 2015 were not just those in the Northeast or just the more urban states. For example, Iowa, Minnesota, and Utah were all on the list. While in the late 20th century, one might have had to venture to a major urban area to find gay acceptance, now in the second decade of the 21st century, the majority of the population seemed to be supportive. Gallup has been polling Americans since 1996 on their attitudes about gay marriage. Starting in 2011, at least 50% of respondents each year approved of gay marriage (Jones, 2013). In 2017, that number had risen to between 62% to 64% of Americans in support of same-sex marriage (McCarthy, 2017; Pew Research Center, 2017b).

Much of the opposition to marriage equality came from (and continues to come from) the religious right and political conservatives. However, it is important to note that many, especially younger, Republicans and religious Americans are supportive of marriage equality. Several prominent public figures known to be either religious or Republican (or both)—such as Marie Osmond, Colin Powell, Laura Bush, and Dick Cheney—have spoken out in favor of gay marriage, often because they have a family member who is gay or lesbian (Stolberg, 2013). Some Americans may confuse a legal marriage—through which tax, health insurance, and other benefits are secured—and a religious marriage, which is up to individual churches to grant or deny for their own reasons and not subject to interference by the state.

Several American churches were performing holy unions between same-sex couples long before the 2015 Supreme Court ruling. United Church of Christ, Unitarian Universalists, and Metropolitan Community Church all performed such marriages nationwide, and most Reform Jewish synagogues and several Lutheran churches (a denomination that allows autonomy of individual congregations) did so as well. The Methodist Church was split in vigorous debate over the matter (Zoll, 2014). Even after the Supreme Court granted civil marriage to same-sex couples, no church could be forced to perform such ceremonies, due to the separation of church and state. Yet sometimes there is confusion on this matter, causing concern for those who oppose marriage equality on moral or religious grounds.

SEXUAL ORIENTATION IN THE U.S. MILITARY

President Harry Truman desegregated the military via executive order in 1948 but only after many years of back-and-forth compromise, political pressure, and influence from the Civil Rights Movement (Moskos & Butler, 1997). Similar maneuvering preceded the eventual repeal in 2010 of the Don't Ask, Don't Tell (DADT) policy that barred nonheterosexuals from the military.

With two ongoing wars (in Afghanistan and Iraq) in the early 2000s, U.S. military forces were strained, and there was even talk of reinstituting a draft. It was becoming more difficult to justify the removal of able-bodied service members, despite the concern over whether having openly gay members would fracture the cohesion of units. Indeed, similar concerns were raised when racial integration of the military was proposed, and in the 1940s, Gallup polls showed that two-thirds of the American public was against such a change (Herek, Jobe, & Carney, 1996).

As more states began to allow same-sex marriage, couples with one partner in the military began seeking the same benefits as heterosexual couples. Moreover, several of the nations allied with the United States—including Great Britain, Canada, Australia, Israel, and the Netherlands—had integrated their military forces by 2010. These countries even discovered unanticipated benefits—what sociologists refer to as positive latent consequences—of this policy change. For example, Great Britain reported that the amount of unfilled positions in its military was cut in half, and retention rates improved because the gay members were less likely to leave the service to start families or have children (Shaughnessy, 2010). Although President Obama could have simply signed an executive order as Truman did in 1948, the bill to repeal DADT went through Congress, getting both Senate and House approval in late 2010, and was signed into law by Obama in 2011 (Bumiller, 2011; Foley, 2010).

One of the advantages of a relatively authoritarian organization such as the military, with a clear chain of command, is that policies such as desegregation can take hold relatively quickly and without extensive protest. While both pro and con voices from within the military spoke out when the policy was being debated, all military leaders made clear that whatever became the law of the land, it would be their duty to enforce it. Although the Pentagon could not extend federal benefits to partners and families of gay service members until the U.S. Supreme Court repealed DOMA in 2013 (with the *U.S. v. Windsor* ruling), the repeal of DADT brought immediate change to the culture of the U.S. military, and by the anniversary of the repeal, there was little contention to report (Tungol, 2012).

The major areas of continued legal battles will be the overturning of dishonorable discharges issued under the DADT years (1993–2011) and the acquisition of veterans' benefits for families/partners of those discharged. A group called OutServe–SLDN (Servicemembers Legal Defense Network) provides legal assistance for such persons, as various cases/bills attempting to remove barriers to these rights continue to move through both the courts and Congress (Reilly, 2013; Terkel, 2011). It remains to be seen whether a glass ceiling for LGBT service members will persist in the highest ranks of the military, as it has done for other minorities (Smith, 2010). As we have seen, there is a difference between legal desegregation and the cultural and structural shifts to full integration at all levels of any organization.

As discussed in Chapter 11, the advances represented by the repeal of DADT may have been comprised in the summer of 2017 by the announcement of President Trump that transgender people would no longer be permitted in the U.S. military. The policy change was announced by Twitter and was apparently not coordinated with the Pentagon. The announcement provoked considerable negative reactions from virtually the full spectrum of political and religious opinion and some observers believe that it is destined for implementation (Miller, 2017). However, the ban has been blocked by at least two federal judges and its fate may be in question (Phillips, 2017).

RACE, RACISM, AND SEXUAL ORIENTATION

When California voters repealed same-sex marriage via a ballot initiative in 2008, the allegation was made that the record turnout of African American voters (due to Obama's presidential candidacy) was in part responsible for this antigay legal setback. Immediately after the vote, LGB activists and their allies gathered to protest the new law (Proposition 8), and black lesbian and gay protesters reported being called racial epithets during the march (Bates, 2008). This incident illustrates a microcosm of a larger and ongoing tension between African American and gay rights groups, despite the fact that both movements share much in common. Not all African Americans see gay liberation as connected with their own struggles against racism, and, conversely, some elements of the gay liberation movement have not been inclusive of racial minorities.

Some conservative religious African Americans have been outspoken about their disagreement with the parallels often drawn between equal rights for people of color and equal rights for LGB people; they contend that being black is not analogous to being gay. When President Obama

Kelly Huston/Flickr

A protest against Proposition 8 in California.

changed his position to support same-sex marriage, a group of black pastors organized in protest (Merica, 2012). Due in part to media coverage of such events, public perception often holds that African Americans are just as, or even more, homophobic than whites. Yet, along with the majority of Americans, blacks have been steadily evolving in their views on this issue. In 2007, just over one fourth (26%) of African Americans supported gay marriage. By 2017, it had nearly doubled to 51% (Pew Research Center, 2017b).

Many contend that framing African Americans as largely antigay is an unfair characterization of a diverse racial community. As early as 1989, black feminist writer bell hooks pointed out that there are certain forms of exaggerated expression among black communities—such as The Dozens, a game in which the participants exchange playful zingers against "your momma," among many other potential targets—that are meant to be taken in fun and not intended with the vitriol that a literal reading of them might suggest. Just as she argued that the "gangsta rap" of that era was no more misogynistic than the "high-culture" films being produced by whites, hooks also maintained that black public talk about gays was doing less harm than the antigay public policies put forth by the predominantly white political institution. And she also pointed out that, in practice, black communities were hardly ignorant of the vital presence of LGB members in their own local neighborhoods, whether or not they were always fully understood (hooks, 1999).

Studies have confirmed the complexity of African American views about homosexuality. In his review of several surveys and polling results over the late 20th and early 21st century, Gregory Lewis (2003) found a consistent trend: Controlling for education and religion, African Americans were no more disapproving of homosexuality than were whites. Regardless of race, religiosity tends to decrease approval and education tends to increase approval of homosexuality. To the extent that African Americans are less educated and more religious than whites as a whole,

their tendency to disapprove of homosexuality can trend slightly higher. Interestingly, though, African Americans were more likely than whites to agree that LGB persons deserved legal protection from employment discrimination, regardless of whether or not they considered homosexuality a sin. In other words, in theory, blacks might disagree slightly more with homosexuality, but in legal and political practice, they are more likely than whites to support public-policy measures for LGB rights (Lewis, 2003).

Indeed, virtually all well-known African American civil rights activists have spoken out in support of the gay liberation movement. Coretta Scott King, late widow of Martin Luther King Jr., spoke out in favor of same-sex marriage as early as 1998 (PBS, 2011). The NAACP in 2012 also issued a public statement supporting Obama's position on same-sex marriage, with Reverend Al Sharpton and other clergy also expressing agreement. And U.S. Attorney General Eric Holder has labeled the current movement for LGB rights as the next phase of the Civil Rights Movement (Apuzzo, 2014). This framing extends the legal struggles for civil rights beyond who marries whom to encompass the equality of all persons before the law, in terms of employment, fair housing, and access to medical care and survivor benefits for one's dependents.

Yet, just as women of color resented racism in the feminist movement, so, too, have black gay and lesbian activists found that the gay liberation movement has not always included them, or understood the unique experiences of their communities. Indeed, some African American LGB people have found that the gay rights movement has "used" them for political support when necessary, yet not reciprocated when it was time to work on the concerns of people of color (Bates, 2008; Warren, 2011). Some LGB people of color feel more comfortable in co-ethnic communities, despite the stigma they may face there due to their sexual orientation, because they have been so badly hurt by racism in the LGB movement (Boykin, 2006).

Philadelphia City Council and Tierney

The eight-color flag designed by the Philadelphia City Hall includes a black and brown stripe to honor people of color.

Because both groups face prejudice and discrimination, some may have elevated expectations of LGB people, thinking they should be more open-minded than others regarding racism. The fact that interracial couples are actually more common in the gay community than in society at large only adds to this expectation (Jayson, 2012). However, research shows that racism can also be present even within close interracial relationships (Childs, 2005; Korgen, 2002; O'Brien & Korgen, 2007). Partners of color may feel "exoticized" and objectified in ways that are dehumanizing. And white partners may see their partner of color as an "exception" (e.g., "You're not like the rest of them") and still hold onto racial prejudices about the rest of their partner's group.

On a macro level, LGB persons of color—not unlike women of color in the feminist movement—can find their unique concerns overshadowed by a white-centered public policy agenda. To counteract this marginalization within the gay liberation movement, several national-level groups—such as the National Black Justice Coalition, founded in 2003 (Keith Boykin, author of the first Narrative Portrait in this chapter, was co-founder of this group), and Gay Men of African Descent, founded in 1986—exist in the United States. Although same-sex marriage may be the public policy campaign getting the most media attention, communities of color have for centuries found creative ways of family formation when the state would not recognize their relationships—such as "jumping the broom" as an indigenous way of recognizing black family ties during slavery. As such, when one visits the websites of LGBT organizations of color, one tends to find less of a focus on same-sex marriage and more of a focus on issues of physical health and safety, such as HIV/AIDS outreach and antibullying and suicide-prevention programs. Far from seeing an either/or question of "racial equality" versus "gay equality," LGBT persons of color in such organizations stress the importance of recognizing the interconnectedness of both types of minority statuses. However, this remains an ongoing struggle for those who refuse to recognize the relationship between the two, whether in blatant or more subtle ways.

QUESTIONS FOR REFLECTION

7. Which of the three issues discussed in this section (Same-Sex Marriage; Sexual Orientation in the U.S. Military; or Race, Racism, and Sexual Orientation) most directly impacts you—through your family and/or your local community? If you became a policymaker, which would you feel was the most urgent to address and why?

8. Do you feel that marriage equality—so often in the news—is the most important issue facing LGB people today? Why or why not? If not, which issue (including those not covered in this section) would you say warrants the most pressing attention in terms of LGB inequality?

9. What role has religion played in the these issues, as well as in the inequalities discussed in other chapters of this text? How has religion fueled continued discrimination? How has it supported movements toward equality?

HOMOPHOBIA AND HETEROSEXISM

As we have seen in previous chapters, prejudice and discrimination exist in many different forms, and the prejudice and discrimination directed at LGB persons is likewise multifaceted.

The term **homophobia** refers to the more attitudinal dimension: It literally means hatred or fear of gays and lesbians. Homophobia can be blatant and overt, but, like other forms of prejudice we have discussed, it can also be subtle and indirect.

Sometimes homophobia manifests itself in the fear of being mistaken as gay or lesbian. Take the case of Charles Butler, in prison for the hate crime of killing Billy Jack Gaither, a gay man. Butler claims that he likes gay people and has even hung out with them. But when Gaither allegedly propositioned Butler and his friend Steven Eric Mullins, the two felt that Gaither had crossed a line, insulted their heterosexual identity, and deserved to be beaten for it. One might expect perpetrators of antigay hate crimes to be filled with feelings of hate and rejection for all gay people, yet this case illustrates a more expansive definition of homophobia. Sociologist Michael S. Kimmel describes this as "the fear that people might get the wrong idea about you" (Malis, 2000).

Some forms of homophobia spring from the inability to deal with one's secret desires and feelings of attraction toward members of the same sex, similar to the inability of highly authoritarian people to deal with their hostility toward their parents (see Chapter 3). People who feel uncomfortable with the idea that others of their sex may be romantically attracted to them may be homophobic and in denial of their own feelings.

Heterosexuality is the dominant ideology in U.S. society, and it can affect even LGB people, who are, after all, socialized into the same culture as are people with a heterosexual orientation. This is called **internalized homophobia**, and it occurs when persons who are attracted to

---

Homophobia is prejudice directed at LGB persons.

Internalized homophobia refers to the repulsion some people feel in response to their own feelings of attraction to other members of their sex.

---

members of the same sex are repulsed in various ways by their own attraction, consciously or subconsciously. In the most extreme cases, internalized homophobia may cause people with an LGB sexual orientation to carry out anti-gay hate crimes, but these feelings can also manifest themselves in more subtle ways, such as not wanting to be seen around other gay people or referring to oneself as a "very straight-acting gay," so as not to be associated with other LGB persons.

These feelings of rejection and even loathing for one's own group can be found in other groups as well, including women who think that men are inherently smarter or better equipped to be leaders and people of color who feel that whiteness is more desirable or attractive (see "Gender and Physical Acculturation: The Anglo Ideal" in Chapter 9). Minorities commonly experience feelings of rejection for their own group because they, too, are exposed to the dominant ideology, which marginalizes and denigrates their own experiences.

Research demonstrates that men are more likely to be homophobic than women (Herek, 1988). Additionally, homophobia tends to increase with age and decrease with education (Lewis, 2003). This suggests that homophobia is learned, like many (possibly all) other forms of prejudice, and can be unlearned, perhaps through education or more frequent equal-status contact situations.

In Chapter 1, we distinguished between the individual (micro) and group or societal (macro) levels of analysis (see Table 1.1). We also said that we would use *prejudice* to refer to individual thoughts and feelings and *ideological racism* to refer to similar phenomena at the macro level of analysis.

In this chapter, we can make an analogous distinction. Homophobia is a form of prejudice and refers to an individual's thoughts and feelings. At the group and societal level of analysis, we will use the term **cultural heterosexism** to refer to the ideology that upholds heterosexuality as the norm and confers societal privilege on heterosexual relationships.

Cultural heterosexism is maintained, in part, by the ways we socialize youngsters to expect heterosexuality in themselves as well as those around them. Adrienne Rich (1980) has referred to this practice as *compulsory heterosexuality*. We socialize young girls to look forward to the day when they will marry their Prince Charming, not necessarily due to homophobia but through an unquestioned adherence to custom. However, this creates a climate in which girls and women who may not be attracted to Prince Charming are made to feel out of place—or may not even realize they are attracted to other women, because they are socialized not to recognize that desire in themselves.

Cultural heterosexism is also encouraged in adults. It is present in water-cooler conversations when coworkers ask each other if they had any dates (implicitly meaning dates with a member of the "opposite" gender) over the weekend. Such conversations are a way of connecting with others, but they have the latent (and probably unintended) consequence of marginalizing individuals who may want to share the news about their same-sex date but are reluctant to do so in an environment where their existence is inadvertently written off or discounted.

When we describe a girl baby as "flirting" when she is affectionate with a boy or man, we are also practicing cultural heterosexism. Teachers who ask their students about their "mom and dad" are another good example (though this practice also excludes a host of other possible family forms, not just those headed by same-sex parents). Cultural heterosexism is present in myriad well-intentioned conversations that inadvertently exclude LGB persons and their experiences.

In Chapter 1, we also identified another dimension of analysis and differentiated "doing" from thinking and feeling. Discrimination refers to the unequal treatment of others by individuals, and at the group or societal level of analysis, institutional discrimination refers to patterns of unequal treatment built into the everyday operations of society. We have seen many examples of institutional discrimination, and, when applied to LGB people, we can also use the term **structural heterosexism**, which refers to ways heterosexual people, relationships, and families receive unequal material and institutional privileges.

To illustrate, the U.S. General Accounting Office concluded that DOMA (the Defense of Marriage Act of 1996) denied more than 1,000 rights, privileges, and benefits to same-sex couples (Bedrick, 1997), including access to Social Security benefits, advantageous tax deductions, and less costly medical insurance plans. Also, as of 2016, only 20 states and the District of Columbia ban discrimination based on sexual orientation and gender identity in employment and housing (ACLU, 2017). Over the years, organizations and companies such as Cracker Barrel and the Boy Scouts of America have made national news for their exclusionary hiring policies, but they are not alone (Chatel, 2013). These patterns of institutional discrimination or heterosexism result in a variety of privileges for heterosexuals. These privileges similar to the those that other dominant group members have (e.g., men, whites).

Cultural heterosexism refers to the ideologies that uphold heterosexuality as normative.

Structural heterosexism refers to the ways heterosexual relationships are allocated more resources, opportunities, and privileges.

Several actual events are listed below. In the space provided, classify each as an example of homophobia, cultural heterosexism, or structural heterosexism, and briefly explain your reasoning. Some incidents may be ambiguous and include elements of more than one concept.

	INCIDENT	CONCEPT	EXPLANATION
1.	A middle school bully uses antigay slurs to taunt another boy on the school bus.		
2.	Making conversation at the sandbox in the local playground, a neighborhood parent asks your child where her "mom and dad" live.		
3.	You receive an offer for free tickets to a local amusement park. The only catch is that you must take a tour of a timeshare development with your spouse.		
4.	The textbook that lists the spouses of all American astronauts, does not include Sally Ride's (woman) partner of 27 years.		
5.	A man's coworker tells him about a place where lots of beautiful women hang out after work: "You'll love it," the coworker says.		
6.	A father does not feel comfortable that one of his 16-year-old son's best friends is gay, and he discourages his son from inviting this friend to his birthday party.		
7.	The local youth baseball league does not allow gay or lesbian coaches.		

NOTE: Your instructor may ask you to complete this assignment as a group discussion.

TURN THE PAGE TO FIND OUR ANSWERS

QUESTIONS FOR REFLECTION

10. Can you identify examples of homophobia, cultural heterosexism, and structural heterosexism from your own experiences or from something you have seen in the news media, in movies, or on television?

11. Which is the most serious problem for LGB individuals: homophobia, cultural heterosexism, or structural heterosexism? Why? Could any one of these exist in the absence of the other two? How?

ASSIMILATION AND PLURALISM

In this section, we use many of the concepts from previous chapters to assess the situation of the LGB minority group. As usual, the discussion is organized around the concepts of acculturation and integration.

ACCULTURATION

In this chapter, as in Chapter 11, we change our usual approach to acculturation. Usually, we have discussed the ways minority groups learn the culture of the dominant group. Here, we reverse directions and examine the increasing inclusion of LGB people in the dominant culture.

The meaningful inclusion of LGB persons into mainstream culture has been quite recent. Historically, mass media either ignored the group or treated it as "comic relief." For example, sitcoms sometimes featured men cross-dressing or using a gay "cover" but only to get closer to women and only for laughs. It was not until the past several decades that mainstream TV shows began to portray gays and lesbians as family members or as people with love interests. At about the same time, talk shows such as *Oprah* and *Donahue* began to include lesbian and gay guests as panelists (Eaklor, 2008).

By the end of the 1990s, the term *culture wars*—popularized by presidential candidate Patrick Buchanan in a 1992 Republican National Convention speech—became

	INCIDENT	CONCEPT	EXPLANATION
1.	A middle school bully use antigay slurs to taunt another boy on the school bus.	Homophobia	This is both an individual action and an expression of negative feelings.
2.	Making conversation at the sandbox in the local playground, a neighborhood parent asks your child where her "mom and dad" live.	Cultural heterosexism	The comment is based on the assumption that everyone has heterosexual parents. It suggests that "opposite-sex" couples are "normal."
3.	You receive an offer for free tickets to a local amusement park. The only catch is that you must take a tour of a timeshare development with your spouse.	Structural heterosexism	Not all gay couples can receive this benefit (the free tickets), especially in states where gay couples have been denied the right to marry or whose marriages are not accepted as legitimate, in spite of the recent Supreme Court ruling.
4.	The textbook that lists the spouses of all American astronauts does not include Sally Ride's woman partner of 27 years.	Cultural heterosexism	The omission illustrates the marginalization of same-sex relationships.
5.	A man's coworker tells him about a place where lots of beautiful women hang out after work: "You'll love it," the coworker says.	Cultural heterosexism	The coworker is making assumptions about sexual orientation.
6.	A father does not feel comfortable that one of his 16-year-old son's best friends is gay, and he discourages his son from inviting this friend to his birthday party.	Homophobia	Like #1, this is both an individual action and an expression of negative feelings.
7.	The local youth baseball league does not allow gay or lesbian coaches.	Structural heterosexism	A benefit (the opportunity to coach) is being denied to lesbians and gays.

widely used to characterize the struggle between increasingly mainstream LGB visibility and those who opposed it. Many well-known public figures were daring to "come out" during the decade—from Candace Gingrich (U.S. House Speaker Newt Gingrich's daughter) to popular musicians such as k.d. lang and Melissa Etheridge and actors such as Nathan Lane and Ellen DeGeneres (Eaklor, 2008; Handy, 1997).

This increasing visibility, including the publication of children's books such as *Heather Has Two Mommies* and *Daddy's Roommate*, prompted a conservative backlash. Sponsors cancelled their support of certain TV shows, and protests were held at public libraries to express disapproval of gay-friendly material and content (The Associated Press, 1998; Taffet, 2013). Yet the groundswell could not be quieted, and Americans of all ages and classes were increasingly exposed to LGB people in a variety of cultural settings.

Perhaps one of the most striking indicators of the vast cultural shift between the 1990s and the present is the difference in the pattern of protesting today. In the 1990s, companies such as Wendy's and JCPenney pulled their advertisements from the Ellen DeGeneres show when she came out. In 2014, in contrast, companies have publically disassociated themselves from organizations that could be seen as antigay. For example, the Disney Corporation pulled its funding from the Boy Scouts of America because of its discrimination against gay troop leaders (Frizell, 2014). Other major companies such as AT&T spoke out about Russia's antigay laws both before and during the Sochi Winter Olympics (Elliott, 2014). Today, it is clear that many corporations perceive it as to their benefit to position themselves as being for gay equality.

Indicators of progress toward LGB cultural assimilation can also be found in an institutional arena especially well-known for homophobia—sports. Previously, most news stories about gay athletes concerned their coming out after retirement. In recent years, in contrast, the focus has been on highly placed athletes coming out while they are still active.

NBA player Jason Collins announced his sexual orientation in *Sports Illustrated* in 2013, and Michael Sam, a college football player and NFL draft prospect, made his sexual orientation public in 2014, prompting an avalanche of mainstream media attention (Branch, 2014). In anticipation of more such announcements in the future, all four of the major professional sports leagues—NBA, NFL, MLB, and NHL—have included sexual orientation in their nondiscrimination policies and have instituted various policies to foster inclusive cultures in their organizations (Klein & Battista, 2013). This inclusion of and support for gay athletes may increase the acceptance of LGB people in the society as a whole, much as African American athletes such as Jesse Owens, Jackie Robinson, and Arthur Ashe assisted in the further integration of their group.

While the media and sports have a tremendous impact on culture, the lives of everyday people—not just superstars—should also be considered. As we have noted earlier, in the past decade alone, American's attitudes have shifted considerably toward support of gay marriage, with youth becoming a driving force in this change. Other surveys have shown increasingly favorable views of LGB Americans and decreases in the percentage of adults who say they would be "very upset" if their children came out to them as gay or lesbian (Drake, 2013), for example, from 89% in 1985 to much less than half that (39%) in 2015 (Gao, 2015).

The pace of cultural change regarding acceptance of the LGBT minority in recent years is clearly unprecedented; however, we must be careful not to mistake a rapid increase with full acceptance. When a sample of LGBT Americans were asked if they felt there was "a lot" of acceptance in society for them, only 19% said yes, and many reported being made to feel unwelcome in various social settings, including places of employment and churches (Drake, 2013).

Also, even though they are encountering a more tolerant society than did prior generations, LGBT youth still face hostile cultural climates in many areas of the United States, as evidenced by their alarmingly high rates of suicide attempts. In a 2012 survey of more than 10,000 youth ages 13 to 17 of all sexual orientations, the LGBT respondents were twice as likely to report some kind of physical bullying and more than 90% of all the youth surveyed said they hear some kind of negative message at school about being gay. Further, nearly half (42%) of all the youth surveyed felt that their particular community was not accepting of gay people (Human Rights Campaign, 2012).

LGB persons live in grave danger of physical attacks and harassment in many parts of the world, including the United States, and the level of cultural heterosexism remains high. Yet the increasing pace of change in the United States has at least given some hope to LGBT youth: Although only 49% of the youth surveyed felt that they could lead a happy life in their current hometown, 83% said they believe they will be happy "eventually" (Human Rights Campaign 2013).

Taken together, these shifts indicate increasing incorporation of LGB minorities into the dominant society. As you will learn in the next section, major issues of inequality remain.

SECONDARY STRUCTURAL ASSIMILATION

In this section, we will assess the status of the LGB minority following our usual format. However, some problems limit the analysis. First, one of our primary sources of information is not available, because the U.S. Census Bureau does not collect information on sexual orientation or sexual identity. It does, however, collect information on same-gender households, as you will see below. Second, an unknown percentage of LGB people are "in the closet," at least to some degree. Thus, it is difficult to ascertain even the most basic information (the size of the group, for example) with certainty.

However, recent studies provide some insight into the extent of secondary structural assimilation for the LGB minority. The studies are also limited in some ways. For example, they use different measures and definitions in their assessment of the LGB community, which makes comparisons difficult. Some are only based on people living together as same-sex couples, not on the entire group (which would include gay single people). Nonetheless, we can draw some conclusions regarding some dimensions of structural integration for the LGB minority group.

Size of Population, Racial and Ethnic Composition, and Residential Patterns. A recent survey estimates the LGBT group at 4.3% of the adult U.S. population. Between 2012 and 2016, the population grew from 8.3 million to almost 10.1 million (Gates, 2017). These results are based on large representative samples of more than 1.6 million people taken over several years. Researchers asked, "Do you personally identify as gay, lesbian, bisexual, or transgender?" While this seems to be a reasonable estimate of group size, it is based on sexual identity, not sexual orientation or sexual behavior. As with any kind of research a different methodology or types of questions might yield somewhat different estimates. A different study, based on household data collected by the Census Bureau, shows that the number of same-sex–couple households increased by 80% between 2000 and 2010, double the rate of growth of opposite-sex married-couple households (Gates, 2012, p. 1). It seems likely that a large part of this very rapid rate of apparent growth reflects greater openness about claiming an LGB identity, as opposed to an actual increase in group size.

Every racial and ethnic group is represented among LGB Americans, in roughly the same proportions as in the general population. We presented information about the racial/ethnic mix of the U.S. population in Figure 1.1, and a recent survey shows that the LGBT population has a similar composition: About two thirds are white, 15% Latino, and 12% African American (Pew Research Center, 2013d, p. 4). As we mentioned previously, a much higher percentage

COMPARATIVE FOCUS

Attitudes Toward LGBT people in Global Perspective

Attitudes about LGBT people vary widely across the globe. Some nations recognize same-sex marriages and have instituted strong civil rights protections for LGBT citizens. In other nations, homosexuality is criminalized and demonized, punishable by harsh prison terms or even death.

The map in Figure 12.2 outlines the diversity in levels of acceptance of nonheterosexuals. It is based on representative samples from 39 nations across the globe. Respondents were asked, "Should society accept homosexuality?"

In the lighter green nations, more than 55% of respondents replied "yes" to the question, with the highest levels of support in Spain (88%) and Germany (87%). Acceptance was generally highest in Western Europe, North America, and Australia. Most Central and South American nations also frequently scored above the 55% mark.

The nations colored in darker green, on the other hand, scored lower than 45% on the question and were strongly opposed to homosexuality. The lowest levels of acceptance were in Asia, the Middle East, and, especially, Africa. The nations of Pakistan (2% "yes"), Senegal (3% "yes"), and Nigeria (1% "yes") were virtually unanimous in their rejection of homosexuality.

Acceptance of homosexuality has increased in recent years in many nations: Levels of acceptance in both the United States and Canada increased about 10% between 2007 and 2013. Other nations have remained consistently opposed. There is no worldwide trend toward greater acceptance.

Russia (16% "yes"), in particular, has repeatedly made world headlines in recent years with its campaign to ban "homosexual propaganda," especially in the run-up to the 2014 Olympics in Sochi. The law goes far beyond what we might think of as propaganda (e.g., printed materials) to prohibit anyone from "creating a distorted image of the social equivalence of traditional and nontraditional sexual relationships." Human rights activists claimed the law gave homophobic police the ability to detain, arrest, and punish LGB people and in 2017, a European court ruled it illegal (Chan, 2017). Chechnya (a federal republic within Russia), in particular, has recently become gravely concerning with reports of gay men being "rounded up," tortured, and killed (Kramer, 2017).

Great resistance to gays and lesbians, also, has been common in the Muslim world and in Africa. In 2014, for example, Nigeria enacted a law that prescribed a 10-year prison term for public displays of same-sex relationships. In the more Muslim areas of northern Nigeria, the penalty for homosexuality is death by public stoning (Nossiter, 2014). Also in 2014, Uganda (4% "yes") passed a law that punishes homosexuality with a life sentence and provides jail terms

FIGURE 12.2 View on Homosexuality Worldwide

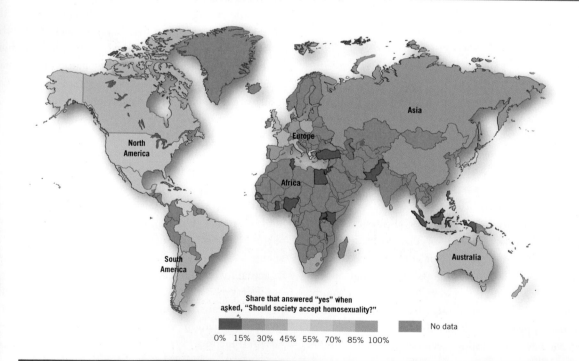

SOURCE: Fisher (2013a).

for groups convicted of "promoting" homosexuality (McConnell, 2014).

What accounts for this mixed pattern of support and rejection? Not surprisingly, religiosity might explain much of the variance: The nations most accepting of homosexuality tend to be more secular, and those most opposed tend to be highly religious. There is a pervasive pattern of greater acceptance among the young, which might suggest a higher level of tolerance in the future. However, in predominantly Muslim nations and African nations, overwhelming majorities of *all* age groups agree that homosexuality should be rejected (Pew Research Center, 2013a, pp. 6–7).

Questions to Consider

1. What other variables besides religiosity might help account for the differences in acceptance of homosexuality? Which of the theories of intolerance and prejudice that we have reviewed might be useful?

2. What predictions can you make about future levels of tolerance for gays and lesbians around the globe? Does the future for greater acceptance appear bright or dim? Why?

---

of same-sex couples (20.6%) than heterosexual couples (9.5%) are interracial or interethnic (Gates, 2012, pp. 2–5).

LGBT persons live in every corner of the United States, from the smallest village to the largest metropolis. Figure 12.3 shows that the percentage of each state's population that identifies as LGBT ranges from a low of 1.7% in North Dakota to highs of 5.1% in Hawaii and 10% in Washington, D.C. The variation from state to state is not large, but there is a pattern in these figures. With the exception of South Dakota, every state in which the percentage of LGBT persons exceeds 4% has laws that prohibit discrimination based on sexual orientation (Gates & Newport, 2013).

Education. LGBT Americans have higher levels of educational attainment than the general population, as displayed in Figure 12.4. They are less likely to be at the lower level of education and, particularly for gay men, more likely to have a college degree or more.

Figure 12.4 refers to all LGBTs. A different study used census data to compare the educational profiles of heterosexual couples with same-sex couples (defined as households in

FIGURE 12.3 Geographic Distribution of the LGBT Population, 2012

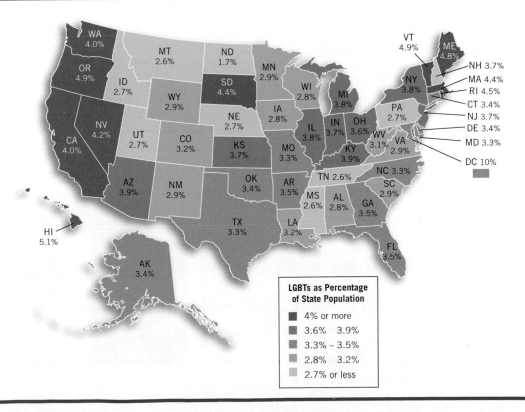

SOURCE: Gates and Newport (2013).

FIGURE 12.4 Educational Attainment for the General Population and LGBT Americans, 2012

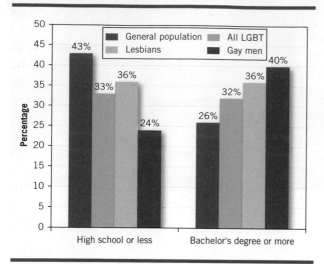

SOURCE: Pew Research Center (2013d, p. 4).

which the same-gender residents describe each other as husband or wife or domestic partner) (Kastanis & Wilson, 2012). The researchers found that same-sex couples were more likely to have a college degree—consistent with Figure 12.4—but that this pattern varied markedly by race or ethnic group. Half the white same-sex couples had completed college compared with about a third of the white heterosexual couples. As we saw in Chapter 9, Asian American couples—both same sex and heterosexual—were the most educated group (p. 3). Also consistent with earlier chapters, the levels of education for African Americans, Native Americans, and Hispanic Americans were markedly lower, although the same-sex couples in each group were more educated than the opposite-sex couples.

Political Power. As such a small minority, LGB Americans have relatively little influence on the political institution. As we have seen, however, political power is a function of group organization as well as sheer numbers, and LGB groups have been able to impact local and city elections, especially in the larger metropolitan areas.

In terms of ideology and party preference, LGBT Americans tend to be liberal and Democrat. However, these preferences are not unanimous, and the community is diverse and split on many issues. A 2012 national survey showed that 44% of LGBT Americans identified themselves as Democrats, but 43% were political independents and 13% identified with the Republican Party. In 2016, those numbers had changed fairly dramatically with 82% of LGB registered voters either identifying with the Democratic Party or leaning in that direction. Just 18% were affiliated with or inclined to vote for the Republican Party (Kiley & Maniam, 2016). As in the general population,

conservative LGBTs are more religious, older, and more likely to be white (Gates & Newport, 2012).

Income and Poverty. Earlier research tended to find that LGBT Americans were at a disadvantage in terms of income and other measures of affluence, consistent with other marginalized groups. Figure 12.5 confirms that LGBT persons are more likely to be low income and less likely to be high income. This is not consistent with the relatively high levels of educational attainment of the group (see Figure 12.4) and suggests that LGBT Americans are getting lower rewards for their investment in human capital. This pattern is similar to the situation for women (see Figure 11.4), and we discuss it in more detail below.

The pattern of income inequality changes when we look at couples as opposed to individuals. Figure 12.6 displays census data showing that, for all racial and ethnic groups except African Americans, same-sex couples average higher incomes than do heterosexual couples. (The difference for African Americans, although contrary to the other groups, was only about $1,700, the smallest difference of the four groups.) Note how the differences between groups echo patterns discussed in previous chapters. For both same- and opposite-sex couples, white and Asian Americans have higher incomes than do African Americans and Hispanic Americans. Thus, the patterns of inequality in the larger society are echoed within the LGB community.

Figure 12.7 displays levels of poverty for couples and repeats the patterns displayed in Figure 12.6: Inequality and economic distress varies by race and ethnicity among LGB Americans as it does in the larger society. White and Asian American couples have lower poverty levels than do

FIGURE 12.5 Annual Family Income for the General Population and LGBT Americans

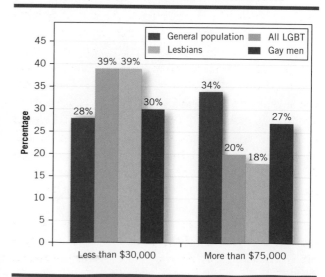

SOURCE: Pew Research Center (2013d, p. 4).

FIGURE 12.6 Median Incomes for Same-Sex and Opposite-Sex Couples by Racial and Ethnic Group, 2010

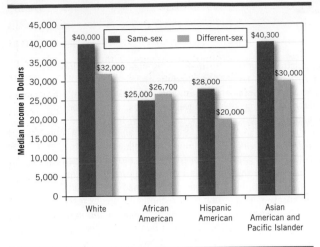

SOURCE: Kastanis and Wilson (2012, p. 8).

African American and Hispanic American couples, and levels of poverty are especially high for gay and lesbian African American couples.

The picture painted by the information in this section is somewhat unclear, in part because the data are based on different units of analysis (couples vs. individuals). However, one idea that may knit the picture together is discrimination and disadvantage, especially in jobs and income.

Consider disposable income, rather than total income. The fact that gay and lesbian couples could not be legally married in so many states until recently meant that they experienced a variety of disadvantages in how they had to spend their income. They had higher costs for medical insurance—a major expense for most Americans—because they couldn't take advantage of the discounts offered by family plans. They also tended to pay higher income taxes. Imagine two families with identical incomes of $45,000 and two children. One family is heterosexual and legally married; the other is a same-sex couple. Using standard deductions for child care and other expenses, the heterosexual couple would have claimed a $50 refund on their federal income taxes. The gay couple would have owed about $2,100 (Capehart, 2012). The two families might be equal in gross salary but not in their actual disposable income. This puts a new perspective on the income data and suggests some of the costs of being gay in America and the significance of the 2015 Supreme Court ruling on marriage equality.

Another major issue for LGBT people is job discrimination. Members of this group sometimes face agonizing choices about revealing their sexual orientation during job searches for fear that it will limit their opportunities, as detailed in the second Narrative Portrait in this

chapter. In fact, there is evidence from research, some using the powerful audit study methodology (see Chapter 5), of a tendency to pass over LGBT candidates for jobs (Movement Advancement Project, Human Rights Campaign, & Center for American Progress, 2013).

On the job, LGBT people often face hostile workplaces, harassment, bullying, and worse. Also, one of the patterns that limits upward mobility for women (see Chapter 11) also applies to gays and lesbians: They may not have the same chance to network with colleagues and bosses, and such contacts can provide crucial links to opportunities to increase skills and knowledge and to prepare for jobs at higher levels. Discrimination in the workplace, both subtle and open, may explain the apparent gap between preparation for work, as measured by education, and actual rewards, as shown in the income data in Figure 12.5.

PRIMARY STRUCTURAL ASSIMILATION

Our version of Gordon's model of assimilation cites marital assimilation as the final stage of the assimilation process, and in previous chapters we have applied this idea to a variety of American minority groups. As with women in Chapter 11, this criterion does not apply to LGBTs. Thus, we will consider other areas of primary assimilation—such as family and friendships—where LGB people still face barriers to full acceptance.

Earlier, we noted the survey result showing that Americans were much less likely to be "very upset" if their child came out to them as gay or lesbian. Nevertheless, LGB

FIGURE 12.7 Poverty Rates for Same-Sex and Opposite-Sex Couples by Racial and Ethnic Group, 2010

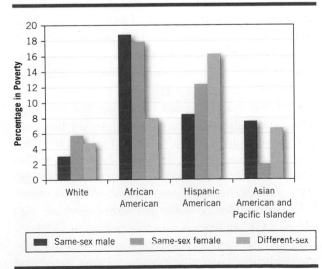

SOURCE: Badgett, Durso, and Schneebaum (2013, p. 11).

Negotiating the Job Market

Jenny Strauss had just graduated college in 1989, but even though she lived in relatively tolerant San Francisco, she feared that her job prospects would be diminished by the fact that she was lesbian. When she got her first job, she remained "in the closet" to her boss and coworkers, but when she began a relationship, she felt that she could no longer live a lie and found the courage to reveal her sexual orientation.

She eventually moved on to jobs with companies that were more open to diversity, and she married and started a family. Today, she and her spouse are happy and secure, but as we saw in the vignette that opened this chapter, this state of affairs was not typical for same-sex families across the nation.

FAMILIES LIKE OURS

Jenny Strauss

My [first] boss, an evangelical woman, openly disapproved of "aberrant" lifestyles. She wasn't unkind, and although I learned a lot from her, I definitely felt that I couldn't be open. About a year into the job I met a woman, and shortly afterward decided that I couldn't hide anymore. Because I had kept this essential part of me a secret (for fear of being treated differently, or worse, mistrusted), no one had a clue, and so I had to formally come out to my boss and coworkers. Palms sweating and heart racing, I went to each of them and said, "I have something to tell you. I'm a lesbian." It was awful! I felt like I was giving them permission to judge me. I felt self-conscious . . . and nervous to the point of feeling sick to my stomach. In fact, my boss, who was shocked, told me she didn't agree with my "lifestyle choices." This is a woman with whom I had built a good relationship, and yet, now there was this strange rift between us. After that, I swore I would be open from the start, and only work where I would be accepted for who I am.

I left that job to work at Levi Strauss & Company . . .—one of the few companies at the time known to be gay-friendly. . . . Altogether, I spent seven years at Levi's. While there, I met my partner, Em, and we've been together 16 years and legally married since 2008.

In the mid-1990s I left Levi's to work for a boutique advertising agency, but was laid off during the dot-com bust when I was pregnant with our first child. Em was also laid off during this period. Thank goodness I was on her benefits . . . or we would have been in terrible shape. In the end, I took an entry-level job and a huge pay cut just to make ends meet and be close to home and my child.

Em and I now have two children. We have good jobs, and a good life. I work for an LGBT-friendly . . . company, SunPower, which has a non-discrimination policy covering both sexual orientation and gender identity/expression. A few transgender employees have transitioned at work, and the company recently added sex reassignment surgery to our health benefits package. SunPower also offers domestic partner benefits. . . .

I feel very grateful that times have changed enough that many companies, not just one, recognize families like ours and I look forward to the day when no matter where someone lives in the country, they feel safe coming out at work.

SOURCE: Movement Advancement Project, Human Rights Campaign, and Center for American Progress (2013, p. 23).

Questions to Consider

1. Are there companies in your area that offer the sorts of benefits that Jenny and Em enjoy? How could you identify these companies?

2. Does your state or city have laws prohibiting discrimination on the grounds of sexual orientation?

adults report that coming out to their parents is extremely difficult. About a third of them have not disclosed their sexual orientation to their mothers, and roughly half have not told their fathers (Drake, 2013).

Between fear of parental rejection and the social stigma and bullying of peers, it is no wonder that LGB youth have a higher risk of attempted suicide, substance abuse, and depression. Yet those who did not report family rejection were less likely to experience those negative outcomes (Ryan, Huebner, Diaz, & Sanchez, 2009). Indeed, when family, peer, and community are supportive, LGB youth grow up to be well adjusted (Savin-Williams, 2001). Thus, acceptance at the primary level is crucial to this particular minority group's mental and physical health, especially at young ages. At any age,

however, being able to be "out" to one's family and friends relieves an enormous amount of stress and avoids a host of difficulties, both psychosocial and physical. Indeed, although reported as stressful initially, most LGB adults found that coming out to their parents did not significantly alter their relationships with them (Drake, 2013).

Having a personal relationship with someone who is gay or lesbian increases support for legal equality (Morales, 2009). One study also found that people who had recently become supportive of same-sex marriage cited knowing someone gay or lesbian as the number one reason for their change of mind (Pew Research Center, 2013b). Even when controlling for other variables known to affect people's views on LGB equality, such as religion and political affiliation, the effect of knowing someone gay or lesbian remains significant, a finding that lends support to the contact hypothesis (Lewis, Emerson, & Klineberg, 2011).

The number of people who say they know someone LGBT has increased in recent years, from 61% of adults in 1993 to 87% in 2016 (Pew Research Center, 2016). Moreover, nearly a quarter of Americans surveyed in 2013 said they know "a lot" of gay or lesbian people (Drake, 2013). Even the social networking site Facebook reported that about 70% of its users have someone gay or lesbian on their friend list (Fowler, 2013). Figures such as these are striking for a minority group that accounts for such a small segment of the total U.S. population.

Although the 2010 U.S. Census found that less than 1% of all households were headed by a same-sex couple, such households are on the rise, and more than 100,000 of them have their own children (Lofquist, Lugailia, O'Connell, & Feliz, 2012). As the number of children who live in households with gay or lesbian parents continues to grow, we can expect the number of adults who know someone who is LGB to increase as well.

Despite the significant headway LGB persons have made in recent decades in terms of coming "out" in their families, building their own families, and developing cross–sexual-orientation friendships, many Americans remain steadfastly antigay. Outside the United States, as our Comparative Focus box demonstrated, there are many places where primary structural assimilation is an elusive goal.

QUESTIONS FOR REFLECTION

12. Would you say that LGB people are now fully included in American culture? Are they more included in popular culture and the media than in everyday life? If so, why does this difference exist?

13. Comparing the evidence presented in this chapter and Chapter 11, are LGB people closer to secondary structural integration than women are? What are the key challenges facing the LGB minority in the quest for equality?

CONCLUSIONS AND IMPLICATIONS FOR DOMINANT–MINORITY RELATIONS

As with many of the groups we have considered over the course of this text, the LGB minority has made a great deal of progress in recent years, but much remains to be done before full acceptance, assimilation, and equality are achieved. Like other minorities, LGB people face discrimination and inequalities in the distribution of material resources (jobs and income, for example) and in the protections offered by civil rights law. Unlike other minorities, however, part of the challenge facing LGB people is moral and cultural.

Fifty years ago, after decades of struggle and turmoil, American society formally rejected the Jim Crow system of segregation and its racist past. Through legislation, court decisions, and the changed thinking of millions of ordinary people, the United States recommitted itself to one of the most fundamental of its founding principles: equal treatment for all under the law, regardless of race, color, creed, national origin, or gender. As we have seen, in many ways our society continues to fall short of actually implementing this principle, but the importance of this moral consensus cannot be understated. The 1960s was a watershed decade in American history, and it is almost impossible to imagine a return to the days of overt racism and state-sponsored group inequality.

A similar moral and cultural debate now faces the nation: Should this same principle of equality be extended to gays and lesbians? Should antidiscrimination laws be extended to include sexual orientation and gender identity? Is this a time when another fundamental shift in America's thinking—another watershed—will occur?

It seems that popular support for gay rights is building in this nation, and some observers argue that full civil rights are just a matter of time. However, there is powerful, well-funded, and well-organized opposition to these changes, and it is clear that the traditional views of homosexuality as sinful and a form of deviance and mental illness retain considerable strength.

The nation is clearly committed to racial and gender equality (at least in principle). Will this moral and cultural consensus be extended to LGB Americans?

SUMMARY

This summary is organized around the Learning Objectives listed at the beginning of this chapter.

 12.1 Identify and analyze the difference between sexual orientation, sexual identity, and sexual behavior or practices.

Sexual orientation refers to the gender or genders to which a person is attracted, while sexual identity refers to how people think about themselves as sexual beings. The two concepts are closely but not perfectly related, and neither is perfectly related to sexual practices or behaviors.

12.2 List and explain the key events that have impacted how lesbian, gay, and bisexual persons are viewed by society and have experienced society.

Same-sex relations are ancient but have been expressed and perceived differently in different eras and types of societies. In ancient Greece, same-sex relations between men were normative and accepted. In agrarian societies, the need for large families placed a huge premium on heterosexual relations, but same-sex relations existed even in the most straight-laced and prudish societies. As societies began to industrialize and urbanize, more social spaces were created where same-sex relations could exist, and gay subcultures emerged in larger cities. In postindustrial society, LGB people are more visible than ever before and have become increasingly accepted, although strong opposition to homosexuality persists among the more religious and conservative.

12.3 Describe key moments in the struggle for gay liberation.

The modern U.S. gay liberation movement began with the formation of several "homophile" organizations in the 1950s. Perhaps the key event in the movement's history was the Stonewall Rebellion in 1969, which marked the beginning of a more activist, confrontational, inclusive approach. After Stonewall, a variety of organizations emerged to lead the struggle and attract allies.

Successes were sporadic in the 1980s and 1990s, but the movement enjoyed a number of successes in the new century, including the Supreme Court decision that legalized marriage equality and various state and local protections against discrimination in work and other institutions.

12.4 Identify and explain the patterns of sexual-orientation inequality in society today.

Information is less available for the LGB minority than for other groups, but patterns of inequality in income and poverty can be documented. As is the case with some other minorities, LGB people seem to enjoy lower returns (income) on their investments in human capital (education). Also, same-sex couples must often spend a higher percentage of their incomes on health care and taxes.

12.5 Describe how race, class, gender, and religion impact sexual-orientation inequality.

The patterns of inequality in the LGB community reflect those in the larger society. For example, African Americans and Hispanic Americans are at a greater disadvantage than white Americans and Asian Americans. The gay and lesbian communities reflect the larger society in other ways as well and are divided by racism and other cultural values. Heterosexism and homophobia affect different subgroups of LGB people in different ways.

KEY TERMS

collective identity 441

coming out 439

cultural heterosexism 450

homophobia 449

internalized

 homophobia 449

queer 444

sexual identity 433

sexual orientation 432

structural heterosexism 450

REVIEW QUESTIONS

1. Define and explain the terms *sexual orientation* and *sexual identity*. How do they relate to sexual practices and behaviors?

2. How has changing subsistence technology affected the LGB minority? What are the key differences between the agrarian, industrial, and postindustrial levels of development for this group?

3. Summarize the history of the gay liberation movement. Why do we distinguish between pre- and post-Stonewall eras? What are the most important victories and setbacks for gay liberation since 1990?

4. Summarize and explain each of the three issues for LGB people analyzed in this chapter (marriage equality; service in the military; and race, racism, and sexual orientation).

5. What are homophobia and heterosexism? How do these compare and contrast with prejudice, discrimination, institutional discrimination, and ideological racism?

6. Apply the concepts of acculturation, secondary structural assimilation, and primary structural assimilation to the LGB minority. How does the application of these concepts differ for this group compared with other groups we have considered?

STUDENT STUDY SITE

Sharpen your skills with SAGE edge at edge.sagepub.com/healey8e

SAGE edge for students provides a personalized approach to help you accomplish your coursework goals in an easy-to-use learning environment.

The following resources are available at SAGE edge:

Current Debates: Whose Rights Should Prevail?

Many Americans, especially the more religious and politically conservative, find homosexuality offensive and believe that it is morally wrong. What should happen when these views clash with laws that require equal treatment? Which should prevail: religious values or civil rights?

On our website you will find an overview of the topic, the clashing points of view, and some questions to consider as you analyze the material.

Public Sociology Assignments

Public Sociology Assignments provide opportunities for students to address directly and personally some of the issues raised in this text.

There are four assignments for Part IV on our website. In the first assignment, students use the information available from the Pew Research Center to examine religion as a source of diversity in American life. In the second assignment, groups of students will analyze the lyrics of popular songs. Do the lyrics reflect stereotypes of racial or ethnic groups? What messages are being conveyed about gender or sexual orientation?

The third assignment focuses on a film and website that probe the reality of bullying in America's schools. The fourth assignment is an analysis of the thousands of languages around the world that are in danger of becoming extinct.

Contributed by Linda M. Waldron

Internet Research Project

This Internet Research Project has two parts, and you are urged to complete both. In the first, you will search the Internet for information on several controversial questions related to this chapter; in the second, you will add to the profiles of LGB people. It is particularly important to rely on trusted, scientifically based sources for these projects. Your instructor may ask you to discuss your findings in small groups.

For Further Reading

Please see our website for an annotated list of important works related to this chapter.

CHAPTER-OPENING TIMELINE PHOTO CREDITS

1948: Library of Congress Prints and Photographs Division

1969: NY Daily News/Getty Images

1979: Wikimedia Commons

1987 (AIDS quilt): National Institutes of Health

1987 (National March on Washington): Associated Press

2008: Wikipedia

2009: Official White House Photo/Pete Souza

2015: jordanuhl7/Wikimedia Commons

2016: WalterPro/Flickr

13

DOMINANT–MINORITY RELATIONS IN CROSS-NATIONAL PERSPECTIVE

LOC

State of Israel's National Photo Collection

timeline

1899
British and Dutch factions fight each other in the Boer War for control of South Africa.

1918
Yugoslavia is created.

1948
The state of Israel is established by the UN as the Jewish homeland, resulting in full-scale wars between Israel and its neighbors in 1948, 1967, and 1973.

| 1890 | 1900 | 1910 | 1920 | 1930 | 1940 | 1950 |

1916
The Easter Rebellion leads to the creation of an independent Republic of Ireland. The new nation encompasses most of the island, but the largely Protestant northern counties remain part of Great Britain.

301

1939–1945
6 million Jews and at least 6 million others, including Roma, Slavs, and the disabled, are murdered by the Nazi German state.

German Federal Archive

1948
The National Party, the primary political vehicle of the Afrikaans, or Dutch, segment of the white community, comes into control of South Africa. The system of apartheid is subsequently constructed to firmly establish white superiority.

1953
Josip Broz Tito, a leader of anti-Nazi guerrilla forces during World War II, becomes Prime Minister of Yugoslavia.

1960s
The Catholics of Northern Ireland begin a civil rights movement, seeking amelioration for their minority status. Protestants, fearing loss of privilege and control, resist attempts at reform, and the confrontation escalates into violence.

I pause in the central square of Uzhgorod, a city on the western edge of Ukraine. It is early evening, and the streets are crowded as people hurry through the cold, on their way home or to one of the numerous bars for an after-work drink. It is 2006, and I am here for a semester at the university, trying to acclimate to this ancient, recently Soviet, formerly Hungarian, formerly Czechoslovakian, strangely (to me) cosmopolitan city.

If I listen closely to the passing crowds, even my untutored ear can hear multiple languages besides Ukrainian: Russian, Czech, Romanian, Hungarian, Slovak, and probably others. I know that almost everyone in the city speaks at least two of these languages, and some, especially the more educated, speak English (thankfully!).

From where I stand, I can see the old synagogue, abandoned after World War II when only a few hundred Jews—survivors of

LEARNING OBJECTIVES

By the end of this chapter, you will be able to do the following:

13.1 State and explain the central themes of this text.

13.2 Summarize the overall pattern of ethnic variability around the globe, and identify which regions are most and least diverse.

13.3 Summarize the dominant–minority situations outlined in this chapter, including the history and present situation, and apply the central concepts developed in this text to each case.

Wikimedia Commons

Getty

Wikimedia Commons

1979
Egypt, formerly committed to the destruction of the Jewish state, signs a peace accord with Israel.

1992–1995
More than 100,000 Bosnian Muslims are killed by Serbs and Croats in Yugoslavia.

1994
Nelson Mandela is elected President of South Africa.

1998
The "Good Friday Agreement" is signed, establishing a new power-sharing arrangement for the governance of Northern Ireland in which both Protestant and Catholic parties participate.

2013
Brazil legalizes gay marriage but also has some of the highest LGBT violence in the world. Since 2012, about 1,600 LGBT people have been murdered.

1960   1970   1980   1990   2000   2010   2020

1960s
A militant pluralistic movement begins in Quebec.

1960s
Canada reforms its restrictive immigration policy that favored whites, leading to a steady influx of newcomers from Latin America, the Caribbean, and Asia.

1980
Referendums supporting a politically autonomous Quebec fail. A similar referendum fails in 1995, but only by a very thin margin.

1990
F. W. de Klerk, the leader of the National Party and the prime minister of the nation, begins a series of changes that eventually ends apartheid in South Africa.

1994
Paramilitary groups of the Republic of Ireland and Northern Ireland declare a cease-fire and begin to negotiate with each other.

1994
Approximately 800,000 ethnic Tutsis are killed by Hutu rebels is Rwanda.

1998
A terrorist attack on a shopping area in Omagh, Northern Ireland, leaves nearly 30 people dead.

2017
The organization Genocide Watch declares 10 countries in a state of "genocide emergency" with mass killing underway. Many other countries appear on the Warning or Watch lists.

2017
Canada amends its Human Rights Act to include "gender identity and gender expression" to the list of federally prohibited grounds for discrimination.

Copyright World Economic Forum

the Holocaust and a tiny remnant of a once large, bustling community—returned to the area. In the 1950s, the Soviets, practicing their brand of anti-Semitism, stripped the building of all religious symbols and turned it into a concert hall.

I can hear a Roma boy of about 10 singing nearby. He belts out a melody and accompanies himself on a beat-up guitar. People mostly ignore him, but he manages to score an occasional coin or two from those not too afraid to get close to a Gypsy. He looks cold and unkempt, but I have learned that he is probably better off than the hundreds of Roma children in the orphanages scattered throughout the countryside.

The group makeup of the city reflects its complicated past and its geographic centrality. For centuries, it has been a crossroads for cultures and languages, armies and traders. The diversity constantly surprises me, but it is just one of the countless ways ethnicity, language, culture, and race are blended around the globe. •

—Joe Healey

Early in this text, we developed a set of concepts and hypotheses to help analyze and understand dominant–minority relations. Our analytical framework has been elaborated and applied to the creation and evolution of a variety of minority groups across U.S. history. Although our concepts have proven their usefulness, up to this point, we have primarily tested them against the experiences of a single nation. Just as you would not accept an interview with a single person as an adequate test of a psychological theory, you should not accept the experiences of a single nation as proof for the sociological perspective developed in this text. However, if our ideas can be applied to dominant–minority situations in other societies, we will have some assurance that the dynamics of intergroup relations in the United States are not unique and that our conclusions have some general applicability.

To that end, in this chapter, we will first briefly review the ideas that have guided our analysis. Then, after looking at an overview of diversity around the world, we will apply our ideas to a variety of societies. It is not possible to investigate every nation in the world, so we will focus on societies with dominant–minority group conflicts that have been widely publicized and are, therefore, familiar to many people. For purposes of comparison, we have also included several societies in which group relations are thought to be generally peaceful.

We want to be very clear as to the limits of this "test." The sample of societies is small and is not representative of all human societies across time and space; therefore, the test will not be definitive. Before final conclusions can be reached, we need much more research on a broad array of societies, drawn from a variety of time periods, regions, levels of development, and cultural backgrounds. Just as important, information about many of our most crucial concepts (e.g., the degree and nature of prejudice or discrimination) is simply not available for many societies. Without precise, trustworthy information, our tests will necessarily be informal and impressionistic. At any rate, you can rest assured that the conclusions reached in this chapter—and in this text—will not be the final word on the subject.

A BRIEF REVIEW OF MAJOR ANALYTICAL THEMES

Before our comparative analysis begins, it seems useful to review the major analytical points developed in this text. We summarized these ideas as seven themes in the introduction to Part 3. Because we have reiterated those themes extensively throughout the text, a brief review should be sufficient here.

One major theme is the importance of the initial contact situation between groups. The characteristics of the initial meeting can shape relations for centuries. The type and intensity of the competition and the balance of power between the groups is particularly significant. Additionally, research suggests that the experiences and outcomes of minority groups created by colonization and conquest are very different from those of minority groups created by immigration. As we have demonstrated, colonized or conquered minority groups, throughout U.S. history, have been subjected to greater rejection, discrimination, and inequality. Positive change is more difficult to accomplish for conquered or colonized groups, especially when the group is racially or physically different from the dominant group.

As this chapter examines the most difficult and explosive group conflicts from around the world, you'll see that their origins often occur in contact situations in which the colonizers were white Europeans and the eventual minority groups were peoples of color. This pattern of dominance and subordination reflects the conditions under which the present world system of societies was created. By the 1400s, the nations of Europe were the most technologically advanced in the world, and they used that superiority to explore, conquer, and sometimes destroy much of the rest of the world. Contemporary conflicts between whites and nonwhites around the world—and many of the conflicts between peoples of color—are just one legacy of these contact situations.

The early days of the Industrial Revolution.

Of course, the present pattern of white dominance is also an accident of history. Nations have been conquering, enslaving, persecuting, and oppressing their neighbors since there were nations. When neighboring societies differed in some visible way, prejudice, racism, and systems of inequality based on group membership often followed military conquest.

The unique contribution of Europeans to this ancient pattern was that their era of conquest and colonization was made possible by breakthroughs in shipbuilding, navigation, and other technologies that enabled them to spread their influence further and more permanently than previous colonizers. The nations of Europe (and the British in particular) were able to rule much of the world until very recent decades, and many ethnic and racial conflicts today were born during the era of European colonialism (see Wallace, 1997).

A second important theme developed in this text is that dominant–minority relationships tend to change most rapidly and dramatically when changes occur in the level of development or the basic subsistence technology of the society. For example, industrialization not only revolutionized technology and modes of production; it also transformed group relationships in Europe, in the United States, and, eventually, around the world. In Europe, the growth of industrial technology stimulated massive waves of immigration, beginning in the 1820s, and the new technology helped European nations dominate the world system of societies in the 19th century and much of the 20th century.

In the United States, the industrial revolution led to a transition from paternalistic to rigid competitive group relations, starting in the 19th century. In the latter half of the 20th century, continuing modernization led to the present era of fluid competitive group relations. The blatant racism and overt discrimination of the past have become (for the most part) more moderate, taking on milder, more ambiguous forms that are more difficult to identify and measure. Importantly, this evolution to less repressive forms of group relations has been energized, in large part, by the protest activities of minority-group members and their allies.

Contact situations, subsistence technology, assimilation and pluralism, prejudice, racism, and institutional discrimination are all central to understanding the past and present situations of U.S. minority groups. To what extent are these themes and concepts applicable to group relations around the world?

QUESTIONS FOR REFLECTION

1. What is a contact situation, and why is it important?

2. Why do group relationships change when a society undergoes a change in subsistence technology?

A SNAPSHOT OF GLOBAL DIVERSITY

Before we consider individual nations, let's examine diversity worldwide. Figure 13.1 presents one type of diversity based on ethnicity. As you can see, the nations of Africa, with their multitude of tribes, languages, and cultures, tend to rank highest on ethnic diversity.

This pattern partly reflects the colonization of the continent by European powers: Virtually all of Africa has

FIGURE 13.1 Ethnic Diversity Around the Globe

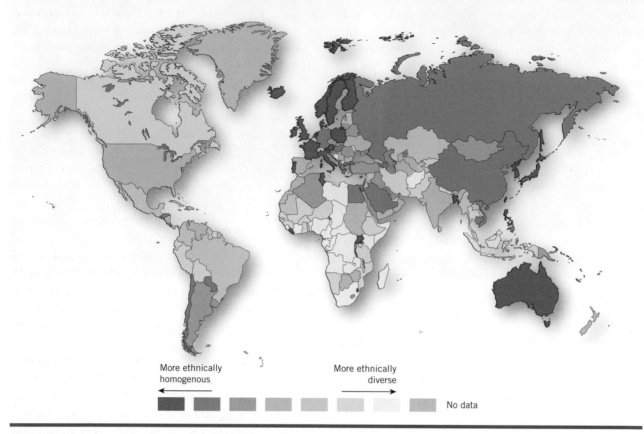

More ethnically homogenous ← More ethnically diverse → No data

SOURCE: Fisher (2013b). This map is based on Alesina, Devleeschauwewr, Easterly, Kurlat, and Wacziarg (2002).

been, at one time or another, a colonial possession of a European nation. The African national boundaries of today were drawn for the convenience of—and sometimes at the whim of—the European leaders.

Also, in many cases, part of the governing strategy of European conquerors was to incorporate different ethnic groups in the same colony and pit one against the other, using a "divide-and-conquer" strategy to solidify European rule. This strategy, as we shall see in the case study of Rwanda, often resulted in prolonged tragedies.

Europe is the least diverse region of the globe, but the most homogeneous nations, according to this measure, are Japan and North and South Korea. The nations of North and South America are fairly diverse. The United States scores in the middle range and Canada scores higher (largely, as we shall see, because of the large French-speaking population).

Maps such as Figure 13.1 are interesting and useful for identifying broad patterns, but they should not be taken too literally. For one thing, the data used to compute the scores are old, sometimes stretching back to the early 1990s. (We would prefer updated data, of course, but this is the most recent available.) Also, as we have seen, ethnicity—like race—is a social construction. Thus, any

attempt to measure it (especially across political, cultural, and social lines) is somewhat arbitrary. Still, the map is a useful starting point and reminds us that the United States is not the only nation to confront issues of group relations.

QUESTIONS FOR REFLECTION

3. Why do African nations tend to be so diverse?

4. All other things being equal, would you prefer to live in a more diverse or less diverse society? Why?

A GLOBAL TOUR

We begin our "world tour" of group relations with Canada, our neighbor to the north, and then continue east, spanning the globe and returning to the Western Hemisphere for a discussion of Brazil.

CANADA

Citizens of the United States sometimes see Canada as simply a colder version of their home society, a perception sustained by the enormous impact the United States has had on everyday social, economic, and political life in Canada. In fact, dominant–minority situations in both countries share some similarities, historically and at present. But the two societies are quite different. For example, although black Africans were enslaved in colonial Canada, the institution of slavery never reached the economic, political, or social significance it achieved in the United States. (For more, see the Comparative Focus in Chapter 4.)

Perhaps the most obvious difference between the two nations is that, for much of its history, the most significant minority-group issue in Canada has been cultural and linguistic, not racial. Virtually since its inception, Canadian society has been divided into two major language groups, French speaking and English speaking. French speakers (or Francophones) are the minority group and are concentrated in the province of Quebec. Nationally, French speakers make up about 21% of the population, but they are about 77% of the population of Quebec (Statistics Canada, 2017).

In our terms, issues of assimilation and pluralism separate the two linguistic and cultural groups. French Canadians have preserved their language and culture in the face of domination by English speakers for more than 200 years, and they continue to maintain their traditions today.

Although French Canadians tend toward pluralism, they are not unanimous about the type of relationship they want with the larger society. At one extreme, some Francophones want complete separation between Quebec and English-speaking Canada: Their goal is to make Quebec an independent nation. Others would be satisfied with guarantees of more autonomy for Quebec and some national recognition of the right of the French-speaking residents to maintain their language and culture.

What caused the conflict between French- and English-speaking Canadians? It will not surprise you that the answer begins with the contact situation between the English and French in Canada. Throughout the 1600s and 1700s, France and England (and other nations) fought for control of North America. The French were eliminated as a colonial power in 1759 when the British captured Quebec City and Montreal and ended the French and Indian War (as it is called in the United States).

The French who remained after the war were largely concentrated in what is now Quebec, and they became the ancestral community to today's Quebecois (French speakers of Quebec). The French community was organized around small farms; a rural, traditional, relatively low-income lifestyle; and the Catholic Church. The victorious British Protestants took control of the economic and political institutions of the region and became the ruling elite classes.

A militant pluralistic movement began in the 1960s in Quebec. The French-speaking residents were still clearly a minority group, and there were marked differences in wealth, education, occupational profile, and political power between French and English speakers in the province. Industrialization and urbanization had tended to raise the educational levels and aspiration of the Quebecois, and a nationalistic movement—with some similarities to the Black Power, Brown Power, and Red Power movements that developed in the United States in the same decade—emerged and began to grow in power.

The Parti Quebec became the major vehicle for the expression of Quebecois nationalism and the movement for a politically autonomous Quebec. Referendums in support of separation were held in 1980 and 1995. Both failed but the latter only by a very thin margin.

The status of Quebec's French-speaking residents has continued to rise in recent decades, and they have gained more economic and political power, but issues of control of resources and wealth continue to animate the struggle. Quebec is still attempting to work out its relationship with the rest of the nation, and the desire for separation is alive and well. Additional referenda on the issue of separation may take place in the near future.

In addition, Canada faces a number of other minority-group issues, most of which will be familiar to citizens of the United States. For example, after years of maintaining a restrictive immigration policy that favored whites, Canada reformed its laws in the 1960s. Since that time, there has been a steady and large influx of newcomers from the same areas that supply immigrants to the United States: Latin America, the Caribbean, and Asia.

Also, the native peoples of Canada share many problems and inequities with American Indians in the United States. Many live on remote reservations (called "reserves") that have high levels of poverty and unemployment and low levels of health care and educational opportunities.

Even though they are different from those of the United States, Canada's problems of group relations can be analyzed in familiar terms. Some Canadian minority groups (French speakers and Canadian Indians, or First Nations people) originated in conquest and colonization and have been victimized by discrimination and rejection for centuries. Especially since the 1960s, members of these groups have actively protested their situations, and some reforms and improvements have been made.

In early 2017, in the wake of rising concerns about the election of Donald Trump, Canadian Prime Minister Justin Trudeau tweeted, "To those fleeing persecution, terror & war, Canadians will welcome you, regardless of your faith. Diversity is our strength #WelcomeToCanada." (Semotiuk, 2017). Not only is Canada seeing an influx of immigrants from outside North America, it has also experienced an increase in people seeking asylum from the United States — such as undocumented immigrants (Paperny & Lampert,

"The Republic Guarantees . . ." by ADW, a Dublin-based artist, commemorating the 1916 Irish Rebellion, completed on the eve of the 100th anniversary of the Easter Rebellion. This is one of six pieces created by Irish artists with their vision of the 1916 events.

2017). Other people seeking to immigrate to Canada share much in common with immigrants to the United States. In fact, despite the clear and important differences between the nations, Canada faces many of the same issues that confront U.S. society: questions of unity and diversity, fairness and equality, assimilation and pluralism.

NORTHERN IRELAND

Other nations face issues similar to those faced by Canada, but with different levels of intensity, urgency, and lethality. In Northern Ireland, the bitter, violent conflict between Protestants and Catholics has some parallels to Canadian and U.S. group relations and has been closely watched and widely reported. Thousands of people have lost their lives during the struggles, many of them victims of terrorist attacks.

The roots of this conflict lie in armed hostilities between England and Ireland that began centuries ago. By the 1600s, England had colonized much of Ireland and had encouraged Protestants from Scotland and England to move to what is now Northern Ireland to help pacify and control the Catholic Irish. The newcomers, assisted by the English invaders, came to own much of the land and control the economy and governing structure of the northern regions of the island.

Over the centuries, the Protestants in the north of Ireland consolidated their position of power and separated themselves from the native Catholic population in the school system, in residential areas, and in most other aspects of society. Law and strong custom reinforced the subordinate position of Catholics, and the system, at its height, resembled Jim Crow segregation. That is, it was a system of rigid competitive relations (see Chapter 5) in which the Protestants sought to limit the ability of Catholics to compete for jobs, political power, housing, wealth, and other resources.

The British ruled Ireland as a colony for centuries but never succeeded in completely subordinating the Irish, who periodically attempted to gain independence through violent rebellions. These efforts came to partial fruition in the 1920s when an uprising that began with the Easter Rebellion of 1916 led to the creation of an independent Republic of Ireland. The new nation encompassed most of the island, but the largely Protestant northern counties, most of the province of Ulster, remained part of Great Britain.

The partition of the island into an overwhelmingly Catholic Republic of Ireland and a largely Protestant Northern Ireland set the stage for the troubles that reached a boiling point in the 1960s. The Catholics of Northern Ireland began a civil rights movement, seeking amelioration for their minority status. Protestants, fearing loss of privilege and control, resisted attempts at reform, and the confrontation escalated into violence.

Decades of riots, assassinations, bombings, British Army occupation, mass arrests, prisoner hunger strikes, and terror attacks ensued. Both the Catholic and Protestant communities produced extremist, heavily armed terrorist groups (e.g., the Irish Republican Army for the Catholics and the Ulster Defence Association for the Protestants) that coordinated attacks on the other side. The level of violence rose and fell over the decades, but there seemed little reason to hope for peace. Until, in the 1990s, it began to happen.

In 1994, the paramilitary groups on each side declared a cease-fire, and the parties began to negotiate with each other. Four years later, in 1998, the Good Friday Agreement was signed, but only after an extremely difficult negotiation process. This accord, made possible in large part by the involvement and support of Great Britain, the Republic of Ireland, and the United States, established a new power-sharing arrangement for the governance of Northern Ireland in which both Protestant and Catholic parties would participate.

The new governing arrangement has survived several difficult crises, including a terrorist attack on a shopping area in Omagh, Northern Ireland, in August 1998 that left nearly 30 people dead. In that same year, a referendum in support of the arrangement passed with overwhelming agreement in both Northern Ireland and the Republic, and a stable and workable solution to the troubles seemed to have been reached. However, in the spring of 2017, conflicts re-emerged and the power-sharing

COMPARATIVE FOCUS

The Roma: Europe's "True Minority"

FIGURE 13.2 Roma Population in Europe, 2009

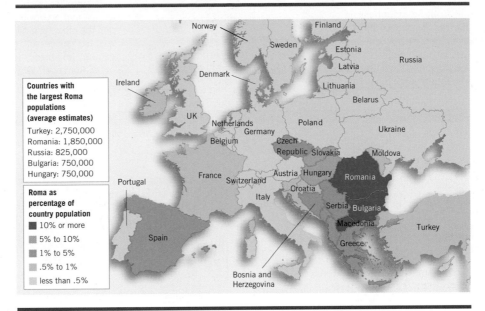

Countries with the largest Roma populations (average estimates)

Turkey: 2,750,000
Romania: 1,850,000
Russia: 825,000
Bulgaria: 750,000
Hungary: 750,000

Roma as percentage of country population

- 10% or more
- 5% to 10%
- 1% to 5%
- .5% to 1%
- less than .5%

Professor Andria D. Timmer studies the Roma of Hungary. She lived and worked in Hungarian Roma communities for several years while conducting research. She has recently published a book summarizing her work.[1]

Dr. Andria D. Timmer

The Roma (often called "Gypsies") live throughout the world, but they are most populous in Europe. They can be found in every European nation, and their geographic distribution is depicted in Figure 13.2. According to many historical documents, the Roma have been part of Central and Eastern European society since at least the 14th century, when they arrived in several migratory waves from India. Despite the fact that they have lived in Europe for more than half a millennium, they are still treated as recent immigrants in many respects. Thus, the Roma illustrate the point made by Gordon (see Chapter 2) and

many others that length of residence in a country is not necessarily related to a group's ability to assimilate and gain acceptance.

The Roma do not form one singular group but comprise several different ethnic enclaves. In most cases, members of these groups have little in common and are more similar to the majority members of the country in which they reside than to one another. However, from a pan-European perspective, they are often considered a single group. To understand how these different peoples get grouped together, it is necessary to return to the definition of *minority group* provided in Chapter 1 of this text. We will use the first two elements of the definition to help us examine the situation of the Roma in Europe.

The first, and most important, defining characteristic of a minority group is disadvantage or inequality, and this is something that all Roma groups have in common. Violence and intolerance toward Roma are an ever-present reality. Roma neighborhoods are often lacking in basic amenities, such as running water and regular trash collection. As an

egregious form of discrimination, Roma youth are frequently educated separately from their majority-group peers and, as a result, receive lower-quality education that leaves them unable to compete in the job market. Unemployment rates for the Roma stand somewhere between 70% and 95%, depending on region.

The second defining characteristic of a minority group is a visible trait or characteristic. Linguistic, genetic, and ethnographic evidence shows that the Roma ancestors migrated out of northern India sometime between the 7th and 10th centuries. Therefore, contemporary populations share physical features with Indian populations, especially in regard to skin color. Otherwise, there is little that culturally ties the Roma to India, and, as mentioned previously, there are few cultural characteristics that tie all Roma groups together. Very few—apart from Traveler groups of England and Ireland, who are not Indian descendants—still practice the stereotypical nomadic lifestyle. Many have lost the use of their native tongue or use it only in the privacy of their homes.

(Continued)

[1] Timmer, Andria. 2016. *Educating the Roma: Nongovernmental Organizations and Minority Rights.* Lanham, MD: Lexington Books.

The deep divide between Roma and non-Roma in Europe is largely the result of a long history of isolation and segregated living. Government and civil-sector programs have done little to address the segregated living but have, for the most part, endeavored to improve living conditions in Roma settlements. They have helped build new houses and sponsored environmental cleanup projects, but there are few programs to integrate Roma families into the larger national communities in which they reside. As long as residential segregation, prejudice, and discrimination persist, Europe will remain divided and the Roma will remain isolated and segregated.

Questions to Consider

1. Are the Roma a "typical" minority group? How do they compare to African Americans or American Indians? What important differences and similarities can you identify?

2. What stereotypes do Americans hold about "Gypsies"? Where do these ideas come from? In Chapter 3, we noted that stereotypes tend to fall into two categories: one for groups that occupy a low status and the other for groups that are "too" successful. Into which category do American stereotypes of the Roma fall? Why?

---

agreement came under heavy stress. At this writing, talks and negotiations to save the government were in a stalemate (Bell, 2017).

Note that in this case, as in the case of relations between Quebec and the rest of Canada, both the dominant and the minority groups are of the same race. The deep divisions are, on the surface, linguistic and cultural (English speaking vs. French speaking) and religious (Protestant vs. Catholic). In both nations, however, these divisions are highly correlated with social class position, access to education and jobs, and political power. That is, Catholics in Northern Ireland—like the French-speaking residents of Quebec—are a minority group that has been victimized by intense, systematic, and persistent discrimination and prejudice.

What was at stake in these struggles was not simply the survival of a culture or religion. These clashes were so bitter, so deadly, and so difficult because they also concerned the distribution of real resources and questions about who gets what and how much.

GERMANY

In the annals of intergroup relations, Germany is infamous as the site of the greatest atrocities against minority groups in history. In the 1930s and 1940s, the Nazi leadership of the nation attempted to eradicate the Jewish community (and several other groups) and nearly succeeded. Six million Jews died in the concentration camps. They also killed thousands of other minority group members such as the Roma, people with disabilities, and LGBT people.

Since the end of World War II, modern Germany has broken from its racist past, democratized, industrialized, and modernized. It is a global leader politically and economically, and has one of the world's best-trained and most-educated workforces. Germany has worked hard to atone for

A Berlin resident places flowers on *stolpersteine*, or stumbling stones. The stones feature small brass plates inscribed with the names and dates of Jewish people killed during the Holocaust. Typically, they are installed in front of houses where the person(s) last lived.

the Nazi's attempted genocide of Jews. It has, for example, paid reparations to the state of Israel in partial compensation for the atrocities of World War II and is Israel's leading trading partner in Europe. Germany also funds a variety of cultural exchange programs between the two nations.

Today, Germany faces new dominant–minority group challenges. Like the United States, Canada, and other Western European nations, Germany has become a highly desirable destination for immigrants, who come to satisfy the demand for both unskilled, cheap labor and "high-tech" professionals (see the Comparative Focus in Chapter 8).

Besides the demand in various parts of the job market, immigrants are also pulled to Germany (and many other European nations) by the low rate of population growth. Birthrates are low throughout Western Europe, and Germany's birthrate is actually lower than its death rate (Population Reference Bureau, 2017). If this condition continues, Germany will begin to lose population.

JOHN MACDOUGALL/AFP/Getty Images

Based on the patterns we have documented in the United States, we would predict that high rates of immigration would be accompanied by episodes of racist violence, and it is easy to find neo-Nazi hate groups, hate crimes, and violent attacks against immigrants and other minority-group members in Germany (and other European nations) in recent years. These attacks include bombings, killings, beatings, and myriad other forms of violence and brutality.

One of the most sensational of these attacks involved a gang of three neo-Nazis who allegedly murdered at least nine people from immigrant backgrounds and robbed at least a dozen banks to finance their activities. Two of the members of the so-called Zwickau Cell of the National Socialist Underground committed suicide as they were about to be captured, but the third, Beate Zschaepe, went on trial for these crimes in December 2013 (Schofield, 2013).

Also, anti-Semitism is still a fact of life in Germany and may be increasing there and across Europe. A recent survey of Jews in eight European nations found that 66% thought that anti-Semitism was a "very big" or "fairly big" problem in their country. Percentages ranged from a high of 85% in France to a low of 48% in the United Kingdom. Germany was intermediate, with a percentage of 61% (European Union Agency for Fundamental Rights, 2013, pp. 15–16).

Another survey found that anti-Semitic sentiments had increased just between 2009 and 2012 in four of the seven nations surveyed. Support for such sentiments ranged from a low of 17% in the United Kingdom to a high of 63% in Hungary. In this survey, Germany ranked toward the bottom, with 21% supporting prejudiced statements (Anti-Defamation League, 2012, p. 18). A more recent survey found that anti-Semitic prejudice in Germany had decreased between 2014 and 2015 (ADL Global, 2016).

Hate crimes, neo-Nazis, and anti-Semitic sentiments are part of everyday life in Germany, other European nations, and the United States, as well as across the globe. They seem to have some common causes: high rates of immigration combined with economic uncertainty for working-class, less educated men and strong traditions of racism and intolerance. Still, the memory of the Holocaust gives special resonance to attacks on minority groups in Germany.

SWITZERLAND

Although our focus is on the ethnic and racial trouble spots, it is also important to consider societies in which group relations are generally peaceful and conflict is comparatively minimal. One such society is Switzerland. Swiss society incorporates three major and distinct language and cultural groups: French speakers, German speakers, and Italian speakers. Each language group resides in a particular region of the country and enjoys considerable control of its local affairs. In our terms, Switzerland is a pluralistic society in which the groups are separate both culturally and structurally. That is, at the local level, the groups have neither acculturated nor integrated. Each group maintains its unique cultural and linguistic heritage, and its separate institutional and organizational structures.

At the national level, political power and economic resources are shared in proportion to the size of each group. The leaders of the different groups are careful to cooperate in national affairs and maintain the sense of proportional sharing and fundamental fairness. With the combination of cooperation at the national level and autonomy at the local level, Switzerland is able to function effectively as a multicultural, multilingual society.

Perhaps the key to Swiss success in combining diversity and unity is that none of the three major groups was forced to join the nation by military conquest or coercion. The groups joined together voluntarily and created this pluralistic nation for mutual advantage. Thus, for the three major groups that make up Swiss society, there is no history of conquest or subordination and no patterns of structured inequality, prejudice, or resentment.

FORMER YUGOSLAVIA

The case of Switzerland indicates that peaceful and prosperous pluralistic societies can be created, but this is not typical of multigroup societies. Conquest and coercion are more common than voluntary cooperation, and the potential for rancor, conflict, and violence tends to be high, as demonstrated by the former nation of Yugoslavia.

As we saw in the introduction to this chapter, Eastern Europe is a region of immense ethnic, linguistic, and religious diversity. Travel, trade, and warfare have mixed and scattered groups, and over the centuries, nations and empires have come and gone. The former nation of Yugoslavia exemplifies both the diversity of the region and the complexities of intergroup conflict and cooperation.

The history of the modern nation of Yugoslavia is both short and complex. When it was created in 1918, at the end of World War I, the nation encompassed a variety of ethnic groups, each with its own language, religion, history, and memories of grievances against other groups. The larger groups include Croats (who are mainly Roman Catholic), Serbs (primarily Eastern Orthodox), and Bosnians (roughly half Muslim, half Christian). Each of these groups had a home territory (see Figure 13.3) in which it was the numerical majority. For example, in 1992, Croatia was 78% Croatian, and Serbia was 85% Serbian. Bosnia was the most diverse of the former Yugoslav states. In 1992, about 44% of the population of Bosnia was Muslim, 39% was Serb, and 17% was Croat (Remington, 1997, p. 275).

During World War II, Yugoslavia was one of the bloody battlegrounds, and each of these groups took sides. German forces invaded the region and created a puppet government in Croatia. The Croatian allies of the Nazis participated not only in the persecution of Jews but also in a campaign against the Serbs residing within their reach. Concentration camps were constructed and mass executions carried out. By the end of the war, the fascist Croatian government had murdered hundreds of thousands of Serbs. However, the Croats were not alone in their atrocities. Their campaign against Serbs provoked anti-Croatian violence in Serbia; hostility and resentment between the two groups had grown to new heights by the end of the war.

World War II also saw the emergence of Josip Broz Tito as a leader of anti-Nazi guerrilla forces. After the war, Tito became the chief architect of the modern nation of Yugoslavia. Tito's design incorporated many of the same elements that make Switzerland a successful pluralistic society. Postwar Yugoslavia comprised several different subnations, or republics, each of which was associated with a particular ethnic group. Power at the national level was allocated proportionately, and each region had considerable autonomy in the conduct of its affairs.

A major difference between Yugoslavia and Switzerland, however, lies in the contact situation. Whereas Switzerland was formed on a voluntary basis, Yugoslavia was first created by post–World War I diplomatic negotiations and then re-created at the end of World War II by the authoritarian regime of Tito. The nation was held together largely by the forcefulness of Tito's leadership. After his death in 1980, little remained to preserve the integrity of the Yugoslavian experiment in nation building. The memories of past hostilities and World War II atrocities were strong, and the separate republics began to secede from the Yugoslav federation in the 1990s.

Self-serving political and military leaders in Serbia and in the other former Yugoslavian states inflamed prejudices and antipathies. Vicious conflicts broke out throughout the region, with the worst violence occurring in Bosnia. Bosnia's attempt to establish its independence was opposed by Serbia and by the Serbian and Croatian residents of Bosnia, both of whom formed armed militias. Bosnia became a killing field as these different contingents confronted each other. The Serbs began a campaign of "ethnic cleansing" in Bosnia in 1992 and committed the worst excesses. In the areas of Bosnia where they could establish control, Serbs mounted a campaign to eliminate non-Serbs by forced relocation or, if necessary, by wholesale massacre. Concentration camps appeared, houses were torched, former neighbors became blood enemies, women were raped, and children were killed along with their parents.

The Serbs were not alone in resorting to tactics of mass terror and murder. Croats used the same methods against Bosnian Muslims, and Bosnians retaliated in kind against Serbs. By the time relative peace was established in Bosnia in 1995, more than 100,000 people had died in the murderous ethnic conflict. Many of these patterns of vicious brutality reappeared in the conflict between Serbia and Kosovo that began in 1999 and was ended by the armed intervention of the United States and its North Atlantic Treaty Organization allies.

The disintegration of the former Yugoslavia into savage ethnic violence is one of the nightmarish episodes of recent history. Unfortunately, it is not unique.

RWANDA

In the spring of 1994, the tiny African nation of Rwanda sprang into international headlines. Rwanda's two ethnic groups, the Hutus and Tutsis, had a long history of mutual enmity and hatred, but the attacks that began in 1994 reached new heights of brutality. Perhaps 800,000 people— perhaps many more—were murdered, and millions fled to neighboring nations (Gourevitch, 1999, p. 83). Accounts by witnesses and survivors told of massacres with rifles, machetes, rocks, and fists. No one was spared in the killing frenzy. Elderly people, pregnant women, and small children were executed along with the men in what became one of the most horrific, unimaginable episodes of intergroup violence in world history.

What caused this outburst? As seems to be the case whenever intense ethnic violence occurs, colonization and conquest are part of the explanation for the brutal confrontation between the Hutus and Tutsis. European nations began colonizing Africa in the 1400s, and the area that became Rwanda did not escape domination. Germany

FIGURE 13.3 States of Former Yugoslavia

established control over the region in the late 1800s. Following its defeat in World War I, Germany lost its overseas possessions, and Belgium became the dominant power in the region. Both European powers valued Rwanda for its mild climate and fertile soil. The native population was harnessed to the task of producing agricultural products, especially tea and coffee, for export.

The European colonizers attempted to ease the difficulty of administering and controlling Rwanda by capitalizing on the long-standing enmity between the Tutsis and Hutus. In a classic case of divide and conquer, Germany placed the Tutsis in a position to govern the Hutus, a move that perpetuated and intensified hostilities between the tribes. The Belgians continued the tradition and maintained the political and economic differentials between the tribes.

Throughout the colonial era, mutual tribal hostilities were punctuated by periodic armed clashes, some of which rose to the level of massacres. In the early 1960s, the era of direct European political colonialism ended, and two nations were created in the region: Rwanda was dominated by the Hutus, and neighboring Burundi by the Tutsis. Hostilities did not stop at this point, however, and the short histories of these two new nations are filled with shared conflicts. What portion of these conflicts is international and what portion domestic is difficult to determine, because a substantial number of Tutsis continued to reside in Rwanda and many residents of Burundi were Hutu. In other words, the borders between the two nations were drawn arbitrarily and do not reflect local traditions or tribal realities.

In the early 1990s, a rebel force led by exiled Tutsis invaded Rwanda with the intention of overthrowing the Hutu-dominated government. The conflict continued until the spring of 1994, when the plane carrying the Hutu president of Rwanda was shot down, killing all aboard. This was the incident that set off the massacres, with Hutus seeking revenge for the death of their president and attempting to eliminate their Tutsi rivals. In another of the great nightmarish episodes of the 20th century, perhaps as many as half the Tutsis in Rwanda died in the confrontation, and millions more fled for their lives. Although surely not a complete explanation for these horrors, the history of intertribal enmity and competition for power and control enhanced and magnified by European colonialism is part of the background for understanding them—if such an understanding is possible.

Since 1994, Rwanda has enjoyed relative calm. Violent ethnic clashes, however, have continued across the African continent, and the nightmare of genocide has struck Darfur, the Central African Republic, and Somalia, among other nations. The year 2014 marked 20 years post-genocide and Rwanda memorialized its victims. In that time, and since, its government and people have taken impressive measures to prosecute those responsible through the court of law—more

than 20,000 of them. Additionally, local community Gacaca courts ("Gacaca" loosely translate to "justice amongst the grass") have taken on almost 1.2 million cases in addition to the cases the formal legal system has tried (New York Times, 2014). Because Rawanda's genocide was largely an instance of neighbors killing neighbors, this local approach seems useful, though it's certainly not without critique. Also, local communities must deal with situations where people convicted of brutal crimes come back to their neighborhoods. To deal with these issues, many people are joining "peace clubs" to acknowledge their responsibility for playing a part in the atrocities and to ask for forgiveness (Hopkins, 2017).

SOUTH AFRICA

Not all stories are nightmares, and the dreary litany of hatred, conflict, and violence occasionally takes a surprising twist. As recently as the late 1980s, the Republic of South Africa was one of the most racist and discriminatory societies in the world. A small minority of whites (no more than 10%) dominated the black African population and enjoyed a level of race-based privilege rarely equalled in the world's history.

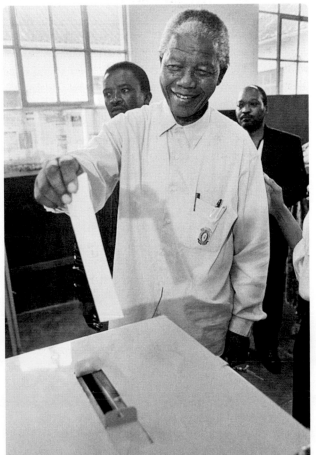

Paul Weinberg/Wikimedia Commons

Nelson Mandela casts his ballot in South Africa's first democratic election. He was elected President and served from 1994 to 1999.

Today, although enormous problems of inequality and racism remain, South Africa has officially dismantled the machinery of racial oppression, enfranchised non-whites, and elected three black presidents. Even in a world where change is rapid and unpredictable, the end of state-supported racism and race-based privilege in South Africa is one of the more stunning surprises of recent times.

Some background will illuminate the magnitude of the change. Europeans first came into contact with the area that became the nation of South Africa in the 1600s, at about the time when the British were establishing colonies in North America. First to arrive were the Dutch, who established ports on the coast to resupply merchant ships for the journey between Asia and Europe. Some of the Dutch began moving into the interior to establish farms and sheep and cattle ranches. The "trekkers," as they were called, regularly fought with indigenous black Africans and tribes moving into the area from the north. These interracial conflicts were extremely bloody and resulted in enslavement for some black Africans, genocide for others, and a gradual push of the remaining black Africans into the interior. In some ways, this contact period resembled that between European Americans and Native Americans, and in other ways, it resembled the early days of the establishment of black slavery in North America.

In the 1800s, South Africa became a British colony, and the new governing group attempted to grant more privileges to blacks. These efforts stopped far short of equality, however, and South Africa continued to evolve as a racially divided, white-dominated society into the 20th century. The white community continued to be split along ethnic lines, and hostilities erupted into violence on a number of occasions. In 1899, British and Dutch factions fought each other in the Boer War, a bitter and intense struggle that widened and solidified the divisions between the two white communities. Generally, the descendants of the Dutch have been more opposed to racial change than have the descendants of the British.

In 1948, the National Party, the primary political vehicle of the Afrikaans, or Dutch, segment of the white community, came into control of the state. As the society modernized and industrialized, there was growing concern about controlling the majority black population. Under the leadership of the National Party, the system of apartheid was constructed to firmly establish white superiority. In Afrikaans, *apartheid* means "separate" or "apart," and the basic logic of the system was to separate whites and blacks in every area of life: schools, neighborhoods, jobs, buses, churches, and so forth. As we pointed out in Chapter 5, apartheid resembled the Jim Crow system of segregation in the United States, except it was even more repressive, elaborate, and unequal.

Although the official government propaganda claimed that apartheid would permit blacks and whites to develop separately and equally, the system was clearly intended to solidify white privilege and black powerlessness. By keeping blacks poor and powerless, white South Africans created a pool of workers who were both cheap and powerless. Whites of even modest means could afford the luxuries of personal servants, and employers could minimize their payrolls and their overhead. Of the dominant–minority situations considered in this text, perhaps only American slavery rivals apartheid for its naked, unabashed subjugation of one group for the benefit of another.

Note that the coming of apartheid reversed the relationship between modernization and control of minority groups that we observed in the United States. As the United States industrialized and modernized, group relations evolved from paternalistic to rigid competitive to fluid competitive forms (see Table 5.2), each stage representing a looser form of control over the minority group. In South Africa after 1948, group relations became more rigid and the structures of control became stronger and more oppressive. Why the difference?

Just as whites in the U.S. South attempted to defend their privileged status and resist the end of de jure segregation in the 1950s and 1960s, white South Africans were committed to retaining their status and the benefits it created. Although South Africans of British descent tended to be more liberal in matters of race than those of Dutch descent, both groups were firmly committed to white supremacy. Thus, unlike the situation in the United States at the end of Jim Crow segregation, in which white liberals and non-Southerners put considerable pressure on the racist South, there was little internal opposition to the creation of apartheid among South African whites.

Furthermore, South African blacks in the late 1940s were comparatively more powerless than blacks in the United States in the 1950s and 1960s. Although South African black protest organizations existed, they were illegal and had to operate underground or from exile and under conditions of extreme repression. In the United States, in contrast, blacks living outside the South were able to organize and pool their resources to assist in the campaign against Jim Crow, and these activities were protected (more or less) by the national commitment to civil liberties and political freedom.

A final difference between the two situations has to do with numbers, as we pointed out in Chapter 5. Whereas in the United States blacks are a numerical minority, they were the great majority of the population in South Africa. Part of the impetus for establishing the rigid system of apartheid was the fear among whites that they would be "swamped" by the numerical majority unless black powerlessness was perpetuated. The difference in group size helped contribute to the "fortress" mentality among some white South Africans: the feeling that they were defending a small (but luxurious) outpost surrounded and besieged by savage hordes who threatened their immediate and total destruction. This strong sense of threat among whites, and the need to be vigilant and constantly resist the least hint of racial change, is part of what made the events of the 1990s so remarkable and unexpected.

The system of racial privilege called apartheid lasted about 40 years. Through the 1970s and 1980s, changes within South Africa and the world in general built up pressure against the system. Internally, protests by blacks against apartheid began in the 1960s and continued to build in intensity. The South African government responded to these protests with violent repression, and thousands died in the confrontations with police and the army. Nonetheless, anti-apartheid activism continued to attack the system from below.

Apartheid also suffered from internal weaknesses and contradictions. For example, jobs were strictly segregated, along with all other aspects of South African society. In a modern, industrial economy, however, new types of jobs are constantly being created and old jobs are continually lost to mechanization and automation, making it difficult to maintain simple, caste-like rules about who can do what kinds of work. Also, many of the newer jobs required higher levels of education and special skills, and the number of white South Africans was too small to meet the demand. Thus, some black South Africans were slowly rising to positions of greater affluence and personal freedom even as the system attempted to coerce and repress the group as a whole.

Internationally, pressure on South Africa to end apartheid was significant. Other nations established trade embargoes and organized boycotts of South African goods. South Africa was banned from the Olympics and other international competitions. Although many of these efforts were more symbolic than real and had only minor impacts on everyday social life, they sustained an outcast status for South Africa and helped create an atmosphere of uncertainty among its economic and political elite.

In the late 1980s, these various pressures made it impossible to ignore the need for reform any longer. In 1990, F. W. de Klerk, the leader of the National Party and prime minister of the nation, began a series of changes that eventually ended apartheid. He lifted the ban on many outlawed black African protest organizations, and, perhaps most significant, he released Nelson Mandela from prison. Mandela was the leader of the African National Congress, one of the oldest and most important black organizations, and he had served a 27-year prison term for actively protesting apartheid.

Together, de Klerk and Mandela helped ease South Africa through a period of rapid racial change that saw the franchise being extended to blacks, the first open election in South African history, and Mandela's election in 1994 to a five-year term as president. After his presidency, Mandela continued to grow in stature on the world stage, hailed as the key individual who prevented a race war in South Africa and as a symbol of racial democracy and justice. His passing in December 2013 was met with virtually universal grief.

In 1999, Mandela was replaced by Thabo M. Mbeke, another black South African. Mbeke was reelected in 2004 but ousted in September 2008 after a bitter struggle with African National Congress rival Jacob Zuma, who became president in 2009. Zuma is a charismatic figure with strong support among the rank-and-file of the party, but his standing has been compromised by allegations of corruption, charges of rape, and other scandals.

The future of South Africa remains unclear. Although the majority black population now has political power, deep racial divisions remain. In many urban and white residential areas, South Africa maintains a First-World infrastructure, but the black population continues to live in Third World poverty.

In 2010, South Africa hosted the soccer World Cup and expanded airports, improved roads, and built hotels and stadiums to provide first-class facilities for the hordes of fans who attended the matches. The event went off smoothly and was generally considered a triumph as South Africa presented its best multiracial, unified face to the world.

What the world didn't see was that much of the black population continues to live in apartheid-era townships—pockets of deep, grinding poverty with no running water, electricity, or sewage, poor or nonexistent medical care, and grossly overcrowded and understaffed schools. Things may be getting better for black South Africans: One report concludes that the black middle class has doubled in size since 1993 and the percentage of blacks in the middle class has increased from 8% to almost 14% in the same time period. Furthermore, the income gap between whites and blacks has declined. Still, the average annual income (in U.S. dollars) for black households was $5,203 in 2015, about one-fifth of the annual income for white households (Statistics South Africa, 2017).

The problems of racial and class inequality facing South Africa are enormous, and this experiment in racial reform might still fail. However, should it succeed in meeting these challenges, the dramatic transition away from massive racism and institutionalized discrimination could still provide a model of change for other racially divided societies.

THE MIDDLE EAST

The tense, often violent relations between Israelis, Palestinians, and other Arabs are yet another example of the complex, long-lasting conflicts that seem to defy the most concerted, best-intentioned efforts at conciliation. Hatred, terrorism, and pledges to fight to the death are common in these conflicts and deeply complicated by the fact that they involve nation-states and global alliances as well as dominant and minority groups. Relations between groups in the Middle East are perhaps the most complex and ancient of any around the globe.

As with many of the situations considered in this chapter, present-day conflicts in the Middle East have their origins in military conquest. Following World War II and the horrors of the Holocaust, European Jews pushed for the establishment of a Jewish state in their traditional homeland. The United Nations and United States strongly supported this cause, and Israel was founded in 1948.

Unfortunately, the Jewish homeland was established on land occupied by Arabs (Palestinians), who also regarded it as their rightful homeland. Thus began the dominant–minority (Israeli–Palestinian) situation that continues today and is further complicated by relations between Israel and the other nations of the Middle East.

One difference between this and other intergroup struggles is the span of time involved. Although the modern state of Israel encompasses the traditional Jewish homeland, few Jews have lived in this area for the past 2,000 years. Jews were exiled from the region during the time of the Roman Empire and resettled in parts of Europe, Africa, and Asia. The Middle East has been Arab land for most of the past thousand years. Jews began to immigrate back to the area early in the 20th century, and especially after World War II and the founding of Israel, but they found a well-entrenched Palestinian Arab society on what they considered to be "their" land.

Warfare between the newly founded Israel and the surrounding Arab nations began almost immediately, and violent confrontations of one sort or another have been nearly continuous. Full-scale wars were fought in 1948, 1967 (the famous Six-Day War), and again in 1973. Israel was victorious in all three instances, and it claimed additional territory from its Arab neighbors (including the Golan Heights, the West Bank, and the Gaza Strip) to reduce the threat and provide a buffer zone. The wars also created a large group of refugees in the Arab countries neighboring Israel.

The Arabs who remained in Israel after the wars and in Israeli-occupied territories became a minority group. Israel has always pursued an official policy of assimilation, and some Arabs eventually became Israeli citizens, although most prefer to be classified as "permanent residents" rather than citizens, as a way of refusing to recognize Israel's sovereignty. Arabs make up about 20% of Israel's population of eight million (Israel Central Bureau of Statistics, 2014). The Palestinian population of Israel is supplemented with millions more living in the surrounding Arab nations.

Part of the complexity and intensity of this situation stems from the fact that the groups involved are separated along so many different lines: nationality, religion, language, ethnicity, history, and social class. In addition, because of the huge oil reserves in the region, the Israeli–Arab conflict has political and international dimensions that directly involve the rest of the world. The U.S. involvement in two separate invasions of Iraq; the war on terror following the September 11, 2001, attacks on the United States; the war in Afghanistan; and the difficult relationship between Iran and the West have added a level of complexity to the already tense relationships between Israel and its Arab neighbors.

There are some indications that a solution to the enmities in the Middle East is possible. In 1979, Egypt, formerly committed to the destruction of the Jewish state, signed a peace accord with Israel. More recently, Israel and representatives of the Palestinians have engaged in occasional peace talks and, most famously, signed an accord intended to lead to Palestinian self-rule in Oslo in 1993. The peace talks have been punctuated with violent uprisings by Palestinians ("Intifadas") and military responses by the Israeli Army. To say the least, negotiations have been extremely difficult and constantly threatened by violence, suicide bombings, attacks, and counterattacks.

The year 2017 marks the 50th year anniversary of the 1967 war, with May 2018 marking the 50th year that Israel has had a homeland—or 50 years that Palestinians have lived under occupation—depending on one's perspective. Negotiations continue sporadically, but few can see an end to the ongoing conflicts. Of course, much the same point was made about South Africa until the dramatic events that led to the release of Mandela and the relatively peaceful transition to a racial democracy. The history of dominant–minority relations is filled with surprises, and, at least theoretically, a peaceful, permanent resolution remains a possibility.

HAWAII

Like Switzerland, Hawaii is often identified as a place that maintains peaceful group relations in the face of great diversity. This reputation justifies the inclusion of the islands in this global survey despite the fact that Hawaii is not a separate, autonomous nation.

The diversity of Hawaiian society is demonstrated, in part, by its racial makeup. The population of Hawaii is much more racially mixed than the general population of the United States. In the 2010 Census, for example, 24% of Hawaiians chose more than one category to describe their race, compared with less than 3% of the U.S. population as a whole.

Whites are a numerical minority on the island, accounting for about a quarter of the population. Asians are the single largest racial group, with Japanese Americans and Filipino Americans the largest Asian subcategories. Native Hawaiians are about 20% of the population. Other groups—Hispanic Americans, African Americans, and

Palestinian activists confront Israeli soldiers during a demonstration.

the population of Native Hawaiians fell from about 300,000 in 1788 to less than 60,000 a century later (Kitano & Daniels, 1995, p. 137).

As relations between the islands and Europeans developed, the land gradually began to be turned to commercial agriculture. By the mid-1800s, white planters had established sugar plantations, an enterprise that is extremely labor-intensive and has often been associated with systems of enforced labor and slavery (Curtin, 1990). By that time, however, there were not enough Native Hawaiians to fill the demand for labor, and the planters began to recruit abroad, mostly in China, Portugal, Japan, Korea, Puerto Rico, and the Philippines. Thus, the original immigrants of the Asian American groups we discussed in Chapter 9 often came first to the Hawaiian Islands, not to the mainland.

The white plantation owners came to dominate the island economy and political structure. Other groups, however, were not excluded from secondary structural assimilation. Laws banning entire groups from public institutions or practices such as school segregation are nonexistent in Hawaiian history. Americans of Japanese ancestry, for example, are very powerful in politics and have produced many of the leading Hawaiian politicians. (In contrast to events on the mainland, Japanese Americans in Hawaii were not interned during World War II.) Most other groups have taken advantage of the relative openness of Hawaiian society and have carved out niches for themselves in the institutional structure.

In the area of primary structural assimilation, rates of intermarriage among the various groups are much higher than on the mainland, reflecting the openness to intimacy across group lines that has characterized Hawaii since first contact. About 42% of all marriages in Hawaii from 2008 to 2010 crossed group lines, a much higher rate than for any other state (Wang, 2012, p. 10). In particular, Native Hawaiians have intermarried freely with other groups (Kitano & Daniels, 1995, pp. 138–139).

Although Hawaii has no history of the most blatant and oppressive forms of group discrimination, all is not perfect in the reputed racial paradise. There is evidence of ethnic and racial stratification, as well as prejudice and discrimination. Native Hawaiians, like Native Americans and other colonized groups, have developed organizations to pursue compensation for lands illegally taken and to resolve other grievances. There have been reports of attacks on whites by Native Hawaiians, incidents that some are calling

Samoans and other Pacific Islanders, among others—are also a part of the island social order.

The cultures and traditions of all these groups are evident in the mix of Hawaiian society and the rhythm of everyday life. The relatively low levels of prejudice, discrimination, and group conflict in the midst of this diversity are the bases for the sometimes glowing (and, many would argue, overstated) depictions of Hawaii as a racial paradise.

The comparatively high levels of tolerance seem unusual in a world that often features just the opposite. A brief review of the history of the islands provides some insight into the development of these peaceful relations, as well as the suggestion that the peaceful facade hides a grimmer reality.

Hawaii first encountered Europeans in 1788, but conquest and colonization did not follow the initial contact. Early relations between the islanders and Europeans were organized around trade and commerce—not agriculture, as was the case in the United States, South Africa, Northern Ireland, and so many other places. Thus, the contact situation did not lead immediately to competition over the control of land or labor.

Also, the indigenous Hawaiian society was highly developed and had sufficient military strength to protect itself from the relatively few Europeans who came to the islands in these early days. Thus, two of the three conditions—competition and a differential in power—stated in the Noel hypothesis (see Chapter 4) for the emergence of a dominant–minority situation were not present in the early days of European–Hawaiian contact. Anglo dominance did not emerge until decades after first contact.

Contact with Europeans did bring other consequences, including smallpox and other diseases to which Native Hawaiians had no immunity. Death rates began to rise, and hate crimes (Kasindorf, 2012). However, the traditions of tolerance and acceptance remain strong in the island state, even though it is not the paradise of mutual respect sometimes alleged.

BRAZIL

As we noted in the Chapter 6 Comparative Focus, Brazilian and U.S. history run parallel in many ways. Both nations emerged from a contact situation that involved three racially distinct groups and a struggle for land and labor. In both cases, the group that became dominant was white, harsh treatment and disease devastated one of the defeated groups (the indigenous population), and the other group (blacks from Africa) was used for slave labor on plantations. Despite these early parallels, the nations developed along different tracks, and race relations in modern Brazil are different from those in the United States.

Brazil is the largest nation in South America and about the same size as the United States. Its territory stretches from the Atlantic Ocean deep into the interior and almost across the width of the continent. Its population of 207 million people (in 2017) is racially and ethnically diverse. About 800,000 indigenous people survive, down from about five million at first contact. Portugal colonized Brazil in 1500 and it remained a colony until 1822. Portuguese remains its primary language.

The colonial history of Brazil began almost a century before Jamestown was established. In fact, the African slave trade on which the British colonies became so dependent in the 1600s and 1700s was originally created to provide slave labor for colonial Brazil in the 1500s (Curtin, 1990). Until 1866, Brazil "imported" 4.9 million enslaved people—more than any other country and about 10 times as many the United States (Bourcier, 2012; Gates, 2014). Although its system of slavery started much earlier than in the United States it evolved for the same reason—to supply labor —in this case for sugar, gold and diamonds, cotton, coffee, cattle, and tobacco production (Wimberly, 2015). In other words, it also had a plantation economy (Bourcier, 2012; Buccifero, 2017).

In both countries, slave experiences were gendered. For example, most enslaved women in both nations worked as domestic servants, were often sexually abused by their masters, and were regarded as useful for their reproductive capabilities (Santos, 2016). However, the overall system of slavery in Brazil tended to be more open than the North American system. Brazilian slaves were freed at a much higher rate than slaves in the United States and free blacks and "mulattos" were allowed to work in most jobs in that society.

The slave trade in both countries declined, in part, due to changing subsistence economies that required fewer slaves. As abolitionist movements gained strength, people in both countries fought to preserve their respective systems of slavery. The abolition of slavery came in gradual stages in Brazil. In the United States slavery ended more suddenly due to the Civil War. In Brazil, preparations for the end of slavery extended over decades, allowing for a smoother transition of slaves to free citizens. For example, Brazil outlawed the importation of slaves in 1831 though slave traders often ignored that law. In 1851, it outlawed the maritime slave trade (again), this time criminalizing it as an act of piracy (Bucciferro, 2017, pp. 176-178; Conrad 1972, p. 106). Enslaved people in the two countries were liberated in different ways. In contrast with the United States, which freed enslaved people all at once with the signing of the Emancipation Proclamation, Brazil freed enslaved people in stages. First, in 1871, through the "Law of Free Birth" which granted freedom to children born to enslaved women. Then, in 1885, slaves over the age of 60 were freed (Conrad 1972, pp. 214–216). Finally, in 1888, Brazil outlawed the ownership of slaves, making it the last country in the Western Hemisphere to abolish slavery (Bourcier, 2012; Bucciferro, 2017, p. 176; Conrad, 1972).

Various scholars (e.g., see Cottrol, 2013; Degler, 1971; Tannenbaum, 1947) have explored the contrasting racial systems of the two nations and, although we cannot examine every issue in these few pages, we can make the point that the foundation for today's race relations may have been laid in the distant past, both before and during the contact situation. At the time Brazil was established, Portugal, unlike England, had had a long acquaintance with African cultures and peoples. In fact, Moors from North Africa ruled Portugal for a time. Thus, darker skin and other African "racial" features were familiar to the Portuguese, which was not the case for early American colonists.

In Brazil, slavery was not so thoroughly equated with race as it was in the United States. Although slave status was certainly undesirable and unfortunate, it did not always carry the presumption of racial inferiority. In contrast, antiblack prejudice and racism developed to rationalize and support the system of slavery in the United States (see Chapter 4). Thus, slavery, blackness, and inferiority were tightly linked in the dominant ideology, an equation with powerful echoes in the present.

The type of colonization during the contact situation has some importance for contemporary race relations. "Colonies of exploitation" are mainly created by single men (Barnhill, 2014, p. 192) who intermarry with other racial groups and help produce a group of "mixed-race" people. The Portuguese who colonized Brazil were, primarily, a colony of exploitation (Novais, 1991) though there was some regional variation (Metcalf, 2005, p. 39). As a result, there

Listed below are some ethnic or racial "trouble spots" that were not covered in this chapter. For each, can you identify the region of the world, the groups involved in the conflict, and at least one key issue? For any given location, there may well be more than one issue, but we have tried to select the most prominent (at least in the headlines). How well do you think most Americans would do on this quiz?

AREA	REGION	GROUPS AND ISSUES
Chechnya		
Scotland		
Nigeria		
China		
Spain		
Mexico		

TURN THE PAGE TO FIND OUR ANSWERS.

were high rates of intermarriage between the Portuguese, Africans, and indigenous people.

"Colonies of settlement" are formed by families who arrive together or plan, at some point, to reunite in the colonies. In colonies of settlement, migrants force indigenous people out. The United States was primarily a colony of settlement (Szirmai, 2005). Interracial marriage between free whites and free blacks first became illegal in Maryland in 1664, and eventually, in all the colonies. Variations of that law remained in place until 1967 when the Supreme Court ruled it unconstitutional in *Loving v. Virginia*. Thus, colonists did not recognize a mixed-race group (even though this group indisputably existed).

Today, in Brazil, whites are less than a majority of the population (47%), and blacks are about 8%. The remainder of the population (about 43%) consists of *pardos*, or people of mixed-race ancestry (Instituto Brasileiro do Geografica e Estatistica, 2013). The results of high intermarriage rates and the large population of pardos are manifold. First, they helped sustain a way of thinking about race that is sharply different from North American practices, as we saw in Chapter 6. In Brazil and other parts of South and Central America, people see race as more fluid and as having somewhat ambiguous, indeterminate boundaries between groups. People in the United States, in contrast, have traditionally seen race as a set of sharply delineated categories with relatively clear boundaries between groups.

Societal life, post-slavery, was also different for both countries. Brazil did not go through a period of legalized racial segregation like the American Jim Crow system. Such a system would be difficult to construct or enforce when race is seen as a set of open-ended categories that gradually fade into one another. Racial segregation requires a simple racial classification system in which people are easily classified into a single category. The more nuanced and subtle perception of race in Brazil is not conducive to such a system of racial inequality. This is not to say that segregation did not occur in Brazil. After the abolishment of slavery, former slaves moved to the tops of mountains where they built separate communities. The key factor for living in these areas today, known as *favelas*, is poverty not race (Nunes & Veloso, 2012, p. 233). This de facto segregation continues today.

Brazil is not the "racial paradise" as some people claim. While race in Brazil is socially constructed in less rigid ways, research suggests that whites felt concern about "darker races" (Oboler & Gonzalez, 2005, p. 194). These fears influenced the country's "racial whitening" (*branqueamento*) policies of the late 19th century. When President Theodore Roosevelt visited Brazil, a government leader advised him to consider it, saying, "Now comes the necessity to devise some method of dealing with it [the Negro problem]. You of the United States are keeping the blacks as an entirely separate element, and you are not treating them in a way that fosters their self-respect . . . they will remain a menacing element . . . With us the question tends

AREA	REGION	GROUPS AND ISSUES
Chechnya	Eastern Europe	Separatism. Since the dissolution of the Soviet Union, Chechnya has fought two wars for independence. Besides cultural differences with Russia, Chechens are predominantly Muslim.
Scotland	Northern United Kingdom	Separatism. Scotland has been part of the United Kingdom for centuries, but there has always been strong sentiment to secede and become an independent sovereign nation. A variety of Scottish groups are pursuing this goal. A referendum on the question was held in 2014. The supporters of separation lost decisively (55% to 45%) but, in the wake of Britain's exit from the European Union, there is renewed interest in independence.
Nigeria	Western Africa	Discrimination against gays and lesbians (see Chapter 12). In January 2014, Nigeria passed a law that criminalized homosexuality and provided up to 14 years in prison for same-sex relationships.
China	East Asia	Separatism. Groups claiming to represent Uyghur, a predominantly Muslim area of western China, wish to gain their independence and make the province a separate, autonomous nation. There is also considerable support for separation and autonomy in Tibet, which has been a part of China since the 1950s.
Spain	Western Europe	Separatism. Many Basques, who live in the mountainous northern regions of Spain, desire their own independent nation. Basques are a distinct cultural and linguistic minority whose "home territory" stretches across the border to France.
Mexico	North America	Indigenous rights. The indigenous population of Mexico (about 15% of the total) is concentrated in the southern states of Oaxaca and Chiapas. They have numerous grievances, including land claims, discrimination, and racism.

Note the frequency of separatism as a goal in these trouble spots. Is this a testimony to the ability of groups to maintain their culture and distinct identity even when they have been part of a larger nation, sometimes for centuries? Will ethnicity ever fade away?

to disappear, because the blacks themselves tend to disappear and become absorbed. You speak of Brazil as having a large Negro population. Well, in a century there will not be any Negroes, whereas you will have 20 or 30 million of them" (Roosevelt, 1914, pp. 410–411).

To facilitate branqueamento the government allowed more than four million (white) Europeans to immigrate to help supply labor from 1884 to 1939 (Gates, 2011). However, they banned African immigrants (Hernandez, 2012). The hope was that, over time, Brazil would become "whiter" as whites and blacks had children. Although many Brazilians (and others) promoted the idea that their country was a "racial democracy," this policy illustrates an ideology that "white blood" is superior (Telles, 2004). (The Chapter 7 Comparative Focus illustrates similar thinking and practice regarding Aboriginal people in Australia.)

The legacy of slavery is still strong, and there is a very high correlation between skin color and social status. Studies consistently show that black Brazilians have higher poverty rates and lower educational attainment, levels of health, and incomes. Whites dominate the more prestigious and lucrative occupations and the leadership positions in the economy and politics, whereas blacks are concentrated at the bottom of the class system (Haan & Thorat, 2012; Marteleto, 2012).

Interestingly, Brazil has made a major commitment to increasing the opportunities available to the poor, a disproportionate number of whom are black or brown. For example, a program called Brazil Without Misery was launched in 2011 with the intent of eliminating extreme poverty by 2014, and the central government has instituted a variety of affirmative action programs intended to increase the enrollment of black students in the nation's universities.

Racial discrimination, inequality, and racism are massive problems in Brazil, as they are in the United States. Still, the comparison between the two nations is instructive. Differences in the contact period and the development of race relations over time have resulted in a notably different form of group relations today.

5. Which, if any, of these dominant–minority situations is new to you? Which was the most surprising to you? Why?

6. Do you think your peers are aware of the situations described in this section? How about most Americans? How would you explain the level of information (or interest) that people have in these matters?

ANALYZING GROUP RELATIONS

Our analysis of group relations around the world has been brief and highly selective. Nonetheless, we can make some conclusions.

Problems of dominant–minority relations are extremely common. It seems that the only nations that lack such problems are the relatively few (such as Sweden) that are homogeneous in their racial, cultural, religious, and linguistic makeup. Still, many of these countries (including Sweden) face challenges related to immigration.

Dominant–minority problems are highly variable in their form and intensity. They encompass genocide in the former Yugoslavia and Rwanda; hate crimes motivated by race, religion, or ethnicity in Germany (and many other nations); and complaints of racism, unfairness, and injustice virtually everywhere. Some long-standing minority grievances remain unresolved, and new problem areas appear on a regular basis. It seems unlikely that all these issues of group relations—and the many others not covered in this chapter—will be settled or otherwise fade away at any point in the near future.

As we have noted on a number of occasions, the most intense, violent, and seemingly intractable problems of group relations almost always have their origins in contact situations in which one group is conquered or colonized by another. Blauner's hypothesis seems well supported by this examination of dominant–minority relations around the globe.

The impact of modernization and industrialization on racial and ethnic relations varies. Whereas these forces led to less rigid group relations in the United States, they had the opposite effect in South Africa until the 1990s. Furthermore, globally, ethnic and racial groups that were thought to have been submerged in the hustle and bustle of modern society have reappeared with some regularity. The former Yugoslavia supplies some of the most dramatic examples of the seeming imperviousness of ethnicity to industrialization and modernization, but others can be found in Scotland, Belgium, Spain, the former Soviet Union, Mexico, China, Nigeria, Iraq, and scores of other nations. In each of these cases, pluralistic or separatist movements based on ethnic, racial, or religious groups are present and, in some cases, thriving.

It seems unlikely that even the most sophisticated and modern of nations will outgrow the power of ethnic loyalties at any point in the near future. In virtually all the cases discussed, whatever tendencies modernization fosters to reduce, prejudice seems to be offset by memories of past injustices, unresolved grievances, a simple yearning for revenge, and continuing struggles over control of land, labor, and other resources. Ethnic and racial lines continue to reflect inequalities of wealth and power, and as long as minority-group status is correlated with inequality, ethnic and racial loyalties will remain powerful motivations for conflict.

As we have noted, ethnic and racial group conflicts are especially intense when they coincide with class divisions and patterns of inequality. For example, minority-group members in Canada, South Africa, and Northern Ireland command lower shares of wealth and political power, and have worse jobs, poorer housing, and lower levels of education. When a conflict arises in these societies, whether the problem is one of economics, politics, or a dominant–minority issue, the same groups face each other across the lines of division. The greater the extent to which issues and lines of fracture coincide and reinforce each other, the greater the threat to society as a whole and the more difficult it will be to manage the conflict and avoid escalation to its extremes.

With respect to the intensity and nature of dominant–minority problems, the United States is hardly in a unique or unusual position. Many nations are dealing with problems of assimilation and pluralism, diversity and unity, and some of these issues seem far more difficult and complex than those facing our society. Societies such as Switzerland and Hawaii help sustain the idea that relatively peaceful, comparatively just, and roughly equal group relations are possible even for very diverse nations. Our tour of the globe also shows that no racial paradises exist; even the multigroup societies with the most glowing reputations for tolerance are not immune to conflict, inequality, discrimination, and racism.

7. Do the case studies in this chapter demonstrate the importance of the contact situation and subsistence technology? How?

8. Which is the most important of the major concepts applied in this text? Why?

SUMMARY

This summary is organized around the Learning Objectives listed at the beginning of this chapter.

 13.1 State and explain the central themes of this text.

Throughout the text, we have stressed the importance of the initial contact situation (especially competition, differential in power, and colonization vs. immigration); subsistence technology; assimilation; pluralism; and prejudice, discrimination, and racism.

 13.2 Summarize the overall pattern of ethnic variability around the globe, and identify which regions are most and least diverse.

The United States is one of many nations dealing with issues of diversity. African nations tend to be the most diverse, and Western European nations tend to be the least.

 13.3 Summarize the dominant–minority situations outlined in this chapter, including the history and present situation, and apply the central concepts developed in this text to each case.

Virtually all these dominant–minority situations began with a contact situation in which one group colonized another. In Canada, the groups were based on language and culture; in Northern Ireland, religion was the obvious dividing line; and in South Africa and Brazil, it was race. In all cases, however, the divisions go deeper and include differences in access to power, property, and prestige.

In all cases, perhaps especially in the Middle East, Northern Ireland, Rwanda, and former Yugoslavia, the group divisions are ancient and carry a heavy burden of history, memory, and old grievances. Unlike the United States, separatism, self-determination, and group autonomy are major themes, especially in Canada, Northern Ireland, and the former Yugoslavia (and in the situations listed in the Applying Concepts exercise in this chapter). Immigration and assimilation are important factors in Germany, Canada, and many other nations.

The cases of Switzerland and Hawaii suggest the possibility that multigroup societies can have relatively peaceful group relations. The other cases seem to suggest the difficulty of achieving that goal.

REVIEW QUESTIONS

1. How do the cases reviewed in this chapter illustrate the importance of the contact situation and subsistence technology? How do modernization and industrialization affect group relations?

2. For each case study in this chapter, list the racial and cultural characteristics of the dominant and minority groups, the nature of the contact situation, and the type of competition that motivated the construction of minority status. What common patterns do you observe? How do the patterns relate to the concepts used throughout this text?

3. Switzerland, Hawaii, and Brazil are often cited as examples of multigroup societies that are relatively harmonious. How accurate are these characterizations? Are there any common characteristics of their contact situations that might help account for the relative harmony?

4. Compare the development of dominant–minority relations in Brazil and the United States. What important differences and similarities can you identify? How do these differences and similarities affect contemporary relations?

5. What does this chapter say to you about the prevalence and persistence of minority inequality, prejudice, and racism? Will there ever be a time when the nations of the world are free of these problems? What would have to happen to achieve this peace?

Sharpen your skills with SAGE edge at edge.sagepub.com/healey8e

SAGE edge for students provides a personalized approach to help you accomplish your coursework goals in an easy-to-use learning environment.

The following resources are available at SAGE edge:

Public Sociology Assignments

Public Sociology Assignments provide opportunities for students to address directly and personally some of the issues raised in this text.

On our website you will find four assignments in Part IV. In the first assignment, students use the information available from the Pew Research Center to examine religion as a source of diversity in American life. In the second assignment, groups of students will analyze the lyrics of popular songs. Do the lyrics reflect stereotypes of racial or ethnic groups? What messages are being conveyed about gender or sexual orientation?

The third assignment focuses on a film and website that probe the reality of bullying in America's schools. The fourth assignment is an analysis of the thousands of languages around the world that are in danger of becoming extinct.

Contributed by Linda M. Waldron

Internet Research Project

For this Internet Research Project, you will select any two of the dominant–minority situations covered in this chapter or listed in the Applying Concepts exercise and use the resources available on the Internet to update information and conclusions. Has the situation improved, or has it gotten worse? What course concepts seem to be of continuing relevance? Which are less relevant? The project will be guided by a series of questions, and your instructor may ask you to discuss your findings in small groups.

For Further Reading

Please see our website for an annotated list of important works related to this chapter.

CHAPTER-OPENING TIMELINE PHOTO CREDITS

1899: Library of Congress Prints and Photographs Division

1916: Library of Congress Prints and Photographs Division

1939–1945: National Archives and Records Administration/Wikimedia Commons

1948: State of Israel's National Photo Collection

1979: Library of Congress Prints and Photographs Division

1990: Copyright World Economic Forum

1992–1995: Wikimedia Commons/Paul Katzenberger

1994: Wikimedia Commons

2013: Cris Faga/NurPhoto via Getty Images

PART V

CHALLENGES FOR THE PRESENT AND THE FUTURE

Chapter 14 Minority Groups and U.S. Society:
Themes, Patterns, and the Future

hapter 14 brings this text to a close. It summarizes the major themes and the information presented in the previous 13 chapters, and it speculates about the future of group relations in the United States and the world.

We begin by revisiting the nine Americans we introduced in Chapter 1 who represent American diversity in terms of race, ethnicity, gender, sexual orientation, and social class. Has your perspective on these individuals changed after reading this text? Are you more aware of how their differences reflect American diversity in general?

Then, we review the major concepts used throughout the text, including subsistence technology, the contact situation, group competition and power, intersectionality, assimilation, and pluralism. How has your understanding of these terms and ideas changed after reading this text? Do you understand their meanings and feel comfortable applying them?

We close by considering the major sociological lessons regarding dominant–minority relations in the United States—including both historical and contemporary forms of racism, prejudice, sexism, and homophobia. How do you respond to our points? How do they enrich your views? What are their limitations?

We are all too aware that we have raised many more questions in this text than we have answered. We hope that we have stimulated your interest in the vast and complex subject matter of dominant–minority relations and enhanced your ability to ask questions and seek answers on your own. If you finish this text with a stronger commitment to analytical thinking and careful evaluation—if you are less willing to settle for the everyday, superficial "explanations" that pass for understanding—we will have accomplished our most important goal.

MINORITY GROUPS AND U.S. SOCIETY

Themes, Patterns, and the Future

timeline

1960
The first U.S. public gathering of lesbians occurs at San Francisco's Daughters of Bilitis national convention.

1963
The March on Washington for Jobs and Freedom is attended by about 250,000 people. Martin Luther King Jr. delivers his famous "I Have a Dream" speech.

1968
The American Indian Movement, an advocacy group, is founded.

1978
The American Indian Movement leads the Longest Walk, a spiritual walk across the country for tribal sovereignty and to protest anti-Indian legislation.

1955   1960   1965   1970   1975   1980

1955
The Daughters of Bilitis, a lesbian organization, is founded.

1955
Rosa Parks refuses to give up her seat on a bus to a white passenger, spurring the Montgomery bus boycott.

1960
Four black students in Greensboro, North Carolina, begin a sit-in at a segregated Woolworth's lunch counter. The event triggers many similar nonviolent protests throughout the South.

1965
César Chávez and Dolores Huerta found the United Farm Workers association.

1969
Patrons of the Stonewall Inn in Greenwich Village riot when police officers attempt to raid the popular gay bar.

1972
The American Indian Movement sponsors the Trail of Broken Treaties, a cross-country protest presenting a 20-point list of demands from the federal government.

Department of Labor

Throughout the previous 13 chapters, we have analyzed ideas and theories about dominant–minority relations, examined the historical and contemporary situations of minority groups in U.S. society, and surveyed a variety of dominant–minority situations around the globe. Now it is time to reexamine our major themes and concepts, and determine what conclusions we can derive from our analysis. •

LEARNING OBJECTIVES

By the end of this chapter, you will be able to do the following:

(14.1) Explain how the people profiled at the beginning of Chapter 1 exemplify the central themes and concepts of this text.

(14.2) Explain the relevance of our central concepts—especially subsistence technology, the contact situation, competition and power, and intersectionality—for American dominant–minority relations.

(14.3) Summarize the situation of each of the groups we have considered in terms of acculturation and integration.

(14.4) Explain the importance of a sociological perspective for understanding American dominant–minority relations.

Associated Press

Corbis

1987
The National March on Washington for Lesbian and Gay Rights draws over 500,000 people, making it the largest civil rights demonstration in U.S. history.

2004
Hispanic Americans become the largest minority group.

2008
The number of undocumented immigrants begins to decline in response to economic hard times in the U.S., falling to less than 11 million in 2012.

2012
Asians surpass Hispanics as the largest group of new immigrants in the U.S.

1990   1995   2000   2005   2010

1979
An estimated 75,000 people participate in the National March on Washington for Lesbian and Gay Rights.

1995
The Million Man March is held in Washington, D.C. to place black issues back on the nation's political agenda.

2007
Massive demonstrations occur around the U.S. in support of immigrant rights.

Wikipedia

©iStockphoto.com/Coast-to-Coast

REVISITING SOME AMERICANS

Let's begin with an exercise. Turn back to Chapter 1 and reread the biographies at the beginning of the chapter, in the Some American Stories section. After reading this book, you may see these nine people differently than you did the first time. These people occupy a variety of positions in American society, and represent a complex mix of privilege and disadvantage. Some are successful and affluent, but others are marginalized because of their sexual orientation, religion, or race. Some are completely integrated into the primary job market, but others drift on the fringes in the informal, underground economy. Some, such as Juan Yancy, are bi- or multiracial and some, such as Hector Gonzalez, have a strong attachment to their cultural heritage. Others are uninterested their ancestors' experiences.

Kim Park lives in an enclave economy, and Shirley Umphlett's life was profoundly affected by the "great migration" of African Americans from the rural South to the urban North. Mary Farrell's family history exemplifies the slow, generation-by-generation rise to middle-class status characteristic of so many European American immigrants, whereas George Snyder and Dennard Umphlett face the urban poverty and underclass marginality that confronts so many racial minority-group members today. William Buford III, in contrast, is wealthy and powerful, and argues that anyone could duplicate his success with sufficient diligence and hard work, conveniently forgetting that his wealth was inherited.

Some people might think that Buford's conclusions are not particularly insightful or informed, but millions of people share his views. Americans traditionally see success or failure as a matter of individual choice and personal effort. Blaming the victims of racism and discrimination for their situations can be comforting because it absolves more fortunate individuals of guilt or complicity in the perpetuation of minority-group poverty and powerlessness.

People who are harmed by systems of oppression may offer us more accurate analyses and compelling conclusions precisely because they have experienced the dynamics of discrimination and may have spent considerable effort trying to avoid victimization. We should recognize, however, that these nine Americans, like all of us, may be victims in some ways and beneficiaries in others. Disadvantage and privilege are distributed in endlessly complex ways across the group matrices that structure our society.

We should also remember that our understandings are limited by who we are, where we come from, and what we have experienced. Our ability to imagine the realities faced by others is never perfect, and what we can see of the world depends very much on where we stand.

If we are to understand the forces that have created dominant–minority relationships in the United States and around the globe, we must find ways to surpass the limitations of our personal experiences and honestly confront the often ugly realities of the past and present. We believe that the information and ideas developed in this text can help liberate our sociological imaginations from the narrow confines of our own experiences and perspectives.

As we look backward to the past and forward to the future, it seems appropriate to paraphrase historian Oscar Handlin (1951): "Once I thought to write a history of the minority groups in America. Then, I discovered that the minority groups were American history" (p. 3).

THE IMPORTANCE OF SUBSISTENCE TECHNOLOGY

One of the most important sociological ideas we have developed is that large social, political, and economic forces shape dominant–minority relations, and they change as these broad characteristics change. To understand the evolution of America's minority groups is to understand the history of the United States, from the earliest colonial settlement to the modern megalopolis. As we have seen throughout the text and in Chapter 13, these same broad forces have left their imprint on many societies around the globe.

Subsistence technology is the most basic force shaping a society and the relationships between dominant and minority groups in that society. In the colonial United States, minority relations were bent to the demands of a land-hungry, labor-intensive agrarian technology, and the early relationships between Africans, Europeans, and American Indians flowed from the colonists' desire to control both land and labor. By the mid-1800s, two centuries after Jamestown was founded, the same dynamics that had enslaved African Americans and nearly annihilated American Indians made a minority group out of Mexican Americans.

The agrarian era came to an end in the 19th century as the new technologies of the industrial revolution increased the productivity of the economy and eventually changed every aspect of life in the United States. The paternalistic, oppressive systems used to control the labor of minority groups in the agrarian era gave way to competitive systems of group relations. These newer systems evolved from more rigid forms to more fluid forms as industrialization and urbanization progressed.

As the United States grew and developed, new minority groups were created, and old minority groups, including women and lesbian, gay, bisexual, and transgender (LGBT) people, were transformed. Rapid industrialization, combined with the opportunities available on the frontier, made the United States an attractive destination for immigrants from Europe, Asia, Latin America, and other parts of the world. Immigrants helped farm the Great Plains, mine the riches of the West, and, above all, supply the armies of labor required by industrialization.

The descendants of the immigrants from Europe benefited from the continuing industrialization of the economy, rising slowly in the social class structure as the economy grew and matured. Immigrants from Asia and Latin America were not so fortunate. Chinese and Japanese Americans survived in ethnic enclaves on the fringes of the mainstream society, and Mexican Americans and Puerto Ricans supplied low-paid manual labor for both the rural and the urban economy. For much of the 20th century, both Asian and Hispanic Americans were barred from higher-paid jobs and widespread access to dominant-group institutions.

The racial minority groups, particularly African Americans, Mexican Americans, and Puerto Ricans, began to enter the urban working class after European American ethnic groups began to move up in the occupational structure, at a time when the supply of manual, unskilled jobs was dwindling. Thus, the processes that allowed upward mobility for European Americans failed to work for the racial minority groups, who confronted urban poverty and bankrupt cities in addition to the continuing barriers of racial prejudice and institutional discrimination.

Immigration to the United States has been quite high for the past several decades. It has supplied our nation with highly educated professionals to help staff the postindustrial economy as well as undocumented immigrants who work in the secondary labor market, the enclaves, and the irregular economy. This stream of people has evoked the usual American nativism and racism, along with intense debates—in the social sciences and in the general public—about the cost and benefits of the immigrants and their ultimate places in American society.

Some of the many people contributing to America's diversity.

We can only speculate about what the future holds, but the emerging information-based, high-tech society is unlikely to offer many opportunities to people with lower levels of education and few occupational skills. It seems highly likely that, at least for the foreseeable future, a substantial percentage of racial and colonized minority groups and some recent immigrant groups will be participating in the mainstream economy at lower levels than will the dominant group, the descendants of the European immigrants, and the more advantaged recent immigrant groups. This outcome would be consistent with the segmented assimilation thesis discussed in Chapter 10. Upgraded urban educational systems, job training programs, and other community development programs might alter the grim scenario of continuing exclusion, but, as we discussed in Chapter 3, current public opinion on matters of race and discrimination makes creation of such programs unlikely.

The perpetuation of the status quo will bar a large percentage of the population from the emerging mainstream economy. Those segments of the African, Hispanic, and Asian American communities currently mired in the urban underclass will continue to compete with some of the newer immigrants for jobs in the low-wage, secondary labor market or in alternative opportunity structures, including crime.

Shifts in subsistence technology also helped transform gender relations and women's lives in particular. In the postindustrial era, women are heavily involved in the paid labor force and, because of the concerted, long-term efforts of the feminist movements, enjoy more opportunities and choices than ever before. However, as we have documented, women still face gender gaps in wages, glass ceilings, sexual harassment, and other gender-related challenges and limitations. Women today are less constrained by institutional barriers, stereotypes, and presumptions of inferiority compared with the past. However, men (as a group) still reap "invisible privileges" from intimate family relations to corporate boardrooms. Globally, women's status continues to depend heavily on subsistence technology, and women in more agrarian societies face especially formidable barriers to gender equality.

As with other minority groups, nonheterosexuals have benefited from the greater acceptance and inclusion associated with more educated, more advanced industrial societies. The relative anonymity of urban spaces provided opportunities for LGB people to find one another, develop a sense of community, and form organizations to fight discrimination based on sexual orientation. In recent decades, after considerable struggle and hard work, gay and lesbian Americans experienced a number of triumphs, including the legalization of same-sex marriage. However, much work remains to be done for LGBT people to achieve full equality, especially in the areas of civil rights and legal protection against job (and other forms of) discrimination.

THE IMPORTANCE OF THE CONTACT SITUATION, GROUP COMPETITION, AND POWER

Many of the positive changes we have discussed in this text were the results of minority-group activism and protest.

Throughout this text we have stressed the importance of the contact situation—the conditions under which the minority group and dominant group first come into contact with each other. Blauner's distinction between immigrant and colonized minority groups is fundamental, a distinction so basic that it helps clarify minority-group situations centuries after the initial contact period. In Part 3, we used Blauner's distinction as an organizing principle and covered American minority groups in approximate order from "most colonized" to "most immigrant." The groups covered first (African Americans and American Indians) are clearly at a greater disadvantage in contemporary society than are the groups covered last (especially immigrants from Asia with high levels of human capital) and the white ethnic groups covered in Chapter 2.

For example, prejudice, racism, and discrimination against African Americans remain formidable forces in contemporary America, even though they may have softened into more subtle forms. In contrast, prejudice and discrimination against European American groups such as Irish, Italian, and Polish Americans have nearly disappeared today, even though they were quite formidable just a few generations ago.

In the same way, contemporary immigrant groups that are nonwhite and bring few resources and low levels of human capital (e.g., Haitians) may experience segmented assimilation and find themselves in situations resembling those of colonized minority groups. Contemporary immigrant groups that are at the opposite end of the continuum (e.g., Asian Indians) are more likely to approximate the experiences of white ethnics and find themselves in some version of middle-class suburbia. The Internet research exercises presented at the ends of Chapters 6 through 10 should have given you information to assess some of these patterns.

Noel's hypothesis states that if three conditions—ethnocentrism, competition, and a differential in power—are present in the contact situation, ethnic or racial stratification will result. The relevance of ethnocentrism is largely limited to the actual contact situation, but the other two concepts help clarify the changes occurring after initial contact.

We have examined numerous instances in which group competition—or even the threat of competition—increased prejudice and led to greater discrimination and more repression. Recall, for example, the opposition of the labor movement (dominated by European American ethnic

groups) to Chinese immigrants. The anti-Chinese campaign led to the Chinese Exclusion Act of 1882, the first significant restriction on immigration to the United States. There are parallels between campaigns for exclusion in the past and current ideas about ending or curtailing immigration. Clearly, some part of the current opposition to immigration is motivated by a sense of threat and the fear that immigrants are a danger not only to jobs and the economy but also to the cultural integrity of U.S. society.

Noel's third variable, differential in power, determines the outcome of the initial contact situation and which group becomes dominant and which becomes minority. Following the initial contact, the superior power of the dominant group helps it sustain the minority group's inferior position.

Minority groups, by definition, have fewer power resources, but they characteristically use what they have in an attempt to improve their situations. Improvements in the situations of American minority groups since the middle of the 20th century have been due in large part to the fact that they (especially African Americans, who typically led the way in protest and demands for change) finally acquired some power resources of their own. For example, one important source of power for the Civil Rights Movement in the South during the 1950s and 1960s was the growth of African American voting strength in the North. After World War II, the African American electorate became too sizable to ignore, and its political power helped pressure the federal government to take action and pass the legislation that ended the Jim Crow era.

Minority status being what it is, however, each of the groups we have discussed (with the exception of the white ethnic groups) still controls relatively few resources and is limited in its ability to pursue its self-interests. Many of these limitations are economic and related to social class; many minority groups simply lack the resources to finance political campaigns for reform or to exert significant political pressure. Other limitations include small group size (e.g., Asian

American groups), language barriers (e.g., many Hispanic American groups), and divided loyalties within the group (e.g., Native Americans separated by tribal allegiances).

At any rate, the relative powerlessness of minority groups today is a legacy of the contact situations that created these groups in the first place. In general, colonized groups are at a greater power disadvantage than immigrant groups. Contact situations set agendas for group relations that continue to exert influence centuries after the initial meeting.

Given all we have examined in this text, it is obvious that competition and differences in power resources will continue to shape intergroup relations (including relations between minority groups themselves) well into the future. Because they are so basic and consequential, jobs will continue to be primary objects of competition, but plenty of other issues will divide the nation. Included on this divisive list will be debates about crime and the criminal justice system, welfare reform, national health care policy, school integration, bilingual education, immigration policy, and multicultural school curricula.

These and other public issues will continue to separate us along ethnic and racial lines because those lines have become so deeply embedded in the economy, in politics, in our schools and neighborhoods, and in virtually every nook and cranny of U.S. society. These deep divisions reflect fundamental realities about who gets what in the United States, and they will continue to reflect the distribution of power and stimulate competition along group lines for generations to come.

Of course, some of our most important concepts do not fit all dominant–minority group situations. For example, there is no "contact situation" for men and women, no time in history when one existed without the other. Similarly, it is impossible to identify a contact situation for heterosexuals and nonheterosexuals.

Still, both women and LGBT people fit Blauner's category of colonized minority group rather well. Patterns of inequality, marginalization, and denigration are easily documented, as we demonstrated in Chapters 11 and 12.

In the case of women, highly visible physical markers of group membership help maintain the system of oppression similar to the ways subordination is maintained for racial minority groups. For LGBT people, the dynamics of social visibility are subtler and variable. However, as anyone who has "come out" can attest, visibility can bring fundamental changes in personal relations, occupational opportunities, and other areas of life.

Blauner's hypothesis may not be literally applicable to women and LGBT people, but Noel's concepts of power and competition are central to both group situations. They have both had to organize, acquire resources, and confront the bastions of privilege in the streets as well as the courtrooms to improve their situations and move closer to equality. Resistance to these movements has been constant and formidable, even though the long-term trend has been toward inclusion.

For women, the society made a formal (and, many would argue, partial and unfulfilled) commitment to equality many decades ago. The struggle for acceptance and an end to stigma and marginalization continues for people who are LGBT. The United States is currently embroiled in a deeply felt controversy over whether that commitment to equality should be extended to them, a struggle that reminds us that competition can be symbolic and cultural, and independent from the distribution of resources such as jobs, income, and political representation.

THE IMPORTANCE OF INTERSECTIONALITY

All too often, and this text is probably no exception, dominant and minority groups are seen as somewhat undifferentiated. Although overgeneralizations are sometimes difficult to avoid, we want to stress again the diversity within each of the groups we have examined. Minority-group members vary from one another by age, sex, region of residence, level of education, urban versus rural residence, political ideology, and many other variables. The experience of one segment of the group (e.g., college-educated, fourth-generation, native-born Chinese American women) may bear little resemblance to the experience of another (e.g., undocumented, Chinese immigrant men with less than a high school education), and the problems of some members may not be the problems of others.

One way we have tried to highlight the importance of this diversity is by stressing gender differentiation within each minority group. Studies of minority groups by U.S. social scientists have focused predominantly on men, and the experiences of minority women have been described in much less depth. Virtually all of the groups we have examined have strong patriarchal traditions. Regardless of race or ethnicity, women have had much less access to leadership roles and higher-status positions compared to men. Thus, they generally have subordinate status, even in their own groups. Researchers are just beginning to fully explore the ways that minority-group women's experiences are different from and similar to those of minority-group men and dominant-group women.

As discussed in Chapter 11, generalizations about "all women" or "all men" seldom conform to reality. We saw that feminist organizations working for gender equality have needed to adopt an intersectional approach and consider variations in girls' and women's experiences as they relate to race, ethnicity, class, sexual orientation, age,

Women have often taken the least desirable, lowest-status jobs, caring for the needs of others rather than their own families.

religion, disability, and other social locations. Although mainstream feminists have begun to frame issues in more inclusive terms, not everyone who might benefit from feminist activism feels that the movement represents them or their concerns. Because gender inequality remains a persistent problem worldwide, the extent to which feminist efforts incorporate an intersectional approach will undoubtedly shape the relative success of the movement domestically and globally.

Likewise, our consideration of gays, lesbians, and bisexual people has also demonstrated that group members vary considerably by race, ethnicity, social class, and gender. Two white men together in a household will tend to elevate that household's income, while the household income for two men of minority racial backgrounds or two women of any background will tend to mirror the patterns of inequality discussed in previous chapters. Moreover, gay liberation movements have faced challenges not unlike those of feminist groups, in that their efforts to alter public policy often privilege white, middle-class concerns over other issues.

Gender, class, race, ethnicity, and sexual orientation can intersect to create especially heavy burdens for some people. Women of every minority group have tended to take the least-desirable, lowest-status positions available in the economy, often while trying to raise children and attend to other family needs. They have been expected to provide support for other members of their families, kinship groups, and communities, often sacrificing their own self-interests for the welfare of others. At the other end of the continuum, white, Anglo, heterosexual, affluent, Protestant men have enjoyed—and continue to enjoy—a system of privilege and advantage so pervasive that it is often invisible to its beneficiaries.

Going back to the biographies in Chapter 1, fully understanding the complexities of inequality requires the recognition that Shirley Umphlett and Mary Farrell have

some different goals in life, despite the fact that both are women. One woman must deal with modern racism, while the other must confront the realities of heterosexism; neither experiences the world as a woman only. Likewise, Juan Yancy and William Buford III share a gender and little else. Similar comparisons and contrasts can be made for all nine of the Americans introduced in Chapter 1. Together, they suggest the outlines of difference and diversity in U.S. society, and the need to recognize the intersecting social locations that shape our experiences.

ASSIMILATION AND PLURALISM

It seems fair to conclude that some of the traditional or "melting pot" views of assimilation do not adequately explain the diversity and complexity of minority-group experiences in the United States. For example, there is little evidence to support the idea that assimilation is a linear, inevitable process. Immigrants from Europe probably fit that model better than other groups, but as the ethnic revival of the 1960s demonstrated, assimilation and ethnic identity can take surprising turns.

Also without support is the notion that there is always a simple, ordered relationship between the various stages of assimilation: acculturation, integration into public institutions, integration into the private sector, and so forth. We have seen that some groups integrated before they acculturated, others have become more committed to their ethnic or racial identity over time, and still others have been acculturated for generations but are no closer to full integration. New expressions of ethnicity come and go, and minority groups emerge, combine, and recombine in unexpected and seemingly unpredictable ways. The 1960s saw a reassertion of ethnicity and loyalty to old identities among some groups, even as other groups developed new coalitions and invented new ethnic identities (e.g., pantribalism among Native Americans). No simple or linear view of assimilation can begin to make sense of the array of minority-group experiences.

Indeed, the very desirability of assimilation has been subject to debate. Since the 1960s, many minority spokespersons have questioned the wisdom of becoming a part of a sociocultural structure that was constructed by the systematic exploitation of minority groups. Pluralistic themes increased in prominence as the commitment of the larger society to racial equality faltered. Virtually every minority group, including women and LGBTs, proclaimed the authenticity of its own experiences, its own culture, and its own version of history, separate from but as valid as those of the dominant groups. From what might have seemed like a nation on the verge of integration in the 1950s (at least for white ethnic groups), America evolved into what might have seemed like a Tower of Babel in the 1960s. The consensus that assimilation was the best solution and the most sensible goal for all of America's groups was shattered (if it ever really existed at all).

Let's review the state of acculturation and integration in the United States on a group-by-group basis:

- African Americans are highly acculturated. Despite the many unique cultural traits forged in America and those that survive from Africa, black Americans share language, values and beliefs, and most other aspects of culture with white Americans. In terms of integration, in contrast, African Americans present a mixed picture. For middle-class, more-educated members of the group, American society offers more opportunities for upward mobility and success than ever before. Without denying the prejudice, discrimination, and racism that remain, this segment of the group is in a favorable position to achieve higher levels of affluence and power for their children and grandchildren. At the same time, a large percentage of African Americans remain mired in poverty, and for them, affluence, security, and power are just as distant as they were a generation ago (perhaps even more so). As a group, African Americans experience high levels of residential and school segregation, and unemployment and poverty remain serious problems, perhaps even more serious than a generation ago.

- Native Americans are less acculturated than African Americans, and some tribes and organizations are trying to preserve American Indian cultures and languages. Overall, however, the strength and vitality of these traditions is probably decreasing. Some measures of integration show improvement, but many American Indians are among the most isolated and impoverished minority-group members in the United States. One possible bright spot for some native communities lies in the further development of the gambling industry, which could allow for the development of tribal infrastructure such as schools, health clinics, job training centers, and so forth.

- Members of the largest Hispanic American groups are also generally less acculturated than African Americans. Hispanic traditions and the Spanish language have been sustained by the exclusion and isolation of these groups within the United States and have been continually renewed and revitalized by immigration. Cubans have moved closer to equality than have Mexican Americans and Puerto Ricans, but they did so by resisting assimilation and building an ethnic enclave economy. Mexican Americans and Puerto Ricans share many of the problems of poverty that confront African Americans, and they are below national norms on measures of equality and integration.

The smaller Hispanic groups consist mostly of new immigrants who are just beginning the assimilation process. Many members of these groups, along with Mexican Americans and Puerto Ricans, are less educated and have few occupational skills, and they face the dangers of becoming part of a permanent underclass. Nonetheless, some evidence suggests that these groups (or, more accurately, their descendants) may eventually find their way into the American mainstream (recall the debate over segmented assimilation in Chapter 10).

- As with Hispanic Americans, the extent of assimilation among Asian Americans is highly variable. Some groups (e.g., third- and fourth-generation Japanese and Chinese Americans) have virtually completed the assimilation process and compare favorably to national norms in terms of integration and equality, at least in terms of group averages. Some Asian American groups (the more elite immigrants from India and the Philippines) seem to be finding a place in the American mainstream. Other groups consist largely of newer immigrants with occupational and educational profiles that often resemble those of colonized minority groups, and these groups face the same dangers of permanent marginalization and exclusion. Still other Asian American groups (e.g., Korean Americans) have constructed ethnic enclaves and pursue economic equality by resisting acculturation.

- Only European American ethnic groups, covered in Chapter 2, seem to approximate the traditional model of assimilation. The development of even these groups, however, has taken unexpected twists and turns, and the pluralism of the 1960s and 1970s suggests that ethnic traditions and ethnic identity, in some form, may withstand the pressures of assimilation for generations to come. Culturally and racially, these groups are the closest to the dominant group. If they still retain a sense of ethnicity, even if merely symbolic, after generations of acculturation and integration, what is the likelihood that the sense of group membership will fade in the racially stigmatized minority groups?

- Different normative expectations continue to shape the experiences of boys/men and girls/women throughout the life cycle. In that sense, "acculturation" has not been accomplished. Women are equal to men on some measures of equality (e.g., education), but large gaps in other areas (e.g., income) persist. The gaps vary by race, ethnicity, sexual orientation, and other factors, but in general we can say that women are disproportionately concentrated in less-well-paid occupations and they continue to confront glass ceilings and other limits to their social mobility.

- As with women, the usual sociological meaning of acculturation does not easily fit the LGBT minority. The patterns of inequality in the LGBT community generally mirror those in the larger society, and, like women, LGBT people seem not to receive rewards proportionate to their degree of preparation for the job market. In most states, major inequalities persist between same-sex and heterosexual couples in terms of taxes and health care costs, and civil liberties and occupational discrimination continue to be issues of major importance. However, mainstream popular culture increasingly includes positive portrayals of LGBT people, which is one area of improvement.

For the racial and ethnic minority groups, assimilation is far from accomplished. The group divisions that remain are real and consequential; they cannot be willed away by pretending we are all "just American." Group membership continues to be important because it continues to be linked to fundamental patterns of exclusion and inequality. The realities of pluralism, inequality, and ethnic and racial identity persist to the extent that the American promise of a truly open opportunity structure continues to fail. The group divisions forged in the past and perpetuated over the decades by racism and discrimination will remain to the extent that racial and ethnic group membership continues to be correlated with inequality and position in the social class structure.

Along with economic and political pressures, other forces help sustain the pluralistic group divisions. Despite evidence to the contrary, some people argue that ethnicity is rooted in biology and can never be fully eradicated (e.g., see van den Berghe, 1981). Although this may be an extreme and increasingly rare position, there is little doubt that many people find their own ancestries to be a matter of great interest. Some (perhaps most) of the impetus behind the preservation of ethnic and racial identity may result from vicious and destructive intergroup competition. In other ways, though, ethnicity can be a positive force that helps people locate themselves in time and space and understand their position in the contemporary world. Ethnicity remains an important aspect of self-identity and pride for many Americans from every group and tradition. It seems unlikely that this sense of a personal link to particular groups and heritages within U.S. society will soon fade.

Can we survive as a pluralistic, culturally and linguistically fragmented, racially and ethnically unequal society? What will save us from balkanization and fractionalization?

Given our history of colonization and racism, can the United States move closer to the relatively harmonious models of race relations found elsewhere?

As we deal with these questions, we need to remember that in and of itself, diversity is no more "bad" than unity is "good." Our society has grown to a position of global preeminence despite, or perhaps because of, our diversity. In fact, many people have argued that our diversity is a fundamental and essential characteristic of U.S. society and a great strength to be cherished and encouraged. Sociologist Ronald Takaki (1993) offers this eloquent endorsement:

> As Americans, we originally came from many different shores and our diversity has been at the center of the making of America. While our stories contain the memories of different communities, together they inscribe a larger narrative. Filled with what Walt Whitman celebrated as the "varied carols" of America, our history generously gives all of us our "mystic chords of memory."
>
> Throughout our past of oppressions and struggles for equality, Americans of different races and ethnicities have been "singing with open mouths their strong melodious songs" in the textile mills of Lowell, the cotton fields of Mississippi, on the Indian reservations of South Dakota, the railroad tracks high in the Sierras of California, in the garment factories of the Lower East Side, the cane fields of Hawaii, and a thousand other places across the country. Our denied history "bursts with telling." As we hear America singing, we find ourselves invited to bring our cultural diversity [into the open], to accept ourselves. (p. 428)

To this heady mix of diversity in race, ethnicity, language, and culture, we must add the dimensions of gender and sexual orientation, and their infinite intersections and

This mural was created by the Public Works of Art Project, a federal program from 1933–1934 that created jobs for artists and yielded more than 15,000 public works of art, all depicting American life. This image shows downtown San Francisco.

combinations with group membership. The "varied carols" of American life are voiced by a complex, diversified chorus: The tune will not be the same for heterosexual, middle-class African Americans as for lesbian, Hispanic immigrants with low levels of human capital. How can we sort out this complexity? How can we answer the question we raised at the beginning of this text: What does it mean to be an American?

The question for our future might not be so much "unity or diversity?" as "What blend of pluralism and assimilation will serve us best in the 21st century?" Are there ways society can prosper without repressing our diversity? How can we increase the degree of openness, fairness, and justice without threatening group loyalties? The one-way, Anglo-conformity mode of assimilation of the past is too narrow and destructive to be a blueprint for the future, but the more extreme forms of minority-group pluralism and separatism might be equally dangerous.

How much unity do we need? How much diversity is most beneficial for society? These are questions you must answer for yourself, and they are questions you will face in numerous ways over the course of your life. We do not pretend that the ideas presented in this text can fully resolve every present issue or others that will arise in the future. As long as immigrants and minority groups are a part of the United States, as long as prejudice and discrimination and inequality persist, the debates will continue and new issues will arise as old ones are resolved.

As U.S. society attempts to deal with new immigrants, the varieties of gender expression, and unresolved minority grievances, we should recognize that it is not diversity per se that threatens stability but, rather, the realities of exclusion and marginalization, split labor markets, racial and ethnic stratification, poverty, and institutionalized discrimination. We need to focus on the issues that confront us with an honest recognition of the past and the economic, political, and social forces that have shaped us. As the United States continues to remake itself, an informed sense of where we have been will help us decide where we should go next and, perhaps, how best to get there.

MINORITY-GROUP PROGRESS AND THE IDEOLOGY OF AMERICAN INDIVIDUALISM

There is so much sadness, misery, and unfairness in the history of minority groups that evidence of progress sometimes goes unnoticed. Lest we be guilty of ignoring the good news in favor of the bad, let us note some ways the situations of American minority groups are better today than they were in the past. Evidence of progress is easy to find for some groups; we need look only to the relative economic, educational, and income equality of European American ethnic groups and some Asian American groups, or recall the election of President Barack Obama. The United States has become more tolerant and open, and minority-group members can be found at the highest levels of success, affluence, and prestige. Women, in large numbers, have entered occupations traditionally filled only by men. Lastly, U.S. society has become increasingly inclusive of sexual-orientation minorities and people with nonbinary gender identities.

Although prejudice in all its forms unquestionably exists, research documents a decline in traditional racism and prejudice, sexism, and homophobia. As we discussed in Chapter 3, the strong racial and ethnic sentiments and stereotypes of the past are no longer the primary vocabulary for discussing race relations among dominant-group members, at least not in public. Similar shifts have occurred in attitudes toward women and LGBT people.

The decrease in blatant bigotry is, without doubt, a positive change. However, in many ways, negative intergroup feelings and stereotypes have not disappeared, they've simply changed form. Many people now express the same racist and sexist feelings in subtler ways—called "modern" or "symbolic" racism and sexism. Key to modern racism and sexism is the belief that routes of upward mobility in American society are equally open to all. (However, it is also clear that the blatant bigotry of the past has not disappeared: hate groups and racist epithets have reappeared in the everyday language of our society, as we noted in Chapter 3 and various other places in the text.)

This individualistic view of social mobility is consistent with the human capital perspective and the traditional, melting-pot view of assimilation. Taken together, these ideologies present a powerful and widely shared perspective on the nature of minority-group problems in modern American society. Proponents of these views tend to be unsympathetic to the plight of minorities and to programs, such as affirmative action, intended to ameliorate these problems. The overt bigotry of the past often has been replaced by blandness and an indifference more difficult to define and harder to measure than "old-fashioned" racism, yet still unsympathetic to change.

This text has argued that the most serious problems facing contemporary minority groups, however, are structural and institutional, not individual or personal. For example, the paucity of jobs and high rates of unemployment in the inner cities are the result of economic and political forces beyond the control not only of the minority communities but also of local and state governments. The marginalization of the minority-group labor force is a reflection of the essence of modern American capitalism. The mainstream, higher-paying, blue-collar jobs available to people with modest educational credentials are controlled by national and multinational corporations, which maximize profits by automating their production processes and moving the jobs that remain to areas, often outside the United States, with abundant supplies of cheaper labor.

We have also seen that some of the more effective strategies for pursuing equality require strong in-group cohesion and networks of cooperation, not heroic individual effort. Immigration to this country is (and always has been) a group process that involves extensive, long-lasting networks of communication and chains of population movement, usually built around family ties and larger kinship groups. Group networks continue to operate in America and assist individual immigrants with early adjustments and later opportunities for jobs and upward mobility. A variation on this theme is the ethnic enclave found among so many different groups.

Survival and success in America for all minority groups has had more to do with group processes than with individual will or motivation. The concerted, coordinated actions of the minority community provided support during hard times and, when possible, provided the means to climb higher in the social structure during good times. Far from being a hymn to individualism, the story of U.S. minority groups—whether based on race, ethnicity, gender, or sexual orientation—is profoundly sociological.

A FINAL WORD

U.S. society and its minority groups are linked in fractious unity. They are part of the same structures but are separated by lines of color and culture and by long histories (and clear memories) of exploitation and unfairness. This society owes its prosperity and position of prominence in the world no

Group processes have been more significant for minorities than heroic individual effort.

American groups celebrate a diversity of traditions and an endless array of realities.

less to the labor of minority groups than to that of the dominant group. By harnessing the labor and energy of these minority groups, the nation has grown prosperous and powerful, but the benefits have flowed disproportionately to the dominant group.

Since the middle of the 20th century, minority groups have demanded greater openness, fairness, equality, respect for their traditions, and justice. Increasingly, the demands have been made on the terms of the minority groups, not on those of the dominant group. Some of these demands have been met, at least verbally, and the society as a whole has rejected the overt, oppressive racism of the past. Yet, minority-group progress has stalled well short of equality and the patterns of poverty, discrimination, marginality, and despair continue to negatively influence millions of people.

As we face the 21st century, the dilemmas of America's minority groups remain perhaps the primary unresolved domestic issue facing the nation. The answers of the past— the simple faith in assimilation and the belief that success in America is open to all who simply try hard enough—have proved inadequate, even destructive and dangerous, because they help sustain the belief that the barriers to equality no longer exist and that any remaining inequalities are the problem of the minority groups, not the larger society.

These issues of equality and access will not solve themselves or simply fade away. They will continue to manifest themselves in myriad ways—through protest activities, rancorous debates, diffused rage, and pervasive violence. The solutions and policies that will carry us through these coming travails are not clear. Only by asking the proper questions, realistically and honestly, can we hope to find the answers that will help our society fulfill its promises to the millions who are currently excluded from achieving the American Dream.

The United States is one of many ethnically and racially diverse nations in the world today. As communication networks, immigration, trade, and transportation increasingly connect people globally, diversity-related challenges will become more international in their scope and implications.

For example, agreements between the United States and the nations of Latin America will have direct impact on immigration patterns, and organizations representing women and sexual-orientation minorities will develop more international ties. In many ways, the patterns of dominant–minority relations discussed in this text have already been reproduced in other parts of the world. The mostly Anglo industrialized nations of the Northern Hemisphere have continuously exploited the labor and resources of the mostly nonwhite, undeveloped nations of the Southern Hemisphere. Thus, the tensions and resentments we have observed in U.S. society are being reproduced in the global system of societies.

The United States is neither the most nor the least diverse country in the world. Likewise, it is not the most or the least successful in confronting the problems of prejudice, discrimination, and racism. However, the multigroup nature of our society, along with the present influx of immigrants from around the world, presents an opportunity to improve on our record. A society that finds a way to deal fairly and humanely with the problems of diversity and difference, prejudice and inequality, exclusion and marginalization, and racism and discrimination can provide a sorely needed model for other nations and, indeed, for the world.

SUMMARY

This summary is organized around the Learning Objectives listed at the beginning of this chapter.

 Explain how the people profiled at the beginning of Chapter 1 exemplify the central themes and concepts of this text.

These brief biographies illustrate both the diversity and complexity of contemporary American society, including the divisions along the lines of class, race, ethnicity, gender, and sexual orientation. They display the varieties of acculturation and integration and the multiplicity of privilege and disadvantage. They also remind us of the often daunting difficulties of communicating across the diverse experiences and perspectives that animate contemporary society.

 Explain the relevance of our central concepts—especially subsistence technology, the contact situation, competition and power, and intersectionality—for American dominant–minority relations.

Subsistence technology is the most basic force shaping society and group relationships. Before the 1800s, agrarian technology created competition for land and labor, resulting in the subjugation of some groups and the near extermination of others. The evolution of subsistence technology through the industrial and postindustrial stages continued to shape the situation of minority groups—including women and LGBTs—and the nature of dominant–minority conflict.

The contact situation creates dynamics that can affect dominant–minority relations for centuries (or longer). We have analyzed these dynamics using Blauner's distinction between immigrant and colonized minority groups and

Noel's concepts of ethnocentrism, competition, and power and we have seen the numerous ways in which minority groups today continue to be affected by their contact situation.

Intersectionality reminds us of the myriad ways in which we are each both privileged and disadvantaged and the multiple realities that shape our lives and opportunities. Although we have often generalized, we need to continually recognize the diversity within groups.

 Summarize the situation of each of the groups we have considered in terms of acculturation and integration.

The extent of acculturation and integration is highly variable from group to group. Of the racial and ethnic minority groups, only the descendants of the European immigrant groups have approached full assimilation. Virtually all of the other groups we have considered ranks below white ethnics in terms of acculturation and integration and some of these groups (Hispanic and Asian groups in particular) have been affected by high rates of immigration in recent decades. Gender norms retain significant strength in American culture and women rank below men on many measures of integration and equality. The LGBT minorities seem to be gaining more acceptance but continue to face significant issues of inequality and marginalization.

 Explain the importance of a sociological perspective for understanding American dominant–minority relations.

The sociological perspective locates the source of minority problems in the structure and everyday functioning of the larger society. It counters the individualistic view shared by

many Americans and rejects the assumption that mobility and opportunity are equally open to all. It takes account of the history of dominant–minority relations, the evolving subsistence technology, globalization, and the changing political, cultural, and economic processes that structure modern societies. It provides a broad view of groups and social structures, grounded in evidence and research and guided by critical thinking and careful reflection.

STUDENT STUDY SITE

Sharpen your skills with SAGE edge at edge.sagepub.com/healey8e

SAGE edge for students provides a personalized approach to help you accomplish your coursework goals in an easy-to-use learning environment.

The following resources are available at SAGE edge:

Public Sociology Assignments

Public Sociology Assignments provide opportunities for students to address directly and personally some of the issues raised in this text.

The first assignment on our website for this final chapter leads students to identify and act on a problem in their neighborhood. The second assignment is a service-learning project in which students will research a local refugee group and then volunteer to help that community.

In the third assignment, students will explore privilege on their campus and engage with an organization that promotes a cause of interest to them. In the final assignment, students will explore the presentation of race, gender, ethnicity, class, and sexuality on the Internet.

Contributed by Linda M. Waldron

CHAPTER-OPENING TIMELINE PHOTO CREDITS

1955: Library of Congress Prints and Photographs Division

1960: Library of Congress Prints and Photographs Division

1963: Library of Congress Prints and Photographs Division

1965: Department of Labor

1969: NY Daily News/Getty Images

1978: Library of Congress Prints and Photographs Division

1987: Associated Press

1995: Wikipedia

2007: ©iStockphoto.com/Coast-to-Coast

2012: Stephanie Keith/Getty Images News/Getty Images

GLOSSARY

abolitionism: The movement to abolish slavery.

acculturation: The process by which one group (generally a minority or immigrant group) learns the culture of another group (generally the dominant group); also called **cultural assimilation**.

affective dimension of prejudice: The emotional or "feeling" dimension of individual prejudice. The prejudiced individual attaches negative emotions to members of other groups.

affirmative action: Programs designed to reduce the effects of past institutional discrimination or increase diversity in workplaces and schools.

Alien Land Act: Bill passed by the California legislature in 1913 declaring that aliens who were ineligible for citizenship (effectively meaning only immigrants from Asia) were also ineligible to own land.

Americanization: The model of assimilation in which groups are pressured to conform to Anglo-American culture (same as **Anglo-conformity**).

androgynous: Refers to a combination of "masculine" and "feminine" traits.

Anglo-conformity: The model of assimilation in which groups are pressured to conform to Anglo-American culture (same as **Americanization**).

anti-Semitism: Prejudice or ideological racism directed specifically toward Jews.

ascribed status: A social position assigned to individuals over which they have little control such as race and sex.

assimilation: The process by which formerly distinct and separate groups come to share a common culture and merge together socially.

authoritarian personality: A theory that links prejudice to childhood experiences with stern, severe parents.

Black Power Movement: A coalition of African American groups that rose to prominence in the 1960s. Some central themes of the movement were Black Nationalism, autonomy for African American communities, and pride in race and African heritage.

Blauner hypothesis: States that minority groups created by colonization will experience more intense prejudice, racism, and discrimination than those created by immigration.

bourgeoisie: The elite or ruling class in an industrial society that owns or controls the means of production; see **proletariat**.

Bureau of Indian Affairs: The agency of the U.S. government that has primary responsibility for the administration of American Indian reservations.

capital-intensive: Replaces hand labor with machine labor. Large amounts of capital are required to develop, purchase, and maintain the machines.

caste system: A closed system of stratification with no mobility between positions. A person's class at birth is permanent and unchangeable.

chattel: An item of personal property. In a system of chattel slavery, slaves were defined by law not as persons but as the personal property of their owners.

Chicanismo: A militant ideology of the Mexican American protest movement that appeared in the 1960s. The ideology took a critical view of U.S. society, made strong demands for justice and an end to racism, expressed a positive image for the group, and incorporated other pluralistic themes.

Chicanos: A group name for Mexican Americans; associated with the ideology of Chicanismo, which emerged in the 1960s.

Chinese Exclusion Act: Passed in 1882 by the U.S. Congress, banned virtually all immigration from China.

cisgender: People whose gender identity "matches" the biological sex they were assigned at birth.

Civil Rights Movement: The effort of African Americans and their allies in the 1950s and 1960s to end de jure segregation in the South.

cognitive dimension of prejudice: The "thinking" dimension of individual prejudice. The prejudiced individual thinks about members of other groups in terms of stereotypes.

collective identity: A shared understanding of one's place in society.

colonized minority groups: Groups whose initial contact with the dominant group was through conquest or colonization.

coming out: The act of a nonheterosexual person publicly disclosing his or her sexual identity.

competition: A situation in which two or more parties struggle for control of some scarce resource.

cultural assimilation: See **acculturation**.

cultural feminism: The movement to change patriarchal values and norms.

cultural heterosexism: Ideologies that uphold heterosexuality as normative.

cultural pluralism: A situation in which groups have not acculturated or integrated and each maintains a distinct identity.

culture: The way of life associated with a group of people, including (but not limited to) language, beliefs, norms, values, customs, and technology.

culture of poverty theory: A theory asserting that poverty causes certain personality traits—such as the need for instant gratification—which, in turn, perpetuate poverty.

Dawes Allotment Act of 1887: A key piece of U.S. government policy that divided Native American land into smaller units for individual ownership and moved indigenous people away from their tribal communities.

de facto segregation: A system of racial separation and inequality that appears to result from voluntary choices about where to live, work, and so forth. Often, this form of segregation is really de jure segregation in thin disguise.

de jure segregation: Racial segregation that is institutionalized in local and state law.

deindustrialization: The shift from a manufacturing economy to a service-oriented, information-processing economy.

detention camps: Camps that held Japanese Americans during World War II. Sometimes called "relocation camps."

differential in power: Any difference between two or more groups in their ability to achieve their goals.

discrimination: The unequal or unfair treatment of a person or persons based on their group membership.

dissimilarity index: A measure of residential segregation. The higher the score, the greater the segregation, and scores above 60 are considered to indicate extreme segregation.

doing gender: The idea that people act to create and assert their gender rather than an innate quality that people are born with. For example, people do gender in how they walk, dress, or express emotion; see **gender displays**.

dominant group: The group that benefits from and, typically, tries to sustain minority-group subordination.

double bind: A situation in which negative consequences ensue regardless of the choice that is made.

enclave minority group: A group that establishes its own neighborhood and relies on a set of interconnected businesses for economic survival.

equal status contact hypothesis: A theory of prejudice reduction asserting that equal status and cooperative contacts between groups will tend to reduce prejudice.

ethclass: The group formed by the intersection of social class and racial or ethnic groups.

ethnic minority groups: Minority groups identified primarily by cultural characteristics, such as language or religion.

ethnic revival: An increase in the interest in heritage that occurred among white ethnics during 1960s and 1970s.

ethnic succession: The process by which white ethnic groups affected one another's positions in the social class structure.

ethnocentrism: Judging other groups, societies, or cultures by the standards of one's own.

extractive (or primary) occupations: Those that produce raw materials, such as food and agricultural products, minerals, and lumber; often involve unskilled manual labor, require little formal education, and are generally low paying.

fatalism: The view that one's fate is beyond one's control.

feminism: A variety of ideas, movements, and organizations that have sought to reduce gender stratification and achieve gender equality.

fluid competitive systems: Systems of group relations in which minority-group members are freer to compete for jobs and other scarce resources; associated with advanced industrialization.

gender: Socially constructed ideas associated with a person's sex (e.g., what people in a society consider "masculine" or "feminine").

gender displays: Behaviors that indicate one's gender status to others; see **doing gender**.

gender fluid: People who identify as more than one gender and easily shift between them.

gender identity: One's sense of being a girl/woman, boy/man, or some other gender.

gender norms: Societal expectations for behavior based on one's gender status (e.g., girl, boy).

gender socialization: The process by which people learn societal beliefs and norms related to gender and through which they develop a gender identity.

gender status: One's position in the social structure based on gender (e.g., girl, boy).

genderqueer: An umbrella term including anyone whose sexual orientation, gender identity, or gender expression deviates from the gender binary.

genocide: The deliberate attempt to exterminate an entire group.

glass ceiling: Discriminatory practices that limit opportunities for women and other minority groups to rise to higher levels in their careers, qualify for promotions, and earn higher salaries.

glass escalator: An occupational setting in which the dominant group (e.g., men) enjoys a distinct advantage.

hate crime: A criminal offense against a person or property motivated in whole or in part by an offender's bias against a race, religion, disability, sexual orientation, ethnicity, gender, or gender identity.

hegemonic masculinity: The privileged, dominant expression of masculinity in a society.

homophobia: Prejudice directed at lesbian, gay, and bisexual persons.

homosocial reproduction: The tendency of elite men to select candidates for advancement who are most like themselves.

huiguan: Associations in Chinese American society based on the region of China from which an individual or the individual's family came. The huiguan performed a number of social and welfare functions.

human capital theory: Consistent with the traditional view of assimilation, this theory considers success to be a direct result of individual efforts, personal values and skills, and education.

ideological racism: A belief system asserting that a particular group is inferior. Although individuals may subscribe to racist beliefs, the ideology itself is incorporated into the culture of the society and passed on from generation to generation.

immigrant minority groups: Groups whose initial contact with the dominant group was through immigration.

indentured servants: Contract laborers who are obligated to serve a particular master for a specified length of time.

Indian Reorganization Act: Federal legislation passed in 1934 that was intended to give Native American tribes more autonomy.

industrial revolution: The shift in subsistence technology from labor-intensive agriculture to capital-intensive manufacturing.

institutional discrimination: A pattern of unequal treatment based on group membership that is built into the daily operations of society.

integration: The process by which a minority group enters the social structure of the dominant society; also called **structural assimilation**.

intermarriage: Marriage between members of different groups; same as **marital assimilation**.

internalized homophobia: The repulsion some people feel in response to their own attractions to members of their same sex.

intersectionality: A theoretical perspective in sociology that stresses the cross-cutting, linked nature of inequality and the multiplicity of statuses all people occupy.

intersex: People with the biological characteristics of more than one sex.

Issei: First-generation immigrants from Japan.

jigsaw method: A learning technique that requires cooperation among students.

Jim Crow system: The system of rigid competitive race relations that followed Reconstruction in the South. The system lasted from the 1880s until the 1960s and was characterized by laws mandating racial separation and inequality.

labor-intensive: A form of production in which the bulk of the effort is provided by human beings working by hand. Machines and other labor-saving devices are rare or absent.

level of development: The stage of societal evolution. The stages discussed in this text are agrarian, industrial, and postindustrial.

machismo: A cultural value stressing men's dominance, virility, and honor.

manufacturing (or secondary) occupations: Occupations involving the transformation of raw materials into finished products ready for the marketplace. An example is an assembly line worker in an automobile plant.

marielitos: Refugees from Cuba who arrived in the United States in 1980.

marital assimilation: Marriage between members of different groups; same as **intermarriage**.

means of production: The materials, resources, and social relations by which the society produces and distributes goods and services.

melting pot: A type of assimilation in which all groups contribute in roughly equal amounts to the creation of a new culture and society.

middleman minority groups: Groups that rely on interconnected businesses, dispersed throughout a community, for economic survival.

minority group: A group that experiences a pattern of disadvantage or inequality, has a visible identifying trait, and is a self-conscious social unit. Membership is usually determined at birth, and group members tend to form intimate relations within the group.

miscegenation: Marriage or sexual relations between members of different racial groups.

modern institutional discrimination: A more subtle and covert form of institutional discrimination that is often unintentional and unconscious.

modern racism: A subtle and indirect form of prejudice that incorporates negative feelings about minority groups but not the traditional stereotypes.

modern sexism: Like modern racism, an indirect, more subtle way of expressing prejudice against women.

multiculturalism: A general term for some versions of pluralism in the United States. Generally, multiculturalism stresses mutual respect for all groups and celebrates the multiplicity of heritages that have contributed to the development of the United States.

New Immigration: Immigration from Southern and Eastern Europe to the United States between the 1880s and the 1920s.

Nisei: Second-generation Japanese Americans.

nonviolent direct action: The central tactic used during the Civil Rights Movement in the South to defeat de jure segregation.

Old Immigration: Immigration from Northern and Western Europe to the United States between the 1820s and the 1880s.

Operation Wetback: A government program developed in the 1950s to deport illegal immigrants from Mexico.

past-in-present institutional discrimination: Patterns of inequality or unequal treatment in the present that are caused by some pattern of discrimination in the past.

paternalism: A form of dominant–minority relations often associated with plantation-based, labor-intensive, agrarian technology. In paternalistic relations, minority groups are extremely unequal and highly controlled. Rates of overt conflict are low.

patriarchy: Men's dominance. In a patriarchal society, men tend to monopolize power and decision making.

pink-collar: Occupations that have been predominately been held by women that are typically low in pay and prestige.

plantation system: A labor-intensive form of agriculture that requires large tracts of land and a large, cheap labor force. This was the dominant form of agricultural production in the American South before the Civil War.

pluralism: A situation in which groups maintain separate identities, cultures, and organizational structures.

postindustrial society: A society dominated by service work, information processing, and high technology.

power: The ability to affect the decision-making process of a social system.

prejudice: The tendency of individuals to think and feel negatively toward others.

prestige: The amount of honor or respect accorded a particular person or group.

primary labor market: The segment of the labor market that encompasses better-paying, higher-status, more-secure jobs, usually in large bureaucracies.

primary sector: Relationships and groups that are intimate and personal. Groups in the primary sector are small.

principle of third-generation interest: The notion that the grandchildren of immigrants will stress their ethnicity much more than the second generation will.

proletariat: The workers in an industrial society who sell their labor; see **bourgeoisie**.

Protestant ethic: Stressed hard work, success, and individualism, and was analyzed by Max Weber in his sociological classic *The Protestant Ethic and the Spirit of Capitalism*.

queer: A term to describe a variety of non-normative gender or sexual identities.

race relations cycle: A concept associated with Robert Park, who believed that relations between different groups would go through predictable cycles, from conflict to eventual assimilation.

racial minority groups: Minority groups constructed primarily based on physical characteristics such as skin color or facial features (e.g., Asian Americans).

rape culture: Beliefs, values, and norms that encourage, condone, or minimize the rape of girls and women by boys and men.

Reconstruction: The period of southern race relations following the Civil War. Reconstruction lasted from 1865 until the 1880s and witnessed many racial reforms, all of which were reversed during de jure segregation, or the Jim Crow era.

relocation camps: The areas where the U.S. government held Japanese Americans during World War II;

sometimes called interment, detention, or prison camps.

repatriation: A government campaign begun during the Great Depression of the 1930s to deport illegal immigrants back to Mexico. The campaign also caused some legal immigrants and native-born Mexican Americans to leave the United States.

revolution: A minority-group goal. A revolutionary group wishes to change places with the dominant group or create a new social order, perhaps in alliance with other groups.

rigid competitive group system: A system of group relations in which the dominant group seeks to exclude minority groups or limit their ability to compete for scarce resources such as jobs.

Sansei: Third-generation Japanese Americans.

scapegoat hypothesis: A theory of prejudice that posits that under certain conditions, people will express their aggressions against substitute targets. When other groups are chosen as substitute targets, prejudice increases.

secondary labor market: The segment of the labor market that includes low-paying, low-skilled, insecure jobs.

secondary sector: Relationships and organizations that are public, task oriented, and impersonal. Organizations in the secondary sector can be large.

segmented assimilation: The idea that assimilation can have a number of outcomes, in addition to eventual entry into mainstream society. Some groups may enter the middle class, but others may be permanently excluded, marginalized, and impoverished.

selective perception: The tendency to see only what one expects to see; associated with stereotyping in individual prejudice.

separatism: A minority-group goal. A separatist group wishes to sever all ties with the dominant group.

service (or tertiary) occupations: Jobs that involve providing services, such as retail clerk, janitor, and schoolteacher.

sex: Physical or biological characteristics such as genitalia, hormones, and chromosomes that are used to classify people as female, male, or intersex; see **gender**.

sexism: Belief systems that label girls/women as inferior to boys/men and rationalize their lower status.

sexual identity: The way people classify themselves sexually—for example, as lesbian, gay, or bisexual.

sexual orientation: The gender to which a person is physically or emotionally attracted.

sexual scripts: Expectations for people's behavior in romantic or sexual situations often related to gender norms.

sharecropping: A system of farming often used in the South during de jure segregation. The sharecropper (often black), or tenant, worked the land, which was actually owned by someone else (usually white), in return for a share of the profits at harvest time. The landowner supplied a place to live and credit for food and clothing.

social classes: Groups of people who command similar amounts of valued goods and services, such as income, property, and education.

social constructions: Perceptions shared by a group. These perceptions become real to the people who share them.

social distance: The degree of intimacy a person is willing to

accept for members of other groups.

social mobility: Movement up and down the stratification system.

social structure: The networks of social relationships, groups, organizations, communities, and institutions that organize the work of a society and connect individuals to one another and to the larger society.

socialization: The process of social development through which a person learns cultural beliefs, values, and norms and develops an identity.

sojourners: Immigrants who intend to return to their countries of origin.

split labor market theory: When the labor force is divided into a higher-paid segment composed of members of the dominant group and a lower-paid segment composed of minority-group members, higher-paid labor uses prejudice and racism to limit the ability of cheaper labor to compete for jobs.

stereotypes: Overgeneralizations that are thought to apply to all members of a group.

stratification: The unequal distribution of valued goods and services (e.g., income, job opportunities, prestige and fame, education, health care) in society; the social class system.

structural assimilation: See integration.

structural heterosexism: Patterns of institutional discrimination whereby heterosexual relations are allocated more resources, opportunities, and privileges.

structural mobility: Rising occupational and social class standing that is the result of changes in the overall structure of the economy and labor market, as opposed to individual efforts.

structural pluralism: A situation in which a group has acculturated but is not integrated.

subsistence technology: The means by which a society satisfies basic needs. An agrarian society relies on labor-intensive agriculture, whereas an industrial society relies on machines and inanimate fuel supplies.

symbolic ethnicity: A sense of ethnicity that is superficial, voluntary, and changeable.

termination: A policy by which all special relationships between the federal government and American Indians would be abolished.

tongs: Secret societies in Chinatowns that sometimes fought with each other and with other organizations over control of resources.

transgender: People who have a gender identity different from their assigned sex.

triple melting pot: The idea that structural assimilation for white ethnic immigrants took place within the context of the three major American religions.

two-spirit: Within indigenous cultures, people who identify as both genders or identify outside of the Western gender binary of girl/woman or boy/man.

urban underclass: The urban lower classes, consisting largely of African Americans and other minority groups of color, which have been more or less permanently barred from the mainstream economy and the primary labor market.

vicious cycle: A process in which a condition (e.g., minority-group inferiority) is assumed to be true and forces are then set in motion to create and perpetuate that condition.

Yonsei: Fourth-generation Japanese Americans.

REFERENCES

Abdo, Geneive. 2017. "Like Most Americans, U.S. Muslims Concerned About Extremism in the Name of Islam." Retrieved August 30, 2017 (http://www.pewresearch.org/fact-tank/2017/08/14/like-most-americans-u-s-muslims-concerned-about-extremism-in-the-name-of-islam/).

Aberson, Christopher, Carl Shoemaker, and Christina Tomolillo. 2004. "Implicit Bias and Contact: The Role of Interethnic Friendships." *Journal of Social Psychology* 144:335–347.

Abrahamson, Harold. 1980. "Assimilation and Pluralism." Pp. 150–160 in *Harvard Encyclopedia of American Ethnic Groups*, edited by S. Thernstrom, A. Orlov, and O. Handlin. Cambridge, MA: Harvard University Press.

Ackerman, Holly. n.d. *The Cuban Rafter Phenomenon.* (http://balseros.miami.edu).

Actions Overview H.R.2867. 2015. Rep. Sewell, Terri A. [D-AL-7]). 114th Congress (2015–2016). (https://www.congress.gov/bill/114th-congress/house-bill/2867/actions).

Acuña, Rodolfo. 1988. *Occupied America.* 3rd ed. New York: Harper & Row.

Acuña, Rodolfo. 1999. *Occupied America.* 4th ed. New York: Harper & Row.

Adams, Natalie, and Pamela Bettis. 2003. "Commanding the Room in Short Skirts." *Gender & Society* 17(1):73–91.

Adarand Constructors Inc. v. Pena, 515 U.S. 200 (1995).

Adorno, Theodore W., Else Frenkel-Brunswick, Daniel J. Levinson, and R. Nevitt Sanford. 1950. *The Authoritarian Personality.* New York: Harper & Row.

Agbayani-Siewert, Pauline, and Linda Revilla. 1995. "Filipino Americans." Pp. 134–168 in *Asian Americans: Contemporary Issues and Trends*, edited by P. G. Min. Thousand Oaks, CA: Sage.

Alba, Richard. 1985. *Italian Americans: Into the Twilight of Ethnicity.* Englewood Cliffs, NJ: Prentice Hall.

Alba, Richard. 1990. *Ethnic Identity: The Transformation of White America.* New Haven, CT: Yale University Press.

Alba, Richard. 1995. "Assimilation's Quiet Tide." *The Public Interest* 119:9–19.

Alba, Richard, and Victor Nee. 1997. "Rethinking Assimilation Theory for a New Era of Immigration." *International Migration Review* 31: 826–875.

———. 2003. *Remaking the American Mainstream: Assimilation and Contemporary Immigration.* Cambridge, MA: Harvard University Press.

Aleiss, Angela. 2005. *Making the White Man's Indian: Native Americans and Hollywood Movies.* Westport, CT: Praeger.

Alesina, Alberto, Arnaud Devleeschauwewr, William Easterly, Sergio Kurlat, and Romain T. Wacziarg. 2002. *Fractionalization* (Harvard Institute Research Working Paper No. 1959). Retrieved July 20, 2002 (http://papers.ssrn.com/sol3/papers.cfm?abstract_id=319762).

Alexander, Michelle. 2012. *The New Jim Crow: Mass Incarceration in the Age of Colorblindness.* New York: New Press.

Allen, Jane E. 2010. "Rutgers Suicide: Internet Humiliation Trauma for Teen." *ABC News*, September 30. (http://abcnews.go.com/Health/MindMoodNews/rutgers-suicide-latest-linked-gay-humiliation/story?id=11766816).

Allen, Paula Gunn. 1992. T*he Sacred Hoop: Recovering the Feminine in American Indian Traditions.* New York: Open Road Integrated Media.

Allison, Rachel and Barbara J. Risman. 2013. "'It Goes Hand in Hand with the Parties': Race, Class, and Residence in College Student Negotiations of Hooking Up." *Sociological Perspectives* 57(1): 102–123.

Allport, Gordon. 1954. *The Nature of Prejudice.* Reading, MA: Addison-Wesley.

Almasy, Steve and Holly Yan. 2014. "Protesters Fill Streets Across Country as Ferguson Protests Spread Coast to Coast." *CNN.* Retrieved August 10, 2017 (http://www.cnn.com/2014/11/25/us/national-ferguson-protests/).

Almasy, Steve, and Holly Yan. 2014. "London Is Latest City to See Protests As Ferguson Dismay Spreads." *CNN.* Retrieved November 26, 2014 (http://edition.cnn.com/2014/11/26/us/national-ferguson-demonstrations/index.html).

Almquist, Elizabeth M. 1979. "Black Women and the Pursuit of Equality." pp. 430–450 in *Women: A Feminist Perspective*, edited by J. Freeman. Palo Alto, CA: Mayfield.

Almukhtar, Sarah, Larry Buchanan, and Michael Gold. 2017. "After Weinstein: The Fallout for 34 Men Accused of Sexual Misconduct, From Lewd Texts to Rape." *New York Times*, November 21. (https://www.nytimes.com/interactive/2017/11/10/us/men-accused-sexual-misconduct-weinstein.html).

Alonso, Alex A. 1998. "Rebuilding Los Angeles: A Lesson of Community Reconstruction." (http://www.streetgangs.com/academic/1998.Alonso-RLAreport-final-001.pdf).

Alvarez, Lizette. 2017. "A Great Migration From Puerto Rico Is Set to Transform Orlando." *New York Times*, November 17. (https://www.nytimes.com/2017/11/17/us/puerto-ricans-orlando.html).

Alvarez, Rodolfo. 1973. "The Psychohistorical and Socioeconomic Development of the Chicano Community in the United States." *Social Science Quarterly* 53:920–942.

Amazon Watch. 2017. "Over 700,000 People Demand Banks Stop Financing the Dakota Access Pipeline." February 3. Retrieved August 18, 2017 (http://amazonwatch.org/news/2017/0203-over-700000-people-demand-banks-stop-financing-the-dakota-access-pipeline).

American Civil Liberties Union. 2013. *The War on Marijuana in Black and White.* (https://www.aclu.org/billions-dollars-wasted-racially-biased-arrests).

_____. 2017. "Past LGBT Nondiscrimination and Anti-LGBT Bills Across the Country." (https://www.aclu.org/other/past-lgbt-nondiscrimination-and-anti-lgbt-bills-across-country).

American Immigration Council. 2017. "The Impact of Immigrant Women on America's Labor Force." March 8. (https://www.americanimmigrationcouncil.org/research/impact-immigrant-women-americas-labor-force).

American Postal Workers Union. 2004. "Sweatshop Tragedy Ignites Fight for Workplace Safety." _The American Postal Work Magazine_, March. Retrieved April 17, 2017 (http://www.apwu.org/labor-history-articles/sweatshop-tragedy-ignites-fight-workplace-safety).

American Sociological Association. 2003. _The Importance of Collecting Data and Doing Scientific Research on Race._ Washington, DC: Author. http://www2.asanet.org/media/asa_race_statement.pdf.

Amir, Yehuda. 1994. "The Contact Hypothesis in Intergroup Relations." Pp. 231–237 in _Psychology and Culture_, edited by W.J. Lonner and R.S. Malpass. Boston, MA: Allyn and Bacon.

Amott, Teresa, and Julie Matthaei. 1991. _Race, Gender, and Work: A Multicultural History of Women in the United States._ Boston, MA: South End.

Andersen, Margaret L. 1993. _Thinking About Women: Sociological Perspectives on Sex and Gender._ 3rd ed. New York: Macmillan.

Anderson, Bridget. 2000. _Doing the Dirty Work?: The Global Politics of Domestic Labour._ New York: Zed Books.

Anderson, Margo J. and Stephen E. Fienberg. 1999. _Who Counts? The Politics of Census-Taking in Contemporary America._ New York: Russell Sage Foundation.

Anderson, Kim. 2016. _A Recognition of Being: Reconstructing Native Womanhood._ 2nd ed. Toronto, Canada: Women's Press.

Andrews, Leslie. 2012. "Why Augusta Matters." _Newsweek_, August 27. (http://www.newsweek.com/why-augusta-matters-64527).

Anglin, Andrew. 2017. "PSA: When the Alt-Right Hits the Street, You Wanna be Ready." Retrieved August 13, 2017 (https://www.dailystormer.com/psa-when-the-internet-becomes-real-life-and-the-alt-right-hits-the-street-you-wanna-be-ready/).

Anonymous. 1924. "The Jew and the Club." _The Atlantic_, October. Retrieved August 3, 2017 (https://www.theatlantic.com/magazine/archive/1924/10/the-jew-and-the-club/306258/).

Anti-Defamation League. 2000. _Anti-Semitism in the United States._ (http://www.adl.org/backgrounders/Anti_Semitism_us.html).

_____. 2012. _Attitudes Towards Jews in Ten European Countries._ New York: Author. (http://archive.adl.org/anti_semitism/adl_anti-semitism_presentation_february_2012.pdf).

Anti-Defamation League Global. 2016. "An Index of Anti-Semitism." (http://global100.adl.org/public/ADL-global-100-Executive-Summary2015.pdf).

Anzaldúa, Gloria. 1999. _Borderlands/La Frontera: The New Mestiza._ San Francisco, CA: Aunt Lute Books. (Original work published in 1987).

Âpihtawikosisân. 2012. "Language, Culture, and Two-Spirit identity." March 29. Retrieved August 18, 2017 (http://apihtawikosisan.com/2012/03/language-culture-and-two-spirit-identity/).

Appelrouth, Scott, and Laura Desfor Edles. 2012. _Classical and Contemporary Sociological Theory: Text and Readings._ Los Angeles, CA: Pine Forge Press.

Aptekar, Sofya. 2015. The _Road to Citizenship: What Naturalization Means for Immigrants and the United States._ New Brunswick, NJ: Rutgers University Press.

Apuzzo, Matt. 2014. More Federal Privileges to Extend to Same-Sex Couples. _The New York Times_, February 8. (http://www.nytimes.com/2014/02/09/us/more-federal-privileges-to-extend-to-same-sex-couples.html?_r=0).

Arab American Anti-Discrimination Committee. 2002. _ADC Fact Sheet: The Condition of Arab Americans Post 9/11._ (http://www.adc.org/terror_attack/9-11aftermath.pdf.

Arciniega, G. Miguel, Thomas C. Anderson, Zoila G. Tovar-Blank, and Terence J. G. Tracey. 2008. "Toward a Fuller Conception of Machismo: Development of a Traditional Machismo and Caballerismo Scale." _Journal of Counseling Psychology_ 55(1): 19–33.

Arizona Daily Star. 2010. "Illegal Immigrant Deaths, by Border Patrol Sector." August 22. (http://tucson.com/online/pdf/pdf_731dc548-ada5-11df-9449-001cc4c03286.html).

Aronson, Eliot, and Alex Gonzalez. 1988. "Desegregation, Jigsaw, and the Mexican-American Experience." Pp. 301–314 in _Eliminating Racism: Profiles in Controversy_, edited by P. Katz and D. Taylor. New York: Plenum.

Aronson, Eliot, and Shelly Patnoe. 1997. _The Jigsaw Classroom: Building Cooperation in the Classroom._ 2nd ed. New York: Addison-Wesley Longman.

Ashmore, Richard, and Frances DelBoca. 1976. "Psychological Approaches to Understanding Group Conflict." Pp. 73–123 in _Towards the Elimination of Racism_, edited by P. Katz. New York: Pergamon.

Asian Americans Advancing Justice. 2017. "Tell Us Your Story." Retrieved August 26, 2017 (https://www.standagainsthatred.org/stories/).

Associated Press. 1998. "After Protest by Pastor, Interest in Gay Books at Library Grows." _New York Times_, May 24. (http://www.nytimes.com/1998/05/24/us/after-protest-by-pastor-interest-in-gay-books-at-library-grows.html).

_____. 2005. "Asian Youth Persistently Harassed by U.S. Peers." _USA Today_, November 13. (http://usatoday30.usatoday.com/news/nation/2005-11-13-asian-teens-bullied_x.htm).

_____. 2015. "U.S. Episcopal Church Installs First Black Leader." _NBC_, November 1. Retrieved August 8, 2017 (http://www.nbcnews.com/news/us-news/u-s-episcopal-church-installs-first-black-leader-n455381).

_____. 2017. "Weinstein's Impact: List of Men Accused of Sexual Misconduct." _ABC_

News, November 24. (http://abcnews.go.com/Entertainment/wireStory/weinsteins-impact-list-men-accused-sexual-misconduct-51365570).

Austin, Algernon. 2010. *Different Race, Different Recession: American Indian Unemployment in 2010* (Issue Brief 289). Washington, DC: Economic Policy Institute. (http://epi.3cdn.net/94a339472e6481485e_hgm6bxpz4.pdf).

Australian Bureau of Statistics. 2014. "What the NATSISS Tells Us." Retrieved August 18, 2017 (http://www.abs.gov.au/AUSSTATS/abs@.nsf/Lookup/4714.0Main+Features100012014-15?OpenDocument#WHAT).

Australian Government. 2015. "The Dreaming." Retrieved August 18, 2017 (http://www.australia.gov.au/about-australia/australian-story/dreaming).

Baca Zinn, Maxine, and Bonnie Thornton Dill, eds. 1994. *Women of Color in U.S. Society.* Philadelphia, PA: Temple University Press.

Baca Zinn, Maxine, and D. Stanley Eitzen. 1990. *Diversity in Families.* New York: HarperCollins.

Badgett, M.V. Lee, Laura E. Durso, and Alyssa Schneebaum. 2013. *New Patterns of Poverty in the Lesbian, Gay, and Bisexual Community.* Los Angeles, CA: Williams Institute, UCLA School of Law. (https://williamsinstitute.law.ucla.edu/wp-content/uploads/LGB-Poverty-Update-Jun-2013.pdf).

Baehr v. Miike, 910 P. 2d 112 (1996).

Bagemihl, Bruce. 2000. *Biological Exuberance: Animal Homosexuality and Natural Diversity.* New York: St. Martin's Press.

Bahadur, Nina. 2014. "Dove 'Real Beauty' Campaign Turns 10: How a Brand Tried to Change the Conversation About Female Beauty." *Huffington Post*, January 21. (http://www.huffingtonpost.com/2014/01/21/dove-real-beauty-campaign-turns-10_n_4575940.html).

Ball, Richard. 2009. "Social Distance in Japan: An Exploratory Study." *Michigan Sociological Review* 23:105–113.

Banner, Stuart. 2005. *How the Indians Lost Their Land: Law and Power on the Frontier.* Cambridge, MA: Harvard University Press.

Barclay, Eliza and Alexia Fernández Campbell. 2017. "New Data Shows Hurricane Deaths In Puerto Rico Could Be 20 Times Higher Than The Government Claims." *Vox*, November 17. (https://www.vox.com/policy-and-politics/2017/11/29/16623926/puerto-rico-death-toll-hurricane-maria-count).

Barnhill, John. 2014. "Colonialism." In *Encyclopedia of World Geography*. Vol. 1, edited by R.W. McColl. New York: Infobase Publishing.

Barnes, Robert and Matt Zapotosky. 2017. "Supreme Court Allows Limited Version of Trump's Travel Ban the Take Effect and Will Consider Case in Fall." *The Washington Post*, June 26. (https://www.washingtonpost.com/politics/courts_law/supreme-court-allows-limited-version-of-trumps-travel-ban-to-take-effect-will-consider-case-in-fall/2017/06/26/97afa314-573e-11e7-b38e-35fd8e0c288f_story.html?utm_term=.3b11d42ba283).

Barreto, Manuela, and Naomi Ellemers. 2005.

"The Perils of Political Correctness: Men's and Women's Responses to Old-Fashioned and Modern Sexist Views." *Social Psychology Quarterly* 68:75–88.

Barringer, Herbert, David Takeuchi, and Michael Levin. 1995. *Asians and Pacific Islanders in the United States.* New York: Russell Sage Foundation.

Bates, Karen Grigsby. 2008. "Racial Divisions Challenge Gay Rights Movement." *NPR*, December 4. (http://www.npr.org/templates/story/story.php?storyId=97826119).

Bauer, M. 2008. "Close to Slavery. Guestworker Programs in the United States." *A Report of the Southern Poverty Law Center.* (https://www.splcenter.org/sites/default/files/d6_legacy_files/downloads/Close_to_Slavery.pdf).

Baumgardner, Jennifer, and Amy Richards. 2000. *Manifesta: Young Women, Feminism, and the Future.* New York: Farrar, Straus & Giroux.

Bayer, Ronald. 1987. *Homosexuality and American Psychiatry: The Politics of Diagnosis.* Princeton, NJ: Princeton University Press.

Bayoumi, Moustafa. 2008. *How Does It Feel to Be a Problem?* New York: Penguin Books.

BBC News. 2013. "Gay Marriage Around the World." Retrieved April 23, 2013 (http://www.bbc.co.uk/news/world-21321731).

Beagle, Christine. 2016. "Siente lenguas: The Rhetorical History of Dolores Huerta and the Rise of Chicana Rhetoric." PhD dissertation, Department of English Language and Literature, University of New Mexico. (http://dspace.unm.edu/bitstream/handle/1928/31702/Garcia_Diss_LoboVault.pdf?sequence=1&isAllowed=y).

Bean, Frank, and Gillian Stevens. 2003. *America's Newcomers and the Dynamics of Diversity.* New York: Russell Sage Foundation.

Beaton, Anne, Francine Tougas, and Stephane Joly. 1996. "Neosexism Among Male Managers: Is It a Matter of Numbers?" *Journal of Applied Social Psychology* 26: 2189–2204.

Becerra, Rosina. 1988. "The Mexican American Family." Pp. 141–172 in *Ethnic Families in America: Patterns and Variations*. 3rd ed., edited by C.H. Mindel, R.W. Habenstein, and R. Wright Jr. New York: Elsevier.

Beck, E. M., and Timothy Clark. 2002. "Strangers, Community Miscreants, or Locals: Who Were the Black Victims of Mob Violence?" *Historical Methods* 35(2):77–84.

Beck, E. M., and Stewart Tolnay. 1990. "The Killing Fields of the Deep South: The Market for Cotton and the Lynching of Blacks, 1882–1930." *American Sociological Review* 55:526–539.

Becker, Howard S. 1963. *Outsiders: Studies in the Sociology of Deviance.* New York: Free Press.

Bedrick, Barry R. 1997. *Letter to Harry J. Hyde, Chairman, Committee on the Judiciary, House of Representatives, on the Defense of Marriage Act.* Washington, DC: U.S. General Accounting Office, Office of the General Counsel. (http://www.gao.gov/archive/1997/og97016.pdf).

Belkin, Lisa. 2012. "Huggies Pulls Ad After Insulting Dads." *Huffington Post*,

March 12. (http://www
.huffingtonpost.com/
lisa-belkin/huggies-pulls-
diaper-ads_b_1339074
.html).

Bell, Daniel. 1973. *The
Coming of Post-Industrial
Society*. New York: Basic
Books.

Bell, Derrick. 1992. *Race,
Racism, and American
Law*. 3rd ed. Boston, MA:
Little, Brown.

Bell, Jonathon. 2017. "British
and Irish Ministers to
'Plot Way Forward' if No
Northern Ireland Power-
Sharing Deal." *Belfast
Telegraph*, November
21. (https://www
.belfasttelegraph.co.uk/
news/republic-of-ireland/
british-and-irish-ministers-
to-plot-way-forward-if-
no-northern-ireland-
powersharing-deal-
varadkar-36341497.html).

Benedict, Ruth. 1946. T*he
Chrysanthemum and
the Sword: Patterns of
Japanese Culture*. Boston,
MA: Houghton Mifflin.

Benjamin, Lois. 2005. *The
Black Elite*. Lanham, MD:
Rowman & Littlefield.

Benowitz, June Melby. 2017.
*Encyclopedia of American
Women and Religion*, 2nd
ed. Santa Barbara, CA:
ABC-CLIO.

Berkowitz, Leonard. 1978.
"Whatever Happened to
the Frustration-Aggression
Hypothesis?" *American
Behavioral Scientist*
21:691–708.

Berndt, Ronald Murray and
Catherine Helen Berndt.
1987. *End of an Era:
Aboriginal Labour in
the Northern Territory*.
Canberra: Australian
Institute of Aboriginal
Studies. Bernheimer,
Charles S. 1908.
"Prejudice Against the
Jews in the United States."
The Independent 65,
November 12.

Bernstein, Robert A. 2008.
*Straight Parents, Gay
Children: Keeping Families
Together*. Cambridge, MA:
Da Capo Press.

Berry, John W. 1980.
"Acculturation as Varieties
of Adaptation." Pp. 9–25
in *Acculturation: Theory,
Models, and Some New
Findings*, edited by
A.M Padilla. Boulder,
CO: Westview.

Bertrand, Marianne, and
Mullainathan, Sendhil.
2004. "Are Emily and
Greg More Employable
Than Lakisha and Jamal? A
Field Experiment on Labor
Market Discrimination."
*American Economic
Review* 94:991–1013.

Bever, Lindsey. 2016.
"The Swedish Stanford
Students Who Rescued
An Unconscious Sexual
Assault Victim Speak Out."
The Washington Post,
June 8. (https://
www.washingtonpost
.com/news/morning-
mix/wp/2016/06/07/
the-swedish-stanford-
students-who-rescued-
an-unconscious-sexual-
assault-victim-speak-out/).

Bibb, Henry. 1849. "Narrative
of the Life and Adventures
of Henry Bibb, An
American Slave, Written
by Himself." With an
Introduction by Lucius
C. Matlack. Written by
Himself. New York: Author.
(http://docsouth.unc.edu/
neh/bibb/bibb.html).

Biskupic, Joan. 1989. "House
Approves Entitlement for
Japanese-Americans."
*Congressional Quarterly
Weekly Report*, October
28, p. 2879.

Blackmon, Douglas A. 2008.
*Slavery by Another Name:
The Re-Enslavement of
Black Americans from the
Civil War to World War II*.
New York: Anchor Books.

Blackmon, Douglas A. 2009.
*Slavery by Another Name:
The Re-Enslavement of
Black Americans from the
Civil War to World War II*.
Knopf Doubleday Publishing
Group. Retrieved August 10,
2017 (https://books.google
.com/books?isbn=0307
472477).

Blackwood, Evelyn 1997.
"Native American Genders
and Sexualities: Beyond
Anthropological Models
and Misrepresentations."
Pp. 284–294 in *Two-spirit
People: Native American
Gender Identity, Sexuality,
and Spirituality*, edited by
S. Jacobs, W. Thomas, and
S. Lang. Champaign, IL:
University of Illinois Press.

Blake, John. 2014. "The New
Threat: 'Racism without
Racists.'" *CNN*, November
27. Retrieved August 9,
2017 (http://www.cnn
.com/2014/11/26/us/
ferguson-racism-or-racial-
bias/index.html).

Blassingame, John W. 1972.
*The Slave Community:
Plantation Life in the
Antebellum South*. New
York: Oxford University
Press.

Blau, Peter M., and Otis
Dudley Duncan. 1967. *The
American Occupational
Structure*. New York: Wiley.

Blauner, Robert. 1972. *Racial
Oppression in America*.
New York: Harper & Row.

Blessing, Patrick. 1965.
Industrialization and Race
Relations. Pp. 200–253 in
*Industrialization and Race
Relations: A Symposium*,
edited by G. Hunter.
London, UK: Oxford
University Press.

Blessing, Patrick. 1980.
"Irish." Pp. 524–545 in
*Harvard Encyclopedia of
American Ethnic Groups*,
edited by S. Thernstrom,
A. Orlov, and O. Handlin.
Cambridge, MA: Harvard
University Press.

Blumberg, Rae Lesser. 2004.
"Extending Lenski's
Schema to Hold up Both
Halves of the Sky: A
Theory-Guided Way of
Conceptualizing Agrarian
Societies That Illuminates
a Puzzle about Gender
Stratification." *Sociological
Theory* 22(2):278–29.

Blumer, Herbert. 1958. "Race
Prejudice as a Sense of
Group Position." *Pacific
Sociological Review* 1:3–7.
_____. 1965.
"Industrialization and Race
Relations." Pp. 200–253
in *Industrialization
and Race Relations: A
Symposium*, edited by G.
Hunter. London: Oxford
University Press.

Bobo, Lawrence. 2001.
"Racial Attitudes and
Relations at the Close of
the Twentieth Century."
Pp. 264–301 in *America
Becoming: Racial Trends
and Their Consequences*.
Vol. 1, edited by N.
Smelser, W. Wilson, and F.
Mitchell. Washington, DC:
National Academy
Press.

Bobo, Lawrence D., Camille
Z. Charles, Maria Krysan,
and Alicia D. Simmons.
2012. "The Real Record
on Racial Attitudes."
Pp. 38–83 in *Social Trends
in American Life: Findings
From the General Social
Survey Since 1973*, edited
by P. Marsden. Princeton,
NJ: Princeton University
Press.

Bobo, Lawrence, and James
Kluegal. 1997. "Status,
Ideology, and Dimensions
of Whites' Racial Beliefs
and Attitudes: Progress
and Stagnation." P. 101
in *Racial Attitudes in the
1990s: Continuity and
Change*, edited by S. Tuck
and J. Martin. Westport,
CT: Praeger.

Bobo, Lawrence, and Mia
Tuan. 2006. *Prejudice in
Politics: Group Position,
Public Opinion, and the
Wisconsin Treaty Rights
Dispute*. Cambridge, MA:
Harvard University Press.

Bobo, Lawrence. 1988.
"Group Conflict, Prejudice,
and the Paradox of
Contemporary Racial
Attitudes." Pp. 85–114
in *Eliminating Racism:
Profiles in Controversy*,
edited by P. Katz and

D. Taylor. New York: Plenum.

Bodley, John H. 2013. *The Small Nation Solution: How the World's Smallest Nations Can Solve the World's Biggest Problems*. Lanham: MD. AltaMira Press.

Bodnar, John. 1985. *The Transplanted*. Bloomington, IN: Indiana University Press.

Bogardus, Emory. 1933. A Social Distance Scale. *Sociology and Social Research* 17:265–271.

Bonacich, Edna. 1972. "A Theory of Ethnic Antagonism: The Split Labor Market." *American Sociological Review* 37:547–559.

Bonacich, Edna, and John Modell. 1980. *The Economic Basis of Ethnic Solidarity: Small Business in the Japanese American Community*. Berkeley, CA: University of California Press.

Bonilla-Silva, Eduardo. 2001. *White Supremacy and Racism in the Post–Civil Rights Era*. Boulder, CO: Lynne Rienner.

Bonilla-Silva, Eduardo. 2003. "'New Racism,' Color-Blind Racism, and the Future of Whiteness in America." Pp. 271–284 in *White Out: The Continuing Significance of Racism*, edited by A. Doane and E. Bonilla-Silva. New York: Routledge.

Bonilla-Silva, Eduardo. 2006. *Racism Without Racists*. 2nd ed. Lanham, MD: Rowman & Littlefield.

Booth, Alan, Douglas Granger, Alan Mazur, and Katie Kivligham. 2006. Testosterone and Social Behavior. *Social Forces* 86:167–191.

Bordewich, Fergus. 1996. *Killing the White Man's Indian*. New York: Doubleday.

Borstelmann, Thomas. 2009. *The Cold War and the Color Line*. Cambridge, MA: Harvard University Press.

Bosman, Julie and Joseph Goldstein. 2014. "Timeline for a Body: 4 Hours in the Middle of a Ferguson Street." *The New York Times*, August 23. Retrieved August 10, 2017 (https://www.nytimes.com/2014/08/24/us/michael-brown-a-bodys-timeline-4-hours-on-a-ferguson-street.html).

Bosman, Julie, Mitch Smith, and Michael Wines, 2017. "Jurors Find Video Isn't Providing 20/20 Vision in Police Shootings." *The New York Times*, June 25. Retrieved July 20, 2017 (https://www.nytimes.com/2017/06/25/us/police-shootings-trials-video-body-cam.html).

Boswell, A. Ayres, and Joan Z. Spade. 1996. "Fraternities and Collegiate Rape Culture: Why Are Some Fraternities More Dangerous Places for Women?" *Gender and Society* 10:133–147.

Boswell, Terry. 1986. "A Split Labor Market Analysis of Discrimination Against Chinese Immigrants, 1850–1882." *American Sociological Review* 51:352–371.

Bolter, Jessica. 2017. "The Evolving and Diversifying Nature of Migration to the U.S.-Mexico Border." *Migration Policy Institute*, February 1. (http://www.migrationpolicy.org/article/evolving-and-diversifying-nature-migration-us-mexico-border).

Boulton, John. 2017. "Destruction of Food Resources at the Colonial Frontier." Pp.150–172 in *Aboriginal Children History and Health: Beyond Social Determinants*, edited by J. Boulton. New York: Routledge.

Bourcier, Nicolas. 2012. "Brazil Comes to Terms With Its Slave Trading Past." *The Guardian*, October 23. Retrieved July 20, 2017 (https://www.theguardian.com/world/2012/oct/23/brazil-struggle-ethnic-racial-identity).

Bouvier, Leon F., and Robert W. Gardner. 1986. "Immigration to the U.S.: The Unfinished Story." *Population Bulletin* 41(November):1–50.

Bowers v. Hardwick, 478 U.S. 186 (1986).

Boyer, Paul S., Clifford E. Clark, Sandra Hawley, Joseph F. Kett, and Andrew Rieser. 2008. *The Enduring Vision: A History of the American People, Concise*. Boston, MA: Cengage Learning.

Boykin, Keith. 2006. *Beyond the Down Low: Sex, Lies and Denial in the Black Community*. Boston, MA: Da Capo Press.

Boykin, Keith. 1997. *One More River to Cross: Black and Gay in America*. New York: Anchor Books.

Branch, John. 2014. "NFL Prospect Michael Sam Proudly Says What Teammates Knew: He's Gay." *The New York Times*, February 9. (http://www.nytimes.com/2014/02/10/sports/michael-sam-college-football-star-says-he-is-gay-ahead-of-nfl-draft.html?_r=0).

Brennan Center for Justice. 2013. "Voting Laws Roundup 2013." (http://www.brennancenter.org/analysis/election-2013-voting-laws-roundup).

Brezina, Corona. 2005. *Sojourner Truth's 'Ain't I a woman?' Speech: A Primary Source Investigation*. New York: The Rosen Publishing Group.

Briggs, Bill. 2013. "Senator Seeks to Reform Military's 'Unacceptable' Sex Abuse Policies." *NBC News*, May 16. Retrieved (http://usnews.nbcnews.com/_news/2013/05/16/18280367-senator-seeks-to-reform-militarys-unacceptable-sex-abuse-policies?lite).

Brilliant, Mark. 2010. *The Color of America Has Changed: How Racial Diversity Shaped Civil Rights Reform in California, 1941–1978*. Oxford, UK: Oxford University Press.

Brittingham, Angela, and G. Patricia de la Cruz. 2004. *Ancestry: 2000*. Washington, DC: U.S. Census Bureau. (http://www.census.gov/prod/2004pubs/c2kbr-35.pdf).

Brody, David. 1980. "Labor." Pp. 609–618 in *Harvard Encyclopedia of American Ethnic Groups*, edited by S. Thernstrom, A. Orlov, and O. Handlin. Cambridge, MA: Harvard University Press.

Bronson, Po, and Ashley Merryman. 2009. "Even Babies Discriminate: A NurtureShock Excerpt." *Newsweek*, September 14. (http://www.newsweek.com/even-babies-discriminate-nurtureshock-excerpt-79233).

Brown v. Board of Education of Topeka, 247 U.S. 483 (1954).

Brown, Anna. 2014. "U.S. Hispanic And Asian Populations Growing, But For Different Reasons." *Pew Research Center*. Retrieved August 26, 2017 (http://www.pewresearch.org/fact-tank/2014/06/26/u-s-hispanic-and-asian-populations-growing-but-for-different-reasons/).

Brown, Anna, and Eileen Patten. 2013a. *Hispanics of Colombian Origin in the United States, 2011*. Washington, DC: Pew Hispanic Center. (http://www.pewhispanic.org/2013/06/19/hispanics-of-colombian-origin-in-the-united-states-2011/).

_____. 2013b. *Hispanics of Cuban Origin in the United States: 2011*. Washington, DC: Pew Hispanic Center. (http://www.pewhispanic.org/files/2013/06/CubanFactsheet.pdf).

_____. 2013c. *Hispanics of Dominican Origin in the United States, 2011*. Washington, DC: Pew Hispanic Center. (http://www.pewhispanic.org/2013/06/19/hispanics-of-dominican-origin-in-the-united-states-2011/).

_____. 2013d. *Hispanics of Salvadoran Origin in the United States, 2011*. Washington, DC: Pew Hispanic Center. Retrieved (http://www.pewhispanic.org/2013/06/19/hispanics-of-dominican-origin-in-the -united-states-2011/).

_____. 2013e. *Statistical Profile: Hispanics of Puerto Rican Origin in the United States, 2011*. Washington, DC: Pew Hispanic Center. Retrieved (http://www.pewhispanic.org/2013/06/19/hispanics-of-puerto-rican-origin-in-the-united-states-2011/).

Brown, Kendrick T., Tony N. Brown, James S. Jackson, and Robert M. Sellers, and Warde J. Manuel. 2003. "Teammates On and Off the Field? Contact with Black Teammates and the Racial Attitudes of White Student Athletes." *Journal of Applied Social Psychology* 33:1379–1403. doi:10.1111/j.1559-1816.2003.tb01954.x.

Brown, Nicholas D. 2015. "The Brotherhood of Sleeping Car Porters: The Civil Rights Movement." Thesis, The University of Toledo, OH. (https://etd.ohiolink.edu/!etd.send_file?accession=toledo1430166476&disposition=inline).

Brown, Rupert. 1995. *Prejudice: Its Social Psychology*. Cambridge, MA: Blackwell.

Brunnerová, Helena . 2016. "The Role of Two-Spirit People as Mediators." Bachelor's Thesis. Retrieved August 18, 2017 (https://is.muni.cz/th/414981/fss_b/Brunnerova_-_BA_Thesis.txt).

Brunsma, David. 2005. "Interracial Families and the Racial Identification of Mixed-Race Children: Evidence From the Early Childhood Longitudinal Study." *Social Forces* 84:1131–1157.

Bruzgulis, Anna. 2015. "Confederate Flag Wasn't Flown at South Carolina Statehouse Until 1961, Pundit Claims." June 22. (http://www.politifact.com/punditfact/statements/2015/jun/22/eugene-robinson/confederate-flag-wasnt-flown-south-carolina -state-/

Bucciferro, Justin R. 2013. "A Forced Hand: Natives, Africans, and the Population of Brazil, 1545–1850." *Revista de Historia Económica/Journal of Iberian and Latin American Economic History* 31(2):285–317.

_____ 2015. "Racial Inequality in Brazil from Independence to the Present." Pp. 171–194 in *Has Latin American Inequality Changed Direction*, edited by L. Bértola and J. Williamson. New York: Springer.

Buchanan, Bruce. 2005. "The Empire of Political Thought: Civilization, Savagery and Perceptions of Indigenous Government." *History of the Human Sciences* 18(2): 1–22.

Budech, Keiko A. 2014. *Missing Voices, Hidden Fields: The Gendered Struggles of Female Farmworkers*. Pitzer College Thesis, Claremont, CA. (http://scholarship.claremont.edu/cgi/viewcontent.cgi?article=1056&context=pitzer_theses)

Bulwa, Demian. 2010. "Mehserle Convicted of Involuntary Manslaughter." *San Francisco Chronicle*, July 9. (http://www.sfgate.com/bayarea/article/Mehserle-convicted -of-involuntary-manslaughter-3181861.php).

Bumiller, Elisabeth. 2011. "Obama Ends 'Don't Ask Don't Tell' Policy." *The New York Times*, July 22. (http://www.nytimes.com/2011/07/23/us/23military.html).

Buriel, Raymond. 1993. "Acculturation, Respect for Cultural Differences, and Biculturalism Among Three Generations of Mexican American and Euro-American School Children." *Journal of Genetic Psychology* 154:531–544.

Burns, Peter, and James Gimpel. 2000. Economic Insecurity, Prejudicial Stereotypes, and Public Opinion on Immigration Policy. *Political Science Quarterly* 115:201–205.

Buzinski, Jim. n.d. "Record-Breaking Six Openly Gay College Football Players Hit the Field This Fall." *Huffington Post*. (http://www.huffingtonpost.com/entry/six-out-gay-football-players_us_59a841f0e4b010ca289b1d90?ncid=inblnkushpmg00000009).

Caldwell, Kia Lilly. 2008. "'Look at Her Hair': The Body Politics of Black Womanhood in Brazil." *Transforming Anthropology* 11(2): 18–29. doi: 10.1525/tran.2003.11.2.18.

Callens, Marie-Sophie, Bart Meuleman, and Marie Valentova. 2015. "Perceived Threat, Contact and Attitudes towards the Integration of Immigrants. Evidence from Luxembourg." Luxembourg Institute of Socio-Economic Research (LISER) Working Paper Series 2015-0. (https://www.liser.lu/publi_viewer.cfm?tmp=3885).

Callimachi, Rukmini. 2005. "Is Nike Campaign Real About Curves?" *Salt Lake Tribune*, August 19. (http://www.sltrib.com/business/ci_2954991).

Camarillo, Albert, and Frank Bonilla. 2001. "Hispanics in a Multicultural Society: A New American Dilemma?" Pp. 103–134 in *America Becoming: Racial Trends and Their Consequences*. Vol. 2, edited by N. Smelser, W. Wilson, and F. Mitchell. Washington, DC: National Academy Press.

Cameron, James. 2001. "Social Identity, Modern Sexism, and Perceptions of Personal and Group Discrimination by Women and Men." *Sex Roles* 45:743–766.

Campbell, Braden. 2017. "Dukes Class Members Hit Walmart With New Pay Bias Suit." *Law360*, November 8. (https://www.law360.com/articles/983223/dukes-class-members-hit-walmart-with-new-pay-bias-suit).

Capehart, Jonathon. 2012. "The Income Inequality Faced by LGBT Families." *Washington Post*, February 2. (http://www.washingtonpost.com/blogs/post-partisan/post/the -income-inequality-faced-by-lgbt-families/2011/03/04/gIQAoInNkQ_blog.html).

Cardenas, Natalie. 2017. "LatinX: Why You Should Start Using The Term." *Her Campus*, February 28.

(https://www.hercampus
.com/school/ufl/latinx-why-
you-should-start-using-
term).

Cardona, Nina. 2015. "50
Years Before Rosa Parks,
A Bold Nashville Streetcar
Protest Defied Segregation.
Podcast." *NPR*,
September 22 (http://
nashvillepublicradio
.org/post/50-years-rosa-
parks-bold-nashville-
streetcar-protest-defied-
segregation#stream/0).

Carlson-Ghost, Mark. "Two-
Spirit Tales–A Berry
Curious Raiding Party."
2016. Retrieved August
18, 2017 (http://www.
markcarlson-ghost.com/
index.php/2016/10/14/
two-spirit-tales-a-berry-
curious-raiding-party/).

Carpenter, Dale. 2012.
*Flagrant Conduct: The
Story of* Lawrence vs.
Texas. New York:
W. W. Norton.

Carter, David. 2005.
*Stonewall: The Riots
That Sparked the Gay
Revolution.* New York:
St. Martin's Griffin.

Carter, Nancy M., and
Christine Silva. 2010.
Pipeline's Broken Promise.
New York: Catalyst.
(http://www.catalyst.org/
publication/372/pipelines-
broken-promise).

Casillas, D. Ines. 2014.
"Speaking 'Mexican' and
the use of 'Mock Spanish'
in Children's Books (or
Do Not Read Skippyjon
Jones)." *Sounding
Out*, May 5. (https://
soundstudiesblog
.com/2014/05/05/
speaking-mexican-and-the-
use-of-mock-spanish-in-
childrens-books-or-do-not-
read-skippyjon-jones/).

CBS News/Associated Press.
2016. "Writer Starts
Social Media Movement
of Women Sharing Sexual
Assault Stories." *CBS*,
October 9. (https://www
.cbsnews.com/news/
kelly-oxford-starts-social-

media-movement-of-
women-sharing-sexual-
assault-stories/).

Center for American Women
and Politics. 2017.
"Gender Differences in
Voter Turnout." (http://
www.cawp.rutgers
.edu/sites/default/files/
resources/genderdiff.pdf).

_____. 2018a. "High-
Level Presidential
Appointments." (http://
www.cawp.rutgers.edu/
levels_of_office/high-level-
presidential-appointments).

Center For American Women
And Politics. 2018b.
"Women in Elective Office
2017." (http://www
.cawp.rutgers.edu/women-
elective-office-2017).

Centers for Disease Control
and Prevention. 2017.
"Lesbian, Gay, Bisexual,
and Transgender Health:
LGBT Youth." (https://www
.cdc.gov/lgbthealth/youth
.htm).

Central Intelligence Agency.
2017. "The World
Factbook." Retrieved April
17, 2017 (https://www.cia
.gov/library/publications/
the-world-factbook/geos/
sf.html).

Central Statistics Office
[Ireland]. 2014.
"Population and
Migration Estimates".
Retrieved April 29, 2014
(http://www.cso.ie/en/
releasesandpublications/
er/pme/
populationandmigrationesti
matesapril2014).

Chan, Sewell. 2017. "Russia's
'Gay Propaganda' Laws Are
Illegal, European
Court Rules." *The New
York Times*, June 20.
*(https://www.nytimes
.com/2017/06/20/
world/europe/russia-gay-
propaganda.html)*.

Chan, Sucheng. 1990.
"European and Asian
Immigrants Into the United
States in Comparative
Perspective, 1820s to
1920s." Pp. 37–75 in
Immigration Reconsidered:

*History, Sociology, and
Politics*, edited by V. Yans-
McLaughlin. New York:
Oxford University Press.

Chapman, George. 2004.
"Geographical Distribution
of Environmental Factors
Influencing Human Skin
Coloration." *American
Journal of Physical
Anthropology*: 292–302.

Chappell, David L. 1996.
*White Southerners in the
Civil Rights Movement.*
Baltimore, MD: Johns
Hopkins University Press.

Charles-Toussaint, Gifflene C.,
and H. Michael Crowson.
2010. "Prejudice Against
International Students: The
Role of Threat Perceptions
and Authoritarian
Dispositions in U.S.
Students." *Journal of
Psychology* 144:413–428.

Chatel, Amanda. 2013. "7
Companies That Don't
Support Gay Rights."
Huffington Post, October
16. (http://www
.huffingtonpost
.com/2013/10/16/anti-gay-
companies_n_4110344
.html).

Chavez-Dueñas, Nayeli Y.,
Hector Y. Adames, and
Kurt C. Organista. 2013.
"Skin-Color Prejudice
and Within-Group Racial
Discrimination." *Hispanic
Journal of Behavioral
Sciences* 36(1):3–26.
doi: 10.1177/073998
6313511306.

Cherry, Kittredge. 2012. "Two-
spirit Native Americans
Bridge Genders on
Columbus Day." October
08. Retrieved August 18,
2017 (http://jesusinlove
.blogspot.com/2012/10/).

Chen, Jenny J. 2017. "First-
Ever Tracker of Hate
Crimes Against Asian-
Americans Launched."
NPR, February 17. (http://
www.npr.org/sections/
codeswitch/2017/02/17/
515824196/first-ever-
tracker-of-hate-crimes-
against-asian-americans-
launched).

Childs, Erica Chito. 2005.
*Navigating Interracial
Borders: Black–White
Couples and Their Social
Worlds.* New Brunswick,
NJ: Rutgers University
Press.

Chinese Railroad Workers in
North American Project
at Stanford University.
n.d. "FAQ." Retrieved
August 26, 2017 (http://
web.stanford.edu/group/
chineserailroad/cgi-bin/
wordpress/faqs/).

Chirot, Daniel. 1994.
How Societies Change.
Thousand Oaks, CA: Sage.

Cho, Sumi. 1993. "Korean
Americans vs. African
Americans: Conflict and
Construction." Pp. 196–211
in *Reading Rodney King,
Reading Urban Uprising*,
edited by R. Gooding-
Williams. New York:
Routledge & Kegan Paul.

Choo, Christine. 2016. "The
Health of Aboriginal
Children in Western
Australia 1829–1960." In
*Aboriginal Children History
and Health: Beyond Social
Determinants*, edited by
John Boulton. New York:
Routledge.

Chou, Rosalind, and Joe
Feagin. 2008. *The Myth of
the Model Minority: Asian
Americans Facing Racism.*
Boulder, CO: Paradigm.

Chowkwanyun, Merlin, and
Jordan Segall. 2012. "The
Rise of the Majority-Asian
Suburb." *CityLab*, August
24. (http://www.citylab
.com/politics/2012/08/
rise-majority-asian-
suburb/3044/).

Chu, Donald, and David
Griffey. 1985. "The
Contact Theory of Racial
Integration: The Case of
Sport." *Sociology of Sport
Journal* 2(4):323–333.

Chung, Maya. 2015.
"Breaking Barriers:
African-American Firsts
in 2015." *NBC News*,
December 22. Retrieved
August 8, 2017 (http://
www.nbcnews.com/news/

nbcblk/breaking-barriers-african-american-firsts-2015-n478556).

Churchill, Ward. 1985. "Resisting Relocation: Dine and Hopis Fight to Keep Their Land." *Dollars and Sense*, December, pp. 112–115.

Civil Rights Act of 1964, Pub. L. 88-352, § 42 U.S.C. 2000 (1964).

Clark, Kenneth B., and Mamie K. Clark. 1940. "Skin Color as a Factor in Racial Identification of Negro Preschool Children." *The Journal of Social Psychology* 11:159–169.

_____. 1950. "Emotional Factors in Racial Identification of Negro Preschool Children." *Journal of Negro Education* 19:341–350.

Clark, M. L., and Willie Person. 1982. "Racial Stereotypes Revisited." *International Journal of Intercultural Relations* 6:381–392.

Clements, Nicholas. 2014. *Black War: Fear, Sex and Resistance in Tasmania.* Brisbane, Australia: University of Queensland Press.

CNN Library. 2017a. "Mexico Drug War Fast Facts." *CNN*, May 16. (http://www.cnn.com/2013/09/02/world/americas/mexico-drug-war-fast-facts/index.html).

_____. 2017b. "Deadliest Mass Shootings in US." *CNN*, June 28. Retrieved July 28, 2017 (http://www.cnn.com/2013/09/16/us/20-deadliest-mass-shootings-in-u-s-history-fast-facts/index.html).

Coates, Ta-Nehisi. 2010. "Small Truth Papering Over a Big Lie." *The Atlantic*, August 9. Retrieved May 5, 2017 (https://www.theatlantic.com/national/archive/2010/08/small-truth-papering-over-a-big-lie/61136/).

Coates, Ta-Nehisi. 2014. "The Case for Reparations." *The Atlantic*, June 24. Retrieved August 10, 2017 (https://www.theatlantic.com/projects/reparations).

Cofer, Judith Ortiz. 1995. "The Myth of the Latin Woman: I Just Met a Girl Named Maria." Pp. 148–154 in *The Latin Deli: Prose and Poetry*. Athens: University of Georgia Press.

Cohen, Adam, and Elizabeth Taylor. 2000. *American Pharaoh, Mayor Richard J. Daley: His Battle for Chicago and the Nation.* New York: Little, Brown.

Cohen, Felix S. 1945. *Handbook of Federal Indian Law: With Reference Tables and Index.* 4th ed. Washington, DC. U.S. Government Printing Office.

Cohen, Jeremy. 1982. *The Friars and the Jews: The Evolution of Medieval Anti-Judaism.* Ithaca, NY: Cornell University Press.

Cohen, Phillip. 2013. The Problem With Mostly Male (and Mostly Female) Workplaces. *Atlantic Monthly*, March 20. (http://www.theatlantic.com/sexes/archive/2013/03/the-problem-with-mostly-male-and-mostly-female-workplaces/274208/).

Cohen, Steven M. 1985. *The 1984 National Survey of American Jews: Political and Social Outlooks.* New York: American Jewish Committee.

Cohen, Tom. 2013. "Obama: 'Trayvon Martin could have been me'." *CNN*. Retrieved July 20, 2017 (http://www.cnn.com/2013/07/19/politics/obama-zimmerman/).

Cohn, D'Vera. 2010. "Census History: Counting Hispanics." *Pew Research Center*, March 3. (http://www.pewsocialtrends.org/2010/03/03/census-history-counting-hispanics-2/).

_____. 2015. "Future Immigration Will Change the Face of America by 2065." *Pew research Center Facttank - Our Lives in Numbers*, October 5. (http://www.pewresearch.org/fact-tank/2015/10/05/future-immigration-will-change-the-face-of-america-by-2065/).

_____. 2017. "Seeking Better Data on Hispanics, Census Bureau May Change How It Asks About Race." *Pew Research Center*, April 20. (http://www.pewresearch.org/fact-tank/2017/04/20/seeking-better-data-on-hispanics-census-bureau-may-change-how-it-asks-about-race/).

Colby, Sandra L., and Jennifer M. Ortman. 2015. "Projections of the Size and Composition of the U.S. Population, 2014 to 2060." *Current Population Reports*. Retrieved April 11, 2017 (https://www.census.gov/content/dam/Census/library/publications/2015/demo/p25-1143.pdf).

College Enrollment in India Expands Rapidly. 2012. *Chronicle of Higher Education*, August 22. (http://chronicle.com/blogs/global/college-enrollment-in-india-expands-rapidly/34342).

Collins, Jason (with Franz Lidz). 2013. "Why NBA Center Jason Collins Is Coming Out Now." *Sports Illustrated*, May 6. (http://sportsillustrated.cnn.com/magazine/news/20130429/jason-collins-gay-nba-player/).

Collins, Patricia Hill. 2000. *Black Feminist Thought: Knowledge, Consciousness, and the Politics of Empowerment.* 2nd ed. New York: Routledge.

Commonwealth of Australia. 1997. "Bringing them Home". Report of the National Inquiry into the Separation of Aboriginal and Torres Strait Islander Children from Their Families. Retrieved August 18, 2017 (http://www.humanrights.gov.au/sites/default/files/content/pdf/social_justice/bringing_them_home_report.pdf).

Congress of Racial Equality. n.d. "What is CORE?" Retrieved June 13, 2017 (http://www.core-online.org/Features/what-is-core.htm).

Congressional Record. 2007. *House of Representatives*, volume 153, part 3, February 12, p. 3721.

Connor, Phillip, and Jens Manuel Krogstad. 2016. "Key Facts About the World's Refugees." *Pew Research Center*, October 5. (http://www.pewresearch.org/fact-tank/2016/10/05/key-facts-about-the-worlds-refugees/).

Conot, Robert. 1967. *Rivers of Blood, Years of Darkness.* New York: Bantam.

Conrad, Robert E. 1972. *The Destruction of Brazilian Slavery, 1850–1888.* Berkeley, CA: University of California Press.

Constitutional Rights Foundation. n.d. "Race and Voting in the Segregated South." Retrieved August 10, 2017 (http://www.crf-usa.org/black-history-month/race-and-voting-in-the-segregated-south).

Conzen, Kathleen N. 1980. "Germans." Pp. 405–425 in *Harvard Encyclopedia of American Ethnic Groups*, edited by S. Thernstrom, A. Orlov, and O. Handlin. Cambridge, MA: Harvard University Press.

Cook, Rebecca J. 2013. "Human Rights and Maternal Health: Exploring the Effectiveness of the Alyne Decision." *Journal of Law, Medicine and Ethics* 41:103–123.

Coontz, Stephanie. 1997. *The Way We Really Are: Coming to Terms With America's Changing Families*. New York: Basic Books.

Corkery, Michael. 2017. "Betty Dukes, Greater Whose Walmart Lawsuit Went to Supreme Court, Dies at 67." *New York Times*. July 18. (https://www.nytimes.com/2017/07/18/business/betty-dukes-dead-walmart-worker-led-landmark-class-action-sex-bias-case.html).

Cornell, Stephen, and Joseph Kalt. 1998. *Sovereignty and Nation-Building: The Development Challenge in Indian Country Today*. Cambridge, MA: Harvard Project on American Indian Economic Development.

Cooper, Helene. 2014. "Pentagon Study Finds 50% Increase in Reports of Military Sexual Assaults." *The New York Times,* May 1. (https://www.nytimes.com/2014/05/02/us/military-sex-assault-report.html?_r=0).

Cornell, Stephen, Joseph Kalt, Matthew Krepps, and Johnathan Taylor. 1998. American Indian Gaming Policy and Its Socioeconomic Effects: A Report to the National Impact Gambling Study Commission. Cambridge, MA: Economics Resource Group.

_____. 1987. "American Indians, American Dreams, and the Meaning of Success." *American Indian Culture and Research Journal* 11:59–71.

_____. 1988. *The Return of the Native: American Indian Political Resurgence*. New York: Oxford University Press.

_____. 1990. Land, Labor, and Group Formation: Blacks and Indians in the United States. *Ethnic and Racial Studies* 13: 368–388.

_____. 2006. *What Makes First Nations Enterprises Successful? Lessons from the Harvard Project*. Tucson, AZ: Native Nations Institute for Leadership, Management, and Policy.

Cornell University. 1911. "Men and Girls Die in Waist Factory Fire; Trapped High Up in Washington Place Building; Street Strewn with Bodies; Piles of Dead Inside." *The New York Times Company*, March 26, p. 1. Retrieved April 17, 2017 (Trianglefire.ilr.cornell.edu/primary/.../nyt_032611.html).

_____. n.d. Legal Information Institute. Department of Defense. Chapter I, Subchapter D - Personnel, Military and Civilian. § 105.3 Definitions. (https://www.law.cornell.edu/cfr/text/32/105.3).

Correll, Shelley J. 2004. "Constraints Into Preferences: Gender, Status, and Emerging Career Aspirations." *American Sociological Review* 69:93–113.

Cortes, Carlos. 1980. "Mexicans." Pp. 697–719 in *Harvard Encyclopedia of American Ethnic Groups*, edited by S. Thernstrom, A. Orlov, and O. Handlin. Cambridge, MA: Harvard University Press.

Cose, Ellis. 1993. *The Rage of a Privileged Class*. New York: HarperCollins.

Coski, John M. 2009. *The Confederate Battle Flag*. Boston, MA: Harvard University Press.

Costner, Kevin (director). 1990. *Dances with Wolves*. TIG Productions, Inc.

Cottrol, Robert. 2013. *The Long Lingering Shadow: Slavery, Race, and Law in the American Hemisphere*. Athens: University of Georgia Press.

Council of Energy Resource Tribes. n.d. *About CERT*. Retrieved October 11, 2015 (http://74.63.154.129/aboutus-philosophyHistory.html).

Cowan, Gloria. 2005. "Interracial Interactions at Racially Diverse University Campuses." *Journal of Social Psychology* 145:49–63.

Cox, Daniel, Juhem Navarro-Rivera, and Robert P. Jones. 2016. "Race, Religion, and Political Affiliation of Americans' Core Social Network." *Public Religion Research Institute*, March 8. Retrieved July 20, 2017 (https://www.prri.org/research/poll-race-religion-politics-americans-social-networks/).

Cox, Oliver. 1948. *Caste, Class, and Race: A Study in Social Dynamics*. Garden City, NY: Doubleday.

Craven, Wesley Frank. 1970. *The Southern Colonies in the Seventeenth Century, 1607–1689: A History of the South*. Vol. 1. Baton Rouge, LA: Louisiana State University Press.

Cribbs, Sarah E., and D. Mark Austin. 2011. "Enduring Pictures in Our Heads: The Continuance of Authoritarianism and Racial Stereotyping." *Journal of Black Studies* 42(3): 334–359.

Cristol, Dean, and Belinda Gimbert. 2008. "Racial Perceptions of Young Children: A Review of Literature Post-1999." *Early Childhood Education* 36:201–207.

Crossley, Paul, Colin Gourlay, and Ben Spraggon. 2017. "Pride, Prejudice and Punishment: Gay Rights Around the World." *Australian Broadcasting Company*, August 1. (http://www.abc.net.au/news/2017-03-04/gay-lesbian-mardi-gras-rights-around-the-world/8126828).

Crow Dog, Mary. 1990. *Lakota Woman*. New York: HarperCollins.

Cuddy, Amy J.C., Susan T. Fiske, Virginia S. Y. Kwan, Peter Glick, Stéphanie Demoulin, Jacques-Philippe Leyens, Michael Harris Bond, Jean-Claude Croizet, Naomi Ellemers, Ed Sleebos, Tin Tin Htun, Hyun-Jeong Kim, Greg Maio, Judi Perry, Kristina Petkova, Valery Todorov, Rosa Rodríguez-Bailón, Elena Morales, Miguel Moya, Marisol Palacios, Vanessa Smith, Rolando Perez, Jorge Vala, and Rene Ziegler. 2009. "Stereotype Content Model Across Cultures: Towards Universal Similarities and Some Differences." *British Journal of Social Psychology* 48:1–33.

Curtin, Philip. 1990. *The Rise and Fall of the Plantation Complex*. New York: Cambridge University Press.

Curtis, Christopher M. 2012. *Jefferson's Freeholders and the Politics of Ownership in the Old Dominion*. New York: Cambridge University Press.

D'Alessio, Stewart, Lisa Stolzenberg, and David Eitle. 2002. "The Effect of Racial Threat on Interracial and Intraracial Crimes." *Social Science Research* 31:392–408.

D'Angelo, Raymond. 2001. *The American Civil Rights Movement: Readings and Interpretations*. New York: McGraw-Hill.

D'Emilio, John. 1998. *Sexual Politics, Sexual Communities: The Making of a Sexual Minority in the United States, 1940–1970*. 2nd ed. Chicago, IL: University of Chicago Press.

D'Orso, Michael. 1996. *Like Judgment Day: The Ruin and Redemption of a Town Called Rosewood*. New York: Putnam.

Dakota Access, LLC. n.d. "About the Dakota Access

Pipeline." Retrieved August 18, 2017 (https://daplpipelinefacts.com/about-the-dakota-access-pipeline/).

Danzer, Gerald A. 1992. *The Americans*. Evanston, IL: McDougal Littell Inc. Retrieved April 17, 2017 (https://books.google.com/books?id=63xJAQAAIAAJ).

Dao, James. 2013. "In Debate Over Military Sexual Assault, Men Are the Overlooked Victims." *The New York Times*, June 23. Retrieved August 30, 2017 (http://www.nytimes.com/2013/06/24/us/in-debate-over-military-sexual-assault-men-are-overlooked-victims.html?pagewanted=all.data-show/).

Davidson, James M. 2004. "Rituals Captured in Context and Time: Charm Use in North Dallas Freedman's Town (1869-1907), Dallas, Texas." *Historical Archaeology* 38(2):22–54.

Davis, Angela Y. 1983. *Women, Race and Class*. New York: Vintage Books.

Davis, Kiri. 2005. "A Girl Like Me." (http://www.youtube.com/watch?v=YWyI77Yh1Gg).

Davis, Simon. 1990. "Men as Success Objects and Women as Sex Objects: A Study of Personal Advertisements." *Sex Roles* 23:43–50.

Dawson, Michael C., and Lawrence D. Bobo. 2009. "One Year Later and the Myth of a Post-Racial Society." *Du Bois Review: Social Science Research on Race* 6(2):247–249.

de la Cruz, Patricia, and Angela Brittingham. 2003. *The Arab Population: 2000*. (http://www.census.gov/prod/2003pubs/c2kbr-23.pdf).

Debo, Angie. 1970. *A History of the Indians of the United States*. Norman, OK: University of Oklahoma Press.

Degler, Carl. 1971. *Neither Black nor White: Slavery and Race Relations in Brazil and the United States*. New York: Macmillan.

Delk, John L., R. Burt Madden, Mary Livingston, and Timothy T. Ryan. 1986. "Adult Perceptions of the Infant as a Function of Gender Labeling and Observer Gender." *Sex Roles* 15: 527–534.

Demby, Gene. 2013. "'Latin@' Offers a Gender-Neutral Choice; But How to Pronounce it?" *NPR*, January 7. (http://www.npr.org/sections/thetwo-way/2013/01/07/168818064/latin-offers-a-gender-neutral-choice-but-how-to-pronounce-it).

Department of Homeland Security. 2016. *Yearbook of Immigration Statistics 2016*. Retrieved from https://www.dhs.gov/immigration-statistics/yearbook/2016.

Deutsch, Barry. n.d. "The Male Privilege Checklist." *Amptoons*. (http://amptoons.com/blog/the-male-privilege-checklist/).

Deutsch, Morton, and Mary Ann Collins. 1951. *Interracial Housing: A Psychological Evaluation of a Social Experiment*. Minneapolis, MN: University of Minnesota Press.

Devine, Patricia, and Andrew Elliot. 1995. "Are Racial Stereotypes Really Fading? The Princeton Trilogy Revisited." *Personality and Social Psychology Bulletin* 21:1139–1150.

Dewan, Shaila. 2013. "Immigration and Social Security." *The New York Times*, July 2. (http://economix.blogs.nytimes.com/2013/07/02/immigration-and-social-security/?_r=0).

Dhingra, Pawan. 2012. *Life Behind the Lobby*.

Redwood City, CA: Stanford University Press.

Diamond, Jared. 1998. *Guns, Germs, and Steel: The Fates of Human Societies*. New York: W. W. Norton & Company.

Dickerson, Caitlin. 2017a. "After Hurricane, Signs of a Mental Health Crisis Haunt Puerto Rico." *New York Times*, November 13. (https://www.nytimes.com/2017/11/13/us/puerto-rico-hurricane-maria-mental-health.html).

_____. 2017b. "Immigration Arrests Rise Sharply as a Trump Mandate Is Carried Out." *The New York Times*, May 17. (https://www.nytimes.com/2017/05/17/us/immigration-enforcement-ice-arrests.html).

Dillard, Joey L. 2014. *A History of American English*. New York: Routledge.

Dinnerstein, Leonard. 1977. The East European Jewish Immigration. Pp. 216–231 in *Uncertain Americans*, edited by L. Dinnerstein and F.C. Jaher. New York: Oxford University Press.

Dixon, Jeffrey. 2006. "The Ties That Don't Bind: Towards Reconciling Group Threat and Contact Theories of Prejudice." *Social Forces* 84:2179–2204.

Dixon, Jeffrey, and Michael Rosenbaum. 2004. "Nice to Know You? Testing Contact, Cultural, and Group Threat Theories of Anti-Black and Anti-Hispanic Stereotypes." *Social Science Quarterly* 85:257–280.

Dolan, Jay P. 2010. *The Irish Americans: A History*. New York: Bloomsbury Publishing USA.

Dollar Times. n.d. "Inflation Calculator." Retrieved August 9, 2017 (http://www.dollartimes.com/inflation/inflation.php?amount=100&year=1946).

Dollard, John. 1937. *Caste and Class in a Southern Town*. New Haven, CT: Yale.

Dollard, John, Neal E. Miller, Leonard W. Doob, O. H. Mowrer, and Robert R. Sears. (with Clellan S. Ford, Carl Iver Hovland, and Richard T. Sollenberger). 1939. *Frustration and Aggression*. New Haven, CT: Yale University Press.

Domonoske, Camila. 2016. "One Tweet Unleashes A Torrent Of Stories Of Sexual Assault." October 11. (https://www.npr.org/sections/thetwo-way/2016/10/11/497530709/one-tweet-unleashes-a-torrent-of-stories-of-sexual-assault).

Donoso, Juan Carlos. 2014. "On Religion, Mexicans are more Catholic and Often More Traditional Than Mexican Americans." *Pew Research Center*, December 8. (http://www.pewresearch.org/fact-tank/2014/12/08/on-religion-mexicans-are-more-catholic-and-often-more-traditional-than-mexican-americans/).

Dovidio, John F., Peter Glick, and Laurie Rudman, eds. 2008. *On the Nature of Prejudice*. New York: John Wiley & Sons.

Doyle, Anna Beth, and Frances E. Aboud. 1995. "A Longitudinal Study of White Children's Racial Prejudice as a Socio-Cognitive Development." *Merrill-Palmer Quarterly* 41:209–228.

Drake, Bruce. 2013. *How LGBT Adults See Society and How Society Sees Them*. Washington, DC: Pew Research Center. (http://www.pewresearch.org/fact-tank/2013/06/25/how-lgbt-adults-see-society-and-how-the-public-sees-them).

Drake, Samuel Gardener. 1845. The *Book of the Indians, or, Biography and History of the Indians of North America, from Its First Discovery to the Year 1841*. 9th ed. Boston, MA: Benjamin B. Mussey.

Drogin, Richard. 2003. *Statistical Analysis of Gender Patterns in Wal-Mart Workforce*. Berkeley, CA: Drogin, Kakiki & Associates. (http://www.walmartclass.com/staticdata/reports/r2.pdf).

Du Bois, W. E. B. 1961. *The Souls of Black Folk*. Greenwich, CT: Fawcett.

Duberman, Martin. 1994. *Stonewall*. New York: Plume.

Dubrulle, Hugh. 2016. "Lies, Damn Lies, and Statistics: Slavery and the 1.6%." Retrieved April 30, 2017 (https://saintanselmhistory.wordpress.com/2016/02/05/lies-damn-lies-and-statistics-slavery-and-the-1-6/).

Dudley, William. 2006. *Reproductive Rights*. Farmington Hills, MI: Greenhaven Press.

Duleep, Harriet O. 1988. *Economic Status of Americans of Asian Descent*. Washington, DC: U.S. Commission on Civil Rights.

Dumont, J.-C., and G. LeMaitre. 2011. "Counting Immigrants and Ex-patriots in OECD Countries: A New Perspective." OECD Working Paper. (http://www.oecd.org/dataoecd/27/5/33868740.pdf).

Dwyer, Rachel E. 2010. "Poverty, Prosperity, and Place: The Shape of Class Segregation in the Age of Extremes." *Social Problems* 57: 114–137.

Dyke and Sparhawk. 1865. "Constitution or Form of Government for the People of Florida, as Revised, / Amended and Agreed Upon, at a Convention of the People, Begun and Holden at the City of Tallahassee, on the 25th Day of October, A.D. 1865, Together with the Ordinances Adopted by Said Convention." Tallahassee, FL: Dyke & Sparhawk. Retrieved August 10, 2017 (https://books.google.com/books?id=nWQpAAAAYAAJ).

Eaklor, Vicki. 2008. *Queer America: A GLBT History of the Twentieth Century*. Chicago, IL: Greenwood Press.

Echavarri, Fernanda, and Marlon Bishop. 2016. "No Mexicans Allowed:' School Segregation in the Southwest." *Latinousa*, March 11. (http://latinousa.org/2016/03/11/no-mexicans-allowed-school-segregation-in-the-southwest/).

Eckholm, Erik. 2010. "Congress Moves to Narrow Cocaine Sentencing Disparity." *The New York Times*, July 28. (http://www.nytimes.com/2010/07/29/us/politics/29crack.html?adxnnl=1&pagewanted=print&adxnnlx=1382103459-x0tOpZ4wq4lKuhvMAc5weg).

The Economist. 2012. "Affirming a Divide.". *The Economist*. Retrieved August 13, 2017 (http://www.economist.com/node/21543494).

EEOC v. WRS Infrastructure and Env't Inc. d/b/a WRS Compass, No. 1:09-cv-4272 (N.D. Ill. consent decree filed Aug. 23, 2012) c.f. Significant EEOC Race/Color Cases (Covering Private and Federal Sectors). (https://www1.eeoc.gov//eeoc/initiatives/e-race/caselist.cfm?renderforprint=1).

Egelko, Bob. 2009. "BART Shooting Draws Rodney King Case Parallels." *San Francisco Chronicle*, January 15. (http://www.sfgate.com/bayarea/article/BART-shooting-draws-Rodney-King-case-parallels-3176756.php).

Eilperin, Juliet. 2013. "What's Changed for African Americans since 1963, By the Numbers." *Washington Post*. Retrieved July 20, 2017 (https://www.washingtonpost.com/news/the-fix/wp/2013/08/22/whats-changed-for-african-americans-since-1963-by-the-numbers/?utm_term=.32e0026761b3).

Eisenstadt v. Baird, 405 U.S. 438 (1972).

Elias, Paul. 2010. "Greeter" Becomes Face of Fight vs Wal-Mart. *Huffington Post*, May 1. (http://www.huffingtonpost.com/huff-wires/20100501/us-betty-v-goliath/).

Elkins, Stanley. 1959/2013. *Slavery: A Problem in American Institutional and Intellectual Life*. New York:

Elliott, James R., and Ryan A. Smith. 2004. "Race, Gender and Workplace Power." *American Sociological Review* 69:365–386.

Elliott, Stuart. 2014. "AT&T Becomes First Major Advertiser to Protest Russia's Antigay Law." *The New York Times*, February 4. (http://www.nytimes.com/2014/02/05/business/media/att-becomes-first-major-advertiser-to-protest-russias-antigay-law.htm).

Ellis, Lee, Donald Burke, and M. Ashley Ames. 1987. "Sexual Orientation as a Continuous Variable: A Comparison Between the Sexes." *Archives of Sexual Behavior* 16:523–529.

Ellsworth, Scott. 1982. *Death in a Promised Land: The Tulsa Race Riot of 1921*. Baton Rouge, LA: Louisiana State University Press.

Emory University. 2013. "Trans-Atlantic Slave Database Voyages: African Names." *Slave Voyages*. Retrieved August 4, 2017 (http://www.slavevoyages.org/resources/names-database).

Engels, Friedrich. 2010. *The Origin of Family, Private Property and the State*. New York: Penguin. (Original work published in 1884).

Ennis, Sharon, Merarys Rios-Vargas, and Nora Albert. 2011. *The Hispanic Population: 2010*. Washington, DC: U.S. Census Bureau. (http://www.census.gov/prod/cen2010/briefs/c2010br-04.pdf).

Erie, Steven P. and Vladimir Kogan. 2016. "Machine Bosses, Reformers, and the Politics of Ethnic and Minority Incorporation." Pp 302–318 in *Handbook of American Immigration and Ethnicity*, edited by Ronald H. Bayor. New York: Oxford University Press.

Equal Employment Opportunity Commission. 2010. "Walmart To Pay More Than $11.7 Million To Settle EEOC Sex Discrimination Suit." *Newsroom*, March 1. (https://www.eeoc.gov/eeoc/newsroom/release/3-1-10.cfm).

Equal Justice Initiative. 2017. *Lynching in America: Confronting the Legacy of Racial Terror*. 3rd ed. New York: New American Library. Retrieved August 10, 2017 (https://lynchinginamerica.eji.org/report/).

Espinosa, Kristin, and Doulas Massey. 1997. "Determinants of English Proficiency Among Mexican Migrants to the United States." *International Migration Review* 31:28–51.

Espiritu, Yen. 1996. "Colonial Oppression, Labour

Importation, and Group Formation: Filipinos in the United States." *Ethnic and Racial Studies* 19:29–48.

Essien-Udom, E. U. 1962. *Black Nationalism.* Chicago: University of Chicago Press.

Estrada, Gabriel S. 2011. "Two Spirits, Nádleeh, and LGBTQ2 Navajo Gaze." *American Indian Culture and Research Journal* 35(4):167–190.

European Union Agency for Fundamental Rights. 2013. *Discrimination and Hate Crimes Against Jews in EU Member States: Experiences and Perceptions of Anti-Semitism.* (http:// fra.europa.eu/sites/ default/files/fra-2013- discrimination -hate-crime- against-jews-eu-member- states_en.pdf).

Evans, Sara M. 1980. *Personal Politics: The Roots of Women's Liberation in the Civil Rights Movement and the New Left.* New York: Vintage Books.

Evans, Sara M. 1989. *Born for Liberty: A History of Women in America.* New York: Free Press.

Evans, Sara M. 1979. *Personal Politics.* New York: Knopf.

Faderman, Lillian. 1991. *Odd Girls and Twilight Lovers: A History of Lesbian Life in Twentieth Century America.* New York: Columbia University Press.

Fadiman, Anne. 1998. *The Spirit Catches You and You Fall Down.* New York: Farrar, Straus, & Giroux.

Falicov, Celia Jaes. 2010. "Changing Constructions of Machismo for Latino Men in Therapy: The Devil Never Sleeps." *Family Process* 49(3): 309–329. doi: 10.1111/ j.1545-5300.2010 .01325.x.

Farivar, Masood. 2017. "U.S. Justice Department Defends Record Against Hate Crimes." *VOA News,* May 2. Retrieved August 9, 2017 (https://www .voanews.com/a/justice- department-defends- record-against-hate- crime/3835580.html).

Farley, John. 2000. *Majority– Minority Relations.* 4th ed. Englewood Cliffs, NJ: Prentice Hall.

Farley, Reynolds. 1996. *The New American Reality.* New York: Russell Sage Foundation.

Fausto-Sterling, Anne. 1993. "The Five Sexes: Why Male and Female Are Not Enough." *The Sciences* (March–April):20–24.

Faux, Jeff. 2004. "NAFTA at 10: Where Do We Go From Here?" *Nation* (February 2):11–14.

Feagin, Joe R. 2001. *Racist America: Roots, Current Realities, and Future Reparations.* New York: Routledge.

Feagin, Joe R., and Clairece Booher Feagin. 1986. *Discrimination American Style: Institutional Racism and Sexism.* Malabar, FL: Robert E. Krieger.

Feagin, Joe R., and Eileen O'Brien. 2004. *White Men on Race: Power, Privilege, and the Shaping of Cultural Consciousness.* Boston, MA: Beacon Press.

Fears, Darryl. 2007. "Hate Crime Reporting Uneven." *Washington Post,* November 20, p. A3.

Fears, Darryl. 2014. *Hate Crimes Report, 2014.* Washington, DC: Author. (http://www.fbi.gov/news/ stories/2014/december/ latest-hate-crime-statistics- report-released/latest-hate- crime-statistics-report- released).

Federal Bureau of Investigation. 2017. *Hate Crime Statistics, 2015. Table 1.* Retrieved August 9,

2017 (https://ucr.fbi .gov/hate-crime/2015/ tables-and-data-declaration s/1tabledatadecpdf).

Federal Glass Ceiling Commission. 1995. *Good for Business: Making Full Use of the Nations Human Capital.* Washington, DC: Author. (http://www.dol .gov/dol/aboutdol/history/ reich/reports/ceiling.htm).

Feinberg, Leslie. 1996. *Transgender Warriors: Making History From Joan of Arc to Dennis Rodman.* Boston, MA: Beacon Press.

Feliciano, Cynthia. 2006. *Another Way to Assess the Second Generation: Look at the Parents.* Washington, DC: Migration Policy Institute. (http:// www.migrationinformation .org/USfocus/display. cfm?ID=396).

Fennell, Christopher C. 2013. "Group Identity, Individual Creativity, and Symbolic Generation in a BaKongo Diaspora." *International Journal of Historical Archaeology* 7(1):1–31.

Fernandes, Deepa. 2017. "Havana's Small Business Boom Exposes a Stark Racial Divide." *PRI,* April 5. (https://www.pri .org/stories/2017-04-05/ havanas-small-business- boom-exposes-stark-racial- divide).

Fetzer, J.S. (2011). *Luxembourg as an immigration success story: the grand duchy in pan-European perspective.* Plymouth: Lexington Books.

File, Thom. 2013. *The Diversifying Electorate: Voting Rates by Race and Hispanic Origin in 2012 (and Other Recent Elections).* Washington, DC: U.S. Census Bureau. (http://www.census.gov/ prod/2013pubs/p20-568 .pdf).

Firefighters Local Union No. 1784 v. Stotts, 467 U.S. 561 (1984).

Fishbein, Harold D. 2014. "Peer Prejudice and Discrimination: The Origins of Prejudice." *Psychology Press,* April 8.

Fisher v. University of Texas at Austin, 570 U.S. 11-345 (2013).

Fisher, Mary. 2008. "Does Campus Diversity Promote Friendship Diversity? A Look at Interracial Friendships in College." *Social Science Quarterly* 89:623–655.

Fisher, Max. 2013a. "A Revealing Map of the Countries That Are Most and Least Tolerant of Homosexuality." *Washington Post,* June 5. (http://www .washingtonpost.com/ blogs/worldviews/ wp/2013/06/05/a- revealing-map-of-the-F).

Fisher, Max. 2013b. "A Revealing Map of the World's Most and Least Ethnically Diverse Countries." *Washington Post,* May 16. (http://www .washingtonpost.com/blogs/ worldviews/wp/2013/ 05/16/a-revealing-map- of-the-worlds-most-and- least-ethnically-diverse- countries).

Fiske, Susan T., Hilary Bergsieker, Ann Marie Russell, and Lyle Williams. 2009. Images of Black Americans: Then, "Them," and Now, "Obama!" *Du Bois Review* 6:83–101.

Fitzpatrick, Joseph P. 1976. "The Puerto Rican Family." Pp. 173–195 in *Ethnic Families in America,* edited by C. H. Mindel and R. W. Habenstein. New York: Elsevier.

Fitzpatrick, Joseph P. 1980. "Puerto Ricans." Pp. 858–867 in *Harvard Encyclopedia of American Ethnic Groups,* edited by S. Thernstrom, A. Orlov, and O. Handlin. Cambridge, MA: Harvard University Press.

Fitzpatrick, Joseph P. 1987. *Puerto Rican Americans: The Meaning of Migration to the Mainland.* 2nd ed. Englewood Cliffs, NJ: Prentice Hall.

Flavia C. Parra, Roberto C. Amado, José R. Lambertucci, Jorge Rocha, Carlos M. Antunes, and Sérgio D. J. Pena. 2003. "Color and Genomic Ancestry in Brazilians". *Proceedings of the National Academy of Sciences of the United States of America* 100(1):177–182. doi: 10.1073/pnas.0126614100.

Foley, Elise. 2010. "Don't Ask Don't Tell Repeal Passes Senate, 65-31." *Huffington Post,* December 18. (http://www.huffingtonpost.com/2010/12/18/dont-ask-dont-tell-repeal_5_n_798636.html).

Follman, Mark. 2014. "Michael Brown's Mom Laid Flowers Where He Was Shot—and Police Crushed Them." *Mother Jones,* August 27. Retrieved August 10, 2017 (http://www.motherjones.com/politics/2014/08/ferguson-st-louis-police-tactics-dogs-michael-brown/).

Foner, Eric. 2011. *Reconstruction: America's Unfinished Revolution, 1863–1877.* New York: Harper Collins.

Fong, Eric, and William Markham. 1991. "Immigration, Ethnicity, and Conflict: The California Chinese, 1849–1882." *Sociological Inquiry* 61:471–490.

Fong, Timothy. 2002. *The Contemporary Asian American Experience.* 2nd ed. Upper Saddle River, NJ: Prentice Hall.

Foraker Act, April 12, 1900. (http://college.cengage.com/history/world/keen/latin_america/8e/assets/students/sources/pdfs/167_foraker_act_of_1900.pdf).

Forbes, Hugh Donald. 1997. *Ethnic Conflict: Commerce, Culture, and the Contact Hypothesis.* New Haven, CT: Yale University Press.

Forner, Philip S. 1980. *Women and the American Labor Movement: From World War I to the Present.* New York: Free Press.

Fowler, Geoffrey A. 2013. "On Facebook, 70% of Americans Have a Gay Friend." *Wall Street Journal,* June 25. (http://blogs.wsj.com/digits/2013/06/25/on-facebook-70-of-americans-have-a-gay-friend/).

Frankel, Jonathan. 1997. *The Fate of the European Jews, 1939–1945: Continuity or Contingency? New York: Oxford University Press. Retrieved April, 28, 2017* (https://books.google.com/books?id=Rzp51R5WHtIC&pg=PA16#v=onepage&q&f=false).

Franke-Ruta, Garance. 2012. "Americans Have No Idea How Few Gay People There Are." *The Atlantic,* May 31. (http://www.theatlantic.com/politics/archive/2012/05/americans-have-no-idea-how-few-gay-people-there-are/257753/).

Franklin, John Hope, and Alfred Moss. 1994. *From Slavery to Freedom.* 7th ed. New York: McGraw-Hill.

Franklin, John Hope. 1967. *From Slavery to Freedom.* 3rd ed. New York: Knopf.

Frazier, E. Franklin. 1957. *Black Bourgeoisie: The Rise of a New Middle Class.* New York: Free Press.

Frederickson, Kari. 2003. *The Dixiecrat Revolt and the End of the Solid South, 1932–1968.* Chapel Hill: University of North Carolina Press.

Freelon, Deen, Charlton D. McIlwain, and Meredith D. Clark. 2016. "Beyond the Hashtags." Center for Media and Social Impact. Washington, DC, American University.

French, Katy. 2015. "The Rape Statistics You Need to Know." *Visual News,* July 28. (https://www.visualnews.com/2015/07/28/the-rape-statistics-you-need-to-know/).

Freyre. 1946. T*he Masters and the Slaves: A Study in the Development of Brazilian Civilization.* New York: Knopf.

Frizell, Sam. 2014. "Disney to End Funding for Boy Scouts Over Gay Leader Ban." *Time,* March 3.

Frost, Alan. 2012. *The First Fleet: The Real Story.* Collingwood, AU: Black Inc.

Fry, Richard. 2007. *The Changing Racial and Ethnic Composition of U.S. Public Schools.* Washington, DC: Pew Hispanic Center. (http://pewhispanic.org/files/reports/79.pdf).

Frye, Marilyn. 1983. *The Politics of Reality: Essays in Feminist Theory.* Freedom, CA: Crossing Press.

Gabaccia, Donna. 1991. "Immigrant Women: Nowhere at Home?" *Journal of American Ethnic History* 10(4): 61–87.

Gabrielson, Ryan, Ryann Grochowski Jones, and Eric Sagara. 2014. "Deadly Force, in Black and White." *ProPublica,* October 10. Retrieved July 20, 2017 (https://www.propublica.org/article/deadly-force-in-black-and-white).

Gallagher, Charles. 2001. "Playing the Ethnic Card: How Ethnic Narratives Maintain Racial Privilege." Paper presented at the Annual Meetings of the Southern Sociological Society, April 4–7, Atlanta, GA.

Gallup. 2017. *Gallup Race Relations Fact Sheet.* Retrieved August 5, 2017 (http://www.gallup.com/poll/1687/race-relations.aspx).

Gamboa, Suzanne. 2017. "History of Racism Against Mexican-Americans Clouds Texas Immigration Law." *NBC News,* June 3. (https://www.nbcnews.com/news/latino/history-racism-against-mexican-americans-clouds-texas-immigration-law-n766956).

Gannon, Megan. 2016. "Race Is a Social Construct, Scientists Argue." Retrieved April 15, 2017 (https://www.scientificamerican.com/article/race-is-a-social-construct-scientists-argue/).

Gans, Herbert. 1979. "Symbolic Ethnicity: The Future of Ethnic Groups and Cultures in America." *Ethnic and Racial Studies* 2:1–20.

_____. 1997. "Toward a Reconciliation of 'Assimilation' and 'Pluralism': The Interplay of Acculturation and Ethnic Retention." *International Migration Review* 31(4):875–892.

Gao, George. 2015. "Most Americans Now Say Learning Their Child is Gay Wouldn't Upset Them." *Pew Research Center,* June 29. (http://www.pewresearch.org/fact-tank/2015/06/29/most-americans-now-say-learning-their-child-is-gay-wouldnt-upset-them/).

Garcia-Navarro, Lulu. 2015. "Dark-Skinned Or Black? How Afro-Brazilians Are Forging A Collective Identity."

NPR, August 12. (http://www.npr.org/sections/codeswitch/2015/08/12/431244962/dark-skinned-or-black-how-afro-brazilians-are-forging-a-collective-identity).

Garvey, Marcus. 1969. *Philosophy and Opinions of Marcus Garvey*. Vols. 1–2, edited by A. Jacques Garvey. New York: Atheneum.

_____. 1977. *Philosophy and Opinions of Marcus Garvey*. Vol. 3, edited by A. Jacques Garvey and E.U. Essien-Udom. London: Frank Cass.

Gates, Gary J. 2013. "LGBT Parenting in the United States. The Williams Institute." (http://williamsinstitute.law.ucla.edu/wp-content/uploads/LGBT-Parenting.pdf).

Gates, Gary. 2012. *Same-Sex Couples in Census 2010: Race and Ethnicity*. Los Angeles, CA: Williams Institute, UCLA School of Law. (http://williamsinstitute.law.ucla.edu/wp-content/uploads/Gates-CouplesRaceEthnicity-April-2012.pdf).

_____. 2017. "In U.S., More Adults Identifying as LGBT." *Gallup Polls*. (http://www.gallup.com/poll/201731/lgbt-identification-rises.aspx).

Gates, Gary, and Frank Newport. 2012. "LGBT Americans Skew Democratic, Largely Support Obama." *Gallup Politics*. (http://www.gallup.com/poll/158102/lgbt-americans-skew-democratic-largely-support-obama.aspx).

Gates Jr., Henry Louis. 2011. "What it Means to Be 'Black in Latin America.'" *NPR*. Retrieved August 10, 2017 (www.npr.org/2011/07/27/138601410/what-it-means-to-be-black-in-latin-america).

_____. 2014. "How Many Slaves Landed in the US?" *The Root*, June 1. Retrieved July 20, 2017 (http://www.theroot.com/how-many-slaves-landed-in-the-us-1790873989).

Gee, Lisa Christiansen, Matthew Gardner, and Meg Wiehe. 2016. "Undocumented Immigrant's State and Local Tax Contributions. Institute on Taxation and Economic Policy." (https://itep.org/undocumented-immigrants-state-local-tax-contributions-1/).

Geiger, Kim. 2012. "Rush Limbaugh's 'Slut' Comment Draws Rebuke from All Sides." *Los Angeles Times*, March 2. (http://articles.latimes.com/2012/mar/02/news/la-pn-rush-limbaugh-draws-rebukes-from-all-sides-20120302).

General Convention. 1976. *Journal of the General Convention of The Episcopal Church, Minneapolis*. New York: Author, 1977, C-109. (http://www.episcopalarchives.org/cgi-bin/acts/acts_resolution.pl?resolution=1976-A069).

Genovese, Eugene D. 1974. *Roll, Jordan, Roll: The World the Slaves Made*. New York: Pantheon.

George-Kanentiio, Douglas M. 2000. *Iroquois Culture & Commentary*. Santa Fe, NM: Clear Light Publishers.

George-Kanentiio, Douglas M. 2006. *Iroquois on Fire: A Voice from the Mohawk Nation*. Westport, CT: Greenwood Publishing Group.

Gerson, Kathleen. 2009. *The Unfinished Revolution: Coming of Age in a New Era of Gender, Work and Family*. Oxford, UK: Oxford University Press.

Gerstenfeld, Phyllis. 2004. *Hate Crime:*

Causes, Controls, and Controversies. Thousand Oaks, CA: Sage.

Gerth, Hans, and C. Wright Mills, eds. 1946. *From Max Weber: Essays in Sociology*. New York: Oxford University Press.

Geschwender, James A. 1978. *Racial Stratification in America*. Dubuque, IA: William C. Brown.

Gibson, Campbell & Jung, Kay. 2015. "Historical Census Statistics on Population Totals by Race, 1790 to 1990, and by Hispanic Origin, 1970 to 1990, for Large Cities and Other Urban Places in the United States." Population Division, U.S. Census Bureau Working Paper No. 76. (https://www.census.gov/population/www/documentation/twps0076/twps0076.pdf).

Gilbert, Dennis L. 2011. *The American class structure in an age of growing inequality*. Thousand Oaks, CA: Pine Forge Press.

Gilley, Brian Joseph. 2006. *Becoming Two-spirit: Gay Identity and Social Acceptance in Indian Country*. Lincoln, NE. University of Nebraska Press.

Glaeser, Edward, and Jacob Vigdor. 2012. *The End of the Segregated Century: Racial Separation in America's Neighborhoods, 1890–2010*. New York: Manhattan Institute, Center for State and Local Leadership. (http://www.manhattan-institute.org/html/cr_66.htm).

Glancy, Jennifer A. 2002. Slavery in Early Christianity. Oxford: Oxford University Press.

Glazer, Nathan, and Daniel Moynihan. 1970. *Beyond the Melting Pot*. 2nd ed. Cambridge, MA: MIT Press.

Gleason, Philip. 1980. "American Identity and Americanization." Pp. 31–57

in *Harvard Encyclopedia of American Ethnic Groups*, edited by S. Thernstrom, A. Orlov, and O. Handlin. Cambridge, MA: Harvard University Press.

Goff, Phillip Atiba, Matthew Christian Jackson, Brooke Allison, Lewis Di Leone, Carmen Marie Culotta and Natalie Ann DiTomasso. 2014. "The Essence of Innocence: Consequences of Dehumanizing Black Children." *Journal of Personality and Social Psychology* 106(4): 526–545. doi: 10.1037/a003566.

Goffman, Erving. 1959. *The Presentation of Self in Everyday Life*. New York: Doubleday.

_____. 1963. *Stigma: Notes on the Management of Spoiled Identity*. New York: Simon & Schuster.

Gold, Steven. 2002. *The Arab American Community in Detroit, Michigan*. Berkeley, CA: University of California Press.

Goldfield, David, Carl Abbott, Virginia DeJohn Anderson, Jo Ann E. Argersinger, Peter H. Argersinger, and William M. Barney. 2002. *The American Journey: A History of the United States*. Upper Saddle River, NJ: Prentice Hall.

Goldstein, Amy, and Robert Suro. 2000. "A Journey on Stages: Assimilation's Pull Is Still Strong but Its Pace Varies." *Washington Post*, January 16, p. A1.

Golway, Terry. 2014. *Machine Made: Tammany Hall and the Creation of Modern American Politics*. New York: W. W. Norton & Company.

Gomez, Laura. 2008. *Manifest Destinies: The Making of the Mexican American Race*. New York: NYU Press.

Gonzalez, Juan. 2011. *Harvest of Empire: A History of Latinos in America*. New York: Penguin Books.

Gonzales, Sara. 2017. "The State of Alabama Could Eliminate Marriage Licenses Completely." *The Blaze*, March 15. (http://www.theblaze.com/news/2017/03/15/the-state-of-alabama-could-eliminate-marriage-licenses-completely/).

Gonzalez-Barrera, Ana. 2015. "More Mexicans Leaving Than Coming to the U.S." *Pew Research Center*, November 19. (http://www.pewhispanic.org/2015/11/19/more-mexicans-leaving-than-coming-to-the-u-s/).

Gonzalez-Barrera, Ana, and Mark Hugo Lopez. 2013. "A Demographic Portrait of Mexican-Origin Hispanics in the United States." *Pew Research Center*, May 1. (http://www.pewhispanic.org/2013/05/01/a-demographic-portrait-of-mexican-origin-hispanics-in-the-united-states/).

Gordon, Milton M. 1964. *Assimilation in American Life: The Role of Race, Religion, and National Origins.* New York: Oxford University Press.

Goren, Arthur. 1980. "Jews." Pp. 571–598 in *Harvard Encyclopedia of American Ethnic Groups*, edited by S. Thernstrom, A. Orlov, and O. Handlin. Cambridge, MA: Harvard University Press.

Gottlieb, Beatrice. 1993. *The Family in the Western World From the Black Death to the Industrial Age.* New York: Oxford University Press.

Goudreau, Isar. 2000. "La semantica fugitiva: 'Raza', color y vida cotidiana en Puerto Rico." *Revista de Ciencias Sociales (Nueva Epoca)* 9:52–71.

Gourevitch, Philip. 1999. *We Wish to Inform You That Tomorrow We Will Be Killed with Our Families: Stories From Rwanda.* New York: Picador.

Gradín, Carlos. 2007. "Why Is Poverty So High Among Afro-Brazilians? A Decomposition Analysis of the Racial Poverty Gap." Discussion Paper Series. Retrieved July 20, 2017 (http://ftp.iza.org/dp2809.pdf).

Grant-Thomas, Andrew, and Gary Orfield, eds. 2008. *Twenty-First Century Color Lines: Multiracial Change in Contemporary America.* Philadelphia, PA: Temple University Press.

Gratz v. Bollinger, 539 U.S. 244 (2003).

Gray, David J. 1991. "Shadow of the Past: The Rise and Fall of Prejudice in an American City." *American Journal of Economics and Sociology* 50:33–39.

Gray, Marion W. 2000. *Productive Men, Reproductive Women: The Agrarian Household and the Emergence of Separate Spheres During the German Enlightenment.* New York: Berghahn Books.

Grebler, Leo, Joan W. Moore, and Ralph C. Guzman. 1970. *The Mexican American People.* New York: Free Press.

Greeley, Andrew M. 1974. *Ethnicity in the United States: A Preliminary Reconnaissance.* New York: Wiley.

Green, Donald. 1999. "Native Americans." Pp. 255–277 in *The Minority Report*, edited by A. Dworkin and R. Dworkin. Orlando, FL: Harcourt-Brace.

Greenberg, Jon. 2015. "Sonia Sotomayor's Family is From Puerto Rico, Not 'Immigrant Family.'" *Politifact*, February 17. (http://www.politifact.com/punditfact/statements/2015/feb/17/laura-ingraham/ingraham-says-sotomayor-comes-immigrant-family/).

Greenwald, Anthony G., and Mahzarin R. Banaji. 1995. "Implicit Social Cognition: Attitudes, Self-Esteem, and Stereotypes." *Psychological Review* 102:4–27.

Greenwald, Anthony G., Mahzarin R. Banaji, Laurie A. Rudman, Shelly D. Farnham, Brian A. Nosek, and Deborah S. Mellott. 2002. "A Unified Theory of Implicit Attitudes, Stereotypes, Self-Esteem, and Self-Concept." *Psychological Review* 109:3–25.

Grey, George. 1841. Journals of Two Expeditions of Discovery in North-west and Western Australia: During the Years 1837, 38, and 39, Under the Authority of Her Majesty's Government. Describing Many Newly Discovered, Important, and Fertile Districts, with Observations on the Moral and Physical Condition of the Aboriginal Inhabitants. Vol. 1. London: T. and W. Boone. Retrieved August 18, 2017 (https://books.google.com/books?id=jfsoAAAAYAAJ).

Griswold v. Connecticut, 381 U.S. 479 (1965).

Griswold, Daniel T. 2012. "Immigration and the Welfare State." *Cato Journal* 32:159–174.

Grundy, Trevor. 2015. "National Anglican Head Expresses Concern About Episcopal Vote On Gay Marriage." *The Washington Post*, July 2. (https://www.washingtonpost.com/national/religion/anglican-head-expresses-concern-about-episcopal-vote-on-gay-marriage/2015/07/02/61dcc656-20e8-11e5-a135-935065bc30d0_story.html).

Grutter v. Bollinger, 539 U.S. 306 (2003).

Guedel, W. Gregory. 2014. "Sovereignty, Economic Development, and Human Security in Native American Nations." *American Indian Law Journal* 3:17–39.

Giuliano, Giuliano, Geoffrey. 2002. *Behind Blue Eyes: The Life of Pete Townshend.* New York, NY: Cooper Square Press.

Guerrero, Diane, and Michelle Burford. 2016. *In the Country We Love: My Family Divided.* New York, NY: Henry Holt and Co.

Gugliotta, Guy. 2008. "The Great Human Migration." *Smithsonian Magazine*, July. Retrieved April 15, 2017 (http://www.smithsonianmag.com/history/the-great-human-migration-13561/).

Guilbault, Rose Del Castillo. 1993. "Americanization Is Tough on 'Macho'." Pp. 163–165 in *American Voices*, edited by D. La Guardia and H. Guth. Mountain View, CA: Mayfield. (First published in "*This World*," San Francisco Chronicle, August 20, 1989).

Gullah Geechee Cultural Heritage Corridor Commission. n.d. "Roots." Retrieved August 5, 2017 (https://www.gullahgeecheecorridor.org).

Gutiérrez, David G. n.d. "An Historic Overview of Latino Immigration and the Demographic Transformation of the United States." (https://www.nps.gov/heritageinitiatives/latino/latinothemestudy/immigration.htm#_edn1).

Gutman, Herbert. 1976. *The Black Family in Slavery and Freedom, 1750–1925.* New York: Vintage.

Haan, Arjan, and Thorat, Sukhadeo. 2012. "Addressing Group Inequalities: Social Policies in Emerging Economies' Great Transformation." *European Journal of Development Research* 24: 105–124.

Hacker, Andrew. 1992. *Two Nations: Black and*

White, Separate, Hostile, Unequal. New York: Scribner's.

Hackman, Rose. 2016. "'It's Like We're Seen as Animals': Black Men on Their Vulnerability and Resilience." Retrieved August 8, 2017 (https://www.theguardian.com/world/2016/jul/12/black-men-america-violence-vulnerable-detroit).

Hagler, Jamal. 2015. "It Is Time to Update the Voting Rights Act." Retrieved November 28, 2016 (https://www.americanprogress.org/issues/race/news/2015/08/06/118888/it-is-time-to-update-the-voting-rights-act/).

Hainmueller, Jens, and Michael Hiscox. 2010. "Attitudes Toward Highly Skilled and Low-Skilled Immigration: Evidence From a Survey Experiment." *American Political Science Review* 104:61–84.

Hakimzadeh, Shirin, and D'Vera Cohn. 2007. *English Language Usage Among Hispanics in the United States.* Washington, DC: Pew Hispanic Center.

Halberstam, David. 1998. *The Children.* New York: Fawcett Books.

Haley, Alex. 1976. *Roots: The Saga of an American Family.* New York: Doubleday.

Hall, Andy. 2011. "Ninety-eight Percent of Texas Confederate Soldiers Never Owned a Slave." *Dead Confederates, A Civil War Era Blog,* April 28. (https://deadconfederates.com/2011/04/28/ninety-eight-percent-of-texas-confederate-soldiers-never-owned-a-slave/).

Hall, Gwendolyn Midlo. 2009. *Slavery and African Ethnicities in the Americas: Restoring the Links.* Chapell Hill: University of North Carolina Press.

Hall, Mia, and Sedria Renee. 2016. "Breaking Barriers in 2016: A Year of Firsts Among African Americans." *NBC News,* December 30. Retrieved August 8, 2017 (http://www.nbcnews.com/news/nbcblk/breaking-barriers-2016-year-firsts-among-african-americans-n701291).

Haller, William, Alejandro Portes, and Scott Lynch. 2011. "Dreams Fulfilled, Dreams Shattered: Determinants of Segmented Assimilation in the Second Generation." *Social Forces* 89:733–762.

Halperin, David. 1989. *One Hundred Years of Homosexuality: And Other Essays on Greek Love.* New York: Routledge.

Hämäläinen, Pekka. 2008. *The Comanche Empire.* New Haven, CT: Yale University Press.

Hamer, Fannie Lou. 1967. *To Praise Our Bridges: An Autobiography of Fannie Lou Hamer.* Jackson, MS: KIPCO.

Hand, Mark. 2017. Ohio sues developer behind Dakota Access Pipeline over pollution issues. Mark Hand. Nov 6, 2017. https://thinkprogress.org/ohio-sues-rover-pipeline-438c4b6b9516/

Handlin, Oscar. 1951. *The Uprooted.* New York: Grosset & Dunlap.

———. 2002. *The Uprooted: The Epic Story of the Great Migrations That Made the American People.* Philadelphia, PA: University of Pennsylvania Press.

Handy, Bruce. 1997. "Roll Over, Ward Cleaver and Tell Ozzie Nelson the News. Ellen DeGeneres Is Poised to Become TV's First Openly Gay Star. Is TV Ready or Not?" *Time,* April 14.

Hansen, Marcus Lee. 1952. "The Third Generation in America." *Commentary* 14:493–500.

Hanson, Jeffery, and Linda Rouse. 1987. "Dimensions of Native American Stereotyping." *American Indian Culture and Research Journal* 11:33–58.

Harjo, Suzan. 1996. "Now and Then: Native Peoples in the United States." *Dissent* 43: 58–60.

Harris, Alex. 2016. "Mateen Said He Slaughtered Club Patrons to Avenge U.S. Airstrikes". *The Miami Herald,* September 24. Retrieved September 28, 2016 (http://www.miamiherald.com/news/state/florida/article103878026.html).

Harris, Angela P. 2008. "From Color Line to Color Chart: Racism and Colorism in the New Century." *Berkeley Journal of African-American Law & Policy* 10: 52–69. doi: 10.15779/Z380C9X.

Harris, John. 1990. *One Blood: 200 Years of Aboriginal Encounter with Christianity: A Story of Hope.* Australia: Concilia Ltd. Retrieved August 18, 2017 (https://books.google.com/books/about/One_Blood.html?id=fF4RAQAAIAAJ).

Discrimination Survey. Washington, DC: National Gay and Lesbian Task Force.

Hartley, E. L. 1946. *Problems in Prejudice.* New York: Kings Crown.

Hartman, Holly. n.d. "Gender Roles in Colonial America." Retrieved August 18, 2017 (http://www.wou.edu/history/files/2015/08/Holly-Hartman-HST-499.pdf).

Hartmann, Margaret. 2014. "In a Stunning Reversal, Police Join Peaceful Protest in Ferguson." (http://nymag.com/daily/intelligencer/2014/08/ferguson-protest-thursday.html).

Hatewatch Staff. 2017. "Flags and Other Symbols Used By Far-Right Groups in Charlottesville." Retrieved August 13, 2017 (https://www.splcenter.org/hatewatch/2017/08/12/flags-and-other-symbols-used-far-right-groups-charlottesville).

Hauser, Christine. 2017. "White Police Officer in St. Louis Shoots Off-Duty Black Colleague." Retrieved July 20, 2017 (https://www.nytimes.com/2017/06/26/us/saint-louis-black-officer.html?action=click&contentCollection=Politics&module=Trending&version=Full&region=Marginalia&pgtype=article).

Havekes, Esther, Michael Bader, and Maria Kryson. 2016. "Realizing Racial and Ehtnic Neighborhood Preferences? Exploring the Mismatches Between What People Want, Where They Search, and Where They Live." *Population Research and Policy Review* 35:101–126.

Hawkins, Hugh. 1962. *Booker T. Washington and His Critics: The Problem of Negro Leadership.* Boston, MA: D. C. Heath.

Healy, Jack. 2016. "From 280 Tribes, a Protest on the Plains." *The New York Times,* September, 11. Retrieved August 18, 2017 (https://www.nytimes.com/interactive/2016/09/12/us/12tribes.html).

Healy, Jack. 2016. "North Dakota Oil Pipeline Battle: Who's Fighting and Why." *The New York Times,* August 26. Retrieved August 18, 2017 (https://www.nytimes.com/2016/11/02/us/north-dakota-oil-pipeline-battle-whos-fighting-and-why.html?smid=pl-share).

Heartland Geopolitical Maps. 2009. "European Immigration to the United States." (http://temi.repubblica.it/limes-heartland/european-immigration-to-the-united-states-2/867).

Heer, David M. 1996. *Immigration in America's Future.* Boulder, CO: Westview.

Hegewisch, Ariane, and Heidi Hartmann. 2014. "Occupational Segregation and the Gender Wage Gap: A Job Half Done." (https://www.dol.gov/wb/resources/occupational_segregation_and_wage_gap.pdf).

Hegewisch, Ariane, Hannah Liepmann, Jeffrey Hayes, and Heidi Hartmann. 2010. *Separate and Not Equal? Gender Segregation in the Labor Market and the Gender Wage Gap.* Washington, DC: Institute for Women's Policy Research. (http://www.iwpr.org/publications/pubs/separate-and-not-equal-gender-segregation-in-the-labor-market-and-the-gender-wage-gap).

Hennesey, James J. 1981. *American Catholics: A History of the Roman Catholic Community in the United States: A History of the Roman Catholic Community in the United States.* New York: Oxford University Press.

Herberg, Will. 1960. *Protestant–Catholic–Jew: An Essay in American Religious Sociology.* New York: Anchor.

Herek, Gregory M. 1988. "Heterosexuals' Attitudes Toward Lesbians and Gay Men: Correlates and Gender Differences." *Journal of Sex Research* 25(4):451–477.

Herek, Gregory M., Jared B. Jobe, and Ralph M. Carney. 1996. *Out in Force: Sexual Orientation and the Military.* Chicago,

IL: University of Chicago Press.

Hernandez, Tanya Katerí. 2007. "Latino Inter-Ethnic Employment Discrimination and the Diversity Defense." FLASH: The Fordham Law Archive of Scholarship and History. 42:259–316. Retrieved August 10, 2017 (http://ir.lawnet.fordham.edu/faculty_scholarship/13).

Hernández, Tanya Katerí. 2012. *Racial Subordination in Latin America: The Role of the State, Customary Law and the New Civil Rights Response.* Cambridge, UK: Cambridge University Press.

Higham, John. 1963. *Strangers in the Land: Patterns of American Nativism, 1860–1925.* New York: Atheneum.

Hill, Jane. 1995. "Mock Spanish: A Site for the Indexical Reproduction of Racism in American English." *Language and Culture: Symposium 2.* (http://language-culture.binghamton.edu/symposia/2/part1/).

Hines, Alice. 2012. "Wal-Mart Sex Discrimination Claims Filed by 2,000 Women." *Huffington Post*, June 6. (http://www.huffingtonpost.com/2012/06/06/walmart-sex-discrimination-women-_n_1575859.html).

Hinrichs, Donal W., and Pamela J. Rosenberg. 2002. "Attitudes Towards Gay, Lesbian and Bisexual Persons Among Heterosexual Liberal Arts College Students." *Journal of Homosexuality* 43:61–84.

Hinton, Elizabeth. 2016. *The War on Poverty to the War on Crime.* Cambridge: Harvard University Press.

Hirschfeld Davis, Julie, and Helene Cooper. 2017. "Trump Says Transgender People Will Not Be Allowed

in the Military." *The New York Times*, July26. (https://www.nytimes.com/2017/07/26/us/politics/trump transgendermilitary.html).

Hirschman, Charles, and Morrison Wong. 1984. "Socioeconomic Gains of Asian Americans, Blacks, and Hispanics: 1960–1976." *American Journal of Sociology* 90:584–607.

Hirschman, Charles, and Morrison Wong. 1986. "The Extraordinary Educational Attainment of Asian-Americans: A Search for Historical Evidence and Explanations." *Social Forces* 65:1–27.

Hirschman, Charles. 1983. "America's Melting Pot Reconsidered." *Annual Review of Sociology* 9:397–423.

Hirst, Kris K. 2017. "Out of Africa Hypothesis – Did All Humans Evolve in Africa?" *ThoughtCo.*, June 26. Retrieved April 15, 2017 (https://www.thoughtco.com/out-of-africa-hypothesis-172030).

His Horse Is Thunder, Deborah, Nate Anderson, and Darlene G. Miller. 2013. *Building the Foundation for Success: Case Studies of Breaking Through Tribal Colleges and Universities.* Boston, MA: Jobs for the Future. (http://www.jff.org/sites/default/files/publications/BuildingFoundation Success_ExSumm_040813.pdf).

Hitsch, Günter J., Ali Hortaçsu, and Dan Ariely. 2010. "Mate Preferences in Online Dating." *Quantitative Marketing and Economics* 8(4):393–427.

Hobson, Will and Steven Rich. 2017. "290 Coaches, Officials Tied to U.S. Olympic Groups Have Been Accused of Sexual Misconduct Since 1982." *Chicago Tribune*, November 18. (http://www

.chicagotribune.com/sports/ct-olympic-sexual-abuse-20171118-story.html).

Hochschild Jennifer L., and Brenna Marea Powell. 2008. "Racial Reorganization and the United States Census 1850–1930: Mulattoes, Half-Breeds, Mixed Parentage, Hindoos, and the Mexican Race." *Studies in American Political Development* 22 (1):59–96. Retrieved August 3, 2017 (https://scholar.harvard.edu/jlhochschild/publications/racial-reorganization-and-united-states-census-1850-1930-mulattoes-half-br#_edn64).

Hochschild, Arlie. 1979. "Emotion Work, Feeling Rules, and Social Structure." *American Journal of Sociology* 85:551–575.

Hoeffel, Elizabeth, Sonya Rastogi, Myoung Ouk Kim, and Hasan Shahid. 2012. *The Asian Population: 2010.* Washington, DC: U.S. Census Bureau. (http://www.census.gov/prod/cen2010/briefs/c2010br-11.pdf).

Hohn, Marcia D., Justin P. Lowry, James C. Witte, and José Ramón Fernández-Pena. 2016. "Immigrants in Health Care: Keeping Americans Healthy Through Care and Innovation." Retrieved August 30, 2017 (http://s3.amazonaws.com/chssweb/documents/22231/original/health_care_report_FINAL_20160629.pdf?1467209316).

Hollinger, David A. 2003. "Amalgamation and Hypodescent: The Question of Ethnoracial Mixture in the History of the United States." *The American Historical Review* 108(5): 1363–1390.

Holmes, Ryan Connelly. 2017. "It's Been 10 Weeks Since Hurricane Maria Hit Puerto Rico. Here's Where Recovery Stands." *PBS News*. (https://www.pbs.org/newshour/nation/its-been-10-weeks-since-hurricane-maria-hit-puerto-rico-heres-where-recovery-stands).

hooks, bell. 1996. *Bone Black*. New York: Henry Holt.

_____. 1999. T*alking Back: Thinking Feminist, Thinking Black*. Boston, MA: South End Press.

_____. 2000. *Feminist Theory: From Margin to Center*. Cambridge, MA: South End Press. (Original work published in 1984)

_____. 2013. "Dig Deep: Beyond Lean In." *The Feminist Wire*, October 28. (http://thefeministwire.com/2013/10/17973).

Hopcroft, Rosemary. 2009. "Gender Inequality in Interaction: An Evolutionary Account." *Social Forces* 87:1845–1872.

Hopkins, Valerie. 2017. "Peace Clubs: Rwanda's Post-Genocide Search For Renewal." *Al Jazeera*, July 10. (http://www.aljazeera.com/indepth/features/2017/06/peace-clubs-rwanda-post-genocide-search-renewal-170604161202872.html).

Horasan, Seçil. 2013. "Code-*Switching in EFL Classrooms: A Case Study On Discourse Functions, Switch Types, Initiation Patterns, and Perceptions.*" *Master Thesis*, The Graduate School of Social Sciences of Middle East Technical University (http://etd.lib.metu.edu.tr/upload/12616052/index.pdf).

Hostetler, John. 1980. *Amish Society*. Baltimore, MD: Johns Hopkins University Press.

Hovland, Carl I., and Robert R. Sears. 1940. "Minor Studies of Aggression: Correlation of Lynchings and Economic Indices." *Journal of Psychology* 9:301–310.

How to Tell Your Friends From the Japs. 1941. *Time*, October–December, p. 33.

Hoxie, Frederick. 1984. *A Final Promise: The Campaign to Assimilate the Indian, 1880–1920.* Lincoln: University of Nebraska Press.

Hraba, Joseph. 1994. *American Ethnicity.* 2nd ed. Itasca, IL: F. E. Peacock.

Hubbard, Thomas K. 2003. *Homosexuality in Greece and Rome: A Sourcebook of Basic Documents.* Oakland: University of California Press.

Huber, Joan. 2007. *On the Origins of Gender Inequality*. Colorado Springs, CO: Paradigm.

Hughes, Michael, and Melvin Thomas. 1998. "The Continuing Significance of Race Revisited: A Study of Race, Class, and Quality of Life in America, 1972 to 1996." *American Sociological Review* 63:785–803.

Hult, John. 2017. *Dakota Access Sued Over Farmland Damage in South Dakota*. (http://www.argusleader.com/story/news/2017/11/01/dakota-access-sued-over-farmland-damage-south-dakota/822273001/).

Human Rights Campaign. 2012. *Growing Up LGBT in America: HRC Youth Survey Report Key Findings.* (http://www.hrc.org/files/assets/resources/Growing-Up-LGBT -in-America_Report.pdf).

Human Rights Campaign. 2013. "The History of Coming Out." (http://www.hrc.org/resources/entry/the-history-of-coming-out).

Huntington, Samuel. 2004. *Who Are We? The Challenges to America's National Identity*. New York: Simon & Schuster.

Hurh, Won Moo. 1998. *The Korean Americans.* Westport, CT: Greenwood.

Hurley, Lawrence. 2013. "Gay Marriage Gets Big Boost in Two Supreme Court Rulings." *Reuters*, June 26 (http://www.reuters.com/article/2013/06/26/us-usa-court-gaymarriage-idUSBRE95P06W20130626).

Hurley, Lawrence. 2016. "Supreme Court leaves Ohio Voting Restrictions in Place." Retrieved August 9, 2017 (http://www.reuters.com/article/us-usa-court-vote-idUSKCN11J1W6).

Hyman, Herbert, and Paul Sheatsley. 1964. "Attitudes Toward Desegregation." *Scientific American* 211:16–23.

IB Times. 2015. "Charleston Shooting Racial Motivation? Dylann Storm Roof Told Black Neighbor He Planned on Killing Clark Mindock." *IB Times*, June 18. Retrieved July 29, 2017 (http://www.ibtimes.com/charleston-shooting-racial-motivation-dylann-storm-roof-told-black-neighbor-he-1974050).

Ibish, Hussein, ed. 2003. *Report on Hate Crimes and Discrimination Against Arab Americans: The Post–September 11 Backlash.* Washington, DC: American-Arab Anti-Discrimination Committee. (http://www.adc.org/hatecrimes/pdf/2003_report_web.pdf).

Iceland, John, Donald Weinberg, and Erika Steinmetz. 2002. *Racial and Ethnic Residential Segregation in the United States: 1980–2000* (U.S. Census Bureau, Series CENSR-3). Washington, DC: U.S. Government Printing Office. (http://www.census.gov/prod/2002pubs/censr-3.pdf).

Ifill, Gwen. 2009. *The Breakthrough: Politics and Race in the Age of Obama.* New York: Doubleday.

Instituto Brasileiro do Geografica e Estatistica. 2013. "Table 1.3.1— Resident Population by Race, Age, and Sex." *Censo 2010*. (http://www.ibge.gov.br/english/estatistica/populacao/censo2010/caracteristicas_da_populacao/tabelas_pdf/tab3.pdf).

International Organization for Migration. 2014. *Fatal Journeys: Tracking Lives Lost During Migration*, edited by T. Brian and F. Lascko. Geneva, Switzerland: Author. (http://www.iom.int/files/live/sites/iom/files/pbn/docs/Fatal-Journeys-Tracking-Lives-Lost-during-Migration-2014.pdf).

International Rescue Committe. 2014. "The Lost Boys of Sudan." *International Rescue Committee*, October 3. Retrieved August 5, 2017 (https://www.rescue.org/article/lost-boys-sudan).

Israel Central Bureau of Statistics. 2014. *65th Independence Day—More Than 8 Million Residents in the State of Israel* [Press release]. (http://www1.cbs.gov.il/www/hodaot2013n/11_13_097e.pdf).

Jablonski, Nina G., and George Chaplin. 2010. "Human Skin Pigmentation as an Adaptation to UV Radiation." Retrieved August 3, 2017 (www.pnas.org/content/107/Supplement_2/8962.full).

Jack, Amani El. 2010. Education Is My Mother and Father: The "Invisible" Women of Sudan. *Refuge* 27(2):19–29.

Jackman, Mary, and Michael J. Muha. 1984. "Education and Intergroup Attitudes: Moral Enlightenment,

Superficial Democratic Commitment, or Ideological Refinement?" *American Sociological Review* 49:751–769.

Jackman, Mary. 1978. "General and Applied Tolerance: Does Education Increase Commitment to Racial Integration?" *American Journal of Political Science* 22:302–324.

Jackman, Mary. 1981. "Education and Policy Commitment to Racial Integration." *American Journal of Political Science* 25:256–259.

Jackson, Beverly. 2000. *Splendid Slippers: A Thousand Years of an Erotic Tradition*. Berkeley, CA: Ten Speed.

Jacobs, David, and Katherine Wood. 1999. "Interracial Conflict and Interracial Homicide: Do Political and Economic Rivalries Explain White Killings of Blacks or Black Killings of Whites?" *American Journal of Sociology* 105:157–180.

Jacobs, Harriet Ann. 1861. *Incidents in the Life of a Slave Girl, Written by Herself (electronic edition, 2003).*, edited by L. Maria Francis Child. Boston, MA: Author. (http://docsouth .unc.edu/fpn/jacobs/jacobs .html).

Jacobs, Margaret D. 2009. *White Mother to a Dark Race: Settler Colonialism, Maternalism, and the Removal of Indigenous Children in the American West and Australia, 1880–1940*. Lincoln, NE: University of Nebraska Press.

Jaher, Frederic C. 1996. *A Scapegoat in the New Wilderness: The Origins and Rise of Anti-Semitism in America*. Cambridge, MA: Harvard University Press.

James, Sandy E., Jody L. Herman, Susan Rankin, Mara Keisling, Lisa Mottet,

and Ma'ayan Anafi. 2016. *The Report of the 2015 U.S. Transgender Survey*. Washington, DC: National Center for Transgender Equality.

James, Susan Donaldson. 2011. "Census 2010: One-Quarter of Gay Couples Raising Children." *ABC News*, June 23. (http://abcnews.go.com/ Health/sex-couples -census-data-trickles- quarter-raising- children/story?id=138 50332).

_____. 2014. "Jason Collins and Michael Sam Redefine Black Manhood." *ABC News*, February 24. (http://abcnews.go.com/ Health/jason-collins -michael-sam-redefine -black-manhood/story? id=22650777.

Jamieson, David. 2012. "Betty Dukes, Renowned Dukes v. Walmart Plaintiff, Takes Her Fight Back to Capitol Hill." *Huffington Post*, June 20. (http:// www.huffingtonpost. com/2012/06/20/betty- dukes-walmart-supreme- court_n_1613305.html).

Japanese American Citizens League. 2009. *Myths and Mirrors: Real Challenges Facing Asian American Students*. San Francisco, CA: Author. (http://www.jacl.org/ leadership/documents/ MythsandMirrorsFinal.pdf).

Jargowsky, Paul. 2015. "The Architecture of Segregation: Civil Unrest, the Concentration of Poverty, and Public Policy." *The Century Foundation*. Retrieved July 20, 2017 (https://tcf.org/ content/report/architecture- of-segregation/).

Jayson, Sharon. 2012. "Census Shows Big Jump in Interracial Couples." *USA Today*, April 26. (http://usatoday30 .usatoday.com/news/ nation/story/2012-04-24/

census-interracial- couples/54531706/1).

Jensen, Gwenn M. 2008. "Dysentery, Dust, and Determination: Health Care in the World War II Japanese American Detention Camps." *Discover Nikkei*, June 21. Retrieved August 26, 2017 (http://www.discovernikkei .org/en/journal/2008/6/21/ enduring-communities/).

Jibou, Robert M. 1988. "Ethnic Hegemony and the Japanese of California." *American Sociological Review* 53:353–367.

Johnson, Colin. 2013. *Just Queer Folks: Gender and Sexuality in Rural America*. Philadelphia, PA: Temple University Press.

Johnson, Jeh. 2014. "'Border Security in the 21st Century' Remarks by Secretary of Homeland Security Jeh Johnson: - As Delivered." *Homeland Security*, October 9, 2014. (https://www.dhs .gov/news/2014/10/09/ remarks-secretary- homeland-security-jeh- johnson-border-security- 21st-century).

_____. 2016. "Statement by Secretary Johnson on Southwest Border Security." *Homeland Security*, October 17, 2016. (https://www.dhs .gov/news/2016/10/17/ statement-secretary- johnson-southwest-border- security).

_____. 2016. "United States Border Patrol Southwest Family Unit Subject and Unaccompanied Alien Children Apprehensions Fiscal Year 2016 'Statement by Secretary Johnson on Southwest Border Security.'" *U.S. Customs and Border Protection*. (https:// www.cbp.gov/newsroom/ stats/southwest-border- unaccompanied-children/ fy-2016).

Johnson, Tim. 2011. "Free Trade: As U.S. Corn Flows South, Mexicans Stop

Farming." *McClatchy Dc Bureau*, February 1. (http://www.mcclatchydc .com/news/nation-world/ world/article24609829 .html).

Jones, Bradley. 2016. "Americans' Views of Immigrants Marked by Widening Partisan, Generational Divides." *Pew Research Center*. Retrieved August 30, 2017 (http://www.pewresearch .org/fact-tank/2016/04/15/ americans-views-of- immigrants-marked- by-widening-partisan- generational-divides/).

Jones, James. 1997. *Prejudice and Racism*. 2nd ed. New York: McGraw-Hill.

Jones, Jeffrey M. 2013. *Most in U.S. Say It's Essential That Immigrants Learn English*. *Gallup*, August 9. Retrieved April 21, 2017 (http://www.gallup.com/ poll/163895/say-essential- immigrants-learn-english .aspx?version=print).

_____. 2013. "Same Sex Marriage Support Solidifies Above 50% in U.S." *Gallup Politics*. (http://www.gallup.com/ poll/162398/sex-marriage- support-solidifies-above .aspx).

_____. 2016. "Americans' Optimism About Blacks' Opportunities Wanes." *Gallup*. Retrieved August 3, 2017 (http://www .gallup.com/poll/193697/ americans-optimism- blacks-opportunities- wanes.aspx).

_____. 2017. "In U.S., 10.2% of LGBT Adults Now Married to Same-Sex Spouse." *Gallup Daily*, June 22. (http://www .gallup.com/poll/212702/ lgbt-adults-married- sex-spouse.aspx?g_ source=position4&g_ medium=related&g_ campaign=tiles).

Jones, N., and Bullock, J. 2012. *The Two or

More Races Population: 2010. Washington, DC: U.S. Census Bureau. (http://www.census.gov/prod/cen2010/briefs/c2010br-13.pdf).

Jordan, Winthrop. 1968. *White Over Black: American Attitudes Towards the Negro: 1550–1812.* Chapel Hill: University of North Carolina Press.

Josephy, Alvin M. 1968. *The Indian Heritage of America.* New York: Knopf.

Joyce, Amy. 2004. "Still Outside the Good Ol' Boys Club: Women Continue to Be Discriminated Against in the Workplace, Study Finds." *Washington Post*, July 18. (http://www.washingtonpost.com/wp-dyn/articles/A56858-2004Jul17.html).

Kahn, Carrie. 2017. Cuba's Small Businesses Brace For New U.S. Trade, Travel Restrictions." *NPR*, June 19. (http://www.npr.org/2017/06/19/533481614/cubas-small-businesses-brace-for-new-u-s-trade-travel-restrictions).

Kaleem, Jaweed. 2011. "Religious Lobbying Groups Have Dramatically Increased in Washington: Study." *Huffington Post*, November 21. (http://www.huffingtonpost.com/2011/11/21/religious-lobbying-groups_n_1105565.html).

Kallen, Horace M. 1915a. "Democracy Versus the Melting Pot I." *Nation* 100(2590):190–194.

_____. 1915b. "Democracy Versus the Melting Pot II." *Nation* 100(2591): 217–222.

Karlins, Marvin, Thomas Coffman, and Gary Walters. 1969. "On the Fading of Social Stereotypes: Studies in Three Generations of College Students." *Journal of Personality and Social Psychology* 13:1–16.

Karskens, Karen. 2003. "Revisiting the Worldview: The Archaeology of Convict Households in Sydney's Rocks Neighborhood." *Historical Archaeology* 37(1):34–55.

Kasarda, John D. 1989. "Urban Industrial Transition and the Underclass." *Annals of the American Academy of Political Science* 501: 26–47.

Kasindorf, Martin. 2012. "Racial Tensions Are Simmering in Hawaii's Melting Pot." *USA Today*, March 6. (http://usatoday30.usatoday.com/news/nation/2007-03-06-hawaii-cover_N.htm).

Kasinitz, Philip, John H. Mollenkopf, Mary C. Waters, and Jennifer Holdaway. 2008. *Inheriting the City: The Children of Immigrants Come of Age.* New York: Russell Sage Foundation.

Kastanis, Angeliki, and Wilson, Blanca. 2012. *Race/Ethnicity, Gender, and Socioeconomic Wellbeing of Individuals in Same-Sex Couples.* Los Angeles: Williams Institute, UCLA School of Law. (http://williamsinstitute.law.ucla.edu/wp-content/uploads/Census-Compare-Feb-2014.pdf).

Katz, Daniel, and Kenneth Braly. 1933. "Racial Stereotypes of One Hundred College Students." *Journal of Abnormal and Social Psychology* 28:280–290.

Katz, Michael B., and Mark J. Stern. 2008. *One Nation Divisible: What America Was and What It Is Becoming.* New York: Russell Sage Foundation.

Katz, Phyllis, and Dalmas Taylor, eds. 1988. *Eliminating Racism: Profiles in Controversy.* New York: Plenum.

Katz, Phyllis. 1976. "The Acquisition of Racial Attitudes in Children." Pp. 125–154 in *Towards the Elimination of Racism*, edited by P. Katz. New York: Pergamon.

Katz, Phyllis. 2003. "Racists or Tolerant Multiculturalists? How Do They Begin?" *American Psychologist* 58:897–909.

Katznelson, Ira. 2005. *When Affirmative Action Was White: An Untold History of Racial Inequality in Twentieth-Century America.* New York: Norton.

Kaufman, Herbert L. 2003. *Lucky To Be Here.* Bloomington, IN: Xlibris Corporation. Retrieved August 5, 2017 (https://books.google.com/books?isbn=1462834663).

Kaw, Eugenia. 1997. "Opening Faces: The Politics of Cosmetic Surgery and Asian American Women." Pp. 55–73 in *In Our Own Words: Readings on the Psychology of Women and Gender*, edited by M. Crawford and R. Under. New York: McGraw-Hill.

Kaye, Jeffrey. 2010. *Moving Millions: How Coyote Capitalism Fuels Global Immigration.* Hoboken, NJ: Wiley.

Kearney, Denis, and H. L. Knight. 1978. "Appeal from California. The Chinese Invasion. Workingmen's Address" *Indianapolis Times*, February 28. (http://historymatters.gmu.edu/d/5046/).

Keels, Micere, and Keisha Harris. 2014. "Intercultural Dating at Predominantly White Universities: The Maintenance and Crossing of Group Borders." *Societies* 4:363–379.

Kelley, Blair L. M. 2010. *Right to Ride: Streetcar Boycotts and African American Citizenship in the Era of Plessy v. Ferguson.* Chapel Hill, NC: University of North Carolina Press. Retrieved August 8, 2017 (https://books.google.com/books?isbn=0807895814).

Kelly, Meghan A. 2012. "Is Spanish Sexist?" *Language Lens*, September 18. (https://languagelens.wordpress.com/2012/09/18/just-how-sexist-is-spanish/).

Kennedy, Randall. 2001a. "Racial Trends in the Administration of Criminal Justice." Pp. 1–20 in *America Becoming: Racial Trends and Their Consequences.* Vol. 2, edited by N. Smelser, W. Wilson, and F. Mitchell. Washington, DC: National Academy Press.

Kennedy, Robert C. 2001b. "On This Day." *The New York Times Company* and *Harper's Weekly.* Retrieved August 3, 2017 (http://www.nytimes.com/learning/general/onthisday/harp/0728.html).

Kennedy, Ruby Jo. 1944. "Single or Triple Melting Pot? Intermarriage Trends in New Haven, 1870–1940." *American Journal of Sociology* 49:331–339.

_____. 1952. "Single or Triple Melting Pot? Intermarriage Trends in New Haven, 1870–1950." *American Journal of Sociology* 58:56–59.

Kephart, William, and William Zellner. 1994. *Extraordinary Groups.* New York: St. Martin's Press.

Kessler, Jason. 2017. "Yes, Virginia (Dare), There Is Such A Thing As White Genocide." Retrieved August 12, 2017 (http://www.vdare.com/articles/yes-virginia-dare-there-is-such-a-thing-as-white-genocide).

Kheel Center, Cornell University. 2017. *The 1911 Triangle Factory Fire.* Retrieved December 10, 2017 (http://www.ilr.cornell.edu/index.html).

Kiley, Jocelyn, and Shiva Maniam. 2016. *Lesbian, Gay And Bisexual Voters Remain A Solidly Democratic Bloc.* Washington, DC: Pew Research Center. (http://www.pewresearch.org/fact-tank/2016/10/25/lesbian-gay-and-bisexual-voters-remain-a-solidly-democratic-bloc/).

Killian, Lewis. 1975. *The Impossible Revolution, Phase 2: Black Power and the American Dream.* New York: Random House.

Kim, Kwang Chung, and Shin Kim. 1999. "The Multiracial Nature of Los Angeles Unrest in 1992." Pp. 17–38 in *Koreans in the Hood: Conflict with African Americans*, edited by K. Chung Kim. Baltimore, MD: Johns Hopkins University Press.

Kime, Patricia. 2014. "Incidents of rape in military much higher than previously reported." *Military Times*, December 4. (https://www.militarytimes.com/2014/12/04/incidents-of-rape-in-military-much-higher-than-previously-reported/).

Kimmel, Michael S. 1996. *Manhood in America: A Cultural History.* New York: Free Press.

Kinder, Donald R., and David O. Sears. 1981. "Prejudice and Politics: Symbolic Racism Versus Racial Threats to the Good Life." *Journal of Personality and Social Psychology* 40:414–431.

King Jr., Martin Luther. 1958. *Stride Toward Freedom: The Montgomery Story.* New York: Harper & Row.
_____. 1963. *Why We Can't Wait.* New York: Mentor.
_____. 1968. *Where Do We Go From Here: Chaos or Community?* New York: Harper & Row.

Kinsey, Alfred. 1948. *Sexual Behavior in the Human Male.* Philadelphia, PA: W. B. Saunders.

Kishi, Katayoun. 2016. "Anti-Muslim Assaults Reach 9/11-Era Levels, FBI Data Show." *Pew Research Center*, November 21. (http://www.pewresearch.org/fact-tank/2016/11/21/anti-muslim-assaults-reach-911-era-levelsfbi).

Kitano, Harry H. L. 1980. "Japanese." Pp. 561–571 in *Harvard Encyclopedia of American Ethnic Groups*, edited by S. Thernstrom, A. Orlov, and O. Handlin. Cambridge, MA: Harvard University Press.

Kitano, Harry, and Roger Daniels. 1988. *Asian Americans: Emerging Minorities.* Englewood Cliffs, NJ: Prentice Hall.
_____. 1995. *Asian Americans: Emerging Minorities.* 2nd ed. Englewood Cliffs, NJ: Prentice Hall.
_____. 2001. *Asian Americans: Emerging Minorities.* 3rd ed. Upper Saddle River, NJ: Prentice Hall.

Klein, Jeff Z., and Judy Battista. 2013. "Major Sports Leagues Prepare for the "I'm Gay" Disclosure." *New York Times*, April 11. (http://www.nytimes.com/2013/04/12/sports/hockey/nhl-announces-initiative-in-support-of-gay-athletes.html).

Kluegel, James R., and Eliot R. Smith. 1982. "Whites' Beliefs About Blacks' Opportunities." *American Sociological Review* 47:518–532.

Kochhar, Rakesh. 2004. *The Wealth of Hispanic Households: 1996 to 2002.* Washington, DC: Pew Hispanic Center. (http://pewhispanic.org/files/reports/34.pdf).
_____. 2006. *Growth in the Foreign-Born Workforce and Employment of the Native Born.* Washington, DC: Pew Hispanic Center. (http://pewhispanic.org/files/reports/69.pdf).

Kochhar, Rakesh, Richard Fry, and Paul Taylor. 2011. *Wealth Gap Rises to Record Highs Between Whites, Blacks, and Hispanics.* Washington, DC: Pew Research Center. (http://www.pewsocialtrends.org/files/2011/07/SDT-Wealth-Report_7-26-11_FINAL.pdf).

Kolchin, Peter. 1993. *American Slavery 1619–1877.* New York: Hill and Wang. Retrieved August 5, 2017 1993 (https://books.google.com/books?id=FaffAAAAQBAJ&q=planter#v=onepage&q&f=true).

Kordunsky, Anna. 2013. "Russia Not Only Country With Anti-Gay Laws." *National Geographic*, August 14. (http://news.nationalgeographic.com/news/2013/08/130814-russia-anti-gay-propaganda-law-world-olympics-africa-gay-rights/).

Korgen, Kathleen. 2002. *Crossing the Racial Divide: Close Friendships Between Black and White Americans.* Westport, CT: Praeger.

Kovaleski, Serge F., Julie Turkewitz, Joseph Goldstein, and Dan Barry. 2016. "An Alt-Right Makeover Shrouds the Swastikas." *The New York Times*, December 10. Retrieved August 13, 2017 (https://www.nytimes.com/2016/12/10/us/alt-right-national-socialist-movement-white-supremacy.html).

Kraditor, Aileen S. 1981. *The Ideas of the Women's Suffrage Movement: 1890–1920.* New York: W. W. Norton.

Kramer, Andrew E. 2017. "'They Starve You. They Shock You': Inside the Anti-Gay Pogrom in Chechnya." *The New York Times*, April 21. (https://www.nytimes.com/2017/04/21/world/europe/chechnya-russia-attacks-gays.html).

Krauss, Michael. 1996. "Status of Native American Language Endangerment." In *Stabilizing Indigenous Languages*, edited by G. Cantoni. Flagstaff, AZ: Center for Excellence in Education, Northern Arizona University.

Kraybill, Donald B., and Carl F. Bowman. 2001. *On the Backroad to Heaven: Old Order Hutterites, Mennonites, Amish, and Brethren.* Baltimore, MD: Johns Hopkins University Press.

Kristofic, Jim. 2011. *Navajos Wear Nikes: A Reservation Life.* Albuquerque, NM: University of New Mexico Press.

Kritz, Mary, and Douglas Girak. 2004. *The American People: Immigration and a Changing America.* New York: Russell Sage Foundation.

Krogstad, Jens. 2017. "Key Facts About the Latino Vote in 2016." Pew Research Center. (http://www.pewresearch.org/fact-tank/).

Krogstad, Jens Manuel, and D'Vera Cohn. 2015. *Multiracial in America: Proud, Diverse and Growing in Numbers.* Washington, D.C.: Pew Research Center. (http://assets.pewresearch.org/wp-content/uploads/sites/3/2015/06/2015-06-11_multiracial-in-america_final-updated.pdf).

Krogstad, Jens Manuel, and Ana Gonzalez-Barrera. 2015. "A Majority of English-Speaking Hispanics in the U.S. are Bilingual." *Pew Research Center.* (http://www.pewresearch.org/fact-tank/2015/03/24/a-majority-of-english-speaking-hispanics-in-the-u-s-are-bilingual/).

Krogstad, Jens Manuel, and Mark Hugo Lopez. 2017. "Black Voter Turnout Fell in 2016, Even as a Record Number of Americans Cast Ballots." *Pew Research Center*, May 12. Retrieved July 20, 2017 (http://www.pewresearch.org/fact-tank/2017/05/12/black-voter-turnout-fell-in-2016-even-as-a-record-number-of-americans-cast-ballots/#).

Krogstad, Jens Manuel, Kelsey Jo Starr, and Aleksandra Sandstrom. 2017. "Key Findings About Puerto Rico." *Pew Research Center*, March 29. (http://www.pewresearch.org/fact-tank/2017/03/29/key-findings-about-puerto-rico/).

Krogstad, Jens Manuel, and Mark Hugo Lopez. 2016. "Hillary Clinton Won Latino Vote But Fell Below 2012 Support for Obama." *Pew Research Center*, November 29. (http://www.pewresearch.org/fact-tank/2016/11/29/hillary-clinton-wins-latino-vote-but-falls-below-2012-support-for-obama/).

Krysan, Maria, and Reynolds Farley. 2002. "The Residential Preferences of Blacks: Do They Explain Persistent Segregation?" *Social Forces* 80:937–981.

Kulikoff, Allan. 1992. *The Agrarian Origins of American Capitalism*. Charlottesville, VA: University of Virginia Press.

Kulish, Nicholas, Caitlin Dickerson, and Ron Nixon. 2017. "Immigration Agents Discover New Freedom to Deport Under Trump." *The New York Times*, February 25, (https://www.nytimes.com/2017/02/25/us/ice-immigrant-deportations-trump.html).

Kuperman, Diane. 2001. "Stuck at the Gates of Paradise." *UNESCO Courier*, September, pp. 24–26.

Labaton, Stephen. 1994. "Denny's Restaurants to Pay $54 Million in Race Bias Suits." *New York Times*, May 25. (http://www.nytimes.com/1994/05/25/us/denny-s-restaurants-to-pay-54-million-in-race-bias-suits.html).

Lacy, Dan. 1972. *The White Use of Blacks in America*. New York: McGraw-Hill.

Lai, H. M. 1980. "Chinese." Pp. 217–234 in *Harvard Encyclopedia of American Ethnic Groups*, edited by S. Thernstrom, A. Orlov, and O. Handlin. Cambridge, MA: Harvard University Press.

Lai, Him Mark, Genny Lim, and Judy Yung. 1991. *Island: Poetry and History of Chinese Immigrants on Angel Island, 1910-1940*. Seattle: University of Washington Press. Retrieved August 26, 2017 (https://www.aiisf.org/).

Lame Deer, John (Fire), and Richard Erdoes. 1972. "Listening to the Air." Pp. 119–121 in *Lame Deer, Seeker of Visions*. New York: Simon & Schuster.

Lamont-Brown, Raymond. 1993. "The Burakumin: Japan's Underclass.' *Contemporary Review* 263:136–140.

Landale, Nancy, and R. S. Oropesa. 2002. "White, Black, or Puerto Rican? Racial Self-Identification Among Mainland and Island Puerto Ricans." *Social Forces* 81: 231–254.

Landrieu, Mitch 2017. "Mitch Landrieu's Speech on the Removal of Confederate Monuments in New Orleans." Retrieved August 12, 2017 (https://www.nytimes.com/2017/05/23/opinion/mitch-landrieus-speech-transcript.html).

Lane, Ben. 2016. "Bancorpsouth Fined $10.6 Million For Discriminatory Lending, Redlining." June 29. (https://www.housingwire.com/articles/37405).

Lang, Sabine. 2010. *Men as Women, Women as Men: Changing Gender in Native American Cultures*. Austin, TX: University of Texas Press.

LaPiere, Robert. 1934. "Attitudes *vs.* Actions." *Social Forces* 13:230–237. (http://academicworks.cuny.edu/cgi/viewcontent.cgi?article=2996&context=gc_etds).

Law, Vincent. 2017. "The Alt-Right Holds MASSIVE Rally to Defend White Heritage in Charlottesville." Retrieved August 12, 2017. (https://altright.com/2017/05/15/alt-right-rallies-to-defend-white-heritage-in-charlottesville/).

Lawrence v. Texas, 539 U.S. 558 (2003).

Lawson, Steven F. 2009. "African American Voting Rights, Part One, 1865-1900" in *Civil Rights in America: Racial Voting Rights*. Washington, DC: A National Historic Landmarks Theme Study. Susan Cianci Salvatore, Project Manager. Retrieved August 10, 2017 (https://www.nps.gov/nhl/learn/themes/CivilRights_VotingRights.pdf).

Le, C. N. 2005. "Fleeing Dragon: The Refugee Experience of a Vietnamese Immigrant Family." Pp. 340–362 in *Minority Voices: Linking Personal Ethnic History and the Sociological Imagination*, edited by J. Myers. Boston, MA: Pearson.

Leadership Council for Education Fund. 2016. "Warning Signs: The Potential Impact of Shelby County v. Holder on the 2016 General Election Races for President, Senate and Governorships at Risk with an Eviscerated Voting Rights Act." Retrieved June 12, 2017 (http://civilrightsdocs.info/pdf/reports/2016-Voting-Rights-Report-FOR-WEB.pdf).

Leake, David, and Rhonda Black. 2005. *Essential Tools: Cultural and Linguistic Diversity: Implications for Transition Personnel*. Minneapolis, MN: University of Minnesota, Institute on Community Integration, National Center on Secondary Education and Transition. (http://www.ncset.org/publications/essentialtools/diversity/partIII.asp).

Lee, Jennifer, and Frank D. Bean. 2007. "Reinventing the Color Line: Immigration and America's New Racial/Ethnic Divide." *Social Forces* 86(2).

Lee, Sharon. 1998. "Asian Americans: Diverse and Growing." *Population Bulletin* 53(2):1–40.

Lee, Shelley Sang-Hee. 2015. *Asian Americans and the 1992 Los Angeles Riots/Uprising*. doi: 10.1093/acrefore/9780199329175.013.15.

Leff, Lisa. 2011. Gay Population in U.S. Estimated at 4 Million, Gary Gates Says. *Huffington Post*, April 7. (http://www.huffingtonpost.com/2011/04/07/gay-population-us-estimate_n_846348.html).

Lefkowitz, Bernard. 1998. *Our Guys: The Glen Ridge Rape and the Secret Life of the Perfect Suburb*. New York: Vintage.

Lenski, Gerhard E. 1984. *Power and Privilege: A Theory of Social Stratification*. Chapel Hill,

NC: University of North Carolina Press.

Lenski, Gerhard, Patrick Nolan, and Jean Lenski. 1995. *Human Societies: An Introduction to Macrosociology*. 7th ed. New York: McGraw-Hill.

Leonard, David J., and Carmen R. Lugo-Lugo. 2015. *Latino History and Culture: An Encyclopedia*. New York: Routledge.

Leslie, Neleen S. 2016. "There's A Difference: Code Switching, Spanglish and Bilingual Advertising." March 8. (https://www.linkedin.com/pulse/theres-difference-code-switching-spanglish-bilingual-leslie-ph-d-).

Levin, Jack, and Jack McDevitt. 1993. *Hate Crimes: The Rising Tide of Bigotry and Bloodshed*. New York: Plenum.

Levine, Lawrence. 1977. *Black Culture and Black Consciousness*. New York: Oxford University Press.

Levy, Jacques. 1975. *César Chávez: Autobiography of La Causa*. New York: Norton.

Lewin, Tamar. 2012. "Black Students Face More Discipline, Data Suggests." *The New York Times*, March 6. Retrieved August 8, 2017 (http://www.nytimes.com/2012/03/06/education/black-students-face-more-harsh-discipline-data-shows.html).

Lewis, Gregory. 2003. Black–White Differences in Attitudes Toward Homosexuality and Gay Rights. *Public Opinion Quarterly* 67:59–78.

Lewis, John (with Michael D'Orso). 1999. *Walking with the Wind: A Memoir of the Movement*. New York: Harvest Books.

Lewis, Oscar. 1959. *Five Families: Mexican Case Studies in the Culture of Poverty*. New York: Basic Books.

_____. 1965. *La Vida: A Puerto Rican Family in the Culture of Poverty*. New York: Random House.

_____. 1966. "The Culture of Poverty." *Scientific American* (October):19–25.

Lewis, Valeria A. 2012. "Social Energy and Racial Segregation in the University Context." *Social Science Quarterly* 93:270–290.

Lewis, Valerie, Michael Emerson, and Stephen Klineberg. 2011. "Who We'll Live With: Neighborhood Composition Preferences of Whites, Blacks, and Latinos." *Social Forces* 89:1385–1408.

Lewy, Guenter. 2004. "Were American Indians the Victims of Genocide?" *Commentary* 118:55–63.

Library of Congress. n.d. "Chronology of Puerto Rico in the Spanish-American War." (http://www.loc.gov/rr/hispanic/1898/chronpr.html).

_____. 1865. "13th Amendment to the U.S. Constitution." Retrieved August 10, 2017 (http://www.loc.gov/rr/program/bib/ourdocs/13thamendment.html).

_____. 2008. "Reconstruction and Its Aftermath." March 21. Retrieved August 10, 2017 (https://memory.loc.gov/ammem/aaohtml/exhibit/aopart5.html).

Lieberman, Robert C. 1998. *Shifting the Color Line: Race and the American Welfare System*. Cambridge, MA: Harvard University Press.

Lieberson, Stanley. 1980. *A Piece of the Pie: Blacks and White Immigrants Since 1880*. Berkeley, CA: University of California Press.

Lieberson, Stanley, and Mary C. Waters. 1988. *From Many Strands*. New York: Russell Sage Foundation.

Light, Ivan, and Edna Bonacich. 1988. *Immigrant Entrepreneurs: Koreans in Los Angeles, 1965–1982*. Berkeley, CA: University of California Press.

Lincoln, C. Eric. 1961. *The Black Muslims in America*. Boston, MA: Beacon.

Ling, Huping. 2000. "Family and Marriage of Late-Nineteenth and Early-Twentieth Century Chinese Immigrant Women." *Journal of American Ethnic History* 9:43–65.

Liptak, Adam, and Michael Wines. 2017. "Strict North Carolina Voter ID Law Thwarted After Supreme Court Rejects Case." *The New York Times*. Retrieved July 20, 2017 (https://www.nytimes.com/2017/05/15/us/politics/voter-id-laws-supreme-court-north-carolina.html).

Liptak, Adam. 2013. "Supreme Court Invalidates Key Part of the Voting Rights Act." *New York Times*, June 25. (http://www.nytimes.com/2013/06/26/us/supreme-court-ruling.html).

_____. 2017. "Gay Couples Entitled to Equal Treatment on Birth Certificates, Justices Rule." *The New York Times*, June 26. (https://www.nytimes.com/2017/06/26/us/politics/gay-couples-entitled-to-equal-treatment-on-birth-certificates-justices-rule.html).

Livingston, Gretchen. 2017. "Among U.S. cohabiters, 18% have a partner of a different race or ethnicity." *Pew Research Center*, June 8. Retrieved August 26, 2017 (http://www.pewresearch.org/fact-tank/2017/06/08/among-u-s-cohabiters-18-have-a-partner-of-a-different-race-or-ethnicity/).

Livingston, Gretchen, and Anna Brown. 2017. *Intermarriage in the U.S. 50 Years After Loving v. Virginia*. Washington, DC: Pew Research Center. Retrieved August 9, 2017. (http://www.pewsocialtrends.org/2017/05/18/intermarriage-in-the-u-s-50-years-after-loving-v-virginia/).

Locust, Carol. 1990. "Wounding the Spirit: Discrimination and Traditional American Indian Belief Systems." Pp. 219–232 in *U.S. Race Relations in the 1980s and 1990s: Challenges and Alternatives*, edited by G. Thomas. New York: Hemisphere.

Loewen, James. 2005. *Sundown Towns: A Hidden Dimension of American Racism*. New York: Simon & Schuster.

Lofquist, Daphne, Terry Lugailia, Martin O'Connell, and Sarah Feliz. 2012. *Households and Families: 2010*. Washington, DC: U.S. Census Bureau. (http://www.census.gov/prod/cen2010/briefs/c2010br-14.pdf).

Logan, John, Richard Alba, and Thomas McNulty. 1994. "Ethnic Economies in Metropolitan Regions: Miami and Beyond." *Social Forces* 72:691–724.

Logan, John, and Brian Stults. 2011. *The Persistence of Segregation in the Metropolis: New Findings From the 2010 Census*. (http://www.s4.brown.edu/us2010/Data/Report/report2.pdf).

Logan, John, Richard Alba, and Thomas McNulty. 1994. "Ethnic Economies in Metropolitan Regions: Miami and Beyond." *Social Forces* 72:691–724.

Lopata, Helena Znaniecki. 1976. *Polish Americans*. Englewood Cliffs, NJ: Prentice Hall.

Lopez, Gustav. 2015a. "Hispanics of Cuban Origin in the United

States, 2013." *Pew Research Center*, September 15, p. 6 (http://assets.pewresearch.org/wp-content/uploads/sites/7/2015/09/2015-09-15_cuba-fact-sheet.pdf).

_____. 2015b. "Hispanics of Mexican Origin in the United States, 2013." *Pew Research Center*, September 15. (http://www.pewhispanic.org/2015/09/15/hispanics-of-mexican-origin-in-the-united-states-2013/).

Lopez, Gustavo, and Kristen Bialik. 2017. "Key Findings About U.S. Immigrants." *Pew Research Center*, May 3. (http://www.pewresearch.org/fact-tank/2017/05/03/key-findings-about-u-s-immigrants/).

Lorber, Judith. 2001. *Gender Inequality: Feminist Theories and Politics.* 2nd ed. Los Angeles, CA: Roxbury.

Los Angeles Times Editorial Board. 2015. "Cuba off the U.S. Terrorism List: Goodbye to a Cold War Relic." *Los Angeles Times*, April 17. (http://www.latimes.com/opinion/editorials/la-ed-cuba-20150417-story.html).

Loving v. Virginia, 388 U.S. 1 (1967).

Lowcountry Digital History Initiative at the College of Charleston. n.d. "New World Labor Systems: American Indians." (http://ldhi.library.cofc.edu/exhibits/show/africanpassageslowcountryadapt/introductionatlanticworld/new_world_labor_systems).

Lowenthall, Terri Ann. 2014. "Race and Ethnicity in the 2020 Census: Improving Data to Capture a Multiethnic America." Leadership Conference Education Fund. (http://civilrightsdocs.info/pdf/reports/Census-Report-2014-WEB.pdf).

Lowery, Wesley, Carol D. Leonnig, and Mark Berman. 2014. "Even Before Michael Brown's Slaying In Ferguson, Racial Questions Hung Over Police." *Washington Post*, August 13. (https://www.washingtonpost.com/politics/even-before-teen-michael-browns-slaying-in-mo-racial-questions-have-hung-over-police/2014/08/13/78b3c5c6-2307-11e4-86ca-6f03cbd15c1a_story.html).

Lundquist, Jennifer Hickes. 2008. "Ethnic and Gender Satisfaction in the Military: The Effect of a Meritocratic Institution." *American Sociological Review* 73:477–496.

Lurie, Julia. 2014. "10 Hours in Ferguson: A Visual Timeline of Michael Brown's Death and Its Aftermath." *Mother Jones*, August 27. Retrieved August 10, 2017 (http://www.motherjones.com/politics/2014/08/timeline-michael-brown-shooting-ferguson/).

Lurie, Nancy Oestrich. 1982. "The American Indian: Historical Background." Pp. 131–144 in *Majority and Minority*, 3rd ed., edited by N. Yetman and C. Hoy Steele. Boston, MA: Allyn & Bacon.

Lyman, Stanford. 1974. *Chinese Americans.* New York: Random House.

Madley, Benjamin. 2016. *An American Genocide: The United States and the California Indian Catastrophe, 1846–1873.* New Haven, CT: Yale University Press.

Maglaty, Jeanne. 2011. "When Did Girls Start Wearing Pink?" *Smithsonian Magazine*, April 7.(http://www.smithsonianmag.com/arts-culture/when-did-girls-start-wearing-pink-1370097/).

Mak, Stephen. 2017. "Japanese Latin Americans. " *Densho Encyclopedia.* Retrieved August 26, 2017 (http://encyclopedia.densho.org/Japanese_Latin_Americans/).

Malcolm X. 1964. *The Autobiography of Malcolm X.* New York: Grove.

Malis, Claudia Pryor (Writer, Producer, and Director). 2000. *Frontline: Assault on Gay America* [Television broadcast]. Washington, DC: PBS. (http://www.pbs.org/wgbh/pages/frontline/shows/assault/etc/script.html).

Mann, Barbara Alice. 2008. "Women in Native Woodland Societies." Pp. 190–196 in *Encyclopedia of American Indian History.* Vol. 1, edited by B.E. Johansen and B.M. Pritzker. Santa Barbara, CA: ABC-CLIO.

Mann, Charles. 2011. *1491: New Revelations of the Americas Before Columbus.* New York: Vintage Books.

Manning, Jennifer E. 2013. "Membership of the 133th Congress: A Profile." *Congressional Research Service.* (http://www.senate.gov/CRSReports/crs-publish.cfm?pid=%260BL%2BR%5CC% 3F%0A).

Manning, Jennifer. 2017 "Membership of the 115th Congress: A Profile." *Congressional Research Service.* p. 7 (https://fas.org/sgp/crs/misc/R44762.pdf).

Mannix, Daniel P. 1962. *Black Cargoes: A History of the Atlantic Slave Trade.* New York: Viking.

Marable, Manning. 2011. *Malcolm X: A Life of Reinvention.* New York: Penguin.

Lanthemann, Marc. 2014. "NAFTA and the Future of Canada, Mexico and the United States." January 7. (https://www.forbes.com/sites/stratfor/2014/01/07/nafta-and-the-future-of-canada-mexico-and-the-united-states/#460f5f10724d).

Marcelli, Enrico, and David Heer. 1998. "The Unauthorized Mexican Immigrant Population and Welfare in Los Angeles County: A Comparative Statistical Analysis." *Sociological Perspectives* 41:279–303.

Marcus, Sharon. 2007. *Between Women: Friendship, Desire and Marriage in Victorian England.* Princeton, NJ: Princeton University Press.

Marosi, Richard. 2005. "Death and Deliverance: The Desert Swallows Another Border Crosser, and Her Father Is Determined to Find Her Body." *Los Angeles Times*, August 7, p. A1.

Marteleto, Leticia. 2012. "Educational Inequality by Race in Brazil, 1982–2007: Structural Changes and Shifts in Racial Classification." *Demography* 49:337–358.

Martin, Michel. 2015. "Fear of Black Men: How Society Sees Black Men and How They See Themselves." *NPR*, March 31. Retrieved August 10, 2017 (http://www.npr.org/2015/03/31/396415737/societys-fear-of-black-men-and-its-consequences).

Martin, Philip, and Elizabeth Midgley. 1999. Immigration to the United States. *Population Bulletin* 54(2):1–44.

Marvasti, Amir, and Karyn McKinney. 2004. *Middle Eastern Lives in America.* Lanham, MD: Rowman & Littlefield.

Marx, Karl, and Friedrich Engels. 1972. *The German Ideology*, edited by C.J. Arthur. New York:

International Publishers Co. Retrieved July 30, 2017 (https://books.google .com/books?isbn=0717 803023).

Marx, Karl, and Friedrich Engels. 1967. *The Communist Manifesto.* Baltimore, MD: Penguin. (Original work published 1848).

Masci, David. 2016. *How Income Varies Among U.S. Religious Groups.* Washington DC: Pew Research Center. Retrieved April 16, 2017 (http:// www.pewresearch.org/fact- tank/2016/10/11/ how-income-varies- among-u-s-religious- groups/).

Masci, David, Elizabeth Sciupac, and Michael Lipka. 2013. *Gay Marriage Around the World.* Washington, DC: Pew Research Religion and Life Project. (http://www .pewforum.org/2013/12/ 19/gay-marriage-around- the-world-2013).

Massarik, Fred, and Alvin Chenkin. 1973. "United States National Jewish Population Study: A First Report." Pp. 264–306 in *American Jewish Committee, American Jewish Year Book, 1973.* New York: American Jewish Committee.

Massey, Douglas. 1995. "The New Immigration and Ethnicity in the United States." *Population and Development Review* 21:631–652.

———. 2000. "Housing Discrimination 101." *Population Today* 28:1, 4.

———. 2007. *Categorically Unequal: The American Stratification System.* New York: Russell Sage Foundation.

Massey, Douglas, and Nancy Denton. 1993. *American Apartheid.* Cambridge, MA: Harvard University Press.

Mastro, Dana, Elizabeth Behm-Morawitz, and Michelle Ortiz. 2007. "The Cultivation of Social Perceptions of Latinos: A Mental Models Approach." *Media Psychology* 9(2):347–365. doi:10.1080/15213260 701286106.

Mastropasqua, Kristina. 2015. Sexual Assault and Rape on U.S. College Campuses: Research Roundup. *Journalist's Resource,* September. (https:// journalistsresource .org/studies/society/public- health/sexual-assault- rape-us-college-campuses- research-roundup).

Matas, Caroline. 2016. "Federal Government Halts Pipeline Construction on American Indian Sacred Grounds." September 13. Retrieved August 18, 2017 (https://rlp.hds .harvard.edu/news/federal- government-halts-pipeline- construction-american- indian-sacred-grounds).

Matheson, Zara. 2011. Reprinted with Permission; Originally Appeared in "The Geography of Hate" in *The Atlantic,* edited by R. Florida. Martin Prosperity Institute. Retrieved July 29, 2017 (https://www.splcenter.org/ get-information/hate-map).

Mathis-Lilley, Ben. 2014. "Police Handler Let Dog Urinate on Michael Brown Memorial the Day He Was Killed." *The Slatest,* August 27. Retrieved August 12, 2017 (http:// www.slate.com/blogs/ the_slatest/2014/08/27/ ferguson_police_dog_ urinated_on_michael_ brown_memorial.html).

Mauer, Marc. 2011. "Addressing Racial Disparities in Incarceration." *The Prison Journal* 91: 875–1015.

McCabe, Katie, and Dovey Johnson Roundtree. 2009. *Justice Older Than the Law: The Life of Dovey Johnson Roundtree.* Jackson, MS: University Press of Mississippi. Retrieved August 9, 2017 (https://books.google.com/ books?isbn=1604 737743).

McCarthy, Justin. 2017. "US Support for Gay Marriage Edges to New High." *Gallup,* May 15. (http:// www.gallup .com/poll/210566/ support-gay-marriage- edges-new-high.aspx?g_ source=position6&g_ medium=related&g_ campaign=tiles).

McConahy, John B. 1986. "Modern Racism, Ambivalence, and the Modern Racism Scale." Pp. 91–125 in *Prejudice, Discrimination, and Racism,* edited by J.F. Dovidio and S. Gartner. Orlando, FL: Academic Press.

McConnell, Tristan. 2014. "Uganda's New Anti-Gay Law: Part of a Broader Trend in Africa." *National Geographic,* February 28. (http://news .national geographic.com/ news/2014/02/140228- uganda-anti-gay-law-smug- homophobia-africa-world).

McCook, Brian. 2011. *The Borders of Integration: Polish Migrants in Germany and the United States, 1870–1924.* Athens, OH: Ohio University Press. Retrieved November 18, 2016 (https://books.google. com/books?isbn=0821 443518).

McDonald, Steve, Nan Lin, and Dan Ao. 2009. "Networks of Opportunity: Race, Gender and Job Leads." *Social Problems* 56:385–402.

McDowell, Amber. 2004. "Cracker Barrel Settles Lawsuit; Black Customers, Workers Reported Discrimination." *Washington Post,* September 10, p. E1.

McGowan, Kevin. 2016. "Wal-Mart Settles Sex Bias Claims, but Class Action Refiled." *Bloomberg News,* July 19. (https://www .bna.com/walmart-settles- sex-n73014444958/).

McGuire, Danielle L. 2010. *At the Dark End of the Street: Black Women, Rape, and Resistance - A New History of the Civil Rights Movement from Rosa Parks to the Rise of Black Power.* New York: Random House. Retrieved August 8, 2017 (https://books.google.com/ books?isbn=0307 594475).

McIntosh, Peggy. 1989. "White Privilege: Unpacking the Invisible Knapsack." (http://www.isr .umich.edu/home/diversity/ resources/white-privilege .pdf).

McKibben, Bill. 2016. "A Pipeline Fight and America's Dark Past." *The New Yorker.* September 6. Retrieved August 18, 2017 (http://www. newyorker.com/news/daily- comment/a-pipeline-fight- and-americas- dark-past).

McKinley, Jesse. 2010. "Officer Guilty in Killing That Inflamed Oakland." Retrieved August 10, 2017 (http://www .nytimes.com/2010/07/09/ us/09verdict.html).

McLaren, Lauren. 2003. "Anti-Immigrant Prejudice in Europe: Contact, Threat Perception, and Preferences for the Exclusion of Migrants." *Social Forces* 81:909–936.

McLemore, S. Dale. 1973. "The Origins of Mexican American Subordination in Texas." *Social Science Quarterly* 53:656–679.

McNickle, D'Arcy. 1973. *Native American Tribalism: Indian Survivals and Renewals.* New York: Oxford University Press.

McPherson, Miller, Lynn Smith-Lovin, and Matthew Brashears. 2006. "Social Isolation in America:

Changes in Core Discussion Networks Over Two Decades." *Social Forces* 71:353–375.

McTaggart, Ninochka, and Eileen O'Brien. 2013. *Challenging the Face of Hip Hop: An Exploration of Gender and Representation in Hip HopCulture.* Annual Meeting of the Association for Asian American Studies, April 18, Seattle, WA.

McWilliams, Carey. 1961. *North From Mexico: The Spanish-Speaking People of the United States.* New York: Monthly Review.

Medoff, Marshall. 1999. "Allocation of Time and Hateful Behavior: A Theoretical and Positive Analysis of Hate and Hate Crimes." *American Journal of Economics and Sociology* 58: 959–973.

Meek, Barbara. 2006. "And the Indian goes "How!": Representations of American Indian English in White Public Space." *Language in Society* 35:93–128.

Meenes, Max. 1941. "American Jews and Anti-Semitism." *The Journal of Negro Education* 10: 557–566.

Meissner, Doris. 2010. "5 Myths about Immigration." *Washington Post*, May 2, p. B2.

Menes, Rebecca. 2001. *Corruption in Cities: Graft and Politics in American Cities At the Turn of the Twentieth Century.* The National Bureau of Economic Research. Fairfax, VA: George Mason University.

Merica, Dan. 2012. "Black Pastors Group Launches Anti-Obama Campaign Around Gay Marriage." *CNN*, July 31. (http://religion.blogs.cnn.com/2012/07/31/black-pastors-group-launches-anti-obama-campaign-around-gay-marriage/).

Merton, Robert. 1968. *Social Theory and Social Structure.* New York: Free Press.

Messner, Michael. 1990. "When Bodies Are Weapons: Masculinity and Violence in Sports." *International Review of the Sociology of Sports* 25:203–218.

Metcalf, Alida C. 2005. *Family and Frontier in Colonial Brazil: Santana de Parnaíba, 1580–1822.* Austin: University of Texas Press.

Meyer, Maureen and Adam Isacson. n.d. "Border Security, Migration, and Humanitarian Concerns in South Texas." (https://www.wola.org/files/1502_stx/index.html)

Meyer, Robinson. 2016. "The Legal Case for Blocking the Dakota Access Pipeline." *The Atlantic*, September 9. Retrieved August 18, 2017 (https://www.theatlantic.com/technology/archive/2016/09/dapl-dakota-sitting-rock-sioux/499178/).

Meyer, Robinson. 2017a. "The Standing Rock Sioux Claim 'Victory and Vindication' in Court." *The Atlantic*, June 14. Retrieved August 18, 2017 (https://www.theatlantic.com/science/archive/2017/06/dakota-access-standing-rock-sioux-victory-court/530427/).

Meyer, Robinson. 2017b. "What's Happening With the Relief Effort in Puerto Rico?" *The Atlantic*, Oct. 4. (https://www.theatlantic.com/science/archive/2017/10/what-happened-in-puerto-rico-a-timeline-of-hurricane-maria/541956/).

Miceli, Melissa. 2005. *Standing Out, Standing Together: The Social and Political Impact of Gay-Straight Alliances.* New York: Routledge.

Midlo Hall, Gwendolyn. 2009. *Slavery and African Ethnicities in the Americas: Restoring the Links.* Chapel Hill, NC: University of North Carolina Press.

Mikulak, Marcia L. 2011. "The Symbolic Power of Color: Construction of Race, Skin-Color, and Identity in Brazil." *Humanity and Society* 35:62–99.

Milkie, Melissa A. 1999. "Social Comparisons, Reflected Appraisals, and Mass Media: The Impact of Pervasive Beauty Images on Black and White Girls' Self Concepts." *Social Psychology Quarterly* 62:190–210.

Miller, Joe, Jennie Miller, and Dorothy Miller. 1994. "Cultural Survival and Contemporary American Indian Women in the City." pp. 185–202 in *Women of Color in U.S. Society*, edited by M. Zinn and B.T. Dill. Philadelphia, PA: Temple University Press.

Miller, Neal E., and Richard Bugelski. 1948. "Minor Studies of Aggression: The Influence of Frustrations Imposed by the In-Group on Attitudes Expressed Towards Out-Groups." *Journal of Psychology* 25:437–442.

Miller, Norman, and Marilyn Brewer, eds. 1984. *Groups in Contact: The Psychology of Desegregation.* Orlando, FL: Academic Press.

Miller, Zeke J. 2017. "President Trump Has Taken a Key Step to Implement His Transgender Military Ban." *Time Magazine*, August 25. (http://time.com/4916871/donald-trump-transgender-military-ban/).

Mills, C. Wright. 1959. *The Sociological Imagination.* New York: Oxford University Press.

Min, Pyong Gap, ed. 1995. *Asian Americans: Contemporary Trends and Issues.* Thousand Oaks, CA: Sage.

_____. 2006. *Asian Americans: Contemporary Trends and Issues.* 2nd ed. Thousand Oaks, CA: Sage.

Mindock 2015. Charleston Shooting Racial Motivation? Dylann Storm Roof Told Black Neighbor He Planned On Killing Clark Mindock. *International business Times*, June 18. Retrieved January 15, 2018 (http://www.ibtimes.com/charleston-shooting-racial-motivation-dylann-storm-roof-told-black-neighbor-he-1974050).

Minnesota Population Center. 2016. National Historical Geographic Information System: Version 11.0 [Database]. Minneapolis: University of Minnesota. (http://doi.org/10.18128/D050.V11.0).

Mirandé, Alfredo, and Evangelina Enríquez. 1979. *La Chicana: The Mexican-American Woman.* Chicago: University of Chicago Press.

Mirandé, Alfredo. 1985. *The Chicano Experience: An Alternative Perspective.* Notre Dame, IN: University of Notre Dame Press.

Mirandé, Alfredo. 2017. *Behind the Mask: Gender Hybridity in a Zapotec Community.* Tuscon, AZ: University of Arizona Press.

Mississippi Band of Choctaw Indians. 2017. *Tribal Profile.* (http://www.choctaw.org/img/tribalprofile.pdf).

Monger, Randall. 2012. *Nonimmigrant Admissions to the United States: 2012.* Washington, DC: U.S. Department of Homeland Security. (https://www.dhs.gov/sites/default/files/publications/ois_ni_fr_2012.pdf).

Monifa, Akilah. 2008. "Interracial or Same Sex

Marriage: Same Core Civil Rights Issues." *The Progressive*, June 12. (http://www.progressive.org/mp_monifa061208).

Montes-Alcalá. 2000. "Attitudes Towards Oral and Written Code-switching in Spanish-English Bilingual Youths." Pp.218-227 in *Research on Spanish in the United States*, edited by A. Roca. Somerville, MA: Cascadilla Press.

Mooney, Linda, David Knox, and Caroline Schacht. 2010. *Understanding Social Problems.* Farmington Hills, MI: Cengage Learning.

Moore, Joan W. 1970. *Mexican Americans.* Englewood Cliffs, NJ: Prentice Hall.

Moore, Joan W., and Harry Pachon. 1985. *Hispanics in the United States.* Englewood Cliffs, NJ: Prentice Hall.

Moore, Joan, and Raquel Pinderhughes. 1993. *In the Barrios: Latinos and the Underclass Debate.* New York: Russell Sage Foundation.

Moquin, Wayne, and Charles Van Doren, eds. 1971. *A Documentary History of Mexican Americans.* New York: Bantam.

Morales, Lymari. 2009. "Knowing Someone Gay/Lesbian Affects Views of Gay Issues." *Gallup.* (http://www.gallup.com/poll/118931/Knowing-Someone-Gay-Lesbian-Affects-Views-Gay-Issues.aspx).

Morales, Lymari. 2010. "Amid Immigration Debate, Americans' Views Ease Slightly." *Gallup Politics.* (http://www.gallup.com/poll/141560/Amid-Immigration-Debate-Americans-Views-Ease-Slightly.aspx).

Morawska, Ewa. 1990. "The Sociology and Historiography of Immigration." Pp. 187–238 in

Immigration Reconsidered: History, Sociology, and Politics, edited by V. Yans-McLaughlin. New York: Oxford University Press.

Morawski, J.G. 1998. "Measurement of Masculinity and Femininity." Pp. 454–476 in *The Gender and Psychology Reader*, edited by B. Clinchy, and J.K. Norem. New York: New York University Press.

Morgan, Edmund. 1975. *American Slavery, American Freedom.* New York: Norton.

Morin, Rich, Kim Parker, Renee Stepler, and Andrew Mercer. 2015. "English Proficiency on the Rise Among Latinos." (http://www.pewhispanic.org/2015/05/12/english-proficiency-on-the-rise-among-latinos/).

Morin, Rich, Kim Parker, Renee Stepler, and Andrew Mercer. 2017. *What Police Think About Their Jobs.* Washington, DC: Pew Research Center. Retrieved August 10, 2017 (www.pewsocialtrends.org/2017/01/11/behind-the-badge/).

Morlin, Bill. 2017. "Extremists' 'Unite the Right' Rally: A Possible Historic Alt-Right Showcase?" Retrieved August 13, 2017 (https://www.splcenter.org/hatewatch/2017/08/07/extremists-unite-right-rally-possible-historic-alt-right-showcase).

Morris, Aldon D. 1984. *The Origins of the Civil Rights Movement.* New York: Free Press.

———. 2015. *The Scholar Denied: W. E. B. Du Bois and the Birth of Modern Sociology.* Oakland, CA: University of California Press.

Morris, Edward. 2005. "Tuck in That Shirt! Race, Class, Gender, and Discipline in an Urban School." *Sociological Perspectives* 48:25–48.

Moskos, Charles, and John Sibley Butler. 1997. *All That We Can Be: Black Leadership and Racial Integration the Army Way.* New York: Basic Books.

Motel, Seth, and Eileen Patten. 2013. *Statistical Portrait of the Foreign-Born Population in the United States, 2011.* Washington, DC: Pew Hispanic Center. (http://www.pewhispanic.org/2013/01/29/statistical-portrait-of-the-foreign-born-population-in-the-united-states-2011).

Movement Advancement Project, Human Rights Campaign, and Center for American Progress. 2013. *A Broken Bargain: Discrimination, Fewer Benefits and More Taxes for LGBT Workers (Full Report).* (http://www.lgbtmap.org/file/a-broken-bargain-full-report.pdf).

Moynihan, Daniel. 1965. *The Negro Family: The Case for National Action.* Washington, DC: U.S. Department of Labor.

Mozingo, Joe, and Angel Jennings. 2015. "50 years After Watts: 'There is Still a Crisis in the Black Community'." *Los Angeles Times*, August 13. Retrieved August 9, 2017 (http://www.latimes.com/local/wattsriots/la-me-watts-african-americans-20150813-story.html).

Mufson, Steven. 2016. " Why Hollywood, Environmentalists and Native Americans Have Converged on North Dakota." *The Washington Post*, October 28. Retrieved August 18, 2017 (https://www.washingtonpost.com/business/economy/why-hollywood-environmentalists-and-native-americans-have-converged-on-north-dakota/2016/10/28/007620c8-9c8f-11e6-9980-50913d68eacb_story.html).

Muhindi, Martin and Kiganzi Nyakato. 2002. "Integration of the Sudanese 'Lost Boys' in Boston Massachusetts." MIT Center for International Studies. (https://cis.mit.edu/sites/default/files/documents/IntegrationOfTheSudaneseLostBoys.pdf).

Mulligan, Thomas S., and Chris Kraul. 1996. "Texaco Settles Race Bias Suit for $176 Million." *Los Angeles Times*, November 16. (http://articles.latimes.com/1996-11-16/news/mn-65290_1_texaco-settles-race-bias-suit).

Murguia, Edward, and Tyrone Foreman. 2003. "Shades of Whiteness: The Mexican American Experience in Relation to Anglos and Blacks." pp. 63–72 in *White Out: The Continuing Significance of Racism*, edited by A. Doane, and E. Bonilla- Silva. New York: Routledge.

Muslim West Facts Project. 2009. *Muslim Americans: A National Portrait.* Washington, DC: Gallup. (http://www.gallup.com/strategicconsulting/153572/report-muslim-americans-national-portrait.aspx).

Murriel, Maria. 2016. "Millions of Americans can't vote for president because of where they live." November 1. (https://www.pri.org/stories/2016-11-01/millions-americans-cant-vote-president-because-where-they-live).

Myrdal, Gunnar. 1962. *An American Dilemma: The Negro Problem and Modern Democracy.* New York: Harper & Row. (Original work published 1944).

Nabakov, Peter, ed. 1999. *Native American Testimony* (Rev. ed.). New York: Penguin.

Nash, Alice N., and Christoph Strobel. 2006. *Daily Life*

of Native Americans from Post-Columbian Through Nineteenth-century America. Westport, CT: Greenwood Publishing Group.

National Academies of Sciences, Engineering, and Medicine. 2017. *The Economic and Fiscal Consequences of Immigration.* Washington, DC: The National Academies Press. (https://doi.org/10.17226/23550).

National Advisory Commission. 1968. *Report of the National Advisory Commission on Civil Disorders.* New York: Bantam Books.

National Association of Korean Americans. 2003. "A Brief History of Korean Americans." Edited by John H. Kim, Esq., with contributions from Prof. Ji-Yeon Yuh, Prof. Elaine H. Kim and Prof. Eui-Young Yu. Retrieved August 30, 2017 (http://www.naka.org/resources/history.asp).

National Center for Health Statistics. 2010. *Health, United States, 2010: With Special Feature on Death and Dying.* Hyattsville, MD: Author. (http://www.cdc.gov/nchs/data/hus/hus10.pdf#061).

National Center for Juvenile Justice. 2017. "Juvenile Arrest Rates by Offence, Race, and Sex, 1980-2015." Retrieved July 20, 2017. (http://www.ojjdp.gov/ojstatbb/crime/excel/JAR_2015.xls).

National Congress of American Indians. n.d. "An Introduction to Indian Nations in the United States." Retrieved August 18, 2017 (http://www.ncai.org/about-tribes/indians_101.pdf).

National Council on Crime and Delinquency. 2007. *And Justice for Some: Differential Treatment of Youth of Color in the Justice System.* (http://www.nccdglobal.org/sites/default/files/publication_pdf/justice-for-some.pdf).

National Gay and Lesbian Task Force. 2014. "Relationship Recognition Map for Same-Sex Couples in the United States." (http://www.thetaskforce.org/reports_and_research/relationship_recognition).

National Geographic Society. 2017. "Reference Populations - Geno 2.0 Next Generation." (https://genographic.nationalgeographic.com/reference-populations-next-gen/).

National Indian Gaming Commission. 2017. "2016 Indian Gaming Revenues Increased 4.4%" (https://www.nigc.gov/news/detail/2016-indian-gaming-revenues-increased-4.4).

_____. 2017. "Growth in Indian Gaming." (https://www.nigc.gov/commission/gaming-revenue-reports).

_____. 2011. "NIGC Tribal Gaming Revenues." (http://www.nigc.gov/LinkClick.aspx?fileticket=1k4B6r6dr-U%3d&tabid=67).

_____. 2014. "Indian Gaming Revenues Increased by 0.5%." (http://www.nigc.gov/linkclick.aspx?fileticket=E3BeULzk1cA%3d&tabid=1006).

_____. 2015. "Growth in Indian Gaming." (http://www.nigc.gov/commission/gaming-revenue-reports).

National Opinion Research Council. 1972–2016. *General Social Survey.* Chicago: Author. (http://www.norc.org/Research/Projects/Pages/general-social-survey.aspx).

National Origins Act, Pub. L. 139, Chapter 190, § 43 Stat. 153 (1924).

National Park Service. 2014. "Indian Reservations in the Continental United States." *U.S. Department of the Interior.* (http://www.nps.gov/nagpra/DOCUMENTS/ResMAP.HTM).

_____. 2016. "Bayard Rustin." Retrieved August 9, 2017 (https://www.nps.gov/people/bayard-rustin.htm).

_____. 2015a. "African Americans at Jamestown." Retrieved April 29, 2017 (https://www.nps.gov/jame/learn/historyculture/african-americans-at-jamestown.htm).

_____. 2015b. "Japanese Americans at Manzanar." Retrieved August 26, 2017 (https://www.nps.gov/manz/learn/historyculture/japanese-americans-at-manzanar.htm).

_____. 2015c. "Veto of the Freedmen's Bureau Bill." Retrieved August 10, 2017 (https://www.nps.gov/anjo/learn/historyculture/freedmens-bureau.htm).

_____. n.d. "Operating the Underground Railroad." Retrieved August 4, 2017 (https://www.nps.gov/nr/travel/underground/opugrr.htm).

National Public Radio. 2004. *Immigration in America: Survey Overview.* (http://www.npr.org/templates/story/story.php?storyId=4062605).

NationMaster. 2014. "Education—Average Years of Schooling of Adults: Countries Compared." (http://www.nationmaster.com/graph/edu_ave_yea_of_sch_of_adu-education-average-years-schooling-adults).

Neal, Derek and Rick Armin. 2014. "The Prison Boom and the Lack of Black Progress after Smith and Welch." NBER Working Paper No. 20283 (http://www.nber.org/papers/w20283).

Neary, Ian. 2003. "Burakumin at the End of History." *Social Research* 70: 269–294.

Nelli, Humbert S. 1980. "Italians." Pp. 545–560 in *Harvard Encyclopedia of American Ethnic Groups*, edited by S. Thernstrom, A. Orlov, and O. Handlin. Cambridge, MA: Harvard University Press.

Nelson, Lynn A. (2008). "Native American Agriculture." Pp. 88–92 in *The New Encyclopedia of Southern Culture: Volume 11: Agriculture and Industry*, edited by M. Walker, and J. Cobb. Chapel Hill: University of North Carolina Press. Retrieved August 18, 2017 (http://www.jstor.org/stable/10.5149/97814 69616681_walker.20).

Newport, Frank. 2013a. "Gulf Grows in Black-White Views of the U.S. Justice System Bias." *Gallup Politics.* (http://www.gallup.com/poll/163610/gulf-grows-black-white-views-justice-system-bias.aspx).

_____. 2013b. "In U.S., 24% of Young Black Men Say Police Dealings Unfair." *Gallup.* (http://www.gallup.com/poll/163523/one-four-young-black-men-say-police-dealings-unfair.aspx?version=print).

_____. 2014. "Gallup Review: Black and White Attitudes Toward Police." *Gallup.* Retrieved July 20, 2017 (http://www.gallup.com/poll/175088/gallup-review-black-white-attitudes-toward-police.aspx?utm_source=tagrss&utm_medium=rss&utm_campaign=syndication&utm_reader=feedly).

_____. 2015. "Americans Greatly Overestimate Percent Gay, Lesbian in U.S." *Gallup Polls*, May 21. (http://news.gallup.com/poll/183383/americans-greatly-overestimate-percent-gay-lesbian.aspx).

_____. 2016a. "In US, Support for Decreasing Immigration Holds Steady." *Gallup Polls*, August 24. (http://www.gallup.com/poll/194819/support-decreasing-immigration-holds-steady.aspx).

_____. 2016b. "Public Opinion Context: Americans, Race, and Police." *Gallup*. Retrieved July 20, 2017 (http://www.gallup.com/opinion/polling-matters/193586/public-opinion-context-americans-race-police.aspx?g_source=attitudes+police+race&g_medium=search&g_campaign=tiles).

The New York Times Editorial Board. 2014. "After Rwanda's Genocide." *The New York Times*, April 8. (https://www.nytimes.com/2014/04/09/opinion/after-rwandas-genocide.html).

The New York Times. 2004. "Utah Supreme Court Rules That Non-Indian Members of Native American Church Can Use Peyote in Church Ceremonies." *The New York Times*, June 23, p. A20.

Ngo, Van Hieu. 2008. "A Critical Examination of Acculturation Theories." *Critical Social Work* 9(1). Rerieved August 5, 2017 (http://www1.uwindsor.ca/criticalsocialwork/a-critical-examination-of-acculturation-theories).

Nichols, Roger L. 1986. "Indians in Nineteenth Century America: A Unique Minority." Pp. 127–136 in *The American Indian: Past and Present*. 3rd ed., edited by R.L. Nichols. New York: Newbury Award Records.

Nieves, Evelyn. 2014. "Surviving Rape in the Military." *The New York Times*, December 17. (https://lens.blogs.nytimes.com/2014/12/17/surviving-rape-in-the-military/).

Nirenberg, David. 2014. *Anti-Judaism: The Western Tradition*. New York: W. W. Norton & Company.

Nishi, Setsuko. 1995. "Japanese Americans." Pp. 95–133 in *Asian Americans: Contemporary Trends and Issues*, edited by P. Gap Min. Thousand Oaks, CA: Sage.

The New York Times. 1994. "Flight from Cuba Exodus Is Very Different From '80 Boatlift." August 24, . (http://www.nytimes.com/1994/08/24/us/flight-from-cuba-exodus-is-very-different-from-80-boatlift.html).

Noel, Donald. 1968. "A Theory of the Origin of Ethnic Stratification." *Social Problems* 16: 157–172.

Nolan, Patrick, and Gerhard Lenski. 2004. *Human Societies*. Boulder, CO: Paradigm.

Norman, Al. 2016. "Sex Discrimination Wal-Mart: The 'Bitches' Story That Won't Go Away." *Huffington Post*, July 17. (https://www.huffingtonpost.com/entry/sex-discrimination-t-wal-mart-dthe-biktches-story_us_578bbafae4b0b107a24147d3).

Norris, Tina, Paul Vines, and Elizabeth Hoeffel. 2012. "The American Indian and Alaska Native Population: 2010." *2010 Census Briefs*. Washington, DC: U.S. Census Bureau. (http://www.census.gov/prod/cen2010/briefs/c2010br-10.pdf).

Nossiter, Adam. 2014. "Nigeria Tries to 'Sanitize' Itself of Gays." *New York Times*, February 8. (http://www.nytimes.com/2014/02/09/world/africa/nigeria-uses-law-and-whip-to-sanitize-gays.html).

Novais, Fernando A. 1991. "Brazil in the Old Colonial System" Pp. 11–56 in *Brazil and the World System*, edited by R. Graham. Austin, TX: University of Texas Press.

Novak, Michael. 1973. *The Rise of the Unmeltable Ethnics: Politics and Culture in the 1970s*. New York: Collier.

Nunes, Brasilmar Ferreira and Leticia Veloso. 2012. "Divided Cities: Rethinking the Ghetto in Light of Brazilian Favelas" Pp. 225–244 in *The Ghetto: Contemporary Global Issues and Controversies*, edited by R. Hutchison, and B.D. Haynes. Boulder, CO: Westview Press.

Oboler, Suzanne, and Deena J. González. 2005. *The Oxford Encyclopedia of Latinos and Latinas in the United States*. Vol. 1. Oxford, U.K: Oxford University Press.

O'Brien, Eileen, and Kathleen Korgen. 2007. "It's The Message, Not the Messenger: The Declining Significance of Black–White Contact." *Sociological Inquiry* 77:356–382.

O'Keefe, Ed. 2010. "Minorities Disproportionately Discharged for Don't Ask Don't Tell Violations." *Washington Post*, August 17. (http://www.washingtonpost.com/wp-dyn/content/article/2010/08/16/AR2010081605153.html).

O'Toole, Molly. 2013. "Military Sexual Assaults Spike Despite Efforts to Control Epidemic." *New York Times*, May 7. (http://www.huffingtonpost.com/2013/05/07/military-sexual-assaults-2012_n_3230248.html).

Obama, Barack. 2008. "Barack Obama's Speech on Race." *New York Times*, March 18. (http://www.nytimes.com/2008/03/18/us/politics/18text-obama.html?pagewanted=all).

_____. 2017. "Statement by the President on Cuban Immigration Policy". *The White House*, January 12.

Obergefell v. Hodges, 576 U. S. ___ (2015).

Odo, F. 2002. "Contact and Conflict: Asia and the Pacific: Through 1900." Pp. 9–126 in *The Columbia Documentary History of the Asian American Experience*, edited by F. Odo. New York: Columbia University Press. (https://books.google.com/books?isbn=0231110308).

Ogrysko, Nicole. 2017. "Under Trump's 2018 Budget Proposal, Here's One Agency That's Hiring." *Federal News Radio*, May 25. (https://federalnewsradio.com/budget/2017/05/under-trumps-2018-budget-proposal-heres-one-agency-thats-hiring/).

Ogunwole, Stella. 2006. *We the People: American Indians and Alaska Natives in the United States*. Washington, DC: U.S. Census Bureau. (http://www.census.gov/prod/2006pubs/censr-28.pdf).

Oldenburg, Ann. 2013. "Miss America Nina Davulari Brushes Off Racist Remarks." *USA Today*, September 16. (http://www.usatoday.com/story/life/people/2013/09/16/miss-america-nina-davuluri-brushes-off-racist-remarks/2819533).

Orfield, Gary, Jongyeon Ee, Erica Frankenberg, and Genevieve Siegel-Hawley. 2016. "Brown at 62: School Segregation, by Race, Poverty, and State." *Civil Rights Project, UCLA*, May 16. Retrieved July 20, 2017 (https://www.civilrightsproject.ucla.edu/research/k-12-education/integration-and-diversity/brown-at-62-school-segregation-by-race-poverty-and-state).

Oliver, Melvin and Thomas Shapiro. 2006. *Black Wealth, White Wealth*. 2nd ed. New York: Taylor and Francis.

Oliver, Melvin, and Thomas Shapiro. 2008. "Sub-Prime

as a Black Catastrophe." *American Prospect* (October): A9–A11.

Olivo, Antonio, and Duaa Eldeib. 2013. "Catholic Church Works to Keep Up With Growing Latino Membership." *Chicago Tribune*, March 17. (http://articles.chicagotribune.com/2013-03-17/news/ct-met-chicago-latino-catholics-20130317_1_latino-appointments-latino-candidates-priests).

Olson, James S., and Raymond Wilson. 1984. *Native Americans in the Twentieth Century*. Provo, UT: Brigham Young University Press.

Omi, Michael, and Howard Winant. 1986. *Racial Formation in the United States From the 1960s to the 1980s*. New York: Routledge & Kegan Paul.

Orfield, Gary, and Chungmei Lee. 2007. *Historic Reversals, Accelerating Resegregation, and the Need for New Integration Strategies*. Los Angeles, CA: Civil Rights Project, UCLA. (http://www.eric.ed.gov/PDFS/ED500611.pdf).

Orfield, Gary, John Kucsera, and Genevieve Siegel-Hawley. 2012. *E Pluribus . . . Segregation: Deepening Double Segregation for More Students*. Los Angeles, CA: Civil Rights Project. (http://civilrightsproject.ucla.edu/research/k-12-education/integration-and-diversity/mlk-national/e-pluribus. . .separation-deepening-double-segregation-for-more-students).

Organization Intersex International. 2015. "How Common is Intersex? An Explanation of the Stats." *Oii-USA*, April 1. (http://oii-usa.org/2563/how-common-is-intersex-in-humans/).

Orser, Charles E. 1994. "The Archaeology of African-American Slave Religion in the Antebellum South." *Cambridge Archaeological Journal* 4(1):33–45. doi: 10.1017/S0959774300000950.

Ortiz, Paul. 2009. "From Slavery to Cesar Chavez and Beyond: Farmworker Organizing in the United States." In *The Human Cost of Food: Farmworkers' Lives, Labor, and Advocacy*, edited by C.D. Thompson, and Jr., M.F. Wiggins. Austin, TX: University of Texas Press.

Osofsky, Gilbert. 1969. *Puttin' On Ole Massa*. New York: Harper & Row.

Oswalt, Wendell, and Sharlotte Neely. 1996. *This Land Was Theirs*. Mountain View, CA: Mayfield.

Padavic, Irene, and Barbara Reskin. 2002. *Women and Men at Work*. Thousand Oaks, CA: Pine Forge Press.

Page, Michelle. 2017. "Forgotten Youth: Homeless LGBT Youth of Color and the Runaway and Homeless Youth Act." *Northwestern Journal of Law & Social Policy* 12(2):17–45.

Pager, Devah, and Hana Shepherd. 2008. "The Sociology of Discrimination: Racial Discrimination in Employment, Housing, Credit, and Consumer Markets." *Annual Review of Sociology* 34:181–209.

Paperny, Anna Mehler, and Allison Lampert. 2017. "Canada Sees 'Unsustainable' Spike in Asylum Seekers at U.S. Border." August 17. (https://www.reuters.com/article/us-canada-immigration/canada-sees-unsustainable-spike-in-asylum-seekers-at-u-s-border-idUSKCN1AX1PO).

Pappas, Stephanie. 2012. "Gay Parents Better Than Straight Parents? What Research Says." *Huffington Post*, January 16. (http://www.huffingtonpost.com/2012/01/16/gay-parents-better-than-straights_n_1208659.html).

Parish, Peter J. 1989. *Slavery: History and Historians*. New York: Harper & Row.

Park, Haeyoun, and Iaryna Mykhyalyshyn. 2016. "L.G.B.T. People Are More Likely to Be Targets of Hate Crimes Than Any Other Minority Group." *The New York Times*, June 16. Retrieved August 9, 2017 (https://www.nytimes.com/interactive/2016/06/16/us/hate-crimes-against-lgbt.html).

Park, Robert E., and Ernest W. Burgess. 1924. *Introduction to the Science of Society*. Chicago: University of Chicago Press.

Parke, Ross, and Raymond Buriel. 2002. "Socialization Concerns in African American, American Indian, Asian American, and Latino Families." Pp. 211–218 in *Contemporary Ethnic Families in the United States*, edited by N. Benokraitis. Upper Saddle River, NJ: Prentice Hall.

Park, Sunmin, Nobuko Hongub, and James W. Daily. 2016. "Native American Foods: History, Culture, and Influence on Modern Diets." *Journal of Ethnic Foods* 3(3):171–177. doi: 10.1016/j.jef.2016.08.001.

Parrillo, Vincent, and Christopher Donoghue. 2013. "The National Social Distance Study: Ten Years Later." *Sociological Forum* 28:597–614.

Passel, Jeffrey, S., and D'Vera Cohn. 2011. *Unauthorized Immigrant Population: National and State Trends, 2010*. Washington, DC: Pew Hispanic Center. (http://pewhispanic.org/files/reports/133.pdf).

_____. 2017. "As Mexican Share Declined, U.S. Unauthorized Immigrant Population Fell in 2015 Below Recession Level." *Pew Research Center*, April 25. (http://www.pewresearch.org/fact-tank/2017/04/25/as-mexican-share-declined-u-s-unauthorized-immigrant-population-fell-in-2015-below-recession-level/).

Passel, Jeffrey, D'Vera Cohn, and Ana Gonzalez-Barrera. 2012. *Net Migration From Mexico Falls to Zero—and Perhaps Less*. Washington, DC: Pew Hispanic Center. (http://www.pewhispanic.org/files/2012/04/Mexican-migrants-report_final.pdf).

_____. 2013. *Population Decline of Unauthorized Immigrants Stalls, May Have Reversed*. Washington, DC: Pew Research Center. (http://www.pewhispanic.org/2013/09/23/population-decline-of-unauthorized-immigrants-stalls-may-have-reversed.

Passel, Jeffrey, Wendy Wang, and Paul Taylor. 2010. *Marrying Out: One-in-Seven New U.S. Marriages Is Interracial or Interethnic*. Washington, DC: Pew Research Center. (http://www.pewsocialtrends.org/2010/06/04/marrying-out/).

Pathela, Preeti, Anjum Hajat, Julia Schillinger, Susan Blank, Randall Sell, and Farzad Mostashari. 2006. "Discordance Between Sexual Behavior and Self-Reported Sexual Identity: A Population-Based Survey of New York City Men." *Annals of Internal Medicine* 145:416–425.

Paul Nabhan, Gary. 2002. *Enduring Seeds: Native American Agriculture and Wild Plant Conservation*. Tuscon: University of Arizona Press.

Payne, Ed, and Botelho, Greg. 2015. "Charleston Church Shooting: Suspect Confesses, Says He Sought Race War." *CNN*, June 19. Retrieved July 29, 2017 (http://www.wjcl.com/article/charleston-church-shooting-suspect-confesses-says-he-sought-race-war/948238).

PBS. 1998a. "Africans in America: Arrival of First Africans to Virginia Colony 1619." Retrieved August 8, 2017 (http://www.pbs.org/wgbh/aia/part1/1p263.html).

_____. 1998b. "1835 Thomas Griggs of Charlestown, South Carolina, Offers the 'Highest Price for Men, Women, and Children'—Paid in Cash." Retrieved August 7, 2017 (http://www.pbs.org/wnet/historyofus/web05/).

_____. 1998c. "Africans in America: Conditions of Antebellum Slavery 1830–1860." Retrieved August 4, 2017 (https://www.pbs.org/wgbh/aia/part4/4p2956.html).

_____. 1998d. "Africans in America: From Indentured Servitude to Racial Slavery." Retrieved August 4, 2017 (http://www.pbs.org/wgbh/aia/part1/1narr3.html).

_____. 1998e. "Indentured Servants in the U.S." Retrieved April 29, 2017 (http://www.pbs.org/opb/historydetectives/feature/indentured-servants-in-the-us/).

_____. 2011. "Timeline: Milestones in the American Gay Rights Movement." (http://www.pbs.org/wgbh/americanexperience/features/timeline/stonewall).

Peck, Emily. 2017. "Sheryl Sandberg Warns Of #MeToo Backlash Against Women." *Huffington Post*, December 3. (https://www.huffingtonpost.com/entry/sheryl-sandberg-sexual-harassment-backlash_us_5a22c2a5e4b03350e0b710eb)

Peck, Tom. 2017. "Northern Ireland Power-Sharing: UK Government Says It May Need to Step in to Approve Budget as Deadline Expires." *The Independent*, July 3. (http://www.independent.co.uk/news/uk/politics/northern-ireland-power-sharing-latest-updates-parliament-budget-approve-deadline-dup-commons-a7821451.html).

Pedraza, Silvia. 1998. "Cuba's Revolution and Exodus." *The Journal of International Institute* 5(2). Winter. (http://hdl.handle.net/2027/spo.4750978.0005.204).

Pego, David. 1998. "To Educate a Nation: Native American Tribe Hopes to Bring Higher Education to an Arizona Reservation." *Black Issues in Higher Education* 15:60–63.

Peña-Talamantes, Abráham E. 2013. "Defining Machismo, No Es Siempre Lo Mismo: Latino Sexual Minorities' Machoflexible Identities in Higher Education." *Culture, Society & Masculinities*, 5(2):166–178.

Perez, Lisandro. 1980. "Cubans." pp. 256–261 in *Harvard Encyclopedia of American Ethnic Groups*, edited by S. Thernstrom, A. Orlov, and O. Handlin. Cambridge, MA: Harvard University Press.

Petersen, Williams. 1971. *Japanese Americans.* New York: Random House.

Peterson, Bill, and Joyce Pang. 2006. "Beyond Politics: Authoritarianism and the Pursuit of Leisure." *Journal of Social Psychology* 146:442–461.

Peterson, Bill, and Eileen Zurbriggen. 2010. "Gender, Sexuality, and the Authoritarian Personality." *Journal of Personality* 78:1801–1826.

Peterson, Mark. 1995. "Leading Cuban-American Entrepreneurs: The Process of Developing Motives, Abilities, and Resources." *Human Relations* 48:1193–1216.

Peterson, Nicholas. 2005. "What Can the Pre-Colonial and Frontier Economies Tell Us About Engagement With the Real Economy: Indigenous Life Projects and The Conditions for Development." In *Culture, Economy and Governance in Aboriginal Australia: Proceedings of a Workshop Held at the University of Sydney*, 30 November–1 December 2004, edited by D.J. Austin-Broos, G. Macdonald. Sydney, Australia: Sydney University Press. Retrieved August 18, 2017 (https://books.google.com/books?isbn=192089 8204).

Pettigrew, Thomas F., and Linda R. Tropp. 2006. "A Meta-Analytic Test of Intergroup Contact Theory." *Journal of Personality and Social Psychology* 90:751–783. doi: 10.1037/0022-3514.90.5.751.

Pettigrew, Thomas F., Linda R. Tropp, Ulrich Wagner, and Oliver Christ. 2011. "Recent Advances in Intergroup Contact Theory." *International Journal of Intercultural Relations* 35: 271–280.

Pettigrew, Thomas, Ulrich Wagner, and Oliver Christ. 2007. "Who Opposes Immigration? Comparing German and North American Findings." *Du Bois Review* 4:19–39.

Pettigrew, Thomas. 1958. "Personality and Sociocultural Factors in Intergroup Attitudes: A Cross-National Comparison." *Journal of Conflict Resolution* 2:29–42.

_____. 1971. *Racially Separate or Together?* New York: McGraw-Hill.

_____. 1980. "Prejudice.' pp. 820–829 in *Harvard Encyclopedia of American Ethnic Groups*, edited by S. Thernstrom, A. Orlov, and O. Handlin. Cambridge, MA: Harvard University Press.

_____. 1998. "Intergroup Contact Theory." *Annual Review of Psychology* 49:65–85.

Pettit, Becky, and Bruce Western. 2004. "Mass Imprisonment and the Life Course: Race and Class Inequality in U.S. Incarceration." *American Sociological Review* 69:151–169.

Pettit, Emily J. 2015. "Aborigines' Dreaming or Britain's Terra Nullius: Perceptions of Land Use in Colonial Australia." *The Iowa Historical Review* 5(1):23–60. Retrieved August 18, 2017 (http://ir.uiowa.edu/cgi/viewcontent.cgi?article=1030&context=iowa-historical-review).

Pew Charitable Trust. 2008. *One in 100: Behind Bars in America 2008.* (http://www.pewtrusts.org/uploadedFiles/wwwpewtrustsorg/Reports/sentencing_and_corrections/one_in_100.pdf).

Pew Hispanic Center. 2004. *Survey Brief: Assimilation and Language.* Washington, DC: Author. (http://pewhispanic.org/files/factsheets/11.pdf).

_____. 2005. *Hispanics: A People in Motion.* Washington, DC: Author. (http://pewhispanic.org/files/reports/40.pdf).

_____. 2013. *A Nation of Immigrants: A Portrait of the 40 Million, Including 11 Million Unauthorized.* Washington, DC: Author. (http://www.pewhispanic

.org/files/2013/01/statistical_portrait_final_jan_29.pdf).

Pew Research Center. 2007. *Muslim Americans: Middle Class and Mostly Mainstream*. Washington, DC: Author. (http://pewresearch.org/assets/pdf/muslim-americans.pdf).

_____. 2011. *Muslim Americans: No Signs of Growth in Alienation or Support for Extremism*. Washington, DC: Author. (http://www.people-press.org/files/legacy-pdf/Muslim%20American%20Report%2010-02-12%20fix.pdf).

_____. n.d. *About Pew Research Center*. Washington, DC: Author. Retrieved August 16, 2017. (http://www.pewresearch.org/about/).

_____. 2012. *The Rise of Intermarriage. Chapter 4: Public Attitudes on Intermarriage*. Washington, DC: Author. Retrieved August 9, 2017 (http://www.pewsocialtrends.org/2012/02/16/chapter-4-public-attitudes-on-intermarriage/).

_____. 2013a. *A Survey of LGBT Americans Attitudes, Experiences and Values in Changing Times*. Washington, DC: Pew Research Center, June 13.(http://www.pewsocialtrends.org/files/2013/06/SDT_LGBT-Americans_06-2013.pdf).

_____. 2013b. *Growing Support for Gay Marriage: Changed Minds and Changing Demographics*. Washington, DC: Author. (http://www.people-press.org/2013/03/20/growing-support-for-gay-marriage-changed-minds-and-changing-demographics).

_____. 2013c. *The Global Divide on Homosexuality*. Washington, DC: Author. (http://www.pewglobal.org/files/2013/06/Pew-Global-Attitudes-Homosexuality-Report-FINAL-JUNE-4-2013.pdf).

_____. 2013d. *The Rise of Asian Americans*. Washington, DC: Author. Retrieved August 30, 2017 (http://www.pewsocialtrends.org/2012/06/19/the-rise-of-asian-americans/).

_____. 2014a. "Mexican President Peña Nieto's Ratings Slip." (http://www.pewglobal.org/2014/08/26/mexican-president-pena-nietos-ratings-slip-with-economic-reform/).

_____. 2014b. *The Party of Nonvoters*. Washington, DC: Author. Retrieved August 9, 2017 (http://www.people-press.org/2014/10/31/the-party-of-nonvoters-2/).

_____. 2014c. *The Shifting Religious Identity of Latinos in the United States*. Washington, DC: Author. (http://www.pewforum.org/2014/05/07/the-shifting-religious-identity-of-latinos-in-the-united-states/).

_____. 2015a. *Multiracial in America Proud, Diverse and Growing in Numbers*. Washington, DC: Author, June 11. (http://www.pewsocialtrends.org/2015/06/11/multiracial-in-america/)

_____. 2015b. *The Many Dimensions of Hispanic Racial Identity*. Washington, DC: Author, June 11. (http://www.pewsocialtrends.org/2015/06/11/chapter-7-the-many-dimensions-of-hispanic-racial-identity/#fn-20523-48).

_____. 2016a. "On Views of Race and Inequality, Blacks and Whites are Worlds Apart." Retrieved July 20, 2017 (http://www.pewsocialtrends.org/2016/06/27/1-demographic-trends-and-economic-well-being/).

_____. 2016b. Vast Majority of Americans know Someone Who is Gay, Fewer Know Someone Who is Transgender. Washington, DC: Author. (http://www.pewforum.org/2016/09/28/5-vast-majority-of-americans-know-someone-who-is-gay-fewer-know-someone-who-is-transgender/).

_____. 2016c. *Where the Public Stands of Religious Liberty vs. Nondiscrimination*. Washington, DC: Pew Research Center, June 13. (http://www.pewforum.org/2016/09/28/5-vast-majority-of-americans-know-someone-who-is-gay-fewer-know-someone-who-is-transgender/).

_____. 2017a. *Americans Express Increasingly Warm Feelings Toward Religious Groups*. Washington, DC: Author. Retrieved August 30, 2017 (http://www.pewforum.org/2017/02/15/americans-express-increasingly-warm-feelings-toward-religious-groups/).

_____. 2017b. *Support for Same Sex Marriage Grows, Even Among Groups That Had Been Skeptical*. Washington, DC: Author, June 26. (http://www.people-press.org/2017/06/26/support-for-same-sex-marriage-grows-even-among-groups-that-had-been-skeptical/).

_____. 2017c. *U.S. Muslims Concerned About Their Place in Society, but Continue to Believe in the American Dream*. Washington, DC: Author, July 26. Retrieved August 30, 2017 (http://assets.pewresearch.org/wp-content/uploads/sites/11/2017/07/25171611/U.S.-MUSLIMS-FULL-REPORT.pdf).

Pfaelzer, Jean. 2008. *Driven Out: The Forgotten War against Chinese Americans*. Berkeley: University of California Press.

Phillips, Dave. 2017a. "Second Judge Blocks Trump's Transgender Ban in the Military." *New York Times*, Nov. 21. (https://www.nytimes.com/2017/11/21/us/transgender-ban-military.html).

_____. 2017b. "Judge Blocks Trump's Ban on Transgender Troops in Military." *New York Times*, Oct. 30. (https://www.nytimes.com/2017/10/30/us/military-transgender-ban.html).

Phillips, Ulrich. 1918. *American Negro Slavery: A Survey of the Supply, Employment, and Control of Negro Labor as Determined by the Plantation Regime*. New York: Appleton.

Pilgrim, David. 2007. "Irene Morgan v. Commonwealth of Virginia." Retrieved August 9, 2017. (http://www.ferris.edu/jimcrow/question/dec07/index.htm).

Pincus, Fred. 2011. *Understanding Diversity: An Introduction to Class, Race, Gender, Sexual Orientation, and Disability*. 2nd ed. Boulder, CO: Lynne Rienner Press.

Pippert, Wesley. 1983. "Detainment Cost Japanese-Americans Upto $6.2 Billion." *UPI*, June 15. Retrieved August 26, 2017 (http://www.upi.com/Archives/1983/06/15/Detainment-cost-Japanese-Americans-up-to-62-billion/7203424497600/).

Pitt, Leonard. 1970. *The Decline of the Californios: A Social History of the Spanish-Speaking Californians, 1846–1890*. Berkeley, CA: University of California Press.

Plessy v. Ferguson, 163 U.S. 537 (1896).

Pollard, Kelvin, and William O'Hare. 1999. "America's Racial and Ethnic Minorities." *Population Bulletin* 54(3): 29–39.

Population Reference Bureau. 2014. *2014 World Population Data Sheet*. Washington, DC: Author. (http://www.prb.org/Publications/Datasheets/2014/2014-world-population-data-sheet/data-sheet.aspx).

_____. 2017. *World Population Data Sheet*. Washington, DC: Author. (http://www.prb.org/Publications/Datasheets/2017/2017-world-population-data-sheet.aspx).

Porter, Eduardo. 2005. "Illegal Immigrants Are Bolstering Social Security With Billions." *New York Times*, April 5, p. A1.

Portes, Alejandro. 1990. "From South of the Border: Hispanic Minorities in the United States." pp. 160–184 in *Immigration Reconsidered*, edited by V. Yans-McLaughlin. New York: Oxford University Press.

Portes, Alejandro, Juan Clark, and Robert Bach. 1977. "The New Wave: A Statistical Profile of Recent Cuban Exiles to the United States." *Cuban Studies* 7(1):1–32.

Portes, Alejandro, and Robert L. Bach. 1985. *Latin Journey: Cuban and Mexican Immigrants in the United States.* Berkeley, CA: University of California Press.

Portes, Alejandro, and Robert Manning. 1986. "The Immigrant Enclave: Theory and Empirical Examples." Pp. 47–68 in *Competitive Ethnic Relations*, edited by S. Olzak, and J. Nagel. New York: Academic Press.

Portes, Alejandro, and Rubén Rumbaut. 1996. *Immigrant America: A Portrait.* 2nd ed. Berkeley, CA: University of California Press.

_____. 2001. *Legacies: The Story of the Immigrant Second Generation.* New York: Russell Sage Foundation.

Portes, Alejandro, and Steven Shafer. 2006. *Revisiting the Enclave Hypothesis: Miami Twenty-Five Years Later* (Working Paper No. 06-10). Princeton, NJ: Center for Migration and Development, Princeton University. (https://www.princeton.edu/cmd/working-papers/papers/wp0610.pdf).

Portland State University. n.d. "Iroquois Man." Retrieved August 18, 2017 (https://www.pdx.edu/iroquois-democracy/iroquois-man).

Posadas, Barbara. 1999. *The Filipino Americans.* Westport, CT: Greenwood.

Potok, Mark. 2013. "The Year in Hate and Extremism." *Southern Poverty Law Center.* (http://www.splcenter.org/home/2013/spring/the-year-in-hate-and-extremism.

Potter, George. 1973. *To the Golden Door: The Story of the Irish in Ireland and America.* Westport, CT: Greenwood.

Poushter, Jacob. 2016. "European Opinions of the Refugee Crisis in 5 Charts." September 16. (http://www.pewresearch.org/fact-tank/2016/09/16/european-opinions-of-the-refugee-crisis-in-5-charts/).

Powers, Daniel, and Christopher Ellison. 1995. "Interracial Contact and Black Racial Attitudes: The Contact Hypothesis and Selectivity Bias." *Social Forces* 74:205–226.

Powlishta, Kimberly K., Lisa A. Serbin, Anna Beth Doyle, and Donna R. White. 1994. "Gender, Ethnic, and Body-Type Biases: The Generality of Prejudice in Childhood." *Developmental Psychology* 30:526–537.

Prabhala, Achal. 2014. "The Whitening of Neymar: How Color Is Lived In Brazil." Retrieved August 13, 2017 (http://deadspin.com/the-whitening-of-neymar-how-color-is-lived-in-brazil-1601716830).

Price, Tom. 2010. "What is Spanglish? The Phenomenon of Code-Switching and Its Impact Amongst US Latinos." *Début: The Undergraduate Journal of Languages, Linguistics and Area Studies* 1(1). (www.llas.ac.uk/debut).

Prois, Jessica. 2013. "Child Marriage on Rise as Global Crises Increase, New Study Says." *Huffington Post*, March 8. (http://www.huffingtonpost.com/2013/03/08/child-marriage-international-womens-day_n_2838421.html).

Protect Our Defenders. 2017. "Facts on United States Military Sexual Violence." (http://www.protectourdefenders.com/factsheet/).

Puzo, Mario. 1993. "Choosing a Dream: Italians in Hell's Kitchen." Pp. 56–57 in *Visions of America*, edited by W. Brown and A. Ling. New York: Persea.

Qian, Zhenchao, and Daniel Lichter. 2011. "Changing Patterns of Interracial Marriage in a Multiracial Society." *Journal of Marriage and Family* 75:1065–1084.

Quaid, Libby. 2008. "Math Class is Tough" No More: Girls' Skill Now Equal to Boys." *USA Today*, July 25. (http://usatoday30.usatoday.com/tech/science/mathscience/2008-07-24-girls-math-skills_N.htm).

Quast, Lisa. 2012. "Thin Is In for Executive Women: How Weight Discrimination Contributes to the Glass Ceiling." *Forbes*, August 6. (http://www.forbes.com/sites/lisaquast/2012/08/06/thin-is-in-for-executive-women-as-weight-discrimination-contributes-to-glass-ceiling/).

Quigley, Mike. 2013. "The Rights of our Daughters: Fighting for Global Reproductive Health." *Huffington Post*, November 1. (http://www.huffingtonpost.com/mike-quigley/reproductive-rights_b_4181828.html).

Quillian, Lincoln, and Mary Campbell. 2003. "Beyond Black and White: The Present and Future of Multiracial Friendship Segregation." *American Sociological Review* 68:540–567.

Quillian, Lincoln. 2006. "New Approaches to Understanding Racial Prejudice and Discrimination." *Annual Review of Sociology* 32:299–328.

Quinones, Sam. 2007. *Antonio's Gun and Delfino's Dream: True Tales of Mexican Migration.* Albuquerque, NM: University of New Mexico Press.

Quiros, Laura. 2009. "The Social Construction of Racial and Ethnic Identity Among Women of Color from Mixed Ancestry: Psychological Freedoms and Sociological Constraints." PhD dissertation, Social Welfare, City University of New York, New York. (http://academicworks.cuny.edu/cgi/viewcontent.cgi?article=2996&context=gc_etds).

Raabe, Tobias, and Andreas Beelman. 2011. "Development of Ethnic, Racial, and National Prejudice in Childhood and Adolescence: A Multinational

Meta-Analysis of Age Differences." *Child Development* 82(6): 1715–1737.

Rader, Benjamin G. 1983. *American Sports: From the Age of Folk Games to the Age of Spectators.* Englewood Cliffs, NJ: Prentice Hall.

Rastogi, Sonya, Tallese Johnson, Elizabeth Hoeffel, and Malcolm Drewery. 2011. *The Black Population, 2010.* Washington, DC: U.S. Census Bureau. (http://www.census.gov/prod/cen2010/briefs/c2010br-06.pdf).

Ray, Nicholas. 2006. *Lesbian, Gay, Bisexual And Transgender Youth: An Epidemic Of Homelessness.* New York: National Gay and Lesbian Task Force Policy Institute and the National Coalition for the Homeless.

Raymer, Patricia. 1974. "Wisconsin's Menominees: Indians on a Seesaw." *National Geographic,* August, pp. 228–251.

Reagan, Timothy. 2018. *Non-Western Educational Traditions: Local Approaches to Thought and Practice.* 4th ed. New York: Taylor and Francis.

Read, Jen'nan Ghazal. 2004. "Cultural Influences on Immigrant Women's Labor Force Participation: The Arab-American Case." *International Migration Review* 38:52–77.

Reaney, Patricia. 2010. "Informal Work Networks New Form of Inequality: Study." *Reuters,* August 16. (http://www.reuters.com/article/2010/08/16/us-women-work-networks-idUSTRE67F49820100816).

Rebecca M. Blank, Marilyn Dabady, and Constance F. Citro, eds. Committee on National Statistics. Division of Behavioral and Social Sciences and Education. 2004. "Measuring Racial Discrimination." *Panel on Methods for Assessing Discrimination.* Committee on National Statistics, Division of Behavioral and Social Sciences and Education. Retrieved August 30, 2017 (https://www.nap.edu/read/10887/chapter/1).

Reich, Michael. 1986. "The Political-Economic Effects of Racism." Pp. 381–388 in *The Capitalist System: A Radical Analysis of American Society.* 3rd ed., edited by R. Edwards, M. Reich, and T. Weisskopf. Englewood Cliffs, NJ: Prentice Hall.

Reichard, Raquel. 2017. "Latino/a vs. Latinx vs. Latine: Which Word Best Solves Spanish's Gender Problem?" *Latina,* March 30. Retrieved August 9, 2017 (http://www.latina.com/lifestyle/our-issues/latinoa-latinx-latine-solving-spanish-genderproblem?utm_source=social_share&utm_medium=twitter&utm_campaign=social_share&page=9,1).

Reid, Michael. 2014. *Brazil: The Troubled Rise of a Global Power.* New Haven, CT: Yale University Press.

Reilly, Ryan J. 2013. "Gay Veterans' Spouses Still Can't Get Benefits." *Huffington Post,* August 27. (http://www.huffingtonpost.com/2013/08/27/gay-veterans_n_3825093.html).

Remington, Robin Alison. 1997. "Ethnonationalism and the Disintegration of Yugoslavia." Pp. 261–280 in *Global Convulsions,* edited by W. Van Horne. Albany: SUNY Press.

Reséndez, Andrés. 2016. *The Other Slavery: The Uncovered Story of Indian Enslavement in America.* Boston, MA: Houghton Mifflin Harcourt.

Reuters. 2017. "Sexual Assault Reports in U.S. Military Reach Record High: Pentagon." *NBC,* May 1. (https://www.nbcnews.com/news/us-news/sexual-assault-reports-u-s-military-reach-record-high-pentagon-n753566).

Reyes, Raul A. 2016. "Are you Latinx? As Usage Grows, Word Draws Approval, Criticism." *NBC,* September 29. (http://www.nbcnews.com/news/latino/are-you-latinx-usage-grows-word-draws-approval-criticism-n651396).

Reyna, Christine, Ovidiu Dobria, and Geoffrey Wetherell. 2013. "The Complexity and Ambivalence of Immigration Attitudes: Ambivalent Stereotypes Predict Conflicting Attitudes Toward Immigration Policies." *Cultural Diversity and Ethnic Minority Psychology* 19:342–356.

Reynolds, Henry. 2000. *Why Weren't We Told?: A Personal Search for the Truth About Our History.* Melbourne, Australia: Penguin.

_____. 2006. *The Other Side of the Frontier: Aboriginal Resistance to the European Invasion of Australia.* Sydney, Australia: University New South Wales Press. Retrieved August 18, 2017 (https://books.google.com/books?isbn=1742240496).

Ricci v. DeStefano, 557 U.S. (2009).

Rich, Adrienne. 1980. "Compulsory Heterosexuality and Lesbian Existence." *Signs: Journal of Women in Culture and Society* 5:631–660.

Richardson, Christopher M., and Ralph E. Luker. 2014. *Historical Dictionary of the Civil Rights Movement.* Lanham, MD: Rowman & Littlefield.

Ridgeway, Cecilia. 2011. *Framed by Gender: How Gender Inequality Persists in the Modern World.* New York: Oxford University Press.

Rifkin, Jeremy. 1996. *The End of Work: The Decline of the Global Labor Force and the Dawn of the Post-Market Era.* New York: Putnam.

Risério, Antonio. 2007. *The Brazilian Utopia and the Black Movements.* San Paolo, Brazil.

Robbins, Liz. 2017. "Number of DACA Applications Stuck in the Mail Tops 900." *New York Times,* November 30. (https://www.nytimes.com/2017/11/30/nyregion/daca-applications-immigrants.html).

Roberts v. Clark Cnty. Sch. Dist. n.d. (https://casetext.com/case/roberts-v-clark-cnty-sch-dist-5).

Roberts, D. 1997. *Killing the Black Body: Race, Reproduction and the Meaning of Liberty.* New York: Vintage Books.

Robertson, Claire. 1996. "Africa and the Americas? Slavery and Women, the Family, and the Gender Division of Labor." Pp. 4–40 in *More Than Chattel: Black Women and Slavery in the Americas,* edited by D. Gaspar, and D. Hine. Bloomington, IN: Indiana University Press.

Robles, Frances. 2017. "23% of Puerto Ricans Vote in Referendum, 97% of Them for Statehood." *The New York Times,* June 11. (https://www.nytimes.com/2017/06/11/us/puerto-ricans-vote-on-the-question-of-statehood.html?_r=0).

Rock, Chris (Producer). 2009. *Good Hair.* HBO Films.

Rockquemore, Kerry Ann, and David Brunsma. 2008. *Beyond Black: Biracial*

Identity in America.
2nd ed. Lanham, MD:
Rowman & Littlefield.

Rodriguez, Arturo. 2011.
"UFW Written Statement
on House Judiciary
Subcommittee on
Immigration Policy and
Enforcement Hearing on
'The H-2A Visa Program—
Meeting the Growing Needs
of American Agriculture?'"
(http://ufwfoundation.org/_
cms.php?mode=view&b_
code=00300200000
0000&b_no=8777&
page=14&field=&key=
&n=717).

Rodriguez, Clara. 1989.
*Puerto Ricans: Born in the
USA.* Boston, MA: Unwin-
Hyman.

_____. 2010. "Parent-Child
Aggression: Association
with Child Abuse Potential
and Parenting Styles."
Violence and Victims
25:728–741.

Rodriguez, Clara, and Hector
Cordero-Guzman. 1992.
"Placing Race in Context."
Ethnic and Racial Studies
15:523–542.

Rodriguez, Junius P. 1997.
*The Historical Encyclo-
pedia of World Slavery.*
Vol. 1. Santa Barbara,
CA: ABC-CLIO. Retrieved
August 6, 2017 (https://
books.google.com/
books?isbn=08743
68855).

Rodriguez, Luis. 1993. *Always
Running: La Vida Loca.*
New York: Touchstone
Books.

Roe v. Wade, 410 U.S. 113
(1973).

Rojas, Leslie Berestein.
2011. "The Forgotten
History of the Filipino
Laborers Who Worked with
Cesar Chavez." *Southern
California Public Radio
(SCPR)*, April 1. (http://
www.scpr.org/blogs/
multiamerican/2011/04/
01/7203/the-asian-
american-
farm-worker-legacy/-).

Romell, Rick. 2012.
"Shooter's Odd Behavior
Did Not Go Unnoticed."
*Milwaukee Journal-
Sentinel*, August 6.
Retrieved July 29, 2017
(http://archive.jsonline
.com/news/crime/shooter-
wade-page-was-army-
vet-white-supremacist-
856cn28-165123946
.html/).

Roosevelt, Theodore. 1906.
"Message Regarding the
State of Puerto
Rico." *Miller Center*,
December 11. (https://
millercenter
.org/the-presidency/
presidential-speeches/
december-11-1906-
message-regarding-state-
puerto-rico).

_____. 1914. "Brazil and
the Negro." *Outlook*. New
York: Outlook Publishing
Company, Inc. Retrieved
August 13, 2017 (http://
www.unz.org/Pub/Outlook-
1914feb21-00409).

The Root. 2016. "Misty
Copeland, Top 100." *The
Root*. Retrieved August 8,
2017 (http://onehundred.
theroot.com/facewall/
the-root-100-2016/#misty-
copeland).

Roper Center. 2012. "U.S.
Elections: How Groups
Voted in 2012." (http://
www.ropercenter.uconn
.edu/elections/how_groups_
voted/voted_12.html).

Rosales, F. Arturo. 1997.
*Chicano! The History of
the Mexican American
Civil Rights Movement.*
Houston, TX: Arte Publico
Press.

Roscoe, Will. 1991. *The Zuni
Man-Woman.* Albuquerque,
NM: University of New
Mexico Press.

_____. 2014. "Native
American Two Spirits at
National Historic Sites."
Retrieved August 18, 2017
(http://www.willsworld.org/
Roscoe-2SpiritAtNational
HistoricSites.pdf).

Rose, Margaret. 1990.
"Traditional and
Nontraditional Patterns
of Female Activism in the
United Farm Workers of
America, 1962 to 1980."
*Frontiers: A Journal of Women
Studies* 11(1):26–32.

Rosenblatt, Kalhan, and
Corky Siemaszko. 2017.
"Confederate Flag
Raised at South Carolina
Statehouse in Protest by
Secessionist Party." *NBC*,
July 10. Retrieved
August 12, 2017
(http://www.nbcnews
.com/news/us-news/
confederate-flag-rises-
south-carolina-statehouse-
protest-secessionist-
party-n781331).

Rosenblum, Karen E., and
Toni-Michelle C. Travis.
2002. *The Meaning of
Difference: American
Constructions of Race,
Sex and Social Class,
and Sexual Orientation.*
3rd ed. New York:
McGraw-Hill.

Rosenfield, Michael. 2002.
"Measures of Assimilation
in the Marriage Market:
Mexican Americans
1970–1990." *Journal of
Marriage and the Family*
64:152–163.

Rosich, Katherine. 2007.
*Race, Ethnicity, and the
Criminal Justice System.*
Washington, DC: American
Sociological Association.
(http://www.asanet.org/
images/press/docs/pdf/
ASARaceCrime.pdf).

Rotella, Sebastian. 1994.
"The Melding Americas:
'Spanglish' Mirrors Hybrid
Culture on U.S.-Mexican
Border: The Incursion of
English Into Spanish Has
Been Driven by Television
and Migration." *Los
Angeles Times*, September
27. (http://articles.latimes
.com/1994-09-27/news/wr-
43707_1_mexican-border-
cities).

Rothstein, Richard. 2014.
"Modern Segregation."
Economic Policy Institute,
March 6. Retrieved June 7,
2017 (http://www.epi
.org/publication/modern-
segregation/).

_____. 2017. *The Color of
Law: A Forgotten History
of How Our Government
Segregated America.* New
York: Liveright Publishing
Corporation. Retrieved
August 10, 2017 (https://
books.google.com/books?
isbn=1631492861).

Rouse, Linda, and Jeffery
Hanson. 1991. "American
Indian Stereotyping,
Resource Competition, and
Status-Based Prejudice."
*American Indian Culture
and Research Journal*
15:1–17.

Royster, Deirdre. 2003. *Race
and the Invisible Hand:
How White Networks
Exclude Black Men From
Blue-Collar Jobs.* Berkeley,
CA: University of California
Press.

Rumbaut, Rubén. 1991.
"Passage to America:
Perspectives on the
New Immigration."
Pp. 208–244 in *America
at Century's End*, edited
by A. Wolfe. Berkeley, CA:
University of California
Press.

Rupp, Leila J., and Verta
Taylor. 1987. *Survival
in the Doldrums: The
American Women's Rights
Movement 1945–1960.*
New York: Oxford
University Press.

Rusin, Sylvia, Jie Zong, and
Jeanne Batalova. 2015.
"Cuban Immigrants in the
United States."
Migration Policy Institute,
April 7. Retrieved
January 12 (http://www
.migrationpolicy.org/article/
cuban-immigrants-united-
states).

Russell, Carrie A. 2010.
"Reckoning with a Violent
and Lawless Past: A
Study of Race, Violence
and Reconciliation
in Tennessee." PhD
Dissertation, Department of
Social Science, Vanderbilt
University, Nashville,
TN. (http://etd
.library.vanderbilt.edu/
available/etd-07262010-

142217/unrestricted/CarrieRussellDissertation.pdf).

Russell, James W. 1994. *After the Fifth Sun: Class and Race in North America.* Englewood Cliffs, NJ: Prentice Hall. Retrieved January 12, 2017. (http://www.migrationpolicy.org/article/cuban-immigrants-united-states).

Rustin, Bayard. 1942. "Non-Violence vs. Jim Crow." *Fellowship.* Reprinted in C. Carson, D.J. Garrow, and B. Kovach. 2003. *Reporting Civil Rights: American Journalism, 1941–1963. Library of America.* Pp. 15–18.

_____. 1947. "Twenty-two Days on the Chain Gang at Roxboro, North Carolina." Retrieved June 13, 2017 (http://documents.law.yale.edu/sites/default/files/Official-report-chain-gang.pdf).

Ryan, Caitlin, David Huebner, Rafael Diaz, and Jorge Sanchez. 2009. "Family Rejection as a Predictor of Negative Health Outcomes in White and Latino Lesbian, Gay, and Bisexual Young Adults." *Pediatrics* 123:346–352.

Saad, Lydia. 2010. "Americans Value Both Aspects of Immigration Reform." *Gallup Politics.* (http://www.gallup.com/poll/127649/Americans-Value-Aspects-Immigration-Reform.aspx).

Saad, Lydia. 2013. "Americans More Pro-Immigration Than in the Past." *Gallup Politics.* (http://www.gallup.com/poll/163457/americans-pro-immigration-past.aspx).

Sadker, David, and Karen Zittleman. 2009. *Still Failing at Fairness: How Gender Bias Cheats Girls and Boys in School and What We Can Do About It.* New York: Simon & Schuster.

Sadler, Anne G., Brenda M. Booth, Brian L. Cook, and Bradley N. Doebbeling. 2003. "Factors Associated with Women's Risk of Rape in the Military Environment." *American Journal of Industrial Medicine* 43(3):262–273. doi:10.1002/ajim.10202.

Saenz, Rogelio. 2005. *The Social and Economic Isolation of Urban African Americans.* Washington, DC: Population Reference Bureau.

Sammon, Alexander. 2016. "A History of Native Americans Protesting the Dakota Access Pipeline." *Mother Jones,* September 9. Retrieved August 18, 2017 (http://www.motherjones.com/environment/2016/09/dakota-access-pipeline-protest-timeline-sioux-standing-rock-jill-stein/).

Salhani, Justin. 2015. "Why People Are Calling Out Cops For Being Racist in Brazil." *ThinkProgress,* September 6. Retrieved July 20, 2017 (https://thinkprogress.org/why-people-are-calling-out-cops-for-being-racist-in-brazil-d26b4dc2076d).

Sanchirico, Andrew. 1991. "The Importance of Small Business Ownership in Chinese American Educational Achievement." *Sociology of Education* 64:293–304.

Sandberg, Sheryl. 2013. *Lean In: Women, Work and the Will to Lead.* New York: Knopf.

Sandfort, T. G. 2005. "Sexual Orientation and Gender: Stereotypes and Beyond." *Archives of Sexual Behavior* 34(6): 595–611.

Santiago, Cassandra, and Doug Criss. "An Activist, a Little Girl and the Heartbreaking Origin of 'Me Too.'" *CNN,* October 18. (http://www.cnn.com/2017/10/17/us/me-too-tarana-burke-origin-trnd/index.html).

Santiago, Charles R. Venator. 2001. "Space, and the Puerto Rican Citizenship." *Denver University Law Review* (http://academic.udayton.edu/race/02rights/PRico02.htm).

Santiago, Esmeralda. 1993. *When I Was Puerto Rican.* Cambridge, MA: De Capo Press.

Santos, Martha S. 2016. "'Slave Mothers,' Partus Sequitur Ventrem, and the Naturalization of Slave Reproduction in Nineteenth-Century Brazil." *Tempo* 22(41):467–487. doi: 10.20509/tem-1980-542x2016v224106.

Sappho and Anne Carson. 2003. *If Not, Winter: Fragments of Sappho.* New York: Vintage.

Sappho and Stanley Lombardo. 2002. *Poems and Fragments.* Cambridge, MA: Hackett.

Sasha M Fountain. 2016. "What is Latinx and AfroLatinx?" August 17. (https://medium.com/heymigente/what-is-latinx-and-afrolatinx-c05a63b5a3d4).

Satter, Beryl. 2009. *Family Properties: Race, Real Estate, and the Exploitation of Black Urban America.* New York: Henry Holt.

Savage, Charles. 2017. "Justice Department to Take on Affirmative Action in College Admissions." *The New York Times,* August 1. Retrieved August 10, 2017 (https://www.nytimes.com/2017/08/01/us/politics/trump-affirmative-action-universities.html).

Savin-Williams, Ritch C. 2001. "A Critique of Research on Sexual Minority Youths." *Journal of Adolescence* 24:5–13.

Sawyer, Nuala. 2017. "Activists Paint Anti-DAPL Mural Outside Wells Fargo." *SFWeekly,* Nov. 6. (http://www.sfweekly.com/news/activists-paint-anti-dapl-mural-outside-wells-fargo/).

Saxton, Alexander. 1966. "Army of Canton in the High Sierra." *Pacific Historical Review* 35(2):141–152.

Sayers, Daniel O., P. Brendan Burke, and Aaron M. Henry. 2007. "The Political Economy of Exile in the Great Dismal Swamp." *International Journal of Historical Archaeology* 11(1): 60–97.

Schachner, Judy. 2003. *Skippy Jon Jones.* New York: Penguin Random House.

Schachter, Ariela. 2016. "From 'Different' to 'Similar' An Experimental Approach to Understanding Assimilation." *American Sociological Review* 81(5):98–1013.

Schafer, John, and Joe Navarro. 2004. "The Seven-Stage Hate Model: The Psychopathology of Hate Groups." *The FBI Law Enforcement Bulletin* 72:1–9.

Schlesinger, Arthur M., Jr. 1992. *The Disuniting of America: Reflections on a Multicultural Society.* New York: Norton.

Schmid, Carol. 2001. *The Politics of Language: Conflict, Identity, and Cultural Pluralism in Comparative Perspective.* New York: Oxford University Press.

Schmidt, von Björn A. 2017. *Visualizing Orientalness: Chinese Immigration and Race in U.S. Motion Pictures, 1910s-1930s.* Retrieved August 26, 2017 (httpss://books.google.com/books?isbn=3412505323).

Schoener, Allon. 1967. *Portal to America: The Lower East Side, 1870–1925.* New York: Holt, Rinehart, & Winston.

Schofield, Janet Ward, Leslie R. M. Hausmann, Feifei Ye, and Rochelle L. Woods. 2010. "Intergroup Friendships on Campus: Predicting Close and Casual Friendships Between White and African American First-Year College Students." *Group Processes and Intergroup Relations* 13:585–602.

Schofield, Matthew. 2013. "Far-Right Hate Crimes Creep Back into German Society." *Miami Herald*, December 24. (http://www.miamiherald.com/2013/12/24/3834799/far-right-hate-crimes-creep-back.html).

Schorr, Daniel. 2008. "A New, 'Post-Racial' Political Era in America." *NPR*. Retrieved August 1, 2017 (http://www.npr.org/templates/story/story.php?storyId=184894).

Schuette v. BAMN, 572 U.S. 12-682 (2014).

Schulman, Michael. 2013. "Generation LGBTQIA." *The New York Times*, January 9. (http://www.nytimes.com/2013/01/10/fashion/generation-lgbtqia.html?_r=0).

Schwartz, Mary Ann, and Barbara Marliene Scott. 1997. *Marriages and Families: Diversity and Change*. 2nd ed. Upper Saddle River, NJ: Prentice Hall.

Schwartzman, Luisa Farah. 2007. "Does Money Whiten? Intergenerational Changes in Racial Classification in Brazil." *American Sociological Review* 72(6):940–963.

Schwarz, A. B. Christa. 2012. *Gay Voices of the Harlem Renaissance*. Bloomington, IN: Indiana University Press.

Sears, David, and P. J. Henry. 2003. "The Origins of Modern Racism." *Journal of Personality and Social Psychology* 85: 259–275.

Sears, David. 1988. "Symbolic Racism." Pp. 53–84 in *Eliminating Racism: Profiles in Controversy*, P. Katz and D. Taylor. New York: Plenum.

Seattle Civil Rights and Labor History Project. "Racially Restrictive Covenants." Retrieved August 26, 2017 (http://depts.washington.edu/civilr/covenants_database.htm).

See, Katherine O'Sullivan, and William J. Wilson. 1988. "Race and Ethnicity." Pp. 223–242 in *Handbook of Sociology*, edited by N.J. Smelser. Newbury Park, CA: Sage.

Sellers, Barney. 2017. "City's Accord with Sanitation Workers a Long-Awaited Victory." *The Commercial*, July 8. Retrieved August 9, 2017 (http://www.commercialappeal.com/story/opinion/2017/07/08/citys-deal-sanitation-workers-huge-win/459324001/).

Selzer, Michael. 1972. *"Kike": Anti-Semitism in America*. New York: Meridian.

Semotiuk, Andy J. 2017. "Illegal Immigrants Flee to Canadian Border as Trump Cracks Down on Immigration in the U.S." *Forbes*, August 12. (https://www.forbes.com/sites/andyjsemotiuk/2017/08/12/illegal-immigrants-flee-to-canadian-border-as-trump-cracks-down-on-immigration-in-the-u-s/#179ff59b715a).

Sen, Rinku, and Fekkah Mamdouh. 2008. *The Accidental American: Immigration and Citizenship in the Age of Globalization*. San Francisco, CA: Berrett-Koehler.

Sengova, John F. 2016. "Gullah." Pp. 139–141 in *African American Folklore: An Encyclopedia for Students*, edited by A. Prahlad. Santa Barbara, CA: ABC-CLIO.

Shaffer, Kirwin R. 2013. *Black Flag Boricuas: Anarchism, Antiauthoritarianism, and the Left in Puerto Rico, 1897–1921*. Champaign, IL: University of Illinois Press.

Shannon, William V. 1964. *The American Irish*. New York: Macmillan.

Shapiro, Thomas, Tatjana Meschede, and Sam Osoro. 2013. *The Roots of the Widening Racial Wealth Gap: Explaining the Black-White Economic Divide*. Waltham, MA: Institute on Assets and Social Policy, Brandeis University. (http://iasp.brandeis.edu/pdfs/Author/shapiro-thomas-m/racialwealthgapbrief.pdf).

Shaughnessy, Larry. 2010. "U.S. Allies Say Integrating Gays in the Military Was Non-Issue." *CNN*, May 20. (http://edition.cnn.com/2010/US/05/19/us.allies.military.gays/).

Sheet Metal Workers v. EEOC, 478 U.S. 421 (1986).

Sherif, Muzafer, O. J. Harvey, B. Jack White, William R. Hood, and Carolyn W. Sherif. 1961. *The Robber's Cave Experiment: Intergroup Conflict and Cooperation*. Norman, OK: University Book Exchange.

Sheth, Manju. 1995. "Asian Indian Americans." Pp. 168–198 in *Asian American: Contemporary Issues and Trends*, edited by P. Gap Min. Thousand Oaks, CA: Sage.

Sigelman, Lee, and Susan Welch. 1993. "The Contact Hypothesis Revisited: Black-White Interaction and Positive Racial Attitudes." *Social Forces* 71:781–795.

Showalter, Brandon. 2017. "Broad Coalition of Evangelicals Releases 'Nashville Statement' on Human Sexuality, Identity." *The Christian Post*, August 30. Retrieved September 3, 2017 (http://www.christianpost.com/news/broad-coalition-of-evangelicals-releases-nashville-statement-on-human-sexuality-identity-197214/).

Siegel, Nathan. 2014. "Dozens of Countries Take in More Immigrants Per Capita Than the U.S." *NPR*, October 29. (http://www.npr.org/2014/10/29/359963625/dozens-of-countries-take-in-more-immigrants-per-capita-than-the-u-s).

Silko, Leslie. 2013. Y*ellow Woman and a Beauty of the Spirit: Essays on Native American Life Today*. New York. Simon & Schuster.

Simmons, Gwendolyn Zoharah. 2011. *Oral history interview conducted by Joseph Mosnier*. Gainesville, FL. Retrieved August 9, 2017 (https://www.loc.gov/item/afc2010039_crhp0049/).

Simon, Julian. 1989. *The Economic Consequences of Immigration*. Cambridge, MA: Blackwell.

Simpson, George, and Milton Yinger. 1985. *Racial and Cultural Minorities: An Analysis of Prejudice and Discrimination*. New York: Plenum.

Simpson, Kelly. 2012. "The Great Migration: Creating a New Black Identity in Los Angeles." *KCET*, February 15. (https://www.kcet.org/history-society/the-great-migration-creating-a-new-black-identity-in-los-angeles).

Singhvi, Anjali and Alicia Parlapiano. 2017. "Trump's Immigration Ban: Who is Barred and Who is Not." *New York Times*, Feb. 3. (https://www.nytimes.com/interactive/2017/01/31/us/politics/trump-immigration-ban-groups.html?mcubz=0).

Skinner, Benjamin. 2008. "A World Enslaved." *Foreign Policy* 165:62–68.

Sklare, Marshall. 1971. *America's Jews*. New York: Random House.

Small, Mario Luis, David J. Harding, and Michèle Lamont. 2010. "Reconsidering Culture and Poverty." *Annals of the American Academy of Political and Social Science* 629:6. (http://ann.sagepub.com/content/629/1/6).

Smedley, Audrey. 2007. *Race in North America: Origin and Evolution of a Worldview*. 3rd ed. Boulder, CO: Westview.

Smith, Andrew F. 2013. *Food and Drink in American History: A "Full Course" Encyclopedia*. Santa Barbara, CA: ABC-CLIO.

Smith, Sara J., Amber M. Axelton, Donald A. Saucier. 2009. "The Effects of Contact on Sexual Prejudice: A Meta-Analysis." *Sex Roles* 61(3–4):178–191. doi: 10.1007/s11199-009-9627-3.

Smith, Barbara. 2000. *Home Girls: A Black Feminist Anthology*. New York: Kitchen Table Women of Color Press. (Original work published in 1983)

Smith, Christopher B. 1994. "Back to the Future: The Intergroup Contact Hypothesis Revisited." *Sociological Inquiry* 64:438–455.

Smith, Irving, III. 2010. Why Black Officers Still Fail. *Parameters* 40(3): 32–47.

Smith, James, and Barry Edmonston, eds. 1997. *The New Americans: Economic, Demographic, and Fiscal Effects of Immigration*. Washington, DC: National Academy Press.

Smith, Kevin, and Wayne Seelbach. 1987. "Education and Intergroup Attitudes: More on the Jackman and Muha Thesis." *Sociological Spectrum* 7:157–170.

Smith, Mitch. 2017. "Standing Rock Protest Camp, Once Home to Thousands, Is Razed." *The New York Times*, February 23. (https://www.nytimes.com/2017/02/23/us/standing-rock-protest-dakota-access-pipeline.html).

Smith, Tom, and Glenn Dempsey. 1983. "The Polls: Ethnic Social Distance and Prejudice." *Public Opinion Quarterly* 47:584–600.

Smithers, Gregory D. 2008. *Science, Sexuality, and Race in the United States and Australia, 1780–1940*. Lincoln, NE: University of Nebraska Press.

Smithsonian National Museum of American History. n.d. "The Promise of Freedom." Retrieved August 10, 2017 (http://americanhistory.si.edu/brown/history/1-segregated/promise-of-freedom.html).

Snipp, C. Matthew. 1989. *American Indians: The First of This Land*. New York: Russell Sage Foundation.

———. 1992. "Sociological Perspectives on American Indians." *Annual Review of Sociology* 18:351–371.

———. 1996. "The First Americans: American Indians." Pp. 390–403 in *Origins and Destinies: Immigration, Race, and Ethnicity in America*, S. Pedraza and R. G. Rumbaut. Belmont, CA: Wadsworth.

Snyder, Christina. 2010. *Slavery in Indian Country: The Changing Face of Captivity in Early America*. Cambridge, MA: Harvard University Press.

Soares, Rachel, Jan Combopiano, Allyson Regis, Yelena Shur, and Rosita Wong. 2010. *2010 Catalyst Census: Fortune 500 Women Board Directors*. New York: Catalyst. (http://catalyst.org/publication/460/2010-catalyst-census-fortune-500-women-board-directors).

Social Science Data Analysis Network. n.d. "Segregation: Dissimilarity Indices." *CensusScope*. (http://www.censusscope.org/us/s40/p75000/chart_dissimilarity.html).

Soennichsen, John. 2011. *The Chinese Exclusion Act of 1882*. Santa Barbara, CA: Greenwood Publishing Group.

Sopel, Jon. 2015. "US Flag Raised over reopened Cuba Embassy in Havana." *BBC*, August 15. (http://www.bbc.com/news/world-latin-america-33919484).

Southern Poverty Law Center. 2010. "Ex-Skinhead Recalls Violent Past." *Intelligence Report* (140). (http://www.splcenter.org/get-informed/intelligence-report/browse-all-issues/2010/winter/dark-angel).

———. 2017a. "Hate Groups Increase for Second Consecutive Year as Trump Electrifies Radical Right." February 15. Retrieved August 30, 2017 (https://www.splcenter.org/news/2017/02/15/hate-groups-increase-second-consecutive-year-trump-electrifies-radical-right).

———. 2017b. Hate Map. Retrieved August 9, 2017. (https://www.splcenter.org/hate-map).

Spicer, Edward H. 1980. "American Indians." pp. 58–122 in *Harvard Encyclopedia of American Ethnic Groups*, edited by S. Thernstrom, A. Orlov, and O. Handlin. Cambridge, MA: Harvard University Press.

Spickard, Paul. 1996. *Japanese Americans: The Formation and Transformations of an Ethnic Group*. New York: Twayne.

Spilde, Katherine, and Jonathan B. Taylor. 2013. "Economic Evidence on the Effects of the Indian Gaming Regulatory Act on Indians and Non-Indians." *UNLV Gaming Research & Review Journal* 17(1): 13–30.

Spilde, Kate. 2001. "The Economic Development Journey of Indian Nations." (http://www.indiangaming.org/library/articles/the-economic-development-journey.shtml).

Stack, Liam. 2016. "In Stanford Rape Case, Brock Turner Blamed Drinking and Promiscuity." *The New York Times*, June 8. (https://www.nytimes.com/2016/06/09/us/brock-turner-blamed-drinking-and-promiscuity-in-sexual-assault-at-stanford.html).

Stainback, Kevin, and Donald Tomaskovic-Devey. 2012. *Documenting Desegregation: Racial and Gender Segregation in Private-Sector Employment Since the Civil Rights Act*. New York: Russell Sage.

Stallard, Karin, Barbara Ehrenreich, and Holly Sklar. 1983. *Poverty in the American Dream: Women & Children First*. New York: South End Press.

Stampp, Kenneth. 1956. *The Peculiar Institution: Slavery in the Antebellum South*. New York: Random House.

Stannard, David E. (1992). *American Holocaust*. New York: Oxford University Press.

Staples, Brent A. 1986. "Black Men and Public Space." *Harper's Magazine* (December). (http://harpers.org/archive/1986/12/black-men-and-public-space/).

Staples, Robert. 1988. "The Black American Family." pp. 303–324 in *Ethnic Families in America*. 3rd ed., edited by C. Mindel, R. Habenstein, and R. Wright. New York: Elsevier.

Statistics Canada. 2017. "Mother Tongue." (http://www12.statcan.gc.ca/census-recensement/2016/dp-pd/dt-td/rp-eng.cfm?

tabid=2&lang=e&
apath=3&detail=0&
dim=0&fl=a&free=0&
gc=0&gk=0&grp=1&
pid=110463&prid=10&
ptype=109445&s=0&
showall=0&sub=0&
temporal=2016&
theme=118&vid=0&
vnamee=&vnamef=).

Statistics South Africa.
2017. "Living Conditions
of Households in South
Africa." p.5 (http://www
.statssa.gov.za/
publications/P0310/
P03102014.pdf).

Stavans, Ilan. 2004.
*Spanglish: The Making of
a New American Language.*
New York: Harper Collins.

Steinberg, Stephen. 1981.
*The Ethnic Myth: Race,
Ethnicity, and Class
in America.* New York:
Atheneum.

Steinberg, Stephen. 2011.
"Poor Reason: Culture Still
Doesn't Explain Poverty."
Boston Review, January
13. (http://www
.bostonreview.net/
steinberg.php).

Steiner, Linda, Fred Fejes,
and Kevin Petrich. 1993.
"Invisibility, Homophobia
and Heterosexism:
Lesbians, Gays and the
Media." *Critical Studies
in Mass Communication*
10(4):395–422. doi:
10.1080/15295039
309366878.

Steinhauer, Jennifer. 2013.
"Sexual Assaults in
Military Raise Alarm in
Washington." *New York
Times,* May 7. (http://www
.nytimes.com/2013/05/08/
us/politics/pentagon-
study-sees-sharp-rise-
in-sexual-assaults.
html?pagewanted=all&_r=0).

Stephens, Alexander H. 1861.
"'Corner Stone' Speech."
Presented on March 21,
Savannah, GA. Retrieved
April 29, 2017 (http://
teachingamericanhistory.
org/library/document/
cornerstone-speech/).

Stephens-Davidowitz, Seth.
2013. "How Many

American Men Are Gay?"
The New York Times,
December 7. (http://www
.nytimes.com/2013/12/08/
opinion/sunday/how-many-
american-men-are-gay.
html?page wanted=all&_
r=0).

Stepick, Alex, Carol Dutton
Stepick, Emmanuel
Eugene, Deborah Teed,
and Yves Labissiere. 2001.
"Shifting Identities and
Intergenerational Conflict:
Growing Up Haitian in
Miami." pp. 229–266 in
*Ethnicities: Children of
Immigrants in America,*
edited by R. Rumbaut and
A. Portes. Berkeley, CA:
University of California
Press.

Stepler, Renee, and Anna
Brown. 2016. "Statistical
Portrait of Hispanics in
the United States." *Pew
Research Center.* (http://
www.pewhispanic
.org/2016/04/19/
statistical-portrait-of-
hispanics-in-the-
united-states-key-
charts/).

Stoddard, Ellwyn. 1973.
Mexican Americans. New
York: Random House.

Stokes, Bruce. 2015. "How
Americans and Japanese
See Each Other."
Washington, DC: Pew
Research Center. Retrieved
July 30, 2017 (http://
www.pewresearch.org/
fact-tank/2015/04/09/how-
americans-and-japanese-
see-each-other/).

Stokes, Bruce. 2016.
"Euroskepticism Beyond
Brexit." *Pew Research
Center,* June 7. (http://
www.pewglobal
.org/2016/06/07/
euroskepticism-beyond-
brexit/#eurefugees).

Stolberg, Sheryl Gay. 2013.
"Prominent Republicans
Sign Brief in Support of
Gay Marriage." *The New
York Times,* February 25.
(http://www.nytimes
.com/2013/02/26/us/
politics/prominent-
republicans-sign-brief-in-

support-of-gay-marriage
.html?pagewanted=all).

Stolberg, Sheryl Gay, and
Brian M. Rosenthal.
2017. "Man Charged After
White Nationalist Rally
in Charlottesville Ends in
Deadly Violence." *The New
York Times,* August 12.
(https://www.nytimes
.com/2017/08/12/us/
charlottesville-protest-
white-nationalist.html).

Stolberg, Sheryl, and Yamiche
Alcindor. 2017. "Trump's
Support for Law to Protect
'Dreamers' Lifts its
Chances." *New York Times,*
September 14. (https://
www.nytimes
.com/2017/09/14/us/
politics/trump-daca-
dreamers.html).

Stoll, Michael. 2004. *African
Americans and the Color
Line.* New York: Russell
Sage Foundation.

Strachey, William, and
Richard Henry Major.
1849. *The Historie of
Travaile into Virginia
Britannia: Expressing
the Cosmographie
and Comodities of the
Country, Together with the
Manners and Customes
of the People.* London:
Hakluyt Society. Retrieved
August 16, 2017 (http://
www.archive.org/stream/
historietravail00majo
goog#page/n134/
mode/1up).

Strother, Logan, Thomas
Ogorzalek, and Spencer
Piston. 2017. "The
Confederate Flag Largely
Disappeared After the Civil
War. The Fight Against
Civil Rights Brought
It Back." *Washington
Post,* June 12. Retrieved
August 12, 2017 (https://
www.washingtonpost.
com/news/monkey-
cage/wp/2017/06/12/
confederate-symbols-
largely-disappeared-after-
the-civil-war-the-fight-
against-civil-rights-brought-
them-back/?hpid=hp_hp-
cards_hp-card-politics
%3Ahomepage%2Fcard).

Stuckey, Sterling. 1987. *Slave
Culture: Nationalist Theory
and the Foundations of
Black America.* New York:
Harper & Row.

Sue, Derald Wing, Jennifer
Bucceri, Annie I. Lin,
Kelvin L. Nadal, and Gina
C. Torino. 2007. "Racial
Microaggressions and the
Asian American Experience."
*Cultural Diversity and
Ethnic Minority Psychology*
13:72–81.

Sullivan, Kirstin Eddings.
2015. "Familiarity,
Religiosity, and
Authoritarianism: The
Acceptability of Gay Rights
and Same-Sex Marriage."
Thesis, Iowa State
University. (http://lib.dr
.iastate.edu/cgi/viewcontent
.cgi?article=5463&
context=etd).

Sumagaysay, Levi, and Martha
Ross. 2017. "As #Metoo
Trends, Here's a List of Sex
Scandals…" *The Mercury
News,* October 16. (http://
www.mercurynews
.com/2017/10/16/as-
metoo-trends-heres-a-list-
of-sex-scandals-in-tech-
and-entertainment/).

Sumner, William G. 1906.
*Folkways: A Study of the
Sociological Importance
of Usages, Manners,
Customs, Mores, and
Morals.* Boston, MA: Ginn
and Company.

Swaine, Thomas, and Richard
S. Nishimoto. 1946. *The
Spoilage.* Berkeley, CA:
University of California
Press.

Swim, Janet, and Laurie
Cohen. 1997. "Overt,
Covert, and Subtle Sexism:
A Comparison Between the
Attitudes Toward Women
and Modern Sexism
Scales." *Psychology of
Women Quarterly* 21:
103–119.

Swim, Janet, Robyn Mallett,
and Charles Stangor.
2004. "Understanding
Subtle Sexism: Detection
and Use of Sexist
Language." *Sex Roles*
51:117–128.

Szirmai, Adam. 2005. *Socio-Economic Development*, 2nd ed. Cambridge, U.K.: Cambridge University Press.

Taffet, David. 2013. "'Heather Has Two Mommies' Author Reflects on 25 Years." *Dallas Voice*, July 26.

Taíno Museum. 2017. "Taino." (http://tainomuseum.org/taino/).

Takaki, Ronald. 1993. *A Different Mirror: A History of Multicultural America*. Boston, MA: Little, Brown.

Takao Ozawa v. United States, 260 U.S. 178 (1922).

Tanenbaum, Leora. 1999. *Slut! Growing Up Female With a Bad Reputation*. New York: Seven Stories Press.

Tannenbaum, Frank. 1947. *Slave and Citizen: The Negro in the Americas*. New York: Knopf.

Taylor, Alan. 2014. "20 Years After the 1994 Cuban Raft Exodus." *The Atlantic*, November 12. (https://www.theatlantic.com/photo/2014/11/20-years-after-the-1994-cuban-raft-exodus/100852/).

Taylor, Dorceta. 2014. *Toxic Communities: Environmental Racism, Industrial Pollution, and Residential Mobility*. New York: New York University Press.

Taylor, Jonathan, and Joseph Kalt. 2005. *American Indians on Reservations: A Databook of Socioeconomic Change Between the 1990 and 2000 Censuses*. Cambridge, MA: The Harvard Project on American Indian Economic Development. (http://www.hks.harvard.edu/hpaied/pubs/documents/AmericanIndianson ReservationsADatabookof Socioeconomic Change.pdf).

Taylor, Paul, D'Vera Cohn, Gretchen Livingston, Cary Funk, and Rick Morin. 2013. *Second Generation Americans: A Portrait of Adult Children of Immigrants*. Washington, DC: Pew Research Center. (http://www.pewsocialtrends.org/files/2013/02/FINAL_immigrant_generations_report_2-7-13.pdf).

Taylor, Paul, Mark Lopez, Jessica Martinez, and Gabriel Velasco. 2012. *When Labels Don't Fit: Hispanics and Their Views of Identity*. Washington, DC: Pew Hispanic Center. (http://www.pewhispanic.org/files/2012/04/PHC-Hispanic-Identity.pdf).

Teen Vogue. "Here's How You Can Help Standing Rock." *Vouge*, November 25, 2016. Retrieved August 18, 2017 (http://www.vogue.com/article/how-you-can-help-standing-rock-donations-dakota-access-pipeline).

Teke, John, and Waleed Navarro. 2016. "Nonimmigrant Admissions to the United States: 2015." Annual Flow Report, Office of Immigration Statistics. (https://www.dhs.gov/sites/default/files/publications/Nonimmigrant_Admissions_2015.pdf).

Telles, Edward E. 2002. "Racial Ambiguity Among the Brazilian Population." *Ethnic & Racial Studies* 25:415–441.

Telles, Edward. 2004. *Race in Another America: The Significance of Skin Color in Brazil*. Princeton, NJ: Princeton University Press.

Telles, Edward, and Vilma Ortiz. 2008. *Generations of Exclusion: Mexican Americans, Assimilation, and Race*. New York: Russell Sage Foundation.

Terkel, Amanda. 2011. "Lawmakers Press Pentagon to Give Veterans' Benefits to Service Members Discharged Under DADT." *Huffington Post*, February 4. (http://www.huffingtonpost.com/2011/02/04/dadt-veterans-benefits-honorable-discharge_n_818555.html).

Terman, Lewis, and Catherine Cox Miles. 1936. *Sex and Personality: Studies in Masculinity*. New York: Russell and Russell.

Theen, Andrew, and Oliver Staley. 2012. "Dartmouth to Create Task Force to Investigate Fraternity Hazing." *Bloomberg*, March 2. (http://www.bloomberg.com/news/2012-03-02/dartmouth-to-create-task-force-to-investigate-fraternity-hazing.html).

Theoharis, Jeanne. 2006. *The Black Power Movement: Rethinking the Civil Rights-Black Power Era*. Pp. 47–49. New York: Routledge.

Theoharis, Jeanne. 2013. *The Rebellious Life of Mrs. Rosa Parks*. Boston, MA: Beacon Press.

_____. 2015. *The Rebellious Life of Mrs. Rosa Parks*. Boston, MA: Beacon Press.

Thernstrom, Stephan, Ann Orlov, and Oscar Handlin, eds. 1980. *Harvard Encyclopedia of American Ethnic Groups*. Pp. 150–160. Cambridge, MA: Harvard University Press.

Thomas, Wesley. 1997. "Navajo Cultural Constructions of Gender and Sexuality." Pp. 156–173 in *Two-spirit People: Native American Gender Identity, Sexuality, and Spirituality*, edited by S.-E. Jacobs, W. Thomas, and S. Lang. Champaign, IL: University of Illinois Press.

Thompson, Becky. 1996. *A Hunger So Wide and So Deep: A Multiracial View of Women's Eating Problems*. Minneapolis, MA: University of Minnesota Press.

Thornton, Russell. 2001. "Trends Among American Indians in the United States." Pp. 135–169 in *America Becoming: Racial Trends and Their Consequences*. Vol. 1, edited by N. Smelser, W. Wilson, and F. Mitchell. Washington, DC: National Academy Press.

Tilly, Charles. 1990. "Transplanted Networks." Pp. 79–95 in *Immigration Reconsidered: History, Sociology, and Politics*, edited by V. Yans-McLaughlin. New York: Oxford University Press.

Tizon, Alex. 2014. *Big Little Man: In Search of My Asian Self*. Boston, MA: Houghton Mifflin Harcourt Publishing.

Tizon, Alex. 2016. "Conversation with Alex Tizon." (http://web.archive.org/web/20161013220455/, http://alextizon.com/big-little-man/)

Toma, Catalina L., and Jeffrey T. Hancock. 2010. "Looks and Lies: The Role of Physical Attractiveness in Online Dating What Makes You Click?" *Communication Research*, 37(3):335–351.

Treuer, Anton. 2012. *Everything You Wanted to Know About Indians But Were Afraid to Ask*. St. Paul, MN: Borealis Books.

Treuer, David. 2012. *Rez Life: An Indian's Journey Through Reservation Life*. New York: Atlantic Monthly Press.

Trevanian. 2005. *The Crazy Ladies of Pearl Street*. New York: Crown Books.

Tribune Wire Reports. 2014. "Riot Erupts Near St. Louis Over Police Shooting of Teen." *Chicago Tribune*, October 11. Retrieved August 10, 2017 (http://www.chicagotribune.com/news/nationworld/chi-missouri-police-shooting-20140810-story.html).

Trotta, Daniel. 2006. "Americans Not Waiting For Manana to Learn Spanish." *redOrbit*, February 15. (http://www.redorbit.com/news/general/393007/

americans_not_waiting_for_maana_to_learn_spanish/#CGuWFcf1J4jaZS79.99).

Tsai, Alexander C., and Atheendar S. Venkataramani. 2015. "The Causal Effect of Education on HIV Stigma in Uganda: Evidence from a Natural Experiment." *Social Science & Medicine* 142:37–46. doi: 10.1016/j.socscimed.2015.08.009.

Tsai, Shih-Shan Henry. 1986. *The Chinese Experience in America*. Bloomington, IN: Indiana University Press.

Tungol, J. R. 2012. "Don't Ask Don't Tell" One-Year Repeal Anniversary: 25 Amazing Moments." *Huffington Post*, September 20. (http://www.huffingtonpost.com/2012/09/20/dont-ask-dont-tell-repeal-anniversary_n_1891519.html).

U.S. Bureau of Labor Statistics. 2013. "Employment Status of the Civilian Non-Institutional Population by Race, Hispanic or Latino Ethnicity, Sex, and Age, Seasonally Adjusted." (http://www.bls.gov/web/empsit/cpseea04.pdf).

———. 2014. "1972–2013: Labor Force Characteristics by Race and Ethnicity." Retrieved July 13, 2017 (http://www.bls.gov/opub/reports/cps/race_ethnicity_2013.pdf).

———. 2015. "Labor Force Characteristics by Race and Ethnicity, 2013." (http://www.bls.gov/opub/reports/cps/race_ethnicity_2013.pdf).

———. 2016. "Employment Status of Civilian Noninstitutionalized Population by Sex, Age, and Race." Retrieved July 13, 2017 (https://www.bls.gov/cps/cpsaat05.pdf).

———. 2017. "Employment Status of Population by Sex, Marital Status and Presence of Children."(https://www.bls.gov/news.release/famee.t05.htm).

U.S. Census Bureau. 1790. *1790 Overview*. Washington, DC: U. S. Bureau of the Census. Retrieved August 3, 1017 (https://www.census.gov/history/www/through_the_decades/overview/1790.html).

———. 1978. *Statistical Abstract of the United States, 1977*. Washington, DC: Author.

———. 1990. "Summary File 3." (http://factfinder2.census.gov/faces/nav/jsf/pages/index.xhtml).

———. 1993. *Statistical Abstract of the United States, 1992*. Washington, DC: Government Printing Office.

———. 1997. *Statistical Abstract of the United States, 1996*. Washington, DC: Government Printing Office.

———. 2000a. "Summary File 1." *Census 2000*. (https://www.census.gov/census2000/sumfile1.html).

———. 2000b. "Summary File 4." *Census 2000*. (https://www.census.gov/census2000/SF4.html).

———. 2002. *Statistical Abstract of the United States, 2001*. Washington, DC: Author.

———. 2004a. "Ancestry." pp. 138–155 in *Census Atlas of the United States*. (http://www.census.gov/population/www/cen2000/censusatlas/pdf/9_Ancestry.pdf).

———. 2004b. "Population by Region, Sex, and Hispanic Origin Type, with Percent Distribution by Hispanic Origin Type, 2004." (http://www.census.gov/population/socdemo/hispanic/ASEC2004/2004CPS_tab19.2.pdf).

———. 2005. *Statistical Abstract of the United States, 2005*. Washington, DC: Author.

———. 2007. *Statistical Abstract of the United States, 2007*. Washington, DC: Author. (http://www.census.gov/compendia/statab/past_years.html).

———. 2008. "1990 Summary Tape File 3." (http://factfinder.census.gov/servlet/DatasetMainPageServlet?_program=DEC&_tabId=DEC2&_submenuId=datasets_1&_lang=en&_ts=222966429406).

———. 2010. *Statistical Abstract of the United States: 2010*. Washington, DC: Author. (http://www.census.gov/compendia/statab/2010/2010edition.html).

———. 2011. *Statistical Abstract of the United States, 2011*. Washington, DC: Author.

———. 2012a. "Most Children Younger Than Age 1 Are Minorities, Census Bureau Reports." News release. (http://www.census.gov/newsroom/releases/archives/population/cb12-90.html).

———. 2012b. *National Population Projections: Summary Tables*. (http://www.census.gov/population/projections/data/national/2012/summarytables.html).

———. 2012c. *Statistical Abstract of the United States, 2012*. Washington, DC: Government Printing Office. (http://www.census.gov/compendia/statab/2012edition.html).

———. 2012d. *2010 Census American Indian and Native Alaska Summary File*. (http://factfinder2.census.gov/faces/nav/jsf/pages/index.xhtml).

———. 2013a. *American Community Survey 3-Year Estimates, 2010–2012*. (http://factfinder2.census.gov/faces/tableservices/jsf/pages/productview.xhtml?pid=ACS_sumfile_2010_2012&prodType=document).

———. 2013b. "Educational Attainment—People 25 Years Old and Over, by Total Money Earnings in 2012, Work Experience in 2012, Age, Race, Hispanic Origin, and Sex (Table PINC-03)." *Current Population Survey*. (http://www.census.gov/hhes/www/cpstables/032013/perinc/pinc03_000.htm).

———. 2013c. "Historical Income Tables: Household." *Current Population Survey*. (http://www.census.gov/hhes/www/income/data/historical/household.

———. 2013d. "Historical Poverty Tables." *Current Population Survey*. (http://www.census.gov/hhes/www/poverty/data/historical/index.html).

———. 2013e. "Household Income Tables." *Current Population Survey*. (http://www.census.gov/hhes/www/cpstables/032013/hhinc/hinc01_000.htm).

———. 2013f. "Selected Characteristics of People 15 Years and Over, by Total Money Income in 2012, Work Experience in 2012, Race, Hispanic Origin, and Sex (Table PINC-01)." *Current Population Survey*. (http://www.census.gov/hhes/www/cpstables/032013/perinc/pinc01_000.htm).

———. 2013g. "Selected Economic Characteristics (Table DP03)." *American Community Survey, 2006–012*. (http://factfinder2.census.gov/faces/tableservices/jsf/pages/productview.xhtml?pid=ACS_10_SF4_DP03&prodType=table).

———. 2014. "Historical Income Tables: People."

Current Population Survey. Table P-36 (http://www.census.gov/hhes/www/income/data/historical/people/).

_____. 2015a. "2014 National Population Projections." Retrieved August 3, 2017 (http://www.census.gov/population/projections/data/national/2014/summarytables.html).

_____. 2015b. "2015 American Community Survey." (https://factfinder.census.gov/faces/tableservices/jsf/pages/productview.xhtml?src=bkmk).

_____. 2015c. "Languages Spoken at Home. American Community Survey, 2009–2013." (https://factfinder.census.gov/faces/tableservices/jsf/pages/productview.xhtml?src=bkmk).

_____. 2015d. "2014 National Population Projections." *Summary Tables* (Table 11). (http://www.census.gov/population/projections/data/national/2014/summarytables.html).

_____. 2015e. "American Community Survey 2015." Retrieved July 20, 2017 (https://factfinder.census.gov/faces/tableservices/jsf/pages/productview.xhtml?pid=ACS_15_1YR_S0201&prodType=table).

_____. 2015f. "American Community Survey, 5-year Estimates." (https://factfinder.census.gov/faces/tableservices/jsf/pages/productview.xhtml?pid=ACS_15_SPT_DP03&prodType=table).

_____. 2015g. "Households by Type and Tenure of Householders for Selected Characteristics (Table H 1)." (http://www.census.gov/hhes/families/data/cps2014H.html).

_____. 2015h. *People Reporting Ancestry.*

Washington DC: American Community. Retrieved August 3, 2017 (https://factfinder.census.gov/faces/tableservices/jsf/pages/productview.xhtml?src=bkmk).

_____. 2015i. "Percent of People 25 Years and Over Who Have Completed High School or College, by Race, Hispanic Origin and Sex." (https://knoema.com/USCBCPSEATB22015/percent-of-people-25-years-and-over-who-have-completed-high-school-or-college-by-race-hispanic-origi).

_____. 2016a. "American Community Survey, 2015." *Comparative Demographic Estimates.* Retrieved April 15, 2017 (https://factfinder.census.gov/faces/tableservices/jsf/pages/productview.xhtml?pid=ACS_15_5YR_CP05&prodType=table).

_____. 2016b. "Table H1: Households by Type and Tenure of Householder for Selected Characteristics, 2016." Retrieved July 14, 2017 (https://www.census.gov/data/tables/2016/demo/families/cps-2016.html).

_____. 2016c. "Table P-36: Historical Income Tables: People, Full-Time Year Round Workers by Median Income and Sex." Retrieved July 14, 2017 (https://www.census.gov/data/tables/time-series/demo/income-poverty/historical-income-people.html).

_____. 2017a. "American Community Survey, 2015, One-year Estimates." (https://factfinder.census.gov/faces/tableservices/jsf/pages/productview.xhtml?src=bkmk).

_____. 2017b. *Educational Attainment in the United States.* Retrieved August 9, 2017 (https://www.census.gov/data/tables/2016/demo/education-attainment/

cps-detailed-tables.html).

_____. 2017c. "Historical Income Tables, Table H-5." Retrieved August 26, 2017 (https://www.census.gov/data/tables/time-series/demo/income-poverty/historical-income-households.html).

_____. 2017d. "Quarterly Residential Vacancies and Home Ownership, Fist Quarter 2017." Retrieved July 20, 2017 (https://www.census.gov/housing/hvs/files/currenthvspress.pdf).

_____. 2017e. "Percent of People 25 years and over who have completed HS or College by Race Hispanic Origin and Sex, Selected Years, 1940–2015, Table A-2." Retrieved July 20, 2017 (https://www.census.gov/data/tables/time-series/demo/educational-attainment/cps-historical-time-series.html).

_____. 2017f. "Selected Characteristics of People 15 Years and Over, by Total Money Income, Work Experience, Race, Hispanic Origin, and Sex." Table PINC-01. (https://www.census.gov/data/tables/time-series/demo/income-poverty/cps-pinc/pinc-01.html#par_textimage_14).

_____. 2017g. "Voting and Registration in the Election of November 2016. Table 4. (https://census.gov/data/tables/time-series/demo/voting-and-registration/p20-580.html).

U.S. Commission on Civil Rights. 1976. *Puerto Ricans in the Continental United States: An Uncertain Future.* Washington, DC: Government Printing Office.

U.S. Commission on Civil Rights. 1992. *Civil Rights Issues Facing Asian Americans in the 1990s.* Washington, DC:

Government Printing Office.

U.S. Congress House of Representatives. *Fair Minimum Wage Act of 2007.* H.R. 2. 110th. (https://www.congress.gov/bill/110th-congress/house-bill/2).

U.S. Department of Education Office for Civil Rights. 2014. "Civil Rights Data Collection." Issue Brief No. 1. Retrieved August 8, 2017 (https://ocrdata.ed.gov/Downloads/CRDC-School-Discipline-Snapshot.pdf).

U.S. Department of Health and Human Services. 2011. *Thirty Years of AIDS.* (http://aids.gov/news-and-events/thirty-years-of-aids).

_____. 2012a. "Yearbook of Immigration Statistics, 2012." (http://www.dhs.gov/yearbook-immigration-statistics-2012-legal-permanent-residents).

_____. 2012b. "Yearbook of Immigration Statistics, 2012." (http://www.dhs.gov/yearbook-immigration-statistics-2012-legal-permanent-residents.

_____. 2013a. "Table 2: Persons Obtaining Legal Permanent Resident Status by Region and Selected Country of Last Residence, 1820–2013. Yearbook of Immigration Statistics, 2013." (http://www.dhs.gov/yearbook-immigration-statistics-2013-lawful-permanent-residents).

_____. 2013b. "Yearbook of Immigration Statistics 2013. Table 1. Persons Obtaining Lawful Permanent Resident Status: Fiscal Years 1820 to 2013." (http://www.dhs.gov/sites/default/files/publications/ois_yb_2013_0.pdf).

_____. 2013c. "Yearbook of Immigration Statistics 2013. Table 2. Persons Obtaining Lawful

Permanent Resident Status by Region and Selected Country of Last Residence: Fiscal Years 1820 to 2013." (http://www.dhs.gov/yearbook-immigration-statistics-2013-lawful-permanent-residents).

_____. 2013d. "Yearbook of Immigration Statistics 2013. Table 3. Persons Obtaining Lawful Permanent Resident Status By Region and Country of Birth: Fiscal Years 2004 to 2013." (http://www.dhs.gov/sites/default/files/publications/ois_yb_2013_0.pdf).

_____. 2014. "Yearbook of Immigration Statistics, 2013. Table 2 Persons Obtaining Lawful Permanent Resident Status by Region and Selected Country of Last Residence: Fiscal Years 1820 to 2013." (http://www.dhs.gov/sites/default/files/publications/ois_yb_2013_0.pdf).

_____.2016. "Yearbook of Immigration Statistics, 2015." Retrieved April 15, 2017 (https://www.dhs.gov/sites/default/files/publications/Yearbook_Immigration_Statistics_2015.pdf).

U.S. Department of Justice Civil Rights Division. 2015. "Investigation of the Ferguson Police Department." Retrieved August 10, 2017 (https://www.courts.mo.gov/file.jsp?id=95274).

U.S. Department of Justice. n.d. "Raising Awareness About Sexual Abuse." (https://www.nsopw.gov/en-US/Education/FactsStatistics?AspxAutoDetectCookieSupport=1).

U.S. Department of Labor. 2014. "Traditional (female-dominated) occupations, 2014 annual averages." (https://www.dol.gov/wb/stats/TraditionalOccupations.pdf).

U.S. Department of Homeland Security. 2009. "Rightwing Extremism: Current Economic and Political Climate Fueling Resurgence in Radicalization and Recruitment." Retrieved August 13, 2017 (https://fas.org/irp/eprint/rightwing.pdf).

U.S. Equal Employment Opportunity Commission. 2017. "EEOC Sues Pizza Studio Restaurant Owner for Violating Equal Pay Act." (https://www.eeoc.gov/eeoc/newsroom/release/9-5-17.cfm).

_____. n.d., "Examples of Court Decisions Supporting Coverage of LGBT-Related Discrimination Under Title VII." (https://www.eeoc.gov/eeoc/newsroom/wysk/lgbt_examples_decisions.cfm).

U.S. Government Accountability Office. 2016. "K-12 Education: Better Use of Information Could Help Agencies Identify Disparities and Address Racial Discrimination." Retrieved July 20, 2017 (http://www.gao.gov/assets/680/676745.pdf).

U.S. Immigration and Naturalization Service. 1993. *Statistical Yearbook of the Immigration and Naturalization Service, 1992.* Washington, DC: Government Printing Office.

_____. 1993. Statistical *Yearbook of the Immigration and Naturalization Service, 1992.* Washington, DC: Author.

U.S. Legislation. "The Act Prohibiting Importation of Slaves of 1807 (2 Stat. 426, enacted March 2, 1807)." Retrieved July 20, 2017 (http://legisworks.org/sal/2/stats/STATUTE-2-Pg426.pdf).

U.S. Office of Juvenile Justice and Delinquency

Prevention. 2015. "Juvenile Arrest Rate Trends." (http://www.ojjdp.gov/ojstatbb/crime/JAR_Display.asp?ID=qa05274).

U.S. Parks Service. "Indian Reservations in the Continental United States." Retrieved January 15, 2017 (https://www.nps.gov/nagpra/DOCUMENTS/ResMAP.HTM).

U.S. v. Windsor, 133 S. Ct. 2675 (2013).

Udry, Richard. 2000. "Biological Limits of Gender Construction." *American Sociological Review* 65:443–457.

United Nations. 1948. *Convention on the Prevention and Punishment of the Crime of Genocide.* New York: United Nations. (http://www.hrweb.org/legal/genocide.html).

_____. 2013. The Millennium Development Goals Report, 2013. New York: United Nations.

_____. 2015. "International Migrant Stock." (http://esa.un.org/migration/).

_____. 2016. "International Migration Report 2015 Highlights." Retrieved August 9, 2017. (http://www.un.org/en/development/desa/population/migration/publications/migrationreport/docs/MigrationReport2015_Highlights.pdf).

United Nations Department of Economic and Social Affairs, Population Division. 2013. "Population Facts (No. 2013/2)." (http://esa.un.org/unmigration/documents/The_number_of_international_migrants.pdf).

United Nations Department of Economic and Social Affairs, Population Division. 2015. "Trends in International Migration, 2015." Population Fact Sheets. (http://www.un.org/en/development/

desa/population/publications/pdf/popfacts/PopFacts_2015-4.pdf).

United Nations Development Programme Human Development Reports. 2016. "Human Development Indicators." (http://hdr.undp.org/en/countries/profiles/MEX).

United Nations Refugee Agency. 2017. "Figures at a Glance." Retrieved August 9, 2017 (http://www.unhcr.org/uk/figures-at-a-glance.html).

United States Congress. 2014. "S.1752 - Military Justice Improvement Act of 2013, 113th Congress (2013-2014)." (https://www.congress.gov/bill/113th-congress/senate-bill/2992/related-bills).

United States Customs and Border Patrol. 2016. "Border Patrol Agent Nationwide Staffing by Fiscal Year." October 1. (https://www.cbp.gov/sites/default/files/assets/documents/2016-Oct/BP%20Staffing20FY1992-FY2016.pdf).

United States Government Accountability Office. 2016. "K-12 Education: Better Use of Information Could Help Agencies Identify Disparities and Address Racial Discrimination." (http://www.gao.gov/assets/680/676745.pdf).

United Steelworkers of America, AFL-CIO-CLC v. Weber, 443 U.S. 193 (1979).

Valentine, Sean, and Gordon Mosley. 2000. "Acculturation and Sex-Role Attitudes Among Mexican Americans: A Longitudinal Analysis." *Hispanic Journal of Behavioral Sciences* 22:104–204.

Varela, Julito. 2011. "The 1917 Jones Act: Puerto Ricans as U.S. Citizens." *Franky Benítez*, January 30. (https://juliorvarela

.com/2011/01/30/the-1917-jones-act-puerto-ricans-as-us-citizens/).

Van Ausdale, Debra, and Joe Feagin. 2001. *The First R: How Children Learn Race and Racism.* Lanham, MD: Rowman & Littlefield.

van den Berghe, Pierre L. 1967. *Race and Racism: A Comparative Perspective.* New York: Wiley.

van den Berghe, Pierre L. 1981. *The Ethnic Phenomenon.* New York: Elsevier.

Van Hook, J. 2010. *The Demographic Impacts of Repealing Birthright Citizenship.* (http://www.migrationpolicy.org/pubs/BirthrightInsight-2010.pdf).

Vargas-Ramos, Carlos. 2012. "Migrating Race: Migration and Racial Identification Among Puerto Ricans." *Ethnic and Racial Studies* 37:383–404. (http://www.mixedracestudies.org/wordpress/?p=22819).

_____. 2005. Vargas-Ramos, Carlos. 2005. Black, Trigueño, White . . . ? Shifting Racial Identification Among Puerto Ricans. *Du Bois Review* 2:267–285.

Vasquez, Jessica M. (2014). "The Whitening Hypothesis Challenged: Biculturalism in Latino and Non-Hispanic White Intermarriage." *Sociological Forum* 29(2):386–407. doi:10.1111/socf.12089.

Veterans Stand For Standing Rock. n.d. (https://www.facebook.com/events/1136540643060285/).

Vicens, A.J. 2016. "Here's What's Happening in the Battle for Voting Rights." *Mother Jones*, August 3. Retrieved June 12, 2017 (http://www.motherjones.com/politics/2016/08/voting-rights-decisions-across-country-update/).

Vincent, Theodore G. 1976. *Black Power and the Garvey Movement.* San Francisco, CA: Ramparts.

Vinje, David. 1996. "Native American Economic Development on Selected Reservations: A Comparative Analysis." *American Journal of Economics and Sociology* 55:427–442.

Vock, Daniel. 2013. "With Little Choice, Alabama Backs Down on Immigration Law." *Stateline*, October 30. Pew Charitable Trusts. (http://www.pewstates.org/projects/stateline/headlines/with-little-choice-alabama-backs-down-on-immigration-law-85899516441).

Von Drehle, David. 2004. *Triangle: The Fire that Changed America.* New York: Grove Press.

von Hippel, William, Lisa A. Silver, and Molly E. Lynch. 2000. "Stereotyping Against Your Will: The Role of Inhibitory Ability in Stereotyping and Prejudice Among the Elderly." *Personality and Social Psychology Bulletin* 26:523–532.

Voting Rights Act, 42 U.S.C. § 1971 (1965).

Wade, Peter. 1997. *Race and Ethnicity in Latin America.* London: Pluto Press. Retrieved August 10, 2017 (https://books.google.com/books?isbn=0745309879).

Wade, Peter. 2008. "Race in Latin America." Pp175–192 in *A Companion to Latin American Anthropology*, edited by D. Poole. Oxford, UK: Blackwell Publishing Ltd.

Wagley, Charles, and Marvin Harris. 1958. *Minorities in the New World: Six Case Studies.* New York: Columbia University Press.

Walker, Alice. 1983. *In Search of Our Mother's Gardens: Womanist Prose.* New York: Harcourt.

_____. 1983/2011. "In Search of Our Mothers' Gardens: Prose." *Open Road Media.* (https://openroadmedia.com/ebook/In-Search-of-Our-Mothers-Gardens/9781453224069).

Wallace, Michael, and Rodrigo Figueroa. 2012. "Determinants of Perceived Immigrant Job Threat in the American States." *Sociological Perspectives* 55:583–612.

Wallace, Walter. 1997. *The Future of Race, Ethnicity, and Nationality.* Westport, CT: Praeger.

Walshe, Shushannah. 2013. "Obama Makes History by Citing Gay Rights in Inaugural Address." *ABC News*, January 21. (http://abcnews.go.com/Politics/obama-makes-history-citing-gay-rights-inaugural-address/story?id=18275341).

Walvin, James. 2011. *A Massacre, the Law and the End of Slavery.* New Haven, CT: Yale University Press.

Wang, Wendy. 2012. *The Rise of Intermarriage: Rates, Characteristics Vary by Race and Gender.* Washington, DC: Pew Research Center. (http://www.pewsocialtrends.org/2012/02/16/the-rise-of-intermarriage).

Ware, Leland. 2013. "'Color Struck': Intragroup and Cross-Racial Color Discrimination." *Connecticut Public Interest Law Journal* 13(1):75–110.

Warren, Kenneth F., eds. 2008. *Encyclopedia of U.S. Campaigns, Elections, and Electoral Behavior.* Thousand Oaks, CA: Sage Publications.

Warren, Tamara. 2011. "Gay Rights vs. Civil Rights." *Black Enterprise*, July 12. (http://www.blackenterprise.com/lifestyle/gay-rights-is-a-civil-rights-issue/).

Warshaw, Robin. 1994. *I Never Called It Rape: The Ms. Report on Recognizing, Fighting and Surviving Date and Acquaintance Rape.* New York: Harper Perennial.

Washington Office on Latin America. 2017. "House Releases Department of Homeland Security Appropriations Bill." July 17. (https://www.wola.org/2017/07/house-releases-department-homeland-security-appropriations-bill/)

Washington, Booker T. 1965. *Up From Slavery.* New York: Dell.

Washington, Reginald. 2005. "Sealing the Sacred Bonds of Holy Matrimony. Freedmen's Bureau Marriage Records." *National Archieves* 37(1). Spring. Retrieved August 10, 2017 (https://www.archives.gov/publications/prologue/2005/spring/freedman-marriage-recs.html).

Waters, Mary, and Tomas R. Jimenez. 2005. "Assessing Immigrant Assimilation: New Empirical and Theoretical Challenges." *American Review of Sociology* 31:105–125.

Waters, Mary. 1990. *Ethnic Options.* Berkeley, CA: University of California Press.

Wax, Murray. 1971. *Indian Americans: Unity and Diversity.* Englewood Cliffs, NJ: Prentice-Hall.

Weeks, Philip. 1988. *The American Indian Experience.* Arlington Heights, IL: Forum.

Weil, Frederick D. 1985. "The Variable Effects of Education on Liberal Attitudes: A Comparative-Historical Analysis of Anti-Semitism Using Public Opinion Survey Data." *American Sociological Review* 50(4):458–474.

Weinberg, Sydney S., Donna Gabaccia, Hasia

R. Diner, and Maxine Schwartz Seller. 1992. "The Treatment of Women in Immigration History: A Call for Change [with Comments and Response]." *Journal of American Ethnic History* 11(4):25–69.

Weitz, Rose, and Leonard Gordon. 1993. "Images of Black Women Among Anglo College Students." *Sex Roles* 28:19–34.

Welcome page. n.d. "Chican@/Latin@ Studies Program at the University of Wisconsin, Madison." (https://chicla.wisc.edu/).

Wellner, Alison. 2007. *U.S. Attitudes Toward Interracial Dating Are Liberalizing.* Washington, DC: Population Reference Bureau. (http://www.prb.org/Publications/Articles/2005/USAttitudesToward InterracialDatingAre Liberalizing.aspx).

Wells, Shawn Alfonso. 1992. "Evolution And Race: Cuban Color Classification and Identity Negotiation: Old Terms In A New World." PhD dissertation, The University of Pittsburgh. (http://d-scholarship.pitt.edu/7737/1/AlfonsoWells_dissertation.pdf).

Welter, Barbara. 1966. "The Cult of True Womanhood: 1820–1860." *American Quarterly*, 18(2):151–174.

Wessell, Thomas R. 1986. "Agriculture, Indians, and American History." Pp.1–9 in *The American Indian: Past and Present.* 3rd ed., edited by R.L. Nichols. New York: Newbury Award Records.

West, Darrel. 2011. "The Costs and Benefits of Immigration." *Political Science Quarterly* 126:427–443.

West, Candice, and Don Zimmerman. 1987. "Doing Gender." *Gender and Society* 1(2):125–151.

Wilson, James. 2000. *The Earth Shall Weep: A History of Native America.* New York. Grove Press.

Whisnant, Rebecca. 2017. "Feminist Perspectives on Rape." *Stanford Encyclopedia of Philosophy.* Retrieved May 4, 2017 (https://plato.stanford.edu/entries/feminism-rape/).

White House. 2005. *Economic Report of the President.* Washington, DC: Government Printing Office. (http://www.gpoaccess.gov/eop/2005/2005_erp.pdf).

White, Deborah Gray. 1985. *Ar'n't I a Woman? Female Slaves in the Plantation South.* New York: Norton.

White, Michael, and Jennifer Glick. 2009. *Achieving Anew: How New Immigrants Do in American Schools, Jobs, and Neighborhoods.* New York: Russell Sage Foundation.

Whiteman, Hilary. 2012. "Akin 'Legitimate Rape' Reaction, From the Congo to the Black Crickets." *CNN*, August 22. (http://www.cnn.com/2012/08/22/world/akin-international-rape- reaction/).

Whiting, Robert. 1990. *You Gotta Have Wa.* New York: Macmillan.

Wilkens, Roger. 1992. "L.A.: Images in the Flames; Looking Back in Anger: 27 Years After Watts, Our Nation Remains Divided by Racism." *Washington Post*, May 3, p. C1.

Williams, Christine L. 2013. "Glass Escalator, Revisited: Gender Inequality in Neoliberal Times." *Gender and Society* 27:609–629.

Williams, Gregory. 1995. *Life on the Color Line.* New York: Dutton.

Wilson, Erika, and Khaled A. Beydoun. 2017. "Charlottesville is America Everywhere." Retrieved August 13, 2017 (http://www.aljazeera.com/

indepth/opinion/2017/08/charlottesville-america-170813071924488.html).

Wilson, John Paul, Kurt Hugenberg, and Nicholas O. Rule. 2017. "Racial Bias in Judgments of Physical Size and Formidability: From Size to Threat." *Journal of Personality and Social Psychology* 113(1):59–80. doi: 10.1037/pspi00.

Wilson, William J. 1973. *Power, Racism, and Privilege: Race Relations in Theoretical and Sociohistorical Perspectives.* New York: Free Press.

———. 1987. *The Truly Disadvantaged: The Inner City, the Underclass, and Public Policy.* Chicago, IL: University of Chicago Press.

———. 1996. *When Work Disappears.* New York: Knopf.

———. 2009. *More Than Just Race.* New York: W. W. Norton.

Wimberly, Samantha. 2015. "The Roots of Slavery Between the United States, and Brazil." *Washington State University.* Retrieved August 10, 2017 (https://history.libraries.wsu.edu/spring2015/2015/01/16/racisms-effect-on-modern-day-society-in-the-united-states/).

Wirth, Louis. 1945. "The Problem of Minority Groups." Pp. 347–372 in *The Science of Man in the World,* edited by R. Linton. New York: Columbia University Press.

Wise, Tim. 2008a. *Speaking Treason Fluently: Anti-Racism Reflections from an Angry White Male.* Berkeley, CA: Soft Skull Press.

———. 2008b. *White Like Me: Reflections on Race From a Privileged Son.* Brooklyn, NY: Soft Skull Press.

———. 2010. *Colorblind: The Rise of Post-Racial Politics and the Retreat from Racial Equity.* San Francisco, CA: City Light Books.

Wittig, Michele Andrisin, and Sheila Grant-Thompson. 1998. "The Utility of Allport's Conditions of Intergroup Contact for Predicting Perceptions of Improved Racial Attitudes and Beliefs." *Journal of Social Issues* 54:795–812.

Wogan, J. B. 2013. "Alabama's Anti-Immigration Law Gutted." *Governing*, November 13. (http://www.governing.com/news/headlines/gov-alabamas-anti-immigration-law-dies-amid-hunger-for-reform.html).

Woldoff, Rachael A. 2011. *White Flight/Black Flight: The Dynamics of Racial Change in American Neighborhood.* Ithaca, NY: Cornell University Press.

Wolf, Naomi. 2002. *The Beauty Myth: How Images of Beauty Are Used Against Women.* New York: Harper Perennial.

Wolfe, Brendan, and Martha McCartney, eds. 2015. "Indentured Servants in Colonial Virginia." in *Encyclopedia Virginia.* Charlottesville, VA: Virginia Foundation for the Humanities. Retrieved August 4, 2017 (http://www.EncyclopediaVirginia.org/Indentured_Servants_in_Colonial_Virginia).

Wolfenstein, Eugene V. 1993. *The Victims of Democracy: Malcolm X.* New York: Guilford Press.

Wolitski, Richard J., Kenneth T. Jones, Jill L. Wasserman, and Jennifer C. Smith. 2006. "Self-Identification as Down Low Among Men Who Have Sex with Men (MSM) From 12 US Cities." *AIDS and Behavior* 10:519–529.

Women's Labor Force Participation. n.d. *Status of Women in the States.* (https://statusofwomendata.org/earnings-and-the-gender-wage-gap/womens-labor-force-participation/).

Wong, Morrison. 1995. "Chinese Americans." pp. 58–94 in *Asian Americans: Contemporary Trends and Issues*, edited by P. Gap Min. Thousand Oaks, CA: Sage.

Wood, Peter, and Michele Chesser. 1994. "Black Stereotyping in a University Population." *Sociological Focus* 27:17–34.

Woodward, C. Vann. 1974. *The Strange Career of Jim Crow.* 3rd ed. New York: Oxford University Press.

World Bank. 2013. "Data: Mexico." (http://data.worldbank.org/country/mexico).

———. 2017. "Education Statistics." Retrieved August 30, 2017 (http://databank.worldbank.org/data/reports.aspx?source=Education-Statistics:-Education-Attainment).

Wormser, Richard. n.d. "The Rise and Fall of Jim Crow." Retrieved August 10, 2017 (http://www.pbs.org/wnet/jimcrow/stories_events_freed.html).

Worsnop, Richard. 1992. "Native Americans." *CQ Researcher*, May 8, pp. 387–407.

Wright, Richard. 1940. *Native Son.* New York: Harper & Brothers.

———.1945. *Black Boy: A Record of Childhood and Youth.* New York: Harper & Brothers.

———. 1988. *12 Million Black Voices: A Folk History of the Negro in the United States.* New York: Viking Press. (Original work published 1941).

Wu, Ellen D. 2015. "The Color of Success: Asian Americans and the Origins of the Model Minority." *Journal of Transnational American Studies* 6(1).

Wu, Frank H. 2012. "Why Vincent Chin Matters." *The New York Times*, June 22. Retrieved August 26, 2017 (http://www.nytimes.com/2012/06/23/opinion/why-vincent-chin-matters.html).

Wyman, Mark. 1993. *Round Trip to America.* Ithaca, NY: Cornell University Press.

Yamato, Alexander. 1994. "Racial Antagonism and the Formation of Segmented Labor Markets: Japanese Americans and Their Exclusion From the Workforce." *Humboldt Journal of Social Relations* 20:31–63.

Yancey, George. 1999. "An Examination of the Effects of Residential and Church Integration on Racial Attitudes of Whites." *Sociological Perspectives* 42(2):279–304.

———. 2007. *Interracial Contact and Social Change.* Boulder, CO: Lynne Rienner.

———. 2003. *Who Is White? Latinos, Asians, and the New Black/Non-Black Divide.* Boulder, CO: Lynne Rienner.

Yardley, William. 2016. "North Dakota Governor Orders Evacuation of Standing Rock Protest Site, But No Forcible Removals Planned." *Los Angeles Times*, November 28. (http://www.latimes.com/nation/la-na-standing-rock-corps-20161128-story.html).

Yinger, J. Milton. 1985. "Ethnicity." *Annual Review of Sociology* 11:151–180.

Yudell, Michael, Dorothy Roberts, Rob DeSalle, and Sarah Tishkoff. 2016. "Taking Race Out of Human Genetics." *Science*, 351(6273):564–565. doi: 10.1126/science.aac4951.

Zacharek, Stephanie, Eliana Dockterman, and Haley Sweetland Edwards. 2017. "The Silence Breakers." *Time Magazine.* (http://time.com/time-person-of-the-year-2017-silence-breakers/).

Zecker, Robert M. 2011. *Race and America's Immigrant Press: How the Slovaks were Taught to Think Like White People.* New York: Bloomsbury Publishing USA. Retrieved August 3, 2017 (https://books.google.com/books?isbn=1441161996).

Zentella, Ana Celia. 1997. *Growing Up Bilingual: Puerto Rican Children in New York.* Malden, MA: Blackwell.

Zentella, Ana Celia. 2003. "'José can You See': Latin@ Responses to Racist Discourse." Pp. 51–68 in *Bilingual Games*, edited by D. Sommer. New York: Palgrave Press.

Zhou, Min, and John R. Logan. 1989. "Returns on Human Capital in Ethnic Enclaves: New York City's Chinatown." *American Sociological Review* 54:809–820.

Zhou, Min. 1992. *Chinatown.* Philadelphia, PA: Temple University Press.

Zillmer, Eric A., Molly Harrower, Barry A. Ritzler, and Robert P. Archer. 1995. *The Quest for the Nazi Personality: A Psychological Investigation of Nazi War Criminals.* New Jersey: LEA Hillside.

Zimmer, Benjamin. 2006. "Mock Spanish or Mock Mock Spanish?" May 12. (http://itre.cis.upenn.edu/~myl/languagelog/archives/003137.html).

Zócalo Public Square. 2009. "Census Counts and Controversies, Past and Present." November 24. Retrieved August 27, 2017 (http://www.zocalopublicsquare.org/2009/11/24/census-counts-and-controversies-past-and-present/events/the-takeaway/).

Zoll, Rachel. 2014. "Methodists in Crisis Over Gay Marriage, Church Law." *MSN News*, February 9. (http://news.msn.com/us/methodists-in-crisis-over-gay-marriage-church-law).

INDEX